After the Australopithecines

World Anthropology

General Editor

SOL TAX

Patrons

CLAUDE LÉVI-STRAUSS
MARGARET MEAD
LAILA SHUKRY EL HAMAMSY
M. N. SRINIVAS

MOUTON PUBLISHERS · THE HAGUE · PARIS
DISTRIBUTED IN THE USA AND CANADA BY ALDINE, CHICAGO

General Editor's Preface

These two volumes provide what for years will be the plateau from which research will continue on the critical "big change" from early hominids to modern man. These were developed at a Wenner-Gren conference at Burg Wartenstein, held immediately preceding the IXth International Congress of Anthropological and Ethnological Sciences; and it was agreed that the results should be reported to, and published with the works of, the Congress. This was fitting, since the Wenner-Gren Foundation's long tradition of international and interdisciplinary conferences furnished a pattern for the numerous other conferences organized directly by the Congress to discuss problems chosen for full discussion before, and publication by, the Congress. And of course the series as a whole includes other closely related books on prehistory, archeology, primatology, and paleanthropology.

We are more than pleased to be able to include *After the Australopithecenes* among the first works of *World Anthropology*.

Chicago, Illinois   SOL TAX
March 17, 1975

Preface

Holding a symposium to discuss the Middle Pleistocene is like doing a jigsaw puzzle with local sequences and individual circumstantial reconstructions as the potentially interlocking parts. Unfortunately most of the pieces are still missing; and of those in the possession of the scientific community, only a small number will fit on the conference table at one time. However, in compensation, the extraordinary ambience of a convivial Burg Wartenstein seminar provided an excellent opportunity to find joins and juxtapositions amongst the available sample of jigsaw pieces. There is hope that in the configurations that developed, perhaps we may have caught glimpses of how the whole picture may one day appear. The diversity of approaches and information that was assembled is apparent from the written contributions to the symposium. With these as a basis, the task before the group in the discussion sessions was to explore aspects of the present state of our knowledge of the middle ranges of Pleistocene time and of the processes of human cultural development that occurred during that interval. Rather one should say, explore the state of ignorance, for as one might expect we found that the complexity of the story is very great when compared with the fragmentary information that we now have available for reconstruction and interpretation.

The middle part of the Pleistocene is the least well understood, both in geological and paleoanthropological terms. At the one end, events of the late Pleistocene are reasonably well documented from a good number of well preserved sedimentary sequences, as well as from biological and archeological assemblages increasingly liable to sound interpretation and stratigraphic interrelation. In fact, within the 30-70,000 year span of radio-carbon dating, the chronometry of physical events and cultural change has been determined for several regions. At the other end of the stratigraphic column, the early Pleistocene has benefited from suites of increasingly satisfactory, potassium-argon dates from many of the key faunal and archeological sites. In addition to this rudimentary yet surprisingly efficient chronometric framework, the early Pleistocene has yielded a comparative wealth of hominid fossils and a small array of informative archeological associations.

Yet, between these two extremities, stratigraphic correlation and chronological resolution of the mid-Pleistocene time range is at present unsatisfactory. Sedimentary sequences are characteristically brief, incomplete, and isolated, with rare opportunities for isotopic dating of any kind. Although a number of complex successions are known, few are resolved in a satisfactory manner, and external correlations by litho- or climato-stratigraphic means are to varying degrees controversial. Consequently, biostratigraphic horizons have assumed ever greater importance at the regional level, although the few available chronometric tools are now revealing that biological assemblages are far from foolproof for purposes of either intra- or intercontinental correlation. It is within this "floating" stratigraphic and paleoenvironmental framework that rare, informative archeological occurrences and even rarer hominid fossils rest, with little precision possible as to temporal or spatial interrelationships.

Yet the mid-Pleistocene was a formative phase in human evolution. However loosely defined, this geological time span saw the transformation from an early Pleistocene situation, involving a "proto-human" level of behavior, to a late Pleistocene situation, involving cultural elaboration analogous with the ethnographic complexity of recent times.

The known archeological record of the history of human behavior begins effectively with the Olduvai Bed I and the Rudolf Basin occupation sites dating from between 1.7 and 2.6 million years ago. These sites and the associated hominid fossils indicate that at least one hominid lineage had already undergone marked evolutionary divergence away from patterns common among related primate stocks. A bipedal gait and stance were coupled with significant intensities of behaviors that are now distinctive of man, namely, dependence on tools, meat-eating (hunted or scavenged), food-sharing, and the occupation of home bases. Despite the "humanness" of this set of fundamental attributes, it is increasingly doubtful that early Pleistocene hominid behaviors involved rule-systems or communication systems with the complexity universal in recent mankind.

By contrast, the archeological record of the Upper Pleistocene shows abundant evidence of elaborate, regionally-differentiated cultural rule-systems that appear to be indicative of a capacity for culture equivalent to that of today. In fact, the late Pleistocene and Holocene archeological and historical records can be viewed as the realization of potentials generated by the evolutionary processes of the mid-Pleistocene.

A decade of comparatively intensive stratigraphical, paleobiological, and paleoanthropological research has turned up much new data on the Middle Pleistocene, but little scholarly attempt has yet been made to identify evolutionary processes distinctive of the period or to plot the trajectory of systemic change. Various general works have offered speculative accounts, but scientists engaged in the primary investigations have as yet made few generalizations, and, what is more important, there has been little attempt to formulate the research questions to be asked or to specify the particular kinds of data needed.

It seemed to us that a multidisciplinary appraisal of the state of information on mid-Pleistocene stratigraphy, ecology, and paleoanthropology would be important for its own sake, and even more so as a potential impetus toward further and more effective studies of the whole range of interrelated interests. If the "muddle in the middle" is to be resolved there must be awareness, problem-formulation, and interdisciplinary collaboration. The Wenner-Gren Foundation for Anthropological Research generously agreed to sponsor a Burg Wartenstein Symposium entitled "Stratigraphy and patterns of cultural change in the Middle Pleistocene." A group of twenty earth scientists, paleobiologists, and paleoanthropologists was invited to prepare pre-conference review papers and participate in the joint discussions which were held at Burg Wartenstein, Lower Austria, July 2-11, 1973. The selection of a maximum of twenty specialists to represent the major lines of subdisciplinary work in key world regions proved a very difficult task. Many innovative and productive scholars could not be invited due to the limitations on space and the need to give as balanced a representation as possible. In the end we were obliged to omit specialists on eastern Asia and North America. Unfortunately, too, several of the original invitees were unable to attend, on relatively short notice, so that eighteen participants finally assembled at Burg Wartenstein. H. D. Kahlke (Weimar), who was also unable to attend, kindly prepared a paper for pre-conference circulation.

One of the themes deliberately omitted from the agenda was radiometric dating as such since the conference took as one of its starting points the material of a recent (1971) Burg Wartenstein symposium that had been addressed to this topic. Copies of the resulting volume[1] were provided as background for the conference participants through the courtesy of the Wenner-Gren Foundation. Instead, our mid-Pleistocene specialists were asked to address themselves to a fresh reassessment of the stratigraphic framework and archeological record. This they did with a vengeance, as the following papers will show.

The conference evolved over eight days, interrupted by a pleasant day of relaxation in Graz and a half-day visit to the pivotal loess exposures on the Danube bluffs above Krems. Our polyglot and polymorphic group was imbued with such an interest in understanding, and possibly resolving, the problems at hand that no single discussion was ever marred by polemic or undue bias. Participants spent many of their "free" hours revising their own papers and incorporating aspects of the material covered in discussion as modifications and additions. The organizers have each prepared a summary of their impression of the configurations which developed during the meetings, and these are presented as the concluding chapters of the volume. Inasmuch as these reports on the discussions treat the interrelationships of the material in the various contributions, they can be used as some sort of guide to the volume and readers may find it helpful to consult them before tackling the body of the book. We feel that the modified papers and the commentaries together will be a more intelligible record of the transactions than a session-by-session account could be. We have therefore not included any other specific reporting of discussions.

As organizers, we have much to be grateful for. First and foremost the participants were magnificent in their dedication and collaboration. The review papers requested were demanding and the response was most gratifying. The pressures of interminable working days were born with a rare, good humor that was shared by the equally-taxed castle staff. Mrs. Lita Osmundsen, Director of Research of the Wenner-Gren Foundation, made the conference possible by her continuing interest and sympathetic encouragement. Sol Tax, President of the IXth-International Congress of Anthropological and Ethnological Sciences (Chicago, 1973), invited us to publish these proceedings in the *World Anthropology* series. Karen Tkach of the Mouton publishing house personally saw the agglomeration of typescripts through the various stages of processing to prompt publication as a finished volume. Elisabeth Butzer and Barbara Isaac worked indefatigably in recording the con-

---

[1]   *Calibration of hominoid evolution*, edited by W. W. Bishop and J. A. Miller, and published 1972 by the Scottish Academic Press, Edinburgh.

ference discussion, organizing the revision of papers, and carrying through the final scientific editing under trying circumstances while the organizers were in the field.

In closing we come away with more than the sense of a communal effort done to the best of our abilities. It was also a unique human experience to discover the warmth of personalities that emerged across the conference round-table and during our social hours. The vigor, rather than quality, of dancing at our *Heurigerfest* amazed even the musicians. On the final evening, our skit "Scenes from Life during the Wenner-Gren Glacial Vascillation," produced unforgettable performances by Jean-Jacques Jaeger as a terminal moraine, Ofer Bar-Yosef and Henri de Lumley as two *Homo erectus,* Charles Turner as a "well-developed Oldowan," and Leslie Freeman as *Anancus alkaselzer.* Perhaps the castle halls are still ringing to the unprintable refrain of our Correlation Song, sung (to misuse the word) to the tune of "Clementine". Our thanks to all.

Chicago, Illinois   KARL BUTZER

Berkeley, California   GLYNN ISAAC

November, 1973

Table of Contents

The Stratigraphic Record of Deep-Sea Cores and Its Implications for the Assessment of Glacials, Interglacials, Stadials, and Interstadials in the Mid-Pleistocene

N. J. SHACKLETON

ABSTRACT

Middle Pleistocene deep-sea sediments possess a virtue for students of continental stratigraphy that is probably unique in the geological column. They can be studied the world over using a common technique (oxygen isotope analysis); this technique provides a stratigraphic resolution equivalent to only a few thousand years; it provides a record that is uniquely related to events in mid-continent, that is, to the quantity of continental ice stored.

The system of numbered stages defined on the basis of the use of this technique nearly twenty years ago appears to be stabilized and useful. The ages of the stage boundaries are known with uncertainties varying between a few thousand, and a few tens of thousand, years; these uncertainties are likely to be reduced below 10,000 years throughout the Middle Pleistocene within a short time.

Within this framework a variety of techniques is available which may give evidence for environmental change on the continents. The extent to which these techniques can be used to distinguish between different glacial or interglacial stages is seriously underexplored, and there may be a potential for continental correlation on this basis. Certainly the Middle Pleistocene is not a cyclic repetition of identical climatic events.

Within each stage there are clearly discernible variations in most parameters investigated. Although adjacent stages may be grossly characterized alternately by extensive and minor quantities of continental ice, separated by easily correlated boundaries, there is no reason to suppose that these stages are time-equivalent to the climatic stages into which any particular continental sequence might be most naturally divided. In particular, palynologically defined interglacials in North-West Europe are probably shorter, and less frequent, than are odd-numbered marine stages.

The terrestrial Pleistocene record is one of erosion, or at best of discontinuous deposition. Uniform sedimentation is extremely rare. The best known estimate of the relative duration of Pleistocene events is based not on the rate of accumulation of rocks, but on the rate of their removal by erosion; this erosion took place under such varying climatic conditions that its rate can only be estimated in the vaguest way. Yet the importance of Pleistocene continental deposits is such that we try and try again to develop quantitative or semiquantitative techniques to place the deposits in a stratigraphic and time framework.

Unfortunately it is still common for workers studying deep-sea deposits to attempt an interpretation of the sequences they find in continental terms, on the quite mistaken assumption that the continental sequence is well known. Terrestrial workers then assume that the given marine sequence, based as it is on regular deposition of deep-sea sediment, provides a firm framework for continental events. It is worth citing an example of this. Ericson and Wollin (1964) in examining a series of cores containing sediments deposited during perhaps the past 2 million years or so, sought the record of the "Great Interglacial," believing this epithet was properly applied to the European Mindel-Riss and to the American Yarmouth. Having sought the episode, they found it and estimated its duration at about 500,000 years (Ericson and Wollin 1964: Figure 23). Emiliani (1955) on the other hand used the oxygen isotope technique and discovered evidence for at least four glaciations in sediments which he showed covered about 300,000 years in all. He too was able to identify a "Mindel-Riss" interglacial lasting somewhat longer than the others, though lasting only a tenth of the time suggested by Ericson and Wollin a few years later. Neither of the papers cited provided evidence for the correlations proposed, while terrestrial workers for their part have made practically no attempt to assess the data presented by the deep-sea workers; rather they have chosen one or other "chronology" on the basis of personal preconceptions.

The purpose of this contribution is to discuss the stratigraphy of deep-sea deposits, and the extent to which the record contained in them is susceptible to correlation with continental deposits.

DEEP-SEA SEDIMENTS

Deep-sea sediments can be sampled for stratigraphic purposes either by drilling or by coring. Deep-sea drilling is a relatively new invention; the main purpose is to sample older sediments and at present it is of little interest in relation to the Middle Pleistocene. Coring is performed by lowering a weighted tube into the sediment from the side of the ship. A piston corer (Kullenberg 1947) commonly takes 10 to 30 meters of sediment, using a piston inside the coring tube which in effect permits the great hydrostatic pressure on the sea bed to be utilized in forcing the sediment into the tube. Coring is not simple, and by no means does every core taken contain a complete and undisturbed record of the sediment penetrated. Currently a new generation of piston corers is being developed; the so-called Giant Piston Corer (Silva and Hollister 1973) promises a significant improvement in sediment recovery.

The constituents of deep-sea sediments may be classified as of organic or inorganic origin. The inorganic component may be precipitated from solution, or may be transported from the continents by wind, by rivers, or by floating ice. The biogenic components may be usefully divided according to chemical composition, carbonate (e.g. foraminifera), silica (e.g. radiolaria), and so forth. A good review article on deep-sea sediments is that by Arrhenius (1963).

As we shall see, the value of a deep-sea sediment core lies in the fact that it may contain a record both of changes in the conditions at the water surface perhaps a mile above the sediment, and of events on the distant continents. On the other hand, the main limitations on the value of the record are imposed by conditions on the sea floor where sediment is accumulating. One should never forget the burrowing organisms which mix the sediment (Berger and Heath 1968); the currents transporting material from one place to another, mixing material of different ages, and so on. Nor can one ignore the chemical properties of the water in which the sediment is deposited: in particular, at great depths, the increased capacity of the water to dissolve calcium carbonate, and in doing so to selectively remove the thinner and more fragile calcium carbonate fossils (Berger 1968). In general these are problems for the person studying the sediment rather than the user of the record, but they do mean that a record based on one core is always liable to modification when a few more cores have been examined. Much of what we know about the Pleistocene in deep-sea sediments is based on the hundreds of cores collected by the major oceanographic institutions of the world and curated by them, notwithstanding the fact that the picture can now be illustrated by reference to a very limited number of cores. Indeed, it is difficult to adequately acknowledge the work that precedes the selection of a particular core as suitable for the application of a particular technique.

It is perhaps a result of this often unmentioned background stratigraphic study, that marine geologists do not usually start off by drawing stratigraphic sections. It is more usual to make correlations between cores treated as time-sequences. If this seems an overhasty approach to workers in other fields, it must be remembered that enormous lateral distances are often involved, so that physical correlation of rock units would be out of the question. Furthermore, there is usually a number of different techniques used in the correlations, even if only a few are specifically mentioned.

Oxygen Isotope Stratigraphy

It is now well known that during the glacial episodes of the Pleistocene, immense ice sheets composed of isotopically light ice accumulated in Northern North America and Europe. When this happened, the oceans shrank in volume, became slightly more saline, their surface level was lowered, and they became isotopically more positive (that is, enriched in ^{18}O). Thus the relatively local glaciations were felt indirectly over two thirds of the earth's surface. For many years it has been obvious that the sea-level record ought to enable a worldwide stratigraphy to be built up, but in practice there are many difficulties; the fact that it is difficult to obtain a continuous record is a serious limitation. Because oxygen isotope studies were originally intended for another purpose (paleotemperature estimation) it was not at first appreciated that they enable the glacial record to be used as a basic stratigraphical framework in sediments all over the oceans.

The first work in this field was performed by Emiliani (1955, 1958, 1966, 1972) on the assumption that paleotemperature measurement was the primary aim. He established a stratigraphic scheme which will be discussed below. The role of ice sheets in determining the record has been discussed by many workers (Olausson 1965; Shackleton 1967; Dansgaard and Tauber 1969; Duplessy, Lalou, et al 1970). Shackleton and Opdyke (1973) obtained a record covering at least the past 800,000 years in which the temperature component appears to be negligible. Correlation between this record and those previously published, and believed to contain a temperature component, is excellent.

Terminology

Emiliani (1955) defined a numbered series of climatic stages on the basis of his oxygen isotope measurements. His later studies of a greater number of cores, using a variety of techniques in addition to oxygen isotope analysis, showed that two of the cores previously used contained stratigraphic breaks; a slight revision became necessary (Emiliani 1966).

Emiliani (1955) defined stage boundaries by reference to a model of sinusoidal paleotemperature changes through time, rather than defining them at specified points in particular cores. Shackleton and Opdyke

(1973) defined the stage boundaries in core V28–238 at given depths. In future it may be considered worthwhile to consider the stage boundaries and their correlation more carefully; for the present, it is only necessary to emphasize that stage boundaries are related to the quantity of ice stored on the continents, not to the climate responsible for that ice.

To some workers Emiliani's definition of a stage (stage 3) corresponding roughly to the interstadial in the 30,000 year time range, was unfortunate (or even wrong). We would emphasize here that there is no difficulty in recognizing this stage in the oxygen isotope record in either the Caribbean or in distant parts of the oceans. Neither is there any doubt that at least in some regions there were climates during this time-interval that were substantially different from those prevailing in the glacial extremes corresponding to stages 2 and 4.

Broecker and van Donk (1970) used a new terminology in a discussion of the oxygen isotope record. These workers envisage the record as predominantly "saw-toothed" in shape rather than sinusoidal; they numbered each rapid deglaciation, such that the stage 2–1 transition was named "Termination I," the stage 6–5 transition "Termination II" and so on. It must be emphasized that this is not to be used as a new stratigraphic nomenclature. It is a nomenclature applied to the oxygen isotope record only on the assumption that it resembles the model (which, in our opinion, it does not).

At least some of the odd-numbered ("interglacial") stages begin with a relatively rapid period of ice melting similar to that between about 16,000 and 6,000 years ago. It may be reasonably argued that the Eemian interglacial of North-West Europe occupied the same position with respect to the stage 6–5 transition, as the present interglacial occupies with respect to the more recent major ice retreat. The position of the end of this interglacial is less easy to relate to the marine record. However, it was reasoned by Shackleton (1969) that the end of the Eemian in the palynologists' sense (the decline of the temperate forests) must have occurred well within stage 5, at the end of what was there named sub-stage 5e. This view is now widely held (see *Quaternary Research* 2 (3)). More generally, it is almost certainly the case that the proportion of Middle Pleistocene time occupied by interglacials as palynologists use that term is small, probably less than one tenth (Emiliani 1972). On the other hand odd-numbered and even-numbered stages occupy roughly equal parts of the marine record.

To some extent this is a function of the asymmetry in the definitions of glacial and interglacial as palynologists use these terms: a glacial may be punctuated by interstadials, but an interglacial is terminated if conditions become so cold that the temperate forests are extinguished. However, this is probably not a complete explanation. There is little doubt that in fact episodes without any Northern Hemisphere ice WERE but a small fraction of Pleistocene time.

On the other hand, there seems little doubt that at least in low latitudes the marine record is most logically divided into approximately equal-duration climate stages. We simply do not know at present how much time was occupied by different climatic regimes in many parts of the world. This point is emphasized because although the oxygen isotope stratigraphy provides a reliable framework within which to discuss the Middle Pleistocene, it does not itself contain enough information to deduce the sequence of climatic events in any region.

Initially workers viewed the number of stages proposed by Emiliani with some dismay. It is now clear that so far as terrestrial correlation is concerned, an even finer subdivision of the isotope record is necessary at least in some sections. However, the scheme proposed by Emiliani (1955) has proved to be stable and easily applied; there is no need to alter it.

It must be emphasized that the stages defined by Emiliani, and discussed above, are not the same as the many other systems of numbering which others have utilized. It is the writer's opinion that many of these have been set up on so weak a basis that they can scarcely bear the strain of inter-core correlation, and on no account should be regarded as stratigraphic units of value in other contexts. In many cases they have been set up under the influence of such strong preconceptions about the "established" continental stratigraphy in Europe as to be positively dangerous (see Olausson 1965: 221–223). Earlier the rather clumsy phrase "isotope stage" was suggested for the sake of clarity (Shackleton 1969). Perhaps a better procedure would be to make a point of referring always to a particular core ("we suggest that unit xxxxx at locality yyyyy may be correlated with the early part of stage 7 in core V28–238"). This might help to counteract the tendency to propose correlation with nebulous ideals (whether "Riss," "Würm" or "5," "7") instead of with actual stratigraphic sequences.

Climatic Sequences Based on "Sensitive Species"

A great deal of the pioneering postwar work on deep-sea sediments and their climatic record was performed by David Ericson and others at the Lamont (now Lamont-Doherty) Geological Observatory. They based their work on the use of a relatively simple approach applied to a large number of cores, although this approach grew out of a much more detailed initial study. Ericson and Wollin (1956a, 1956b) showed that the abundance of a single species group, *Globorotalia menardii*, was very low or zero in Atlantic sediments of the last glacial, and high in post-glacial sediments. They compared the down-core record of the abundance of this group with the climatic record obtained by Emiliani (1955) on the basis of oxygen isotope analysis on the same cores, and found that the agreement between the two methods at the top of the cores broke down in lower sections, initiating a dispute which has continued, not without acrimony.

As a stratigraphic tool this approach has the disadvantage of being too simple; one zone with abundant *Globorotalia menardii* may look much like another. For this reason the application of paleomagnetic studies to Atlantic sediments (Glass, et al. 1967) necessitated serious revision to the earlier stratigraphy (Ericson, et al. 1964). Subject to this reservation, it is clear that the use of this simple technique has been of immense stratigraphic value in the Atlantic region. It must be emphasized, how-ever, that zone boundaries may be, and in this case probably are, time-transgressive (Kennett and Huddleston 1972). Moreover, there is no doubt that the relationship between these zones and worldwide climatic change is not the same right through the Middle Pleistocene (for ex-ample, "interglacial" stage 15 falls within "glacial" zone U). For these reasons, this system of nomenclature should certainly not be used at all except in sediments in which the zones are recognized.

A further disadvantage of this approach, as far as detail is concerned, is that stratigraphic breaks are likely to go unnoticed. For example, much of the work which went into dating the U–V zone boundary in the Carib-bean was performed on a core, V12–122, which is now known (Imbrie, et al. 1973) to lack about a meter of sediment near this boundary. Cer-tainly for meaningful stratigraphic correlation to the continents a more subtle approach is essential.

Climatic Sequences Based on Total Fauna

There have been a great number of different approaches made to the climatic record left in the faunal variations found in sediment cores. In general, the more sophisticated methods utilize a greater proportion of the total fauna (and involve more work). An interesting piece of work by Lidz (1966) generated climatic curves based on the ratios of a group of species rather than single species; the curves were compared with an oxygen isotope sequence in the same core. As Lidz pointed out, curves using several species gave better agreement with the oxygen isotope sequence than curves based on the abundance of a single species. Since the oxygen isotope method can be applied with virtually identical precision right through the Pleistocene, it is perhaps not surprising that in general the more sophisticated methods give agreement with the oxygen isotope record over a longer period of time than the less sophisticated. The more we can learn from all sources about the Upper Pleistocene, the more reliably we will be able to use the oxygen isotope technique for environmental reconstruction in the Middle and Lower Pleistocene.

A particularly interesting recent development has been the quantitative approach of Imbrie and his co-workers (Imbrie and Kipp 1971). A large array of core-tops (recent sediment) is analyzed in terms of present-day summer temperature, winter temperature, salinity, and so forth, and this information is used to derive estimates of these variables through time by analyzing sediment cores. In detail the method is subject to continuing improvement as more core-top (recent) data is fed in and as better mathematical techniques are used. The approach is now being used in all the world oceans and in the next few years we may expect very detailed paleoclimatic reconstructions at least for the Upper Pleistocene to be evolved by the CLIMAP project (*Quaternary Research* 3 (1)).

As far as the Middle Pleistocene is concerned, it is not at present clear to what extent the method will break down in older sediments; the record in core V12–122 (Imbrie and Kipp 1971) is only partly convincing. Interglacial stage 15 clearly registers a higher temperature than the glacials before and after, but stage 11 seems not to be detected, although the oxygen isotope record for the core shows that it is present. Put another way, the particular version used in the publication cited appears to start diverging from the oxygen isotope record around 200,000 years ago, although there is still a general resemblance at 400,000 years. Comparison with the next version to be used (Imbrie, van Donk, and Kipp 1973) is particularly interesting in this connection; agreement with the oxygen isotope record in the older part of the core is considerably better, although the improvements made were founded only on an expanded range of core-top data. A long-term trend in temperature maxima and minima is still present; it is the writer's opinion that this reflects evolutionary change in the fauna rather than a real temperature shift (it is not seen in the oxygen isotope records through this interval). This means that at present it is not possible to use faunal methods, however sophisticated, to make detailed climatological comparisons between different "glacial" or "interglacial" stages, although the faunal methods may be of great assistance in delineating climatic changes within each stage.

Faunal Extinctions in the Middle Pleistocene

Although rough stratigraphic subdivision on the basis of extinction of individual species has been extremely useful in some regions, there are plainly not enough extinctions to provide a stratigraphy of the degree of refinement that we require. Furthermore, it is only with the increase in the use of oxygen isotope analysis as a stratigraphic tool that it is becoming possible to discover to what extent any extinction is synchronous over a wide area, and particularly over a wide latitudinal range. Up to the present, comparison of extinction points between cores has only been possible on the basis of comparison of interpolated and extrapolated absolute ages. Recently Gartner (1972) demonstrated the extinction of the coccolith *Pseudoemiliania lacunosa* in stage 13 in Caribbean core P6304 –9, and Geitzenauer (Personal communication) demonstrated the extinction of the same species in the same stage in Pacific core V28–238.

With this one exception, it remains to be seen whether any nonclimatic biostratigraphical zonation of deep-sea sediments will have resolution even as good as ± half a climatic cycle (or say ± 50,000 years), whereas the resolution of the oxygen isotope stratigraphic record is probably better than ± 5,000 years. On the other hand, it is essential that biostratigraphy is used to ensure that there are no errors greater than one cycle, as Emiliani (1966) demonstrated. Since, particularly if sedimentation is slow, one cycle looks much like another in oxygen isotope terms, the use of oxygen isotope analysis alone is almost powerless to recognize a lacuna of one or more complete climatic cycles. Thus the whole Middle Pleistocene deep sea stratigraphy is based on enormous amounts of biostratigraphic work, and this will certainly continue to be the case, yet insofar as the continental record is concerned this biostratigraphic work can only be treated as the invisible infrastructure on which the oxygen isotope record is based.

Carbonate Percentage Curves

In a monumental study of sediment cores from the Equatorial Pacific, Arrhenius (1952) showed that quasi-cyclic variations occur in the pro-

Table 1.   Depths and estimated ages of stage boundaries in core V28–238

Boundary	Depth, centimeters	Age, years
1–2	22	13,000
2–3	55	32,000
3–4	110	64,000
4–5	128	75,000
5–6	220	128,000
6–7	335	195,000
7–8	430	251,000
8–9	510	297,000
9–10	595	347,000
10–11	630	367,000
11–12	755	440,000
12–13	810	472,000
13–14	860	502,000
14–15	930	542,000
15–16	1015	592,000
16–17	1075	627,000
17–18	1110	647,000
18–19	1180	688,000
19–20	1210	706,000
20–21	1250	729,000
21–22	1340	782,000

Ages are estimated on the basis of a uniform sedimentation rate of 1.71×10^{-3} centimeters per year, calibrated by the presence of the Brunhes-Matuyama magnetic epoch boundary, age 700,000 years, at 1200 centimeters.

portion of calcium carbonate in the sediment. Arrhenius deduced correctly that these cycles were related to glacial-interglacial climatic changes. However, he was not able to establish the precise relationship between carbonate percentage and temperature, or ice volume. Indeed, this is a question that has not yet been solved. Attention is drawn to this

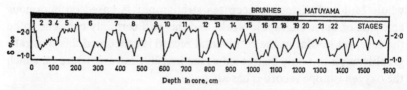

Figure 1.   Oxygen isotope record of core V28–238, from Shackleton and Opdyke (1973). Stages 1 to 22 are defined in this core. Estimated ages of stage boundaries are given in Table 1. The range in isotopic composition is about 1.3 per mil, and should probably be attributed entirely to change in ocean isotopic composition caused by the accumulation of Northern-Hemisphere ice sheets. This implies that the entire record may also be read as a depiction of glacio-eustatic changes in world sea level.

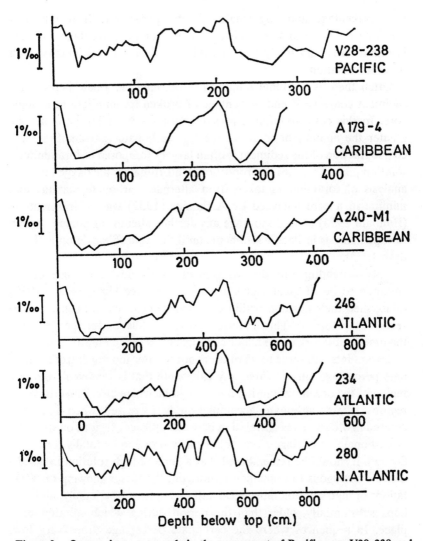

Figure 2. Oxygen isotope records in the upper part of Pacific core V28–238 and in a number of Atlantic cores described by Emiliani. The cores have been plotted at various sedimentation rate scales, so as to coincide at the stage 6–5 boundary. Clearly the extent to which detailed inter-core correlation is possible depends on the sedimentation rate, which is in fact, a more important factor than the distance between the cores correlated. In most or all regions there have been changes in sedimentation rate in response to the direct and indirect results of climatic change. To this extent, dating by interpolation or extrapolation is always suspect in detail.

matter for the reason that the factors governing the proportion of carbonate in the sediment are varied, complex and often opposed in effect. Thus there is no reason to expect a simple relationship between carbonate percentage and any single climatic parameter. It is relatively speaking a simple matter to determine carbonate percentage, and the information is very likely to be useful — but only in conjunction with other information.

Often there is a simple relationship between carbonate percentage, sediment coarseness, and percentage of broken foraminifera in a single core. In this case, solution is presumably the controlling variable; the greater the amount of solution, the less carbonate remains. Since the coarse fraction of the sediment is often largely composed of foraminifera, solution plainly reduces its proportion. Unfortunately the oxygen isotope analysis of foraminifera taken from alternate carbonate maxima and minima in a core analyzed by Arrhenius (1952) was so inconclusive (Emiliani 1955) as to discourage any further attempt to pursue oxygen isotope analysis in Pacific sediments until this year (Shackleton and Opdyke 1973).

Notwithstanding this discouragement, Arrhenius' carbonate curves continue to be of great value, the more so since Hays, et al. (1969) established their position within the framework of earth magnetic field reversals (Figure 3). This important work established for the first time the time-framework of the major climatic cycles of the Pleistocene.

Two points will serve to warn users not to infer too much from carbonate percentage curves. First, any carbonate that is removed from one region of the ocean by solution has to go somewhere else. Thus there are regions where carbonate accumulation is increased when it is decreased in others. Thus correlation between different regions on the basis of carbonate percentage alone could easily prove to be totally incorrect. Second, it should be remembered that a zone of high solution in a sediment is analogous to a weathering horizon; the fossils showing manifestations of high solution must necessarily be at least fractionally, and perhaps substantially, older than the period during which solution took place. In sequences where the carbonate percentage drops very low, there may be no carbonate fossils preserved characterizing the episode of intense dissolution. Thus deposits showing extreme variations in carbonate percentage may be very unsuitable vehicles for detailed stratigraphical studies, particularly those based on carbonate fossils. This may explain the relatively disappointing oxygen isotope data obtained by Emiliani from the Pacific.

For this reason, the attractive numbering scheme put forward by Hays, et al., whereby peaks and troughs in the graph of carbonate percentage were numbered B1, B2, ... in the Brunhes Normal Magnetic Epoch, M1, M2 ... in the Matuyama, and so forth, cannot be used as a

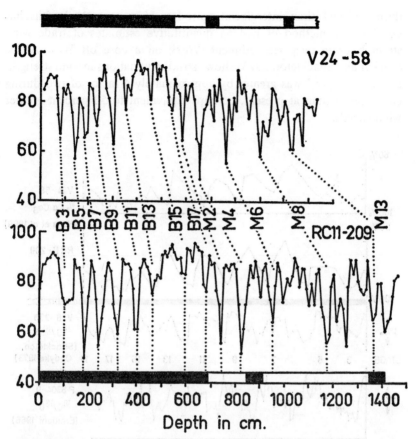

Figure 3. The record of changing calcium carbonate percentage in two Pacific cores (Hays, et al. 1969, with their numbering scheme for carbonate minima). Arrhenius (1952) showed that high-carbonate sediment was deposited in glacials, and low-carbonate during interglacials, at least in an approximate sense. In placing these variations in a magnetic framework, Hays, et al. were the first workers to establish the duration of the major climatic cycles of the Middle Pleistocene. Note that there is not necessarily any relationship between the magnitude of the carbonate low "peaks" and the interglacial "intensity." Luz (1973) argues that the carbonate minima occur at the onset of glaciations, rather than at interglacial maxima. See also Figure 4.

stratigraphic scheme except in cores where these carbonate "zones" can be recognized.

Wind Strength Studies

Several workers (Arrhenius 1952; Hays and Peruzza 1972) have deduced from deep-sea core studies that there were stronger trade winds during glacial than interglacial episodes. Very recently Parkin has developed a method of making quantitative estimates of trade wind strength using deep-sea sediment. Work on a core off West Africa (Parkin and Shackleton 1973) shows striking variations in wind strength; the wind "vigor" was greater by approximately a factor of two during each glacial than at present, perhaps equivalent to 50 percent greater wind speeds.

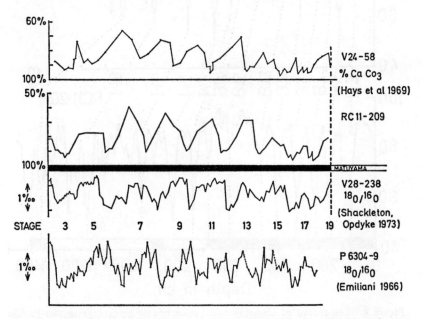

Figure 4.   The oxygen isotope record of core V28–238, the calcium carbonate record of cores RC11–209 and V24–58 (see Figure 3), and the oxygen isotope record of Caribbean core P6304–9 (Emiliani 1966). Here the two records of calcium carbonate variation have been re-plotted for illustrative purposes, on the assumption that the rate of accumulation of the non-carbonate fraction is uniform, instead of making the assumption that the thickness of sediment deposited in unit time remained constant. For the numbering system of Hays, et al., see Figure 3. The chief value of this exercise is that it demonstrates the fact that the two carbonate peaks numbered B14 and B16 by Hays, et al. may not have occupied more time than the later "glacial" carbonate peaks; they contain a greater thickness of sediment, most of which is carbonate. Note however that the assumption of constant non-carbonate accumulation may be incorrect (Broecker 1971). Core P6304–9 has been plotted on the basis of uniform sedimentation rate, which plainly is not correct if the assumption of uniform sedimentation in V28–238 is valid. There is some evidence suggesting that there was generally a lower sedimentation rate in the Caribbean (? and Equatorial Atlantic) during the Middle Pleistocene than during the last 150,000 years or so (Emiliani and Shackleton 1974).

Palynology in Middle Pleistocene Deep-Sea Sediments

One promising area for the study of Middle Pleistocene terrestrial pollen grains in deep-sea sediments seems to be in the sapropel layers found in Eastern Mediterranean sediments. Unfortunately these are formed discontinuously, and indeed rather rarely. It seems that from time to time, probably during times of glacial ice melting (Olausson 1967) the Mediterranean deep water stagnates. There is then no benthonic activity and organic matter is not oxidized on the sea floor. Three such horizons are found in stage 5, and four in stage 7. Pollen is well preserved and studies by Rossignol-Strick (1974) show that they contain abundant information. In addition, Leg 13 of the Deep-Sea Drilling Project (Ryan, et al. 1973) was able to drill a long Pleistocene section (about 70 meters) at Hole 132, in which sapropel layers are found, so that the outlook in this direction is encouraging. The chief interpretational difficulty is the uncertainty as to the origin of the pollen. However, by studying the stratigraphically identical sapropel in different cores this difficulty can be reduced.

Chronology

The dating of the stage boundaries in the marine Middle Pleistocene presents some problems, and there remain some difficulties; we propose to treat the matter briefly. The only radiometric method of directly dating Middle Pleistocene sediments is the decay of excess ^{230}Th. This is produced in sea water by the decay of ^{234}U, so that the rate of accumulation of ^{230}Th in the sediment should depend on the thickness of the water layer above (that is the ocean depth) and on the amount of uranium in solution. In the sediment, ^{230}Th decays with a half-life of about 75,000 years, so that an estimate of the sedimentation rate can be obtained by measuring the ^{230}Th content as a function of depth in the core. The method can never be precise, because the amount of ^{230}Th in unit quantity of sediment depends on the rate of sediment accumulation (which is unlikely to be constant) as well as on the time that has elapsed since the sediment was deposited. Moreover detailed studies (Ku, et al. 1972) reveal disconcerting gaps in our understanding of ^{230}Th accumulation.

There remain two options: to date by extrapolation from the top of the core where alternative methods of age determination are available, or to date by interpolation to the position of the Brunhes-Matuyama magnetic reversal, if the core is long enough to contain it.

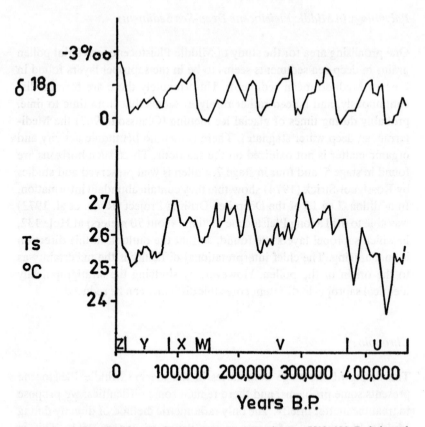

Figure 5.   A faunal estimate of summer temperature in core V12–122 (Imbrie and Kipp 1971) compared with the oxygen isotope record from the same core (by van Donk). The timescale is that of Broecker and van Donk (1969). This illustrates the long-term trends in temperature values obtained in this version of the faunal method; oxygen isotope records generally give the impression that each inter-glacial maximum, and each glacial minimum, is about the same. A later version of the faunal method (Imbrie, et al. 1973) displays a smaller long-term trend. The letters U, V, W, X, Y, Z represent the *Globorotalia menardii* zones, which were formerly regarded as climate-stratigraphic units, in this core.

The means which have been used to date the Upper Pleistocene section of the deep-sea record are outside the scope of this contribution. The age of stage 5, and particularly of the peak in substage 5e, is generally considered to be reliably dated at about 124,000 years on the basis of a number of different lines of reasoning (Broecker, et al. 1968; Broecker and van Donk 1970; Shackleton 1969; Duplessy et al. 1974; Shackleton and Opdyke 1973). Unfortunately, extrapolation from this point is not straightforward. Emiliani (1966) dated the oxygen isotope record by extrapolation (using a different age for stage 5) but there is a great deal

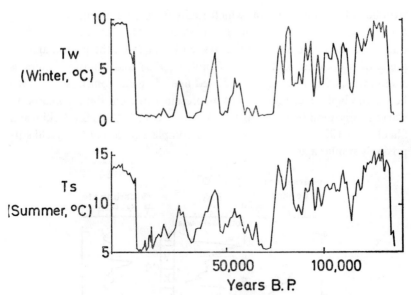

Figure 6. Faunal estimates of winter and summer temperature in core V23–82 (off Ireland), from Sancetta, et al. (1973). The timescale is based on Broecker and van Donk (1969). The record between about 75,000 and 125,000 years (see also Sancetta, et al. 1972) is particularly pertinent. This section is time-equivalent to stage 5 in core 280 from a similar latitude (illustrated in Figure 2) and shows the great variability of climate when looked at in detail. It appears that in this region there were episodes of extreme cold within the marine "interglacial" stage 5. The oceanographic changes documented (McIntyre, et al. 1972) about 110,000 years ago certainly did not occur within the Ipswichian Interglacial in Britain, which must have been terminated by this episode.

of evidence that there have been systematic longterm trends in sedimentation rate in the Caribbean, so that extrapolation is inescapably unreliable at least in this region (Emiliani and Shackleton 1974). A careful reading of the much quoted paper by Broecker and van Donk (1970), in which the estimated age of the U–V zone boundary was revised upwards from 320,000 years to 400,000 years, reveals that although further [230]Th determinations implied that the previous estimate was too low, the value actually adopted was based not on these determinations, nor on the very complete and reliable set of age determinations in the upper part of the core, V12–122, under discussion, but on interpolation in an entirely separate group of cores.

Since the first report of a magnetic reversal being located in a deep-sea sediment core, the application of paleomagnetic stratigraphy has revolutionized the stratigraphic study of Pleistocene and Tertiary sediments. There is little doubt that at present, it is only the lack of a reasonable number of complete and detailed sequences through to the

Brunhes Matuyama reversal which limits detailed agreement regarding ages in the Middle Pleistocene. In the Pacific, core V28–238 is the only one so far studied from both the oxygen isotope and the paleomagnetic point of view (Shackleton and Opdyke 1973) and although there is some evidence that some interpolated ages derived from this core may be on the high side, there is not at present sufficient data available to warrant any modification. In the Atlantic, core V23–100 (Parkin and Shackleton 1973) appears to contain a complete record and to yield surprisingly similar ages.

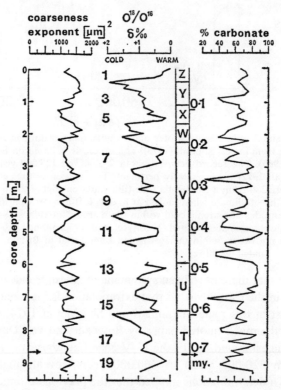

Figure 7. Variation in trade-wind strength, and oxygen isotope record, in Atlantic core V23–100 (Parkin and Shackleton 1973).

IMPLICATIONS FOR SEA-LEVEL VARIATIONS

Clearly if the record of oxygen isotope variations in the oceans through the Middle Pleistocene depicts changing ice volume on the continents, it also represents a glacio-eustatic sea-level curve. As such, it plainly has something to tell us. First, that the presence of raised marine terraces of

Middle Pleistocene age on many coasts is not due to there having been more water in the oceans. Thus it is probably due to coastal uplift. The exception to this statement concerns the beginning of stage 5, at which time it appears that some ice (Greenland or Antarctic) melted to increase ocean volume above the present value. Even on non-uplifted coasts a terrace of this age (about 120,000 years) is preserved, and has been dated in innumerable localities.

On a coast that is undergoing a fairly regular uplift, the use of the oxygen isotope record enables us not only to estimate the possible age ranges within which the preserved marine terraces must lie (roughly speaking, the odd-numbered stages in the record), but also enables us to estimate the relative altitudes to which the transgression or transgressions within each stage might be expected to have reached, and predicts to a certain degree the complexity within each stage.

On Barbados, Matthews (1973), has taken the opposite approach: taking carefully dated coral terraces at measured altitudes on several traverses, he has estimated the relative ocean volumes represented by the 80,000, 100,000, and 124,000 year old terraces. These estimates agree very well with the oxygen isotope data (Shackleton and Opdyke 1973). This agreement led the writer to speculate (Shackleton and Opdyke 1973: 50) that on most coasts the beaches deposited during stage 7 are unlikely to be preserved above later ones; if there is any

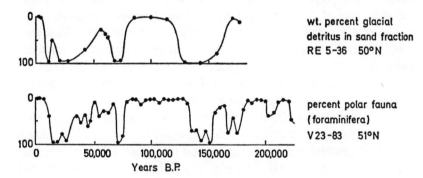

wt. percent glacial detritus in sand fraction
RE 5-36   50°N

percent polar fauna (foraminifera)
V 23-83   51°N

Years B.P.

Figure 8.   The record of events in the North Atlantic during the past 225,000 years, from McIntyre, et al. (1972). This detailed study documents elegantly the complex history of oceanographic changes over this time interval (ages derived from Broecker and van Donk 1969). The investigation has now been extended to cover the past 600,000 years (Ruddiman and McIntyre, unpublished materials). Although oxygen isotope stratigraphy is not available for any of the long cores described, there is very good internal stratigraphic control, and correlation with the oxygen isotope record seems secure. This may be attributed to the fact that the major oceanographic changes in this ocean are clearly directly linked with the advance of Northern ice sheets, as is the oxygen isotope record.

sense at all in the concept of a "penultimate interglacial" associated with a raised beach, it is older than stage 7. It may be interesting to consider this argument in more detail.

Let us consider a coast on which the transgression of 120,000 years ago reached 15 meters (e.g. parts of Majorca; Butzer, this volume: Table 2). Of this, 6 meters may be regarded as the "norm" for non-uplifted coasts (Broecker, et al. 1968), leaving 9 meters uplift in 120,000 years, a rate of 7.5 meters per 1,000 years. Let us consider the highest beach deposited in Stage 7, which should have an age around 220,000 years (about 380 centimeters in Figure 1), representing an uplift of 16.5 meters. Inspection of Figure 1 shows that there was probably still a little more ice on some continents during stage 7, as compared with the Holocene, so that the expected position of the terrace deposited at this time is somewhat less than 16.5 meters. Allowing (10 ± 5) meters for this difference predicts an altitude today of 5 ± 5 meters above present sea level. Agreement between this estimate and the observed height of the XI terrace cited by Butzer as having an age of $210,000 \pm 10,000$ years is excellent, suggesting that the assumption of uniform uplift is valid for this segment of time in Majorca. If we assume that this rate of uplift was preserved during the earlier part of the Middle Pleistocene, we may investigate the possible presence of deposits of stages 9 and 11. According to Figure 1, these should have ages about 330,000 and 420,000 years, representing uplifts of about 25 meters and 32 meters at this same rate of 7.5 meters per 1,000 years. The peaks at these points in Figure 1 are probably not significantly different from the Holocene peak, so that these figures are probably reasonable estimates for these stages. From these estimates it appears that while the altitudes cited for W2 and W3 in Butzer's table are entirely consistent with their having been deposited during stage 9, an alternative position in stage 11 might be considered for W1. On the other hand it is plain that there may well have been a gradual or sudden change in uplift rate, so that it would be pointless to extend the discussion beyond this stage. However, the fact that a projection of a rate of uplift established for the past 300,000 years back for somewhat over twice that interval implies that beaches over about 50 meters might be older than the Brunhes-Matuyama boundary, supports Butzer's suggestion that magnetic measurements should be made in these deposits.

A similar calculation may be made for the Mont Boron near Nice (de Lumley, this volume). The most significant and immediate result is that it is clear that the age of the beach in the back of the Grotte du Lazaret must be somewhat greather than generally assumed, as a stage 7 age is excluded by any reasonable estimates of uplift rate. Thus this beach probably has an age of about 330,000 years. Within the limits of resolution of this type of calculation, the position of the Terra Amata sequence seems to be entirely consistent with its spanning at least stages 13 and 11, and quite possibly stage 15 as well. Clearly this is a locality where a discontinuity in uplift rate is indicated, since the Grotte du Vallonet, situated over 100 meters above present sea level, is unlikely to be much older than 1 million years according to current thinking (uniform uplift would imply an age in excess of 1.5 million years). This may be taken as a warning as to the limitations of this approach.

REFERENCES

ARRHENIUS, G.
  1952 *Sediment cores from the East Pacific.* Reports of the Swedish Deep-Sea Expedition 5.
  1963 "Pelagic sediments," in *The Sea*, volume three. Edited by M. N. Hill, 655–727. New York and London: Interscience.
BERGER, W. H.
  1968 Planktonic foraminifera: selective solution and palaeoclimatic interpretation. *Deep-Sea Research* 15:31-43.
BERGER, W. H., G. R. HEATH
  1968 Vertical mixing in pelagic sediments. *Journal of Marine Research* 26:134–142.
BROECKER, W. S.
  1971 "Calcite accumulation rates and glacial to interglacial changes in oceanic mixing," in *The Late Cenozoic glacial ages.* Edited by K. K. Turekian, 239–265. New Haven: Yale University Press.
BROECKER, W. S., D. L. THURBER, J. GODDARD, T-L. KU, R. K. MATTHEWS, K. J. MESOLELLA
  1968 Milankovitch hypothesis supported by precise dating of coral reefs and deep-sea sediments. *Science* 159:297–300.
BROECKER, W. S., J. VAN DONK
  1970 Insolation changes, ice volumes, and the O^{18} record in deep-sea cores. *Reviews of Geophysics and Space Physics* 8:169–198.
DANSGAARD, W., H. TAUBER
  1969 Glacier oxygen-18 content and Pleistocene ocean temperatures. *Science* 166:499–502.
DUPLESSY, J. C., C. LALOU, A. C. VINOT
  1970 Differential isotopic fractionation in benthic foraminifera and palaeotemperatures reassessed. *Science* 168:250–251.
DUPLESSY, J. C., L. CHENOUARD, J. L. REYSS
  1974 Paléotemperatures isotopiques de l'Atlantique Equatorial. *Col. loque Centre National de la Recherche Scientifique* 219:251–258.
EMILIANI, C.
  1955 Pleistocene temperatures. *Journal of Geology* 63:149–158.

1958   Palaeotemperature analysis of core 280 and Pleistocene correlations. *Journal of Geology* 66:264–275.

1966   Palaeotemperature analysis of Caribbean cores P 6304-8 and P 6304-9 and a generalized temperature curve for the last 425,000 years. *Journal of Geology* 74: 109–126.

1972   Quaternary paleotemperatures and the duration of the high-temperature intervals. *Science* 178:398–401.

EMILIANI, C., N. J. SHACKLETON
1974   The Brunhes epoch: isotopic paleotemperatures and geochronology. *Science* 183:511–514.

ERICSON, D. B., G. WOLLIN
1956a Micropalaeontological and isotopic determinations of Pleistocene climates. *Micropalaeontology* 2:257–270.

1956b Correlation of six cores from the Equatorial Atlantic and the Caribbean. *Deep-Sea Research* 3:104–125.

1964   *The deep and the past.* London: Cape.

ERICSON, D. B., M. EWING, G. WOLLIN
1964   The Pleistocene epoch in deep-sea sediments. *Science* 146:723–732.

GARTNER, S.
1972   Late Pleistocene calcareous nannofossils in the Caribbean and their interoceanic correlation. *Palaeogeography, Palaeoclimatology, Palaeoecology* 12:169–191.

GLASS, B., D. B. ERICSON, B. C. HEEZEN, N. D. OPDYKE, J. A. GLASS
1967   Geomagnetic reversals and Pleistocene chronology. *Nature* 216:437–442.

HAYS, J. D., T. SAITO, N. D. OPDYKE, L. H. BURCKLE
1969   Pliocene-Pleistocene sediments of the Equatorial Pacific: their palaeomagnetic, biostratigraphic, and climatic record. *Geological Society of America Bulletin* 80:1481–1514.

HAYS, J. D., A. PERUZZA
1972   The significance of calcium carbonate oscillations in eastern Equatorial Atlantic deep-sea sediments for the end of the Holocene warm interval. *Quaternary Research* 2:355–362.

IMBRIE, J., N. G. KIPP
1971   "A new micropalaeontological method for quantitative palaeoclimatology: application to a late Pleistocene Caribbean core," in *The late Cenozoic glacial ages.* Edited by K. K. Turekian, 71–183. New Haven: Yale University Press.

IMBRIE, J., J. VAN DONK, N. G. KIPP
1973   Oxygen isotope and palaeomagnetic stratigraphy of Equatorial Pacific core V28–238. *Quaternary Research* 3:10–38.

KENNETT, J. P., P. HUDDLESTON
1972   Late Pleistocene palaeoclimatology, foraminiferal biostratigraphy and tephrochronology, western Gulf of Mexico. *Quaternary Research* 2:38–69.

KU, T-L., J. L. BISCHOFF, A. BOERSMA
1972   Age studies of mid-Atlantic ridge sediments near 42°N and 20°N. *Deep-Sea Research* 19:233–247.

KULLENBERG, B.
1947   The piston core sampler. *Svenska Hydrografisk-Biologiska Kommissionens Skrifter*, Band 1, Heft 2. Tredje Series.

LIDZ, L.
1966   Deep-sea Pleistocene biostratigraphy. *Science* 154:1448–1452.

LUZ, B.
1973   Stratigraphic and palaeoclimatic analysis of late Pleistocene tropical southeast Pacific cores. *Quaternary Research* 3:56–72.

MATTHEWS, R. K.
1973   Relative elevation of late Pleistocene high sea level stands: Barbados uplift rates and their implications. *Quaternary Research* 3: 147–153.

MC INTYRE, A., W. F. RUDDIMAN, R. JANTZEN
1972   Southward penetrations of the North Atlantic polar front: faunal and floral evidence of large-scale surface water mass movements over the last 225,000 years. *Deep-Sea Research* 19:61–77.

OLAUSSON, E.
1965   Evidence of climatic changes in North Atlantic deep-sea cores, with remarks on isotopic palaeotemperature analysis. *Progress in Oceanography* 3:221–252.
1967   Climatological, geoeconomical and paleooceanographical aspects on carbonate deposition. *Progress in Oceanography* 5:245-265.

PARKIN, D. W., N. J. SHACKLETON
1973   Trade wind and temperature correlations down a deep-sea core off the Saharan coast. *Nature* 245:455–457.

ROSSIGNOL-STRICK, M.
1974   Analyse pollinique de sapropèles Quaternaires marins en Méditerranée Orientale. *Colloque C.N.R.S.* 219:93–102.

RUDDIMAN, W. F., A. MC INTYRE
1975   Northeast Atlantic paleoclimatic changes over the last 600,000 years. *Geological Society of America Memoir* 145.

RYAN, W. B. F., K. J. HSU, et al.
1973   *Initial reports of the deep-sea drilling project*, volume thirteen. Washington, D.C.: U.S. Government Printing Office.

SANCETTA, C., et al.
1972   Climatic record of North Atlantic deep-sea core V23–82: comparison of the last and present interglacials based on quantitative time series. *Quaternary Research* 2:363–367.

SANCETTA, C., J. IMBRIE, N. KIPP
1973   Climatic record of the past 130,000 years in North Atlantic deep-sea core V23–82: correlation with the terrestrial record. *Quaternary Research* 3:110–116.

SHACKLETON, N. J.
1967   Oxygen isotope analyses and Pleistocene temperatures re-assessed. *Nature* 215:15–17.

1969   The last interglacial in the marine and terrestrial records. *Proceedings of the Royal Society London*, B, 174:135–154.
SHACKLETON, N. J., N. D. OPDYKE
1973   Oxygen isotope and palaeomagnetic stratigraphy of Equatorial Pacific core V28–238. *Quaternary Research* 3:39–55.
SILVA, A. J., C. D. HOLLISTER
1973   Geotechnical properties of ocean sediment recovered with Giant Piston Corer, part one: Gulf of Maine. *Journal of Geophysical Research* 78:3597–3616.

Pleistocene Littoral-Sedimentary Cycles of the Mediterranean Basin: A Mallorquin View

KARL W. BUTZER

De Tempé la vallée un jour sera montagne
et la cyme d'Athos une large campagne,
Neptune quelque fois de blé sera couvert,
la matière démeure mais la forme se perd.

PIERRE DE RONSARD (1524–1585)

ABSTRACT

Littoral-sedimentary cycles are defined for the Mallorquin coast. Each consists of a marine hemicycle with superimposed transgressive beaches and interbeach, argillic paleosols, followed by a continental hemicycle comprising several sets of colluvial silts, each followed by an eolianite and interrupted or followed by pedocal formation. The Pleistocene sequence of Mallorca is revised with 6 littoral-sedimentary cycles (marine hemicycles Z-U, continental hemicycles A-F, identified and partly calibrated by uranium-series dating. The last (Y) and next-to-last (X) marine hemicycles date 125,000–75,000 and about 220,000–180,000 B.P. respectively, but the Senegalese *Strombus* fauna first appeared no later than 220,000 B.P. and was eliminated shortly after 100,000 B.P. during a cool, minor regression at which time the last relict *terra rossas* of the Mediterranean Basin formed. Various paleoenvironmental interpretations and implications are discussed. Finally, the Mallorquin cycles are correlated with the Mediterranean pollen stratigraphy and deep-sea cores, with the Moroccan coastal sequence, and with the Rhine terraces and central European loesses.

This paper would not have been possible without repeated discussions I have enjoyed with Charles Stearns (Tufts University) and continued field collaboration with my dear friend and colleague Juan Cuerda (Palma de Mallorca). The illustrations were drafted by Douglas B. Cargo and C. Mueller-Wille.

INTRODUCTION

Many coastal sectors of the Mediterranean Basin record well-defined cyclical sequences of marine and terrestrial deposits. These cycles consist of (a) protracted transgressive intervals, marked by superimposed oscillations and leading to shore erosion or deposition at multiple levels near and above modern sea level; and (b) equally protracted and complex regressive intervals during which several generations of terrestrial deposits accumulated near or seaward of the contemporary littoral zone. These cycles were primarily generated by glacial-eustatic fluctuations of the sea level, although the specific facies of transgressive or regressive phenomena reflect on environmental changes. Isotopic composition of shell or deep-sea oozes, ecological interpretation of molluscan faunas, and radiometric correlations all show that, since late Lower Pleistocene times, transgressions marked planetary interglacial climates while regressions reflected glacial regimes. The facies shifts and environmental changes accompanying local development of the associated sedimentary cycles are clearly patterned and, in their essential characteristics, repetitive. Consequently, the sedimentary sequences have direct bearing on the direction and nature of environmental change on a regional or hemispheric scale.

In the ideal case, these cyclic sedimentary patterns of the Mediterranean littorals provide a means of deciphering complex, sequential change representative of the regional ecosystem. In other words, the cycles are comparable in scope to the traditional glacial and loess sequences or to the more recent deep-sea stratigraphies. Although "high" sea levels have been studied and correlated for many decades, the results have been far from satisfactory. This apparent impasse has been due to the prevailing emphasis on altimetry of isolated beaches and, above all, to the neglect of interrelated terrestrial sediments. An integrated approach to the study of littoral sedimentary sequences can first be recognized in the 1930's fieldwork of Blanc in Italy and of Neuville and Ruhlmann in Morocco and, during the 1940's and 1950's, by investigations along the Gulf-Atlantic coastal plains of the United States and in the Mediterranean Basin (Mallorca, the Provence, Lebanon, Tunisia, and Algeria). Nonetheless, the full stratigraphic and paleoenvironmental implications of a holistic and systematic approach to unraveling cyclic sedimentary patterns have not been fully exploited, and littoral sequences today play a minor role in hemispheric assessments of the Pleistocene record.

The traditional stratigraphic approach applied through most of the

Mediterranean Basin has been based on a suite of successively lower marine transgressions, reflecting on glacial-eustatic oscillations presumably superimposed on a declining late Cenozoic sea level. Such transgressive shorelines were identified on the basis of relative or absolute elevation, molluscan and other faunas, artifactual associations, and, more recently, on radiometric dating. Evidence of local deformation was possibly circumvented by more rigorous morphostratigraphic fieldwork, but an implicit belief in the temporal implications of absolute sea-level stages persists quite widely. When the evidence did begin to point to multiple, oscillating sea levels during each "stage", some of these being repeated at similar elevations during different stages (Butzer and Cuerda 1962a, 1962b), it became necessary to reexamine the assumptions made to establish the simple, downward progressions of "terraces" described from almost all coastal sectors. Yet this work of reassessment has been curiously lagging in the Mediterranean Basin, despite rapid advances in the study of a few other world coastal areas. In general, the great majority of the regional Mediterranean sequences outlined at the Eighth INQUA Congress (*Quaternaria* 15 [1972]) are incredibly simplistic. In particular, archeological sites continue to be "dated" with reference to shorelines that are at best controversial.

Theoretically, littoral sedimentary sequences can be studied along most coastal sectors of the Mediterranean Basin. However, complex faulting and folding unnecessarily complicate the record in unstable areas such as the Provence, much of Italy, Greece, and Anatolia. Major rivers may provide invaluable complementary information, but their study is difficult, and few deltaic, estuarine, or alluvial sequences are without their major lacunae, and controversy is generally rampant. The best examples, therefore, come from depositional coasts of low to moderate relief, interrupted by few large streams, and preferentially with limestone bedrock: a calcareous environment provides opportunity for cementing beach deposits, retards leaching of lime sands and mollusca, and provides more biogenic sands for eolian processes. Two such cases are the Atlantic littoral of Morocco and the Balearic island of Mallorca.

Clear indications of informative Pleistocene sequences on Mallorca were first provided by Muntaner-Darder (1957) and Cuerda (1957). During the years 1959–62 the writer consequently spent seven months studying the Mallorquin Pleistocene, much of this work in close collaboration with Juan Cuerda. A complex suite of transgressions was recognized, fortunately related directly or indirectly to at least nine major generations of terrestrial deposits. This scheme, as described in 1961–

62 — prior to the completion of the field and laboratory work, map and air photo interpretation, and radiometric dating — can be summarized as follows (Butzer and Cuerda 1960, 1962a, 1962b, 1962c; Butzer 1962):

Minor Holocene Transgressions (+2–4 meters)

"Last" Regression (three phases)

Tyrrhenian III Transgression (+0.5–2.8 meters)

Minor Regression

Tyrrhenian IIb Transgression (successive, apparent sea levels at +8–9 meters, +6–7.5 meters and +2–4 meters)

Tyrrhenian IIa Transgression (+10.5–12.5 meters)

"Penultimate" Regression (four phases)

Tyrrhenian I Transgressive Complex (successive, apparent sea levels at +33–34 meters, +29–30 meters, +23–25 meters, +15.5–19 meters, and +4–5 meters)

"Antepenultimate" Regression (two phases)

Pre-Tyrrhenian Transgressions (successive, apparent sea levels at +100–110 meters, +70–72 meters, +60–62 meters, and +48–50 meters)

This summation paid little attention to the early Pleistocene record. Furthermore, the interrelationships of most beach deposits with terrestrial deposits were primarily based on horizontal rather than vertical stratigraphic links. Subsequently, some fifteen Th/U dates were obtained for Mallorca (Stearns and Thurber 1965, 1967; Stearns 1970, n.d.; also Kaufman, et al. 1971), the largest number yet from a restricted area with reasonably good stratigraphic control (see Table 1). No matter how much or how little confidence was placed in these shell dates, they indicated that the Butzer and Cuerda scheme of Tyrrhenian I, II, and III was basically sound, but that the Tyrrhenian II may have been even more complex than we had anticipated in our once controversial revision of the Mediterranean sea level stratigraphy. Further study of new sites on the southwestern coast of Mallorca (Cuerda and Sacarés 1965, 1966) simultaneously provided direct links for beach and terrestrial deposits in the mid-Pleistocene time range, adding important precisions to our original scheme. Finally, a decade of continuing geomorphological and paleobiological research by various workers in many parts of the Mediterranean Basin required a reassessment of the assumptions underlying our interpretations.

In view of these concurrent developments, the seventy site stratigraphies studied by the writer on Mallorca, Ibiza, and Formentera were critically reevaluated. The results leave no doubt that the Mallorquin record is of unique significance in the Mediterranean Basin, matching that of Atlantic Morroco, as well as that of Latium and Tuscany.

CYCLIC SEDIMENTARY PATTERNS OF THE MEDITERRANEAN LITTORAL

The Sedimentary Cycle Defined

Stated in basically descriptive terms, the standard sedimentary cycle of the Mallorquin littoral can be outlined as follows:

a.   BEACH deposits, commonly with one or more thermophile molluscan species, normally resting on several abrasional benches at distinct levels. These are considered to represent several transgressive oscillations superimposed on a single, "positive" sine curve of sea level, unless separated by a major unit of eolian sands. In at least several instances such beaches transgress over reddish, argillic soil profiles that imply pedogenesis of clayey paleosols during the minor regressive oscillations. The marine deposits *per se* include strict beach or nearshore sands and sandy conglomerates with marine fauna, terrestrial silts with mixed marine and terrestrial mollusca, and interbedded, backshore eolian sands or colluvial beds with terrestrial mollusca. Such beach deposits are normally cemented, with secondary calcite recrystallization common; sometimes they show evidence of laminated microlenticles or capping crusts of caliche; occasionally, they are overlain by amorphous calcite, rich in colloidal silica, and contain peds of reworked soil aggregates; rarely, caliche crusts or massive calcite lenses may grade laterally into banded, vertically crystallized tufas or travertines.
b.   COLLUVIAL horizons of crudely stratified silty or clayey sediments are sometimes interbedded with, and generally overlie terminal transgressive beach deposits. These materials include terrestrial mollusca, *terra rossa* soil derivatives, or other rubefied, pedogenetic residues, as well as fresh, angular bedrock debris; they form extensive swale and slope veneers or mantles. Whereas typical colluvia are readily attributed to sheetwash, with ancillary creep or slow earthflow movements, such "red silts" (*limons rouges*) may grade laterally into linear channels with

true alluvial deposits and abundant crude detritus, or into pale, massive-bedded silts with vertical ("loessic") structure but lacking the strong, coarse-silt maxima and associated good sorting of true loess. They also commonly include bedrock rubble to some degree or other. Colluvial silts are characteristically cemented with calcite, or they show calcareous concretions and terminal development of laminated crusts. Although colluvial silts may be found at all elevations, possibly grading upwards into "periglacial" screes, in coastal proximity their gradients can commonly be projected to below modern sea level.

c.   Cemented EOLIAN deposits, consisting predominantly of ground-up marine shell, normally rest on colluvial silts and extend from below modern sea level well inland. These "eolianites" contain terrestrial mollusca, show dunal topography, and in the case of well-sorted bioclastic sand grains, exhibit crossbeds of topset/backset and foreset stratification. Many eolianites form part of a conformable sequence underlain by beach deposits and colluvial silts, and the basal sands are very coarse grained in such cases, including large, abraded fragments of marine shell. More often than not, several generations of eolianites are represented, in each case grading down into colluvial silts that rest on cemented or rubefied interfaces. Such multiple silts and eolianites are best considered indicative of regressive oscillations superimposed on a single, "negative" sine curve of sea level.

Beach Deposits and Associated Phenomena

Interpretation of the beach deposits involves comparatively little controversy.

a.   The presence of locally extinct, Senegalese mollusca in many "high" beaches has traditionally been interpreted as indicating Mediterranean surface waters at least as warm as those of today; furthermore, the migration of these Senegalese forms through the now cool, upwelling waters of the Moroccan Atlantic coast presupposes readjustment or modification of the major ocean currents. Other beaches, lacking in Senegaleze forms *sensu stricto*, commonly include one or other mollusca that, in the western Mediterranean, are presently rare and near their northernmost limit of distribution. This established habit of equating "high" sea levels with interglacial climates has subsequently found support in the oxygen isotopic composition of associated mollusca from a large variety of sites and stages, while the cooler surface waters of the intervening regressions is now clearly shown by isotopic temperatures and foraminiferal composition of mollusca and deep sea sediments (see, for example, Emiliani and Mayeda 1964; Vergnaud-Grazzini and Herman-Rosenberg 1969; Letolle, et al. 1971).

b. Genesis of deep, red, argillic soils, whether *terra rossa*s on calcareous bedrock (see Durand 1959), or red-yellow podsolics on silicate parent materials (see Fränzle 1965), continues to be linked to periods of very moist (even if markedly seasonal) and warm climate in the Pleistocene, in default of any substantive evidence of comparably intensive, hydrolytic weathering in Holocene contexts (see also discussion by Vaudour 1972). On Mallorca three episodes of *terra rossa* pedogenesis on eolianite parent material can be demonstrated, during minor regressive intervals late within three different transgressions (see below); Holocene pedogenesis on identical parent materials has produced nothing more than rendzina profiles. Similar stratigraphic context and pedogenetic properties have also been described from eolianite paleosols on Bermuda (Ruhe, et al. 1961) and Madeira (Lietz and Schwarzbach 1971).

c. The development of calcrete phenomena such as lenticular caliche, capping calcareous crusts, amorphous calcite sediments, or general cementation remains a highly controversial subject. Durand (1959) outlined five major types of genesis, each of which has specific validity in one situation or another, and Butzer (1963a) suggested two additional subtypes. There can be no question that laminated tufas are or were deposited directly as primary sediments by subaerial runoff in such diverse environments as Algeria, the Libyan Desert, South Africa, and northeastern Brazil (see Durand 1959; Butzer and Hansen 1968: Chapter 7; Butzer 1974b). Several subcontemporary instances of organic, valley floor tufas can also be cited from northeastern Mallorca, where algal tufas are still being deposited in some perennial streams. Nonetheless, the writer's subsequent experience in the southwestern United States and South Africa showed that our initial interpretation of the lenticular caliche and calcareous crusts of Mallorca incorrectly downplayed the role of vertical, and above all lateral, translocation of carbonates well within the subsoil; such Ca-horizons become surface duricrusts only after erosion of the overlying A-horizon. Consequently, the diverse Mallorquin examples must be attributed to a multiplicity of factors such as pedogenetic carbonate horizons, to primary, subaerial or subaqueous sedimentation, and in some instances to the equally controversial formation of "beach rock". Our initial argument (Butzer 1963a, following Durand 1959), was that these calcretes, whatever their origin, spoke for morphostatic conditions — with soil development outweighing the effects of geomorphic denudation. This argument still holds.

Colluvial Silts

Interpretation of the colluvial silts or *limons rouges* has necessarily been modified during the last decade as a result of ongoing palynological studies of Pleistocene vegetation in the Mediterranean Basin (see below) and by interdisciplinary study of loessic sediments.

a. As originally argued (Butzer 1963a), colluvial silts reflect extensive, accelerated denudation accompanied by sheetwashing and valley alluviation, by streams with a greater competence than today. Such deposits reflect on a drastic rupture of geomorphic "steady state", inaugurating a morphodynamic pattern of landscape evolution, as first conceived by Erhart (1956). Any explanation must allow for (1) greater rainfall intensity to permit effective erosion; (2) rainfalls of sufficient duration to permit thorough soaking of the soil, extended transportation by sheetwash, and greater stream competence; and (3) a pronounced dry season, to account for the incomplete nature of the vegetation mat. A simple decrease of temperature will not reduce the proportion of evaporative losses for heavy rainfalls of the type that produce sheetwash. Consequently, the accelerated geomorphic processes indicated by the colluvial silts of the Mediterranean Basin require a change of rainfall regime, with more frequent rainstorms of high intensity and considerable duration. Nonetheless, palynological evidence (Frank 1969; Wijmstra 1969; Florschütz, et al. 1971) shows that an open semiarid vegetation had largely replaced the Mediterranean woodlands at the times that colluvial silts were accumulating. This now firmly rules out a "pluvial" interpretation, by demonstrating that absolute precipitation must have been substantially less.

b. Loess has been periodically claimed from various parts of the Mediterranean lowlands, primarily on the basis of massive silty deposits with prismatic structure and vertical cleavage. Such loessic sediments from Mallorca and Catalonia have already been discussed by the writer (Butzer 1963a: Table 3; Butzer 1964b: 39ff.): textural spectra are all poorly sorted, with some 53–61 percent of the samples in the 2–60 micron grade, and 15–37 percent sands in the 60–2000 micron size class. Brunnacker and Ložek (1969) studied other profiles in Catalonia and southeastern Spain, identifying a wide range of sediments as loesses, although only 40–75 percent in the 2–60 micron grade.

Mechanically, almost all of the Spanish examples cited fall outside of the range of even "deluvial", stratified slope loesses as defined by Pecsi (1965), while a comprehensive study of loessic sediments in the lower Illinois Valley (Butzer, unpublished) shows that redeposited, colluvial loesses range from 60–90 percent in the 6–63 micron grade. In our opinion the Spanish loesses, despite their "loess mollusca", are colluvial silts with a significant but not necessarily dominant component of reworked, eolian dust. In our own experience, these are littoral phenomena that may intergrade laterally with silty eolianites. Where studied by Brunnacker and Ložek (1969), the Catalonian lowland examples are attributed to deflation from dry stream beds, while those from the Granadine highlands are ascribed to deflation from a postulated, montane "periglacial" environment. Whatever the problems of terminology and genesis, these semieolian silts with loessic structure underscore the relatively arid nature of the environment contemporary with the colluvial silts. It is, however, premature to posit correlations between the paleosols identified from such loessic sediments and the loess paleosols of mid-latitude Europe.

Eolianites

Interpretation of eolianites has traditionally invoked deflation of freshly exposed marine sediments during glacio-eustatic regressions. In many coastal areas such eolianites extend to well below sea level, and they frequently occur along coasts that have no beach sands today. In the Mallorquin case, eolianites are frequently found in conformable sequences, with eolianites resting on top of silts and beach deposits. Median diameter tends to decrease with time in vertical sections, while multiple eolianite generations within one hemicycle commonly become finer grained. Finally, eolianites of a single cycle are finer grained inland than they are in modern coastal proximity. For these reasons, all or almost all of the Mallorquin eolianites can only be considered as regressional rather than transgressional (Butzer 1962, 1963a), and they are correlated with the major episodes of rapid glacier growth. In this way, successive eolianite generations within each regressive hemicycle would reflect the several key phases of glacier advance during a single glacial complex.

Land, et al. (1967) and Vacher (1973) have recently argued that the comparable eolianites of Bermuda accumulated at times of relatively high sea level and that, furthermore, they are of interglacial age. Lietz and Schwarzbach (1971), on the basis of their Madeira work, have shown that the arguments for an interglacial interpretation are at best ambiguous, and we concur with all points of their counterargument. Particularly convincing are C^{14} dates of 21,570 and 13,480 B.P. from Madeira eolianites (Lietz and Schwarzbach 1971). However, we do not claim that all eolianites are regressional, and some South African examples indeed formed as dune cordons in front of a transgressive sea (Butzer and Helgren 1972). Similarly, we agree that deflation was most active just as sea level began to fall, and that deflation ceased when the shoreline dropped below the outer margin of the continental shelf. Finally, there are well-developed coastal dunes in parts of Mallorca during the present, transgressive stages of the Holocene "interglacial". Nonetheless, the Bermudan evidence offers no general rule why Mediterranean eolianites should be of interglacial rather than glacial age.

Marine and Continental Hemicycles

For our purposes here, an informal nomenclature of marine and continental hemicycles is proposed. Marine hemicycles are numbered Z, Y, X, etc., backwards from the Holocene transgressions (Z), along with multiple, subsidiary, arabic numbers (Z1, Z2, etc.). Similarly, continental hemicycles are numbered A, B, C, etc., backwards from the Holocene coastal dunes (A) and Upper Pleistocene (B) silt-and-eolianite complexes; subsidiary numbers are used for each generation (B1, B2, etc.) within a single hemicycle.

BASIC MALLORQUIN SEDIMENTARY CYCLES

The Banc d'Ibiza Profile

The most complete Pleistocene sequence known from the Balearic Islands is found west of Palma de Mallorca on the peninsula known as Banc d'Ibiza (Figure 1). Brief mention of these exposures is made by Muntaner-Darder (1957) and Solé-Sabarís (1962). They were studied by Butzer and Juan Cuerda in 1961–1962 (unpublished), and the stratigraphy can be summarized as follows, the deposits resting disconformably on late Miocene limestones (Figure 2):

a. OVER 15 METERS Alternating beds of white to very pale brown

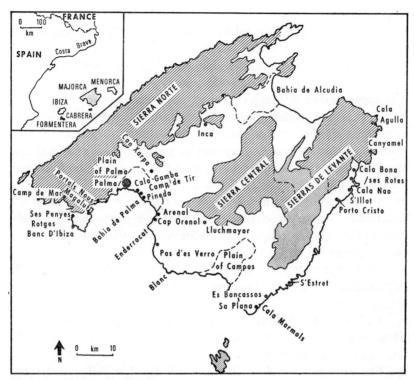

Figure 1. The Island of Mallorca

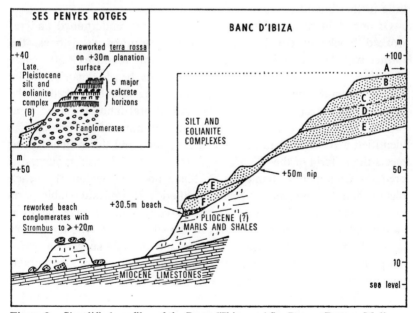

Figure 2. Simplified profiles of the Banc d'Ibiza and Ses Penyes Rotges, Mallorca

marly limestones and light yellow-brown to red-yellow shales; mainly massive bedded, with units 0.6–3.0 meters thick, including one thin-bedded, topmost limestone. The calcareous beds have proliferations of oysters (*Ostrea* cf. *mirabilis*) and *Pecten jacobeus*. Moderately warped, and upper contact disconformable.

b. 1 METER Conglomerate of flat, well-rounded pebbles and some subangular rubble, with a matrix of red-yellow silty sandstone, and containing *Patella ferruginea*, *Spondylus gaederopus*, and derived oysters. This bed pinches out at a little above 30.5 meters above modern sea level. Followed by erosional contact.

c. 5.5 METERS (Continental Hemicycle F). Minor sand and silts units followed by two major eolianites, separated by a major silt. As all subsequent deposits, these beds are undeformed and rise inland. Followed by planation with cutting of a +50 meter littoral nip.

d. 7.8 METERS (Continental Hemicycle E). A major silt with *Helix* impressions, followed by three major eolianites with two minor, intervening silt units.

e. 12.3 METERS (Continental Hemicycles C and D, incomplete). Three major eolianites, each resting conformably on silts with caliche lenticles or crude detritus.

f. 4.6 METERS (Continental Hemicycle B). Silt followed by one major eolianite. Unconsolidated, Holocene cover sands (A) are found a little further inland.

Of uncertain relationship to this sequence are undermined and reworked blocks of conglomerate and well-stratified sandstones, the former with *Strombus bubonius*. These are now found to +20 meters elevation, and represent the highest *Strombus* beach deposits of the Balearic Islands; unfortunately they cannot be directly linked to the continental deposits. However, a younger littoral fauna is mixed in at the base of a fossil talus apron at +2 meters; none of the five species identified here pertains to the Senegalese fauna, and this beach deposit meets the criteria of the "Tyrrhenian III"; field relationships suggest it predates Continental Hemicycle B. Since no "Tyrrhenian II" beach higher than +15 meters has been identified in tectonically stable parts of Mallorca, the +20 meter *Strombus* conglomerate may be even earlier, although stratigraphic links to the silt and eolianite complexes cannot be reconstructed. The +50 meter nip strongly suggests a wave-cut platform, and similar, extensive slope inflections accompany other, unequivocal +50 meter shorelines on Mallorca. The +30.5 meter beach (b) is indisputable and represents one of the very oldest Pleistocene littoral deposits of the Balearic Islands. Finally, the marly limestones and shales (a) constitute a classic epicontinental sequence that could be either of Pliocene or Pleistocene age; its vertical development remains to be studied, and foraminiferal analysis may provide more precise biostratigraphic definition.

The Banc d'Ibiza provides a unique record for five major, littoral sedimentary cycles. On the basis of intensive study around the circumference of the Bahia de Palma, the continental Complex B pertains to a variety of outcrops of poorly developed, post-"Tyrrhenian III" deposits of Upper Pleistocene age, while Complex D is identical to the "Gran Duna", immediately underlying the "Tyrrhenian II" beaches. By extrapolation, Complex E must be related to the silts and eolianites underlying "Tyrrhenian I" beaches at Cap Orenol and Sa Plana, although the record of three major eolianites at Banc d'Ibiza is the most complete known so far. Finally, Complex F appears to be unique in the Balearic Pleistocene.

Assuming that the Banc d'Ibiza gives a reasonably representative Pleistocene marine-littoral sequence for Mallorca, the earliest transgressive deposits and subsequent eolianite appear to find parallels at Pas d'es Verro, some 6 kilometers south of Cap Enderrocat. Here a +70 meter beach sand, dominated by *Patella ferruginea, Ostrea* sp., *and Glycimeris violacescens*, was followed by a massive eolianite complex, and then by cutting of marine caves at +90 meters into this eolianite (Cuerda and Sacarés 1966, 1971). Cuerda and Sacarés (1965, 1966) have conclusively shown that this sector of coastal Miocene has been uparched 30 meters, at the very least, along the southwest-northeast anticline followed by the Mallorquin central sierras, although deformation of the late Cenozoic abrasional surfaces is much less readily quantified. However, if a differential uplift of 40 meters were assumed, the +30 and +70 meter *Patella ferruginea* beaches at Banc d'Ibiza and Pas d'es Verro are equalized, the subsequent eolianite complex becomes coeval, and the +50 meter marine platforms and grottoes at Banc d'Ibiza, in the Plain of Palma (Can Sharpa: see Butzer and Cuerda 1962b), and in the stable, southernmost part of Mallorca (Butzer 1962) can be correlated with the identical forms in +90 meter at Pas d'es Verro. Nonetheless, beaches at +35 meters and lower elevations are readily traced, as morphological forms, from one sector of the island to the next, and we can conclude that any Pleistocene warping had ceased before that time.

Piedmont Alluvia of the Sierra Norte

Important, complementary information for the early Pleistocene time
range is provided by continental sequences exposed by the cliffs of Ses
Penyes Rotges and Portals Nous, as well as by borings around Palma.
The Ses Penyes Rotges section, first referred to by Muntaner-Darder
(1957: 91, and folding map), was examined by the writer in 1960 (see
Butzer 1964a). A simplified, as yet unpublished, section is given in
Figure 2 and the basic units can be outlined as follows:

a.   OVER 19 METERS   Coarse, angular to subangular conglomerate of
Mesozoic limestone detritus, with a matrix of red-yellow silts and
sands, interrupted by lenses of finer texture but by no major disconformities, despite the presence of a large channel in section. The gravels
and cobbles are intensively corroded, and were to a large extent mechanically fractured during or after transport, although rounding increases noticeably in the upper half of the deposit (Butzer 1964a). In
addition to general cementation, the top one meter is conspicuously
calcreted with caliche development.

b.   4.5 METERS   Red-yellow siltstone interrupted by one caliche horizon and capped by a second.

c.   3.5 METERS   Red-yellow, gravelly siltstone, capped by major caliche horizon. Pebbles intensively corroded.

d.   2 METERS   Pink, sandy siltstone with caliche, and truncated lower
B horizon of red-yellow color.

e.   VENEER   Red, clayey siltstone, derived from a *terra rossa* soil.

The surface of the Ses Penyes Rotges exposure is planed off at +30
meters, although this platform cannot be linked with any unequivocal
marine features. It is, however, locally overlain by over 5 meters of
eolianite complex C or D, while complex B deposits are elsewhere em-
banked against the face of the cliffs. Consequently, the above sequence
antedates the "Tyrrhenian I" and the related *terra rossa* paleosol. Although beds (b) to (d) may relate to complex E at Banc d'Ibiza — only
2.2 kilometers south — the frost-shattered fanglomeratic deposits (a)
find no link with the littoral-epicontinental sequence. However, more
complex intergradations of fanglomerates and eolianites are apparent
at Portals Nous and will potentially elucidate that aspect of the record.
Rohdenburg and Sabelberg (1972) have studied the Ses Penyes Rotges
section in detail (but have not published their findings), and claim the
existence of well over thirty paleosols, almost exclusively Ca-horizons.
The significance of these features remains to be scrutinized, although we
lack confidence that any such caliches can be correlated with specific

mid-latitude European paleosols, as is implied by Rohdenburg and Sabelberg (1972).

A more complex record of continental deposits than that of Ses Penyes Rotges is suggested by bore profiles from below the plain of Palma (Muntaner-Darder 1954, 1957: 88ff.). The log data indicate that the bedrock base of this alluvial plain is at variable depths, with as much as 118 meters of Pleistocene (and Pliocene?, see Colom [1967]) sediments overlying Miocene limestones and calcarenites. The deepest boring, from Palma itself, reached bedrock at –113.5 meters and rudimentary sediment identifications are as follows, from top to bottom (Muntaner-Darder 1954):

a. 1.5 METERS   Marine-littoral deposits, including gravels and eolianite.
b. 3 METERS   Brown red sandy clays.
c. 4 METERS   Gravelly alluvium.
d. 6 METERS   Clays with caliche horizons.
e. 10 METERS   Alluvium alternating with gravelly sands and conglomerates.
f. 89 METERS   Red sandy clays.

Unfortunately, the writer was not privileged to carry out a detailed study of this boring, which has since been destroyed. Poorly, if at all, represented in this profile are the surface fanglomerates of the plain of Palma which have conspicuous terrace morphology in the foothills, and which interfinger with eolianites that are locally weathered by a *terra rossa* soil and elsewhere overlapped by "Tyrrhenian II/III" beaches. At Inca these same fanglomerates, weathered by a relict *terra rossa* soil, rest on older fanglomerates with a deep *terra rossa* paleosol that has a truncated B/BC/CCa profile over 2.7 meters thick, and which is best correlated with the "Tyrrhenian I" soils elsewhere.

In overview, including Ses Penyes Rotges and Portals Nous, where at least two *terra rossa* paleosols interrupt the alluvial sequence, there are no fewer than three major complexes of fanglomeratic deposits in the piedmont of the Sierra Norte. Each dates from marine regressions older than the "Tyrrhenian II", and all presumably reflect on intensive, glacial age denudation that may be linked with the "periglacial" phenomena of the higher mountains (Butzer 1964a). The tectonic framework for the oldest fanglomerates remains uncertain, but the younger piedmont deposits are clearly undeformed.

TYRRHENIAN TELECONNECTION

The use of quotation marks with all Tyrrhenian designations above reflects the sweeping stratigraphic revisions to be proposed here:

a.   The oldest presumably Pleistocene shorelines are at +100–105 meters, +75–80 meters, and +60–65 meters, in what appear to be undeformed contexts. All are developed as broad planation surfaces with slopes of less than 0.5°, cut across subhorizontal Miocene calcarenites in step-like echelons that run roughly parallel to the coastal contours and are separated by distinct bedrock inflections that suggest low cliffs. These old platforms all post-date Pliocene littoral beds with *Strombus coronatus* and *Ostrea* cf. *lamellosa* found in 150–160 meters elevation in the foothills north and east of Lluchmayor (Colom, et al. 1968). The 75 meter platform may well correlate with the wave-cut platform just above +70 meters at Pas d'es Verro, where Cuerda and Sacarés (1966, 1971) have recovered a considerable fauna including *Fasciolaria lignaria*, *Purpura plessisi*, *Patella aspera* var. *spinosula*, *Patella ferruginea*, and *Ostrea cucullata*. These forms would be compatible with the Maarifien or Messaoudien faunas of western Morocco (see Biberson 1970, with references), and may therefore be of early Pleistocene age. Marine caves at +60 meters or so are found in Miocene cliffs below Pas d'es Verro (Cuerda and Sacarés 1966, 1971), suggesting correlations with the 60–65 meter platforms elsewhere. However, altimetric correlation of these early shorelines is seriously complicated by a multiplicity of stands at similar elevations as well as by possible early Pleistocene tectonics.

b.   The oldest beach in stratigraphic context is the +30 meter deposit underlying the full sedimentary sequence at Banc d'Ibiza and containing the relatively thermophile limpet *Patella ferruginea*, a form rare in the modern Mediterranean but documented in high Pleistocene beaches of Senegal (see Cuerda and Sacarés 1966). Thus this +30 meter beach records, a relatively high, nonglacial sea level, indicating that the subsequent, well-defined sea level oscillations of Mallorca reflect primarily on glacial-eustatic mechanisms.

c.   The second, ancient beach at the base of the entire littoral-sedimentary sequence is found at two localities in only +11–12 meters, east of Cap Blanc (Els Bancals, Vallgornera) (Cuerda and Sacarés 1966, 1971). Here a rich fauna includes *Balanus concavus*, *Purpura* cf. *gallica*, *Haliotis tuberculata*, *Patella caerulea* var. *intermedia*, *Patella ferruginea*, *Patella* cf. *ambroggi*, *Ostrea virleti*, *Ostrea lamellosa*, *Chlamys* cf. *inaequicostalis*, *Chlamys glabra* var. *sulcata*, and *Mytilus edulis.* This assemblage of Plio-Pleistocene leitfossils as well as Atlantic ecoforms is older than and ancestral to that of the +70 meter beach at Pas d'es Verro, according to Cuerda and Sacarés (1971), although this coastal sector, mapped by the writer, is not deformed. The beach in question is separated by two units of overlying terrestrial deposits from a +14–15 meter beach (see below) that in turn underlies typical deposits of terrestrial Hemicycle E. Consequently the older +11–12 meter beach antedates what must be Hemicycle F and may therefore be coeval with the +30 meter beach deposits at Banc d'Ibiza. Until these seemingly contradictory early Pleistocene sites achieve greater resolution in the field, it is imperative that time-stratigraphic correlations be avoided. In all probability the temporal ranges of the key mollusca are greater than had once been anticipated, and de Lumley indicates the presence of both *Ostrea cucullata* and *Ostrea virleti* in unquestionable mid-Pleistocene deposits of the Provence (see de Lumley's article in this volume).

d.   Shore forms and scanty deposits at +45–50 meters can be seen in various parts of Mallorca. Whether or not they represent one stratigraphic entity is uncertain, but they do predate eolianite complex E at Banc d'Ibiza and south of the Plain of Campos.

e.   Eolianite complex E, southeast of Cap Blanc, is underlain by a +15 meter beach platform with marine deposits and a *faune banale* (Cuerda and Sacarés 1966, 1971). This second continental complex consists of three sets of silts and eolianites near Cap Blanc and at Banc d'Ibiza, or two sets as incompletely exposed in southernmost Mallorca ("Antepenultimate" dunes of Butzer and Cuerda 1962a). Mapping of this complex of eolianities in southern Mallorca at 1:25,000 shows a conspicuous alignment on the offshore platform of the +45–50 meter shoreline (see Butzer 1962: Figure 15), demonstrating that at least +15 meter and +50 meter sea levels immediately preceded the second silt-and-eolianite complex. Furthermore, these continental deposits locally rest on a truncated *terra rossa* soil as little as 4 meters above modern sea level (e.g. under two eolianite generations at Cap Orenol: Butzer and Cuerda 1962b), implying effective pedogenesis at a time of relatively low sea level prior to the full-scale regression. However, the exact stratigraphic position (see, e.g. Figure 3) of this *terra rossa* is uncertain.

f.   The second silt-and-eolianite complex was subsequently truncated by a broad +30–35 meter shore platform (Plain of Campos: Butzer 1962: Figure 16) and then notched by narrow beaches with deposits at +22–24 meters and +15–18 meters, both with abundant *Patella ferru-*

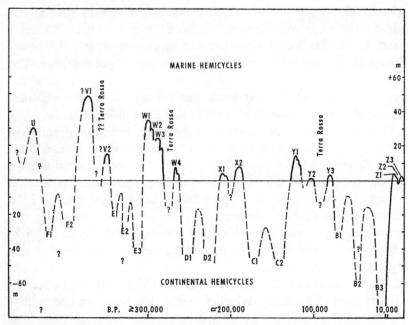

Figure 3.   Mediterranean sedimentary cycles and relative sea levels, as recorded on Mallorca. (There is no time scale prior to 300,000 B.P., and the earlier record is both incomplete and chronologically distorted.)

ginea (at Cap Blanc: Cuerda and Sacarés 1966; also Cala Marmols: Butzer unpublished), and +4–8 meters (at Cap Orenol and Sa Plana: Butzer and Cuerda 1962a, 1962b). At some point or other, each of these beaches is directly overlain by one or more units of eolianite complexes D or E, thus confirming their stratigraphic position. Eolianite complex E is always deeply rubefied, often shows the base of, or derived sediments from, an argillic *terra rossa* B horizon, and is commonly cemented secondarily with calcite recrystallization. Specifically, truncated soil pipes of a *terra rossa* soil at only +2.5 meters were admixed with marine shell and sand during the final +4–8 meter transgression (Sa Plana, also Cap Orenol: Butzer and Cuerda 1962a, 1962b). This shows that deep chemical weathering rather than colluviation or dune formation separated nonglacial, transgressive oscillations.

One Th/U date of "greater than 250,000 B.P." (see Table 1) is available for the final, transgressive oscillation of +4–8 meters at Cap Orenol. In view of the stratigraphy of the continental hemicycles, and by extrapolation from other, younger dated shorelines on Mallorca, this MINIMUM date is quite acceptable.

g.   The next clearly defined marine horizon is the classic Mallorquin

Strombus beach, found from below sea level to +4.5 meters, and in association with the full complement of thermophile Senegalese species (*Conus testudinarius, Tritonidea viverrata, Natica lactea, N. turtoni* Smith, *Ostrea hyotis, Mytilus senegalensis, Arca plicata, Cardita senegalensis*), four extinct subspecies or varieties of *Thais haemostoma* (*consul* Chemnitz; var. *nodulosa, minor,* and *laevis* Monterosato), and two extinct varieties of species now found at great depth but formerly also encountered in littoral assemblages (*Triton costatus* var. *minor* Segre, *Ranella scrobiculata* var. *trinodosa-nodulosa* Bors (Cuerda 1957, 1959b, 1968, 1972; Butzer and Cuerda 1962b; Cuerda and Sacarés 1965; Gasull and Cuerda 1971).

Table 1. Apparent thorium-uranium dates of fossil marine shell from Mallorca*

| Sample number | Locality | Stratigraphy | | | Apparent age (.10^3 B.P.) | Comments |
		(Old)	(in meters)	(New)		
L-884E	Cap Orenol	T-I	(7–8)	W4	> 250	
L-9340	Cap Orenol	T-IIa	(11.5)	Y1	125 ± 10	
L-884D	Torre s'Estallella	T-IIa	(10.5)	Y1	135 ± 10	Excess thorium
L-934G	S'Illot	T-IIb	(7.5)	X2	190 ± 20	
L-934D	Cala Agulla	?T-IIb	(5.5)	X1	220 ± 20	
L-942	Camp de Tir 'A'	T-IIb	(4)	X1	200 ± 20	
L-944	ditto 'B'	T-IIb	(4)	X1	> 300	Excess thorium
L-934I	Cala Agulla	?T-IIb	(6.3)	X1	> 300	
L-934K	Canyamel	T-IIb	(3.3)	X1	> 300	Excess thorium
L-884C	Ses Rotes de sa Cova	T-IIb	(1.6)	Y2	115 ± 15	Excess thorium
L-941	ditto	T-IIb	(1.6)	Y2	120 ± 10	Excess thorium
L-943	Camp de Tir 'B'	T-III	(2.2)	Y3	220 ± 20	Derived shell
L-884G	ditto	T-III	(2.2)	Y3	75 ± 5	
L-934H	La Pineda	T-III	(1.6)	Y2	105 ± 15	
L-934A	Magaluf	T-III	(2.1)	Y3	88 ± 5	

* After Stearns and Thurber 1965, 1967; Stearns 1970, n.d.; stratigraphy after Butzer and Cuerda 1960, 1962a, 1962b, 1962c, and unpublished.

Although preserved as eroded remnants in sheltered inlets, and commonly lacking in diagnostic overlying sediments, these beach deposits are massive and characteristically show several sharp facies variations between well-stratified beach sands and backshore sands or detrital silts. In fact, these are the only beach deposits that commonly attain 1–2 meters or more in thickness. Similarly, no other Pleistocene beaches of Mallorca show such an abundance of *Strombus,* nor such a wide array of Senegalese forms. The +2–4 meter *Strombus* beaches of Mallorca indisputably rest on two generations of silts or eolianites of hemicycle D along much of the Bay of Palma (also near Cap Enderrocat: Cuerda and Sacarés 1965; at Camp de Mar: Butzer, unpublished). In turn, these beaches are separated from superposed Pleistocene beaches ("Tyrrhenian III" in the classical sense) by two major generations of eolianites at Arenal (Can Vanrell: Butzer and Cuerda 1962b) and a variety of new sites between capes Enderrocat and Blanc (Cuerda and Sacarés 1965). At Cala Agulla a similar beach, lacking in Senegalese forms, is positioned between two unweathered eolianites, the younger of which is overlain by a +3.8 meter beach conglomerate ("Tyrrhenian III") (Butzer, unpublished). Paleowind measurements of the eolianites immediately underlying and overlying the *Strombus* beaches at Camp de Mar, Arenal, Cap Blanc, and Cala Agulla are all within 15° of each other, although preliminary measurements of local wind vectors for the D (topmost eolianite) and C (lowest eolianite) cycles of Mallorca show significant differences (Butzer and Cuerda 1962a: Table 8). Consequently, there can now be no doubt that the classic +2–4 meter *Strombus* fits midway between eolianite complexes C and D.

Examining the Th/U dates (Table 1), and barring the aberrant values of "greater than 300,000 B.P.", it can be argued that the type beach of Camp de Tir, as well as Cala Agulla, indicate an age of 200–220,000 B.P. (also Stearns n.d.). A relatively high sea level in several other world regions is indicated for the same span of time by less circumspect uranium series dates on coral (e.g. Mesolella, et al. 1969; Veeh and Chappell 1970).

h.   The +2–4 meter *Strombus* beach appears to have been followed by a slightly higher transgression. The primary evidence comes from a number of abrasional platforms, low cliffs, and notches cut into bedrock at +6.5–8.5 meters, and generally lacking any covering sediments (see Butzer and Cuerda 1962a: Figure 4). Beach sediments preserved at Arenal (Torrente Son Veri: Cuerda, et al. 1959), near Cap Blanc (Pedrera Blanca: Cuerda and Sacarés 1965), and at S'Illot (Butzer and Cuerda 1962c) at least locally include *Conus testudinarius, Tritonidea viverrata, Thais haemostoma laevis, Triton costatus* (in littoral association), *Natica lactea, Mytilus senegalensis,* and *Arca plicata.* A Th/U date of 190,000 B.P. (Table 1) suggests that this +7.5 meter shoreline may follow the classic *Strombus* beach, with an intervening cold phase marked by impoverishment of the Senegalese elements. High sea levels with comparable dates are recorded from the Riviera, southern Italy, and other world areas (Stearns and Thurber 1967; Stearns n.d.; Kaufman, et al. 1971; Mesolella, et al. 1969; Veeh and Chappell 1970). Since the +7.5 meter beach cannot be directly tied in to the eolianite sequences, its stratigraphic position is no more than probable.

i.   Following the two major eolianite generations of complex C, there is clear evidence of several relatively brief shorelines in the range of +9–15 meters. These have cut shallow abrasional forms across bedrock or complex C eolianite — e.g. Sa Plana (Butzer and Cuerda 1962a) and near Cap Blanc (Cuerda and Sacarés 1966). Relatively thin beach accumulations at Cap Orenol (Cuerda and Muntaner-Darder 1960; Butzer and Cuerda 1962b), near Cap Blanc (Cuerda and Sacarés 1966), and at Torre de S'Estalella (Butzer and Cuerda 1960, 1962a) have yielded a fauna with most, but not all, of the Senegalese forms: *Conus testudinarius, Tritonidea viverrata, Triton costatus* (in littoral association), *Strombus bubonius, Mytilus senegalensis, Arca plicata,* and *Cardita senegalensis* — although the proportions, particularly those of *Strombus,* are lower than in the +2–4 meter beach. *Thais haemostoma* is present in its *laevis* and *nodulosa* varieties, the latter showing significant morphological differences from similar forms of the +2–4 meter beach (Butzer and Cuerda 1962b). Thus, all indications point to a new, major transgressive phase. The Th/U date of 125,000 B.P. from Cap Orenol (Table 1) is here accepted as representative and finds ample confirmation from other world regions. For example, it corresponds to the first of three "Last Interglacial" sea level stages on Barbados that is dated 124,000 ±6000 B.P. (see Mesolella, et al. 1969).

j.   Evidence continues to grow for a poorly developed +1.5–2.0 meter beach with some Senegalese faunal elements, which postdates the major *Strombus* stages, but predates the *faune banale* of the traditional Tyrrhenian III. This apparent stage is represented by badly corroded abrasional platforms with very shallow beach deposits, but, again, unfortunately lacking in covering eolianites. Key problematical examples are found at Ses Rotes de sa Cova, Porto Cristo, S'Illot, Cala Nao, and Cala Bona (Butzer and Cuerda, 1962b, 1962c) as well as La Pineda (Muntaner-Darder, 1957 Cuerda 1957). The fauna includes *Conus testudinarius, Tritonidea viverrata, Thais haemostoma* with *laevis* and *nodulosa* varieties, *Triton costatus* (in littoral association), *Strombus bubonius, Natica lactea, Mytilus senegalensis,* and *Arca plicata.* Although uncertainties concerning this last +1.5–2 meter Senegalese beach persist, none of these sites matches the morphological, sedimentological, and ecological patterns evident in the +2–4 meter "classic" *Strombus* beaches. At the same time, no arguments can be mustered against such a young date. Finally, the Th/U dates of 120,000 and 105,000 B.P. (Table 1) add considerable support to the view that this proposed stage probably corresponds with the second high "Last Interglacial" sea level of Barbados, dated 103,000 ±6000 B.P. (see Mesolella, et al. 1969).

k. Detailed reexamination of all local site stratigraphies of the so-called Tyrrhenian III were undertaken as a result of the stratigraphic and faunal precisions made possible by the work of Cuerda and Sacarés (1965) between Cap Enderrocat and Punta Plani. These sites, where Tyrrhenian III beds rest in notches or nips cut into complex C eolianites, were compared with the key sections where the Tyrrhenian III forms the base of the subsequent B complex (see Butzer and Cuerda 1962a, 1962b). It was found necessary to eliminate a number of low-level beaches, but the remaining examples show conspicuous regional faunal similarities and, wherever a full stratigraphic context is present, conform to discriminating sedimentary criteria. In regard to the latter, beds are moderately shallow, seldom attaining 75 centimeters in thickness, and rest on truncated *terra rossa* soils or incorporate eroded soil sediments; only rarely is a true marine facies present, and most beds consist of terrestrial silts or gravels intermixed with marine or marine-terrestrial faunas. Such deposits extend from below sea level to +3 meters and are followed conformably by detrital silts and eolianites of complex B. In other words, this beach forms the base of the continental sequence, a transgression at the time of environmental changes heralding the onset of a glacial episode.

Some thirty faunal sites that match the revised minimal definition of the "Tyrrhenian III", as presently used, lack convincing evidence of any Senegalese fauna, with *Thais haemostoma laevis* the only extinct form. Several of these have yielded single, fragmentary and abraded shells of one or other Senegalese form, but these are almost certainly derived. At the original site of Camp de Tir "B", all Senegalese forms are conspicuously rolled and abraded, derived from the +4 meter *Strombus* beach below (Butzer, unpublished), as verified by the aberrant date L-943 (Table 1) on such a *Strombus* shell. Finally, the stratigraphy of certain other Bahia de Palma sites, originally attributed to be the equivalent of the Tyrrhenian III by Muntaner-Darder (1957) and Cuerda (1957), is either uncertain, or multiple beach levels have been combined in the faunal lists (e.g. Cala Gamba, Magaluf). Thus, the "Tyrrhenian III" appears to lack thermophile Senegalese forms in any unequivocal context.

Two chemically sound and stratigraphically secure Th/U dates of 88,000 and 75,000 B.P. (Table I) are available for the "Tyrrhenian III" of Mallorca. They concur well with a scatter of dates from the same time range obtained in numerous other regions, and suggest correlation with the final, high "Last Interglacial" sea level established for Barbados at 82,000 ±4000 B.P. (see Mesolella, et al. 1969).

Abrasional or depositional features related to Holocene transgressions are very poorly developed and only locally recorded. Nonetheless, post-Pleistocene sea levels at +2 and +4 meters are commonly and unequivocally represented, in sound stratigraphic context resting disconformably on Pleistocene beaches, cut into late Pleistocene eolianites, or linked with valley floor alluvia (see Butzer and Cuerda 1960, 1962a, 1962b). There were at least two stands at +2 meters, one lacking archeological associations, the other of post-Roman age, with pottery; the +4 meter level also lacks specific dating possibilities. All of the Holocene beaches are quite unconsolidated, and may include as much as a meter or more of littoral gravels intercalated between eolian sands. The molluscan fauna is sparse, with only eleven marine species identified from Mallorca thus far, and seldom more than two or three species present at any one site; Senegalese forms are decidedly absent (Butzer and Cuerda 1962b).

A NEW STRATIGRAPHY OF PLEISTOCENE TRANSGRESSIONS

The preceding section has outlined the basic site-specific arguments for revision of the "Tyrrhenian" and pre-"Tyrrhenian" sea level stratigraphy. The sequence of "high" shorelines documented is schematically shown by Figure 3 and summarized in Table 2. The history of sea level fluctuations that emerges is considerably more complex than any previous "sea level curve" for the Mediterranean Basin or other oceanic area. Yet our scheme reflects minimum solutions for all recorded beaches and eolianites, and the true complexity is undoubtedly even greater, particularly for the first half of the time range represented. Such a picture of repeated glacial-eustatic fluctuations, crudely superimposed on an apparent, relative downward trend of Pleistocene sea level, now comes much closer to the degree of stratigraphic resolution evident in the deep-sea cores and continental loesses.

Several general observations can be made.

Altimetric Criteria

The multiplicity of sea levels converging at several identical (but relative) elevations reduces the stratigraphic value of suites of erosional shorelines to a minimum, unless informative sedimentary sequences are associated with them. Allowing that shoreline elevations are often

Table 2. "High" Pleistocene sea levels and marine cycles of the western Mediterranean based on the Mallorquin evidence

Marine cycle	Apparent sea level (in meters)	Faunal characteristics	Radiometric age
Z3	2	Banal	Post-Roman
Z2	2	Banal	
Z1	4	Banal	
Three eolianite generations		HEMICYCLE B	
Y3	0.5–3	Probably banal	80,000 ± 5000 B.P.
Y2	1.5–2	Partial *Strombus* fauna	110,000 ± 5000 B.P.
Y1	9–15	Partial *Strombus* fauna	125,000 ± 10,000 B.P.
Two eolianite generations		HEMICYCLE C	
X2	6.5–8.5	Impoverished Senegalese fauna	190,000 ± 10,000 B.P.
X1	2–4.5	Full *Strombus* fauna	210,000 ± 10,000 B.P.
Two eolianite generations		HEMICYCLE D	
W4	4–8	Banal	> 250,000 B.P.
W3	15–18	*Patella ferruginea*	?
W2	22–24	*Patella ferruginea*	
W1	30–35	?	
Three eolianite generations		HEMICYCLE E	
V (?2)	ca. 15	Banal	
V (?1)	45–50	Banal	
Two eolianite generations		HEMICYCLE F	
U	30 (other levels?)	*Patella ferruginea*	
?	60–65	?	
?	75–80	(? *Purpura plessisi, Ostrea cucullata*)	
?	100–105		

comparable through extensive regions of "undeformed" bedrock, it is precisely the multiplicity of sea levels at a few convergent points of elevation that renders altimetric correlations next to useless. So, for example, on Mallorca there were at least seven stands in +1.5–4 meters, at least four at +8–15 meters, and at least two at +30 meters. What, under these circumstances, does a "4 meter sea level" mean? Clearly the traditional, simplistic sea level "markers" should not be used for attempts to link local or regional stratigraphies with planetary glacial or interglacial episodes.

Faunal Criteria

Strombus is present in many but not all beaches of three substages between marine phases X1 and Y2, and may well have been present locally in substage W2 or W3 at Banc d'Ibiza. Similarly, a broad spectrum of Senegalese faunal elements is present in most beach exposures of four or more substages that span a time range of over 100,000 years. *Patella ferruginea* provides a marker of sorts for at the very least three marine hemicycles prior to the appearance of the Senegalese faunal assemblage. These realizations of Juan Cuerda's are the product of the most intensive regional molluscan studies ever undertaken in the Mediterranean Basin; they are valuable stratigraphic aids, but even so they can only be used with caution. As new sites are found and studied, the picture changes constantly, and there can be no such thing as a definitive faunal stratigraphy of marine stages. Similar reservations must be expressed for the mammalian assemblages of archeological levels in marine caves at specific elevations, which are all then "dated" by circular reasoning, whereas the true time spans of most Pleistocene mammals are far more equivocal. Again, the seemingly brilliant micropaleontological and oxygen-isotopic definition of the Plio-Pleistocene boundary in the marine Calabrian of Italy (see the most recent revisions of Poag 1972) has yet to resolve any general problems of Mediterranean stratigraphy, and the Calabrian remains to be directly correlated with a littoral sedimentary sequence, let alone with the Villafranchian mammalian faunas.

Despite these disappointments, systematic faunal investigations remain indispensable. Cuerda's studies on the Balearic Islands have included relative proportions of various species as well as considerations of depth preferences of each form, to a degree of sophistication matched only recently for a single Lebanese assemblage (Fleisch, et al. 1972). Yet the Mallorquin ecoassemblages, as qualitatively defined, can seldom be applied stratigraphically — partly because individual sites commonly include too few specimens or species, partly because faunal facies vary from site to site and coast to coast, and not in the least because it is difficult to hammer statistically significant samples out of cemented beach rock.

Radiometric Criteria

It need not be emphasized here that C^{14} dating of Pleistocene beaches has been disastrous, creating untold high beaches at 30,000–40,000 B.P. that owe their age only to minimal contamination of molluscan shell. As a consequence, uranium-series dating has revolutionized Pleistocene sea level stratigraphy, despite the serious geochemical problems involved. Unfortunately, the geochemists have unilaterally decided that molluscan dating by Th/U is of no value (Kaufman, et al. 1971), ignoring the field geologist's predicament. Admittedly, many dates are unreasonable, but a high proportion of supposedly aberrant dates are a result of faulty stratigraphy. The great majority of patently unacceptable dates come from mollusca embedded in poorly consolidated sands, e.g. in California and Italy, whereas the Mallorquin and Moroccan samples, derived from indurated beach rock, are generally as consistent and reasonable as dates on coral. This suggests that coralline limestone and indurated bioclastics provide similar geochemical systems, a fact apparently overlooked in the premature obituary of Kaufman, et al. (1971).

While the prospects for further open-minded research of Th/U dating possibilities remain slim, other exploration must be attempted. In particular, the littoral-sedimentary sequences offer considerable possibilities for paleomagnetic investigation, with reference to the K/Ar-dated, "standard" paleomagnetic stratigraphy. Considering the conjectural time concept applied to Figure 3 prior to 250,000 B.P., the position of the Matuyama/Brunhes reversal of ca. 690,000 B.P. will assume a critical chronostratigraphic role.

Nomenclature

The revised, informal nomenclature of sedimentary cycles proposed and applied here has advantages as well as disadvantages.

On the positive side, it avoids the continued use or re-use of such debased, ambiguous, or incorrect appellations as "Tyrrhenian" (including substages I, II, and III), let alone "Monastirian" (including substages I, II, and "Epi-Monastirian"), "Milazzian", "Sicilian", etc. Time-stratigraphic concepts have undoubtedly proved invaluable in geology, but the existing litho- or biostratigraphic terms of the Mediterranean Pleistocene are beyond redemption.

On the negative side of the ledger, identification of cycles raises serious semantic problems. Strictly speaking, a regressive hemicycle would span the time from maximum transgression to minimum regression, while the inverse transgressive hemicycle would continue until the next peak transgression. As implicitly used here, a transgressive hemicycle is approximately equated with an oscillating sea level generally higher than that of the present, while a regressive hemicycle would refer to an oscillating, but generally low, sea level. This usage is eminently practicable in view of the nature of the sedimentary cycle; nonetheless, it is semantically incorrect. Consequently, we have maintained the idea but explicitly refer only to marine or continental hemicycles, depending on whether marine or terrestrial processes dominated near the contemporary shore zone. Also, with deference to potential semantic problems, we have not overformalized our definition of a full cycle, although in practice we find that our sedimentary sequences normally run through from maximum transgression to minimum regression with a sedimentation break thereafter.

Ecological Interpretation of Beach Deposits

The Pleistocene beach sequences of Mallorca pertain primarily to beach-ridge, shingle-beach, nip, and low-cliff coasts, as systematized by Butzer (1962: Figure 10). Depth of marine nearshore or offshore sediments varies accordingly, as does the local availability of submerged or partly emerged rock and the possible development of backshore deposits of mixed wave, splash, and wind origin or exclusively eolian provenance. The molluscan assemblages vary accordingly in most instances (Cuerda 1957, 1968, 1972; Butzer and Cuerda 1960, 1962a, 1962b, 1962c; Cuerda and Sacarés 1965, 1966, 1971). Other examples reflect thanatocoenoses, i.e. death assemblages that appear to combine forms characteristic of distinct water depths and sand or rock preference, as has been explicitly argued for a Lebanese *Strombus* beach by Fleisch, et al. (1972). Further sedimentary and faunistic studies may thus ultimately provide information on the dynamics of the littoral zone, including possible differences of wave energy and better guestimates of geomorphic rates.

Continuing productive work on the zoogeography of thermorphile mollusca, on foraminiferal assemblages, and on oxygen isotopes can also be envisaged. The available evidence presently suggests that most but not necessarily all of the transgressive phases were characterized by surface water temperatures at least as high as todays', and there are possible hints of substantially warmer waters on some occasions (see Letolle, et al. 1971), as might be surmised from the Senegalese faunas. Another point of interest, the apparent elimination of Senegalese fauna between substages Y2 and Y3, finds an explanation in the French cave of Orgnac, where isotopic temperatures have been determined on stalagmite precipitates whose accretion was dated by Th/U (Duplessy, et al. 1970). The results provide a capsuled statement of the "Last Interglacial": temperatures increased slowly (4° C) between 130,000 and 120,000 B.P., then remained almost constant until 97,000 B.P., when a

2.5° C drop took place in a millennium; after a minimum ca. 95,000
B.P., temperatures again rose 4° C by 92,000 B.P. Thus, 5000 years of
glacial-age temperatures are documented in the Languedoc between Y2
and Y3, although there is no corresponding record of regressional
eolianites in Mallorca.

For the main part, the complex beach sedimentary sequences suggest
terrestrial processes much the same as today, with local coastal dunes
but no evidence of significant fluvial denudation — corresponding to
the model of a warm-dry climate as proposed by Butzer (1963b). However, at certain times, particularly in substage Y3, colluvial detritus is
commonplace, suggesting a warm-moist climate, or perhaps better an
accelerating geomorphic dynamism with effective denudation.

Ecological Interpretation of Interbeach Paleosols

All stratigraphically verified *terra rossa* paleosols from the Mallorquin
littoral date from minor regressive oscillations within the marine hemicycles (see above). Three bona fide soils are indicated in such situations, which is compatible with the minimum number of argillic paleosols recorded from the partly older piedmont alluvial sequence of
Palma and Ses Penyes Rotges. It therefore appears reasonable (1) that
the morphostatic, warm-humid situations (see Butzer 1963b) favoring
deep soil development were limited in number, (2) that most or all intensive pedogenesis coincided with relatively cool oscillations within
interglacial time spans, and (3) that such argillic soils developed in
brief intervals comprising only a fraction of any one marine hemicycle.
In the case of the Y2–Y3 *terra rossa*, the Orgnac paleotemperature
curve suggests development in some 5000 years. Further precisions on
terra rossa paleosol morphology, genesis, and stratigraphy are clearly
possible and promise to provide valuable insights into what may be
paleoenvironmental situations not fully replicated anywhere in the Eurafrican subtropics during Holocene time.

DEVELOPMENT OF THE CONTINENTAL SEQUENCES

The Es Bancassos and Sa Plana Profiles

The full complexity of littoral-continental sedimentary sequences can
only be illustrated by actual sections. Two of the most detailed and
continuous Pleistocene profiles come from the southeastern coast of
Mallorca.

The first of these sections is exposed in a former bedrock incision 800 meters northeast of Cala Figuereta, next to a headland and reef known as Es Bancassos. This 25.5 meter, quasi-horizontal sequence has not yet been published and is shown in Figure 4. Corresponding to the topographic location in a drainage line, mixed colluvial-alluvial silts, with lenses of crude detritus, are well developed. Some eleven eolianite generations are recorded, at least one truncated argillic paleosol, and multiple horizons of reworked, reddish soil. There are eight major Ca-horizons and at least another eight minor Ca-horizons, in addition to an undetermined number of zones of significant calcification along eolianite interfaces. Altogether Es Bancassos provides a fairly complete record of the continental hemicycles from mid-E to the close of B (see Figure 3). Apparently, long intervals of nondeposition followed each eolianite, and the carbonate horizons provide a partial clue to the geomorphic environment at such times.

The second section is part of the complex cliff stratigraphy exposed 800 meters southeast of Cala Marmols, beyond a natural arch known as Es Pont de Sa Plana. The profile presented here (Figure 5) comes from one of several measured sections that is reasonably complete, but where thickness of units is only moderate. Partial details have been published (Butzer and Cuerda 1962a), and field revisions are incorporated in Figure 5. As can be expected on an open stretch of coast, colluvia tend to be thin, except where they interfinger laterally with stream deposits, while eolianites are developed in profusion. Two argillic B-horizons, eight major and at least four minor Ca-horizons are present. Although the Sa Plana profile is less complete than that of Es Bancassos, it shows valuable interfingering with transgressions W4, X1, Y1, and Y2, as well as informative intergrading of silts and eolianites.

Clearly, the number of Ca-horizons can be augmented with further sections not discussed here, while the A and B hemicycles can be added or completed. Accordingly, a synthetic discussion of the individual hemicycles follows.

Hemicycle E

The terrestrial deposits of hemicycle E are widespread under mantles of younger eolianities, but good exposures are relatively few — so very few that the full complement of three dunal generations is only seen at Banc d'Ibiza and Pas d'es Verro. These sediments are mainly cemented,

ES BANCASSOS

	PEDOGENESIS	THICKNESS	SEDIMENTS
B3	Ca-horizon	190 cm.	Weathered sandy silt
B2	Ca-horizon	110 cm.	Silt with occasional angular gravel, grading laterally into eolianite
B1	Ca-horizon	100 cm.	Coarse eolianite (direction of bedding N 85° W)
		80 cm.	Weathered sandy silt
		50 cm.	Silt with angular gravel
		120 cm.	Silt
		170 cm.	Coarse eolianite (N 110–115° W) interbedded with Ca-horizons, thickening locally to 14m, and resting on silty rubble
C2	Major disconformity Ca-horizon	110 cm.	Weathered eolianite
		130 cm.	Silt with terminal, angular gravel
	Ca-horizon	60 cm.	Silt with angular gravel
C1	Ca-horizon	50 cm.	Sandy silt with some angular gravel
		120 cm.	Weathered eolianite with Helix
	Ca-horizon	50 cm.	Silt with rounded gravel
		240 cm.	Silt with some angular gravel
D2	Disconformity Ca-horizon	50 cm.	Silt with lenticles of angular gravel
		150 cm.	Eolianite (N 45° W) interbedded with Ca-horizons
D1	Ca-horizon	20 cm.	Silt
		40 cm.	Sandy Silt
	Ca-horizon	20 cm.	Silt
	Ca-horizon	60 cm.	Eolianite with Ca-horizons
		20 cm.	Silt
		150 cm.	Sandy Silt
	Ca-horizon	20 cm.	Silt
	Abrasional Platform	160 cm.	Sandy silt
E3	BC-horizon Ca-horizon	220 cm.	Eolianite
		30 cm.	Silt with angular gravel
E2	Ca-horizon	> 50 cm.	Eolianite

Figure 4.   Sedimentary column at Es Bancassos, southeast coast of Mallorca, near Cala Figuereta. ("Silt" and "eolianite" are used in the genetic sense.)

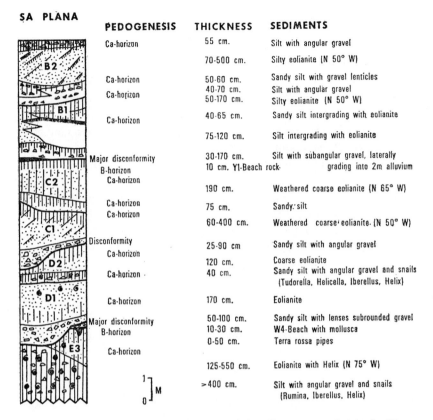

SA PLANA	PEDOGENESIS	THICKNESS	SEDIMENTS
	Ca-horizon	55 cm.	Silt with angular gravel
B2		70-500 cm.	Silty eolianite (N 50° W)
	Ca-horizon	50-60 cm.	Sandy silt with gravel lenticles
	Ca-horizon	40-70 cm.	Silt with angular gravel
		50-170 cm.	Silty eolianite (N 50° W)
B1	Ca-horizon	40-65 cm.	Sandy silt intergrading with eolianite
		75-120 cm.	Silt intergrading with eolianite
	Major disconformity	30-170 cm.	Silt with subangular gravel, laterally
	B-horizon	10 cm. Y1-Beach rock	grading into 2m alluvium
C2	Ca-horizon		
		190 cm.	Weathered coarse eolianite (N 65° W)
	Ca-horizon	75 cm.	Sandy silt
	Ca-horizon	60-400 cm.	Weathered coarse eolianite (N 50° W)
C1			
	Disconformity	25-90 cm	Sandy silt with angular gravel
	Ca-horizon	120 cm.	Coarse eolianite
D2		40 cm.	Sandy silt with angular gravel and snails
	Ca-horizon		(Tudorella, Helicella, Iberellus, Helix)
D1	Ca-horizon	170 cm.	Eolianite
	Major disconformity	50-100 cm.	Sandy silt with lenses subrounded gravel
	B-horizon	10-30 cm.	W4-Beach with mollusca
		0-50 cm.	Terra rossa pipes
E3	Ca-horizon		
		125-550 cm.	Eolianite with Helix (N 75° W)
		>400 cm.	Silt with angular gravel and snails
			(Rumina, Iberellus, Helix)

Figure 5. Representative section of terrestrial sediments recorded at Sa Plana, southeastern Mallorca, near Cala Marmols

with secondary calcite recrystallization, and they are also intensively rubefied. Induration is such and residual soils are so sparse that out-crops are seldom cultivated or even quarried; instead these eolianite landscapes stand out by their undulating topography and scrub vegeta-tion. As a result of such alteration to reddish limestones, hemicycle E sediments are often difficult to differentiate, paleowind directions can seldom be measured, and intraformational paleosols remain almost im-possible to decipher.

Hemicycle E eolianites are found from below modern sea level to over +100 meters, locally sweeping onto the edge of the upland plain of Mallorca, both from the west and from the north. Orientation of related dune fields is best defined with respect to the +45–50 meter shoreline around the Plain of Campos and again east of the Plain of Palma. Direction of bedding in these areas is directly related to former sources of sand and the alineation of contemporaneous coasts. No informative bedding structures and few organic casts were noted.

The silts of Hemicycle E are poorly exposed. However, at Sa Plana (Figure 5; Butzer and Cuerda 1962a) they include unusually large snails. In particular, the most common snail, *Rumina* cf. *decollata*, was of unusual maturity (five whorls compared with four in C and D deposits or modern samples), having an average length near 5 centimeters (compared with 3 centimeters for specimens from younger contexts) and an average maximum diameter of over 1.75 centimeters (compared with 1.0 centimeters for more recent examples). Variations in *Rumina decollata*, a moisture-loving form, are mainly determined by ecological factors (Frömming 1956), and a luxuriant vegetation is implied for at least one of the E-silt generations. The Hemicycle E *Rumina* of Sa Plana is identical to that identified as *Rumina* aff. *atlantica* Pallary by Colom, et al. (1968) from old ("Pliocene") silts at Lluchmayor, suggesting that this variety or distinct species may have stratigraphic value for the older continental deposits of Mallorca.

In the piedmont of the Sierra Norte, the same hemicycle is represented by massive, partly cryoclastic fanglomerates, indicating long periods of intensive highland denudation with torrential runoff and high competence along piedmont watercourses. The degree of frost weathering suggests a mid-winter temperature depression of 10° C or more (Butzer 1964a). Ultimately, here as elsewhere, a deep argillic soil developed as cold climate deposition came to a close and warm, morphostatic conditions resumed.

Hemicycles C and D

The sediments of hemicycles C and D are generally extensive and well exposed, although vertical development is seldom great and only two eolianite generations are exposed at most localities. Whereas paleowind vectors differ markedly from one eolianite to the next, stratigraphic differentiation of C versus D sediments in the interior is seldom possible with any degree of confidence. Compaction and partial cementation, as well as a variable but intermediate degree of rubefaction are also similar at any one locality. As a result, the deposits of the two hemicycles are best considered together.

Eolianites C and D are found in the same general areas as those of hemicycle E. However, bedding is conspicuous and interior distribution far more extensive, while there is no alignment with any particular shoreline. The most continuous eolianites owe their primary disposition to northwesterly winds that evidently swept across the interior plains at high velocities. Specific regional patterns cannot be represented since the paleowind plots are insufficiently certain by stratigraphic criteria. However, significant differences in prevailing winds are indicated for the major episodes of eolian activity. Only below the cliffs of the eastern coast are coeval dunes with easterly vectors represented. South of the Bay of Alcudia, present dunes and tree deformation are oriented to N 125–135° W, as a result of northeasterly winds; however, C/D eolianites are bedded N 95–140° E in the same areas. It would appear that northwesterly to westerly winds, presumably gales related to intense storms over the Gulf of Valencia, were able to sweep sands right across the island. Unusual aridity and storminess are indicated.

The silts of hemicycles C and D were inaugurated by extensive denudation and colluvial reworking of once-friable paleosols on hemicycle E materials. Apart from such derivatives of older argillic soils, the C and D silts are generally sandy, commonly interbedded with eolian materials, and little intraformational hydrolysis is indicated. On the other hand, Ca-horizons formed repeatedly within the silt units, and a major pedocal developed on top of each eolianite. These indications of a persistence of relatively dry conditions are borne out by the molluscan faunas. These are always poor in numbers of specimens, although a wide array of *Helix* and *Helicella* is represented, and helicidae account for 60–100 percent of the snail faunas. *Iberellus minoricensis* and its subspecies *companyoii* are by far the most common forms. In general, specimens of extant species are of the same size as those found in rocky, coastal garrigue today.

Coeval piedmont deposits are moderately well developed, and like the crude detritus of the coastal silts, there is evidence of frost weathering. Similarly, most of the highland "periglacial" phenomena must be attributed to this same time span (Butzer 1964a), and a January temperature depression of at least 6° C is inferred. This underscores the harsh nature of the Mallorquin environment during the accumulation of continental deposits C and D.

Although almost all C or D eolianites show the effects of rubefaction and hydrolysis during marine hemicycle Y, no comparable paleosols have been found between C and D deposits, implying the lack of a warm-humid, morphostatic phase during the X transgression.

Hemicycle B

Eolianites of hemicycle B are shallow and restricted in development. Except where locally blown into thick coastal dunes, exposures on the upland surfaces are unusually rich in primary silts, root drip, and snails (almost exclusively helicidae), whereas bedding is poorly developed. Moderate calcification is the rule. Paleowinds not only vary internally but differ substantially from those of hemicycles C and D: eolianites are best developed on the eastern rather than the southwestern littoral, and upland dunes are evenly divided with respect to westerly and easterly bedding components. Vector deviations on the southwestern coasts are westerly, probably reflecting a higher incidence of westerly Llebeig gales, while on the eastern littoral, easterly deviations are strong, suggesting a secondary storm center over the open Mediterranean southeast of the Balearic Islands.

Silts of hemicycle B are distributed over much of the Mallorquin lowlands. They incorporate local soil derivatives and, in coastal proximity, include eolian components and eolianite interbeds, as well as Ca-horizons suggestive of repeated episodes of semiarid pedogenesis. At S'Estret des Temps (Butzer and Cuerda 1962a) and other sites, there also is direct evidence of rubefaction and cambic paleosols following the first two eolianite generations. The snail faunas are slightly more mesic than those of the C and D silts, being dominated by *Tudorella ferruginea* and including the only examples of *Mastus pupa* (see Cuerda 1959a) in the Balearic record. However, the truely mesic *Rumina* cf. *decollata* and *Archelix* cf. *punctata* of the E hemicycle are totally absent, while the xeric form *Eobania vermiculata* is present (see discussion of modern snail ecology in Colom 1957: 475ff.).

Colluvial screes of comparable age are poorly developed in the Mallorquin high country where, despite frost weathering suggestive of a winter temperature depression of 6° C (Butzer 1964a), "periglacial" type deposits are barely, if at all, developed. Piedmont alluvia are restricted to narrow, silty terraces along major streams. Everywhere the evidence suggests comparatively subdued geomorphic activity.

In overview, the B hemicycle was characterized by a relatively dry and cool climate, with widespread denudation and eolian activity. But conditions were far less severe than during the preceding two stages. The silty upland eolianites were partly a result of deflation from colluvial silts, and occasional outcrops of semieolian silts with loessic structure are present.

Whenever eolianite B3 is preserved with conspicuous eolian bedding, there is no evidence of rubefaction and the deepest post-depositional soil profiles are of rendzina type. Similarly, the E silts have been humified and slightly decalcified, but there is no evidence of hydrolytic weathering, oxidation, or illuviation in the subsoil. Consequently, it must be assumed that post-B3 pedogenesis has amounted to calcification, followed by formation of several edaphic varieties of loamy rendzina.

Hemicycle A

The youngest terrestrial sediments of the Balearic Islands comprise (a) the products of accelerated soil erosion, and (b) coastal dunes.

Soil wash, intermixed with medieval potsherds, can be found in a few isolated piedmont channels, as well as interbedded with the +1–2 meter historical beach deposits (Butzer 1974a). These features are of limited significance, and indicate only limited human interference with the geomorphic "steady state". Older mixed colluvial-alluvial fills may be found in some smaller coastal streams, where they interfinger with +2 meter beach deposits that are archeologically sterile. These fills may be of "prehistoric" age and of noncultural origin.

Holocene coastal dunes include two generations. The older is fragmentarily preserved under contemporary dune fields, and is poorly consolidated yet cohesive, with conspicuous bedding. The overlying, undulating sheets and low dunes of loose sands are only weakly bedded (Butzer 1962). At one critical section they include Roman republican-age pottery, and it appears that major accumulation dates from a minor glacial-eustatic regression in Greco-Roman times. Modern soils are limited to sandy rendzinas with A1–Ca profiles with a total thickness of 50–100 centimeters.

Fortunately, some concrete information on the natural, mid-Holocene vegetation of Mallorca can be gleaned from a 2 meter pollen core obtained from marsh clays and peats near Magaluf by Menéndez-Amor and Florschütz (1961). Oak and pine woodland were characteristic, with subordinate hygrophile hardwoods and oleaceae, although prior to 3000 B.P., grasses, sedges, and chenopodiaceae were prominent near the coast. This picture of an open oak-pine woodland, with intermixed wild olive and riverine hardwoods, closely matches the "spontaneous" vegetation mapped by Rosselló-Verger (1964: 96ff.) in southern Mallorca. It circumscribes the environmental parameters governing Holocene pedogenesis — before the disrupting influences of intensive settlement —

and provides the datum against which Pleistocene paleosols must be measured.

Environmental and Stratigraphic Generalizations

The preceding stratigraphic summation leads to a number of conclusions concerning the continental sedimentary sequences:

1. The basic mechanics of the individual sedimentary hemicycles are remarkably repetitive.

2. In detail, the development of each hemicycle varied, with different intensities of chemical weathering, different degrees of aridity, eolian activity, and cold, and different paleoclimatic patterns.

3. The E hemicycle was characterized by cold yet relatively moist conditions, particularly during the mobilization of colluvial silts; the C and D hemicycles were cold and very dry, with harsh environmental conditions prevailing even during phases of accelerated fluvial activity; the B hemicycle was somewhat intermediate between the relatively mesic E and the emphatically xeric C and D hemicycles. The Holocene A hemicycle does not represent a typical continental development, and reflects warm but relatively dry conditions.

4. The combined total of multiple colluvial silts, eolianites, and semiarid pedocals accounts for most of the time elapsed between successive marine hemicycles. Less commonly documented but equally basic were minor phases of rubefaction, with development of fresh, reddish cambic soil profiles at some point prior to each new generation of silts.

5. In terms of geomorphologic and stratigraphic definition: (a) each basal unit of silts marks the transition from a terminal transgressive oscillation to a major regression with eolianite development; (b) each subsequent silt unit appears to document a shift from pedogenesis to accelerated erosion and deposition during a renewed, major regression; (c) each major eolianite seems to record a major regressive oscillation of sea level; and (d) each pedocal marks dry morphostatic conditions with dune stabilization and limited fluvial denudation.

6. As here described and defined within specific stratigraphic constraints and with specific geomorphologic attributes, the silt-eolianite-pedocal hemicycles refer to relatively dry and cool glacial stages. Presumably, the minor reddish soils formed during the key interstadials, with each stadial advance paralleled by renewed colluviation and eolianite formation. However, until this particular hypothesis can be tested by a carefully designed C^{14}-dating program on the eolianites of hemi-

cycle B, any teleconnection of paleosols across latitudinal zones is premature and irresponsible.

EXTERNAL CORRELATIONS

The minimum of five complete and one incomplete littoral-sedimentary cycles outlined here for Mallorca provide an unusually detailed and relatively complete record for much of the Pleistocene of the coastal regions of the western Mediterranean Basin.

Pollen Stratigraphy of the Mediterranean Pleistocene

Several long pollen cores have contributed greatly to our understanding of the Mediterranean Pleistocene in recent years. These include the following:

a. CUEVA DEL TOLL, 750 meters elevation, 41° 50′ N, near Barcelona; 2 meters of cave sediments;
b. PADUL, 740 meters, 37° 1′N, near Granada; 72 meters of polliniferous peats and lake marls, over sterile sands;
c. LAKE VICO, 507 meters, 42° 20′ N, near Rome; 8 meters of organic clay;
d. TENAGHI PHILIPPON, 44 meters, 41° 10′ N, near Salonika; almost 200 meters of peat, gyttja, and lake marl, topmost 30 meters analyzed;
e. IOANNINA, Epirus, 500 meters, 40° 46′N; 12 meters of clay and peat;
f. GHAB VALLEY, Syria, 190 meters, 35° 41′ N; 11 meters of clay;
g. LAKE HULA, 25 meters, 33° 7′ N, Dead Sea-Jordan Rift; 125 meters of peat, lake marl, and clay.

With the exception of the Padul core, which extends down well into mid-Pleistocene deposits (Florschütz, et al. 1971), these profiles all span the Upper Pleistocene and Holocene.[1] Except for Lake Hula, each records a long period of open vegetation that began prior to 60,000 B.P.

---

[1] Preliminary analyses of the Tenaghi Philippon core from 30–120 meters depth are shown in a very much simplified graph by Van der Hammen, et al. (1971: Figure 7). The pollen zones recognized by these authors appear arbitrary in view of the diagram's complexity, and the time-stratigraphic correlations are quite premature. Ultimately, however, this core promises to open much of the mid-Pleistocene.

(minimum dates extrapolated from C^{14} dates and allowing for no compaction or disconformities) and terminated ca. 15,000–10,000 B.P. This period was essentially coeval with the Würm Glacial as radiometrically defined.

In both the Padul and Toll profiles, nonarboreal pollen (NAP) fluctuated between 15 and 50 percent during the Würm Glacial, with *Pinus silvestris* the dominant tree (Florschütz, et al. 1971; Butzer and Freeman 1968). At Lake Vico the NAP component was between 45 and 90 percent (Frank 1969), at Ioannina 45–75 percent (Bottema 1967), and at Tenaghi Philippon 75–95 percent (Wijmstra 1969), each with pine the principal arboreal representative. For the low mountains of the Spanish mainland, this evidence suggests an open *Artemisia*-chenopodiaceae vegetation, with stands of pine, during the most severe phases of the Würm Glacial. For most of Italy and Greece, it implies an *Artemisia*-chenopodiaceae steppe although, as in the case of Spain, it is uncertain whether arboreal vegetation was best developed in the warm lowlands or in a mesic belt of intermediate elevation between cold montane and arid lowland zones. The contrast of Ioannina and Tenaghi Philippon supports the latter hypothesis. The Lake Hula profile differs fundamentally in that arboreal pollen at almost all times exceeded NAP (excluding marsh species), while oak was the dominant tree (Horowitz 1971). Similarly, the AP-NAP pollen trends of the Ghab profile (Niklewski and van Zeist 1970) show little correspondence with those at either Greek site. This would suggest different environmental anomalies along the southeastern margins of the Mediterranean Basin.

Concentrating on the "typical" Mediterranean profiles, the apparent interstadial episodes ca. 60,000–15,000 B.P., saw only limited increases of arboreal pollen, and pine and oak remained dominant trees at all times. Determining the glacial/interglacial interface in these profiles is a matter of opinion. The Dutch authors prefer to correlate one or more woodland phases preceding the glacial steppe vegetation with Early Würm interstadials. However, this is incompatible with any reasonable extrapolation of the available, consistent C^{14} dates to adjusted sedimentation rates. Far more probable is that the tripartite maximum of warm-temperate forests, clearly delineated at some time earlier than 60,000 B.P. in the Padul and Tenaghi Philippon profiles, represents the "Last Interglacial", specifically the Mallorquin hemicycle Y. If this view is accepted, the period 125,000–75,000 B.P. saw considerable variation of vegetation through time, with at least thirteen and fifteen distinct vegetation zones represented in pollen zones Q through U at Padul and Tenaghi Philippon, respectively. No such variability of ecoassemblages and inferred temperature and moisture factors has characterized the Holocene.

Without elaborating on the details, the available Mediterranean pollen cores, seen in conjunction with other biological evidence (see review in Butzer 1971: 299ff.), show significant environmental changes paralleling the Y and B hemicycles of the Mallorquin Upper Pleistocene. Woodland vegetation characterized the mediterranean ecozone throughout the marine hemicycles, even though environmental parameters varied repeatedly and within relatively wide margins. Open vegetation, steppe or parkland, dominated throughout the continental hemicycles, again with repeated but moderate oscillations of climate and as yet poorly understood contrasts in vertical ecozonation.

Table 3. External correlations of the Mallorquin sequence*

Radiometric dates	Mallorquin cycle	Padul zone	Deep-sea stages	Moroccan formation	Rhine sequence	Loess cycle
Since 10,000 B.P.	Z	Z	1	Mellahian	Soil	B-1
10,000–70,000	B	V, X, Y	2–4	Soltanian	Low Terrace	L-B
75,000–125,000	Y	Q, S, U	5	Ouljian	Soil; Eem transgression	B-3
	C	N	6	Presoltanian	M.T. IV	L-C
180,000–220,000	X	L, M	7	(?)	Soil	B-5
	D	K	8	Tensiftian Anfatian/	M.T. III Drenthe moraines	L-D
> 250,000 B.P.	W	H, I, J	9 (?)	Harounian	Soil	B-7
	E	G		Amirian	M.T. IIb/IIIa	L-E
	V				Soil	B-9
	F			Maarifian M.T. I/IIa		L-F
	U				Soil	B-11

* Padul pollen zones after Florschütz, et al. 1971; deep-sea core stages after Shackleton, this volume; Moroccan formations after Biberson 1970, also Stearns 1970; lower Rhine sequence after Brunnacker, this volume, with M.T. = Middle Terrace; Central European loess cycles after Kukla, this volume.

Only the Padul core (see Table 3) sheds some specific light on the systematic, long-term alternations of open and woodland vegetation that presumably span the whole Pleistocene record of the Mediterranean Basin. Interestingly, the lower 45 meters of this core have values of *Artemisia* and chenopodiaceae (15–75 percent) seldom attained in

Upper Pleistocene times, and arboreal pollen never reaches the levels of the Holocene and "Last Interglacial" (see Florschütz, et al. 1971). However, the prominence of oak and the presence of other thermophile species both speak for two major warm episodes with open but warm-humid woodland, alternating with exceedingly dry intervals of *Artemisia*-chenopodiaceae steppe. It would appear that the three steppe phases (N, K, G) correlate with Mallorquin hemicycles C, D, and E; an open and ericaceous, *Quercus ilex-Q. pubescens* woodland (zone M) appears to mark the climax of hemicycle X, and an open woodland with deciduous oak, pine, fir, hemlock, cedar, beech, ash, walnut, holly, wild grape, and mediterranean shrubs (zones H, I, J) is characteristic of hemicycle W. This would seem to corroborate the aridity of hemicycles C and D on Mallorca, the very warm but relatively dry nature of hemicycle X, and the more temperate seas of hemicycle W.

The earliest steppe phase at Padul (zone G) was probably coeval with the long record of alternating open vegetation and pine woodland from the mid-Pleistocene deposits of Torralba and Ambrona, at 1100–1140 meters on the central Iberian plateau (Florschütz and Menéndez-Amor unpublished; also Freeman, this volume; Butzer 1971: 458ff.). The Torralba-Ambrona sediments were subsequently altered by a deep argillic soil and then dissected before new valley bottom deposits with an interglacial pollen profile were laid down. The basal 2.5 meters of this younger fill include appreciable quantities of *Castanea* (up to 10.4 percent of the total pollen), with a little oak and alder and abundant pine. Since chestnut does not grow in the Spanish sierra today, its presence indicates a warmer climate. At a later point in the same profile, the warm deciduous species were totally displaced by pine, and the overall floral picture suggests a cold grassland. Consequently, the Torralba-Ambrona pollen sequence predates two classical interglacials, whatever their names; in terms of arboreal composition the second of these interglacials more closely resembles the open, thermophile woodland of Padul zone M than it does zones Q, S, and U. The fortunate preservation of key interglacial horizons at Torralba-Ambrona underscores the incomplete nature of standard alluvial histories (Gladfelter 1971).

Mediterranean Deep-Sea Cores

The Mallorquin littoral-sedimentary cycles cover a much longer range of Pleistocene time than do the available Mediterranean deep-sea cores.

The Swedish Deep-Sea Expedition of 1947–1948 obtained fifteen deep cores in the central and eastern parts of the Mediterranean, between Sicily and the Nile Delta. These have been comprehensively reported by Olausson (1961), who recognizes five faunal zones, partly dated by C^{14}. For purposes of correlation with the Mallorquin sequence, it seems preferable to consider the better calibrated isotopic curve of Shackleton (this volume). Correlations are readily made (Table 3) and discussed further by Shackleton in this volume.

Recent detailed isotopic and foraminiferal analyses of a new core in the eastern Mediterranean suggest surface waters 5–10° C cooler than today's during the cold faunal zone of the Upper Pleistocene (Vergnaud-Grazzini and Herman-Rosenberg 1969); however, actual temperatures may have been a little less severe since changes of water salinity and density were not fully compensated for.

Cores in the western Mediterranean Basin have generally proved to be disappointingly young, and the oldest sediments available date to ca. 30,000 B.P. (Eriksson 1965). Detailed physical analyses of one core show that loessic sediments, with a strong 15–30 micron maximum, were being dispersed over the open sea during parts of hemicycle B. Furthermore, carbonized microorganic detritus indicates that grassy vegetation was well developed on parts of the adjacent land surface (Eriksson 1965).

Thus the Mediterranean deep-sea cores cannot substitute for the littoral-sedimentary sequence of Mallorca, but they do provide valuable complementary information. The greater sedimentation rates and abundant terrestrial detritus in cores of the western Mediterranean Basin speak for more intensive denudation of the surrounding land surfaces than in the eastern basin.

The Atlantic Coast of Morocco

The concept of littoral-sedimentary cycles has been specifically applied on the Atlantic coast of Morocco since 1956 (see Biberson 1970), and the well-known sequence of Casablanca (Biberson 1970, with references; also Freeman, this volume; Jaeger, this volume) requires no introduction. Correlations between Mallorca and Morocco are now readily made for certain cycles, but remain problematical for others. The latter situation is unfortunate because the Moroccan sequence is linked to a variety of faunas, both molluscan and mammalian, as well as Paleolithic industries and fossil hominids.

There is no difficulty equating the continental Soltanian and hemicycle B, while the tripartite, marine Harounian and Anfatian — with sea levels ranging from +16–34 meters, a comparably "modern" molluscan fauna with the first *Patella haemostoma*, and Th/U dates of "greater than 200,000 B.P." (125–145,000 B.P. dates do NOT apply to these substages, see Stearns and Thurber 1965, 1967; Stearns 1970) — are readily equated with Mallorquin hemicycle W. Although there is as yet no demonstrable correlative for hemicycle X, the continental Presoltanian and Tensiftian are logically related to hemicycles C and D, respectively. Finally, at least part of the continental Amirian must have been contemporaneous with hemicycle E.

Relationships of the earlier cycles are dubious, since the scale of the Moroccan sequence from the Amirian back to the Plio-Pleistocene Maghrebian is simply too large to allow one-to-one correlation, while the Mallorquin sequence is unsatisfactory for the early Pleistocene time range. Conceivably, the Amirian includes both hemicycles E and F, while the multiple-stage, marine Maarifian — which has complex contacts with the Amirian — may include U and V, if not some of the even older Mallorquin marine phenomena.

These potential points of correlation, particularly relevant both for the paleontology and archeology of the Maghreb, are summarized in Table 3.

Mid-Latitude Europe

Comparisons can be readily made with the lower Rhine stratigraphy (terraces, loesses, moraines, pollen) of Brunnacker (this volume) and the central European loess stratigraphy of Kukla (this volume); they show a surprisingly close correspondence of warm-climate paleosols in mid-latitude Europe with marine hemicycles in Mallorca on the one hand, and of gravels, moraines, or loesses with silts and eolianites on the other (Table 3). Marine hemicycles W, X, and Y, as tentatively dated by Th/U, show a satisfactory correlation with European paleosols ca. 300,000; 200,000; and 100,000 B.P. (see Table 3). Hemicycle D can therefore be related to the Saale-Drenthe Glacial in the type area and, by implication, hemicycle C is of Saale-Warthe Glacial age. However, at least some uncertainty remains whether the Holsteinian and Eemian transgressions are temporal equivalents of all paleosols and interglacial pollen horizons currently labelled Eemian and Holsteinian. Accordingly, correlation of hemicycles X, Y, and Z with the standard European time-stratigraphic designations is uncertain. The oldest Mallorquin unit, U, would appear to be equivalent to the soil on the youngest Rhine High Terrace ("Cromerian III") and to carbonate cycle B-11 in the central European stratigraphy. If these inferences are correct, the Mallorquin cycles now documented span approximately a half million years.

REFERENCES

BERGGREN, W. A.
1973   Late Neogene biostratigraphy, chronostratigraphy and paleoclimatology. *Earth Science Reviews.*

BIBERSON, PIERRE
1970   Index-cards on the marine and continental cycles of the Moroccan Quaternary. *Quaternaria* 13:1–76.

BOTTEMA, S.
1967   A late Quaternary pollen diagram from Ioannina, northwestern Greece. *Proceedings, Prehistoric Society* 33:26–29.

BRUNNACKER, KARL, VOJEN LOŽEK
1969   Löss-Vorkommen in Südost-Spanien. *Zeitschrift für Geomorphologie* 13:297–316.

BUTZER, K. W.
1962   Coastal geomorphology of Majorca. *Annals, Association of American Geographers* 52:191–212.

1963a Climatic-geomorphologic interpretation of Pleistocene sediments in the Eurafrican subtropics. *Viking Fund Publications in Anthropology* 36:1–27.

1963b The last "pluvial" phase of the Eurafrican subtropics. *Arid Zone Research* (UNESCO) 20:211–221.

1964a Pleistocene cold-climate phenomena of the Island of Mallorca. *Zeitschrift für Geomorphologie* 8:7–31.

1964b *Pleistocene geomorphology and stratigraphy of the Costa Brava region (Catalonia)*. Abhandlungen, Akademie der Wissenschaften und der Literatur (Mainz), Mathematisch-Naturwissenschaftliche Klasse, 1, 1–51.

1965   Acheulian occupation sites at Torralba and Ambrona, Spain: their geology. *Science* 150:1718–1722.

1971   *Environment and archeology: an ecological approach to prehistory*. Chicago: Aldine-Atherton.

1974a "Accelerated soil erosion: a problem of man-land relationships," in *Perspectives on Environment*, Association of American Geographers, Commission on College Geography, 57–78.

1974b Paleo-ecology of South African australopithecines: Taung revisited. *Current Anthropoly* 15:367–382, 413–426.

BUTZER, K. W., J. CUERDA
1960   Nota preliminar sobre la estratigraphia y paleontologia del Cuaternario marino del Sur y S.E. de la Isle de Mallorca. *Boletin, Sociedad de Historia Natural de Baleares* 6:9–30.

1962a   Coastal stratigraphy of southern Mallorca and its implications for the Pleistocene chronology of the Mediterranean Sea. *Journal of Geology* 70:398–416.
1962b   Nuevos yacimientos marinos cuaternarios de las Baleares. *Notas y Communicaciones, Instituto geológico y minero de españa* 67:25–70.
1962c   Formaciones cuaternarias del litoral este de Mallorca (Canyamel-Porto Cristo). *Boletin, Sociedad de Historia Natural de Baleares* 7(1961):3–30.

BUTZER, K. W., L. G. FREEMAN
1968   Pollen analysis at the Cueva del Toll, Catalonia: a critical reappraisal. *Geologie en Mijnbouw* 47:116–120.

BUTZER, K. W., C. L. HANSEN
1968   *Desert and river in Nubia: geomorphology and prehistoric environments at the Aswan Reservoir*. Madison: University of Wisconsin Press.

BUTZER, K. W., D. M. HELGREN
1972   Late Cenozoic evolution of the Cape Coast between Knysna and Cape St. Francis, South Africa. *Quaternary Research* 2:143–169.

COLOM, G.
1957   *Biogeografia de las Baleares*. Estudio General Luliano, Seria Cientifica 1. Palma.
1967   Sobre la existencia de una zona de hundimientos, plioceno-cuaternarios situada al pie meridional de la Sierra Norte de Mallorca. *Acta Geológica Hispanica* 2:60–64.

COLOM, G., J. SACARÉS, J. CUERDA
1968   Las formaciones marinas y dunares pliocénicas de la région de Lluchmayor (Mallorca). *Boletin, Sociedad de Historia Natural de Baleares* 14:46–57.

CUERDA, J.
1957   Fauna marine del Tirreniense de la Bahia de Palma (Mallorca). *Boletin, Sociedad de Historia Natural de Baleares* 3:3–76.
1959a   Presencia de *Mastus pupa* Bruguière en el Tirreniense de las Baleares orientales. *Boletin, Sociedad de Historial Natural de Baleares* 5:45–50.
1959b   Tritónidos fósiles del Cuaternario de Mallorca. *Estudios Geológicos* 15:119–130.
1968   Nuevos yacimientos cuaternarias marinos en el Termino de Palma de Mallorca y su paleogeografia. *Boletin, Sociedad de Historia Natural de Baleares* 14:145–170.
1972   Sur la distribution et l'écologie des espèces de signification stratigraphique du Pléistocène supérieur marin de Majorque. *Rapports et Communications Internationales du Mer Méditerranéen* 20:541–543.

CUERDA, J., A. MUNTANER-DARDER
1960   Nota sobre diversos niveles tirrenienses localizados en las cercanias del Cap Orenol (Mallorca). *Boletin, Sociedad de Historia Natural de Baleares* 6:37–48.

CUERDA, J., J. SACARÉS
1965 Nuevos yacimientos cuaternarios en la costa de Lluchmayor (Mallorca). *Boletin, Sociedad de Historia Natural de Baleares* 10 (1964):89–132.
1966 Nueva contribución al estudio del Pleistoceno marino del Termino de Lluchmayor (Mallorca). *Boletin, Sociedad de Historia Natural de Baleares* 12:63–98.
1971 Formaciones marinas correspondientes al limite plio-cuaternario y al Pleistoceno Inferior de la costa de Lluchmayor (Mallorca). *Boletin, Sociedad de Historia Natural de Baleares* 16:10–41.

CUERDA, J., J. SACARÉS, M. DE MIRÓ
1959 Nota sobre un nuevo yacimiento cuaternario marino. *Boletin, Sociedad de Historia Natural de Baleares* 5:31–32.

DUPLESSY, J. C., J. LABEYRIE, C. LALOU, H. V. NGUYEN
1970 Continental climatic variations between 130,000 and 90,000 B.P. *Nature* 226:631–633.

DURAND, J. H.
1959 *Les sols rouges et les croûtes en Algérie*. Service des Études Scientifiques, Algiers.

EMILIANI, C., T. MAYEDA
1964 Oxygen isotopic analysis of some molluscan shells from fossil littoral deposits of Pleistocene age. *American Journal of Science* 262:107–113.

ERHART, H.
1956 *La genèse des sols en tant que phénomène géologique*. (Second edition 1967). Paris: Masson.

ERIKSSON, K. G.
1965 The sediment core No. 210 from the western Mediterranean Sea. *Reports of the Swedish Deep-Sea Expedition* 8(7):395–594.

FLEISCH, H., J. COMATI, P. REYNARD, P. ÉLOUARD
1972 Gisements à *Strombus bubonius* Lmk.(Tyrrhénien) à Naamé (Liban). *Quaternaria* 15(1971):217–238.

FLORSCHÜTZ, F., J. MENÉNDEZ-AMOR, T. A. WIJMSTRA
1971 Palynology of a thick Quaternary succession in southern Spain. *Palaeogeography, Palaeoclimatology and Palaeoecology* 10:233–264.

FRANK, A. H. E.
1969 Pollen stratigraphy of the Lake of Vico (Central Italy). *Palaeogeography, Palaeoclimatology and Palaeoecology* 6:67–85.

FRÄNZLE, O.
1965 *Die pleistozane Klima- und Landschaftsentwicklung der nördlichen Po-Ebene*. Abhandlungen, Akademie der Wissenschaften und der Literatur (Mainz), Mathematisch-Naturwissenschaftliche Klasse (1965) 8, 1–141.

FRÖMMING, E.
1956 Experimentelle Untersuchungen über den Einfluss von Umweltfaktoren auf das Gedeihen der Lungenschnecke *Rumina decollata*. *Systematisches Zoologisches Jahrbuch* 84:577–602.

GASULL, L., J. CUERDA
1971   Observaciones sobre la distribución geografica y estratigrafica de *Thais (Stramonita) haemostoma* L. s. sp. *consul* (Chemnitz). *Boletin, Sociedad de Historia Natural de Baleares* 16:143–164.

GLADFELTER, B. G.
1971   *Meseta and campiña landforms in central Spain: a geomorphology of the Alto Henares Basin.* University of Chicago Department of Geography Research Papers 130, 1–204.

VAN DER HAMMEN, T., T. A. WIJMSTRA, W. H. ZAGWIJN
1971   "The floral record of the Late Cenozoic of Europe," in *The late Cenozoic ice ages.* Edited by K. K. Turekian, 391–424. New Haven: Yale University Press.

HOROWITZ, A.
1971   Climatic and vegetational developments in northeastern Israel during Upper Pleistocene-Holocene times. *Pollen et Spores* 13: 255–278.

KAUFMAN, A., W. S. BROECKER, T. L. KU, D. L. THURBER
1971   The status of U-series methods of mollusk dating. *Geochimica et Cosmochimica Acta* 35:1155–1183.

LAND, L. S., F. T. MACKENZIE, S. J. GOULD
1967   Pleistocene history of Bermuda. *Bulletin, Geological Society of America* 78:993–1006.

LETOLLE, R., H. DE LUMLEY, C. VERGNAUD-GRAZZINI
1971   Composition isotopique de carbonates organogènes quaternaires de Méditerranée occidentale. *Comptes Rendués, Académie des Sciences de Paris* 273-D:2225–2228.

LIETZ, J., M. SCHWARZBACH
1971   Quartäre Sedimente auf der Atlantik-Insel Porto Santo (Madeira) und ihre paläoklimatische Deutung. *Eiszeitalter und Gegenwart* 22:89–109.

MACKENZIE, F. T.
1964   Bermuda Pleistocene eolianites and paleowinds. *Sedimentology* 3:52–64.

MENÉNDEZ-AMOR, J., F. FLORSCHÜTZ
1961   La concordancia entre la composición de la vegetación durante la segunda mitad del Holoceno en la costa de Levante y en la costa W. de Mallorca. *Boletin, Real Sociedad Española de Historia Natural* (G) 59:97–100.

MESOLELLA, K. J., R. K. MATTHEWS, W. S. BROECKER, D. L. THURBER
1969   The astronomical theory of climatic change: Barbados data. *Journal of Geology* 77:250–274.

MUNTANER-DARDER, A
1954   Nota sobre los aluviones de Palma de Mallorca. *Boletin, Sociedad de Historia Natural de Baleares* 1:36–48.
1957   Las formaciones cuaternarias de la Bahia de Palma (Mallorca). *Boletin, Sociedad de Historia Natural de Baleares* 3:77–118.

NIKLEWSKI, J., W. VAN ZEIST
1970   A late Quaternary pollen diagram from northwestern Syria. *Acta Botanica Neerlandica* 19:737–754.

OLAUSSON, ERIC
1961 Sediment cores from the Mediterranean Sea and the Red Sea. *Reports of the Swedish Deep-Sea Expedition* 8(6):335–391.

PECSI, M.
1965 Genetic classification of the deposits constituting the loess profiles of Hungary. *Acta Geologica Hungarica* 9:65–84.

POAG, C. W.
1972 Correlation of early Quaternary events in the U.S. Gulf Coast. *Quaternary Research* 2:447–469.

ROHDENBURG, H., U. SABELBERG
1972 Quartäre Klimazyklen im westlichen Mediterrangebiet und ihre Auswirkungen auf die Relief und Bodenentwicklung. *Zeitschrift für Geomorphologie* (Supplement) 15:87–92.

ROSSELLÓ-VERGER, J. M.
1964 *Mallorca: el sur y sureste.* Palma: Graficas Miramar.

RUHE, R. V., J. G. CADY, R. S. GOMEZ
1961 Paleosols of Bermuda. *Bulletin, Geological Society of America* 72:1121–1142.

SOLÉ-SABARÍS, L.
1962 Le quaternaire marin des Baléares et ses rapports avec les côtes méditerranéennes de la Péninsule Ibérique. *Quaternaria* 6:309–342.

STEARNS, C. E.
1970 The Ouljian stage, Atlantic coast of Morocco. *Abstracts, Geological Society of America* 2:694.
n.d. "Mediterranean strand lines." Unpublished final report to National Science Foundation, for grant GP-2899.

STEARNS, C. E., D. L. THURBER
1965 Th[230]/U[234] dates of late Pleistocene marine fossils from the Mediterranean and Morocan littorals. *Quaternaria* 7:29–42.
1967 Th[230]/U[234] dates of late Pleistocene marine fossils from the Mediterranean and Morocan littorals. *Progress in Oceanography* 4:293–305.

VACHER, LEN
1973 "Coastal dunes of younger Bermuda," in *Coastal geomorphology.* Edited by D. R. Coates, 355–391. Publications in Geomorphology, State University of New York.

VAUDOUR, JEAN
1972 Chronique de pédologie méditerranéenne. *Méditerranée* 1:117–127.

VEEH, H. H., J. CHAPELL
1970 Astronomical theory of climatic change: support from New Guinea. *Science* 167:863–865.

VERGNAUD-GRAZZINI, C., Y. HERMAN-ROSENBERG
1969 Étude paléoclimatique d'une carotte de Méditerranée orientale. *Revue, Géographie Physique et Géologie Dynamique* 11:279–292.

WIJMSTRA, T. A.
1969 Palynology of the first 30 m of a 120 m deep section in northern Macedonia. *Acta Botanica Neerlandica* 18:511–527.

The Contribution of the Volcanic Massif Central of France to European Quaternary Chronology

PIERRE BOUT

ABSTRACT

The earliest Pleistocene mammalian fauna of the Volcanic Massif Central of France is distinguished from the local Pliocene fauna by the appearance of new species of cervids and of a rhino (*Dicerorhinus jeanvireti*) that is different from the Pliocene rhino (*Rhinoceros megarhinus*). Pleistocene subdivisions are proposed, above all, by taking into account the evolution of proboscidians, horses, and cervids.

The Pliocene taxodiaceae forests (*Taxodium, Glyptostrobus*, with *Sciadopitys* and *Sequoia*) as well as other genera (*Liquidambar, Nyssa*) disappeared at the beginning of the Pleistocene. As reconstructed from the flora, the early Pleistocene climate of the Massif Central of France seems to have been comparable to that of today, sometimes showing a Mediterranean influence. Several warmer phases were accompanied by a few recurrences of Pliocene forms, until mid-Villafranchian time. Frequent periglacial deposits help establish phases of cold climate together with the Villafranchian floral changes.

The important faunal changes seem to coincide with cold intervals as well as changes of magnetic polarity. Absolute dates cover the majority of these variations. Thanks to the correlation possibilities of the mammalian faunas, the results from the Massif Central appear to be of wider applicability to the European Pleistocene, particularly for purposes of subdivision.

With its fossiliferous deposits, including floral and faunal fossil remains, and volcanic formations susceptible to paleomagnetic and radiochronologic determinations, the Massif Central of France contributes significantly to the subdivision of the Quaternary period in Europe. The first problem to be resolved regarding this period is when it began. Subdivisions are examined subsequently.

The Beginning of the Quaternary Period

This problem has been discussed elsewhere (Bout 1968). The criteria used for determining the beginnings of the Pleistocene include the concept of the sedimentary cycle, important changes undergone, by flora and fauna as well as climate and paleomagnetism. Radiochronologic datings complement these data.

1. THE CONCEPT OF THE SEDIMENTARY CYCLE refers to marine formations, but it would be nonetheless reasonable to examine it in this context if it is compatible with the classification of the Quaternary and, more generally, of the geological past. In fact, it provides correlations of European continental faunas, related to those of the Massif Central, with interdigitated fossiliferous marine formations of the Mediterranean coast (Italy, France) or North Sea (Holland, England).[1]

2. CHANGES OF MAMMALIAN FAUNAS: Haug (1911) held that the Quaternary began with the arrival of the horse in Europe, as well as the advent of the elephant and Bos (Leptobos). These three genera, which emigrated from Asia to western Europe, represent a paleontological event of great importance. According to Hopwood (1935), the presence of only one of the three is a sufficient criterion. Kurtén (1963) determines the beginning of the European Villafranchian only by the presence of Leptobos. Elephas and Equus did not arrive until much later, the latter preceding the former by a short time.

Rhinoceros etruscus, which replaced Rhinoceros megarhinus in the Pliocene fauna of Montpellier-Roussillon, appeared in our region towards the beginning of the Pleistocene. However, the rhino of Vialette (Haute-Loire) is both different from that at Montpellier and from the Rhinoceros etruscus. According to Guérin (1972), who named this animal Rhinoceros jeanvireti, the Vialette rhino is also part of the fauna of Perrier-les-Etouaires (Puy-de-Dôme), where it is associated with Rhinoceros etruscus, although it is never associated with Rhinoceros megarhinus.

According to Heintz (1967, 1970), the cervidae are different on either side of the Plio-Pleistocene boundary; those of Montpellier-Roussillon are found neither at Vialette nor at Etouaires.[2]

---

[1]   The notion of the sedimentary cycle is not readily applicable to the Pleistocene. The continental shelf of shifting shorelines is also narrow or even nonexistent along the coasts of Europe.

[2]   According to Hürzeler (1967), the mammalian fauna collected at Villafranca d'Asti, the Villafranchian stratotype, since 1945 includes fifteen species known for the most part from Montpellier-Roussillon, Vialette, and Perrier-Roca Neyra. This fauna would belong to the Pliocene. Azzaroli (1967) notes that for paleontological reasons the stratotype of Villafranca d'Asti can only represent the Lower Villafranchian, which belongs within the Upper Pliocene or Astian. Lona and Bertoldi (1972) seem to be inclined to a different option, basing the Plio-Pleistocene boundary on the disappearance of taxodiaceale forests (Taxodium, Glyptostrobus, Sciadopitys, Sequoia), apparently midway in the thick sequence of Villafranca d'Asti.

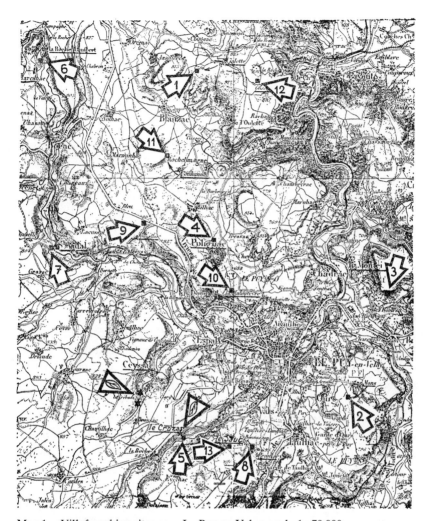

Map 1.   Villafranchian sites near Le Puy-en-Velay, scale 1 : 70,000
1 to 4:   Lower Villafranchian (fauna from Vialette)
5 to 8:   Middle Villafranchian (fauna with mixed *Mastodon arvernensis* and *Elephas meridionalis*)
9 to 13: Upper Villafranchian (fauna with evolved *Elephas meridionalis*)
Pollen spectra are associated with mammalian stages 6 and 7 and with the Ceyssac macroflora.

3.   FLORAL CHANGES: Depape wrote (1928):

"The Plaisancian still shows a large number of exotic plants in our aea. These rapidly disappear after the upper Astian. With the glacial crises of the northern hemisphere, the flora of Europe was decimated. The Quaternary floras now consist mainly of species which have remained indigenous."

The pollen record already studied[3] in several European countries
(Holland, Germany, Poland, France, Spain, Italy, and so forth) suggests a Plio-Pleistocene boundary marked by the disappearance of
Liquidambar, Nyssa, Sciadopitys, Sequoia, or *Cryptomeria,* and cf.
Taxodium. But some Pliocene forms such as *Pterocarya, Carya, Tsuga,*
and *Pinus* of the *haploxylon* type persisted into the Pleistocene. This
second group, which died out in the Cromerian, is considered to be
typical of the Tiglian (Villafranchian). However, this pattern has
proved to be oversimplified. At least in our latitudinal zone (45°),
there are some recurrences of Pliocene elements in *Elephas meridionalis* sites of the Haute-Loire — at Saint-Vidal and Senèze, for example —
which are already much younger than the Plio-Pleistocene boundary.
Another genus, *Eucommia,* known from the Mio-Pliocene of the Dore
Mountains (Puy-de-Dôme), persisted into the Tiglian in northwestern
Europe (Glangeaud, Sauvage, and Manhes 1965).

Accordingly the Plio-Pleistocene boundary as based on floral changes
is less clearcut than had been expected.

4.   CLIMATE: At the International Geological Congress of London
in 1948, it was recommended that the Plio-Pleistocene boundary
should coincide with the first indication of climatic deterioration evident in the marine faunas of the Italian Neogene. It was also decided
to avoid any ambiguity by including within the Pleistocene, as a basal
unit, the Calabrian and its continental equivalent, the Villafranchian.
It goes without saying that continental faunas were also affected by
climatic deterioration, as is obvious from the arrival in Europe of
Leptobos, Equus, and *Elephas,* which emigrated from Asia, as noted
above. The flora also reacted to such climatic changes.

However, it is not at all certain that each of these categories –
marine faunas, continental faunas, flora – reached simultaneously to
the first cold spells. It must have taken some time for northern mollusca (*Cyprina islandica*) and foraminifera (*Anomalina balthica*) to
penetrate the Mediterranean and spread out there. In fact, Italian geologists such as Ruggieri (1954), in the Santerno valley, and Selli (1954),
in the Marches, Romania, and below the eastern Po basin, place the
Plio-Pleistocene boundary in marine sediments at the level where
certain species of Pliocene mollusca or foraminifera are either reduced
in number or are completely absent. This would be below the levels
with *Cyprina islandica* and *Anomalina balthica.*[4] As for the Asiatic

[3]   The literature on this theme is very abundant, in the main part Dutch (e.g.
Florschütz and van Someren 1950, van den Vlerk and Florschütz 1953, Zagwijn
1957). A short recounting is given in Lona (1971).

mammalian faunas, these only appeared in western Europe in successive waves of migration, as we have seen. Some representatives of
these faunas never succeeded there. This was the case for *Elasmotherium*, which was confined to North Eurasia, and for the 400 camels
found in the karst of Odessa.[5] As for the flora, it seems that these
must have immediately proved sensitive to cooling and, except for a
few refuges, soon lost their most thermophile elements.

It is therefore probable that the Calabrian, with its marine fauna,
and the Villafranchian, with its continental fauna, were initially out
of phase. And it is equally probable that the changes undergone by
the flora and fauna of western Europe at the beginning of the Quaternary were not contemporaneous.

5. PALEOMAGNETISM: This must be taken into consideration to the
extent that it may have been able to influence the composition of
flora and fauna. In effect, those periods when the earth's magnetic
field was reversed were critical for life, as cosmic radiation then
reached the earth's surface unimpeded, decimating species or leading
to mutations.

If, on the other hand, it is correct that the mean temperature varies
inversely with the carbon-14 level of the atmosphere, then with the
latter increasing as the magnetic field approaches zero, the paleomagnetic reversals may have corresponded to decreases in temperature
which caused the disappearance or migration of plant or animal
species.[6]

6. ABSOLUTE DATING: This is relevant only to fix in time those paleontological or paleomagnetic events significant for Quaternary chronology and to permit, in association with other criteria, correlations between distant areas.

Considering the diverse data furnished by the volcanic Massif Central of France and the criteria applicable to them, it seems possible

---

[4] Lona, Bertoldi, and Ricciardi (1971) now shorten this interval at Castell d'Arquato and at Stirone.
[5] The karst of Odessa consists of narrow, low galleries forming a network developed through approximately perpendicular fissures within Sarmatian sandstone.
Abundant fauna, embedded in silt, has been collected there along with remains of
camels. Species such as *Hyaenarctos* sp., *Ursus arvernensis, Machairodus crenatidens, Anancus arvernensis*, etc. have led some Russian paleontologists to place this
fauna within the Lower Villafranchian (*Livret-Guide des Excursions du Colloque
international sur la Géologie et la faune du Pléistocène inférieur et moyen
d'Europe*, Moscow, May-June 1969). Nonetheless, Nikiforova (1969) and Tobien
(1970) believe that the karst fauna of Odessa, which lacks horse, elephant, and
Leptobos, and which includes primitive rodents such as *Mimomys*, should be
attributed to the Pliocene (Astian).
[6] See the periodical *Diagrammes* 123 (May 1967): 41.

to us to place the beginning of the Pleistocene at Perrier-les-Etouaires and Vialette, for the following reasons:

1. The FAUNA of these sites include, along with species inherited from the Pliocene (*Mastodon* [*Zygolophodon*] *borsoni, Mastodon* [*Anancus*] *arvernensis, Tapirus arvernensis*), cervids such as *Cervus cusanus, Croizetoceros ramosus, Cervus pardinensis, Cervus perrieri*, all distinct from Pliocene forms. *Rhinoceros jeanvireti* replaced *Rhinoceros megarhinus* in the Montpellier-Roussillon fauna, and is found associated with the older *Rhinoceros etruscus* as at Etouaires. *Leptobos,* absent at Vialette, is present at Etouaires. The fauna of this last site should therefore be a little more recent than that of Vialette.

2. With regard to FLORA, the forest contemporaneous with *Dicerorhinus jeanvireti* in Vialette includes (Meon-Vilain 1972) *Pinus* (*diploxylon* 25 percent, *haploxylon* 4 percent), *Abies,* some *Cupressacea* (*Juniperus*?), *Tilia, Betula, Corylus, Alnus, Ulmus, Juglans, Quercus,* and *Fagus.* This flora is rather different in composition from that of late Pliocene sites. Even if not characterized by a renewal of species, as is the case for some of the fauna (*Cervus, Rhinoceros*), there is a clear change that seems to culminate its Pliocene evolution.

The unique, broadleaved flora of Perrier cannot be compared with the pre-Tiglian and Tiglian pollen floras. Of eleven species recovered,[7] seven are of forest type: *Populus canescens, Betula alba, Alnus orbicularis* and *stenophylla, Fagus pliocenica, Quercus ilex, Ulmus brauni, Zelkova crenata.* To these can be added two common forms, *Hedera* and *Buxus,* as well as *Punica* and *Smilax.* The only genus which became exotic is *Zelkova,* currently a Caucasian form but frequently found in Villafranchian floras and possibly able to withstand the present climate of the Cantal.[8] The vegetation community of Perrier provides no evidence for Pliocene characteristics.

3. The CLIMATE that permitted a reconstitution of the Vialette and Perrier floras was temperate, with a mediterranean aspect at the second locality.[9] It certainly was not the warm-humid climate sug-

[7]   The list set up at an early stage by Marty (Bout and Marty 1932; and in Bout 1960b) included eleven species. Two of them, *Acer polymorphum* and *Bambusa lugdunensis,* cited by Munier-Chalmas and Michel-Lévy (1889), have been dropped, as their location among the clays and tuffs of Perrier had not been clarified by the authors. In addition, Marty (Bout and Marty 1936) eliminated *Taxodium dubium* and *Grewia crenata,* whose determination seemed to him to be uncertain.
[8]   On his Caillac property near Arpajon (Cantal), Marty was able to exhibit two *Zelkova* in 1933, ones which he had planted himself and which, three meters tall, proved to be quite robust.
[9]   Colonies of Mediterranean xerophytes are now growing on the coasts of Limagne (Luquet 1947), and Chassagne (1956) notes live oaks — *Quercus ilex,* or

gested by the Plaisancian tuff floras of the Cantal (Laurent and Marty 1904-1905), nor the extremely cold climate with which the Congress of London wished to begin the European Pleistocene. But at both Vialette and Perrier the exotic Pliocene forms have disappeared and the remaining species are somewhat more similar to present-day ones. With about three million years of perspective, this fact seems to us to be rather exceptional and quite effective to mark the beginning of the most recent geological era.

4. ABSOLUTE DATING: The fossil mammal sites of Vialette and Etouaires have been dated by the potassium/argon method as applied to volcanic formations associated with bone beds.

At Vialette, a basalt flow covering fossil deposits is dated 3.8 million years (Savage and Curtis 1970).[10] At Etouaires, sanidines from a pumice conglomerate — lahar or mudflow — overlie the faunal beds and date at 3.4 million years (Savage and Curtis 1970).

The Perrier plateau area has been dated at several stratigraphic levels (Bout 1970), by several authors working independently. Although some results agree with one another, such as at Pardines, where Mc-Dougall established a date of 4 million years and Lippolt 4.2 million (Bout 1972), this is not always the case. The flow of Roca Neyra, for instance, has been dated at 3.1 million years by Lippolt, at 3.9 by Curtis (Bout 1966a), and at 3.5 by Savage and Curtis (1970).

As the flow of Roca Neyra is earlier than the fossil beds at Etouaires (Bout 1960b, 1970), the age of the latter — if we take Lippolt's results into consideration — should be in the order of 3 million years old or 400,000 years younger than proposed by Savage and Curtis.

In order to assemble the hundred or so dates obtained by the potassium/argon method for the volcanic formations of the Massif Central of France, it seemed to us that each researcher or laboratory had

---

holly oaks — acclimatized to conditions atop the peak of Pileyre, near Vertaizon (Puy-de-Dôme), at an elevation of 500 meters.
[10] Viret's section (1942) does not show precisely how the Vialette beds relate to the adjacent basalts. The Azanières flow, which dominates the site, is linked to the adjacent Devès basalts to the west in terms of situation and elevation. The Devès flows presently give the oldest dates, 1.8 million years at Vazeilles (Curtis, in Bout 1966a) and 1.92 million at Coupet (Savage and Curtis, in Azzaroli 1967). The basalts of Azanières, Vazeilles, and Coupet maintain the same mesaform topography and show an identical petrography; in each case the basalts show numerous peridotite nodules. We believe that these different basalts are of the same age so that the 3.8 million age obtained by Savage and Curtis (1970) for the Azanières flow seems too high. On the other hand, the stratigraphy of the Vialette area is complex and the strata of this site may be much earlier than the lava sheets that cover them and the dyke that cuts them (see Bout 1960b: 18).

his own individual calibration method, because ages determined by some are rather consistently greater or smaller than those obtained by others. The difference is sometimes quite significant: for example, 800,000 years between the extremes of the ages obtained for the Roca Neyra basalt. In some cases there is reason to choose between these dates (Bout 1970), but several criteria must be used, which are not available at Vialette. We will simply retain an age of between 3.4 and 3 million for Etouaires, with the lower value being preferred. The obvious conclusion is that it is still difficult to fix a precise date for the beginning of the Pleistocene in the Massif Central of France.

5. *Paleomagnetism*: The available absolute datings should place Vialette within the Gilbert period of reversed polarity but within the normal Cochiti event (3.70 to 3.92 million years). Etouaires might be placed just on the border between the Gilbert reversed and the Gauss normal (3.32 million years) and could also correspond with the reversed Mammoth event (2.94 to 3.06 million years), if Lippolt's determination is chosen.

In each case, however, it is obvious that the faunas are contemporaneous with magnetic reversals.

THE DIVISIONS OF THE PLEISTOCENE PERIOD

The same criteria used to determine or characterize the beginning of the Pleistocene (fauna, flora, climate, paleomagnetism) allow us to establish its subdivisions.

Fauna

Proboscidians, horses, and families of *Cervus* yield the most data. However, each faunal group appearing produces some data.

PROBOSCIDIANS At the beginning of the Pleistocene, *Mastodon(Zygolophodon) borsoni* and *Mastodon (Anancus) arvernensis* survived from the Pliocene. The former then disappeared while the latter remained and, after a while, occupied the area in company with the first elephants. Eventually *Mastodon arvernensis* disappeared, to leave the scene to *Elephas (Archidiskodon) meridionalis* which developed into an evolved form before being replaced by *Elephas (Palaeloxodon) antiquus*. Much later, this form in turn gave way in the Auvergne to *Elephas primigenius,* preceded in one site — Saint-Hippolyte — by *Elephas trogontherii*. Thus, the proboscidians alone of the French Massif Central characterize the following five Pleistocene faunas:

1. *Mastodon borsoni* and *Mastodon arvernensis*, together;
2. *Mastodon arvernensis* and *Elephas meridionalis*, in association;
3. *Elephas meridionalis*, archaic and later, evolved;
4. *Elephas antiquus*;
5. *Elephas trogontherii* and *Elephas primigenius*.

The Villafranchian or Lower Pleistocene can be terminated with the evolved *Elephas meridionalis*, thus including three subdivisions (faunas 1, 2, and 3). The Middle Pleistocene can be characterized by *Elephas antiquus* in the Massif Central. The Upper Pleistocene has both an older phase, with *Elephas trogontherii* (fauna 4), and a more recent one, with *Elephas primigenius* (fauna 5).

HORSES   In the Villafranchian, horses were represented by two different forms (Prat 1968): *Equus stenonis* and *Equus* cf. *bressanus*. The first of these had several sub-varieties, notably *Equus stenonis vireti* at Saint-Vidal, la Roche-Lambert, and Chilhac; and *Equus stenonis senezensis* at Senèze. Other types both preceded and followed these, the last of which were found in the Middle Pleistocene at Solilhac.

Recently discovered at Blassac (Haute-Loire) (Beden and Guth 1970a), *Equus* cf. *bressanus* did not go beyond our Villafranchian.

Next, we have those forms known from Germany, *Equus sussenbornensis* and *Equus mosbachensis*, whose representatives are found at Solilhac (Middle Pleistocene) and Saint-Hippolyte (Upper Pleistocene), respectively. The first of these was found together with the last survivor of the *Equus stenonis* lineage, the second associated with *Equus caballus germanicus*. *Equus caballus germanicus* subsequently spread to Les Rivaux near Le Puy (Haute-Loire) only to be replaced by *Equus caballas gallicus* in the alluvia of the low terrace of Allier at Pont-du-Château (Puy-de-Dôme).

CERVIDS   The cervids of Perrier-les-Etouaires and Vialette which, as noted above, mark the beginning of the Pleistocene in our area (fauna 1) include the following forms: *Cervus cusanus, Croizetoceros ramosus ramosus, Cervus pardinensis, Cervus perrieri*, and *Arvernoceros ardei* (Heintz 1969, 1970).

Then, at Chilhac (fauna 2) there is a site for which we have the most recent identification possible (Beden and Guth 1970): *Croizetoceros ramosus minor, Cervus philisi schaubi, Eucladoceros senezensis depe-*

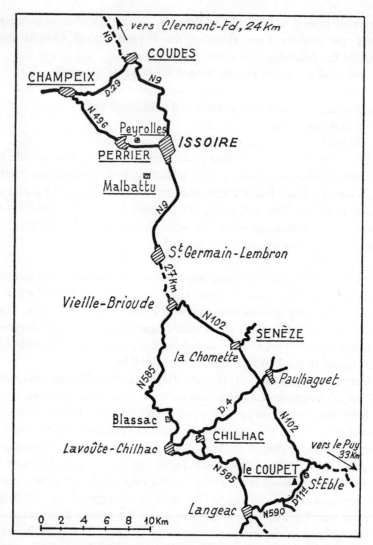

Map 2.   Location of Villafranchian Mammalian sites of the Allier valley (Puy-de-Dôme and Haute-Loire) (fossiliferous sites capitalized)

reti. The first two species evolved from *Croizetoceros ramosus* and *Cervus pardinensis* at Perrier-les-Etouaires. These three forms appear at Senèze along with an elk (*Libralces gallicus*). With respect to the cervids, therefore, Senèze would be classified within fauna 2 save its elk. Later, *Cervus perolensis* and *Eucladoceros tetraceros* (fauna 3), appearing at Blassac (Haute-Loire) and Peyrolles (Puy-de-Dôme) mark the end of the Villafranchian. As early as or since the Solilhac (Haute-Loire) level (fauna 4), red deer lived in the area along with a large *Megaceros* of the *verticornis* type, *Megaceros solilhacus* (Azzaroli 1952).

Reindeer has been found in the low terrace of Pont-du-Château (Puy-de-Dôme).[11] It also appears in prehistoric sites of Magdalenian age in the Auvergne (Neschers) and the Haute-Loire (Cottier, Chanteuges, Saint-Arcons, Rond du Barry [fauna 5]). It is missing at Rivaux, however, where only red deer is present.

OTHER GROUPS *Rhinoceros etruscus* spans the entire Villafranchian from Etouaires on, and persisted in the area until the Middle Pleistocene, at Coudes (Puy-de-Dôme) and at Solilhac.[12] *Rhinoceros tichorhinus* is absent at Saint-Hippolyte. It does appear along with *Elephas primigenius,* however, at Rivaux and in the low terrace alluvia of Allier. Until now it was not known from any of the Magdalenian sites at Velay. But a questionable occurrence has been cited (T. Poulain, in de Bayle 1972), among the fauna of the Rond du Barry cave, near Polignac (Haute-Loire), where *Elephas primigenius* also appears.

Antelopes died out after Senèze and are absent from the evolved *Elephas meridionalis* fauna of the later Villafranchian. It was not until the very end of the Pleistocene that a final reappearance from the group occurred, the chamois of Rivaux and certain Magdalenian sites (Cottier near Retournac, Haute-Loire). Gazelles disappeared with fauna 2.

Although difficult to distinguish in many cases, *Bison priscus* and *Bos primigenius* are common to the Middle and Upper Pleistocene. But the former seems to have already been present at the end of the Villafranchian in the Malbattu fauna, near Issoire (Puy-de-Dôme) (Bout 1960b).[13]

Noted at Senèze (Jung 1946), *Hippopotamus major* came on the scene later and is certainly present at Sinzelles (Haute-Loire), near the end of the Villafranchian. *Hippopotamus amphibius* followed in the Middle Pleistocene, at Solilhac.

[11] Two reindeer antlers were found near the top of the Saint-Hippolyte deposits, whose thickness attains about fifteen meters (G. Gaudron, personal communication). However, the fauna of this area come from beds which, according to the owner and our own studies, are situated lower down in this sequence of sand lenses and thin clay beds.

[12] *Rhinoceros mercki* has been noted by Boule (1892) among the Solilhac fauna, but this determination has not been retained by S. Schaub. A well-preserved metapodial that we found has been classified as *Rhinoceros etruscus* by paleontologists from Lyon.

[13] Bouillet and Dévèze de Chabriol (1827) described a skull fragment with two horn cores that must have come from Malbattu, near Issoire. It seems that this fossil may pertain to *Bison.*

Finally, it should be noted that the tapir (*Tapirus arvernensis*), persisting from Pliocene times, spans fauna 1, with further remains in two sites — le Crozas and le Coupet — of fauna 2. Although of little help in determining Pleistocene subdivisions, this form at least permits us to fix the Coupet fauna at the beginning of fauna 2. The absence of *Gazella* has in fact led Heintz (1969) to alter his dates rather significantly for the fauna of Coupet, estimating it as being much younger and placing it after Saint-Vidal and Roche-Lambert (Haute-Loire), where tapir is absent.

Thus, all of the groups of fauna of the volcanic Massif Central of France contribute to the establishment of valid Pleistocene subdivisions. The classification proposed here can certainly be disputed; it might, for example, seem surprising to see Senèze, because of the disappearance of the mastodon of Auvergne, at the basis of fauna 3, whereas the deer and antelope of this site would seem to assign it to fauna 2. Nonetheless Senèze, the most carefully excavated site of the region, is a special case. Two monkeys, *Dolichopithecus* and *Macacus*, lived in this region with elk and possibly *Hippopotamus*. The flora (see below) proves that the fossiliferous beds are contemporaneous with a cold climate on numerous occasions interrupted by warmer conditions. Senèze thus seems to have served as a refuge where species of differing ecological preferences were associated.

In the volcanic Massif Central, rodents have been found only in small numbers. Thus, they cannot play an important role in Pleistocene subdivision of the region.

Comparisons with other Pleistocene mammalian sites in Europe show some dissimilarities. Some faunas found in peripheral locations show species lacking in the more central parts of Europe. At the beginning of the Pleistocene, *Dinotherium* — known from the Pontian of Cantal at Puy Courny and at Joursac, but absent since — lived together in Moldavia with *Mastodon borsoni, Mastodon arvernensis,* and the first representatives of the genus *Elephas (Archidiskodon)* (Alexeeva 1965). Near Kharkow, the remains of a *camelid* were associated with horses, elephants, and rhinoceros — the three latter providing an analogy to the corresponding species of Senèze (Alexeeva 1966). In Transylvania, a giraffid (*Mitilanotherium*) is known from the Upper Villafranchian (Samson and Radulesco 1966). On the other side of Europe, the mammalian fauna was enriched with an African form in Miocene times, namely *Hesperoceras*, which never crossed the Pyrenees but rather stayed in the valley of the Ebro at Villaroya, along with species similar to those of Perrier and Senèze.

There are also some animals which, in the Massif Central of France, have been shown to have appeared in succession, although in other countries they have proved to be contemporaneous or at least capable of being substituted for each other. Thus, *Elephas meridionalis* and *Elephas antiquus* coexisted in the Cromer Forest Bed, while in Central Europe, in the Middle Pleistocene, *Elephas trogontherii* occupies the place held in the Massif Central of France by *Elephas antiquus*.

Flora

Abundant in Upper Miocene, Pliocene, and Villafranchian times, both macrobotanical remains and pollen of the volcanic Massif Central subsequently became scarce, because the volcanic eruptions that buried and preserved these floras tapered off. Thus, although the floras contribute towards a discussion of the Plio-Pleistocene boundary, they no longer allow determination of precise Pleistocene subdivisions, at least not after the Villafranchian. Leaf impressions discovered at Saint-Saturnin (Puy-de-Dôme) under a basalt flow and studied by Braun-Blanquet (1921) provide little additional help: dating from 7,650 B.P. by carbon-14, they pertain to the Holocene.

Climate

The floras register climate fluctuations at the beginning of the Villafranchian, while the faunal associations, including the abundance of cervids or the disappearance of antelopes, furnish complementary data for the beginning and end of the Villafranchian.[14]

However, the most complete data we have on the Pleistocene climate of the high Massif Central of France come from the periglacial deposits of the Velay (Bout 1952, 1957, 1960b). During the Pleistocene glacials the elevation attained by the volcanic masses permitted glaciation of the mountains of Mont Dore, the Cantal, Cezallier, Aubrac, and locally on Forez, Margeride, and the southeastern Velay. At the same time, the

[14] It is always risky to draw paleoclimatic conclusions from fossil mammals. However, the abundance of *Cervus* animals suggests the presence of woodland, and the complete disappearance of a group such as the antelope implies significant ecological changes. Additionally, some isolated species such as *Megaceros hibernicus* of the Irish peat bogs or *Megaceros solilhacus* from Solilhac slope deposits argues in favor of a cold climate at some time. Does the fossil megacerid from Etouaires, *Arvernoceros ardei*, carry similar implications?

surrounding areas were subject to periglacial conditions. Volcanic activity assured the preservation of former slope deposits, either by sealing them under lava flows or by impeding dissection of the valleys and hillsides. Volcanic rocks, having always made up a large part of the surface, were more widely spread in slope deposits by disintegration of basalt ridges and subsequently resulted in cementation of the clastic slope debris, principally by soluble iron.

The preceding discussion points out that periglacial deposits corresponding to different Pleistocene cold phases are preserved in the volcanic Massif Central of France. The earliest indication of their presence appears at Cheyrac (Haute-Loire), in the "mastodon sands" of the Puy basin: a subsiding series of sediments dating from the earliest Villafranchian infilling (Bout 1960b), at the base of which the Vialette fauna is found. However, the exact connections between this fauna and the first cold-climate deposits cannot be determined. The pollen diagram of the Ceyssac clays, intercalated with the mastodon sands, indicates that there were alternating temperate and cooler fluctuations of climate (F. Florschütz, in Bout 1960b). A macroflora collected from the base of these same clays shows, as does the Perrier flora, rather cold species mixed with temperate-mediterranean forms such as *Zizyphus, Acer cretensis*, and *Acer monspelianensis*.

The Coupet fauna comes from periglacial deposits contemporaneous with the base of the second Villafranchian infilling (Bout 1960b), which the pollen record of Roche-Lambert (Florschütz, in Bout 1960b) shows to have been intermittently cold. Deposits of similar age and type at Vazeilles are cryoturbated.[15]

[15] We have already described the periglacial deposits of Velay and argued their attribution to different Pleistocene intervals (Bout 1957, 1960b). Their composition naturally varies according to the bedrock of the slopes they cover. There are no *"grèzes litées"* such as are known from other French regions around the Massif Central (Dordogne, Charentes, Causses) or in Lorraine, where these are developed in relation to mid- or upper-Jurassic limestones. There is, in effect, no Mesozoic bedrock at the heart of the Massif Central.

At Coupet these slope deposits consist of tuffs covered by crude ejecta of a nearby volcanic cone. Analyses show 6 to 11 percent fines (colloids or silts), 7 to 25 percent fine sands, 15 to 52 percent coarse sands, and 16 to 72 percent coarser than 2 millimeters. The sediments were deposited by repeated slope transfer, and at the base of each bed is a horizon of angular basalt blocks or clusters of unweathered scoria from the slope.

The slope deposits of Senèze include gneissic debris and basalt ejecta from an explosion breccia (that dominates the maar to the west). They cover diatomitic and polliniferous lake beds, and the upper units of the latter yield fine, complete skeletons of deer, rhino, elk, horse, and *Leptobos*.

At Malouteyre the periglacial deposits rest on basanite breccias, disaggregated by frost-weathering to a depth of two meters. There are crudely stratified beds

The Senèze fauna is found at the top of a lacustrine series whose pollen diagram indicates initial warmth, becoming colder in three stages (Elhai 1969), while superposed slope deposits subsequently prove the establishment of a very cold climate.

The Malouteyre fauna (Haute-Loire) (Bout 1960a) was also recovered from periglacial deposits and probably also those of Malbattu and Peyrolles. With no antelopes present, the faunal assemblages of these three sites — to which we might also add Blassac — indicate important biotopical changes subsequent to Senèze. This was also the time, contemporary with the Calabrian and the Sicilian, that the Mediterranean was invaded by mollusca and foraminifera from the subarctic seas.

A new cold wave of periglacial intensity affected Solilhac, whose fossils are found both in slope deposits and clayey lacustrine sands (Bout 1964a).

At Rivaux, mammalian remains are found in sands and silts with humic beds or lenses of solifluction material on top of a sheet of basalt rubble produced by frost-weathering (Bout 1960a, 1964b; Bout, Dufau, and Laborde 1966). Flint artifacts associated with fossils indicate a late Mousterian age. After deposition of the low terrace alluvium, at the time of a warming trend responsible for the accelerated retreat of glaciers in the Massif Central (Bout 1963), the Magdalenian period brought with it another spell of intense cold.[16]

We are, therefore, rather well-informed about the Pleistocene cold climate fluctuations in the Massif Central. It is remarkable that many of the faunas that we have commented upon are found only in peri-

---

above, including blocks of breccia and basalt, with clays and cracking marls developed marginally.

Finally, at Solilhac there is an agglomerate of angular, frost-weathered, basalt blocks, cemented by a clayey, sandy, and ferruginous matrix. The sand and clay were derived from Villafranchian sediments (mastodon sands) and Tertiary marls, underlying a sheet of basalt that forms a conspicuous ledge.

In each case there is no evidence of cryoturbation since these are slope deposits little suitable for frost deformation. A Villafranchian cryoturbation has, however, been described (Bout 1949) from below the Vazeilles flow (dated 1.8 million years), where a silt pocket is squeezed into a coarser, poorly-stratified sediment that consists of weathered explosion breccia.

[16] Indeed, a renewed cold episode coincided with the Aurignacian, which began 32,000 years B.P. (Movius 1961). In France and elsewhere in Europe, sites of this period are rarely found above 200 meters elevation (Movius, personal communication), doubtless because of the harshness of the climate. Consequently, the Aurignacian has left no traces in the Massif Central, except in the form of cryoturbated silt visible at Sarliève, near Clermont-Ferrand, on top of alluvia with *Elephas primi-*

glacial deposits; this is the case for the faunas of Coupet, Malouteyre, Rivaux, and of the Magdalenian sites. Other types come from both lacustrine beds and from superposed periglacial deposits; this is the case at Senèze and Solilhac. As for the low terrace with its mammoth and woolly rhinoceros remains, it immediately follows on one cold phase and is succeeded by other cold periods (Bout 1973).

Only the faunas of Vialette and Etouaires offer no cold characteristics although we have considered them contemporaneous with a relatively cool climate, compared with previous conditions. As for the fauna of Saint-Hippolyte, preserved in the lacustrine sands and clays of a small, subsiding basin on the western edge of the Limagne de Clermont, we are completely ignorant of the associated climate.

But in the main part these were cold spasms that are best dated by the various faunas of the volcanic Massif Central. And this is not surprising. Life is compatible with extremely rigorous climate conditions as the fauna now living in the barren grounds of Canada, or even that of Europe during the Aurignacian and the terminal Magdalenian, seems to indicate. Moreover, such climatic conditions are favorable for the formation of slope deposits which, with each summer thaw, flowed rapidly downhill covering or incorporating — and thus protecting from destruction — the remains of the dead animals, some of which were perhaps killed by the severity of preceding winters.

But it is quite obvious that temperate or warm phases alternated with such periods of severe climate. The floras show this as far into the Pleistocene as Senèze, at the beginning of the upper Villafranchian. Thereafter, there are no further faunas found in sediments that could be interpreted by a warm or temperate climate. However, as our absolute dates will show, the intervals separating the various faunal horizons were quite long. Numerous climatic fluctuations naturally took place between the cold spasms contemporaneous with many of these faunas.

---

genius (Rudel and Lemée 1955), or in the form of slope deposits alternating with sand and pebble horizons in the low terrace of the Allier, near Coudes Station (Puy-de-Dôme). In Perigord (Razac-sur-l'Isle, Dordogne), in the Charente (at Montignac) and in other locations on the western edge of the Massif Central, where the climate was less severe than in the mountains, the topmost alluvia of the low terrace interdigitate with slope deposits. This suggests that lateral sediment influx replaced longitudinal stream discharge, i.e. when the low terrace had been built up, intense cold returned to the area.

Absolute Dates

Absolute age determinations by the potassium/argon method, as applied to volcanic formations related to our fossil mammals sites, are due to G. Curtis (see Bout 1966a), H. J. Lippolt (see Bout, Frechen, and Lippolt 1966), Savage and Curtis (1970), and Prevot and Dalrymple (1970).

It so happens that the faunas are contemporaneous with lavas or related beds within which they are found. This was the case at Coupet (1.92 million years) and at Malouteyre, whose age is probably close to that of Sinzelles (1.3 million years), a nearby site.

In other cases, the faunas rest on top of dated volcanic formations. This is the case with the fossiliferous beds of Roca Neyra, which are younger than the second pumiceous horizon of Perrier that was dated at 2.5 million years by Curtis.

The pumiceous alluvia and associated faunas at Champeix and Coudes (Puy-de-Dôme) (Bout 1966b), on the contrary, underlie a basalt flow whose age has been evaluated at 0.50 million years by Lippolt. The fauna of Vialette is in an identical position with respect to a basalt dated at 3.8 million years by Savage and Curtis.

Finally, some mammalian faunas fit between two volcanic horizons that are radiochronologically dated. Thus, the fauna of Perrier-les-Etouaires is placed between the basaltic extrusion of Roca Neyra, which was dated at 3.5 million years by Savage and Curtis, but at only 3.1 million years by Lippolt, and a pumiceous bed dated at 3.4 million years by Savage and Curtis.

The chronology of Senèze remains rather more uncertain, with numerous datings leading to considerable discrepancies. The result which seems to us to be the closest approximation is that of Dalrymple and Prevot: 2.33 million years for a basalt clearly preceding the fauna. Considering that the first eruptions of Devès have been dated at 1.8 million years at Vazeilles and 1.9 at Coupet, it seems reasonable to give a comparable age to the Senèze basalt flow. Then, at a later time, an explosion crater (maar) opened up within the volcanic system of Senèze and fauna was preserved high up in a 140-meter lacustrine deposit filling a crater with a diameter of 1,000 meters. Furthermore we suggest around 1.6 million years for the fauna of Senèze, taking into account the time needed — 200,000 to 300,000 years (Ehrlich 1968) — for the accumulation of seasonal diatomites that filled the crater. Elsewhere, Heintz (1970) estimates that the Pleistocene evolution of the subspecies of *Cervus* required 500,000 years, and he dates the Senèze fauna at 1.4 million years with the Coupet fauna (1.9 million years) as reference. There is also the degree of evolution of the two rodent species of the same lineage (see Chaline and Michaux 1969) and which Jánossy (this volume) uses to support the chronologic position of Senèze with respect to Perrier-les-Etouaires.[17]

The fauna from the slope deposits at Solilhac is contemporaneous with the basalt flow of Rochelimagne, for which no dates are yet available. However, because of its reversed paleomagnetism (Roche 1956), the flow itself and therefore the fauna can be dated prior to 0.7 million years, and prior to the normal Brunhes epoch.

The fauna from the low terrace dates from 35,000 B.P. The sites of Rivaux and the Magdalenian sites of the Auvergne and the Haute-Loire are found on both sides of the low terrace.

Paleomagnetism

As has been seen, changes in the geomagnetic field took place at the beginning of the Pleistocene. Later changes included the Olduvai event, recently assessed somewhat younger (1.71 to 1.85 million years) by Curtis and Hay (1971) and closely followed by the Gilsa event (1.61 to 1.63 and 1.64 to 1.79 million years). The Coupet fauna is older than these intervals while that of Senèze may correspond to their end. The Jaramillo (0.89 to 0.95 million years) could mark the end of the Villafranchian, together with the Blassac site, covered by a basalt flow with normal polarity (Prevot, personal communication, November 1969).

The Solilhac faunas seem to be close to the 0.7 million year date of the Matuyama-Brunhes reversal.

The Laschamp episode (0.02 to 0.03 million years) is younger than the low terrace, and corresponds to the Aurignacian, known to have been quite cold on occasion.

The relationships established between the paleomagnetic data and the fauna of the volcanic Massif Central are drawn from local mea-

---

[17]   Jánossy has provided the following comments:

"Three species of *Mimomys* have been described from the Senèze locality by Kormos (1937): *Mimomys pliocaenicus* Forsyth-Major, *Mimomys newtoni* Hinton, and *Mimomys pusillus* Mehely. Their presence suggests a mid-Villafranchian age.

"Michaux (1972) described *Mimomys polonicus* Kowalski and *Mimomys reidi* Hinton from Perrier-les-Etouaires. This suggests an essentially early Villafranchian age.

"The minimal differences in evolutionary divergence between *Mimomys pliocaenicus* and *polonicus* hardly matches the long time intervals between Senèze and Perrier that are suggested by the absolute dates."

surements mostly determined by Roche (1956, 1963) and more recently by Bonhommet and Zähringer (1969), as well as Prevot and
Dalrymple (1970).

In many cases, the correspondence of the fauna with paleomagnetic
and climatic variations — cold spasms — is apparent (See table, p. 92).

CONCLUSIONS

In terms of Pleistocene fauna, the volcanic Massif Central of France
provides numerous localities with fossil mammals. These sites include
the characteristic species of faunal assemblages from several European
countries: Italy, Spain, Rumania, the Soviet Union, and so on.

With regard to the floras, some are essential for a discussion of the
Plio-Pleistocene boundary, while those which would document the
decline of the Villafranchian, and those which occurred between the
Villafranchian and our Holocene peatbogs, are missing.

Climate is important here because it was due to the combined factors
of altitude and volcanic activity that the Massif Central of France saw
the development of various Pleistocene glaciations and was able to
preserve a succession of cold-climate deposits, which no other European area has yet been able to match.

It was also the local vulcanism that allowed correlations with the
Pleistocene faunas, together with the sets of paleomagnetic and radiochronologic data that are for the most part lacking from other European areas.

While certain discrepancies remain in the composition of the Pleistocene faunas of different parts of the continent — with some areas exhibiting species lacking elsewhere — the difficulty is not a major one.
The most typical common forms — the proboscidians, for example —
are found in all of the sites and when the successions of foreign faunas
are compared, they can usually be correlated with the Massif Central
of France without much difficulty.

Although there is abundant climatic data, the classification proposed
here does not include correlations with the Pleistocene glacials and
interglacial periods of Central Europe. Although it may be easy to
attribute the most recent cold spasms to Würm — those of Rivaux
(Würm II) and of the Magdalenian (Würm III or IV) — it is more
difficult to see just how to place properly the older ones within the
glacial chronologies. First, it is probable that, in the high Massif Central, only the most extensive glaciations were represented by periglacial

Table 1. Pleistocene chronology of the Massif Central, France

"events"a   M : Mammoth, K : Kaena, R : Réunion, O : Olduvai, G : Gilsa, J : Jaramillo, L : Laschamp.

	Lower Pleistocene or Villafranchian			Middle Pleistocene	Upper Pleistocene		
	Lower	Middle	Upper				
Absolute Paleo ages in magne- million tism years (Vulcanism)	3.1 3.3	2.5	1.92	1.3 1.6?	0.9	>0.7 0.5	0.02 0.03
		I I		+ I I +	I	+	I
Fossil mammal sites	Perrier (Etouaires) Vialette	Perrier (Roca Neyra) Le Crozas Le Coupet	Chilhac La Roche-Lambert	Saint-Vidal Seneze Sinzelles La Malouteyre Malbattu Blassac	Peyrolles	Solilhac Champeix-Coudes	Saint-Hippolyte Les Rivaux (Le Puy) Paix (Issoire) Pont-du-Château La Ponélie (Aurillac) Gites magdaléniens
Probos-cidians							
Mastodon borsoni	▬▬						
Mastodon arvernensis	▬▬▬▬▬						
Elephas meridionalis		▬▬▬▬▬▬					
Elephas antiquus					▬▬▬		
Elephas trogontherii							▬▬
Elephas primigenius							▬▬▬
Tapir							
Tapirus arvernensis	▬▬▬	▬					
Rhino-ceroids							
Rhinoceros jeanvireti	▬▬						
Rhinoceros etruscus	▬						?
Rhinoceros tichorinus							▬▬
Equids							
Equus stenosis		▬▬▬▬▬▬▬▬▬▬▬▬					
Equus cf. bressanus			▬▬				
Equus cf. süssenbornensis						▬	
Equus cf. mosbachensis						▬	
Equus caballus germanicus							
Equus caballus gallicus							
Cervids							
Cervus cusanus	▬▬▬						
Croizetoceros ramosus ram.	▬▬▬▬						
Croizet. ramosus medius			▬▬▬				
Croizet. ramosus minor				▬			
Cervus pardinensis	▬▬▬▬						
Cervus philisi valliensis		▬					
Cervus philisi philisi			▬				
Cervus perolensis				▬			
Cervus perrieri	▬▬						
Eucladoceros senez. vireti	▬▬▬▬▬▬						
Eucladocerus senez. senez.			▬▬				
Eucladoceros tetraceros							
Cervus elaphus							▬
Arvernoceros ardei	▬▬▬						
Libralces gallicus	▬						
Megaceros solilhacus						▬	
Rangifer tarandus							▬▬
Antilopes							
Antilopes (tous genres)	▬▬▬▬▬▬▬▬▬						
Gazelles							
Gazella	▬▬▬▬▬▬▬						
Leptobos							
Leptobos	▬▬▬▬▬▬						
Bovids							
Bison priscus					▬		
Bos primigenius							▬▬
Hippo-potamus							
Hippopotamus major				? ▬▬			
Hippopotamus amphibius							▬▬
Rodents							
Mimomys stehlini	▬▬▬						
Mimomys polonicus	▬▬▬						
Mimomys reidi	▬▬						
Mimomys pliocaenicus			▬▬				
Mimomys newtoni				▬			
Mimomys pusillus				▬			
Periglacial deposits							
	•	•	•	••	•	•	•
Dates of reversal in million years (Paleomagnetism)	3.32	3.06 2.8 2.43	2 1.85	1.71 1.79 1.61	0.95 0.9	0.7	0.03 0.02
Epochs and "events"a	Gilbert (reversed)	K M Gauss (normal)	R	O Matuyama (reversed) J	Q	Brunhes (normal)	L

deposits. The most northerly and briefest cold phases left no traces at all. It might equally be supposed that vulcanism did not always intervene to preserve the evidence in identical fashion.

REFERENCES

ALEXEEVA, L. I.
1965   Stratigraphical review of the Proboscideans of Eopleistocene according to the materials of the European South of the U.S.S.R. *Academy of Sciences of U.S.S.R. Commission d'étude du Quaternaire*, 69–90. Moscow.
1966   Nouveaux gisements de la faune éopléistocène de mammifères dans la région de Kharkov. *Academy of Sciences of U.S.S.R. Commission d'étude du Quaternaire*, 122–127. Moscow.

AZZAROLI, AUGUSTE
1952   La sistematica dei cervi giganti e i cervi nani delle isole. Note préliminaire. *Atti della Società Toscana di Scienze Naturali*, Mémoire, series A, 59:3–11.
1967   Villafranchian correlations based on large mammals. *Commission of Mediterranean Neogene Stratigraphy*, IVe Session, Bologna 1967, 15.

BEDEN, M., C. GUTH
1970a Nouvelles découvertes de restes de Mammifères dans le gisement villafranchien de Chilhac (Haute-Loire). *Comptes rendus de l'Académie des Sciences de Paris* 270:2065–2067.
1970b Un nouveau gisement de vertébrés du Villafranchien de la vallée de l'Allier. *Comptes rendus de l'Académie des Sciences de Paris* 271:168–171.

BONHOMMET, N., J. ZÄHRINGER
1969   Paleomagnetism and potassium age determinations of the Laschamp geomagnetic polarity. *Earth and Planetary Science Letters* 6:43–46. Amsterdam.

BOUILLET, J. B., DÉVÈZE DE CHABRIOL
1827   Essai géologique et minéralogique sur les environs d'Issoire et principalement sur la montagne de Boulade. Clermont-Ferrand.

BOULE, MARCELLIN
1892   Description géologique du Velay. *Bulletin du Service de la carte géologique de la France* 4(28):1–259.

BOUT, P.
1949   Sur un dépôt de pente villafranchien cryoturbé à Vazeilles (Haute-Loire.) *Bulletin de la Société géologique de France*, series 5, 19: 427.
1952   Le climat du Velay au Quaternaire et au Postglaciaire. *Comptes rendus sommaires des Séances de la Société de Biogéographie* 249:17–41.
1957   Actions périglaciaires en Velay (France) au Quaternaire. *Biuletyn Peryglacjalny* 5:161–173.

1960a De la basse terrasse aux faits morphologiques actuels dans le Velay et la région de l'Allier supérieur. *Revue d'Auvergne* 74:1-28.

1960b *Le Villafranchien du Velay et du bassin hydrographique moyen et supérieur de l'Allier.* Le Puy: Imprimerie Jeanne d'Arc.

1963 Observations sur la basse terrasse de l'Allier à Pont-du-Château (Puy-de-Dôme). *Actes du 88e Congrès national des Sociétés savantes à Clermont-Ferrand,* Geography Department, 45–58.

1964a Etude stratigraphique et paléogéographique du gisement de mammifères fossiles pléistocène moyen de Solilhac, près Le Puy-en-Velay (Haute-Loire). *Geologie en Mijnbouw* 43:83–93.

1964b Des restes de marmotte dans le gisement des Rivaux. *Bulletin de la Société académique du Puy* 42:233–238.

1966a Problèmes du volcanisme, 1: Les méthodes de datation des formations éruptives. *Revue d'Auvergne* 80:55–67.

1966b Un épisode des éruptions sancyitiques du Mont-Dore enregistré à Coudes (Puy-de-Dôme). *Bulletin de la Société géologique de France* 8(7):263–273.

1968 La limite Pliocène-Quaternaire en Europe occidentale. *Bulletin de l'Association française pour l'étude du Quaternaire* 1:55–78.

1970 Absolute ages of some volcanic formations in the Auvergne and Velay areas and chronology of the European Pleistocene. *Palaeogeography, Palaeoclimatology, Palaeoecology* 8:95–106.

1972 Problèmes du volcanisme, VII: Datations des formations éruptives. *Revue d'Auvergne* 86:54–59.

1973 *Les volcans du Velay. Itinéraires géologiques et géomorphologiques en Haute-Loire.* Brioude: Imprimerie Watel.

BOUT, P., A. AZZAROLI
1952 Stratigraphie et faune du Creux-de-Peyrolles près Perrier (Puy-de-Dôme). *Annales de Paléontologie* 38:37–56.

BOUT, P., F. DUFAU, A. LABORDE
1966 Nouvelles découvertes au gisement des Rivaux. *Bulletin de la Société académique du Puy* 44:157–162.

BOUT, P., J. FRECHEN, H. J. LIPPOLT
1966 Datations stratigraphiques et radiochronologiques de quelques coulées basaltiques de Limagne. *Revue d'Auvergne* 80:207–231.

BOUT, P., P. MARTY
1932 Sur la découverte d'un gisement de plantes fossiles dans la formation pliocène de Perrier, près d'Issoire (Puy-de-Dôme). *Comptes rendus de l'Académie des Sciences de Paris* 195 (September 12).

1936 Flore astienne de Perrier (Puy-de-Dôme). *Annales du Musée d'Histoire naturelle de Marseille,* Mémoire 1, 28:5–39.

BRAUN-BLANQUET, J.
1921 L'origine et le développement des flores dans le Massif Central de France. *Annales de la Société linnéenne de Lyon,* n.s. 68:113–143.

CHALINE, J., J. MICHAUX
1969 Evolution et signification stratigraphique des arvicolidés du genre Mimomys dans le Plio-Pléistocène de France. *Comptes rendus de l'Académie des Sciences de Paris* 268:3029–3032.

CHASSSAGNE, M.
1956 *Inventaire analytique de la Flore d'Auvergne et contrées limitrophes des départements voisins,* volume one, 229. Paris: Paul Lechevalier.

CURTIS, G. H., R. L. HAY
1971 "Further geological studies and potassium-argon dating at Olduvai Gorge and Ngorongoro Crater," in *Calibration of hominoid evolution.* Edited by W. W. Bishop and J. A. Miller, 289–301. Edinburgh: Scottish Academic Press.

DE BAYLE DES HERMENS, R.
1972 Le Magdalénien final de la grotte du Rond du Barry, commune de Polignac (Haute-Loire). *Extraits du Congrès préhistorique de France,* XIXe session, Auvergne 1969, 37-69.

DEPAPE, G.
1928 Le monde des plantes à l'apparition de l'homme en Europe occidentale. *Annales de la Société scientifique de Bruxelles,* series B, 48:39.

EHRLICH, A.
1968 Les diatomées fossiles des sédiments villafranchiens de Senèze (Haute-Loire, Massif Central français). *Bulletin de l'Association française pour l'étude du Quaternaire* 5(17):267–280.

ELHAI, H.
1969 La flore sporo-pollinique du gisement villafranchien de Senèze (Haute-Loire, Massif Central français). *Pollen et Spores* 11(1):127–139.

FLORSCHÜTZ, F., A. M. H. VAN SOMEREN
1950 The palaeontological boundary Pliocene-Pleistocene in the Netherlands. *International Geological Congress' Report of the 18th Session, Great Britain* 9:40–46.

GLANGEAUD, L., J. SAUVAGE, F. MANHES
1965 Stratigraphie et tectonique des formations prétigliennes du massif volcanique du Mont-Dore. *Comptes rendus de l'Académie des Sciences de Paris* 260:1689–1692.

GRANGEON, P.
1951 Etude d'un nouveau gisement de plantes fossiles tertiaires et de quelques nouvelles espèces découvertes à Ceyssac. *Bulletin de la Société géologique de France* 6(1):75.

GUÉRIN, C.
1972 Une nouvelle espèce de rhinocéros (*Mammalia, Perissodactyla*) à Vialette (Haute-Loire, France) et dans d'autres gisements du Villafranchien inférieur européen: *Dicerorhinus jeanvireti* n.sp. *Documents du Laboratoire de Géologie de la Faculté des Sciences de Lyon* 49:53–150.

HAUG, E.
1911 *Traité de géologie,* II: *Les périodes géologiques.* Paris.

HEINTZ, E.
1967 "Données préliminaires sur les cervidés villafranchiens de France et d'Espagne," in *Problèmes actuels de paléontologie (evolution des vertébrés),* 539–552. Colloques internationaux du Centre Na-

tional de la Récherche Scientifique 163.

1968   Principaux résultats systématiques et biostratigraphiques de l'étude des cervidés villafranchiens de France et d'Espagne. *Comptes rendus de l'Académie des Sciences de Paris* 266:2184–2186.

1969   Signification stratigraphique du genre *Gazella* (*Bovidae, Artiodactyla, Mammalia*) dans les formations villafranchiennes de France. *Comptes rendus sommaires des Séances de la Société géologique de France* 4:127–129.

1970   "Les cervidés villafranchiens de France et d'Espagne," in *Sciences de la terre*, two volumes. *Mémoires du Muséum national d'Histoire naturelle*, series C, n.s. 12.

HOPWOOD, A. T.
1935   Fossil elephants and man. *Proceedings of the Geologists' Association* 46(1):46–60.

HÜRZELER, J.
1967   "Nouvelles découvertes de mammifères dans les sédiments fluviolacustres de Villafranca d'Asti," in *Problèmes actuels de paléontologie (evolution des vertébrés)*, 633–636. Colloque internationaux du Centre National de la Recherche Scientifique 163.

JUNG, J.
1946   Géologie de l'Auvergne et de ses confins bourbonnais et limousins. *Mémoire du Service de la carte géologique de France.*

KURTÉN, B.
1963   Villafranchian faunal evolution. *Commentationes Biologicae Societas Scientiarum Fennica* 26(3).

LAURENT, M., P. MARTY
1904–   Flore pliocène des cinérites du Pas de la Mougudo et de Saint-
1905   Vincent-la-Sabie. *Annales du Musée d'Histoire naturelle de Marseille, Géologie* 9:313.

LONA, F.
1971   Correlazioni tra alcune sequenze micropaleobotaniche plio-pleistoceniche, continentali, e marine dell'Italia Centrosettentrionale ed Europa Centro-occidentale con riferimento al Limite Tiberiano. *L'Ateneo Parmense. Acta Naturalia* 7(2):145–157.

LONA, F., R. BERTOLDI
1971   Rinvenimento di Arctica (Cyprina) islandica in una serie continua plio-pleistocenica presso Castell'Arquato (Piacenza) in connessione con sequenze pollinologiche. *L'Ateneo Parmense. Acta Naturalia* 8(1):35–44.

1972   La storia del plio-pleistocene italiano in alcune sequenze, vegetazionali lacustri, e marine. *Atti della Accademia dei Lincei*, Memorie, Classe di Scienze fisiche, matematiche e naturali; series eight, volume nine. Sezione IIIa (Botanica, zoologia, fisiologia e patologia). Fascicle one, 1–46.

LONA, F., R. BERTOLDI, E. RICCIARDI
1971   Synchronization of outstanding stages of some Italian Upper Pliocene and Lower Pleistocene sequences especially by means of palynological researches. *Comm. V Congrès du Néogène méditerranéen, Section de Paléobotanique.* Lyon.

LUQUET, A.
1947   *Les colonies xérothermiques de la Limagne.*

MEON-VILAIN, H.
1972   Analyse palynologique du gisement villafranchien de Vialette (Haute-Loire). *Documents du Laboratoire de Géologie de la Faculté des Sciences de Lyon* 49:151–155.

MOVIUS H. L.
1961   More on Upper Palaeolithic archaeology. *Current Anthropology* 2(5):427–454.
1963   "L'âge du Périgordien, de l'Aurignacien et du Proto-Magdalénien en France sur la base des datations au Carbone 14," in *Aurignac et l'Aurignacien. Centenaire des fouilles d'Edouard Lartet. Bulletin de la Société méridionale de Spéléologie et de Préhistoire,* 131–142.

MUNIER-CHALMAS, A. MICHEL-LÉVY
1889   Etude sur les environs d'Issoire. *Bulletin de la Société géologique de France* 18(3).

NIKIFOROVA, K. V.
1969   *International colloquium on Lower and Middle Pleistocene geology and fauna of Europe: guide-book.* Moscow: Nauka.

PRAT, F.
1968   "Recherches sur les Equidés pléistocènes en France." Unpublished thesis, Faculté des Sciences de Bordeaux.

PREVOT, M., G. B. DALRYMPLE
1970   Un bref épisode de polarité géomagnétique normale au cours de l'époque inverse de Matuyama. *Comptes rendus de l'Académie des Sciences de Paris* 271:2221–2224.

ROCHE A.
1956   Sur la date de la dernière inversion du champ magnétique terrestre au cours du Quaternaire. *Comptes rendus de l'Académie des Sciences de Paris* 243:812–814.
1963   Elaboration d'une stratigraphie paléomagnétique des formations volcaniques. *Bulletin de la Société géologique de France* 7:182–187.

RUDEL, A., G. LEMÉE
1955   Würmien et Post-Würmien en Limagne de Clermont. *Revue des Sciences naturelles d'Auvergne* (1–2) 27–37.

RUGGIERI, G.
1954   La limite entre Pliocène et Quaternaire dans la série plio-pléistocène du Santerno. *Comptes rendus de la 19e Session du Congrès géologique international,* Alger 1952, 13(15):235–240.

SAMSON, P., C. RADULESCO
1966   Sur la présence de girafidés dans le Villafranchien supérieur de Roumanie. *N. Jahrbuch f. Geologie und Paläontologie, Monatshefte* 10:588–594.

SAVAGE, D. E., G. H. CURTIS
1970   "The Villafranchien stage-age and its radiometric dating," in *Radiometric dating and paleontologic zonation,* 207–231. Geological Society of America, Special Paper 124.

SELLI, R.
1954   La limite plio-pléistocène dans les environs d'Ancone (Marche). *Compte rendus de la 19e Session du Congrès géologique international*, Alger 1952, 13(15):241–247.
TOBIEN, H.
1970   Biostratigraphy of the mammalian faunas at the Plio-Pleistocene boundary in Middle and Western Europe. *Palaeogeography, Paclimatology, Palaeoecology* 8:77–93.
VAN DEN VLERCK, I. M., F. FLORSCHÜTZ
1953   The palaeontological base of the subdivision of the Pleistocene in the Netherlands. *Verhandeling van de Koninklijke Nederlandse Akademie van Wetenschappen, Afdeling Natuurkunde*, series one, 20(2).
VIRET, J.
1942   Fouilles paléontologiques à Vialette (Haute-Loire). *Bulletin mensuel de la Société Linnéene de Lyon* 11(1):13.
ZAGWIJN, W. H.
1957   Vegetation, climate and time-correlations in the Early Pleistocene of Europe. *Geologie en Mijnbouw*, n.s. 19(7):233.

Loess Stratigraphy of Central Europe

GEORGE J. KUKLA *

ABSTRACT

Eight glaciations of Brunhes age are recorded in deep-sea sediments but only four are recognized on land. Sequences of loess beds and soils resting on river terraces in Czechoslovakia and Austria, close to the former fronts of the Scandinavian and Alpine glaciers, shed more light on the dilemma as they enable a correlation to be made between oceanic record and the classical glacial stages of Europe. They show seventeen major glacial-interglacial shifts within the last 1.6 million years (cf. Figure 6). Eight of them are of Brunhes age. However, only four times did the continental glacier advance far enough to leave behind end moraines undestroyed by subsequent glaciation. According to the best estimates available at present, this occurred 20,000 years ago during the Weichsel advance; about 140,000 years ago during the Warthe advance; about 350,000 years ago during the Saale, *sensu stricto* (Drenthe), and about 550,000 years ago during the main Elster *sensu stricto* advance. Weichsel moraines broadly correlate with the oceanic 0^{18} stage 2, Warthe with stage 6, Saale with stage 10, and Elster with stage 16 (cf. Figure 29).

Unlike the short-lived ice advances representing the north European classical glacial stages, the *Würm* terraces in the Alps apparently formed during a long interval covering the last glacial, a substantial part of the next-to-last glacial, the last interglacial, and the Holocene. It probably correlates with 0^{18} stages 1 through 6. Correspondingly the *Riss* terrace probably correlates with 0^{18} stages 12 through 7; *Mindel* with 18 through 13, and *Günz* terrace with 22 through 19. The RW, MR, GM, and DG erosional episodes of the alpine rivers are of glacial rather than interglacial origin. They seem to represent morphostratigraphic correlation horizons of wide regional significance with approximate ages of 180, 450, 650, and 850 millenia (within 0^{18} stages 6, 12, 18 and 22). They are supposed to be primarily of

* With contributions of Alois Kočí, Czechoslovak Academy of Sciences, Bočni II, Prague.

The research was supported by the NSF grant GX-28671-K as a part of CLIMAP (Climate Long-range Investigation Mapping and Prediction) program and by the donation of Roger B. Morrison, Denver, Colorado.

For the reading of the manuscript my thanks to Karl Butzer, W. S. Broecker, N. D. Opdyke and J. D. Hays.

tectonic rather than climatic origin. Evidently the classical glacial stages of Penck and Brückner based on the alpine terraces cover the last 850,000 years fully, but their climatic concept is in error.

Interglacials are defined as intervals of continuous presence of mixed broadleaf forest in northwestern and central Europe. There were at least three such interglacials locally labeled as Eem (120, 230, and about 330 thousand years ago), two which were described as Holstein, and three labeled, or mislabeled, as Cromer.

Our conclusions are based on three highly probable assumptions that still cannot be directly proved: (1) that the eight glacial cycles of Brunhes age, recognized in the semicontinuous loess-soil sequences around Brno and Prague and labeled as L-B to L-I in an order of increasing age, are the products of roughly synchronous, gross global climate changes which left a record of eight similar cycles in deep-sea sediments; (2) that the development of river terraces around Brno was roughly synchronous with that of the terraces around Ulm and Munich; and (3) that the development of terraces around Prague was roughly synchronous with those around Leipzig.

Needless to say, the misinterpreted climatic and time stratigraphic concept of classical European glacial stages and the broad use of corresponding labels in world-wide correlations far away from the original type localities contributed greatly to the remarkable confusion which reigns in the jungles of Pleistocene stratigraphy today. The use of classical Pleistocene stage names should be restricted to their type areas and to the intervals of time truly represented by their type units. The meaningful world-wide climatostratigraphic subdivision of the Pleistocene must be based on continuous depositional sequences.

INTRODUCTION: THE NATURE OF THE LOESS RECORD

Deep-sea stratigraphers find six to eight glacial-interglacial cycles in the Brunhes, while land geologists recognize only four. There is no doubt that the climatic oscillations inferred from oceanic records really did occur and that they affected the continents as well as the oceans. Thus, it must be concluded that paleoclimatic events in glaciated areas on land are either incompletely recorded or preserved, or that some of the recorded oscillations were not recognized. The latter may have occurred because of the well known, repetitive nature of the geologic record in glaciated areas and because of the natural tendency of stratigraphers to interpret their findings in terms of the most simple climatostratigraphic schemes already published. (This tendency was described as the "Reinforcement Syndrome" by Watkins 1971).

It is the periglacial area around Prague, Brno, and Nitra in Czechoslovakia, as well as around Krems and Vienna in Austria, which sheds more light on this dilemma (cf. Figure 1). This part of Central Europe was never glaciated. When the Alpine and Fennoscandinavian ice sheets reached their maximum extents, loess accumulated in this region that was influenced by highly continental periglacial climate. During the interglacials the climate was of atlantic type, similar to the present one, or warmer and wetter. Deciduous forests developed, leaving behind the characteristic parabraunerde soils. Thus in favorable depositional basins, glacial-interglacial cycles were recorded by repeated alternation of loess and forest soils. The deposits are frequently associated with river terraces, because the steep cliffs of abandoned river banks provided ideal sedimentary traps for the windblown dust. The terraces around Prague were formed by a tributary of the Labe (Elbe) River, that flows through the region of Fennoscandinavian glacial deposits. The terraces around Brno, Nitra, Krems, and Vienna belong to the tributaries of the Danube. This river also drains the Alpine foothills. The classical Alpine glacial stages were defined by Penck and Brückner (1909) on terraces in the vicinity of Munich and Ulm (Figure 1). Thus, the correlation of loess sequences with glacial deposits in Northern Europe and in the Alps is possible.

Magnetostratigraphy and close parallels in climatic history have enabled the correlation of the loess sections with deep-sea sediments, so that now these can be correlated with reasonable confidence with the classical European glacial stages.

The Bohemian and Moravian loess area is special because it has a greater variety of climate-indicative sediments and soils than any other part of Europe. As Zeuner (1959) observed, it is located close enough to the Atlantic Ocean to show its influence of atlantic-type climates during interglacials, but at the same time it is far enough inland to develop continental chernozem steppes during interstadials.

Because of their high sensitivity in recording the regional climate change, the loesses of central Europe have been intensively studied. Unlike North America or Russia, where for the most part only extensive loess sheets and subdividing soils are recognized and utilized in geological mapping, in central Europe the best subdivided loess and soil sequences have been traditionally approached and viewed as the sources of paleoclimatic information.

More than one hundred selected localities, with especially well-developed sequences, have been described in Czechoslovakia and Austria during this century (among others: Penck and Brückner 1909; Götzinger 1936; Soergel 1939; Schönhals 1951, Žebera 1943, 1944; Fink 1954, 1956, 1969; Musil, et al. 1955; Demek and Kukla 1969; Kukla 1970). Several hundred more localities of this nature are described in unpublished reports of the Geological Surveys.

The localities best known in literature are Paudorf and Göttweig in Austria, and Věstonice (Unterwisternitz) in Czechoslovakia, but the

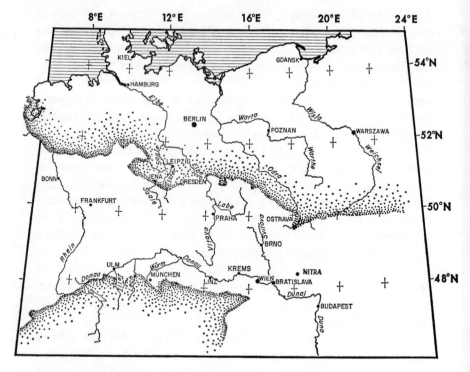

Figure 1.   Location of the main area of study around Praha, Brno and Krems. Maximum extent of Pleistocene glaciers dotted.

two most important key localities are Červený Kopec (Red Hill) in Brno, and the Kremser Schiesstätte in Krems.

THE PALEOCLIMATIC VALUE OF LOESS SERIES

What type of environment and climate is recorded by loess and its associated sediments and soils? The comparative sedimentologic and pedologic observations, as well as studies of the embedded abundant snail assemblages, prove that mixed-oak woodlands, steppes, barren badlands, and loess tundras on permafrost alternately occupied this part of central Europe (Figure 2).

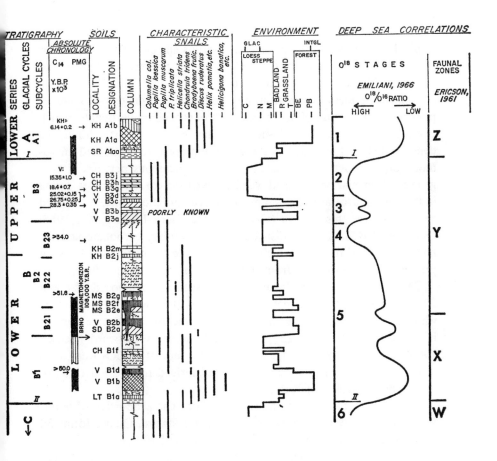

Figure 2. Summarized stratigraphy of the loess sequences from the last 130,000 years in the area around Prague and Brno.

PMG: polarity of remanent magnetization, black: normal, stripped: interpreted as reversed (after Kukla and Koči 1972). Radiocarbon ages from Kutná Hora (KH) and Věstonice (V) (see Figures 17 and 18); abbreviations of type localities of soils are the same as in Figure 12, lithologic column with same signs as in Figure 15.

Curve of reconstructed environment shows cold (C), normal (N) and mild (M) loess steppe; badlands characterized by hillwash deposits; sparse or ephemeral grasslands favoring rendzinas (R); rich or persistent grasslands favoring cherno-zems (T); coniferous or short-lived mixed forests favoring braunerde (BE); and deciduous, long lasting forest favoring parabraunerde (PB). Cold and normal loess steppe in studied area is characteristic for full glacial (GLAC.), parabraunerde for full interglacial (INTGL.).

Roman numerals under glacial cycles designate marklines, under O[18] stages, terminations. Vertical scale is proportional to relative thickness (NOT a time scale).

Loess

Typical loess is a yellow, calcareous, porous silt of eolian origin. It is relatively homogenous, non-bedded, breaks in prismatic columns, and is remarkably stable in vertical walls.

Pleistocene loess differs from any known eolian deposit of contemporary origin because of its fine network of secondary carbonate, which coats the rock detritus and sheets of clay minerals, partly filling the dense system of fine grass rootholes. Stratigraphic relations and micromorphology prove beyond doubt that the calcareous network is syngenetic. A special type of arid weathering called LOESSIFICATION, acting in both the source area as well as in the accumulation zone, is believed responsible for this feature (Ganssen 1922; Berg 1932; Ložek 1965; Obruchev 1945). It is the distribution of secondary carbonate and the high porosity of the rock which makes possible the distinction between primary windblown loess from redeposited hillwash or floodloam.

The loesses in Czechoslovakia and Austria are composed of about 30-40 percent of grains between 0.01 and 0.05 millimeters in size, while 30-40 percent are less than 0.01 millimeters. Carbonate content is frequently between 7-15 percent and increases eastward (Pelíšek 1969). An exceptionally high content of 40 percent $CaCO_3$ was found in the so called "white loess" which was derived from the detritus of marlstones (Ložek and Kukla 1959).

The leading clay mineral in loesses is illite. The proportion of montmorillonite is low in the west but increases eastward. Quartz forms 30 to 50 percent of the silt fraction, feldspar around 10 percent, mica (including weathered biotite) some 5 to 10 percent. The remaining constituents are various silicates, oxides, and occasional fragments of shale or limestone (Pelíšek 1969).

Next to the loess basins, in the bordering highlands, the so called loessloams ("Loesslehm" in German) are found. They are light brown, rusty, mottled, noncalcareous, wind blown, clayey silts or silty clays with frequent limonite and manganolimonite concretions. They have only approximately 1 percent calcium carbonate, and less silt and more clay than typical loess (around 50 percent of fraction below 0.01 millimeters). Frequent constituents are tiny spherules of limonite and manganolimonite and rootcasts of amorphous silica (Ambrož 1947). In Czechoslovakia and Austria the loess typically occupies elevations from 150 to 350 meters above sea level while the loessloams lie between 300 and 600 meters and as high as 1,000 meters.

While it is possible that part of the loessloam was deposited with a very low content of primary carbonate, the overwhelming majority of the deposits bear the marks of secondary decalcification. Thus it is highly probable that during the cold phases of the Pleistocene, carbonate rich loesses covered a much larger area than they do today. During the Holocene their distribution was restricted to relatively warm and dry environment.

Loess stretches in discontinuous bodies from southern England and the coast of Brittany toward the Paris basin, the lower Rhine Valley, central and South Germany, Bohemia, Moravia, Austria, Slovakia to Poland, Hungary, Bulgaria, Rumania, Ukraine and central Asia. In eastern Europe and Asia the loess sheets attain their maximum thickness of over 100 meters. Calcareous loess in its present distribution is restricted to dry lowlands with elevations of not more than 300 to 400 meters above sea level, and with a mean annual rainfall below 700 millimeters.

The northeastern limit of loesses and loessloams in central Europe lies some fifty miles south of the margin of the Late Weichselian ice. It was formerly believed that the extensive plains of glacial outwash were the main source of the European loess, and that the dust was transported by wind for fairly long distances. It is now believed that the bulk of the sediment was picked up by wind from the seasonally dried floodplains of the intermittent Pleistocene rivers (Lauterborn 1912; Schönhals 1944) and from the mechanically weathered hard rock outcrops in the neighbouring highlands (Ambrož 1947; Ložek 1965).

Even though a recent replica of Pleistocene loess is not known from any part of the world, its depositional environment can be fairly well reconstructed. Extensive, bare or poorly vegetated, seasonally-dry surfaces exposed to loessification must have existed in the deflation areas. Sparse patches of grass and sedges in the accumulation areas were necessary to pick up the dust and prevent further erosion of the surface. Indeed, pollen of *Gramineae* and *Cyperaceae* were reported from the Moravian and Austrian loesses by Frenzel (1964). The frequent sandy interlayers and wind-moved cobbles on the slopes prove that winds were occasionally strong.

The most valuable information on the loess environment is provided by the gastropods. Calcareous loesses in Czechoslovakia and Austria are very rich in snail shells. These are found largely intact and there is no doubt that snails lived at the time of loess deposition.

The typical autochthonous assemblage of central european loesses is one dominated by the group *Pupilla* and called the *Pupilla* fauna by Ložek (1964). It is a monotonous association, poor in numbers of species. Some of these still live in the steppes of Europe, while others such as *Pupilla loessica* are extinct. No place is known today where the living elements of the *Pupilla* fauna dwell together.

The temperature requirements of the *Pupilla* group are difficult to estimate, but they seem to be higher than those of the *Columella* fauna (see below). The type of environment corresponding to loesses with a *Pupilla* fauna could be best referred to as COLD LOESS-STEPPE (Büdel 1951; Ložek 1969), indicating a highly continental climate with a large daily and seasonal temperature range.

The *Columella* faunas (Ložek 1964, 1969) are dominated by a cold resistant species *Columella columella*, frequently accompanied by *Vertigo parcedentata, Vallonia tennuilabris*, or *Pupilla loessica*. Elements of wet-cold environments such as *Succinea putris* or *Vertigo arctica* and *Vertigo pseudosubstriata* are also present. The latter today lives in the alpine zone of the Tien Shan Mountains of central Asia, under an extremely cold and highly continental climate.

At the Paleolithic sites of Věstonice and Pavlov, the wet *Columella* fauna is accompanied by lynx, wolverine (*Gulo gulo*), arctic fox (*Alopex lagopus*), reindeer, mammoth and woolly rhinoceros (Musil 1959), and in Bojnice by lemming (*Dicrostonyx torquatus*) (Prošek and Ložek 1957). Also related to this assemblage are the frost-gley soils of cycles B, C, and E (see below) indicative of permafrost.

Evidently the *Columella* fauna was able to persist in a subarctic environment, with very low winter temperatures. This kind of environment was referred to by Büdel (1951) as *Loess-tundra*, even though the designation may be inappropriate.

The *Striata* fauna of Ložek (1964, 1969) is represented, among others, by *Helicopsis striata, Chondrula tridens, Pupilla muscorum, Vallonia costata* and in some areas by *Abida frumentum*. All its elements today live in central Europe, and the assemblage as a whole is closely related to the Holocene steppe faunas of southeastern Europe. This assemblage, characteristic of what we could call the WARM LOESS-STEPPE (Ložek 1969), is frequent in the loess interlayers separating the humus-rich early glacial chernozems, and in loesses interlayed by pellet sands. A *Striata* fauna does not necessarily imply that the climate was mild. It may resist harsher winters than those occurring today in eastern Europe. Nevertheless, it probably indicates relatively warm and dry summers. It is also interesting to note that the Czech and Austrian *Striata* faunas closely resemble the assemblages of full glacial loesses known from Spain and southern France.

In conclusion the loess of central and eastern Europe was deposited under a variety of climatic conditions which have only one thing in common: expressed continentality, with low precipitation and a short rainy season. Mean annual temperatures may have been as low or even lower than in northern Siberia today but also as high as they are now in the Black Sea Basin.

Marker and the Pellet Sands

Loess comes together with almost any kind of sediment, including fluvial sands and gravels, volcanic ash or glacial varves. There are, however, two very specific types of sediments fairly common within the loess filled depressions of Bohemia and Moravia: pellet sands and "markers" (Kukla 1961b).

Both have a high climate-indicative value. The pellet sands, sediments at least partly contemporaneous with gravel aggradation in neighbouring rivers, are the slope deposits of torrential rains that followed a prolonged warm and dry season. "Markers" are probably a deposit of dust storms of continental magnitude.

PELLET SANDS (*Lehmrockelsand* in German as proposed by the late F. E. Zeuner) are the well-bedded hillwash loams composed entirely or partly of the sand-size pellets of older reworked clayey soils. These were redeposited by flash currents so quickly that they did not have time to disintegrate; an eight-meter, single layer of fossil pellet sand is known from Mnešice. Two or three meter-thick deposits are quite common.

Recent pellet sands were formed, for example, during the torrential rain in May of 1960 in Ünětice, Prague, following three weeks of hot dry weather with daily maximum temperatures of 25 to 29 ° centigrade. The bare surface of an artificially-stripped beet field dried and crumbled. Loose, angular loam fragments were then picked up by water and deposited on nearby grassy slopes and at the foot of the hill. The inclination of pellet sand layers, where held by grass, was 35°, but only 1° on the foothill, where a 25 centimeter-thick deposit was laid down 100 meters from the source area. The middle part of the layer was the coarsest. Loam pellets here were up to 8 millimeters in diameter and rock fragments up to 30 millimeters. Out of the total 18.3 millimeters of precipitation, 13.4 fell during the first fifteen minutes, and maximum intensity was 2.8 millimeters per minute.

Judging from actual observations the formation of pellet sands requires: (1) almost bare surface with very sparse vegetation upslope;

(2) clayey loams that crack into hard fragments when slowly dessicated; and (3) a sufficiently long period of dry, warm weather followed by intensive torrential rains. In addition, some grass must be present in places where the fossil pellet sands accumulate on steep slopes.

The autochthonous snail fauna of the fossil pellet sands seems to belong to the *Helicopsis striata group*, but has no typical loess elements such as of the *Pupilla* family. The fauna could live today in the temperate steppes of Europe.

Storms during late spring and early summer do occur in central Europe today, but under normal circumstances they are preceded by frequent spring rains which keep the ground wet and the grass flourishing. Thus the pellet sand climate in some ways suggests a monsoon-like pattern, with low cloudiness and absence of rain in spring or early summer, followed by a period or rainstorms.

The principal problem in explaining the occurrence of fossil pellet sands is in determining why and how the upper parts of the slopes were stripped of vegetation. Were the spring seasons too dry to support the dense grass of chernozem steppes? Were rainstorms displaced from late spring to late summer? Or was the deterioration of grasslands a result of other phenomena?

In this respect the regular occurrence of "markers" at the base of pellet sand layers becomes suspect.

MARKERS are thin (2 to 30 centimeters thick) bands of light brown, fine grained, mostly calcareous silt that separate underlying black, rich humus steppe soil from overlying pellet sands (Kukla 1961b). The upper section is bedded and shows signs of hillwash redeposition. Markers are generally finer grained than normal loess, but no significant differences in petrographical composition were found. Their base is often reworked by worms. By their sharp lower boundary, airborne base, and hillwash top, markers resemble some of the Pearlette occurrences of the American Midwest.

The intriguing problem of markers is the source of the dust. It could not have been the close vicinity of localities, as the surface there was covered by black, mostly decalcified and degraded chernozems under dense grass cover, while the local rivers carried decalcified detritus from surrounding wooded highlands.

Thus dust storms of continental magnitude seem to be the most logical explanation for the deposition of markers. On April 5, 1960, such a storm deposited 3 centimeters of dust in Romania, carried from the Kalmyk steppe in central Asia, a distance of over 2,000 kilometers. Whether this explanation is correct or not, markers provide an excellent correlation horizon, subdividing the autochthonous soils from overlying sediments. Within Bohemia and Moravia these horizons were very probably strictly synchronous.

Soils

Soils do record the principal character of vegetation established at a locality for a period of least several centuries. The quality of soil horizons depends directly on the type, density, and duration of vegetational cover. Only indirectly is it affected by variations of climate. Thus, once a thick grassland or forest is established in the area, sedimentation slows down and eventual fluctuations in temperature or precipitation are no longer recorded. Most of the localities studied lie on slopes. Under such conditions the soils are para-autochthonous. Surfaces did not become fully stabilized, but slow redeposition of soil materials from higher elevations into depressions proceeded constantly. Leached soils with clay-rich B-horizons have the highest stratigraphic value. They are the product of deciduous forests, which in this part of Europe are, by definition, interglacial. Characteristic of the full glacials are frost-gleys — pseudo-gleyed raw soils developed on top of the frozen substratum.

The soils in the loess areas of central Europe are of two main groups: (1) BIOLOGICALLY REWORKED STEPPE (PRAIRIE) SOILS, showing an accumulation of organic matter but little chemical change of mineral matrix; and (2) LEACHED or BRAUNERDE TYPE SOILS with evidence of *in situ* redeposition of carbonate, iron and manganese compounds as well as clay, but are only slightly reworked by the pedofauna.

Some authors (eg. Smolíková 1971) distinguish a third group called RAW SOILS that are in initial phases of development, and may later become either braunerdes or chernozems.

The original Holocene soils in central Europe were, for the most part, heavily disturbed by intensive and long lasting agriculture. Undisturbed profiles, however, can be found in natural gullies, on rocky hilltops, under forests, or in caverns.

Two climax soil types developed on the calcareous loesses of the studied area: (1) CHERNOZEMS — rich in humus, calcareous, well granulated, occupying the dry central parts of loess basins north of Prague, south of Brno, and east of Vienna and Bratislava; and (2) PARABRAUNERDES — decalcified, brown soils with clay illuviation in the B-horizon. Clay fills the rootholes and coats the peds, while there is a thick *C-ca* horizon. Parabraunerdes border the chernozem belt.

Chernozems are closely bound on the loess belt, and stretch from central Germany and Czechoslovakia to the Urals and central Asia. Here they reach as far north as 57° latitude, in the vicinity of Perm. Chernozems are, at present, characteristic of continental climates with cold to very cold winters, rainy springs, and dry summers.

The parabraunerdes and related forest soils, with illuvial clays in their B-horizons, border the southern periphery of the loess belt. Contrary to chernozems, which reach their northernmost limit in the Asian interior, parabraunerde-type soils find their northern limits in central Europe.

A variety of less intensively developed soils may locally represent the climax of Holocene pedogenesis. Shallow, light brown rendzinas, relatively poor in humus, but strongly reworked by pedofauna, are common on southward slopes in Austria and Slovakia.

Bordering the northern perimeter of the loess belt, deep PSEUDO-GLEYS developed during the Holocene on the loessloam substratum. These and related, humid forest soils extend from central Europe northeastward to approach 60° North latitude in the vicinity of the Urals.

Under natural conditions, the loess belt today would be thoroughly vegetated, its surface stabilized, and the occasional limited airborn increments reaching the surface would be assimilated in soils without interrupting the pedogenetic process. Actually, however, large areas have been denuded by man and are now subject to extensive soil erosion and redeposition. Thus, modern allochthonous soils are frequent in the region.

Snail faunas in the driest parts of the basins, with thick chernozems, are dominated by such species as *Chondrula tridens* and *Abida frumentum*. They differ from similar Pleistocene interstadial faunas by the presence of some exothermic elements like *Cepea vindobonensis* or *Oxychilus inopinatus*, and by the presence of southern immigrants, like *Helicella cecilioides*, whose expansion was facilitated by man (Ložek 1972).

At the forested borders of the loess basins there are the richly diversified faunas of deciduous forests. Among their numerous elements are *Monachoides incarnata*, *Ena montana*, *Discus perspectivus*, *Helicodonta obvoluta*, and *Helix pomatia*. With respect to this last species, Ložek (1964) refers to these assemblages as the *Helix* faunas.

Related to the *Helix* faunas are the so-called *Banatica* faunas typical for Pleistocene interglacials. In addition to forms known from recent broadleaf forests in the region, species such as *Helicigona banatica,*

Soosia diodonta, and *Aegopinella rossmani* are present. Some require higher winter temperatures and wetter summers than presently exist on these sites.

The parabraunerde of Czechoslovakia and Austria, which developed on calcareous loess of the last glacial age, is always associated with an undisturbed environment of mixed hardwood forests and *Helix* faunas. Fossil parabraunerde are also associated with *Banatica* snail assemblages. Gastropods are typically found in krotowinas reaching into *Cca* horizons of this soil or in carbonate-rich, hillwash loams, immediately underlying such soils. They are not present within the soil itself, since it is strongly leached.

In the parabraunerde of cycle *B1* (see below), Frenzel (1964) found a relatively rich pollen assemblage with oak, linden, elm and hazel, providing an independent proof of an interglacial origin for this soil. Stones of *Celtis*, a subtropical form, are common in the older parabraunerdes and braunlehms (Ložek 1969).

Only two types of soil known from the Pleistocene sections did not form within the loess belt during Holocene times: braunlehms, strongly weathered, argillic forest soils of the Mediterranean province, and the FROST-GLEYS (frost-pseudogleys), initial soil formations bound to permafrost.

A BRAUNLEHM in Kubiena's micromorphologic system (1956) is the soil with secondary clay plasma forming the major component of the B-horizon. It develops by ongoing weathering from an initial parabraunerde. Within the Eurasian loess belt, a braunlehm of unquestionable Holocene age has not yet been described. Braunlehms are common in the Mediterranean, but here also they are, in the main part, evidently fossil.

The snail assemblages associated with braunlehms are essentially the same as those of the parabraunerde, *Banatica* group. There are no faunistic or floristic indications of a substantially warmer climate during the formation of braunlehm as compared to the parabraunerde environment.

On the other hand, all fossil braunlehms in the study area are polygenetic and show marks of repeated pedogenesis. Thus, rather than providing indications of extreme warmth and humidity of the corresponding intervals, braunlehms are tentatively interpreted as products of relatively long and probably repeated presence of deciduous forest. The wide rootholes of xerophytes, filled with clayey soil plasma (*Lehmstangen*), that are common in Slovakia and Austria, suggests that during the formation of braunlehms, phases of seasonally-dry savanna-type climate were succeeded by forest readvances.

Still unclear is the terminology and climatic interpretation of the so-called frost-gleys (initial pseudo-gleys, also micro-gleys). These are horizons that differ from the surrounding loess only by the greenish-gray stains of reduced iron compounds and by frequent limonitic concentrations. These features are believed to be due to repeated saturation of the soil by groundwater. As these initial, soil developmental stages are often associated with cold-tolerant *Columella* faunas, and since the gley phenomena run parallel to the surface and are accompanied by small involutions and signs of solifluction, it is probable that they formed at the base of the seasonal Thaw zone, on top of the permafrost.

Also important as paleoclimatic indicators are the common BRAUN-ERDE soils. Braunerde *B3a* horizons (see below on the labeling of units) with deep leaching and oxidation, do not show signs of clay illuviation. Temperate snails were not found accompanying this soil in any of the studied localities. Smolíková (1968a, 1968b, 1971) studied the micro-morphology of this soil in the neighborhood of Brno and Prague and compared it to artic braunerdes, commonly found under taiga. The *B2a* horizon is similar in appearance, rarely yielding reworked remains of concentrated BLP (braunlehm plasma). Judging by the accompanying snail assemblages with *Bradybaena fruticum*, it formed under parkland or open forest, in the relatively temperate climate of early glacial inter-stadials.

Paleoclimatic Indicators: Concluding Remarks

As the preceding discussion indicates, the paleoclimatic information that can be derived from loess sequences comes from characteristic types of sediments or soils and, independently, from snail assemblages. Both soils and snails depend upon the type of established vegetation cover and its persistence. They are specific to the loess belt, which is relatively narrow in Europe. Thus, unlike marine faunas, which can be followed moving north and south during the glacial cycles, the characteristic soils and gastropod assemblages of the loess belt alternately appeared and disappeared.

Interglacials are defined as intervals of warm and wet climate, during which temperate deciduous forests were established in northwestern Europe (Turner and West 1968; Fairbridge 1972; Turner, this volume). In the neighbourhood of Prague, Brno, and Krems the development of hardwood forests was practically synchronous with the type region

(Frenzel 1968). Thus parabraunerdes, braunlehms and the accompanying *Helix* and *Banatica* faunas are the approximate time equivalents of the II and III temperate phases of interglacials as described from palynological records. Their presence in the sequence is the stratigraphic proof of an interglacial proper.

On the other hand, the presence of some other, less developed soil or of some less demanding snail assemblage does not in itself rule out the possible interglacial age of the corresponding level. In this respect we must remember that today, almost at the end of the Holocene interglacial, soils of both basic groups, braunerdes and chernozems, in various stages of development and degradation, coexist within the area as local climax soils. As a consequence, unequivocal recognition of interglacials from soils is not possible within the dry, central parts of the loess belt, such as Vienna, southern Slovakia or Hungary, where the climax soils of interglacials as well as of temperate interstadials were chernozemic.

Full glacial conditions, during which the glaciers in the Alps, north Germany and Poland reached their last maxima, although well recorded in the Prague and Brno area by frost-gley soils and *Columella* snail faunas, can barely be detected within the dry core of the loess belt.

CYCLIC PATTERNS IN THE LOESS SEQUENCES

A surprisingly close correspondence of sedimentation sequences of different ages has been observed in the region around Prague and Brno. This observation led to the definition of sedimentary cycles of the first and second order (Kukla 1961a) and, later, to a regional lithostratigraphic system based on the cyclic position of soils within the sequence (Kukla 1969). Cycles of the first order are called GLACIAL CYCLES and are delimited by marklines. Those of the second order, STADIAL CYCLES or SUBCYCLES, are delimited by submarklines. Each cycle and subcycle starts with a thin deposit of hillwash loam (phase 1), succeeded by a forest soil of braunerde type (phase 2), steppe soil of chernozem type (phase 3), marker (phase 4), pellet sand (phase 5), and loess (phase 6). Some members of the sequence may be missing, but within the studied area the successive order of the phases always remains identical. The detailed, cyclic repetitions of the early glacial chernozems, markers, and pellet sands were not observed in glacial cycles older than *D*, but this may reflect the fact that only a few localities of this age are known.

Marklines

The basic framework for the cyclic subdivision is provided by mark-lines. They are the boundaries between a thick layer of "cold" loess, of the type containing the *Columella* or *Pupilla* faunas and found between successive interglacial parabraunerdes or braunlehms, or their imme-diately underlying hillwash sediments of phase 1.

Each unit delimited by two successive marklines is a glacial cycle. It is labeled by a capital letter. The elapsed interval of the first Holocene glacial cycle is labeled *A*, the last completed Pleistocene cycle *B*, the next older one *C*, and so on, in order of increasing age.

Within each glacial cycle, an oscillatory but gradual change is evident between a pronounced climatic optimum (marked by a forest soil and snail assemblage) and the most severe continental climate. Whereas the optimum occurs at the beginning of each cycle, the coldest environment is recorded shortly before its end. In this respect the loess cyclothems resemble glacial cycles in marine O^{18} records (Broecker and Van Donk 1970) or the oscillations of foraminiferal assemblages and coccoliths in the North Atlantic (Ruddiman and McIntyre 1973). The stratigraphic sequence of the last glacial cycle *B* is a good example of such a development (Figure 3).

Submarklines

Submarklines (Kukla and Koči 1972) are the boundaries between loess of any kind and braunerdes or chernozems (or underlying hill-wash loams of phase 1).

Each unit delimited by two successive submarklines is called a stadial cycle (or subcycle) and labeled by a capital letter of the corre-sponding glacial cycle as well as an arabic numeral.

Designation of Soil Units

Individual soils and lithologic units recognized in the studied area are so numerous that the original attempt of naming them after the type localities (Klíma, et al. 1962) was fully abandoned in Czechoslovakia. Instead, the soils are labeled by a minor letter combined with the de-signation of the corresponding stadial or glacial cycle. The intention is to use the same designation for horizons considered to be of equal age throughout the region. However, because a correct correlation cannot always be guaranteed, the complete reference needs to include the abbreviated symbol of the locality. Also, where correlations are made with units from outside the loess system, the affix *L* (for loess) is used to avoid confusion with similar labels of other authors.

Thus the designation *L-CK-C3j* refers to the soil observed within the subcycle *C3* (youngest section of glacial cycle *C*) at the locality Červený Kopec (symbol CK). Correspondingly, the soil *L-DK-C3j* in Dolní Kounice (symbol DK) shows the same stratigraphic position and presumably is of the same age. In discussions of the general stratigraphy of the loess belt, the reference to *C3j* soil is explicit enough and symbols of the type sections and the loess area are not necessary.

Also frequently used is a consecutive roman numbering of whole soil groups called *Pedokomplexes* (PK) (Kukla and Ložek 1961). PKO refers to all soils of Holocene age, *PK-I*, *PK-II*, and *PK-III* to the soils of subcycles *B3*, *B2*, and *B1*, *PK-IV* to all soils of glacial cycle *C*; *PK-V* to all soils of glacial cycle *D* and so on (Figure 3).

The development of individual subcycles within each glacial cycle systematically differs one from another. In the oldest subcycle the sediments of phase 1 and 2 are best preserved and developed; in the middle phase, chernozems and pellet sands (phases 3 and 5) are dominant; and in the youngest one, loess (phase 6) prevails, while phases 1, 4, and 5 are completely missing.

Thus apart from multidivision of the glacial cycle into five or three stadial cycles, there also are good reasons for a two-fold subdivision. Under such a scheme, the sedimentary sequence of every glacial cycle is divided into a LOWER and UPPER SERIES. In the lower one, dark-colored soils and soil sediments predominate, while in the Upper one, light-colored loess is the predominant deposit.

Figure 3 shows the relation between the various subdivisions of the deposits of one glacial cycle. Unlike the multidivisions, the two-fold subdivision is applicable for young as well as old deposits, and is useful outside Czechoslovakia and Austria. Typical arctic vertebrates like arctic fox, lemming, or wolverine are either missing or very rare in the Lower Series, but are abundant in the Upper one, giving it a pronounced glacial character. Thus the composition of vertebrate faunas in this part of Europe parallels the two-fold rather than the multifold subdivision of the glacial cycle. Generally speaking, the following conclusions can be drawn in regard to the stratigraphic utility of the various subdivisions of a glacial cycle:

1. Suitable depressions filled with sediments of cycles *D*, *C*, and *B* in

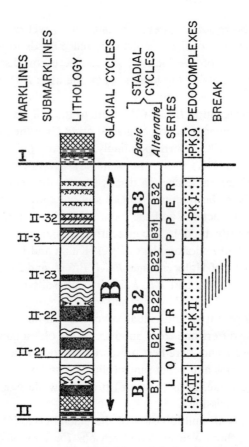

Figure 3.   Different stratigraphic subdivisions of the last glacial cycle *B*. Lithologic column: crosshatched: parabraunerde; full black: rendzinas and chernoze hatched: braunerde; crossed: frostgley soils; wavy lines: pellet sands; dotted: marker; dashed: hillwash loams.

the regions around Prague and Brno. These frequently show detailed, three-fold subdivisions that allow separate recognition of subcycles 1, 2, and 3.

2. Outside such suitable depressions, on platforms or in sequences older than cycle *E*, or away from the Prague and Brno areas, glacial cycle can only be subdivided into Upper and Lower Series, the latter being composed of a complicated polygenetic soil or of pseudo-gleyed, truncated basal B-horizon of a forest soil. Similar two-fold units are common in loess areas of the United States and Soviet Union and are widely utilized in geologic mapping.

The Megacycles

As will be discussed later, the soils of some of the glacial cycles are exceptionally strongly developed and the loesses are thicker than normal. Also within such cycles (*F* and *K*), intervals of major erosion produce disconformities. As far as the available evidence shows, the glaciers reached their extreme extent one cycle later, that is during *J* and *E*.

Thus it is possible to subdivide the loess sequence into major units, labeled tentatively as megacycles and delimited by disconformities. Following the suggestion of John Imbrie, the last two such megacycles are labeled by the Greek letters α and β. Each lasted for several hundred thousand years (cf. Figure 28). Compared to the *F* and *K* disconformities, the *C* break is less significant.

THE TIME CONTROL

The chronostratigraphic setting of the loess sequence (Figure 29, page 169) is based on:

1. Finite radiocarbon dates of charcoal and soils extending back to about 30,000 years B.P., with infinite radiocarbon dates on soils over 50,000 years old.
2. Positions of magnetostratigraphic boundaries: the Brunhes/Matuyama and Olduvai/Matuyama reversals, and the Blake event.
3. Inferred, general temporal coincidence of marklines with the terminations in oceanic sediments. The ages of terminations obtained upon assumption of regular sedimentation rates in the deep-sea can be directly used as age estimates for corresponding marklines.

Radiocarbon age determinations were performed on samples of charcoal and soil from several localities: Věstonice (Klíma, et al. 1962; Vogel and Zagwijn 1967), Paudorf and Göttweig (Fink 1969; Vogel and Zagwijn 1967), and several others in the area. The youngest, well developed, Pleistocene chernozem was found to be over 51,800 years old at Věstonice and 43,000 years old at Oberfellabrunn. In the latter locality, strong contamination by younger materials was observed, so that the obtained date, similarly to Věstonice, was classified as a minimum age (Vogel and Zagwijn 1967). The summary of the available radiocarbon control is shown in Figure 2, page 103.

Oriented paleomagnetic samples of loess and related soils and sediments have shown fairly stable and strong depositional remanence. A

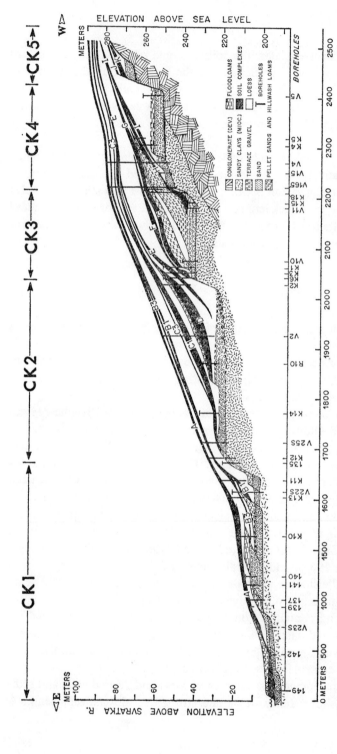

Figure 4.   Section of Červený Kopec (CK — Red Hill) at Brno, Czechoslovakia, showing semicontinuous sequence of soils and sediments of Brunhes and Late Matuyama age, cut into Miocene clays and Devonian conglomerates. Horizontal scale shows distance from the Svratka River. *CK 1–5* are individual terraces, *A* to *K* baselines of corresponding glacial cycles. Section exposed by brick-loam excavations or boreholes. (See location in Figures 12 and 13; detailed stratigraphic column in Figure 5.)

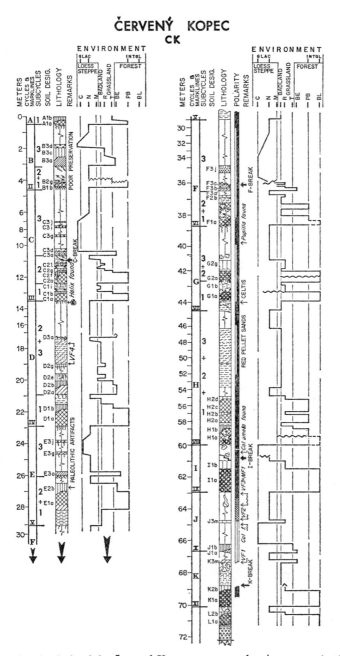

ČERVENÝ KOPEC
CK

Figure 5. Analysis of the Červený Kopec sequence, showing segments of highest stratigraphic resolution from Figure 4. Symbols as in Figure 2; *BL* marks repeated pedogenesis under deciduous forests. Polarity measured by A. Koči (unpublished) and Bucha, et al. (1969) (Details of B/M boundary given by Figure 14). Snail assemblages after Ložek (unpublished), classification of polygenetic soils partly after Smolíková (1967, 1971). Other symbols are the same as in Figure 15.

120   GEORGE J. KUKLA

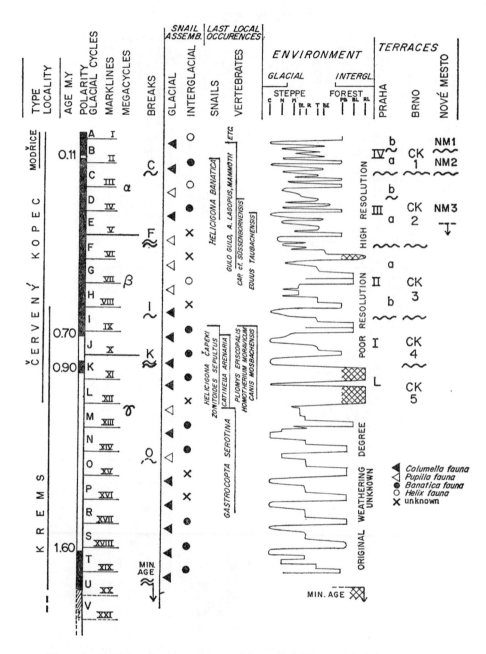

Figure 6.   Environment changes around Brno and Krems as reconsrtucted from
the loess record. Symbols as in Figure 2, with *RL* (crosshatched) marking warm, wet
climate with prolonged, warm, dry seasons (exceptionally red, polygenetic soils).
Terrace stratigraphy of the Vltava at Prague according to Záruba (1942).

magnetostratigraphic unit characterized by southseeking remanent declination, but downpointing inclination, was found in Modřice, close to Brno (Figure 4; Kukla and Kočí, 1972); it has been correlated with the Blake event of some 110,000 years ago. The Brunhes/Matuyama reversal of 0.7 ±0.05 million years was located in two sequences in Krems, Austria (Fink, et al. i.p.; cf. Figures 8 and 9), two at Červený Kopec, Czechoslovakia (Bucha, et al. 1969; Bucha 1973; Kočí, un-

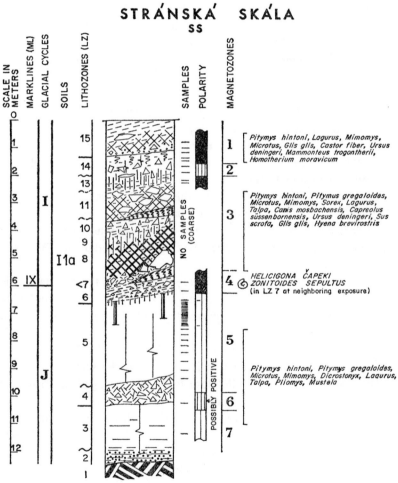

Figure 7. Stratigraphic column of the main excavation of Biharian vertebrates at Stránská Skála. All soils are partly or wholly reworked. Lithozones and characteristic vertebrates after Musil (1969); polarity after a/f demagnetization on 150°e partly after Kočí (unpublished) and Bucha and Horáček (unpublished). Double vertical line shows closely sampled paleomagnetic sections. Snails after Ložek and Fejfar (1957) (see also Figures 13 and 16).

published; cf. Figures 4 and 5), one on Stránská Skála (cf. Figure 1) (Koči, unpublished; cf. Figure 1), and one in Únětice (Koči, unpublished; cf. Figure 24).

It must be stressed that the independent intercorrelation confirms the contemporaneousness of five of the mentioned locations, namely those in Červený Kopec, Stránská Skála, and Krems. The two sites with detected transition at Červený Kopec occur below a soil which (1) can be traced continuously from one location to the other, (2) contains a Biharian fauna of a type similar to that of Stránská Skála, (3) is the same braunlehm as at Stránská Skála, and (4) covers the same terrace level as that on Stránská Skála (Figure 7). In a similar way, the layer with the B/M transition at Krems is continuously exposed between both sampled sites (Figure 8), while the capping soil contains a snail assemblage typical for Stránská Skála.

The magnetohorizon interpreted as the Matuyama/Olduvai transition has so far been located in only one place, at Krems (Figure 9). Because of possible gaps in the record below the Brunhes/Matuyama level, this interpretation is uncertain and should be considered as a minimum age estimate (Figure 6).

Marklines — boundaries where the "cold" loess with *Pupilla* or *Columella* faunas meet with interglacial forest soils, and a product of rapid deglaciation at the end of glacial cycles — broadly correlate with terminations in the O^{18} isotopic record of deep-sea sediments (Broecker and Van Donk 1970).

Global synchroneity of gross climate changes was the original, basic argument for synchroneity of terminations and marklines (Kukla 1970). Today, new facts support this correlation. There are eight O^{18} glacial cycles and thus eight terminations in the Brunhes section of the Pacific deep-sea core V 28-238 (Shackleton and Opdyke 1973). The corresponding number of marklines in loess series is the same.

The age of Markline I falls close to 10,000 B.P., judging from the last occurrences of autochthonous wind-blown loesses at the Magdalenian cave sites (Kukla and Koči 1972; Valoch 1968). Termination I was dated in the cores of the equatorial Atlantic to about 11,000 B.P. (Broecker, et al. 1960). Ruddiman and McIntyre (1973) showed that this is really the case in the central zone of the North Atlantic, but that the termination occurred two thousand years earlier in the eastern part and some four thousand years later in the western part of the North Atlantic. Thus the age of markline I falls within the age range of termination I.

Termination II, 127,000 years old, predates by about 5,000 years the

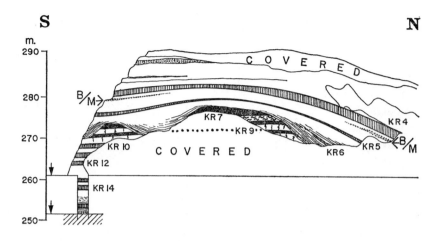

Figure 8. The Krems (Kremser Schiesstätte) brickyard section, showing loess (blank), rotlehms of the "Kremser soil complex" (*KR 7–9*): gray; other soils: vertical lines or dots; pellet sands: wavy lines. After Fink, et al. (i.p.).

last interglacial peak in the O^{18} record. Markline II is more than 115,000 years old, assuming that the correlation of reversed magneto-stratigraphic unit in Modřice with the Blake event is correct. Also Markline II predates, by a few thousand years, the climax soil of the last interglacial deciduous forests. These relations make the synchroneity of Markline II with termination II highly probable.

Pacific core V23-238 correlates very closely with the long cores P 6304-4, P 6304-7, P 6304-9 of Emiliani (1966, 1972) in the Caribbean. Using these four cores, the ages of terminations III-VIII were estimated (Tables 1 and 2) in the following five steps:

1. The intervals between successive terminations were expressed as the percentage of the sediment column separating terminations II and VII. (Termination VII is the oldest reached in all cores).
2. Mean values were calculated (Table 1).
3. Set *A* of apparent ages was obtained by downward EXTRAPOLATION from Termination II, assuming a constant sedimentation rate between the Terminations I (10,000 years old) and VII. The age of Termination II is taken as 127,000 years Old and between Termination IX, close to 700,000 years old.
4. Set *B* of apparent ages was obtained by INTERPOLATION between Termination II taken as 127,000 years (Broecker and Van Donk years old (Shackleton and Opdyke 1973). The sedimentation rate within the interval was considered constant.

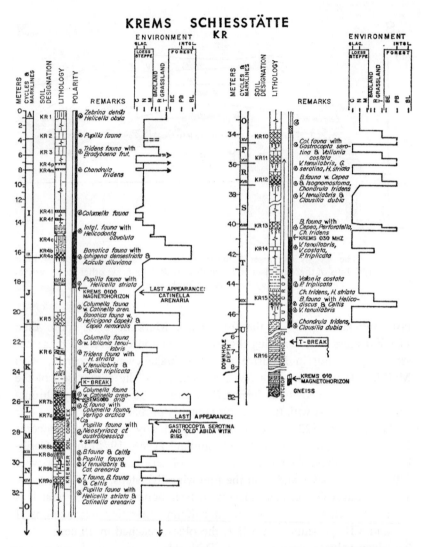

Figure 9. Summary column of Kremser sequence, composed of sediments and soils of Matuyama age. Informal local soil designations *KR 1–16* do not follow the cyclic system. Gaps in the record exist above the soils of the *KR 4* group and below *KR 15*, possibly also at the *K*-break. *KR 7a* and *KR 7b* are deep red rotlehms. Vertical wiggly lines: "Lehmstangen" (root holes). Paleomagnetic determinations by A. Koči and partly J. Kukla (Fink, et al. i.p.). Snail assemblages after Ložek (unpublished). Other symbols are the same as in Figure 15.

Table 1. Mean depth of terminations I to VII in the four long cores analysed for delta O^{18} by Emiliani (1966, 1972) and Shackleton and Opdyke (1973). a = depth in centimeters; b = sediment thickness between T I and VII; c = expressed as percent of b; d = sediment thickness between successive terminations as percent of b; f = mean values of d. Numbers in parentheses refer to poorly expressed terminations.

Glacial Terminations / cycles	Pacific V23-238				Caribbean P-6309-9				P-6304-4				P-6304-7				Means	
	a_1	b_1	c_1	d_1	a_2	b_2	c_2	d_2	a_3	b_3	c_3	d_3	a_4	b_4	c_4	d_4	$e=(d_1+d_2+d_3+d_4)$	$f=e \div 4$
A				24.7				30.3				38.2				35.9	129.1	32.5
I	22		2.8		40		4.2		25		3.2		30		3.2			
B				26.5				26.0				31.2				31.4	115.1	28.8
II	220		27.5		330		34.5		325		41.4		350		39.3			
C				20.8				20.2				20.4				22.5	83.9	21.0
III	430		54.0		580		60.5		570		72.6		630		70.7			
D				20.1				18.8				18.5				20.8	77.9	19.5
IV	595	795	74.8		775	960	80.7		730	785	93.0		830	890	93.2			
E				17.1				10.0				12.5				13.5	53.1	13.3
V	755		94.9		955		99.5		875		111.5		1015		114.0			
F				15.5				25.0				17.4				11.8	69.7	17.4
VI	(890)		112.0		(1050)		109.5		(975)		124.0		1135		127.5			
G				12.3				11.5									23.8	÷ 2) 11.9
VII	1015		127.5		1290		134.5		1110		141.4		1240		139.3			
H				12.2				11.5									23.7	÷ 2) 11.9
VIII	(1110)		139.8		(1400)		146.0											
IX	1210		152.0		Extrapolated 1510*		157.5											

Table 2. Approximate ages of terminations I to IX based on data of Table 1. A = extrapolated past termination II, assuming constant sedimentation rate between T I and T IX; B = intrapolated between T II and T IX assuming constant sedimentation rate within this interval; C = arithmetic means of A and B. Taken as the best estimates back to T V (C-b). Terminations VIII and IX are probably close in ages to C-c, ages of T VI and T VII are uncertain between Cb and Cc columns. Dates for T I and II after Broecker and Van Donk (1970). Best estimates in bold figures.

		In 10³ years							
		Known age	A		B		C a	b	c
Terminations	Mean relative thickness (cm) (from Table 1)		Duration 10³ years	Approximate age	Duration	Approximate age	Means: (A+B)/2	a; rounded	a; assuming constant sedimentation rate from V-IX
I		11	11		11		**11**		
II	32.5	128	117		117		**128**		
III	28.8		104	232	133	261	246	245	
IV	21.0		76	308	97	358	333	335	
V	19.5	123.8	70	378	90	448	413	415	
VI	13.3		48	426	572 61	509	467	465	480
VII	17.4		63	489	81	590	540	540	575
VIII	11.9		43		55	645			**635**
IX	11.9	700	43		55	700			**700**

5. Finally set C of the best age estimates was obtained by averaging sets A and B.

The age of Termination II as used here is considered relatively accurate, since it is consistent with the uranium ages of interglacial coral reefs (Mesollela, et al. 1969).

DEPOSITIONAL ENVIRONMENT AND QUALITY OF RECORD

The number of distinguishable layers developed and preserved in the sequence, and thus the quality of climatostratigraphic information, depends critically on the local morphology.

Serious miscorrelations were frequent in the loess belt in former decades, when Pleistocene stratigraphers did not pay sufficient attention to this fact. In the absence of independent correlation criteria, the authors dated the strata by counting them down from the surface and labeling them in terms of Soergel's and Milankovitch's chronology. This "count from the top" method produced, for instance, the notorious "type" soil of the Riss-Würm interglacial, the Kremser paleosol (Gross

1957; Brandtner 1956; Movius 1960). As we now know, this soil is about one million years old, older than the whole of Penck's classical Pleistocene (see below). Also, by similar miscorrelations, apparent evidence was produced for an oscillating climate within the last interglacial (Musil and Valoch 1966), and a complex, polygenetic soil at Paudorf was chosen to represent a Late Pleistocene interstadial 30,000 years old. (It later yielded one of the richest known snail assemblages of the last interglacial). Much of the reknowned stratigraphic *Würmwirwarr* (Würm-mess), as commented on by Büdel (1949) and still extant among Pleistocene stratigraphers in parts of Europe, has its origins in the loess area.

If counting from somewhere is the only method that the stratigrapher wishes to utilize, then a "count from the bottom" rather than a "count from the top" method should be used. The age of the depression and the age of the uppermost fluvial member in the sequence are clues to the age of a fill. It must be realized that, like any other kind of sediment, loess and hillwash loams require a depression in which to accumulate. This must be favorably located if the sequence is to remain preserved.

Most of the studied sections in Czechoslovakia and Austria rest on abandoned river terraces and fill sheltered depressions cut deep into the subsurface by meandering streams. As the streams gradually cut deeper, the high-lying relief becomes increasingly exposed to denudation and the subsurface zones are largely removed. As a result, loess and soils immediately overlying fluvial sediments are thicker, better subdivided, and less affected by retrograde weathering or destruction than the younger layers deposited closer to the present surface. The westerlies were the prevailing winds throughout the Pleistocene, and therefore the most complete sequences developed on footslopes exposed toward the east and southeast. The layers in such depressions dip under about 2 to 10°.

Favorable conditions cease to exist when a depression is filled and the mean dip of the slope is restored. Meanwhile, however, the river has cut deeper to provide space for the younger fill. Thus, a so-called "telescopic superposition" of strata (Kukla 1961b), exemplified in Figure 4, is commonly observed in the western banks of Czech and Moravian rivers.

The poor subdivision of the sequence is caused by (1) sedimentary undernourishment, and (2) subsequent erosion.

A typical example of "undernourishment" are the polygenetic soils reworked by burrowing animals or by percolating waters. On platforms or on hilltops where no new sediment could be incorporated, except for eolian dust, a forest soil frequently survives cold phases during which it is covered by only sparse vegetation. It may later be reactivated several times under forest before it is ultimately covered with loess or removed by erosion. The polygenetic soils in loess areas can be readily recognized by the layers of carbonate concretions interbedded within decalcified B-horizons. Micromorphologic investigation (Kubiena 1956) can detect the traces of redeposited clay plasma, excrements of characteristic groups of pedofauna, as well as features due to gleying or frost action. However, in practice, no more than four or five successive phases in the soil development can be detected by the micromorphologic study of a single polygenetic soil, and often only the last phase can be recognized. Thus, for instance, at Červený Kopec, over twenty-five individual soils including four interglacial forest soils from glacial cycles E, D, and C merge gradually into one frost-gley horizon, indistinguishable from a raw soil of full glacial age (Figure 4).

This kind of retrograde weathering is a common feature in loess areas, so that determination of a "climax" environment through which a soil has passed, always includes interpretative uncertainties. For example, a braunerde with the structure of an arctic soil has to be interpreted as a climax soil of taiga, when accompanied by a cold-tolerant snail fauna. But essentially the same soil, with residual accretions of clay plasma or accompanied by an interglacial snail assemblage, must be recognized as the trace of a former interglacial parabraunerde. Reliable conclusions on the soil forming paleoenvironment can only be reached when information from several localities is combined.

Once deposited, layers may be destroyed by erosion or solifluction. Such disturbances can take place at any time during the glacial cycle, but are most frequent at the time of deposition of the pellet-sand of subcycle 2, and of the basal part of the Upper Series. Also, the frost wedges and involutions of the B, C and E cycles are most common at this level.

At numerous sites the sediment of the Upper Series rests directly at the base or on the surface of terrace gravels, suggesting that major denudation had taken place during the middle of a glacial cycle. For the sake of convenience, such intervals of exceptionally active, periglacial erosion are called BREAKS.

The most probable stratigraphic composition of incomplete sequences can be determined with the use of the diagram in Figure 10. It was constructed from combined observations made on numerous localities where gradual merging and partial destruction of the horizons of glacial cycle B are seen in long exposures, as at Věstonice, Modřice, Mšené, Chabry, Ždánice, Sedlec, Letky, Kutná Hora, and Nové Mesto. As observed, this section (composed of braunerde, chernozem and loess) in all probability does not represent an exceptionally well-developed, terminal subcycle *B3*, but a commonplace remnant of the last glacial cycle, with the retrogradely weathered B-horizon of the *B1b* soil, interstadial chernozem *B2g*, and the merged loess of subcycles *B2* and *B3*.

The merging of soils of the older glacial cycles is well exposed in Červený Kopec. Here the soils of cycles *C*, *D*, and *E* merge into one polygenetic horizon, as well as the soils of *G* and *F* cycles and *I* and *H* cycles (Figure 4, page 20). A question arises whether such a reduced sequence is discontinuous. It may well be. On the other hand, the slow continuous deposition could have also produced such a profile lacking in detailed resolution. In this respect, loess sequences are similar to deepsea sediments.

Deposition within one lithologic unit can best be described as semi-

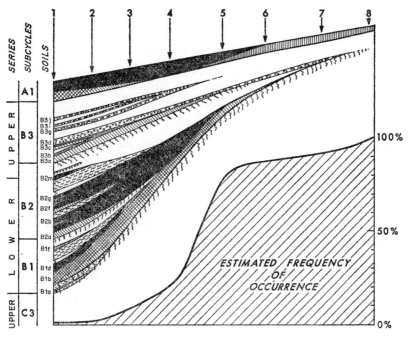

Figure 10. A relative preservation diagram for cycle B phenomena. Complete profiles like that of case 1 are rare; parabraunerdes (*B 1b*), with chernozems (*B 2g*) and braunerdes (*B 2a*) (cases 4 and 5) can be recognized in about a half of the studied sections, whereas the loess of the last and the penultimate glacial cycles was found in all instances.

continuous. A layer of pellet sand frequently shows numerous minor unconformities, proving that deposition alternated with local removal of sediment. A similar internal structure is also anticipated in loess. The wind blown silt accumulated in the lee of grass patches was simultaneously removed elsewhere. Thus the absolute synchroneity between any two distant sections of one unit is improbable, a fact that must be recognized in the interpretation of paleomagnetic data (Figure 11). Markers are the only exception to this rule.

The uneven sedimentation rate of the loess series is exemplified in the section from Věstonice. The youngest loess in this section was deposited at a rate of about 50 centimeters per 1,000 years, whereas the accretion of the forest soil proceeded at a mean rate of only 2 to 5 centimeters per 1,000 years.

STRATIGRAPHY ON SELECTED LOCALITIES

Stratigraphic columns shown in Figures 5, 7, 9, 14, 15, 17, and 18 are a small selection from many described. The location of the sites is shown by Figures 12 and 13. For further information consult Demek and Kukla (1969). The two most complete sections providing the framework of the Standard Loess Sequence (Figure 6) are at Červený Kopec and in the Kremser Schiesstätte. Additional comments to individual localities can be provided as follows.

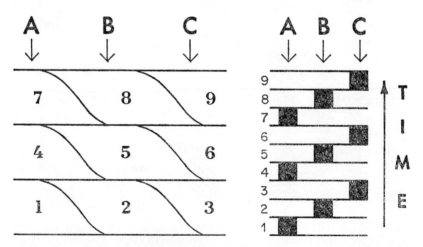

Figure 11. Scheme showing semicontinuous deposition of loesses and terrace gravels so that parallel sections A, B, and C are not fully synchronous. Spatial relations of subunits 1–9 on left, temporal relations on right.

Principal Exposures of the Brno Area

Červený Kopec (symbol CK, translation from Czech: Red Hill). The exposure is in the SW section of Brno City, in an operational brickyard 1 kilometer long and 0.7 kilometers wide. The superposition of the strata was continuously followed in the excavation fronts, and the underlying terraces were investigated by auger boreholes. Figure 6 shows the stratigraphic relation along the highway Brno-Prague at the southern border of the brickyard. The sequence in this area was proclaimed a Czechoslovakian nature monument. It is planned to make it permanently accessible through a strip exposure, enclosed in a future city park.

The stratigraphic column in Figure 5 is composed of segments with the highest resolution. The newly investigated profile ZZ, with the rich snail assemblage of early interglacial and with vertebrate fauna *VF3* which just overlies the B/M transition, was magnetically studied by Kočí (unpublished, see his results in Figure 14). *Pitymys*, the vole typical of Biharian vertebrate age, was determined in *VF3* by Musil (unpublished).

The vertebrate remains in the pellet sands of cycle *D* (VF4) were studied by Musil (1960) and their evolutionary position has been compared to that of Ehringsdorf. Characteristic interglacial elements are missing, however.

An interglacial *Helix* fauna was found in the pockets below the *C1a* soil, and *Celtis* stones below the *G1a soil*. Snails from glacial intervals are more common. *Columella* faunas were found in the loesses of *C3*, *E3*, *I3*, and *J3* subcycles. Depressions with red burned soil and charcoal found in the eluvial horizon of the *E1a* soil yielded several pieces of quartz fragments, described by Klíma (1963) as probable Paleolithic artifacts.

The sequence at Červený Kopec covers five terrace levels of the Svratka River that are labeled *CK 1-5*. These terraces will be discussed later.

The paleomagnetic determination of the Brunhes/Matuyama reversal in CK was confirmed at the same stratigraphic level at two distant sites, namely the southern ZZ site and the original station 04 described in Bucha, et al. (1969) and Kukla (1970). Whether the normal polarity found in the strongly rubefied braunlehms of cycles *K* and *L* is the depositional remanence or the secondary magnetization is less certain. The data published so far (Bucha 1973) do not exclude the second possibility. Additional localities in direct relationship to CK are

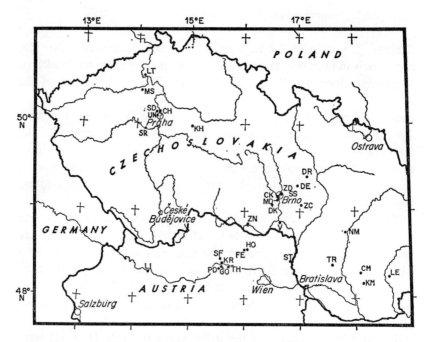

Figure 12.   Site locations. CM: Čermáň; CK: Červený Kopec; CH: Chabry; DE: Dědice; DK: Dolní Kounice; DR: Držovice; FE: Fellabrunn; GO: Göttweig soil in Furth; HO: Hollabrunn; KM: Komjatice; KR: Krems; KH: Kutná Hora; LE: Levice; LT: Litoměřice; MD: Modřice; MS: Mšené; NM: Nové Mesto; PD: Paudorf; SD: Sedlec; SF: Senftenberg; ST: Stillfried; SS: Stránská Skála; SR: Srbsko: TH: Thallern; TR: Trenčín; UN: Únětice; ZC: Ždánice; ZD: Židenice; ZN: Znojmo.

Modřice (MD), Galašova (GA), Židenice (ZD), and Stránská Skála (SS).

Modřice (MD) lies in clear morphostratigraphic relation to terrace CK1. The interglacial and early glacial soils here are overlain by younger, fluvial sands and gravels in the same manner as on Červený Kopec. A unit with reversed declination was found in Modřice (Kukla and Kočí 1972) and correlated with the Blake event. On the GA site the black pellet sands of B2 subcycle interfinger with the uppermost gravels of the CK1 terrace.

Stránská Skála (SS) is a reknowned site of Biharian vertebrates (Stehlík 1934; Kurtén 1960; Musil 1969; Ložek and Fejfar 1957; Jánossy, this volume). The bones are found in the caves and in the fan at the foot of a limestone cliff, cut out by the Svitava River while flowing at the terrace level CK 4 (Figures 13 and 16). Paleomagnetic study was made in three parallel vertical sampling lines by Kočí (unpublished) and Horáček (unpublished). The B/M boundary lies in the uppermost part of the loess, about 0.5 meters below the early inter-

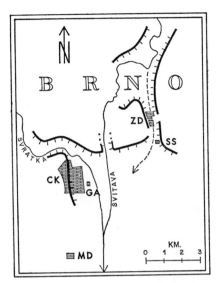

Figure 13. Location of sites around Brno. CK: Červený Kopec, MD: Modřice, GA: Galašova, ZD: Židenice, SS: Stránská Skála. River valley during stage *CK 3* shown by full black line, with contemporary eastern branch of the Svitava shown by dashed line.

glacial tufa with *Helicigona čapeki* and *Zonitoides sepultus* (Prošek and Ložek 1957). The basal, semi-autochthonous soil cementing the limestone debris is a braunlehm (Smolíková, personal communication). Questionable fragments of local chert believed to be Paleolithic artifacts were reported by Valoch (1968). Stránská Skála lies in the eastern bank of the Nová Hora narrows, abandoned by the Svitava River during cycle *F* (Figure 13).

Židenice (ZD)is the name of the exposure in two neighbouring brickyards, now quarrying the fill of the abandoned Nová Hora narrows of the Svitava River (Žebera 1943; Pelíšek 1954; Musil, et al. 1955). The oldest soil developed on the abandoned terrace *CK 3* is *Ela* (Figures 13, 15, and 16).

Dolní Kounice (DK), three interglacial complexes in direct superposition, each with an interglacial snail fauna, cover the sands of the middle terrace of the Dyje, now found some 20 meters above the river (Figures 12 and 15).

Principal Exposures in the Krems Area

The *Kremser Schiesstätte* (Krems, Symbol KR) is the exposure in the loess fill of an abandoned river meander with an elevation of 60 meters above the Danube (Figures 8 and 9). The site was described by Göt-

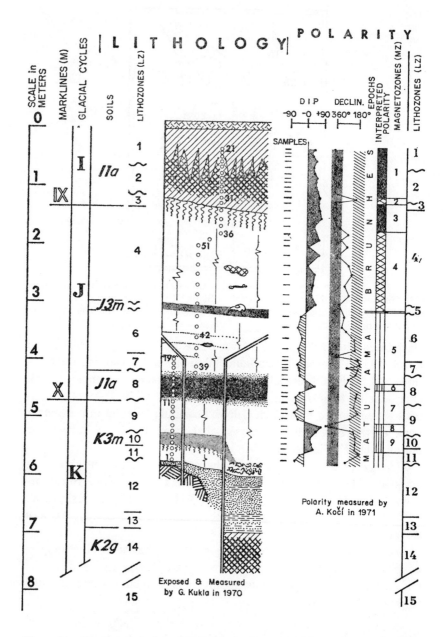

Figure 14.   Stratigraphy of the ZZ site in the Červený Kopec (CK) exposure (see Figure 5). Braunlehm (*LZ 2*) and rotlehm (*LZ 14*) crosshatched; chernozem (*LZ 8*) black, low-humus biogenic soils (*LZ 5* and *LZ 10*) in gray. Paleomagnetic samples shown by circles.

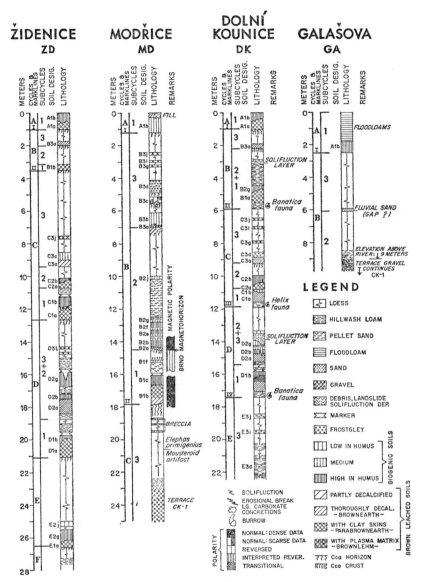

Figure 15. Stratigraphic columns for selected sites near Brno. For Židenice section, above *CK 3* terrace, see Figure 16.

zinger (1936), Fink (1955), Brandtner (1956) and the two best developed soil groups were considered to represent the R/W interglacial (soils KR7-9) and the so-called Göttweiger interstadial (Soil KR4) Kukla (1969) and Fink, et al. (i.p.), showed that the main soil complex KR 7-9 is of Matuyama age. The interglacial snail assemblage at the base of *KR 4* (with *Helicigona čapeki*) is closely related to the assemblage in the basal interglacial soil at Stránská Skála. The depositional remanent magnetization of the *KR 7* soil is unclear at present, as the normal and transitional polarities were found in the top of this horizon. Weathering of the *KR 7b* soil during the Jaramillo normal polarity interval could be responsible for the phenomenon, but other explanations are still possible. The *KR 6* soil is interpreted as an interstadial feature because of the presence of snails with low climatic demands and a poor degree of weathering. Below this level, large unrecognized gaps may exist in the record.

The Krems soil complex consists of rubefied braunlehms, representing the most intensively weathered Pleistocene soil horizon known from central Europe.

The Cca horizon, at the base of *KR 7a*, is a hard, compacted limestone crust, penetrated only by the vertical cavities with red braunlehm fill (*Lehmstangen*). Practically no loess, only pellet sand developed at the end of glacial cycle *M*. Remainders of *Columella* fauna in the calcareous interlayer between *KR 7a* and *KR 7b* points to an existence of the peak cold climate break separating the development of the two forest soils. In our interpretation a thin loess blanket developed originally on *KR 7a* but later has been mostly eroded or weathered. Thus, cycles *K*, *L*, and *M*, seem to comprise an exceptionally prolonged interval (possibly about 250,000 years) of predominantly mild and warm climate in this part of the world.

The loess separating the soils *KR 9* and *KR 10* and the soils *KR 12* and *KR 13* seem to be, on the average, thicker than the other loess beds of the early Pleistocene segment of this sequence. This may eventually indicate the existence of unrecognized breaks in the development of the river at corresponding levels. The top of a relatively thick, positively magnetized unit found under the soil *KR 13*, is interpreted as correlative with the top of the Olduvai event in deep-sea sediments (Opdyke 1972).

At *Paudorf* (PD), a small, abandoned brickyard on a relatively steep hillside, 30 meters above the local stream which forms the type of soil, the so-called Paudorf interstadial (Götzinger 1936; Gross 1957) is exposed. It is a complicated, highly calcareous, polygenetic soil of the chernozem group, intensively reworked by worms. Scattered charcoal fragments and a rich snail fauna are embedded in the soil. Radiocarbon dates from humus range between 29,250 and 43,300 B.P. (Vogel and Zagwijn 1967). The snails are one of the richest known assemblages of interglacial deciduous forest (Ložek 1969).

North of *Göttweig* (G0), west of Furth, is a steep road cut through the vineyards, exposing the B-horizon of a typical parabraunerde embedded in loess overlying the gravel terrace. In the Cca horizon, there is an interglacial snail assemblage. It is different from those in Paudorf soil, but lacks any characteristic Biharian species (Ložek 1969).

The Localities of Stillfried Type

Dolní Věstonice (also Věstonice, Unterwisternitz, symbol *V*), is a classic profile found in the abandoned brickyard on the southern bank of the Dyje River (Lais 1951; Knor, et al. 1953; Klíma, et al. 1962; cf. Figures 12 and 17). The Gravettian (Upper Paleolithic) occupation layer (25,000 to 27,000 B.P.) was directly exposed here and its relative stratigraphic position fixed. Radiocarbon dates on soil humus originally performed by de Vries (Klíma, et al. 1962) and later revised by Vogel (Vogel and Zagwijn 1967) are considered to be relatively reliable, but because of possible younger contamination they should be interpreted as minimum ages only. Thus, the chernozem *B 2g* could be many thousands of years older than the stated age. Vertebrate remains found at the neighbouring sites of Gravettian mammoth hunters include the bones of 200 mammoths, the arctic species *Gulo gulo* (wolverine), *Alopex lagopus* (arctic fox), and *Rangifer tarandus*. More demanding elements such as *Equus, Bos, Ursus arctos, Ursus spelaeus* and *Panthera spelaea* are also present (Musil 1959).

Stillfried (ST) in Austria, the type locality of the Stillfried B and Stillfried A soil complexes, is a close equivalent of Věstonice (Fink 1955). It is in a similar morphologic position above the river Morava (March). Charcoal of *Larix decidua* from the loess 10 centimeters above Stillfried B is 28,340 ±220 years old.

Oberfellabrunn (FE) and neighbouring *Hollabrunn* (HO) are two other sites with stratigraphy closely equivalent to Věstonice, but with the basal interglacial braunerde poorly preserved (Brandtner 1954; Felgenhauer, et al. 1959; Movius 1960). The Fellabrunn complex of Brandtner is equivalent to the Stillfried A complex of Fink (1954) as well as the PK III with PK II complexes of Klíma, et al. (1962). The radiocarbon ages of the soil samples were affected by much contamination and should be considered much too young (Vogel and Zagwijn 1967).

Principal Exposures in the Prague Area

At *Sedlec* (SD), in the active brickyard, a well-subdivided loess series is

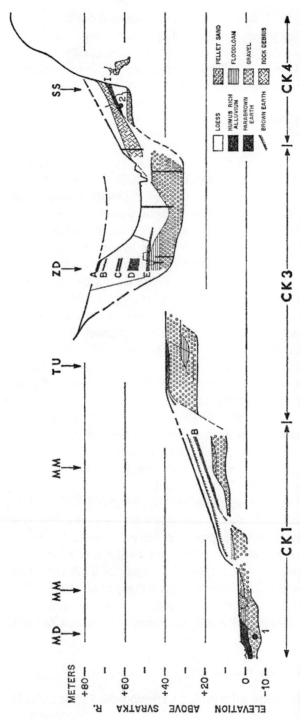

Figure 16. Schematic profile for Brno, combining terrace observations from the eastern bank of the Svitava River. Stratigraphy of *CK 1* in Maloměřice (MM) partly after Musil, et al. (1955). Position of *Megaceros* in Modřice (MD) shown as 1, position of Brunhes/Matuyama boundary at Stránská Skála (SS) shown as 2 (see Figure 7; also Figure 15 for Židenice section). Vertical lines: boreholes. A to E and I designate soil complexes of corresponding glacial cycles.

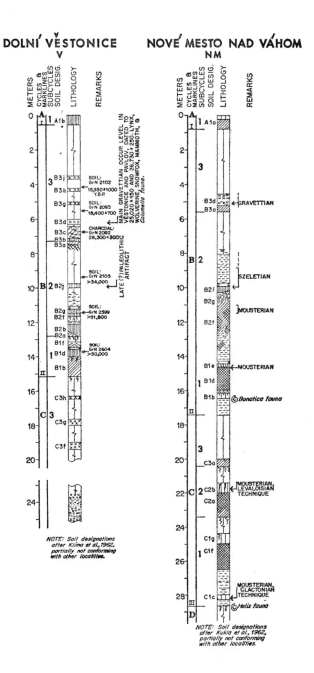

Figure 17. Stratigraphic columns of Věstonice brickyard after Klíma, et al. (1962) with revised radiocarbon ages after Vogel and Zagwijn (1967), and of Nové Mesto brickyard after Kukla, et al. (1962). Relation to river terraces in Nové Mesto shown by Figure 22. Other symbols are the same as in Figure 15.

exposed in a profile several hundred meters long. It covers five terraces of the Vltava River (Figures 18 and 19). The soils of cycles *E* to *B* were here micromorphologically studied by Smolíková (1967a). At the highest elevation, there are banded clays several meters thick, which are underlying the polygenetic forest soil (Kukla 1961b). The stratigraphic relationship of this part of the sequence to the sediments of cycle *E* to *B* is still unknown.

The Paleolithic artifacts of mousteroid character, accompanied by lenses of charcoal and red, fired soil, were found in the glacial sediments of cycles *D* and *E* (Prošek and Ložek 1954; Žebera 1949; Kukla 1961c).

Letky (LT) is an abandoned brickyard pit, north of Sedlec, in the western bank of the Vltava, with a morphologic and stratigraphic setting similar to that of Sedlec. The oldermost loess exposed here is of the E3 subcycle. Soils were microscopically studied by Smolíková (1967b). Early Paleolithic pebble tools and flakes associated with charcoal lenses were described from the soils of *C* cycle by Prošek (1946), Prošek and Ložek (1951, 1954), and Kukla (1961c).

Chabry (CH), is the exposure in the active brickyard pit in the northern outskirts of Prague that cuts the fill of the young depression formerly excavated into Precambrian shists (Figure 18). A relatively rich snail fauna is present in most of the layers and there are two levels with vertebrate remains: *VF 1* with *Mammuthus primigenius* and *VF 2* with *Coelodonta antiquitatis* (woolly rhino), *Equus sp.*, and *Bos sp.* Vertebrates of *VF 2* are accompanied by the *Pupilla* snail assemblage with *Pupilla loessica*. The interglacial *Banatica* snail fauna is found redeposited within the *B 1* pellet-sands. At the pseudogleyed base of the *B 3* loess are snails of the *Columella* assemblage (details in Demek and Kukla 1969).

Kutná Hora (KH), the active brickloam pit in the filling of a river meander ceased to accumulate during the *C 2* or *C 3* subcycle. The loesses of *D 3* cover the gravels of higher terrace of the Vrchlice, tributary of the Elbe. Two interglacial snail assemblages of deciduous forest type were found in pockets below soils *B1b* (*Banatica* fauna) and *C1a* (*Helix* fauna with the demanding species *Iphigena densestriata*). *Celtis* stones occur in the latter horizon (details in Demek and Kukla 1969; Ložek 1969; the stratigraphic column is shown in Figure 18).

Other Selected Localities

Držovice (DR), is a 100-meter exposure into the loess cycles *F*, *E*, *D*,

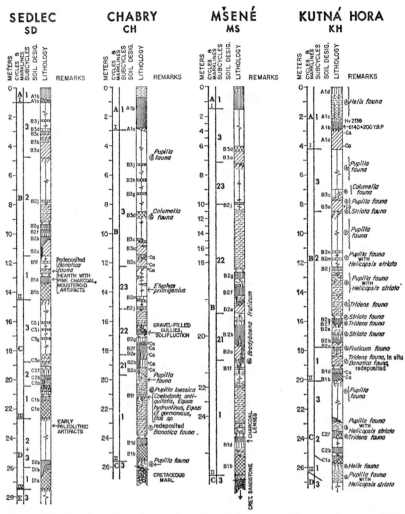

Figure 18. Stratigraphic columns for selected sites around Prague. Other symbols are the same as in Figure 15.

C, and *B*, that rest on a subhorizontal erosional plane cut into sandy clays of probable early Pliocene age. No gravel was found on the boundary, so that the surface covered by *F 3* loess may have been a pediment. Scattered charcoal is frequent in the steppe soil of the cycle *E*.

Ždánice (ZC) is the active brickyard extracting loess that covers the lower terrace and an upper terrace of the local stream. Whereas the gravels of the lower terrace interfinger with *B 2* pellet-sands, the upper terrace is covered by *D 3* loess.

Dĕdice (DE) is the active brickloam pit where a gravel body, correlated with the terrace of the Saale (Drenthe) advance in the Ostrava region, is overlain by the decalcified braunerde of the *D 3* subcycle and by subsequent soils of the *C* and *B* cycles (Zeman 1966).

Nové Mĕsto (NM) is a recently-abandoned brickloam pit where loesses of *E, D, C,* and *B* cycles cover terraces *NM-1, NM-2,* and *NM-3* of the Váh river (Vaškovský 1970; Figures 17 and 22).

The relatively abundant collection of Gravettian artifacts was localized in the pseudogley of the *B 3* subcycle. A laurel leaf blade of red radiolarian chert, typical for the local Late Paleolithic Szeletian, was found in the top of the upper humus soil, close below *B 2* marker. A few chert artifacts of mousteroid appearance were found in the *B1a, C2g,* and *C1b* layers (Kukla, et al. 1962; Demek and Kukla 1969). Frequent charcoal lenses can also be seen in the *B1d* and the *C2g* soils (Figure 17).

Linz (LI), Grabnerstrasse, Austria. In excavations recently made in the bottom of an abandoned brickyard, the terrace gravel of Günz terrace (Penck and Brückner, 1909; Kohl, 1955) was found weathered in a red, decalcified ferretto. It is overlain by a fluvial, gleyed silt that gradually passes into a windblown loess interbedded with several soils (Figure 21).

Samples of the lowermost portion of the flood loam are reversely magnetized, whereas the higher levels of the flood loam and the overlying loess show normal polarity. The specimens were a/f demagnetized on 150°e and measured on the spinner magnetometer by Kočí (unpublished).

Mšené (MS) is an active brickloam pit in north central Bohemia (Figure 18), where the complex subdivided series of the last glacial cycle shows one with the thickest known layers of pellet-sands. It is also the only known site where the *B1b* parabraunerde is separated from the *B1d* steppe soil by the stratified layer of sandy hillwash, demonstrating an interval of local surface instability, after the disappearance of the forest and before the development of the steppe soil.

THE RELATION OF THE LOESS SEQUENCE TO THE TERRACES

With suitable exposures, it is possible to establish age of river downcutting and aggradation relative to a loess sequence. By age of a terrace, we understand the time span during which the fluvial sediments were continuously or at least seasonally incorporated into its body. The

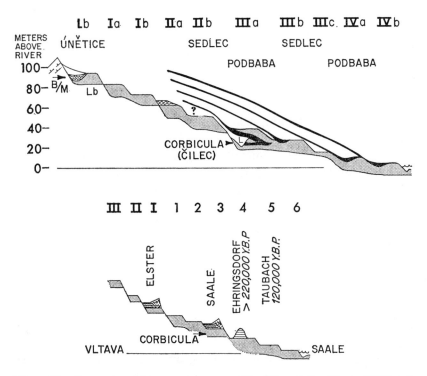

Figure 19. Comparison of terrace sequences of the Vltava (after Záruba 1942) and the Saale Rivers (after Soergel 1939; Toepfer 1933). Stratigraphic details from Podbaba (Figure 23), Sedlec (Figure 18), and Únětice (Figure 24) added by author. *Corbicula fluminalis* level in Čilec described by Smetana (1935) and correlated with III terrace by Záruba (1942). Position of Elster and Saale fluvioglacial and glaciolacustrine deposits after Soergel (1939), radiometric ages from Ehringsdorf and Taubach travertines after Goddard, et al. (i.p.). Terrace gravel in gray, floodloams and varves in wavy lines, soil complexes black, loess blank, travertine horizontally shaded.

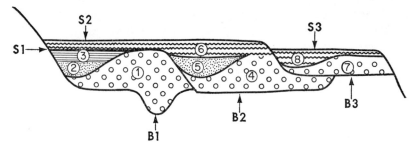

Figure 20. Schematic diagram showing time relations of sediments (1–8), surfaces (S1–S3), and bedrock platforms (B1–B3) within an alluvial terrace recognized as a single morphological unit. Numbering in order of decreasing age.

terrace itself is identified in a given area, in both a horizontal and vertical sense, as an independent morphostratigraphic unit. The areas of deposition at any given interval represent only a fraction of the total extent of the terrace. Simultaneously, in another section of the terrace, there is erosion. These areas of net deposition and erosion shift irregularly with time. As a result, most terraces in the study area have complicated internal structures, such as the one illustrated by the schematic model in Figure 20.

Obviously, sediments of greatly divergent ages may be present at the same level in a terrace body. If the gravels are sterile, there is only one way to recognize their relative age — through the dating of their overlying strata. A statistical approach must be used and observations from several localities combined to fix the age of the regionally significant episodes in terrace history.

The age of the terrace is given by (1) THE BEDROCK DATE, the time when the river first cut into the new level, abandoning the older one and (2) THE SURFACE DATE, the last episode of fluvial deposition within the terrace body. The time which separates the surface date of the higher terrace from the bedrock date of the subsequent younger one could be labeled the (3) TERRACE BREAK.

On several localities it was found that the local deposition of terrace gravels ceased or became largely restricted toward the end of the main pellet-sand phase (for instance on CK, GA, ZC). The most frequent upper boundary of buried terraces is a contact with the loess of the third or second subcycle or sometimes with the intervening windblown sands. Hitherto no case is known where the members of the Lower Series (that is, the soils and sediments of the first half of the glacial cycle), are separated by a terrace break. As for the rivers of both the Prague and Brno areas, it is unlikely that substantial downcutting occurred during the pellet-sand phase of subcycle 1. Judging from the stratigraphic circumstances, Figures 4 and 19), the probable cyclic equivalent of intensive downcutting seems to have been the main pellet-sand and the subsequent gleyed section in the loess deposits of subcycle 2.

It was during stormy episodes of torrential rains, beating on a weathered surface stripped of vegetation, that the climate and environment were ideally suited to produce extreme but ephemeral river floods. It also seems likely that the bulk of the coarse gravel load was carried into the river beds at this time. Vertical erosion and lateral erosion/accumulation may have alternated on a timescale of millenia, and perhaps even on a seasonal basis. The fast modern gravel aggradations,

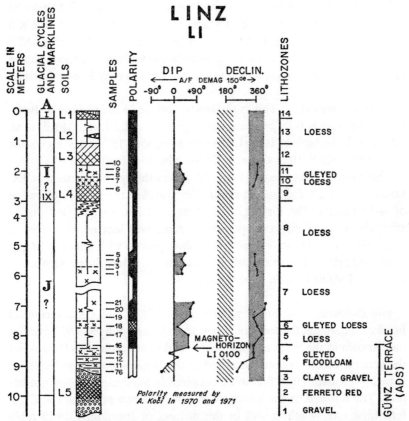

Figure 21. Reversely magnetized, gleyed floodloams in the top of the "Günz" terrace at Linz. Exposed in abandoned brickyard and in construction pits between Grabner and Kudlich streets. Further stratigraphic details in Kohl (1955) and Fink (1969). Other symbols are the same as in Figure 15.

causing river beds to rise several meters in a few decades, are known from the Cordillera of northwestern Argentina (for instance, the Humahuaca Valley) or from northern Sicily. Sparse vegetation and a short rainy season, represented by a few intensive downpours, is characteristic of this environment. Extensive Pleistocene solifluction is likely to have contributed to the blocking of rivers with sediment during aggradation phases.

The Age of the Terraces in the Brno Area

Numerous exposures and boreholes exist in the terraces of the Svitava and the Svratka Rivers in the vicinity of Brno (Zapletal 1931; Musil, et al. 1955; cf. Figure 13). The relation of the terraces to the loess cover is best known at Červený Kopec and around Nová Hora and Stránská Skála. On Červený Kopec the terraces were labeled as *CK 1* to *CK 5* (Figure 4). In the Nová Hora narrows the terraces are labeled as *SS 1* to *SS 3*. The combined terrace sequence in the vicinity of Brno is shown in Figure 16 and labeled with reference to the Červený Kopec system.

THE CK 1 TERRACE   This is the lowest terrace in the vicinity of Brno. Its known base is 6 to 7 meters below present water level (Musil, et al. 1955) and the highest fluvial deposits are about 15 meters above the river (Borehole K 10 at Červený Kopec, also Modřice).

The bedrock date is equal to or older than the age of the main pellet-sands of subcycle *C 2*, which covers the gravel at the relative elevation of +11 meters. The highest level of aggradation was reached during subcycle *B 3* and the corresponding surface was labeled as terrace A by Zapletal (1931). Some time before that, gravels with bones of *Megaceros* and reindeer were deposited a few meters below the present water level at Modřice (Musil, et al. 1955).

THE C-BREAK   The break separating the *CK 1* and *CK 2* terrace is bracketed between the loess of subcycle *D 3* (the youngest *CK 2* surface date known in the area) and the pellet-sand of subcycle *C 2*. Because of the general considerations discussed at the beginning of this chapter, it is highly probable that the break occurred in subcycle *C 2* and not before. The *C-break* is the youngest one in the Brno area and the *CK 1* terrace is one which is still in the process of forming. Considerable downcutting occurred during the *B 2* subcycle. The reindeer gravels at Modřice were probably deposited during this period. Nevertheless, because subsequent aggradation returned to previous and even higher levels, a separate morphostratigraphic unit did not develop.

THE CK 2 TERRACE   This is the middle terrace with the surface from about 20 to 30 meters above the river. Its oldest gravels are older than the loess *E 3* and younger than the floodloam *G-1* (Figure 4). In the Nová Hora gorge the terrace level correlative with *CK 3* was abandoned during the *F* cycle and the gorge remained dry thereafter (Figure 16). Thus the bedrock date of *CK 2* falls very probably within the cycle *F*. The youngest proved surface date coincides with the deposition of banded basal *D 3* loess, but it is probable that the fluvial deposition continued in this level during the whole Lower Series of *C*-cycle. The characteristic feature of terrace *CK 2* is that its surface remained essentially in the same general level during at least two successive interglacials represented by *D 1a* and *C 1a* soils. A terrace, with a similar relation to the soils of *D* and *C* cycles, is known at Nové Mesto as *NM3* (Figure 22; Vaškovský 1970), and around Prague as the III terrace (Figure 23).

THE F-BREAK   The age of downcutting from *CK 3* to *CK 2* level, dated to *F* cycle at Nová Hora (Figure 16), is probably coincident with deep gullies, cutting through the sediments of cycles *F* and *G* at Červený Kopec. The base of the Pleistocene loess sequence in Držovice (DR) has the same age, suggesting that the F-break has a regional significance.

THE CK 3 TERRACE   The surface of this terrace lies 40 to 50 meters high above the river. It is best developed in the vicinity of Stránská Skála (Figure 16) and in the Nová Hora gorge. The bedrock date of this terrace is bracketed by the *J 3* waterlaid loess and by the highly humic gley deposited in the buried oxbow found by boring *K 18* at Červený Kopec. The gley is older than the red pellet-sands of cycle *H* and possibly of *H 1* age. The probable time of the break between *CK 4* and *CK 3* terrace would than fall within cycle *I*. This determination is tentative and uncertain since the critical level was reached in one borehole only. What we do know is that the terrace already existed when the red pellet-sands of the *H* cycle formed. The river probably still occupied this level at the time of braunlehm formation of cycle *G* and of the red polygenetic soil of cycle *F*.

THE CK 4 TERRACE   It lies 60 meters above the river on Červený Kopec and at Stránská Skála. The base of the overlying loess of cycle *J* (reversely magnetized) is seen at both locations, reworked by water (Figures 4 and 7).

The "basement" date could not be bracketed with confidence at any of the studied localities. It is probable that this event is roughly synchronous with the deep *K* cycle gullying at Krems.

The Age of the Terraces around Prague

Terraces of the Vltava were described by Záruba (1942, 1960), in perhaps the most accurate work ever published on Pleistocene terraces. Results of hundreds, precisely leveled, engineering excavations and boreholes were analysed. The gravel deposits were then divided into five

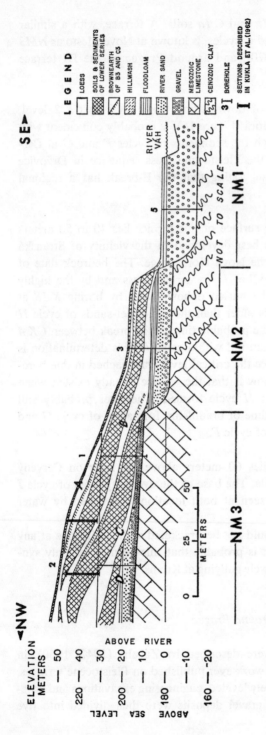

Figure 22. Loesses and soils covering the terrace sequence *NM—3* of the Váh River at Nové Mesto (NM). Partly after Vaškovský (1970). A to D: baselines of corresponding glacial cycles (see Figure 17).

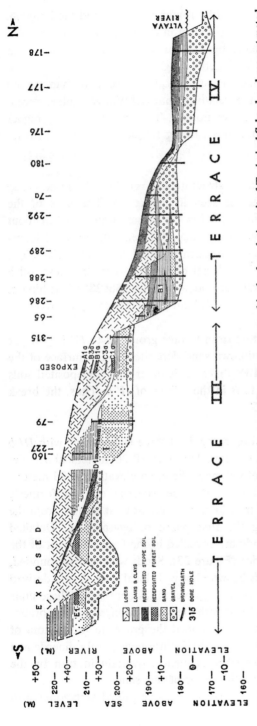

Figure 23. Terraces of Vltava at Podbaba and Dejvice, near Prague, as exposed in the foundation pit of Technical School and reconstructed from boreholes (heavy lines and numerals). Segment shown is about 1.5 kilometer long. Climax soils of individual subcycles shown by corresponding letters and numerals.

groups and eleven stages, labeled by roman numerals and the letters *a*, *b*, and *c*. Ten of the terraces are shown in the schematic section combining the observations made by Záruba with those made by us at Dejvice, Podbaba, Sedlec, and Letky (Figure 19). Accurate dating of the terraces relative to the loess cover is more difficult here than around Brno. This is because in the relatively narrow Vltava valley, recent floods reach to 15 meters above normal. They were probably higher still during Pleistocene times thus causing frequent removal of earlier terrace deposits.

TERRACE GROUP IV   Detailed structure and relation of terrace group IV overlying loess sequence is seen in Figure 23. The base of the gravels rises from about 6 meters below the present water level to about 5 meters above it. Whereas only young, Holocene humic flood loams rest on the *IV b* terrace, loess is frequently found on the *IV a* level. The allochthonous soils of the last glacial cycle *B*, covered by loess, fill a deep oxbow in the *IV a* terrace at Podbaba (holes 286, 288). The highest fluvial deposit of the *IV a* terrace is about 15 meters above the river.

THE C-BREAK   Downcutting from terrace group *III* to *IV* is younger than the *D 3* loess and windblown sand deposited on the surface of the *III b* terrace in Sedlec and Podbaba. It is older than redeposited soils of the Lower Series of cycle *B* in the oxbow of *IV a*. Thus, the break occurred within the cycle *C*.

TERRACE GROUP III   Záruba recognized three stages (*a-c*), with *III b* the main one. Base of the accumulation is 18-20 meters above the river, and the highest fluvial sediments lie at an elevation of 35 meters. The recent excavation in Dejvice (Prague) suggests that the formerly recognized high *III a* stage may have resulted, at least locally, from the lateral erosion terminating the first phase of aggradation. Detailed structures of the terrace body are revealed in the foundation pit of the Technical Institute in Dejvice (Figure 23). Sands with poorly rounded, local detritus and a reddish brown clay with local rock debris derived from reworked forest soils, covered gravel of distant origin. These units were cut by a deep channel filled with loess. A thin layer of dark braunerde, possibly of interstadial age, capped the gravel in the bottom of the channel. Semi-autochthonous and allochthonous parabraunerde and humic sand covered the described sequence, overlain in turn by the fluvial sands, terminated by a thin layer of fine sand.

The two allochthonous forest soils were interpreted as belonging to the *D* and *E* cycles. They must be older than the *C* soils covering the terrace at considerably lower elevations.

At the base of *III b* terrace at Čilec (Labe) is a layer with the bivalve *Corbicula fluminalis* (Smetana 1935). Higher in the section, gastropods of loess steppe type were found redeposited in the fluvial sequence. The *Corbicula* bed is the well-known marker of the "O" terrace of the Elbe (Labe) watershed (after Grahmann 1933), and is supposed to correlate with the Late Holstein. Preceding the deposition of the *Corbicula* terrace, the Elbe in Germany cut far below the present water level and left the *Rinnenschotter* behind.

TERRACE GROUPS II AND I   A several meters-thick deposit of varved clay was found in Sedlec (Kukla 1961b), at the level of terrace *II* (Figure 19). Similar sediments in a similar position were found some 50 kilometers further downstream in Brozany (Šibrava 1972). The clays are not of glaciolacustrine origin, because Sedlec is too far south from the Elster ice front. They nevertheless indicate a sudden change in river gradient, possibly caused by the partial blocking of the Elbe further north. The stratigraphic position and the geomorphologic significance of the Sedlec varves require further studies.

Both terraces of group I accumulated on a common bedrock surface (Záruba, personal communication). The same is probable for the terraces of group *II*.

TERRACE GROUP L   The older *L-a* and younger *L-b* terraces are the two oldest members of Záruba's system. At this time the valley was wide and shallow, surrounded by the Pliocene peneplain. The depression in the *L-b* gravel at Únětice, probably an oxbow channel, is filled with Early Pleistocene fossiliferous marls and freshwater chalk (Figures 19 and 24). Characteristic snails of the Biharian faunal stage were found in the marl (Ložek 1964). The sequence starts with reversely magnetized sandy clays of late glacial age and continues into a normally magnetized, probably early interglacial deposit (Koči, unpublished). Samples were a/f demagnetized. The oxbow fill is covered by the loess. No flood loams or sands intervene in the channel fill. This calm environment of deposition may indicate that the river occupied a lower level, probably that of the *I a+b* terraces. If this assumption is correct, the bedrock date of *I a+b* terraces is older than the B/M boundary and possibly correlates with the *K*-break.

It is evident from the above discussion that in the vicinity of Prague the correlation of the bedrock date of terrace *IV a+b* with the *C*-break,

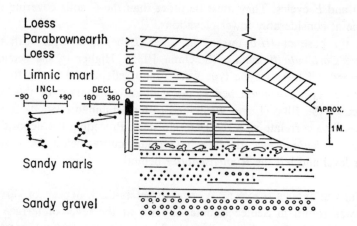

Figure 24.   Section through the oxbow fill cut in the *L-b* terrace at Ünĕtice, Prague. Sketch only, since original field data no longer available. This is the youngest known reversely magnetized sediment within the terrace system of Záruba (1942). (See Figure 19.)

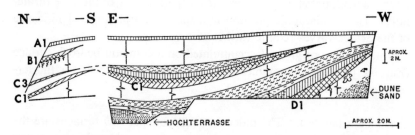

Figure 25.   Excavation faces of the Thallern brickyard, Austria, exposing loess and soils of B, C, and D cycles that rest on the Alpine Hochterrase and merge with its floodloams. As exposed in Nov. 1970.

of *III a+b* with the *F*-break, and *I a+b* with the *K*-break, is reasonably well supported by the available evidence. The *II a+b* bedrock date remains unclear.

Thus the *IV* group of Vltava terraces correlates with *CK 1*, the *III* group with *CK 2*, the *II* and *I* groups with *CK 3* and *CK 4* (Figure 29).

Relation of the Vah and Donau Terraces to the Loess Cover

Figure 22 is adapted from Vaškovský (1970) and Kukla, et al. (1962) and shows the relation of the loess sequence (*E* to *B* cycles) to the three terraces of the Váh (Waag) River, labeled *NM 1, 2,* and *3*.

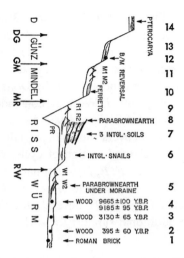

Figure 26. Hypothetical composite diagram of the "classical" alpine and sub-alpine terraces from the Iller-Lech Platte, from around Zurich, and from lower Austria. Gravel shown blank, soils heavily dotted or black, loess lightly dotted, end moraines marked W1, W2, R1, R2, and M1, M2. Full circles: position of radiometrically dated logs, Roman brick, and the paleomagnetic reversal. See text.

Evidently the relation of the *D* and *C* soils to the *NM 3* terrace is the same as to the *CK 2* terrace at Červený Kopec. The *B* soils cover the *NM 2* level in the same way as the *CK 1* terrace. The break separating the aggradation of the *NM 2* and *NM 3* levels occurred in cycle *C*.

The surface of the Hochterrasse of the Donau in the brickyard of Thallern is covered by loess with 3 fossil soil complexes. The lowermost one (*D*) merges with the floodplain sediments (Figure 25). Similar stratigraphic circumstances accompany the *CK 2* terrace at Červený Kopec. In the Senftenberg brickyard above the Krems River, the low terrace, considered to be a Hochterrasse, is overlain by loess with soils of *D*, *C*, and *B* cycles, two of them accompanied by interglacial snail assemblages (Ložek, personal communication).

CORRELATION OF THE LOESS SEQUENCE WITH CLASSICAL ALPINE GLACIAL STAGES

Four major terraces *CK 1*, *CK 2*, *CK 3*, and *CK 4* underlie the eight glacial cycles of the Brunhes epoch at Červený Kopec in Brno. The highest one is of Matuyama age. Four terraces: Niederterrasse (NT), Hochterrasse (HT), Jüngerer Deckenschotter (JDS), and Älterer Deckenschotter (ADS) represent the four classical alpine glacials — Würm, Riss, Mindel, and Günz — of Penck and Brückner (1909). The oldest, Günz terrace in the exposure of Linz on the Danube, was found to be of Matuyama age (Figures 21 and 26). Both Brno and Linz lie in a similar tectonic position at the border of the Bohemian Massif with the forealpine depression, and both belong to the Danube watershed. Therefore the broad correlation of three Brunhes terraces at Brno with the three terraces of the alpine tributaries of the Donau in Austria and Bavaria is reasonably well justified. We may conclude that with high probability the alpine Würm (as represented by the Niederterrasse) correlates with the $CK\,1$ and covers the younger half of loess cycle C, the whole cycle B and the clapsed section of cycle A. Riss correlates with $CK\,2$, and thus with cycles F, E, D, and a part of C. Mindel probably, correlates with $CK3$ and thus cycles F, G, H, I, and Günz with K, J, and a part of cycle I (Figure 29). Several observations, discussed further below, provide additional support for such a correlation.

The Litho- and Morphostratigraphic Content of Alpine Glacial Stages

The four classical glacial stages, Würm, Riss, Mindel, and Günz were named by Penck (in Penck and Brückner 1909) after the four Bavarian rivers joining the Danube (Donau) and Isar around Ulm and Munich. The system was later extended by adding two older stages: Donau (Eberl 1930) and Biber (Schaefer 1953). The type locality of all the stages is the Iller-Lech Platte in the northern foothills of the Alps, south of Ulm, Augsburg, and Munich (Figure 1).

The first four stages defined by Penck are known as "classical." Their type units are gravels and moraines connected with one of the terraces called Niederterrasse (NT - Würm), Hochterrasse (HT - Riss), Jüngerer Deckenschotter (JDS - Mindel) and Älterer Deckenschotter (ADS - Günz). Eberl's Donauschotter (Donau glacial) and Schaefer's Höhenschotter (Biber glacial) are not known to be connected with any moraine.

Although Penck clearly stated that each of the four glacials is documented by the corresponding "glacial series," which include moraines and glacier outwash deposited during the outermost stands of piedmont glaciers in the type area, his stratigraphic system rests entirely on the four gravel terraces. Penck believed that their formation was fully contemporaneous with the glaciations (Penck and Brückner 1909: 107–113). Unlike moraines, the terraces have the advantage of being well defined and mappable morphostratigraphic units, ideal for regional extension of the system all over the Alps. And Penck's principal working method was geomorphologic mapping.

Thus, in practice, Penck and Brückner in their basic work (1909) as well as work of their numerous followers, established the gravel terraces as units representing the Würm, Riss, Mindel, Günz, Donau and Biber glaciations (see discussion by Zeuner 1946: 116).

The erosional intervals separating the terrace levels were believed to correspond to the interglacials. They were labeled Riss-Würm (R/W), Mindel-Riss (M/R), Günz-Mindel (G/M), Donau-Günz (D/G), and Biber-Donau (B/D). It was observed that the surfaces of Mindel and Günz terraces, contrary to the younger two, are strongly weathered into the red clayey zone called *Ferretto*. The vertical distance of Riss and Mindel terraces was in many areas found to be especially great. Because the depth of the incision from one terrace to the next was considered to be a measure of time, the obvious conclusion was that the M/R interglacial was substantially longer than the others.

There is no doubt today that the terraces of Penck and Brückner are real features, and represent widespread morphostratigraphic correlation units. The morphostratigraphic value of Penck's Alpine stages within certain valleys of the Alpine foreland remains intact after several decades of intensive study and revisions. Finer local subdivisions were proposed (cf. Eberl 1930), but these could not be safely extended outside the type areas.

The Climatostratigraphic Content of Alpine Glacial Stages

Whereas the geomorphologic setting of the Alpine terraces was properly described and stratigraphically exploited, their climatic interpretation was incorrect.

As we now know, the gravels accumulated not only during glacials, but also during interglacials (Heim 1919; Penck 1922; Nathan 1953). The erosional intervals which separate the terraces are, for the most part, glacial rather than interglacial features (Schaefer 1953). Spectacular illustrations of interglacial accumulation are the C^{14} dated logs of Holocene age in the Niederterrasse at Ulm, Linz and Krems (Graul 1973; Piffl 1971) or the rolled Roman bricks at the base of Niederterrasse, overlain by several meters of coarse gravel in Vienna (Fink, personal communication). Interglacial snail assemblages within the Hochterrasse around Munich (Brunnacker and Brunnacker 1962), or the warm-water molluscs *Melanopsis acicularis* and *Pisidium amnicum* in the Hochterrasse at Moosburg, Bavaria (Nathan 1953), demonstrate interglacial accumulation as well. Buried interglacial soils were also found in the gravel of Niederterrasse at Murnau (Kaiser 1963) and

Hörmating (Ebers 1960; Brunnacker 1962; Figure 26).

The authority of Penck was respected to such a degree that the inter-glacial layers within the terrace bodies were interpreted as local anomalies rather than proof of the partly interglacial age of all the Alpine terraces. Because fossils within gravels are very rare, and because only a few species of vertebrate fauna are really characteristic for inter-glacials, many geologists still believe in the glacial origin of any coarse river gravel. For instance, the gravels of the lower terrace (Nieder-terrasse) close to Ostrava (north central Czechoslovakia), were for many years mapped as being of Würm age, which they really are. But after the famous Czech Quaternary stratigrapher, Tyráček, unearthed a rusty bicycle steering rod from the intact gravel, this level was recharted as Holocene alluvium, which it is also. In this manner a shocking conflict with established stratigraphic schemes was avoided. But the logical conclusion escaped: the gravels of the Niederterrasse are by definition Würm gravels, whether or not they contain bicycles and Roman bricks, because the Würm gravel terrace is a morphostratigraphic, not a time-stratigraphic unit.

So defined, Würm can correlate and actually does correlate with the Late Pleistocene as well as with the Holocene. What holds true for the Würm also holds for the older terraces which contain gravels from glacial as well as from interglacial epochs.

A question could now be raised as to whether the use of terms Würm, Riss, Mindel, and Günz should be restricted only to sediments de-posited during the glacial phases and thus temporally correlative with the corresponding moraines. This probably was the original climato-stratigraphic concept of Penck. Unfortunately (1) there is no way to distinguish sterile interglacial from glacial gravels within one terrace body, and (2) it is too late for any substantial revision of the system since terraces were extensively used as type units of the four glaciations for several decades.

To avoid further confusion, the terms Würm, Riss, Mindel, and Günz as well as Donau and Biber should only be used in connection with the terraces or moraines in the Alps, and reference should be made in full to either *Würm terrace* or *Würm moraine*. Wherever the use of classical Alpine stages is found to be necessary, the different time-stratigraphic and climatostratigraphic setting of moraines and ter-races has to be specified. While the terrace sequence completely covers time, irrespective of glacials or interglacials, the moraines and their related outwash fans formed only during a few millenia of maximum expansion of the piedmont glaciers.

The Alpine "Vollgliederung"

The so-called "Vollgliederung" is the "full" delineation of Alpine Pleistocene system as attempted by Eberl (1930) under the influence of Milankovitch's insolation chronology. Within the original type area he recognized three substages of the Würm, two of the Riss, two of the Mindel, two of the Günz, and three of the Donau. Eberl's approach combined geomorphic mapping with litho-stratigraphic observations. Even though some of his conclusions were later found to be based on miscorrelations, the main part of his work is still valid. Thus it is now widely agreed that there were at least two generations of Riss gravels separated by a weathering interval of possibly interglacial rank (Woldstedt 1958). Also, the existence of two moraine generations in the Würm and two in the Mindel, each pair separated by a non-glacial interval of considerable length, seems to be reasonably well-demonstrated. What remains mostly unclear, however, is the stratigraphic relation of the warm climate interlayers within the terrace bodies to individual end-moraines and to individual terrace surfaces.

Present knowledge on the stratigraphy of the forealpine terraces in Bavaria and Switzerland, and the Niederterrasse in Lower Austria, can be combined in the composite diagram shown in Figure 26. Numbered in the same order as in the figure, the observed features are:

1. Rolled Roman brick, made in the first centuries A.D., dredged from the submerged base of coarse gravels of the Würm terrace in Vienna during recent engineering operations (Fink, personal communication).

2. Logs C^{14} dated at 395 ±60 B.P. on the base of Niederterrasse, under 6 meters of relatively coarse gravel, two meters below the groundwater level in the gravel pit in Frauendorf a.d. Au, 25 kilometers east of Krems (Piffl 1971).

3. Logs of oak (*Quercus* cf. *robur*), C^{14} dated at 3165 ± 115 B.P. and 3130 ±65 B.P., and found 4 meters below the groundwater level in the gravel pit of Trübensee, 35 kilometers east of Krems. The logs were underlain by 2 meters of gravel with huge boulders at the bottom, and overlain by 4 meters of relatively coarse gravel (Piffl 1971).

4. Logs of pine up to 8.5 meters long, C^{14} dated at 9660 ±115 B.P. and 9665 ±100 B.P., and of birch dated at 9185 ±95 B.P., found 6 meters below the surface in the Neustift gravel pit, 23 kilometers east of Krems. They are overlain by 4 meters of gravel and underlain by 7 meters of coarse and medium gravel (Piffl 1971). Also of similar age, are the logs in the gravels of Niederterrasse around Ulm and Linz (Graul 1973).

5. The subhorizontal layer of parabraunerde at the top of the Würm gravel in the Murnau area and overlain by a moraine of Würm age (Kaiser 1963). Separation of Würm gravels by till has already been described from this area by Penck (1922). Also interglacial peats within the Laufen gravel at Zeifen are correlative with the Eemian (Frenzel 1973a).

6. Three localities in the München area where gastropods of deciduous forest type were found in fine-grained interlayers of the Riss terrace (Brunnacker and Brunnacker 1962).

7. Localities of Senftenberg and Thallern where the forest soils (parabraunerdes) of glacial cycles D, C, and B, interbedded with loess and partly accompanied by the interglacial snail fauna, overlie the Riss terrace (Hochterrasse), or merge with its floodloams.

8. The deep weathering horizon capping the thick accumulation of so-called pre-Riss gravels of Zink (1940), northern Switzerland (Basel, Bodensee, and Zürich area). The gravels of the R-I stage (Altriss) are stratigraphically younger. During the latter period, the glaciers attained their maximum extent in this part of Switzerland. The gravels of the R-II (Jungriss) stage follow.

The Riedmatt forest bed is believed to fall into the Pre-Riss/Riss-I interval and the Grünholz black clays with the remains of temperate flora should correspond to a RI/RII interval (Woldstedt 1958).

9. The M/R erosion, which at Zürich cuts 500 meters under the Mindel terrace, far below the present river alluvia, was followed by rapid aggradation of the so-called "Rinnenschotter" (Zink 1940).

10. The Mindel terrace is covered by a red weathering zone, the so-called Ferretto, at numerous locations throughout the Alps (Penck and Brückner 1909). This is by an order of magnitude more intensively developed than any younger soil known in the region.

11. Two generations of Mindel moraines and two levels of the Mindel gravels (not necessarily temporally related) in the Iller-Lech Platte described by Eberl (1930).

12. A reversely magnetized layer in the flood loam (redeposited loess), covering the ferretto in the top of the Günz terrace gravel, at Grabnerstrasse in Linz on the Danube (LI), determined by Kočí and Kukla (unpublished).

13. Two surfaces of the Günz terrace found by Eberl (1930) in the type area.

14. The lignite lenses in clays deposited at the top of the Donau gravel at Uhlenberg, west of Augsburg. Interglacial flora with Pterocarya and Carya, elements known in abundance in the Waalian inter-

glacial (but not in the following Cromer-type interglacials I and II) of the Netherlands (Zagwijn 1961), were found here (Filzer and Scheuenpflug 1970).

Correlation of the Alpine Terraces with the Loess Region: Supporting Evidence

RISS AND RISS/WÜRM   The terrace *CK-2* at Červený Kopec (Figure 4), the terrace of the Dyje River at Dolní Kounice (DK) brickyard, and the *NM 3* terrace of the Váh at Nové Mesto (NM) (Figure 22), show the same relation to the soils of cycle *D* and *C* as the Hochterrasse in Thallern and Senftenberg by Krems (Figure 25), and as the terrace group III of Vltava.

Therefore it seems probable that in the northern foothills of the Alps the formation of the Hochterrasse proceeded in the same way as the accumulation of *CK 2* terrace around Brno and the III terrace group around Prague, and that it lasted from the end of cycle *F* through the first half of cycle *C*. Judging from Červený Kopec (Figures 6 and 23) and also Podbaba (Figure 15), this level was abandoned before the beginning of subcycle *C 3*, probably during the pellet-sand phase of *C 2*.

Thus the R/W erosion which separates the Hochterrasse from Niederterrasse with high probability correlates with the *C*-break and therefore is the glacial event of *C 2* age. However, as the breaks must be expected to behave in a time-transgressive manner, this correlation may not be valid throughout the whole of the Alpine foreland.

MINDEL AND MINDEL/RISS   The flood loams and silty interlayers in the Mindel gravels of several localities between Salzburg and Linz in Austria were measured by Kočí (unpublished) and found to be normally magnetized. The gravels are weathered into red ferretto, the youngest intensively decomposed horizon in the Alpine forelands. Soils which developed at the top of terrace *CK 3* in Červený Kopec as well as their related sediments are normally magnetized, and form the youngest intensively weathered polygenetic soils of braunlehm type in the section. Thus the correlation of the Mindel terrace, the third in the alpine system, with *CK 3*, third in the Red Hill sequence, as well as its counterpart *SS 1* at Židenice, is highly probable. The river abandoned the *SS 1* level during the cycle *F* (Figure 16). Thus the MR erosion of Penck and Brückner with high probability correlates with the *F*-break.

GÜNZ AND GÜNZ/MINDEL   The *CK 4* terrace at Červený Kopec and the *SS-2* terrace at Stránská Skála were covered by waterlaid loess of subcycle *J 3*, a few millenia before the Brunhes/Matuyama reversal (Figures 3 and 7). At Linz Grabnerstrasse the same situation was found above the Günz terrace of the Danube — mapped as such in the vicinity by Penck and Brückner (1909) and later by Kohl (1955). There is no reason to question the validity of morphostratigraphic correlation between the Iller-Lech Platte and Linz. Thus it is highly probable that *CK 4* and *SS 2* at Brno are the Günz terraces. Furthermore, such correlation is strongly supported by the presence of a Biharian fauna with *Pitymys* and *Mimomys savini* at Stránská Skála (Musil 1969; Jánossy, this volume) and Červený Kopec in the interglacial soils immediately overlying the reversal. The approximate synchroneity of the Biharian faunas with the Günz/Mindel interglacial and with the Cromer forest bed, is well known (Woldstedt 1958; Zeuner 1946; Musil 1969; Jánossy, this volume).

The G/M erosion which cuts down from the Günz to the Mindel terrace level is thus likely to correlate with the incision from the *CK-4* to the *CK-3* levels. This seems to have occurred during the second half of cycle *I*. Because the critical segment at Red Hill was explored only by boreholes, the identification of soils is not as certain as in the exposures.

The timing of the G/M erosion with the *I*-break is at present only tentative. More certain is its bracketing between the *J 3* loess and *H 3* pellet sand. No other locality is known today where the conclusions from Red Hill could be checked for regional significance.

THE DONAU/GÜNZ EROSION   Deep erosion at Červený Kopec cuts the loamy sands of the *CK 5* terrace and the overlying soils of the *K* and *L* cycles. The exposed front is not sufficiently long to conclude whether the *K* and *L* soils were deposited within the reach of a floodplain or at a higher elevation on the dry slope. Thus it is not known whether the observed erosion immediately followed the soil formation or not. In Krems the deep gullies cutting into the surface of *K* and *L* rotlehms are of *K* age. Although highly probable, it cannot be proven whether they correlate with the downcutting of the river (Figure 8).

The floral assemblage with *Pterocarya* and *Carya* in Uhlenberg is similar to the one of Waalian interglacial in the Netherlands. This interglacial, because of its position in the paleomagnetic time scale (van Montfrans and Hospers 1969) is correlative with the *KR 7* soil in Krems (Fink, et al. i.p.). Thus the D/G incision, which is younger than the lignite in Uhlenberg, probably correlates with the K-break in much the same way as the M/R erosion coincides with the F-break.

THE MID-MATUYAMA BREAK   The Kremser meander was cut into gneiss either during the Olduvai event or some time before it. Thick, red pellet-sands covering the slopes and the basal terrace gravel were assigned to cycle R, but this is a minimum rather than a definite age because the record below the B/M boundary is likely to be interrupted by gaps. The depositional circumstances and morphological position of the oldest sediments in Kremser Schiesstätte are indicative of an important break in the development of relief, perhaps similar in intensity to the F-break (M/R erosion). The same as during cycles K and F, the surface was stripped of an extensive and probably strongly weathered soil cover, including rubefied braunlehms. Since Krems is the only locality in the loess region where the studied level was safely recognized, checks could not be made on its regional significance and stratigraphic value. The apparent close chronostratigraphic relation of this break to the Plio-Pleistocene boundary in Italy is nevertheless intriguing.

Breaks older than the D/G erosion and younger than the Mid-Matuyama break may have passed unrecognized. Therefore, a correlation, however tentative, of the loess sequence with the Donau and the Biber terraces, has not been attempted.

CORRELATION BETWEEN THE STANDARD LOESS SEQUENCE AND THE CLASSICAL GLACIALS AND INTERGLACIALS OF NORTH-CENTRAL EUROPE

Eight terraces of the Vltava (Moldau) formed during the Brunhes geomagnetic epoch. Their relation to the loesses of glacial cycles B to E is known from the exposures in Sedlec, Letky, and Podbaba. The correlation of the Vltava terraces by Záruba (1942) with terraces of the Saale River and of its tributaries, the Unstruht and Elster in central Germany (Soergel 1939; Toepfer 1933), is supported today by several independent criteria and must be considered generally correct. Thus deposits of the Elster and Saale glaciations in the type area, clearly related to the local river terraces, can be correlated with the loess system. Independent cross-checks of the correlation is possible in Bad Kosen, where the loesses and soils of three glacial cycles directly overlie the glacial lacustrine varves of main advance of Saalian glaciation (Saale-Drenthe;

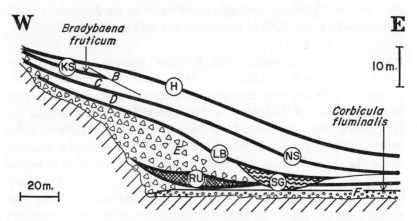

Figure 27.   Exposure in Bad Kosen, near Leipzig, showing loess (blank) with soil complexes: Kosener (KS), Naumburger (NS), Laugenburger (LB) and Rudelsburger (RU), as resting on *Corbicula fluminalis* terrace. Glaciolacustrine varves of lake dammed by Saale ice shown as (SG). Rock debris with loess admixture shown by triangles. Glacial cycles *B, C, D, E,* and *F* as interpreted by author. After Mania and Altermann (1970).

cf. Figure 27). Furthermore, taking into account the available radiocarbon dates obtained on samples from last glacial sediments, the conclusion was reached that the Weichsel moraines correlate with subcycle *B 3,* the Warthe moraines with *C 3,* the Drenthe (Saale *sensu stricto*) advance with *E 3,* while the main Elster glacial advance occurred during subcycle *H 3.* This conclusion is in agreement with independent evidence indicating the existence of more than one warm interval widely described as Eem, and of at least two individual warm intervals described as Holstein. Several observations, discussed further, support the correlation.

The Morphostratigraphic Content of the North European Glacial and Interglacial Stages

The classical glacial stages of the Fennoscandinavian continental ice sheet are the Weichsel, Warthe, Saale, and Elster. These were recognized from the semi-continuous end-moraine systems crossing Denmark, northern Germany, and Poland and are named after the rivers of this area. Moraines of the Weichsel and Warthe have fresh hummocky constructional topography. Moraines of the Saale are dissected and flattened, while moraines of the Elster have lost their original morphology completely. As the type formations of each of the four glaciations are moraines, the resulting system is a morphostratigraphic one. It should be observed that progressively older moraines lie progressively further south. This was a principal condition aiding their preservation and recognition.

The labeling of the moraines (except Warthe) is attributed to Keilhack (1926), who mapped them in north-central Germany. Unlike the Alps, frequent interglacial deposits are known in the area. Deposits of three marine transgressions and temporally equivalent lake beds were mapped, stratigraphically studied, and assigned to the Eem, Holstein, and Cromer interglacials. The stratigraphic position of the Eem transgression is established by the fact that it cuts through Saale or Warthe moraines, but was overridden by the Weichsel. Similarly, the Holstein beds cut into Elster deposits and are overlain by Saale sediments. The pollen sequences in the lake beds of the Holstein interglacial are indicative of deciduous forests with a high proportion of conifers. This distinguishes them from the Eem and Cromer, whose vegetational histories resemble that of the Holocene (see review in Turner, this volume). Marine molluscs and foraminifers of the Holstein epicontinental sea point to relatively chilly waters similar to those of the modern North Sea. In contrast, the Eem marine fauna with a "lusitanian" assemblage of molluscs indicates a warmer ocean than today.

Vertebrate faunas associated with Cromer and Elster deposits belong to the Biharian faunal stage (formerly called "Cromerian") and exhibit numerous extinct elements. They are readily distinguished from the younger faunal wave that accompanied the post-Elster deposits.

This is in short, the basic framework of classical Pleistocene stratigraphy of the glaciated part of northern Europe. A few years ago, with local subdivisions here and there, it was still sufficient to explain and describe the Pleistocene sequences known to exist between England and Russia (cf. Woldstedt 1958; Flint 1971). Deep boreholes made in recent years complicated this picture. Today, the existence of two successive transgressions with "Eemian" type of marine fauna is well established (Wiegank 1972), as well as the presence of two interglacials with vegetational characteristics of Holstein type (Dücker 1969). The older interglacial correlates with the Holstein marine transgression and possibly with the river gravels containing *Corbicula fluminalis*, the well known marker bed of the German Pleistocene.

Several buried till sheets with differing petrographical composition have been found lying in a superposition that allowed further local subdivisions of the Saale and Elster glacial deposits (Lüttig 1964; Cepek

1969). In addition, buried tills of supposedly early Würm age were claimed from Finland and Poland, although in both places the evidence is questionable. While there could be no doubt that more than two interglacials lie between Elster and Weichsel, it remains unclear what the relation of the buried till sheets to the surface moraine tracks is, and which of these represent the first order glacial advances (cf. Duphorn, et al. 1973). For this reason we have not attempted to correlate the various subsurface till occurrences with the loess system, but have instead concentrated on the classical units defined by the end-moraine tracks.

The Relation of Saale Terraces with those of the Vltava

The terraces of the Elbe river (Engelmann 1938; Grahmann 1933; Genieser 1962) and of its tributaries Saale (with the Elster, Ulm, and Unstruht) (Soergel 1939; Toepfer 1933), are directly or indirectly connected with the end-moraines of the Weichsel, Saale and Elster glacial advances (Figure 19).

The marker horizon of the Elbe (Labe) watershed is the terrace with the mollusc *Corbicula fluminalis*. It is interconnected with the Holstein transgression and overlain by the moraine of the southernmost advance of Saale glaciation (the Drenthe or the Saale *sensu stricto* advance). This is the so-called Hauptterrasse of the Saale drainage ("Main Terrace," also the third terrace of Soergel), the terrace "O" and the Čilec terrace of the Elbe, and the terrace III of the Vltava (Záruba 1942).

The correlation of the Vltava terraces with the Saale system (Figure 19) is furthermore supported by another observation. The Ehringsdorf travertine, with its rich, warm-climate flora and fauna, is considered to be of Eemian age, yet rests conformably upon the flood loams of terrace 4 of the Ilm (Kahlke 1958). Both the upper and lower "warm" members of this travertine — separated by the "Pariser" loam with a continental, cool steppe fauna — were uranium-dated to about 220,000 years B.P. by Goddard, et al. (i.p.). The neighbouring Taubach travertine, with similar fauna and flora but without a cold Pariser, was found to be 100,000 years younger. The soils of the next to last Pleistocene cycle *C*, which temporally correlate with the Ehringsdorf travertines, are not preserved lower than on terrace *III b* of the Vltava system. This suggests that this terrace correlates with terrace *4* of the Saale watershed.

The Loess Sequence in Bad Kosen

In the quarry of Bad Kosen, Saale Valley, the glaciolacustrine varved clays of the main Saale advance are directly overlain by the Laugenburger soil complex, with snails frequent in early interglacial deposits. Two younger polygenetic soils interbedded with loess are present: the Naumburger and Kosener soil complexes (Figure 27). To comply with the established stratigraphic model, Mania and Altermann (1970) labeled the Naumburger complex as Eem, and the Laugenburger and Kosener complexes as interstadial soils of the Weichsel and Saale glaciations. However, the Kosener soil yielded the gastropod *Bradybaena fruticum*, a common element of early interglacials. This species is more demanding than the snail fauna now reported from the site, and it is unknown in proven mid- and late-Weichselian interstadial deposits of the European loess belt.

Thus taking into account the morphology of the site and the observations made in Czechoslovakia on incompletely developed sequences (Figure 10), we must interpret the Kosener soil as the poorly preserved remainder of the *B 1b* interglacial soil and the Laugenburger soil as that of the *D* cycle. The Saale varves then correlate with subcycle *E 3*.

Time-stratigraphic Position of the Eem Interglacial

The Eem interglacial is recognized and named after the marine clays with the mollusc *Tapes aureus* var. *eemiensis*, accompanied by other elements of the thermophile lusitanian fauna (Madsen 1929). The Eem River region in The Netherlands is one of several known locations of the Eem marine clays on the western coast of Europe. Because it was widely believed that the marine beds at all these sites were contemporaneous, no special effort was made to define the type locality. Most workers nevertheless consider this to be in the Netherlands. The location, in close vicinity of the town Amersfoort, has several boreholes that demonstrate how sediments of the Eemian transgression overlie the Saale ground moraine (Zagwijn 1961). A thick layer of sand, believed to be of glacial-fluvial origin, separates the till from interglacial peat and sand. Pollen content in the clayey interlayers found between the till and marine series indicates a progressive warming, from glacial to interglacial climate, during a single deglaciation (Van der Hammen, personal communication).

The Eem deposits are overlain by coversands that contain lenses of peat. The Amersfoort interstadial and the local equivalent of the Brörup interstadial, both of Weichselian age *sensu lato,* are represented by the peats.

There is no doubt that the Saale moraines around Amersfoort are older than the end-moraines of the Warthe and Weichsel. There is also no reason to question their geomorphologic correlation with the main Saale advance in central Germany. As this one correlates with the *E 3* subcycle, which is some 350,000 years old, and was followed by several gross oscillations of climate, it can be concluded that the climatostratigraphic record in The Netherlands must have gaps.

The gaps could be either below the marine sequence or above it. In the first case the image of a continuous climatic improvement could be an artifact of contamination of the sediments by unrecognized, reworked pollen. In such a case the Eem of The Netherlands could correlate in time with the Eemian of Schleswig-Holstein. But the gap may also exist in the coversands overlying the Eem sequence. Then the Eem transgression would have immediately followed the main Saale deglaciation and would correlate with the start of the glacial cycle *D.* The close morphologic relation of the Eemian embayment in the Netherlands with the moraines of Amersfoort stage, speaks in favor of the second rather than the first alternative. However, much more work is needed before the stratigraphic position of type Eemian can be reliably fixed.

In northern Germany, Wiegank (1972) showed the existence of the two transgressive marine sequences with Eemian type fauna. One is older and the other is younger than the Warthe moraines. Whereas the younger must correlate with the *B 1b* forest soil, it is probable that the older one correlates with the *D 1a* or *C 1a* soil.

Some peat bogs with interglacial flora, assigned to the Eem, fill kettles in the main Saale moraine. These are the depressions left by the melted ice, and deposits of this kind (also Rabutz) must have immediately followed the Saale-Drenthe deglaciation and thus correlate with the *D 1a* forest soil.

On the other hand, similar kettles in Warthe moraines originated during the younger, *C 3* deglaciation and their pollen sequences, also asigned to Eem, must be younger. They have to be correlated with the *B 1b* forest soil of last interglacial age.

The Ehringsdorf travertines, also described as Eemian but recently dated by uranium isotopes (Goddard, et al. i.p.), belong neither to the last, nor to the third to last interglacial but correlate with the soils of *C 1* and *C 2* cycles.

Thus in Figure 29 three time positions of the "Eem" interglacial are shown: *"Eem 1,"* correlative with *L-D 1a* soil, and with the fills of kettles in Saale-Drenthe moraines; *"Eem 2,"* correlative with *L-C 1a* and *L-C 2a* soils and with the travertines of Ehringsdorf; and *"Eem 3,"* correlative with *L-b 1b* soil and with the marine unit and freshwater peats overlying the Warthe moraines of Schleswig-Holstein and on numerous sites in northern Germany. All are in quotation marks to indicate that their time relation to the type Eemian is not yet known.

The Time-stratigraphic Position of the Holstein Interglacial

The HOLSTEIN marine transgression is morphologically related to the Elster advance, whose glaciofluvial sands and presumably glacio-lacustrine Lauenburger clays it overlies. The terrestrial Holstein peats demonstrate a characteristic dominance of conifers with relatively unimportant deciduous elements in northwestern Germany. Some diagrams indicate a short cool spell approximately in the middle of the interglacial. The climatic conditions in Europe in Holstein times are considered to be cooler than during the Eem, although several thermophilous exotic taxa such as *Azolla filiculoides, Salvinia, Pterocarya, Buxus, Trapa,* or *Vitis* reached much further north than in Holocene times.

The duration of the temperate part of the Holstein interglacial was estimated from varve counting to be 12,000 to 15,000 years (Duphorn, et al. 1973). The Marks-Tey interglacial in England which supposedly correlates with Holstein was estimated by the same method to be about 10,000 years long (Turner 1970; Turner, this volume).

At Wacken (Dücker 1969) and Prignitz (Erd 1970), Germany, a younger interglacial sequence (called Wacken or Dömnitz interglacial or "Holstein-II") has been found. It is separated from the main Holstein layer by sediments of a subarctic climate (Mehlbeck or Fuhne glacial). Except for *Abies*, which is present in the Holstein *sensu stricto* but missing in the younger interglacial, the composition and development of the floras is very similar in both intervals. The characteristic *Azolla filiculoides* is also common to both of them.

The predominantly coniferous Holstein forests with its scattered, highly demanding species, somehow resembled the Late Pliocene vegetation of northwestern Europe (Menke and Behre, 1973).

Correlation of the Holstein and Dömnitz interglacials with the loess sequence is based on the following observations:

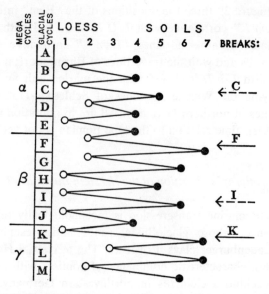

Figure 28.   Subdivision of loess sequence into megacycles by marklines. Observe that the soils preceding the breaks in cycles K and F are strongly weathered and reddened to an exceptional degree (7). Other designations: "cold" loess (1); "normal" loess (2); hillwash (3); parabraunerde (4); doubled parabraunerde or parabraunerde strongly developed toward a braunlehm (5); braunlehm (6). Only environmental extremes of each cycle are shown.

1.   It is older than subcycle *E 3* (correlative with Saale-Drenthe), and younger than the Brunhes/Matuyama boundary.

2.   It is temporally close to the deposition of the *Corbicula* terrace, which according to Bad Kosen (Figure 27) and Podbaba (Figure 23) falls within cycle *F* or is older.

3.   The vegetational successions of the Holstein and Wacken-Dömnitz interglacials are the youngest distinctly differing from the Holocene and Eemian successions. Soils of the *F* and *G* cycles are the youngest that differ distinctly from the last interglacial and Holocene soils in the area. Thus the complicated polygenetic soils of the *G* and *F* cycles — with large carbonate concretions, substantially different from any younger soil, and thought to be a product of prolonged or repeated weathering in one horizon — tentatively correlate with the type Holstein and with the Dömnitz interglacial.

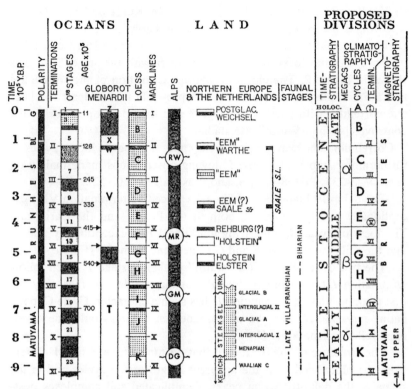

Figure 29. Correlation of the oceanic and terrestrial paleoclimatic record of the last million years. Normal polarity black, reversed white, transitional crosshatched. G: Gothenburg "event," BL: Blake event. Deep-sea sediments after Emiliani (1966), Shackleton and Opdyke (1973), and Ericson and Wollin (1968). Presumed cold stages with heavy dots, cool intervals with light dots, warm stages blank. Terminations marked by Roman numerals, their ages estimated from interpolated thickness (see Tables 1 and 2). Glacial cycles in loess after this report: loess steppe with *Columella* fauna and frostgley shown in heavy dots, temperate intervals with predominant soil formation blank, others lightly dotted. See text for details.

CORRELATION OF THE LOESS SEQUENCE WITH DEEP-SEA SEDIMENTS

Correlation of the standard loess sequence for the past one million years with the deep-sea sediments is shown in Figure 29. It is based upon assumed synchroneity of glacial cycles and marklines, alias terminations in both systems (Kukla 1970), strongly supported by paleomagnetic data.

Detailed correlation of the last four completed glacial sycles *B, C, D,* and *E* between the loess area and the Caribbean Sea has been discussed by Kukla (1970). It was further supported by Kukla and Koči (1972), who found the reversed magnetic unit probably correlative with the Blake event that separates soils $B\ 1b$ and $B\ 2a$ (Figure 15). Correlation of the composite loess sequence of cycle B with 0^{18} stages 2 to 5 is shown in Figure 2. The chronostratigraphic position of the soils $B\ 2m$ and $B\ 3a$ is questionable, but it seems probable that at least the later one correlates with part of 0^{18} stage 3 and thus developed during the controversial "mid-Würm" interstadial.

Correlation between glacial cycles and the loess glacial cycles is furthermore supported by the following observations made mainly on cores V23-238, P6308-4, 7, 8, and 9 as well as V12-122:

1. The delta-0^{18} high (= "cold" peak) preceding termination VI is exceptionally poorly expressed, both in the Pacific and the Caribbean. The loess of cycle G, underlying markline VI, is exceptionally thin so that the soil complexes of F and G cycles tend to merge (Figure 4).

2. The two delta-0^{18} lows (= "warm" peaks) of stage 7 which follow termination III are both of interglacial magnitude, whereas only the first peak postdating termination II has such a character. Cycle C, postdating markline III has two parabraunerdes, whereas only one developed following markline II.

3. The structure of the 0^{18} record that postdates termination V differs from the older section in the apparent length of the cycles and in the shape of the delta-0^{18} warm peaks. Complicated soil complexes postdating the markline V differ substantially from the older ones, where braunlehms represent climax soils.

The Mid-Brunhes Episode

The interval between about 420,000 and 550,000 years, that of cycles F and G, and 0^{18} stages 12 to 15, is interesting in many respects. Three characteristic abundance peaks in left-coiling *Globorotalia truncatulinoides* occurred during three subsequent intrusions of cold waters into the Caribbean (stages 16, 14, and 12). The first of these is temporally related with the disappearance of the thermophile *Globorotalia menardii* group (Stage 16). The second apparently almost coincides with its reappearance in the Atlantic and Caribbean (the U/V boundary of Ericson and Wollin 1968) as well as with the extinction of *Pseudoemiliania lacunosa* in the Pacific and the Atlantic (stage 14 and, in some cores, perhaps 12). Closely related in time is the F-break, during which the hydrographic network of Europe was partly rearranged, the salinity of the Elbe River temporally increased (indicated by the occurrence of *Corbicula fluminalis*), and crustal movements reached an especially large scale in the Swiss Alps and in north-central Germany (*Rinnenschotter*). Few cores and loess sequences were hitherto studied in necessary detail to enable an accurate reconstruction of what actually but to us, the most plausible tentative explanation of what actually happened involves an episode of speeded crustal movements in the young mountain belts, changing the morphology of the continents as well as the ocean floor during cycle *F* and possibly already *G*. If this was the case, it is probable that circulation patterns as well as sedimentation rates in parts of the ocean changed at the same time. Correspondingly, caution is advised when interpreting the age and climatic significance of deep-sea sediments older than the F-break. Paleoclimatic criteria based on the analysis of the younger layers may not be valid below that level.

The B/M Boundary

The Brunhes-Matuyama magnetohorizon correlates with the end of a glacial and shortly precedes markline *IX*. The deep-sea cores for the most part do not have sufficient resolution along the boundary, but they do not contradict observations made in the loess areas. The magnetic transition is found close to termination *IX* (Shackleton and Opdyke 1973; Hays et al. 1969).

The Matuyama Section

No detailed O^{18} record has been published covering this interval. Long cores with faunal paleoclimatic indicators are still too scarce to enable meaningful comparisons with the sequence from Krems. Generally, however, as in the loess areas, the basic patterns of cold and warm oscillations and their frequency seem to have been similar to those of the Brunhes epoch (Hays, et al. 1969).

PALEOCLIMATIC HISTORY OF CENTRAL EUROPE AS RECONSTRUCTED FROM THE LOESS SEQUENCE

Combining the evidence discussed in the previous paragraphs, the paleoenvironmental and gross paleoclimatic changes that affected central Europe during the Pleistocene can be reconstructed and approximately dated (Figure 29). The reconstruction is fairly reliable for the past 350,000 years. Continuous sedimentary records of this period are known in considerable detail from more than fifteen loess localities. Climatic oscillations with a period on the order of 20,000 years or less, are characteristic for this young, best-known section of the standard loess sequence.

The resolution of the loess record below 400,000 years is still insufficient to detect the detailed internal structure of glacial cycles such as revealed by the deep-sea cores. It is not known whether this limitation stems from an unfavorable depositional environment of the few available localities, or whether the study area was insensitive to minor climate changes prior to 0.4 million years.

Eight glacial cycles labeled *B-I* were completed within the Brunhes epoch, and at least nine more between the Olduvai and the B/M boundary. As each of them starts with a deciduous forest soil, the presence of which in neighbouring parts of Europe by definition marks an interglacial, at least seventeen interglacials must have affected Europe during the Pleistocene. In addition to that, numerous temperate interstadials occurred within the past two million years.

Climate During the Last Pleistocene Glacial Cycle

The last glacial cycle, that is the interval from about 125,000 to about 10,000 years ago, started with the last interglacial. During this interglacial the environment of Europe was in general similar to that of today but, at the same time, comparatively warmer, wetter and less continental than during the Holocene altithermal. The "Eemian" Sea of Schleswig-Holstein was then inhabited by lusitanian molluscs, an assemblage that today is found along the coast of Portugal and northwest Africa. Detailed paleomagnetic sampling of the loess section in Modřice (Kukla and Kočí 1972), and the varve counting on interglacial diatomites in the Luhe Valley of western Germany (Müller, cited in Duphorn, et al. 1973), both demonstrate convincingly that the interglacial was only about 10,000 years long and was already over by about 115,000 B.P. This finding is in complete agreement with the deep-sea record (Shackleton 1969).

During the following, 10,000-year episode, climate was continental and cold. Badlands with loess steppe developed around Brno and Prague, probably at the same time as the cover-sands originated in The

Netherlands and Denmark (Van der Hammen, et al. 1971) and open vegetation became established in Macedonia (Wijmstra 1969). At this time, cold subpolar waters of the northern Atlantic, similar to those off Iceland and northern Norway, expanded as far south as the Bay of Biscay (McIntyre and Ruddiman 1972).

Two temperate interstadials followed. During the older one, forest existed in central Europe (soil *L-B 2a*). A coniferous forest with strikingly low numbers of thermophilous trees is also known from Denmark (type Brörup) and from The Netherlands (the Amersfoort "interstadial," of Brörup age, cf. discussion by Menke and Behre 1973). The younger interstadial is represented by the *B 2f* and *B 2g* soils of Czechoslovakia. The remainder of the forest soil from this interval is found only at one site (Mšené), whereas grassland was by far the dominant type of vegetation. Soil development was interrupted once or twice by periods of intensive dust deposition. The Odderade interstadial in northwestern Germany (Averdieck 1967) and the Elevtheroupolis interstadial in Macedonia (Van der Hammen, et al. 1971) probably correlate with this episode. Vegetation in northern Germany during Odderade was similar to that during the Brörup, except that the forest possibly was more open (Menke and Behre 1973).

Correlation of both interstadials with the late 0^{18}-stage 5 in the deep-sea sediments, and with the terraces Barbados I and II (Mesollela, et al. 1969), places the end of the development of the *B 2g* soil, and correspondingly of the Odderade interstadial, at about 75,000 B.P., which is consistent with the minimum age determined by radiometric dating.

Following the *B 2g* soil interval, the full glacial environment of the loess area of central Europe began to develop in much the same way as that of the early glacial — by formation of a marker and badlands, and by deposition of loess. This time, however, indications of intensive periglacial action are present, and the rate of river downcutting and/or aggradation seems to have substantially changed. Whether these features alone could be interpreted as a sign that glacier fronts were relatively close, is doubtful. Nevertheless the vertebrate fauna, which includes distinct arctic species, favors such a deduction.

There is no conclusive evidence of a closed forest younger than Odderade and older than the Late Glacial in northern Europe. The *B 3a* braunerde of the loess area may have developed under a taiga vegetation. Whatever the true original environment of the soil was, it must have represented a considerable change in a local climate, toward a less continental and wetter type. This change occurred earlier than 30,000 years ago, sometime during the 0^{18}-stage 3. No such substantial climatic break during the full glacial is known from vegetational successions of northwestern and western Europe, or from Macedonia. However, Coope (1973) concluded from the Late Pleistocene beetles that at about 40,000 to 43,000 years ago, the summers of western Europe were as warm, if not warmer than today and climate was maritime. This is in striking contrast to the preceding phase of cold continental climate as well as to the following one. It is not unlikely that the *B 3a* soil actually developed during the same episode.

The decalcified soil *B 3c* probably formed under grassland or tundra, with several millenia of stabilized surface. Around 24,000 to 26,000 years ago, when Paleolithic men hunted mammoths around Pavlov and Věstonice, the formation of these soils was already over and loess was accumulating at least intermittently (Klíma, et al. 1962). Before 18,000 B.P., and at three later occasions prior to 15,000 years ago, frost-gleys formed on the loess, indicating cold-humid episodes that seem to correlate with the main advances of the continental ice sheet (soils *B 3d-j*).

The climatic history of the Late Glacial and of the Holocene is best recorded in the pollen bearing bogs and lake beds and extensively described elsewhere. In the loess belt of central Europe the deposition of loess terminated about 10,000 years ago and soils formed thereafter. From the spatial relation of the parabraunerdes to the pseudochernozems, it can be concluded that deciduous forests covered larger portions of the loess belt prior to about 5,000 B.P. and that they then retreated toward the bordering highlands. Such a move would indicate increased continentality during the Late Holocene, but the interference of Man is another factor possibly involved.

Climate during the Glacial Cycles C to E

Between about 245,000 and 125,000 years ago, during glacial cycle C, the succession of sediments and soils in Czechoslovakia closely followed the pattern of younger cycle *B*. There are, nevertheless, two fundamental differences: (1) Soil *C 2a* is a fully developed deciduous forest soil, which means that cycle *C* (in contrast to cycle *B*) has two interglacial horizons separated by a glacial interlayer. The floral content of the "Eemian" travertine of Ehringsdorf in central Germany, and the stratigraphy of some deep-sea cores (Hays and Perruzza 1972), suggest that this feature had an interregional validity. The pollen evidence from the interglacial type areas in northwestern Europe is either still missing or remains unrecognized. (2) The rivers of central and northern Europe as well as the Alps cut down deeper during the *C 2* than during the *B 2* subcycle. This led to a separation of the younger and older terrace units and to minor rearrangements of hydrography. Deep sedimentary traps formed by the rivers as well as a large amount of transported detritus may have led to a generally greater observed thickness of the *C* loesses, compared to the loesses of cycle *B*.

It is interesting to note that the number and relative stratigraphic position of the *C 3* frost-gleys parallels those of the *B 3* subcycle, indicating that the readvances of Warthe ice may have followed the same pattern as those of the Weichsel.

There are no frost-gley soils nor *Columella* fauna assemblages known within the *D* cycle, in striking contrast to cycles *C*, *B*, and *E*. A reasonable interpretation of this phenomenon is that the kind of cold-humid weather oscillations that probably marked the advances of Weichsel and Warthe ice did not affect the study area during cycle *D* and that the glacier fronts may have remained further north. Also, no significant downcutting was observed along the rivers, and the *C* and *D* soils in the Elbe as well as the Donau watersheds merge into one single terrace body. This makes the presence of an extensive continental glacier sheet in Europe during the *D* cycle highly improbable. The *D 2a* soil at Kounice reaches the development stage of a parabraunerde, but it is only a simple braunerde at all other known localities. Thus the *D 2a* soil should be interpreted as representing an interstadial rather than a full interglacial.

Columella faunas and frost-gley soils in the loesses of the *E 3* subcycle point to a severe, cold-continental climate similar to the Weichsel and Warthe full glacials. The northern ice front stood in the Ostrava Gate, one of its closest positions to the study area. The wet-cold episodes represented by the frost-gleys were at least as numerous and frequent as during the younger glacial cycles *C* and *B*. The interglacial soil *D 1a* points to the presence of a similar kind of deciduous forest as that which produced the younger soils *C 1a* and *B 1b*.

Climate during Cycles I to F

There is no proof that the cold and warm maxima of European climate during the Early Brunhes differed substantially from the subsequent time span. However, numerous observations show that the geomorphology of the Alps and their foothills, as well as of northern Europe, changed substantially during cycle *F* (and possibly during *G*), when the modern details of the drainage network were established. In general, mean elevation and degree of dissection of the European subcontinent were less before the F-break than they were afterwards. It may be for this reason that polygenetic interglacial forest soils, with large carbonate concretions indicative of savanna-type microclimate episodes, developed. On the other hand chernozems, so characteristic for the post-F loess sequence are practically missing in the study area.

It is also possible that the apparently different reliefs of the Alpine mountain belt, and the different setting of land bridges contributed to differences in vertebrate fauna of central Europe which in Biharian interglacials includes such species as *Hippopotamus* and monkey. It remains questionable how far south the continental glacier advanced during the F-pleniglacial. Frost-gley soils and *Columella* faunas have not yet been observed in the *F 3* loess of the few localities hitherto studied. Thus it is probable that the fronts of the continental glacier stood farther north at that time than during the Saale-Drenthe glaciation. The moraines of the so called Rehburger stage overridden by Saale-Drenthe ice, may possibly have been deposited during the F cycle.

Climate of Cycles M to J

The deep weathered rubefied soils of the cycles *M*, *L*, and *K*, known both from Krems and Červený Kopec, are exceptional features of the loess sequence. Chances are that the corresponding warm intervals were, at least locally, more favorable than during any later interglacial, and that each soil developed under oscillating forest and savanna covers for an exceptionally long time. For reasons previously discussed, the interglacial of Uhlenberg in southern Germany and the Waalian in The Netherlands are probable time equivalents for at least a part of the *M*, *L*, and *K* sequence. Predominantly coniferous forest, with "Tertiary relicts" such as *Tsuga, Pterocarya* and *Carya*, is known to have existed at both sites. This type of vegetation has broad affinities to the Pliocene, Tegelen, and Holstein forests, but differs substantially from the deciduous woodlands of Eemian or Holocene age. It is interesting to note that the red polygenetic soil of cycle *F*, correlated with the Holstein and so different from younger soils, is the closest equivalent to *M*, *L*, and *K* rotlehms. Thus, some links seem to exist between the presence of coniferous woodlands with *Pterocarya* in western and central Europe, and the development of rubefied soils in the loess area.

Following the *K*-break, cold loess steppes, similar to those of the

Late Pleistocene, develop in central Europe. The change of environment, and probably also the shift in climatic regimes that occurred during the K-break (alias D/G) about 850,000 years ago, seems to have been by far the most prominent on record. What we now often call the classical or the glacial Pleistocene began at this time. There are numerous indications that fundamental rearrangements of morphology accompanied the shift. The Alps as well as the smaller mountain ranges in the Bohemian Massif were probably uplifted at this time (Genieser 1962). Thus geomorphologic primary causes may have set conditions permitting large-scale glaciation of Europe during the subsequent glacial episodes. Furthermore, the rearrangement of land bridges that probably occurred at this time may have contributed to the rapid modernization of European vertebrates as represented by the replacement of Late Villafranchian assemblages through Biharian faunas.

Climate Before Glacial Cycle M

Our knowledge of the early Pleistocene in the study area is rather poor. Available data come from the vicinity of Krems in Austria. The only safe conclusion to draw is that an alternation of forest and loess steppe was already taking place, possibly with the same or similar periodicity as during the later part of Pleistocene. The equivalents of the *Columella* faunas hitherto found. Provide indirect indications of major glaciations in the area. The loesses of cycles N (about 1.2 million years old), and S and T (about 1.5–1.6 million years old) would be the most likely correlatives of exceptional deep downcuttings of the river, as they seem to be exceptionally thick.

CONCLUSIONS

Summarizing our evidence, the following general conclusions can be made:
1. The frequency and amplitude of climatic changes during at least the past 1.5 million years probably followed the same basic complex pattern observed during the Late Pleistocene. This supports the conclusion of modern stratigraphic studies in the world oceans (Shackleton and Opdyke 1973; Emiliani 1972; Ruddiman 1971) and on the continents (Van der Hammen, et al. 1971; Kukla 1970; Butzer, this volume).

2. The simplistic subdivision of the Mid- and Late Pleistocene into three classical interglacials and four glacials is incorrect. The apparent evidence produced in favor of such subdivision is mainly the result of:
a. Climatic misinterpretation of geomorphologic features, especially of the Alpine terraces. It now appears that the Pleistocene environment of Europe was under the influence of two largely independent processes, climatic cycles and the crustal movements. Interference of the two led to a substantial differentiation of the morphostratigraphic evidence created during the individual glacials and interglacials. Such a separation did not affect the oceans.
b. A lamentable lack of physical evidence, and its repetitive nature in the glaciated areas of northern and western Europe. The cumulative time actually represented by the type units of the classical North European glacials and interglacials accounts for only about 100,000 years — out of the 700,000 years known to have elapsed since the Brunhes-Matuyama reversal.
c. The persistent and common practice of violating basic stratigraphic principles in the use of classical Pleistocene subdivisions. Specifically, stratigraphic terms are used outside their type areas and so acquire different meanings than were originally intended by their authors.
3. Confusion in Pleistocene stratigraphy today has reached such a degree that the sooner the classical terminology is abandoned in interregional correlations, the better. Future, global stratigraphic subdivision of the Quaternary must be based on continuous sequences such as exist for example in the oceans of the world (Cooke 1973).

The present article has attempted to show how the classical glacials and interglacials of Europe may possibly correlate with the deep-sea record. Our model, as summarized in Figure 29, is limited by scarcity of observations and it is far from final or perfect. We would like to propose it as a basic working hypothesis, calling for further checks and improvements, rather than as a definitive climatostratigraphic model for the Middle Pleistocene.

Without doubt, extremely valuable sets of basic data have been accumulated by European Pleistocene students during the past hundred years or so. However, before these can be fully utilized, the local stratigraphic systems must be critically revised and the local marker-beds reliably correlated with available sequences of continuous deposition, such as those in the deep-sea.

Painful as it may seem to us stratigraphers of the continental Pleistocene, the time has come to accept a sad reality: a complete paleoclimatic history cannot be reconstructed from incomplete evidence.

REFERENCES

AMBROŽ, V.
1947 Spraše pahorkatin. *Sborník Státního ústavu geologického ČSR.* 14:225–280. Prague.

AVERDIECK, F. R.
1967 Die Vegetationsentwicklung des Eem-Interglazials und der Früh-würm-Interstadiale von Odderade/Schleswig-Holstein. *Fundamenta* B/2, 101–125. Cologne, Graz.

BERG, L.
1932 Löss als Produkt der Verwitterung und Bodenbildung (in Russian). *Transactions of the Second International Conference of Association for Quaternary* 1. Moscow.

BRANDTNER, F.
1954 Jungpleistozäner Löss und Fossile Böden in Niederösterreich. *Eiszeitalter und Gegenwart* 4/5:49–82.
1956 Löss Stratigraphie und paläolithische Kulturabfolge in Nieder-österreich und den angrenzenden Gebieten. *Eiszeitalter und Gegenwart* 7:127–175.

BROECKER, W. S., M. EWING, B. C. HEEZEN
1960 Evidence for an abrupt change in climate close to 11,000 years ago. *American Journal of Science* 258:429–448.

BROECKER, W. S., J. VAN DONK
1970 Insolation changes, ice volumes, and the O^{18} record in deep-sea cores. *Review of Geophysics and Space Physics* 8:169–198.

BRUNNACKER, K.
1962 Bemerkungen zum Profil Hörmating/Obb. *Eiszeitalter und Gegenwart* 13:125–128.

BRUNNACKER, M., K. BRUNNACKER
1962 Weitere Funde pleistozäner Molluskenfaunen bei München. *Eiszeitalter und Gegenwart* 13:129–137.

BUCHA, V.
1973 Correlation between field variations and precession of the earth in the Quaternary. *Nature* (Physical Science) 244:137, 108–109.

BUCHA, V., J. HORÁČEK, A. KOČÍ, J. KUKLA
1969 "Palaomagnetische Messungen in Loessen," in *Periglazialzone, Löss und Paläolithikum der Tschechoslowakei.* Edited by J. Demek and J. Kukla, 123–131. Tschechoslowakische Akademie der Wissenschaften, Geographisches Institut in Brno.

BÜDEL, J.
1949 Die räumliche und zeitliche Gliederung des Eiszeitklimas. *Die Naturwissenschaften* 36:105–112, 133–139. Berlin.
1951 Die Klimazonen des Eiszeitalters. *Eiszeitalter und Gegenwart* 1:16–26.

CEPEK, A. G.
1969 Zur Bestimmung und stratigraphischen Bedeutung der Dolomit-geschiebe in den Grundmoränen im Nordteil der DDR. *Geologie* 18, 6:657–673. Berlin.

COOKE, H. B. S.
1973   Pleistocene chronology: long or short?. *Quaternary Research* 3: 206–220.

COOPE, G. R.
1973   "A reinterpretation of Mid-Weichselian climatic changes in western Europe, based on fossil coleopteran assemblages," in *INQUA, Ninth Congress International Union for Quaternary Research Abstracts. Christchurch, New Zealand 2-10 December*, 67–68.

DEMEK, J., J. KUKLA
1969   *Periglazialzone, Löss und Paläolithikum der Tschechoslowakei.* Tschechoslowakische Akademie der Wissenschaften, Geographisches Institut in Brno.

DÜCKER, A.
1969   Der Ablauf der Holstein-Warmzeit in Westholstein. *Eiszeitalter und Gegenwart* 20:46–57.

DUPHORN, K., F. GRUBE, K.-D. MEYER, H. STREIF, R. VINKEN
1973   Area of the Scandinavian glaciation. *Eiszeitalter und Gegenwart* 23/24:222–250.

EBERL, B.
1930   *Die Eiszeitenfolge im nördlichen Alpenvorlande.* Augsburg.

EBERS, E.
1955   Hauptwürm, Spätwürm, Frühwürm und die Frage der älteren Würmschotter. *Eiszeitalter und Gegenwart* 6:96–109.
1960   Drumlinkerne, ältere Würmschotter und das Würm-Interstadial Profil von Hörmating/Obb. *Eiszeitalter und Gegenwart* 11:64–76.

EMILIANI, C.
1966   Paleotemperature analysis of the Carribean cores P 6304–8 and P 6304–9, and a generalized temperature curve for the past 425,-000 years. *Journal of Geology* 74:109–124.
1972   Quaternary paleotemperatures and the duration of the high-temperature intervals. *Science* 178:398–400.

ENGELMANN, R.
1938   Der Elbedurchbruch, geomorphologische Untersuchungen im oberen Elbegebiet. *Abhandlungen geographischen Gesellshaft Wien* 13:1–139. Vienna.

ERD, K.
1970   Pollen-analytical classification of the Middle Pleistocene in the German Democratic Republic. *Palaeogeography, Palaeoclimatology, Palaeoecology* 8:129–145.

ERICSON, D. B., G. WOLLIN
1968   Pleistocene climates and chronology in deep-sea sediments. *Science* 162:1227–1234.

FAIRBRIDGE, R. W.
1972   Climatology of a glacial cycle. *Quaternary Research* 2:283–302.

FELGENHAUER, F., J. FINK, H. DE VRIES
1959   Studien zur absoluten und relativen Chronologie der fossilen Böden in Österreich, I: Oberfellabrunn. *Archaeologia Austriaca* 25:35–73.

FILZER, P., L. SCHEUENPFLUG
1970 Ein frühpleistozänes Pollenprofil aus dem nordlichen Alpenvorland. *Eiszeitalter und Gegenwart* 21:22–32.

FINK, J.
1954 Die fossilen Böden im österreichischen Löss. *Quartär* 6:85–107. Bonn.
1955 Das Marchfeld. Beitrage zur Pleistozänforschung in Österreich. *Verhandlungen d. Geologischen Bundesanstalt*, Sonderheft D.
1956 Zur Korrelation der Terrassen und Lösse in Österreich. *Eiszeitalter und Gegenwart* 7:49–77.
1969 "Les progrés de l'étude des loess en Europe," in *La stratigraphie des loess d'Europe. Bulletin de l'Association Française pour l'Etude du Quaternaire*, Supplément, 3–12. Bordeaux.

FINK, J., A. KOČÍ, G. J. KUKLA, V. LOŽEK, L. PIFFL
i.p. Pleistocene climates in central Europe: at least 17 interglacials after Olduvai.

FLINT, R. F.
1971 *Glacial and Quaternary Geology*. New York: Wiley and Sons.

FRENZEL, B.
1964 Zur Pollenanalyse von Lössen. *Eiszeitalter und Gegenwart 15:5–39*.
1968 The Pleistocene vegetation of northern Eurasia. *Science* 161:637–649.
1973a Some remarks on the Pleistocene vegetation. *Eiszeitalter und Gegenwart* 23/24:281–292.
1973b On the Pleistocene vegetation history. *Eiszeitalter und Gegenwart* 23/24:321–332.

GANSSEN, R.
1922 Die Entstehung und Herkunft des Löss. *Mitteilungen a. d. Labor. d. Preuss. Geol. Landes-Anstalt* 4:1

GENIESER, K.
1962 Neue Daten zur Flussgeschichte der Elbe. *Eiszeitalter und Gegenwart* 13:141–156.

GERASIMOV, I. P., editor
1964 *Fiziko — geograficheskii Atlas Mira*. Moscow. Akademia Nauk SSSR I Glavnoe Upravlenie Geodezii I Kartografii GGK SSSR.

GODDARD, J., W. S. BROECKER, G. J. KUKLA
i.p. The age of Eemian travertines in Ehringsdorf.

GÖTZINGER, G.
1936 Das Lössgebiet um Göttweig und Krems an der Donau. Führer f. d. Quartär-Exkursionen in Österreich. 1:1–11. Vienna.

GRAHMANN, R.
1932 Der Löss in Europa. *Mitteilungen d. Gesellshaft für Erdkunde zu Leipzig, Jahrgang, 1930–1931,* 5–24. Leipzig.
1933 Die Geschichte des Elbtales von Leitmeritz bis zu seinem Eintritt in das norddeutsche Flachland. *Mitteilungen Vereins f. Erdkunde Dresden,* N. F. 1933:133–194. Dresden.

GRAUL, H.
1973 Foreland of the Alps. *Eiszeitalter und Gegenwart* 23/24:268–280.

182   GEORGE J. KUKLA

GROSS, H.

1957   Die Fortschritte der Radiokarbon Methode 1952–1956. *Eiszeitalter und Gegenwart* 8:141–180.

HAYS, J. D., A. PERRUZZA
  1972   The significance of calcium carbonate oscillations in eastern Atlantic deep-sea sediments for the end of the Holocene warm interval. *Quaternary Research* 2:355–362.

HAYS, J. D., T. SAITO, N. D. OPDYKE, L. H. BURCKLE
  1969   Pliocene-Pleistocene sediments of the equatorial Pacific: their
paleomagnetic, biostratigraphic, and climatic record. *Geological
Society of America Bulletin* 80:1481–1514.

HEIM, A.,
  1919   *Geologie der Schweiz*, volume one: *Handbuch der Gletscherkunde*. Tauchnitz, Leipzig.

KAHLKE, H. D.
  1958   Die jungpleistozänen Säugetierfaunen aus dem Travertingebiet
von Taubach —Weimar — Ehringsdorf. *Alt-Thüringen* 3:97–130.
Weimar.

KAISER, K.
  1963   Zur Frage der Würm Gliederung durch einen "Mittelwürm-Boden"
im nordlichen Alpenvorland bei Murnau. *Eiszeitalter und Gegenwart* 14:208–215.

KEILHACK K.
  1926   "Das Quartär," in *Grundzüge der Geologie,* volume two. Edited
by W. Salomon. Stuttgart.

KLÍMA, B.
  1963   Altpaläolithischer Fund auf Červený Kopec/Roter Berg/bei Brno.
Přehled výzkumů 1962. *Archeologický ústav ČSAV,* 1–2. Brno.

KLÍMA, B., J. KUKLA, V. LOŽEK, H. DE VRIES
  1962   Stratigraphie des Pleistozäns und Alter des pälaeolithischen Rast-
platzes in der Ziegelei von Dolní Věstonice (Unter-Wisternitz).
Anthropozoikum 11:93–145.

KNOR, A., V. LOŽEK, J. PELÍŠEK, K. ŽEBERA
  1953   Dolní Věstonice. Výzkum tábořiště lovců mamutů v letech 1945–
1947. *Monumenta Archeologica* 2:1–87, Prague.

KOHL, H.
  1955   Die Exkursion Zwischen Lambach und Enns. — Beiträge zur
Pleistozänforschung in Österreich. *Verhandlungen d. geologischen
Bundesanstalt,* Sonderheft D.

KUBIENA, W. L.
  1956   Zur Mikromorphologie, Systematik und Entwicklung der rezen-
ten und fossilen Lössboden. *Eiszeitalter und Gegenwart* 7:102–112.

KUKLA, G. J., A. KOČÍ
  1972   End of the last interglacial in the loess record. *Quaternary Research* 2:374–383.

KUKLA, J.
  1961a Quaternary Sedimentation Cycle — Survey of Czechoslovak
Quarternary — Czwartorzed Europy srodkovej i wschodniej.
INQUA VIth International Congress. Instytut Geologiczny, Prace.

34:145–154. Warsaw.
1961b Lithologische Leithorizonte der tschechoslowakischen Lössprofile. *Věstník Ústředního ústavu geologického* 36:369–372.
1961c Stratigrafická posice českého starého paleolitu/Stratigraphische Position des tschechoslowakischen Altpaläolithikums. *Památky archeologické* 52:18–30.
1969 "Die zyklische Entwickung und absolute Datierung der Lösserien," in *Periglazialzone, Löss und Paläolithikum der Tschechoslowakei.* Edited by J. Demek and J. Kukla, 75–95. Tschechoslowakische Akademie der Wissenschaften, Geographisches Institut in Brno.
1970 Correlations between loesses and deep-sea sediments. *Geologiska Föreningen i Stockholm Förhandlingar* 92:148–180. Stockholm.

KUKLA, J., V. LOŽEK
1961 Loess and related deposits. Survey of Czechoslovak Quaternary. Czwartorzed Europy Srodkowej i Wschodniej. *INQUA VIth International Congress.* Institut Geologiczny, Prace. 34:11–28. Warsaw.

KUKLA, J., V. LOŽEK, J. BÁRTA
1962 Das Lössprofil von Nové Město im Waagtal. *Eiszeitalter und Gegenwart* 12:73–91.

KURTÉN, B.
1960 Chronology and faunal evolution of the earlier European glaciations. *Commentationes Biologicae* 21:3–62.

LAIS, R.
1951 Über den jüngeren Löss in Niederösterreich, Mähren und Böhmen. *Berichte Naturforschenden Gesellschaft Freiburg i. Braunschweig* 41:119–168. Freiburg.

LAUTERBORN, R.
1912 Über Staubbildung aus Schotterbanken im Flussbett des Rheins. *Verhandlungen naturhist.-med. Ver. Heidelberg, N.F.11.*

LOŽEK, V.
1964 *Quartärmollusken der Tschechoslowakei.* Rozpravy Ústředního ústavu geologického 31. Prague.
1965 Das Problem der Lössbildung und die Lössmollusken. *Eiszeitalter und Gegenwart* 16:61–75.
1969 "Paläontologische Charakteristik der Löss-Serien," in *Periglazialzone, Löss und Paläolithikum der Tschechoslowakei.* Edited by J. Demek and J. Kukla, 43–60. Tschechoslowakei Akademie der Wissenschaften, Geographisches Institut, Brno.
1972 Holocene Interglacial in Central Europe and its land snails. *Quaternary Research* 2:327–334.

LOŽEK, V., O. FEJFAR
1957 K otázce staropleistocénní fauny ze Stránské skály u Brna [A contribution to the question of the Early Pleistocene fauna from the Stránská Skála near Brno]. *Věstník Ústředního Ústavu geologického* 32:290–294.

LOŽEK, V., J. KUKLA
1959 Das Lössprofil von Leitmeritz an der Elbe, Nordböhmen. *Eiszeitalter und Gegenwart* 10:81–104.

LÜTTIG, G.
1964   Prinzipielles zur Quartärstratgraphie. *Geologisches Jahrbuch* 82: 177–202.

MADSEN, V.
1928   Übersicht über die Geologie von Dänemark. *Danmarks Geologiske Undersögelse* 5 R., 4:1. Copenhagen.

MANIA, D., M. ALTERMANN
1970   Zur Gliederung des jüngeren Mittelpleistozäns im mittleren Saaletal bei Bad Kosen. *Geologie* 19:1161–1184.

MCINTYRE, A., W. F. RUDDIMAN
1972   Northeast Atlantic post-Eemian paleooceanography: a predictive analog of the future. *Quaternary Research* 2:350–354.

MENKE, B., K.-K. BEHRE
1973   History of vegetation and biostratigraphy. *Eiszeitalter und Gegenwart* 23/24:251–267.

MESOLELLA, K. J., R. K. MATHEWS, W. S. BROECKER, D. L. THURBER
1969   The astronomical theory of climatic change. Barbados data. *Journal of Geology* 77:250–274.

MOVIUS, H L., JR.
1960   Radiocarbon dates and Upper Paleolithic archeology in central and western Europe. *Current Anthropology* 1:355–391.

MUSIL, R.
1959   Osteologický materiál z paleolitického sídliště v Pavlově. Část II. *Anthropozoikum* 8:83–106.
1960   Palaonthologische Funde in Sedimenten der letzten Zwischeneiszeit. *Acta Musei Moraviae* 45:99–136.
1969   "Stratigraphische Korrelation im Pleistozän auf Grund der Vertebratenentwicklung," in *Periglazialzone, Löss und Pälaolithikum der Tschechoslowakei.* Edited by J. Demek and J. Kukla, 61–73. Tschechoslowakische Akademie der Wissenschaften, Geographisches Institut in Brno.

MUSIL, R., K. VALOCH
1966   Beitrag zur Gliederung des Würms in Mitteleuropa. *Eiszeitalter und Gegenwart* 17:131–138.

MUSIL, R., K. VALOCH, V. NEČESANÝ
1955   Pleistocénní sedimenty okolí Brna. *Anthropozoikum* 4:107–142. Prague.

NATHAN, H.
1953   Ein interglazialer Schotter südlich Moosburg in Oberbayern mit Fagotia acicularis Férussac (Melanopsenkies). *Geologia Bavarica* 19:315–334. Munich.

OBRUCHEV, V. A.
1945   Loess types and their origin. *American Journal of Science* 243: 256–262.

OPDYKE, N. D.
1972   Paleomagnetism of deep-sea cores. *Reviews of Geophysics and Space Physics* 10:213–249.

PELÍŠEK, J.
1942   Pohřbené půdy v aluviích svrateckého úvalu. *Příroda* 35.

1954 Kvartér východního okolí Brna. *Anthropozoikum* 4:107–168. Prague.

1969 "Lössablagerungen der trockenen Niederungsgebiete," in *Periglazialzone, Löss und Paläolithikum der Tschechoslowakei.* Edited by J. Demek and J. Kukla. Tschechoslowakische Akademie der Wissenschaften Geographisches Institut in Brno.

PENCK, A.
1922 Die Terrassen des Isartales in den Alpen. *Sonderberichte d. preussischen Akademie d. Wissenschaften.* Phys.-math., Kl.

PENCK, A., E. BRÜCKNER
1909 *Die Alpen im Eiszeitalter.* Bd 1–3. Chr.-Herm. Tauchnitz, Leipzig.

PIFFL, L.
1971 Zur Gliederung des Tullner Feldes. *Ann. Naturhistor. Mus. Wien* 75:293–310. Vienna.

PROŠEK, F.
1946 Nález clactonienského úšťěpu v Letkách nad Vltavou. *Památky archeologické* 42, Nová řada 9-16 (1939–46) 132–136. Prague.

PROŠEK, F., V. LOŽEK
1951 Zpráva o výzkumu kvartéru v Letkách nad Vltavou. *Věstník Ústředního ústavu geologického* 26:101–104.

1954 Stratigrafické otázky československého paleolitu. *Památky Archeologické* 45:35–74. Prague.

1957 Stratigraphische Übersicht des tschechoslowakischen Quartärs. *Eiszeitalter und Gegenwart* 8:37–90.

RUDDIMAN, W. F.
1971 Pleistocene sedimentation in the equatorial Atlantic: stratigraphy and faunal paleoclimatology. *Geological Society of America Bulletin* 82:283–302.

RUDDIMAN, W. F., A. MCINTYRE
1973 Time transgressive deglacial retreat of polar waters from the North Atlantic. *Quaternary Research* 3:117–130.

SCHAEFER, I.
1950 Die diluviale Erosion und Akkumulation. *Forschungen zur deutschen Landeskunde* 49:1–154. Landshut.

1953 Die donaueiszeitlichen Ablagerungen an Lech und Wertach. *Geologia Bavarica* 19:13–64. Munich.

SCHÖNHALS, E.
1944 Spätglazialer Löss in Lettland. *Neues Jahrbuch für Mineralogie (Geologie und Paläontologie)*, Monatsheft 1944B, 241–250. Stuttgart.

1951 Über fossile Böden im nichtvereisten Gebiet. *Eiszeitalter und Gegenwart* 1:109–130.

SHACKLETON, N. J.
1969 The last interglacial in the marine and terrestrial records. *Proceedings of Royal Society London B* 174:135–154.

SHACKLETON, N. J., N. D. OPDYKE
1973 Oxygen isotope and paleomagnetic stratigraphy of equatorial Pacific cores V28–238: Oxygen Isotope temperatures and ice volumes on a 10^5 year-10^6 year scale. *Quaternary Research* 3:39–55.

186   GEORGE J. KUKLA

ŠIBRAVA, V.
1972   Zur Stellung der Tschechoslowakei im Korrelierungssystem des Pleistozäns in Europa. Sborník Geologických Věd. *Anthropozikum.* Řada A. 8:1–218.

SMETANA, A.
1935   Corbicula fluminalis Müller a fauna třebestovické plistocénní terasy v Čilci u Nymburka. *Rozpravy II. tř. České akademie* 49 (4). Prague.

SMOLÍKOVÁ, L.
1967a Mikromorphologie der altpleistozänen Fossilböden von Červený Kopec bei Brno (Brünn). (Vorläufige Mitteilung) *Věstnik Ústředního ústavu geologického* 42:369–373. Prague.
1967b Zur Mikromorphologie der jungpleistozänen Böden von Sedlec bei Praha. *Časopis pro Mineralogii a Geologii* 12:277–286. Prague.
1968a Polygenese der fossilen Lössböden der Tschechoslowakei im Lichte mikromorphologischer Untersuchungen. *Geoderma* 1:315–324. Amsterdam.
1968b Genese mladopleistocénních půd v Modřicích u Brna na základě půdní mikromorfologie. *Časopis pro Mineralogii a Geologii* 13: 199–209. Prague.
1971   Gesetztmässigkeiten der Bodenentwicklung im Quartär. *Eiszeitalter und Gegenwart* 22:156–177.

SOERGEL, W.
1939   Das diluviale System. *Fortschritte d. Geologie u. Paläontologie* 7: Heft 39. Berlin.

STEHLÍK, AL.
1934   Fosilní ssavci ze Stránské skály u Brna. *Práce Moravské přírodovědecké společnosti* 9:1–94. Brno.

TOEPFER, V.
1933   *Die glazialen und präglazialen Schotterterrassen im mittleren Saaletal.* Ber. natforsch. Ges. Freiburg i. Br. 32.

TURNER, C.
1970   The Middle Pleistocene deposits at Marks Tey, Essex. *Philosophical Transactions of the Royal Society of London B* 257:373–440.

TURNER, C., R. G. WEST
1968   The subdivision and zonation of interglacial periods. *Eiszeitalter und Gegenwart* 19:93–101.

VALOCH, K.
1968   Evolution of the Palaeolithic in Central and Eastern Europe. *Current Anthropology* 9:351–390.

VAN DER HAMMEN, T., T. A. WIJMSTRA, W. H. ZAGWIJN
1971   "The floral record of the Late Cenozoic of Europe," in *Late Cenozoic glacial ages.* Edited by K. K. Turekian, 391–424. New Haven and London: Yale University Press.

VAN MONTFRANS, H. M., J. HOSPERS
1969   A preliminary report on the stratigraphical position of the Matuyama-Brunhes geomagnetic field reversal in the Quaternary sediments of the Netherlands. *Geologie en Mijnbouw* 48:565–572.

VAŠKOVSKÝ, I.
1970 Geological profile of the Quaternary near Nové Mesto nad Váhom. *Věstnik Ústředního ústavu geologického* 45:41–44.

VOGEL, J. C., W. H. ZAGWIJN
1967 Groningen radiocarbon dates VI. *Radiocarbon* 9:63–106.

WATKINS, N. D.
1971 Geomagnetic polarity events and the problem of "The Reinforcement Syndrome." *Comments on Earth Sciences: Geophysics* 2: 36–42. London.

WIEGANK, K. F.
1972 Ökologische Analyse quartärer Foraminiferen. *Geologie* 21. Beiheft 77, 1–111. Berlin.

WIJMSTRA, T. A.
1969 Palynology of the first 30 metres of a 120 m deep section in Northern Greece. *Acta Botanica Nederland.* 18:511–527.

WOLDSTEDT, P.
1954 *Das Eiszeitalter,* Band 1. Stuttgart: Ferdinand Enke Verlag.
1958 *Das Eiszeitalter,* Band 2. Stuttgart: Ferdinand Enke Verlag.

ZAGWIJN, W. H.
1961 Vegetation, climate and radiocarbon datings in the Late Pleistocene of the Netherlands, Part 1: Eemian and Early Weichselian. *Mededelingen v. d. Geol. Stichting,* N.S. 14:15–45.

ZAGWIJN, W. H., H. M. VAN MONTFRANS, J. G. ZANDSTRA
1971 Subdivision of the "Cromerian" in the Netherlands. Pollen analysis, palaeomagnetism and sedimentary petrology. *Geologie en Mijnbouw* 50:41–58.

ZAPLETAL K.
1931 Štěrkové terasy, spraše a jeskynní usazeniny ve vztazích. *Příroda* 24:206.

ZÁRUBA, Q
1942 Längsprofil durch die Moldauterrassen zwischen Kamaik und Weltrus. *Mitteilungen tschechoslowakischen Akademie Wissenschaften.* 52, no. 9, 1–38, Prague.
1960 Stáří přehloubené brázdy na dně vltavského údolí pod Prahou. *Věstník Ústředniho ústavu geologického* 35:55–59. Prague.

ŽEBERA K.
1943 Devět sprašových pokryvů fosilními půdními typy pod Novou horou na líšeňském katastru u Brna. *Příroda* 36:83–89. Brno.
1944 *Povšechný přehled, roztřídění a zhodnocení čtvrtohorních pokryvů v Čechách.* Rozpravy II třídy České akademie 52. Prague.
1949 K současnému výzkumu kvartéru v oblasti Českého masivu (À propos de l'exploration actuelle des terrains quaternaires dans le domaine du Massif Bohémien). *Sborník Státního geologického ústavu ČSR* 16:731–781. Prague.

ZEMAN, A.
1966 Neotektonika a její souvislost s vývojem podloží sedimentů čelní karpatské hlubiny ve Vyškovském úvalu, mezi Vyškovem a Vrchoslavicemi. *Věstník Ústředního ústavu geologického* 41:37–43. Prague.

ZEUNER, F. E.
1946   *Dating the past: an introduction to geochronology.* London: Methuen.
1959   *The Pleisocene: its climate, chronology and faunal successions* (second edition). London: Hutchinson.
ZINK, F.
1940   Zur diluvialen Geschichte des Hochrheines. *Mitteillungen Reichsst. f. Bod. Zweigst. Freiburg i. Brnsw.* 1:1.

The Mid-Pleistocene of the Rhine Basin

KARL BRUNNACKER

ABSTRACT

The beginning of the Middle Pleistocene should be set in the time between Cromerian I-Interglacial and the following glacial period. Observations in the lower Rhine area now suggest that this was the seventh-to-last glacial. The Matuyama/Brunhes geomagnetic boundary also coincides with this limit, which immediately preceded the development of significant permafrost indications in the lower Rhine basin. Slightly younger, but still pertaining to the Cromer-complex, there is a terrace south of the Rheinisches Schiefergebirge with two cold-climate facies interrupted by a paleosol. This indicates that the sixth-to-last glacial period was less severe than either the preceding or the following one.

Younger than the base of the Mosbach and Kärlich beds (with reversed paleomagnetism) are the Cromerian fossiliferous sites of the Main River near Würzburg, at Mauer near Heidelberg, and at Mosbach near Wiesbaden (normal magnetism). Steinheim-on-the-Murr, like the Holstein Interglacial, belongs to the younger part of the Middle Pleistocene. Both the Saale as well as the Elster glacials include two distinct glacial periods.

INTRODUCTION

In the southern Rhine River Basin there are several sites important to the mid-Pleistocene geology of the area on account of their macromammalian deposits. In addition to Jockgrim, Mosbach and Randersacker — Mauer and Steinheim also belong to this group of internationally significant sites. The mammalian assemblages of this area suggested stratigraphic subdivisions to K. D. Adam (1953, 1966) as shown in Table 1.

Yet, the apparently clear division of the mid-Pleistocene is considerably more complicated according to Heller (1967) who, for exam-

Table 1. Stratigraphic subdivisions of the Rhine Basin, according to Adam (1953, 1966)

Upper Pleistocene	Würm/Weichsel Glacial Taubachian Woodland Phase (Eem)		
Middle Pleistocene	Riss/Saale Glacial Steinheimer Woodland Phase (Holstein)		Diluvium
Lower Pleistocene	Mindel/Elster Glacial Younger Steppe Phase Mauerian Woodland Phase Older Steppe Phase	Mosbachian	
Basal Pleistocene	Villafranchian		

ple, places the Cromerian Upper Freshwater Bed fauna somewhat older than that from Mauer. Furthermore, according to Zagwijn, et al. (1971), who base themselves primarily on palynology, a further distinction of three, separate Cromerian (I, II, and III) Interglacials must be envisaged. However, this also suggests a key to the solution of the problem of division, namely that no matter where the boundary to the older Pleistocene is set, there are several more cold-warm cycles within the mid-Pleistocene than was originally supposed. This suggestion becomes increasingly plausible if we consider the succession of loessic paleosols at Červeny Kopec, near Brünn. Here Kukla (in Demek and Kukla 1969) recognized some eight distinct cold-warm cycles younger than the last paleomagnetic reversal, i.e. dating from the past 700,000 years. Their relation to the "Cromerian" complex is given by van Montfrans' paleomagnetic work (1971), whereby this reversal followed the Cromer I Interglacial.

Based on the comprehensive work of Kaiser (1961), there is a multiple terrace sequence along the Middle and Lower Rhine which can be used to subdivide the mid-Pleistocene. However, the deficiency of precise information makes detailed interpretation difficult. Consequently, the Ice Ages research group of the University of Cologne has been continuing this work over the past years. Emphases here have been the terraces of the southern Lower Rhine, and key profiles of the Middle Rhine. This research was only made possible by substantial financial support from the Deutsche Forschungsgemeinschaft and the Landesamt für Forschung in Düsseldorf. In addition, many colleagues from home and abroad have helped us. Few results have been published so far and study of the mid-Pleistocene is still in its initial stages.

PLEISTOCENE SUBDIVISION IN THE RHINE BASIN

To begin with, it is necessary to outline the position of the mid-Pleistocene within the Pleistocene sequence. The middle and lower Rhine are particularly suited for this purpose.

Tectonic evolution of the Rhine was marked by uplift of the Rheinisches Schiefergebirge and subsidence of the lower Rhine basin. The ideal model of a Quaternary terrace sequence is thereby modified, with vertical distances between individual terraces relatively large in the area of uplift (see Figure 2), while in the area of subsidence, terrace deposits overlie one another. The zone where the terraces intersect is between Cologne and Nijmegen (see Figure 3). Furthermore, this hinge line and the area just downstream are complicated by fragmentation into tectonic blocks with further individual movements. In addition to the tectonic and climatic developments, evolution of the other Rhine catchment (e.g. the Alpine Rhine and the Main) are also important (see Figure 1). Insofar as the variable position of the North Sea coast plays a special role in the development of these terraces, it also must be considered.

Older Views of Terrace Subdivision

The textbook representation of the structure and division of the Rhine terraces as shown in Table 2 is generally well known.

Table 2. Traditional division of the Rhine terraces

South	North	
— Low Terrace a —		Weichselian Glacial
— Lower "Middle Terrace" —	{Krefeld Middle Terrace {Push moraines of Lower Rhine}	Saale Glacial
	Krefeld beds	Holsteinian Interglacial
— Middle "Middle Terrace" — — Upper "Middle Terrace" — — Younger Main Terrace — — Older Main Terrace —	Channel gravels	Elsterian Glacial

a In German nomenclature it is common practice to subdivide alluvial bodies and river-cut platforms with superposed alluvium into stratomorphologic entities, locally described as "Low", "Middle" and "High" Terraces. In the case of the Rhine, the "High" Terrace is so extensive and dominant that it is generally designated as the "Main" Terrace, while the "Middle" Terrace is subdivided into further relative subdivisions labelled low, middle and high.

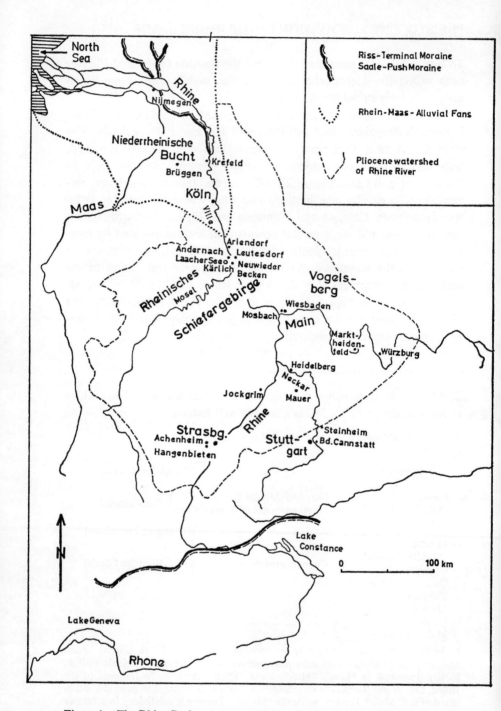

Figure 1. The Rhine Basin

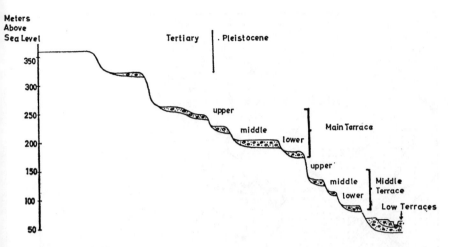

Figure 2. Schematic terrace suite of the Lower Middle Rhine (modified after Quitzow 1961)

Further subdivisions, such as the tripartite Upper Middle Terrace of Kaiser (1961), can be subsumed in the same framework.

Towards a New Subdivision in the Southern Lower Rhine

The following account is intended as an interim statement based primarily on the region of Cologne (Figure 4). A schematic differentia-

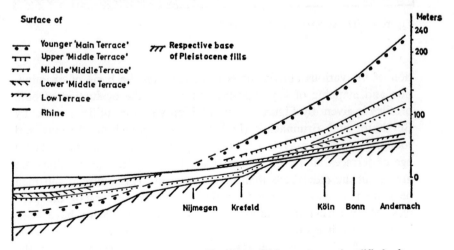

Figure 3. Schematic longitudinal profile of the Rhine terraces (modified after Zonneveld in Woldstedt 1958)

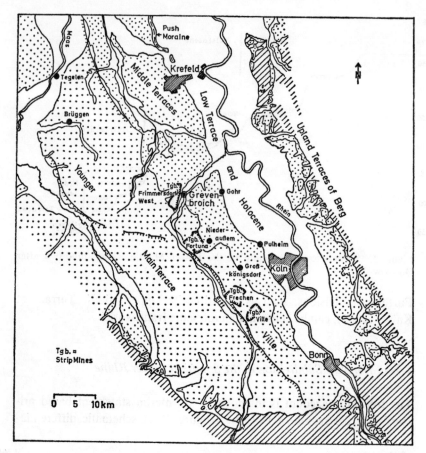

Figure 4.   The southern Lower Rhine Basin

tion of the various alluvial units recognized on the basis of examination and mapping of key exposures as well as the evaluation of bore
profiles is given by Figure 5. In addition we have utilized work by
Burghardt and Brunnacker (i.p.) on quartz gravel proportions and
rounding. Quartz gravels provide a crude indication of the relative
age of terraces along the lower Rhine, because their proportions are
greater in the older beds than in the younger. This estimate can then
be compared with visually-determined rounding indices of the pebbles. Many earlier designations of these terrace segments have been
ignored since it is often impossible to combine older and newer views.

The following Pleistocene subdivisions can be recognized in the
terrain around Cologne:

I. Fluvial deposits underlying the Main Terraces (Basal Pleistocene)
   cene)
II. Main Terrace Suite
III. Middle Terrace Suite
IV. Low Terraces (Upper Pleistocene)

The Tertiary/Quaternary Boundary

The Plio-/Pleistocene boundary has been chronostratigraphically defined, by geobotanical criteria, between the Reuverian and the Pretiglian (Zagwijn 1959). Further stratigraphic aids are provided. In the
Reuverian "B", a tourmaline-zircon-staurolite association (below)
is replaced by epidote-alterite-garnet-green hornblende as "Rhine facies"
above (Boenigk 1969, Boenigk, et al. 1972). Likewise the proportion of
heavy minerals increases about tenfold. This change is due to growth
of the Rhine catchment. In the Ville area, this boundary coincides with
the base of Clay Horizon A2 (Figure 5), and further indications are
evident higher in the profile, within Gravel Horizon b (Figure 5).
    Paleomagnetic orientation of Clay Horizons A1 and A2 is gener-
ally normal (Koči); and only in the Fortuna strip mine was reversed
polarity detected in the upper section. A related interesting feature of
Clay Horizon A2 is the Pliocene nature of its mollusca (Gliese and
Strauch 1969).

Basal Pleistocene

Basal Pleistocene sediments were temporarily exposed in recent years
within the former sediment trap recorded by the subsided tectonic
block along the western periphery of the Ville (Figure 5):
1. Gravel b: The main erosion and disconformity of the entire profile runs through Gravel Horizon b. The basal Gravel b1 still exhibits Pliocene character while the upper b2 gravel is typically Pleistocene.
It is, however, unclear whether this bed or a part of it belongs to the
Pretiglian cold phase.
    Figure 6 indicates a gap between Upper Piocene gravels and the
Basal Pleistocene Gravel c. Whether this gap is filled with Gravels b1
and b2, remains uncertain and it was not possible to make definitive
determinations in either horizon.
2. Clay Horizon B: The overlying clay contains a warm Pleistocene

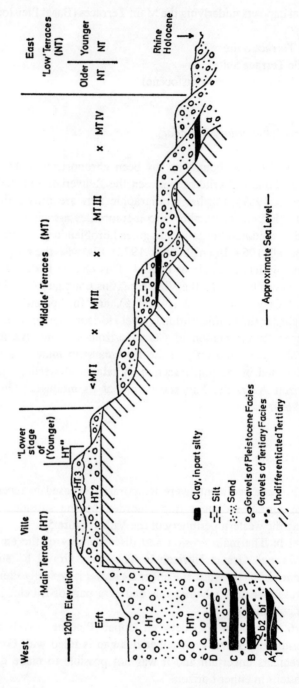

Figure 5.   West-East profile through the Rhine terraces near Cologne (partly generalized)

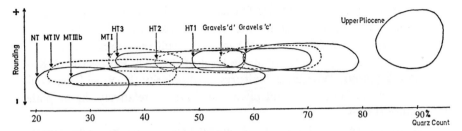

Figure 6.   Relationship between quartz ratio and rounding of quartz pebbles in alluvia of the southern Lower Rhine Basin (after Burghardt and Brunnacker i.p.)

molluscan fauna (Ložek). In addition, the macro flora retrieved are clearly of Pleistocene type (Kempf). The clay exhibits reserved paleomagnetism (Koči).

3.   Gravel c: This is a relatively quartz-poor gravel.

4.   Clay Horizon C: In this clay there also are remains of thermophile mollusca (Ložek) and the same is true of the flora (Kempf). Other studies have shown that this clay horizon apparently has normal magnetic polarity above, but reversed polarity below. Clay Horizon C can be correlated with the Tiglian C of the Dutch sequence since garnet, epidote, alterite and green hornblende are clearly dominant among the heavy minerals down to this level.

5.   Gravel d: This relatively sand-rich horizon contains large ice-rafted blocks. The heavy mineral component indicates an increase of reworked older Tertiary elements.

6.   Clay Horizon D: The heavy mineral spectrum is again similar to the underlying clay unit. The mollusca are still thermophile and Pleistocene (Ložek), while the flora includes several Tertiary elements (Kempf). This bed has normal magnetic polarity in the area of the Ville, and is correlated with the Waalian complex.

Main Terrace Suite

A variety of studies on the Main Terrace Complex (HT 1, HT 2, HT 3) is nearing completion (Boenigk: heavy minerals; Schnütgen: gravel petrography; Musa: peripheral facies). As a result this presentation falls back on the geological investigations of the Ville by Kowalzyk (1969).

Above Gravel c the quartz component decreases up to HT 3 at a more or less constant rate, and only in locally-preserved unit HT 3 is the quartz gravel count lower due to quartz-low Eifel contributions. From this we infer the following subdivisions:

1. Main Terrace 1 (HT 1): On the basis of a relatively high quartz component one can identify the basal horizon as HT 1. Locally it is followed by a few meters of sand. It is still uncertain whether this local sand is approximately at the level of the Clay Horizon E of Kowalzyk (1969). This clay exhibits reversed polarity (Koči) and also contains, in addition to several plants, molluscs of relatively thermophile nature (Ložek).

2. Main Terrace 2 (HT 2): A gravel veneer contains conspicuously fewer quartz pebbles, while in the Ville strip mines the upper boundary is given by a silty-clayey lense.

3. Main Terrace 3 (HT 3): Over a clay layer destroyed by ice, also in the Ville strip mines, there is a notably quartz-poor gravel above clayey units disturbed by cryoturbation. Its high content of Eifel minerals shows that the main Rhine discharge was increasingly derived from its present catchment. Terminal sedimentation shows a very pronounced floodplain soil. Shallow channels, also underlain by this paleosol, are filled with sand, which was altered by another floodplain soil. A general eastward shift of the Rhine is indicated during this time, and ice-rafted blocks occur throughout the Main Terrace. Deposits are either rare or lenticular. Uniequivocal cryoturbations are known only from Main Terrace 3, however. This horizon shows the oldest, certain syngenetic ice-wedges. Main Terraces 1 and 2 are composed of several cyclic coarse gravel/sandgravel alternations.

4. Lower Horizon of the (younger) Main Terrace: Quitzow (1956) has demarcated a lower horizon on the eastern side of the Ville; its base is cut some 20 meters into the Main Terrace surface. Quartz proportions are about as high as those of Main Terrace 2. This gravel was also modified by a well-developed floodplain soil. From this point in time the Rhine channel remained east of the Ville horst blocks.

The Middle Terrace Suite

There have been several attempts to subdivide the Middle Terraces of the southern, lower Rhine. But such attempts have been hindered by a cover mantle of up to 20 meters of loess and by man-made disturbances. Our recent investigations of the Middle Terraces, obviously beginning on the foundations of earlier work (see literature cited by Kaiser 1961, Winter 1968), were first based on geomorphologic mapping (nearing completion, Mentzen). This work is complemented by study of the thickness of the alluvial bodies proper (in association with Dolezalek), and the results of the profile investigations are integrated with this. Since only part of this work is finished we must again refer to Figure 5, as well as to the heavy mineral investigations of Vinken (1959).

The Middle Terrace is morphologically subdivided into four major surfaces:

Middle Terrace I — topographically highest
Middle Terrace II
Middle Terrace III
Middle Terrace IV — topographically lowest.

These surfaces can in part be subdivided further as a result of lower, minor surfaces created by denudation.

1. Middle Terrace I (MT 1): Middle Terrace I is developed downstream of Grosskönigsdorf. In the literature it is also called Upper Middle Terrace, Upper Middle Terrace₁, and Upper Middle Terrace₂ (Ahorner 1962; Quitzow 1956, 1959; Breddin 1968). The base of the 10-meter thick alluvium terrace is at about 70–75 meters above sea level near Grosskönigsdorf; quartz ratios are between 36 to 47 percent, similar to Main Terrace 2; the associated heavy minerals are basically similar to those of the Main Terrace, according to Vinken (1959), although brown hornblende derived from relatively acidic vulcanics of the middle Rhine also provides a distinguishing criterion.

2. Middle Terrace II (MT II): This terrace occupies a long arc near Niederaussem, as well as the bend of the strip mine at Frimmersdorf West. From this it is apparent that its margin forms broad, meander-like bends. It has been known as Upper Middle Terrace₂, Upper Middle Terrace₃, and likewise Lower Middle Terrace (Breddin 1968; Heller and Brunnacker 1966; Kaiser 1961; Quitzow 1956, 1959). The base of the related gravels lies about 50 meters above sea level at Niederaussem, and begins with gravel as much as 5 meters thick, with syngenetic ice-wedges. Above this there are 4 meter thick clay plugs which, similar to Frimmersdorf, can be associated with an interglacial (v.d. Brelie, et al. 1959). These fine-grained layers exhibit normal magnetization (Koči). Above them is a 15-meter thick flood silt with syngenetic ice-wedges. As a result of such superposition this unit is subdivided into a basal MT IIa and an upper MT IIb; between them is the interglacial clay. The quartz ratio of MT IIa in the former Rhine arm near Niederaussem is high: 52–56 percent, suggesting a reworked gravel component from the Main Terraces. The same holds for gravel lenticles in the local MT IIb terrace.

3. Middle Terrace III (MT III): Previously known as Lower Middle Terrace, MT III is extensively developed between Gohr and Greven-

broich with its base at highly variable elevations, e.g. at 5 meters above sea level east of Gohr and 45 meters north of Gohr. The basal part of the accumulation (MT IIIa) is known as the Channel Gravels (*Rinnenschotter*, Middle Middle Terrace) in the literature. These are overlain by the Krefeld beds of Holsteinian interglacial age; remnants of similar beds may also occur near Cologne (Kaiser and Schütrumpf 1960). The upper gravel (MT IIIb) lies on top.

The heavy mineral association in MT IIIa and above is characterized by minerals related to balsaltic vulcanism (pyroxenes) (Vinken 1959).

Near Gohr-Broich, MT IIIb rests on an ancient, sandy gravel with a quartz ratio of between 65 and 73 percent.

The complete MT III sequence near Krefeld was laterally compressed by the Drenthe-age continental glacier.

4. Middle Terrace IV (MT IV): The terrace runs along the Ville between Bonn and Pulheim. In the literature this terrace is known as the Lower Middle Terrace south of Cologne, while further downstream a distinct Krefeld Middle Terrace is supposed to be present. Nonetheless, Winter (1968) was able to show that these terraces are identical and the gravel surface lies at about 50–55 meters above sea level near Cologne; only the variable thickness of cover mantles simulates distinct surface elevation.

The terrace alluvium is topped by a patchy, gleyed flood silt which is convoluted together with the underlying gravel as a result of cryoturbation. This zone is altered by an interglacial soil. Above it lies the cover mantle, which is often remarkably thick along the inner terrace margins due to alluvial fans originating in the Ville. The superposed loess is up to 15 meters thick.

LOESS MANTLES OF THE MIDDLE TERRACES Information is due to several authors (Mückenhausen 1954; Paas 1961; Brunnacker 1967). According to them the Lower Terrace lacks a loess mantle, while MT IV has a single loess veneer. Two generations of loess rest on MT III, and near Niederaussem, three on MT II. Obviously these generations of loess covers only provide a minimum number of redated glacials.

OVERVIEW Conventionally, two Middle Terraces have been distinguished in the southern part of the lower Rhine basin, but recent work now establishes the existence of four individual Middle Terraces according to morphology, surface (and in part also base) elevations, as well as quartz ratios, heavy mineral associations, and number of superposed loess mantles. Those alluvia known as MT II and MT III are further subdivided according to the intercalated, interglacial clayplug deposits. The gravels of MT IIa have syngenetic ice wedges. MT III is subdivided by the interstratified Krefeld beds and their basal Channel Gravel (MT IIIa).

Lower Terraces

Results of Thoste (1972) are available for the Low Terraces. The vicinity of Cologne apparently lacks evidence of the Eemian Interglacial and, instead, cobble gravels with a cold fauna underlie the Low Terrace. The subsequent alluvium has syngenetic ice wedges. Even before the Alleröd, in part during the Oldest Dryas, the Rhine had already begun to downcut. At first the Rhine was still able to veneer the abandoned gravel surfaces with flood silts that contain mollusca suggestive of slightly warmer and moister conditions than the full glacial loess fauna (Ložek and Thoste 1972).

At the beginning of the Upper Dryas the floodplain was about 10 meters below the original Low Terrace gravel surface. The subsequent accumulation approached this old level before the Rhine began to downcut rapidly once again. This occurred during the Upper Dryas as is evidenced by cryoturbation along a related erosional surface, which was then altered by a floodplain soil at the beginning of the Holocene.

This valley evolution during the last glacial may serve as a model for the older terraces in terms of genetic relationships between climate and aggradation or downcutting.

The Neuwied Basin and the Lower Middle Rhine

In the Neuwied Basin and along the lower middle Rhine, it is possible to interrelate terrace remnants, loess mantles, and vulcanism. First the volcanic heavy minerals allow correlations with the lower Rhine (Frechen and Heide 1970). In addition, macromammalian fossils are not rare whenever new quarrying observations can be monitored. In any case, however, the Pleistocene stratigraphy of this sector is based on isolated sections.

THE KÄRLICH CLAY PITS   The Pleistocene of Kärlich consists of fluvial strata and overlying, multiple loess strata continuing right up to Holocene colluvium (Figure 7). At the same time, it provides an exemplary case of both the possibilities and problems of stratigraphic subdivision by means of loesses and paleosols (Brunnacker, et al. 1969; Brunnacker 1971).

The fluvial succession of Unit A consists of gravel, flood silts, and paleosols. Above this lies Unit B, consisting of gravels with ice-rafted blocks as well as ice-wedges in the upper part of the profile.

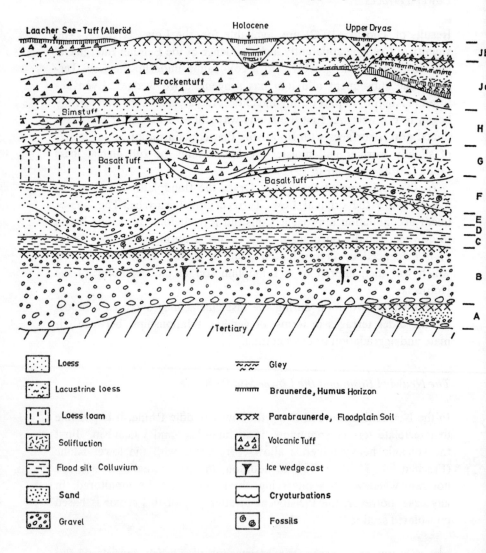

Figure 7.   Profile of Kärlich and the Neuwied Basin

Sandy flood silts are altered by a floodplain soil. In the upper part of the gravels there are heavy minerals related to a phonolithic (selbergitic) vulcanism. The transition to the cover mantle is given by Unit C, a thin flood silt modified by a weak gley.

The strikingly greenish loess of Unit D is only weakly gleyed above and is therefore included with the loess of Unit E. The end of the sequence is formed by traces of a Parabraunerde whose development is comparable to the modern soil.

In and above Unit F there are volcanic tuffs interlayered with the loesses, while ice-wedge casts are once again common.

As has been recently determined, the major erosional disconformity of the cover mantle complex lies at the base of Unit G. This bed begins with humic, solifluction-like deposits that are yielding increasing numbers of mammalian fossils.

Next to the base of Unit H there are channels filled with basalt tuff. Somewhat higher, pumice follows together with some basalt tuff. This section is also much disturbed by ice wedges, cryoturbations and pocket soils. The uppermost facies consist of a calcareous brown soil, with full interglacial mollusca. These beds are preserved by a very coarse pumiceous tuff *(Brockentuff)*, derived from vents within the area of exposures.

On the edge of a recently exposed vent are Units Ja and Jb, overlying the Brockentuff. Jb begins with three humic horizons, followed by loess. The upper interface of Ja is formed by a paleosol, originally held to represent an interstadial. More recently the views of Schirmer (1970), that this is a clearcut Parabraunerde, have been confirmed.

The top of the loess sequence is marked by Unit Jb. Locally, Lake Laach tuff of Alleröd age rests on Jb.

Originally Units Ja and Jb were combined to represent a single glacial with the soil of Unit E ascribed to an admittedly important interstadial. These interpretations must be abandoned in view of the better exposures now available.

Climatic indicators suggest that at least the upper part of Unit B was deposited during a glacial period. The loesses also indicate glacial episodes.

Fauna and Flora   Full interglacial mollusca were found in the Unit H paleosol. Traces of reworked, interglacial molluscs are also found in C, D, and E (Ložek). Micromammals are occur in F (lacustrine loess facies) and indicate a post-Cromerian age in the sense of Heller. *Chletrionomys* was recovered from the base of G (Heller). Earlier discoveries of large mammals cannot be localized beyond doubt, but recently-found molars of *Elephas trogontherii* in C and a fragment of a molar in B, suggestive of *meridionalis,* are of great interest. A trogontheroid molar is also known from F (Poplin).

Paleomagnetism   The flood silt of A exhibits reversed magnetism (Koči). In addition, a silt lense in the upper part of the B gravel shows reversed magnetism, in contrast to the paleosol of B, to the flood silt of C, to the loesses of D, E, and F, as well as to the solifluction material of G (Heye).

Paleosol Stratigraphy   Paleosols of interglacial type, supported by faunal remains, are found at the top of Units A, B, E, F, G, H, Ja, and Jb (contemporary soil). Above the fluvial sequence A to C (C — linking flood silt), the cover mantle consequently records six different cold periods. If one places the soil of A in the Cromerian-I Interglacial, the paleomagnetic reversal of about 700,000 years ago (Matuyuma-Brunhes) occurred during the seventh-to-last cold period.

THE ARIENDORF PROFILE   The Ariendorf gravel pit provides another model for the Middle Terrace. Some 10 meters over the base of the gravel, heavy minerals resulting from basaltic vulcanism first appear in a sandy horizon (Frechen and Heide 1970). A phonolitic tuff is found 2 to 3 meters beneath the top of this fluvial unit.

The cover mantle of the terrace begins with a layer of phonolitic tuff up to two meters thick. A channel which cuts through it is filled with loess-like material containing macro-mammalian fossils, e.g. mammoth crania older than the Würm Glacial (Poplin). The associated molluscan fauna is of cold type despite isolated elements of interglacial type (Puissegur).

Disconformably above this is a first loess mantle with two lenticles of basalt tuff, partly disturbed by cryotrubation. Above this is a Parabraunerde. A second loess mantle shows a basal humic zone containing pumice.

The stratigraphy can be argued as follows. The basalt tuff of the terrace alluvium is more recent than that of Unit B at Kärlich or MT I of the lower Rhine, since both these gravels contain components deriving from acidic vulcanism, in contrast to the more recent terraces with minerals of basaltic origin. At least two separate loess mantles are present, and the fill of the channel, which contains fossil mammals, is also composed of loessic material. There may therefore be

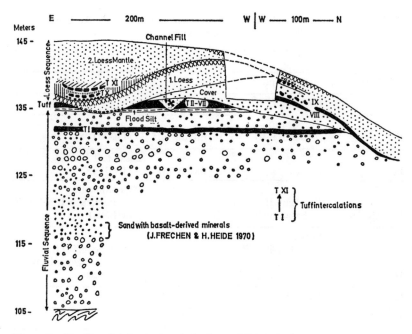

Figure 8.　Profile of Ariendorf and the lower Middle Rhine

an important erosional disconformity between the tuffs and the channel fill. The Ariendorf terrace can therefore be correlated with MT III (or II) of the lower Rhine; a phonolitic tuff can be found near the top of MT III (Paas 1961).

TEPHROCHRONOLOGY　In the Lake Laach region, Quaternary vulcanism played an important role, and the Alleröd tuff is readily identifiable. However, the Eltville tuff horizon (formerly Kärlich tuff) in the Würm loess is only developed locally, even in the type area. Older tuffs are well enough known along the middle Rhine, but their correlations remain an open problem, as the profiles of Table 3 show.

ABSOLUTE DATING　Similar tephrochronological problems exist for the K/Ar datings of vulcanic rocks in the vicinity of Lake Laach by Frechen and Lippolt (1965). Table 4 illustrates the key difficulty of relating the vulcanic deposits to specific terraces. The alternative interpretations of Table 4 underscore the stratigrajphic uncetainties. Either the dates are too young, or their correlations with the terraces are faulty, or the inferences from Kärlich are not generally applicable.

Table 3. Volcanic Intercalations in Pleistocene profiles near Lake Laach (T = tuff in loess, colluvium, or terrace alluvium)

Kärlich (Figure 7)		Leutesdorf	Ariendorf (Figure 8)
Subdivisions	Intercalation		
Alleröd	Pumice tuff	Pumice tuff	
Jb	Eltville tuff (Basalt tuff)	Eltville tuff	Pumice tuff (TX-XI)
Ja		Basalt tuff	Basalt tuff (TVIII-IX)
Interglacial	Brockentuff (Basalt tuff)		Phonolitic tuff (+ Pumice or Basalt tuff) (TII-VII)
H	Pumice (+ Basalt) tuff Basalt (+ Pumice) tuff	Basalt tuff	Phonolitic tuff (TI); basaltic heavy minerals in gravels
G	Basalt tuff	Basalt tuff	
Interglacial	↓ ?	Basalt tuff	
F	Basalt tuff		
C-D-E			
B	Phonolitic heavy minerals in gravels		

Table 4. K/Ar dates on volcanics of the Lake Laach area and their potential stratigraphic positions

J. Frechen and H. J. Lippolt (1965):		Alternative possibilities within the terrace stratigraphy outlined here
K/Ar dates B.P.	Correlation	(approximations only)
140/150,000	Holsteinian interglacial	Penultimate interglacial or younger
220/260,000	Middle "Middle" Terrace	Middle Terrace III b?
300,000	Older "Middle" Terrace	
320,000	Cromerian interglacial	
340/350,000	Younger Main Terrace	Middle Terrace II b?
405/420,000	Older Main Terrace	Basal substage of Main Terrace? up to Middle Terrace I?
570,000		

Problems of Correlation

The interrelationships of the unlike categories of data are not particularly easy to determine. The central problem remains the number of cold-warm cycles within a particular time span. Above all, this applies to evaluation of Middle Terraces IIa and IIIa of the lower Rhine. Does each of these represent cold-climate basal facies of the subsequent interglacials? Or does each represent an independent cold episode? These questions were already posed earlier without a satisfactory answer (Brunnacker 1967, 1971), when we attempted to find analogues with other terrace systems of the interior. If one instead considers the lower Rhine basin independently, it appears that the former alternative is more likely (cf. Brunnacker 1965; Thoste 1972). Figure 9 shows the results of a corresponding attempt to link the lower Rhine terraces with the Kärlich profile, as based on the following arguments:

The upper gravels of Unit B as well as HT 3 first exhibit large numbers of clear-cut ice-wedges. Furthermore, the overlying generations of loess or alluvia speak for an identical number — six — of subsequent cold periods. All other criteria, which are only fragmentary or incomplete at the moment (e.g. fauna, heavy minerals, paleomagnetism), do not contradict this. Yet the following points remain unresolved or methodologically equivocal:

1. The actual position of the Plio-Pleistocene boundary and its absolute age, as well as the temporal span of the sedimentary gap within the Basal Pleistocene.

2. The exact number of climatic cycles recorded by the Main and Middle terrace suites.

The results of work in other areas give almost no clue to the answer to these two questions. The same even applies for correlations with the adjacent Netherlands, where rather thorough investigations of the Pleistocene are available. Insofar as possible, the Netherlands terminology is entered on Figure 9. However, this demonstrates that subdivision of the Middle Terrace complex in the Netherlands still is incomplete (compare Zagwijn, et al. 1971).

Climatic History

Pleistocene climatic evolution in the study area is documented by numerous types of evidence of variable reliability. The most typical rock category for each of the known cold periods, except for the Pretigian, is loess, with characteristic mollusca during at least the later Pleistocene.

A first paleoclimatic span is malacologically demonstrated between the Upper Pliocene (Clay Horizon A 2) and the oldest warm period known on the Rhine (Clay Horizon B). Ice-rafted blocks follow in Gravel d and the subsequent gravel units. Apparently, at about the same time or a little later, fluvial accumulations changed from thin, extensive strata to massive units some ten meters thick. Each subsequent warm interval was represented by deep floodplain soils developed on the preceding terrace. Correspondingly, major dissection must be attributed to the beginning of the next cold period. This is the case back to the earliest substage of the Main Terrace. Consequently the patterns of Pleistocene downcutting and accumulation became increasingly complicated, probably as a result of cold-climate permafrost. This is first documented in HT 3.

An archaic form of a lemming is present in MT IIb (Heller and Brunnacker 1966). Furthermore, quartz-pebble rounding decreases rapidly in the younger Middle and Lower Terraces. The great glacial advances that began with the Elster further demonstrate an increasingly harsh climate, so that intensification of cold from one glacial episode to the next is apparent for the later Pleistocene, with an additional trend from cool-humid to cold-arid. The same is true of the maxima of the warm periods, namely a change from warm-humid to temperate-drier.

The warm episodes of the Basal Pleistocene saw the disappearance of Tertiary floral elements. Nonetheless, Clay Horizon D, contemporary with the Waalian, is exceptional by again containing fruits and seeds of Tertiary plants. These findings are not, as yet, supported by palynology. The succeeding Cromerian Interglacial of the Netherlands is treated by Zagwijn, et al. (1971), who indicate that the Cromerian–II–interglacial was warmer. Correlated with the Mauer Forest Phase, this might help explain the presence of hippopotami. An interglacial of Cromerian type (which?) is also found interrelated with the Main River Valley fill (compare Frenzel 1967; see our Table 6). The interglacial of Frimmersdorf West (v.d. Brelie, et al. 1959) is placed at the base of MT II b; noteworthy there is the abundance of *Juglans* and *Pterocaras*. Previously this deposit was correlated with the Holsteinian Interglacial. The true Holsteinian has been determined palynologically from the region of push-moraines along the lower Rhine (Kampf 1966), while the Eemian Interglacial was established at Weeze on the lower Rhine by a characteristic pollen succession (v.d. Brelie, et al. 1955).

On the basis of these paleoclimatic interpretations, the last epoch of normal magnetic polarity of about 700,000 years ago began during

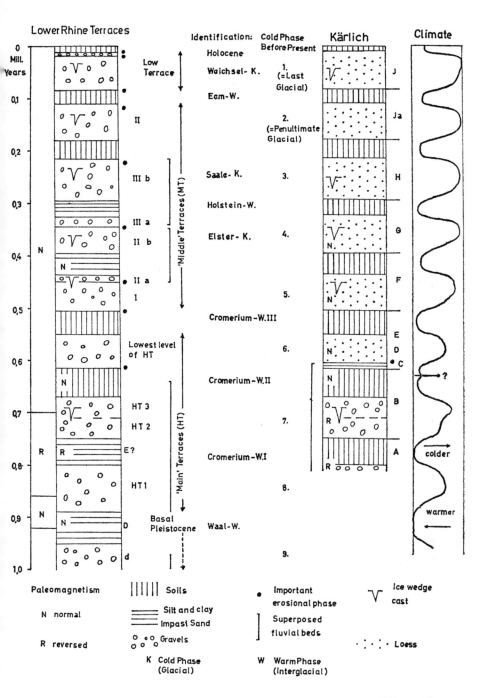

Figure 9. Attempt to correlate the terraces of the southern Lower Rhine with the Pleistocene sequence of Kärlich, with climatic interpretations

the seventh-to-last glacial. The subsequent climatic cycles consequently spanned about 100,000 years each (Figure 9). However, the proportional duration of the cold and warm episodes gradually shifted in favor of the glacials (from relative lengths of five-to-five to seven-to-three?)

A key position for the genetic development of the older mid-Pleistocene appears to be occupied by the earliest substage of the (Younger) Main Terrace (Figure 9), a feature thus far given little attention. Ice-wedge casts are strikingly absent from this alluvial unit, while these beds primarily include reworked gravels along the lower Rhine. This can be related to an absence of permafrost. If one accept Büdel's theory (1969), that downcutting in hard rocks is primarily due to the effects of a frozen subsoil, then the incision of the Rhine into the rising Rheinisches Schiefergebirge was much inhibited. Upstream massive fluvial beds were deposited, e.g. the 60 meters of gravels in the middle Main River Valley (cf. Figure 11; Körber 1962). According to these considerations this particular glacial was then less cold, particularly in comparison with later glacials.

THE MID-PLEISTOCENE

The lower boundary of the mid-Pleistocene needs to be determined more precisely. A marker should be chosen that can be readily recognized within the limits of available techniques in at least some regions. At the same time this marker should also coincide with a paleoclimatic or evolutionary break. The Matuyama/Brunhes geomagnetic reversal fulfills such requirements. This would locally coincide with the appearance of frequent ice-wedge casts — and implicitly of permafrost — in the deposits of the seventh-to-last glacial. Obviously a terminology such as "seventh-to-last, sixth-to-last, etc. glacial" is a clumsy expedient that needs to be replaced as soon as possible.

The Loess Sequence

The only apparently unbroken loess succession of comparable length in Central Europe, fortunately well investigated, is found as Červeny Kopec, near Brünn. Admittedly Kukla (in Demek and Kukla 1969) determined the paleomagnetic reversal in the eighth-to-last glacial, but the relative position of the Cromerian coincides with that adopted here. This discrepancy in the number of climatic cycles should not be overemphasized since we are assuming further gaps in the Rhine terrace sequence, as well as underevaluation of particular horizons. On the other hand, a highly differentiated loess profile is equally susceptible to overevaluation.

The Glacial Sequence

Time-stratigraphic terminologies derived from glacial stratigraphy have been deliberately avoided here. This has been done because of the highly controversial, in part even inadequate definitions. In addition, correlations of North European and Alpine glacials are often debatable, while the traditional application of the Alpine terminology — from an area where there are next to no fossils — to biostratigraphic horizons elsewhere is hardly justifiable. Finally, the necessarily incomplete nature of successions based on glacier advances can hardly be ignored.

Alpine Glaciations A practicable subdivision of the later Pleistocene in the Alpine region is still based on the work of Albrecht Penck, who established successive "glacial series". For example, from this point of view the Riss glaciation cannot be considered as a complex of several glaciations, interrupted by interglacials, but must be defined as that single glaciation younger than the Mindel but older than the Würm glaciation. Admittedly Penck anticipated that additional glaciations might have to be added between these "glacial series." In practice, however, one must necessarily define the Würm as the last, the Riss as the penultimate glaciation, and so on. Otherwise even the correlation of contiguous glacial lobes in the Alpine Piedmont is impossible. The four classic glacials can therefore only be correlated with the four youngest terrace alluvia of the lower Rhine, if this system is applied in Penck's sense. The earlier Donau glacial complex is represented by a gravel plain west of the Lech, comparable to the Main Terrace surface of the lower Rhine. One can further subdivide the Donau gravels, e.g. by molluscan criteria (Schröder and Dehm 1951; cf. also Graul 1962). Then Schaefer's oldest Biber glacial complex (1956) might be correlated with the incomplete Basal Pleistocene of the Rhine sequence.

The North European Glaciations These discouraging comments on the Alpine glaciations should not delude the reader into thinking that the record of the North European glaciations is any more reliable. To the contrary. Nonetheless, this area is crucial since the continental glacier reached the lower Rhine during the Saale glacial (Thomé 1959; Kempf 1966). If extrapolation from the region of Cologne is permissible, one can associate MT IIIa with the "Channel Gravel" (see Table 5). Furthermore the Lower Middle Terrace is identical with MT III b. The ice advance therefore belongs to the antepenultimate glacial.

In the adjacent Netherlands, the Pottery Clay Formation is correlated with the Elster Glacial (de Jong 1965), and a connection with Lauenburg Clay appears to be indicated. Correlation with MT IIa is not impossible, since the erosional base of each is exceptionally deep (Table 5). The even older glaciofluvial (?) Hattem complex is considered to be the first indication of a northern glaciation, younger than the Waalian. Perhaps it corresponds to our HT 1, or HT 2 and 3.

The Fluvial Sequence

As suggested, a characterization of Pleistocene river development by the argument of "warm climate downcutting versus cold climate alluviation" is hardly accurate. Such an idealized scheme most closely

Table 5.   Terrace stratigraphy on the lower Rhine and glacial deposits of the Netherlands

Rhine Terraces	Netherlands	Glacial
— — — — Low Terrace — — — —		Weichselian
	Eemian interglacial	
Middle Terrace IV Middle Terrace III b	Drenthe advance	Saale
Krefeld beds	Holsteinian interglacial	
Middle Terrace III a (deep incision of channel) Middle Terrace II b	Pottery Clay Form	(Late Elster) Elsterian
Middle Terrace I to Main Terraces 2 + 3	glacial deposits unknown in area (?)	
	Cromerian-I interglacial	
Main Terrace I	Glaciofluvial (?) Hattem Complex	

Identification of :

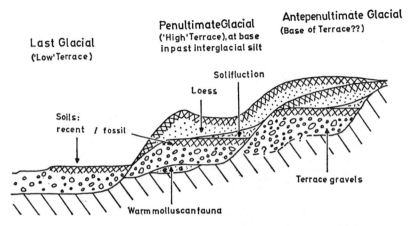

Figure 10.   Generalized terrace sequence of the later Pleistocene, with loess cover mantles

matches observations in immediate proximity to the Alpine glaciers where, locally, there may be multiple Pleistocene terrace sequences (compare Fink 1965).

Regional contrasts in terrace development are due to extensive or localized movements of the earth's crust, as well as distance from marine transgressions. Another possibility is the influence of bedrock contrasts on river downcutting (for example, the hard Paleozoic rocks of the middle Rhine, in contrast to the Cenozoic, partly unconsolidated and sandy beds of the lower Rhine). In addition, the detailed climatic history is relevant, particularly the development of permafrost.

South of the Schiefergebirge the pattern of terraces is shown in Figure 10 (Brunnacker 1971). Curiously, this sector lacks an older unit with three generations of loess mantles. Instead there are terraces with at least four loess veneers. In this case the terrace alluvia exhibit unique features, for example in the Main River Basin and at Regensburg (Brunnacker 1964 b; our Figure 11). The terraces of fourth-to-last and third-to-last glacials are superposed in this model (as a rule?), so that only two loess strata are present (Figure 10). The next oldest sequence is again superposed and therefore exhibits four or more loess veneers (Figure 10).

It is tempting to correlate such a system with MT II and MT III of the lower Rhine, but a satisfactory solution is not yet available.

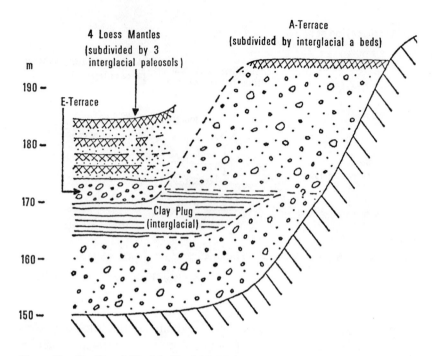

Figure 11.   Profile of Marktheidenfeld, Maintal

The Marine Sequence

In regard to interdigitation of North Sea transgressions in the embouchure of the Rhine, it can only be stated that the Eemian seas correlate with the last interglacial, while the Holstein seas predated the antepenultimate glacial. Only in the Basal and perhaps also the Lower Pleistocene record are marine facies again found in what is now a terrestrial environment. This means that the shoreline was generally located further seawards during the mid-Pleistocene. Not without interest are similar discoveries on the Mediterranean coast (Brunnacker 1973).

IMPORTANT MID-PLEISTOCENE SITES

There are several important mid-Pleistocene sites in the Rhine Basin. Key fossiliferous horizons are shown in Table 6.

Table 6.   Key fossiliferous horizons according to Adam and Heller

Heller (1967)	Adam (1953, 1954)
	Taubach Forest Phase (Eemian)
	Steinheim Forest Phase (Holsteinian)
Mosbach (Main faunal level)	Mosbach (Main faunal level)
Mauer Forest Phase	Mauer Forest Phase
Upper Freshwater Bed	

It is interesting to combine or compare these biostratigraphic subdivisions with our own succession of alluvial terraces, paleosols, and loess mantles, and the more recent paleomagnetic dates:

Step 1.   Correlation of terraces and cover mantles for the later Pleistocene (cf. Figure 10; Brunnacker 1957).

Step 2.   Superposed terrace alluvia with very deep soils are covered by at least four loess veneers, for example at Regensburg, Marktheidenfeld, Kärlich, Mosbach, Mauer (see Figure 11, Brunnacker 1964 a, 1964 b, 1971).

Step 3.   Subdivision of the above localities (step 2) by means of paleomagnetism (Koči, et al. 1973) into (Table 7):

a.   An older group: Kärlich and the Mosbach sands, with reversed magnetism in the lower or lowest sections;

b.   An intermediate group: Marktheidenfeld, Mauer, with normal magnetization in the interglacial beds subdividing cold-climate alluvia; a minimum age is given by four overlying loesses;

c.   A younger group: Steinheim-on-the-Murr as the key locality; a minimum age is indicated by two loess mantles.

A fourth step is suggested, insofar as the intermediate group of sites (3b) can be subdivided on the basis of alluvial stratigraphy. In particular, the interglacial in MT II could well be younger than Mauer and Marktheidenfeld.

The Mosbach Sands at Wiesbaden

The Mosbach sands in the limestone quarry of the Dyckerhoff Company were systematically recorded during the last few years by Brüning (1970, 1972) (see Table 7):

IV.   Rust-red Mosbach (cold-climate, modified by soil);

III.   Grey Mosbach delta: sand and gravel (cold-climate);

„   gamma: sand and gravel (cold-climate), primary fossil horizon with transitional fauna at base;

„   beta: reworked horizon

„   alpha: periglacial phase (colluvial loess)

Table 7. An attempt to correlate key mid-Pleistocene localities of the Rhine Basin

Glacial before the present	Kärlich	Mosbach Sands	Mauer	Marktheidenfeld	Steinheim	Achenheim-Hangenbieten
1. Eemian	J b	Loess		Loess	Loess	loess recent
	Ja	Soil		Soil	Soil	eroded
2.		Loess		Loess	Loess	loess ancien supérieur
	H	Soil		Soil	Soil (in part)	loess ancien moyen
3.		Loess		Loess	Main mammoth gravels	loess ancien inférieur
Holsteinian	G	Soil		Soil	Steinheim Forest Phase Gravels	
4.		Loess		Loess		
	F	Soil IV		eroded?		
5.		III δ-ε?		E-Terrace?		
Cromer III?	D-E	eroded? III γ	Soil	Soil		
6.			Upper beds	Upper beds		
	C	Main fauna	Mauer Forest Phase (N)	Interglacial (N)		
Cromer II?	(N) B	III β (local)	Lower beds	Lower beds		
7.	(R)	III α (local)				
Cromer I	A	II				
8.		I (R)				

(N) Normal magnetization
(R) Reversed magnetization

Cover Mantles
Alluvial } Boundary

II. Flood silts with soil (warm climate); reversed magnetism;
I. Coarse-grained Mosbach (cold-climate).

Semmel (1968) has found up to four loess generations on top of this sequence.

The Mosbach profile illustrates the dilemma facing any extensive parallelizations within the mid-Pleistocene. Alluvial development is largely analogous with that at Kärlich (Brunnacker 1971; Semmel 1972) and the paleomagnetism appears to indicate a similar age for the basal deposits. However, if one considers that the paleontological evidence provides a younger date for the main Mosbach fauna than that at Mauer, one must shift the upper part of the Dyckerhoff profile upwards (as in Table 7), since Mauer exhibits normal polarity. However, it must also be questioned whether the Kärlich terrace sequence is not incomplete. This is certainly not impossible.

Mauer near Heidelberg

The position of the Mauer Forest Phase and with it, the age of *Homo heidelbergensis*, is established by paleotological associations and a normal magnetic polarity (Koči, et al. f.c.). Of additional interest is that Müller-Beck (1964) reported no permafrost indicators from the upper part of the profile. This suggests that the Mauer Forest Phase is older than the fifth-to-last and younger than the seventh-to-last glacial. A localization in the sixth-to-last glacial can be disputed since cold-climate indicators are absent (Table 7).

The Middle Main River Valley

A whole series of Cromerian fossil mammal sites has been found in the Main Valley in recent years, both above and below Würzburg (Wurm 1955; Rutte 1958, 1971). Clear associations with the massive valley fill are given.

Steinheim-on-the-Murr

The gravel beds with the Steinheim interglacial are the most important feature of their kind for the younger part of the mid-Pleistocene. The sequence, according to Adam (1954) and Freising (1952), is as follows:

Loess

Interglacial Soil

Loess

Gravel
↓
Steinheim Forest Phase

Gravel

This sequence can be modified to include a further but localized interglacial paleosol between the gravel and loess (see Table 7). This requires a correction, whereby the position of the Holsteinian Interglacial must be shifted back to coincide with the next oldest interglacial.

The Cannstatt Travertine

The oligohaline tufas of Bad Cannstatt belong to various Pleistocene interglacials (Reiff 1965). Stratigraphic dating is difficult since erosion has destroyed the original surface of the deposits. No paleontological correlations can presently be made with Steinheim-on-the-Murr.

Achenheim-Hangenbieten

The long-famous loess quarries of Achenheim-Hangenbieten have provided a substantial collection of mammalian remains and Paleolithic material, as the result of many years of collecting by Wernert (1957). These classic exposures nonetheless provide an exemplary case of erroneous interpretation on the dictum "loess *in situ* and reworked, soil *in situ* and reworked, in addition to mammalian faunas", as Guenther (1971) had clearly shown. Beyond this the profile is representative of all others in that faunas are a necessary condition in biostratigraphy for subdividing glacial deposits. Yet interglacial fossils are only available where sedimentation was originally possible and where these sediments have indeed been preserved. Consequently, whenever there are big discrepancies in the number of glacials and interglacials obtained by litho- and biostratigraphic approaches, there certainly are reasons to explain the absence of interglacial megafaunas in the average exposure.

RESULTS

The Pleistocene sequence established from alluvial sequences for the southern lower Rhine includes a gap of unknown duration in the earliest Pleistocene. Moreover, there is a larger number of distinct Middle Terraces. Comparisons with the Kärlich profile, composed of alluvial sediments, loesses, and paleosols with volcanic intercalations, complements the results of the terrace stratigraphy. However, an unequivocal correlation remains open. In light of other evidence from Central Europe, one can now only say that the Matuyuma-Brunhes reversal, which is dated at about 700,000 years, occurred somewhere between the fifth-to-last and eighth-to-last glacials or, in the Netherlands sequence, between the Cromerian-I and Cromerian-II interglacials. The results from the Rhine indicate that this reversal dates from the seventh-to-last glacial. Furthermore, in the lower Rhine, this boundary is located within the upper part of the Main Terrace sequence (HT 2 and HT 3). In the long run this should provide a useful marker for the beginning of the Middle Pleistocene, since this cold period first produced ice-wedges in the study area.

The next cold period, the sixth-to-last by our reckoning, is also individualistic due to weaker development. It is correlated with the basal part of the Main Terrace, a terrace that, with its loess equivalent, lacks the evidence for permafrost present in each subsequent glacial. In addition, the gravels of this terrace were largely reworked from older terraces, which can be interpreted by Büdel's concept that permafrost would be necessary for effective bedrock downcutting in the Schiefergebirge. This allows a hypothesis that the massive, superposed alluvial fills of the Main and Neckar rivers, at least in their upper part — and thus the interglacial of "Cromerian vegetation type" at Marktheidenfeld and the Mauer Forest Phase — were a result of alluviation upstream of a major bedrock barrier. According to the cover mantles this upper part of the Main River fill is older than the fourth-to-last glacial. At both localities normal magnetization was found. A satisfactory correlation for the Mosbach sands remains impossible in spite of the systematic study of Brüning. Possibly there were special conditions here due to the tectonic instability of the Mainz basin.

For the lower Rhine it has been established that Middle Terrace I corresponds with the fifth-to-last glacial. Middle Terrace IIa contains a particular species of lemming, until recently known only from Upper Biharian. This terrace is linked with the fourth-to-last glacial, although others consider it to be of Elsterian age. This is supported by a period of very deep incision during the later glacial and that is probably related to the very deep base of the Lauenburg clay. This channel was filled with gravels of the terminal glacial as well as younger deposits of the Holstein Interglacial. MT III rests on top of this complex and, together with the basal units, was overrun by the Drenthe-age (Saalian) ice advance and incorporated into the resulting push moraines. Younger yet is MT IV and the Low Terrace (last glacial), which is also subdivided into two alluvial units as a result of late glacial downcutting, followed by alluviation.

REFERENCES

ADAM, K. D.
  1953 Die Bedeutung der altpleistozänen Säugetier-Faunen Südwestdeutschlands für die Gliederung des Eiszeitalters. *Geologica Bavarica* 19:357–363.
  1954 Die zeitliche Stellung der Urmenschen-Fundschicht von Steinheim an der Murr innerhalb des Pleistozäns. *Eiszeitalter und Gegenwart* 4/5:18–21.
  1966 Zur Grossgliederung des mitteleuropäischen Pleistozäns. *Zeitschrift der deutschen geologischen Gesellschaft* 115:751–757.
AHORNER, L.
  1962 Untersuchungen zur quartären Bruchtektonik der Niederrheinischen Bucht. *Eiszeitalter und Gegenwart* 13:24–105.
BOENIGK, W.
  1969 "Zur Kenntnis des Altquartärs bei Brüggen (westlicher Niederrhein)." Unpublished dissertation, University of Cologne.
BOENIGK, W., G. KOWALCZYK, K. BRUNNACKER
  1972 Zur Geologie des Ältestpleistozäns der Niederrheinischen Bucht. *Zeitschrift der deutschen geologischen Gesellschaft* 123:119–161.
BREDDIN, H.
  1968 Die unterirdische Oxydation der Braunkohle im Kölner Revier während der Pleistozänzeit. *Fortschritte in der Geologie von Rheinland und Westfalen* 2:683–720.
BRÜNING, H.
  1970 Zur Klima-Stratigraphie der pleistozänen Mosbacher Sande bei Wiesbaden (Hessen). *Mainzer Naturwissenschaften Archiv* 9:204–256.
  1972 *Die eiszeitliche Tierwelt im Rhein-Main-Gebiet-Mosbacher Sande.* Naturhistorischer Museumsführer 4. Mainz.

BRUNNACKER, K.
1957 Die Geschichte der Böden im jüngeren Pleistozän in Bayern. *Geologica Bavarica* 37.
1964a Böden des älteren Pleistozäns bei Regensburg. *Geologica Bavarica* 54:148–160.
1964b Über Ablauf und Altersstellung altquartärer Verschüttungen im Maintal und nächst dem Donautal bei Regensburg. *Eiszeitalter und Gegenwart* 15:72–80.
1965 Die Entstehung der Münchener Schotterfläche zwischen München und Moosburg. *Geologica Bavarica* 55:341–359.
1967 Grundzüge einer Löß- und Bodenstratiphie am Niederrhein. *Eiszeitalter und Gegenwart* 18:142–151.
1971 Beiträge zur Stratigraphie des Quartär-Profils von Kärlich am Mittelrhein. *Mainzer Naturwissenschaften Archiv* 10:77–100.
1973 Bemerkungen zu quartären Strandterrassen des Mittelmeers. *Neues Jahrbuch Für Geologie und Paläontologie*, Monatshefte 1973: 129–135.
BRUNNACKER, K., R. STREIT, W. SCHIRMER
1969 Der Aufbau des Quartär-Profils von Kärlich/Neuwieder Becken (Mittelrhein). *Mainzer Naturwissenschaften Archiv* 8:102–133.
BÜDEL, J.
1969 Der Eisrinden-Effekt als Motor der Tiefenerosion in der exzessifen Talbildungszone. *Würzburger Geographische Arbeiten* 25: 1–41.
BURGHARDT, E., K. BRUNNACKER
i.p. Quarzzahl und -rundung in Schottern der Niederrheinischen Bucht. *Decheniana* 126.
DE JONG, J. D.
1965 Quaternary sedimentation in the Netherlands. *The Geological Society of America, Special Paper* 84:95–123.
DEMEK, J., J. KUKLA, *editors*
1969 Periglazialzone, Löß und Paläolithikum der Tschechoslowakei. Brno: ČSAV Geogr. Inst. Brno.
FINK, J.
1965 The pleistocene in eastern Austria. *The Geological Society of America, Special Paper* 84:179–199.
FRECHEN, J.
1959 Die Tuffe des Laacher Vulkangebietes als quartärgeologische Leitgesteine und Zeitmarken. *Fortschritte in der Geologie von Rheinland und Westfalen* 4:363–370.
FRECHEN, J., H. HEIDE
1970 Tephrostratigraphische Zusammenhänge zwischen Vulkantätigkeit im Laacher See-Gebiet und der Mineralführung der Terrassenschotter am unteren Mitttelrhein. *Decheniana* 122:35–74.
FRECHEN, J., H. J. LIPPOLT
1965 Kalium-Argon-Daten des Laacher Vulkanismus, der Rheinterrassen und der Eiszeiten. *Eiszeitalter und Gegenwart* 16:5–30.
FREISING, H.
1952 Die Deckschichten der eiszeitlichen Flußkiese von Steinheim an

der Murr (Landkreis Ludwigsburg). *Jahrbuch der geologischen Abteilung für württembergische statistische Landesanstalten* 2: 66–72.

FRENZEL, B.
1967   *Die Klimaschwankungen des Eiszeitalters.* Braunschweig: Vieweg und Sohn.

GLIESE, J., F. STRAUCH
1969   Eine Pliozän-Fauna in den Deckschichten der rheinischen Braunkohle — Eine vorläufige Mitteilung. *Neues Jahrbuch für Geologie und Paläontologie,* Monatsheft 1969: 446–448.

GRAUL, H.
1962   Eine Revision der pleistozänen Stratigraphie des schwäbischen Alpenvorlandes. *Petermanns Geographische Mitteilungen* 1962: 253–271.

GUENTHER, E. W.
1971   Die Faunen von Achenheim-Hangenbieten im Elsaß und ihre Aussage zur Altersdatierung der Lößprofile. *Quartär* 22:57–71.

HELLER, FL.
1967   Die Alterstellung des Villafranchium und seiner Fauna. *Quartär* 18:9–23.

HELLER, FL., K. BRUNNACKER
1966   Halsbandlemming-Reste aus einer Oberen Mittelterrasse des Rheins bei Niederaußem. *Eiszeitalter und Gegenwart* 17:97–112.

KAISER, KH.
1961   "Gliederung und Formenschatz des Pliozäns und Quartärs am Mittel- und Niederrhein sowie in den angrenzenden Niederlanden unter besonderer Berücksichtigung der Rheinterrassen," in *Festschrift XXXIIII. Deutscher Geographentag.* Edited by K. Kayser and Th. Kraus, 236–278. Wiesbaden: F. Steiner.

KAISER, KH., R. SCHÜTRUMPF
1960   Zur Gliederung mittel- und jungpleistozäner Schichten in der Niederrheinischen Bucht. *Eiszeitalter und Gegenwart* 11:166–185.

KEMPF, K. E.
1966   Das Holstein-Interglazial von Tönisberg im Rahmen des niederheinischen Pleistozäns. *Eiszeitalter und Gegenwart,* 17:5–60.

KOČÍ, A., W. SCHIRMER, K. BRUNNACKER
f.c.   Paläomagnetische Daten aus dem mittleren Pleistozän des Rhein-Main-Gebietes.

KÖRBER, H.
1962   Die Entwicklung des Maintales. *Würzburger Geographische Arbeiten* 10.

KOWALCZYK, G.
1969   "Zur Kenntnis des Altquartärs der Ville (südliche Niederrheinische Bucht)." Unpublished dissertation, University of Cologne.

LOŽEK, V., V. THOSTE
1972   Eine spätglaziale Molluskenfauna aus dem Bereich der Niederterrasse südlich von öln. *Dacheniana* 125:55–61.

MÜCKENHAUSEN, E.
1954   Über die Geschichte der Böden. *Geologisches Jahrbuch* 69:501–516.

MÜLLER-BECK, HJ.
1964   Zur stratigraphischen Stellung des Homo heidelbergensis. *Jahrbuch der Römisch-Germanischen Zentralmuseums* Mainz 11:15–33.

PAAS, W.
1961   Rezente und fossile Böden auf niederrheinichen Terrassen und deren Deckschichten. *Eiszeitalter und Gegenwart* 12:165–230.

QUITZOW, H. W.
1956   Die Terrassengliederung im niederrheinischen Tieflande. *Geologie en Mijnbouw* 18:357–373.
1959   Hebung und Senkung am Mittel- und Niederrhein während des Jungtertiärs und Quartärs. *Fortschritte in der Geologie von Rheinland und Westfalen* 4:389–400.
1961   Mittelrhein und Niederrhein. *Beitrage Rheinkunde.* 14:27–39.

REIFF, W.
1965   Das Alter der Sauerwasserkalke von Stuttgart — Münster — Bad Cannstatt — Untertürkheim. *Jahresberichte und Mitteilungen des oberrheinischen geologischen Vereins.* 47:111–134.

RUTTE, E.
1958   Die Fundstelle altpleistozäner Säugetiere von Randersacker bei Würzburg. *Geologisches Jahrbuch* 73:737—754.
1971   Pliopleistozäne Daten zur Änderung der Hauptabdachung im Main-Gebiet, Süddeutschland. *Zeitschrift für Geomorphologie.* Supplement 12:51–72.

SCHAEFER, I.
1956   Geologische Karte von Augsburg und Umgebung 1:50 000 mit Erläuterungen, München.

SCHIRMER, W.
1970   Das Jüngere Pleistozän in der Tongrube Kärlich am Mittelrhein. *Mainzer Naturwissenschaften Archiv* 9:257–284.

SCHRÖDER, J., R. DEHM
1951   Die Molluskenfauna aus der Lehm-Zwischenlage des Deckenschotters von Fischach, Kreis Augsburg (Resumé). *Geologica Bavarica* 6:118–120.

SEMMEL, A.
1968   Die Lößdecken im Dyckerhoff-Steinbruch bei Wiesbaden-Biebrich. *Mainzer Naturwissenschaften Archiv* 7:74–79.
1972   Fragen der Quartärstratigraphie im Mittel- und Oberrhein-Gebiet. *Jahresberichte und Mitteilungen des oberrheinischen geologischen Vereins* 54:61–71.

THOMÉ, K. N.
1959   Die Begegnung des nordischen Inlandeises mit den Rhein. *Geologisches Jahrbuch* 76:261–308.

THOSTE, V.
1972   "Die Niederterrassen des Rheins vom Neuwieder Becken bis in

die Niederrheinische Bucht." Unpublished dissertation, University of Cologne.

V. D. BRELIE, G., K. KILPPER, R. TEICHMÜLLER

1959 Das Pleistozän-Profil von Frimmersdorf an der Erft. *Fortschritte in der Geologie von Rheinland und Westfalen* 4:179–196.

V. D. BRELIE, G., E. MÜCKENHAUSEN, U. REIN

1955 Ein Torf aus dem Eiszeitalter im Untergrund von Weeze. *Der Niederrhein* 22:80–83.

VAN DER HAMMEN, T., T. A. WIJMSTRA, W. H. ZAGWIJN

1971 The floral record of the late Cenozoic of Europe. In The late Cenozoic Ice Age. Edited by K. K. Turekian, 391–424. New Haven and London: Yale University Press.

VAN MONTFRANS, H. M.

1971 "Palaeomagnetic dating in the North Sea basin." Unpublished dissertation, Amsterdam University.

VINKEN, R.

1959 Sedimentpetrographische Untersuchungen der Rheinterrassen im südlichen Teil der Niederrheinischen Bucht. *Fortschritte in der Geologie von Rheinland und Westfalen* 4:127–170.

WERNERT, P.

1957 Stratigraphie paléontologique et préhistorique des sédiments quaternaires d'Alsace. Achenheim. *Mémoires de la Service de la Carte Géologique d'Alsace et de Lorraine* 14.

WINTER, K.-P.

1968 "Die Untere Mittelterrasse im Südteil der Niederrheinischen Bucht." Unpublished dissertation, University of Cologne.

WOLDSTEDT, P.

1958 *Das Eiszeitalter, II* (Second edition). Stuttgart: Enke.

WURM, A.

1955 Beiträge zur Flußgeschichte des Mains und zur diluvialen Tektonik des Maingebietes. *Geologica Bavarica* 25:1–25.

ZAGWIJN, W. H.

1959 Zur stratigraphischen und pollenanalytischen Gliederung der pliozänen Ablagerungen im Roertal-Graben und Venloer Graben der Niederlande. *Fortschritte in der Geologie von Rheinland und Westfalen* 4:5–26.

ZAGWIJN, W. H., H. M. VAN MONTFRANS, J. G. ZANDSTRA

1971 Subdivision of the "Cromerian" in the Netherlands; pollenanalysis, paleomagnetism and sedimentary petrology. *Geologie en Mijnbouw* 50:41–58.

Middle Pleistocene Sedimentary Sequences in East Anglia (United Kingdom)

BRUCE G. GLADFELTER

ABSTRACT

Informative sequences of Middle Pleistocene deposits are only occasionally available for study in the East Anglian hinterland; consequently, the stratigraphic column is fragmentary when compared to the more accessible and better known Norfolk coastal sections. The biostratigraphic nature of present correlations of the sedimentological record is apparent from a review of the published studies and this succession is subject to revision based on current geologic mapping. Such revision most notably involves the appropriate age of the penultimate interglacial (Hoxnian) and the East Anglian till succession, within which complex the Lower Paleolithic (Acheulian) industries in Britain occur. The evidence now shows that the last glacial radiometric dates obtained from Hoxnian age materials are not reliable in the case of Hoxne itself and probably not for other dated sites as well.

Revision of the till succession recognizes the classical Lowestoft and Gipping chalky boulder clays simply as different expressions of the same glaciation, followed by the penultimate interglacial. Current excavations of this type-site demonstrate the complexity of post-Hoxnian geomorphic events. Morphogenetic environments recorded at Hoxne and in the surrounding vicinity unquestionably hold answers relevant to the age of this phase of the Pleistocene. The stratigraphic age of the Clactonian and Acheulian assemblages and hominid material at Swanscombe, as well as other lower Thames artifacts sites must be re-established since

Field work on which much of this discussion is based was conducted during the summers of 1970 and 1972 with the kind cooperation of Ronald Singer, Department of Anatomy, University of Chicago. Financial support was provided by several grants to Professor Singer: United States Public Health Service, National Institute of Health, No. GM10113; National Science Foundation, No. GS-1658, No. GS-2907; Wenner-Gren Foundation for Anthropological Research; Dr. Wallace C. and Clara A. Abbott Memorial Fund of the University of Chicago, and the Hinds Fund of the University of Chicago. This support is gratefully acknowledged. Several people have been most helpful in providing data unpublished at the time of this writing. I am particularly indebted to Peter Banham, Department of Geology, University of London (Regents Park), and to William Corbett, University of East Anglia (Soils Survey of England and Wales).

that terrace sequence usually is held to post-date the East Anglian till succession. The Clactonian assemblages at Clacton-on-Sea can be shown to be independent of the till stratigraphy.

INTRODUCTION

The many geologic sections scattered across East Anglia together comprise the most complete Pleistocene succession in Britain. The chronology, based on biostratigraphical and lithological units that use nomenclature derived from type locations (West 1963), is the system of subdivision most widely adopted by workers in the British Quaternary. Some fundamental problems exist because the few sites where successive units are superimposed have yet to be properly interrelated by detailed mapping. Furthermore, until recently, Drift Series maps for this area dated from the last century. The Institute of Geological Sciences, however, has remapped superficial deposits of small areas of the region and introduced a more detailed subdivision of the lithostratigraphical units. The new interpretation of the East Anglian stratigraphy proposed by Bristow and Cox (1973) is the first of numerous revisions that promise to emerge from this work. Detailed mapping by the Soils Survey of England and Wales also furnishes valuable data for Pleistocene scientists, while the extensive use of pollen analytical studies emphasizes further the interdisciplinary nature of Quaternary research and, at the same time, underscores the need to include other lines of evidence that are developing in the earth sciences.

The Pleistocene stratigraphic column for England is shown in Table 1. Terminology follows revised stratigraphic usage with the conventional nomenclature listed parenthetically. The Lower Pleistocene is recorded by deep borings and several sections of the Crag deposits, shelly sands with northern marine Mollusca, and a wide range of mammalian fauna (Cambridge 1970) that give the first indications of colder conditions. Pollen and foraminifera studies of borehole samples from the interior of the Crag basin of East Anglia (West 1962; Funnell 1970; Beck, Funnell, and Lord 1972) have permitted assignment of the Crags to stages in the Lower Pleistocene (Table 2).

The Middle Pleistocene begins with the temperate freshwater peats and muds of the Cromer Forest Bed Series and terminates with the penultimate interglacial. Within this time period, glaciers first inundated most of Britain, and man the toolmaker appeared. Proper recording and clear deciphering of the stratigraphic record is critical for an understanding of the interchange between these spatially and temporally dynamic developments. This is borne out by the recent revision of the

Table 1. British Quaternary stratigraphy (after Schotton and West 1969)

Holocene		Flandrian	postglacial	
Quater-nary	Pleistocene	Upper	Devensian (Weichselian)	cool (till)
			Ipswichian	temperate
			Wolstonian (Gippingian)	cool (till)
		Middle	Hoxnian	temperate
			Anglian (Lowestoftian)	cool (till)
			Cromerian	temperate
		Lower	Beestonian	cool
			Pastonian	temperate
			Baventian	cool
			Antian	temperate
			Thurnian	cool
			Ludhamian	temperate

upper part of this time range as a consequence of field mapping and laboratory (radiometric) study that have challenged the conventional stratigraphic interpretation (Bristow and Cox 1973; Page 1972). In the discussion that follows, primary attention is given to penultimate interglacial sites with which the author has firsthand knowledge, and which are fundamental for the understanding of the stratigraphic and archeological records. Ironically, at the time of this writing correlation of the Hoxnian interglacial with the penultimate interglacial of the Continental sequence (Turner, this volume) seems more secure than the glacial-interglacial succession within East Anglia. Finally, throughout the following discussion there is an intentional effort to enumerate both kinds of evidence on which stratigraphic interpretations have been based and the underlying methodologies implemented.

THE HOXNIAN TYPE-SITE

The Hoxnian Interglacial type-site is located near the village of Hoxne, Suffolk, 60 kilometers inland and south of the Lower and Middle Pleistocene coastal cliff sections of Norfolk. The deposits at Hoxne accumulated in a depression, possibly a kettle, formed on the surface of of Chalky Boulder Clay of Anglian age (Baden-Powell 1950). The lacustrine deposits, now buried by younger sediments, are situated at 36 meters above sea level on the upland flat overlooking the River Waveney, 2 kilometers to the north. Low order tributaries of the Waveney

Table 2. Compilation of East Anglian Coastal Sequences

South Coastal ————————————————————————————————————→ sequences North

Stage	Corton	Happisburgh	Bacton	Mundesley	Sidestrand	Overstrand	The Runtons	Sheringham	Some correlations
?	Plateau Gravel		Bacton Gravels	Bacton Gravels		Brick Kiln Dale Gravels			Chalky Boulder Clay
Anglian — Lowestoft Stadial	Pleasure Gardens Till; Oulton Beds; Lowestoft Till								
Anglian — Gunton Stadial	Corton Beds b; Cromer Till	Second Till; Intermediate Beds; First Till	Gimingham Sands; Third Till; Mundesley Sands; Second Till	Gimingham Sands; Third Till; Mundesley Sands; Second Till		Gimingham Sands; Third Till; Mundesley Sands; Second Till; Intermediate Beds; First Till	Estaurine Silts; Marine Gravels		Norwich Brickearth a; North Sea Drift
Cromerian	Cromer Forest Bed Series	Cromer Forest Bed Series	Cromer Forest Bed Series	Cromer Forest Bed Series		Cromer Forest Bed Series	Cromer Forest Bed Series		
Beestonian								Beestonian	
Pastonian					Pastonian		Weybourne Crag (Pastonian)	Pastonian	Norwich, Weybourne Crags; Chillesford Clay; Westleton Beds
Baventian					Baventian			Baventian	
(base)		Chalk		Chalk	Chalk		Chalk		

have incised shallow valleys 12 to 15 meters deep to the east (Gold-brook) and west (River Dove) of the interfluve.

The sections at Hoxne originally were uncovered by excavations for brickearth at the end of the eighteenth century. The stone tools unearthed were correctly recognized for the first time in Britain as prehistoric stone implements (Frere 1800). Aperiodic excavations on eight seperate occasions over the next century and a half have yielded the Acheulian industry from Hoxne (West and McBurney 1954) *in situ* within geologically and palynologically datable deposits. The overall stratigraphic sequence of the deposits at Hoxne was established by Richard West (1956), and his thorough study of that site and recognition of its palynological interglacial status have been reaffirmed by similar pollen and or macroflora evidence obtained from Hoxne (Turner 1968a; 1968b) and nearby at Saint Cross South Elmham (West 1961), and in Essex at Marks Tey (Turner 1970). The sequence of deposits interpreted by West was established from a series of more than one hundred boreholes and a few vertical sections (Table 3).

The pollen data were obtained from a ten-centimeter (four-inch) borehole (number 36) sunk near the presumed center of ancient Lake Hoxne, so as to include as complete a stratigraphic sequence as possible. This core penetrated the bottom of Stratum C, Strata D, E, F, and the top of G. Pollen analysis was performed (Diagram I in West 1956) on material taken from the center of successive ten-centimeter cores, each about 50-centimeters long, but the "general conformity" of the individual diagrams was felt to show that no significant gaps occur between adjoining cores. Additional diagrams were constructed from samples obtained along the margins of the lake, either from excavated sections (Diagrams II, III, IV, and V) or from auger boreholes (Diagram VI). Pollen grains could not be reclaimed from Strata B, A2, or A1, yet the underlying deposits span pre-temperate (Ho I) to post-temperate (Ho IV) time.

◀

The table lists vertical sequences as recorded at the respective locales. Although horizontal equivalences may be suggested, these are assured only in those cases where the same terminology is used. Other lithologic correlations (e.g. Bacton Gravels – Brick Kiln Dale Gravels) have yet to be demonstrated.
Sources: Banham 1971; Banham and Ranson 1970; Beck, Funnell, and Lord 1972; Hey 1967; Nickless 1971; West 1972; West and Banham 1968.
a   Correlated with the Lowestoft Chalky Boulder Clay (Lowestoft Stadial) by Bristow and Cox (1973) and Cox and Nickless (1972).
b   The Corton Beds with cold flora are not regarded as an interstadial by West (Sparks and West 1972: 146). The interpretation cited here follows Banham (1971).

Table 3. Summary of Sequence at Hoxne, Suffolk, According to West (1956)

Bed	Maximum thickness	Deposit	Pollen	Archeology
A1	0.6 meters	Gray or brown fine sand with stones up to 5 cm. This stratum overlies the entire Hoxne sequence and except for floodplains, comprises the surface mantle of the entire area; "derived from A2" and includes frost shattered and aeolian polished flint.	No pollen recovered	Derived artifacts
A2	2.5 meters	Clay, sand, and till. Unsorted, noncalcareous including water laid deposits and unstratified, unsorted gravel ("hoggin") interpreted as till and not part of the lacustrine sequence.	No pollen recovered	Current excavations yield artifacts (Layer 7). Equivalent of West's A2. Industry?
B	2.0 meters	Stratified clay, sand, and gravel. The final lacustrine infilling preserved but includes clastic deposits brought into the lake by fluvial activity and solifluction; little brecciation of deposits, little or no organics.	No pollen recovered	Derived artifacts
C	3.5 meters	Gray brown, sandy silt, brecciated clay-mud, and pebbles. A highly variable series of interlayered lenses of clastics reaching considerable thickness (3.5 m). Interpreted as deposits of a fluctuating lake level with aperiodic introduction of larger clastics by solifluction from the lake margin.	Early — glacial (IV)	
D	0.4 meters	Brown, noncalcareous, detritus mud. A richly organic layer up to 40 cm thick with profuse macroflora and well preserved wood chunks. Succeeded by pollen disconformity, with drying up of lake and erosional unconformity.	Late — temperate (III)	Some artifacts
E	6.5 meters	Brown green, calcareous, lacustrine clay-mud, deposited in thickness at both the center and margins of the lake without evidence of addition of older or reworked material, although water currents and channels may have moved across this stratum. Upper zone is "weathered" (decalcified).	Early — temperate (II)	Major archeological horizon at top
F	0.5 meters	Gray lacustrine clay-mud and marl. Contains some "laminae" near top and "drift mud" or this clastic layers near the bottom interpreted as solifluction debris.	Late — glacial (I)	
G		Chalky Boulder Clay. A blue gray sandy clay with many chalk pebbles and erratics, usually as pebbles. Comprises the subsurface and attains thickness in excess of 20 m. Equivalent of the Lowestoft Till of Baden-Powell (1948, 1951).		

Current Excavation at Hoxne

Excavation now in progress at Hoxne allows redefinition and extension of certain aspects of the sequence recognized by West (1956) based entirely upon several new sections. Much data remain to be studied and properly interpreted from the 1971–1973 field seasons of the University of Chicago, but even at this initial stage, significant implications are emerging, most particularly concerning the post-pollen zone III time period recorded by the upper part of the sequence. The sections shown in Figure 1 correspond to Strata D, C, and A2 in Table 3; Strata B is not recognized at this exposure, and Strata A1 overlies the entire sequence as recorded in additional sections at the site. The sections were exposed in the southwest corner of the Oakley Park pit of the Hoxne Brickworks and present a complex sequence of partially faulted lacustrine, deltaic, and alluvial beds with internal disconformities. The abbreviated description of the deposits illustrated by these sections is given in Table 4*, which is preliminary and subject to revision pending further field and laboratory study.[1] Bed 9 was artificially removed from the top of Cutting XXIX by commercial brickearth operations; this deposit completes the Upper Sequence and is the surface material of the Hoxne area. It comprises 1.0 to 1.3 meters of unstratified sands and angular-to-subangular pebbles, with a high fine sand-silt content in the top 40 centimeters.

The relationship of the archeological materials to the Hoxne geologic sequence is shown in Table 5*. Since the Main excavation area was completely exploited by the conclusion of the 1972 season, that artifact inventory is more precise; excavation of the Upper Sequence was still in progress during the 1973 field season. The need to determine the pollen stratigraphic position and paleoenvironmental conditions during alluviation of Beds 4, 5, and 6 is apparent from Table 5.

Stratum C as recorded in these sections is a fluvial deposit with several discharge regimes, and probably distinctive climatic conditions as well, indicated by clastic components stripped from a surrounding chalk or boulder clay surface interlayered with fine textured sediments. This stratum no longer can be interpreted as lacustine lenses with solifluction debris, which obviates the necessity of explaining the accumulation of up to 3.5 meters of Stratum C with soliflucted stones in the CENTER of the lake (West 1956: 285f., Figure 8). Pollen from Stratum C was mixed and undoubtedly derived and, although macrofossils sug-

---

[1] Samples collected in the field in 1972 had not yet been received for laboratory study at the time of this writing.
* *Tables 4 and 5, see foldout between pp. 240–241*

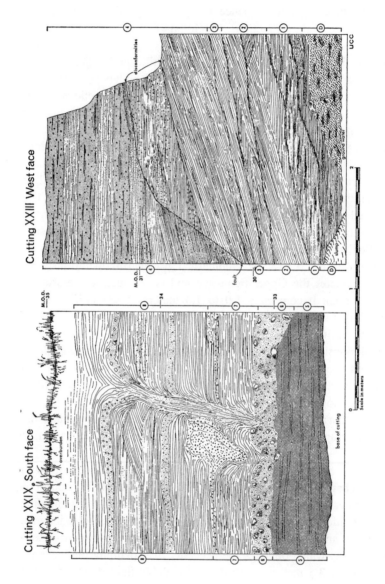

Figure 1.   Upper sequence, Hoxne 1972. This series of deposits equates with West's strata D, C, and A 2 (see Table 4). Identification and terminology of particular beds are subject to revision, pending conclusion of the excavations still in progress

gest cooler conditions, the "periglacial" climate implied for this deposit now must be demonstrated from other evidence. The relationship of the sedimentation of beds shown in Figure 1 to changing lake levels also needs to be established, as this may implicate climatic change and paleomorphogenesis of the surrounding landscape. The suggestion at this point is that the lower fluvial and deltaic layers (Beds 1 to 3) record the stream system that fed Lake Hoxne and a final high water-level phase. However, the latter phases of the sequence (Beds 4 to 8) indicate very different conditions, and one possible interpretation is that these deposits relate to a post-Lake Hoxne river system, perhaps ancestral to the Waveney or the River Dove.

The upper part of the sequence (Figure 1, Beds 5 to 8) corresponds to the clay, sand, and "hoggin" (till) series described by West (Stratum A2). The coarse gravel, Bed 6, is the stratum studied by West and Donner (1956) for macrofabric analysis and sampled for erratics by Baden-Powell (1956), who considered the deposit to be derived from Gipping Till (Wolstonian), rather than an actual till. More than two hundred boulders from this strata, mostly larger than 15 centimeters in diameter, were examined by the writer for stria, but none could be found. Futhermore, the gravel can be seen to be crudely stratified with bedded sand lenses in the order of 10 cm thick near the base. These aspects all indicate a fluvial origin for this stratum. Sedimentological evidence of post-temperate (Ho IV) glacial till, consequently, does not appear to be recorded by West's A2 stratum; however, periglacial or permafrost conditions now can be documented by at least two distinct generations of ice wedge casts developed in these sediments. The earlier of these occurred soon after aggradation of Bed 7 and accretion of the 2 to 5 centimeter thick gley band near the top of this bed. This wedge formation phase involved approximately 45 centimeters of sediments including the top of the coarse gravel (Bed 6). The second generation of ice wedge formation was considerably more intense (see Figure 1) and is well recorded by numerous casts more than 1.5 meters in length.

It does not appear that the Bed 9 surface deposits of the Upper Sequence (i.e. Stratum A1 discussed below) were involved in this period of periglacial activity. Stratum A1, as defined by West, has been found to mantle every section thus far extended to the surface. This pebbly brown sand (Bed 9) can be mapped as a surface deposit and seen in section throughout the Hoxne vicinity. It completes the lacustrine-fluvial sequence at Hoxne and elsewhere caps Chalky Boulder Clay and massive gravel deposits in the Waveney valley. Therefore, this is not just a local deposit to be explained as head or as a weathered residual of underlying "tills" since it overlies several "parent materials." A similar deposit, described by Catt, et al. (1971), mantles a larger portion of northeast Norfolk and is thought to comprise at least in part Hunstanton till-derived loess, but the origin of larger clasts is uncertain. Pebble constituents rule out eolian origins, although the large silt-fine sand fraction suggests an eolian component; nowhere has the deposit displayed bedding characteristics. Recently completed detailed, soil mapping of the Harleston area, immediately northeast of Hoxne, shows that the upland plateau parent materials chiefly comprise Chalky Boulder Clay or "surface sands" (Corbett i.p.). The mapping was based on four hundred boreholes located in clusters around points established by a systematic grid over a 100 square kilometer area. These sand pockets apparently are not restricted to the area mapped but occur elsewhere in East Anglia on Chalky Boulder Clay (Corbett and Tatler 1970). The patches with depths of up to three meters have been interpreted as surface sand, possibly of Weichselian age, but their origin and/or age are by no means certain for this area. This deposit may be equivalent to the surface sand and pebbles at the Hoxne site (i.e. Bed 9, of West's A1) and/or variant of a post-Chalky Boulder Clay till.

The conventional stratigraphic dating of the Hoxnian Interglacial derives from the situation of these deposits between two tills (Moir 1926). These tills are further differentiated on the basis of erratics (Baden-Powell 1948) and pebble orientation (West and Donner 1956). The lower till is equated with the upper till overlying the Cromer Forest Beds of the Norfolk coast (Lowestoft Till). The top till at Hoxne is older than the till of the last glaciation (Hunstanton Till) of the Norfolk northwest coast, and therefore is considered Gipping Till of Wolstonian age. However, this interpretation now is questioned.

Reappraisal of the Gipping Till

The proposed revision of the East Anglian till succession is based upon remapping at a scale of 1:10,560 by the Institute of Geological Sciences. The project covered approximately 1900 square kilometers in the Chelmsford ,Essex) and Norwich (Norfolk) areas and included examination of 200 kilometers of temporarily exposed sections and more than one thousand boreholes. The workers (Bristow and Cox 1973) conclude that nowhere in East Anglia do Hoxnian Interglacial deposits SEPARATE two glacial tills. Hoxnian deposits can be shown to rest on Chalky Boulder Clay till, usually called the Lowestoft Till, and post-Hoxnian cold conditions can be demonstrated by pollen evidence or periglacial related features, but nowhere can a true till burying Hoxnian materials be recognized. They conclude, therefore, that there is only one Chalky Boulder Clay in Essex and East Anglia, overlain by river terrace deposits or temperate lacustrine sediments (Hoxnian). The conventional division of Anglian and Wolstonian aged tills is unwarranted; these deposits were formed during only one glacial episode.

The authors further conclude that the East Anglian and Essex Chalky Boulder Clay is Wolstonian (Saale) in age. Consequently: (1) the Hoxnian and Ipswichian "Interglacials" were not separated by a major time span although colder conditions probably intervened; (2) much less time has elapsed since the Hoxnian than is usually held. This seems confirmed by the "relatively undissected" condition of the Chalky Boulder Clay plateau in East Anglia, the "little weathered" aspect of the Chalky Boulder Clay surface itself, and the limited development of terrace sequences in valleys which generally are thought to postdate the Chalky Boulder Clay.

Two separate issues are posed by the interpretation outlined above: the succession of the tills in East Anglia and Essex, and the actual chronology and correlation of this sequence. Only the first is of concern here, and although it may be appropriate to recognize only one Chalky Boulder Clay glacial episode in East Anglia, certain unresolved relationships outlined below need to be kept in mind.

Bristow and Cox (1973: 10) conclude that the Plateau Gravels (Cannonshot Gravels), Chalky Boulder Clay, and Mid-Glacial Gravels comprise an essentially syndepositional series of deposits, and that these are "penecontemporaneous" with the Norwich Brickearth. Since conventional interpretations equate the Norwich Brickearth with the Cromer Till (Table 2), Bristow and Cox appropriately indicate that correlation of the coastal sections and hinterland sequence needs to be established.

Clarification of the upper sequence at Hoxne is required also. West (1956: 287) regarded only the coarse gravel as a till, not the entire 2.5 meters of Stratum A2, as stated by Bristow and Cox (1973: 11); this stratum, also interpreted as a solifluction deposit (Sparks and West 1972), now is shown to be a fluvial deposit. Furthermore, the statement that West subsequently considered the A2 Stratum and the overlying A1 as periglacial deposits (Bristow and Cox 1973: 11) is incorrect and an unjustified conclusion on the basis of the very general diagram presented by West (1963: Figure 2). Finally, the well-sorted sands and occasional small flint pebbles referred to as part of the A1 stratum (Bristow and Cox 1973: 11) are in fact the A2. West (1956: 290–291) indicates that the A1 deposit forms the superficial mantle, about 60 centimeters thick, for the entire area.

These clarifications are not insignificant. The current excavations at Hoxne reaffirm the importance of the upper sequence and the need to determine the origin and geographical distribution of Bed 9, as implied above, and the upper sequence itself must be related to local paleo-geomorphic developments. It is relevant to note also that gravels "similar to the outwash gravels seen at the margins of the chalky till of Norfolk" (Bristow and Cox 1973: 10) DO occur south of the Norwich region, as at Hoxne (Gladfelter, unpublished), but as yet these are not related to the local stratigraphy.

Finally, it has been pointed out that Ipswichian and Hoxnian sites occupy distinctive topographic positions, the former relating to contemporary valley patterns while the latter are situated on interfluves (Sparks and West 1968). However, Bristow and Cox (1973: 14) emphasize that, in fact, Hoxnian sites "are on the sides of or within the present day valleys." It is difficult to understand how this can be concluded in the case of Hoxne itself, whether one wishes to relate the Brickworks site to the neighboring River Dove, the Goldbrook which has incised its valley through the lacustrine sequence, or to the Waveney. The Waveney Valley provides, in fact, valuable stratigraphic associations for the Hoxnian type site.

As many as three terrace levels have been identified in the Waveney Valley. The highest, the Upper Terrace, is recorded by gravel deposits overlying the Chalky Boulder Clay at sites along the upland edge. This terrace possibly records a retreat stage of Anglian ice (Corbett i.p.). The Main Terrace comprises several meters of gravels with erratics, best preserved as a platform along the valley midslope in the Wortwell-Hommersfield region. This terrace is reported to contain Late Pleistocene fauna — aurochs, woolly rhino, and woolly mammoth (Spencer, in Baden-Powell, 1950) — and has been interpreted as glaciofluvial in origin. A Wolstonian age is suggested on the basis of its morphology, elevation, and texture as compared with the Upper Terrace (Funnell 1955; Corbett i.p.). The Main Terrace, 7.5 to 12 meters above the floodplain, is also termed the Homersfield Terrace and is higher than a downstream feature, the Broome Terrace, although both may relate to Wolstonian events. At Wortwell, deposits below the Homersfield Terrace but above the modern floodplain have yielded fauna (*Elephas antiquus*), Mollusca and five grab samples that characterize the Ipswichian (Ia–IIb) Interglacial (Sparks and West 1968). This platform probably corresponds to the Lower Terrace feature locally recognized in that area, and possibly to a section with Late Pleistocene fauna briefly exposed in the Waveney floodplain at Oakley (Wymer, personal communication).

A series of five borings by the University of East Anglia indicates that the Lower-Middle Pleistocene stratigraphy in the Hoxne vicinity consists of Norwich Crag, Corton Beds, and Lowestoft Till (see Lord 1972, with references). Both Hoxnian and Ipswichian Interglacial pollen has been obtained from deposits later than the Anglian Chalky Boulder Clay; the latter interglacial deposits are associated with the post-Anglian terrace sequence in the Waveney Valley, and the former (Hoxnian) are covered by a series of fluvial "surface sands and gravel." The stratigraphic relation of this strata to the topmost sequence at the Hoxne site needs to be confirmed, but the evidence from the Waveney supports the hypothesis that it is Wolstonian in age, since terrace features in that valley postdate Anglian but predate Ipswichian deposits. Almost regardless of the age ultimately confirmed for these features and developments, it is directly relevant to emphasize that interglacial deposits at Hoxne accumulated originally in a low spot or depression, but now occur on an upland surface.[1] Only younger interglacial deposits have been located in the neighboring lowlands. In light of these facts, a post-Saale age for the Hoxnian type-site sequence does not appear reasonable or likely.

Radiocarbon Dates

Five radiocarbon dates on wood from Hoxne have been published. Page (1972) obtained finite C^{14} dates of 24,500 ±560 B.P. (T–932) and and 24,100 ±400 B.P. (T–1030). On the basis of these and five other dates he proposed that the Hoxnian Interglacial belongs within the "Last Glaciation." A similar date of 26,930 ±975 B.P. (IGS 104–St–3830) has been obtained from Hoxne by the Institute of Geological Sciences, and will be published in the journal *Radiocarbon*. All of these dates are from material taken from questionable contexts and are unreliable. This is verified by infinite C^{14} dates obtained independently by Singer, Wymer, and Gladfelter (1973) and by Shotton (1973) from freshly exposed wood samples of pollen zone III at Hoxne. The radiocarbon chronology for East Anglia proposed by Page (1972), which ascribes all deposits of Cromer age and younger to the last glacial, is based on a total of fifteen C^{14} dates. The provenance of each of these must be

---

[1] These deposits are buried by up to 7 meters of fluvial sediments at the type-site which evidence at least two generations of periglacial environments.

carefully reviewed since the obtained dates by Page and the Institute of Geological Sciences from Hoxne itself are now discredited.

THE HOXNIAN SITE AT CLACTON-ON-SEA

Excavations at the Clacton Golf Course have exposed a series of fluvial sediments related to the channel deposits (Singer, Wymer, Gladfelter, and Wolf 1973). As many as six different channels were noted by Hazzledine Warren (1923, 1955) over a period of several decades, occurring from Walton-on-Naze southwestward to Lion Point. Aspects of the deposits and series of channels have been uncovered only occasionally in section: (1) at Clacton-on-Sea where Warren's West Cliff sequence (1955), now covered over, was exposed along the backshore by wave erosion and cliff recession; (2) at Jaywick Sands where the buried channels were located by borings and excavated by Oakley and Leakey (1937); and (3) at the Clacton Golf Course where the channels were first unearthed and studied under the controlled circumstances of an archeological excavation (Wymer and Singer 1970). These exposures demonstrate the horizontal and vertical variability of the deposits. While at Clacton more than 10 meters of freshwater AND overlying estuarine sediments are preserved, less than 3.5 meters of freshwater sediments have been excavated at Jaywick Sands and the Clacton Golf Course, but, as yet, without firm evidence of transgressional estuarine aggradation. In the Jaywick-Clacton Golf Course vicinity, the channels are buried between approximately −3.0 and 4.5 meters above sea level and present no surface morphological expression, while just a few kilometers away at Clacton, Warren (1955) recorded the overall Freshwater-Estuarine sequence overlying London Clay at between −3.7 and 9.4 meters O.D. The series of freshwater deposits excavated at the Clacton Golf Course is situated approximately 200 meters northeast of the pit excavations of Oakley and Leakey (1937), and approximately 1.9 kilometers southwest of the West Cliff section described by Warren (1955) and cored for pollen by Pike and Godwin (1953).

Less than 1 meter of unstratified to crudely stratified, weakly consolidated gravel occurs at the base of the channel sequence preserved at the Clacton Golf Course site. These materials rest on a gently undulating London Clay surface and, judging from borings, define a bed load channel about 16 to 25 meters wide that at this point assumes a general east-west direction. Flint is the predominant gravel constituent (94 percent), and it served as the raw material for artifacts. Flint stones consist of subrounded or fractured buff, black, and mahogany pebbles

Table 6. Stratigraphy at the Clacton Golf Course site

Bed	Thickness	Cold-climate features	Archeological material
Modern soil	0.1–0.3 meters		Occasional flint artifacts, probably thrust up from lower deposits
Brown clay; leached, eolian in part	0.6–0.8 meters	Upended pebbles; *in situ* thermo-clastic shattering	
		———Discontinuity———	
Variegated marl, with sand lenses, pebbly zones	0.6–1.05 meters	Deformed sand lenses; base partially penetrated by ice-vein cast; cryoturbate mixing with London Clay	Clactonian flint flakes and cores (frequently mint); bone fragments
		———Discontinuity———	
Gravel; predominantly flint, with quartzite and chert	0.5–0.6 meters	Penetrated by ice-vein; severely contorted; cryoturbate mixing with London Clay	Flint tools on and in the gravel; mammalia fauna

both with and without cortex. Other lithologies are Lower Greensand chert (3.8 percent), Bunter quartzite (1.5 percent) and sandstone (0.7 percent). Yellowish-brown coarse sand comprises the gravel matrix that also includes freshwater mussel (undifferentiated) and partially decomposed septarian nodes. Inclusion in the gravel of Lower Greensand chert from Kent and blue tourmoline and pale green augite in the heavy mineral assemblage of overlying sediments at Jaywick Sands serves as the basis for assigning provenance of the Clacton channels to drainage systems related to a proto-Thames-Medway system (Soloman 1937). The greater portion of the artifacts and mammalian materials occur in association with the basal gravel bed (Table 6).

Up to 1.05 meters of consolidated (dry), medium subangular, blocky marl overlies the gravel with an abrupt, wavy boundary. The body of the calcareous sediment is yellowish brown; color variation derives from a coarse lattice of slightly more calcareous, white or light gray marl. Origin of this network is not entirely apparent, but vertical components may represent calcite filling and precipitation in dehydration cracks. Isolated flint pebbles and occasional pebble seams occur within the marl along with a very few artifacts and bone fragments. Laterally, the variegated marl interdigitates with shelly sand (Wymer and Singer

1970), which may be correlated with the pebbly silver sand noted 200 meters west of the golf course by Oakley and Leakey (1937).

The sedimentary sequence is completed by about 60 to 80 centimeters of yellowish-brown or brown, silty clay separated from the marl by a clear, wavy boundary. Flint stones dispersed throughout the sediment indicate fluvial origins for the silty clay, with an additional incorporation of eolian brickearth silts. The brown clay is almost entirely leached of carbonates; redox potential values and the occurrence of slickensides indicate waterlogging beyond that experienced under present conditions. Heavy mineral constituents suggest that the silty clay may be locally derived, in contrast to the hinterland provenance of the gravel and marl (Oakley and Leakey 1937).

Channel deposits exposed by the golf course excavation have been subjected to postdepositional deformation under more rigorous conditions of Pleistocene environments (Gladfelter 1972). A number of distinctive features record the fossil cold-climate activity. Along the channel margins, basal gravels are intermixed with London Clay and the overlying marl which records cryoturbate heaving. Similar disturbance was more severe along the channel north bank where gravel has been pushed in anticlinal-like form into the overlying marl, causing realignment of pebbles to conform with the surface trend of this feature. Elsewhere the gravel is penetrated by a slightly calcareous, pale yellow or olive fine sand vein with some pebbles up to 15 centimeters wide, which is interpreted as a fossil ice wedge cast. This feature extends into the base of the overlying marl, indicating development during or after that alluviation phase. Basal sand lenses of the marl also show this deformation by plications involving up to 20 centimeters of vertical distortion. *In situ* conformable halves of shattered flint pebbles in the brown silty clay demonstrate intensive frost activity, conditions that further suggest a silt/loess/brickearth component of the sediment.

The gravels of the Clacton Golf Course sequence comprise bed load of a high energy channel system probably active throughout several morphogenetic environments, since the pollen assemblage includes both cold and thermophile species. Bed load alluviation in a laterally migrating channel with variable discharge and periods of overbank flow could account for the general contemporaneity of the mint and "derived" condition of artifacts occurring together both in and on the gravel. Intense cold at this or a later period is shown by heaving of the gravel and cryoturbate intermixing along the channel margin. The succeeding marl may be interpreted as overbank alluvium with local sand lenses or pebbly layers, although solifluction also has been suggested

(Singer, Wymer, Gladfelter, and Wolff 1973). Cold conditions during early phases of marl alluviation intermixed the London Clay, gravel, and marl along the channel edges and formed the ice wedge cast that penetrates the gravel and marl base. Severe cold conditions apparently prevailed, therefore, as late as the pre-temperate pollen zone (Ho I) to which the marl is related (see below). Somewhat drier conditions, with a lower precipitation/evaporation ratio, are indicated by the calcareous aspect of the marl itself and by the variegation. Frost shattering of pebbles in the brown silty clay occurred during a later, less intensive cold period, since a protracted period of subaerial erosion, removing all aspects of estuarine beds recorded at the Clacton West section, is thought to have intervened between marl and brown silty clay alluviation. Pollen analysis should contribute greatly to the ultimate interpretation of this aspect of the sequence.

The pollen evidence shows that the series of Clacton channels is indeed a rather complex system of alluvial beds. In addition to horizontal and vertical facies variability now recognized, the time range of the deposits also can be expanded. The Freshwater-Estuarine beds of the Clacton West Cliff section are late-temperate (Ho IIIa) in age, according to Pike and Godwin (1953); recent analysis of sediments related to this series has extended the age of that sequence to early temperate (Ho IIb) conditions (Turner and Kerney 1971). Preliminary results of pollen study of the gravel, marl, and brown clay by William Mullenders (Louvain) indicate several distinctive climatic situations throughout alluviation of this series (Singer, Wymer, Gladfelter, and Wolff 1973). Conditions most likely were variable (cool to temperate) during alluviation of the gravel. A pollen diagram obtained from the marl suggests conditions earlier than the early-temperate pollen zone (Ho I?), while results from the brown clay are incomplete but indicate a hiatus between the marl and brown clay (Mullenders and Desair-Coremans 1973). The evidence, therefore, shows that the golf course site predates the Clacton West Cliff sections and may represent the earliest dated archeological industry in Britain.

The actual Clacton channel system is supposed to belong to proto-Thames drainage. The heavy mineral and erratic contents determined by Soloman (1937) imply that the gravel deposit does not contain derivatives of the Chalky Boulder Clay (Anglian), but that the overlying deposits do. The marl and brown clay also contain locally derived minerals. Alluviation of the channel can therefore be tied to Anglian-Hoxnian times. Since the proto-Thames system conventionally has been invoked, the temporal and paleogeomorphic relationship between that

Table 7.   River Thames courses in the London Basin

Thames stage	Feature-deposit	Some suggested correlations
Stage III Modern Thames Valley	Lower Floodplain Terrace (buried) Upper Floodplain Terrace Middle Terrace ("Taplow") (Lynch Hill Terrace) High Terrace ("Boyn Hill")	Weichselian; buried channels of Roach, Crouch Ipswichian (at Ilford, Aveley, ?Grays) Hoxnian (at Swanscombe)
Stage II Finchley Depression — Blackwater estuary	(Black Park Terrace) C. Winter Hill Terrace B. Harefield Terrace — Lower Gravel Trains A. Higher Gravel Train	Lake Hertford; Lowestoftian Westleton Beds
Stage I Vale of St. Albans — Mid-Essex (?)	C. Westland Green Gravels B. Pebble Gravels A. High Plateau Gravel	(pre-Westleton Beds) Red Crag

Compiled from several sources including Greensmith and Tucker (1971), Hey (1967), Hey, Krinsley, and Hyde (1971), West (1969), and Wooldridge (1960).

system and the Clacton channels should be examined.

The Clacton Channels and Proto-Thames Courses

Wooldridge spent more than a quarter century studying the ancient Thames courses north of London. The succession established by him (Wooldridge 1927, 1957, 1960; Wooldridge and Linton 1939; Wooldridge and Henderson 1955) is based primarily upon the physiography (distribution and altitude) of deposits, but also on lithology; this sequence is shown in Table 7. Diversion from the earlier Stage I and Stage II courses was caused by the Chiltern drift and Chalky Boulder Clay, respectively; terrace development in the modern Thames valley therefore entirely postdates the Chalky Boulder Clay (Anglian) glaciation. An additional Stage I unit called the Westland Green gravels is recognized by Hey (1965); these gravels postdate deposition of the 400 foot level Pebble Gravel (Stage IB) but predate the Higher Gravel Train (Stage IIA). The Westland Green gravels can be traced to the vicinity of the Westleton (Suffolk), where they are higher and therefore older than the Westleton gravels (Hey 1967). The Stage I gravels appear, then, to be older than the Westleton Beds, and the highest level marine deposits seem contemporary with the Red Crag of East Anglia (Hey, Krinsley, and Hyde 1971).

Table 8. Stratigraphy of Essex according to different authors and different times

	Clayton (1957)	Clayton (1960)	Turner (1970)	Bristow and Cox (1973)
Older drift Wolstonian	Springfield Till Chalky Boulder Clay (Saale) Chelmsford Gravels, Mid-glacial gravels Maldon Till (Saale)	Springfield Till	Springfield Till	Springfield Till (Followed by Hoxnian) Chelmsford Gravels Maldon Till (locally)
Hoxnian	Erosion	Chelmsford Gravels (Boyn Hill Terrace)	Marks Tey and Clacton Deposits	
Anglian	Hanningfield Till, possibly Danbury gravels and Chiltern drift (Elster)	Maldon Till, the second glaciation; pre-Hoxnian (Late Elster) Rejuvenation, erosion and leading (Corton Beds) Hanningfield Till and Danbury Gravel (outwash), the first glaciation. Overlies the pebble gravel (Elster)	Springfield Till Chelmsford Gravels (recessional outwash) Maldon Till	Hanningfield Till not recognized as a till Wolstonian

A relationship of these various stages to the till sequence in Essex is proposed by Clayton (1957), who identified three tills in Essex, interlayered with gravel deposits and all postdating the preglacial pebble gravels (Table 8). These are named: First Glaciation (Hanningfield Till and Danbury gravels), followed by a period of major erosion and leaching (up to 3.4 meters); Second Glaciation (Maldon Till) and the Chelmsford outwash gravels; Third Glaciation (Springfield Till). The last two units are stratigraphically superimposed and readily identified in the field, but relation of this sandwich of deposits to the older Hanningfield Till hinges upon altimetric and morphologic differences, the latter till displaying a "patchy" distribution, reaching lower elevations and showing greater depths of leaching. The Hanningfield Till is reported to overlie the Pebble gravel (Clayton 1964). The second till (Maldon) is identified by Clayton as causing diversion of the proto-Thames from the Middlesex loop, while the Springfield till comprises the drift mantle of the "youthful" Essex plateau surface and was the last ice lobe to reach the London basin.

Correlation of the Essex deposits with the London Basin via glacial deposits in the vicinity of Hertford has been proposed by Clayton and Brown (1958). Three tills and interbedded lacustrine silts and sands and gravels reoccur in numerous sections in the Hertford-Harlow area. These workers postulate a proglacial lake Hertford at the convergence of the Vale of St. Albans and the Finchley depression, formed by blockage of the Middlesex loop-Mid Essex-proto Thames routes by the second ice sheet to reach this area. The invasion diverted the Thames southward to its present valley, and the lacustrine sequences eventually were partially overriden by the last ice sheet to reach the London Basin, represented by the Springfield Till. The history indicated by this sequence shows that after deposition of the Lower Gravel Train (Harefield Terrace), base level lowering tied to a glacial regression allowed the proto-Thames to further downcut; the associated ice invasion into the Hertford area dammed the Thames and formed Lake Hertford, diverting the proto-Thames southward to the modern Thames valley.

The correlation of the Lake Hertford deposits and associated tills is in question. Clayton and Brown (1958) were unable to discern any major temporal breaks in the sedimentary record of this area and, therefore, considered this complex of three tills and interbedded silts, sands, and gravels to relate to the oscillating frontal margin of a single ice sheet. The top, or third, till is contiguous with the Springfield Till that mantles the Essex plateau surface eastward and northward, and a Wolstonian age is assigned to the deposits in the Hertford region.

Clayton (1960) subsequently reinterpreted this sequence and recognized an interglacial stage between the second (Maldon) and Third (Springfield) tills. In western Essex, division of a tripartite till sequence cannot be recognized so that the various tills probably relate to a single glaciation involving fluctuations of the frontal lobe (Baker 1971).

The occurrence of several stages within these deposits is borne out by pollen study (Sparks, West, Williams, and Ransom 1969). A Hoxnian pollen profile was obtained from silty clay and marl pond deposits overlying a till and buried by cryoturbated deposits near Hatfield. By implication, the basal till is Anglian in age, and the topmost deposits are considered Wolstonian. The sections studied are a few miles west of the sites investigated by Clayton and Brown, which would suggest that these exposures may be broadly correlated. Consequently, at this point the evidence is that both the Maldon and Springfield Tills recognized elsewhere in Essex are recorded in the Hertford vicinity, and an interglacial sequence (Hoxnian) also is preserved overlying a till and buried by cryoturbated deposits. However, it cannot be concluded with certainty to which of the three tills identified by Clayton and Brown the basal till of the Hatfield sections of Sparks, et al. (1969) relates.

Correlation of the Hanningfield-Maldon-Springfield sequence with the stratigraphic series recognized in East Anglia is provisional, since several interpretations are offered. Clayton (1960) has proposed equating this sequence with the Cromer, Lowestoft, and Gipping Tills, respectively; Turner (1970) regarded all tills in southeast Essex as Anglian in age. This is based on a late glacial-interglacial-early glacial pollen profile obtained from a lacustrine setting at Marks Tey, Essex. Turner identified the underlying till at the base of this sequence as the Springfield Till. These disparate interpretations emphasize a fundamental problem of East Anglian Pleistocene stratigraphy — the need for uniform criteria for identification and stratigraphic subdivision of the glacial deposits.

If the sequence outlined above is adopted, rather significant conclusions emerge with regard to the age of the Clacton channels. Subsurface drift contours reconstructed by Wooldridge and Henderson (1955) indicate a mid-Essex buried proto-Thames valley leading via Chelmsford to the Blackwater estuary, or via Chelmsford-Colchester to the River Colne estuary, either route of which would have traversed the Clacton-on-Sea region. The Clacton channels with their Weald erratics must relate to this route, rather than a Thames-Medway system as proposed earlier (Oakley and Leakey 1937). This channel might be noted as a Mole-Thames system (after Wooldridge 1960: Figure 3). The Clacton

deposits and the type site of the Clacton industry, therefore, are interpreted here as equating with the proto-Thames Stage II and predate
the Clacton-Acheulian industries recorded in the Boyn Hill Terrace at
Swanscombe. This conclusion is consistent with the pollen evidence
from Clacton already noted above.

THE LOWER THAMES: SWANSCOMBE

The section in the High Terrace at Swanscombe is probably the best-
known Pleistocene section in Britain. This 30-meter terrace, the Boyn
Hill Terrace, is the oldest of the Lower Thames, and despite its continued study for more than sixty years, fundamental questions remain
unanswered regarding the precise age of this feature, and the relationship of the Clactonian and Acheulian industries it contains to other key
Lower Paleolithic sites in Essex and East Anglia.

The stratigraphic sequence at Barnfield's Pit, Swanscombe, has been
widely discussed in the literature (Smith and Dewey 1914; Marston
1937; Baden-Powell 1951; Dines, et al. 1964; Howell 1966). The
Barnfield sections comprise more than 11 meters of Pleistocene deposits in a channel cut into Thanet sand (Eocene) and, in places, the
Chalk (Cretaceous). Sections periodically exposed in the Swanscombe
area, usually as a result of chalk excavation, show that the thalweg of
the channel varies between 23 and 27 meters O.D. over a horizontal
cross section of about 500 meters. The modern surface of the terrace
ranges between 30 and 35 meters O.D. Several channel segments have
been inferred in the Swanscombe area because of the different evolved
state of the contained artifacts (Globe Pit, Ingress Vale Pit, New Cray-
lands Lane Pit, Colyers Pit, Rickson's Pit), although molluscan fauna
allow some reliance on aspects of this archeological dating. The Lower
Gravel, comprising the base of the sequence at Barnfield Pit, is mostly
flint; it is horizontally bedded, with Clactonian artifacts throughout and
molluscan and mammalian fauna. Most recently, "nests" of the "thermally
fractured pebbles" at the base and the top of this layer have been interpreted as a solifluction material (Conway 1969, 1970). The Lower Loam
is essentially a clayey sand (fluviatile) with gravel patches. In the past,
artifacts have been sparse, but now this loam has yielded a "floor" with
artifacts and a variety of mammal bone (Waechter 1970). The loam is
interpreted as a pond or marsh deposit, enduring aperiodic flooding
and minor channeling, desiccation, and, ultimately, subaerial weathering. Evidence for the last development consists of complete decalcifi-

cation to varying depths reaching 45 centimeters (Conway 1972), but others have argued that decalcification can be attributed to postdepositional leaching (Kerney 1971). Detailed textural analyses, clay-mineral studies, or redox properties have yet to be published for this "weathered" zone, so that paleosol implications must be withheld. Nevertheless, a disconformity, if not hiatus, is almost universally recognized between the Lower Loam and Lower Middle Gravels (see below).

The Lower and Upper Middle Gravels contain the earlier Acheulian industry, and the Upper Middle Gravel yielded the Swanscombe skull. The Lower Middle Gravel is a horizontally bedded, medium, flint gravel similar to the Lower Gravel and difficult to distinguish from it unless a stratigraphic context can be seen. It contains a mix of Clactonian and Acheulian elements (Waechter 1971). The Upper Middle Gravel is distinctive because of the several meters of cross-bedded sands ("current bedded") that typify this sediment. This unit has been observed to cut a channel into the Lower Middle Gravel (Marston 1937); a skull was uncovered in the lower beds of this unit. Erosion of the older deposits by the Upper Middle Gravel has been questioned with the suggestion that solution hollows in the underlying chalk may have been mistaken for erosional troughs (Conway 1972), although the report and sections (Figure 11) of J. Wymer seem to substantiate the former interpretation (Wymer 1964).

The Upper Middle Gravel grades into the overlying Upper Loam without a distinct boundary; the latter comprises a discontinuous horizon of a sandy clay with some patches of gravel and is not unlike the Lower Loam. The Upper Gravel is a clayey, medium gravel that is silty in upper parts and has been referred to as a brickearth. According to Conway (1972: 84), the lower part of this gravel "can be shown on lithological and structural grounds to be a solifluction deposit." It contains Middle Acheulian implements and possibly tundra-steppe fauna *(Ovibos?).*

Current excavations at the Barnfield Pit have revealed additional interesting aspects of the Boyn Hill Terrace sequence (Conway 1972). A series of new vertical sections spanning more than 70 meters of an east-west cliff-face: (1) showed lateral pinching out of the Lower Loam, (2) failed to uncover evidence of channels of Upper Middle Gravel cut through the older sequence, and (3) disclosed a new sediment — a "loamy sand with horizontal or undulating bedding" intervening between the Upper Middle Gravel and Upper Loam (see Figure 2).

The age of the Boyn Hill Terrace traditionally has been established by altimetric, faunal, and select geologic means. It is the first terrace of

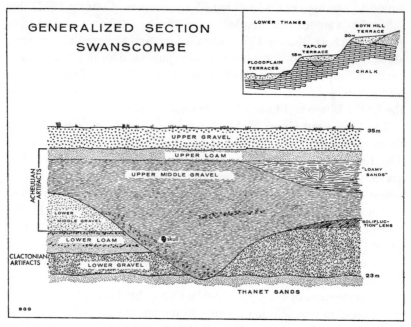

Figure 2.   Generalized section, Swanscombe. Compiled from several sources including Dines, et al. (1964), Howell (1966), and Conway (1972)

the lower Thames to have formed after diversion of the river to its present valley (Wooldridge's Stage III) by Anglian ice; the faunal assemblage has been compared with that of Clacton-on-Sea and Steinheim (Sutcliffe 1964). Derivation of the erratic assemblage has been used to suggest that post-Chalky Boulder Clay (Anglian) but pre-Wolstonian clastic materials are preserved at Swanscombe (Baden-Powell 1951).

Unfortunately, there are no sections within the Lower Thames Valley that directly record Chalky Boulder Clay-Boyn Hill Terrace associations. According to Wooldridge (1957), the Chalky Boulder Clay glaciation advanced to the northern edge of the Thames valley, and Boyn Hill deposits generally are two or more miles beyond this margin. However, a relationship may be established in the Ingrebourne Valley, at Hornchurch. There, river gravels thought to be related to the Thames Boyn Hill, because of similar elevation, overlie a Chalky Boulder Clay (Holmes 1894), the age of which now is generally held to be Anglian. Baden-Powell (1951) assigned this till to the Anglian glaciation of East Anglia on the basis of erratics derived from a western provenance. Clayton (1964) identified the Hornchurch till as Maldon Till, the second glaciation of his sequence which also is equated with the Anglian. Turner (1970) considers that both the Second and Third glaciations in Essex (Maldon and Springfield, respectively) date to the Anglian glacial, because the Hoxnian lacustrine beds at Marks Tey overlie a chalky boulder clay he correlates with the Springfield Till. Consequently, the till-gravel sequence at Hornchurch for various reasons is assigned an Anglian age.

Independent lines of evidence, now beginning to converge, allow a more preicise dating of the Barnfield Pit. Solifluction deposits between the Thanet Sands and Lower Gravel (Conway 1972) suggest a colder phase (with Clactonian implements) prior to the more temperate conditions otherwise indicated for the Lower Gravel and Lower Loam. However, this interpretation is not incontrovertible since the molluscan fauna assemblage yields no evidence for cold conditions. The body of the Lower Gravel reflects woodland conditions because of the abundant woodland mammalian species (Sutcliffe 1964). Woodland conditions probably persisted through the period recorded at the base of the Lower Loam, as suggested by preliminary pollen study (Hubbard 1972) with temperate conditions and mild winters as indicated by the inclusion of frost-sensitive mollusc species (Kerney 1971). The base of the Lower Loam has been suggested as being no older than the early-temperate substage (Ho IIb) of the Hoxnian Interglacial (Hubbard 1972; Kerney 1971). The transition to a grassland situation probably occurred sometime during alluviation of the Lower Loam, which is suggested by preliminary pollen (Hubbard 1972) and shell and bone fragments obtained near the top of this unit (Conway 1972). This also is indicated by a complete pollen diagram from the Lower Loam which shows a break in the pollen sequence in the upper part and an influx of more open-habitat plants (Desair-Coremans and Myllenders, unpublished). Temperate grassland situations may have persisted through Lower Middle Gravel times (Sutcliffe 1964; Kerney 1971), but by the Upper Middle Gravel time cold conditions returned, signaled by terrestrial, open grassland molluscs, *Lemmus*, and cryoturbations (interpreted as solifluction) in sands below the Upper Loam (Dines, et al. 1964). The recent section opened by the Royal Anthropological Institute (Conway 1972) confirms these earlier observations; bona fide ice wedge casts are developed in the loamy sand horizon now recorded between the Upper Middle Gravel and Upper Loam (personal observation). Hoxnian post-temperate conditions (Ho IV) have been proposed for the Upper Middle Gravel, perhaps even early Wolstonian (Kerney 1971). Additional aspects of this cold stage may extend into the Upper

Gravel with tundra-steppe conditions and solifluction phenomena (Conway 1972).

In summary, these data indicate that the Boyn Hill deposits at Barnfield Pit span at least the early-temperate to post-temperate Hoxnian Interglacial time. If corroborated by additional evidence, cryoturbations at the base of the Lower Gravel may record pre-temperate conditions (Ho I). Cold conditions indicated in the top of the sequence (Upper Middle Gravel to Upper Gravel) possibly herald the next glacial, but this, then, causes other stratigraphic problems for the Lower Thames valley, since if the higher section of the aggradational sequence is assigned to the penultimate glacial, conflicts arise with the conventional interpretation of the Thames terrace sequence.

Terraces of the Lower Thames have been outlined in some detail by King and Oakley (1936), but not mapped. Two aggradational phases of the Boyn Hill Terrace were recognized: the Early and Late Boyn Hill stages, equated with the Lower units, and the Middle and Upper units, respectively, the interval of alluviation between having witnessed weathering of the Lower Loam surface and uplift. This interval of interrupted alluviation rejuvenated the Thames which dissected to about 7 meters O.D. at Little Thurrock (Grays) and to about 3.7 meters below sea level at Clacton, and truncated the top of the Lower Loam at Barnfield. Reversal of this trend and renewed aggrading then accounted for alluvation of the terrace with Clactonian implements at Clacton-Jaywick Sands (Oakley and Leakey 1937) and Little Thurrock (Grays), and the Ilford brickearth and sands. Lastly, deposition of the Middle and Upper sequences at the Barnfield Pit, Swanscombe, completed the Boyn Hill stage. Therefore, according to Oakley and Leakey, all the aforementioned sites are of comparable ages, falling within the same interglacial; the Clactonian industry of the Lower Gravel-Loam at Swanscombe would necessarily predate those of Clacton-on-Sea and Little Thurrock (Grays); and aggrading of the Middle and Upper units in the same terrace at Barnfield Pit and the contained Acheulian implements somehow post-date the Clactonian of Clacton and Little Thurrock. Note that the magnitude of uplift during the penultimate interglacial proposed by this hypothesis is at least equivalent to the eustatic sea level fluctuation of the subsequent entire cut-fill cycle (Taplow Terrace).

The terrace sequence of the Lower Thames could be restudied with profit since many of the archeological and stratigraphic relationships King and Oakley tried to resolve can now be shown, on the basis of new evidence, to be based on faulty interpretations. The Clactonian industry at Clacton-on-Sea, for example, in all likelihood predates the Swanscombe Clactonian (Singer, Wymer, Gladfelter, and Wolff 1973). In addition, aspects of Middle Terrace (Taplow) deposits at Ilford can be placed in the Ipswichian Interglacial (West, Lambert, and Sparks 1964), but the Little Thurrock (Grays) site remains problematic. The Clactonian industry there occurs in a 15 meter Middle Terrace at an elevation below the Lower Gravel bench developed at Swanscombe, about 3 kilometers distant. Wymer (1957) embraces Oakley's hypothesis regarding this stage, but partial analysis of pollen from Grays has led West (1969) to conclude that these deposits cannot yet be assigned an appropriate interglacial age, although he favors an Ipswichian age on the basis of altimetric correlatives with pollen-dated deposits at Ilford and Aveley.

A final problem can be noted with regard to the Lower Thames terrace stratigraphy. If, as the present evidence indicates, the Upper Middle Gravel unit and Upper Loam and Gravel denote a cold period, it then becomes problematic to relate the 30 to 35 meter above sea level deposits (Wolstonian) to the Middle Terrace (15 m), also alleged to belong to a Wolstonian-Ipswichian cut-fill hemicycle. As Brunnacker (this volume) has shown to be the case for the Lower Rhine, the complexity of alluvial terrace sequences may be disguised by the confusion of distinctive morphologic and lithologic entities. What is needed is thorough study of the Lower Thames terraces based on minerology, sedimentology, pebble morphology/lithology, and paleontological and paleogeomorphic data as appropriate. Only then can an objective picture be formulated that may enable us to understand beyond hypothetical models the disparate elevation and contextural aspects of the Thames Valley terraces.

AN OVERVIEW

This discussion has focused on only a few aspects of the Middle Pleistocene succession in East Anglia, but the implicit emphasis is upon the multidisciplinary nature of Pleistocene studies. In the past, the Pleistocene sequence of this region has been based largely on biostratigraphic data. Now, with the active involvement of earth scientists, the conventional framework is challenged, and the most immediate need is to integrate the various lines of evidence, perhaps independently, but not in ignorance, of Pleistocene developments across the Channel. Because of the numerous Paleolithic sites in southeastern Britain and the opportunity to study superimposed archeological assemblages — such as at Swanscombe and Hoxne — the stratigraphic record assumes special importance.

A fundamental, necessary component of subsequent research is the continuation of mapping of superficial deposits and stratigraphic units. Such programs must apply consistently reliable, objective criteria for identifying tills and statistically reliable sampling methods in the field and in the laboratory. These efforts might best be made in: (1) relating the coastal and hinterland sequences, (2) establishing the glacial-interglacial succession, and (3) mapping moraine systems and other morphological features including terraces of the major valleys. Correlation of discontinuous terrace features has been too dependent upon altimetric relationships which, in order to be consistently reliable, requires: (1) understanding of the historic stability of a region and where terraces are nonclimatic in origin (2) knowledge of regional isostatic/eustatic changes. Neither of these requisites is fulfilled in the case of the London Basin-southern North Sea region.

Revision of the traditional East Anglian Middle Pleistocene succession is now required. Any such proposal must recognize the following: (1) there is no firm basis for differentiating tills of two distinct glacials, both the Gipping and Lowestoft Tills, for example, may pertain to a single Chalky Boulder Clay glacial phase succeeded by Hoxnian Interglacial conditions; (2) a post-Hoxnian cold phase is documented by periglacial geomorphic features and a pre-Ipswichian cold period also is indicated; (3) the duration of elapsed time between these temperate periods is disputed; (4) the implication that a post-Hoxnian till is not recorded in most of East Anglia, with the exception of the Hunstanton Till (Devensian) along the northwest coast of Norfolk, is not completely justified as certain surface deposits, such as at Hoxne itself, need to be understood; and (5) correlation of the East Anglian Chalky Boulder Clay (Lowestoft Till) to the continental sequence is uncertain.

With regard to the "Hoxnian" Interglacial sites discussed above, effects of the revised interpretation are varied. Hoxne itself promises to hold some of the answers. Interpretation of the age of the Clacton-on-Sea golf course site does not depend on the till stratigraphy and can be interpreted as the oldest dated archeological site in Britain. The situation in the Lower Thames is problematic, since the terrace system usually is thought to post-date the Lowestoft Chalky Boulder Clay. But, as yet, there is no direct stratigraphic link to the till sequence. If a penultimate interglacial age is to be retained for Swanscombe, it is apparent that the Thames terrace sequence must be reevaluated.

Stratigraphic correlations, past and present, that implement archeological dating need to be supplanted by reliable, conventional strati-graphic procedures. The illusion of archeological "dating" should be dispelled by the inability to construct an archeological time scale, a reasonable if not expected circumstance in view of the time transgres-siveness of human adaptation and culture change. The considerable temporal and geographic differences of cultural levels or traditions il-lustrate the inherent fallacy of archeological dating. Time comparisons based on selected artifacts are even more problematic as there is hardly agreement on typological terminology or even the cultural implications of the same assemblage. It has been argued that it is valid to use arti-facts as time indicators just as we use bones, but there is a major dis-tinction because, in the case of bones, modern species provide analogies for Pleistocene species such that paleodistributions, habitat, and ecology can be reconstructed, frequently on a zonal basis. Such large-scale, broadly based reconstructions hold greater stratigraphic reliability and significance than reconstructions inferred from typologies or collections, the time transgressiveness of which generally is an unknown (intra- or interregionally), the environmental-ecological context for which needs to be established, and the implications of which frequently are less well understood than other forms of contextual evidence.

REFERENCES

BADEN-POWELL, D. F. W.
1948   The chalky boulder clays of Norfolk and Suffolk. *Geological Magazine* 85:279–296.
1950   Field meeting in the Lowestoft District. *Proceedings of the Geologists' Association* 61:191–197.
1951   The age of interglacial deposits at Swanscombe. *Geological Magazine* 88:344–354.
1956   "Glacial erratics from the upper glacial bed at Hoxne," in *The Quaternary deposits at Hoxne, Suffolk*. R. G. West, 349–351.
BAKER, C. A.
1971   A contribution to the glacial stratigraphy of west Essex. *The Essex Naturalist* 32:317–329.
BANHAM, P. H.
1971   Pleistocene beds at Corton, Suffolk. *Geological Magazine* 108: 281–285.
BANHAM, P. H., C. E. RANSON
1970   A guide to the Pleistocene geology of the Mundesley Cliffs. *Transactions of the Norfolk and Norwich Naturalists' Society* 21:383–386.

BECK, R. B., B. M. FUNNELL, A. R. LORD
1972   Correlaton of Lower Pleistocene Crag at depth in Suffolk. *Geological Magazine* 109:137–139.
BRISTOW, C. R., F. C. COX
1973   The Gipping Till: a reappraisal of East Anglian glacial stratigraphy. *Journal of the Geological Society* 129:1–37.
CAMBRIDGE, P. G.
1970   *A review and guide to the Neogene and Lower Pleistocene deposits of East Anglia.* Norwich: School of Environmental Sciences, University of East Anglia.
CATT, J. A., W. M. CORBETT, C. A. H. HODGE, P. A. MADGETT, W. TATLER, A. H. WEIR
1971   Loess in the soils of north Norfolk. *Journal of Soil Science* 22: 444–452.
CLAYTON, K. M.
1957   Some aspects of the glacial deposits of Essex. *Proceedings of the Geologists' Association* 68:1–21.
1960   The landforms of parts of southern Essex. *The Institute of British Geographers, Transactions and Papers* 28:55–74.
1964   The glacial geomorphology of southern Essex. *Guide to London Excursions, 20th International Geographical Congress* 25.
CLAYTON, K. M., J. C. BROWN
1958   The glacial deposits around Hertford. *Proceedings of the Geologists' Association* 69:103–119.
CONWAY, B. W.
1969   Preliminary geological investigation of Boyn Hill terrace deposits at Barnfield pit, Swanscombe, Kent, during 1968. *Proceedings of the Royal Anthropological Institute* (1968):59–61.
1970   Geological investigation of Boyn Hill terrace deposits at Barnfield pit, Swanscombe, Kent, during 1969. *Proceedings of the Royal Anthropological Institute* (1969):90–93.
1971   Geological investigation of Boyn Hill terrace deposits at Barnfield pit, Swanscombe, Kent, during 1970. *Proceedings of the Anthropological Institute* (1970):60–64.
1972   Geological investigation of Boyn Hill terrace deposits at Barnfield pit, Swanscombe, Kent, during 1971. *Proceedings of the Royal Anthropological Institute* (1971):80–85.
CORBETT, W. M.
i.p.   *Soil survey of England and Wales.* TM28.
CORBETT, W. M., W. TATLER
1970   *Soils in Norfolk.* Sheet TM49 (Beccles North). Soil Survey 1. Harpenden.
COX, F. C., E. F. P. NICKLESS
1972   Some aspects of the glacial history of central Norfolk. *Bulletin of the Geological Society of Great Britain* 42:79–98.
DINES, H. C., W. B. R. KING, K. P. OAKLEY
1964   "A general account of the 100-ft. terrace gravels of the Barnfield Pit," in *The Swanscombe skull.* Edited by C. D. Ovey, 5–10. London: The Royal Anthropological Institute.

FRERE, J.
1800   Account of flint weapons discovered at Hoxne in Suffolk. *Archaelogia* 13:204–205.

FUNNELL, B. M.
1955   An account of the geology of the Bungay district. *Suffolk Naturalists' Transactions* 9:115–126.
1970   "The Palaeogene and early Pleistocene of Norfolk," in *The Geology of Norfolk*. Edited by G. P. Larwood and B. M. Funnell, 340–364. Norwich: The Geological Society of Norfolk.

GLADFELTER, B. G.
1972   Cold-climate features in the vicinity of Clacton-On-Sea, Essex (England). *Quaternaria* 16:121–135.

GREENSMITH, J. T., E. V. TUCKER
1971   The effects of late Pleistocene and Holocene sea level changes in the vicinity of the River Crouch, East Essex. *Proceedings of the Geologists' Association* 82:301–322.

HEY, R. W.
1965   Highly quartzose pebble gravels in the London Basin. *Proceedings of the Geologists' Association* 76:403–420.
1967   The Westleton beds reconsidered. *Proceedings of the Geologists' Association* 78:427–445.

HEY, R. W., D. H. KRINSLEY, P. J. W. HYDE
1971   Surface textures of sand-grains from the Hertfordshire pebble gravels. *Geological Magazine* 108:377–382.

HOLMES, T. V.
1894   Further notes on some sections on the new railway from Romford to Upminster, and on the relations of the Thames valley beds to the boulder clay. *Quarterly Journal of the Geological Society* 50:443–452.

HOWELL, F. C.
1966   "Observations on the earlier phases of the European Lower Paleolithic," in *Recent studies in Paleoanthropology*. Edited by J. D. Clark and F. C. Howell, 88–201. American Anthropological Association Special Publication 68(2). Menasha, Wisconsin.

HUBBARD, N. L. B.
1972   An interim report on the pollen record at Swanscombe. *Proceedings of the Royal Anthropological Institute* (1971):79.

KERNEY, M. P.
1971   Interglacial deposits in Barnfield pit, Swanscombe, and their molluscan fauna. *Journal of the Geological Society* 127:69–93.

KING, W. B. R., K. P. OAKLEY
1936   The Pleistocene succession in the lower parts of the Thames valley. *Proceedings of the Prehistoric Society* 2:52–76.

LORD, A. R.
1972   A preliminary account of a research borehole at Syleham, Suffolk. *Bulletin of the Geological Society of Norfolk* 21:25–28.

MARSTON, A. T.
1937   The Swanscombe skull. *Journal of the Royal Anthropological Institute* 67:339–406.

MOIR, J. R.
1926 The silted-up lake Hoxne and its contained flint implements. *Proceedings of the Prehistoric Society* 5:137–165.

MULLENDERS, W., M. DESAIR-COREMANS
1973 "Preliminary report on the pollen analysis of a marl section at Clacton-on-Sea (Essex, England)," Unpublished manuscript.

NICKLESS, E. F. P.
1971 *The sand and gravel resources of the country southeast of Norwich, Norfolk.* Institute of Geological Sciences Report 71/20:1–93.

OAKLEY, K. P., M. LEAKEY
1937 Report on excavations at Jaywick Sands, Essex (1934), with some observations on the Clactonian industry, and on the fauna and geological significance of the Clacton Channel. *Proceedings of the Prehistoric Society* 3:217–260.

PAGE, N. R.
1972 On the age of the Hoxnian Interglacial. *Geological Journal* 8: 129–142.

PIKE, K., H. GODWIN
1953 The interglacial at Clacton-on-Sea, Essex. *Quarter Journal of the Geological Society* 108:261–272.

SHOTTON, F. W.
1972 A reply to 'On the age of the Hoxnian Interglacial' by N. R. Page. *Geological Journal* 8:387–394.

SHOTTON, F. W., R. G. WEST
1969 Recommendations on stratigraphical usage. *Proceedings of the Geological Society of London* 1656:155–157.

SINGER, R., J. WYMER, B. GLADFELTER, R. WOLFF
1973 Excavation of the Clactonian industry of the golf course, Clacton-on-Sea, Essex. *Proceedings of the Prehistoric Society* 39:6–74.

SINGER, R., J. WYMER, B. GLADFELTER
1973 Radiocarbon dates from Hoxne, Suffolk. *Journal of Geology* 81:508–509.

SMITH, R. A., H. DEWEY
1914 The high terrace of the Thames: report on excavations made on behalf of the British Museum and H.M. Geological Survey. *Archaeologia* 65:187–212.

SOLOMAN, J. D.
1937 "Report on heavy minerals of Clacton channel deposits from Jaywick Sands, and of sand from the Holland gravel pit," in *Report on excavations at Jaywick Sands, Essex (1934), with some observations on the Clactonian industry, and on the fauna and geological significance of the Clacton channel.* K. P. Oakley and M. Leakey, 257–258. *Proceeding of the Prehistoric Society* 3.

SPARKS, B. W., R. G. WEST
1968 Interglacial deposits at Wortwell, Norfolk. *Geological Magazine* 105:471–481.
1972 *The Ice Age in Britain.* London: Methuen.

SPARKS, B. W., R. G. WEST, R. B. G. WILLIAMS, M. RANSOM
1969   Hoxnian interglacial deposits near Hatfield Herts. *Proceedings of the Geologists' Association* 80:243–267.

SPENCER, H E. P.
1967   A contribution to the geological history of Suffolk. *Suffolk Naturalists' Transactions* 13:366–389.

SUTCLIFFE, A. J.
1964   "The mammalian fauna," in *The Swanscombe skull*. Edited by C. D. Ovey, 85–111. London: The Royal Anthropological Institute.

TURNER, C.
1968a   A Lowestoftian late-glacial flora from the Pleistocene deposits at Hoxne, Suffolk. *New Phytologist* 67:327–332.
1968b   A note on the occurrence of *Vitis* and other new plant records from the Pleistocene deposits at Hoxne, Suffolk. *New Phytologist* 67:333–334.
1970   The Middle Pleistocene deposits at Marks Tey, Essex. *Philosophical transactions of the Royal Society of London*, B, 257:373–440.

TURNER, C., M. P. KERNEY
1971   A note on the age of the freshwater beds of the Clacton Channel. *Journal of the Geological Society* 127:87–93.

TURNER, C., R. G. WEST
1968   The subdivision and zonation of interglacial periods. *Eiszeitalter und Gegenwart* 19:93–101.

WAECHTER, J. D'A.
1969   Swanscombe 1968. *Proceedings of the Royal Anthropological Institute* (1968):53–58.
1970   Swanscombe 1969. *Proceedings of the Royal Anthropological Instute* (1969):83–85.
1971   Swanscombe 1970. *Proceedings of the Royal Anthropological Institute* (1970):43–49.
1972   Swanscombe 1971. *Proceedings of the Royal Anthropological Institute* (1971):73–78.

WARREN, S. H.
1923   The Elephas-Antiquus bed of Clacton-on-Sea (Essex) and its flora and fauna. *Quarterly Journal of the Geological Society* 79:606–634.
1955   The Clacton (Essex) channel deposits. *Quarterly Journal of the Geological Society* 111:287–307.

WEST, R. G.
1956   The Quaternary deposits at Hoxne, Suffolk. *Philosophical Transactions of the Royal Society*, B, 239:265–356.
1961   The glacial and interglacial deposits of Norfolk. *Transactions of the Norfolk and Norwich Naturalists Society* 19:365–375.
1962   Vegetational history of the early Pleistocene of the Royal Society borehole at Ludham, Norfolk. *Proceedings of the Royal Society*, B, 155:437–453.
1963   Problems of the British Quaternary. *Proceedings of the Geologists' Association* 74:147–186.

1968   *Pleistocene Geology and Biology.* New York: John Wiley and Sons.
1969   Pollen analyses from interglacial deposits at Aveley and Grays, Essex. *Proceedings of the Geologists' Association* 80:271–282.
1970   "The glacial and interglacial deposits of Norfolk," in *The Geology of Norfolk.* Edited by G. P. Larwood and B. M. Funnell, 365–376. Norwich: The Geological Society of Norfolk.
1972   The stratigraphical position of the Norwich Crag in relation to the Cromer Forest Bed Series. *Bulletin of the Geological Society of Norfolk* 21:17–23.

WEST, R. G., P. H. BANHAM
1968   Short field meeting on the north Norfolk coast. *Proceedings of the Geologists' Association* 79:493–512.

WEST, R. G., J. J. DONNER
1956   The glaciation of East Anglia and the East Midlands: a differentiation based on stone orientation measurements of the tills. *Quarterly Journal of the Geological Society of London* 112:69–91.

WEST, R. G., C. A. LAMBERT, B. W. SPARKS
1964   Interglacial deposits at Ilford, Essex. *Philosophical Transactions of the Royal Society,* B, 247:185–212.

WEST, R. G., C. M. B. MCBURNEY
1954   The Quaternary deposits at Hoxne, Suffolk, and their archaeology. *Proceedings of the Prehistoric Society* 20:131–154.

WOOLDRIDGE, S. W.
1927   The Pliocene history of the London Basin. *Proceedings of the Geologists' Association* 38:49–132.
1957   Some aspects of the physiography of the Thames valley in relation to the ice age and early man. *Proceedings of the Prehistoric Society* 23:1–19.
1960   The Pleistocene succession in the London Basin. *Proceedings of the Geologists' Association* 71:113–129.

WOOLDRIDGE, S. W., H. C. K. HENDERSON
1955   Some aspects of the physiography of the eastern part of the London Basin. *Institute of British Geographers, Transactions and Papers* 21:19–31.

WOOLDRIDGE, S. W., D. L. LINTON
1939   *Structure, surface and drainage in Southeast England.* London: George Philip and Son.

WYMER, J.
1957   A Clactonian flint industry at Little Thurrock, Grays, Essex. *Proceedings of the Geologists' Association* 68:159–177.
1964   "Excavations at Barnfield Pit, 1955–1960," in *The Swanscombe skull.* Edited by C. D. Ovey, 19–61. London: The Royal Anthropological Institute.

WYMER, J., R. SINGER
1970   The first season of excavations at Clacton-on-Sea, Essex, England: a brief report. *World Archaeology* 2:12–16.

The Correlation and Duration of Middle Pleistocene Interglacial Periods in Northwest Europe

CHARLES TURNER

ABSTRACT

Interglacials of Middle Pleistocene age in northwest Europe, which have been investigated by means of pollen analysis, are considered from the standpoint both of their stratigraphic relationships and of their paleobotany.

The base of the Middle Pleistocene is taken as the top of the Menapian or Baventian glacial period. There is evidence of at least three post-Menapian, pre-Elsterian interglacial stages. The fullest sequence so far promises to come from the Netherlands, nevertheless it is at present almost impossible to correlate the so-called "Cromerian Complex" interglacials of either Britain or Germany with this sequence. Both the stratigraphical and the botanical evidence are tantalizingly incomplete. There is still no good paleobotanical evidence from interstadial periods within the Elsterian glacial period. Since there was clearly an earlier ice advance into Northern Germany, subdivision of the Elsterian needs careful reconsideration.

There is good evidence for the Holsteinian interglacial from many sites in the region. These suggest a rather uniform and well defined vegetational succession across the area, with particularly characteristic features in zone III, when *Abies* forest with *Vitis*, *Buxus* and later *Pterocarya*, developed. Stratigraphically the position of this interglacial is reasonably clear. There is, however, increasing evidence for a further short interglacial period, the Dömnitzian, before the main Saale glaciation of northern Europe. Between the Holsteinian and the Dömnitzian, which had a vegetational succession initially resembling the Holsteinian, ice may have reached southern Scandinavia. More evidence is needed to confirm these stages. For the Saalian glacial period there is still remarkably little evidence for well-developed interstadial periods, let alone any interglacial development within this stage. The only certain interglacial deposit at Kap Arkona, Rügen, may be of Dömnitzian age, whereas of other once-claimed intra-Saalian deposits, the "Ohe interglacial" is certainly Holsteinian, and the Bederkesa and Treene deposits certainly Eemian.

The study of laminated lacustrine deposits can be used to estimate the duration of interglacial periods. The nature of this lamination is discussed, and methods by which annual cycles of deposition can be demonstrated. On evidence of this kind a duration of 28,000–36,000 years has been suggested for the pre-Elsterian interglacial of Bilshausen (Müller 1965), of 17,000–25,000 for the Holsteinian (Turner 1970, Meyer i.p., Müller i.p.a) and of 9,000–11,000 for the Eemian (Müller i.p.b).

INTRODUCTION

During the Middle Pleistocene, northwest Europe seems to have experienced an intensification of the climatic oscillations which characterized the Pleistocene period, such that periods cold enough to occasion extensive glaciation of the north European lowlands, probably for the first time, alternated with temperate periods of varying duration with climatic regimes not dissimilar to that of the present day. Indeed, this general pattern of alternating glacial and interglacial periods has persisted from the Middle Pleistocene through the Late Pleistocene to the present Flandrian temperate stage. The object of this paper is to review the paleobotanical evidence from Middle Pleistocene deposits in northwest Europe, partly as a means of correlating the sequences of warm climatic oscillations, interglacial and interstadial, in different regions of the area, and partly in order to assess the environmental development, both vegetational and climatic, during the temperate interglacial stages. Such developments can now be set against a timescale derived from studies of annual lamination structures in a small number of interglacial deposits in Germany and England.

In more detailed stratigraphical terms the Middle Pleistocene is deemed to cover that period between the end of the Menapian cold or glacial stage of the Netherlands (Zagwijn 1960), the probable equivalent of the Baventian of the British Pleistocene succession (West 1961), and the end of the Saalian glacial period. It thus includes what have traditionally been regarded as two major interglacial complexes, the Cromerian and the Holsteinian, which recent work is now leading to a more definite subdivision, and the intervening Elsterian glacial stage, which is certainly imperfectly understood. Most, but not all, workers wish to include the Saalian also within the Middle Pleistocene, but here such a point is academic, because the discussion naturally leads to cover that stage and in some particulars even the succeeding Eemian interglacial. Firstly, however, it is desirable to clarify some fundamental points, assumptions which have been developed over the years about the definition, nomenclature, and zonational subdivision of interglacial periods both by stratigraphers and by paleobotanists.

INTERGLACIAL AND INTERSTADIAL PERIODS

Minor climatic oscillations occur within the periods of major ones. During interglacial times there seem to have been relatively few such fluctuations (see Müller i.p.a), but the glacial stages were certainly interrupted for short periods by milder interstadial phases. The distinction between interglacial and interstadial periods must necessarily be an arbitrary one, since the differences are those of degree and not of kind. Nevertheless, in the northwest European area the most generally acceptable definition of an interglacial period seems to depict an interval of relatively warm climate both temperate enough and of long enough duration to permit (a) a rise in ocean levels equivalent to those of today and (b) the immigration and establishement of mixed-oak forest as a climax vegetation in the north European lowlands.

The definition of interstadial periods is much more difficult because of the complexity of climatic change in terms of temperature and precipitation. Differing lines of evidence have been used, both biostratigraphic and lithostratigraphic, to define interstadial periods during the Weichselian glacial stage, and this has caused confusion. Thus the study of pollen zones and beetle assemblages have led to the formulation of "interstadials" during that period, which in some cases overlap, but in others do not coincide in time. Even though this may be explained by the two groups of organisms having differing rates of response to environmental change, it is exceedingly troublesome for stratigraphers unless these biozones are typified by a prefix denoting the organisms on which they are based — thus pollen-interstadial or beetle-interstadial (West, et al. 1974). Occasionally an interstadial period is defined simply on the presence of peat beds within an inorganic sequence. These need have no climatic significance *per se*, and in that case the term is simply misused and can again give rise to stratigraphic confusion.

Nomenclature of Interglacial Stages

Attempts at developing a stratigraphical framework for the Pleistocene period in Europe have consistently placed greater stress on glacial rather than interglacial periods. Penck and Brückner (1909) recognized four major periods of glaciation in the Alpine region, and Keilhack subsequently recognized three glaciations of north Germany, but both the zonation schemes of these authors gave distinctive names only for the glacial periods. These names, in a loose context, did indicate local regions, where actual deposits could be found, which these authors assigned to particular stratigraphic horizons within the Pleistocene. The intervening interglacial periods, on the other hand, were indicated merely by a conjunction of the names of the preceding and succeeding glacial stages. It follows that such terms as Mindel-Riss, Riss-Würm, Es (Elster-Saale), and Saw (Saale-Weichsel) interglacial periods were set up much more as concepts than as stratigraphical entities based on deposits which could be used as a firm basis for correlation. There are in effect no type areas or localities for such units. Terms such as Es and Saw are now almost defunct, but the Alpine terminology has acquired a highly suspect, if not entirely spurious, worldwide usage. Terms such as Mindel-Riss are still being applied by many authors quite out of context, either because of uncritical habit or of an unwillingness to set up local stage names or else use such neutral terms as penultimate interglacial. This practice should cease, unless the Alpine sequence itself is being discussed.

At the time that these stratigraphic schemes were erected, many of the more important interglacial strata then recognized, such as the Hötting breccia and the *Paludina* beds of the Berlin area, were of uncertain stratigraphical position. As more information about interglacial strata accumulated, so the need for a better defined scheme of stratigraphical nomenclature became apparent, and this need was crystallized in a paper by Woldstedt (1953), in which he proposed the formal adoption of the stage names Eem interglacial, Holstein interglacial, and Cromer interglacial for the last three major interglacial periods. It is from these names that the current widely accepted terms Eemian, Holsteinian, and Cromerian have been derived. Woldstedt stressed the necessity for these terms to refer in the first instance to a type region or locality where actual deposits could be studied and used as a basis for wider correlation. For this reason the first two terms are related to deposits of interglacial marine transgressions, because it was felt that these offered a possibility of correlation on a global as well as a regional scale. Since that time a further refinement of interglacial stratigraphy has been achieved as a result of the widespread, detailed application of pollen analysis and other micropaleontological techniques to interglacial sediments. It is now possible to subdivide interglacial periods on the basis of biostratigraphic evidence, and this approach now necessitates the setting up of a fresh and finer network of type localities for deposits of the various interglacial and interstadial periods in each of the subregions of northwest Europe. Ideally such type localities should be defined in detail and be based on permanent sections or borehole cores which can be conserved for re-evaluation at any future time. Where possible they should provide as full and typical a biostratigraphic record as is available. In the British Isles an attempt has been made to set up such type localities for the various stages of the Quaternary era (Mitchell, et al. 1973), but on the European mainland this has yet to be done. One aim of this paper is to promote that development as speedily as possible.

The Zonation of Interglacial Periods

The correlation of interglacial deposits in northwest Europe is fraught with complications, because there are almost as many zonation schemes as authors. Virtually all subdivision of interglacial periods has been based on palynological evidence, that is on the zonation of pollen diagrams. Because pollen diagrams reflect both regional and local vegetation conditions, local zonation schemes have been set up for many different sites as well as for different interglacial stages. The problems of correlating these zonation schemes were reviewed by Turner and West (1968); their paper has provoked further useful informal discussion.

The zonation of a pollen diagram fulfills two main functions. The most important of these is to provide an analytical framework for the description of the palynological record and for the discussion of the vegetational history of the site. The zones themselves are therefore essentially assemblage zones, in fact pollen biozones and, as biostratigraphic units, must be based on defined pollen assemblage characters. The best code of practice suggests that authors should give their biozones not only numbers or letters but also names defining the dominant or characteristic pollen types present, thus "Zone IX: *Corylus-Picea (Alnus-Pinus)*-zeit" (Müller i.p.a) or "Subzone Ho IIb: *Alnus-Quercus-Corylus* subzone" (Turner 1970).

A subsidiary function is that the zonation scheme will be used when comparing and attempting to correlate one site with another, whether neighboring or distant. In this, the two functions are frequently at variance, because the first generally requires an emphasis on local detail, and therefore local vegetational fluctuations, whereas the second requires such fluctuations to be disregarded in the tracing of broad regional trends of vegetational change.

How, therefore, can these two functions best be served? In particular, the study of interglacial deposits has emphasized the strong parallelism of vegetational, climatic, and edaphic development during all the interglacial periods of the Middle and Late Pleistocene and likewise in the Flandrian postglacial period. This parallelism has been discussed in particular by Iversen (1958) and by Andersen (1966). Andersen has described the similarity in the general features of interglacial vegetational succession and lake development from both the Eemian and Harreskovian interglacial periods. This similarity is very great, despite the differences in detail which characterize the individual interglacial periods. As a result of his analyses of the behavior of different components of the vegetation as ecological indicators, he divides the vegetational successions into three main stages, a protocratic, a mesocratic, and an oligocratic stage, the last-named being conditioned by soil evolution rather than by climatic change. Finally interglacial conditions are drawn to a close during a "telocratic" stage as described by Iversen (1958), though the term "telutocratic" (Firbas 1949) is probably more appropriate.

On the basis of these divisions, of their own investigations into interglacial deposits in Britain, and of an evaluation of pollen diagrams from other parts of northwest Europe, Turner and West (1968) suggested that during each of the interglacial periods of the Middle and Late Pleistocene a series of four more or less distinct subperiods of vegetational development could be recognized within that area. These they defined as zones I-IV on pollen assemblage characters. The vegetational implications are described below.

ZONE I: THE PRE-TEMPERATE ZONE   This zone is characterized by the development and closing-in of forest vegetation after a late-glacial period. The forest dominants are generally boreal trees, particularly *Betula* and also *Pinus*, but light-demanding herbs and shrubs are also significant elements of the vegetation. This zone approximates closely to Andersen's protocratic stage.

ZONE II: THE EARLY-TEMPERATE OR MESOCRATIC ZONE   This shows the establishment and expansion of mixed-oak forest vegetation, typically with *Quercus*, *Ulmus*, *Fraxinus*, and *Corylus*. During this zone the forest is thriving on rich soil conditions and achieves its maximum denseness and luxuriance.

ZONE III: THE LATE-TEMPERATE OR OLIGOCRATIC ZONE   The onset of this zone is marked by the expansion of late-immigrating temperate trees, especially of *Carpinus* and *Abies*, sometimes of *Picea*, and perhaps, in terms of Flandrian vegetational history, of *Fagus*. This expansion is usually, though not always, accompanied by a progressive decline in dominance of the mixed-oak forest tree species.

Changes of this type can be demonstrated to have occurred regularly in every interglacial period later than the earliest such periods of the Middle Pleistocene, certainly from the Cromerian interglacial *sensu stricto* onwards. The causes of these changes are not agreed. On the one hand, trees such as *Carpinus*, *Fagus*, and *Tilia* are "shade trees," that is they are able to reproduce and grow to dominance even in dense woodland, whereas *Ulmus* and *Quercus* require considerably more light when young saplings if they are to survive. It can therefore be argued that, under the right climatic and soil conditions, ultimately such shade trees will largely replace the mixed-oak forest as a climax vegetation. On the other hand at the same time there are various indications of degenerating soil conditions; these include the more regular appearance of pollen of calcifuge plants, especially Ericaceae, changes in lacustrine sedimentation, and often, though not at all sites, an expansion of *Picea*. Andersen, studying Danish sites where these conditions were apparent, drew attention to the tendency of *Picea* to promote the accumulation of raw humus. No doubt, locally this is a very important factor in the podsolization of soils, but the same trends may occur even if *Picea* is rare. Finally, there is really very little evidence for major changes in temperature or rainfall at this horizon from any interglacial period, so that specific climatic changes do not appear to offer an explanation.

ZONE IV: THE POST-TEMPERATE ZONE   This shows a return to dominance of boreal trees, in particular of *Pinus*, *Betula*, and *Picea*, together with a thinning of the forest and the gradual development of open communities, particularly damp heathland. Temperate trees become virtually extinct. Ericaceous heathland may be particularly characteristic of this zone, but it also often persists into the succeeding early-glacial periods.

One anomaly of this scheme, which has been brought to the attention of the authors, is that although the four vegetational subperiods are labelled as zones, and are indeed defined on very broad pollen assemblage characteristics, they are nevertheless also given names which bear climatic implications. It is therefore debatable whether the subperiods should be regarded technically as zones or as substages of interglacial periods.

Some workers fear that the scheme might act as a strait-jacket, which would hinder or distort the description of local interglacial vegetational successions, particularly where pollen zones intermediate between those typical of the subperiods described above occur (cf. the difficulty of defining a clear I/II boundary in Holsteinian pollen diagrams from Denmark [Andersen 1965]). Here it should be emphasized that the scheme was never intended to replace or restrict a framework of local biozones for describing particular pollen diagrams in detail. It has already been suggested that such zones should be given a precise definition based on their pollen content. But for the purpose of regional correlation, the scheme outlined above does seem to offer a framework within which different sites can be discussed, bearing in mind that there is no absolute means of dating interglacial deposits, and that biozone boundaries of almost any kind are unlikely to be exactly synchronous across Europe. There certainly seems to be a case for authors to discuss their diagrams within this framework, whether or not they wish to make use of it in setting up their local pollen-biozones. Certainly in the present paper it provides, additionally, the only consistent means for comparing vegetational successions from different interglacial periods as well as from sites belonging to the same stage.

Table 1. Comparison of different Holsteinian zonation schemes

	Elsterian	Holsteinian				Saalian
Proposed general zonation (Turner and West 1968)	/E1	HoI	HoII	HoIII	HoIV	eSa
England						
West (1956)	I	IIa	IIb-d	III	←IV →	
Turner (1970)	/Lo	HoI	HoIIa-c	HoIIIa-b	HoIVa-b	eGi
Ireland						
Jessen, Andersen, and Farrington (1959)		1	2	3	4 5 6	
Watts (1967)	G1 G2	G3	G4	G5	G6→	
Netherlands						
de Ridder and Zagwijn (1962)		1	2a	2b-c,?3		
Denmark & Germany						
Jessen and Milthers (1928)	a b	c d	e f	g h	i	k
Selle (1955)		I II	III	IV V	VI	
Andersen (1963)		1 2	← 3	→4 5		
Andersen (1965)		1 2	3 4	5 6 7	8 9	
Menke (1968)		HI HII	HIII			
Erd (1970)		1	2 3	4 5 6	7	
Müller (i.p.a)		I-VI	VII-IX	X-XIII	XIV-XV	
Poland						
Szafer (1953)		I	← II	→III	IV	
Środoń (1957)	IV	V	VIa-b	VII		
Środoń (1972)		I	II	→	←III	IV

As an example of both the need for and the uses of this scheme, and also its limitations, Table 1 provides a comparison of different zonation schemes used by various authors to describe Holsteinian vegetational successions, set within the framework suggested above.

PRE-ELSTERIAN INTERGLACIALS OF THE MIDDLE PLEISTOCENE

Interglacials of this age have very frequently been called Cromerian, since Woldstedt (1953) proposed the stage names Weybourne-Kaltzeit and Cromer-Warmzeit for two stages which preceded the Elster glaciation.

Both the Weybourne Crag and the Cromer Forest Bed Series are deposits occurring along the north coast of Norfolk, England, beneath the oldest glacial deposits of Britain. The antiquity of the Cromer Forest Bed Series is emphasized by a mammalian fauna containing such elements as *Dicerorhinus etruscus*, *Mimomys* and *Archidiskodon meridionalis*, as well as *Paleoloxodon antiquus*. Both studies of plant macrofossils (E. M. Reid 1920) and preliminary pollen analyses of the Cromer Forest Bed Series (Thomson in Woldstedt 1951; Duigan 1963) suggested, however, a vegetation of comparatively modern aspect with little evidence of species extinct or not living in Western Europe today. In the Netherlands Zagwijn and Zonneveld (1956) investigated an interglacial clay at Westerhoven, which, as well as containing *Dicerorhinus etruscus*, yielded a pollen diagram broadly similar to those of the British sites, that is, with almost no evidence of exotic elements and notably an absence of such genera as *Carya*, *Pterocarya*, and *Tsuga* which are so characteristic of the Lower Pleistocene Tiglian and Waalian interglacial periods of the Dutch succession. In consequence, palynologists have come to place the Lower/Middle Pleistocene boundary at the top of the Menapian glacial stage, the Baventian in Britain, since this seems to have been the cold period which finally was severe enough to suppress these three genera and prevent their reappearing, at least as a consistent assemblage together, in the vegetation of succeeding interglacial periods in Northwest Europe.

BRITAIN

The Cromer Forest Bed Series is now being reinvestigated by West and Wilson; in a preliminary report (1966) they reject the stratigraphic divisions of C. Reid (1882, 1890) and propose a division into two temperate interglacial periods separated by a severe cold period. The details of their provisional stratigraphic scheme are given in Table 2. Details of the type localities for these stages are given in Mitchell, et al. (1973). The type locality of the Cromerian interglacial *sensu stricto* is the Upper Freshwater Bed at West Runton, Norfolk. The name Cromerian should no longer be used for any deposits which cannot be correlated definitely with this horizon.

Stratigraphic Control

The above sequence has been built up partly from paleobotanical indications of climate and partly from stratigraphic observations of highly transient sections of this very complex series of marine, estuarine, and freshwater sediments. These outcrop intermittently along the coast of East Anglia for almost 100 kilometers from Weybourne to Kessingland. Perhaps the most extraordinary feature of the series is that deposits of two distinct interglacial periods, both containing evidences of marine transgression, and separated in time by a severe, probably truly glacial stage, should nevertheless be preserved in association at a number of sites at approximately the same height, close to modern sea level. Nevertheless, there is no doubt that two such interglacial stages are present; furthermore, it must be borne in mind that this stratigraphy is provisional and it is possible that an even more complex sequence may eventually emerge.

Everywhere these beds are overlain by glacial deposits of Anglian (formerly Lowestoftian = Elsterian) age, the Cromer Tills (West and Banham 1972). It is for this reason that the uppermost deposits of the series, which yield indications of arctic conditions — ice-wedge casts involutions, and an arctic-type flora, are ascribed to the early Anglian. There could, of course, be a somewhat larger hiatus in the stratigraphical succession here.

Table 2.   Provisional stratigraphic divisions (from West and Wilson 1966)

Stage	Deposit	Environment	Identified by C. Reid as:
Anglian	till	glacial	Cromer Till
(Lowestoftian)	mossy silts, sands ice wedge casts and involutions	cold freshwater permafrost	Arctic Freshwater Bed
Cromerian	silts, sands	temperate estuarine, marine	*Leda-myalis* Bed Forest Bed (estuarine)
	soil	temperate	
	muds, peats	temperate freshwater	Upper Freshwater Bed
Beestonian	silty marls	late-glacial freshwater	
	silts	cold freshwater	Arctic Freshwater Bed
	gravels, sands, clay-conglomerates	cold	Forest Bed (estuarine)
	ice wedge casts and involutions	permafrost	
Pastonian	silts and sands	temperate estuarine, marine	Weybourne Crag

Sediments of Beestonian glacial age lie well stratified between deposits of the two temperate interglacial stages in the cliffs between West Runton and Sheringham. The severity of the climate is indicated not only by arctic plant beds, containing *Betula nana*, *Salix* cf. *polaris*, *Salix* cf. *reticulata*, *Oxyria digyna*, and *Saxifraga oppositifolia*, but also by sediments showing festooning and a network of ice-wedge casts.

The so-called Weybourne Crag is a facies deposit of variable age. At its type site, at Weybourne, it is of Pastonian interglacial age, though believed by Woldstedt (1953) to fall within a glacial stage. At Beeston, Pastonian marine sediments rest on earlier marine and freshwater sediments formed during a preceding cold climatic stage. West (West and Wilson 1966; West 1972) believes that the Pastonian interglacial is represented not only by sediments within the Cromer Forest Bed Series on the Norfolk coast but also by the uppermost part of the fully marine Norwich Crag as at Ludham (West 1961) and by the Chillesford Crag much further south in East Anglia. In these latter areas and at Easton Bavents, type site of the Baventian (Funnell and West 1962), the Pastonian sediments rest unconformably on sediments of Baventian age. This indicates not only a widespread marine transgression during the Pastonian, but also the possibility, perhaps even the likelihood, of a major hiatus in the British Quaternary succession at this horizon.

Paleobotanical Characteristics

Unfortunately the pollen diagrams illustrating the vegetational development of these new stages are still unpublished. A limited amount of new information may be found in West (1972; Sparks and West 1972). Further, it is not easy to ascribe more than a few of Duigan's earlier pollen diagrams to horizons within this scheme.

In general the vegetational succession of both interglacial periods followed the typical interglacial pattern already outlined. Both begin with a pre-temperate zone with *Pinus, Betula,* and also *Picea.* In the Pastonian, zone II is dominated by mixed-oak forest trees, particularly *Ulmus* and *Quercus,* but *Carpinus* is also present from the onset of the zone so that a zone II/III boundary is rather difficult to recognize. *Corylus* is present, but not important. *Tilia* and *Abies* appear to be virtually absent during this interglacial, as are *Pterocarya, Carya,* and *Eucommia.* On the other hand, a few grains of *Tsuga* have been recorded from zone III at a number of sites, and it may be that this tree survived into the Pastonian in Britain at a very low frequency in the forests. For the Cromerian interglacial, pollen diagrams have been published from the type site at West Runton both by Thomson and by Duigan. These diagrams are somewhat inaccurate, because it was at first not realized that the lower part of the Upper Freshwater Bed is finely brecciated, so that the pollen spectra of the lower zones are confused by redeposition. The early-temperate zone, zone II is again dominated by *Ulmus* and *Quercus* in approximately equal amounts with quite high values of *Alnus* and again a very moderate amount of *Corylus*. *Tilia* appeared briefly towards the end of this zone. In zone III both *Carpinus* and later *Abies* became important; finally *Picea* expanded, leading into a post-temperate zone dominated by *Pinus* and *Betula*. Above this follow sediments with pollen spectra and plant macrofossils indicating a return to cold climatic conditions.

A thorough study of the plant macrofossils (Wilson 1973) has confirmed that relatively few plant taxa occur which are not found in Britain or elsewhere in northwest Europe today. In the Pastonian *Azolla filiculoides* and *Chamaedaphne calyculata* occur, in the Beestonian *Corispermum* and *Swertia perennis* and in the Cromerian *Azolla filiculoides*, *Alnus incana*, *Corema album*, and *Staphylea*.

THE NETHERLANDS

In the Netherlands the latest information (Zagwijn, v. Montfrans, and Zandstra 1971) suggests that at least three post-Menapian, pre-Elsterian interglacials can be recognized. Provisionally these are called Interglacials I, II, and III of the "Cromerian Complex", the intervening glacial periods are referred to as Glacial A and Glacial B. No doubt they will shortly receive local stage names.

Stratigraphic Control

All these divisions are based on palynological evidence from clay lenses within the thick marine and fluviatile sand and gravel formations of the Netherlands. The lower two interglacials lie within the Sterksel Formation, the uppermost near the base of the overlying Urk Formation, of which the younger sediments are of Elsterian and Holsteinian age. Deep boreholes at Waardenburg and Doordrecht suggest the following well stratified sequence of stages through the Sterksel Formation:

7.   An interstadial period near the top of the Sterksel Formation, characterized palynologically by a dominance of *Betula* and *Pinus* and low values for herbaceous pollen.

6.   Glacial B: high percentages of herbaceous pollen.

5.   Interglacial II: a fully temperate interglacial stage with dominant mixed-oak forest vegetation.

4.   Glacial A: high pollen percentages of *Juniperus* and herbaceous plants, indicating at least subarctic conditions.

3. Interglacial I: also a fully temperate interglacial stage with well-developed mixed-oak forest, but with zone III possessing a very characteristic *Carpinus-Eucommia* assemblage.

2. Menapian glacial period: partly within the Sterksel Formation and partly within the underlying Kedichem Formation, this possesses a characteristic cold-climate pollen flora dominated by herbaceous elements. This is the typical stratigraphic position of the Menapian at other sites.

1. Waalian interglacial (entirely within the Kedichem Formation): temperate pollen spectra not only with mixed-oak forest elements, but also with the *Pterocarya-Tsuga-Carya-Eucommia* assemblage characteristic of Lower Pleistocene temperate or interglacial periods in the Netherlands (Zagwijn 1960).

Zagwijn, v. Montfrans, and Zandstra (1971) put forward one particularly important piece of evidence concerning the dating of this sequence. Paleomagnetic studies show that the Matuyama-Brunhes boundary (0.7 million years) is situated between Interglacial I and part of Interglacial II, most probably within Glacial A. Interglacial I can be firmly correlated with the pollen spectra described from Loenermark (Polak, Maarleveld, and Nota 1962), and Interglacial II with the deposit already mentioned from Westerhoven (Zagwijn and Zonneveld 1956).

Interglacial III is less firmly substantiated. It appears that an interglacial horizon, not yet studied in detail, occurs in the northern part of the Netherlands in the basal part of the Urk Formation, but below the Elsterian fluvioglacial "Potklei" and certainly at a much deeper level than the Holsteinian beds usually found in that area. Such deposits occur for example in the borehole at Bergumerheide from 45–65 meters (Brouwer 1949) and at other unpublished sites, where in the past they have been confused with sediments of the Holsteinian.

Paleobotanical Characteristics

The full paleobotanical evidence from these deposits has not yet been published, but the most important features are summarized below.

INTERGLACIAL I   At Loenermark (Polak, Maarleveld, and Nota 1962) the pollen spectra cover zones II and III. The vegetational succession shows a full development of mixed-oak forest with abundant *Quercus* (up to 40 percent), *Ulmus* (up to 30 percent in zone II) and also *Alnus*. *Carpinus* occurs in both zones but is most abundant in zone III (up to 25 percent) together with *Eucommia* (10–15 percent), a type found otherwise only in earlier, Lower Pleistocene interglacials in the Netherlands. *Celtis* and *Abies* are both recorded and also *Carya*, but these taxa may or may not be diagnostic for the vegetation of this period.

INTERGLACIAL II Mixed-oak forest elements, especially *Quercus* (up to 60 percent) and *Ulmus* (up to 30 percent) are dominant. Other elements present are *Taxus, Corylus* and, sparsely, *Abies. Eucommia* is absent, and *Carpinus* is only present in some samples (less than 0.5 percent).

INTERGLACIAL III "As far as we can say now, this interglacial is similar to the Holsteinian in its vegetational sequence, except for *Ulmus* being more important in its lower part and *Abies* missing in its upper part" (Zagwijn, v. Montfrans, and Zandstra 1971).

Massulae and megasporangia of the water fern *Azolla filiculoides* have been recovered from both Loenermark and Westerhoven and from another deposit within the same complex at De Duno near Oosterbeek (Teunissen and Florschütz 1957).

DENMARK

Interglacial deposits occur at several sites in Denmark, which differ in their pollen record from typical Holsteinian and Eemian deposits. They are believed to be older and are referred to as the Harreskovian interglacial, since the most detailed published pollen diagrams are from lacustrine sediments at Harreskov in West Jutland (Jessen and Milthers 1928; Andersen 1965). Almost identical diagrams were obtained from similar sediments in the same region at Ølgod (Andersen 1965) and at Starup (Jessen and Milthers 1928).

Stratigraphic Control

The stratigraphical position of these deposits is still unclear. At Harreskov they are overlain by boulder clay and at Ølgod actually disturbed by ice-pushing. At Starup, Jessen and Milthers reported that they were further underlain by glacial clay. It would be of the greatest interest to know whether any of these deposits ultimately rests on a boulder clay deposit.

Paleobotanical Characteristics

The vegetational development of the Harreskovian interglacial has been analyzed in detail by Andersen (1966). A record from zones I-IV is present, almost the full span of the interglacial period. Percentages of *Ulmus* are particularly high at the onset of zone II (up to 55 percent) and so are those of *Taxus* in the same zone later on. The major dominant in both zones II and III is *Quercus*, but there are significant percentages of *Corylus* (up to 25 percent). *Carpinus* and *Eucommia* are both completely absent. *Picea*, present throughout the interglacial, increased in importance during zones III and IV.

At Ølgod, Andersen has described two interstadial periods from thin bands of organic sediment in the clay overlying the main interglacial deposit. The first interstadial, heralded by a peak of *Juniperus* pollen, shows a vegetational development with an incipient expansion of temperate trees, *Quercus*, *Ulmus*, *Taxus*, *Corylus*, and particularly *Alnus*. The second interstadial, again beginning with an expansion of *Juniperus* appears less temperate, the pollen spectra being dominated by *Betula* and *Pinus* with *Picea*, *Alnus* and a small amount of *Quercus*. The main difficulty in regarding these horizons as true interstadial periods is that the pollen spectra from the intervening thin clay bands do not really indicate any cooling of the climate between them. Bearing in mind the difficulty that the deposits at Ølgod have been affected by ice-pushing, clearly more information about these interstadial horizons is required.

The dating of these strata depends entirely on palynological evidence.

NORTHERN GERMANY

In the Harzvorland at least four sites are known where interglacial deposits ascribed to the "Cromerian Complex" have been investigated palynologically. One of these, Voigtstedt (Erd 1965), lies within the German Democratic Republic, the remainder, Bilshausen (Lüttig and Rein 1955; Müller 1965), the Elm (Goedeke, Grüger, and Beug 1966; Grüger 1968) and the Osterholz (Grüger 1968), in West Germany.

Stratigraphic Control

At all four sites the deposits lie within solution hollows of varying size and extent, associated with cavitation or salt solution of the underlying

Triassic strata. In this position they have escaped subsequent denudation. From a stratigraphical point of view, the most interesting site is the Elm, where organic interglacial deposits are not only overlain by till but also underlain by a strongly weathered till, both tills containing erratics of Scandinavian origin. On palynological grounds a Holsteinian age is excluded, and so, on stratigraphic grounds, is an Eemian age. The stratigraphy must, therefore, imply a major pre-Elsterian glaciation of North Germany, an event long suspected ("Elbe glaciation") but previously unproven. At the Osterholz, unfortunately, no glacial deposits were detected below the interglacial stratum, but overlying it is a till undoubtedly of Elster age, so that on stratigraphic grounds alone it must be pre-Elsterian. The palynological results in turn excluded a Lower Pleistocene age.

At Bilshausen a fuller and more complicated sequence of deposits occurs. The overlying strata consist of an upper and lower loess separated by a soil horizon. These have been ascribed to the Weichselian and Saalian glacial periods respectively. The composite sequence of older water-laid deposits is:

5. "Geröllage," perhaps a fluviatile gravel.
4. "T_2-Ton" (Gelkenbach Ton), grey organic silts.
3. Upper red clay, reddish-grey finely laminated clays and silt.
2. "Kohleton," finely laminated, dark grey, organic clay mud.
1. Lower red clay, reddish-grey, partly laminated clays, silts, and sands.

Beneath them lies brecciated and then solid Buntsandstein (Trias). The age of the deposit was not determined on stratigraphic grounds but indicated by finds of *Alces latifrons* and *Dicerorhinus etruscus* within the "Kohleton" and only later supported by palynological evidence.

The Voigtstedt sequence is certainly capped by glacial deposits of Elsterian age. The succession described by Krutzsch (1965) consists of:

8. Boulder clay — Elsterian.
7. Glacial laminated clays.
6. Fine silty sand (?loess).
5. Upper, pale gravel.
4. "Lehmschichten".
3. Lower, reddish gravel.
2. Muscheltone: clays and silts with freshwater molluscan remains.
1. Basal sands and gravels.

These in turn rest on Oligocene or Triassic sediments.

The "Lehmschichten," a series of alternating sands and clays, have been the subject of particular attention (Ruske 1965), because at their base occurs the main horizon from which a rich mammalian fauna has been recovered (see *Paläontologische Abhandlungen* A, 2[2–3] for 1965).

Periglacial phenomena are reported from several horizons within the Voigtstedt sequence. There are certainly well developed involutions and ice-wedge casts in the upper part of the "Lehmschichten," though the features reported by Krutzsch and Reichstein (1956) from the lower part of this stratum are not accepted as periglacial by Ruske. Finally, Krutzsch and Reichstein also believed that the upper and lower gravels showed evidence of being formed under permafrost conditions. The question, whether or not this is the case, must be of critical importance in the interpretation of the sequence at this site.

The important indications of the age of the site come from the stratigraphy and mammalian paleontology. However, Erd (1965, 1970) has proposed a more detailed subdivision of the lower part of the sequence, into three glacial and two interglacial stages, based on palynological evidence from the Muscheltone, the lower part of the "Lehmschichten," and on the evidence of the periglacial phenomena. He does not exclude the possibility of a more complex sequence.

Table 3. Stages of the Middle Pleistocene at Voigtstedt (after Erd 1965)

Stage	Evidence
Elsterian glacial period	Boulder clay, laminated clays etc.; cold climate phenomena in the upper gravel; involutions and ice-wedge casts in the upper part of the "Lehmschichten"; uppermost pollen spectrum (13) from the "Lehmschichten."
Voigtstedtian interglacial	Lower pollen spectra (2–10) from the "Lehmschichten" profile; weathering of lower gravel.
Helmian glacial period	Cold climate phenomena in lower gravel; uppermost pollen spectrum (16) of the Muscheltone.
Arternian interglacial	Pollen spectra (17–19) from the Muscheltone.
Unstrutian glacial period	Lower pollen spectra (20–25) from the Muscheltone.

Paleobotanical Characteristics

The vegetational successions indicated by the pollen diagrams from the Elm and the Osterholz are relatively straightforward, whereas at Voigtstedt the interpretation is more difficult; at Bilshausen the vegetational succession appears to be more complex than at any of the other sites in northwest Europe. The pollen diagrams from the Elm cover zones I and II of an interglacial vegetational succession, those from Osterholz early zone I to early zone IV. Fluctuating values for herbaceous pollen and perhaps for *Betula* at the Osterholz may be ascribed to local vegetational fluctuations within the basin of deposition due to changes in water level. At both sites, zones I and II show vegetational features characteristic of early Middle Pleistocene interglacial periods; *Picea* plays a minor role in zone I, *Ulmus* immigrates early and achieves joint dominance with *Quercus* in zone II. There is little else of note except for an expansion of *Tilia* at the Elm (though not at the Osterholz site) in the upper part of zone II, just below the horizon where the deposits are truncated by the overlying till. However, in the upper zones, which survive only at the Osterholz, there occurs a highly characteristic *Carpinus-Eucommia* assemblage very similar to those already described from Interglacial I in the Netherlands. From this zone there is virtually no trace of *Tsuga*, *Pterocarya*, or *Carya*, and only very occasional grains of *Abies*.

At Voigtstedt Erd (1965, 1970) believes that he has a pollen record from two interglacial periods. In the stratigraphically lower diagram (Arternian), widely spaced pollen samples suggest a vegetational development from a subarctic period characterized by high herbaceous pollen, including Gramineae, *Artemisia*, and Chenopodiaceae, through a pre-temperate zone with *Pinus*, *Betula*, and *Picea*, to a temperate zone with *Quercus* and *Ulmus*; this last zone also contains a persistently high amount of Gramineae and Chenopodiaceae pollen, perhaps representing local halophyte sites in the vicinity. There is no sign of a late-temperate zone; but this is not surprising since samples could only be recovered at meter intervals. However, at the top of the sequence a single pollen sample shows even higher values of Gramineae with very little thermophilous pollen, so that Erd has put this forward as evidence for a return to subarctic conditions. Above the intervening lower gravels Erd has found evidence of a further segment of an interglacial period which he calls Voigtstedtian. Thermophilous pollen indicative of a zone III, late-temperate vegetation is found, namely *Ulmus*, *Tilia*, *Abies*, *Carpinus*, and *Alnus* but no *Quercus*. The pollen is in a poor state of preservation and the absence of the latter taxon is attributed to this cause. Higher in the diagram occurs a transition to a zone IV dominated by *Pinus* and *Picea* with, above this, once again, a single pollen sample suggesting a transition to a steppe or glacial climate. Above this horizon, however, there is good evidence of periglacial phenomena in the sediments.

It is clear that a further borehole through the lower part of the Voigtstedt sequence would be rewarding. Until this is done there will be continuing speculation as to whether the Arternian in fact represents only the early part of the Voigtstedtian interglacial. The stratigraphical evidence against this, the occurrence of permafrost phenomena reported in the lower gravels, also needs further investigation.

A number of workers have published pollen diagrams from Bilshausen (Lüttig and Rein 1955; Chanda 1962; Averdieck and v. d. Brelie 1963; Müller 1965). The relationship of these diagrams has been discussed by Müller. His results suggest that the site is more complex in its vegetational development than other lower Middle Pleistocene sites, and that in the early part of the interglacial the succession was definitely different; therefore it is difficult to describe it under the zonal system so far employed.

The interglacial succession is found entirely within the "Kohleton." The pollen record from the underlying Lower red clay suggests a preceding cold period with a vegetation dominated by herbaceous vegetation and by *Betula nana*. During this stage, Müller (i.p.a) recognizes three interstadial intervals. Above the "Kohleton" Chanda described a succeeding cold period, during which time the "T$_2$-Ton" was deposited. This too was characterized by herbaceous vegetation, with two interstadial periods, showing a re-expansion of *Betula* and *Pinus*.

A superficial look at Müller's pollen diagram from the "Kohleton" suggests a subdivision into two distinct episodes of vegetational succession, from the upper and lower parts of the stratum respectively. The lower succession is unusual; instead of beginning with a *Betula-Pinus* assemblage, the interglacial appears to have had a pioneer tree vegetation of *Ulmus*, *Picea*, *Pinus*, and *Alnus*. Furthermore these trees persisted at much the same frequency into undoubtedly temperate times, when they were joined by *Tilia* cf. *cordata*. During this period *Quercus* was present (ca. 5 percent) but failed to expand until the final zone of this lower succession, when *Abies*, freshly immigrated, *Picea*, and *Quercus* became the most important trees. Only low values of *Carpinus* are found.

In the middle of the "Kohleton" succession, with apparently no signs of any stratigraphical break, this vegetational developmental sequence was interrupted by a sudden short expansion of *Betula* and *Picea* at the expense of almost all the temperate trees. From then onwards a more typical series of interglacial pollen zones can be traced. First came a zone dominated by *Quercus*, also with maxima for *Ulmus* and *Tilia*, i.e. a typical zone II, next a zone of late-temperate aspect, dominated by *Carpinus*, *Abies*, and *Quercus* and finally a transition through a *Picea* zone into a post-temperate zone dominated by *Pinus* and *Betula*.

The entire "Kohleton" sequence was laminated in the borehole studied by Müller. As described in more detail later, he considers that the complete interglacial succession here at Bilshausen lasted for 28,000 to 36,000 years.

THE CORRELATION OF PRE-ELSTERIAN INTERGLACIAL PERIODS

It is clear that there are considerable difficulties in the correlation of deposits of this age. They are much less frequent than those of younger interglacial periods, often lie in either uninformative or complex stratigraphical positions, and the pollen diagrams, where they have been published, are by no means easy to interpret. Most of these diagrams seem to share particular features of zones I and II which, taken together, make them readily distinguishable from those of Holsteinian or Eemian age. *Picea* first appears in zone I, *Ulmus* immigrates early and is particularly abundant and often dominant in zone II; during the temperate zones mixed-oak forest species are generally far more abundant than *Pinus*. These common features, however, make it virtually impossible to distinguish isolated fragments of a pollen record of these zones as belonging to particular early Middle Pleistocene stages. Clearly the Elm diagram is a case in point.

In zone III though, the different diagrams do exhibit distinct differences. Some show *Carpinus-Eucommia* assemblages, in others *Carpinus* is distinctively absent or very sparse, some have *Abies* in abundance, others only as traces. In the interpretation of these differences matters such as local habitats, regional distribution patterns, sediment source, have to be taken into account.

Finally there are the differing kinds of evidence that evoke some notion of the existence of a glacial stage above, below or between temperate pollen sequences; these are boulder clay, gravels with periglacial features stratified within them, sequences of pollen spectra yielding high herbaceous pollen values, single spectra showing the same thing, and pollen spectra which indicate sharp periods of cooling, but not below the threshold for forest growth. How reliable are these, and can they be used for correlation purposes with any real certainty?

The most reliable stratigraphical sequence at present seems to be that from the Netherlands, indicating at least three temperate interglacial periods during the interval under discussion. This stratigraphy is supported by evidence of superposition, of differing pollen records and of association with gravel suites which are sedimentologically distinctive. A very good case can be made for a correlation of the Osterholz deposit with Interglacial I (the "Loenermark interglacial") on the grounds of the distinctive *Carpinus-Eucommia* assemblage in zone III. A plausible correlation can be made between the Harreskovian deposits of Denmark and Interglacial II (the "Westerhoven interglacial") on the grounds of a general similarity of the vegetational succession and particularly the absence of *Carpinus* and *Abies* in Denmark, and the very small amounts of these two pollen types which occur in the Westerhoven diagram. Grüger correlated the fragmentary pollen diagram from the Elm with that from the Oster-holz. This is possible but no more likely than a correlation with any other interglacial stages of this general age reported from the Netherlands. In fact, since this deposit overlies a highly significant till deposit, it is more important to note a failure to pinpoint the exact age of this deposit than to make speculations.

Although Britain is, in terms of distance, close to the Netherlands, it is not yet possible to suggest any firm correlation between the British sequence and the one suggested by Zagwijn, v. Montfrans, and Zandstra. Both the Pastonian and the Cromerian contain appreciable amounts of *Carpinus*, the Cromerian also contains fairly high values of *Abies*. No trace of *Eucommia* has been found in spectra from either age. Without the evidence of detailed pollen diagrams, it is not easy to maintain a critical discussion on these points.

Again, neither Voigtstedt nor Bilshausen can be correlated satisfactorily with the Dutch sequence. The former site yields evidence which is too fragmentary and stratigraphically too uncertain to be used satisfactorily in what is clearly a very complicated matter anyway. Nevertheless the site certainly is important and might yield vital evidence. Tentative correlations have naturally been put forward between Voigtstedt and Bils-hausen. The vegetational sequence at the latter site clearly cannot be correlated at all, at least in its lower part, with the Osterholz or the Nether-lands sites, nor certainly with Britain and Denmark. We must ask whether a quite different interglacial period from those recorded elsewhere is re-presented here, or whether this part of Germany lay within or on the borders of a different climatic and vegetational province during the early Middle Pleistocene. Certainly the indications of rather high percentages of herbaceous pollen at both Bilshausen and Voigtstedt even during ap-parently temperate zones, give rise to thoughts of steppe plant communi-ties at no great distance as much as of the suggested local halophyte sites. On the other hand some of this herbaceous pollen may, as has recently been proposed (Turner i.p.), be ascribed to the effects on the vegetation of local grazing pressures around water-holes frequented by large mam-mals.

ELSTERIAN INTERSTADIAL DEPOSITS

In the pollen record, there is as yet very little if any evidence for intra-

Elsterian interstadial periods. The interstadial pollen spectra overlying the Bilshausen and Ølgod deposits have already been mentioned. Really, there are no good reasons for placing these within the Elsterian stage rather than in some pre-Elsterian cool or glacial interval. They surely do not postdate the first Elsterian ice advance. With the discovery of glacial till actually underlying pre-Elsterian interglacial deposits at the Elm, the whole question of the subdivision of the Elster glaciation needs careful re-examination.

THE HOLSTEINIAN INTERGLACIAL PERIOD

Interglacial deposits of Holsteinian age have been found at numerous localities in Northwest Europe. Unlike the pre-Elsterian deposits, they are strongly characterized by a number of features that seldom leave their age in doubt, particularly if any substantial palynological evidence is available. For these reasons, individual sites will seldom be discussed in detail, as they were for the earlier interglacial periods.

Stratigraphically it is certain that the Holsteinian lies between the Elsterian and Saalian glacial periods. Whether or not the Saalian directly follows the Holsteinian, will be discussed in the next section. Rarely, as at Ummendorf, Germany (Selle 1941), and in the neighborhood of Berlin (Erd 1960), may interglacial layers of Holsteinian age actually be found stratified between Elsterian and Saalian tills. Often Holsteinian deposits are preserved, laid down in deep troughs within the Elster till (cf. Weichselian tunnel valleys in Denmark), and these indicate clearly that the onset of interglacial lacustrine conditions followed very rapidly on deglaciation.

At various sites in northern Germany, Denmark, England, and France, interglacial deposits of this age are associated with a major marine transgression (the Holsteinian transgression) which reached levels well above both modern sea level and that of the Eemian transgression.

Because of the great number of sites which have been studied, the vegetational development of the interglacial is well known. Over much of the region there was a uniformity both of the dominant taxa and of the succession in which the major forest trees immigrated. Nevertheless, distinctive trends between the relatively oceanic west and the more continental east of the region are very much apparent in the major features of the vegetational succession.

ELSTERIAN LATE-GLACIAL   Soon after the melting of the ice sheets, a dwarf shrub vegetation developed, characterized by *Salix* spp., *Juniperus* and, particularly in the west, *Hippophaë*. At Hoxne, England, Coope (personal communication) reports that thermophilous species of beetles already appear in a stratum of this age (Turner 1968), suggesting a very rapid rise in mean annual temperatures in the late Elsterian, similar to that known to have taken place during pollen zone I of the late-Weichselian, prior to the Allerød interstadial. Under these late-glacial conditions certain elements of beetle faunus appear to have been able to migrate in reaction to environmental changes much more swiftly than the vegetation belts.

ZONE I Everywhere this zone was dominated by *Betula* and *Pinus*. From the southeast Netherlands eastwards, *Picea* was present at least at a low frequency reaching values of 2–4 percent in pollen diagrams from Denmark and Poland. To the west, elsewhere in the Netherlands, in England and in Ireland, there is almost no trace of *Picea*, which did not immigrate there until zone II, indeed, to some parts of Ireland not until zone III. At most sites, the earliest thermophilous trees to immigrate during zone I were *Ulmus*, *Quercus*, and *Alnus*. It is not certain whether *Alnus glutinosa* or possibly *Alnus incana*, was the species involved. Later in the interglacial the former species was certainly the important one. No particular order of immigration can be recognized as of general occurrence for these taxa.

ZONE II Characteristically the vegetation of zone II was dominated by *Pinus* and *Alnus*, with the mixed-oak forest trees, *Quercus*, *Ulmus*, *Tilia*, and *Taxus* expanding a little but never becoming the true dominants of the vegetation, at least in the area from the Netherlands eastwards. This feature above all separates the vegetational development of the Holsteinian interglacial from that of the pre-Elsterian and the Eemian interglacials and likewise of the Flandrian; during all these periods mixed-oak forest trees were dominant in this zone. At the same time, *Picea* achieved its maximum participation in the forest in all those areas into which it had successfully immigrated in zone I. Andersen (1969) has suggested that the failure of mesocratic, mixed-oak forest species to expand at this time was due to a widespread occurrence of sandy soils, poor in lime, following the Elsterian glaciation. These could have been rapidly leached and podzolized, particularly if they were colonized at an early stage by *Picea*.

Certainly there was a great vegetational contrast in the west, in England and in northwest France, where *Picea* was never important in zones I or II; here the soils, particularly where the ice had left behind spreads of chalky boulder clay, were highly calcareous. In these areas, *Pinus* declined rapidly after zone I, and, although *Alnus* became widespread and important, the dominant forest trees were, as in other interglacial periods, the mixed-oak forest species, *Quercus, Ulmus,* and *Corylus,* with *Taxus* and *Tilia* locally fairly abundant.

Even farther west, however, in Ireland, the situation — at most though not all sites — unexpectedly resembles not that of England, but continental Europe with again *Pinus* and *Alnus* greatly exceeding the mixed-oak forest elements.

ZONE III   This again shows a generally uniform stage in the vegetational succession from sites right across northwest Europe. Everywhere it is characterized by the expansion of *Carpinus* and *Abies,* except that the former tree failed to reach Ireland. This developed into a vegetation type characterized in pollen diagrams by an *Abies-Alnus* assemblage. With this assemblage are found small amounts of *Buxus* and *Vitis* pollen at many sites, and of pollen of *Celtis* type in Germany. At the Polish and some German sites this zone contains the maximum expansion of *Quercus* and *Corylus,* which elsewhere took place in zone II.

One of the most important features for the correlation of the Holsteinian interglacial period across Europe is the immigration of the "Tertiary relic" *Pterocarya* into the region during the latter part of this zone. This tree is not known to have occurred in northwest Europe in any other Middle Pleistocene interglacial period, although it was characteristic of the Lower Pleistocene temperate stages. So far its pollen has been found at virtually identical horizons in diagrams from Poland, Germany, Denmark, the Netherlands, and England. At some of these sites small amounts of *Fagus* pollen have been detected at about the same level. Fruits of *Pterocarya* have been recorded from a single deposit of this age in the Rhineland (v. d. Brelie, Kilpper, and Teichmüller 1959). The record of *Keteleeria* from that site is no longer accepted.

Because of the maximum development of *Quercus* in their area in zone III, eastern European workers have tended to regard this zone as the thermal maximum of the interglacial. In the west, zone II has been regarded as so, for the same reason. The evidence from indicator species such as *Hedera, Ilex,* and particularly *Vitis* suggests that both these zones had summer temperatures at least as warm as today, if not warmer. The vegetational changes are to be seen as principally a response to seral and edaphic factors rather than temperature. At the same time, particularly from western evidence, a case can be made for an increase in rainfall having taken place during zone III.

At this point the question must be raised as to how synchronous the vegetation-zone boundaries are likely to have been during this stage across the breadth of Western Europe, in particular the zone II/III boundary.

Clearly an exact answer cannot yet be given, though it may lie in the future development of a lamination chronology. The general pattern of development of the pollen diagrams suggests that the differing age of the *Quercus* maximum across the area must be a reality. On the other hand, in Poland and much of Germany *Carpinus* and *Abies* can be shown to have both immigrated at approximately the same time. Further west, in the Netherlands, Britain and in Denmark, *Carpinus* appears to have arrived distinctly in advance of *Abies*. One interpretation is that this *Carpinus* advent is more or less synchronous across the area, with *Carpinus* migrating northwards from southern Europe, but with *Abies*, like *Picea* earlier in the interglacial, and perhaps like *Pterocarya* later, expanding from refugia in southeast Europe, in the Balkans or Carpathians and therefore reaching the eastern part of the region first. Alternatively, the immigration of *Carpinus* into Western Europe may simply have taken place earlier than in the east, for quite other reasons, with the advent of *Abies* taking place from the south, perhaps including oceanic biotypes which became extinct during later glaciations, and thus being broadly synchronous across northwest Europe.

ZONE IV The expansion of *Pinus* and, to a lesser extent, of *Betula* which is found in pollen diagrams of this age from right across Europe must indicate a fairly severe climatic deterioration. At first *Abies* and *Pterocarya* persisted, though thermophilous trees dwindled rapidly. Likewise *Picea* persisted in some areas. In the west, particularly in Britain and in Ireland but to a lesser extent elsewhere, there is evidence of the temporary development of oceanic heathland, dominated by Ericaceae and *Empetrum* and with an extension of bogs. In Ireland such vegetation, particularly characterized by *Rhododendron ponticum*, probably persisted into the succeeding early glacial period, but elsewhere, as colder, drier conditions spread, open subarctic grassland with herbs such as *Artemisia* and dwarf shrub vegetation with *Salix* spp. and *Juniperus* replaced the forest.

A characteristic feature of the vegetation of the Holsteinian interglacial which has not so far been mentioned is the presence, often in abundance, of the water fern *Azolla filiculoides*. This has been identified from Ireland, England, the Netherlands, Germany, and Poland. It probably occurs in almost all suitable freshwater deposits of this age but in the past has frequently been overlooked. Its major stratigraphic importance is that it has never been recorded from Eemian deposits anywhere in Europe, except in a context which suggested redeposition from earlier strata. It seems certain that this species was exterminated from the flora of northwest Europe by the severe conditions of the Saalian glacial period.

GERMANY

The type area for the Holsteinian interglacial, as defined by Woldstedt (1953), is the neighborhood of Lauenburg, where marine deposits of the Holstein sea occur. The following important sites of this age have been investigated by means of pollen analysis: in the German Democratic Republic, the *Paludina* beds of Berlin (Erd 1960), Pritzwalk (zones I-III), Granzin (zones I-IV) (Erd 1970); in the Federal Republic of Germany, Hamburg-Hummelsbüttel (zones I-III) (Hallik 1960), Münster-Breloh (zones II-IV) (Müller i.p.a), and Wacken (zones I-II) (Menke 1968).

Stratigraphical Control

The stratigraphical position of these deposits between the Elster and Saale ice advances is generally undisputed. Some deposits actually lie stratified between tills of this age, others in troughs floored by Elster till. In the lower Rhine valley, both the Krefelder Schichten (Kaiser and Schütrumpf 1960), which are ice-pushed, and the deposits at Frimmers-dorf (v. d. Brelie, Kilpper, and Teichmüller 1959) have been ascribed to this interglacial. But, according to Brunnacker (this volume), they belong to terraces of different ages. At present, the pollen assemblage with *Pterocarya* from Frimmersdorf suggests that it is this deposit which is most likely to be of Holsteinian age. At Hummelsbüttel, Pritzwalk, and Granzin there is good evidence for a rise of sea level in zone II and a gradual regression of the sea in the latter part of zone III. The maximum height of the transgression is not clear from these investigations. At Wacken there is evidence of an earlier marine interlude during the El-sterian late-glacial, presumably as a result of continuing isostatic depression of Schleswig-Holstein at that period.

Paleobotanical Characteristics

There is an urgent need for an agreed biostratigraphical type site in this area. Historically the most important site is that at Hummelsbüttel, but the pollen diagram, lacking evidence for *Taxus* and herbaceous pollen, needs revision. A very detailed pollen diagram has recently been prepared by Müller (i.p.a), which unfortunately lacks zone I (but see Meyer i.p.). Nevertheless it is taken from laminated sediments which, when counted, yielded an estimate of 16,000–17,000 years for the total duration of the interglacial.

The Münster-Breloh diagram shows a number of particularly interesting features. Firstly, zone II was interrupted by a brief expansion of *Pinus*, *Betula*, and Gramineae at the expense of thermophilous trees. Müller correlates this interval, which had a duration of 200–400 years, with the similar high non-tree pollen phase, with about the same duration, which West (1956) and Turner (1970) recorded from sites in East Anglia during the same zone. Müller believes that these represent a short, sharp period of climatic deterioration. A similar but possibly composite phase, again with *Pinus*, *Betula*, and Gramineae expanding suddenly, is repeated during zone III, when *Carpinus* received a severe, though temporary setback. This second phase has not been identified elsewhere with certainty. At this site the maximum expansion of *Quercus* is attained after this second phase during zone III.

Finally Müller suggests that the pollen diagram indicates two interstadial periods which occurred after the completion of the main interglacial succession or possibly during zone IV. They are said to be separated by periods when heathland developed. However, although at least the lower of these so-called interstadials lay within undisturbed laminated sediment, the pollen flora of both so strongly resembles in all respects that of late zone III, with a repetition of the spectra for *Abies*, *Picea*, *Quercus*, and even *Pterocarya*, *Celtis*, and *Fagus*, that there seems to be some probability that these horizons are greatly enriched by reworked sediment rather than representing episodes of climatic change.

DENMARK

Only two interglacial deposits of this age are known from Denmark. The first, from Tornskov (zones I-IV) (Andersen 1963) are entirely marine sediments, the other at Vejlby (zones I-IV) (Andersen 1965) freshwater lacustrine sediments, stratified between two tills. In both these pollen diagrams it is difficult to make a clear separation between zones I and II. In particular at Vejlby there appears to be an interesting early expansion of *Fraxinus*. Since the deposits at this site are in part laminated, it is to be hoped that a fuller and more detailed account of the site will eventually be published.

POLAND

A comparatively large number of pollen diagrams, as well as studies of plant macrofossils, have been published from sites of this stage, locally called the Masovian interglacial. Again the stratigraphical position is generally undisputed. Amongst the many sites on which excellent investigations have been carried out, special mention might be made of Nowiny Zukowskie (zones I-IV) (Dyakowska 1952), Wylezin (zones I-IV) (Dyakowska 1956), Olszewice (zones I-IV) (Sobolewska 1956a) and Syrniki (zones I-III) (Sobolewska 1956b). A recent review of the period has been published by Środoń (1972). The most important features of the vegetational succession of the interglacial in Poland have already been covered in the previous discussion.

THE NETHERLANDS

Not many Holsteinian pollen diagrams have been published from the Netherlands, and most of these are fragmentary, since they come from clay-layers found in borings through fluviatile gravels. One site that is particularly important, however, is that at Bantega (Brouwer 1949; Zagwijn 1973), where the pollen record covers virtually the whole interglacial. The local stage name for the interglacial is Needian, because deposits of zone III age were long recognized from the clay pit at Neede (van der Vlerk and Florschütz 1953). Stratigraphically this exposure was very significant, because the interglacial deposits were ice-pushed during the succeeding Saalian ice-advance, the only certain period of glaciation in the Netherlands. The strata at Rosmalen (de Ridder and Zagwijn 1962), formerly ascribed to the Holsteinian, are now believed to belong to Interglacial III of the "Cromerian Complex" (Zagwijn, personal communication).

In some respects the Holsteinian vegetational succession in the Netherlands resembles that of Germany, for example in the dominance of *Pinus* and *Alnus* in zone II, which is not surprising in view of the generally non-calcareous nature of the soils there. On the other hand, other features, such as the late immigration of *Picea* form a link with the English successions.

ENGLAND

In England the equivalent of the Holsteinian interglacial is believed to be the Hoxnian interglacial period. The major sites which have been investigated palynologically are Hoxne (zones I-III) (West 1956), Marks Tey (zones I-IV) (Turner 1970) and Nechells, Birmingham (zones I-IV)

(Kelly 1964), but the deposit at Clacton-on-Sea (zones II-III) (Pike and Godwin 1953) is also of considerable interest.

Stratigraphical Control

At Hoxne, Marks Tey and a number of minor sites, deposits of Hoxnian age rest directly on boulder clay of Anglian (Elsterian) age. Mostly they were formed as lake sediments in basins and troughs left behind on the deglaciated land surface of East Anglia. In Britain the Anglian glaciation was certainly more extensive than the Wolstonian (Saalian). Indeed, the precise limits of the latter glaciation are still uncertain and a matter of debate. Nowhere in eastern England can boulder clay be seen overlying Hoxnian deposits, but at Nechells the interglacial deposit is said to lie within a sedimentary sequence which elsewhere underlies the oldest Wolstonian till of the Midlands. It is probable that other unpublished interglacial deposits of this age in that area will be shown to lie between the two tills.

In the Nar Valley, north Norfolk (Stevens 1960), at Clacton, and at an unpublished site at Walton-on-the-Naze, Essex, very close to the latter town, there is evidence of a major marine transgression during zone III which reached a height of some 20 meters above present sea level.

Paleobotanical Characteristics

At first sight pollen diagrams from the Hoxnian interglacial look strikingly different from Holsteinian ones on the Continent. These differences, when examined in detail, consist of the expansion to dominance of mixed-oak forest trees during zone II and the failure of *Picea* to immigrate early or make any substantial impact on the zone II forest, as it had done in more easterly regions. An explanation already discussed for the former feature has been put forward by Andersen (1966), and the latter can be set in the context of a much wider trend across Europe. On the other hand, the Hoxnian is the youngest known interglacial period in Britain from which *Azolla filiculoides* has been recovered; indeed, it has occurred at almost every site of this age; the general succession in which the major forest taxa immigrated is virtually identical to that found in sites from Denmark and north Germany; zone III is characterized by abundant *Abies* pollen, a feature common to all Holsteinian pollen diagrams for this zone, but not of Eemian pollen diagrams from approximately the area west of the river Elbe (Selle 1960); together with *Abies* immigrated *Buxus* and *Vitis*, both typical components of the *Abies-Alnus* pollen assemblage of this stage from Germany, Denmark, and Poland; finally the most striking piece of evidence is the appearence of *Pterocarya* in the pollen record from zones III and IV at Marks Tey. This pollen type has now also been recovered from an unpublished Hoxnian site in the Midlands (Herbert-Smith, personal communication).

A recent paper by Bristow and Cox (1973) has suggested that, because no boulder clay can be discovered overlying the Hoxnian deposits of eastern England, the Anglian tills should be correlated with Saalian tills on the Continent, both representing the glaciation of maximum extent. On this reasoning they suggest an Eemian age for both the Hoxnian and Ipswichian interglacial periods in Britain. Clearly this view is quite untenable, both on the paleobotanical evidence and on that of a high-level marine transgression. The problem of the relative extent of different glaciations, which will again be apparent in the discussion of Ireland, is certainly bound up with the fact that, except for a very local area along the east coast of Britain, the ice sheets which covered Britain had a different source of supply from those of the Netherlands and north Germany, which originated in Scandinavia.

Paleobotanical Evidence for the Age of Archeological Horizons

At two sites in Britain, which are considered in more detail in another paper in this volume (Gladfelter), it has been possible to locate archeological horizons within the framework of pollen stratigraphy of the Hoxnian interglacial. The first of these sites is at Hoxne where West (West and McBurney 1954; West 1956) showed that the earliest handaxe industry at this site came from a level near the top of zone II (subzone Ho IIc) where a high non-tree pollen phase occurred, already mentioned in connection with a similar phase from Münster-Breloh. Turner (1970) has investigated this phase further, showing that teeth of *Paleoloxodon antiquus* found in the Hoxne pits also came from this level, and that the same phase, in which a fall in the percentages of certain thermophilous trees is followed by an expansion of herbs and then of *Betula* and *Pinus*, could be identified in the pollen record from Marks Tey, some 60 kilometers distant; here the onset of the phase was associated with finely disseminated charcoal in the sediments, which at this site are also laminated. Neither West nor Turner believe that Paleolithic man was directly responsible for the deforestation that appears to have taken place. Indeed, the phase has now been identified at yet another site equally distant from the first two, so that it bears more than just a local significance. Nevertheless, the detailed succession of ecological changes which appear to have taken place at Hoxne and at Marks Tey during this short interval — some 300 years according to the lamination chronology at the latter site — do not fully support Müller's hypothesis of a climatic deterioration. A further handaxe industry is found on the surface, or just below the surface of the coarse detritus mud forming West's Stratum D. This stratum is known to belong to subzone Ho IIIa, when *Alnus, Quercus,* and *Carpinus* dominated the forest. Here, at this level, no period of open conditions in the forest has yet been proved, so that it is important to try to confirm whether man was living in a forest environment or whether the artifacts derive from a later period, perhaps at the end of the interglacial or in the succeeding early-glacial, before younger deposits were laid down unconformably on this surface. Certainly, further archeological horizons occur in the overlying strata described by Gladfelter (this volume).

The second site, at which the age of an archeological horizon has been indicated by palynological studies, is at Clacton-on-Sea, where Kerney and Turner (Kerney 1971) have shown that in the now concealed West Cliff section the famous Clactonian industry came from subzone Ho IIb or earlier and certainly predated the earliest handaxe industry at Hoxne. Their work, based on both pollen and molluscan stratigraphy, enables a correlation to be made with Swanscombe, where the Clactonian industry also falls within the early zones of this interglacial.

At the golf course site at Clacton-on-Sea (Singer, et al. 1973), attempts have been made to date both the basal gravel and the marl by means of pollen analysis using a flotation method to extract small quantities of pollen from large samples of sediment. Pollen in the marl is both very sparse and highly corroded. Because *Pinus* pollen is relatively far more resistant to destruction than that of thermophilous pollen, the tentative conclusions (based on relative frequencies of these pollen types) that the marl is of zone Ho I age should be treated with great caution. Neither these results nor the faunal evidence would exclude a zone Ho II age. The pollen analyses from the basal gravels are fraught with problems. First, the age of fine-grained material emplaced within gravels in a region of fluctuating water levels is open to doubt. Second, the stratum is described as having a "mixed flora" because three samples yielded dominantly herbaceous pollen spectra with few tree types and a single further sample fair amounts of temperate tree pollen, including *Fagus*, normally a good indicator of the late-Flandrian. In considering the validity of these spectra, it must be remembered that the pollen concentration in these sediments is, at any reckoning exceedingly low, perhaps 1/10,000 of that from the fine-grained lacustrine and fluviatile sediments to which pollen analysis is normally applied. Clearly such samples are many times more liable to distortion by contamination, post-depositionally, during sampling, or within the laboratory. Flotation methods are normally used in pollen analysis of loesses or cave deposits, where it is recognized that the original rate of sedimentation of pollen was very low. The uncritical use of such methods on sediments where the low pollen frequency is due to post-depositional destruction can only give rise to misleading results and bring this whole method of analysis into disrepute. In this case there seems little doubt that it is better to rely on the faunal and geomorphological rather than the palynological evidence in assessing the age and climate during which these basal gravels with their contained Clactonian industry were deposited.

NORTHERN FRANCE

Few interglacial deposits have been recorded from anywhere in this area. However, at Trez-Rouz, Finistère, Morzadec-Kerfourn (1969; cf. Kerfourn 1965) has described interglacial deposits belonging to zones II and III. Although she suggests that deposits of both Eemian and Holsteinian age are present, it seems probably that the interglacial sediments are all of one age, but have been subject to disturbance within the cliff sequence. The general aspect of the diagram, particularly the high values for *Abies*, suggest a Holsteinian age.

IRELAND

Virtually all the well-stratified interglacial deposits which have been discovered in Ireland appear to belong to the same stage, which has been named the Gortian. Several sites are known, of which four have been published in detail: Gort (Jessen, Andersen, and Farrington 1959), Kilbeg (Watts 1959), Baggotstown (Watts 1964), and Kildromin (Watts 1967). Stratigraphically only the Baggotstown deposit is believed to rest on till, but almost all are overlain by glacial moraine. This is clearly the reverse of the stratigraphical situation in England, and yet on biostratigraphical grounds the Hoxnian and the Gortian are believed to belong to the same interglacial period.

Paleobotanical Characteristics

As has been discussed earlier, the dominance of *Pinus* even during zone II of this interglacial in Ireland makes the vegetational succession there appear more akin to that of continental deposits than that of England. Nevertheless Watts (1959) has pointed out several features which link Gortian sites to the Hoxnian as well. Common to both areas are: a very great abundance of *Hippophaë* during the preceding late-glacial; the presence of *Azolla filiculoides*; the presence of a period when *Alnus* and *Taxus* were important elements in the pollen rain; a rapid expansion of *Abies*. Likewise, there is a common problem in the presence of an unidentified tricolpate reticulate pollen type (Type X of Turner 1970), which occurs in these Irish sites and at Hoxne, Marks Tey, and Clacton.

Particularly striking local features of the Gortian vegetational succession are the luxuriant evergreen communities, with *Abies*, *Taxus*, *Ilex*, *Picea*, and particularly *Rhododendron ponticum* which occurred during the latter part of zone III, and the presence even in Gortian times of some of the Lusitanian vegetational elements such as *Daboecia cantabrica*, *Erica mackaiana*, *Erica ciliaris*, and *Eriocaulon septangulare* which are characteristic today of the extreme oceanic Altantic fringe of Europe.

During the Holsteinian-Hoxnian interglacial it seems unlikely that any marine channel separated Britain from the contnental mainland. It is clear that *Carpinus*, *Abies*, and *Pterocarya* were all able to reach Britain without difficulty. *Abies* also managed to reach Ireland, but *Carpinus*, and more strikingly *Tilia*, apparently did not, nor did exotic species like *Rhododendron* reach England even when oceanic heathland existed. There seems a much greater likelihood, therefore, that Ireland remained an island even in Holsteinian times.

THE DÖMNITZ INTERGLACIAL

At two sites recently, in Northern Germany, both stratigraphic and paleobotanical evidence has been put forward for the existence of a fully temperate interglacial period during the interval between the end of the Holsteinian and the first ice advance of the Saale glaciation. At Pritzwalk (Erd 1970), a borehole passed through Saalian till and successively into an upper interglacial deposit showing zones I to early III of a distinctive vegetational succession, next into glaciolacustrine sands, then down into a fully developed Holsteinian interglacial deposit capped by an early-glacial zone where Gramineae steppe and shrub tundra were indicated.

Distinctive characteristics of the upper interglacial deposit are: low values of Pinus in zone II, but high *Quercus* and *Alnus*; in this area this alone serves to distinguish the succession from the Holsteinian. However it also contains *Azolla filiculoides*, with *Carpinus*, *Corylus*, and *Taxus* all immigrating in zone III. This clearly excludes any remote possibility of an Eemian age.

A somewhat similar pollen diagram has been published also by Erd (1970) from Kap Arkona on the island of Rügen. According to Cepek (1967) this deposit is stratified within the Saale tills and is younger than the so-called Dömnitzian interglacial of Pritzwalk. Erd nevertheless points out that many of the characteristics of the Rügen pollen diagram are the same as those of the Dömnitzian, although *Azolla filiculoides* was not detected.

At Wacken in Schleswig-Holstein, Menke (1968) has also demonstrated two interglacial deposits, separated by sands, and both involved in an ice-pushed complex of supposed Saalian age. Again, whereas the lower interglacial deposit is unquestionably of Holsteinian age, the upper also contains *Azolla* and shows some, but not all, of the features of the Dömnitzian diagram of Erd. For example *Picea* is very sparse, and Carpinus is present without any trace of *Abies*. In zone II, however, Quercus is generally well subordinate to *Pinus*.

Erd suggests that the cold period separating the Holsteinian and Dönnitzian (Fühne glacial period) might have supported glaciation as far south as southern Scandinavia. Clearly more study of this interval is necessary, as these interglacial deposits cannot easily be dismissed as belonging to either the Eemian or the Holsteinian.

In Denmark at Vejlby, Andersen (1965) has demonstrated pollen evidence for two small interstadial intervals following the Holsteinian, but these are weak oscillations characterized mainly by the expansion of *Juniperus*. Likewise Zagwijn (1973) in The Netherlands has been investigating two post-Holsteinian interstadials seen in the pollen diagram from Bantega (Brouwer 1949). At other localities, further evidence of these two interstadial phases is found. The earlier or Hoogeveen interstadial shows a vegetational development towards thermophilous forest with *Quercus*, *Corylus*, and even *Carpinus*. Whether this phase can be related to the Dömnitzian interglacial is not yet clear; it was separated from the Holsteinian by a period with severe permafrost. The younger or Bantega interstadial followed, after a period of open vegetation, *Pinus* and *Betula* were the dominant trees, with just a few thermophilous elements. The sequence is capped by sediments indicating renewed permafrost and eventually by Saalian till.

THE SAALIAN GLACIAL PERIOD

Virtually all the interglacial deposits formerly suspected of being intra-Saalian have now been discredited or assigned to other interglacial periods. Thus the "Ohe interglacial" of v. d. Brelie (1955) is clearly Holsteinian, the "Bederkesa interglacial" of Hallik (1968) Eemian, and the Treene deposits and soil horizon (Picard 1962) Eemian or early Weichselian.

At High Lodge, Mildenhall, in England, a possible Saalian interstadial with *Picea* and *Pinus* dominant (Turner, unpublished) is of particular interest as it is associated with a classic Paleolithic industry. Unfortunately the stratigraphy is unclear. The interstadial horizon is believed to overlie Anglian (Elsterian) till but be severely disturbed by Wolstonian (Saalian) ice-pushing.

Clearly the most significant feature of Saalian stratigraphy is that paleobotanical evidence of interstadial periods is virtually absent.

THE EEMIAN INTERGLACIAL

This interglacial period is only treated briefly in this paper. Many sites have been investigated across Europe. They have generally been correlated on the grounds of the vegetational succession demonstrated from pollen diagrams. This succession is even more uniform than that of the Holsteinian. In zone I, only *Pinus* and *Betula* were important and *Picea* absent. In zone II, mixed-oak forest trees were overwhelmingly dominant, particularly *Quercus*, while towards the end of the zone *Corylus* and *Tilia* were especially abundant. *Carpinus*, sometimes reaching values of over 50 percent in the pollen spectra, was everywhere the dominant of zone III being gradually replaced by *Picea*. Only east of the river Elbe did *Abies* play any significant role in the forests. In zone IV, *Picea* forest gave way to *Pinus* and *Betula* and to heathland vegetation dominated by Ericaceae. Regional variation was small, even the succession of immigration of the forest trees being similar. In Britain, however, neither *Tilia* nor *Picea* was ever abundant. Evidence from the fruiting of water plants suggests that the thermal optimum of this interglacial was warmer than that of either the Holsteinian or the Flandrian. Nevertheless Müller (i.p.b) suggests that the total span of this stage was only 9,000 to 11,000 years, less than that of the Flandrian at present.

Such a pollen record has been obtained chiefly from lake deposits in valleys eroded during the Saalian glaciation. Important sites in Germany have been recorded by, among others, Selle (1962), Behre (1962) and

Müller (i.p.b), and in Denmark by Andersen (1965). However, these deposits are also linked by pollen evidence with transgressional deposits of the Eemian Sea in the Netherlands (Zagwijn 1961). Both the Lusitanian elements in the molluscan fauna of the Eemian Sea and the paleobotanical evidence from England would suggest that Britain was severed from the Continent by straits linking the English Channel and North Sea during this period.

In the British Isles, the stratigraphical position of Eemian deposits differs significantly from that on the Continent. In Ireland, there is almost a complete lack of known deposits of this age, whereas in England, such deposits only occur stratified within river terrace systems and never associated with tills of Saalian age.

THE COMPLETENESS OF THE POLLEN RECORD

Clearly the pollen record can only be fragmentary in an area such as northwest Europe, which has been repeatedly invaded by ice sheets. Nevertheless, the rejuvenation of the landscape initiated by these invasions does provide new geomorphic situations in which freshwater deposits are laid down, and, where these are preserved, a fresh fragment of the record is also conserved.

The record is becoming more complete year by year as further studies are carried out. It is now certain that there were at least three pre-Elsterian, Middle Pleistocene interglacial periods, separated by significant intervals of cold climate. At least one, if not more, of these intervals brought a glacial advance into the north European plain. Little is known of the detailed pollen stratigraphy of the glacial periods of the Middle Pleistocene. Some information is becoming available on interstadial periods preceding the Saalian, which could compare with the much fuller record from the Weichselian, but virtually nothing is known about the Elsterian glacial period in this respect.

For post-Elsterian interglacial periods, the situation is becoming more, rather than less, confusing. Five years ago, it seemed clear that only two interglacial periods were involved, the Holsteinian and the Eemian, each with a well characterized vegetational succession. This contrasted with indications of a more complicated climatic record suggested by early work on deep-ocean cores. Since the discovery of the Dömnitzian interglacial, which now seems well-established, both palynologists and stratigraphers must look more carefully at their records. Nevertheless, as has already been indicated in this paper, the great bulk of the many pollen diagrams relating to this time range of the Middle Pleistocene does seem to fall, both on vegetational and stratigraphical evidence, within these two interglacial periods, whereas the Dömnitzian had its own distinctive vegetational characteristics. Part of the problem may be that palynologists prefer to work on lake sediments, which give long, uninterrupted pollen records covering large spans of interglacial time. Lake deposits of this kind tend to form in basins left behind following major rapid periods of deglaciation. Presumably, if a glacial phase ends less drastically, such basins are less likely to survive to be available for sedimentation in intervening temperate periods. In other words, it may have been that geomorphic conditions only favored the development of lakes in our region after particular glacial stages. If this is true, then palynologists must turn their attention to the more difficult and initially less rewarding study of terrace deposits, which also contain sediments suitable for pollen analysis.

At present there is no good palynological evidence for any major temperate period other than the Eemian, between the Saalian and Weichselian glacial periods, although a series of several mild interstadial periods occurred in the early-Weichselian, prior to the first really severe glacial conditions. In Britain, however, where virtually all studies of last interglacial deposits have been on terrace sediments, and where, consequently, no full record of the period is known, there is disagreement from some mammalian paleontologists ((Sutcliffe 1960, Kurten 1968) as to whether interglacial deposits from Ilford and from Trafalgar Square belong to the same interglacial age or terrace. Nevertheless, West (West, Lambert, and Sparks 1964) ascribes both sites on palynological grounds to the Ipswichian (Eemian) interglacial. Clearly this is the kind of debate which needs to be taken up with vigor and fresh investigations in other parts of Europe, where complex successions of terrace deposits exist.

THE DURATION OF INTERGLACIAL PERIODS

At present the Middle Pleistocene interglacial periods lie outside the range of sensitivity of any isotopic method of dating, which might indicate not merely their absolute age but also their duration. It has long been realized that varved clay sequences, laid down in former pre-glacial lakes in Scandinavia, could be used to give an estimate of the duration of the Flandrian post-glacial period (de Geer 1912, Sauramo 1923), but the occasional residual deposits of varved clays from earlier Pleistocene periods to be found at more southerly latitudes in northwest Europe can offer nothing more than vague chronologies of a few thousand years at most, with a minimum local significance and no chance of correlation. From 1920 onwards, however, it has been realized that even under temperate climatic conditions, laminated sediments, showing a definable seasonal periodicity have been and presumably are still being laid down in lakes under certain rather specialized environmental conditions. Laminated sequences of such lake sediments have been recorded not only from the Flandrian but also from interglacial sediments of at least three different ages in northwest Europe. The advantage of studying these lamination structures lies in the fact that, although they can give no idea of the absolute age of the sediments, they can not only be used to estimate the duration of sedimentation in years but also to calibrate the pollen record from those sediments, which may be useful for correlation over a much wider area.

THE FORMATION OF LAMINATED LACUSTRINE SEDIMENTS

Sediments which preserve seasonal lamination structures can only accumulate on the floor of a lake, provided that the bottom-living fauna, the burrowing and mud-feeding organisms which normally churn up and homogenize the bottom sediments of lakes and ponds, is very sparse or absent. This is only likely to happen under anaerobic conditions. Although the hypolimnion of many lakes may become stagnant, when a thermocline develops during the summer months, there is usually a mixing of the upper and lower waters at least in spring and autumn, so that any deoxygenization that takes place is purely temporary. In meromictic lakes, on the other hand, the lake waters become permanently stratified, not because of temperature differences but because of substances in solution which affect the density of the water. The simplest case is that of lakes formerly flooded by the sea which retain a basal layer or monimolimnion of saline water. Saline springs or biogenic processes which also produce an excess of electrolytes can similarly set off a meromictic development in a lake, which once begun is increasingly likely to persist. In these cases the monimolimnion normally becomes permanently anaerobic, and if the sedimentary cycle favors seasonal lamination than this lamination is likely to be preserved.

In general it is lakes where production is high and circulation low, which are most likely to become meromictic. Typical features of such lakes are:

1. A small surface area, relative to their depth (small, steep-sided, deep lakes).
2. Lake surfaces well sheltered from winds, which might encourage mixing.
3. Only small inflow streams.

4. An abrupt winter/summer transition (i.e. a rather continental climate).

5. High productivity of organisms in the surface waters of these lakes.

To the naked eye these lamination structures generally appear to consist of thin alternating bands of pale and dark sediment, each pair of laminae having a thickness in the order of 1-2 millimeters or less. Most usually the light laminae consist of $CaCO_3$ or sometimes of very concentrated layers of diatom frustules, whereas the dark laminae are organic.

The sedimentation pattern, structure, and composition of these laminated deposits has been studied in detail at a number of sites, principally of Flandrian age (see Brunskill 1969; Müller 1962; Geyh, Merkt, and Müller 1971). An important facet of such investigations is the demonstration that the lamination is seasonal, and that an annual rhythm can be detected. This has been achieved not only through sedimentological studies, e.g. from examination of thin sections of resin-impregnated sediment, but principally through detailed analysis of the pollen, diatom, Cladocera, and Chrysophyceae cyst content of individual laminae.

As an example, the sediments of Flandrian Boreal and Atlantic age from the Schleinsee (Müller 1962; Geyh, Merkt, and Müller 1971) showed repeated fine sedimentary sequences consisting of a thin lamina of carbonate sediment, formed largely of calcite crystals 1-70 meters in diameter, overlain by a lamina with many Chrysophyceae cysts set in a structureless organic groundmass, in turn overlain by a lamina rich in diatom frustules. Above this began the carbonate lamina of the next sedimentary unit. A total of about 3,500 lamination units were counted lying in a consecutive sequence in this deposit. Although the lake is still meromictic today, apparent exhaustion of the $CaCO_3$ supply led to the cessation of lamination formation in the more recent sediments. Very fine pollen analyses of the laminae showed that the darker organic sediments contained pollen dominantly of plants flowering in the autumn and early spring, such as *Hedera*, *Corylus*, *Ulmus*, *Alnus*, and *Fraxinus*, whereas the pale carbonate laminae contained the bulk of the pollen of summer-flowering taxa such as *Quercus*, *Picea*, *Abies*, *Tilia*, and Gramineae. The diatom-rich layers usually contained spring-blooming species, though occasionally extra laminae with autumn-blooming diatom species could be detected between the carbonate and organic laminae. From this it was hypothesized that the dark organic laminae were deposited during the autumn and winter months, the main diatomaceous laminae generally in the spring, the exact period each year being dependent on the nutrient status of the lake, and the carbonate laminae during full summer. The summer precipitation of calcite in the similarly meromictic Fayetteville Green Lake today is described in detail by Brunskill (1969).

INTERGLACIAL LAMINATED SEDIMENTS

Ruhme Interglacial — Bilshausen

At Bilshausen the bulk of the "Kohleton" contains lamination structures, in part distinct, in part faint. So too do the underlying and overlying red clays. Müller made counts of the full sequence of lamination pairs in the cores from which he obtained his pollen samples. At the same time he made a series of pollen analyses from adjacent fine laminae forming these structures, as he had done earlier on the deposits of the Schleinsee.

The lamination of the Bilshausen deposits appears to be different in origin from that of the Schleinsee. The pale laminae consist of silty grey clay and are normally not calcareous, the dark laminae of organic detritus. No detailed sedimentological study has been carried out. From palynological work, however, it is clear that these lamination pairs were deposited in an annual cycle. Here the evidence shows that it is the pale laminae which contain most pollen of such early-spring-flowering trees as *Alnus* and *Ulmus*, whereas the dark organic laminae contain most of the pollen of summer-flowering types such as *Quercus, Pinus, Picea, Abies, Tilia,* and Gramineae. This is the reverse of the situation in the Schleinsee, but a very different sedimentary regime was evidently taking place.

The total number of lamination cycles actually counted by Müller was somewhat over 25,500 from 11.24 meters of sediment. To this he added a further estimate of 3,400 cycles for portions of the cores which were disturbed or too weakly laminated to be countable. He lists a number of uncertainties for these counts: loss of sediment between cores, disturbances during boring or from brick-making operations or from post depositional settling, counting errors due to weakly developed laminae and the impossibility of checking that the lamination was really annual throughout the whole length of the borehole. Nevertheless he puts forward a broad estimate of 28,000 to 36,000 years for the total length of the Ruhme interglacial and a narrower span of 30,000 to 32,000 as the most probable.

The duration of the individual vegetational zones of this complex interglacial succession he estimates as follows:

Picea-Betula-Pinus zone   ca. 2,200 years
Picea zone   ca. 1,000 years
Quercus-Abies-Carpinus zone   ca. 9,300 years
     (but because of disturbances
     might be 6,000–14,000 years)

Abies-Carpinus-Quercetum mixtum zone ca. 1,200 years
Quercetum mixtum zone ca. 1,800 years
Betula-Pinus expansion ca. 400 years
Picea-Abies-Quercetum mixtum zone ca. 4,000 years
Late *Ulmus-Picea-Pinus* zone ca. 6,000 years
Early *Ulmus-Picea-Pinus* zone ca. 4,500 years

Holstein Interglacial

Laminated interglacial deposits of this age have been investigated at three sites: Hetendorf (Meyer i.p.), Münster-Breloh (Müller i.p.a) and Marks Tey (Turner 1970). The first two sites are both located in Niedersachsen and can be discussed together.

Following Nipkow's observations (1920) that annual lamination structures were being deposited in the highly polluted Zürichsee, several workers turned their attention to the laminated interglacial diatomite deposits of the Lüneburger Heide. Giesenhagen (1925) examined the diatomite from Ober-Ohe and concluded from a very small number of counts that the deposition period of the 10–15 meters of diatomite had lasted 11,000 to 12,000 years. Later van Dewall (1929) examined the actual structure of the laminations. These consisted of dark laminae of organic material, alternating with light laminae consisting chiefly of frustules of the large diatom *Melosira*. V. Dewall believed this to be *M. italica* and proposed that these pale laminae were formed in autumn, and the dark laminae during the rest of the year.

New investigations by Benda and Brandes (i.p.) of similar lamination structures at the nearby site of Münster-Breloh now suggest that the lamination is in fact caused by frustules of a different species of *Melosira M. granulata*, which has flushes of great abundance in lakes in early- to mid-spring, when nutrients in the lake waters build up in concentration. These diatomite deposits are not calcareous, so lamination of the type described from the Schleinsee does not occur.

Müller has not only confirmed that the lamination structures are annual, by means of the fine palynological techniques which he used on the deposits from the Schleinsee and from Bilshausen, but has also counted the lamination pairs from the cores and open sections, from which his pollen diagrams have been produced. In this way it has been possible to check lamination counts for the same subzones from different profiles.

A summary of Müller's results is given in Table 4. Unfortunately boreholes through strata of zone I age at Münster-Breloh only yielded material too badly disturbed for either pollen analysis or lamination counting. However, Meyer's results from a similar study of the deposits at Hetendorf can be used to fill this gap.

Table 4. Lamination counts for local subzones
(from Müller [i.p.])

Turner and West (1968)	Müller (i.p.) local subzones	Lamination pairs counted
Zone III	XIII Decline of *Quercus* and *Alnus*	ca. 1,000–1,500*
	XII *Quercus-Pinus*	ca. 4,000–5,000*
	XI 2nd. *Betula-Pinus* expansion	ca. 300–500
	X *Carpinus*	ca. 1,600
Zone II	IX *Corylus-Picea*	ca. 1,000 +
	VIII 1st. *Betula-Pinus* expansion	ca. 200–400
	VII *Taxus-Corylus-Picea*	ca. 2,500 +
Zone I	II–VI (*Betula-Pinus*)	ca. 3,300*

* Considerable estimates have been made for these subzones.

In total Müller estimates a period of 12,500–13,500 years for the temperate zones of the interglacial, and 16,000–17,000 for its full span.

At Marks Tey, the lamination structures closely resemble those described from the Schleinsee, at least where they are best developed, in sediments of subzones Ho IIc and Ho IIIa and b. The pale laminae are composite, consisting usually of a thin stratum formed largely by the frustules of the diatom, *Stephanodiscus astraea* var. *minutula*, overlain by an even finer layer of calcite crystals. The dark layers into which the carbonate laminae grade consist of organic detritus. *Stephanodiscus* is a diatom which flushes in early spring, and consequently it was assumed that the calcite laminae represented early summer deposition, and the organic laminae that of late summer, autumn, and winter. This view is confirmed by unpublished pollen analyses of the type carried out by Müller.

It was only possible to make accurate counts on sediments of zones II and III, and not even in their entirety. Sediments from zone I and the early part of zone II were laminated, but too finely to be countable; therefore, a very broad estimation was made of the number of lamination pairs present. The onset of countable lamination coincided almost exactly with the spread of the diatom *Stephanodiscus* in the lake (Evans 1972). Sediments of the upper part of zone III, the *Abies-Alnus* subzone were also clearly laminated but, unfortunately, in the borehole investigated, were too slumped and brecciated to give any possibility of an accurate count. The counted cores from the Marks Tey deposits gave the following numbers of lamination pairs:

Zone III   subzone IIIa   *Alnus-Corylus-Quercus-Carpinus*   ca. 2,025
Zone II   subzone IIc   *Alnus-Corylus-Ulmus-Taxus-Quercus* ca. 2,500

Approximately 5,000–10,000 pairs were estimated to cover zone I and subzones IIa and IIb. Originally Shackleton and Turner (1967) suggested a duration of 30,000–50,000 years for the interglacial. This is certainly too long, especially if the lengthy early-glacial zone at Marks Tey is excluded. Comparative sedimentation rates from other boreholes through the deposits suggest a total duration on the order of 20,000 years, at most perhaps 25,000, a figure in the same general order as that suggested by Müller.

Eemian Interglacial

Müller has also extended his investigations to the Eemian diatomite deposits at Bispingen (Müller i.p.b). Briefly, the lamination structures here are confined to the lower part of the deposit, covering zone I and parts of zone II. This leads to an estimate of 3,000 years for zones I and II, and, after a comparison of sedimentation rates at other Eemian sites in Germany and adjacent areas, to a total estimate of 10,000 years ±1,000 for the whole Eemian interglacial period.

The conclusions to be drawn from these studies are that interglacial periods vary considerably in their length, though they all lie within the same general order of magnitude. More promising fields of interest will be opened if and when a sufficient number of laminated deposits are studied from individual interglacial periods to enable the development of a true lamination chronology.

REFERENCES

ANDERSEN, S. T.
   1963   Pollen analysis of the Quaternary marine deposits at Tornskov in South Jutland. *Danmarks Geologiske Undersøgelse* IV Raekke 4 (8): 1–23.
   1965   Interglacialer og interstadialer i Danmarks kvartaer. *Meddelelser fra Dansk Geologisk Forening* 15: 486–506.
   1966   Interglacial succession and lake development in Denmark. *The Palaeobotanist* 15: 117–127.

1969   Interglacial vegetation and soil development. *Meddelelser fra Dansk Geologisk Forening* 19:90–102.

AVERDIECK, F.-R., G.V.D. BRELIE
1963   Neue Beiträge zur pollenanalytischen Untersuchung des Interglazials von Bilshausen (Unter-Eichsfeld). *Geologisches Jahrbuch* 80:437–446.

BEHRE, K.-E.
1962   Pollen- und diatomeenanalytische Untersuchungen an letztinterglazialen Kieselgurlagern der Lüneburger Heide. *Flora* 152:325–370.

BENDA, L., H. BRANDES
i.p.   Verbreitung, Alter und Entstehung der niedersächsischen Kieselgur-Vorkommen. *Geologisches Jahrbuch.*

BRISTOW, C. R., F. C. COX
1973   The Gipping Till: a reappraisal of East Anglian glacial stratigraphy. *Journal of the Geological Society* 129:1–37.

BROUWER, A.
1949   Pollenanalytisch en geologisch onderzoek van het Onder- en Midden-Pleistoceen van Noord-Nederland. *Leidse Geologische Mededelingen* 14B:259–346.

BRUNSKILL, G. J.
1969   Fayetteville Green Lake, New York. II Precipitation and sedimentation of calcite in a meromictic lake with laminated sediments. *Limnology and Oceanography* 14:830–847.

CEPEK, A. G.
1967   Stand und Probleme der Quartärstratigraphie im Nordteil der DDR. *Bericht der Deutschen Gesellschaft der geologischen Wissenschaften. A, Geologie, Paläontologie* 12:375–404.

CHANDA, S.
1962   Untersuchungen zur Pleisozänen Floren- und Vegetationsgeschichte im Leinetal und im südwestlichen Harzvorland (Untereichsfeld). *Geologisches Jahrbuch* 79:783–844.

DE GEER, G.
1912   A geochronology of the last 12,000 years. *Eleventh International Geological Congress, Stockholm, 1910, Compte Rendu* 1:241–253.

DE RIDDER, N. A., W. H. ZAGWIJN
1962   A mixed Rhine-Meuse deposit of Holsteinian age from the South-Eastern part of the Netherlands. *Geologie en Mijnbouw* 41:125–130.

DUIGAN, S. L.
1963   Pollen analysis of the Cromer Forest Bed Series in East Anglia. *Philosophical Transactions of the Royal Society of London* B 246:149–202.

DYAKOWSKA, J.
1952   Pleistocene flora of Nowiny Zukowskie on the Lublin Upland. *Biuletyn Instytutu geologicznego* 67:115–181.
1956   Pleistocene profile from Wylezin (Central Poland). *Biuletyn Instytutu geologicznego* 100:193–216.

ERD, K.
1960   Die bisherige botanische Erforschung des Paludinen-Interglazials in Brandenburg. *Wissenschaftliche Zeitschrift der Pädagogischen Hochschule Potsdam* 6 (1-2):59–68.

1965 Pollenanalytische Untersuchungen im Altpleistozän von Voigtstedt in Thüringen. *Paläontologische Abhandlungen* A, II (2-3):259–272.

1970 Pollen-analytical classification of the Middle Pleistocene in the German Democratic Republic. *Palaeogeography, Palaeoclimatology, Palaeoecology* 12:129–145.

EVANS, G. H.
1972 The diatom flora of the Hoxnian deposits at Marks Tey, Essex. *New Phytologist* 71:379–386.

FIRBAS, F.
1949 *Waldgeschichte Mitteleuropas I.* Jena: Fischer

FUNNELL, B. M., R. G. WEST
1962 The Early Pleistocene of Easton Bavents, Suffolk. *Quarterly Journal of the Geological Society of London* 98:125–141.

GEYH, M. A., J. MERKT, H. MÜLLER
1971 Sediment-, Pollen- und Isotopenanalysen an jahreszeitlich geschichteten Ablagerungen im zentralen Teil des Schleinsees. *Archiv für Hydrobiologie* 69:366–399.

GIESENHAGEN, K.
1925 Kieselgur als Zeitmass für ein Interglazial. *Zeitschrift für Gletscherkunde* 14: 1–10.

GOEDEKE, R., E. GRÜGER, H.-J. BEUG
1966 Zur Frage der Zahl der Eiszeiten im Norddeutschen Tiefland. Erdfalluntersuchungen am Elm. *Nachrichten der Akademie der Wissenschaften in Göttingen. II: Mathematisch-physikalische Klasse* 15:207–212.

GRÜGER, E.
1968 Vegetationsgeschichtliche Untersuchungen an cromerzeitlichen Ablagerungen im nördlichen Randgebiet der deutschen Mittelgebirge. *Eiszeitalter und Gegenwart* 18:204–235.

HALLIK, R.
1960 Die Vegetationsentwicklung der Holstein-Warmzeit in Nordwestdeutschland und die Alterstellung der Kieselgurlager der südlichen Lüneburger Heide. *Zeitschrift der Deutschen Geologischen Gesellschaft* 112:326–333.

1968 Organogene Serie einer Pleistozänen Warmzeit vom Typ Bederkesa. *Eiszeitalter und Gegenwart* 19:244–249.

IVERSEN, J.
1958 The bearing of glacial and interglacial epochs on the formation and extinction of plant taxa. *Uppsala Universitets Årsskrift* 6:210–215.

JESSEN, K., S. T. ANDERSEN, A. FARRINGTON
1959 The interglacial deposit near Gort, Co. Galway, Ireland. *Proceedings of the Royal Irish Academy* 60B:1–77.

JESSEN, K., V. MILTHERS
1928 Stratigraphical and palaeontological studies of interglacial fresh-water deposits in Jutland and Northwest Germany. *Danmarks Geologiske Undersøgelse* II Raekke 48:1–380.

KAISER, K.-H., R. SCHÜTRUMPF
1960 Zur Gliederung mittel- und jungpleistozäner Schichten in der Niederrheinischen Bucht. *Eiszeitalter und Gegenwart* 11:166–185.

KELLY, M. R.
1964   The Middle Pleistocene of North Birmingham. *Philosophical Transactions of the Royal Society of London* B 247:533–592.

KERFOURN, M.-T.
1965   Le dépôt tourbeux de l'anse de Trez-Roux à Camaret (Finistère) peut être rapporté à l'Interglaciaire Mindel-Riss. *Compte rendu hebdomadaire des séances de l'Académie des sciences, Paris* 260:2024–2026.

KERNEY, M. P.
1971   Interglacial deposits in Barnfield pit, Swanscombe and their molluscan fauna. *Journal of the Geological Society* 127:69–93.

KRUTZSCH, W.
1965   Das geologische Profil von Voigtstedt in Thüringen. *Paläontologische Abhandlungen* A, II (2–3):235–248.

KRUTZSCH, W., H. REICHSTEIN
1956   Das Pleistozänprofil von Voigtstedt-Edersleben. *Geologie* 5 (4–3); 327–349.

KURTEN, B.
1968   *Pleistocene mammals of Europe*. London: Weidenfeld and Nicholson.

LÜTTIG, G., U. REIN
1955   Das Cromer-(Günz-Mindel) Interglazial von Bilshausen (Unter-Eichsfeld). *Geologisches Jahrbuch* 70:159–166.

MENKE, B.
1968   Beiträge zur Biostratigraphie des Mittelpleistozäns in Norddeutschland. *Meyniana* 18:35–42.

MEYER, K.-J.
i.p.   Pollenanalytische Untersuchungen und Jahresschichtenzählungen an der holsteinzeitlichen Kieselgur von Hetendorf. *Geologisches Jahrbuch*.

MITCHELL, G. F., L. F. PENNY, F. W. SHOTTON, R. G. WEST
1973   *A correlation of Quaternary deposits in the British Isles*. Geological Society of London, Special Report 4.

MORZADEC-KERFOURN, M.-T.
1969   Le Quaternaire de la plage de Trez-Rouz. *Bulletin de l'Association française pour l'étude du Quaternaire* (1969–2):129–138.

MÜLLER, H.
1962   Pollenanalytische Untersuchung eines Quartärprofils durch die spät- und nacheiszeitlichen Ablagerungen des Schleinsees (Südwestdeutschland). *Geologisches Jahrbuch* 79:493–526.

1965   Eine pollenanalytische Neubearbeitung des Interglazial-Profiles von Bilshausen (Unter-Eichsfeld). *Geologisches Jahrbuch* 83:327–352.

i.p. a   Pollenanalytische Untersuchungen und Jahresschichtenzählungen an der holsteinzeitlichen Kieselgur von Münster-Breloh. *Geologisches Jahrbuch*.

i.p. b   Pollenanalytische Untersuchungen und Jahresschichtenzählungen an der eemzeitlichen Kieselgur von Bispingen/Luhe. *Geologisches Jahrbuch*.

NIPKOW, F.
1920   Vorläufige Mitteilungen über Untersuchungen des Schlammabsatzes im Zürichsee. *Zeitschrift für Hydrologie, Hydrographie, Hydrobiologie, Fischereiwissenschaft* 1:1–23.

PENCK, A., E. BRÜCKNER
1909 *Die Alpen im Eiazeitalter.* Leipzig.

PICARD, K.
1960 Zur Untergliederung der Saalevereisung im Westen Schleswig-Holsteins. *Zeitschrift der deutschen geologischen Gesellschaft* 112: 316–325.
1962 Gletscherrandlagen im Westen Schleswig-Holsteins. *Neues Jahrbuch für Geologie und Paläontologie. Monatshefte* 6:273–281.

PIKE, K., H. GODWIN
1953 The interglacial at Clacton-on-Sea, Essex. *Quaterly Journal of the Geological Society of London* 108:261–272.

POLAK, B., G. C. MAARLEVELD, D. J. G. NOTA
1962 Palynological and petrological data of a section in ice-pushed deposits (Southern Veluwe, Netherlands). *Geologie en Mijnbouw* 41: 333–350.

REID, C.
1882 The geology of the country around Cromer. *Memoirs of the Geological Survey of the United Kingdom.*
1890 The Pliocene deposits of Britain. *Memoirs of the Geological Survey of the United Kingdom.*

REID, E. M.
1920 A comparative review of Pliocene floras, based on the study of fossil seeds. *Quarterly Journal of the Geological Society of London* 76: 145–161.

RUSKE, R.
1965 Zur petrographischen Ausbildung und Genese der "Lehmzone" von Voigtstedt in Thüringen. *Paläontologische Abhandlungen* A, II (2–3): 249–258.

SAURAMO, M.
1923 Studies on the Quaternary varve sediments in southern Finland. *Bulletin de la Commission géologique de la Finlande* 60:1–164.

SELLE, W.
1941 Beiträge zur Mikrostratigraphie und Paläontologie der Nordwestdeutschen Interglaziale. *Jahrbuch der Reichsstelle für Bodenforschnung* 60:197–231.
1955 Die Vegetationsentwicklung des Interglazials vom Typ Ober-Ohe. *Abhandlungen herausgegeben vom Naturwissenschaftlichen Verein zu Bremen* 34:33–46.
1960 Das Interglazial von Praschnitz. *Geologisches Jahrbuch* 77:319–328.
1962 Geologische und vegetationskundliche Untersuchungen an einigen wichtigen Vorkommen des letzten Interglazials in Nordwestdeutschland. *Geologisches Jahrbuch* 79:295–352.

SHACKLETON, N. J., C. TURNER
1967 Correlation between marine and terrestrial Pleistocene successions. *Nature,* London 216:1079–1082.

SINGER, R., J. WYMER, B. GLADFELTER, R. WOLFF
1973 Excavation of the Clactonian industry of the golf course, Clacton-on-Sea, Essex. *Proceedings of the Prehistoric Society* 39:6–74.

SOBOLEWSKA, M.

1956a Pollen analysis of the interglacial deposits of Olszewice. *Biuletyn Instytutu geologicznego* 100:271–289.

1956b Pleistocene vegetation of Syrniki on the river Wieprz. *Biuletyn Instytutu geologicznego* 100:143–192.

SPARKS, B. W., R. G. WEST

1972 *The Ice Age in Britain.* London: Methuen.

ŚRODOŃ, A.

1957 Interglacial flora from Gościęcin near Kozle, Sudeten Foreland. *Biuletyn Instytutu geologicznego* 118:7–60.

1972 "Róslinność polski w czwartozedzie," in *Szata Roslinna Polski*, volume one, 527–569. Warsaw: PWN.

STEVENS, L. A.

1960 The Interglacial of the Nar Valley, Norfolk. *Quarterly Journal of the Geological Society of London* 115:291–316.

SUTCLIFFE, A. J.

1960 Joint Mitnor Cave, Buckfastleigh. *Transactions of the Torquay Natural History Society* 13:1–28.

SZAFER, W.

1953 Pleistocene stratigraphy of Poland from the floristic point of view. *Annales de la Société Géologique de Pologne* 22:1–99.

TEUNISSEN, D., F. FLORSCHÜTZ

1957 Over een pollenhoudende kleilaag op de "Duno" bij Oosterbeek. *Tijdschrift van het Koninklijk Nederlandsch Aardrijkskundig Genootschap* 76:413–421.

TURNER, C.

1968 A Lowestoftian late-glacial flora from the Pleistocene deposits at Hoxne, Suffolk. *New Phytologist* 67:327–332.

1970 The Middle Pleistocene deposits at Marks Tey, Essex. *Philosophical Transactions of the Royal Society of London* B, 257:373–440.

i.p. The influence of large mammals on interglacial vegetation. *Quartärpaläontologische Abhandlungen und Berichte* Weimar 1.

TURNER C., R. G. WEST

1968 The subdivision and zonation of interglacial periods. *Eiszeitalter und Gegenwart* 19:93–101.

V.D. BRELIE, G.

1955 Die pollenstratigraphische Gliederung des Pleistozäns in Nordwestdeutschland, 2: Die Pollenstratigraphie im jüngeren Pleistozän. *Eiszeitalter und Gegenwart* 6:25–38.

V.D. BRELIE, G., K. KILPPER, R. TEICHMÜLLER

1959 Das Pleistozän-Profil von Frimmersdorf an der Erft. *Fortschritte in der Geologie von Rheinland und Westfalen* 4:179–196.

VAN DER VLERK, I. M., F. FLORSCHÜTZ

1953 The palaeontological base of the subdivisions of the Pleistocene in the Netherlands. *Verhandelingen der Koninklijke Akademie van Wetenschappen, Otd. Natuurkunde* I, 20(2):2–58.

VAN DEWALL, H. W.

1929 Geologisch-biologische Studie über die Kieselgurlager der Lüneburger

Heide. *Jahrbuch der Preussischen geologischen Landesanstalt und Berg-akademie zu Berlin* 1928 49 : 641–684.

WATTS, W. A.

1959   Interglacial beds at Kilbeg and Newtown, Co. Waterford. *Proceedings of the Royal Irish Academy* 60B:79–134.

1964   Interglacial deposits at Baggotstown, near Bruff, Co. Limerick. *Proceedings of the Royal Irish Academy* 63B:167–189.

1967   Interglacial deposits at Kildromin Townland near Herbertstown, Co. Limerick. *Proceedings of the Royal Irish Academy* 65B:339–348.

WEST, R. G.

1956   The Quaternary deposits at Hoxne, Suffolk. *Philosophical Transactions of the Royal Society of London* B, 239:265–356.

1961   Vegetational history of the Early Pleistocene of the Royal Society borehole at Ludham, Norfolk. *Proceedings of the Royal Society of London* B, 155:437–453.

1972   The stratigraphical position of the Norwich Crag in relation to the Cromer Forest Bed Series. *Bulletin of the Geological Society of Norfolk* 21:17–23.

WEST, R. G., P. H. BANHAM

1972   Short field meeting on the north Norfolk coast. *Proceedings of the Geologists' Association* 79:493–512.

WEST, R. G., C. A. DICKSON, J. A. CATT, A. H. WEIR, B. W. SPARKS

1974   Late Pleistocene deposits at Wretton, Norfolk, II: Devensian deposits. *Philosophical Transactions of the Royal Society of London* B, 267: 337–420.

WEST, R. G., C. A. LAMBERT, B. W. SPARKS

1964   Interglacial deposits at Ilford, Essex. *Philosophical Transactions of the Royal Society of London*, series B, 247:185–212.

WEST, R. G., C. M. B. MCBURNEY

1954   The Quaternary deposits at Hoxne, Suffolk, and their archaeology. *Proceedings of the Prehistoric Society* 20:131–154.

WEST, R. G., D. G. WILSON

1966   Cromer Forest Bed Series. *Nature*, London 209:497–498.

WILSON, D. G.

1973   Notable plant records from the Cromer Forest Bed Series. *New Phytologist* 72:1207–1234.

WOLSTEDT, P. W.

1951   Das Vereisungsgebiet der Britischen Inseln und seine Beziehungen zum festländischen Pleistozän. *Geologisches Jahrbuch* 65:621–640.

1953   Über die Benennung einiger Unterabteilungen des Pleistozäns. *Eiszeitalter und Gegenwart* 3:14–18.

ZAGWIJN, W. H.

1960   Aspects of the Pliocene and Early Pleistocene vegetation in the Netherlands. *Mededelingen van de Geologische Stichting* (Serie C-III), 1(5):78.

1961   Vegetation, climate and radiocarbon datings in the Late Pleistocene of the Netherlands, Part I: Eemian and Early Weichselian. *Mededelingen van de Geologische Stichting*, n.s. 14:15–45.

1973   Pollenanalytic studies of Holsteinian and Saalian Beds in the northern Netherlands. *Mededelingen Rijks Geologische Dienst*, n.s. 24:139–156.

ZAGWIJN, W. H., H. M. V. MONTFRANS, J. G. ZANDSTRA
1971   Subdivision of the "Cromerian" in the Netherlands: pollen analysis, palaeomagnetism and sedimentary petrology. *Geologie en Mijnbouw* 50:41–58.
ZAGWIJN, W. H., J. I. S. ZONNEVELD
1956   The Interglacial of Westerhoven. *Geologie en Mijnbouw*, n.s. 18:37–46.

The Macro-faunas of Continental Europe During the Middle Pleistocene: Stratigraphic Sequence and Problems of Intercorrelation

H. D. KAHLKE

The last ten years have seen a remarkable enrichment of our knowledge of continental European Middle Pleistocene fossil associations, making possible a discussion of the stratigraphic sequence and the problems of intercorrelations on a much wider scale than was possible before.

Before discussing the stratigraphic sequence of "Middle Pleistocene" faunas, however, we must first locate the boundary between the Lower Pleistocene and the Middle Pleistocene, which, in turn, demands a review of the Lower Pleistocene boundary as it is accepted today. The Commission appointed to advise on the Plio/Pleistocene boundary (International Geological Congress 1948, London) recommended "that the Lower Pleistocene should include as its basal member in the type area the Calabrian formation (marine) together with its terrestrial (continental) equivalent the Villafranchian." This boundary was proposed and finally accepted as a geological horizon where, for the first time, climatic depressions initial to the Ice Age could be traced by paleontological materials. In accordance with the classical method of grouping fossiliferous strata, the Commission based the boundary on changes in marine faunas. In following this classical method we will have to consider the suggestion that an acceptable Lower Pleistocene-Middle Pleistocene boundary also be based on changes in marine faunas in a type area as well.

The exact boundary between the Lower Pleistocene and the Middle Pleistocene is not yet fixed by an International Geological Congress (IGC). According to different fields of research or according to different local conditions, some students have suggested that the Lower Pleisto-cene-Middle Pleistocene boundary be drawn between the Villafranchian and the "Cromerian" stages, others between the "Cromerian" and the Mindel, others still later. We, therefore, want to draw the attention of the President of the INQUA Stratigraphical Commission to the question of appointing a subcommission within the Stratigraphical Commission of INQUA to advise on a Lower-Middle Pleistocene and on a Middle-Upper Pleistocene boundary.

In 1965, based on the sequence of Continental European fossil macrofaunas (land mammal ages), we preliminarily suggested that the Lower-Middle Pleistocene boundary be marked, in accordance with the principle of London 1948, by the first appearance of "arctic," that is, real "glacial," mammals in the temperate zones of the Palearctic region. This would correspond to a worldwide climatic depression of high intensity. Paleontologically, this horizon is characterized by the earliest typical associations of the *Mammonteus-Coelodonta-Rangifer-Ovibos* faunal block and its different chronological associations with the Middle Pleistocene-Upper Pleistocene sequence of the whole Palearctic area. This horizon can today be traced, in its earliest stages, from the Tajo (Spain) to the Chukotija (northeast-Siberia) River areas.

The typical element of all "early Middle Pleistocene" fossil associa-tions, even though locally varied, is *Mammonteus trogontherii* (Pohlig). These Mammontoid populations, in different stages of evolution, specialization, and differentation, occur in the open Palearctic continen-tal area between the Iberian peninsula and northeast-Siberia, associated in the central European area with the earliest reindeer *Rangifer arcticus stadelmanni* Kahlke, the earliest musk-ox *Ovibos moschatus süssen-bornensis* Kahlke, and the earliest Coelodonta populations, *Coelodonta tologoijensis* Beliajeva and *Coelodonta* cf. *tologoijensis* Beliajeva.

These earliest associations of the *Mammonteus-Coelodonta-Rangifer-Ovibos* faunal block at the transition between the Lower Pleistocene and the Middle Pleistocene, although still associated with archaic elements like *Dicerorhinus etruscus* (Falconer) and *Praemegaceros verticornis* (Dawkins), lead, in a biostratigraphical sense, to the first real "glacial" faunal associations in the Eurasian temperate zone and mark the be-ginning of a new phase in Pleistocene glacial progress. The sequence of glacial deposits at Süssenborn near Weimar and Voigtstedt-Edersleben near Sangerhausen shows these associations to be of early Elster I (= early Mindel I) age.

Thus, land mammal horizons make it possible to draw the Lower Pleistocene-Middle Pleistocene boundary either between the Villafranchian and the Cromerian or between the Cromerian and the Mindel of the Alpine sequence. The boundary between the Middle Pleistocene and the Upper Pleistocene may be drawn between the Riss of the Alpine sequence and the Eemian or between the Eemian and the Würm of the Alpine sequence. A decision by an IGC about this problem is necessary as soon as possible.

THE SEQUENCE OF MIDDLE PLEISTOCENE MACROFAUNAS AND THE DIFFERENT FAUNAL PROVINCES OF THE CONTINENTAL EUROPEAN AREA

For Pleistocene times we may divide the European continent into three faunal subareas: a western province of Atlantic facies, an eastern province of continental facies, and a southern province of Mediterranean affinities. Between these European faunal provinces, however, we must distinguish transitional zones of more or less mixed characters: in the Rhine River valley, there is a mixed association with *Hippopotamus antiquus* Desmarest and "continental" elements, and in the eastern province, there are increasing Asian affinities (*Elasmotherium, Camelus, Struthio*).

I. UPPERMOST LOWER PLEISTOCENE, LATE *ARCHIDISKODON* ASSOCIATIONS

A. *Western Province (Selected Macrofaunas)*

1. Basin of Granada (Granada), Spain
    (Aguirre 1957; Crusafont-Pairo 1960, 1965; Kahlke 1969)
    Carnivora
       Hyaenidae gen. et sp. indet.
    Proboscidea
       Archidiskodon meridionalis (Nesti)
    Perissodactyla
       Dicerorhinus etruscus (Falconer)
       Equus sp.
    Artiodactyla
       Praemegaceros verticornis (Dawkins)
       Cervidae gen. et sp. indet.
       Capreolus capreolus ssp.
       Gazella sp.
       Leptobos sp.

2. Valverde de Calatrava (Ciudad Real), Spain
(Hernández-Pacheco 1921; Schlösser 1921; Crusafont-Pairó
1960, 1965)
Proboscidea
   Archidiskodon meridionalis (Nesti)
Perissodactyla
   Equus cf. *mosbachensis* von Reichenau
Artiodactyla
   Hippopotamus antiquus Desmarest
   Eucladoceros cf. *dicranios* (Nesti)
   Leptobos cf. *etruscus* (Falconer)

3. Mestas de Con (Cangas de Onis), Spain
(Llopis and Fraga 1958; Crusafont-Pairó 1959, 1960, 1965)
Carnivora
   Homotherium crenatidens (Fabrini)
   Ursus cf. *etruscus* Cuvier
Perissodactyla
   Dicerorhinus etruscus (Falconer)
   Equus cf. *süssenbornensis* Wüst
Artiodactyla
   Praemegaceros sp.
   Cervus cf. *elaphus* ssp.
   Capreolus capreolus ssp.
   Bison sp.

4. Llobregat River area (Barcelona), Spain (eighty to ninety-meter
terrace)
(Masachs and Villalta 1953; Solé Sabaris 1963; Crusafont-
Pairó, 1953, 1960, 1965)
Proboscidea
   Archidiskodon meridionalis (Nesti)
Perissodactyla
   Dicerorhinus etruscus (Falconer)
   Equus stenonis Cocchi
Artiodactyla
   Hippopotamus antiquus Desmarest

All of these Spanish fossil associations of macromammals, thought to
be initial to the northern Elster glaciation (= Mindel of the Alpine
system), are obviously of different chronological horizons. The species

record is very scanty, and some of the materials also need modern revision. Still, they seem close to the faunal boundary between the late *Archidiskodon* and the subsequent *Mammonteus* complex which is suggested as a preliminary characterization of the beginning of the Middle Pleistocene in the Palearctic region.

5. Saint-Prest (Chartres), France
    (Laugel 1862; Gaudry 1876; Depéret 1902; Haug 1911; Stehlin 1912; Lacassagne 1943; Azzaroli 1953; Bourdier and Lacassagne 1963; M. F. Bonifay 1969, 1971)
    Carnivora
    Ursus arvernensis Croizet and Jobert
    Proboscidea
    Archidiskodon meridionalis cromerensis Depéret and Meyet
    Palaeoloxodon antiquus (Falconer)
    Perissodactyla
    Dicerorhinus etruscus (Falconer)
    Equus stenonis Cocchi
    Artiodactyla
    Hippopotamus antiquus Desmarest
    Praemegaceros verticornis (Dawkins)
    Cervus elaphus ssp.
    Alces latifrons (Johnson)
    Bos or *Bison* sp.

6. Abbeville area (Somme River terraces), France
    (Commont 1910, 1912; Pontier 1910, 1928, 1940; Depéret and Mayet 1923; Breuil and Koslowski 1931, 1932, 1934; Bourdier, et al. 1957; Prat 1968; M. F. Bonifay 1969, 1971)
The deposits of Abbeville (forty to forty-five meter terrace system) are obviously from different horizons. The lower part (Abbeville I), with *Archidiskodon meridionalis* (Nesti) and archaic *Palaeoloxodon antiquus* (Falconer), may be correlated to the late "Cromerian" stage, the middle part (Abbeville II) to the Mindel s. l., and the upper part (Abbeville III) to the Holsteinian.
Abbeville I to III
    Carnivora
    Homotherium latidens (Owen)
    Mustela sp.
    Proboscidea
    Archidiskodon meridionalis (Nesti)

Mammonteus cf. *trogontherii* (Pohlig) primitive type
Palaeoloxodon antiquus (Falconer) primitive type
Perissodactyla
  Dicerorhinus etruscus (Falconer)
  Dicerorhinus kirchbergensis (Jäger)
  Equus stenonis Cocchi
  Equus cf. *hydruntinus* Regalia
Artiodactyla
  Hippopotamus antiquus Desmarest
  Sus scrofa ssp.
  Praemegaceros verticornis (Dawkins)
  Praemegaceros solilhacus (Robert)
  Cervus elaphus ssp.
  Dama cf. *clactoniana* (Falconer)
  Capreolus capreolus ssp.
  Bison sp.

7. Rosières (Saint-Florent, Cher.), France
   (Grossouvre and Stehlin 1912; Stehlin 1914; M. F. Bonifay 1969, 1971)
   Carnivora
     Cuon dubius stehlini Thenius
     Felis (Lynx) sp.
   Perissodactyla
     Dicerorhinus etruscus (Falconer)
     Dicerorhinus cf. *kirchbergensis* (Jäger)
     Equus stenonis Cocchi
   Artiodactyla
     Sus sp.
     Praemegaceros verticornis (Dawkins)
     Bos sp.

8. Sainzelles (Le Puy), France
   (Aymard 1846; Boule 1893; Commont 1910; Depéret, Mayet, and Roman 1923; Bout 1960; Prat 1968 Kurtén 1968; M. F. Bonifay 1969, 1971)
   Carnivora
     Canis sp.
     Felis (? Lynx) sp.
     Homotherium cf. *crenatidens* (Fabrini)
     Hyaena brevirostris (Aymard)

Proboscidea
Archidiskodon meridionalis (Nesti)
Perissodactyla
Dicerorhinus etruscus (Falconer)
Equus stenonis Cocchi
Artiodactyla
Hippopotamus antiquus Desmarest
Praemegaceros sp.
"Cervus" pardinensis Croizet and Jobert
"Cervus" sp.
Leptobos sp.

9. Grotte du Vallonnet (Alpes-Maritimes), France
(Gagnière 1963; E. Bonifay 1964, 1969, 1971; Guérin 1966; M. F. Bonifay 1971)
Carnivora
Canis cf. *lupus* ssp.
Felis sp.
Panthera leo ssp.
Acinonyx pardinensis Croizet and Jobert
Ursus cf. *arctos* ssp.
Hyaena perrieri Croizet and Jobert
Proboscidea
Archidiskodon meridionalis (Nesti)
Perissodactyla
Dicerorhinus etruscus (Falconer)
Equus stenonis Cocchi
Artiodactyla
Hippopotamus antiquus Desmarest
Sus sp.
Eucladoceros senezensis (Depéret)
"Cervus" philisi Schaub
Bos cf. *primigenius* Bojanus
Memorhaedus philisi Schaub

10. Soave (Verona), Italy
(Pasa 1950; Kretzoi 1965)
The fossils of this locality seem to be mixed with those of later horizons, or their determination may not always be correct (cf. Kretzoi 1965). Given here, therefore, are only those species of uppermost Lower Pleistocene affinities which serve to characterize the geological horizon until a modern revision is available.

Carnivora
   Canis lupus mosbachensis Soergel
   Vulpes alopecoides Forsyth Major
   Ursus arctos mediterraneus (Forsyth Major)
Proboscidea
   Archidiskodon meridionalis cromerensis Depéret and Mayet
   Palaeoloxodon antiquus (Falconer)
Perissodactyla
   Dicerorhinus sp.
   Equus stenonis major Boule
Artiodactyla
   Hippopotamus antiquus Desmarest
   Sus scrofa ssp.
   Cervus elaphus ssp.
   Dama cf. *clactoniana* (Falconer)
   Capreolus capreolus ssp.

11. Monte Oliveto (S. Gimignano), Italy
     (Ambrosetti, et al. 1972)
     Proboscidea
        Palaeoloxodon antiquus (Falconer)
     Perissodactyla
        Equus cf. *mosbachensis* von Reichenau
     Artiodactyla
        Hippopotamus antiquus Desmarest
        Praemegaceros verticornis (Dawkins)
        Bos sp.

B.   *Transitional Zone, Rhine River Area s. 1.*

Between the zoogeographical western province of Atlantic character and
the eastern province of continental facies we must distinguish a transitional zone of Atlantic affinities but with an increasing number of "continental" species. Fossiliferous localities of this type are mainly found in
the area of the Rhine River and in the western part of the Main and
Donau Rivers, in localities with *Hippopotamus antiquus* Desmarest.
The classical locality of this type ("lower Middle Pleistocene") is Mosbach near Wiesbaden.

12. Mosbach area (Wiesbaden), West Germany
     (Römer 1887, 1895; Kinkelin 1889; Schröder 1898; von Reiche-

nau 1900, 1903, 1904, 1905, 1906, 1912, 1915; Soergel 1912, 1914, 1927; Schmidtgen 1910, 1922, 1929, 1932, 1938; Geib 1915; Kuthe 1932; Bachofen-Echt 1930; Heller 1932; Beninde 1937, 1939; Zeuner 1937; Adam 1953, 1959; Thenius 1954; Tobien 1957; Kurtén 1957, 1962, 1968, 1969; Kuss 1957; Kahlke 1960, 1961; Schütt 1969, 1970, 1971; Guenther 1968, 1969; Hemmer and Schütt 1969; Hemmer 1971)

Mosbach I (Lower Sands)
  Proboscidea
    Archidiskodon meridionalis (Nesti)
    Mammonteus trogontherii (Pohlig) primitive type
    Palaeoloxodon antiquus (Falconer) primitive type
  Perissodactyla
    Dicerorhinus etruscus (Falconer)
    Equus sp.
  Artiodactyla
    Hippopotamus antiquus Desmarest
    Praemegaceros verticornis (Dawkins)
    Cervus elaphus acoronatus Beninde
    Alces latifrons (Johnson)
    ?*"Cervus" elaphoides* Kahlke

13. Jockgrim (Pfalz), West Germany
    (Freudenberg 1909, 1911, 1914; Soergel 1925; Schwegler 1935; Grüner 1950; Küss 1955)

  Carnivora
    Canis lupus mosbachensis Soergel
    Ursus deningeri von Reichenau
  Proboscidea
    Archidiskodon meridionalis (Nesti)
    Mammonteus trogontherii (Pohlig)
  Perissodactyla
    Dicerorhinus etruscus (Falconer)
    Equus robustus Pomel
  Artiodactyla
    Hippopotamus antiquus Desmarest
    Praemegaceros verticornis (Dawkins)
    Cervus elaphus ssp.
    Alces latifrons (Johnson)
    Capreolus capreolus ssp.
    Bison sp.

14. Goldshöfer Sande (Stuttgart), West Germany
     (Hennig 1952; Adam, 1953)

     Proboscidea
       Archidiskodon meridionalis (Nesti)
       Mammonteus trogontherii (Pohlig)
     Perissodactyla
       Equus süssenbornensis Wüst
     Artiodactyla
       Alces latifrons (Johnson)

15. Stuttgart-Rosenstein (Stuttgart), West Germany
     (Berckhemer 1930; Adam 1953)

     Carnivora
       Ursus sp.
     Proboscidea
       Archidiskodon meridionalis (Nesti)
       Mammonteus trogontherii (Pohlig)
     Perissodactyla
       Dicerorhinus etruscus (Falconer)
       Equus süssenbornensis Wüst
     Artiodactyla
       Cervus elaphus ssp.
       Alces latifrons (Johnson)
       Bison cf. *priscus* (Bojanus)

16. Würzburg-Schalksberg (Würzburg), West Germany
     (Rutte 1967)

     Carnivora
       Canis lupus mosbachensis Soergel
       Felis sp.
       Homotherium moravicum (Woldrich)
       Meles sp.
     Proboscidea
       Elephantidae gen. et sp. indet.
     Perissodactyla
       Dicerorhinus etruscus (Falconer)
       Equus mosbachensis von Reichenau

Artiodactyla
Hippopotamus antiquus Desmarest
Cervidae gen. et sp. indet.
Alces sp.
Bison schoetensacki Freudenberg
Bison priscus (Bojanus)

C. *Eastern Province*

17. Bilshausen (Unter-Eichsfeld), West Germany
   (Sobotha 1923; Schmidt 1930; Bismarck 1942; Lüttig and Rein 1954; Kahlke 1958)

   Perissodactyla
   Dicerorhinus etruscus (Falconer)
   Artiodactyla
   Praemegaceros verticornis (Dawkins)
   Alces latifrons (Johnson)
   Capreolus capreolus cf. *süssenbornensis* Kahlke

18. Voigtstedt (Sangerhausen), East Germany
   (Dietrich 1965; Guenther 1965; Fischer 1965; Hünermann 1965; Jánossy 1965; Kahlke 1965; Kretzoi 1965; Musil 1965; Thenius 1965)

   Carnivora
   Canis lupus mosbachensis Soergel
   Felis sp.
   Panthera pardus ssp.
   Homotherium moravicum (Woldřich)
   Ursus deningeri von Reichenau
   Martes cf. *martes* Linnaeus
   Mustela (Putorius) cf. *eversmanni* Lesson
   Meles meles cf. *atavus* Kormos
   Lutra simplicidens Thenius
   Proboscidea
   Archidiskodon meridionalis voigtstedtensis Dietrich
   Perissodactyla
   Dicerorhinus etruscus (Falconer)
   Equus altidens von Reichenau

Artiodactyla
  Sus scrofa ssp.
  Praemegaceros verticornis (Dawkins)
  Praemegaceros sp.
  Praedama sp.
  Cervus elaphus acoronatus Beninde
  "Cervus" sp.
  Alces latifrons (Johnson)
  Alces sp. (cf. *Libralces gallicus* Azzaroli)
  Capreolus capreolus süssenbornensis Kahlke
  Bison schoetensacki voigtstedtensis Fischer

19. Csarnóta I (Villany), Hungary
     (Kormos 1911, 1937; Kretzoi 1956)

Carnivora
  Canis lupus mosbachensis Soergel
  Nyctereutes petenyii (Kormos)
  Panthera sp.
  Homotherium moravicum (Woldřich)
  Mustela palerminea Petenyi
  Baranogale helbingi Kormos
  Pannonictis pliocaenica Kormos
Perissodactyla
  Dicerorhinus etruscus (Falconer)
Artiodactyla
  Praemegaceros verticornis (Dawkins)
  "Cervus" (*Rusa?*) sp.
  Alces sp.
  Capreolus capreolus ssp.
  Gazellospira cf. *torticornis* (Aymard)
  Procamtoceras cf. *brivatense* Schaub
  Hemitragus jemlahicus cf. *bonali* Harlé and Stehlin

20. Betfia V (Crişana), Romania
     (Kormos 1911, 1914; Kretzoi 1956, 1962, 1965; Terzea and
     Jurczak 1968, 1969)

Carnivora
  Canis lupus mosbachensis Sorgel
  Canis sp.

Vulpes sp.
Vulpes praecorsac Kormos
Felis sp.
Felis (Lynx) cf. *issiodorensis* Croizet and Jobert
Panthera gombaszögensis (Kretzoi)
Homotherium moravicum (Woldřich)
Crocuta sp.
Ursus gombaszögensis Kretzoi
Ursus Stehlini Kretzoi
Martes vetus Kretzoi
Mustela palerminea Petenyi
Putorius cf. *stromeri* Kormos
Gulo schlosseri Kormos
Pannonictis pliocaenica Kormos
Meles meles atavus Kormos
Perissodactyla
    Dicerorhinus etruscus (Falconer)
    Equus sp.
Artiodactyla
    Praemegaceros sp.
    Alces latifrons (Johnson)
    Capreolus capreolus süssenbornensis Kahlke
    Bison schoetensacki Freudenberg

21. Buguilesti II (Oltenia), Romania
    (Bolomey 1965; Samson and Radulesco 1968)
The younger phase of the Buguilesti sequence (Buguilesti II) in Oltenia
(Tetes, Valea Caselor, Dealul Viilor, Dealul Sasei) has to be placed in
the late Cromerian (Buguilesti I = late Villafranchian and early post-
Villafranchian).

Proboscidea
    Archidiskodon or *Mammonteus* sp.
Perissodactyla
    Equus süssenbornensis Wüst
    Equus aluticus Radulesco and Samson
Artiodactyla
    Soergelia elisabethae Schaub
    Bison cf. *schoetensacki* Freudenberg

22. Rotbav-Silvestru (Transylvania), Romania
    (Necrasov, Samson, and Radulesco 1961; Liteanu, Mihaila, and

Bandrabur 1962; Samson and Radulesco 1963, 1965; Radulesco, Samson, Milhăila, and Kovács 1965; Radulesco and Kovács 1966; Samson and Kovács 1968; Radulesco and Samson 1967, 1968; Alimen, Radulesco, and Samson 1968)
From the lower part of horizon III of the depression of Baraolt and Sf. Gheorghe (Rotbav-Silvestru, Rotbav-Cariera de Sub Brazi, lower horizon, and Feldioara-Cetate), an uppermost Lower Pleistocene association has been reported:

Proboscidea
    Archidiskodon meridionalis (Nesti)
Perissodactyla
    Dicerorhinus etruscus (Falconer)
    Equus cf. *stenonis* Cocchi
    Equus süssenbornensis Wüst
    Equus aluticus Radulesco and Samson
Artiodactyla
    "Allocaenelaphus" arambourgi Radulesco and Samson
    "Cervus" sp.

23. Split (Marjan Peninsula), Yugoslavia
    (Vuletić 1953; Malez 1959)
    Carnivora
        Ursus etruscus Cuvier
        Ursus cf. *deningeri* von Reichenau
        Martes sp.
    Perissodactyla
        Dicerorhinus etruscus (Falconer)
    Artiodactyla
        Cervus sp.
        Capreolus capreolus süssenbornensis Kahlke

24. Kair (Cherson), USSR
    (Topačevski 1957, Kretzoi 1965)
    Proboscidea
        Archidiskodon meridionalis (Nesti)
    Perissodactyla
        Equus cf. *sivalensis* Falconer
    Artiodactyla
        Paracamelus alutensis Simionescu
        Cervidae gen. et sp. indet.
        Bos sp.
        Bison sp.

25. Siniaya Balka (Taman Peninsula. Black Sea), USSR
(Oswald 1915–1916; Andrusov 1926; Archangelski and Strachov 1938; Beliajeva 1925, 1933; Gromov 1948; Vereščagin 1957, 1959; Alexeeva 1961; Dubrovo 1963)
The fossil fauna of the Taman Peninsula is the type-association of the Taman faunistic complex (Gromov 1948). It correlates with the associations of middle and late "Cromerian." Other localities are Fontalovskaya, Kapustina Balka, Shutnovtsy, Tikhonovka, Nogaisk, etc.

Taman Penisula
Carnivora
Canis tamanensis Vereščagin
Panthera sp.
Proboscidea
Archidiskodon meridionalis tamanensis Dubrovo
Mammonteus trogontherii (Pohlig)
Perissodactyla
Dicerorhinus cf. *etruscus* (Falconer)
Elasmotherium caucasicum Borissiak
Equus cf. *süssenbornensis* Wüst
Artiodactyla
Sus tamanensis Vereščagin
Praemegaceros verticornis (Dawkins)
?Eucladoceros sp.
?Megaloceros sp.
"Tamanalces" caucasicus Vereščagin
Camelus cf. *kujalnikensis* Khomenko
Gazella sp.
Strepsicerotini gen. et sp. indet.
Bison schoetensacki ssp.
Bison sp.

26. Nogaisk (Sea of Azov, northern shore), USSR
(Garutt 1954; Topačevski 1957; Kretzoi 1965)
Carnivora
Canis sp.
Mustela cf. *nivalis* Linnaeus
Mustela palerminea Petenyi
Hyaena sp.
Proboscidea
Archidiskodon meridionalis (Nesti)

Perissodactyla
Elasmotherium caucasicum Borissiak
Equus sp.
Artiodactyla
?*Megaloceros* sp.
Bison sp.

II.   LOWERMOST AND LOWER "MIDDLE PLEISTOCENE"

Early *Mammonteus* associations

A.   *Western Province (Selected Macrofaunas)*

27.   Toledo (Tajo River), Spain
(Gómez de Llarena 1913; Ismael del Pan 1918; Perez de Barradas 1920; Roman 1922; Aranegui 1927; Hernández-Pacheco 1930, 1955 Medina and Riba 1957; Aguado 1962, 1963; Aguirre 1965)
Important Quaternary field research in Spain has been continued in recent years by Professor M. M. Aguado in the vicinity of Toledo (Buenavista, Campo de Tiro, Pinedo). With these fossil associations, it has become possible to trace the lower Middle Pleistocene early *Mammonteus* complex from the Tajo as far as to the Chukotija River (northeast Siberia) areas.

Proboscidea
Mammonteus trogontherii (Pohlig)
Palaeoloxodon antiquus (Falconer)
Perissodactyla
Dicerorhinus sp.
Equus sp.
Artiodactyla
Hippopotamus antiquus Desmarest
Praedama cf. *süssenbornensis* Kahlke
Cervus elaphus ssp.
Bos primigenius ssp.

28.   Manzanares I (Madrid), Spain
(Prado 1864; Villanova 1873; Obermaier, Wernert, and Perez de Barradas 1957; Riba 1957; Crusafont-Pairó 1960, 1965)

Proboscidea
Palaeoloxodon antiquus platyrhinchus Graells

Perissodactyla
Dicerorhinus cf. *kirchbergensis* (Jäger)
Equus sp.
Artiodactyla
?Megaloceros sp.
Cervus elaphus ssp.
Bos sp.

29. Solilhac (Velay), France
(Boule 1892; Commont 1910; Freudenberg 1914; Woldstedt 1958; Prat 1968; M. F. Bonifay 1969, 1971)
Carnivora
Hyaena sp.
Proboscidea
Archidiskodon cf. *meridionalis* (Nesti)
Palaeoloxodon antiquus (Falconer)
Perissodactyla
Dicerorhinus kirchbergensis (Jäger)
Equus cf. *süssenbornensis* (Wüst)
Artiodactyla
Hippopotamus antiquus Desmarest
Praemegaceros solilhacus (Robert)
Cervus elaphus ssp.
Dama cf. *clactoniana* (Falconer)
Capra sp.
Bison priscus ssp.

30. Grotte de l'Escale (Saint-Estève-Janson, Bouches-du-Rhône), France
(M. F. Bonifay and E. Bonifay 1963; E. Bonifay 1968, 1969; M. F. Bonifay 1969, 1971; Jánossy 1969)
Carnivora
Canis lupus cf. *mosbachensis* Soergel
cf. *Cuon dubius stehlini* Thenius
Vulpes vulpes jansoni Bonifay
Felis (Lynx) pardina spelaea Boule
Panthera gombaszögensis (Kretzoi) (= *Jansofelis vaufreyi* Bonifay)
Hyaena prisca de Serres
Ursus deningeri von Richenau
Mustela palerminea Petenyi

Gulo schlosseri Kormos
Meles sp.
Perissodactyla
   Dicerorhinus cf. *kirchbergensis* (Jäger)
Artiodactyla
   Sus sp.
   ?Megaloceros sp. (*?Praemegaceros* sp.)
   Hemitragus sp.
   Bos sp.

31. Chalon-Saint-Cosme (Chalon), France
   (Bourdier, Combier and Gauthier 1952; Bourdier 1954; Woldstedt 1958)
   Perissodactyla
      Equus cf. *stenonis* Cocchi
   Artiodactyla
      Praemegaceros sp.
      Cervus elaphus ssp.
      ?Rangifer sp.
      Bos sp.

32. Chatillon-Saint-Jean (Drôme), France
   (Bourdier, Combier, and Gauthier 1952; Bourdier 1954; Chauvire 1962; M. F. Bonifay 1969, 1971)
   Perissodactyla
      Equus sp.
   Artiodactyla
      ?Megaloceros sp.
      Cervus elaphus ssp.
      "Cervus" sp.
      ?Rangifer sp.
      Capreolus capreolus ssp.

33. Caya Arnoldi (Ponte Galeria), Italy
   (Ambrosetti 1967; Bonnadonna 1968; Azzaroli and Ambrosetti 1970; Ambrosetti, Azzaroli, Bonnadonna and Follieri 1972)
   Proboscidea
      Mammonteus cf. *trogontherii* (Pohlig)
      Palaeoloxodon antiquus (Falconer)
   Artiodactyla
      Hippopotamus antiquus Desmarest
      Praedama savini (Dawkins)

Praemegaceros verticornis (Dawkins)
Cervus elaphus acoronatus Beninde
Dama cf. *dama* Linnaeus
Bos primigenius Bojanus

B. Transitional Zone, Rhine River Area s. 1.

In the transitional-zone between the Atlantic and the continental zoogeographical provinces, the mixed character of the lower Middle Pleistocene associations is two-fold: together with archaic elements like *Cuon dubius stehlini* Thenius, *Panthera gombaszögensis* (Kretzoi), *Hyaena perrieri* Croizet and Jobert, and *Dicerorhinus etruscus* (Falconer) we find more progressive species of these families like *Cuon alpinus priscus* Thenius, *Panthera leo fossilis* (von Reichenau), *Crocuta crocuta praespelaea* Schütt, and *Dicerorhinus kirchbergensis* (Jäger). Together with species with "Atlantic" affinities like *Hippopotamus antiquus* Desmarest we find "northern-continental" elements like *Mammonteus trogontherii* (Pohlig), *Rangifer arcticus stadelmanni* Kahlke and *Praeovibos schmidtgeni* Schertz, as well as the "continental" equid *Equus süssenbornensis* Wüst.

34. Mosbach II (Wiesbaden), West Germany
   (For references, see Mosbach I, Number 12)
Middle layers, "main fauna"
   Carnivora
      Canis lupus mosbachensis Soergel
      Cuon dubius stehlini Thenius
      Cuon alpinus priscus Thenius
      Felis (Lynx) issiodorensis Croizet and Jobert
      Panthera gombaszögensis (Kretzoi)
      Panthera leo fossilis (von Reichenau)
      Panthera pardus ssp.
      Acinonyx pardinensis Croizet and Jobert
      Homotherium sp.
      Hyaena perrieri Croizet and Jobert
      Crocuta crocuta praespelaea Schütt
      Ursus stehlini Kretzoi
      Ursus deningeri von Reichenau
      Mustela nivalis Linnaeus
      Mustele (Putorius) putorius Linnaeus
      Gulo schlosseri Kormos

Meles meles ssp.
Proboscidea
    Mammonteus trogontherii (Pohlig)
    Palaeoloxodon antiquus (Falconer)
Perissodactyla
    Dicerorhinus etruscus (Falconer)
    Dicerorhinus kirchbergensis (Jäger)
    Equus mosbachensis (von Reichenau)
Artiodactyla
    Hippopotamus antiquus Desmarest
    Sus scrofa mosbachensis Küthe
    Praemegaceros verticornis (Dawkins)
    Praemegaceros sp.
    Praedama sp.
    Cervus elaphus acoronatus Beninde
    "Cervus" elaphoides Kahlke
    Rangifer arcticus stadelmanni Kahlke
    Alces latifrons (Johnson)
    Alces sp.
    Capreolus capreolus süssenbornensis Kahlke
    Bison schoetensacki Freudenberg
    Bison priscus Bojanus
    Praeovibos schmidtgeni Schertz
35. Steinheim I (Murr), West Germany
    (Berckhemer 1927, 1933, 1934, 1940, 1941; Beninde 1937;
    Rode 1933; Adam 1952, 1953, 1954, 1961)
Lower Mammoth gravels
Proboscidea
    Mammonteus trogontherii (Pohlig)
Perissodactyla
    Dicerorhinus kirchbergensis (Jäger)
    Equus cf. *mosbachensis* von Reichenau
Artiodactyla
    Cervus elaphus ssp.
    Bison priscus (Bojanus)

36. Mauer (Heidelberg), West Germany
    (von Richenau 1906; Schoetensack 1908; Freudenberg 1911,
    1914, 1929; Soergel 1912, 1914, 1922, 1928; Wurm 1912, 1913;
    Rüger 1928, 1929; Voelcker 1930, 1931; Beninde 1937;
    Schmidt 1940; Schütt 1969; Hemmer 1971)

Carnivora
  Canis lupus mosbachensis Soergel
  Felis cf. *Silvestris* Schreber
  Felis (Lynx) issiodorensis Croizet and Jobert
  Panthera leo fossilis (von Reichenau)
  Panthera pardus sickenbergi Schütt
  Homotherium sp.
  Hyaena arvernensis Croizet and Jobert
  Ursus stehlini Kretzoi
  Ursus deningeri von Reichenau
Proboscidea
  Mammonteus trogontherii (Pohlig)
  Palaeoloxodon antiquus (Falconer)
Perissodactyla
  Dicerorhinus etruscus (Falconer)
  Equus mosbachensis von Reichenau
Artiodactyla
  Hippopotamus antiquus Desmarest
  Sus scrofa priscus Goldfuss
  Cervus elaphus acoronatus Beninde
  Alces latifrons (Johnson)
  Capreolus capreolus ssp.
  Bison priscus (Bojanus)

37. Randersacker (Würzburg), West Germany
    (Rutte 1958, 1967)
    Carnivora
      Ursus cf. *deningeri* von Reichenau
    Proboscidea
      Mammonteus trogontherii (Pohlig)
      Palaeoloxodon antiquus (Falconer)
    Perissodactyla
      Dicerorhinus etruscus (Falconer)
      Equus mosbachensis von Reichenau
    Artiodactyla
      ?Praemegaceros verticornis (Dawkins)
      ?Megaloceros sp.
      ?Alces sp.
      Capreolus capreolus ssp.
      Bison priscus (Bojanus)
      Bison schoetensacki Freudenberg

38. Herxheim (Pfalz), West Germany
     (Voelcker 1937; Plewe 1938; Kuss 1961)
     Proboscidea
        Palaeoloxodon antiquus (Falconer)
     Perissodactyla
        Dicerorhinus etruscus (Falconer)
     Artiodactyla
        Sus scrofa ssp.

C. *Eastern Province*

The eastern zoogeographical province of continental Europe seems to
us to be an important area to correlate both the faunal sequence of
Middle Pleistocene Europe and Asia and the faunal sequence and the
sequence of glacial deposits of the northern glaciations. In this area it
was possible to prove that the first *Mammonteus* associations correlate
with the Elster glacial complex and that the early *Mammonteus-Coelodonta-Rangifer-Ovibos* associations reached the temperate zones of
central Europe within the beginning of the early Elster (= early Mindel
of the alpine sequence). The character of the associations is distinct
northern-continental with glacial (arctic) components like *Rangifer* and
Ovibos.

39. Edersleben (Sangerhausen), East Germany
     (Herter 1850; Kayser 1884; Wüst 1901; Kammholz 1955;
     Krutzsch and Reichstein 1956)
     Proboscidea
        Mammonteus trogontherii (Pohlig)
     Artiodactyla
        Cervus elaphus ssp.
        Bison priscus (Bojanus)

40. Bornhausen (Harz), West Germany
     (Bode and Schröder 1913; Sickenberg 1962)
     Proboscidea
        Mammonteus trogontherii (Pohlig)
     Perissodactyla
        Coelodonta antiquitatis (Blumenbach) (?*C. tologoijensis*
        Beliajeva)
        Equus sp. (cf. *germanicus* Nehring)

Artiodactyla
Rangifer tarandus ssp.

41. Neuekrug (Harz), West Germany
(Bode and Schröder 1913; Sickenberg 1962)
Proboscidea
Mammonteus ?*trogontherii* (Pohlig)
Perissodactyla
Coelodonta antiquitatis (Blumenbach) (?*C. tologoijensis*
Belia-Jeva)
Artiodactyla
Rangifer tarandus ssp.

42. Süssenborn (Weimar), East Germany
(Baumer 1763; Wüst 1900; Soergel 1911, 1912, 1913, 1919,
1926, 1928, 1936, 1939, 1941; Freudenberg 1914; von Reichenau 1915; Zeuner 1937; Thenius 1948; Schaub 1951; Kahlke
1951, 1956–1959, 1958, 1960, 1961, 1963, 1964, 1969; Koby
1952; Adam 1956; Flerov 1969; Guenther 1969; Hünermann
1969; Kurtén 1969; Musil 1969; Schäefer 1969)

Carnivora
Canis lupus mosbachensis Soergel
Panthera cf. *gombaszögensis* (Kretzoi)
Homotherium sp.
Hyaena brevirostris Aymard
Crocuta crocuta (Erxleben)
Ursus deningeri von Reichenau
Lutra cf. *simplicidens* Thenius
Proboscidea
Mammonteus trogontherii (Pohlig)
Perissodactyla
Dicerorhinus etruscus (Falconer)
Equus süssenbornensis Wüst
Equus marxi von Reichenau
Equus altidens von Reichenau
Artiodactyla
Sus scrofa priscus Goldfuss
Praemegaceros verticornis (Dawkins) (= *Orthogonoceros)*
Praemegaceros sp.
Praedama süssenbornensis (Kahlke) (= *Polichodoryceros*)

Cervus elaphus acoronatus Beninde
"Cervus" elaphoides Kahlke
Rangifer arcticus stadelmanni Kahlke
Alces latifrons (Johnson)
Capreolus capreolus süssenbornensis Kahlke
Soergelia elisabethae Schaub
Bison schoetensacki schoetensacki Freudenberg
Bison schoetensacki lagenocornis Flerov
Bison priscus priscus (Bojanus)
Ovibos moschatus süssenbornensis Kahlke

43. Bad Frankenhausen (Kyffhäuser), East Germany
    (Schmidt 1923; Sickenberg 1962; Kahlke 1963)
    Carnivora
       Ursus sp.
    Perissodactyla
       Coelodonta antiquitatis ssp.
       Equus süssenbornensis Wüst
       Equus sp.
    Artiodactyla
       Rangifer sp.
       ?*Soergelia elisabethae* Schaub
       Praeovibos priscus Staudinger

44. Hundsheim (Deutsch-Altenburg), Austria
    (Toula 1902, 1906, 1907; Freudenberg 1908, 1914; Ehrenberg
    1929, 1933; Sickenberg 1933; Kormos 1935, 1937; Breuer 1938;
    Zapfe 1939, 1946, 1948; Bachofen-Echt 1941; Thenius 1947,
    1948, 1949, 1951, 1953, 1954, 1965; Adam 1961; Daxner and
    Thenius 1965; Daxner 1968; Schütt 1971)

    Carnivora
       Canis lupus mosbachensis Soergel
       Cuon priscus Thenius
       Vulpes angustidens Thenius
       Felis cf. *silvestris* Schreber
       Panthera pardus ssp.
       Homotherium moravicum (Woldřich)
       Acinonyx pardinensis intermedius Thenius
       Hyaena sp.
       ?*Crocuta crocuta* ssp.

Ursus deningeri hundsheimensis Zapfe
Mustela sp.
Putorius sp.
Lutra simplicidens Thenius
Proboscidea
   Elephantidae gen. et sp. indet.
Perissodactyla
   Dicerorhinus etruscus hundsheimensis Toula
Artiodactyla
   Sus scrofa ssp.
   Cervus elaphus ssp.
   Capreolus capreolus ssp.
   Hemitragus jemlahicus bonali Harlé and Stehlin
   Bison priscus (Bojanus)
45. Zlaty Kon-Cave (C 718, Koneprusy), Czechoslovakia
   (Fejfar 1956, 1961; Prošek and Ložek 1957; Heller 1958)

Carnivora
   Canis lupus mosbachensis Soergel
   Xenocyon spelaeoides Kretzoi
   Vulpes angustidens Thenius
   Felis (Felis) sp.
   Felis (Lynx) sp.
   Panthera gombaszögensis (Kretzoi)
   Panthera pardus ssp.
   Homotherium moravicum (Woldřich)
   Hyaena brevirostris Aymard
   Ursus mediterraneus Forsyth Major
   Ursus deningeri von Reichenau
   Mustela palerminea Petenyi
   Meles meles atavus Kormos
Proboscidea
   Mammonteus trogontherii (Pohlig)
Perissodactyla
   Dicerorhinus etruscus (Falconer)
   Equus cf. *mosbachensis* von Reichenau
   Equus sp.
Artiodactyla
   Sus scrofa priscus Goldfuss
   Preemegaceros sp.
   Cervus elaphus acoronatus Beninde

Alces latifrons (Johnson)
Soergelia sp.
Bison schoetensacki Freudenberg
Praeovibos priscus Staudinger

46. Holštejn (Brno), Czechoslovakia
(Musil 1966)

Carnivora
  Panthera gombaszögensis (Kretzoi)
  Ursus sp.
  Putorius cf. *stromeri* Kormos
  Meles meles Linnaeus
Artiodactyla
  Sus scrofa priscus Goldfuss
  Cervidae gen. et sp. indet.
  Capreolus capreolus süssenbornensis Kahlke
  Bison priscus (Bojanus)

47. Stránská skála (Brno), Czechoslovakia
(Woldřich 1916, 1917; Knies 1925, 1926; Capek 1917, 1921;
Schirm-Eisen 1926, 1930, 1932, 1935; Jaros 1926; Jaros and
Zapletal 1928; Stehlik 1928, 1934, 1935, 1936; Skutil 1930,
1932; Kormos 1933; Musil 1965, 1968, 1971; Fejfar 1961, 1971;
Hemmer 1971; Flerov 1971; Kahlke 1971; Kurtén 1971)

Carnivora
  Canis lupus mosbachensis Soergel
  Cuon sp.
  Xenocyon spelaeoides Kretzoi
  Vulpes praeglacialis (Kormos)
  Vulpes angustidens Thenius
  Vulpes sp.
  Nyctereutes cf. *petenyii* (Kormos)
  Panthera gombaszögensis (Kretzoi)
  Panthera pardus ssp.
  Homotherium moravicum (Woldřich)
  Hyaena brevirostris Aymard
  Crocuta crocuta (Erxleben)
  Ursus deningeri von Reichenau
Proboscidea
  Mammonteus trogontherii (Pohlig)

Perissodactyla
  Dicerorhinus etruscus (Falconer)
  Equus süssenbornensis Wüst
Artiodactyla
  Praemegaceros verticornis (Dawkins)
  Praemegaceros sp.
  Cervus elaphus ?*acoronatus* Beninde
  "Cervus" cf. *elaphoides* Kahlke
  Alces latifrons (Johnson)
  Capreolus capreolus süssenbornensis Kahlke
  Bison schoetensacki Freudenberg

48. Gombasek (= Gombaszög) (Slovakia), Czechoslovakia
    (Suf 1931; Tasnády-Kubacska 1935; Kretzoi 1938, 1941, 1956;
    Fejfar 1961; Dietrich 1968; Kurtén 1969; Jánossy 1969)

    Carnivora
      Canis lupus mosbachensis Soergel
      Xenocyon spelaeoides Kretzoi
      Vulpes vulpes ssp.
      Alopex sp.
      Felis (Felis) sp.
      Felinae gen. et sp. indet.
      Panthera gombaszögensis (Kretzoi)
      Panthera pardus ssp.
      Homotherium moravicum (Woldřich)
      Hyaena brevirostris Aymard
      Crocuta sp.
      Ursus mediterraneus Forsyth Major
      Ursus gombaszögensis Kretzoi
      Mustela palerminea (Petenyi)
      Gulo schlosseri Kormos   '
      Meles meles atavus Kormos
    Proboscidea
      Mammonteus trogontherii (Pohlig)
    Perissodactyla
      Dicerorhinus etruscus (Falconer)
      Equus robustus Pomel
    Artiodactyla
      Sus scrofa priscus Goldfuss
      Praemegaceros verticornis (Dawkins)
      Cervus elaphus ssp.

49. Vértesszöllös, Location I and II (Tata), Hungary
    (Kormos 1913; Freudenberg 1914; Kretzoi 1926–1927, 1965;
    Schréter 1953; Kretzoi and Vértes 1965; Thoma 1966; Jánossy
    1969)

Carnivora
  Canis lupus mosbachensis Soergel
  Vulpes sp.
  Panthera gombaszögensis (Kretzoi)
  Panthera leo fossilis (von Reichenau)
  Hyaena brevirostris Aymard
  Ursus stehlini Kretzoi
  Ursus deningeri von Reichenau
  Mustela cf. *erminea* Linnaeus
Perissodactyla
  Dicerorhinus cf. *etruscus* (Falconer)
  Equus mosbachensis von Reichenau
Artiodactyla
  Cervus elaphus cf. *acoronatus* Beninde
  Capreolus capreolus süssenbornensis Kahlke
  Bison priscus ssp.

50. Várhegy (Budapest), Hungary
    (Horusiatzky 1938; Mottl 1942, 1943; Schréter 1953; Jánossy
    1969)

Carnivora
  Canis lupus mosbachensis Soergel
  Panthera leo fossilis (von Reichenau)
  Homotherium latidens (Owen)
Proboscidea
  Mammonteus trogontherri (Pohlig)
Perissodactyla
  Dicerorhinus etruscus (Falconer)
  Equus stenonis Cocchi
  Equus mosbachensis von Reichenau
Artiodactyla
  ?Praemegaceros sp.
  Cervus elaphus ssp.
  Capreolus capreolus major Regalia
  Bison priscus (Bojanus)

51. Betfia VII (Crisana), Romania
(For references, see Betfia V, Number 20)
Carnivora
Canis lupus mosbachensis Soergel
Ursus sp. (*?deningeri* von Reichenau)
Proboscidea
Mammonteus trogontherii (Pohlig)
Artiodactyla
Bison schoetensacki Freudenberg

52. Rotbav-Dealul (Brasov, Transylvania), Romania
(Radulesco and Kovács 1966, 1968; Radulesco, Samson, Mihăilă and Kovács 1965; Samson and Radulesco 1963, 1965; Alimen, Radulesco and Samson 1968)
From the Brasov area (Rotbav-Dealul, Tiganilor, Feldioara-Cariera, and Araci-Cariera) a "lower Middle Pleistocene" association is known:

Proboscidea
Mammonteus trogontherii (Pohlig) primitive type
Perissodactyla
Dicerorhinus kirchbergensis (Jäger)
Equus cf. *mosbachensis* von Reichenau
Artiodactyla
Praedama savini (Dawkins)
Cervus elaphus ssp.
Alces latifrons (Johnson)
Capreolus capreolus ssp.
Bison cf. *priscus* (Bojanus)

53. Petralona (Saloniki), Greece
(Kannelis 1962; Sickenberg 1964, 1971; Kannelis and Marinos 1969)

Carnivora
Canis lupus mosbachensis Soergel
Cuon sp.
Vulpes marinoso Sickenberg
Felis ?silvestris Schreber
Felis ?chaus Goldenstaedt
Panthera leo fossilis (von Reichenau)

Hyaena perrieri Croizet and Jobert
Crocuta crocuta cf. *praespelaea* Schütt
Ursus deningeri von Reichenau
Perissodactyla
    Dicerorhinus sp.
    Equus sp. (?*mosbachensis* von Reichenau)
    Equus cf. *hydruntinus* Regalia
Artiodactyla
    Sus scrofa ?*priscus* Goldfuss
    Praemegaceros verticornis (Dawkins)
    Cervus elaphus ssp.
    Dama cf. *dama* Linnaeus
    Capra ibex macedonica Sickenberg
    Bos primigenius Bojanus

54. Tiraspol (Moldavia), USSR
(Barbot de Marny 1869; Pavlova 1906, 1910, 1925; Gromova 1932, 1935, 1949; Gromov 1939, 1948, 1970; Vereščagin 1957, 1959, 1961; Pidopličko 1954; David 1962, 1965, 1971; Vereščagin and David 1968; Dubrovo 1971; Gromov and Dubrovo 1971; Beliajeva and David 1971; Alexeeva 1971; Kahlke 1971; Flerov and David 1971; Vereščagin, Alexeeva, David, and Baigusheva 1971)
The fossil association of Tiraspol (alluvial deposits of Kolkotova terrace V of the Dniester River) is the type-association of the Tiraspol faunal complex (Gromov 1948), typical for the "Mindel" of the southern area of the European part of the Soviet Union. Tiraspol is the most important locality in the Soviet Union for correlating Middle Pleistocene Europe and Asia by means of biostratigraphy.

Carnivora
    Panthera leo ssp.
    Hyaena sp.
    Crocuta sp.
    Ursus deningeri von Reichenau
Proboscidea
    Hammonteus trogontherii (Pohlig)
Perissodactyla
    Dicerorhinus etruscus (Falconer)
    Dicerorhinus kirchbergensis (Jäger)
    Dicerorhinus sp.

Equus aff. *süssenbornensis* Wüst
Equus aff. *mosbachensis* von Reichenau
Equus sp.
Artiodactyla
  Praemegaceros verticornis (Dawkins)
  Praedama cf. *süssenbornensis* Kahlke
  Cervus elaphus acoronatus Beninde
  "Cervus" elaphoides Kahlke
  Alces latifrons (Johnson)
  Gazella sp.
  Pontoceros ambiguus Veresčagin, Alexeeva, David and Baigusheva
  Bison schoetensacki schoetensacki Freudenberg
  Bison schoetensacki lagenocornis Flerov

55. Achalkalaki (Georgia), USSR
   (Vekua 1962)
Recently, an important lower Pleistocene-Middle Pleistocene boundary association was discovered by Professor Vekua at Achalkalai, in Transcaucasia.

Carnivora
  Canis tengisi Vekua
  Panthera (Tigris) tigris ssp.
  Crocuta cf. *sinensis* Zdanski
  Ursus sp.
  Lutra lutra ssp.
  Meles meles ssp.
  Vormela cf. *peregusna* Güldenstaedt
Proboscidea
  Archidiskodon sp.
  Mammonteus trogontherii (Pohlig)
Perissodactyla
  Dicerorhinus etruscus (Falconer)
  Equus süssenbornensis Wüst
  Equus hipparionoides Vekua
Artiodactyla
  Hippopotamus antiquus georgicus Vekua
  Praemegaceros cf. *verticornis* (Dawkins)
  Capra sp.
  Bos sp.

III.   "MIDDLE PLEISTOCENE"

A.   Western Province (Selected Macrofaunas)

56. Torralba, Ambrona (Soria province), Spain
     (Cerralbo 1909, 1911, 1913; Breuil 1910; Harlé 1909, 1910,
     1911; Obermaier 1925; Aguirre 1962; Butzer 1962; Howell
     1962, 1968; Aguirre and Fuentes 1969)
     Carnivora
         Canis lupus cf. *mosbachensis* Soergel
         Panthera leo spelaea Goldfuss
     Proboscidea
         Mammonteus trogontherii (Pohlig)
         Palaeoloxodon antiquus (Falconer)
     Perissodactyla
         Dicerorhinus hemitoechus (Falconer)
         Equus sp.
     Artiodactyla
         Cervus elaphus ssp.
         Dama cf. *clactoniana* (Falconer)
         Bos primigenius Bojanus
         Bovidae gen. et sp. indet.

57. Manzanares II (Madrid), Spain
     (For references, see Toledo, Number 27)
     Middle terrace
     Proboscidea
         ?*Archidiskodon meridionalis* ssp. (?*Mammonteus trogonthe-rii*)
         Palaeoloxodon antiquus (Falconer)
     Perissodactyla
         Dicerorhinus kirchbergensis (Jäger)
         Equus sp.
     Artiodactyla
         Cervus elaphus ssp.
         Bos primigenius Bojanus
         Bison priscus (Bojanus)

58. Abbeville III (Somme River), France
     (For references, see Abbeville, Number 6)

Proboscidea
  Mammonteus trogontherii (Pohlig) progressive type
  Mammonteus primigenius (Blumenbach) franco-italian type
  Palaeoloxodon antiquus (Falconer)
Perissodactyla
  Coelodonta antiquitatis (Blumenbach)
  Dicerorhinus kirchbergensis (Jäger)
  Equus sp.
  Equus cf. *hydruntinus* Regalia
Artiodactyla
  Sus scrofa Linnaeus
  Cervus elaphus Linnaeus
  Capreolus capreolus (Linnaeus)
  Bos primigenius Bojanus
  Bison priscus (Bojanus)

59. Bruges (Gironde, Bordeaux), France
  (Viret and Balland 1938)
  Proboscidea
    Palaeoloxodon antiquus (Falconer)
  Perissodactyla
    Dicerorhinus kirchbergensis (Jäger)
  Artiodactyla
    Sus scrofa Linnaeus
    Cervus elaphus ssp.
    Capreolus capreolus ssp.

60. Mas des Caves (Lunel-Viel, Hérault), France
  (de Serres 1827; de Serres, Dubreuil, and Jeanjean 1828;
  Christol and Bravard 1828; Harlé 1910; M. F. Bonifay and E.
  Bonifay 1965; E. Bonifay 1968; M. F. Bonifay 1969, 1971;
  Kurtén 1968, 1969; Jánossy 1969)

  Carnivora
    Canis lupus lunellensis Bonifay
    Cuon alpinus priscus Thenius
    Vulpes vulpes ssp.
    Felis (Felis) monspessulana Bonifay
    Felis (Lynx) cf. *pardina* Temminck
    Felis (Lynx) spelaea Boule
    Panthera leo ssp.

Panthera pardus lunellensis (Bonifay)
Hyaena prisca de Serres
Crocuta crocuta spelaea Goldfuss (*intermedia* de Serres)
Ursus cf. *deningeri* von Reichenau
Mustela palerminea Petenyi
Lutra sp.
Meles thorali spelaeus Bonifay
Perissodactyla
   Dicerorhinus cf. *kirchbergensis* (Jäger)
   Equus sp.
   Equus hydruntinus Regalia
Artiodactyla
   Sus sp.
   Eucladoceros mediterraneus (Bonifay)
   Cervus elaphus ssp.
   Capreolus cf. *süssenbornensis* Kahlke
   Bos primigenius Bojanus
   Bison priscus (Bojanus)

61. Montereau I (Seine), France
    (Chaput 1924, 1927)

    Proboscidea
       Palaeoloxodon antiquus (Falconer)
    Perissodactyla
       Dicerorhinus kirchbergensis (Jäger)

62. Mainxe I (Charente), France (thirty meter terrace)
    (Guillien 1941, 1943)

    Proboscidea
       Palaeoloxodon antiquus (Falconer)
    Perissodactyla
       Dicerorhinus kirchbergensis (Jäger)
    Artiodactyla
       Hippopotamus antiquus Desmarest

B.   *Transitional Zone, Rhine River Area s. 1.*

63. Heppenloch (Gutenberg, Schwäbische Alb), West Germany
    (Nehring 1890, 1891; Hedinger 1891; von Reichenau 1906;

Koken 1912; Freudenberg 1914, 1932; Thies 1926; Bachofen-Echt 1931; Adam 1959, 1961, 1963)

Carnivora
    Canis lupus ssp.
    Cuon alpinus fossilis Nehring
    Vulpes vulpes ssp.
    Panthera leo ssp.
    Ursus arctos Linnaeus
    Ursus spelaeus Rosenmüller and Heinroth
Proboscidea
    Mammonteus sp.
Perissodactyla
    Equus cf. *steinheimensis* von Reichenau
Artiodactyla
    Sus scrofa Linnaeus
    Cervus elaphus ssp.
    Capreolus capreolus (Linnaeus)
    Bison priscus (Bojanus)

64. Steinheim II (Murr), West Germany
    (For references, see Steinheim I, Number 35)
    "*Palaeoloxodon antiquus* gravels"
    Carnivora
        Ursus spelaeus Rosenmüller and Heinroth
        Panthera cf. *leo* (Linnaeus)
        Homotherium sp.
        Meles meles (Linnaeus)
    Proboscidea
        Palaeoloxodon antiquus (Falconer)
    Perissodactyla
        Dicerorhinus kirchbergensis (Jäger)
        Dicerorhinus hemitoechus (Falconer)
        Equus steinheimensis von Reichenau
    Artiodactyla
        Sus scrofa Linnaeus
        Megaloceros giganteus antecedens (Berckhemer)
        Cervus elaphus angulatus Beninde
        Capreolus capreolus (Linnaeus)
        Bos primigenius Bojanus
        Bison cf. *schoetensacki* Freudenberg

Bison priscus (Bojanus)
Buffelus murrensis Berckhemer

65. Steinheim III (Murr), West Germany
(For references, see Steinheim I, Number 35)
"Main Mammoth gravels"

Carnivora
  Canis lupus Linnaeus
  Panthera cf. *leo* (Linnaeus)
  Ursus spelaeus Rosenmüller and Heinroth
Proboscidea
  Mammonteus trogontherii (Pohlig)
  Mammonteus primigenius (Blumenbach)
Perissodactyla
  Coelodonta antiquitatis (Blumenbach)
  Equus steinheimensis von Reichenau
Artiodactyla
  Megaloceros giganteus ssp.
  Cervus elaphus Linnaeus
  Bison priscus (Bojanus)

C. *Eastern Province*

66. Schönebeck (Elbe River), East Germany
(Schertz 1936, 1937)

Proboscidea
  Palaeoloxodon antiquus (Falconer)
Perissodactyla
  Equus sp.
Artiodactyla
  Cervus elaphus ssp.
  Bison priscus (Bojanus)
  Buffelus wanckeli Schertz

67. Ördöglyuk (Solymár, Budapest), Hungary
(Kretzoi 1933, 1944, 1956; Vèrtes 1950; Jánossy, 1969)

Carnivora
  Canis lupus Linnaeus

Perissodactyla
  Dicerorhinus kirchbergensis (Jäger)
  Equus sp.
Artiodactyla
  Cervus elaphus ssp.
  Alces brevirostris Jánossy

68. Sindominic (Intra-Carpathian Basin), Romania
  (Samson and Radulesco 1969)

Carnivora
  Ursus spelaeus Rosenmüller and Heinroth
Perissodactyla
  Coelodonta cf. *antiquitatis* (Blumenbach)
  Equus cf. *steinheimensis* von Reichenau
  Equus sp.
Artiodactyla
  Cervus elaphus Linnaeus
  Rangifer tarandus (Linnaeus)
  Bison cf. *priscus* (Bojanus)

69. Drăghici (Muntenia), Romania
  (Athanasiu 1914; Samson and Radulesco 1968)

Carnivora
  Hyaena sp.
  Homotherium cf. *moravicum* (Woldřich)
Artiodactyla
  Sus scrofa Linnaeus
  Cervus cf. *elaphus* Linnaeus
  Dama sp.
  Bison cf. *schoetensacki* Freudenberg

70. Tusnad-Sinmartin (Intra-Carpathian Basin), Romania
  (Samson and Radulesco 1969)

Proboscidea
  Mammonteus trogontherii (Pohlig) progressive type
  Mammonteus primigenius (Blumenbach) primitive type
Perissodactyla
  Equus sp.

Artiodactyla
Bison priscus (Bojanus)

71. Sfintu-Gheorghe, Malnas, Bodoc, and Ghindfalau (Braşov),
Romania
(Jekelius 1932; Poovici 1959; Radulesco, Samson, Mihaila, and
Kovács 1965; Liteanu, Mihaila, and Bandrabur 1962; Samson
and Radulesco 1963, 1965, 1968; Alimen, Radulesco, and Sam-
son 1968)

Proboscidea
Mammonteus trogontherii (Pohlig) progressive type
Mammonteus primigenius (Blumenbach) primitive type
Perissodactyla
Coelodonta antiquitatis (Blumenbach)
Equus steinheimensis von Reichenau
Equus sp.

72. Khazar faunal complex (Volga River), USSR
(Gromov 1948; Nikiforova 1960; Vasilyev 1961; Fedorov 1961;
Alexandrova 1965)

In this faunal complex we have the representatives of a relatively long
faunal sequence including the uppermost parts of the Great Interglacial Period (Mindel/Riss of the alpine sequence), as well as the Riss
(= Saale) glacial complex. In recent publications this faunal complex
has been divided into a lower and an upper Khazar complex (Vasilyev
1961; Fedorov 1961). Modern revisions of the different local associations (as we have from Taman, Tiraspol, and Binagady) are necessary
for detailed subdivisions and correlations.

Carnivora
Canis lupus Linnaeus
Vulpes vulpes (Linnaeus)
Vulpes corsac (Linnaeus)
Panthera leo spelaea (Goldfuss)
Crocuta crocuta spelaea (Goldfuss)
Ursus arctos Linnaeus
Proboscidea
Mammonteus trogontherii (Pohlig) progressive type
Mammonteus primigenius (Blumenbach) primitive type

Palaeoloxodon antiquus (Falconer)
Perissodactyla
Dicerorhinus kirchbergensis (Jäger)
Coelodonta antiquitatis (Blumenbach)
Elasmotherium sibiricum Fischer von Waldheim
Equus chorsaricus Gromov
Equus missi Pavlova
Artiodactyla
Sus scrofa Linnaeus
Megaloceros giganteus ssp.
Cervus elaphus Linnaeus
Alces alces (Linnaeus)
Rangifer tarandus (Linnaeus)
Capreolus capreolus (Linnaeus)
Camelus knoblochi Nehring
Saiga tatarica Linnaeus
Bison priscus longicornis Gromov

73. Syngyl faunal complex (Southern Zavolzhie, lower Volga River), USSR
(Gromov, Alexeev, Vangengeim, Kind, Nikiforova and Ravsky 1965; Nikiforova 1968; Alexeeva 1968)

In the European part of the Soviet Union, fossil associations suggested to be correlated with the Schönebeck-Steinheim (*Palaeoloxodon antiquus* gravels) associations are reported from an area near Raygorod (Volga River). These fossil associations have been discovered in the Syngyl layers succeeding the marine Bakinian (=Baku series). Near Chernojarsk, the Syngyl horizons are overlain by fossiliferous Khazar layers. The faunal complex of Syngyl obviously represents an intermediate stage between the Tiraspol and the Khazar faunal complexes (Nikiforova 1968).

Proboscidea
Palaeoloxodon antiquus (Falconer)
Perissodactyla
Dicerorhinus kirchbergensis (Jäger)
?*Elasmotherium sibiricum* Fischer von Waldheim
Artiodactyla
Bos volgensis (Gromov)

IV.   UPPERMOST   MIDDLE   PLEISTOCENE   AND   LOWER UPPER PLEISTOCENE

A.   *Western Province (Selected Macrofaunas)*

74.   Cueva de Castillo I and II (Santander), Spain
(Carballo 1910; Obermaier 1925, 1934; Breuil and Obermaier 1935; González Echegaray 1951, 1962; Crusafont-Pairó 1960; Altuna 1971)
Lower horizon
Carnivora
Ursus spelaeus Rosenmüller and Heinroth
Artiodactyla
Rangifer tarandus (Linnaeus)

Middle horizon
Carnivora
Canis lupus Linnaeus
Panthera leo spelaea (Goldfuss)
Crocuta crocuta spelaea (Goldfuss)
Ursus spelaeus Rosenmüller and Heinroth
Proboscidea
Palaeoloxodon antiquus (Falconer)
Perissodactyla
Dicerorhinus kirchbergensis (Jäger)
Equus sp.
Artiodactyla
Sus scrofa Linnaeus
Cervus elaphus Linnaeus
Rupicapra rupicapra (Linnaeus)
Bos primigenius Bojanus
Bison priscus (Bojanus)

75.   Cueva de Morin I (Villanueva, Villaescusa), Spain
(Vega del Sella 1921; Carballó 1923; González Echegaray and Freeman 1971; Altuna 1972)
Perissodactyla
Dicerorhinus kirchbergensis (Jäger)
Equus sp.
Artiodactyla
Cervus elaphus Linnaeus
Bos primigenius Bojanus

76. Olazagutia Cave (Yacimiento de Coscobilo, Navarra), Spain
    (Ruiz de Goana 1941, 1952, 1958; Maluquer de Motes 1957;
    Crusafont-Pairó 1960; Barandiarán 1967; Altuna 1972)

Carnivora
  Canis lupus Linnaeus
  Vulpes vulpes (Linnaeus)
  Felis sp.
  Panthera pardus (Linnaeus)
  Crocuta crocuta spelaea (Goldfuss)
  Ursus spelaeus Rosenmüller and Heinroth
  Ursus arctos Linnaeus
  Mustela sp.
Perissodactyla
  Dicerorhinus ?*megarhinus* de Christol (= *Dicerorhinus kirch-
  bergensis)*
  Equus sp.
Artiodactyla
  Hippopotamus antiquus Desmarest
  Sus scrofa Linnaeus
  Cervus elaphus Linnaeus
  Capreolus capreolus (Linnaeus)
  Capra sp.

77. Cueva de Lezetxiki (Garagarza, Mondragón), Spain
    (Altuna 1972)
    Layer VIII

Carnivora
  Panthera leo spelaea (Goldfuss)
  Ursus cf. *deningeri* von Reichenau (= *U. spelaeus*?)
Perissodactyla
  Dicerorhinus sp.
Artiodactyla
  Bos primigenius Bojanus
  Bison priscus (Bojanus)
  Layers V to VII

Carnivora
  Canis lupus Linnaeus
  Vulpes vulpes (Linnaeus)
  Felis (Lynx) lynx Linnaeus
  Panthera leo spelaea (Goldfuss)

Panthera pardus (Linnaeus)
Ursus spelaeus Rosenmüller and Heinroth
Ursus arctos Linnaeus
Perissodactyla
  Dicerorhinus kirchbergensis (Jäger)
  ?*Dicerorhinus hemitoechus* (Falconer)
  Equus sp.
Artiodactyla
  Sus scrofa Linnaeus
  Megaloceros giganteus ssp.
  Cervus elaphus Linnaeus
  Capreolus capreolus (Linnaeus)
  Capra sp.
  Rupicapra rupicapra (Linnaeus)
  Bison priscus (Bojanus)

78. Fontéchevade (Dordogne), France
  Alimen, Arambourg and Schreuder 1958; Chaline 1965; Jánossy 1969)
  Carnivora
    Canis lupus Linnaeus
    Cuon alpinus Pallas
    Vulpes vulpes (Linnaeus)
    Vulpes cf. *lagopus* (Linnaeus)
    Crocuta crocuta (Erxleben)
    Ursus spelaeus Rosenmüller and Heinroth
    Martes sp.
    Putorius putorius (Linnaeus)
    Mustela erminea Linnaeus
    Mustela nivalis Linnaeus
    Meles meles (Linnaeus)
  Perissodactyla
    Dicerorhinus kirchbergensis (Jäger)
    Equus sp.
    Equus hydruntinus Regalia
  Artiodactyla
    Sus scrofa Linnaeus
    Cervus elaphus Linnaeus
    Dama cf. *grimaldensis* Patte
    Capreolus capreolus (Linnaeus)
    Bovidae gen. et sp. indet.

79. Montereau II (Seine), France
    (For references, see Montereau I, Number 61)

    Proboscidea
    Palaoloxodon antiquus (Falconer)
    Perissodactyla
    Dicerorhinus kirchbergensis (Jäger)
    Artiodactyla
    Hippopotamus antiquus Desmarest

80. Montereau III (Seine), France
    (For references, see Montereau, Number 61)

    Proboscidea
    Mammonteus primigenius (Blumenbach)
    Perissodactyla
    Coelodonta antiquitatis (Blumenbach)

81. Grotte du Prince (Ligurie italienne), France
    (Boule 1910–1919; M. F. Bonifay 1962, 1971; M. F. Bonifay
    and E. Bonifay 1962; Sickenberg 1965; Jánossy 1965)
    "Foyer D"
    Carnivora
    Canis lupus Linnaeus
    Felis (Lynx) lynx Linnaeus
    Panthera pardus (Linnaeus)
    Crocuta crocuta spelaea (Goldfuss)
    Ursus spelaeus Rosenmüller and Heinroth
    Ursus arctos Linnaeus
    Proboscidea
    Palaeoloxodon antiquus (Falconer)
    Perissodactyla
    Dicerorhinus kirchbergensis (Jäger)
    Equus cf. *stenonis* Cocchi
    Equus sp.
    Artiodactyla
    Hippopotamus antiquus Desmarest
    Cervus elaphus Linnaeus
    Dama grimaldensis Patte
    Capreolus capreolus (Linnaeus)
    Capra ibex (Linnaeus)
    Bovidae gen. et sp. indet.

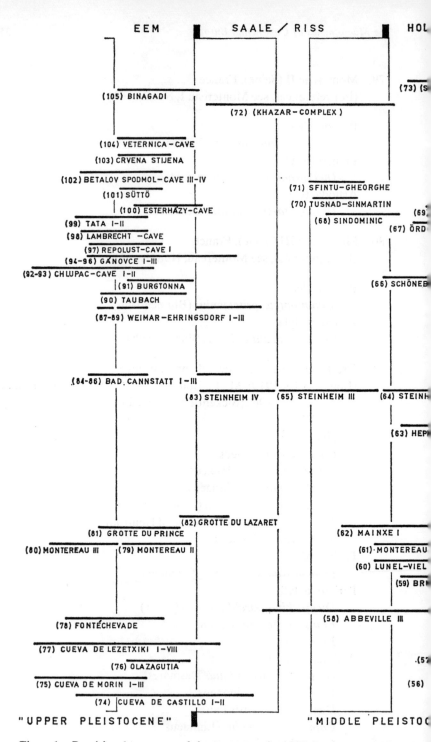

Figure 1. Provisional summary of the sequence of mid-Pleistocene macrofaunas o

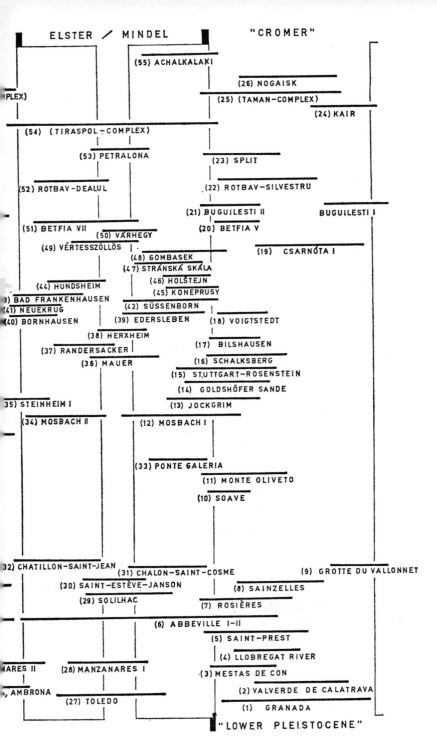

ELSTER / MINDEL   "CROMER"

(55) ACHALKALAKI

(26) NOGAISK

(PLEX)   (25) (TAMAN-COMPLEX)

(24) KAIR

(54) (TIRASPOL-COMPLEX)

(53) PETRALONA   (23) SPLIT

(52) ROTBAV-DEALUL   (22) ROTBAV-SILVESTRU

(21) BUGUILESTI II   BUGUILESTI I

(51) BETFIA VII   (20) BETFIA V
(50) VÁRHEGY
(49) VÉRTESSZÖLLÖS   (19) CSARNÓTA I
(48) GOMBASEK
(47) STRÁNSKÁ SKÁLA
(44) HUNDSHEIM   (46) HOLŠTEJN
(45) KONEPRUSY
3) BAD FRANKENHAUSEN
(41) NEUEKRUG   (42) SÜSSENBORN
(40) BORNHAUSEN   (39) EDERSLEBEN   (18) VOIGTSTEDT
(38) HERXHEIM
(37) RANDERSACKER   (17) BILSHAUSEN
(36) MAUER   (16) SCHALKSBERG
(15) STUTTGART-ROSENSTEIN
(14) GOLDSHÖFER SANDE
35) STEINHEIM I   (13) JOCKGRIM
(34) MOSBACH II   (12) MOSBACH I

(33) PONTE GALERIA
(11) MONTE OLIVETO
(10) SOAVE

32) CHATILLON-SAINT-JEAN   (9) GROTTE DU VALLONNET
(31) CHALON-SAINT-COSME
(30) SAINT-ESTÈVE-JANSON   (8) SAINZELLES
(29) SOLILHAC   (7) ROSIÈRES
(6) ABBEVILLE I-II
(5) SAINT-PREST
(4) LLOBREGAT RIVER
ARES II   (28) MANZANARES I   (3) MESTAS DE CON
, AMBRONA   (2) VALVERDE DE CALATRAVA
(27) TOLEDO   (1) GRANADA
"LOWER PLEISTOCENE"

ental Europe

82. Grotte du Lazaret (Alpes-Maritimes), France
(Gagnière 1957, 1969; de Lumley 1965; E. Bonifay 1968; M. F. Bonifay 1969, 1971)

Carnivora
Canis lupus Linnaeus
Vulpes vulpes (Linnaeus)
Felis (Lynx) spelaea Boule
Felis sp., cf. *Felis (Lynx) pardina* Temminck
Panthera sp.
Perissodactyla
Equus sp.
Artiodactyla
Cervus elaphus Linnaeus
Dama sp.
Rupicapra rupicapra (Linnaeus)
Capra ibex Linnaeus
Bovidae gen. et sp. indet.

B. *Transitional Zone, Rhine River Area s. 1.*

83. Steinheim IV (Murr), West Germany
(For references, see Steinheim I, Number 35)
Proboscidea
Mammonteus primigenius (Blumenbach)
Perissodactyla
Coelodonta antiquitatis (Blumenbach)

84. Bad Cannstatt I (Stuttgart), West Germany
(Frank 1950; Soergel 1929; Berckhemer 1930, 1950; Staesche 1941; Adam 1953)
"*Auemergel* and *Nagelfluh*"
Proboscidea
Mammonteus primigenius (Blumenbach)
Perissodactyla
Coelodonta antiquitatis (Blumenbach)
Equus cf. *germanicus* Nehring
Artiodactyla
Megaloceros giganteus germaniae (Pohlig)

85. Bad Cannstatt II (Stuttgart), West Germany
(For references, see Bad Cannstatt, Number 84)

"Main Travertine and Travertine sand"
Carnivora
  Ursus arctos Linnaeus
Proboscidea
  Palaeoloxodon antiquus (Falconer)
Perissodactyla
  Dicerorhinus hemitoechus (Falconer)
  Equus cf. *germanicus* Nehring
Artiodactyla
  Sus scrofa Linnaeus
  Megaloceros giganteus ssp.
  Cervus elaphus Linnaeus
  Bos primigenius Bojanus

86. Bad Cannstatt III (Stuttgart), West Germany
    (For references, see Bad Cannstatt, Number 84)
    Uppermost Travertine and Travertine sand
    Proboscidea
      Mammonteus primigenius (Blumenbach)
    Perissodactyla
      Equus cf. *germanicus* Nehring
    Artiodactyla
      Bison cf. *priscus* (Bojanus)

C. *Eastern Province*

87. Weimar-Ehringsdorf I (Weimar), East Germany
    (Wüst 1908, 1909, 1910, 1922; Hahne and Wüst 1908; Soergel
    1912, 1917, 1922, 1926, 1927, 1939, 1940; Freudenberg 1914;
    Wiegers, Weidenreich, and Schuster 1928; Rode 1931, 1935;
    Stehlin 1933; Stehlin and Graziosi 1935; Schertz 1936, 1937;
    Zotz 1951; Kahlke 1958)
    Lower Gravels
    Proboscidea
      Mammonteus primigenius (Blumenbach)
    Perissodactyla
      Coelodonta antiquitatis (Blumenbach)

88. Weimar-Ehringsdorf II (Weimar), East Germany
    (For references, see Weimar-Ehringsdorf I, Number 87)

Lower Travertine
Carnivora
  Canis lupus Linnaeus
  Vulpes vulpes (Linnaeus)
  Felis (Lynx) lynx (Linnaeus)
  Panthera leo spelaea (Goldfuss)
  Ursus cf. *spelaeus* Rosenmüller and Heinroth
  Martes martes (Linnaeus)
  Meles meles (Linnaeus)
Proboscidea
  Palaeoloxodon antiquus (Falconer)
Perissodactyla
  Dicerorhinus kirchbergensis (Jäger)
  Dicerorhinus hemitoechus (Falconer)
  Equus cf. *germanicus* Nehring
Artiodactyla
  Sus scrofa Linnaeus
  Megaloceros giganteus germaniae (Pohlig)
  Cervus elaphus Linnaeus
  Alces latifrons postremus Vangengeim and Flerov
  Capreolus capreolus (Linnaeus)
  Bison priscus (Bojanus)

89. Weimar-Ehringsdorf III (Weimar), East Germany
(For references, see Weimar-Ehringsdorf I, Number 87)
"Upper Travertine I and II (including "Pariser" and "Pseudo-pariser")

Carnivora
  Crocuta crocuta spelaea (Goldfuss)
  Ursus cf. *spelaeus* Rosenmüller and Heinroth
  Putorius eversmanni (Lesson)
  Martes martes (Linnaeus)
  Lutra lutra (Linnaeus)
Proboscidea
  Mammonteus primigenius (Blumenbach)
Perissodactyla
  Coelodonta antiquitatis (Blumenbach)
  Dicerorhinus hemitoechus (Falconer)
  Equus cf. *germanicus* Nehring
  Equus hydruntinus Regalia

Artiodactyla
   Bison priscus (Bojanus)
   Megaloceros giganteus germaniae (Pohlig)
   Cervus elaphus Linnaeus
   Rangifer tarandus (Linnaeus)
   Capreolus capreolus (Linnaeus)

90. Taubach (Weimar), East Germany
    (Meyer 1857, 1859; Portis 1878; Pohlig 1889, 1892; Wüst 1908,
    1909, 1911, 1922; Hahne and Wüst 1908; Soergel 1911, 1912,
    1922, 1926; Freudenberg 1914; von Reichenau 1915; Wiegers,
    Weidenreich, and Schuster 1928; Schroeder 1930; Rode 1931,
    1935; Schmid 1940, 1949; Kahlke 1958, 1961)
    "Lower Travertine"
    Carnivora
       Canis lupus Linnaeus
       Felis (Lynx) lynx Linnaeus
       Panthera leo spelaea (Goldfuss)
       Panthera pardus (Linnaeus)
       Crocuta crocuta spelaea (Goldfuss)
       Ursus arctos taubachensis Rode
    Proboscidea
       Palaeoloxodon antiquus (Falconer)
    Perissodactyla
       Dicerorhinus kirchbergensis (Jäger)
       Equus germanicus taubachensis Freudenberg
    Artiodactyla
       Sus scrofa Linnaeus
       Megaloceros giganteus germaniae (Pohlig)
       Cervus elaphus Linnaeus
       Dama dama (Linnaeus)
       Alces latifrons postremus Vangenheim and Flerov
       Capreolus capreolus (Linnaeus)
       Bison priscus (Bojanus)

In materials excavated from Taubach before 1900, a series of *Mammonteus primigenius* molars was found showing a typical travertine fossilization. It seems possible that these molars were excavated by quarrymen from the uppermost travertine layers of Taubach (*plattiger* travertine). In this case, we see, in the uppermost layers of Taubach, equivalents of the upper travertine of Weimar-Ehringsdorf and the uppermost

travertine of Bad Cannstatt, corresponding to an earliest Weichsel (=
earliest Würm) stage.

91. Burgtonna (Gotha), East Germany
(Collegium Medicum Gothanum 1696, 1697; Tentzel 1696, 1697;
Florschütz 1905; Schäfer 1909; Schroeter 1930; Dietrich 1968)
Carnivora
Vulpes vulpes (Linnaeus)
Panthera leo spelaea (Goldfuss)
Crocuta crocuta spelaea (Goldfuss)
Ursus arctos Linnaeus
Proboscidea
Palaeoloxodon antiquus (Falconer)
Perissodactyla
Dicerorhinus kirchbergensis (Jäger)
Equus cf. *germanicus* Nehring
Artiodactyla
Sus scrofa Linnaeus
Megaloceros giganteus ssp.
Cervus elaphus Linnaeus
Dama sp.
Capreolus capreolus (Linnaeus)
Bison priscus (Bojanus)

92. Chlupac cave I (Coneprusy), Czechoslovakia
(Schubert 1900, Petbrok 1953, 1954; Zazvorka 1954; Mostecký
1961, 1963, 1964, 1966, 1969)
Carnivora
Vulpes sp.
Panthera leo spelaea (Goldfuss)
Crocuta crocuta spelaea (Goldfuss)
Ursus arctos taubachensis Rode
Meles meles (Linnaeus)
Perissodactyla
Dicerorhinus kirchbergensis (Jäger)
Equus sp.
Artiodactyla
Sus scrofa Linnaeus
Cervus elaphus Linnaeus
Dama dama (Linnaeus)
Capreolus capreolus (Linnaeus)
Bison priscus (Bojanus)

93. Chlupac cave II (Coneprusy), Czechoslovakia
(For references, see Chulpac cave, Number 92)
Carnivora
  Canis lupus Linnaeus
  Vulpes vulpes (Linnaeus)
  Vulpes sp.
Perissodactyla
  Equus cf. *mosbachensis* von Reichenau
  Equus germanicus Nehring
Artiodactyla
  Rangifer sp.
  Rupicapra rupicapra (Linnaeus)
  Bison priscus (Bojanus)

94. Gánovce I (Proprad, Slovakia), Czechoslovakia
(Staub 1893; Vlček 1950, 1953; Jánossy 1969)
"Lower layers (sand and clays)"
Proboscidea
  Mammonteus primigenius (Blumenbach)
Perissodactyla
  Coelodonta antiquitatis (Blumenbach)
Artiodactyla
  Rangifer tarandus (Linnaeus)

95. Gánovce II (Poprad, Slovakia), Czechoslovakia
(For references, see Gánovce I, Number 94)
"Travertine"
Proboscidea
  Palaeoloxodon antiquus (Falconer)
Perissodactyla
  Dicerorhinus kirchbergensis (Jäger)
  Equus sp.
Artiodactyla
  Sus scrofa Linnaeus
  Cervus elaphus Linnaeus

96. Gánovce III (Poprad, Slovakia), Czechoslovakia
(For references, see Gánovce I, Number 94)
"Upper layers"
Carnivora
  Canis lupus Linnaeus

Proboscidea
   Mammonteus primigenius (Blumenbach)
Perissodactyla
   Coelodonta antiquitatis (Blumenbach)
   Equus sp.
   Equus hydruntinus Regalia
Artiodactyla
   Rangifer tarandus (Linnaeus)

97. Repolust cave I (Peggau), Austria
    (Mottl 1951, 1955, 1960, 1967)
    "Rostbraune Schicht"
    Carnivora
       Canis lupus Linnaeus
       Canis sp.
       Cuon alpinus ssp.
       Vulpes vulpes (Linnaeus)
       Vulpes vulpes ssp.
       Felis silvestris Schreber
       Panthera leo spelaea (Goldfuss)
       Panthera pardus (Linnaeus)
       Ursus arctos Linnaeus
       Ursus spelaeus Rosenmüller and Heinroth
       Martes martes (Linnaeus)
       Putorius putorius (Linnaeus)
       Meles meles (Linnaeus)
    Proboscidea
       Elephantidae gen. et sp. indet.
    Artiodactyla
       Sus scrofa Linnaeus
       Megaloceros giganteus ssp.
       Cervus elaphus Linnaeus
       Rangifer tarandus (Linnaeus)
       Capreolus capreolus (Linnaeus)
       Rupicapra rupicapra (Linnaeus)
       Capra ibex Linnaeus
       Bison priscus (Bojanus)

98. Kálmán Lambrecht Cave (Bükk Mountains), Hungary
    (Jánossy 1953, 1963, 1964; Mottl, 1967)
    Carnivora
       Canis lupus Linnaeus

Vulpes vulpes (Linnaeus)
Felis silvestris Schreber
Panthera leo spelaea (Goldfuss)
Panthera pardus (Linnaeus)
Crocuta crocuta spelaea (Goldfuss)
Ursus arctos Linnaeus
Ursus spelaeus Rosenmüller and Heinroth
Mustela nivalis Linnaeus
Putorius putorius (Linnaeus)
Martes martes (Linnaeus)
Meles meles (Linnaeus)
Proboscidea
  Mammonteus primigenius (Blumenbach)
Perissodactyla
  Coelodonta antiquitatis (Blumenbach)
  Equus sp.
  Equus hydruntinus Regalia
Artiodactyla
  Sus scrofa Linnaeus
  Megaloceros giganteus ssp.
  Cervus elaphus Linnaeus
  Alces alces (Linnaeus)
  Rangifer tarandus (Linnaeus)
  Capreolus capreolus (Linnaeus)
  Ovis sp.
  Bison priscus (Bojanus)

99. Tata I (Tata), Hungary
(Townson 1973; Kiss 1818; Kormos 1912; Kretzoi 1964)
Carnivora
  Canis lupus spelaeus Goldfuss
  Crocuta crocuta spelaea (Goldfuss)
  Ursus arctos Linnaeus
  Ursus spelaeus Rosenmüller and Heinroth
  Putorius sp.
  Mustela sp.
  Meles meles (Linnaeus)
Proboscidea
  Mammonteus primigenius (Blumenbach)
Perissodactyla
  ?Dicerorhinus kirchbergensis (Jäger)
  Coelodonta antiquitatis (Blumenbach)

Equus sp. (cf. *steinheimensis* von Reichenau)
Equus hydruntinus Regalia
Artiodactyla
  Sus scrofa Linnaeus
  Megaloceros giganteus ssp.
  Bos or *Bison* sp.

100. Esterházy Cave (Csákvár, Hungary
  (Kadic and Kretzoi 1930; Kretzoi 1952; Jánossy 1969)
  Carnivora
    Crocuta crocuta (Erxleben)
    Ursus cf. *arctos* Linnaeus
  Perissodactyla
    Coelodonta antiquitatis (Blumenbach)
    Equus cf. *steinheimensis* von Reichenau
    Equus hydruntinus Regalia
  Artiodactyla
    Sus scrofa Linnaeus
    Megaloceros giganteus ssp.
    Cervus elaphus Linnaeus
    Dama cf. *somomensis* (Desmarest)

101. Süttö (Transdanubia), Hungary
  (Kormos 1925; Kretzoi 1938, 1953; Jánossy 1969)
  Carnivora
    Canis lupus Linnaeus
    Vulpes vulpes (Linnaeus)
    Panthera leo ssp.
    ?Crocuta sp.
  Perissodactyla
    Equus sp.
  Artiodactyla
    Sus scrofa Linnaeus
    Cervus elaphus Linnaeus
    Dama sp.
    Capreolus capreolus (Linnaeus)
    Bovidae gen. et sp. indet.

102. Betalov Spodmol Cave III-IV (Postojna), Yugoslavia
  (Anelli 1933; Brodar 1947, 1948, 1949, 1950, 1952, 1954, 1956;
  Rakovec 1952, 1955, 1959; Dietrich 1957)

Carnivora
Canis lupus Linnaeus
Vulpes vulpes (Linnaeus)
Crocuta crocuta spelaea (Goldfuss)
Ursus spelaeus Rosenmüller and Heinroth
Perissodactyla
Dicerorhinus kirchbergensis (Jäger)
Artiodactyla
Sus scrofa Linnaeus
Megaloceros giganteus ssp.
Cervus elaphus Linnaeus
Alces alces (Linnaeus)

103. Crvena Stijena XXVIII–XXIX (Bileća), Yugoslavia
(Benac and Brodar 1957, 1958; Rakovec 1958; Brodar 1959;
Malez 1962, 1965, 1966; Basler and Malez 1966)
Carnivora
Ursus arctos Linnaeus
Perissodactyla
Dicerorhinus kirchbergensis (Jäger)
Equus germanicus Nehring
Artiodactyla
Sus sp.
Megaloceros giganteus ssp.
Cervus elaphus Linnaeus
Dama sp.
Capreolus capreolus (Linnaeus)
Capra sp.
Ovis sp.
Bovidae gen. et sp. indet.

104. Veternica cave (Zagreb), Yugoslavia
(Malez 1963; Mottl 1967)
Carnivora
Canis lupus Linnaeus
Canis sp.
Cuon alpinus europaeus Bourguignat
Vulpes vulpes (Linnaeus)
Vulpes cf. *lagopus* (Linnaeus)
Felis silvestris Schreber
Felis (Lynx) pardina Temminck
Panthera leo spelaea (Goldfuss)

    Panthera pardus (Linnaeus)
    Crocuta crocuta spelaea (Goldfuss)
    Ursus arctos Linnaeus
    Ursus spelaeus Rosenmüller and Heinroth
    Mustela erminea Linnaeus
    Putorius putorius (Linnaeus)
    Martes martes (Linnaeus)
    Martes foina (Erxleben)
    Gulo gulo (Linnaeus)
    Meles meles (Linnaues)
Perissodactyla
    Dicerorhinus kirchbergensis (Jäger)
Artiodactyla
    Sus scrofa Linnaeus
    Megaloceros giganteus ssp.
    Cervus elaphus Linnaeus
    Dama cf. *dama* (Linnaeus)
    Cervidae gen. et sp. indet.
    Alces alces (Linnaeus)
    Capreolus capreolus (Linnaeus)
    Rupicapra rupicapra (Linnaeus)
    Capra ibex Linnaeus
    Capra sp.
    Ovis sp.
    Bos primigenius Bojanus
    Bovidae gen. et sp. indet.

105. Binagadi (Caspian Sea), USSR
    (Burshak-Abramowitsch and Dzhafarov 1951, 1953, 1955;
    Veresčagin 1947, 1951, 1953, 1959; Alekperova 1952, 1959;
    Burshak-Abramowitsch 1953; Dzhafarov 1955)
    Carnivora
        Canis lupus apscheronicus Veresčagin
        Canis sp.
        Vulpes vulpes aff. *alpherakyi* Satunin
        Vulpes corsac (Linnaeus)
        Felis sp.
        Panthera leo spelaea (Goldfuss)
        Acinonyx jubatus Schreber
        Crocuta crocuta spelaea (Goldfuss)
        Ursus arctos binagadensis Veresčagin

Vormela peregusna Guldenstaedt
Meles meles minor Satunin
Perissodactyla
    Dicerorhinus binagadensis Dzhafarov
    Equus sp.
    Equus cf. *hydruntinus* Regalia
Artiodactyla
    Sus apscheronicus Burschak-Abramowitsch and Dzhafarov
    Megaloceros giganteus ssp.
    Cervus elaphus binagadensis Alekperova
    Saiga tatarica binagadensis Alekperova
    Ovis cf. *ammon* Linnaeus
    Bos mastan-zadei Burschak-Abramowitsch

PROBLEMS OF INTERCORRELATION WITH CONTINENTAL ASIA AND THE FAR EAST

In trying to correlate "Middle Pleistocene" fossil macrofaunas of Europe and continental Asia, we find a key association in the alluvial deposits of Kolkotova terrace V of the Dniestr River, near Tiraspol, Moldavian Soviet Socialist Republic. These are generally known as the Tiraspol Gravels. The fossil association of this locality in general is considered to be contemporaneous with the main fauna of Süssenborn, East Germany. In both horizons we find almost identical species aside from, in Tiraspol, *Dicerorhinus etruscus* (Falconer) and the younger *Dicerorhinus kirchbergensis* (Jäger), as well as a progressive type of caballine horse (*Equus* aff. *mosbachensis* von Reichenau). On the other hand, the Tiraspol elephant, *Mammonteus trogontherii* (Pohlig) (= *Elephas wüsti* Pavlova), is less advanced than the Süssenborn elephant, but this may reflect ecological differentations between southern and northern populations of the *Mammonteus trogontherii-primigenius* evolution line. On the basis of this analysis, the Tiraspol faunal complex seems to correlate with the central European fossil localities of Süssenborn (Elster/Mindel I) and Mosbach (Elster/Mindel I and II).

    Further to the East, in western and eastern Siberia, there are only some fifteen fossil localities showing "Süssenborn-Tiraspol affinities" (Alekseev 1970; Vangengeim and Sher 1970), and these are irregularly distributed throughout this vast area. Most of these localities have only one or a few species — if they have any specimens at all. Two exceptions, however, are to be mentioned: the type-locality of the Tologoy faunal complex (Vangengeim and Ravsky 1965; Vangengeim, et al. 1966), Tologoy Mountains (Ulan-Ude), and the type-association of the Olyor faunal complex, the Olyor suite deposits at Chukotija River, Kolyma Lowlands (Sher 1971). As has been demonstrated by Vangengeim and Sher (1970) we may distinguish, within the limits of Siberia, four paleozoogeographical subregions: western Siberia showing "European elements" (*Praemegaceros verticornis* and *Equus* aff. *mosbachensis*), eastern Siberia, the extreme Northeast, and Transbaikalia with central Asiatic endemics. A correlation of these faunas belonging to different paleogeographical regions is difficult and possible only within wide stage boundaries (see Figure 1, between pp. 352–353).

According to our present knowledge, we may refer all Siberian fossil associations of "Süssenborn-Tiraspol affinities" to the "Elster/Mindel" s. 1, in order to characterize prelimininarily their tentative position in the geochronological sequence. In Kazakhstan, the Koshkurgan faunal complex (Bashanov and Kostenki 1961; Bashanov 1962; Khisarova 1963; Kojamkulova 1969) seems to be correlated to the central European-East European Süssenborn-Tiraspol faunal complex suggesting a second line of land mammal correlations from Europe to the Far East.

Today, by means of land mammal associations, we may distinguish three correlation lines. These link continental Europe with:
a.   continental Asia, Bering land bridge, and Alaska,
b.   continental Asia, Transbaikalia, the Far East (Southeast Asia and India), and
c.   Ponto-Caspian region, Kazakhstan, Dzungaria (Northwest China).

The first correlation line runs from continental Europe through West Siberia, East Siberia, extreme Northeast Asia, and via the Bering land bridge to Alaska. This first correlation line of "Middle Pleistocene" mammalian associations, beginning with the continental European "Süssenborn-Tiraspol faunal complex," can be extended by means of the West and East Siberian Middle Pleistocene fossil localities at Tobolsk (Ishim-Irtish) region (Tobolsk suite) (Volkova 1966; Vangengeim and Sher 1970), by the fossil locality at the Yenisey River Basin, near the Bachta River mouth (Vangengeim 1961; Vangengeim and Sher 1970) via the Olyominsk (Vangengeim 1960) and localities at the mouth of the Chebede River (Alexseev 1961; 1970) to the extreme Northeast (Indigirka-Kolyma River region) localities of the Bereliach River (Vangengeim 1961) and Olyor suite (Chukochija River) (Sher 1969; 1971). Typical members of these Middle Pleistocene Siberian fossil sites are *Mammonteus trogontherii* (Pohlig) (= *Elephas wüsti* Pavlova), *Dicerorhinus kirchbergensis, Dicerorhinus hemitoechus, Dicerorhinus binag-*

adensis group s. 1.; *Equus stenonis, Equus süssenbornensis, Equus verae* group s. 1.; *Alces latifrons* (Johnson), *Praeovibos*, and *Soergelia*. The second correlation line extends from continental Europe through West Siberia, East Siberia, and Transbaikalia, to the Far East (Southeast Asia and India). This second line of Middle Pleistocene mammalian associations begins with the continental European Süssenborn-Tiraspol faunal complex and can be extended through the fossil sites of the upper Irtish River area fossil localities of Krasnokutskoje (Vangengeim and Zazhigin 1965; Vangengeim and Sher 1970), the upper Ob River region Kochkov suite (subaerial loams), via the Angara River "Middle Pleistocene" sites (Vangengeim and Sher, 1970) to the Tologoy faunal complex (Ravsky et al. 1964; Vangengeim and Ravsky 1965). The sites at Tologoy (upper part of the middle member of the Tologoy Mountain section not far from Ulan Ude) and Dodogol (Vangengeim and Sher 1970) link the Soviet Union Transbaikalian sites with those of Inner Mongolia, the Province of Hopei, China, and especially, the classical "Middle Pleistocene" (post-Villafranchian, Lower Sanmenian of local stratigraphy) locality of Nihowan (Teilhard de Chardin and Piveteau 1930). Typical members of this southern correlation line are hyenas of the *Crocuta* group, an early *Mammonteus* sp., *Palaeoloxodon* of the *namadicus* group, the *Equus sanmeniensis* group, *Coelodonta tologoijensis* Beliajeva (Tologoy and Nihowan), primitive *Bison* and *Spiroceros* cf. *peii* Young, and species which are present in general in both faunistic associations at Tologoy and Nihowan.

The third correlation line extends from continental Europe through the Ponto-Caspian region and Kazakhstan to Dzungaria, Northwest China. The third European-Asiatic correlation line makes it possible to correlate the Tiraspol faunal complex with the Kazakhian-Koshkurgan faunal complex of which some twenty localities are known today. The main areas of distribution are Central Kazakhstan, Southern Altai, and the Tien-shan areas (Kojamkulova 1969). The line leads from the upper Irtish River sites of Chernojarka, Krasnojarka, Maraldy, Podpusk, and Ostraja Sopka (Kojamkulova 1969) to the northern Sinkiang fossil locality of Ulanbulan (Dzungaria Basin), China (Chow 1957; Kahlke 1968).

PROBLEMS OF INTERCORRELATION WITH THE MIDDLE EAST

To link the Central European-East European "Lower Middle Pleistocene"

Süssenborn-Tiraspol faunal complex with the faunal sequence of the Middle East we can make use of a key association in the "Middle Pleistocene" (Mindel) gravels of the Orontes Valley at Latamme, Syria (Hooijer 1962). At this site we find *Mammonteus trogontherii* (Pohlig) associated with *Praemegaceros verticornis* (Dawkins), a first-class correlation species with a distribution (only "Cromer" and Mindel) extending from southern Spain (Granada) (Kahlke 1969) to as far as Achalkalaki, Transcaucasia (Vekua 1962) and Latamne, Orontes Valley, Syria (Hooijer 1962). The fossil association of Jisr Banat Yaqub, Israel (Hooijer 1960) is closely related to this horizon, which is perhaps late Mindel or early Mindel-Riss of the Alpine sequence. Following this correlation line to the south we find the fossil association of 'Ubeidiya in Israel (Haas 1966), a typical early Middle Pleistocene, not Lower Pleistocene (Villafranchian), association as has already been noticed by D. A. Hooijer (1968).

SELECTED REFERENCES[1]

ADAM, K. D.

1952 Die altpleistozänen Säugetierfaunen Südwestdeutschlands. *Neues Jahrbuch für Geologie und Paläontologie,* Monatshefte 5:229–236. Stuttgart.

1953 Säugetierfunde im württembergischen Pleistozän. 1–10 (verbreitet anläßlich der 5. Hauptversammlung der Deutschen Quartärvereinigung in Stuttgart, Maschinenschrift).

1954 Die mittelpleistozänen Faunen von Steinheim an der Murr. *Quaternaria* (Storia naturale e culturale del Quaternario) 1:131–144. Rome.

1958 *Dicerorhinus kirchbergensis (Jager)* aus einer Karsthöhle bei Črni Kal (Istrien, Jugoslawien). Academia Scientiarum et Artium Slovenica, Classis IV: Historia Naturalis, Dissertationes 4:437–440. Ljubljana.

1959 Mittelpleistozäne Caniden aus dem Heppenloch bei Gutenberg (Württemberg). *Stuttgarter Beiträge zur Naturkunde* 27:1–46. Stuttgart.

AGUADO, M. M.

1962 El hombre primitivo en Toledo. *Toletum* 3:175–206. Toledo.

1963 *El yacimiento prehistorico de Pinedo (Toledo) y su industria triedrica.* Publicaciones del Instituto Provincial de Investigationes y Estudios Toledanos, second series, 1:1–70. Toledo.

1968 Versuch eines chrono-stratigraphischen Vergleichs des Unteren und Mittleren Pleistozäns beiderseits des Tajo. *Berichte der Deut-*

---

[1] Papers not cited are included in more recent publications given here.

schen Gesellschaft für geologische Wissenschaften, Reihe A: *Geologie und Paläontologie* 13(3):289–298. Berlin.

AGUIRRE, E.

1965   Los elefants de las terrazas medias de Toledo y la edad de estos depositos. *Cátedra de Paleontologia, Facultad de Ciencias, Madrid* 4:1–2. Zaragoza.

ALEKSEEV, M. N.

1961   Stratigraphy of continental Neogene and Pleistocene deposits in the Vilyuy Basin and the Lena downstream valley. *Trudy geologičeskogo Instituta, Akademia Nauk SSSR* 51:1–118. Moscow (in Russian).

1970   An occurrence of Tiraspolian fauna at the Vilyuy river (Eastern Siberia). *Palaeogeography, Palaeoclimatology, Palaeoecology* 8: 209–214. Amsterdam.

ALEXANDROVA, L. P.

1965   Rodentia of Chazar-deposits of the lower Pavolsha (Černij Jar). *Publication VII. INQUA-Congress, 1965. Akademia Nauk SSSR* 149–157. Moscow (in Russian).

ALEXEEVA, L. I.

1968   Die asiatischen Elemente in der Säugetierfauna des osteuropäischen Anthropogens. *Berichte der deutschen Gesellschaft für geologische Wissenschaften*, Reihe A: *Geologie und Paläontologie* 13(3): 299–303. Berlin.

1969   The habitat of faunal assemblages of the Anthropogene of Eastern Europe. *Résumés des Communications, VIIIe Congres INQUA:* 117. Paris.

ALTUNA, J.

1971   Fauna de mammiferos de los yacimientos prehistoricos de Guipuzcoa. *Munibe* 24(1–4):1–464. San Sebastian.

AMBROSETTI, P., A. AZZAROLI, F. P. BONADONNA, M. FOLLIERI

1972   A scheme of Pleistocene chronology for the Tyrrhenian side of central Italy. *Bolletino della Società Geologica Italiana* 91:169–184. Rome.

AZZAROLI, A., P. AMBROSETTI

1970   Late Villafranchian and early mid-Pleistocene faunas in Italy. *Palaeogeography, Palaeoclimatology, Palaeoecology* 8:107–111. Amsterdam.

BASHANOV, V. S., N. N. KOSTENKO

1962   Atlas of the Anthropogene mammals of Kazakhstan: 1–110. Alma-Ata (in Russian).

BASLER, D., M. MALEZ

1966   Die Rote Höhle (Crvena Stijena) bei Bileća/Jugoslawien. *Eiszeitalter und Gegenwart* 17:61–68. Öhringen.

BIBERSON, P.

1964   Torralba et Ambrona: Notes sur deux stations acheuléennes de chasseurs d'éléphants de la Vieille Castille. *Instituto de Prehistoria y Arqueología Monografías* 6:201–231. Barcelona.

BONIFAY, E.

1968a   Aperçu sur le Quaternaire de Grenoble à Marseille. *Bulletin de l'Association française pour l'étude du Quaternaire* 1:3–18. Paris.

1968b Stratigraphie et industries lithiques de la grotte n° 1 du Mas des Caves à Lunel-Viel (Hérault). *La Préhistoire* (1968):37–46. Paris.

1969 Grottes et Abris prehistoriques dans le Sud-Est de la France. *Etudes françaises sur le Quaternaire VIIIe Congres INQUA*, Paris 1969):81–83. Paris.

BONIFAY, M. F.

1962 Sur la valeur specifique de l'*Ursus praearctos* M. Boule de la Grotte du Prince (Ligurie italienne). *Bulletin du Musée d'Anthropologie prehistorique de Monaco*, Fascicule 9:65–72. Monaco.

1969a Faunes quaternaires de France. *Etude françaises sur le Quaternaire, VIIIe Congres INQUA*, Paris, 1969: 127–142. Paris.

1969b Principales formes charactéristiques du Quaternaire moyen du Sud-Est de la France (grand mammifères). *Bulletin du Musée d'Anthropologie préhistorique de Monaco* 14:49–62. Monaco.

1971 Carnivores quaternaires du Sud-Est de la France. *Mémoires du Musée Nationale d'Histoire Naturelle*, series C, 21(2):43–377. Paris.

BONIFAY, M. F., E. BONIFAY

1962 Sur l'existence de dépôts quaternaires pré-würmiens dans la Grotte du Prince (Ligurie italienne). *L'Anthropologie* 66(1–2):90–99. Paris.

1963 Un gisement à faune épi-villafranchienne à Saint-Estève-Janson (Bouches-du-Rhône). *Comptes Rendus de l'Academie des Sciences, Paris* 256; 1136–1138. Paris.

1965 Age du gisement de mammifères fossiles de Lunel-Viel (Hérault). *Comptes Rendus de l'Academie des Sciences, Paris* 260:3441–3444. Paris.

BOURDIER, F., H. LACASSAGNE

1963 Précisions nouvelles sur la stratigraphie et la faune du gisement villafranchien de Saint Prest (Eure-et-Loire). *Bulletin de la Société Géologique de France*, seventh series, 5(4):407–650. Paris.

BOUT, P.

1960 *Le Villafranchien du Velay et du Bassin hydrogeographique moyen et supérieur de l'Allier.* Le Puy.

CHOW, M. M.

1957 Notes on some mammalian fossils from the Late Cenozoic of Sinkiang. *Vertebrata Palasiatica* 1(1):33–41. Peking.

COMMONT, V.

1910 Les gisements paléolithiques d'Abbeville. Excursion de la Société Géologique du Nord et de la Faculté des Sciences de Lille, à Abbeville le 11. Juin:249–291. Lille.

CRUSAFONT-PAIRO, M.

1960 Le Quaternaire espagnol et sa faune de mammifères. Essai de synthése. *Mammalia pleistocaenica, Anthropos* Supplement 1:55–64. Brno.

1965 Zur Obergrenze des Villafranchiums in Spanien. *Berichte der geologischen Gesellschaft in der DDR* 10(1):19–48. Berlin.

DSHAFAROV, R. D., *editor*
1951– *Binagady localities of Quaternary fauna and flora,* volume one
1955 (1951); volume two (1952); volume three (1953); volume four (1955). Akademia Nauk Azerbaidshanskaja SSSR. Baku (in Russian).

DUBROVO, I. A.
1957 On *Parelephas wüsti* (Pavl.) and *Rhinoceros mercki* Jäger remains from Yakutia. *Byulletin Komisii iszuscheniju Chetvertičnogo Perioda* 21:94–104. Moscow (in Russian).
1969 The Anthropogene proboscideans of the USSR. *Résumés des Communications, VIIIe Congres INQUA:* 122. Paris.

FEJFAR, C.
1961 "Review of Quaternary Vertebrata in Czechoslovakia," in *Czwartorzed Europy środkowej i wschodniej.* Instytut Geologiczny, Tome 34, (VI. INQUA-Kongres): 109–118. Warsaw.

FREUDENBERG, W.
1914 *Die Säugetiere des älteren Quartärs von Mitteleuropa mit besonderer Berücksichtigung der Fauna von Hundsheim und Deutschaltenburg in Niederösterreich.* Jena: Fischer.

GROMOV, V. I.
1948 Palaeontological and archaeological evidence on the stratigraphy of continental Quaternary deposits on the territory of the USSR. *Trudy geologičeskogo Instituta, Akademia Nauk SSSR* 64, Geology Series, 17:1–521. Moscow (in Russian).

GROMOV, V. I., K. V. NIKIFOROVA
1965 Über die Grenze zwischen dem Unter- und dem Mittelpleistozän. *Berichte der geologischen Gesellschaft in der DDR* 10(1):13–18. Berlin.

GROMOV, V. I., K. V. NIKIFOROVA, E. V. SCHANZER, *editors*
1961 Problems of the Anthropogene Geology. *Akademia Nauk SSSR, Geologičeski Institut,* 1–224. Moscow (in Russian, English summary).

GUENTHER, E. W.
1968 Elefantenbackzähne aus den Mosbacher Sanden, Teil I. *Mainzer Naturwissenschaftliches Archiv* 7:55–73; Teil II, *Mainzer Naturwissenschaftliches Archiv* 8:77–89. Mainz.

HAAS, G.
1966 On the vertebrate fauna of the Lower Pleistocene site 'Ubeidiya. *Israel Academy of Sciences and Humanities:* 1–68. Jerusalem.

HEMMER, H.
1971 Zur Kenntnis pleistozäner mitteleuropäischer Leoparden. *Neues Jahrbuch für Geologie und Paläontologie, Abhandlungen* 138(1): 15–36. Stuttgart.
1971 Zur Charakterisierung und stratigraphischen Bedeutung von *Panthera gombaszoegensis* (Kretzoi, 1938). *Neues Jahrbuch für Geologie und Paläontologie,* Monatshefte 12:701–711. Stuttgart.
1972 Zur systematischen Stellung von *"Jansofelis vaufreyi"* Bonifay, 1971, und *"Felis lunellensis"* Bonifay, 1971, aus dem Pleistozän Südfrankreichs (Carnivora, Felidae). *Neues Jahrbuch für Geologie*

und Paläontologie, Monatshefte 4:215–223. Stuttgart.

HEMMER, H., G. SCHÜTT

1969   Ein Unterkiefer von *Panthera gombaszoegensis* (Kretzoi, 1938) aus den Mosbacher Sanden. *Mainzer Naturwissenschaftliches Archiv* 8:90–101. Mainz.

HOOIJER, D. A.

1962   Middle Pleistocene mammals from Latamne, Orontes Valley, Syria. *Annales archéologiques de Syrie* 11:117–132. Damascus.

1968   "The Middle Pleistocene fauna of the Near East," in *Evolution and hominisation*. Edited by G. Kurth, 82–85. Stuttgart: Fischer.

JÁNOSSY, D.

1963a   Letztinterglaziale Vertebraten Fauna aus der Kálmán Lambrecht-Höhle (Bükk-Gebirge, Nordost-Ungarn) I. *Acta Zoologica Academiae Scientiarum Hungaricae*, 9(3–4):293–331; II, *Acta Zoologica Academiae Scientiarum Hungaricae* 10(1–2):139–195 (1964). Budapest.

1963b   Die altpleistozäne Wirbeltierfauna von Köresvárad bei Répáshuta (Bükk-Gebirge). *Annales Historico-Naturales Musei Nationalis Hungarici, Pars Mineralogica et Palaeontologica* 55:109–141. Budapest.

1969   Stratigraphische Auswertung der europäischen mittelpleistozänen Wirbeltierfauna, Teil I. *Berichte der deutschen Gesellschaft für geologische Wissenschaften*, Reihe A: *Geologie und Paläontologie* 14(4):367–438; Teil II, *Berichte der deutschen Gesellschaft für geologische Wissenschaften*, Reihe A: *Geologie und Paläontologie* 14(5):573–643. Berlin.

KAHLKE, H. D.

1958   Die jungpleistozänen Säugetierfaunen aus dem Travertingebiet von Taubach-Weimar-Ehringsdorf. *Alt-Thüringen* 3:97–130. Weimar.

1961   Revision der Säugetierfaunen der klassischen deutschen Pleistozän-Fundstellen von Süßenborn, Mosbach und Taubach. *Zeitschrift Geologie*, Jahrgang 10(4–5):493–532. Berlin.

1965   Zur Grenze Unterpleistozän/Mittelpleistozän. *Berichte der geologischen Gesellschaft in der DDR* 10(1):5–6. Berlin.

1969   Die Soergelia-Reste aus den Kiesen von Süßenborn bei Weimar. *Paläontologische Abhandlungen*, A, 3(3–4):547–610. Berlin.

1969   Die Cerviden-Reste aus den Kiesen von Süßenborn bei Weimar. *Paläontologische Abhandlungen*, A, 3(3–4);547–610. Berlin.

KOJAMKULOVA, B. S.

1969   The Anthropogene fossils of Kazakhstan. *Akademia Nauk Kazakhstanskaja SSR:* 1–149. Alma-Ata (in Russian).

KRETZOI, M.

1938   Die Raubtiere von Gombaszög nebst einer Übersicht der Gesamtfauna. *Annales Musei Nationalis Hungarici, Pars Mineralogica, Geologica et Palaeontologica* 31:88–157. Budapest.

1941   Weitere Beiträge zur Kenntnis der Fauna von Gombaszög. *Annales Musei Nationalis Hungarici, Pars Mineralogica, Geologica et Palaeontologica* 34:105–139. Budapest.

1956   Die altpleistozänen Wirbeltierfaunen des Villányer Gebirges. *Geologica Hungarica, Series Palaeontologica,* Fasciculus 27:1–264. Budapest.

1965   Die Nager und Lagomorphen von Voigtstedt in Thüringen und ihre chronologische Aussage. *Paläontologische Abhandlungen,* A, 2(2–3):584–660. Berlin.

KURTÉN, B.

1960   Chronology and faunal evolution of the earlier European glaciations. *Societas Scientiarum Fennica, Commentationes Biologicae* 21(5):1–62. Helsingfors.

1965   Die untere Grenze des Mittleren Pleistozäns. *Berichte der geologischen Gesellschaft in der DDR* 10(1):7–11. Berlin.

KUSS, S. E.

1961   Ein Beitrag zur Pleistocän-Fauna von Herxheim/Pfalz. *Berichte der Naturforschenden Gesellschaft Freiburg im Breisgau* 51(2): 145–148. Freiburg.

MOSTECKÝ, V.

1969   Jungpleistozäne Säugetiere aus der "Chlupáč-Höhle" auf dem Hügel "Kobyla" bei Koněprusy (Böhmischer Karst). *Sborník Národního Muzea v Praze* 25, B, 1:1–54. Prague.

MOTTL, M.

1967   Neuer Beitrag zum *Hystrix*-Horizont Europas. *Annalen des Naturhistorischen Museums Wien* 71:305–327. Vienna.

MUSIL, R.

1966   Holštejn, eine neue altpleistozäne Lokalität in Mähren. *Acta Musei Moraviae* (Scientiae naturales) (1966): 133–168. Brno.

MUSIL, R., *editor*

1972   Stránská skála I:1910–1945. *Anthropos* 20, 1–204. Brno.

NIKIFOROVA, K. V.

1965   Die Korrelation der unter- und mittelpleistozänen Ablagerungen im nördlichen Eurasien. *Berichte der deutschen Gesellschaft für geologische Wissenschaften,* Reihe A: *Geologie und Paläontologie* 13(3):367–374. Berlin.

NIKIFOROVA, K. V., *editor*

1965   Correlation of Anthropogene deposits of Northern Eurasia. *Akademia Nauk SSSR, Geologičeski Institut:* 1–112. Moscow (in Russian, with English summaries).

1971   Pleistocene of Tiraspol. *Academia Nauk SSSR i Akademia Nauk Moldavskaja SSR:* 1–187. Kishinev (in Russian).

NIKIFOROVA, K. V., I. K. IVANOVA, N. A. KONSTANTINOVA

1970   Tiraspol as a type locality for the Pleistocene of eastern Europe. *Palaeogeography, Palaeoclimatology, Palaeoecology* 8:175–185. Amsterdam.

PIDOPLIČKO, I. G.

1954   On the Ice-age. *Akademia Nauk Ukrainskol SSR;* 1–220. Kiev (in Russian).

1955   New data on the Anthropogene vertebrate-fauna of Ternopol. *Doklady Akademia Nauk SSSR* 100:989–991. Moscow (in Russian).

PONTIER, G.
1928   Les éléphants fossiles d'Abbeville. *Annales de la Société géologique du Nord* 53:20–46. Lille.

RADULESCO, C., P. SAMSON
1965   *Soergelia elisabethae* Schaub dans le Pléistocène moyen de l'Olténie (Roumanie). *Eclogae geologicae Helvetiae* 58(2):1107–1110. Basel.
1967   Sur un nouveau cerf mégacérin du Pléistocène moyen de la Dépression de Braşov (Roumanie). *Geologica Romana* 6:317–344. Bucharest.

RADULESCO, C., P. SAMSON, N. MIHĂILĂ, A. KOVÁCS
1965   Contributions à la connaissance des faunes de mammifères pléistocènes de la Dépression de Braşov (Roumanie). *Eiszeitalter und Gegenwart* 16:132–188. Öhringen.

RAKOVEC, I.
1958   Pleistocenski sesalci iz jame pri Črnem Kalu. *Dissertationes Academia Scientiarum et Artium Slovenica, Classis IV, Historia naturalis* 4:367–433. Ljubljana.
1959   Kvartana sesalska fauna iz Betalovega Spodmola pri Postojni. *Dissertationes Academia Scientiarum et Artium Slovenica, Classis IV, Historia naturalis* 5:289–348 Ljubljana.

RAVSKY, E. I., L. P. ALEXANDROVA, E. A. VANGENGEIM, V. G. GERBOVA, L. V. GOLUBEVA
1964   *Anthropogene deposits in the South of Eastern Siberia* (in Russian). Moscow: Nauka.

RUTTE, E.
1958   Die Fundstelle altpleistozäner Säugetiere von Randersacker bei Würzburg. *Geologisches Jahrbuch* 73:737–754. Hannover.
1967   Die Cromer-Wirbeltierfundstelle Würzburg-Schalksberg. *Abhandlungen des Naturwissenschaftlichen Vereins Würzburg* 8:1–26. Würzburg.

RYASINA, V. E.
1962   On the origin and the stratigraphy of Quaternary deposits of the steppe plateau of the upper Ob region. *Bjulletin Komisii iszuscheniju Chetvertičnogo Perioda* 27:86–97. Moscow (in Russian).

SAMSON, P., C. RADULESCO
1965   Die Säugetierfaunen und die Grenzen Pliozän/Pleistozän und Unterpleistozän/Mittelpleistozän in Rumänien. *Berichte der geologischen Gesellschaft in der DDR* 10(1):67–76. Berlin.
1968   Das mittlere Pleistozän in Rumänien. *Berichte der deutschen Gesellschaft für geologische Wissenschaften*, Reihe A: *Geologie und Paläontologie* 13(3):375–379. Berlin.

SCHÄFER, H. F.
1909   Über die pleistocäne Säugetierfauna und die Spuren des paläolithischen Menschen von Burgtonna in Thüringen. *Zeitschrift der Deutschen geologischen Gesellschaft* 61(4):445–469. Stuttgart.

SCHERTZ, E.
1936   "Die eiszeitliche Tierwelt in der Umgebung Schönebecks." Schönebeck.

SCHÜTT, G.

1969   *Panthera pardus sickenbergi* n. subsp. aus den Maurer Sanden. *Neues Jahrbuch für Geologie und Paläontologie*, Monatshefte, Jahrgang 1969, Heft 5:299–310. Stuttgart.

1970a   Nachweis der Säbelzahnkatze *Homotherium* in den altpleistozänen Mosbacher Sanden (Wiesbaden/Hessen). *Neues Jahrbuch für Geologie und Paläontologie*, Monatshefte, Jahrgang 1970, Heft 3:187–192. Stuttgart.

1970b   Ein Gepardenfund aus den Mosbacher Sanden (Altpleistozän, Wiesbaden). *Mainzer Naturwissenschaftliches Archiv* 9:118–131. Mainz.

1971   Die Hyänen der Mosbacher Sande (Altpleistozän, Wiesbaden, Hessen) mit einem Beitrag zur Stammesgeschichte der Gattung *Crocuta. Mainzer Naturwissenschaftliches Archiv* 10:29–76. Mainz.

SHER, A. V.

1969   Early Pleistocene mammals of extreme northeastern Asia and their environment. *Résumés des Communications, VIIIe Congres INQUA* (1969): 135. Paris.

1971   Säugetierfunde und Pleistozänstratigraphie in der Kolyma-Niederung. *Berichte der deutschen Gesellschaft für geologische Wissenschaften*, Reihe A: *Geologie und Paläontologie* 16(2):113–125. Berlin.

1971   *Mammals and stratigraphy of the Pleistocene of the extreme northeast of the USSR and of North America* (in Russian). Moscow: Nauka.

SICKENBERG, O.

1962   Die Säugetierreste aus den elsterzeitlichen Kiesen (Pleistozän) von Bornhausen am Harz. *Geologisches Jahrbuch* 79:707–736. Hannover.

1966   Die Wirbeltierfauna der Höhle Petralona (Griechenland). *Eiszeitalter und Gegenwart* 17:214–215. Öhringen.

1971   Revision der Wirbeltierfauna der Höhle Petralona (Griech. Mazedonien). *Annales géologiques des pays Helléniques* 23:230–264. Athens.

TERZEA, E., T. JURCSAK

1968   Bemerkungen über die mittelpleistozänen Faunen von Betfia. *Berichte der deutschen Gesellschaft für geologische Wissenschaften*, Reihe A: *Geologie und Paläontologie* 13(3):381–390. Berlin.

TOBIEN, H.

1968   *Anancus arvernensis* (Croizet and Jobert) und *Mammut borsoni* (Hays) (Proboscidea, Mamm.) aus den pleistozänen Sanden bei Wiesbaden (Hessen). *Mainzer Naturwissenschaftliches Archiv* 7: 35–54. Mainz.

VANGENGEIM, E. A.

1961   Palaeontological basis of the stratigraphy of the Anthropogene deposits of Northeast Siberia. *Trudy geologičeskogo Instituta, Akademia Nauk SSSR* 48:1–182. Moscow (in Russian).

VANGENGEIM, E. A., E. I. RAVSKY

1965   "On the intracontinental type of natural zonality of Eurasia in the Quaternary Period (Anthropogene)," in *Problems of Cenozoic stratigraphy* (in Russian), 128–141. Moscow: Nedra.

VANGENGEIM, E. A., A. V. SHER
1970   Siberian equivalents of the Tiraspol faunal complex. *Palaeogeography, Palaeoclimatology, Palaeoecology* 8:197–207. Amsterdam.

VANGENGEIM, E. A., V. S. ZAZHIGIN
1965   "Some results of the study of Quaternary mammals of West Siberia," in *Principal problems for the study of the Quaternary Period* (in Russian), 301–310. Moscow: Nauka.
1969   "Eopleistocene mammals of Siberia as compared to those of Eastern Europe," in *The main Problems of Anthropogene geology in Eurasia* (in Russian), 47–58. Moscow: Nauka.

VANGENGEIM, E. A., E. I. BELIAJEVA, V. E. GARUTT, E. L. DMITRIJEVA,
V. S. ZAZHIGIN
1966   Eopleistocene mammals of western Transbaikalia. *Trudy geologičeskogo Instituta, Akademia Nauk SSSR* 152:1–162. Moscow (in Russian).

VASILYEV, Y M.
1961   "Anthropogene deposits of southern Zavolzhie," in *Problems of Anthropogene geology* (in Russian, English summary), 107–116. Moscow: Akademia Nauk SSSR, Institut geologii (INQUA, Warszawa).

VEKUA, A. K.
1962   Lower Pleistocene mammalian fauna of Achalkalaki. *Akademia Nauk Gruisinskoi SSR:* 1–207. Tbilisi (in Georgian, English summary).

VERESČAGIN, N. K.
1957   Remains of fossil mammals from the lower Quaternary deposits of the Taman peninsula. *Trudy zoologičeskogo Instituta Akademii Nauk SSSR* 22:9–74. Moscow (in Russian).
1959   Mammals of the Caucasus. The history of faunal evolution. *Akademia Nauk SSSR i Akademia Nauk Azerbaidshanskoi SSR:* 1–704. Moscow-Leningrad (in Russian).

VOLKOVA, V. S.
1966   Quaternary deposits of the Lower Irtisch region and their biostratigraphic characteristic. *Akademia Nauk SSSR, Sibirski:* 1–173. Novosibirsk (in Russian).

Mid-Pleistocene Microfaunas of Continental Europe and Adjoining Areas

DÉNES JÁNOSSY

ABSTRACT

The author subdivides the Middle Pleistocene of temperate Europe and adjoining areas into four larger and nine smaller "faunal waves" on the basis of small vertebrates. This stratigraphic sketch is based chiefly on the only irreversible event, the evolutionary stages of microvertebrates. Included are considerations of their allometric relations and the predominance of different forms. By these means a much more detailed subdivision of the corresponding time span is possible than formerly, when only large mammals were used. The climatic significance of the microvertebrates is also dealt with in a critical fashion.

As I have discussed in detail in previous papers (Jánossy 1969, 1970a, 1970b, etc.), recent research has increasingly shown that the Middle Pleistocene, formerly considered a "nonexistent" time interval, must have been an important period from the evolutionary and biostratigraphic point of view. There are few absolute chronological data from this interval which lies between the classical Lower and Upper Pleistocene in Europe; we divide it by the only irreversible event of geochronology: the evolution of life. This demands a comprehensive investigation of microvertebrate successions, together, of course, with the macromammals of somewhat slower evolutionary rates.

In this respect, we can say that, according to the newer absolute chronological data, the same generalization is valid for the Pleistocene as is applied to some previous geological periods: the older parts of the time unit are, on an absolute chronological scale, regularly longer than the younger ones (e.g. the Paleozoic was longer than the Mesozoic and Cenozoic together, the Eocene was much longer than the Pliocene, etc.). Therefore, we may approximate the ratio of Lower to Middle to Upper Pleistocene, in absolute chronology, as three: two: one. We are able to use the classical method of "guide fossils" of microvertebrates for the subdivision of lower parts of the time span. Because the evolutionary rates of small mammals are quicker, their fossils yield a more detailed subdivision of the earlier parts of the Pleistocene than we have previously been able to achieve.

The differences in the faunal levels in the upper parts of this period, which covers geologically a very short time, are, however, so subtle and hidden that we cannot use the conventional method of "guide fossils" to solve the problem of providing events in the evolution of microvertebrates. Rather, we must apply complex methods. Besides investigating macro- and microvertebrates, we must examine mollusks and pollen, and use sediment petrography as well as other physical methods. Last, but no less important, statistical means may help us to see those very subtle differences in the microfauna not uncovered by morphological investigations. From this point of view, percentage relationships of different species to each other, that is, phases of predominance instead of successions of "hemeras" of the different species, together with changes in size or allometry within one taxonomical unit are important aids. Allometric evolutionary stages also may be followed through extensive geographical regions.

It is regrettable that we are still far from having an exact correlation of biostratigraphic successions with those provided by geology, archeology, or astronomy. Nevertheless, recent investigations have yielded more and more data connecting geomorphologic units with those of faunal stratigraphy. Such results are chiefly connected with undislocated fluvial terraces or moraine deposits, the microfaunas of which are discussed in detail below. Some examples are the animal remains of the travertine of Vértesszöllős, Hungary, overlaying the gravels called Mindel ("High Terrace") by geomorphologists, the moraine deposits in Voigstedt, Germany, likewise designated as Mindel gravels and overlaying the microfauna-bearing clays, and the microfauna-bearing clays in Přezletice, Czechoslovakia, also connected with Mindel terrace deposits, etc. In western Hungary, we have recently discovered a rich microfauna at Gencsapáti, a deposit of the highest terrace of the Würm glacial, and therefore the oldest.

On the basis of recent boring samples (Brielle) obtained in the Netherlands, it is possible to correlate the Eburonian glacial stage with the *Allophaiomys* microfaunal phase (A. van Meulen, personal communication; see Table 1). Of special interest are the vertebrate microfaunas discovered in deposits of the Caspian Sea transgression, especially at Kushkuna in Transcaucasia (Akchagylian transgression, Lower to Middle Villafranchian with *Mimomys pliocaenicus*), and at Cherniy Yar (Volga

Bank, Chosarian transgression, Middle Pleistocene). Regrettably, we still have no microfaunas connected with deposits unambiguously identified as Riss. The gravels of Steinheim, Germany, for example, are tectonically dislocated; Swanscombe, England, shows local features in its animal remains; both have yielded few if any of a microfauna. The stratigraphic position of faunas older than Mindel is also uncertain. For instance, the "loess durci" of Saint Vallier, France, has only *Mimomys pliocaenicus*, which may be Günz or Donau or perhaps something else.

Table 1.   Stratigraphic sketch of the mid-Pleistocene in Europe, based on microvertebrates (italics indicate archaeological sites, small capitals anthropological data only)

Stratigraphic unities		Characteristic microvertebrates	Localities
Middle Würmian		*Lagopus lagopus + mutus* *Microtus arvalis-gregalis* ∞ = *oeconomus*	
	Tokod Phase	*Lyrurus* (Hungary) *Dicrostonyx* *Allactaga* *Microtus gregalis*	*Tokod*, 36,000, Gencsapáti, *Erd*, 38–44,000, *Tata*, 40,000, *Sirgenstein*, *Cotencher,? Buchenloch*, *Breitenfurter Höhle* etc.
Lower Würmian		*Lyrurus* (Hung.) *Lagurus lagurus* (dominant)	*Régourdou*, 45,000; *Subalyuk*, Burgtonna
	Subalyuk Phase	*Microtus arvalis* *Allactaga* (*Lagopus*)?	(Upper) *Nordhessen*, ?*Ehringsdorf* (Upper), ?*Raj Cave*, etc.
± Brörup-Loopstedt, etc.	Varbó Phase	*Tetrao urogallus* (dominant) *Hystrix vinogradovi* *Lagurus lagurus* (few) *Microtus arvalis* (dominant) *Allactaga*	*Lambrecht Cave, Repolust Cave,? Ehringsdorf* (Lower), *Veternica*.
Eemian (Riss-Würmian)	Süttő Phase	*Testudo graeca* (south) *Emys orbicularis* (north) *Sorex araneus* ssp. (large) *Microtus arvalis* (dominant) *Lagurus lagurus* (few)	*Süttő, Fontéchevade,* *Grotte du Prince* (Lower L), Taubach
?Riss	Solymár Phase (Steinheim Phase)	*Lagopus lagopus + mutus* *Sorex araneus* (large) *Dicrostonyx, Lemmus* *Lagurus lagurus* ssp. *Microtus arvalis* (dominant) *M. gregalis, oeconomus*, etc. *Pitymys gregaloides*(relict)	*Solymár, Hunas*, Tornewton Cave (Glutton Stratum) *Swanscombe*, STEINHEIM
?Mindel-Riss Holsteinian		data unknown	
Oldenburgian	Uppony Phase	*Lagopus* cf. *lagopus* *Sorex macrognathus* *Dicrostonyx*	Uppony,? *Lunel Vie.* ? Heppenloch

Stratigraphic unities		Characteristic micro-vertebrates	Localities
		Pliomys posterior	
		Microtus sp. > *Pitymys* sp.	
Biharian	Tarkő Phase	*Lagopus* cf. *lagopus*	Tarkő (above), *Vértess-*
(finish)	(=Vértess-	*Francolinus*	*zöllős, Várhegy,* Brassó,
?Mindel	zöllős Phase	*Sorex subaraneus*	Gombaszög, MAUER,
	(Mosbachian)	*Dicrostonyx, Lemmus*	Mosbach, Hundsheim,
		Lagurus transiens	etc.
		Pitymys sp. = *Microtus* sp.	Khadshibej, Chernij Yar
		Pliomys episcopalis	Stránská Skála, Tir-
		Pl. lenki	aspol, Saint Estève,
		Mimomys savini (below)	Janson, Konieprusy,
			Erpfingen
?Günz-	Templomhegy	*Sorex runtonensis*	Süssenborn Sackdilling,
Mindel	Phase	*Lagurus pannonicus*	Voigtstedt, *Prežletice,*
	("Cromerian"	*Pitymys* sp. = *Microtus* sp.	Villány 8, Kövesvárad,
	part).	*Pliomys episcopalis*	Urömhegy, Budakalász,
		Pl. lenki	Cromer Forest Bed(?),
		Mimomys savini	Hochensülzen, etc.
?Günz	Betfia Phase	*Petenyia hungarica*	Les Valerots, *Vallonet,*
	("Upper Villa-	*Dicrostonyx, Lemmus*	Balaruc, Monte Peglia,
	franchian")	(west and north)	Holstyn,? Marian,
		Lagurus arankae	Kamyk, Shirak, Steppe,
		Allophaiomys	Mamontowa Betfia,
	(±Eburonian)	*Mimomys pusillus*	Nagyharsánynegy 2,
	Biharian	*M. newtoni*	Osztrames 2 and 6,
	(beginning)	*M. savini*	Nogaisk, Soave Chort-
			kow, Dodogol,' *Ubeidiya*
			Brielle.

The almost continuous tradition of investigations of fossil microverte-brates in Hungary includes the intense activity of Petényi (1864), Méhely (1914), Kormos (1937), and Kretzoi (1956, 1962). This has led to the Hungarian microstratigraphic series justly being regarded as a classic succession, chiefly of Lower and Middle Pleistocene, in Europe. During the last decade I have correlated these successions with those from temperate climatic areas in both western and eastern continental Europe and England. The results of these investigations form the rough sketch given below.

First however, it should be borne in mind that when we construct the stratigraphical succession in Europe, the Middle East, northern Asia, and North America, we depend chiefly on the evolutionary rates of the rodent group of voles, which has an exceptionally quick pace of evolution, large numbers, and a rapid distribution. We have to take into consideration the geologically contemporaneous evolutionary stages in the whole area of their distribution. The absence of this group on other continents causes difficulties at present in extending the correlation beyond the well-constructed and finely stratified successions of the Holarctic region, chiefly Europe. Although the evolutionary rates of some groups of insectivorous mammals, especially of some shrews (Soricids), are nearly as rapid as that of the voles, the voles are more numerous and occur more regularly. The evolutionary rates of shrews may, however, open new vistas in extending the correlation of microvertebrate faunas, because the shrews are more characteristic of subtropical and tropical areas than of temperate climatic zones. It is to be hoped that their evolutionary successions may help solve some stratigraphical problems in those areas, especially Africa.

The Pleistocene microstratigraphy of temperate Europe, based on microfaunas, is so detailed that the term Villafranchian appears to be too wide. This term, established by Pareto (1865), was clearly based on the large mammalian fauna; newer revisions have made problematic even the stratotype. Further, one part of the Villafranchian falls into the uppermost Pliocene, another in the lowest Pleistocene. In the future, we must replace "Villafranchian" with one or more new terms. For the adjoining areas of Europe, however, this term is still convenient because information on this time interval in these areas is very incomplete.

The first well-defined microfaunal wave which may conventionally be called Middle to Upper Villafranchian, is characterized, among other events, by the invasion of Europe by two voles having at present only Asiatic relatives. At Kisláng the vole *Lagurus arankae* is found, together with the last mastodons and with a more modern form of *Archidiskodon meridionalis*. *Allophaiomys pliocaenicus* Kormos was present in the eastern part of the continent as far as the Middle East, accompanied by *Lagurus* (*Lagurodon*) *arankae* Kretzoi. An autochthonous evolution of both forms may be assumed in the same area. The transition of *Allophaiomys* into different species of *Microtus*, and *Lagurus arankae* into *L. pannonicus*, may be accepted.

The microfauna of this wave, first defined by Kretzoi (1941) as the Betfia Phase was characterized chiefly from Central Europe by the last survival of a population of ancient shrews, significant as Tertiary relicts (e.g. *Petényia hungarica* Kormos, *Beremendia fissidens* Petényi), and the vanishing of another group of shrews (*Episoriculus, Petényiells*). This phase includes the last small *Mimomys* species in Central Europe (*M. newtoni* Major and *M. pusillus* Méhely). In the Templomhegy Phase there was a similar final appearance of the larger form, *M. savini*. There is also proof of intrusion of arctic elements into the microfauna of what is today the temperate climatic belt of Europe: *Lemmus* is found in northern Hungary in Locations 2 and 8 at Osztramos (Jánossy 1972b).

This well-defined phase can be followed in different localities in France

(Les Valerots, Vallonet, Mas Rambault, Balaruc, etc.), through northern Italy (Verona-Soave, Monte Peglia), Yugoslavia (Marian near Split), Czechoslovakia (Holstyn), Hungary (Kisláng, Locations 2 and 8 at Osztramos; Location 2 at Nagyharsányhegy), Rumania (Betfia), the Ukraine (Chortkrow, Nogaisk), Transcaucasia (Shirak Steppe), to the Middle East ('Ubeidiya), the middle Ural at the northernmost locality (Akkulaewo), and also in eastern Asia (Transbaykalia, Dodogol, Yakutia, Mamontowa Gora) etc. (see Jánossy 1972a; Buachidze 1968; Chaline 1972; Erbaewa 1970; Haas 1966; Kretzoi 1954, 1956; Malez 1961; van Meulen 1972; Agadzanian 1972; Suhow 1970).

This phase is also very important from an archeological point of view. Two localities have yielded the oldest unambiguous evidence of human occupation in Europe and the adjacent areas connected with the micro-fauna we are discussing. Both sites are within the Mediterranean climatic belt, namely, Vallonet, Nice, and 'Ubeidiya, Israel. The newly discovered microfauna of the archeologically important North African locality, Ternifine, has yielded only one vole-like element, the so-called Quetta Mole, *Ellobius fuscocapillus* Blyth (Jaeger 1969). Today, the Quetta Mole is only found in Middle Asia. Related species of *Ellobius* were widespread beginning with the Lower Pleistocene in the eastern parts of Europe and northern Asia; however their stratigraphic significance is still unknown.

The newly discovered microfaunas from different localities of the Lower and mid-Pleistocene of North Africa have shown how entirely isolated this area was during that time. There are almost no zoogeographical connections either with Eurasia or with Africa south of the Sahara (Jaeger 1969, 1970). Only recently have investigations proved a connection between northern Africa and southern Spain in the lowest Pleistocene as evidenced by common rodent species (de Bruijn and van Meulen, personal communication).

For the European succession in the uppermost Villafranchian assemblages, it is remarkably fortunate that even at this level we can establish a connection with the classical Villafranchian large mammalian faunas, the typical animal assemblage on which the term Villafranchian is based. Firstly there is the macrofauna of the Grotte du Vallonet in France (de Lumley, et al. 1963) where however the taxonomic status of the large mammalian material is in need of revision; secondly there is the macro-fauna of Kisláng in Hungary (Kretzoi 1954).

The most recent investigations in Hungary and the Netherlands (Jánossy 1972c; van Meulen 1972) have shown that the Betfia phase may be separated into two units: one with only the more primitive *Allo-phaiomys* among the small voles, and the other characterized by the appearance of the first *Microtus* forms, together with a more evolved form of *Allophaiomys*.

After a short, not very clearly defined faunal period, the Nagyharsány-hegy phase (Kretzoi 1956), a new, very sharp wave of microfauna occurred. This agrees partially with the classical Lower Pleistocene succession published during the last century, which includes the Cromer Forest Bed or Interglacial in England. This was formerly designated as a part of the Upper Pliocene or Preglacial. We would conventionally correlate this faunal wave, named Biharian by Kretzoi (1941) with the Günz-Mindel Interglacial, along with the Mindel or Antepenultimate Glacial. (But see Butzer's article in this volume, Chapter 19.)

Among the very few remnants of ancient shrews (*Beremendia fissidens* Petényi, *Drepanosorex savini* Hinton) the modern forms of Soricid of temperate Europe prevail: first, *Sorex runtonensis* Hinton, then, *Sorex praearaneus* Heller.

The guide fossils among the voles of this period are *Pliomys episcopalis* Méhely and *P. lenki* Heller, together with the last representatives of the genus *Mimomys*, as shown in *M. savini* Hinton in the lower level. This wave may be divided into at least two subwaves, the older one characterized by *Mimomys savini*, accompanied by *Lagurus pannonicus* Kormos (Templomhegy phase; Kretzoi 1956), the second without *Mimomys* but with *Lagurus transiens* Jánossy (Tarko phase; Jánossy 1962 = Vértess-zöllös phase; Kretzoi and Vértes 1965a, 1965b). An equilibrium of

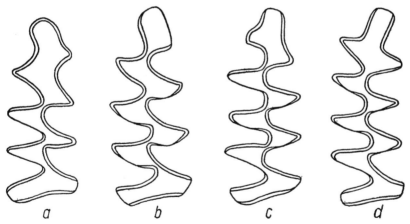

a   *b*   *c*   *d*

Figure 1. Occlusal view of enamel patterns of the first lower molars of the most important guide fossils among the voles in the Middle Pleistocene of Europe: (a) *Lagurus arankae* Kretzoi, Location 8, Osztramos (Upper Villafranchian, Betfia phase); (b)*Lagurus pannonicus* Kormos, Location 14, Osztramos (Templomhegy phase); (c) *Lagurus transiens* Jánossy, Tarkő Rockshelter (Tarkő phase); (d) *Lagurus lagurus* Pallas, Subalyuk (Subalyuk phase)

Pitymys/Microtus species is characteristic of both levels. Among the middle-sized mammals, the last appearance of the giant beaver, *Trogontherium*, is very characteristic in Eurasia throughout the whole period. This faunal wave can be traced through the whole of Europe. In the Templomhegy phase we probably can include a part of the classical terrace deposits of the Cromer Forest Bed in England; Sackdilling, Voigstedt, Süssenborn, and Hochensülzen in Germany; Prežletice in Czechoslovakia; and Locations 6 and 8 in Villány, Kövesvárad, Urömhegy, and Budakalász in Hungary. In 1973 *Archidiskodon meridionalis* cromerensis was found together with *Mimomys savini* at Urömhegy. In the Tarkö phase (Mosbachian *sensu stricto*) we can place a part of the Mauer sequence, the middle layers (Hauptfauna) of Mosbach, Erpfingen 7, Jockgrim, Petersbuch in Germany; the majority of the Hundsheim sequence in Austria; Tarkö, Várhegy (Castle Cave), Vértesszöllös, Gombaszög, Brassó in the Carpathian Basin; Stranská Skála and a part of Konieprusy in Czechoslovakia; and Tiraspol, Khadshibey, and Cherniy Yar in the Russian Plain (see especially Kretzoi 1965; Jánossy 1969, 1970a, 1970b; Alexandrowa 1967, 1971; Fejfar 1969; Koenigswald 1970).

It is well known that we have obtained during recent years not only the classical human remains from Mauer, but also unambiguous evidence of human occupations in Europe from the two cited levels of the Biharian: Prežletice with *Mimomys savini* and *Trogontherium*, and Vértesszöllös without *Mimomys* but with *Pliomys* and *Trogontherium*.

For this period we are accumulating more and more physical and faunal evidence of considerable changes in climate. Red clays which show a gradual transition into loesses (Location 8 at Villány, Konieprusy) are, for instance, physical arguments for these changes. Later I shall discuss the assemblages of small mammals which indicate similar conditions. Here I would like to mention only my recent investigations into birds originating in these deposits. There is an appearance of birds with Mediterranean, that is tropical, affinities at Prežletice: the spoonbill *Platalea* and the ruddy duck *Oxyura*. These constitute a contrast with the distinctly northern ptarmigan, *Lagopus*, at Vértesszöllös.

In the Tarkö phase at Vértesszöllös there is a very good stratigraphical connection between the micro- and macrofauna and the archeological material. The human occupation sites at Locations 1 and 3 contain remains relating to human diet: there are ungulates, chiefly the horse, *Equus mosbachensis* Reichenau; rhinoceros, *Dicerorhinus etruscus* Falconer; and deer, *Cervus acoronatus* Beninde. The fauna of Location 2 however is in striking contrast: there are very few traces of human activity and carnivorous mammals prevail. Perhaps it was a natural CO_2 trap. Lion is

present, *Leo spelaeus wurmi* Freundenberg; bear, *Ursus deningeri* Reichenau; wolf, *Canis mosbachensis* Soergel, etc. The microfauna, independent
of the activities of man, is practically the same in the two localities. The
last representative of the giant beaver, *Trogontherium*, was found, accompanied by an indifferent vole fauna which included equal numbers of
Microtus/Pitymys species. *Pliomys* was found in the lowest levels but
Mimomys is entirely lacking.

The Tiraspol complex of the Russian Plain showed the same connection
of micro- and macrofaunas with eastern elements in both, such as the
jumping mouse *Allactaga* and an antelope. *Mimomys savini* Hinton and
Lagurus transiens Jánossy are found in the microfauna. Evidence of
human occupation is not apparent in this locality.

The above-mentioned level may be followed, using the index fossil
Lagurus transiens through Siberia to Transbaykalia (*Lagurus transiens*
from Chikoi, Erbaewa in litteris). *Trogontherium* and *Beremendia*, etc.
may be followed as far east as the classic site of Location 1, Choukoutien
near Peking as well.

In the literature I have designated the next faunal wave as the Uppony
phase. This was closely connected with its predecessor. The type profile of
this phase is the stratigraphical series 1 to 4 of the rockshelter at Uppony,
northern Hungary (see Jánossy, et al. 1968). Especially characteristic of
the shrews of this phase is a very large form of the European common
shrew, *Sorex araneus macrognathus* Jánossy. Among the voles, a special
Pliomys form, *Pliomys posterior* Jánossy, seems to be the guide fossil of
this period, but *Microtus* species predominate at first over *Pitymys* forms.
The upper levels of Uppony represent not only in their fauna but also in
the sediment, a severe fluctuation in cold. In the upper layers the Siberian,
narrow skulled, vole, *Microtus gregalis*, predominates, while the loess
fraction also prevails in the sediments. The first excavator of the locality,
Vértes, therefore considered the site to be Upper Pleistocene. My latest
investigations of this animal assemblage have demonstrated that there are
elements which contradict the Würm-like appearance of the fauna. Besides
the aberrant *Sorex* and *Pliomys* forms, there is present the carapace fragments of a European pond tortoise, *Emys orbicularis* Linné, and a rich
reptile (lizard and snake) material, quite lacking in the last glacial of our
recently temperate Europe. This argues for a special stratigraphic position
for this site. Moreover, the bird fauna is especially characteristic. Despite
the small number of bones, it is remarkable that it is a typically glacial one.
Among the banal elements is present the long-eared owl, *Asio flammeus*,
and the bullfinch, *Pyrrhula pyrrhula*, together with the willow ptarmigan,
Lagopus cf. *lagopus*. This fauna is similar to the previously known Mindel

bird faunas (Stranská Skála, see Jánossy 1972c; Konieprusy, and Vértess-zöllös). However, there is in the Czechoslovakian localities the last Tertiary relict of a chicken-like bird, the ancient francolin, *Francolinus capeki* Lambrecht, which today is represented only by Ethiopian-Oriental forms. *F. capeki* Lambrecht is entirely lacking at Vértesszöllös and Uppony.

Without entering into more detail we can see that despite the difficulties of resolving stratigraphic correlations for this period, we can attempt to establish that Uppony is different from, and at the same time, very closely related to other Biharian faunas of temperate Europe. We know of very few related localities in Europe. Some similarity may exist with Lunel-Viel, where there are also traces of archeological material. Unfortunately no microfauna has been found at this latter site. Heppenloch in Germany may also belong to the Uppony phase, as well as some levels of Achenheim and La Fage in France (Jánossy 1969, 1970a, 1970b; Chaline 1972). A geomorphological interpretation of the Uppony phase must remain an open question.

As I have pointed out before, a considerable gap in the succession of microfaunas follows the Uppony phase in Europe. We know of very few, if any, fillings of carst holes, representing this period, or even a part of it. The microfauna of this time interval is especially unknown. This gap must have had a geomorphologic reason; we have increasing evidence which implies that the upper part of the mid-Pleistocene was a period of extensive erosion. A series of faunal material originating from borings to depths of several hundred meters or more in the Great Plains of Hungary shows a clear break between the *Mimomys savini* and the *Microtus* faunal associations; and two periods of sedimentation are separated by one of erosion (Krolopp 1970; Kretzoi and Krolopp 1972). Though hitherto unnamed, this period may be called Oldenburgian, a name created by Lüttig (1958) and apparently intended to refer to this time interval.

From the next phase, the so-called Solymár phase (Kretzoi 1969) there are, as with the previous case, only a small number of localities known in Europe. These are chiefly caves which were sheltered against erosion, such as the shaft of the Solymár cave in Hungary, or the ruins of the Hunas cave in Germany, which is completely filled with sediment, or the similar Tornewton cave in England.

I have characterized this phase (Jánossy 1969, 1970a, 1970b) as follows: especially in the rich microfauna of the Solymár cave near Budapest, Hungary, there is a large form of shrew, not identical with *Sorex araneus macrognathus*, but nearly so. For the allometric relations of different *Sorex* species during the Pleistocene, see Figure 2. Among the rodents, the appearance of a relative of the domestic mouse, *Mus* sp., is characteristic. In the vole fauna, *Mimomys* and *Pliomys* forms are wholly absent, while the *Microtus arvalis* group predominates. The only atavistic element remaining from the Lower Pleistocene is *Pitymys gregaloides* Hinton. We also find a subspecies of *Lagurus lagurus* instead of *Lagurus transiens* among the sagebrush voles.

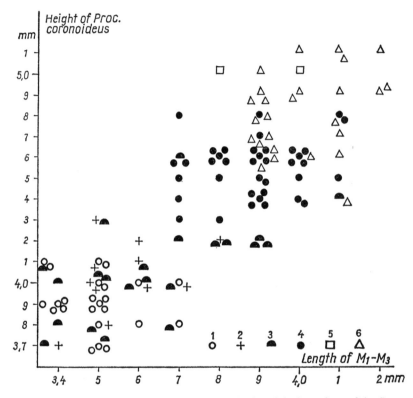

Fig. 2.　Scatter diagram showing the differences in size of the lower jaws of the *Sorex araneus* group vs. time during the Middle Pleistocene; 1. *Sorex runtonensis* Hinton, Loc. 8, Villány; 2. *S. runtonensis* Hinton, Cromer Forest Bed (both= Templomhe Phase); 3. *S. subaraneus* Heller Rockshelter of Tarkő (Tarkő Phase); 4. *S. araneus* Linné, recent Hungary; 5. *S. araneus macrognathus* Jánossy, Rockshelter of Uppony (Uppyon Phase); 6. *S. araneus* ssp., Cave Solymár (Solymár Phase)

The large mammalian fauna is, from a chronological point of view, also distinct: the presence of *Dicerorhinus kirchbergensis* in the covering layers, as well as an aberrant elk, *Alces brevirostris* Kretzoi, is very important.

Solymár has yielded no unambiguous proof of human occupation, although charcoal is abundant and may be from wood fires. The charcoal originated from *Picea* and *Larix*, which are chiefly found today in Siberia,

together with the bald cypress *Taxodium*. At this point, the very interesting succession from the cave fill at Hunas (Heller 1963) merits our attention. We have only a preliminary elaboration of its microfauna, but there
is unambiguous evidence of human occupation: more than two hundred
flints and tool fragments were found. The chief argument for assigning a
younger Middle Pleistocene age to the animal assemblage is based not
only on the microfauna, but also on the presence of the small cave bear.

Most interesting are levels G 1 to 3, which consist of a sediment that
petrographically and botanically gives proof of a cold phase of the upper
Middle Pleistocene, and which contains, besides the common and root
voles, *Microtus arvalis* and *M. oeconomus*, the collared lemming, *Dicrostonyx*, the pika, *Ochotona*, and a small hamster, *Allocricetus*. The bird
fauna of these levels is of a similarly cold character. The most interesting
result from this determination of bird bones is the first known European
appearance in a rich osteological material of two ptarmigan species,
Lagopus lagopus and *L. mutus*. As mentioned above, from the beginning
of the Plio-Pleistocene boundary (Rębielice in Poland) and up to the
Middle Pleistocene (*sensu stricto*) (Stránska Skála and Konieprusy in
Czechoslovakia; Vértesszöllös and Uppony in Hungary) I have only
found the ancient form of the willow ptarmigan. This first evidence of the
divergence into two mountain and lowland forms of *Lagopus* at Hunas is
portentous not only from evolutionary and taxonomic points of view, as
it indicates long isolation of mountain and lowland populations during the
Great Interglacial, but also because it represents an argument for the
stratigraphically independent position of Hunas from Vértesszöllös and
older localities. The higher levels of Hunas (layers E and F) containing deer,
roedeer, beaver, and rhinoceros, together with the snail *Helix*, may indicate
only the Last Interglacial and not an Interstadial of the Last Glacial.

The microfauna of the Glutton stratum of the Tornewton cave in
England (Kowalski 1967) along with Solymar, is also very interesting.
Although strongly modified by local features, it clearly indicates a cold
wave with a strong Atlantic influence. Especially striking features of this
fauna are the first proofs of some steppe or Aralo-Caspian (Turanic)
elements in England: the modern form of the sagebrush vole, *Lagurus
lagurus* Pallas, a large hamster, *Cricetus cricetus* cf. major Woldřich, and
the migratory hamster, *Cricetiscus*. Besides some trivial forms, the presence of the collared and wood lemmings, *Dicrostonyx* and *Lemmus*, and
the absolute predominance of the root vole, *Microtus oeconomus* Pallas,
of which there are more than one thousand specimens, are significant and
quite unusual in European Pleistocene microfaunas. This is a special
Atlantic feature of the British Islands. The stratigraphic position of this

layer is made more clear by the locally overlying sediments containing *Hippopotamus* and *Dama*, and should be interpreted as in the cave of Hunas, as being only Last Interglacial (see also Sutcliffe and Zeuner 1962). Through the courtesy of Sutcliffe I had the opportunity of revising the bird faunas of the same levels at Tornewton. I established, among banal forms, the absolute predominance of an Aralo-Caspian element, as in the case of the mammalian microfauna, namely that of the shelduck, *Tadorna*. Ptarmigans are lacking in this fauna, perhaps a local feature.

Although the two classical European localities apparently representing most of the evolutionary events of the missing late mid-Pleistocene time interval, namely the gravels of Steinheim and the lower gravels of Swanscombe, have yielded very important evidence of the presence of man, we have too few data concerning microfaunas. From Steinheim we have nothing, and the few pieces originating from Swanscombe are insufficient for further inferences. The wood lemming, *Lemmus* sp. (one specimen) and the presence of the Atlantic root vole, *Microtus* aff. *oeconomus* Pallas (one specimen) are mere indications of a faunal connection with the animal assemblages of the Tornewton cave outlined above.

In Hungary the microfaunal connection between the Solymár phase and the subsequent Süttő phase, one of the warmest periods of the Last Interglacial, is very close (see Jánossy 1969, 1970a, 1970b). Among the shrews, a large form of the *Sorex araneus* groups and a relative of the domestic mouse, *Mus* sp., as well as an atavistic hare, *Lepus praetimidus* Kretzoi, are held in common with the fauna of Solymár. Among the voles, the common vole *Microtus arvalis* predominates, but *Pitymys gregaloides* is still unknown in these faunas. The modern form of the sagebrush vole, *Lagurus lagurus*, is rare but present. We will return later to the very important stratigraphic significance of these voles, especially in the Last Interglacial of temperate Europe. The Süttő phase may be characterized by the presence, and locally by the predominance of the European land turtle, *Testudo graeca-hermanni* group, in the southern parts of Europe and by the appearance of the European pond tortoise, *Emys orbicularis* Linné, in the more nothern regions. These guide fossils strengthen the correlations given by the vertebrate fauna and some rich European microfaunas, such as the lower layers of the caves at Grimaldi, and more importantly the Grotte du Prince (*T. greca*) and Fontéchevade (*T. greca* and also *Lagurus lagurus*). Perhaps the lower travertines of Ehringsdorf, Taubach and Burgtonna in Germany, which contain *Emys orbicularis* may be similarly correlated. Last year, together with W. D. Heinrich, I discovered in the covering loess of the travertine of Burgtonna, near Weimar, the first evidence in Central Europe of the absolute predominance of the sagebrush vole, *Lagurus lagurus*. The fossils were in an unambiguous stratigraphic position. This discovery is of some importance, because previously the microfauna of the Last Interglacial could not be separated from that of the Holocene, since the soricid or vole taxa are practically the same, and today inhabit the corresponding area. Among the small vole species, the absolute predominance of the common vole, *Microtus arvalis* Pallas, is characteristic, as it still is today of the cultivated steppes of the same region in Europe. Recent exhaustive investigation into microfaunas of the Last Interglacial in the temperate belt of Europe have increasingly shown that we have to take into account the more or less intense intrusion of the sagebrush vole, an Aralo-Caspian element. This species is certainly present in all faunas of temperate Europe where there is a rich microfauna, but it was previously unrecognized owing to the great morphological resemblance of its teeth to those of the common vole, *Microtus arvalis*. We must also reckon with the intrusion of *Lagurus lagurus* in small numbers, beginning with the so-called Riss Glacial, as shown at Tornewton Cave in England and Solymár Cave in Hungary, and continuing through the warmer and colder parts of the Last Interglacial, starting with Süttő and Fontéchevade, and including Lambrecht Cave in Hungary and the Raj Cave in Poland (Kowalski 1972). The absolute predominance of *Lagurus lagurus* indicates a strong continental climatic change before the beginning of the first true glacial wave of the Würm. We may include in this last level the high Mousterian levels of the Subalyuk Cave in Hungary, the covering layers of Burgtonna, and the new finds, also accompanied by Mousterian cultural remains, in Nordhessen, Germany (Malez personal communication), or Régourdou in France (Couche 4: 45,500 B.P.; see Chaline 1972). Moreover the sagebrush vole survived east of the Carpathians during the whole Würm, and still occurs east of the Dnieper river. Thus the stratigraphic significance of this vole is valid only west of this line in temperate Europe.

Returning to the stratigraphic series of Europe, we may close this mid-Pleistocene succession, *sensu lato*, with the so-called Pre-Würmian cold waves, intercalated with the Anmersfoort, Brörup Interstadials, etc. According to the most recent investigations this period seems to have been longer and also more detailed than formerly supposed. It began with a relatively warmer phase containing Mediterranean relicts, such as the porcupine, *Hystrix vinogradovi* Argyropulo, in Hungary. This is the Varbo phase, or Hystrix horizon (Jánossy 1964). Among birds were the capercaillie, *Tetrao urogallus* Linné, which prevailed absolutely, and the hazel hen, *Tetrastes bonasia* Linné. In the upper parts of the series, we may observe the already mentioned cold waves of the Eemian, indicated at first by *Lagopus* at the Lambrecht cave, and later by the first known appearance of the collared lemming, *Dicrostonyx* in the Last Glacial, in the so-called Tokod Phase. The radiocarbon dating of the type locality is 36,000 B.P. (Jánossy 1972). This level is characterized by the presence of the jumping mouse, *Allactaga jaculus* Pallas. Amongst the birds the black grouse, *Lyrurus tetrix* Linné, is present but the ptarmigan and lemming are lacking. In Hungary this phase is represented at the archeological localities of Tokod, Gencsapáti, Tata (circa 40,000 B.P.), and Érd (42,000 B.P.-38,000 B.P.) (Vértes, et al. 1964; Gábori-Csánk, et al. 1968).

After this period there follows the rich series of relatively well-known Last Glacial faunas of Europe, assemblages beyond the scope of the present discussion.

Finally, the microvertebrate faunas of Mediterranean Europe are very incompletely known. Except for the faunas of this region, discussed above, which are attributable to the Allophaiomys phase at the Grotte du Vallonet, Monte Peglia, Sirak Styep, and 'Ubeidiya, we only know that a *Pliomys lenki*-like form also lived during this period or perhaps later. Its range extended to Spain, perhaps during the Pre-Würmian, at Lezetxiki (Chaline 1970). The appearance of the relict snow vole, *Dolomys* (*Dinaromys*) *bogdanovi* Miller, confined today to some higher Balkan mountains (Bartolomei 1964) seems to be characteristic of the upper parts of the mid-Pleistocene of northern Italy.

Before summarizing the chief results of our investigation into the faunal succession of the European mid-Pleistocene, we should touch on one of the most difficult problems of this field. This is the real climatological significance of the so-called warm and cold elements of the different microfaunas. Our present knowledge of the faunal succession of Europe, although it shows considerable gaps, is sufficient for the drawing of certain conclusions about this question. We can establish that impoverishment of the faunas as a result of early glaciations during the Pleistocene seems to be considerably more acute than in the later phases of this period. This impoverishment opened more ecological niches for intrusion by extraterritorial elements in the European theater; I refer to the large-scale extinction of chiefly Tertiary relict shrews, or to that of most vole species of the *Mimomys* group, etc. On the other hand, we should consider with great caution the climatic indication of the so-called cold elements of the earlier parts of the Pleistocene. In this respect, the significance of the exclusively northern modern forms cited so often in the present work, e.g. the ptarmigans, the genus *Lagopus*, or the lemmings, the genera *Lemmus* or *Dicrostonyx*, is quite different at the Plio-Pleistocene boundary than for the Last Glaciation. These forms seem to have become more

Table 2. Stratigraphical distribution of some microvertebrates of the Middle Pleistocene of temperate Europe

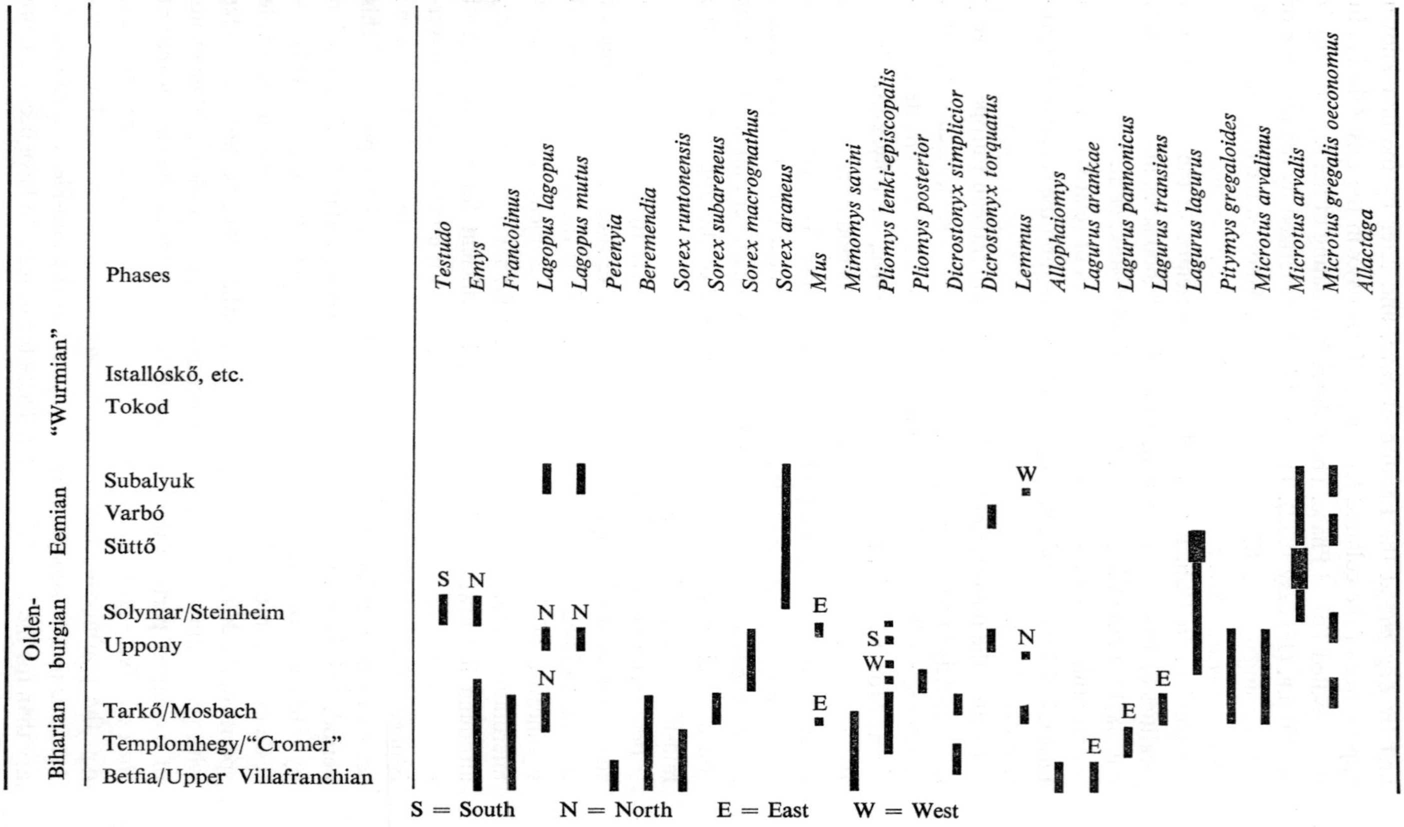
Phases
"Wurmian"
Istallóskő, etc.
Tokod
Eemian
Subalyuk
Varbó
Süttő
Olden-burgian
Solymar/Steinheim
Uppony
Biharian
Tarkő/Mosbach
Templomhegy/"Cromer"
Betfia/Upper Villafranchian
Testudo
Emys
Francolinus
Lagopus lagopus
Lagopus mutus
Petenyia
Beremendia
Sorex runtonensis
Sorex subareneus
Sorex macrognathus
Sorex araneus
Mus
Mimomys savini
Pliomys lenki-episcopalis
Pliomys posterior
Dicrostonyx simplicior
Dicrostonyx torquatus
Lemmus
Allophaiomys
Lagurus arankae
Lagurus pannonicus
Lagurus transiens
Lagurus lagurus
Pitymys gregaloides
Microtus arvalinus
Microtus arvalis
Microtus gregalis oeconomus
Allactaga
S = South N = North E = East W = West

truly arctic from one cold wave to the other, and their numerical increase may also be observed. In the earliest Pleistocene only *Lemmus* was present; in the mid-Pleistocene *Lemmus* was accompanied by the arctic or collared lemming, *Dicrostonyx*, an eastern Asiatic/northwest American invader according to recent investigations (Matthew 1971). We should remember that the oldest known lemming and ptarmigan remains of the Plio-Pleistocene boundary in Europe originate from Poland (Rębielice with both forms), from northernmost Hungary (Osztramos Locality 7; Jánossy 1973), and north of Latitude 50° North. The situation is the same for the later parts of the Lower and Middle Pleistocene; *Lemmus* occurs in the Russian Plain (Tchortkow) at Latitude 50° North, in Poland (Kamyk), Germany (Schernfeld, Deinsdorf), and Localities 2, 3, and 8 at Osztramos in northern Hungary. At the same time, these elements are entirely absent from the contemporaneous and very rich localities in the Villány mountains of southern Hungary, at Latitude 45°, as well as in the northern confines of the Mediterranean. This fact proves clearly that beginning with the lowest part of the Pleistocene, northern forms were confined to the northern parts of Europe, even if they had not been the most decidely arctic forms at that time. More southern localities are known, but only in the atlantic climatic belt of France (Chaline 1972).

The results of complex investigations allow the drawing of further conclusions. For example, I was able to prove that the *Lemmus* of the mid-Pleistocene was a forest dweller rather than an arctic form (Jánossy 1969). This forest may have been a taiga-like coniferous wood with northern features that was regularly stocked with Tertiary "Mediterranean" relicts, such as *Celtis* seeds and a richer reptilian fauna. Similarly the results of complex investigations into the sediments and petrography of different stratigraphic series, prove unambiguously that the presence of the other species, the arctic or collared lemming, *Dicrostonyx*, indicates from its first appearance in the Lower to mid-Pleistocene of Europe, a rather tundra-like climate.

On the other hand, we have an indirect argument for the ecological character of these arctic elements not having changed fundamentally during the Pleistocene. *Lagopus, Lemmus*, and other recent northern forms originating from the Plio-Pleistocene boundary, perhaps three million years ago, are, osteologically and ondontologically, not different or hardly different from their recent representatives. No evolutionary change can be observed in these forms, while most of the small mammals and many other bird forms changed entirely during these times. It is an obvious assumption that species living throughout the entire period under the same cool to cold environmental conditions remained more stable than those surviving extensive environmental changes which stimulated a much quicker tempo of evolution.

My purpose with this seemingly over-detailed discussion of the climatic significance of the microfauna is to emphasize that we still know very little about this field. We must be extremely careful when drawing climatological conclusions which are based chiefly on faunal elements of the earlier parts of the Pleistocene. A caveat must also be given against deductions drawn from Last Interglacial fauna.

Summarizing the chief results, we may conclude that on the basis of microfauna and as far as our present knowledge goes we may subdivide the period of time discussed in this paper, that is to say from the end of the Villafranchian up to the end of the Last Interglacial, into the following more or less well-defined faunal waves, or stratigraphic units. To avoid repetitions, I submit here only a recapitulation of the stratigraphic arrangement of localities, chiefly of archeological significance, without detailing the microfauna (see also the stratigraphic table).

1.   The middle Upper Villafranchian, the boundary between the Villanyian and Biharian of Kretzoi, also called the Betfia phase or Allophaiomys level, may be correlated conventionally with the Günz and perhaps Pre-Günz levels of the astronomical and geomorphological system. As discussed previously we can follow this well-defined microfaunal stage from Western Europe to the Middle East, Transcaucasia, and eastern Asia. The first important archeological sites in this area are only found near the Mediterranean (Grotte du Vallonet and 'Ubeidiya).

2.   The next well-defined stratigraphic unit, the period of the first development of the modern European vole fauna, corresponds partially with the classical Cromer, and it may be correlated with the Günz-Mindel and Mindel in the astronomical and geomorphological system, which also includes the Biharian of Kretzoi. We can distinguish some subdivisions within this period:

a.   The Templomhegy phase.

b.   The Tarkő phase (Mosbachian *sensu stricto*, Saint-Prestian, etc. of earlier literature).

c.   Closely related to this is the Uppony phase, well-represented in Hungary but with very few correlations in the whole of Europe, excepting Lunel-Viel.

It is possible to follow these phases from England through Europe and northern Asia to Transbaikalia and China.

Besides the classical human remains from Mauer, we may include two well-defined human occupations in this time interval: Prežletice in the Templomhegy phase, and Vértesszöllös in the Tarkő phase. Further investigations must prove the presence of human activity in Lunel-Viel, as well as its stratigraphic correspondence with the Uppony phase. Choukoutien seems also to belong in |one level of this period. Whether Ternifine, North Africa, belongs in this or in the former unit is still unknown.

3. After a considerable gap, there follows a period whose designation is very problematic, and for which we have selected the term Oldenburgian. This interval may include in conventional terms the Holsteinian or Hoxnian Interglacial and the Penultimate or Riss Glacial. Steinheim phase is used in earlier literature, Solymár phase in the more recent, for parts of this level. As pointed out above, a period of erosion is supposed to have occurred at the beginning of this time interval.

Very few localities can be securely relegated to this period, but most of them have traces of human activity. Steinheim represents a warmer part with its human skull remains, and is without microfauna. Swanscombe, which is approximately the same age, with only traces of microvertebrates, is the most important archeological locality. Almost of equal significance for future study are Hunas in Germany and the Glutton stratum of Tornewton Cave in England, until now only preliminarily described. In the type locality of the Solymár phase, traces of human activity are uncertain.

4. The animal assemblage of the Last Interglacial, the last microfaunal wave we have to take into account, may be called a prelude to the faunas of the Last Glacial and the Holocene. The modernization of European microfaunas is accomplished in this period. The alternation of predominately warmer or colder faunal elements indicates the climatic events of these times. We designate this global period with technical terms borrowed from geomorphology as the Last or Eemian or Riss-Würm Interglacial. We can also divide this period into certain subdivisions:

a. A warmer period represents the Süttő phase in Hungary. Seemingly contemporaneous are the important localities of Fontéchevade and Grotte du Prince in France, as well as Ehringsdorf and Taubach in Germany.

b. After a greater or smaller gap, there follows the series of the so-called Pre-Würmian cold waves, intercalated by the Interstadials Brörup and Loopstedt. The first of these is perhaps the Varbó phase in Hungary, also called by the present author the Hystrix horizon. The most important archeological localities of this wave are, besides Lambrecht cave in Hungary, Repolust cave in Austria and perhaps a part of Ehringsdorf, etc.

c. Very closely following the Varbó phase in temperate Europe is the Subalyuk phase. Besides Subalyuk in Hungary, there are the upper layers in Burgtonna, the chief Mousterian in Nordhessen in Germany, and

Régourdou in France which belong to this level. Régourdou, layer 4 is dated to 45,000 B.P.

d. We may finish the series with the Tokod phase in Hungary, which is perhaps the first cold phase in the Last Glacial, Würm, beginning with the archeological localities of Tata, at circa 40,000 B.P., and Érd, from 44,000 to 38,000 B.P. The type locality is Tokod, which shows traces of human activity and is dated by the radiocarbon method to 38,000 B.P.; a further corresponding locality in Hungary is Gencsapáti. Also there are the lower layers of the classical localities of Sirgenstein, Buchenloch, Breitenfurter Höhle, etc., in Germany, Cotêncher in Switzerland, and so forth.

This short recapitulation shows clearly that the chronological succession of Pleistocene microfaunas in Europe, although having gaps both large and small, may be regarded as one of the best elaborated chronological series of the world. The gaps become smaller year by year, and they increasingly prove the uninterrupted human occupation of the region at least from the uppermost Villafranchian to recent days, accompanied with much more climatic change, and a succession of environmental changes, than was formerly believed.

REFERENCES

AGADZANIAN, A. K.
1972 "Rodents from the Pleistocene deposits of the Mamontow Mountains," in *Pleistocene mammals.* in Russian. Edited by Markow and Naumow, 24–69. Moscow: Isdateljswo Moskowskogo Universiteta.
ALEXANDROWA, L. P.
1967 "Fossil Eopleistocene voles (rodentia, microtinae) of southern Moldavia and south-western Ukraine," in *Stratigraphic importance of small mammalian anthropogen fauna.* in Russian. Edited by Nikiforova, 98–110. Moscow: Academy of Sciences of the USSR, Geological Institute.
1971 "Rodentia," in *Pleistocene of Tiraspol.* in Russian. Edited by Nikiforova, et al., 71–90. Kishinev: Academies of Sciences of the USSR and the Moldavian SSR.
BARTOLOMEI, G.
1964 Mammiferi di brecce pleistoceniche dei Colli Berici (Vicenza). *Memorie del Museo Civico di Storia Naturale* 12:221–290.
BUACHIDZE, T. I.
1968 On the finding of fossil vole remains in the Shirak Steppe. *Soohshchenije Akademii Nauk Grusinskij SSR* 52(2):503–508. in Russian.
CHALINE, J.
1970 *Pliomes lenki,* forme relique dans la Microfaune du Würm ancien de la Grotte de Lezetxiki (Guipuzcoa-Espagne). *Munibe, San Sebastian* 22: 43–49.
1972 *Le Quaternaire. L'histoire humaine dans son environnement.* Paris: Doin.

DE LUMLEY, H., S. GAGNIÈRE, L. BARRAL, R. PASCAL
1963 La Grotte du Vallonet Roquebrune-Cap-Martin (A.-M.). *Bulletin du Musée d'Anthropologie Préhistorique de Monaco* 10:5–20.

ERBAEWA, M. A.
1970 *The history of lagomorphs and rodents during the anthropogen of the Selenga Range.* Moscow: Nauka.

FEJFAR, O.
1969 Human remains from the Early Pleistocene in Czechoslovakia. *Current Anthropology* 10(2–3):170–173.

GÁBORI-CSÁNK, V., et al.
1968 *La station du paléolithique moyen d'Erd Hongrie.* Monumenta Historica Budapestinensia 3. Budapest: Hungarian Academy of Sciences.

HAAS, G.
1966 "On the vertebrate fauna of the Lower Pleistocene Site 'Ubeidiya," in *The Lower Pleistocene of the Central Jordan Valley, the excavations at 'Ubeidiya, 1960–1963.* Edited by M. Stekelis, 3–68. Jerusalem: Israel Academy of Sciences and Humanities.

HELLER, F.
1963 Ein bedeutsames Quartärprofil in einer Höhlenruine bei Hunas (Hartmannshof) (Nördliche Frankenalb). *Eiszeitalter und Gegenwart* 14:111–116.
1966 Die Fauna von Hunas Nördliche Frankenalb im Rahmen der deutschen Quatärfaunen. *Eiszeitalter und Gegenwart* 17:113–117.

JAEGER, J.-J.-M.
1969 Les rongeurs du Pleistocène Moyen de Ternifine (Algérie). *Comptes rendus des séances de l'Academie des Sciences,* Série D. 269:1492–1495.
1970 Découverte au Jabel Irhoud des premières faunes de rongeurs du Pleistocène Inférieur et Moyen du Maroc. *Comptes rendus des séances de l'Académie des Sciences,* Série D. 270:920–923.

JÁNOSSY, D.
1962 Vorläufige Mitteilung über die Mittelpleistozäne Vertebratenfauna der Tarkö-Felsnische, NO-Ungarn, Bükk-Gebirge. *Annales Historico-Naturales Musei Nationalis Hungarici. Pars Mineralogica et Palaeontologica* 54:155–176.
1964 Letztinterglaziale Vertebratenfauna aus der Kálmán-Lambrecht-Höhle (Bükk-Gebirge, NO-Ungarn) I-II. *Acta Zoologica Hungarica* 10:139–177.
1969 Stratigraphische Auswertung der europäischen mittelpleistozänen Wirbeltierfauna, 1. *Berichte der Deutschen Gesellschaft für Geologische Wissenschaften, Geologie und Paläontologie,* Serie A. 14:367–438.
1970a Stratigraphische Auswertung der europäischen mittelpleistozänen Wirbeltierfauna, 2. *Berichte der Deutschen Gesellschaft für Geologische Wissenschaften, Geologie und Paläontologie,* Serie A. 14:519–589.
1970b The boundary of Lower-Middle Pleistocene on the basis of microvertebrates in Hungary. *Palaeogeography, Palaeoclimatology, Palaeoecology* 8:147–152.
1972a Der erste Nachweis einer Kalt-Moustérien Vertebratenfauna in Ungarn (Tokod-Nagyberek, Kom. Komárom). *Vertebrata Hungarica* 12 (1970–71):103–110. Budapest.

1972b Ein kleiner Hystrix aus dem Altpleistozän der Fundstelle Osztramos 8. (Nordostungarn). *Vertebrata Hungarica* 13:163–182. Budapest.
1972c Die Mittelpleistozäne Vogelfauna der Stránská Skála. *Anthropos, Studia Musei Moraviae* 20 (n.s. 12):35–64.
i.p. The boundary of the Plio-Pleistocene based on the microvertebrates in North Hungary (Osztramos Locality 7). *Vertebrata Hungarica* 14. Budapest.

JÁNOSSY, D., E. KROLOPP, K. BRUNNACKER
1968 Die Felsnische Uppony I. (Nordungarn). *Eiszeitalter und Gegenwart* 19:31–47.

KOENIGSWALD, V. W.
1970 Mittelpleistozäne Kleinsäugerfauna aus der Spaltenfüllung bei Eichstätt. *Mitteilungen der Bayerischen Staatssammlung für Paläontologie und historische Geologie* 10:407–432.

KORMOS, T.
1937 "Zur Frage der Abstammung und Herkunft der quartären Säugetierfauna Europas," in *Festschrift zum 60ten Geburtstage von Professor Dr. Embrik Strand* 3:287–328.

KOWALSKI, K.
1967 *Lagurus lagurus* (Pallas, 1773) and *Cricetus cricetus* (Linnaeus, 1758); rodentia, mammalia in the Pleistocene of England. *Acta Zoologica Cracoviensia* 12:111–122.
1972 "Fossil fauna," in *Studies on Raj Cave near Kielce (Poland) and its deposits.* Folia Quaternaria, Polska Akademia Nauk 41:45–59.

KRETZOI, M.
1941 Die unterpleistozäne Säugetierfauna von Betfia bei Nagyvárad. *Földtani Közlöny* 71 (7–12):308–335. Budapest.
1953 Quaternary geology and the vertebrate fauna. *Acta Geologica Academiae Scientiarum Hungaricae* 2:67–76. Budapest.
1954 Bericht über die calabrische (villafrankische) Fauna von Kisláng, Komitat Fejér. *Jahresberichte der ungarischen Geologischen Anstalt für 1953*, 2:213–264. Budapest.
1956 Die altpleistozänen Wirbeltierfaunen des Villányer Gebirges. *Geologica Hungarica, Series Paleontologica* 27:1–123.
1962 Fauna und Faunenhorizont von Csarnéta. *Jahresberichte der ungarischen Geologischen Anstalt für 1959*, 344–382. Budapest.
1965 Die Nager und Lagomorphen von Voigtstedt in Thüringen und ihre chronologische Aussage. *Paläontologische Abhandlungen, Abteilung A, Paläozoologie* 2:585–661.
1969 Sketch of the Late Cenozoic (Pliocene and Quaternary) terrestrial stratigraphy of Hungary. *Földrajzi Közlemények* 1969/3:179–204. Budapest.

KRETZOI, M., L. VÉRTES
1965a Upper Biharian (Intermindel) pebble-industry occupation site in northern Hungary. *Current Anthropology* 6:74–87.
1965b The role of Vertebrate faunae and Palaeolithic industries of Hungary in Quaternary stratigraphy and chronology. *Acta Geologica Hungarica* 9:125–143.

KRETZOI, M., E. KROLOPP
1972 Oberpliozäne und quartäre Stratigraphie des Alföld Grosse Ungarische Tiefebene auf Grund paläontologischer Angaben. *Földrajzi Értesítő* 21 (2–3):133–158. Budapest.

KROLOPP, E.
1970 Paläontologische Beiträge zur Stratigraphie der pleistozänen-oberpliozänen Schichtenfolge der Ungarischen Tiefebene. *Őslénytani Viták. Discussiones Palaeontologicae, Földtani Társulat* 14:5–44. Budapest.

LÜTTIG, G.
1958 Eiszeit – Stadium – Phase – Staffel. Eine nomenklatorische Betrachtung. *Geologisches Jahrbuch* 76:235–260.

MALEZ, M.
1961 Die altpleistozäne Brekzienfauna der Halbinsel Marian bei Split. *Palaeontologica Jugoslavica* 4:5–37.

MATTHEWS, Jr., J., R. D. GUTHRIE
1971 The Cape Deceit fauna – early Pleistocene mammalian assemblage from the Alaskan Arctic. *Quaternary Research* 1:474–510.

MÉHELY, L.
1914 Fibrinae Hungariae – Die Ternären und Quartären wurzelzähnigen Wühlmäuse Ungarns. *Annales Musei Nationalis Hungariae* 12:155–243.

PARETO, L.
1865 Note sur les subdivisions que l'on pourrait établir dans les terrains de l'Appenin septentrional. *Bulletin de la Société géologique de France* 22(2):262.

PASA, A.
1947 I mammiferi di alcune antiche brecce Veronesi. *Memorie del Museo Civico di Storia Naturale di Verona* 1:1–111.

PETÉNYI, S. J.
1864 A beremendi mészkőbánya, természetrajz és őslénytanilag leirva. *Hátrahagyott Munkái*, 37–81.

SHEVCHENKO, A. I.
1965 "Key complexes of small mammals from Pliocene and Lower Anthropogene in the south-western part of the Russian plain," in *Stratigraphic importance of small mammalian anthropogen fauna.* Edited by Nikiforova, 7–59. Moscow: Academy of Sciences of the USSR, Geological Institute.

SUHOW, V. P.
1970 *Late Pliocene Micromammalia from the Locality Akkulaewo in Bashkiria* (in Russian). Moscow: Nauka.

SUTCLIFFE, A. J., F. E. ZEUNER
1962 Excavations in the Torbryan Caves, Devonshire, 1. Tornewton Cave. *Proceedings of the Devon Archeological Exploration Society* 5:127–145.

VAN MEULEN, A. J.
1972 "Middle Pleistocene smaller mammals from the Monte Peglia (Orvieto, Italy), with special reference to the phylogeny of *Microtus* (*Arvicolidae, Rodentia*)." Unpublished dissertation, Utrecht.

VÉRTES, L., et al.
1964 Tata, eine Mittelpaläolithische Travertin-Siedlung in Ungarn. *Archaeologica Hungarica, Series Nova* 43:1–253.

The Mammalian Faunas and Hominid Fossils of the Middle Pleistocene of the Maghreb

JEAN-JACQUES JAEGER

ABSTRACT

The stratigraphic framework established for the continental Pleistocene of Morocco represents a valuable yardstick for the whole Maghreb. Yet within this framework it is difficult to define the lower limit of the Middle Pleistocene so that two different limits, the one geomorphological, the other paleontological, can be suggested.

The megafaunas, still poorly known, allow the distinction of three successive marker horizons — Ain Hanech, Ternifine, and Sidi Abderrahman (Presoltanian). Study of the rodent faunas allows confirmation of this succession and establishes that a significant time-gap separates Ternifine from the Tensiftian and Presoltanian sites. There is no evidence for direct faunal exchange between the Maghreb and Western Europe, and for the majority of the palearctic immigrants it is possible to show that an east-west migration route was likely.

The presence of hominids is directly attested to since the time of Ternifine. An almost complete skull recently discovered in Morocco, from the later Middle Pleistocene (Tensiftian), confirms the attribution of these hominids to *Homo erectus*.

INTRODUCTION

In 1956 Choubert, et al. proposed a general stratigraphic framework for the continental Pleistocene of Morocco the principal elements of which were redefined by Biberson (1971) (Table 1). This framework was the object of important criticism on the part of certain authors with regard to the choice of some of the type sites. In the case of the Saletian, Beaudet (1969) pointed out that the type site actually seemed to pertain to an older horizon, predating the phase of post-Villafranchian incision, whereas the fifth terrace is generally attributed to the Saletian. Furthermore, in some places and, in particular, adjacent to the type site two "Saletians" have been recognized, and it seems difficult to know which of these is represented at Casablanca. Nonetheless, for Biberson (1961) the identity of the lithic artifact assemblage between the upper formation at Salé and that of Casablanca demonstrates that these two horizons were contemporary.

Table 1. Stratigraphic framework of the Pleistocene of Atlantic Morocco

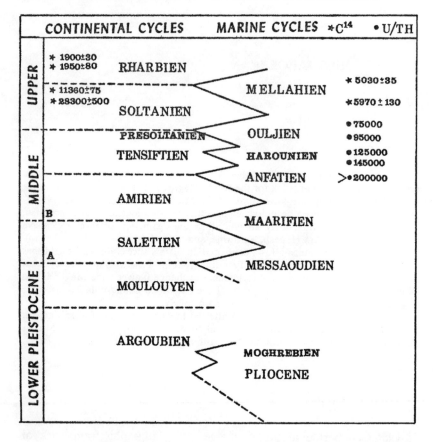

A related problem has been raised by Beaudet in regard to the Amirian. But despite these divergences, the now-classic scheme remains the only valid stratigraphic framework for the Pleistocene and, although defined for Morocco, its usefulness for all of the Maghreb follows.

The problem of the lower limit of the Middle Pleistocene is directly linked to that of the Saletian. From a geomorphological perspective one can place this lower limit at the beginning of the valley downcutting that succeeded the phase of Plio-Villafranchian aggradation (A, Table 1).

From the paleontological viewpoint one can define this limit by the appearance of a cold marine fauna after the close of the Villafranchian (middle Maarifian), more or less synchronous (?) with the establishment of a new mammalian fauna, represented by the beds of Ternifine which are attributed by Biberson (1971) to the early Amirian. Arambourg (1962) adopts such a limit (B, Table 1).

It is generally accepted that the upper limit of the Middle Pleistocene corresponds to the beginning of the Soltanian.

THE SUCCESSION OF MEGAFAUNAS

This outline of the megafaunal succession (Table 2) is not intended to review the whole inventory of large mammals of mid-Pleistocene age recovered from the Maghreb. In effect, many of the older discoveries were made under uncontrolled situations in regard to geographical localization or stratigraphic precision, or in matters of specific or generic determination. Our stratigraphic framework is based only on faunas recently determined or which were recovered from horizons the age of which is clearly established. An important synthesis of the older discoveries made in Algeria is given by Romer (1928).

1. The Ain Hanech fauna (Arambourg 1970; Jaeger i.p.a):

Elephas moghrebiensis; Ceratotherium simum mauritanicum; Equus (Asinus) tabeti; Stylohipparion lybicum; Omochoerus phacochoeroides; Hippopotamus amphibius; Gazella sitifensis; Bos bubaloides; Bos praeafricanus; Oryx el eulmensis; Alcelaphus sp.; Gorgon mediterraneus; Numidocapra crassicornis; Libytherium maurusium; Giraffa pomeli; Crocuta crocuta; Canis cf. atrox.

This site has also yielded numerous polyhedrals (Arambourg 1949) and, in view of its fauna, has been attributed to the Upper Villafranchian. Nonetheless, it should be stratigraphically placed at the base of the Middle Pleistocene because it derives from beds cutting into the underlying Villafranchian (Ain Boucherit) and conformably overlain by deposits that, a few meters higher up, include numerous archaic bifaces (Arambourg and Balout 1952; Camps 1964; Arambourg 1970). This observation places in doubt the origin of the Villafranchian elements (e.g. *Stylohipparion, Omochoerus*) collected at this site, since they may have been derived from the richly fossiliferous horizons below. Associated with these Villafranchian species of doubtful origin there are four panchronic forms that follow throughout the Pleistocene *(Ceratotherium simum,*

Table 1. Mid-Pleistocene megafaunal succession of the Maghreb

Stage groupings: **Amirien** — Inf. (S.T.I.C.), Sup. (Grotte des Ours et al.); **Anfatien** — G1, G2; **Tensiftien** — D0, D1.

	Aïn Hanech	Ternifine	S.T.I.C.	Grotte des Ours et al.	G1	G2	D0	D1	Gres de Salé	Grès de Rabat	D2 Présoltanien
Elephas moghrebiensis	•										
Elephas iolensis			•	•	•						
Loxodonta atlantica		•								•	
Ceratotherium simum	•	•	•	•	•	•	•	•	•	•	•
Equus mauritanicus		•	•	•	•	•	•	•	•	•	•
Equus (Asinus) tabeti	•										
Stylohipparion lybicum	•										
Omochoerus phacochoeroïdes	•										
Afrochoerus cf. nicoli		•									
Phacochoerus aethiopicus										•	
Sus scrofa											•
Hippopotamus amphibius	•	•	•		•	•					
Gazella sitifensis	•										
Gazella sp.		•									
Gazella atlantica				•		•	•			•	•
Gazella dorcas							•				•
Gazella cuvieri						•					•
Bos bubaloïdes	•										
Bos praeafricanus			•								
Bos primigenius				•				•		•	•
Oryx el eulmensis	•										
Oryx sp.			•								
Hippotragus sp.					•	•					
Redunca maupasi				•				•			
Alcelaphus probubalis			•	•	•	•	•			•	•
Alcelaphus sp.	•	•									
Connochaetes taurinus			•				•	•	•		
Connochaetes sp.			•								
Taurotragus sp.			•								
Taurotragus derbianus				•							
Gorgon mediterraneus	•										
Numidocapra crassicornis	•										
Rabaticeras arambourgi										•	
? Cervus sp.					•	•					
Libytherium maurusium	•										
Giraffa pomeli	•										
Giraffa sp.			•								
Camelus thomasi			•								
Crocuta crocuta	•	•		•		•				•	•
Hyaena hyaena		•		•		•	•				•
Canis aureus		•		•		•				•	
Canis cf. atrox	•	•									
Vulpes atlantica									•		
Mellivora sp.		•									
Mellivora cf. capensis						•					
Ursus arctos		•	•	•							
Panthera leo		•									
Panthera pardus		•									
Homotherium cf. latidens		•									
Cercopithecinae indet.		•									
cf. Simopithecus ?		•									
Homo erectus		•				•				•	•

Hippopotamus amphibius, Crocuta crocuta, Alcelaphus), as well as several species also found at Ternifine (*Giraffa, Canis* cf. *atrox, Taurotragus*). Finally, others (*Elephas moghrebiensis* and many bovid species still not published) appear to be characteristic of this horizon itself. The Ain Hanech fauna is generally attributed to the Saletian (Biberson 1961) because of the similarity between the lithic industries. Yet there is no paleontological proof for this date — since the Saletian has yielded a single fossil mammal (*Elephas* cf. *recki*, Arambourg 1970) — and a younger age than the type formation seems to be amply indicated.

2.   The fauna of Bel-Hacel (Algeria) (Arambourg 1970): *Elephas moghrebiensis, Ceratotherium simum, Equus* sp., antelopes (?). The stratigraphic position of this site remains to be narrowed down (Post-Astian, pre-Middle Pleistocene).

3.   The fauna of Ternifine (Arambourg and Hoffstetter 1954, 1955; Arambourg 1955):
Loxodonta atlantica; Ceratotherium simum mauritanicum; Equus mauritanicus; ?*Afrochoerus* sp.; *Hippopotamus amphibius; Gazella* sp.; *Oryx* sp.; *Alcelaphus* sp.; *Connochaetes* sp.; *Taurotragus* sp.; *Giraffa* sp.; *Camelus thomasi; Crocuta* cf. *crocuta; Hyaena* cf. *hyaena; Canis* cf. *aureus; Canis* cf. *atrox; Mellivora* sp.; *Panthera* cf. *leo; Panthera* cf. *pardus; Homotherium* cf. *latidens; Ursus* cf. *arctos*; cf. *Simopithecus;* Cercopithecinae indet.; *Homo erectus mauritanicus.*

The fauna of this site has not yet been studied in detail, making comparisons with older or younger faunas difficult. It is distinguished from that of Ain Hanech by the appearance of several species that characterize the remainder of the Middle Pleistocene as well as the Upper Pleistocene (*Loxodonta atlantica, Equus mauritanicus, Connochaetes, Hyaena, Ursus*) as well as by the disappearance of numerous typical species of the earlier horizon. The uniqueness of Ternifine is due to the survival of certain "Villafranchian" species, leading Arambourg to attribute this fauna to the early Middle Pleistocene (B limit, Table 1).

4.   The fauna of the lower Amirian levels at Casablanca (S.T.I.C.) (Biberson 1961):
Elephas iolensis; Ceratotherium simum; Equus mauritanicus; Hippopotamus amphibius; Bos primigenius; Alcelaphus probubalis; Connochaetes taurinus prognu; Taurotragus derbianus.

For Biberson this fauna is contemporary with that of Ternifine, and he seeks support for this argument in the degree of evolution of the lithic industry, which is similar. Yet Arambourg (1962) considers this fauna younger than that of Ternifine because, on the one hand, it includes *Bos primigenius* (an Asiatic immigrant according to Arambourg) while, on the other, there are none of the "Villafranchian" species of Ternifine. Since no rodent faunas have been collected from the early Amirian of Atlantic coastal Morocco, it is not now possible to confirm or contradict this correlation. The different species of elephants can be explained by the ecological contrasts between the Atlantic littoral and the high plateaus.

5.   The fauna of the upper Amirian levels at Casablanca, including the Grotte des Ours (Biberson 1961):

Elephas iolensis; Ceratotherium simum; Equus mauritanicus; Gazella atlantica; Redunca maupasi; Alcelaphus probubalis; Crocuta crocuta spelaea; Ursus arctos bibersoni.

This fauna, almost identical to that of the earlier Amirian, includes the oldest locality with *Gazella atlantica.*

6.   The fauna of the early Anfatian (G1) (Biberson 1961):

Elephas iolensis; Ceratotherium simum; Equus mauritanicus; Hippopotamus amphibius; Hippotragus sp.; *Alcelaphus probubalis; Cervus* sp.; *Hyaena hyaena; Canis aureus; Ursus arctos bibersoni.*

This fauna is characterized by the first appearance of the genus *Cervus* in North Africa, if the determination can be upheld.

7.   The fauna of the later Anfatian (G2) of Casablanca (Biberson 1961):

Ceratotherium simum; Equus mauritanicus; Hippopotamus amphibius; Gazella atlantica; Gazella sp.; *Alcelaphus probubalis; ? Cervus* sp.

8.   The fauna of the Tensiftian (D0) of Casablanca (Biberson 1961):

Ceratotherium simum; Equus mauritanicus; Gazella atlantica; Gazella dorcas; Gazella cuvieri; Bos primigenius; Hippotragus sp.; *Alcelaphus probubalis; Connochaetes taurinus; Crocuta crocuta spelaea; Hyaena hyaena; Vulpes atlantica; Canis aureus; Mellivora* cf. *capensis; Monachus albiventer; Homo* cf. *erectus.*

The gazelles, represented by three distinct species, suggest a relatively arid climate and an open environment. This is confirmed by the presence of *Phacochoerus aethiopicus,* which first appears in this horizon (Grès de Rabat) (Arambourg 1938).

9.   The fauna of the Presoltanian (D2) of Casablanca (Biberson 1961):

Ceratotherium simum; Equus mauritanicus; Sus scrofa algeriensis; Hippopotamus amphibius; Gazella atlantica; Gazella dorcas; Gazella cuvieri; Gazella sp.; *Bos primigenius; Redunca maupasi; Alcelaphus probubalis; Connochaetes taurinus prognu; Crocuta crocuta; Hyaena hyaena; Canis aureus.*

This fauna is enriched in comparison to the previous one by the arrival of a supplementary element of Eurasiatic origin, *Sus scrofa.*

European or Eurasiatic faunal elements appear gradually during the course of the Middle and Upper Pleistocene. This step-wise increment suggests an ecological filter between their area of origin and the Maghreb. *Ursus* cf. *arctos* is already present at Ternifine, and unpublished documents suggest the presence of *Ursus etruscus* at the very base of the Middle Pleistocene (or at the top of the Villafranchian) in Algeria. *Bos primigenius* appeared in the early Amirian, followed during the Tensiftian by ? *Cervus* sp. (if this determination is correct) and during the Presoltanian by *Sus scrofa*. In regard to *Bubalus antiquus* there is no undisputed find now attributed to levels earlier than the Soltanian. During that epoch, new Eurasiatic elements include *Dicerorhinus kirchbergensis* (= *Rhinoceros mercki*), *Cervus (Megaceroides) algericus,* and *Ammotragus lervia*, even though the Sudanese forms do not disappear. The proportion of forms in the Maghreb derived from Eurasiatic sources is highest during this period.

Seen in the context of the materials discussed above, there are very few data useful for an external biostratigraphic zonation: the presence of *Elephas atlanticus* and *Hippopotamus amphibius* is known from the Tyrrhenian *(sensu lato)* of Bizerta (Solignac 1927), with *Elephas iolensis* recorded in the Tyrrhenian of the littoral near Algiers (Pomel 1896). Even on a relative stratigraphic level only three faunal horizons can be distinguished: (a) Ain Hanech, (b) Ternifine, and (c) the Tensiftian-Presoltanian.

Little has been said about evolutionary lineages, and among the rare examples is that of *Elephas atlanticus atlanticus* — *E. atlanticus maroccanus* (Arambourg 1938), with sparse documentation, as well as that of the hominids (see below). Finally, some important faunas do not fit into the composite table. This is particularly so in the case of Lake Karar, Algeria (Boule 1900), which provided a lithic industry generally attributed to the early Acheulian (Vaufrey 1955) and was associated with *Sus scrofa* and *Bubalus antiquus*, species first appearing on the Moroccan coast during the Presoltanian and Soltanian, respectively. Is this a faunal mixture including several distinct horizons or is it a matter of a poorly-detailed biostratigraphic yardstick? No answer can be given until detailed faunal analysis and descriptions of evolutionary lineages are available.

THE SUCCESSION OF RODENT FAUNAS

As in the case of the large mammals, the succession of rodent faunas (Table 3) permits the establishment of a stratigraphic synopsis based on faunal association. Three successive stages can be recognized: (a) the fauna of Sidi Abdallah (Morocco); (b) the fauna of Ternifine (Algeria); c) the fauna of the Presoltanian (Morocco).

Species	SIDI ABDALLAH	TERNIFINE	AIN MEFTA	THOMAS	SALE	IRHOUD D.V.	SIDI ABDERHAMAN (Présoltanien)
Ellobius cf. fuscocapillus	*						
Ellobius barbarus			*	*	*	*	*
Paraethomys sp,	*						
Paraethomys cf. filfilae		*	*		*	*	*
Arvicanthis sp.		*	*		*		
Praomys sp.	*	*	*			*	*
Mus cf. musculus	*		*		*		
Mus (Leggada) sp.						*	
Eliomys sp.			*		*	*	*
Meriones sp.		*		*	*		
Meriones cf. shawi			*		*	*	*
Genus indet (cf. Meriones ?)	*	*					
Gerbillus sp.	*	*		*	*		*
Gerbillus cf. campestris						*	*
Atlantoxerus getulus	*					*	
Jaculus sp.	*					*	
Irhoudia bohlini	*						
Hystrix cf. cristata		*					

Table 2. Rodent faunal succession of the mid-Pleistocene of the Maghreb

1.   The fauna of Sidi Abdallah (Jaeger i.p.a; and unpublished):
Paraethomys sp.; *Praomys* sp.; *Mus* cf. *musculus;* Gerbillidae gen. and sp. indet.; *Gerbillus* sp.; *Atlantoxerus getulus; Jaculus* sp.; *Irhoudia bohlini.*

This fauna again includes Villafranchian elements (Ctenodactylids and Gerbillidae) but is distinguished from earlier Villafranchian faunas by the small number of such species and by the presence of a species *Parae-thomys* more evolved than *P. anomalus*.

2. The fauna of Ternifine (Jaeger 1969):
Ellobius cf. *fuscocapillus; Paraethomys* cf. *filfilae; Arvicanthis* sp.; *Praomys* sp.; *Meriones* sp.; Gerbillidae gen. indet.; *Gerbillus* sp.; Hystrix cf. *cristata*.

This rodent fauna comes from the lower levels of the site and appears to be homogeneous. There still are certain lineages of the earlier stage but also a large number of new elements, making their first appearance. Some of the latter are of Asiatic origin *(Ellobius, Meriones)*, others of Sudanese origin *(Arvicanthis)*. These new elements remained to characterize all later faunas of the Middle Pleistocene.

3. The Presoltanian fauna of Sidi Abderrahman (Jaeger i.p.a; and unpublished):
Ellobius barbarus; Paraethomys cf. *filfilae; Mus* cf. *musculus; Eliomys* sp.; *Meriones* cf. *shaw; Gerbillus* sp.; *Gerbillus* cf. *campestris*.

This fauna is represented in the Maghreb by a dozen sites. It is characterized by the presence of an *Ellobius* more evolved than that of Ternifine, by a characteristic Eurasiatic element (*Eliomys* sp.), and by a modern gerbil fauna (*Meriones* cf. *shawi, Gerbillus* cf. *campestris*).

Study of the rodents allows the introduction of a supplementary dimension on the bias of the evolutionary lineages. In particular, that of the murid *Paraethomys* allows precise assignment of the different Lower Pleistocene sites (Figure 1) (Jaeger i.p.a). At the same time, certain species first appearing in the Ternifine level underwent rapid evolution of their molar dimensions and sometimes even morphology during the course of the Middle Pleistocene: *Arvicanthis, Meriones, Ellobius, Praomys*. Thus detailed analysis of the evolutionary lineage of *Ellobius* cf. *fuscocapillus* to *Ellobius barbarus* should allow accurate placing of the various rodent populations of the Middle Pleistocene into relative stratigraphic position. These accordingly provide the first arguments (Figures 2 and 3) to show that the Ternifine form is smaller and more primitive than that of the Tensiftian-Presoltanian. One can observe the same phenomenon with *Arvicanthis* and *Praomys*. These preliminary results seem to show the existence of a sufficiently long time span between Ternifine and the group of younger Middle Pleistocene sites to allow for appreciable evolutionary change in at least four distinct lineages. This observation matches that of Arambourg (1962) to confirm the greater age of the Ternifine fauna.

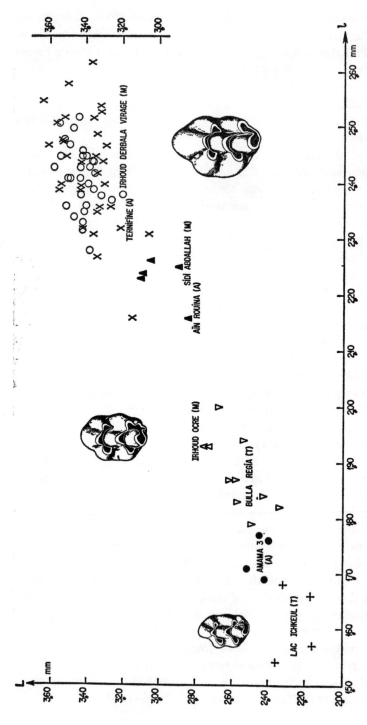

Figure 1.   Evolutionary lineage of *Paraethomys* cf. *anomalus* to *Paraethomys filfilae* from the Lower to Middle Pleistocene (diagram of length-width ratios of upper M1)

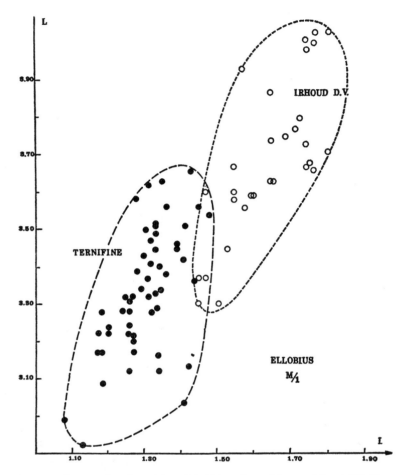

Figure 2. Scatter diagram of length/width ratios of lower M1 of *Ellobius* at Ternifine and from the Presoltanian (Irhoud Derbala Virage)

HOMINIDS OF THE MIDDLE PLEISTOCENE OF THE MAGHREB

Numerous hominid fragments have been recovered in the Maghreb, primarily in Morocco.

1. Ternifine (Arambourg and Hoffstetter 1954, 1955, 1963; Arambourg 1955, 1956, 1963):

This site has provided three hominid mandibles, a fragment of a parietal, and several isolated molars. It is attributed to the base of the Middle Pleistocene (limit B, Table 1), a position confirmed by the micromam-

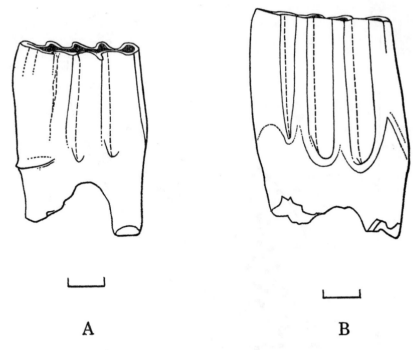

Figure 3.   Lateral view of two lower M1 of *Ellobius*
A) Ternifine, B) Irhoud Derbala Virage (Presoltanian) (note the differences of width and hypsodonty)

mals. In fact, at present, Ternifine represents the most ancient site with a typical Middle Pleistocene fauna (*Elephas atlanticus, Ellobius, Meriones*). Although Biberson (1961) correlates it to the early Amirian on the basis of development of the lithic industry, the megafauna unfortunately does not allow such a correlation while no micromammals are available from the early Amirian of the Moroccan coast. Consequently that problem remains unresolved.
2.   Sidi Abderrahman (Grotte des Littorines):
This site was studied by Biberson (1956) who attributed it to the early Tensiftian. It has yielded two mandibular fragments (Arambourg and Biberson 1955, 1956) attributed to a *Homo erectus*.
3.   The Mifsud Giudice Quarry in the Grès de Rabat (Vallois 1945, 1959):
This site yielded a mandibular fragment, a piece of the upper left maxilla, and several cranial fragments (Marçais 1934). The stratigraphy, acrimoniously argued by numerous authors, allows assignment of this horizon to the Middle Tensiftian or to the regression following the Harounian,

i.e. the Presoltanian (Biberson 1961). The associated fauna allows no choice between these possibilities.

4.   Temara (Grotte des Contrebandiers) (Vallois and Roche 1958): An almost complete mandible was recovered from a cave fill attributed by Choubert to the Presoltanian (Biberson 1961).

5.   The Thomas "I" Quarry, Casablanca (Ennouchi 1969): A left mandibular fragment was collected at this site by P. Beriro and published by Ennouchi, who attributes it to the Amirian eolianite.

However, sedimentological study of the attached matrix does not confirm this provenience (F. Sausse, personal communication). Instead, there is an important solution hollow at the spot the mandible was found, and the infilling is comparable to the matrix. This cave, dissolved into the Amirian eolianite, provided a rodent fauna (see Table 3) that indicates a somewhat younger age than Ternifine, closer to the Presoltanian. The absence of precise data on the derivation of the supposedly associated megafauna deprives that of any stratigraphic value.

6.   The Thomas "2" Quarry, Casablanca (Ennouchi 1972): A cave cut into the Amirian eolianite and exposed by quarry operations has recently yielded a cranial piece including part of the face, the frontal, the temporal, and several upper teeth of a *Homo erectus*. The associated (?) fauna corresponds to the Tensiftian *(Ursus arctos bibersoni, Canis aureus, Phacochoerus africanus, Hystrix cristata, Alcelaphus bubalis, Gazella atlantica, Elephas sp.)*.

It consequently appears clear that, apart from whether Ternifine is attributed to the early Amirian or to an older level, all the other Middle Pleistocene human remains of the Maghreb come from Tensiftian or younger horizons (Temara). Arambourg (1955, 1963) attributed the Ternifine materials to a *Homo erectus mauritanicus* resembling *Sinanthropus*, whereas the Tensiftian forms were considered as slightly more evolved descendants of this form. The advanced degree of evolution attained by some fossils, notably Rabat Man, had already been emphasized by Vallois (1945), who attributed these remains to a "preneanderthaler," distinct from those of Europe. This interpretation of a *Homo erectus* lineage evolving in place was retained by Howell (1960). Other authors, notably Cabot Briggs (1968), even prolonged this endemic lineage to the early North African *sapiens* forms. However, Leakey (1960) expressed reservations on the basic identification of *Homo erectus* traits (occipital, frontal, temporal) on materials from the Maghreb. It is therefore significant that the present writer discovered an almost complete calvarium that provides important new information.

7.   Salé, Morocco (Jaeger i.p.b):

A quasi-complete calvarium, associated with a fragment of the upper left maxilla (I^2–M^2) and a natural endocranial cast, were recovered in July 1971 in eolianite near Salé. This outcrop is located 1.5 kilometers from the modern coast at an elevation of thirty to forty meters, inshore of the maximum transgression of a $+25$ to 30 meter shoreline stage. This marine level corresponds to the second observable along the Salé littoral and probably represents the Anfatian.

The skull was isolated, but the same bed yielded the following mammalian fauna: *Connochaetes taurinus, Ceratotherium simum,* Canidae indet. The eolianite is locally overlain by a bone breccia yielding a rodent fauna of Presoltanian character.

The human fossils were briefly described by Jaeger (i.p.b). The cranium belongs to an adult of short stature with a small cranial capacity (930–960 cubic centimeters). The upper teeth resemble those of Rabat Man. The M^1 and M^2 are similar, but the M^3 is narrower at the mesiodistal end than the first two molars, but larger bucco-lingually. The backside and labial of the M^3 shows a strong cingulum, also present on the labial side of the M^2. The cusps of the upper teeth are strongly worn and most of the details obscured. The face is missing and the frontal is broken just behind the supraorbital ridge. What is left of the frontal shows the characteristics of *Homo erectus,* with strong postorbital constriction and sagittal ridge. Altogether, the front part of the cranium corresponds well with *Homo erectus.* The back part shows a different aspect, completely characteristic. The occipital "neck" is weakly developed. An occipital torus is present, surmounted by a supratoral depression, although both structures are reduced. The inion is situated below the opisthocranion, which is not the case with *Homo erectus.* From the occipital view the greatest length is at the submastoid level but the parietal bosses are well developed and give the skull a quasi-rectangular shape. The mastoid processes are also well developed. In the context of these various characteristics, the occipital gives a fairly modern impression. There is no sylvan crest on the internal face of the skull. The arterial network of the brain cast is simple and shows a poorly developed temporal branch.

This skull can be interpreted in two different ways. It could be an evolved *Homo erectus* characterized by opening of the occipital angle, a shift of the inion, reduction of the occipital torus, and development of parietal bosses. Or it could be a *Homo* sp., forming part of an individualistic North African group.

The characteristics of the front part of the skull (dentition and frontal), the cranial capacity, and the high stratigraphic position within the Middle

Pleistocene, together with the vestigial nature of the occipital torus, make the first alternative more likely, confirming earlier interpretations of the Maghrebian hominid materials.

Cabot Briggs' hypothesis can also be reexamined thanks to this new data. Comparison with the Jebel Irhoud I skull (Soltanian) of Ennouchi (1962a, 1962b) shows an interesting general resemblance. This is above all apparent in the very high position of the maximal biparietal diameter of the Irhoud specimen, a disposition already suggested on the Salé skull. The Irhoud I cranium is nontheles larger and more evolved than that of Salé; another important difference is that the inclination of the posterior root of the zygomatic arch is much more inclined on the Salé skull than in that of Irhoud I. Despite its interest, Cabot Briggs' hypothesis is still not fully acceptable, at least not on presently available information.

Comparison with the Ternifine material is essentially restricted to the parietal, which seems more primitive than that of Salé, particularly in regard to the transverse curvature and the impression of the arterial network. Recent data suggest that the Ternifine parietal belonged to a hominid with a large cranial capacity (1300 cubic centimeters, Kochetkova 1970). This does not match the information provided by the smaller hominid skulls of Tensiftian age (Ennouchi 1972; Jaeger i.p.b), while it remains premature to generalize from such limited evidence, even while contradicting the early stratigraphic position of Ternifine.

The origin of the Middle Pleistocene hominids of the Maghreb remains totally unknown. Are these descendants of a human group present in the Maghreb since the Middle Villafranchian (Biberson 1961) or are they, like the genera *Ursus* and *Ellobius,* immigrants of Asiatic origin? The evidence still is insufficient and the apparent continuity in the development of the lithic industries does not allow a strong argument to reject an indigenous development of these Middle Pleistocene hominids in the Maghreb.

BIOGEOGRAPHIC AND CLIMATIC EVIDENCE

The Pleistocene faunas of the Maghreb are individualistic, with only few Eurasiatic elements that gradually increase in number through the course of the Pleistocene. The majority of these Eurasiatic immigrants are represented in the Pleistocene of the Middle East and their penetration can be explained by the existence of a corridor for migration, situated along the North African coasts of the eastern Mediterranean Sea. Many examples serve to support this interpretation. Thus *Dicerorhinus kirchbergensis* and *Sus Scrofa* are present in the Middle East during the late mid-Acheulian (Bar-Yosef and Tchernov 1972). *Ellobius* cf. *fuscocapillus*, which appears at the Ternifine horizon, is a rodent presently living in central Asia and which undoubtedly moved from east to west. The history of the genus *Apodemus* in North Africa also fits this scheme. This genus appeared in the Maghreb at the end of the Upper Pleistocene and is still present; it was identified by Bate (1955) from the Upper Paleolithic of Cyrenaica, and is represented in the Middle East since the earliest Middle Pleistocene (Haas 1966). These findings again suggest an east-west rather than west-east dispersal.

At the present stage of research there is no proof whatsoever of direct faunal exchanges between Europe and the Maghreb across the Straits of Gibraltar during the Middle and Upper Pleistocene.

The presence of Sudanese species among the mid-Pleistocene megafaunas of the Maghreb suggested a savanna of subsaharan type to Arambourg (1962). This logical interpretation is confirmed by the presence of the murid rodent *Arvicanthis,* characteristic of the tropical savanna, but contradicted by the presence of a rodent characteristic of the Asiatic steppe *(Ellobius).* Since the megafauna is more independent of its environment than is the microfauna, it seems to us that a steppic environment cannot be lightly excluded, at least for the Ternifine stage. In any event, such interpretations must remain speculative in the absence of palynological data.

The Ternifine fauna was preceded by major faunal replacements that seem to have been caused, at least in part, by a significant climatic change. This led to the disappearance of several "Villafranchian" species, among which some groups are temperature-sensitive (Ctenodactylids) and clearly point to a cooling trend. Once established, by the time of Ternifine, the Middle Pleistocene fauna does not exhibit evidence of climatic alterations such as took place in Western Europe, persisting to the end of the Middle or even into the Upper Pleistocene.

The majority of the rodent evolutionary lineages were subject to rapid speciation that appears to have been caused, at least in part, by increasing aridity. This is independently suggested by the increasing number of species of gazelle appearing during the Tensiftian-Presoltanian time span.

Climatic contrasts between the Atlantic littoral (with *Elephas iolensis)* and the interior *(Elephas atlanticus)* are also indicated. Among the rodent faunas this phenomenon is paralleled by the absence of *Arvicanthis* in the littoral zone. Nonetheless the data still are insufficient to establish such an hypothesis.

CORRELATIONS

Two epochs can be separated within the Middle Pleistocene, an upper part with radiometric dates (Th/u.c.), and a lower-to-middle segment for which only paleontological, archeological, and geomorphological criteria are available.

Correlations were suggested by Choubert (1957) for the Atlantic and Mediterranean shorelines:

Anfatian — Mindel-Riss (Holstein) interglacial

Harounian — Riss interstadial

Ouljian — Riss-Würm (Eem) interglacial.

These appeared to be supported in large measure by isotopic analyses (Stearns and Thurber 1965) (see Table 1). Yet these results are not fully in agreement with all observations (Biberson 1961; Houzay, et al. 1973) and new radiometric measures are presently being obtained. Correlations for the older marine levels are still inadequate and allow no discussion on the age of the key site of Ternifine. Furthermore, the faunal assemblage of Ternifine cannot be directly compared with any Middle Eastern sites.

However, the 'Ubeidiya fauna (Haas 1966; Bar-Yosef and Tchernov 1972), attributed to the beginning of the Biharian by Jánossy (this volume), includes several forms in common with that of Ternifine: *Ursus, Panthera*, a machairodont, cercopithecoids, *Equus, Hippopotamus* cf. *amphibius, Giraffa, Hystrix, Meriones, Gerbillus*, even though the species are generally different. Yet, the rodents *Ellobius* and *Arvicanthis* are not represented at 'Ubeidiya, despite an abundance of microfauna. Since *Ellobius* is represented in the Acheulian and early Levalloiso-Mousterian horizons of the Middle East (Tchernov 1968), this suggests an immigration later than 'Ubeidiya. These data consequently imply that Ternifine was younger than 'Ubeidiya.

REFERENCES

ARAMBOURG, C.
    1938   Mammifères fossiles du Maroc. *Mémoires de la Société des Sciences Naturelles et Physiques du Maroc* 46:1–74.
    1949   Sur la présence dans le Villafranchien d' Algérie de vestiges éventuels d'industrie humaine. *Comptes Rendus de l'Académie des Sciences*, Paris 229:66–67.
    1955   Récentes découvertes de paléontologie humaine réalisées en Afrique du Nord française (l'*Atlanthropus* de Ternifine — l'hominien

de Casablanca). *Actes du Troisième Congrès Panafricain de Préhistoire*. Edited by J. D. Clark, 186–194. London.

1956   Le gisement Pléistocène de Ternifine et l'*Atlanthropus. Bulletin de la Société Belge de Géologie, Paléontologie et Hydrologie* 65 (1):132–136.

1962   Les faunes mammalogiques du Pléistocène d'Afrique. *Colloque International du CNRS, Evolution des Vertébrés*, Paris, 369–376.

1963   Le gisement de Ternifine: l'*Atlanthropus* de Ternifine. *Archives de l'Institut de Paléontologie Humaine*, Paris 32:37–190.

1970   Les vertébrés du Pléistocène de l'Afrique du Nord. *Archives du Muséum National d'Histoire Naturelle*, Paris 10:1–126.

ARAMBOURG, C., L. BALOUT

1952   Du nouveau à l'Aïn Hanech. *Bulletin de la Société d'Histoire de l'Afrique du Nord*, Algiers 43:152–159.

ARAMBOURG, C., P. BIBERSON

1955   Découverte de vestiges humains acheuléens dans la carrière de Sidi Abderrahman près de Casablanca. *Comptes Rendus de l'Académie des Sciences*, Paris 240:1661–1663.

1956   The fossil human remains from the Palaeolithic site of Sidi Abderrahman (Morocco). *American Journal of Physical Anthropology* 14(3):467–490.

ARAMBOURG, C., R. HOFFSTETTER

1954   Découverte en Afrique du Nord, de restes humains du Paléolithique inférieur. *Comptes Rendus de l'Académie des Sciences*, Paris 239:72–74.

1955   Le gisement de Ternifine: résultats des fouilles de 1935 et découverte de nouveaux restes d'*Atlanthropus. Comptes Rendus de l'Académie des Sciences*, Paris 241:431–433.

1963   Le gisement de Ternifine: historique et géologie, *Archives de l'Institut de Paléontologie Humaine*, Paris 32:1–36.

BAR-YOSEF, O., E. TCHERNOV

1972   On the palaeo-ecological history of the site of 'Ubeidiya. The Israel Academy of Sciences and Humanities, Jerusalem, 5–35.

BATE, D. M. A.

1955   "Vertebrates faunas of Quaternary deposits in Cyrenaica," in *Prehistory and Pleistocene geology in Cyrenaican Libya*. Edited by C. B. M. McBurney and R. W. Hey, 284–291. Cambridge.

BEAUDET, G.

1969   "Le plateau central marocain et ses bordures. Etude géomorphologique." Thesis, Université de Paris. Inframa, Rabat.

BIBERSON, P.

1956   Le gisement de l'Atlanthrope de Sidi Abderrahman (Casablanca). *Bulletin d'Archéologie Marocaine* 1:39–91.

1961   Le cadre paléogéographique de la préhistoire du Maroc atlantique. *Publication du Service des Antiquités du Maroc*, Rabat 16:1–235.

1966   Réflexions sur de nouvelles datations du Quaternaire marocain. *Comptes Rendus sommaires de la Société Géologique de France* 4:161–162.

1971   Essai de redéfinition des cycles climatiques du Quaternaire continental du Maroc. *Bulletin de l'Association Française pour l'étude du Quaternaire*, Paris 1(26):3–13.

BOULE, M.
1900   Etude paléontologique et archéologique sur la station paléolithique du lac Karar (Algérie). *L'Anthropologie*, Paris 11:1–21.

CABOT BRIGGS, L.
1968   Hominid evolution in Northwest Africa and the question of the North African "Neanderthaloids." *American Journal of Physical Anthropology* 29:377–386.

CAMPS, G.
1964   Recherches récentes sur le Paléolithique inférieur des Hautes Plaines constantinoises. *Libyca* 12:9–42.

CHOUBERT, G.
1957   Essai de corrélation entre les cycles marins et continentaux du Pléistocène du Maroc. *Comptes Rendus de l'Académie des Sciences*, Paris 245:1066–1069.

CHOUBERT, G., F. JOLY, M. GIGOUT, J. MARÇAIS, J. MARGAT, R. RAYNAL
1956   Essai de classification du Quaternaire continental du Maroc. *Comptes Rendus de l'Académie des Sciences*, Paris 243:504–506.

ENNOUCHI, E.
1962a   Un crâne d'homme ancien au Jebel Irhoud (Maroc). *Comptes Rendus de l'Académie des Sciences*, Paris 254:4330–4332.
1962b   Un Néanderthalien: l'homme du Jebel Irhoud (Maroc). *L'Anthropologie*, Paris 66:279–299.
1969   Découverte d'un Pithécanthropien au Maroc. *Comptes Rendus de l'Académie des Sciences*, Paris 269:763–765.
1972   Nouvelle découverte d'un Archanthropien au Maroc. *Comptes Rendus de l'Académie des Sciences*, Paris 274:3088–3090.

HAAS, G.
1966   On the vertebrate fauna of the lower Pleistocene site ʿUbeidiya. The Israel Academy of Sciences and Humanities, Jerusalem 1–68.

HOUZAY, J. P., E. CAIRE, G. CHOUBERT, A. FAURE-MURET
1973   Le Quaternaire marin du bassin de Boudinar (Temsamane), Rif Oriental, Maroc. *Comptes Rendus de l'Académie des Sciences*, Paris 276:897–900.

HOWELL, F. C.
1960   European and northwest African Middle Pleistocene hominids. *Current Anthropology* 1:195–232.

JAEGER, J.-J.
1969   Les rongeurs du Pléistocène moyen de Ternifine (Algérie). *Comptes Rendus de l'Académie des Sciences*, Paris 269: 1492–1495.
i.p.a   Les rongeurs (Mammalia, Rodentia) du Plio-Pléistocène d'Afrique. Intérêt biostratigraphique et paléoclimatique. *Actes du Septième Congrès Panafricain de Préhistoire et de Géologie du Quaternaire*, Addis Ababa.
i.p.b   Découverte d'un crâne d'Hominidé dans le Pléistocène moyen du Maroc. *Colloque International du CNRS, Evolution des Vertébrés*, Paris.

KOCHETKOVA, V. I.
1970   Reconstruction de l'endocrâne de l'*Atlanthropus mauritanicus* et de l'*Homo habilis*. *Proceedings of the Eighth International Congress of Anthropological and Ethnological Sciences* 1:102–104.

LEAKEY, L. S. B.
1960   "The origin of the genus Homo," in *Evolution after Darwin*, volume two. Edited by Sol Tax. Chicago: University of Chicago Press.

MARÇAIS, J.
1934   Découverte de restes humains fossiles dans les grès quaternaires de Rabat (Maroc). *L'Anthropologie*, Paris 44:579–583.

POMEL, A.
1896   Les éléphants quaternaires. *Carte géologique d'Algérie, Paléontologie, Monographie*, 1–68. Algiers.

ROMER, A. S.
1928   In: A contribution to the study of prehistoric man in Algeria, North Africa. *Bulletin of the Logan Museum*, Beloit, Wisconsin: 81–133.

SOLIGNAC, M.
1927   Etude géologique de la Tunisie septentrionale. *Direction générale des travaux publics, Service des Mines, carte géologique*. Tunis.

STEARNS, C. E., D. L. THURBER
1965   Th^{230}/U^{234} dates of late Pleistocene marine fossils from the Mediterranean and Moroccan littorals. *Quaternaria* 7:29–42.

TCHERNOV, E.
1968   "Succession of rodent faunas during the Upper Pleistocene of Israel," in *Mammalia depicta*, 1–152. Hamburg and Berlin: Paul Parey.

VALLOIS, H. V.
1945   L'homme fossile de Rabat. *Comptes Rendus de l'Académie des Sciences*, Paris 221:669–671.
1959   L'homme de Rabat. *Bulletin d'Archéologie Marocaine* 3:87–91.

VALLOIS, H. V., J. ROCHE
1958   La mandibule Acheuléenne de Temara, Maroc. *Comptes Rendus de l'Académie des Sciences*, Paris 246:3113–3116.

VAUFREY, R.
1955   *Préhistoire de l'Afrique*, volume one (Maghreb). Publication de l'Institut des Hautes Etudes 4. Tunis.

Pleistocene Faunal Evolution in Africa and Eurasia

VINCENT J. MAGLIO

ABSTRACT

On each of the three continents of the Old World — Africa, Europe, and Asia — a distinct succession of faunal events can be traced from the Late Pliocene through the Early, Middle, and Late Pleistocene. These events can be characterized by the concomitant immigration of groups not previously represented, the *in situ* origin of new adaptive types, and the extinction of old lineages. Even though the time divisions used here are extremely broad, it can be demonstrated that no faunal criteria apply universally enough to serve as time synchronous markers. Rather, patterns of faunal evolution prove most useful in the establishment of local biostratigraphic sequences each of which may be tied into non-biological criteria of world-wide applicability, such as paleomagnetic changes or absolute dates.

The most reliable faunal data for intercontinental correlation are single evolving lineages in which successive stages can be recognized, and which were rapidly expanding over large geographic areas. But too few groups are sufficiently well studied to allow such application.

The analysis of faunal evolution also shows that the establishment of an essentially modern fauna occurred in Africa by the Early Pleistocene. In Europe and northern Asia this was not achieved until the mid-Pleistocene. This seems to have been the result of more stable conditions in Africa as compared with dramatic climatic fluctuation and habitat fragmentation in the north.

INTRODUCTION

Man's understanding and appreciation of the earth as it is today depends in part upon his unraveling of complex past events. The interplay of such events shaped the modern landscape, gave rise to the biological diversity so familiar to us, and juxtaposed floras and faunas into the distinct biogeographic assemblages that characterize the recent world. The geological and biological processes that structured this world are far from firmly understood, and in many cases we remain today as ignorant as ever of specific events or of their causation.

Yet considerable progress has been made as workers throughout the world have begun to close the great gaps that plague what is at best an inadequate record. The broadest outlines of a history do emerge, and may allow, with caution, a further filling in of details.

Our present concepts of Pleistocene faunal evolution in the Old World suggest greater interrelationships between the continental land masses of Europe, Asia, and Africa than would have been supposed several decades ago. Although evidence is far from complete, recent studies on patterns of faunal evolution in Africa indicate phases during which relatively rapid faunal interchange occurred between that continent and Eurasia. Such events must certainly have proceeded in the reverse direction also, and must reflect periods of relaxation of climatic or of physical barriers. Similar phases of enhanced communication can be recognized between Europe and Asia, even though east-west expansion of faunal distributions between these two areas are not now, and probably were not in the recent past, of major proportions. Indeed one can detect periods of relative faunal isolation in every area interspaced with episodes of intercontinental migration on a much larger scale.

The extent to which the recent biogeographic zonation of the entire Old World persists, and the degree of faunal unity within each area, is precisely the result of these episodic events in animal distributions. Although we can never really understand the causes of these events, it is important to comprehend their nature. Were any of these of intercontinental proportions or synchronous over vast areas and therefore useful for correlating non-radiometrically dated assemblages? Do these events reflect world-wide abiotic crises which can more directly establish common time horizons? And can biological events in one group or in one continent be used to predict those in another? These are questions which we have so far been unable to answer, but which are critical for understanding the Old World not as its isolated components, but as a unified entity.

The processes which shaped the Old World of today are significant in the present context for another reason. It is presumed on good evidence that the Old World, and probably Africa, was the place of origin of the human species. Our subsequent physical and cultural evolution can now be traced through three million or more years from roots in the later Pliocene of Africa, to the emergence of modern types in Europe. To what extent did faunal events of the Pleistocene, documented for other groups of animals, include our own ancestry and in what ways did human cultural patterns interrelate with these changing ecological relationships? The answers to this will come only from the clarification of detailed patterns of relationships between these vast land masses and only from a consideration of many independent lines of evidence. But it is clear that answers to questions that must be asked here cannot be given without consideration of worldwide patterns of change that transcend local geographic and temporal limits.

Of necessity, studies on such a broad scale cannot achieve the degree of resolution possible with more local problems. Recognition of time-synchronous events on any but geophysical means becomes extremely inaccurate with distance. Species generally do not occur over very large areas so that a rather crude generic level consideration must be relied upon in most cases. Also, the life span of many species is greater than even our broad subdivisions of Pleistocene time. In spite of these problems, some tentative analyses are possible and indeed necessary.

CORRELATION AND TIME FRAMEWORK

Faunal correlation must be approached with great caution, especially when dealing with isolated, even though intermittently continuous, biogeographic regions. Such correlations are best made with geophysical data such as radiometric dating or paleomagnetic stratigraphy. Such data are now providing excellent scales against which local faunal and sedimentary occurrences can be measured (e.g. Savage and Curtis 1970; Bout 1970; Ambrosetti, et al. 1972; Cox 1968, 1969; Cox, et al. 1968; and others). Climatic fluctuation records have been utilized, but these must be approached with even greater caution until the degree of synchronism of Pleistocene events and their relative intensities are better known. It is clear from other chapters in this volume that such events were far more complex than previously believed. Nevertheless, some important complementary data are coming to light (e.g. Kukla 1970) which may prove to be valuable yardsticks for correlation of climatic events.

Perhaps least reliable is the vertebrate fossil record, if only because we as yet know too little about the detailed evolution of most mammals. Like the dog chasing his tail, the paleontologist can too easily operate in circles, using his faunas to establish a time framework within which to study these same organisms. The uncritical use of fossils for the determination of time synchronous horizons has in the past been a major contributor toward the perpetuation of a false sense of precision. The fossil record can indeed be a powerful tool, but only with a realization of its limitations as well as its assets.

Large vertebrates present preplexing problems. Local populations typically evolve in partial isolation for greater or lesser periods, and in so doing accumulate morphological characteristics which may differ from other groups. The meaning of such features can too easily be misinterpreted as species level distinctions, or worse, as chronological stages along a lineage.

The use of first or last appearances in the known record is fraught with difficulty, especially when applied to broad geographical regions. No species immigrates into a continental area instantaneously. Depending upon the distribution of ecologically favorable conditions or the pressures of competing species (or their absence), a group may spread very rapidly or exceedingly slowly. Between adjacent land masses problems of ephemeral barriers complicate the situation.

Neither can extinction be viewed as a time marker, as it so often has, for populations may trickle out over many tens of thousands of years as local populations survive in favorable settings.

The use of faunal assemblages for correlation may be equally difficult unless adequate attention is paid to the community structures from which the samples were drawn. Even minor ecological changes in one area may significantly alter faunal composition, but such changes do not necessarily occur synchronously over wide regions.

A further major problem is that identifications of fossil species are not always consistent unless made by the same worker, and not always then. It thus becomes difficult, if not impossible, to evaluate faunal evidence reported from widely separated localities. Since correlations are often based on numbers of identified taxa in common to two or more horizons, or on the presence or absence of "key" groups, it is clear that consistent taxonomic usage is essential. Yet we are still very far from this goal.

Geographic assumptions can and do influence taxonomic usage. As a result many genera and species appear to be found at times over all parts of the Old World, whereas others are highly endemic. Until more groups are studied throughout their entire ranges, and their geographic histories tied more securely to evolutionary events, such assumptions as have been used for faunal correlation will remain suspect.

As an an example, we may cite the appearance of "*Elephas*", *Equus*, and *Leptobos* originally proposed by Haug (1911) as index fossils for the Villafranchian in Europe and used by numerous authors ever since. These taxa certainly proved useful on a crude level, but it is now clear that their appearance was not synchronous, and one or all may be lacking from a deposit strictly for ecological reasons. It is now clear that *Elephas, sensu stricto,* first appeared in Africa more than four million years ago (Maglio 1970), but did not reach Asia until about three million years ago, nor Europe until one million years ago. An elephant with primitive dentition was certainly present earlier in Europe, but this was an early *Mammuthus,* not *Elephas.* Thus correlation based on the first appearance of *"Elephas",* sensu lato (as usually used) has little biological reality since two different and non-synchronously evolving lineages are involved. Likewise, at present we know too little about what we call *Equus* and *Leptobos,* their place of origin, their evolution, and their rate and extent of dispersal, to use such identifications uncritically for intercontinental correlations.

It would seem that we have eliminated any possible use we can make of faunas for purposes of relative correlation. This is not true. Great caution is indeed needed here, but some degree of confidence may be had if we use total faunas, not the presence or absence of "key" taxa, and especially if we use selected groups for which reasonable phyletic sequences can be determined. Thus for regional sequences one may rely more heavily on successions such as the *Mimomys-Arvicola* groups of European voles worked out in recent years by Fejfar (1964), Kowalsky (1966), Chaline and Michaux (1969), and Jánossy (1965, 1970, see also his article in this volume), or the *Lagurus* succession in eastern Europe and Siberia (Zazhigin, 1970). Useful successional sequences have also been described for hyaenids (Kurtén 1957, 1960), bears (Kurtén 1959a), elephants (Maglio 1970, 1973; Aguirre 1969), suids (Thenius 1970), cervids (Heintz 1968), rhinoceroses, horses, and bison (Flerov 1971). These series represent a combination of evolution and immigration so that taken with total faunal similarity, they can result in a reasonable correlation within local biogeographic regions. Correlation over greater distances may be distorted by the presence of polytypic species where geographic morphs may simulate temporal morphs. A form may have a more advanced character in one geographic area than in another even when contemporaneous (Kurtén 1954). The same problem exists between different species in the same genus. It is fallacious to compare evolutionary stages in related but phyletically independent species and expect these to reflect their relative ages. The best approach would appear to be a combination of the criteria of total faunal similarity, plus stages in the phyletic evolution and unchecked migration of new and highly successful species into wide geographic regions (Kurtén 1957).

Our purpose here is to examine the patterns of mammalian evolution within and between Africa and Eurasia, and to gain an idea of their value for relative faunal correlation in the Pleistocene. However, such patterns cannot be examined without some relative time succession which can serve as a temporal framework for faunal studies. It is invariably necessary that any such study utilize some scheme for synchronizing faunal events over vast geographic distances, even if this is only approximate and tentative.

The kinds of broad patterns sought here do not require accurate levels of correlation for analysis. We will attempt only to divide the Pleistocene into four major units — Early, early mid-, late mid-, and Late Pleistocene. Although the exact placement of individual fauna-yielding deposits is often a matter of debate, most workers can usually agree as to which of the above major units any given fauna belongs. Error in placing those that lie on or near our arbitrary boundaries will, of course, yield similar error in range tabulations. Nevertheless, if the Pleistocene was characterized by significant faunal events, then these should be detectable.

In Table 1 some of the more important mammal localities are given for each division of the Quaternary as used here. Individual sites are given in alphabetical order and their placement does not reflect their relative ages.

PATTERNS OF FAUNAL EVOLUTION

Europe and Western Asia

The faunal succession in Europe can be traced from the Pliocene forest type assemblages of the Roussillon-Montpellier type, characterized by sub-Himalayan and Oriental elements that may have spread westward with early expansion of the forest habitat (Kretzoi 1961). During the later Pliocene (pre-Villanyian of Kretzoi [1956]) a wave of new elements entered from the east as the presumed forest environments continued to expand. Typical faunas of this age include those of the lower Val d'Arno, Praetiglian beds, Etouaires, Vialette, Mălușteni, and, in the Middle East, Bethlehem.

The succeeding Villanyian stage witnessed a marked ecological alteration from forest to open grassland, especially in Central Europe, as evidenced by the influx of a nonforest microfauna. Kretzoi and Vértes (1965) have argued for placing the Tertiary-Quaternary boundary at the base of the Villanyian because of this ecological shift. On other evidence, Azzaroli (1970) has suggested a boundary of roughly com-

Table 1. Approximate distribution of principal vertebrate faunal localities in the Late Pliocene and the four major divisions of the Pleistocene as used here. These are not intended as definitive boundaries, nor does the sequence of names in each unit represent a temporal succession

EUROPE

Late Pliocene	Early Pleistocene	Early mid-Pleistocene	Late mid-Pleistocene	Late Pleistocene
Chagny	l'Aquilla	Abbeville I	Abbeville III	Burg Tonna
Ivanovce	Apsheron	Achalkalaki	Akhshtryskaya	Duruthy
Mǎluşteni	Beremend I	Ambrona	Binagady	Ehringsdorf II
Montopoli	Betfia	Bacton	Bruges	Fontechavade
Olivola	Farnetta	Bugiuleşti I-II	Clacton	Gvardzhiles
Pardines	Grotte du	Cromer Forest	Ganovce	La Colombiére
Roca Neyra	Vallonnet	Dubci	Grays Thurrok	Montereau III
Red Crag	Hajněčka	Erpfingen	Grimaldi	Prědmosti
St. Vallier	Imola	Gombasek	Grotte du Prince	
Tuluceşti	Layna	Granada	Heppenloch	
Villaroya	Leffe	Hundsheim	Hunas	
Wolfersheim	Norwich Crag	Karlobag	Hoxne	
	Pietris	Kislang	Il'skaya	
	Psekups	Kuban	Kudaro I	
	Puebla de	Mastas de Con	Lunel Viel	
	Valverde	Mosbach I-II	Sakazhia	
	Sainzelles	Plesivěc	Solymar	
	Sandaja	Podumci	Spessa II	
	Senèze	Püspükfürdö	Steinheim II–IV	
	Severin	Sackdilling	Sütto	
	Soave	Saint-Prest	Swanscombe	
	Stavropol	Solilhac	Tarkö 1	
	Strmica	Steinheim I	Taubach	
	Tegelen	Stránská Skála	Tornetown Cave	
	Upper	Süssenborn	Uppony 3, 5	
	Val d'Arno	Taman Complex	Vertessöllös	
	Villany 3, 5	Tarkö 2, 5		
		Tiraspol		
		Torralba		
		Uppony 9–12		
		Valverde		
		de Calatrava		
		Vertessöllös		
		Villany 6–8		
		Voigtstedt		
		Zlatý Kún		

AFRICA AND THE MIDDLE EAST

Aïn Boucherit	Aïn Hanech	Cornelia	Isimila	Broken Hill
Aïn Brimba	Bel Hacel	Elandsfontein	Jisr Banot	Eyasi
Aïn Jourdel	Koobi Fora	Kanam (part)	Yaqub	Florisbad
Bethlehem	(upper)	Kanjera	Kibish	Gamble's Cave
Brown Sands	Kromdraai	Lac Karâr	Latamné	Haua Fteah

Table 1 (continued)

Late Pliocene	Early Pleistocene	Early mid-Pleistocene	Late mid-Pleistocene	Late Pleistocene
Fouarat	Olduvai I-III	Olduvai IV	Olorgesailie	Hearths
Ichkeul	Peninj	Rawe	Rabat	Jebel Irhoud
Kebili	Shungura G-J	Sidi Abder	Temara	Kibish
Koobi Fora	Swartkrans	Rahman	Yayo	Kom Ombo
Laetolil	ʿUbeidyia	Ternifine		Oumm Qatata
Makapansgat				Skūhl
Ouadi Derdemi				Tabūn
Oued Akrech				Wadi El
Shungura C-F				Mughara
St. Arnaud				
Sterkfontein				

ASIA				
Hsiachaohwan	Boulder Congl.	Angara	Bin Gia	Choukoutien
Irrawaddy beds	Choukoutien 18	Godavari	Choukoutien 1, 3	Upper Cave
Kali Glagah	Djetis	Hsinganhsien	Fungmen	Ngandong
Ma Kai	Karewa beds	Hoshangtung	Heiching-	Potwar Loess
Pinjor	Kochkov	Irtish River	lungtsun	Sjaro-osso-Gol
Tatrot	Lingyi	Kolymor	Hsingan	
Tji Sande	Liucheng	Narbadda	Ko Ho	
Tjidoelang	Mogok caves	Transbaikalia	Koloshan	
	Nihowan	Trinil	Kwelin	
	Yüshe	Viluy River	Lang Son	
		Yenchingkou	Lantien	
			Lingyen	
			Lishih Loess	
			Pa River	
			Se Tchouen	
			Tan Van	
			Tanyang	
			Tungshen	
			Wan Hsien	

parable position. However, for convenience in comparing these faunas with those of Africa and Asia, this boundary is arbitrarily placed within the Villanyian stage, at about 2.0 million years on the absolute time scale. The Early Pleistocene as applied here, therefore, includes the later Villanyian and the Betfia phase of the central European Biharian faunal stage as used by Jánossy (this volume).

The boundary between Early and mid-Pleistocene may be placed approximately at the Brunhes/Matuyama magnetic event. This now appears to lie within the classical Cromerian complex and is radiometrically dated at about 0.7 million years (van Montfrans and Hospers 1969). The limit of the Late Pleistocene is far more difficult to set, but, as an initial procedure we may use the classical boundary between the last interglacial warm phases (Eemian of northern European stratigraphy) and the last major series of cold pulses (Weichselian glacial complex). On radiometric criteria this boundary seems best placed at about 75,000 years B.P. (Butzer 1971).

Between these last two boundaries is the long period of the mid-Pleistocene. For faunal analysis we may further divide this into two parts, an early phase including the classical Cromerian and Elster stages, and a late phase which includes the Holsteinian, Saalian, and Eemian of classical terminology. This two-fold division corresponds with the faunal stages used by Jánossy (this volume), the early mid-Pleistocene being equivalent to the Biharian (except for the Betfia phase), and the late mid-Pleistocene equivalent to the Oldenburgian plus "Eemian" (Figure 1).

The mid-Pleistocene in Europe was characterized by massive faunal changes and climatic fluctuations in which the first truly arctic elements were seen. Adam (1952, 1953) analyzed the faunas of southwestern Germany and confirmed a succession of steppe/forest/steppe/periglacial-forest faunal types which appeared to correlate with the classical glacial-interglacial stages of northern European stratigraphy. Although these climatic events are now known to be more complex, the marked faunal changes characteristic of the mid-Pleistocene must have resulted, at least in part, from ephemeral ecological discontinuity and the resultant establishment of isolating climatic and physical barriers.

LATE PLIOCENE. The Late Pliocene faunas of Europe form the starting point for Pleistocene events that were to follow. This was in many ways a period of transition between the older Tertiary mammalian assemblages and the essentially modern types that were to characterize the Pleistocene (Kowalski 1971). An Oriental and sub-Himalayan forest biotope invaded Europe during the Csarnotian and earlier Pliocene, bringing many new forms that were not represented previously. These included the cercopithecoid primates *Dolichopithecus arvernensis* and *Macaca florentina*. The primitive vole groups *Ungaromys* (= *Germanomys*), *Stachomys* (= *Leukaristomys*), and *Mimomys* were common. The latter group is represented by early species of Fejfar's group I (1961) — *M. hassiacus* and *M. proseki* — plus *M. stehlini* and *M. pliocaenicus*. Among the cricetine rodents *Trilophomys pyrenaicus* carries through from earlier times and the genus *Apodemus* appears in Europe for the first time. The porcupine *Hystrix* is represented by the early species *H. etrusca* and *H. refossa*. An extinct beaver *Trogonthe-*

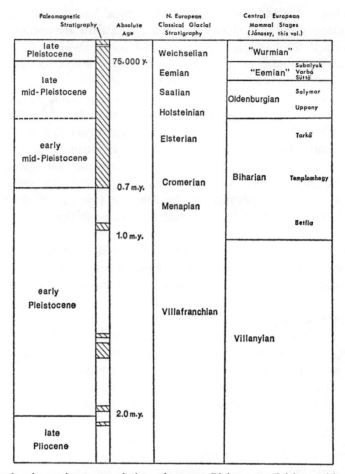

Figure 1.   Approximate correlation of present Pleistocene divisions with paleo-magnetic and radiometric criteria, with classical glacial stratigraphy and with Central European faunal stages

rium minus is also present along with the earliest occurrence of the living form, *Castor fiber*.

Both ochotonid and leporid lagomorphs are known in Europe at this time, the latter family by *Hypolagus* sp. and *Oryctolagus lacosti*.

A number of now extinct carnivore groups persisted from earlier in the Pliocene, among them the machairodonts *Machairodus crenatidens*, *Megantereon megantereon*, an early cheetah *Acinonyx pardinensis*, the extinct lynx *Felis issiodorensis*, and *Nyctereutes megamastoides*, all of which are present at Villaroya (Crusafont-Pairó 1960). The dog, *Canis etruscus*, is also a typical element, and this appears to be the earliest record of the genus in Europe.

Several genera of carnivores which became extinct during the Early Pleistocene were still important elements of Pliocene faunas. Among them were the procyonid *Parailurus*, the ursid *Agriotherium*, and the mustelid *Enhydrictis*. Bears of the *Ursus* group include the primitive species *U. ruscinensis* and *U. etruscus*. *Hyaena brevirostris* is a widespread species during the Late Pliocene, as is *H. perrieri*, the typical species in Europe.

Among the Proboscidea both mammutids (*Mammut borsoni*) and late gomphotheres (*Anancus arvernensis*) persisted, suggesting widespread woodland conditions (Kurtén 1963). The first true elephant, possibly a woodland to savanna form, entered Europe as a very early stage of *Mammuthus meridionalis*, probably from North Africa. This early stage appears as far east as Greece (Melentis 1966), but does not appear to have spread into Asia.

A variety of perissodactyls were present including the tapir, *Tapirus arvernensis*, several early species of *Hipparion*, and the earliest good European record of a caballine horse, *Equus bressanus*, at Pardines. *Equus* apparently made its European debut much earlier (at Montopoli), but the material is too incomplete for identification. A second branch, contemporary with *E. bressanus*, was *E. stenonis*, known from various localities in Tuscany and France. The latter form shows no close relationship to later horses (Azzaroli 1966), but exhibits a number of zebrine features (Thenius 1962). The Pliocene rhinoceros, *Dicerorhinus megarhinus*, makes its last appearance during the close of the Tertiary.

The Asiatic and African suid, *Potamochoerus*, has recently been identified in Turkey at Akçaköy (Sickenberg and Tobien 1971), but the common pigs remain *Sus strozzi* and *S. arvernensis*.

EARLY PLEISTOCENE   The transition from Pliocene to Pleistocene in Europe witnessed several important but not major faunal changes. A number of new insectivores, such as *Beremendia, Blairinoides,* and *Petenyia* are typical elements, as are the extinct moles *Talpa praeglacialis* and *T. minor*. Sciurid rodents of the genera *Citellus* and *Sciurus* appear, and we see now a dominance of the microtine cricetids *Allophaiomys, Dolomys,* and *Lagurus*. A very primitive form of *Microtus* is now recorded in European deposits, but is relatively uncommon (Kretzoi and Vértes 1965). *Mimomys* of Fejfar's vole groups II and III (1961) occur here; these include *M. pusillus, M. hintoni,* and *M. hajnackensis*. Although some earlier species still persist here, none appear to survive this stage. The typical Pliocene genus *Trilophomys* continues, but becomes extinct before the close of the stage. *Pliomys episcopalis*, a characteristic species of the Biharian, supposedly makes its appearance here (Tobien 1970). Among the murids, *Apodemus atavis* is common. *Hystrix etrusca* and *H. refossa* survive, but only until the end of the Early Pleistocene. *Trogontherium minus* is succeeded by two other species, the typical *T. cuvieri* in the latest Pliocene and *T. schmerlingi* in the earliest Pleistocene. Both will survive into the mid-Pleistocene.

Lagomorphs of the genus *Lepus* first appear here as *L. terraerubrae* and *L. etruscus*, neither of which survives the stage. The Pliocene relict, *Oryctolagus lacosti*, likewise disappears before the end of the Early Pleistocene.

The Villanyian witnessed little major change in the carnivore fauna. The genus *Megantereon* disappears toward the end of the period as does *Parailurus* and *Enhydrictis*. The early lynx, *Felis issiodorensis*, is replaced by *F. lynx*, and among the machairodonts only *Homotherium sainzelli*, *H. crenatidens*, and *H. latidens* occur through most of the stage. The mustelid, *Gulo schlosseri*, appears during the latter half of this period.

The Pliocene dog, *Canis etruscus*, becomes extinct before the close of the Early Pleistocene but is replaced by several new species including *C. armensis* and *C. falconeri*. The genus *Cuon* is recorded here for the first time in Europe, as *C. majori*, in the upper Val d'Arno.

Typical bears of the European Pleistocene are now common. These include *Ursus arvernensis* and an early subspecies of the brown bear, *U. arctos deningeri*. *Hyaena brevirostris* and *H. perrieri* remain the common hyaenids into the Biharian.

Among the Proboscidea both *Anancus* and *Mammut* become extinct, although *Anancus arvernensis* may have persisted into the earliest mid-Pleistocene at Gmunden in Austria (Kurtén 1968). The mammoth, *M. meridionalis*, evolves through a series of grades so that by the middle of the Biharian it is commonly referred to under a different species name.

Among the perissodactyls the tapir does not persist beyond the early Pleistocene. *Equus stenonis* survives and a more modern caballine horse, *Equus caballus mosbachensis*, is now common, as is the wild ass, *E. hydruntinus*. *Hipparion* becomes extinct in Europe during the earlier part of this stage. Among the rhinocerotids, *Dicerorhinus etruscus* is still the typical form, but in western Asia *Elasmotherium causicum* appears also to have been present.

The Pliocene pigs, *Sus strozzi* and *S. arvernensis*, disappear from the record, the former species being replaced by the extant *Sus scrofa*. The still relatively warm Villanyian climates supported two species of hippopotamus, *H. amphibius* and *H. antiquus*, both recorded in Europe for the first time.

The large cervids *Euctenoceros dicranius* and *Megaloceros verticornis* are typical elements, as are persistent Pliocene species of deer, *Cervus ramosus* and *C. philisi*. *Alce gallicus*, typical of the Late Pliocene, remains but is replaced by *A. latifrons* before the close of the stage. Both *Capreolus sussenbornensis* and the living roe deer, *C. capreolus*, are first recorded before the beginning of the mid-Pleistocene. At the end of this stage, during a pre-Biharian cold phase, the reindeer, *Rangifer tarandus*, and the musk-oxen, *Ovibos moschatus* and *O. priscus*, penetrated into Europe, presumably from northern Asia. Bovids typical of the European Early Pleistocene were *Bison schoetensacki*, *Leptobos etruscus*, and *L. stenometopon*, the latter two forms marking the last appearance of that genus in Europe. The final occurrences in Europe of both *Deperetia* and *Gazella* are also recorded here.

EARLY MID–PLEISTOCENE The lower boundary of the Middle Pleistocene in Europe can conveniently be placed between the Betfia and Templomhegy phases of the Biharian faunal stage of Kretzoi (1956) (see Figure 1). This boundary was characterized in Europe by a faunal change of major proportions, perhaps the most significant such transition of the European Cenozoic.

The Biharian stage witnessed the extinction of both *Beremendia* and *Blairinoides* and a flowering of modern soricid insectivores. Among the latter *Sorex savini*, *S. runtonensis*, and *S. minutus* were typical forms as were the talpids *Desmana mosbachensis* and *Talpa praeglacialis*. The earlier and contemporary species, *T. minor*, become extinct during this phase. Characteristic of the Middle Biharian in eastern Europe is *Lagurus pannonicus*, known from as far west as Yugoslavia (Marković-Marjanović 1970). Among the primates *Dolichopithecus* did not survive into the Biharian, but *Macaca florentina* occurred at least through the earlier warm phases (Kowalski in Flint [1971]).

Allophaiomys disappears before or at the beginning of the Templomhegy phase (see Jánossy, this volume). Lemmings are now common, although both *Lemmus* and *Dicrostonyx* now appear to have been present in eastern Europe as early as the earliest Biharian.

A significant change is seen in the European vole faunas, and this has been used as a basis for mid-Pleistocene faunal stratigraphy by a number of workers (Fejfar 1961; Kretzoi 1961; Jánossy 1970). The most important new elements are the arvicoloid voles which suddenly appear in Europe during the Early Biharian. A variety of species of the genus *Arvicola* is now recorded, presumably of Asiatic origin. These include *A. cantiana, A. greeni, A. mosbachensis,* and *A. terrestris.* *Pitymys,* the pine mouse, appears during the Biharian, with a diverse group of related species. Among them are *Pitymys arvalidens, P. schmidtgeni,* and *P. hintoni.* The dominance of the genus *Microtus* in Biharian faunas is also characteristic, especially *M. arvalinus, M. raticepoides,* and the *M. nivalinus-nivaloides* group. With the expansion of these new elements, *Mimomys* becomes less dominant with only a few species surviving through the stage (*M. newtoni, M. pusillus,* and *M. intermedius*). Among the Cricetini, *Trilophomys* did not survive into the Biharian.

Both of the Early Pleistocene species of porcupine, *Hystrix etrusca* and *H. refossa,* became extinct before the opening of this stage. The characteristic Biharian glirids, *Glis sackdillingensis* and *G. sussenbornensis,* are known from only this period.

The Pliocene leporid *Hypolagus* is seen for the last time in Europe, recorded at Podumci (Kowalski 1958). *Lepus* and several species of *Ochotona* persisted throughout the stage. Of the three species of *Homotherium* that are known from this time only *H. latidens* survives into later ages; *H. crenatidens* and *H. moravicum* disappear during the Late Biharian. Cats such as *Felis cattus, F. leo spelaea,* and *F. pardus* make their first appearance here along with typically Early Pleistocene species such as *F. issiodorensis,* but the latter does not survive into the Oldenburgian. Among the canids, *Canis lupus* is characteristic. *Nyctereutes* is known only in the earliest Biharian, and thus is not represented in mid-Pleistocene faunas.

The Pliocene bears *Ursus etruscus* and *U. arvernensis,* as well as the brown bear, *U. arctos deningeri,* all survive into the Biharian. By the later Tarkö phase the more progressive form, *U. arctos arctos,* and the cave bear, *U. arctos spelaeus,* have already differentiated. A more specialized hyaenid, *Crocuta crocuta,* is now common during this phase, but the earlier species, *H. perrieri* and *H. brevirostris,* are also recorded throughout the remainder of the stage.

A more progressive species of mammoth, the steppe-adapted form *Mammuthus armeniacus* (= *trogontherii*), is present in colder faunas and is often identified as a late stage of the Early Pleistocene *M. meridionalis,* from which it undoubtedly was descended. A new immigrant into Europe is the forest elephant, *Elephas namadicus* (= *antiquus*) becoming widely distributed in interglacial deposits of the earlier Biharian.

Of the equids, *Equus stenonis* is last recorded during the Middle

Biharian and *Equus sussenbornensis* persists only until the end of the stage. *E. caballus mosbachensis* and the ass *E. hydruntinus*, become characteristic species for the rest of the mid-Pleistocene.

During the latter part of the Biharian *Dicerorhinus etruscus* was replaced by *D. kirchbergensis* and *D. hemitoechus*, the former probably a forest form, the latter adapted to cooler steppe conditions (Thenius 1962). *Elasmotherium* disappeared before the onset of Late Biharian glacial conditions.

The European cervid fauna witnessed several important modifications during the earlier Middle Pleistocene. *Alce latifrons* was the typical moose, but became extinct during the Late Biharian. Both *Capreolus sussenbornensis* and *C. capreolus* persisted throughout the stage, but only the latter survived beyond it. None of the typical Early Pleistocene deer is recorded here; rather the living *Cervus elaphus* is the common widespread species. The Lower Pleistocene *Dama nestii* persisted into the Middle Biharian where it was quickly replaced by the living *Dama dama*. The giant deer *Euctenoceros dicranius* became extinct before the close of the Templomhegy warm phase, but *Megaloceros* remained common as *M. verticornis*, *M. savini*, and *M. giganteus anectens*.

Bovidae are represented by rather different groups than those that characterized the Early Pleistocene. *Bos* appeared during the Early Biharian as *B. primigenius*, and the earlier Pleistocene species *Bison schoetensacki* is joined here by the characteristic mid-Pleistocene *Bison priscus*. The goat, *Capra*, and the musk-ox, *Ovibos*, are now fairly common elements, the latter represented by the extinct Biharian species *O. priscus* and *O. schmidtgeni*, as well as the extant *O. moschatus*.

LATER MID-PLEISTOCENE   As used here, the later mid-Pleistocene encompasses the Oldenburgian and "Eemian" stage of Jánossy (this volume) and includes the classical Holsteinian, Saalian, and Eemian stages of northern European glacial stratigraphy. By the opening of this period, the earlier Pleistocene cercopithecoid *Macaca florentina* had already been replaced by several different species, among them *M. sylvana* and *M. suevica*. The vole genus *Mimomys*, so abundant in the Early Pleistocene, does not survive into this part of the mid-Pleistocene. The great diversity of arvicoloid voles declines as many species of *Pitymus* and *Arvicola* become extinct. These are survived by *A. terrestris*, *Clethrionomys glareolus*, and *Pitymys gregaloides* as characteristic Oldenburgian forms. Typical mid-Pleistocene species of *Microtus* are *M. arvalinus*, *M. gregalis*, and *M. ratticepoides*, with *M. arvalis* appearing during the last interglacial phases. Several other species, including *M. oeconomus* and *M. socialis*, appear only late in this period. *Hystrix vinogradovi*, an immigrant from Asia, appears in the record during the later phases of the mid-Pleistocene. The same is true of *H. cristata* and *H. hirsutirostris*. The giant beaver, *Trogontherium*, did not survive beyond the Biharian.

The late mid-Pleistocene of Europe is characterized by the appearance of the living lagomorphs, *Lepus europaeus* and *Oryctolagus cuniculus*.

Typical later mid-Pleistocene canids include *Alopex lagopus*, *Cuon alpinus*, *Vulpes vulpes* and *V. corsac*, and *Canis lupus*. *Ursus arctos* is the common bear, with the cave variety, *U. a. spelaeus*, widespread during glacial advances. The cave hyaenid, *Crocuta crocuta spelaea*, appears during the late Oldenburgian cold phase (= "Saalian"), and the striped hyaena, *Hyaena hyaena*, is known in Europe only during this part of the mid-Pleistocene.

The forest elephant, *Elephas namadicus*, occurred over wide areas of Europe during warmer periods, while the mammoth, *Mammuthus armeniacus*, appears to have been restricted to cooler conditions and is seen to pass transitionally into the more specialized *M. primigenius* during the Saal glacial complex equivalent.

Equus caballus plicidens is typical of the late mid-Pleistocene, persisting until the end of this period along with *E. hydruntinus*. The Asiatic *E. hemionus* makes its first appearance in Europe during the late Oldenburgian. The genus *Dicerorhinus* persists throughout this period, but a new rhinoceros, *Coelodonta antiquitatis*, is suddenly recorded only from "Holsteinian" and later deposits.

Essentially modern cervids are now typical; these include *Alce alces*, *Capreolus capreolus* and *Cervus elaphus*. Both *Dama dama* and the extinct *D. clactoniana* are present, as are *Megaloceros giganteus* and *M. euryceros*, the latter characteristic of late Oldenburgian and "Eemian" faunas.

Little change is seen among the Bovidae except for the appearance of the buffalo, *Bubalus murrensis*, and the modern goats, *Capra caucasica* and *C. ibex*, and the chamois *Rupicapra rupicapra*.

LATE PLEISTOCENE   The Late Pleistocene, including only the last glacial complex, was characterized in Europe by the appearance of numerous extant species and the concomitant extinction of typical mid-Pleistocene forms. Among the modern taxa recorded here are the moles *Talpa europaea* and *T. caucasica*, the jerboa *Allactaga jaculus*, the living cheetah *Acinonyx jubatus,* the tarpan *Equus caballus caballus,* the wisent *Bison priscus,* and the adjag*Cuon alpinus.* Those species typical of, but not surviving, this phase in Europe include *Homotherium latidens, Ursus arctos spelaeus, Crocuta crocuta spelaea, Mammuthus primigenius, Equus (Asinus) graziosii, Dicerorhinus kirchbergensis, Coelodonta antiquitatis,* and *Megaloceros giganteus.* These Late Pleistocene faunas were primarily of the steppe and arctic type with temperate forest forms, such as *Elephas namadicus,* still surviving in southern Europe (Crusafont-Pairó 1960).

Africa and the Middle East

Prior to the last decade, patterns of faunal evolution on the African continent during the late Tertiary and Quaternary were essentially unknown. Only a few adequate fossiliferous deposits were available and fewer still were securely dated by absolute radiometric means. The standard of comparison for Plio-Pleistocene continental faunas was Olduvai Gorge where studies on fossil successions, human cultural evolution, and associated sedimentary environments could be traced from 1.8 million years to about 0.5 million years.

Since 1965 a remarkable increase in knowledge of the African Pleistocene has occurred. This has followed from the uncovering of major new faunal localities that have permitted re-evaluation of numerous more poorly known sites previously worked. Also, a vast increase in radiometric analyses, paleomagnetic determinations, and more sophisticated faunal methods of relative dating have given a firmer basis for correlation without which faunal evolutionary patterns could not be attempted.

Tertiary-Quaternary faunas of Africa are still very incompletely represented for many groups of vertebrates, particularly among micromammals. It is not yet possible, for example, to state with accuracy that a particular taxon was confined to one or another time period or region of the continent, as the evidence is, for the most part, too scanty. Nevertheless, some interesting patterns are now emerging for the faunas as a whole, although it is difficult to correlate these with faunal events in Europe and Asia. This is less true for North Africa where the most complete stratigraphic sections, in Morocco, contain faunas closely resembling those of the mid-Pleistocene of the Iberian Penninsula; these do not, however, exhibit faunal discontinuities as in the north (Biberson 1970).

For purposes of the present discussion, the African Pliocene will be taken to end at approximately 2.0 million years ago on the absolute time scale. Thus, the base of the African Pleistocene coincides roughly with that used here for Europe and Asia. Principal faunas of late Pliocene age include those from the Shungura Formation up to member F, the lower member of the Koobi Fora Formation, Brown and White Sands, and Laetolil in East Africa, Ouadi Derdemi and Koulá in Chad, Sterkfontein, Makapansgat and Bolt's Farm in southern Africa, Ichkeul, Aïn Brimba, St. Arnaud, Aïn Jourdel and others in northern Africa, and Bethlehem in the Middle East.

As in Europe, our Early Pleistocene is taken to end at the Brunhes/ Matuyama boundary, about 0.7 million years ago. Faunas of this Early Pleistocene period include those from the uppermost Shungura Formation, the upper and Ileret members of the Koobi Fora Formation, and Beds I to III (reversed polarity) at Olduvai Gorge in eastern Africa, Kromdraai and Swartkrans in southern Africa, and Bel Hacel and Aïn Hanech in North Africa, and 'Ubeidiya in Israel.

The mid-Pleistocene is rather more difficult to define, but arbitary limits have been chosen for approximate coincidence with Eurasiatic stratigraphy. On this basis the early mid-Pleistocene begins at the base of the Brunhes event and includes faunas from Bed IV (normal polarity, Cooke [1972] Kanam (in part), Kanjera, the lower Kibish formation, Cornelia, Elandsfontein, Ternifine, Lac Karar, and Sidi Abder Rahman. The later mid-Pleistocene should probably encompass Olorgesailie, Yayo, Rabat, Termara, and Jisr Benot Jaqub.

Least satisfactory to define is the African Late Pleistocene. It is nearly impossible to utilize faunal or other criteria in setting limits to this period on any but completely arbitary grounds; accordingly, its limits as used here are rather broader than elsewhere in the Old World. Nevertheless, the faunas encompassed here should approximately belong to what we are calling Late Pleistocene in Eurasia, and certainly any terminal Pleistocene events, if of major proportion, should be detected. This does not significantly alter conclusions drawn here, at least within the limits of accuracy possible in faunal studies of this kind. We may thus take as Late Pleistocene (*sensu lato*) those faunas from Eyasi, Broken Hill, Florisbad, Gambles Cave, Cave of Hearths, Jebel Irhoud, Oumm-Qatafa, Kom Ombo, Haua Fteah, Wadi-el-Mughara, Skūhl, and Tabūn, among others.

In the first half of this century knowledge of climatic fluctuations during the European Pleistocene led to the development of the pluvial-interpluvial climatic theory for sub-Saharan Africa in which worldwide climatic episodes were supposedly recognized (e.g. Simpson 1934).

Fluctuation in lake levels can clearly be established for several sedimentary basins such as Lake Chad (Franz 1967) or Lake Rudolf (Behrensmeyer i.p.), and phases of widespread high lake stands can be demonstrated for the Late Pleistocene or Holocene of East Africa (Bishop 1971; Butzer et al. 1972). However, it is now clear that the continental-scale climatological implications of a pluvial-interpluvial succession as previously conceived can no longer be accepted. There is thus little climatic basis for intercontinental correlation between tropical Africa and north-temperate to arctic Eurasia, and we must rely, where possible, on faunal, radiometric, and paleomagnetic stratigraphy to tie these areas together.

LATE PLIOCENE   Adequate faunas of the African Pliocene have only recently been uncovered. As these are emerging, they are unique in that they differ significantly from known Miocene assemblages and represent the earliest phase in the development of what is known today as the Ethiopian fauna. Micromammals are only modestly represented, mainly in North Africa and from cave deposits in southern Africa, but they already show a diverse assemblage of the modern type. Various insectivores such as *Erinaceus, Macroscelides, Mylomygale, Crocidura, Myosorex, Suncus, Elephantulus,* and *Chlorotalpa* are repesented south of the Sahara, mainly in southern Africa. More than two dozen typically African rodent genera are less adequately known, but were obviously important elements of these Pliocene communities. The more important elements of these includes *Xerus, Thryonomys, Arvicanthus, Mystromys,* and *Pedetes.* A number of non-endemic genera, such as *Gerbillus, Tatera, Hystrix,* etc., are already significantly elements in Africa, having communicated between here and northern continents much earlier.

The extant aardvark, *Orycteropus afer,* is now recorded from Pliocene deposits in East Africa (M. Leakey, personal communication), and the extinct species, *O. aethiopicus,* is present at several other localities. The living species of hare (*Lepus capensis*) and hyrax (*Procavia capensis*), are both known in southern Africa. Other Pliocene hyracoids include *P. antiqua* and the South African species *P. transvaalensis.*

Primates are represented by the modern genera *Cercocebus, Cercopithecus, Colobus, Papio,* and *Homo,* plus the now extinct genera *Cercopithecoides, Paracolobus, "Parapapio", Theropithecus (Simopithecus),* and *Australopithecus.* Species typical of the late Tertiary include *Cercopithecoides williamsi, Paracolobus chemeroni, Papio robinsoni, "Parapapio" jonesi* and *Theropithecus (Simopithecus) oswaldi.* Both *Australopithecus africanus* and *A. robustus* are present in southern

Africa, but *A. boisei* and an early species of *Homo* are the common hominids north of the Zambesi.

Among carnivores Pliocene faunas already include extant species of the cheetah (*Acinonyx jubatus*), several jackals (*Canis mesomelas* and *C. aureus*), the lion (*Felis leo*), wild cat (*F. libyca*), caracal (*F. caracal*), the meerkat (*Cynictis penicillata*), the bat-eared fox (*Otocyon megalotis*), and two hyenas (*Crocuta crocuta* and *Hyaena hyaena*). The saber-tooth felids *Homotherium aethiopicum*, *Machairodus transvaalensis*, and *Megantereon gracile* carry through from the earlier Pliocene. The extinct dogs, *Canis megamastoides* and *C. brevirostris*, common during this epoch, occur here for the last time. Several rather primitive hyenids still persisted; these included *Lycyaena silberbergi* and early species of living genera, *Crocuta brevirostris* and *Hyaena bellax*. An extinct mongoose, *Herpestes caffer*, did not survive the epoch.

Early proboscideans abounded in a variety of forms with the bizarre *Deinotherium bozasi* and the gomphothere *Anancus osiris* surviving as hold-overs from the African Tertiary, the latter in northern Africa only. True elephants are repesented by three distinct groups, *Loxodonta adaurora*, *Elephas recki* (early stage), and *Mammuthus africanavus*. A stegodon, which apparently made it to Africa earlier in the epoch, did not persist for very long; only a single Pliocene record is known south of the Sahara (Cooke and Coryndon 1970).

Perissodactyla were an important group, more so than today, with a number of additional genera and many now extinct species. *Hipparion* remained abundant, represented by at least six species from the large *H. albertense*, to the tiny *H. sitifense*. Equally numerous were true horses of the genus *Equus* known from another half dozen species including the living zebra *E. burchelli*. *Equus stenonis* and *E. numidicus* were North African in distribution, whereas *E. plicatus* and *E. helmei* are known only from southern Africa.

A single chalicothere, *Ancyclotherium hennigi*, persisted but was rare on the continent, known only from a handful of sites in southern and eastern Africa (Butler 1965, i.p.).

Extant species of both the white and the black rhinoceroses, *Ceratotherium simum* and *Diceros bicornis*, were already widespread. The European *Dicerorhinus etruscus* and the extinct *D. africanus* were known only north of the Sahara, and do not appear to have penetrated further south.

A large suid fauna was very widespread throughout the continent, but the group is badly in need of revision and the validity of many genera is open to question. The forest or woodland genus *Nyanzachoerus* is the dominant Early Pliocene suid throughout the continent and survived into the late Pliocene of East Africa (Shungura Formation; White and Brown Sands). Possibly derived from it was *Mesochoerus*, represented by several species, among them *M. limnetes* in East Africa, and *M. phacocheroides* in the south. The more open country savannah forms, *Notochoerus euilus*, *Phacochoerus aethiopicus*, *Metridiochoerus andrewsi*, and "*Pronotochoerus" jacksoni*, were very abundant south of the Sahara. The living forest hog, *Hylochoerus meinertzhageni*, made its first appearance in the record at this time, as did the bush pig *Potamochoerus porcus*. A European genus, *Sus*, is known only from northern Africa as *S. falconeri* and *S. strozzi*, but several specimens recently discovered in East Africa may also belong to this group (Cooke, personal communication).

Hippopotamus was far more diverse than at present with at least four or five species represented. Among them was a pygmy, *H. imagunculus*, which persisted from the Early Pliocene until well into the mid-Pleistocene. Recent evidence demonstrates the existence of *Camelus* in sub-Saharan Africa as early as the Late Pliocene (Gentry and Gentry 1969; Howel, et al. 1969). This discovery emphasizes the uncertainty of faunal deductions based on negative evidence alone.

The diversity of giraffids was more extensive than today with two species of *Giraffa*, the extant *G. camelopardalis* and the extinct *G. gracilis*, an early okapi *Okapia stilleri*, and several species of the large *Sivatherium*. The latter is represented in North Africa by *S. maurusium* and in East Africa by *S. olduvaiensis*. A third as yet undescribed species has recently been discovered near Lake Rudolf (J. Harris, personal communication). A molar fragment from southern Africa demonstrates the presence of this large giraffe there as well.

Cervidae are unknown in Africa during the Pliocene, but Bovidae are remarkably abundant and are represented by nearly thirty genera and over fifty species. Of these, a number of now living taxa are already present. These include the impala *Aepyceros melampus*, the hartebeest *Alcelaphus buselaphus*, the springbok *Antidorcas marsupialis*, the duiker *Cephalophus monticola* (= *caeruleus*) and *Sylvacapra grimmia*, the wildebeest *Connochaetes taurinus*, the sassaby *Damaliscus lunatus*, Grant's gazelle *Gazella granti*, the roan *Hippotragus equinus*, the oryx *Oryx beisa*, the gemsbok *Oryx gazella*, the reedbuck *Redunca arundinum*, two nyalas *Tragelaphus angasi* and *T. buxtoni*, the kudu *T. strepsiceros*, the sitatunga *T. spekei*, the bushbuck *T. scriptus*, the eland *Taurotragus oryx*, and the buffalo *Syncerus caffer*.

A number of now extinct members of these and related groups were also present, so that typical Late Pliocene bovid faunas also included such species as *Alcelaphus helmei* and *A. robustus, Antidorcas recki, Capra primaeva, Cephalophus silvicultor* and *C. parvus, Damaliscus korrigum* and *D. pygargus, Gazella atlantica* and *G. setifensa, Gorgon gadjingeri, Hippotragus gigas, Kobus sigmoidalis, Parmularius angusticornis,* and *Redunca ancystrocera* and *R. darti.*

Among Pliocene genera no longer living in Africa were several that appear to have been endemic to that continent. These include the giant alcelaphine *Megalotragus (M. kattwinkeli),* as well as *Menelikia (M. lyrocera),* and *Pelorovis (P. olduvaiensis).* Several genera persist today elsewhere in the Old World and include *Antilope, Bison,* and *Gazellospira* (in the Pliocene of North Africa or the Middle East), *Selenoportax nakuae* (in East Africa), and a questionable identification of cf. *Hemibos* sp.

It is interesting to note here one major distinction between Late Tertiary faunas of Africa and those of Europe. In the latter only a few percent of known Pliocene species are now extant, whereas in Africa more than 25 percent of Pliocene mammalian species are still living. Thus, where the complexion of the European Late Tertiary is one of generic similarity to the Recent, that of Africa is more nearly modern in species composition. We will return to this point in the concluding section.

EARLY PLEISTOCENE   The African Early Pleistocene is represented in far fewer deposits than was the Late Pliocene. Two major sites for vertebrate fossils are the Olduvai Gorge and East Rudolf, both in East Africa; less complete faunas are known from both the northern and southern parts of the continent. This time period is of necessity, then, biased in favor of the East African evidence.

The micromammal fauna is only poorly recorded here and it is clear that only a very partial picture is presently available. Primates remain essentially unchanged from the late Pliocene record. Many other Pliocene elements also carry through unchanged, while a number of others become extinct during the period. Thus, *Procavia antiqua* and *P. transvaalensis* do not survive the Early Pleistocene, although they do occur here along with the extant species. Several new carnivores seemingly make their first appearance at this time. Among them are the living serval cat *Felis serval,* the hunting dog *Lycaon pictus,* the ratel *Mellivora capensis,* and the brown hyena *Hyaena brunnea.* Also recorded for the first time are the extinct species *Felis crassidens, Machairodus latidens, Megantereon eurynodon,* and *M. piveteaui,* the wolf *Canis lupus* (only in northern Africa), *Vulpes pulcher, Lycyaena forfex,* and *L. nitidula.*

The proboscidean assemblages of Africa during the Early Pleistocene remain diverse, as *Deinotherium* continues in the east and *Anancus* in the north. *Elephas recki* (stage 2) has succeeded earlier stages and the living *Loxodonta africana* has replaced its ancestor, *L. adaurora.* The mammoth is no longer represented south of the Sahara, but in Mediterranean Africa a late survivor (*"Elephas" moghrebiensis* of Arambourg [1970]) is virtually indistinguishable from the European *M. meridionalis* (early stage).

Among the perissodactyls, *Hipparion* remains common, with Pliocene species still persisting. *Equus stenonis* does not occur this late, but most other Pliocene species remain. Two additional forms appear: Grevy's zebra, *E. grevyi,* and *E. oldowayensis.* The chalicothere, *Ancylotherium,* is recorded here for the last time in Africa, and this is also its last known occurrence in the Old World.

In northern Africa the rhino *Dicerorhinus* is no longer recorded but this may be due only to the paucity of localities of this age. An earlier subspecies of the white rhino, *Ceratotherium simum germanoafricanum,* occurs now in East Africa as does the black rhino, *Diceros bicornis.*

Suids remain abundant. *Nyanzachoerus* did not survive into the Pleistocene and we see the last occurrences of *Metridiochoerus* (as *M. andrewsi* progressive), *Mesochoerus limnetes, Notochoerus scotti, Phacochoerus antiquus, Potamochoerus* (as *P. shawi*), and *"Pronotochoerus" jacksoni.* Another typical early Pleistocene species is the advanced metridiochoere which has been called *"Afrochoerus nicoli"* (L. S. B. Leakey 1942), but which probably represents a high-crowned descendant of *M. andrewsi.*

Camelus is known only from fragmentary remains in East Africa, but the species *C. thomasi* is rather common north of the Sahara. *Giraffa camelopardalis* and *G. gracilis* persist and are joined by a third species, *G. jumae,* the latter apparently confined to East Africa. Among the bovids the only significant changes are in the new occurrence of a number of extant species including *Hippotragus niger* and *Kobus kob.* Other typical taxa are *Antidorcas wellsi, Bos bubaloides* (in northern Africa), *Connochaetes africanus, Damaliscus antiquus, Gorgon semiticus* and *G. mediterraneus.* Other species are identical to the Pliocene forms already mentioned.

MID-PLEISTOCENE   Perhaps even less understood than the Early Pleistocene is the succeeding Middle Pleistocene. Although a number of localities have been discovered from northern to southern Africa, the faunas are generally poor, so that accurate data on species distributions are still lacking. Therefore, no attempt will be made here to divide this period into subunits as was done for Europe. Instead, we will attempt to diagnose its faunal profile as distinguished from earlier and later times.

Almost no data are available concerning Middle Pleistocene micro-mammals in Africa. Several exceptions include the first records of the extant rodents *Bathyergus, Georychus, Cryptomys,* and *Otomys.* A num-ber of primate genera apparently did not survive beyond the Early Pleistocene; at least they have not been recorded here. The most im-portant of these were *Cercopithecoides, Paracolobus,* and *"Parapapio".* *Theropithecus (Simopithecus) oswaldi* persists into the earlier part of this period but was later replaced by *T. (S.) jonathani.* Of the australo-pithecines, only *Australopithecus boisei* appears to have survived into the mid-Pleistocene (Carney, et al. 1971; Walker, personal communica-tion). By the latter part of this period an advanced *Homo, H. erectus,* makes its appearance in eastern and southern Africa associated with a Chellean-Acheulian culture (M. D. Leakey 1971).

Most of the carnivores of the mid-Pleistocene carry through from earlier times. The machairodont *Homotherium* does not survive, how-ever, although both *Megantereon gracile* and *Machairodus latidens* persist in South Africa and in North Africa respectively. The European brown bear, *Ursus arctos,* is seen for the first time in the Middle East but never penetrated into Africa proper. *Herpestes ichneumon,* the Egyptian Mongoose, is recorded for the first time and is known from several localities in southern Africa. Of the hyaenids only the three living species *Hyaena brunnea, H. hyaena,* and *Crocuta crocuta* remain; several earlier forms of these two genera, plus the more primitive *Lycyaena,* became extinct during the early Pleistocene.

The proboscidean fauna of the African Middle Pleistocene is far less diverse than previously; *Deinotherium, Anancus,* and *Mammuthus* do not survive into this time period. The latter does persist as *Mammuthus armeniacus* (= *trogontherii*) in the Middle East (Hooijer 1959; 1961), but is not known from North Africa. The only species remaining on continental Africa are *Loxodonta africana* occurring only rarely, *L. atlantica* dominating mid-Pleistocene faunas of both southern and northern Africa, and an advanced stage (stage 4) of *Elephas recki* known from East Africa.

The three-toed *Hipparion* (including *Stylohipparion*) survived throughout the mid-Pleistocene as *H. stetleri, H. libycus,* and *H. alber-*

tense, but became extinct before the close of this time period. The true horse, *Equus,* persists in a variety of species with *E. mauritanicus* appearing for the first time north of the Sahara. *Equus caballus* is known from the Middle East but has not been recorded further south.

The European rhinoceros, *Dicerorhinus kirchbergensis,* has been found in the Middle East (Hooijer 1961), but not in Mediterranean Africa. South of the Sahara the modern subspecies of the white rhino, *Ceratotherium simum,* has replaced its earlier stage.

A variety of advanced suid species are common during the mid-Pleistocene (Cooke and Maglio 1972). Among them are *Mesochoerus olduvaiensis, M. latigani,* and *M. paiceae* with larger and higher crowned molars than in the earlier *M. limnetes.* The common Early Pleistocene *Notochoerus scotti* has been completely replaced by the narrower and higher-crowned form *N. compactus.* *"Pronotochoerus"* makes its last appearance here and the specialized genus *"Orthostonyx"* seems to have evolved from an earlier notochoerine ancestor. In the Middle East the European suid *Sus scrofa* is represented at several localities.

Both *Sivatherium maurusium* and *S. olduvaiensis* persist throughout this period as do *Giraffa jumae* and the living *G. camelopardalis.* The smaller *G. gracile* has not been recorded and presumably became extinct during the earlier Pleistocene.

Among the Bovidae a number of modern species now appear, including *Alcelaphus caama, Connochaetes gnou, Gazella dorca, Kobus venterae,* and *Redunca redunca.* The mid-Pleistocene marks the last known appearances of several important earlier Pleistocene species of which the best known are *Antidorcas recki, A. wellsi, Damaliscus antiquus, Gazella gazella, Hippotracus niro, Megalotragus kattwinkeli, Pelorovis olduvaiensis, Parmularius angusticornis,* and *Tragelaphus grandis.* The genera *Gorgon* and *Rabaticeras* do not survive into the Late Pleistocene, being recorded here for the last time as *Gorgon olduvaiensis, G. semiticus,* and *Rabaticeras arambourgi.* Several new species typical of this period first appear here but do not survive into the present. The most important are *Connochaetes laticornutus, Megalotragus priscus, M. eucornutus, Hippotragus antiquus,* and *H. leucophaeus.* The extinct genus *Homoioceras* is recorded for the first time in both eastern and southern Africa as *H. baini* and *H. nilssoni.*

LATE PLEISTOCENE With the Late Pleistocene the African record becomes a little more complete, although still underrepresented. It is likely that many of the taxa recorded here for the first time actually evolved earlier in the epoch, but remained undetected; the sudden development of a modern fauna is probably only apparent.

Among the micromammals a dozen or more genera are known, some distributed only in North Africa and clearly of Eurasiatic origin. These latter include *Sciurus*, *Microtus*, *Spalax*, and *Nesokia*. Several endemic murid genera, such as *Lophuromys*, also are seen for the first time, although this is certainly an accident of preservation.

The primate record is very poor. The subgenus *Theropithecus* (*Simopithecus*) has become extinct and *Homo sapiens* is the only hominid represented. The latter occurs as neanderthaloid races from southern and northern Africa.

The carnivore fauna remains unchanged from earlier times except for the lack of the machairodont genus *Megantereon*. *Machairodus* has been recorded at Broken Hill, but is unknown elsewhere in Africa. Among the extant species first appearing here are the side-striped jackal *Canis adustus*, the European red fox *Vulpes vulpes* (only in the Middle East and North Africa), and the Cape Grey mongoose *Herpestes pulverulentus*. *Ursus arctos* persists in northern Africa but was to disappear before the beginning of the Holocene.

Of the Proboscidea, *Loxodonta atlantica* is still common in northern Africa but does not survive beyond the Pleistocene. A late survivor of the *Elephas* lineage in Africa, *E. iolensis* (= *transvaalensis*), is known throughout the continent and is dated to within about 40,000 years B.P. in the Sudan. For the first time during the Pleistocene the genus *Stegodon* is again recorded in this region, known only from the Middle East and identified as the common Asiatic species, *Stegodon trigonocephalus* (Hooijer 1961).

The perissodactyls include the extant *Equus quagga*, *E. grevyi*, and *E. burchelli* as well as a survivor from the Early Pleistocene, *E. helmei*, in southern Africa. *Equus hemionis* is recorded only from the Middle East and *E. hydruntinus* occurs in South Africa. Neither survives into the Holocene. *Hipparion* is unknown here. In Palestine *Dicerorhinus hemitoechus* occurs along with *D. kirchbergensis:* the latter spread across North Africa, but neither species penetrated south of the Sahara.

Among the Suidae only the living species of *Phacochoerus* and *Potamochoerus* are common here, but *Notochoerus compactus* and a few other now extinct species also occur. *Sus scrofa*, still present in northern Africa, does not appear to have crossed the Sahara until later introduced by man, although this has been questioned (Dorst and Dandelot 1970). Only a single species of hippopotamus, *H. amphibius*, is known later than the Middle Pleistocene; this taxon is today found throughout the continent.

In North Africa *Camelus thomasi*, the Early Pleistocene species, still occurs at a number of localities but becomes extinct before the close of the epoch. A new form, *C. dromedarius*, has been recorded questionably from Latamné (Hooijer 1961) and was subsequently introduced into Africa, presumably by man.

For the first time, cervids such as *Capreolus*, *Cervus*, *Dama*, and *Orthogonoceros* appear in the Middle East, but none seem to have spread further southward.

Of the giraffids only the okapi and the living *Giraffa camelopardalis* survive into this period. Extant species of bovids not recorded earlier include *Alcelaphus lichtensteini*, *Capra ibex*, *Damaliscus dorcus*, *Gazella cuvieri*, *Kobus ellipsiprymnus*, and *Oreotragus oreotragus*. The European species *Bos primigenius* is now widespread in northern Africa and *Bison priscus* has been recorded from several localities in the Middle East (Hooijer 1961). Neither genus remains in these areas today. The Late Pleistocene marks the last known occurrence of a number of species, many of which were important elements in the middle and late parts of the epoch. These include *Alcelaphus helmei*, *A. robustus*, *Cephalophus laticornutus*, *Damaliscus niro*, *Gazella arabica*, *G. bondi*, *Hippotragus gigas*, *H. antiquus*, and *Megalotragus priscus*, plus the genera *Pelorovis and Homoioceras*.

Asia

Interpreting the sequence of Pleistocene faunas of Asia has been complicated by the recognition of two distinct vertebrate assemblages separated by the Tsinling Range. To the north is the "Sino-Siberian" palearctic fauna containing many European elements mixed with a typically Asiatic assemblage. The difference between these Siberian faunas and those typical of Europe is not great, and demonstrates the climatic and ecological continuity between this and other parts of the continent (Sher 1971). By the early mid-Pleistocene two distinct faunal complexes are evident, a European-Siberian assemblage in western and eastern Siberia in which mainly European elements predominate, and a central Asiatic province in southern Siberia with many Asiatic endemics (Vangengeim and Sher 1970).

To the south of the Tsinling Range during the Pliocene and Early Pleistocene was the "Sivamalayan" fauna, in which typically Indian elements predominated. This extended from West Pakistan through Burma and South China to Java. During the late Early and mid-Pleistocene a number of distinctive southern Chinese elements extended southward into Burma, India, and Java, resulting in the so-called "Sinomalayan" fauna. The significance of the Siva- and Sinomalayan assemblages has been overworked and their distinctions are generally less impressive than those involving faunal changes in Europe at about the same time. This Asiatic turnover, as in Europe, represents *in situ* evolution of several distinctive types plus the influx of several genera from the west, both resulting in a general increase in the proportion of modern taxa in the fauna.

Thus we can realistically view these Asiatic fossil vertebrates as essentially comprising the northern and southern Tsinling assemblages, with distinctive patterns of faunal change occurring in each. Although some mixing between these faunas was possible during warm phases, Pleistocene glaciation in the Tsinling Range undoubtedly provided an effective barrier against migration, even if an ephemeral one.

The Pleistocene of China has been divided into several phases based on climatic and faunal criteria. For our purposes, the Late Pliocene will be taken as represented by those faunas of pre-Sanmenian age. This includes Asiatic faunas from the Tatrot and Pinjor horizons of the Siwalik series, the Irrawaddy beds of Burma, the Tjidoelang and Kali Glagah deposits of Java, and from Ma Kai and Hsiachaohwan in southern China. Northern Asiatic faunas of this age remain very poorly known.

Early Pleistocene deposits in northern China directly overlie the Pao-Teh (= Pontian) beds in disconformity (Chang 1968). They include faunas represented by the lower Sanmenian *Euctenoceros-Megaloceros* complex of Kahlke (1968) known from Nihowan, Yüshe, Lingyi, and Choukoutien locality 18 in the north, and from the Liucheng *Gigantopithecus* faunal localities in the south. Also included are the Mogok cave deposits of Burma, the Karewa beds of Kashmir, and the Boulder Conglomerate of the Siwalik series in India.

Climatic phases have been recognized within this period, one characterized by lowered temperatures and ice advance in the highlands (Poyang Glacial of Lee [1937]). Fossil pollen from correlative deposits in Shansi and Sinkiang, in areas not covered by ice, suggest moist climatic conditions (Chang 1968). Attempts have been made to correlate such phases with classical glacial stages of European stratigraphy, but on present evidence any such relationships remain highly suspect. Nevertheless, it has been suggested (Chang 1968) that Lee's Poyang phase is an approximate equivalent of the Menapian complex of northern Europe.

What is called the early mid-Pleistocene here includes Lee's Poyang-Taku Interglacial and Taku Glacial stages (Lee 1937). The former warm phase was characterized by general aridity, and on faunal evidence may possibly correlate with the "Cromerian" warm phases of Europe. The following Taku highland glacial stage is represented in the lowlands by pluvial sediments of cold, moist environments. Faunas provisionally included here are the upper Sanmenian assemblages of Hoshangtung, Hsinganhsien, and Yenchingkou-I in southern China, and the faunas of the Angara River, Kolymar, the Lower Irtish, and Transbaikalia series in Siberia, the Djetis faunas of Java, and those of the Narbadda and Godavari Valley deposits of northern India.

The late mid-Pleistocene as used here includes the Taku-Lushan Interglacial of Lee (possibly broadly equivalent to the Holsteinian of Europe), the Lushan Glacial, and the Lushan-Tali Interglacial erosional cycle. Typical faunas of northern China are those from Choukoutien locality 1, Ko-Ho, and Lantien. Both the Gongwangling and Chen'chiawo sites at Lantien contain nearly identical faunas close to that of Choukoutien 1, not that of Nihowan. Presumably all three are nearly contemporaneous in the later mid-Pleistocene (Chow 1964; Wu, et al. 1965). Floral analyses at Choukoutien suggest cool temperate steppe conditions for at least part of the time represented, thus probably not equivalent to a full interglacial phase (Kurtén 1959b). In the south is the Wan Hsien or *Ailuropoda-Stegodon* fauna so characteristic of this period (Kahlke 1961), typically from Hsingan, Tanyang, Koloshan, Tan-Van, Bin Gia, Trinil, and, late in the stage, Kwelin.

The Late Pleistocene here includes the Tali Glacial of Lee. Perhaps belonging to the earliest part of this phase or to the latest mid-Pleistocene are the loess deposits of northern China with the Sjaraosso-Gol fauna, as well as the Tzuyang fauna of southern China (Chang 1968). The Upper Cave deposits at Choukoutien are latest Pleistocene or perhaps Early Holocene in age, and contain a greater number of warm adapted species. We also may include here the Ngandong beds of Java.

LATE PLIOCENE   The Pliocene record of micromammals, both in the northern and southern faunas, is remarkably poor. A number of rodent genera such as *Rhizomys, Myospalax, Hystrix,* and *Nesokia* are known, but clearly this record is not representative. Among the primates, *Macaca, Presbytis,* and *Gigantopithecus* are known from India, but here too the record is certainly under-represented. The extinct leporid,

Hypolagus, is present, but other genera are not yet recorded. The giant beaver, *Trogontherium*, makes its earliest Asiatic appearance during this phase as in Europe.

The carnivore genera *Felis* and *Sivapanthera* are known from the Pliocene of India, represented by a variety of species. The machairodonts *Machairodus* and *Megantereon* are found throughout the Asiatic region, but *Homotherium* is so far unknown. *Canis* is the typical canid, appearing in northern China and in India during the latter part of the epoch. *Agriotherium* is the only bear present and is known only from the Indian subcontinent. Many other Recent genera such as *Martes*, *Meles, Mellivora, Mustela, Enhydriodon, Lutra*, and *Viverra* are known from the general Asiatic region. Of the hyaenids only *Crocuta* is represented in India as *C. sivalensis*.

A variety of Proboscidea characterized these early faunas, mainly in southern Asia. The last of the Asiatic gomphotheres persisted in the Indian subcontinent. These have been placed in a variety of genera such as *Pentalophodon, Tetralophodon*, or *Gomphotherium*, of which the latter is probably best used until a revision of the group is available. The last species that are typical of the Asiatic Pliocene are *G. falconeri* and *G. sivalensis*, neither of which survive the epoch. An early stage of *Elephas*, *E. planifrons*, is present primarily in the southern faunas from India to Java, but is recorded also from scattered finds in northern China. The genus *Stegodon*, so characteristically Asiatic, is known at this time from India and southern China as the primitive *S. bombifrons* and an early stage of the more progressive *S. insignis*. Several other species have been described, but their validity requires investigation. In addition to these, the structurally more primitive mammutid genus *Stegolophodon* occurs here for the last time.

Among the perissodactyls, tapirs (*Tapirus*) carry through from the earlier Pliocene, and *Hipparion* makes its last appearance in Asia as *H. antelopinum* and *H. theobaldi*, both occurring in India and Burma. The true horse, *Equus*, is recorded for the first time in Asia during the latest part of the Pliocene with *Equus yunnanensis* in southern China and *E. namadicus* in the Siwaliks. The genus probably also existed north of the Tsinlings but has so far not been recorded here.

Chalicotheres are present as two distinct genera, *Chalicotherium* and *Nestoritherium*, both in southwestern Asia. The rhinoceros *Aceratherium* carries through from the earlier Pliocene as *A. lydekkeri*, but became extinct before the close of the Pliocene. Both *Dicerorhinus* and *Rhinoceros* are represented, the latter as *R. sivalensis* and *R. palaeindicus* in India.

This period marks the last occurrence of a number of pigs in Asia — *Hypohyus, Potamochoerus, Sivachoerus,* and *Tetraconodon.* Only *Sus* persists into the Pleistocene. Anthracotheres of the genus *Merycopotamus* are still recorded from the Siwalik Pliocene series, but the group's former diversity is much reduced. Both *Hexaprotodon iravaticus* and *Hippopotamus sivalensis* are known, again from the Siwalik succession. The camel, *Camelus sivalensis,* is known in southwestern Asia, but the Pleistocene *Paracamelus* is not yet recorded.

Cervids are abundant throughout Asia, mainly as species of *Cervus;* the typical Pliocene species are *C. punjabicus, C. triplidens,* and *C. unicolor.* Asiatic giraffids are still a varied group during this time with *Giraffa, Vishnutherium, Sivatherium,* and *"Indratherium"* known only from southwestern Asia.

Of the Bovidae, typical Pliocene species include *Antilope subtorta, Bison sivalensis, Bos acutifrons, B. planifrons, B. sondaicus, B. palaeindicus, Capra sivalensis, Hemibos acuticornis, H. triquetricornis, Hippotragus sivalensis,* and *Leptobos falconeri.*

EARLY PLEISTOCENE   The Early Pleistocene, equivalent here to the lower Sanmenian of Asiatic stratigraphy, is still rather poor in known microfauna, but a number of elements do appear, many of which must have been present earlier. These include *Erinaceus, Sorex, Citellus, Arvicola, Microtus, Mimomys,* and *Pitymys.* Among the more important species are *Arvicola terraerubrae, Microtus oeconomus, Mimomys intermedius, Pitymys hintoni-gregaloides* complex, and *Apodemus sylvaticus,* all members of northern Asiatic faunas. The porcupine, *Hystrix subcristata,* and other species occur at this time throughout the Asiatic region. The Early Pleistocene marks a significant change in the lagomorph assemblage with the last record of *Hypolagus* and the earliest occurrence of *Lepus, Ochotona (O. thibethana),* and *Ochotonoides.* The latter two genera were seemingly confined to the north Chinese faunas.

Of the primates the gibbon *Hylobates lar* makes its first appearance and is confined to southern faunas. *Gigantopithecus* occurs here for the last time as *G. blacki,* again known only from south of the Tsinlings.

Among the carnivores *Machairodus* is common both in southern and northern faunas, whereas *Megantereon* appears to survive only north of the Tsinling Range. *Sivapanthera, Enhydriodon,* and *Agriotherium* disappear before or during the opening of the Pleistocene. Of those genera recorded here for the first time, we may list *Cuon (C. dubius), Nyctereutes (N. sivalensis), Ursus (U. cf. etruscus; U. thibethanus),* and *Hya-*

ena (H. brevirostris) as typical of both northern and southern faunas. Those elements still confined to the Sino-Siberian fauna include *Vulpes, Martes, Meles,* and *Mustela.* Typical of the south China or Indian Early Pleistocene assemblages are *Ailuropoda melanoleuca, Arctonyx collaris, Lutra larvata,* and *Viverra.* The genus *Mellivora* apparently became extinct in northern Asia during the Early Pleistocene.

Of the Proboscidea, *Gomphotherium* continues in northern faunas and *Elephas planifrons* has been replaced by the more progressive *E. hysudricus* in India and south China. A new lineage, possibly derived from Africa, is an early stage of *E. namadicus,* which now makes its first appearance in southern Asia. The same species has also been reported from Shansi, north of the Tsinlings (Chow and Chow 1965). *Stegodon* persists as part of the southern mainland assemblages as *S. insignis* and *S. praeorientalis. Stegolophon* did not survive into the Pleistocene.

To those Pliocene species of *Equus* already mentioned is added *E. sanmeniensis,* typical of the Early Pleistocene of northern China. *Equus namadicus* and *E. yunnanensis* remain the characteristic forms of southern faunas. *Hipparion* is not recorded beyond the terminal Pliocene. The chalicothere *Nestoritherium* is no longer present, but *Chalicotherium sivalensis* is the typical form known only from southern localities. *Coelodonta antiquitatis* is the first member of the genus occurring in northern Asiatic faunas during the early Pleistocene at Lingyi, and *Rhinoceros sivalensis* persists in India.

Sus (S. scrofa and *S. falconeri)* is the only genus of suid to survive the Pliocene, and, of the anthracotheres, *Merycopotamus* makes its last Asiatic appearance in the south. The large cervid *Euctenoceros* becomes a typical element of northern assemblages at this time as *E. boulei,* and appears to be related to large European cervids (Kahlke and Hu 1957). The reindeer, *Rangifer,* is recorded for the first time in Siberia.

Among the giraffids the genus *Giraffa* does not persist into the Quaternary but both *"Indratherium"* and *Sivatherium* remain as typical southwestern Asiatic elements. *Bison* appears in the north, and *Bos* remains extremely diverse in India and Java with such typical forms as *B. namadicus, B. sondaicus, B. bubalus,* and *B. palaeindicus. Gazella* is known throughout Asia, but *Hemibos* occurs for the last time in India as *H. antelopinum* and *H. triquetricornis.*

MID-PLEISTOCENE   The mid-Pleistocene in Asia was witness to the appearance of a number of new elements which gave to the faunas a far more modern aspect. Many European genera of micromammals are recorded north of the Tsinling Range, but none so far among the southern faunas. Among these are *Scaptochirus, Crocidura, Lagurus, Neomys, Marmota, Sciurus, Clethrionomys, Mus,* and a number of bats.

Typical species such as *Arvicola terraerubrae, Cricetulus varians, Gerbillus roborowskii, Lagurus simplicidens, Microtus arvalinus* and *M. epiratticeps, Mimomys intermedius,* and *Myospalax wongi* occur in northern China and in Siberia. Others, such as *Rhizomys szechuanensis* and *R. sumatranus, Rattus edwardsi,* and *Echinosorex, Anourosorex, Nectogale,* and *Nesokia,* appear at southern localities. The lemming *Dicrostonyx,* makes its first appearance in Siberia at this time, about the same time as in Europe, but it is not recorded further south. *Trogontherium sinensis* has now been replaced by *T. cuvieri,* the same species as in Europe. For the first time in southern Asia the pangolin, *Manis,* is recorded from mid-Pleistocene deposits of Java.

Primates become rather abundant in the record as new elements of the "Sinomalayan" fauna spread southward. The most important of these are the orangutan *Pongo,* the siamang *Symphalangus,* and several extinct species of *Hylobates* — *H. leuciscus* in Java and *H. sericus* in southern China. Several additional genera, including *Rhinopithecus* and the now extinct *Szechuanopithecus,* are also new elements in southern faunas. The baboon *Macaca* is reported only during this time period in north China. Of great importance is the first appearance in Asia of the genus *Homo; H. erectus* has been recovered from deposits in Java and north of the Tsinling Range, at Choukoutien and Lantien.

A great number of carnivore species are characteristic of the mid-Pleistocene of Asia. A cheetah, *Acinonyx pleistocaenicus,* is a new element in the north, and the saber-tooth, *Homotherium,* is known for the first time in the south. Both *Machairodus* and *Megantereon* are still present in the north. The genus *Felis* is diverse throughout the continent with *F. tigris* and *F. pardus* as typical elements. Similar wide-ranging canids are *Cuon* and *Canis,* with *C. lupus* as a typical element of northern assemblages. *Nyctereutes* persists in both faunas until the end of this time period.

Ailuropoda, the panda, is now widespread south of the Tsinlings, and is a very typical member of this new southern Wan Hsien fauna of China. *Agriotherium* is not known to have persisted into the mid-Pleistocene, but bears of the genus *Ursus* are common throughout Asia. *Ursus thibethanus* is characteristic of southern China, *U. malayanus* in Java, and *U. arctos* in the north. Later in this period the cave bear, *U. arctos spelaeus,* appears in the north, suggesting the onset of colder climatic conditions.

Among the hyaenids *Crocuta crocuta* is known here for the first time in China, on both sides of the Tsinling Range. *Hyaena* is sympatric in range, but also extends southward into Java.

Another characteristic element of the Wan Hsien and "Sinomalayan" faunal complexes is the proboscidean genus *Stegodon*. This group now becomes widespread and very common in all southern faunas from India to Java, but remains very rare in the north. Typical species are *Stegodon insignis* and *S. trigonocephalus*. Several specimens of a gomphothere have been reported from northern China, but this group was clearly much reduced and became extinct before the close of this time unit. The most common proboscideans after *Stegodon*, were the elephants *Elephas namadicus*, represented in all parts of Asia from northern China southward, and *E. hysudrindicus* toward the end of the period in Java. A pygmy elephant, *E. celebensis*, is known from probably mid-Pleistocene deposits on Celebes and Java (Hooijer 1949). The mammoth, *Mammuthus armeniacus*, is known from the mid-Pleistocene of Siberia where it is succeeded toward the end of this period by *M. primigenius*.

The tapir, *Tapirus (Megatapirus)*, survives in south China and Java as *T. augustus* until the end of the mid-Pleistocene, but *Tapirus indicus*, the living species, appears for the first time only in India. Most of the archaic equids have disappeared, but *Equus sanmeniensis* persists throughout China. The European tarpan, *E. caballus*, is found now in Siberia. Chalicotheres of the species *Chalicotherium sinensis* and *Nestoritherium sinensis* are still represented in southern China, while *N. javanesis* occurs only in Java.

The rhinoceros fauna remains diverse with *Coelodonta* cf. *antiquitatis*, which appears to be slightly different from the European form (Kahlke and Chow 1961), and the newly appeared *Dicerorhinus kirchbergensis* in northern faunas. In addition we see *Rhinoceros unicornis* in India, *R. sinensis* in south China, and *R. sondaicus* in Java and elsewhere in southern Asia.

Of the former suid fauna, only *Sus* remains — *Sus scrofa* and *S. brachygnathus* in the south and *S. lydekkeri* to the north. Anthracotheres did not survive the Early Pleistocene, and the hippo, *Hexaprotodon*, is known only from the earlier part of the mid-Pleistocene in India. *Hippopotamus namadicus* is widespread across southern Asia from India to Java.

The camel, *Paracamelus*, appears for the first time in Asia, presumably immigrating from North America, and now becomes a typical element in northern faunas. Of the Cervidae new genera unknown here previously include *Alce, Capreolus,* and *Megaloceros,* all in northern assemblages. The latter is represented at Choukoutien locality 1 by *M. pachyosteus,* a specialized species different from that of the European "Cromerian" (Kahlke and Chow 1961). The living deer *Cervus elaphus* is widespread in Siberia and north China.

None of the genera of Giraffidae is known to have persisted into the mid-Pleistocene of Asia. Of the Bovidae, newly recorded genera include *Capricornis* in the south and *Boopsis, Praeovibos,* and *Spiroceros* in the north, but it is unlikely that these were not present earlier. Other new elements known from both sides of the Tsinlings during this phase are the muntjak, *Elaphodus,* and the goral, *Naemorhedus.* The banteng, *Bos banteng,* is first recorded in Java and other species are widespread throughout the southern regions. *Hemibos* is unknown in this and later time periods, but *Leptobos* is still present throughout the continent, thus surviving its more westerly congeners.

LATE PLEISTOCENE   The Late Pleistocene fossil record of Asia is not well known and where data are available the record appears to be close to that of the living fauna. Most of the mid-Pleistocene micromammals apparently persisted here since they are also represented in the Recent fauna. The giant beaver *Trogontherium* survived here long after it disappeared in Europe, but apparently became extinct just prior to or during this phase, for it is unknown in any of the available faunas. The lagomorph *Ochotonoides* likewise is no longer present, but both *Ochotona* and *Lepus,* the latter as the western species *L. europaeus,* remain.

The primates *Macaca, Presbytis,* and *Rhinopithecus* are still present, and of the pongids *Hylobates lar, Pongo pygmaeus,* and *Symphalangus sp.* persist as typical southern elements. *Szechuanopithecus* is no longer represented, and *Homo sapiens* is now present as the neanderthal-like populations from Ngandong (Java) and a true sapiens type from the Upper Cave site at Choukoutien.

Little is known of carnivore evolution during this period. Species of *Canis, Cuon, Felis, Vulpes,* and many others carry through from the earlier Pleistocene, but none of the machairodonts survive. *Crocuta crocuta* is reported for the last time in Asia, with only *Hyaena* surviving into the Recent. The panda, *Ailuropoda,* persists in South China to the present day, but its distribution and abundance are much reduced. Of the ursids, *Ursus arctos spelaeus,* the cave bear, remains common in the north.

Stegodon trigonocephalus is still a typical element in Javanese faunas and a new pygmy species, apparently derived from it, is known from probable Late Pleistocene deposits on Celebes, Timor, and Flores. The living *Elephas maximus* ranges now from India to south China, and was presumably derived from the earlier *Elephas hysudrindicus* or something close to it. *Elephas namadicus* persists in Asia until the end of the epoch. In Siberia the woolly mammoth, *Mammuthus primigenius*, is also known until the opening of the Holocene.

Only the living species of tapir is known in Late Pleistocene deposits of India and south China, and *Equus hemionus* is recorded for the first time in north China. Chalicotheres do not appear to continue into the late in the epoch. Neither *Paracamelus* nor *Spiroceros* appears to be *Coelodonta*. The living *Dicerorhinus* and *Rhinoceros* persist in various parts of southern Asia.

The hippopotamus, no longer known in Asia, survived in Java until late in the epoch. Neither *Paracamelus* nor *Spiroceros* appears to be present in deposits of this age. In northern Asia *Bos primigenius* and *Cervus canadensis* are known, and other artiodactyls were presumably the same as in the modern fauna. *Megaloceros ordosianus* marks one of the last records of the genus in the north (Sjara-osso-Gol).

FAUNAL RELATIONSHIPS

If we now re-examine the faunal evidence, this time on an intercontinental level, several interesting relationships seem to emerge. Although all such analyses must be approached with the greatest of caution because of the incompleteness of the record, it is possible to give at least the broadest outlines of Old World faunal evolution during the Pleistocene. In order to see more clearly these transcontinental ties, the following discussion will take each major vertebrate group separately.

Insectivora

The evolutionary and zoogeographic history of the insectivores remains essentially unknown because dozens of Old World extant genera lack a known fossil record. From those few types that do occur as fossils, only a very blurred picture emerges. Genera such as *Sorex, Talpa, Desmana*, and *Scaptochirus* were present in the Pliocene records of Europe, but appear on other continents only much later, suggesting expansion from that region. The common shrew *Sorex* does not appear to have ever reached Africa, but by the early mid-Pleistocene had already spread across to Siberia and into northern China. Today, it is represented also in southern Asia. The mole *Talpa* is unknown in the Pliocene of Asia and Africa, but apparently spread eastward from Europe during the earlier Pleistocene, and southward into the Middle East only in the Late Pleistocene. *Desmana*, the desman, is exclusively European in fossil distribution, apparently extending into central western Asia only in Recent times. The hedgehog, *Erinaceus*, occurs in Africa and Europe during the Pliocene, but probably did not spread across northern Eurasia until late in the Pleistocene. The shrew *Suncus*, again widespread in Africa and Europe during the Tertiary, appears in southern Asia only during the Recent, probably by human introduction (Walker 1968). *Anourosorex*, appearing in southern Asia only since the mid-Pleistocene, is apparently now known in Pliocene deposits of eastern Europe (Jánossy, personal communication), and this again underscores the need for extreme caution when dealing with negative evidence. Expansion from Asia westward must also have been significant during the Quaternary. The water shrew, *Neomys*, appearing during the mid-Pleistocene in northern Asia, spread into Europe where it is known only in the Recent fauna.

In addition to these few records a number of genera originated in, and remained endemic to, single continental areas. In Africa the endemics *Elephantulus*, *Palaeothentoides*, *Macroscelides*, *Myosorex*, *Sylvisorex*, *Chlorotalpa*, and *Amblysomus* are already known by the earliest Pleistocene. In Asia *Nectogale* and *Echinosorex* appear only during the mid-Pleistocene in southern faunas, but never expanded beyond that region of the continent.

Thus, although it is unwise to make judgments on so little data, there appear to be two main post-Pliocene phases of faunal interchange among these insectivores — one in the mid-Pleistocene and another in the Late Pleistocene or Early Holocene. Obviously a great deal more evidence is needed here.

Rodentia

Again the fossil record is less than adequate as a representation of true Pleistocene rodent faunas. When we initially pick up the record of such groups as *Marmota*, *Pitymys*, and *Microtus* in the Early Pleistocene and of *Clethrionomys*, *Ellobius*, and *Mus* in the mid-Pleistocene, they are already distributed across the palearctic zone from Europe to northern Asia. Some of these genera are cold-adapted forms living today in cool or moist climates suggesting spread during early pulses of lowered temperatures. Other groups clearly spread from one center of distribution into others somewhat later in their histories. The genera *Citellus*, *Sciurus*, *Mimomys*, and *Apodemus* were already present in European Pliocene deposits, but are not detected in Siberia and northern China until the Early or mid-Pleistocene. Many of them subsequently dispersed southward across the Tsinling Range into southern Asia. This assemblage in general is indicative of the spread of woodland to steppe conditions across northern Eurasia. None of these groups appear to have gained access to the African continent except for *Apodemus* which today is known only along the African Coast of the Mediterranean.

Similarly, several Asiatic groups spread eastward during warm, dry periods. The most important of these is the vole *Arvicola*, known in the Early Pleistocene of northern China and Siberia, but appearing suddenly in Europe only at the beginning of the mid-Pleistocene, during the Templomhegy (= "Cromerian") phase. The mole rat *Nesokia*, which is well represented as fossil in southern Asia from India to China, occurs today eastward to Egypt. It is known at Kom Ombo (Churcher 1972), and apparently dispersed into Africa in Late Pleistocene times. The large beaver *Trogontherium cuvieri*, undoubtedly a moist woodland or forest animal, is known in Europe during the Late Pliocene, but is first recorded in northern China during a warm mid-Pleistocene phase (= "Holsteinian" equivalent).

Not all groups expanded to other continents, however, and a large number of endemic genera are known throughout the Pliocene and Pleistocene on all three land masses.

Primates

Little can be said here about the relationships among the Old World Primates as most known groups in the Quaternary fossil record appear to have been endemic to one continent or another. Thus, such groups as *Cercopithecus*, *Cercopithecoides*, *Theropithecus (Simopithecus)*, *Cercocebus*, and *Australopithecus* do not appear to have spread beyond Africa. Likewise, *Presbytis*, *Rhinopithecus*, *Szechuanopithecus*, *Hylobates*, *Pongo*, *Symphalangus*, and *Gigantopithecus* appear always to have been Asiatic in distribution. One notable exception is *Macaca* which is represented on more than one continent from nearly the earliest time it appears in the fossil record. *Macaca* is identified from southern Asia, northern Africa, and Europe, but does not occur south of the Sahara. It has a wide ecological tolerance, but its preferred forest or woodland habitat was possibly responsible for its failure to cross the

Sahara region. The genus *Homo* is first recorded during the Pliocene in sub-Saharan Africa (R. Leakey 1972, 1973), spreading into southern and northern Asia during the earliest mid-Pleistocene and into Europe possibly as early as the beginning of the Oldenburgian.

Carnivora

Three genera of machairodonts, *Homotherium*, *Megantereon*, and *Machairodus*, were already widespread during the Pliocene, the first two occurring only in Africa and Europe, and the last in Asia as well. By latest Pliocene times, *Megantereon* had spread across into Asia, and by the Early to mid-Pleistocene *Homotherium* had already penetrated south of the Tsinlings. Of the large cats, *Felis* had already spread throughout the Old World before the end of the Pliocene. *Felis Pardus*, after first appearing in Africa during the latest Tertiary, is later recorded from Europe and Asia beginning in the early phases of the mid-Pleistocene. Similarly, the lion, *F. leo*, represented in the African Pliocene did not apparently spread to Europe until the mid-Pleistocene. Although the cheetah, *Acinonyx*, is known from both Africa and Europe during the Pliocene, it was apparently the African form, *A. jubatus*, that spread from that continent northward into Europe; it is represented later in the Caucasus (Vereshchagin 1968). This species is represented in terminal mid- and Late Pleistocene deposits of the palearctic region where open savannah conditions presumably prevailed during drier climatic episodes.

The genus *Canis* was already widespread throughout the Old World by the end of the Tertiary with at least one species, *C. megamastoides*, extending from Europe to the Middle East. Another species widespread in the Old World was the woodland wolf, *C. lupus*. It is first known from the Middle East during the Early Pleistocene, then later from Europe during the earliest Biharian, and finally in northern Asia during the latter half of the mid-Pleistocene. The related form, *Cuon*, appears nearly synchronously in Asia and Europe during the latest Pliocene, with at least two Asiatic species, *C. dubius* and *C. alpinus*, seemingly entering Europe during the Biharian. The Pliocene "raccoon" dog *Nyctereutes*, known in Europe from the Pliocene and becoming extinct during the Templomhegy phase, did not appear further east in Asia until the Early Pleistocene. It persists there to the present day.

The fox, *Vulpes*, had already dispersed between Africa and Europe during the latest Tertiary, and quickly extended its range into northern

Asia soon after the beginning of the Pleistocene, presumably when more open woodland habitats spread across Eurasia. Other apparent movements between continents involved the cold-adapted wolverine, *Gulo*, which expanded from Europe across the forest-tundra of northern Asia during the mid-Pleistocene. Reverse dispersions are seen in the marten, *Martes*, which moved from Asia into Europe along the coniferous forests of the early Pleistocene and into North Africa only recently, possibly during the last extensive pulse of glacial conditions. Of the Eurasiatic Pliocene genera that later spread southward into Africa, we may note that *Mustela* spread into North Africa during the Holocene, *Viverra* and *Lutra* during the Early Pleistocene, and the honey badger, *Mellivora*, spread from southern Asia into Africa, presumably via Arabia, where the animal is found today.

Of the hyaenids the primitive genus *Lycyaena* is known throughout the Old World Pliocene, surviving into the Early Pleistocene only in Africa. *Crocuta* obviously moved into all three continents during the Pliocene. The living African species, *C. crocuta*, is recorded from sub-Saharan Africa in Late Pliocene deposits, but does not appear in Eurasia until the beginning of the warm mid-Pleistocene Templomhegy phase, when it seemingly dispersed northward. The related genus *Hyaena* appears originally to have been African and European in range during the Pliocene, and it was not until the Early Pleistocene that the western species, *H. brevirostris*, spread eastward into Asia. The latter species is close to the African Late Pliocene and Recent *H. brunnea* (Kurtén 1959b) and it may have dispersed southward into Africa as well as eastward. During the early part of the mid-Pleistocene the African species *H. hyaena* apparently moved into Asia Minor and across into India along the warm southern corridor.

Proboscidea

Among these large herbivores only the African *Loxodonta* failed to disperse into other parts of the Old World. During the Pliocene the bizarre *Deinotherium* was already widespread through Eurasia and Africa, but persisted into the Quaternary only in Africa. The middle Tertiary genus *Gomphotherium* survived in Asia until the end of the Pliocene, but was replaced earlier in Africa and Europe by its more specialized descendant *Anancus*. This latter group persisted in North Africa and in Europe until the Early Pleistocene, when the last of the family (Gomphotheriidae) became extinct. The true mastodon, *Mammut*, persisted in Europe and North Africa until the end of the Tertiary.

The demise of both the gomphotheres and mammutids may have resulted from advancing Quaternary climatic deterioration, from the expansion of the true elephants, or from both.

The Asiatic *Stegodon* remained a common form until nearly the close of the Quaternary without significant intercontinental expansion. A single specimen from the Late Pleistocene of the Middle East (Hooijer 1961) seems to represent such an expansion, undoubtedly along southern Asia.

Although the true elephants had gained access to Eurasia during the Pliocene, additional faunal interchange continued into the Pleistocene. The mammoth is not recorded in northern Asia until the mid-Pleistocene when steppe conditions prevailed during several cold episodes. The genus *Elephas* had spread from Africa into southern Asia during the Middle Pliocene, but it appears to have been a second immigration that resulted in the appearance of the forest elephant, *Elephas namadicus*. This seems to have occurred during the Early Pleistocene in southern Asia and the earliest Templomhegy phase in Europe.

Perissodactyla

Soon after the appearance of *Equus* in the late Pliocene, the group spread rapidly throughout the Old World. The close faunal relationship between North Africa and Eurasia, also seen in other groups, is evidenced here with *Equus stenonis* distributed on both sides of the Mediterranean. Subsequent faunal interchange involved a number of species whose ecological requirements remain unknown. The tarpan, *Equus caballus*, spread from temperate Europe into northern Asia and the Middle East during the mid-Pleistocene. During the Late Pleistocene the ass, *E. hemionus*, followed a similar plan, spreading southward and eastward from Europe.

The two-horned rhinoceros, *Dicerorhinus*, was already widespread in Asia, Europe, and northern Africa during the late Tertiary, with a common species both north and south of the Mediterranean. During the Tarkö cold phase the steppe species *D. kirchbergensis* arose and quickly spread throughout northern Eurasia. Both this species and the related forest rhinoceros, *D. hemitoechus*, spread southward into the Middle East during cold phases of the Late Pleistocene. The Asiatic form *Coelodonta* moved into Europe, probably during the late Biharian cold phase.

Artiodactyla

Most suid groups tended to be endemic to one or another part of the
Old World during the Pleistocene so that they offer little in establishing faunal relationship. One exception is the wild hog, *Sus*, which by
Late Pliocene times had already spread throughout Eurasia and into
the Middle East. The Early Pleistocene Asiatic species *S. scrofa* did
not appear in Europe until the Middle Biharian. At about the same
time or perhaps a little later the same species is recorded in the Middle
East, but, presumably because of its requirements for watered grasslands and brush, it did not penetrate into Africa until it was introduced later by man. The region of Palestine appears to have been a
meeting ground for European and Asiatic elements, for we find here
both the Pliocene *Sus falconeri*, known otherwise only from southern
Asia, and *Sus strozzi*, which occurs elsewhere in the Pliocene of Europe.

The hippo, *Hippopotamus amphibius*, is now known from Pliocene
deposits of East and South Africa and, toward the end of that epoch,
from Europe also. The species is restricted to warm, wet habitats.

Of the Bovidae and Cervidae several groups suggestive of cool and
sparsely wooded or tundra conditions, such as *Alce*, *Capra*, and *Rangifer*, spread across Eurasia during the mid-Pleistocene, some of them
certainly during glacial advances. Others, preferring more heavily
wooded habitas (*Bos, Cervus*), seem to have expanded through Eurasia
and the Middle East during the warm Templomhegy phase when woodland and forest conditions seemingly dominated in southern portions
of the continent.

BIOSTRATIGRAPHIC ZONATION OF THE PLEISTOCENE

The establishment of faunal sequences serves two essential functions.
First, such sequences provide basic data on the evolution of particular
groups, their origin, phyletic history, and biogeography. Second, they
give a stratigraphic framework against which new faunas can be measured and placed into a relative temporal succession. Neither function
is divorced from the other, however, and both must be interrelated if
any meaningful conclusions are to be drawn. To be sure, the process
involves a certain degree of circular reasoning as conclusions on each
side depend upon those of the other. Nevertheless, studies on individual
groups of animals taken together with data on absolute dating, palynological and climatic evidence, stratigraphic successions, etc. can give
reasonable, if only tentative, interpretations.

Attempts at establishing biostratigraphic zonations of the Pleistocene are not new. Many schemes have been in use, some based on total faunas (e.g. Cooke and Kowalski, tables in Flint [1971]; Takai 1952; Kretzoi 1961; Kurtén 1963; Kahlke 1961, 1968; Tobien 1970), but others have been based on major elements of these faunas such as the large mammals (Thenius 1962; Azzaroli 1970), micromammals (Fejfar 1961; Jánossy 1970), or on individual vertebrate groups (Azzaroli 1966; Heintz 1968; Flerov 1971). Equally important have been the stratigraphic successions established on nonbiological evidence which provide additional, and in most cases more reliable, data for Pleistocene zonation.

The faunal ranges given in Figure 2 are not intended to give a fine scale means of correlating the Pleistocene. The subdivisions used are those discussed above and only the crudest patterns of vertebrate distributions can be seen. Even so, some biostratigraphic zonation is clearly seen as specific assemblages seem to characterize each broad time unit. The limits of accuracy in the figure are the same as those discussed earlier for correlations, and must be approached with caution.

GENERAL CONCLUSIONS

A number of conclusions, even if only provisional ones, seem to emerge from the above data. The most obvious one on current evidence is that major faunal metamorphoses, which so characterized the Quaternary epoch, were not synchronous nor of equal magnitude in the three continents of the Old World. In Europe the most dramatic biological changes coincided approximately with the commencement of the mid-Pleistocene, that is, with the Brunhes/Matuyama boundary. This was by no means a sharply defined change, but rather one that spanned a broad, fuzzy zone. During this transition well over a hundred characteristic species appeared in or vanished from local faunas, very significantly altering the composition of vertebrate life. A far less impressive transformation attended the Plio/Pleistocene boundary, and indeed all other periods of the Neogene. Faunal evolution in these earlier faunas consisted more or less of slow attrition as new elements were added by immigration and/or *in situ* evolution. Following the early mid-Pleistocene, European faunas again displayed a rather slow depletion of archaic groups, while essentially modern species rose to dominance.

In contrast to Europe, a major faunal transformation is seen in sub-Saharan Africa to accompany the opening of the Pleistocene; here a faunal change nearly as dramatic as that of the European mid-Pleistocene seems to have occurred. A large number of archaic, typically Tertiary elements disappeared at about this time and were replaced by new forms. Subsequent changes were relatively gradual in comparison. These data must be regarded with extreme caution, however, and may be due principally to ecological factors.

Interestingly, the data seem to suggest a major revolution in faunal composition in northern Africa during the Late Pleistocene, when many European or Asiatic elements appear for the first time. Presumably this was correlated with the opening of migration corridors during the last glacial episodes.

For Asia, major periods of faunal change are less readily apparent. In northern Asia much of the faunal alteration of the Early and mid-Pleistocene seems to have resulted more from immigration of new elements than from extinction of archaic forms. The late mid-Pleistocene witnessed a significant change in basic faunal composition, during which many more modern types emerged for the first time. The situation in southern Asia was rather different with a significant number of archaic elements disappearing during the Plio/Pleistocene transition, and a major influx of new elements occurring principally during the early mid-Pleistocene. This new faunal composition was to dominate the southern region for the remainder of the Quaternary with subsequent mid- and Late Pleistocene changes influenced primarily by the extinction of old genera. As with the African data, these are suggestive only and require far more evidence.

It is clear from this that there were no universal faunal events that transcend geographic barriers or that prove useful for broad Old World correlations. The dramatic faunal turnover that fortuitously accompanied the Brunhes/Matuyama boundary in Europe cannot be matched elsewhere, nor can any other less obvious event. Evolution here, as everywhere, represents a continuum with greater or lesser faunal episodes definable by the immigration of new forms, the extinction of old ones, or the *in situ* origin of different adaptive types. Climatic fluctuations influence the succession of vertebrate communities without regard to genetic change. All of these events, however, are local phenomena, and for these data there is no biological basis for the assumption of synchroneity over continental, let alone intercontinental, fields.

Such events do prove useful for local biostratigraphic zonation, even within an area the size of Europe. But even here it is clear that climatic alterations did not have the same influence on faunas in the south as in the north. In the Ethiopian region, both north and south Africa seem to have had a certain degree of faunal independance from the equatorial zone, although it is still uncertain to what extent this phenomenon reflects the isolation of taxonomists rather than that of the animals they study. Likewise in Asia, two distinct faunal provinces were clearly established by the beginning of the mid-Pleistocene. In each of these areas vertebrate successions can be used to stratigraphic advantage, but it is not wise to uncritically correlate seemingly related events, such as the first appearance of *Elephas*, or the onset of cool conditions.

If these local units can be tied to universally applicable criteria, as for example, paleomagnetic events, then we have a firm basis for intercontinental correlation of these regional sequences. Today we are closer than ever to this goal.

One of the purposes of this conference was to determine whether there were any criteria, faunal or otherwise, for the recognition of boundaries around and within the Middle Pleistocene. From a paleontological point of view, the answer seems to be no. Whatever arbitrary criteria we ultimately employ for these time divisions, these must be applicable the world over. Such events that can now be established will be found to correlate, in each local region, to some specific faunal change. Thus, we may be able to objectively define these boundaries for faunas within each continent or region.

In Figure 2, the ranges of selected groups are given for major divisions of Pleistocene time. Based on this, we may characterize Quaternary events as a succession of faunal types. Where evolutionary stages are recognized within species lineages, more precise divisions will eventually be possible.

Another interesting observation is the time of appearance of the modern type of fauna on each of these three continents. In both Europe and Asia, earlier Quaternary assemblages were not significantly modern in aspect since so many Tertiary elements persisted well into the Pleistocene. African faunas, on the other hand, contained a greater proportion of essentially modern species at an earlier date. The reasons for this phenomenon may relate to local taxonomic procedures employed in the two regions. More likely, however, it was the prevalence of more stable environmental conditions in tropical Africa than in northern continents. Thus, we might expect longer lived species in Africa, with many more Pliocene and earlier Pleistocene taxa persisting into the Recent. In northern continents, intense climatic and ecological fluctuations with attendant isolating effects seem to have resulted in more rapid evolutionary rates and a more continuous faunal turnover. The distinction between Africa and Europe, then, is not any fundamental difference in the fauna of the early Pleistocene, but a later acceleration in faunal evolution in Europe than in Africa.

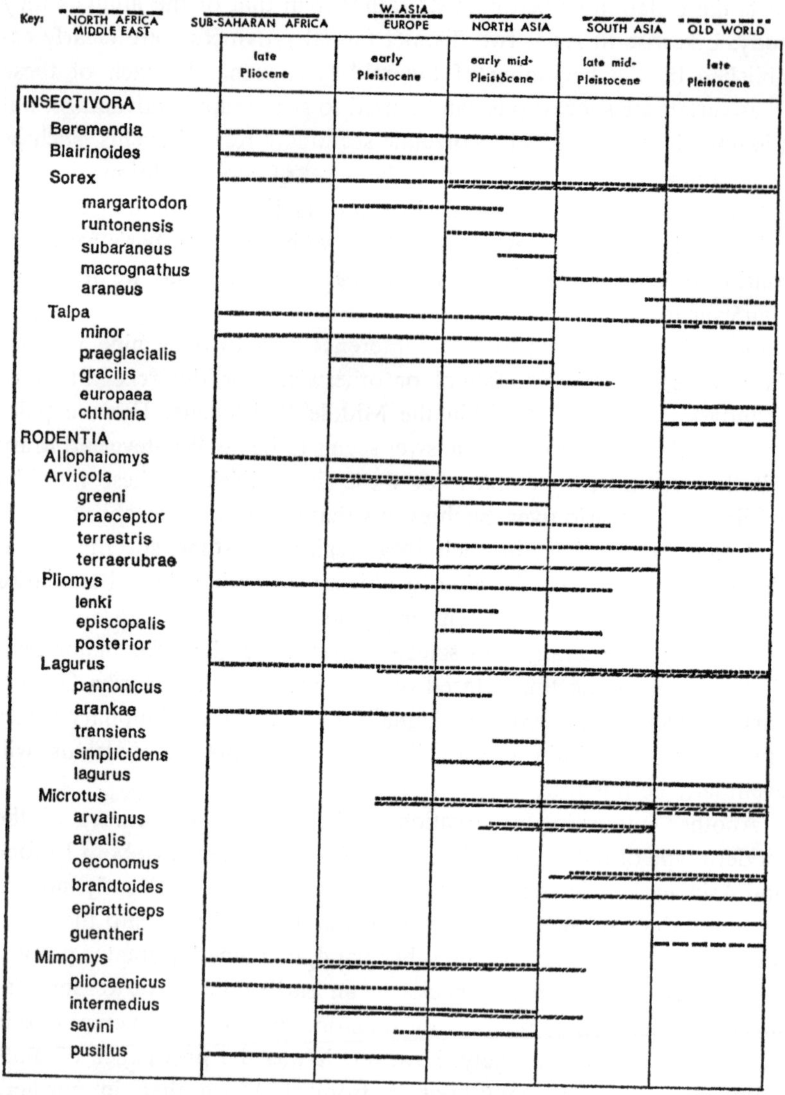

Figure 2. Time distribution in the Pleistocene for selected vertebrate species useful for local biostratigraphic zonation

Figure 2 (continued)

	late Pliocene	early Pleistocene	early mid-Pleistocene	late mid-Pleistocene	late Pleistocene
Pitymys					
gregaloides					
arvalidens					
simplicidens					
Dicrostonyx					
simplicior					
torquatus					
Lemmus					
Trilophomys					
Myospalax					
tingi					
armandia					
Mus					
Hystrix					
etrusca					
leucura					
subcristata					
cristata					
galeata					
Trogontherium					
minus					
cuvieri					
sinensis					
LAGOMORPHA					
Hypolagus					
Lepus					
terraerubrae					
praetimidus					
nigricollis					
europaeus					
Ochotonoides					
Oryctolagus					
lacosti					
cuniculus					
CARNIVORA					
Acinonyx					
pardinensis					
jubatus					
pleistocaenicus					
Felis					
issiodorensis					
pardus					
cristata					
subhimalayana					
leo spelaea					
tigris					
sylvestris					

Figure 2 (continued)

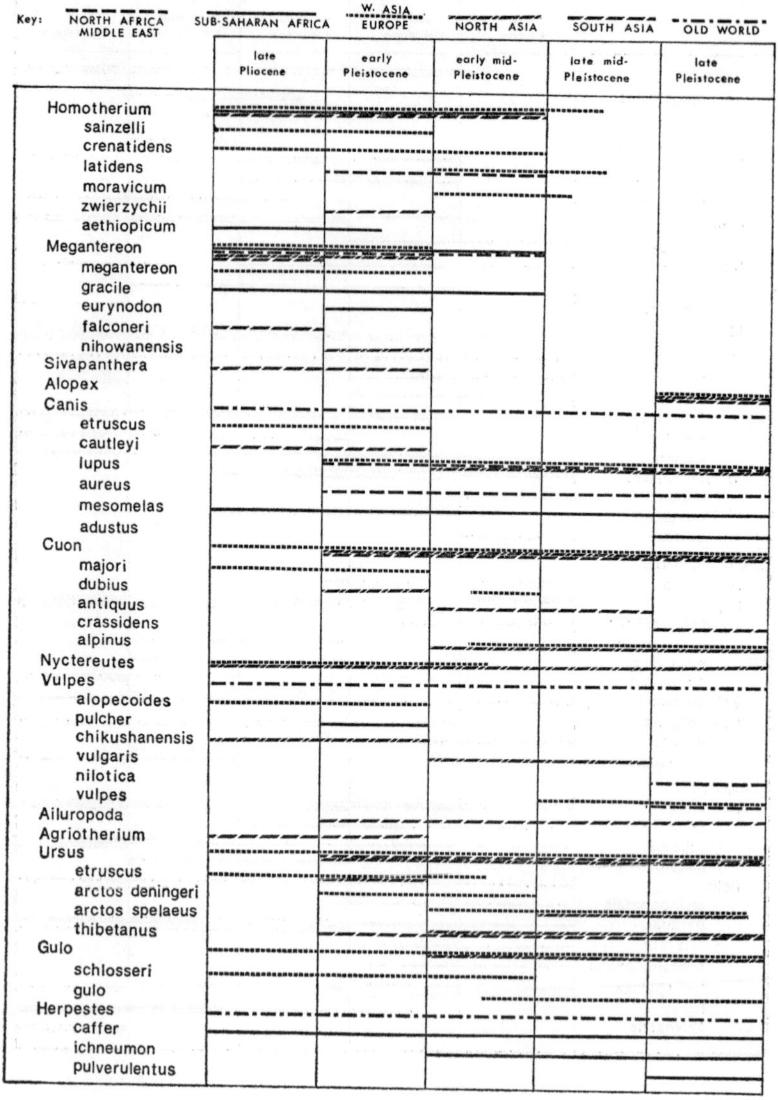

Key:	NORTH AFRICA MIDDLE EAST	SUB-SAHARAN AFRICA	W. ASIA EUROPE	NORTH ASIA	SOUTH ASIA	OLD WORLD
	late Pliocene	early Pleistocene	early mid-Pleistocene	late mid-Pleistocene	late Pleistocene	

Homotherium
  sainzelli
  crenatidens
  latidens
  moravicum
  zwierzychii
  aethiopicum
Megantereon
  megantereon
  gracile
  eurynodon
  falconeri
  nihowanensis
Sivapanthera
Alopex
Canis
  etruscus
  cautleyi
  lupus
  aureus
  mesomelas
  adustus
Cuon
  majori
  dubius
  antiquus
  crassidens
  alpinus
Nyctereutes
Vulpes
  alopecoides
  pulcher
  chikushanensis
  vulgaris
  nilotica
  vulpes
Ailuropoda
Agriotherium
Ursus
  etruscus
  arctos deningeri
  arctos spelaeus
  thibetanus
Gulo
  schlosseri
  gulo
Herpestes
  caffer
  ichneumon
  pulverentus

Figure 2 (continued)

	late Pliocene	early Pleistocene	early mid-Pleistocene	late mid-Pleistocene	late Pleistocene
Hyaena					
brevirostris					
hyaena					
bellax					
brunnea					
Crocuta					
crocuta					
c. spelaea					
c. ultima					
PROBOSCIDEA					
Anancus					
"Gomphotherium"					
Mammut					
Elephas					
recki					
iolensis					
planifrons					
hysudricus					
hysudrindicus					
maximus					
namadicus					
Loxodonta					
adaurora					
atlantica					
africana					
Mammuthus					
africanavus					
meridionalis					
armeniacus					
primigenius					
Deinotherium					
PERISSODACTYLA					
Tapirus					
Chalicotherium					
Nestoritherium					
Ancyclotherium					
Coelodonta					
Elasmotherium					
Dicerorhinus					
etruscus					
kirchbergensis					
hemitoechus					
Rhinoceros					
sivalensis					
unicornis					
Hipparion					
crusafonti					
antelopinum					
gracile					
albertense					

Figure 2 (continued)

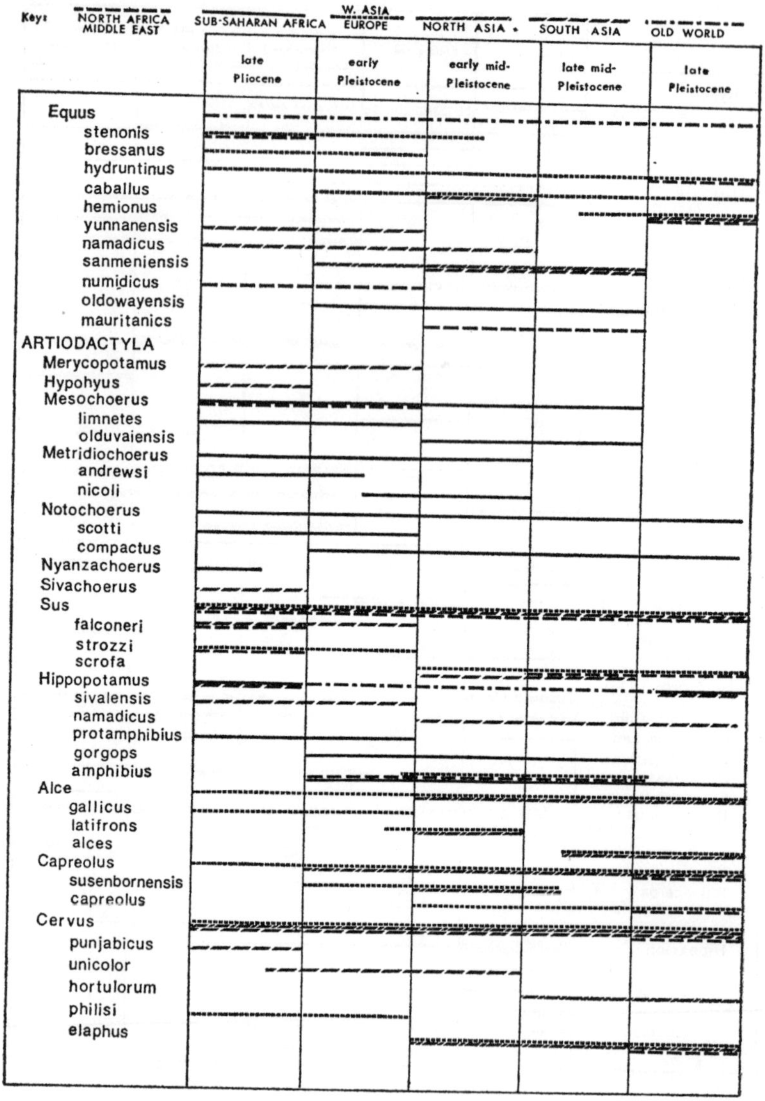

Key:

NORTH AFRICA MIDDLE EAST	SUB-SAHARAN AFRICA	W. ASIA EUROPE	NORTH ASIA •	SOUTH ASIA	OLD WORLD
late Pliocene	early Pleistocene	early mid-Pleistocene	late mid-Pleistocene	late Pleistocene	

Equus
  stenonis
  bressanus
  hydruntinus
  caballus
  hemionus
  yunnanensis
  namadicus
  sanmeniensis
  numidicus
  oldowayensis
  mauritanics

ARTIODACTYLA
Merycopotamus
Hypohyus
Mesochoerus
  limnetes
  olduvaiensis
Metridiochoerus
  andrewsi
  nicoli
Notochoerus
  scotti
  compactus
Nyanzachoerus
Sivachoerus
Sus
  falconeri
  strozzi
  scrofa
Hippopotamus
  sivalensis
  namadicus
  protamphibius
  gorgops
  amphibius
Alce
  gallicus
  latifrons
  alces
Capreolus
  susenbornensis
  capreolus
Cervus
  punjabicus
  unicolor
  hortulorum
  philisi
  elaphus

Figure 2 (continued)

	late Pliocene	early Pleistocene	early mid-Pleistocene	late mid-Pleistocene	late Pleistocene
Dama		▬▬▬	▬▬▬	▬▬▬	▬▬▬
nestii		····	····		
dama			····	····	····
clactoniana			····	····	
mesopotamica			‒ ‒	‒ ‒	‒ ‒
Euctenoceros	▬▬	▬▬	····		
senezensis	····	····			
dicranius		····	····		
mediterraneus				····	
boulei		▬			
Megaloceros	▬▬	▬▬	▬▬	▬▬	▬▬
verticornis	▬▬	▬▬	····		
savini		····	····		
giganteus			····	····	····
pachyosteus				▬▬	
ordosianus					‒ ‒
Rangifer		▬▬	▬▬	▬▬	▬▬
Antidorcas					
recki					
marsupialis					
Bison	‒ ‒	▬▬	▬▬	▬▬	▬▬
schoetensacki		····	····		
priscus			····	····	‒ ‒
bonasus				····	····
sivalensis	‒ ‒	‒ ‒	‒ ‒	‒ ‒	‒ ‒
sondaicus	‒ ‒	‒ ‒	‒ ‒	‒ ‒	‒ ‒
Bos	▬▬	▬▬	▬▬	▬▬	▬▬
acutifrons	‒ ‒	‒ ‒			
namadicus		‒ ‒	‒ ‒	‒ ‒	‒ ‒
banteng			‒ ‒	‒ ‒	‒ ‒
makapani					
primigenius			····	····	▬▬
Connochaetes			‒ ‒	‒ ‒	
africanus			‒ ‒	‒ ‒	
laticornutus					
Damaliscus					
korrigum					
niro					
antiquus					
dorcas					
Hemibos	‒ ‒	‒ ‒			
Hippotragus	‒ ‒	‒ ‒	‒ ‒	‒ ‒	‒ ‒
gigas					
leucophaeus					
niro					
Homoioceras					
baini					
vignardi					

Figure 2 (continued)

	late Pliocene	early Pleistocene	early mid-Pleistocene	late mid-Pleistocene	late Pleistocene
Kobus					
sigmoidalis					
kob					
venterae					
ellipsiprymnus					
Leptobos					
etruscus					
falconeri					
Megalotragus					
kattwinkeli					
eucornutus					
priscus					
Menelikia					
Pelorovis					
olduvaiensis					
antiquus					
Redunca					
ancystrocera					
redunca					
Soergelia					
Giraffa					
sivalensis					
gracilis					
jumae					
Vishnutherium					
Sivatherium					
PRIMATES					
Australopithecus					
africanus					
boisei					
Cercopithecoides					
Dolicopithecus					
Homo					
"habilis"					
erectus					
sapiens					
Gigantopithecus					
Macaca					
florentina					
falconeri					
subhimalayanus					
irus					
Szechuanopithecus					
Theropithecus					
(Simopithecus)					
oswaldi					
jonathani					

REFERENCES

ADAM, K. D.
1952 Die altpleistocänen Säugetierfaunen Südwestdeutschlands. *Neues Jahrbuch für Geologie und Paläontologie*, Monatshefte 5: 229–236.
1953 Die Bedeutung der altpleistozänen Säugetierfaunen Südwestdeutschlands für die Gleiderung des Eiszeitalters. *Geologica Bavarica* 19:357–363.

AGUIRRE, E.
1969 Evolutionary history of the elephant. *Science* 164:1366–1376.

AMBROSETTI, P., A. AZZAROLI, F. P. BONADONNA, M. FOLLIERI
1972 A scheme of Pleistocene chronology for the Tyrrhenian side of central Italy. *Bollettino Societa Geologia Italica* 91:169–184.

ARAMBOURG, C.
1970 Les Vértebrés du Pleistocène de l'Afrique du Nord. *Archives Muséum National d'Histoire Naturelle*, Paris, *séries* 7, 10:1–126.

AZZAROLI, A.
1966 Pleistocene and living horses of the Old World: an essay of a classification based on skull characters. *Palaeontographia Italica* 61:1–15.
1970 Villafranchian correlations based on large mammals. *Giornale di Geologia*, series 2, 35(1):1–21.

BANDY, O. L.
1972 Neogene planktonic foraminiferal zones, California, and some geologic implications. *Paleogeography, Paleoclimatology, Paleoecology* 12:131–150.

BEHRENSMEYER, A. K.
i.p. Late Cenozoic sedimentation in the Lake Rudolf Basin, Kenya. *Egyptian Geological Survey Symposium 1971*.

BIBERSON, P.
1970 The problem of correlations between south Europe and North Africa during the Pleistocene. *Paleogeography, Paleoclimatology, Paleoecology*, 8:113–127.

BISHOP, W. W.
1971 "The late Cenozoic history of East Africa in relation to hominoid evolution," in *The late Cenozoic glacial ages*. Edited by K. K. Turekian, 493–527. New Haven: Yale University Press.

BOUT, P.
1970 Absolute ages of some volcanic formations in the Auvergne and Velay areas and chronology of the European Pleistocene. *Paleogeography, Paleoclimatology, Palaeoecology* 8:95–106.

BUTLER, P.
1965 Fossil mammals of Africa No. 18: East African Miocene and Pleistocene chalicotheres. *Bulletin British Museum (Natural History) Geology* 10(7):165–237.
i.p. "Chalicotheriidae," in *Evolution of mammals in Africa*. Edited by V. J. Maglio.

BUTZER, K. W.
1971   *Environment and archaeology.* Chicago: Aldine.
BUTZER, K. W., G. L. ISAAC, J. L. RICHARDSON, C. WASHBOURN-KAMAU
1972   Radiometric dating of East African lake levels. *Science* 175:1069–1076.
CARNEY, J., A. HILL, J. A. MILLER, A. WALKER
1971   Late australopithecine from Baringo District, Kenya. *Nature,* London 230:509–514.
CHALINE, J., J. MICHAUX
1969   Evolution et signification stratigraphique des arvicolidés du genre Mimomys dans le Plio-Pleistocène de France. *Comptes rendus de l'Académie des Sciences de Paris* 268:3029–3032.
CHANG, K. C.
1968   *The archaeology of ancient China.* New Haven: Yale University Press.
CHOW, M.
1964   Mammals of "Lantien Man" locality at Lantien, Shensi. *Vertebrata Palasiatica.* 8(3):301–307.
CHOW, M., BEN-SHUN CHOW
1965   Notes on Villafranchian mammals of Lingyi, Shansi. *Vertebrata Palasiatica* 9(2):223–234.
CHURCHER, C. S.
1972   *Late Pleistocene vertebrates from archaeological sites in the plain of Kom Ombo, Upper Egypt.* Contributions of the Life Sciences Division, Royal Ontario Museum 82.
COOKE, H. B. S.
1972   Pleistocene chronology: long and short. *Maritime Sediments* 8(1):1–12.
COOKE, H. B. S., S. CORYNDON
1970   Pleistocene mammals from the Kaiso Formation and other related deposits in Uganda. *Fossil Vertebrates of Africa* 2:107–224.
COOKE, H. B. S., V. J. MAGLIO
1972   "Plio/Pleistocene stratigraphy in East Africa in relation to proboscidean and suid evolution," in *Calibration of hominoid evolution.* Edited by W. W. Bishop and J. A. Miller, 303–329. Edinburgh: Scottish Academic Press.
COX, A.
1968   Lengths of geomagnetic polarity intervals. *Journal of Geophysical Research* 73:3247–3260.
1969   Geomagnetic reversals. *Science* 163:237–245.
COX, A., R. R. DOELL, G. B. DALRYMPLE
1968   Radiometric time-scale for geomagnetic reversals. *Quarterly Journal of the Geological Society,* London 124:53–66.
CRUSAFONT-PAIRÓ, M.
1960   Le Quaternaire espagnol et sa faune de mammifères-essai de synthèse. *Mammalia pleistocaenica* 1:55–64.
DORST, J., P. DANDELOT
1970   *A field guide to the large mammals of Africa.* Boston: Houghton Mifflin.

FEJFAR, O.
1961   Review of Quaternary vertebrata in Czechoslovakia. *Prace Institute of Geology*, Warsaw 34(1):109–118.
1964   The lower Villafranchian vertebrates from Hajněčka. *Rozpravy Ustredni Ustavu Geologickeho, Praha*, 30:1–115.

FLEROV, C. C.
1971   "The evolution of certain mammals during the late Cenozoic," in *The late Cenozoic glacial ages*. Edited by K. K. Turekian, 479–491. New Haven: Yale University Press.

FLINT, R. F.
1971   *Glacial and Quaternary geology*. New York: John Wiley and Sons.

FRANZ, H.
1967   "On the stratigraphy and evolution of climate in the Chad basin during the Quaternary," in *Background to evolution in Africa*. Edited by W. W. Bishop and J. D. Clark, 273–284. Chicago: University of Chicago.

GENTRY, A. W., A. GENTRY
1969   Fossil camels in Kenya and Tanzania. *Nature*, London 222:898.

HAUG, E.
1911   *Traité de géologie*, volume two: *Les périodes géologiques*. Paris: Colin.

HEINTZ, E.
1968   Principaux résultats systématiques et biostratigraphiques de l'étude des cervidés villafranchiens de France et d'Espagne. *Comptes rendu de l'Académie des Sciences de Paris*, séries D, 266(22): 2184–2186.

HOOIJER, D. A.
1949   Pleistocene vertebrates from Celebes. IV. *Archidiskodon celebensis* nov. spec. *Zoologische Mededeelingen Museum*, Leiden 30(14):205–226.
1959   Fossil mammals from Jisr Banot Yaqub, south of Lake Huleh, Israel. *Bulletin of the Research Council of Israel* 8G(4):177–199.
1961   Middle Pleistocene mammals from Latamné, Orontes Valley, Syria. *Annales Archaeologie de Syrie* 11:117–132.

HOWELL, F. C., L. S. FICHTER, R. WOLFF
1969   Fossil camels in the Omo Beds, southern Ethiopia. *Nature*, London 223:150–152.

JÁNOSSY, D.
1965   Vertebrate microstratigraphy of the Middle Pleistocene in Hungary. *Acta Geologica, Magyar Tudomanyos Akademiae*, Budapest 9:145–152.
1970   The boundary of lower-middle Pleistocene on the basis of microvertebrates in Hungary. *Palaeogeography, Palaeoclimatology, Palaeoecology* 8:147-152.

KAHLKE, H. D.
1961   On the complex of the *Stegodon-Ailuropoda*-fauna of southern China and the chronological position of *Gigantopithecus blacki* v. Koenigswald. *Vertebrata Palasiatica* 5(1):83–108.
1968   "Zur relativen chronologie ostasiatischer mittelpleistozänen Fau-

nen und Hominoidea-Funde," in *Evolution and hominization.* Edited by G. Kurth, 91–118. Stuttgart: Gustav Fischer.

KAHLKE, H. D., BEN-SHUN CHOW
1961   A summary of stratigraphical and paleontological observations in the lower layers of Choukoutien locality 1, and on the chronological position of the site. *Vertebrata Palasiatica* 5:212–240.

KAHLKE, H. D., CHANG-KANG HU
1957   On the distribution of *Megoceros* in China. *Vertebrata Palasiatica* 1(4):273–283.

KOWALSKI K.
1958   Insectivores, Chiroptera, Lagomorphs and Rodentia from Podumci in Dalmatien, Yugoslavia. *Paleontologica Yugoslavia* 2: 312–325.
1966   Stratigraphic importance of rodents in the studies on European Quaternary. *Folia Quaternaria* 22:1–16.
1971   "The biostratigraphy and paleoecology of late Cenozoic mammals of Europe and Asia," in *The late Cenozoic glacial ages.* Edited by K. K. Turekian, 465–477. New Haven: Yale University Press.

KRETZOI, M.
1956   Die altpleistozänen Wirbeltierfaunen des Villányer Gebirges. *Geologica Hungarica, Series Paleontologica* 27:1–23.
1961   Stratigraphy and chronology. Stand der ungarischen Quatärforschung. *Prace Institute of Geology,* Warsaw 34(1):313–332.
1965   Die Nager und Lagomorphen von Voigstedt in Thüringen und ihre chronologische Aussage. *Palaeontologische Abhandlungen, Abteilung A, Paläozoologie* 2:585–661.

KRETZOI, M., L. VÉRTES
1965   The role of vertebrate faunae and palaeolithic industries of Hungary in Quaternary stratigraphy and chronology. *Acta Geologica Hungarica, Magyar Tudomanyos Akademiae* 9:125–144.

KUKLA, J.
1970   Correlations between loesses and deep-sea sediments. *Geologiska Föreningens i Stockholm Förhandlingar* 92:148–180.

KURTÉN, B.
1954   Observations on allometry in mammalian dentitions; its interpretation and evolutionary significance. *Acta Zoologica Fennica* 85: 1–13.
1957   The bears and hyaenas of the interglacials. *Quaternaria* 4:69–81.
1959a On the bears of the Holsteinian interglacial. *Acta Universitatis Stockholmiensis* 2(5):73–102.
1959b New evidence on the age of Peking man. *Vertebrata Palasiatica* 3(4):173–175.
1960   Chronology and faunal evolution of the earlier European glaciations. *Societas Scientiarum Fennica, Commentationes Biologicae* 21(5):1–62.
1963   Villafranchian faunal evolution. *Societas Scientiarum Fennica, Commentationes Biologicae* 26(3):1–18.
1968   *Pleistocene mammals of Europe.* Chicago: Aldine.

LEAKEY, L. S. B.
1942   *Some East African Pleistocene Suidae.* British Museum (Natural History), Fossil Mammals of Africa 14.

LEAKEY, M. D.
1971   *Olduvai Gorge: excavations in beds I and II, 1960–1963.* Cambridge: Cambridge University Press.

LEAKEY, R. E.
1972   Further evidence of Lower Pleistocene hominids from East Rudolf, north Kenya, 1971. *Nature*, 237:264–269.
1973   Further evidence of Lower Pleistocene hominids from East Rudolf, north Kenya, 1972. *Nature*, 242:170–173.

LEE, J. S.
1937   Quaternary glaciation in the Yangtze Valley. *Bulletin of the Geological Society of China* 13:2–15.

MAGLIO, V. J.
1970   Early Elephantidae of Africa and a tentative correlation of African Plio-Pleistocene deposits. *Nature*, 225:328–332.
1973   Origin and evolution of the Elephantidae. *Transactions of the American Philosophical Society* 63(3):1–149.

MARKOVIĆ-MARJANOVIĆ, J.
1970   Data concerning the stratigraphy and the fauna of the lower and middle Pleistocene of Yugoslavia. *Paleogeography, Paleoclimatology, Paleoecology* 8:153–163.

MELENTIS, J. K.
1966   Studien über fossile vertebraten Griechenlands. 13. *Archidiskodon meridionalis proarchaicus* n. ssp. Die geologisch ältesten elephantenreste aus griechenland. *Annales du Géologie des Pays Helleniques* 17:211–220.

SAVAGE, D. E., G. H. CURTIS
1970   *The Villafranchian stage-age and its radiometric dating.* Geological Society of America, Special Paper 124.

SHER, A. V.
1971   Säugetierfunde und Pleistozän-stratigraphie in der Kolyma-Niederung (UdSSR). *Bericht der Deutches Gesellschaft Geologische Wissenschaft* 16(2):113–125.

SICKENBERG, O., H. TOBIEN
1971   New Neogene and lower Quaternary vertebrate faunas in Turkey. *Newsletter Stratigraphie* 1(3):51–61.

SIMPSON, G. C.
1934   Studies in world climate. *Quarterly Journal of the Royal Meteorological Society* 60:425–478.

TAKAI, F.
1952   The historical development of mammalian faunae of eastern Asia and the interrelationships of continents since the Mesozoic. *Japanese Journal of Geology and Geography* 22:169–205.

THENIUS, E.
1962   Die Grossäugetiere des Pleistozänes von Mitteleuropa. *Zeitschrift für Säugetierkunde* 27:65–83.
1970   Zur Evolution und Verbreitungsgeschichte der Suidae (Artiodac-

tyla, Mammalia). *Zeitschrift für Säugetierkunde* 35(6):321–342.

TOBIEN, H.

1970   Biostratigraphy of the mammalian faunas at the Plio-Pleistocene boundary in middle and western Europe. *Paleogeography, Paleoclimatology, Paleoecology* 8:77–93.

VAN MONTFRANS, H. M., J. HOSPERS

1969   A preliminary report on the stratigraphic position of the Matuyama-Brunhes geomagnetic field reversal in the Quaternary sediments of the Netherlands. *Geologie en Mijnbouw* 48(6):565–572.

VANGENGEIM, E. H., A. V. SHER

1970   Siberian equivalents of the Tiraspol faunal complex. *Paleogeography, Paleoclimatology, Paleoecology* 8:197–207.

VERESHCHAGIN, N. K.

1968   *The mammals of Caucasus: a history of the evolution of the fauna.* Israel Program of Scientific Translations, Jerusalem. (Originally published 1958. Moscow and Leningrad: Izdatel'stovo Akademii Nauk.

WALKER, E. P.

1968   *Mammals of the world* (second edition). Baltimore: Johns Hopkins Press.

WU, XIN-ZHI, A. YUAN, D. HAN, T. QI, Q. LU

1965   Report of the excavation at Lantien. *Vertebrata Palasiatica* 10(1): 23–29.

ZAZHIGIN, V. S.

1970   Significance of *Lagurus* (Rodentia, Microtinae, Lagurini) for the stratigraphy and correlation of Eopleistocene deposits of eastern Euope and western Siberia. *Paleogeography, Paleoclimatology, Paleoecology* 8:237–249.

Cultural Patterns in the Olduvai Sequence

M. D. LEAKEY

ABSTRACT

The Olduvai sequence has yielded the longest known record of stone artifacts and hominid fossils, covering a period of about 1.5 million years. The earliest remains are above the basalt in Bed I that has been dated at 1.89 million years.

Artifacts from Bed I and basal Bed II belong to the Oldowan industrial complex, but in the overlying Beds there appear to be two industrial traditions, the Developed Oldowan and the Acheulean. The former is a continuation of the Oldowan from Bed I, but with a more varied tool kit including a small number of bifaces that are technologically different from those of the Acheulean. This industry is found through Beds II, III, and IV.

The earliest Acheulean occurrence is in Bed II and has an estimated age of 1.2 million years. Acheulean assemblages from various sites and levels in Bed IV and the Masek Beds differ substantially from one another, particularly in the nature of the bifaces, but exhibit no progressive refinement in technique of manufacture.

Stone industries are found throughout the Olduvai sequence (Figures 1 and 2). The earliest are from deposits just above the basalt that has been dated at 1.89 million years (Evernden and Curtis 1965) and the youngest from the Masek Beds that are estimated to be in the region of 200,000 years B.P. The record of hominid activities thus covers a time span of over one and a half million years and is the longest known sequence of stone age cultural material.

The industries from Beds I and II have been described in volume three of the Olduvai monographs (Leakey 1971). A summary will be included in the present paper, as well as a brief account of the material that has been obtained from Beds III, IV, and the Masek Beds during the last field season.

The upper part of the Olduvai sequence to the end of the Middle Pleistocene, that is Beds III, IV, and the Masek and lower Ndutu Beds, has yielded substantially less information than Beds I and II. The principal reason for this lies in the mode of occurrence of the archeological material. Whereas the majority of occupation sites in Bed I and a proportion of those in Bed II appear to be in virtually undisturbed contexts, this is not the case for Beds III and IV, nor for the single site known in the Masek Beds. Without exception, the artifacts and associated occupational debris from these levels have been found in conglomeratic deposits in former stream and river channels. At some sites all the material is uniformly sharp, so that it can be assumed transportation was minimal and that the assemblages are homogeneous. At other sites, however, there are both heavily rolled and fresh specimens, indicating the possibility that all the material may not be contemporaneous.

The current nomenclature for the deposits at Olduvai must be stated briefly before describing the industries from various levels, since a number of names have been changed in recent years.

Bed I now includes the sediments in the western part of the gorge that are above the Naabi ignimbrite, as well as the basalt and the sediments that overlie the basalt in the eastern part of the gorge, up to and including the marker Tuff IF. Bed II consists of the sediments above Tuff IF, up to the base of the red bed (III), wherever it is present. A tuff unit in the lower part of Bed II that is largely of eolian origin and that was formerly known as the Eolian Tuff Member (Tuff IIA) is now designated the Lemuta Member of Bed II. The definition of Bed III remains unaltered in the eastern part of the gorge and in the side gorge, where it is red, but to the west, Beds III and IV are lithologically indistinguishable, and the two units are termed Beds III-IV (undivided). Bed IV was known for a time as IVA but this term has been abandoned and it is known once more as Bed IV without the letter "A." Two marker tuffs are now recognized in Bed IV. These are Tuffs IVA and IVB, and the latter has been taken as a datum to subdivide the bed into upper and lower units. The deposits that overlie Bed IV, consisting largely of eolian tuffs that were formerly termed Bed IVB, have now been given separate status and are known as the Masek Beds; the upper tuff being termed the Norkilili Member.

The eolian tuff deposits formerly designated Bed V, deposited during as well as after the cutting of the gorge, have now been subdivided into two distinct units, termed the Ndutu and Naisiusiu Beds. The Ndutu Beds comprise a lower and an upper unit. Deposits of the former are scantily represented in the gorge but have yielded sufficient faunal material to indicate a Middle Pleistocene age. The upper unit of the Ndutu Beds, on the other hand, is substantially more recent;

it is widely distributed on the plains and has also accumulated to a considerable thickness within the gorge itself. Only living species of mammals are known in these deposits.

The Naisiusiu Beds overlie the upper unit of the Ndutu Beds. No fault displacements have been observed in the Naisiusiu Beds, and they appear to be younger than the last phase of faulting. Radiocarbon dates of 17,550 and 17,000 ±1,000 B.P. were obtained on ostrich eggshell and bone collagen from these beds (Leakey, Hay, et al. 1972.)

Although our subject is, strictly speaking, the Middle Pleistocene, it will be necessary to describe briefly the deposits at Olduvai that fall within the upper part of the Lower Pleistocene, i.e. Bed I and lower Bed II, in order to provide background for the Middle Pleistocene industrial patterns.

During Bed I times there was a perennial lake in the Olduvai area. Where the shore lines have been cut through by the gorge the lake was about fourteen miles wide. The southern and eastern margins are likely to have been along the slopes of the volcanic mountains Lemagrut, Ngorongoro, and Olmoti. To the north, the lake was probably bounded by the hills of Precambrian rocks known as Ol Donyo Ogol. The occupation sites now exposed in the gorge lie along the southern margin of the lake, and it appears that man lived on the flats along the shore, probably at places where freshwater streams from the highlands drained into the lake. Localities where fresh water was available near the home base were probably essential in view of the alkalinity of the lake itself, as evidenced by the presence of flamingo bones at several lake margin sites. In addition to the flamingos, other families of birds present in the fossil avifauna from Bed I are strikingly similar to the bird populations found today around the soda lakes in East Africa; it is likely that conditions were not very different during the Pleistocene.

There was still a permanent lake in the Olduvai area during Bed II times, but it was considerably reduced in size, probably on account of earth movements that began in lower Ber II, shortly before the deposition of the Lemuta Member, which caused the Bed I lake to be partially drained.

Only the Oldowan is known in Bed I. It is present in lower Bed II, where the Developed Oldowan begins. One further Oldowan site occurs later than this (MNK Skull Site, in the lower part of middle Bed II). From Middle Bed II, however, the important industrial traditions are Developed Oldowan and Acheulean, which exist side by side until upper Bed IV.

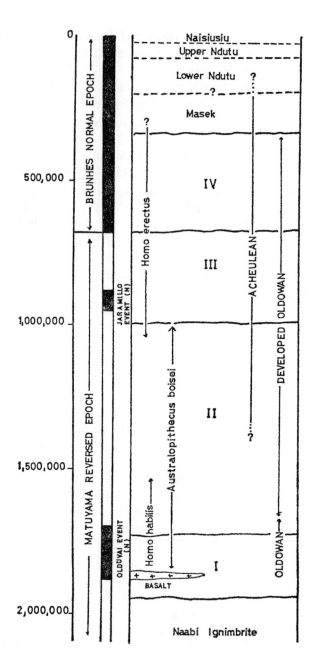

Figure 2. Provisional chart to show the time span of cultural traditions and hominid lineages at Olduvai

In general, the classification of the cultural material put forward at
the 1965 symposium (Leakey 1967) and later in volume three of the
Olduvai monographs (Leakey 1972) still holds good. Additional information, obtained during the current season of fieldwork, suggests,
however, that the Developed Oldowan persisted into upper Bed IV.
It also now seems possible that the industries from two sites in Bed II
(MNK and the Lower Floor at TK), that were classed as Developed
Oldowan, should perhaps be included in the Acheulean, since, although
they are exceedingly rare, the bifacial tools are Acheulean in character
and technique of manufacture. These two industries were originally
classified as Developed Oldowan because the writer formerly considered that a proportionate abundance of bifaces was a diagnostic
character of the Acheulean and followed the suggestion put forward
by M. R. Kleindienst (1962) that an industry should have 40 percent
or more bifaces to qualify as Acheulean. More detailed work on the
Acheulean and Developed Oldowan from Olduvai indicates that other
features are as important, in particular the technique of manufacture
evident in the bifaces.

THE OLDOWAN

The geological evidence, as now interpreted by R. L. Hay, indicates
that Bed I spanned a relatively short period of time, perhaps in the
region of 100,000 years (Hay 1972). This probably accounts for the
fact that no significant changes can be observed in the stone industries
throughout Bed I and even in the lower part of Bed II.

There are ten occurrences of the Oldowan that have been excavated,
eight of which are in Bed I, namely: DK, FLKNN, FLK, and FLK
North Levels 1/2, 3, 4, 5, and 6. An Oldowan industry was also
recovered from the lowest level at HWK East, at the very base of
Bed II, as well as from the MNK Skull site in the lower part of middle
Bed II, about one meter above the Lemuta Member. At all these sites
except FLK, choppers and other heavy-duty tools are more common
than light-duty tools, but at FLK, on the occupation floor that yielded
the cranium of *Australopithecus boisei*, light-duty scrapers outnumber
any other tool category.

The tools recovered from the above sites amounted to 537 specimens
(Figure 3). They consist of the following categories: choppers, including
side, end, pointed, and two-edged (51 percent), protobifaces (1.3 percent),
polyhedrons (10 percent), discoids (9.1 percent), spheroids and sub-

spheroids (6 percent), heavy-duty scrapers (8.6 percent), light-duty scrapers (10.2 percent), burins (1.7 percent), and sundry tools (2 percent).

Some of the choppers from the lowest artifact-bearing level in Bed I (Site DK) are smaller than those from the higher levels. It is also evident that the zenith of chopper manufacture was reached in upper Bed I, at Site FLK North; here the bold, accurate flaking of these tools is unparalleled elsewhere, even in Bed II.

The heavy-duty tools clearly were not manufactured at the Oldowan living sites. They are usually made from waterworn lava pebbles and cobbles, and the amount of lava waste with which they are associated is never sufficient to account for the number of flakes that were detached from the tools. Unlike the heavy-duty tools, the majority of light-duty tools and flakes are of quartzite, which seems to have been the preferred material for small tools. Many of the flakes show chipping and wear on the edges indicating that they were used, even if not shaped into tools. It is interesting to note that the flakes from Koobi Fora, East Rudolf, that are considerably earlier than any from Olduvai, show little evidence of utilization.

The Oldowan industry from the base of Bed II at HWK East most closely resembles that from the highest levels at FLK North, from which, in fact, it is only separated stratigraphically by Tuff IF. Similarly, the industry associated with the hominid skull H. 13 at the MNK Skull Site can only be described as Oldowan, although it occurs at a higher stratigraphic level than the Developed Oldowan at HWK East. It consists of forty-five tools of which 57.8 percent are choppers, the balance being polyhedrons, discoids, spheroids and subspheroids, heavy- and light-duty scrapers. Awls and laterally trimmed flakes, known in the earliest phase of the Developed Oldowan, are not present. The sorting of material by water action, which might explain the absence of small tools, can probably be excluded since the site is on a paleosol and there is no apparent orientation of the occupational debris. It seems, therefore, that this is an instance of the Oldowan industry persisting into a time when contemporary hominids elsewhere had acquired an enlarged tool kit.

THE DEVELOPED OLDOWAN

The Developed Oldowan A is restricted to lower Bed II and the lower part of Middle Bed II, where there are three occurrences that have yiel-

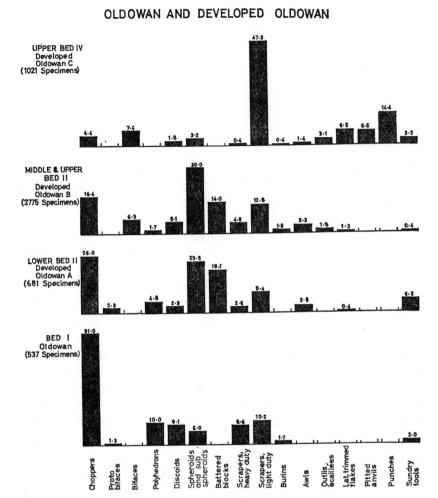

Figure 3. Histograms of tool categories in the Oldowan and Developed Oldowan

ded a total of 682 tools (Figure 3). These are at FLK North, in the Sandy Conglomerate, which is just above the level of the Lemuta Member, and at HWK East, where the industry likewise occurs in the Sandy Conglomerate, as well as in a claystone that immediately underlies the Lemuta member; this industry, therefore, transgresses the level at which the faunal change occurred.

Chert became available for making tools during the time of the Developed Oldowan A; it seems likely that the superiority of this material over those that had been available previously gave a stimulus to tool manufacture, particularly light-duty tools.

There are no true bifaces in this industry, but the number of proto-bifaces is proportionately greater than in the Oldowan. Heavy-duty tools other than choppers are also more numerous, so that choppers amount to only 29.5 percent of the total, instead of 51 percent in the Oldowan.

The term Developed Oldowan B has been applied to a continuation of the same industry (Figure 3), with the same heavy-duty tools, but with the addition of some poorly made and generally small bifaces, as well as a proportionately greater number of light-duty tools. These consist of scrapers, burins, awls, *outils écaillés*, and laterally trimmed flakes. The industry is found in middle and upper Bed II and probably also in Bed III. A later occurrence of the same industry, in upper Bed IV, has provisionally been termed Developed Oldowan C.

The industries from six occurrences in Bed II were described as Developed Oldowan B in volume three of the Olduvai monographs. These are MNK Main Site, FC West, SHK, BK, and the Upper and Lower Floors at TK. The same tool categories are present in each assemblage and in very similar proportions, while bifaces are always scarce and never amount to more than 13 percent of the tools, some-times being only 2 percent. The nature of the bifacial tools at MNK and the Lower Floor at TK, however, is strikingly different from that of SHK, BK, and the Upper Floor at TK. The bifacial tools from MNK and the Lower Floor at TK compare favorably with the bifaces of the early Acheulean; they are of fair size, some indeed, are larger than average, and they also exhibit bold and accurately directed trim-ming scars. It would appear that the makers had full mastery of their materials. This is far from the impression made by the bifacial tools from SHK, BK, and the Upper Floor at TK in which the trimming scars often appear to have been misdirected, as well as being very variable in dimensions, suggesting unskilled workmanship. (The bifa-cial tools from FC West stand closest to those from MNK, but are so poorly represented that it is impossible to indicate the status of this industry.)

The industry recovered from Bed III at JK East by Kleindienst in 1962 is undescribed, but on preliminary examination it appears to be within the Developed Oldowan tradition rather than the Acheulean, although the latter occurs at JK West at approximately the same horizon.

Upper Bed IV has yielded what appears to be a still later phase of the same cultural tradition. As noted above, this has provisionally been termed Developed Oldowan C (Figure 3). It was obtained from a series of sites on the south side of the gorge (WKE, A and C and PDK I–III) and amounts to a total of 979 tools. The bifaces constitute 7.2 percent and are remarkably similar to those from SHK, BK, and the Upper Floor at TK: they are small, asymmetrical, and heavily step-flaked. Light-duty scrapers are by far the most numerous tools (48.7 percent), and many are microlithic in size. There are also certain elements not known in the earlier stages of this industry, notably pitted anvils, a few bifacially trimmed points, and small, thickset, pointed tools that have been termed "punches."

Similar pitted anvils are known from Acheulean sites in lower Bed IV, but they are not common, whereas in the industry under review, they amount to 14.2 percent of the tools; they are also numerous in an Acheulean context that is approximately contemporaneous. The anvils are on stones that range in size from small boulders to large pebbles; they are generally of lava. The hollows or pits vary in width from a few millimeters to several centimeters, with a corresponding variation in depth. They may occur singly or be as many as six on the same stone; specimens with a pair of hollows set close together are common.

It has been suggested by Professor J. D. Clark that the pitted anvils and the small, pointed, quartzite tools may be the result of employing the bi-polar technique for detaching flakes, i.e. that the "punches" represent the residual piece of stone that had been flaked, after it became too small to be of further service. This is a possible explanation, and if this technique were generally employed, it might account for the noticeable lack of large flakes in this industry. However, it does not explain the disposition of the pits on the anvils, particularly those that are in close-set pairs. These are often on the smaller stones that presumably were used to hammer the upper end of the piece of stone while it was held against the lower anvil. Whatever their purpose may have been, these pitted stones are characteristic of all the industries so far found in upper Bed IV.

According to the evidence available at present, it seems that the cultural tradition that has been termed Developed Oldowan, which evolved from the Oldowan of Bed I, persisted through Beds II, III, and IV. It is difficult to explain why this tradition should have remained distinct from the Acheulean, which was comtemporaneous from middle Bed II onwards, and from which the concept of bifacial tools was almost certainly borrowed. Basically, the factor that distinguishes the two traditions is an inability to detach large flakes in the Developed Oldowan — as in the Oldowan itself — whereas from Bed II onwards the Acheulean bifaces were generally made on large flakes.

It has been suggested that the Developed Oldowan and Acheulean should be lumped together in view of the presence in both of bifacial tools. However, the overall pattern of the Developed Oldowan, besides the nature of the bifacial tools, seems to the writer sufficiently distinct from the Acheulean, as it is represented at Olduvai, to justify separating the two. The characteristic features of both traditions are also largely consistent within themselves, with the exception of the industries from MNK and the Lower Floor at TK, which must remain in suspense for the present.

THE ACHEULEAN

Leaving aside the industry from MNK, which probably dates to about 1.4 million years, the earliest known occurrences of the Acheulean at Olduvai are in middle Bed II, a few feet above the limestone that overlies the Lemuta Member in the eastern part of the gorge. These sites have been estimated to be approximately 1.2 or 1.3 million years by R. L. Hay (personal communication). One has been excavated (EF-HR) and has yielded a total of nintey-one tools. Most of the handaxes and the single cleaver are made on large flakes, either end- or side-struck. The primary surface usually shows a minimum of trimming, no more than was required to reduce to some extent the striking platform and bulb of percussion. The trimming scars are bold and well directed, but there is no refined retouch; the scar count is consequently low, with an average of 9.7 per specimen. There are no light-duty tools, with the exception of three scrapers, and these are larger than the majority of such tools in the Developed Oldowan (see Figure 4).

The next Acheulean occurrence in the stratigraphic sequence is at JK West. The site is low in Bed III, not more than five meters above the top of Bed II. Paleomagnetic determinations have consistently shown reversed polarity for Bed III, indicating that it is within the Matuyama Reversed Epoch and therefore not later than 700,000 B.P. An age of not less than 800,000 million years can, therefore, be estimated for this site. The artifacts occur in a coarse river sand, and there are both heavily abraded and comparatively fresh specimens, suggesting the possibility of different origins. The assemblage is thus of doubtful value in assessing the Acheulean of Bed III.

The stratigraphy of Bed IV and the relationship of its archeological

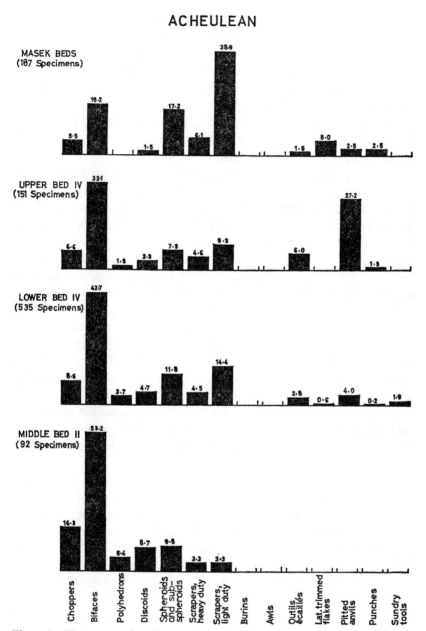

Figure 4.   Histograms of tool categories in the Acheulean

occurrences has presented many problems, since the two marker tuffs mentioned earlier are very localized in distribution. Until 1971, no means of relating sites in different areas was known. In that year F.

H. Brown observed that gray siltstones are diagnostic of the lower part of Bed IV, beneath Tuff IVB. These can be used to demonstrate that the sites at HEB are older than the principal ones at WK (Figure 5).

These two localities have yielded the bulk of the Acheulean material from Bed IV. HEB is on the south side of the gorge, just below the museum, and the WK/PDK gullies are also on the south side of the gorge but 2.5 kilometers further east. Sites HK and TK Fish Gully, which had previously yielded Acheulean material, have now been shown to be in disturbed contexts.

What appears to be the earliest Acheulean occurrence in Bed IV is at PDK IV. This site is at the very base of Bed IV, virtually on the III-IV junction. Only thirty-eight tools were recovered of which the bifaces amounted to 50 percent of the total. Cleavers with flared cutting edges, formed by a notch on either lateral edge, are characteristic of the industry, but are almost unknown at other sites. Both cleavers and handaxes are made on large flakes struck from boulders, with areas of cortical surface often remaining on the dorsal aspects.

There are five artifact-bearing horizons at HEB and HEB W, four of which are below a gray siltstone. The lowest Level 4, consists of a conglomerate within a small stream channel, approximately one meter above the top of Bed III; this channel is younger than Tuff IV A since it contains pieces of it. Some of the artifacts from this channel are considerably abraded, while others are quite fresh, so that the possibility that this is a mixed assemblage cannot be overlooked. The handaxes are of medium size, with noticeable stepflaking. The bifacial tools amount to 21.7 percent of the total; cleavers are represented only by three doubtful specimens.

The succeeding level, is thirty centimeters higher in the sequence. It has yielded the most highly finished handaxes and cleavers known from Bed IV which amount to 75 percent of the tools. They are made almost exclusively on large flakes of fine-grained green phonolite, but both faces have generally been flaked all over, so that little of the primary surface remains. The scar count is high, with an average of twenty per specimen: the two following higher archeological levels, 2a and 2b, occur only at the western end of the site. Both appear to be within a channel and are in fine to medium-coarse sand, separated by about sixty centimeters of relatively barren deposits, the uppermost level being about fifty centimeters below a gray siltstone. The bifaces in both levels are again made on large flakes and are generally of basalt or trachy-andesite. They are shaped with a minimum of large, bold trimming flakes, in contrast to the series from the underlying level. Small tools

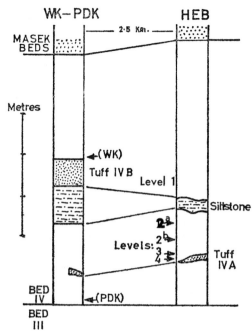

Figure 5. Schematic stratigraphic sections for HEB and WK-PDK showing the basis for correlation between these areas and the relative positions of the excavated levels (after R. L. Hay)

are rare and the bifaces, including both handaxes and cleavers, amount to 46 percent of the tools. The highest occurrence. Level 1, just above the gray siltstone, contained very few artifacts and is not described here.

The total number of tools from the four levels at HEB amounts to 414. Light-duty tools are rare, but there are a few examples of the pitted anvils that become so common in upper Bed IV. The bifacial tools amount to 79 percent of the total.

Thus, at HEB there are four stratigraphically distinct "units" of the Acheulean in lower Bed IV, in three of which the bifaces amount to 40 percent or more of the tools. Each "unit" has distinguishing features, and it is to be noted that the most highly finished unit is near the bottom of the series and does not come last in the series — a typological advance on earlier, more crudely made tools.

The main occurrence at WK in upper Bed IV is situated in a former river channel that has cut through Tuff IVB down to the underlying deposits of lower Bed IV. Fragments of the tuff can be identified in the lower part of the conglomerate in the channel. A gray siltstone is seventy-five centimeters below the channel here. An abundant industry was obtained from this site, as well as the left half of a hominid pelvis and the shaft of a left femur that have been attributed to *Homo erectus* (Leakey and Day 1971). These bones lay on the higher part of the former surface, while the artifacts and majority of fossil bones had accumulated in the deeper part of the channel and in other depressions.

So far it has only been possible to study the artifacts from a single trench. These are estimated to amount to approximately half the total. Although the tools occurred in a conglomerate and there is some difference in the degree of abrasion, the series appears to be entirely homogeneous.

There is a total of 151 tools, in which bifaces and pitted anvils are the most common categories. Cleavers are unusually plentiful and in the material from this trench outnumber handaxes. The majority of both handaxes and cleavers are made on large flakes with minimal trimming of the primary surface, resulting in an average scar count of only 10.5 per specimen. Light-duty scrapers, *outils écaillés*, trimmed flakes, and punches are the only small tools present.

In many respects this industry closely resembles the early Acheulean of Bed II. The similarity is probably accentuated by the fact that in both industries the primary flakes on which the handaxes are made were struck from boulders and often retain areas of cortex.

The last Acheulean assemblage to be described is from the Masek Beds at FLK. This is the only site of the period known at Olduvai; it is in a channel that cuts down through the lower eolian tuff of the Masek Beds into the top of Bed IV and is overlain by the Norkilili Member. Part of a hominid mandible (H. 23), that has provisionally been attributed to *Homo erectus*, was also found at this site. The bifacial tools are exceptionally large and consist entirely of handaxes. They are made almost exclusively on pieces of tabular white quartzite and not on flakes, as is usual in other Acheulean assemblages at Olduvai. They show great refinement of trimming, but in view of the difference in size, it is not possible to compare the scar count with other series in which the bifaces are smaller. It is hoped that a formula will be worked out shortly that will enable surface area to be related to scar count. Small scrapers are particularly abundant in this industry and amount to 38.9 percent of the tools. Many are microlithic in size and are in marked contrast to the handaxes, some of which weigh up to three kilograms.

In the eight Acheulean occurrences briefly reviewed above, the ratio of cleavers to handaxes varies greatly (Figure 6). Only a single cleaver is known in the early Acheulean of Bed II; cleavers vary from

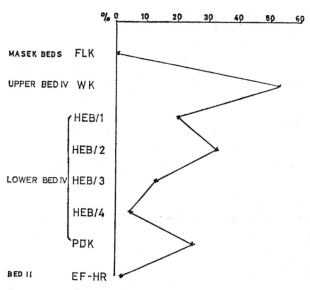

Figure 6.   Ratio of cleavers to handaxes in Acheulean assemblages

5 percent to 33 percent in lower Bed IV; they reach 53 percent in upper Bed IV, and none at all are known from the Masek Beds.

When the later occurrences of both the Developed Oldowan and Acheulean are considered, it is evident (Figure 4) that there is a marked proportional increase in small scrapers in both traditions. Small scrapers reach 47.3 percent of the tools in the Developed Oldowan from upper Bed IV, and they amount to 38.9 percent of the tools in the Acheulean from the Masek Beds. Choppers, on the other hand, progressively decrease. They amount to 51 percent of the Oldowan tools, but have dwindled to 4.4 percent in the Developed Oldowan C of upper Bed IV. In the Acheulean, they are likewise most abundant at EF-HR in Bed II and decrease in the later occurrences. As regards light-duty tools other than scrapers, *outils écaillés* and laterally trimmed flakes occur in both traditions, but the burins and awls of the Developed Oldowan are not known in any Acheulean industry.

Very little information concerning the living conditions was obtained during the excavations in Beds III, IV and the Masek Beds, although it is evident that there was a close connection between camp sites and water courses not only at Olduvai, but also elsewhere in East Africa.

R. L. Hay's interpretation of the paleogeography of the Olduvai region indicates that a permanent lake was in existence during Bed II times, although it was considerably smaller than the Bed I lake. During Bed IV it is likely that there were numerous streams and rivers, with small, seasonal lakes. If the rivers were comparable to the sand rivers found today in the semi-desert areas of East Africa, man may well have chosen to live in the river beds themselves during the dry season since water can often be obtained there by digging. Plentiful remains of catfish at nearly all sites in Bed IV indicate that freshwater rivers or lakes existed at the time, since catfish do not tolerate water with high salinity.

The Acheulean culture complex, as revealed at Olduvai, covered a time span of approximately one million years, possibly slightly more, if the lower Ndutu Beds also prove to contain Acheulean tools. Each of the Acheulean assemblages revealed at Olduvai has been typologically consistent within itself, but distinct from the rest. It can be stated that there is no progressive trend, in the manufacture of bifaces, from Bed II to the Masek Beds, nor does the degree of trimming become more refined in the later occurrences. Indeed, the Acheulean from WK, in upper Bed IV, stands closest to the early Acheulean from Bed II, in the technical simplicity displayed in the manufacture of the bifacial tools.

The Acheulean material now available for study suggests that the artifacts from each site or level were made by a group of people who had their own tradition in toolmaking and standard tool kit, from which they did not deviate to any appreciable extent. Such groups may, perhaps, have consisted of clans or tribes or even family units.

REFERENCES

BROCK, A., R. L. HAY, F. H. BROWN
    1972   Magnetic Stratigraphy of Olduvai Gorge and Ngorongoro, Tanzania. *Geological Society of America Abstracts*, page 457.
EVERNDEN, J. F., G. H. CURTIS
    1965   Potassium-argon dating of late Cenozoic rocks in East Africa and Italy. *Current Anthropology* 6:343–385.
HAY, R. L.
    1972   In *Excavations in Beds I and II, Olduvai Gorge*, volume three, by M. D. Leakey. Cambridge: Cambridge University Press.
KLEINDIENST, M. R.
    1962   Components of the East African Acheulean assemblage: an analytical approach. *Actes du IVe Congrès Panafricain de Préhistoire et de l'Etude du Quaternaire*, volume three. Edited by G. Mortelmans and J. Nenquin, Tervuren, 81–111.
LEAKEY, M. D.
    1967   "Preliminary survey of the cultural material from Beds I and II,

Olduvai Gorge, Tanzania," in *Background to evolution in Africa*. Edited by W. W. Bishop and J. D. Clark, 417–446. Chicago: University of Chicago Press.

1972 *Excavations in Beds I and II Olduvai Gorge*, volume three. Cambridge: Cambridge University Press.

LEAKEY, M. D., M. H. DAY

1971 Discovery of postcranial remains of *Homo erectus* and associated artifacts in Bed IV at Olduvai Gorge, Tanzania. *Nature* 232:380–383.

LEAKEY, M. D., R. L. HAY, *et al.*

1972 Stratigraphy, archaeology and age of the Ndutu and Naisiusiu Beds, Olduvai Gorge, Tanzania. *World Archaeology* 3(3):328–341.

Stratigraphy and Cultural Patterns in East Africa During the Middle Ranges of Pleistocene Time

GLYNN LL. ISAAC

> The White Rabbit put on his spectacles. "Where shall I begin, please, your Majesty?" he asked. "Begin at the beginning," the King said gravely, "and go on till you come to the end; then stop."
>
> LEWIS CARROLL, *Alice in Wonderland*

ABSTRACT

Geophysical measures of age have indicated that the segment of the East African sequence commonly designated as "Middle Pleistocene" dates back to about 1.6 million years. Since this is clearly out of line with usage in most other regions, adjustment of the boundary in Eastern Africa is recommended. The same dating evidence demonstrates that in East Africa several paleoanthropological phenomena normally associated with the "Middle Pleistocene" belong in fact in the Lower Pleistocene (Villafranchian equivalent). These are fossils classifiable as *Homo erectus* and artifact assemblages including true bifaces and designated as Acheulian. This in turn suggests that there may have been a prolonged Lower Pleistocene (Villafranchian) phase when hominid evolution and cultural development was largely confined to Africa and perhaps the warmer parts of Asia. The colonization

This review has been made possible by the friendship and cooperation that exists among those who work in Eastern Africa. Much of the material, and comprehension of it, springs from conversations and field visits in the company of such scholars as W. W. Bishop, J. Chavaillon, J. D. Clark, Glen Cole, Y. Coppens, F. C. Howell, C. M. Keller, M. R. Kleindienst, M. D. Leakey, R. E. Leakey, and H. V. Merrick.

Preparation of the review took place in part during the tenure of a Miller Research Professorship at the University of California, Berkeley. Research reported here includes work done with the aid of National Science Foundation GS 2344 and 28607 and also with the aid of grants from the Wenner-Gren Foundation.

Barbara Isaac has contributed immeasurably by discussion, drawings, and editorial help.

I was recruited into research in this field by the late Louis B. Leakey, who was effectively the founder of the researches reviewed here. I would hope that this summary can in a small way pay tribute to his memory.

of cool, temperate Eurasia may well not have commenced until after the last major paleomagnetic changeover at about seven hundred thousand years ago: that is during the very early Middle Pleistocene of European authors.

Pleistocene sedimentary formations in East Africa are often on a large scale in terms of area and thicknesses. They tend to be associated with tectonically formed basins along the Rift systems. This has created a rich and well-resolved record of cultural and biological evolution. However this record differs from the classic European sequences in as much as climatic fluctuations are less conspicuous. It has transpired that it is perfectly feasible to correlate amongst segments of the record without recourse to inferences regarding climatic events.

The problem with an account of the Middle Pleistocene is that it has no beginning and no end. The term is a label applied to an arbitrarily delimited segment of geological time. However, this vague period of past time has the singular interest that during its passage, hominid behavior underwent crucial, formative transformations. The origin of mankind dates to the late Tertiary; that is to say, the inception of the evolutionary divergence between men and apes took place in this time range. By two to three million years ago, hominids existed who were probably involved in all the most basic distinctive human behavior patterns; archeology documents the making of tools, hunting, food-sharing, and the organization of activities around a home base. (M. D. Leakey 1967, 1971a; Isaac 1969, 1971, 1972a.) Paleontological evidence suggests that the rate of growth and maturation was already greatly retarded relative to the apes (Mann 1968), and this, together with the archeological indicators, strongly suggests that linguistic communication was beginning to be important. However, in spite of similarities due to a common basic organization, there appear to be profound differences between the adaptation and behavior of very early hominids and that of the late Quaternary and recent peoples. Archeological manifestations of important differences include a great expansion of geographic distribution; an extension of the range of staple foods; great elaboration of the maximum level of technology and material culture; increasingly pronounced geographic differentiation; growing specificity of regional adaptation; and more and more substantial material traces of 'spiritual' and 'symbolic' activity. These contrasts presumably have common causation in a great increase of hominid capacity for culture. This greatly expanded cultural potential of mankind began to be really conspicuous only during the last glacial, and we do not yet know its limits. Clearly the evolutionary origins of the capabilities for culture must have preceded its flowering, and it is in this sense that the middle reaches of Pleistocene time constitute a formative period for human evolution. A clearer understanding of the chronology, biogeography, and paleoanthropology of the period thus has vital importance.

The foregoing constitutes a personal view of broad issues in the study of the Middle Pleistocene; let me now turn to the specific contribution of East Africa to this kind of research.[1]

As a region, East Africa has particular importance in that it provides the longest known record of occupation by hominids and their closest relatives. The fossil record itself like all others is discontinuous, but begins with twenty-million-year-old Miocene hominoid fossils, and extends with gaps to the present. During the past decade, the scale and scope of fieldwork have greatly expanded, and current research is steadily filling in many lacunae. A useful scattering of paleoanthropological data is now available covering the last three million years. More fragmentary finds only have been made from the time range three to fourteen million years, but fossiliferous formations of this age are now known and are being explored (Bishop 1971). The singular importance of the region for the study of human evolution stems from a combination of factors:

1. The region lies within the biogeographic zone which supported mankind's hominoid ancestors.

2. Environmental diversity, both at the local and the subregional level, is so great that no climatic fluctuations have been sufficient to obliterate any major biotope (Figure 1).

3. Earth movements associated with the rift valleys have repeatedly created basins of sedimentation in which fossils, and archeological sites, could be preserved with a minimum of disruption, prior to fossilization.

4. Continued earth movements break up and elevate a proportion of the ancient formations, exposing them to erosion and the natural exhumation of their contents.

5. Continual volcanic activity provides a basis for K/Ar dating and a geophysical chronology.

These factors did not operate equally all over East Africa. Figure 2 shows that the majority of important paleoanthropological sites are associated with the eastern or Gregory Rift Valley. Association with a rift valley is related to factors 3 and 4, but the fact that no definitely early material has yet been found in the Western Rift may reflect hominid preferences for the drier eastern zones rather than the wetter, more densely vegetated conditions which would seem to have prevailed in the west. Exploration in the west has not yet been sufficiently intense to establish this difference with certainty.

---

[1] For general reviews of the history of Pleistocene stratigraphic studies in East Africa, see Cooke (1958) and Bishop (1971).

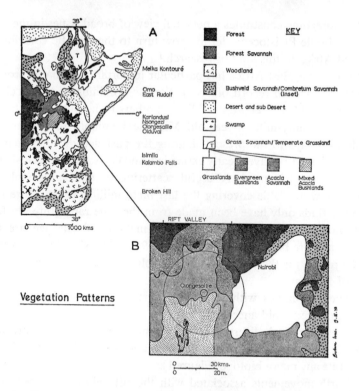

Vegetation Patterns

Figure 1.   Two maps of vegetation patterns in eastern Africa provide effective
illustration of the environmental diversity of the region, which includes the full
range from desert to tropical forest of both lowland and montane types. The patterns involved are complex mosaics, quite unlike the relatively clear-cut latitudinal
zones familiar in Europe. In "A," selected important Middle Pleistocene sites are
shown in relation to vegetation types. Apart from the absence of known sites in the
forested areas, there is little consistency between sites. The inset "B" is presented
as an example of vegetation patterning around one of these sites. It can be seen
that superimposed on the large scale pattern shown in "A" is a finer-grained
mosaic of local differentiation of vegetation and that within thirty kilometers of a
site such as Olorgesailie representatives of as many as five vegetation types may
occur. Most of the sites shown in "A" occur within regions of similar diversity.

   It seems probable that complex environmental situations of these kinds would
exert a buffering action on the effects of climatic changes on faunal elements such
as early men. The relative proportions of desert, savannah, and forest may have
fluctuated without any of these biotypes entirely disappearing even at a local level.
"A" is a slightly simplified rendering of part of Map 5 in Clark (1967b). "B" is
based on Trump (1967).

GEOLOGY

Time and Terminology

The term "Middle Pleistocene" is a geologic-time term. As such it ought to have the same significance all over the world. However, until very recently, time-equivalence between regions could only be judged from the evidence of related evolutionary changes, which can be time-transgressive, or from inferences concerning the nature, synchronization, and identity of climatic events. Because of the imprecisions and imperfections of these modes of determining relations, the term "Middle Pleistocene" has come to be applied to rather different, though overlapping, spans of time in different major areas. Terminological definition and usage is a matter which must eventually be sorted out in stratigraphic tribunals, but meanwhile it is important to recognize that the discrepancies exist. In any event, the increasing availability of geophysical dates is gradually resulting in the replacement of classifications of geologic-time, by measurements of it; so that terms such as "Middle Pleistocene" will eventually become obsolete.

"Middle Pleistocene" has acquired by association various archeological and human paleontological connotations. In Europe, this is the time span characterized *par excellence* by the Acheulian complex of industries, and by pre-Mousterian flake industries such as the "Clactonian" and "Tayacian." In default of other evidence, it has generally been assumed when comparable industries have been found elsewhere, that they too were of Middle Pleistocene age. In a like manner, a sense of association has developed between the taxon now known as *Homo erectus* and the Middle Pleistocene. Table 1 illustrates aspects of the term in question in East Africa.

It is apparent from this table that Olduvai Gorge occupies a pivotal position in East African Pleistocene stratigraphy and paleontology. At Olduvai, an apparent discontinuity in the composition of the fossil faunas has long been recognized (L. S. B. Leakey 1951, 1965) and has come to be known as "the faunal break." Within Bed II, an eolian tuff, the Lemuta Member (M. D. Leakey 1971a: 12, 18), appears to form the dividing line between a very diverse fauna with archaic elements such as deinotheres and calichotheres, and a later fauna which lacked some of the archaic and exotic elements. The earlier fauna has been rated as being a late Villafranchian equivalent, and is usually classified into the Lower Pleistocene. In addition to the faunal change, above the Lemuta Member new stone industries appear alongside con-

Table 1.   Usages of the term "Middle Pleistocene" in the classification of East African strata

	L. S. B. Leakey (1953)	Cooke (1963)	S. Cole (1963)	Bishop (1963)	Proposed as an outcome of this symposium
"Upper Pleistocene" — Gamblian	Gamblian Beds	"Early Gamblian Beds"	Gamblian / Kanjeran	Nsongezi MN	~ .125 million years
"Middle Pleistocene" — Kanjeran	Bed IV, Olorgesailie, Kanjera	Bed IV / Kanjera, Olorgesailie, Semiliki	Bed IV etc.	Bed IV, Kariandusi, Isimila, Olorgesailie, Paraa, Kanjera / Bed III	Isimila, Olorgesailie, Kariandusi, Kanjera etc.
— Kamasian	Bed III, Bed II	Bed III, Rawe Beds	Bed III / Kamasian	Bed III	Bruhnes / Matuyama
	Bed I	Bed II	Bed II	Bed II	Bed IV Olduvai
"Lower Pleistocene" — Kageran	(Kaiso)	Bed I	Bed I	Bed I	Beds I — Lower IV

tinuations of the older Oldowan kinds of tradition. Some of the new industries involve large percentages of bifaces and cleavers and can only be termed "Acheulian." (M. D. Leakey 1971a: 269–70.) These and other considerations have resulted in a tendency for strata above the Lemuta Member to be treated as Middle Pleistocene, and this Member is widely used as a regional boundary marker between the Lower and the Middle Pleistocene. As a result of the data assembled for this symposium it has become abundantly clear that previous notions of time equivalence were in error and the traditional East African usage is out of line. It is therefore proposed that from henceforth the boundary will be drawn to coincide with the Brunhes-Matuyama boundary.

The upper boundary of the Middle Pleistocene is almost impossible to define at present in East Africa. For convenience I will treat formations with Acheulian archeological contents and exclude those which

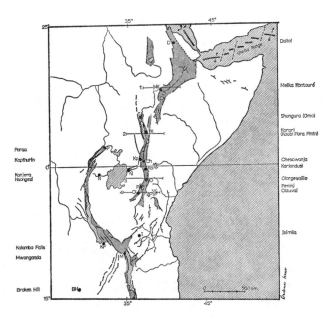

Figure 2a. Important "Lower" and "Middle Pleistocene" localities shown in relation to the Rift system of eastern Africa (base plot after McConnell 1972 and Baker, et al. 1972). Only sites from which complete artifact assemblages have been recovered by excavation are plotted. The tendency to association between these sites and the Rift system is clear, with Broken Hill and Nsongezi as exceptions. Surface collections of bifaces etc. of presumably Middle Pleistocene age have been made in many other localities (see Clark 1967b; overlays 12 and 13), but are not included in this review on account of the incompleteness of archeological and stratigraphic data.

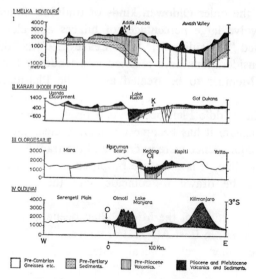

Figure 2b.   Four profiles across the Eastern Rift (after Baker, et al. 1972: Figures 13 and 17). Each profile selected is in the vicinity of one of the sites covered in this review. The high intensity of tectonism is apparent, as is the considerable thickness of sediments and volcanics which have accumulated in and around the graben.

have exclusively "Middle Stone Age" or "Later Stone Age" archeological contents. This probably coincides fairly closely with the "Last Interglacial" boundary ($\sim$. 125 million years) favored by participants at the symposium.

Geophysical Dates[2]

Table 2 and Figures 3 and 4 summarize available geophysical age data for the time range with which we are concerned. It can be seen that, in spite of gaps, the region is perhaps better endowed with such data than almost any other with fossiliferous Quaternary deposits. While the chronology depended solely on K/Ar dates, there was perhaps some legitimate grounds to doubt its validity; but now that paleomagnetic data provide an effectively independent check on the dating of several columns, the basics of the time scale indicated in the chart can be regarded as established.

The geophysical data indicate that the span of time hitherto regarded as Middle Pleistocene in East Africa actually extends from about

[2]   For full treatment of Lower Pleistocene dating, see Howell (1972); for an annotated list of dates associated with archeological evidence, see Isaac (1972a).

1,600,000 years ago to about 100,000 years ago. This does not mean that the time represented by the usage of the term Middle Pleistocene elsewhere has a comparable magnitude; this problem is taken up in the concluding comparative section.

Stratigraphy and Intraregional Correlations[3]

Figure 3 presents a graphic summary of estimated time relations between the various paleoanthropologically important Middle Pleistocene sedimentary formations in eastern Africa. The chart is based on a combination of geophysical, paleontological, and stratigraphic information. It seems reasonably clear that the available stock of excavated evidence and stratigraphically controlled surface finds are scattered through the vast time span. Some formations such as Koobi Fora Upper Member, Olduvai, Olorgesailie, or Isimila may themselves provide quasi-continuous sequences spanning several hundred thousand years; but the sequence as a whole need not be complete or fully representative. Certainly the available sample of paleoanthropological data is minute when one considers the magnitude of the space-time continuum which is being studied (Isaac 1972a: Figure 3; 1972b: 180).

Faulting and Tectonics

As Figure 2 shows, the majority of paleoanthropologically important formations in East Africa are associated with the zones of crystal deformation known as the Rift System. Faulting and volcanic eruption began to be intensified during the mid-Tertiary (Miocene) and continued through the entire Pleistocene (Bishop 1971; Baker, Mohr, and Williams 1972). Displacements occurring during or since the Middle Pleistocene have often been profound. For example, at Olduvai the cumulative displacement on the faults which created the Bal Bal depression amounts to two hundred meters (Hay 1971, and personal communication). At Natron the Peninj Group of Middle Pleistocene sediments have in places been cut by faults with a throw of more than three hundred meters (Isaac 1967). One edge of the former Olorgesailie

[3] The attention of this essay is narrowly focused on fossiliferous or artifact-bearing stratigraphic sections. It ignores a great deal of basic geological research which has been done in the past decade on Pleistocene volcanic stratigraphy and tectonics. For reviews covering these topics, see Baker, Mohr, and William (1972); McCall, Baker, and Walsh (1967); Baker and Wohlenberg (1971); McConnell (1972).

Table 2. A list of geophysical age determinations relevant to the late Lower and Middle Pleistocene chronology of East Africa

x 10^6 years	Lab. Number or Reference	Formation	Stratum	Association with Paleoanthropological evidence	Source
				EARLY UPPER PLEISTOCENE	
0.042 ± .002	GRN 3237 C^{14}	Kalambo Falls	MKamba Member	"Sangoan" Horizon	Clark 1969
0.042 ± .003	L 399 C C^{14}				
0.043 ± .003	L 399 C C^{14}				
> 0.052	GRN 1396 C^{14}	Kalambo Falls	MKamba Member	"Late Acheulian" Horizon	Clark 1969
> 0.060	GRN 2644 C^{14}				
> 0.19	Racemisation date by Bada				Clark, this volume
~ 0.13	Lamont Th/Ur	Kibish Formation	Member 1	Three Hominid crania	Butzer, et al. 1969
				"MIDDLE PLEISTOCENE"	
~ 0.2	Mean of three Th/Ur	Dallol (Afar)	Coral reef	One biface and several flakes	Roubet 1969
0.23	Cambridge K/Ar	Baringo sequence	Baringo trachyte	BELOW beds with mandible and industry	Bishop 1971
0.26	Th/Ur on bone	Isimila Beds	Sands 4	"Acheulian industry"	Howell, et al. 1972
0.486 ±	B 1965 K/Ar	Olorgesailie Formation	Member 4	"Acheulian industry"	Evernden and Curtis 1965; Miller 1967
0.425 ± .009			Member 10	Varied "Acheulian" industries	
(1.45, 1.64, 2.9)^a					
0.928	B 695	Kariandusi Beds		"Acheulian" industry	Evernden and Curtis 1965
0.946	B 1035				
1.1	B 1061				
(8.1)	B 415				

Age	Sample	Unit	Formation	Relationship	Reference
1.33 ± 0.5 1.38 ± 0.1	B 2410 B 2589	Basalt flow	Moinik Formation (Peninj Group)	OVER an early Acheulian industry	Isaac and Curtis 1974
2.27 ± 0.06 1.55 1.21 ± .09 1.21 ± .24 0.97 0.96 ± .14	B 1754 R B 1754 B 2646 B 2832 R B 2578 B 2382	WaMbugu Basalt with normal polarity	Humbu Formation (Peninj Group)	UNDER an early Acheulian industry, OVER an australopithecine mandible	Isaac and Curtis 1974
≥ 1.4	F-M	Karari Tuff with reversed polarity	Koobi Fora Formation (Upper Member)	OVER an industry with heavy-duty scrapers and some bifaces	Fitch and Miller, personal communication
				LOWER PLEISTOCENE	
1.4 — 1.7	F-M	Koobi Fora Tuff with reversed polarity	Koobi Fora Formation (Upper Member)	OVER hominid fossils	Fitch and Miller, personal communication
1.81 ± .09 1.87 ± .09	LKA 2187 LKA 2085	Tuff I 2	Shungura Formation		
1.93 ± .10	LKA 9	Tuff G	Shungura Formation	Interstratified with hominid fossils and artifacts	Brown 1972
1.99 ± 1.10 2.06 ± .10	LKA 11 LKA 21	Tuff F	Shungura Formation		
1.786 ± .029	Mean of nine dates	Bed I, Tuff B	Olduvai Gorge		
1.82 ± .13	Mean of thirty-five dates	Bed I, including Tuff I B and lava flow	Olduvai Gorge	Interstratified with artifacts and hominids	Curtis and Hay 1972

a Ages shown in parentheses are incompatible with other evidence regarding the regional sequence.

lake basin has been faulted and warped down three hundred meters below the topographic level where it could form a barrier. Deformation on a similar scale has certainly occurred at Baringo (Kapthurin) and in the Rudolf basin. A complex history of warping and drainage reversal has been demonstrated for the Kagera Valley at Nsongezi (Bishop 1969). In fact, the only formations under consideration in this essay for which tectonic control and deformation are not known to have been important are the Isimila Formation and the Kalambo Falls Formation. Even in these cases the possibility of subtle effects cannot be eliminated.

Fault dislocations and tectonic deformation have sometimes been treated as "events" and used for correlation from one locality to another within the region. As stratigraphy and chronology have been established in more and more detail, it has become clear that faulting is a process, not an event. Rates and intensities vary widely from site to site and tectonics cannot be used for establishing time lines or correlations except with great caution.

Mammal Faunas

The last comprehensive review of data on East African faunal assemblages was that of Cooke (1963). New discoveries and taxonomic revisions made since then certainly necessitate re-examination. In the meantime it is still perhaps possible to distinguish some four vaguely perceived divisions which can be designated as follows (cf. Bishop and Clark 1967; Maglio, this volume):

3. Late Quaternary (formerly 'Gamblian')
   — very poorly known.
2. "Middle Pleistocene" (1.0–.10? m.y.)
   — Olduvai Bed IV, Olorgesailie, Kanjera, etc.
1b. Early Pleistocene (1.5–1.0 m.y.)
   — Olduvai Bed II, Peninj, *Loxodonta africana* zone at East Rudolf.
1a. Early Pleistocene (2.0–1.5 m.y.)
   — Olduvai Bed I, *Metridiochoerus andrewsi* zone at East Rudolf.

If a site yields a fauna but no geophysical dating evidence, it can probably be assigned with reasonable confidence to one of these gross divisions, but in the present state of knowledge, greater precision is difficult.

There are various mammal groups that show pronounced evolution-

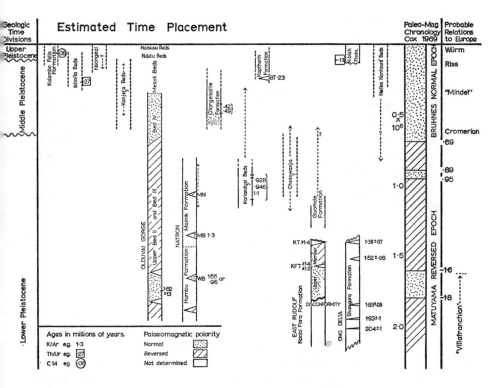

Figure 3. A correlation diagram showing inferred time relationships and estimated dates for important fossiliferous Middle Pleistocene formations in eastern Africa. This diagram is based on a combination of radiometric age determinations (Table 1), paleomagnetic data, and faunal correlations (Cooke 1963; Cooke and Maglio 1972). Uncertainty regarding dating is shown by dotted lines and arrows. The figure has been drawn to reflect the consensus of opinion that the boundary should be moved up to the Bruhnes-Matuyama polarity changeover.

ary changes during the relevant time span. The developmental stages of elephants have been worked out (Maglio 1973) and can be used as chronological indicators. The suids (Cooke and Maglio 1972) and such primate genera as *Simopithecus* (Meave Leakey, personal communication) may also prove useful in this regard.

Paleoclimate and Paleoenvironment

Until the beginning of the last decade, it was customary in East Africa, as elsewhere, to attempt to identify major climatic fluctuations from the lithology and fossil contents of each Quaternary sedimentary formation.

Then, following critical reviews by Cooke (1958), Flint (1959a, 1959b) and others, the practice fell into abeyance. It has become recognized that the basic control on sedimentation in this region has been tectonic. Under these circumstances climatic change cannot be inferred until tectonic factors have been eliminated.

The modern pattern of climatic zonation in East Africa appears to be reflected throughout Late Cenozoic sediments and this also suggests limits for the magnitude of past change. Thus, there exists today a marked contrast between the hydrographic regimes of the eastern and the western Rifts; the lake basins of the latter are normally filled to an overflow level, and they drain ultimately into major river systems such as the Nile or the Congo (Figure 2). By contrast, the eastern Rift Valley lake basins tend to support isolated pools of saline water which fluctuate and only occasionally overflow. The patterns of Pleistocene sedimentation so far reported from each Rift imply that this contrast is one of long standing. There is no evidence of any PROLONGED period of Quaternary time when the eastern Rift Valley was occupied by larger and more stable lakes than those of today, nor is there clear evidence of a time when all the lakes in either Rift Valley were dried up.

These comments apply to the Middle Pleistocene; there is abundant evidence that during the Upper Pleistocene and early Holocene there were several short period and high amplitude fluctuations in lake levels along the Gregory Rift. An early Holocene fluctuation has been particularly well documented and dated and is known to have been synchronous all along the Rift and to have been out of phase with either the glacial maximum or the climatic optimum (Butzer, Isaac, et al. 1972). It is quite possible that such fluctuations characterized Middle Pleistocene times, but as yet they have only been identified in a few instances. For example, there is clear evidence of a short term expansion of the proto-Natron lake during Humbu Formation times (Isaac 1967: 242–243), and at Olduvai, Hay has demonstrated fluctuations in the size of the saline lake and in the intensity of eolian sediment transport (Hay 1971). However, the totality of evidence at Olduvai is unambiguous; there were oscillations from more dry to less dry, but these were never of such an amplitude as to take the basin out of a semi-arid hydrological regime (Hay 1967a, 1967b, 1971).

In the present state of knowledge, mid-Pleistocene climatic change in East Africa cannot be used as a basis either for internal or external correlations, nor can it readily be invoked in relation to cultural or evolutionary change. One suspects that the diversity of zones within the region, and the complexity of the microenvironmental mosaic within the zones, have formed a buffer against overly drastic effects by climatic fluctuations on biogeography (see Figure 1).

HOMINID PALEONTOLOGY

Figure 4 shows that East Africa has yielded numerous hominid fossils and that these are scattered through the full range of Quaternary time. However, the evolutionary pattern indicated by these fossils is still the subject of lively debate. In the divergent opinions of various scholars,

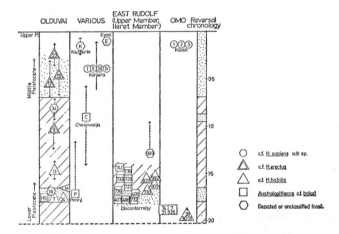

Figure 4. Diagrammatic representation of the time distribution of late Lower and Middle Pleistocene hominid fossils from East Africa. Selected relatively complete or diagnostic specimens only are shown for Olduvai, Koobi Fora, and Shungura. The classificatory symbols relate to the informal groupings discussed in the text rather than to rigorously defined formal taxonomic categories. Reversal chronology zones are shown along the right hand margin as in Figure 3.

the numbers of distinct "lineages" represented range from one to three or even more. At a conversational level, the following sets are often implicitly or explicitly distinguished:
1. "Robust australopithecines," e.g. Olduvai hominid 5 (*"Zinjanthropus"*).
2. "Early Homo," often termed *"H. habilis"*: early subset, e.g. Olduvai hominids 7 and 24; relatively advanced later subset, e.g. Olduvai hominid 13, E.R. 992. For the early subset there is some debate regarding the degree of distinctness vis-à-vis *A. africanus*.

3.   *Homo* cf. *erectus,* notably Olduvai hominids 9, 28 and 12.

4.   *Homo* cf. *sapiens,* various later Middle Pleistocene fossils such as the Kanjera crania, the three Omo (Kibish) skulls. These fossils are variously classified in relation to subspecific divisions and stages of *H. sapiens.* Classifications of the fossils into these informal divisions is shown on the figure.

Proponents of the one lineage viewpoint (e.g. Wolpoff 1971; Brace 1967) treat the marked contrast between robust and contemporaneous non-robust early Quaternary fossils as having been due either to subspecific, racial differentiation or to pronounced sexual dimorphism.

For many other workers, perhaps a majority, the robust australopithecine fossils appear as representatives of at least one separate genetic system, with distinctive adaptations. This divergent lineage, if such it was, seems to have become extinct during the early Middle Pleistocene (L. S. B. Leakey 1966; Pilbeam 1970; Robinson 1972; Tobias 1972). Among those who recognize the robust australopithecines as an extinct lineage, opinion is divided on how many other lineages there are. For some authorities, the *Homo erectus* fossils of East Africa, and those of East Asia, represent a separate lineage which died out without contributing significantly to the ancestry of modern man. It is sometimes considered that this lineage may have originated elsewhere and have been intrusive into East Africa (e.g. M. D. Leakey 1971a: 272–273). Other authorities would consider that given the time and space involved, the diversity of Middle Pleistocene fossils could perfectly well have arisen within a single genetic system (= evolving species) as a result of drift and subspecific, regional differentiation. In this view, differences arise both from local evolution and from the kaleidoscopic change caused by intermittent migration and gene diffusion.[4]

There is as yet no clear outcome to this debate and the details of evidence and argument lie outside the competence and ambitions of this paper. However, two things emerge which are of particular importance for the general review attempted here:

1.   There may have been two or more coexistent species of toolmaking hominids during part of the Middle Pleistocene. We have to contemplate the possible effects of this on the patterning of archeological traces of economy and material cultures.

2.   At the outset of the period under review there was a highly varied

---

[4]   Recent discoveries have been made at East Rudolf of hominid fossils for the 2.5 to 3 million year time range. These do not fit into any of the categories listed above and may require extensive modifications to ideas about phylogenetic relations (R. E. Leakey and Wood i.p.).

suite of hominids. None of these is known to have had a cranial capacity larger than about 800 cubic centimeters. One and a half million years later, at the end of the period, variation was reduced to a level perhaps comparable with that seen in mankind today, and cranial capacities had risen by 50 to 100 percent.

ARCHEOLOGY[5]

Archeological research in East Africa has two principal directions: first, there are field and excavation studies of the traces of hominid diet, land use, and campsite patterning. These can conveniently be termed studies of activities. Second, there are laboratory studies of artifact morphology, typology, assemblage composition, etc. While, in my view, the activity evidence has greater relevance for understanding human evolution, at the present time, the larger volume of published research results and the most active debates relate to artifact studies. As might be expected, the two kinds of study overlap when questions such as the role of artifacts in economy and adaptation are discussed — or when the implications of diversity among artifact assemblages are considered in regard to the kinds of social and cultural systems which may have existed (see below, and M. D. Leakey 1971a: 269–275; Isaac 1969, 1972b).

The archeological traces of Middle Pleistocene ways of life may be listed as follows:

1. Patterns of site locations in relation to paleogeography.
2. Characteristics of sites: size, density, and disposition of materials.
3. Composition of food, refuse, and excreta; currently mainly bone refuse, but potentially also plant remains and organic chemical residues.
4. Derivation of exotic materials from more or less remote sources.

Accumulation of these kinds of data began effectively with Mary Leakey's excavations of occupation sites at Olorgesailie in 1943 (see Isaac 1972b: 171–172 for a brief history of this research movement). While we have as yet only a small fraction of the volume of evidence

[5] The last comprehensive reviews of Middle Pleistocene archeology appeared ten years ago (Kleindienst 1961; Howell and Clark 1963). Since that time, the Olduvai report (M. D. Leakey 1971a) has profoundly altered the situation, both with regard to information and interpretation. Other new research includes the discovery and excavation of Middle Pleistocene sites at Natron (Peninj), Melka Kontouré, Kapthurin (Baringo), and East Rudolf, as well as more detailed work at Olorgesailie, Isimila, Nsongezi, and Olduvai. The researches at Melka Kontouré are not represented in this report to a degree commensurate with their importance.

we need, we can perhaps start to address ourselves to some of the basic questions.

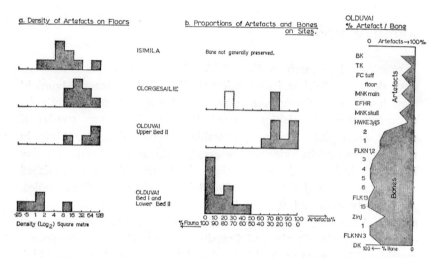

Figure 5 (a, b, c).   Comparative data on the density of artifacts on East African occupation sites and on the proportion of artifacts to bone fragments

(a)   Density per square meter of all artifacts including debitage, but excluding manuports.

(b)   Percentage proportion of artifacts and bone.

$$(\% \text{ Artifacts} = \frac{n \text{ Artifacts}}{n \text{ Artifacts} + n \text{ Bones}} \times 100. \quad \% \text{ Bone} = 100 - \% \text{ Artifacts.})$$

(c)   Changing proportions of artifacts and bones in the Olduvai Beds I and II sequence. Olduvai data from tables in M. D. Leakey (1971a).

In (a) densities have only been computed for occurrences where the encasing deposits are less than six inches (fifteen centimeters thick), i.e. "floors." The Olorgesailie data is from Isaac (1968b); Isimila from Kleindienst (1961).

Note: The high proportion of bone to artifacts at two Olorgesailie sites is due to the presence of very numerous small splinters (one gram average) and is therefore misleading.

Subsistence and Ecology

In man, as in other animals, diet and the means of acquiring food constitute the cornerstone of adaptation. Questions to which we would. like an answer for East Africa and all other regions include how much variation there was in hominid subsistence patterns during the Middle Pleistocene. And then if we begin to perceive variety, can any of the variants be related to such other major variables as time, hominid taxonomy, artifact assemblage type, or geographic zonation? Or alternatively, can variety be related to such fine grained variables as seasons or microenvironments?

I have recently reviewed aspects of the East African evidence for the development of human subsistence patterns and need not repeat my arguments or the details of the evidence (Isaac 1971). However, since that review the publication of Mary Leakey's volume on Olduvai has provided a crucial corpus of fresh numerical data (M. D. Leakey 1971a). Figures 5 and 6 and Table 4 show aspects of these data in relation to other sites. Mary Leakey's current work on Beds III and IV at Olduvai will clearly continue to be the major source of new data.

The figures and tables make it clear that Lower and Middle Pleistocene sites in East Africa vary greatly in the character and quantity of bone-food refuse which they contain. The diversity makes generalization difficult, but the variety itself may be an important feature in its own right, rather than merely a complication. I have argued elsewhere (Isaac 1971, 1972a) that the wide range of densities of bone refuse may reflect varied and opportunistic subsistence patterns of the kind recorded for recent tropical hunter-gatherers. (See papers by Lee, Turnbull, and Woodburn in Lee and DeVore 1968.) Presumably, in spite of its archeological invisibility, gathered vegetable foods were always important as staples or as crucial supplements to meat obtained by hunting.

In spite of the complexity of the data, certain changes through time can perhaps be discerned. East Africa's contribution to the history of human subsistence can be summarized as follows:

Lower Pleistocene

During the period from 2.5 to 1.5 million years B.P., some hominids were effective in acquiring meat, almost certainly by hunting at least in part. The full size range of ungulate and other fauna was exploited. The evolutionary processes by which hominids intensified a taste for meat and developed skill in acquiring it must date to the Tertiary. Indeed, the common ancestors of hominids and chimpanzees may well have been opportunistically carnivorous as are modern chimps (Van Lawick-Goodall 1971: 181–194; Geza 1973). In spite of its popularity in general accounts, there is at present no archeological evidence for a phase of hominid behavior involving the consumption only of small

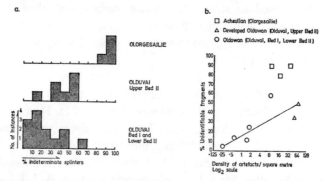

Figure 6 (a, b).   (a) Frequency distributions for the percentages of bone splinters which are indeterminate with regard both to body part and to taxon. This percentage is proportional to the intensity with which the bone has been smashed and/or weathered.

(b) Plot showing an apparent relationship between percentage of indeterminate bone and the density of artifacts. These two attributes may conceivably be interrelated as aspects of "intensity" of usage of the sites. The line shown joins extreme points and is not a regression line. Data from M. D. Leakey (1971a) and Isaac (1968b).

game and young animals. The early sites contain a varied series of ungulate and pachyderm remains.

Also well-established by the Lower Pleistocene was the distinctively human characteristic of carrying meat back to a home base — presumably for the purpose of sharing it. This last practice is a cornerstone in the development of human behavior and created evolutionary possibilities otherwise paralleled only in the social insects.

Lower and Middle Pleistocene Compared

There is almost complete overlap between the character of bone-food refuse accumulations in these two periods; but some differences may prove significant:

1.   Mary Leakey detects a slight rise in the relative proportion of very large mammals in the bone refuse of the later Lower Pleistocene sites at Olduvai (M. D. Leakey 1971a: 260).

2.   Prior to the late Lower Pleistocene there are no sites yet known that are characterized by the presence of remains of numerous individuals of a single species of gregarious animal. Examples of this phenomenon in East Africa include the following:

a.   Olduvai BK *Pelorovis*, a large bovine (L. S. B. Leakey 1957).

b. Olduvai SHK *Antidorcas (Phenacotragus) recki*, a gazelle (M. D. Leakey 1971a, and personal communication).
c. Olorgesailie DE/89 B *Simopithecus oswaldi*, a large gelada-type baboon (Isaac 1968a, 1971).

It is thought that this kind of bone refuse pattern may be indicative of organized cooperative hunting. More examples of this kind are known also in European Middle Pleistocene sites such as Torralba and Ambrona (Howell 1966). The pattern becomes prominent in late Quaternary sites of some regions (e.g. Saltzgitter-Lebenstedt, Molodova, Pincevint, Solutré, Dolni Vistonice, Kostienki, etc.).
3. There are indications that animal bones were more intensively smashed and comminuted at Middle Pleistocene sites than at Lower Pleistocene sites. This is best discerned in the ratio of identifiable to unidentifiable specimens (M. D. Leakey 1971a: Table 3; Figure 6a in this paper). There are signs that the degree of comminution of bone and gross artifact density are correlated (Figure 6b), and both might be taken as indicative of increasing intensity of site usage (i.e. duration of stay and/or frequency of reoccupation).

Middle and Upper Pleistocene Compared

Data on the later periods in East Africa are sporadic and, in general, are not comparable to those of the early periods, so a fair comparison is impracticable. However, it is apparent that Upper Pleistocene sites in Africa are seldom characterized by the spectacular bone concentrations familiar in contemporary European sites. There are hints in East Africa of a broadening of the spectrum of subsistence economies. Thus, the oldest sites where very intensive collections of aquatic foods, such as fish and shellfish, can be specifically documented are late Quaternary sites. However, Mary Leakey informs me that the turtle and fish remains at such Olduvai sites as FLK NN I, TK IV, or PLK may well represent hominid food refuse.

The Possible Influence of "Big Game Hunting" on Human Evolution

Several general works on human evolution have advanced the view that the inception of big game hunting had a decisive influence on the selection pressures channeling genetic change (e.g. Campbell 1966; Pfeiffer

1969). In a sense, these works imply that big game hunting is the key to understanding the transformation in human cultural capacity, consideration of which is one of our concerns here. It should be apparent from the foregoing brief review that the East African evidence is not compatible with this view in its simplest form. The Lower Pleistocene does not emerge as a small game hunting stage — nor is the contrast between Lower and Middle Pleistocene that marked. These are questions which will be taken up again in the concluding sections which compare East Africa with other regions. (For a general discussion of the possible influence of "hunting" on human evolution see Washburn and Lancaster 1968.)

Site Locations in Relation to Paleoenvironments

There is mounting awareness among archeologists that patterns of site location can be an important indicator of human ecology and land use. Table 3 provides a rather oversimplified summary of information from East Africa. Interpretation of the data is difficult; we clearly have a sample which is highly biased in as much as the evidence is drawn entirely from inside sedimentary basins (lacustrine and fluvial, etc.), and we lack comparable documentation of site density and location in the hills and uplands outside zones of deposition. Within the basins hitherto surveyed, there is a marked tendency for Acheulian and other Middle Pleistocene sites to be preferentially located along the courses and banks of seasonal water stream beds (Isaac 1966a; M. D. Leakey 1971a: 259). In some basins (e.g. Olorgesailie), it actually appears that the Acheulians avoided the margins of the lake. At one stage in research it appeared that very early Pleistocene sites, then known only at Olduvai, differed from Middle Pleistocene sites by being predominantly situated on lake margin flood plains. However, the discovery of Lower Pleistocene sites at Koobi Fora, and others at the Omo which are associated with channel situations, suggests that the site preference patterns of the two periods overlap more extensively (Isaac 1972c; Merrick, et al. i.p.).

The reasons for selective use of seasonal stream beds for placing a base camp are probably varied, but a crucial set of factors probably stems from the fact that such channels commonly support dense lines of trees fingering out into the floodplain grassland. The trees provide among other things shade, cover, something to climb as a retreat, and a source of fruits. In some senses it might be argued that the practice of using camps situated along tree-lined streams represents a way in which evolving hominids retained a base in the arboreal environment

Table 3.   Topographic context of Pleistocene sites in East Africa

	Lacustrine associations		Riverine associations — floodplain and alluvial fans		Basin margins	Hills and plateaus
	Floodplain, marsh, and mudflats	Stream channels near margin	In or near channels	On flood plain soils		
Early Lower Pleistocene	Olduvai (1) DK FLKNN FLK FLKN HWKE 1 2	Koobi Fora (2) Koobi Fora FxJj 1 3 4 10	Omo (3)	FtJj 1 Omo	FtJj 2 No records (? lack of preservation)	Virtually none known: circumstances for preservation rare or nonexistent
Later Lower Pleistocene	Olduvai FC West SHK annex MNK main	(Ileret) FwJj 1 Olduvai SHK main	Olduvai EF-HR CK Elephant K Peninj RHS (4) MHS Koobi Fora FxJj 16 FxJj 18	Koobi Fora FxJj 11 FxJj 20	Ditto?	
Middle Pleistocene	Olorgesailie three sites	Olorgesailie twelve sites Olduvai WK (Playa)	Isimila (6) various K 13 sands Kalambo (7) (all Acheulian occurrences) Melka Kontouré (8) (most major concentrations)	Isimila various K 13 silty clay Baringo (9) (LHR)?	Olorgesailie four sites	? Broken (10) Hill

Sources: (1) Hay 1971; (2) Isaac, et al. 1971, and unpublished; (3) Merrick, et al. i.p.; (4) Isaac 1967, 1972c; (5) Isaac 1968a, 1968b; (6) Howell, et al. 1962; Hansen and Keller 1971; Isimila is an "mbuga" that is to say a swampy, choked valley with minimal current action; (7) Clark 1969; (8) Chavaillon 1967, 1971; (9) M. C. Leakey, et al. 1969; (10) Clark 1959.

of the ancestral hominoids, while infiltrating savannah country and exploiting more varied resources.

Site Sizes

At present, in East Africa and many other regions it appears that where the sizes of individual hunter-gatherer camps can be discerned, they are of much the same magnitude regardless of age. However, very few sites, as yet, have been excavated sufficiently completely for rigorous measurement (e.g. Olduvai FLK I). The most notable exceptions are the Upper Pleistocene mammoth hunting stations of eastern Europe (Klima 1962). Other Pleistocene sites seem generally to be of a size that would be appropriate for ten to fifty persons. Some larger accumulations of material occur, but these are suspected to be geologically

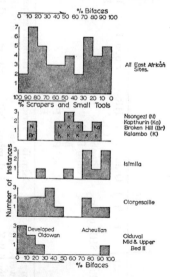

Figure 7.   Frequency distributions for the relative proportions of "bifaces" (large cutting tools) versus light duty scrapers and other small tools. These two major tool families have been treated here in the manner of binomial proportions, i.e.

$$\% \text{ Bifaces} = \frac{n \text{ Bifaces}}{n \text{ Bifaces} + n \text{ small Tools}} \times 100.$$

% small Tools = 100 — % Bifaces.

The top frame shows the overall distribution for forty-one assemblages for which data are available. Other frames show distributions separately for groups of sites. Some sets show bimodality of the kind used by M. D. Leakey as part of the basis for inferring separate Developed Oldowan and Acheulian cultures. Others do not. The overall distribution could be regarded either as weakley bimodal or as non-modal. Data from M. D. Leakey (1971a), Kleindienst (1961), Clark (1964), Cole (1967), M. C. Leakey, et al. (1969) and Isaac (1968b).

disturbed or, in effect, partially overlapping palimpsests of successive occupations, the aggregate size of which therefore does not reflect the size of the occupying group. While there may have been fluctuations or progressive changes in either the usual or the maximum sizes of social groups, archeology does not document this in a way that can usefully be involved in accounts of the formative processes of Middle Pleistocene evolution.

Inferences from Assemblages of Artifacts

As in the case of the hominid fossils, there is marked variability among Middle Pleistocene assemblages of artifacts which have been recovered by excavation. The interpretation of the diversity of tool kits has proved no less controversial than that of the hominid fossils. In fact, East Africa has been a testing ground for new methods of research into Lower Paleolithic archeology. Variation between assemblages is complex and involves both differences in the presence and percentage of typological categories and differences in the modal morphology of the same category in different assemblages. Figures 7 and 8 and Table 5

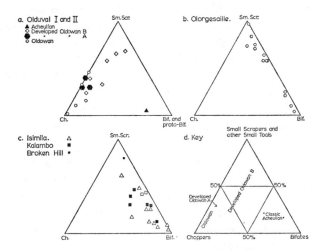

Figure 8. As an illustration of aspects of variation among East African assemblages ternary diagrams are presented showing the relative proportions of (1) bifaces, (2) small scrapers and other small tools, and (3) choppers. Each of these tool families has been regarded by some or all authors as having significance in the taxonomy of artifact assemblages. Mary Leakey's culture-historic entities are indicated in (a) and (c). As in Figure 7 contrasts between the extremes are great, but clear-cut divisions are hard to detect. For further data on variability, see Table 5, and Isaac (1972b). Data from the same sources as for Figure 7.

have been included to provide illustration of aspects of the situation.

The principal axis of variation which has been perceived by most workers concerns the relative proportions of large Acheulian tools, such as handaxes and cleavers, to small scrapers, awls, and other forms which are not specifically Acheulian. The observed range of proportion of bifaces extends from 0 to 95 percent (Figure 7). The frequency distribution of this index is clearly not unimodal; that is, there is no normal or usual value. It is not yet clear whether the frequency distribution is really bimodal as now appears or whether it could more usefully be described as nonmodal. Hitherto, it has proved impossible to demonstrate any clear time or space correlates for the two poles of this variable and many others. Thus, sites in the same sedimentary basin which are close to being contemporaneous may show widely different values for these variables (Figure 7). This constitutes an "anomaly" in as much as the observations deviate from the expectation of linear evolution which arose in the early days of Paleolithic archeology. Confronted with this dilemma, archeologists have experimented with explanations of three different kinds:

1.   Variants can be explained as the products of two or more different cultural systems; for instance, one in which bifaces dominate the equipment and the other in which choppers, spheroids, and small scrapers predominate. Each of these material culture systems, it is argued, may have been associated with a separate hominid species, and the differences may have remained in existence over hundreds of thousands of years, while the hominid species themselves coexisted. This view has been most compellingly advanced by M. D. Leakey (1971a: 262–275). She has termed the variants "Acheulian" and "Developed Oldowan," respectively, and tentatively associates them with *Homo erectus* and *Homo habilis*, respectively.

2.   Differences in activity have also been advanced as a line of explanation; that is, it argued that different tool kits are appropriate in differing situations and that, therefore, one cultural system can be expected to generate a wide diversity of assemblages. Since there would have been long-term continuity in such basic activities as making spears, butchering carcasses, or gathering plant food, the spectrum of variation can be expected to persist and to lack correlation with time or macrogeography. There have been several exponents of activities as a complete or partial explanation of variation (Clark 1959, 1970; Kleindienst 1961; Howell and Clark 1963; Isaac 1969: 16; Binford 1972).

3.   There exists also the possibility that there is a wide degree of lati-

Table 4. Relative abundance of bifaces and of bone refuse

	Abundant bone		Moderate quantities of bone	Low density of well preserved bone	Bone not well preserved
	Butchery sites	*Home base*			
Bifaces dominant > 50 percent bifaces	?? Olorgesailie Hippo	Olorgesailie DE/89 B ?←Ternifine		Olorgesailie H/6 A, Meng, Mid Olduvai EF–HR Peninj RHS ?, MHS ? Melka Kontouré various Cave of Hearths Sidi Zin 1, 2, and 3 Latamne	Isimila K 19, LH 15, J 12, K 6, J 6–7 Lower, K 14, H9–J8, J6–7 upper Kalambo all sites Kapthurin
Intermediate (25 to 50 percent)			Olorgesailie DE/89 A, H/9 A, M 10 Tr Tr Olduvai WK		Isimila K 18
Bifaces subordinate < 25 percent bifaces	Mwanganda Torralba Ambrona upper lower Olduvai SHK channel	?←Olduvai BK Olorgesailie I 3 ←Olduvai SHK annex →	Olduvai FC tuff, MNK Isimila H 20–21 Terra Amata ——→?	Olduvai TK upper, TK lower FC occupation	Broken Hill

tude in the morphological configuration of stone tool assemblages, which will none the less be adaptive. If this is so, then it is also possible that a significant part of the observed variation is of a stochastic or "random walk" nature, and will lack correlation with major divisions of time and space (Isaac 1968b; 1969: 19; 1972b: 185). This is, in a sense, a nonexplanation: it must be treated as a null hypothesis, acceptable only in the absence of evidence for other kinds of patterns.

Binford (1972) has performed a multivariate factor analysis on a modified version of published percentage tables for East African Acheulian assemblages. He argues in this case, as he has done in his experiments with Mousterian assemblages (Binford and Binford 1966, 1969), that sets of artifact categories which covary represent toolkits which had a tendency to be preferentially used for specific tasks or activities. This is an interesting proposition, but it still requires to be tested against independent evidence of the activities; that is, by the demonstration of regularities in the relationship between toolkits (covariant sets of categories) and their context (season, microenvironmental location, food refuse characteristics, site size, etc.).

The most definite suggestion made by Binford constitutes a development of a point previously made by J. Desmond Clark; namely, that small scrapers and other small tools are much more likely to be found in association with traces of butchering large animals than are bifaces and other large cutting tools (Clark and Haynes 1969). Binford's analysis confirms the previous impression that the frequency of these two families of tools tends to vary inversely (see Figure 7). Binford goes on to suggest that handaxes, bifacial knives, etc., may have been preferentially associated with sites where butchery and meat consumption were not important. He points out that this hypothesis could help to account for the rarity of handaxes from areas north of the Alps, Caucasus, and Himalayas, since ethnography strongly suggests that meat is the primary staple of nonagricultural peoples in northerly zones with a continental climate (e.g. Lee 1968: 42–43).

The hypothesis remains to be tested, but Table 4 presents some available information on the relationship between relative abundance of bone at Middle Pleistocene sites and the proportion of bifaces in the accompanying artifact assemblage. The data are in general far from precise and no clear-cut dichotomy emerges. However, it does appear to be true that numerous biface-dominated assemblages are associated with low densities of bone, while I know of only very few where bone is abundant. It is hard to assess the possible effects of differential preservation in causing bias to the data.

I admit to finding the observed variation perplexing and do not think that any one of these lines of explanation is sufficient in itself. It is probable that several of these factors have interacted to produce the complex configuration which has been observed, but since I have summarized my views of the issues involved in this debate elsewhere, there is no need to repeat them (Isaac 1972: 175–186). It is reasonably clear that culture history in the traditional sense is neither a practicable nor a profitable pursuit in Lower Paleolithic studies.

Analogous problems exist in Europe and Asia, and controversy about the meaning of differences among Acheulian, "Clactonian," "Tayacian," etc., has many ingredients in common with the debate reported for Africa.

Gaps in Knowledge

Analyses have been reported for about forty excavated Middle Pleistocene assemblages, and perhaps almost as many more analyses are currently in progress (e.g. Olduvai, East Rudolf area 30, Melka Kontouré, etc.). By many standards this might appear as an impressive array of data; but it must be remembered that these samples are drawn from a vast space-time continuum, one which spans 1.5 million years and some six to eight million square kilometers. The density of information available as a basis for culture historic interpretation is thus very low indeed. There is no certainty at all that we have even established in outline the overall range of variation.

This point has been dramatically brought home by the discovery in recent years of novel kinds of assemblages falling entirely outside the patterns delineated in the various reviews which were based on the first thirty or so assemblages (Kleindienst 1961; Howell and Clark 1963; M. D. Leakey 1967; Isaac 1968b, 1969). Most remarkable among these contrasting assemblages has been that recovered by Margaret and Richard Leakey from the Kapthurin Beds, Baringo (M. C. Leakey, et al. 1969) and those recovered from the early Middle Pleistocene beds of the Karari Escarpment in the upper Member of the Koobi Fora Formation. The Kapthurin industry appears to be a different variant of the Acheulian, displaying a combination of a giant levallois technique and the production of very delicate blades. It may possibly be related to the Acheulio-Levallois described from the Horn by J. D. Clark (1954) and believed to be of early Upper Pleistocene age. Studies of the Karari Escarpment industry are only just beginning, but the assemblages so far obtained all show a tendency to be dominated by distinctive heavy-duty scrapers with scalloped edges. Well-made bifaces seem to be present but are extremely rare.

Time Trends in Material Culture

Given this puzzling state of knowledge, it is necessary to anticipate the question: do the artifacts contribute anything to our understanding of human evolution in the Middle Pleistocene?

In spite of the complexity of pattern, certain trends can be discerned, and several of these appear to have a bearing on our understanding of changes in hominid capacity for culture:

1.   Early in the Middle Pleistocene, there seems to have been a rise in the density of artifact material which accumulated at sites, especially flakes and flaking debris. Figure 5 illustrates this by presenting data for Olduvai and other sites. It is unclear what this means in terms of human behavior — perhaps an increase in the prevalence of stone knapping as a habit, or perhaps an increase in the duration and intensity of campsite occupation, or both. In either case this measurable archeological change seems likely to reflect increased importance for distinctively human behavior: dependence on equipment and organization of behavior around a home base.

2.   There seems to be a rise in the degree of internal differentiation of artifact assemblages. That is, there was an increase in the number of design modalities and/or the degree of precision with which they were executed. I have argued elsewhere that there may have been a quantum jump early in the Middle Pleistocene which gave rise to the new set of tool designs that characterize the Acheulian (Isaac 1969: 16). Archeology has not yet developed objective methods for discerning the number of design modalities intrinsic to an assemblage or for measuring the overall dispersal pattern of interrelated forms, but one can perhaps use the number of intuitively perceived analytic categories as a rough index (e.g. M. D. Leakey 1971a: Figure 5), and a rising degree of internal differentiation seems to be implied by this. The contrast between the Middle and later Pleistocene in Europe is particularly marked in this regard and would seem to be indicative of rising complexity in both technology and rule systems (Isaac 1972a: Figure 5).

3.   Within some segments of the assemblages there was A RISE IN THE MAXIMUM DEGREE OF REFINEMENT attained by craftsmen, though some late assemblages continued to be about as "rough" as the early ones.

This is illustrated by the data in Table 5 (see also Isaac 1969: 17, and Figure 3). However, consideration of new data presented by Mary Leakey (this volume) shows that the trend, if real at all, is not universally detectable.

4. Quantitative study of variation between assemblages is in a state of experimental flux — but the trend to increasing geographic differentiation seems none the less real and is discernible all over the world at this time. Thus, labels such as Oldowan and Acheulian can be applied without undue difficulty to Lower and Middle Pleistocene industries over the whole of Africa and adjoining areas, but regional labels have proved indispensable for the Upper Pleistocene (Isaac 1972a: Figure 6).

COMPARISON WITH OTHER AREAS

The advent of potassium argon dating and, more particularly, of paleomagnetic dating has disrupted old ideas regarding time relations between Pleistocene sequences in different areas — and regarding the timetable of human cultural development.

It is now definitely established that in East Africa a large segment of the sequence which has been classified as "Middle Pleistocene" antedates the last major change of geomagnetic polarity, namely the Matuyama-Brunhes reversal of circa 700,000 years ago. Further, representatives of the family of stone tool assemblages widely known as Acheulian began to be made in East Africa well before the Matuyama-Brunhes polarity change, perhaps as much as 1.4 million years ago.

Europe

Many scholars including myself have, in the absence of specific evidence to the contrary, tended to the view that early Acheulian industries, including Abbevillian industries, were likely to be of much the same age in Africa and Eurasia. Being aware of the lengthened chronology of East Africa, it seemed probable that European estimates of the age of Acheulian industries were in general far too low. However, the Matuyama-Brunhes boundary has now been identified in several European sequences and it begins to appear that the maximum antiquity and duration of the Acheulian in Africa may be greater than that of Europe by a factor of three or four.

Van Montfrans (1971) places the Matuyama-Brunhes boundary in beds assigned to the Cromerian complex, specifically to Cromerian I, or a zone indicative of a cold fluctuation locally termed Glacial A. The biostratigraphy of Europe as currently understood would interpose a long multistage faunal "span," the Biharian, between some time around the beginning of the Brunhes-Matuyama boundary and most of the early Acheulian sites (Terra Amata, Torralba, Torre in Pietra, etc.). A possible exception to this may be the site of Abbeville.[6] (For further information see de Lumley, Freeman, Jánossy, and Shackleton, this volume, and also the post-conference review and its contained correlation chart.) The paleomagnetic evidence reported by Kukla (1970) and others for eastern Europe seems to have the same implications. If these findings are confirmed by subsequent work, then it follows that the Acheulian in western Europe cannot be older than 700,000 years and that, in fact, an estimate of between 400,000 and 500,000 is more likely.

Traces of hominid presence in Europe are extremely rare in well-dated strata that definitely precede those traditionally assigned to the "Mindel-Elster" complex. As a consequence, the possible adjustment of chronological relations is of more than technical interest to paleoanthropology. The implication may be that the first hominid colonization of the temperate zone took place only during the last 20 percent of the timespan for which we have an archeological record of evolving human behavior.[7]

South Africa

The famous Transvaal cave sites do not contribute as much as one might hope to our understanding of the Middle Pleistocene, because of abiding and at present irremediable uncertainty about their age relationship to East Africa and elsewhere. The faunal evidence indicates that Swartkrans and Kromdraai are of late Lower or early Middle Pleistocene data. Swartkrans has yielded an industry comparable in many ways to the Developed Oldowan of Olduvai Bed II (M. D. Leakey

[6]   The site of Abbeville may antedate most strata and fossil assemblages classified as Mindel, but the data were gathered in the late nineteenth century and the exact associations between artifacts, fossils, and lithostratigraphy are obscure (Howell 1966).
[7]   One has the impression that some Middle Pleistocene Eurasiatic sites, such as Torralba, Grotte du Lazaret, Vértesszöllös, Choukoutien, etc., show higher densities of bone refuse than is common in early sites in Africa. However, there are not yet sufficient numerical data to permit rigorous comparisons. This is an urgent need in future researches.

1970). As in East Africa, there is debate about how many kinds of hominids are represented (Clarke, et al. 1970; Wolpoff 1970). Some authorities have argued that the Sterkfontein type site faunal assemblage and the *Australopithecus africanus* fossils it contains are appreciably older than Olduvai Bed I; that is, three to four million years old. However this may be, a different portion of the site has yielded an artifact assemblage which has close resemblances to some of the Bed II archeological materials. (M. D. Leakey 1971b; Isaac, personal observation.) Although the hominid-bearing and the artifact-bearing deposits are infilling in the same cave system, there are no clear stratigraphic indications as to whether they are contemporary. Robinson and Mason (1962) believed the artifacts to be younger than the majority of hominid fossils. Tobias and Hughes (1969) seemed to imply that the absence of a dramatic disconformity meant that the two were of similar age. Until we have more independent indications of date or correlation, it is difficult to incorporate these assemblages into our understanding of human evolution.

Northwest Africa

This region has perhaps furnished an archeological record as long as that being studied in East Africa (Balout 1955; Biberson 1961; Balout, et al. 1967). The sequence begins with the *"civilisation du Galet Amenagé"* (= Oldowan) and spans a long developmental sequence of Acheulian industries. At present the chronology is tied on the one hand to the sea level fluctuation evident in the Casablanca sequence and on the other to rather loosely defined faunistic correlations.

The Ain Hanech occurrence has conventionally been regarded as Pebble Culture (Balout 1955), but the abundance of spheroids and the presence of bifaces in the beds immediately overlying it make comparison with the Developed Oldowan of Olduvai Bed II tempting. New information assigns this site to an immediately post-Villafranchian age (Jaeger, this volume).

Ternifine has yielded a fine Acheulian assemblage (Balout, et al. 1967) and informative hominid fossils which are commonly assigned to a regional variant of *Homo erectus* (Arambourg 1955; Howell 1960). These are "dated" by the associated early Middle Pleistocene fauna, but no great precision seems possible. Studies of paleomagnetic stratigraphy in North Africa could be extremely informative.

The Levant

This area is transected by a continuation of the same Rift system that affects East Africa, and, indeed, the major site complex of 'Ubeidiya in the Jordan Rift in some respects resembles East African occurrences more closely than it resembles any other known Eurasian occurrences.

I regard 'Ubeidiya as the prime candidate for being the oldest known archeological site in Eurasia. This view has received support recently from a K/Ar date of about 600,000 for a basalt associated with the 'Ubeidiya Formation (Horowitz, et al. 1973). While they have many distinctive and idiosyncratic features, the 'Ubeidiya assemblages show intriguing resemblances to those of Bed II at Olduvai (Stekelis 1966; Stekelis, et al. 1969; Bar-Yosef and Tchernov 1972; Isaac, personal observation.) Not only are the basic compositions of assemblages similar, but the pattern of variability seems to be analogous. This may have a bearing on our interpretation of the variation in general.

The Levant has yielded a full sequence of Acheulian industries and is perhaps one of the areas of the world where the passage from Middle Pleistocene kinds of stone industries to Upper Pleistocene stone industries can best be studied.

Java

Java has yielded a large assemblage of late Lower and early Middle Pleistocene *Homo erectus* fossils. Unfortunately, we really do not know how old these are (see Pilbeam this volume). There is good circumstantial evidence that the Kabuh Beds yielding the Trinil fauna and some hominids are as old or older than a tektite shower that is well dated to about 700,000 years. The underlying Putjangan Beds with Djetis faunal assemblages are also said to have yielded *Homo erectus* fossils (e.g. the Modjokerto child and Pithecanthropus IV), as well as *Meganthropus* remains. A K/Ar date of 1.9 ± 0.4 million years on these beds has been obtained by G. Curtis (Jacob 1972), but in the absence of more dates and a thorough revision of information on the stratigraphy and on the provenance of the fossils, its significance is hard to assess. None the less, the Java fossils could well be contemporaneous with the deposition of Beds II and III at Olduvai (1.5 to 0.7 × 10^6 years).

China

Choukoutien remains one of the most important localities for paleoanthropology. Clearly it is a Middle Pleistocene site *sensu lato*, but if we discount as methodologically unsound the dating of the deposits by means of teleclimatic consideration (Kurten and Vassari 1960), then we have to admit that we do not really know how old it is. If one accepts the correlation of the faunal assemblages with late Cromerian or Biharian faunas of Europe, then this site, like Mauer, Vértesszöllös, and Torralba, may belong to an early phase of hominid encroachment into the temperate zone.

CONCLUSION

In summary then, East Africa has yielded the longest known paleoanthropological record. The segment of that record formerly designated as "Middle Pleistocene" is of the order of one to one and a half million years long, but there are no signs in the archeological sequence of any dramatic changes. There was endless variation, but, for the most part, it has the aspect of variations on a theme, a failure of craft practice and economic behavior to transcend certain limits. And yet, for all the potentially monotonous aspects of this stretch of time, there are indications of the consolidation of distinctively human behavior patterns. Toolmaking became more habitual; the maximum attainments of at least some craftsmen became more elaborate and more refined; the prowess of at least some hunting groups came to exceed the levels known for earlier times. Comparison of the chronologies of traces of hominids in East Africa and in Eurasia strongly implies that hominids were restricted to the tropics and warm temperate regions until a comparatively late stage in human evolution. The biogeographic colonization of colder regions by hominids may, from our point of view, have been one of the most important processes of the Middle Pleistocene. This expansion of ecological range may itself be indicative of rising levels of capacity for culture, social organization, and technology. Certainly, the new environments involved fresh adaptive challenges, and some of them certainly encouraged or required more reliance on hunting than is necessary for those living among the more varied and less seasonal resources of the African savannah. The possible influence of these adjustments on human evolution requires further investigation and consideration.

POSTSCRIPT

In discussion of this paper at Burg Wartenstein, the question was raised: is it really true that one can only divide the time span between 1.5 million years and .1 million years into only two or three divisions? Is resolution really that poor? The answer is that at present some faunal and artifact occurrences do "float" with very wide margins of uncertainty about their ages. This seems rather shocking to many European workers, but at least it can be said that we are avoiding in East Africa the pseudoprecision which has so long characterized European work. The statement that a certain site is of Mindel age may be just as imprecise as assignment to the kinds of broad zones recognizable in East Africa.

Meanwhile it should be realized that at present, East Africa has a larger number of geophysical dates for the mid-Pleistocene than any other region of comparable paleoanthropological interest (Table 1). It can confidently be expected that as the study of well-documented faunal samples advances, so the precision of biostratigraphic dating will increase.

Discussion also turned to the question of how one might seek to get a well-resolved record of oscillations in climate through the Pleistocene. Because of the overriding importance of tectonics in many Rift Valley lake basins and because temperature changes are much less critical at low altitudes on the equator than they are in the temperate zone, it will always be hard to resolve climatic changes from sedimentological studies alone. The best chance of getting long well-resolved sequences would be from pollen, diatoms, etc. recovered from boreholes into waterlogged deposits in major basins. This will be an expensive operation but is urgently needed.

Table 5a.   Mean lengths of handaxes

Length in centimeters	Lower Pleistocene	Middle Pleistocene (undifferentiated)	?Late Middle Pleistocene or early Upper	For comparison: Mediterranean and Europe
8				
9				Derby Road (Roe 1964)
10	Olduvai SHK TK upper			
11				Ma Ayan Barukh
12	Olorgesailie LSS			Atelier Commont
13				ʿUbeidiya
14	Olduvai EFHR FC	Isimila H 20 K 18		Baringo (LHR) Ternifine
15	Olduvai TK lower	Kariandusi Olorgesailie Meng	Kalambo A 5 B Kalambo B 6	
16		Olorgesailie M/10 H/9 A	Nsongezi MN Kalambo A 5	Latamne
17	Peninj Olduvai MNK	Olorgesailie DE/89 C Isimila J 12		
18		Olorgesailie Mid Olorgesailie DE/89 B Isimila K 6	Kalambo A 6 Kalambo B 5	
19		Isimila K 14 Olorgesailie DE/89 A		
20		Olorgesailie H/6 A		
21				
22		Olorgesailie Cat Walk		

Table 5 (a, b, c).
The three sections (a–c) display rank orderings of mean values of a dimension, a shape defining ratio, and scar counts for a series of samples of handaxes recovered from various East African sites. The columns indicate tentative assignment of the samples into "Early," "Middle," and "Late," so that trends, if any exist, would be seen as a shift in the zonation of entries in the columns.

Table 5b.   Mean relative thickness indices (thickness/breadth) of handaxes

Th/Br	Lower Pleistocene	Middle Pleistocene (undifferentiated)	Late Middle or early Upper Pleistocene	Mediterranean and France	Britain (after Roe 1968)
.40			Baringo (LHR)		
.41					Oldbury
.42			Kalambo A 6		
.43		Kariandusi			
.44		Olorgesailie Mid			High Lodge
.45		Olorgesailie DE/89A Mid			
.46		Olorgesailie DE/89B	Kalambo A 5 Kalambo B 5		
.47		Olorgesailie C. W.		St. Acheul	
.48		Isimila H 9	Kalambo B 6		Hoxne
.49		Isimila K 14			
.50		Olorgesailie Meng	Kalambo A 5 B	Ma Ayan B.	
.51		Olorgesailie I 3			
.52		Isimila K 6			
.53		Olorgesailie H/6 Isimila H 20			
.54	Olduvai TK lower	Isimila K 18 Olorgesailie DE/89C		Ternifine	Swanscombe MG
.55			Nsongezi MN		
.56					
.57	Olduvai EFHR Olduvai TK upper	Isimila L 19			Furz Platt
.58					
.59					
.60	Olduvai SHK				
.61	Olduvai BK				
.62					
.63	Peninj				
.64					
.65	Olduvai MNK main				
.66	Olduvai FC				
.67					Fordwich
.68					
.69				Latamne	
.70					
.80				Abbeville	

As can be seen, the data available might be taken to indicate some tendency toward a decline in relative thickness and a rise in the maximum mean number of trimming scars in successive phases. These are both trends in the direction of craft "refinement," but their reality requires checking in sequences such as the Olduvai sequence before they are accepted as established.

Mean values for certain well known sites in Europe and the Mediterranean basin are presented in the left hand column(s) for comparison.

Table 5c. Mean scar counts on handaxes

Number	Lower Pleistocene	Middle Pleistocene	Late Middle or early Upper Pleistocene	Other areas
8				
10	Olduvai EFHR Peninj			
12				
14				
16				
18		Olorgesailie LSS		Ternifine
20				
22				
24				Montagu L 5 (small sample)
26		Olorgesailie MSS		
28				
30				
32		Olorgesailie USS		
34				
36				
38				
40				Tabun Ea (small sample)
42				
44				
46			Kalambo various (small sample)	
48				
50				
52				
54				
56			Baringo (LHR)	

Notes and Sources:
Sources: Olduvai — M. D. Leakey (1971a, 1971b); Peninj — Isaac (1967); Kariandusi, Isimila, Kalambo Falls — Kleindienst (1959); Olorgesailie — Isaac (1968b); Baringo — M. C. Leakey, et al. (1969); Mayan Burukh — Stekelis and Gilead (1966); Atelier Commont — Alimen and Vignal (1952); ʿUbeidiya — Stekelis (1966); Ternifine — Balout, et al. (1967, and personal observation) Scar counts: Latamne — Clark (1967b); Kalambo, Montagu Cave, and Tabun scar counts were made by Isaac on small samples in the laboratory at Berkeley; Nsongezi — Cole (1967).

Note: Olorgesailie LSS, MSS, and USS means the lower, middle, and upper stratigraphic set of sites, respectively.

REFERENCES

ALIMEN, H., A. VIGNAL
1952 Etude statistique de bifaces acheuléens. Essai d'archéométrie. *Bulletin de la Société Préhistorique Française* 49:56–72.

ARAMBOURG, C.
1955 Une découverte récente en paléontologie humaine, L'Atlanthropos de Ternifine (Algérie). *Quaternaria* 2:5–13.

BAILLOUD, G.
1965 *Les gisements paléolithiques de Melka-Kontouré.* Cahiers de l'Institut Ethiopien d'Archéologie 1. Addis Ababa.

BAKER, B. H.
1958 *Geology of the Magadi Area.* Geological Survey of Kenya, Report 42. Nairobi: Government Printer.

BAKER, B. H., J. WOHLENBERG
1971 Structure and evolution of the Kenya Rift Valley. *Nature* 229:538.

BAKER, B. H., P. A. MOHR, L. A. J. WILLIAMS
1972 *Geology of the eastern rift system of Africa.* Geological Society of America, Special Paper 136.

BALOUT, L.
1955 *Préhistoire de l'Afrique du nord.* Paris: Arts et Métiers Graphiques.

BALOUT, L., P. BIBERSON, J. TIXIER
1967 L'acheuléen de Ternifine (Algérie). Gisement de l'Atlanthrope. *L'Anthropologie* 71:217–237.

BAR-YOSEF, O., E. TCHERNOV
1972 *On the palaeo-ecological history of the site of 'Ubeidiya.* Jerusalem: Israel Academy of Sciences and Humanities.

BIBERSON, P.
1961 *Le Paléolithique Inférieur du Maroc Atlantique.* Publications du Service des Antiquités du Maroc 17.

BINFORD, L. R.
1972 "Contemporary model building: paradigms and the current state of palaeolithic research," in *Models in archaeology.* Edited by D. L. Clarke, 109–166. London: Methuen.

BINFORD, S. R., L. R. BINFORD
1966 "A preliminary analysis of functional variability in the Mousterian of Levallois facies," in *Recent studies in paleoanthropology.* Edited by J. D. Clark and F. C. Howell, 238–295. American Anthropologist Special Publication 68(2):2.
1969 Stone tools and human behaviour. *Scientific American* 220:70–82.

BISHOP, W. W.
1963 "The later Tertiary and Pleistocene in eastern equatorial Africa," in *African ecology and human evolution.* Edited by F. C. Howell and F. Bourlière, 246–275. Chicago: Aldine.
1965 "Quaternary geology and geomorphology in the Albertine Rift Valley, Uganda," in *International studies on the Quaternary.* Edited by H. E. Wright, Jr. and D. G. Frey, 295–321. Geological Society of America Special Paper 84. Boulder, Colorado.

1967   "Associated lexicon of Quaternary stratigraphic nomenclature in East Africa," in *Background to evolution in Africa*. Edited by W. W. Bishop and J. D. Clark, 375–392. Chicago: University of Chicago Press.

1969   *Pleistocene stratigraphy in Uganda*. Geological Survey of Uganda, Memoir 10. Entebbe.

1971   "The Late Cenozoic history of East Africa in relation to hominoid evolution," in *The Late Cenozoic glacial ages*. Edited by K. Turekian, 493–527. New Haven: Yale University Press.

1972   "Stratigraphic succession 'versus' calibration in East Africa," in *Calibration of hominoid evolution*. Edited by W. W. Bishop and J. A. Miller, 219–246. Edinburgh: Scottish Academic Press.

BISHOP, W. W., J. D. CLARK, *editors*
1967   *Background to evolution in Africa*. Chicago: University of Chicago Press.

BONNEFILLE, R., M. TAIEB
1971   "Quaternaire de la région de Melka Kontouré: géologie et palynologie." VII Pan African Congress of Prehistory and Quaternary Studies, Addis Ababa. Mimeographed guide-pamphlet.

BOUT. P.
1969   Datations absolues de quelques formations volcaniques d'Auvergne et du Velay et chronologie du Quaternaire européen. *Revue d'Auvergne* 83:267–280.

BRACE, C. L.
1967   *The stages of human evolution*. Englewood Cliffs: Prentice-Hall.

BROCK, A., G. LL. ISAAC
i.p.   "Palaeomagnetic stratigraphy and the chronology of hominid bearing deposits at East Rudolf, Kenya." Unpublished manuscript, to be submitted to *Nature*.

BROWN, F. H.
1972   "Radiometric dating of sedimentary formations in the lower Omo Valley, Ethiopia," in *Calibration of hominoid evolution*. Edited by W. W. Bishop and J. A. Miller, 273–288. Edinburgh: Scottish Academic Press.

BUTZER, K. W., F. H. BROWN, D. L. THURBER
1969   Horizontal sediments of the lower Omo Valley: the Kibish formation. *Quaternaria* 11:15-29.

BUTZER, K. W., G. LL. ISAAC, J. L. RICHARDSON, C. WASHBOURN-KAMAU
1972   Radiocarbon dating of East African lake levels. *Science* 175: 1069–1076.

CAMPBELL, B. G.
1966   *Human evolution: an introduction to man's adaptations*. Chicago: Aldine.

CARNEY, J., A. HILL, J. A. MILLER, A. WALKER
1971   A late australopithecine from Baringo District, Kenya. *Nature* 230:509–514.

CHAVAILLON, J.
1967   *Gisement de Melka Kontouré*. Rapport d'Activité du Laboratoire de Géologie du Quaternaire, Oct. 1966 à Oct. 1967.

1967   La préhistoire éthiopienne à Melka Kontouré. *Archéologia* (November-December): 56–63.

1970   Découverte d'un niveau oldowayen dans la basse vallée de l'Omo (Ethiopie). *Bulletin de la Société Préhistorique Française* 67:7–11.

1971   "Prehistorical living-floors of Melka Kontouré in Ethiopia." VII Pan African Congress of Prehistory and Quaternary Studies, Addis Ababa. Mimeographed guide-pamphlet.

CHAVAILLON, J., M. TAIEB

1968   Stratigraphie du Quaternaire de Melka Kontouré (vallée de l'Aouache, Ethiopie): premiers résultats. *C.R. Acad. Sc.*, Paris 226:1210–1212.

CLARK, J. D.

1954   *The prehistoric cultures of the Horn of Africa*. Cambridge: Cambridge University Press.

1959   Further excavations at Broken Hill, Northern Rhodesia. *Journal of the Royal Anthropological Institute* 89:201–232.

1964   The influence of environment in inducing culture change at the Kalambo Falls prehistoric site. *South African Archaeological Bulletin* 19:93–101.

1967a   The middle Acheulian occupation site at Latamne Northern Syria. (First Paper). *Quaternaria* 11:1–68.

1967b   *The atlas of African prehistory*. Chicago and London: University of Chicago Press.

1969   *Kalambo Falls Prehistoric Site*, volume one. (With contributions by G. H. Cole, E. G. Haldemann, M. R. Kleindienst and E. M. van Zinderen Bakker.) Cambridge: Cambridge University Press.

1970   *The prehistory of Africa*. London: Thames and Hudson.

CLARK, J. D., C. V. HAYNES

1969   An elephant butchery site at Mwanganda's village karonga, Malawi and its relevance for palaeolithic archaeology. *World Archaeology* 1:390–411.

CLARKE, R. J., F. C. HOWELL, C. K. BRAIN

1970   More evidence of an advanced hominid at Swartkrans. *Nature* 225:1217–1222.

COLE, G. H.

1961   "Culture change in the middle-upper Pleistocene transition in Africa south of the Sahara." Dissertation submitted to Department of Anthropology, University of Chicago. Microfilm Thesis 8411.

1967   "The later Acheulian and Sangoan of southern Uganda," in *Background to evolution in Africa*. Edited by W. W. Bishop and J. D. Clark, 481–528. Chicago: University of Chicago Press.

COLE, S.

1963   *The prehistory of east Africa*. New York: Macmillan.

COOKE, H. B. S.

1958   Observations relating to Quaternary environments in east and southern Africa. Alex I. Du Toit Memorial Lecture 5. *Geological Society of South Africa*, Annexure to volume 60:1–73.

1963   "Pleistocene mammal faunas of Africa with particular reference to southern Africa," in *African ecology and human evolution*.

Edited by F. C. Howell and F. Bourlière, 65–116. Chicago: Aldine.

COOKE, H. B. S., V. J. MAGLIO
1972 "Plio-Pleistocene stratigraphy in relation to proboscidean and suid evolution," in *Calibration of hominoid evolution.* Edited by W. W. Bishop and J. A. Miller, 303–329. Edinburgh: Scottish Academic Press.

COX, A.
1969 Geomagnetic Reversals. *Science* 163:237–245.

CURTIS, G. H., R. L. HAY
1972 "Further geological studies and potassium-argon dating at Olduvai Gorge and Ngorongoro Crater," in *Calibration of hominoid evolution.* Edited by W. W. Bishop and J. A. Miller, 289–301. Edinburgh: Scottish Academic Press.

DE LUMLEY, H., S. GAGNIÈRE, L. BARRAL, R. PASCAL
1963 La Grotte du Vallonet, Roquebrune-Cap-Martin (A-M). (Note préliminaire.) *Bulletin du Musée d'Anthropologie Préhistorique de Monaco* 10:5–20.

EVERNDEN, J. F., G. H. CURTIS
1965 The potassium-argon dating of Late Cenozoic rocks in east Africa and Italy. *Current Anthropology* 6:343–385.

FLINT, R. F.
1959a On the basis of Pleistocene correlation in east Africa. *Geological Magazine* 96:265–284.
1959b Pleistocene climates in east and southern Africa. *Bulletin of the Geological Society of America* 70:343–374.

GEZA, T.
1973 The omnivorous chimpanzee. *Scientific American* 228:32–42.

HANSEN, C. L., C. M. KELLER
1971 Environment and activity patterning at Isimila karongo, Iringa District, Tanzania: a preliminary report. *American Anthropologist* 73:1201–1211.

HAY, R. L.
1967a "Hominid-bearing deposits of Olduvai Gorge," in *Time and stratigraphy in the evolution of man.* A symposium sponsored by the Division of Earth Sciences, National Academy of Sciences, National Research Council, Washington D.C.
1967b "Revised stratigraphy of Olduvai Gorge," in *Background to evolution in Africa.* Edited by W. W. Bishop and J. D. Clark, 221–228. Chicago: University of Chicago Press.
1971 "Geologic background of Beds I and II: stratigraphic summary," in *Olduvai Gorge,* volume three. Edited by M. D. Leakey, 9–18. Cambridge: Cambridge University Press.

HOROWITZ, A., G. SIEDNER, O. BAR-YOSEF
1973 Radiometric dating of the 'Ubeidiya Formation, Jordan Valley, Israel. *Nature* 242:186–187.

HOWELL, F. C.
1960 European and northwest African Middle Pleistocene hominids. *Current Anthropology* 1:195–232.

1961   Isimila: a paleolithic site in Africa. *Scientific American* 205: 118–129.
1966   "Observations on the earlier phases of the European lower Paleolithic," in *Recent studies in paleoanthropology*. Edited by J. D. Clark and F. C. Howell, 88–201. American Anthropologist Special Publication 68(2):2.
1969   Remains of hominidae from Pliocene/Pleistocene formations in the lower Omo basin, Ethiopia. *Nature* 223:1234–1239.
1972   "Pliocene/Pleistocene hominidae in eastern Africa — absolute and relative ages," in *Calibration of hominoid evolution*. Edited by W. W. Bishop and J. A. Miller, 331–368. Edinburgh: Scottish University Press.

HOWELL, F. C., G. H. COLE, M. R. KLEINDIENST
1962   "Isimila, an Acheulian occupation site in the Iringa highlands," in *Actes du IVe. Congrès Panafricain de Préhistoire et de l'Étude du Quaternaire. Annales — séries IN-8 Sciences Humaines 40*. Edited by G. Mortelmans and J. Nenquin, 43–80. Tervuren: Musée Royal de l'Afrique Centrale.

HOWELL, F. C., J. D. CLARK
1963   "Acheulian hunter-gatherers of sub-Saharan Africa," in *African Ecology and human evolution*. Edited by F. C. Howell and F. Bourlière, 458–533. Chicago: Aldine.

HOWELL, F. C., G. H. COLE, M. R. KLEINDIENST, B. J. SZABO, K. P. OAKLEY
1972   Uranium series dating of bone from the Isimila prehistoric site, Tanzania. *Nature* 237:51–52.

ISAAC, G. LL.
1965   The stratigraphy of the Peninj beds and the provenance of the Natron Australopithecine mandible. *Quaternaria* VII:101–130.
1966a "New evidence from Olorgesailie relating to the character of Acheulian occupation sites," in *Actas del V Congreso Panafricano de Prehistoria y el Estudio de Cuaternario*. Publicaciones del Museo Arqueologico 6(2):135–145. Santa Cruz de Tenerife.
1966b "The geological history of the Olorgesailie area," in *Actas del V Congreso Panafricano de Prehistoria y de Estudio del Cuaternario*. Publicaciones del Museo Arqueologico 6(2):125–133. Santa Cruz de Tenerife.
1967   "The stratigraphy of the Peninj Group — early middle Pleistocene formation west of Lake Natron, Tanzania," in *Background to Evolution in Africa*. Edited by W. W. Bishop and J. D. Clark, 229–257. Chicago: University of Chicago Press.
1968a "Traces of Pleistocene hunters: an east African example," in *Man the hunter*. Edited by R. B. Lee and I. DeVore, 253–261. Chicago: Aldine.
1968b "The Acheulean site complex at Olorgesailie, Kenya: a contribution to the interpretation of Middle Pleistocene culture in East Africa." Unpublished doctoral dissertation, Cambridge University.
1969   Studies of early culture in East Africa. *World Archaeology* 1:1–28.
1971   The diet of early man: aspects of archaeological evidence from

Lower and Middle Pleistocene sites in Africa. *World Archaeology* 2:278–298.

1972a "Chronology and the tempo of cultural change during the Pleistocene," in *Calibration of hominoid evolution.* Edited by W. W. Bishop and J. A. Miller, 381–430. Edinburgh: Scottish Academic Press.

1972b "Early phases of human behaviour: models in Lower Palaeolithic archaeology," in *Models in archaeology.* Edited by D. L. Clarke, 167–199. London: Methuen.

1972c "Comparative studies of Pleistocene site locations in East Africa," in *Man, settlement and urbanism.* Edited by P. J. Ucko, R. Tringham, and G. W. Dimbleby, 165–176. London: Duckworth.

ISAAC, G. LL., G. H. CURTIS
1974 "The age of early Acheulian industries in East Africa — new evidence from the Peninj Group, Tanzania." *Nature* 249:624–627.

ISAAC, G. LL., R. E. F. LEAKEY, A. K. BEHRENSMEYER
1971 Archaeological traces of early hominid activities east of Lake Rudolf, Kenya. *Science* 173:1129–1134.

ISAAC, G. LL., H. V. MERRICK, C. M. NELSON
1972 "Stratigraphic and archaeological studies in the Lake Nakuru basin, Kenya," in *Palaeoecology of Africa,* volume six. Edited by E. M. van Zinderen Bakker, 225–232. Cape Town: A. A. Balkema.

JACOB, T.
1972 The absolute date of the Djetis Beds at Modjokerto. *Antiquity* 182:148.

KENT, P. E.
1942 The Pleistocene Beds of Kanam and Kanjera. *Geological Magazine* 79:117–132.

KLEINDIENST, M. R.
1959 "Composition and significance of a Late Acheulian assemblage based on an analysis of East African occupation sites." Dissertation submitted to the Department of Anthropology, University of Chicago. Microfilm Thesis 4706.

1961 Variability within the late Acheulian assemblage in eastern Africa. *South African Archaeological Bulletin* 16:35–52.

KLIMA, B.
1962 "The first ground-plan of an Upper Palaeolithic loess settlement in Middle Europe and its meaning," in *Courses towards urban life.* Edited by R. J. Braidwood and G. R. Willey, 193–210. Chicago: Aldine.

KUKLA, J.
1970 Correlations between loesses and deep-sea sediments. *Geologiska Föreningen i Stockholm Forhandlingar* 92(2):148–180.

KURTEN, B.
1968 *Pleistocene mammals of Europe.* Chicago: Aldine.

KURTEN, B., V. VASARI
1960 On the date of Peking Man. *Societas Scientiarum Fennica, Commentationes Biologicae* 23(7):3–10.

LEAKEY, L. S. B.

1931   *The stone age cultures of the Kenya Colony.* Cambridge: Cambridge University Press.

1935   *The stone age races of Kenya.* Oxford: Oxford University Press.

1951   *Olduvai Gorge. A report on the evolution of the handaxe culture in Beds I–IV.* Cambridge: Cambridge University Press.

1953   *Adam's ancestors.* London: Methuen.

1957   "Preliminary report on a Chellean I living site at BK II, Olduvai Gorge, Tanganyika Territory," in *Proceedings of the Third Pan-African Congress of Prehistory, Livingstone 1955.* Edited by J. D. Clark, 217–218. London: Chatto and Windus.

1965   *Olduvai Gorge 1951–61,* volume one: *A preliminary report on the geology and the fauna.* Cambridge: University Press.

1966   *Homo habilis, Homo erectus* and the australopithecines. *Nature* 209:1279–1281.

LEAKEY, M. C., P. V. TOBIAS, J. E. MARTYN, R. E. F. LEAKEY

1969   An Acheulean industry and hominid mandible, Lake Baringo, Kenya. *Proceedings of the Prehistoric Society* 35:48–76.

LEAKEY, M. D.

1967   "Preliminary summary of the cultural material from Beds I and II, Olduvai Gorge, Tanzania," in *Background to evolution in Africa.* Edited by W. W. Bishop and J. D. Clark, 417–442. Chicago: University of Chicago Press.

1970   Stone age artefacts from Swartkrans. *Nature* 225:1222–1225.

1971a   *Olduvai Gorge,* volume three: *Excavations in Beds I and II, 1960–1963.* Cambridge: Cambridge University Press.

1971b   Discovery of postcranial remains of Homo erectus and associated artefacts in bed IV at Olduvai Gorge, Tanzania. *Nature* 232:380–383.

LEAKEY, R. E., B. A. WOOD

i.p.   New Homo remains from East Rudolf, Kenya (II). *American Journal of Physical Anthropology.*

LEE, R. B.

1968   "What hunters do for a living or, how to make out on scarce resources," in *Man the hunter.* Edited by R. B. Lee and I. DeVore, 30–48. Chicago: Aldine.

LEE, R. B., I. DEVORE, *editors*

1968   *Man the hunter.* Chicago: Aldine.

MAGLIO, V. J.

1972   Vertebrate faunas and chronology of hominid-bearing sediments east of Lake Rudolf, Kenya. *Nature* 239:379–385.

MANN, A. E.

1968   "The paleodemography of Australopithecus." Unpublished doctoral dissertation, University of California, Berkeley.

MC CALL, G. J. H.

1967   *Geology of the Nakuru-Thomson's Falls-Lake Hannington Area.* Geological Survey of Kenya, Report 78.

MC CALL, G. J. H., B. H. BAKER, J. WALSH
1967 "Late Tertiary and Quaternary sediments of the Kenya Rift Valley," in *Background to evolution in Africa.* Edited by W. W. Bishop and J. D. Clark, 191–220. Chicago: University of Chicago Press.

MC CONNELL, R. B.
1972 Geological development of the rift system of eastern Africa. *Geological Society of America Bulletin* 83:2549–2572.

MERRICK, H., P. HAESAERTS, J. DE HEINZELIN, F. C. HOWELL
1973 Archaeological occurrences of early Pleistocene age from the Shungura Formation, Lower Omo, East Africa. *Nature* 242: 572–575.

MILLER, J. A.
1967 "Problems of dating east African Tertiary and Quaternary volcanics by the potassium-argon method," in *Background to evolution in Africa.* Edited by W. W. Bishop and J. D. Clark, 259–272. Chicago: University of Chicago Press.

PFEIFFER, J. E.
1969 *The emergence of man.* New York: Harper and Row.

PILBEAM, D.
1970 *The evolution of man.* London: Thames and Hudson.

RICHARDSON, J.
1972 "Paleolimnological records from rift lakes in central Kenya," in *Palaeoecology of Africa,* volume six. Edited by E. M. van Zinderen Bakker, 131–136. Cape Town: A. A. Balkema.

ROBINSON, J. T.
1972 The bearing of East Rudolf fossils on early hominid systematics. *Nature* 240:239–240.

ROBINSON, J. T., R. J. MASON
1962 Australopithecines and artefacts at Sterkfontein. *South African Archaeological Bulletin* 17:87–125.

ROE, D. A.
1964 The British Lower and Middle Palaeolithic: some problems, methods of study and preliminary results. *Proceedings of the Prehistoric Society* 30:245–267.
1968 British Lower and Middle Palaeolithic handaxe groups. *Proceedings of the Prehistoric Society* 34:1–82.

ROUBET, C.
1969 Essai de datation absolue d'un biface-hachereau paléolithique de l'Afar (Ethiopie). *L'Anthropologie* 73:503–524.

SAVAGE, D. E., G. H. CURTIS
1970 *The Villafranchian stage-age and its radiometric dating.* Geological Society of America, Special Paper 124:207–231.

SHACKLETON, R. M.
1955 Pleistocene movements in the Gregory Rift Valley. *Geologische Rundschau* 5:43:257–263.

STEKELIS, M.
1966 *Archaeological excavations at 'Ubeidiya 1960–63.* Jerusalem: The Israel Academy of Sciences and Humanities.

STEKELIS, M., D. GILEAD
  1966   Ma'ayan Barukh: a lower Palaeolithic site in Upper Galilee. *Met-qufat Ha-even* 8.
STEKELIS, M., O. BAR-YOSEF, T. SCHICK
  1969   *Archaeological excavations at 'Ubeidiya 1964–1966.* Jerusalem: Israel Academy of Sciences and Humanities.
TOBIAS, P. V.
  1972   "Progress and problems in the study of early man in sub-Saharan Africa," in *Functional and evolutionary biology of primates.* Edited by R. Tuttle, 63–93. Chicago: Aldine-Atherton.
TOBIAS, P. V., A. R. HUGHES
  1969   The new Witwatersrand University excavation at Sterkfontein. *South African Archaeological Bulletin* 24:158–169.
TRUMP, E. C.
  1967   "Vegetation," in *Nairobi, city and region.* Edited by W. T. W. Morgan, 39–47. Nairobi/London: Oxford University Press.
VAN DER HAMMEN, T., T. A. WIJMSTRA, W. G. ZAGWIJN
  1971   "The floral record of the late Cenozoic of Europe," in *The late Cenozoic glacial ages.* Edited by K. Turekian, 391–424. New Haven: Yale University Press.
VAN LAWICK-GOODALL, J.
  1971   *In the shadow of man.* Glasgow: Wm. Collins' Sons.
VAN MONTFRANS, H. M.
  1971   Palaeomagnetic dating in the North Sea basin. *Earth and Planetary Science Letters* 11:226–235.
VONDRA, C. F., G. D. JOHNSON, B. E. BOWEN, A. K. BEHRENSMEYER
  1971   Preliminary stratigraphical studies of the East Rudolf basin, Kenya. *Nature* 231:245–248.
WASHBURN, S. L., C. S. LANCASTER
  1968   "The evolution of hunting," in *Man the hunter.* Edited by R. B. Lee and I. DeVore, 293–303. Chicago: Aldine.
WOLPOFF, M. H.
  1970   The evidence for multiple hominid taxa at Swartkrans. *American Anthropologist* 72:576–607.
  1971   Competitive exclusion among lower Pleistocene hominids: the single species hypothesis. *Man* 6:601–614.

Demography, Subsistence, and Culture During the Acheulian in Southern Africa

H. J. DEACON

ABSTRACT

Artifact occurrences that can be integrated within the Acheulian Industrial Complex were recognized and described from Southern Africa towards the end of the
last century. It was appreciated on geomorphological grounds even at that time
that these Acheulian occurrences are of high antiquity despite the fact that they
are frequently exposed at or near the present day surface. The earliest relatively
dated artifact occurrences are known from the Australopithecine breccia sites of
Sterkfontein and Swartkrans although there is the strong possibility that artifact
occurrences of like or greater age exist elsewhere, as for example in the Vaal River
basin. The Sterkfontein and Swartkrans occurrences have been variously described
as Developed Oldowan and as Acheulian, but indicate an age in excess of 1 million
years for the appearance of a stone tool manufacturing tradition in Southern Africa.
At the other end of the time scale, the Acheulian is defined in terms of the consistent manufacture of bifaces. It persisted until some 100,000 years ago when
replaced by a complex of the flake industries, some occurrences of which can be
related to marine deposits of last interglacial age. The primary focus of initial
Acheulian studies was on discerning evolutionary time trends in biface manufacture.
Many of the sites studied were occurrences in geological context which perforce
have proved limited in allowing discussion of content and inter-assemblage variability. Recently, more occurrences have been excavated in a primary or semiprimary context and make it possible to begin to discuss some aspects of the
demography, subsistence, and behavior of the Acheulian populations through the
Middle Pleistocene in Southern Africa. A limiting factor, however, is still the
paucity of occurrences with preserved faunas or floras in association with artifactual materials. The Pleistocene faunas of southern Africa are known in general
terms only and primarily indicate long-term environmental stability. Indeed as a
stable, large geographical area presenting a mosaic of suitable habitats for Acheulian populations, southern Africa may have been an important population center
in the Middle Pleistocene.

The dispersal of early human populations throughout the southern part
of Africa in the mid-Pleistocene is well attested. Clear and incontro-

vertible evidence for Lower Pleistocene populations is lacking although australopithecine hominids are well represented. The principal evidence of human activities in the Middle Pleistocene time range is in the form of surface and buried occurrences of the more durable stone artifacts. These populations then are the earliest with reasonable archeological visibility and are known principally in terms of their stone technology.

From the latter part of the last century, occurrences with a bifacial component were recognized as Paleolithic and were later given formal designation as the Stellenbosch or Pniel type (Péringuey 1911) and, subsequently, as the Stellenbosch Culture (Goodwin and van Riet Lowe 1929), terms which have now been superseded. The general similarity to other Lower Paleolithic industries was appreciated at the time, but the question seemed to be whether they could be as old as those in western Europe (e.g. Haddon 1906). An answer was provided by Fielden (1905), Johnson and Young (1906), and Lamplugh (1906) among others, and they pointed out the geomorphological evidence for the high antiquity of what would now be termed Acheulian occurrences in southern Africa, despite the artifacts being found abundantly even on the present-day surface.

Initial awareness of Acheulian occurrences encouraged unsystematic collecting only, and it was primarily with the investigations of implementiferous gravels and alluvial sites in the major river valleys that research in the Middle Pleistocene time range and the Acheulian gained its stimulus in southern Africa. The paucity of accumulations of Pleistocene deposits in general drew attention to fluviatile deposits as offering the greatest potential for the study of changes in artifact technology through "long" time. The Vaal River was the focus for studies in South Africa, likewise the Zambezi River in south central Africa. Climatostratigraphic correlations between units in different drainage basins were widely accepted and allowed observations to be fitted into a wide framework embracing the whole of southern Africa and even further afield. In respect to the Acheulian, interest was primarily centered on tracing the perfection of the biface through a succession of time-sequential stages. This appeared to confirm man's halting steps along a path of improving technology. Climatic inferences drawn from evidence of aggradation and degradation cycles provided not only a basis for long range correlations, but also a means for deterministic explanation of culture change in denoting periods of equilibrium under equable climate and periods of stress and the appearance of new adaptations under adverse climate.

There are two factors that led to the collapse of this conceptual framework for viewing the Acheulian in southern Africa. Firstly, the reviews of H. B. S. Cooke (1958) and Flint (1959a, 1959b) questioned the basis for the climatic inferences made in a number of key sequences, and further, these authors pointed out the weakness in the use of second order concepts in correlation. Second, the emphasis in Lower Paleolithic studies changed from a technological evolution model, considering essentially only the large biface component, to an activity pattern model with stress laid on the excavation and study of artifact samples from occupation occurrences in primary context. Most artifact occurrences then best known and studied in southern Africa were from contexts involving disturbance or fluvial transport (see Kleindienst 1961). There has been continued emphasis laid on the importance of occupation occurrences and their excavation, and this has been reinforced to some degree by a broadening of the activity concept to include settlement patterns and ecology. While the full potential for information to be derived from the study of such minimal occurrences is still being explored (see Isaac [1972: 172] for discussion on this point) — they have primarily been analyzed as unbiased or homogeneous unit samples — it is implied that occurrences from disturbed contexts will be of marginal interest or lacking in essential data.

The effect of these factors on Middle Pleistocene research in southern Africa has been stultifying. The lessons of the past have been learned well, if with difficulty. Awareness that generalizations on climatic interpretation have been too ready and cultural terminology often misused (Kleindienst 1967) has had a sobering effect, and future progress should be much sounder for this. There are signs of renewed interest in the problems of the Middle Pleistocene in southern Africa. A good start was afforded by the clarification of the artifact occurrences in the older stratigraphic units of the Vaal basin (Mason 1961b). Progress, however, has been and is likely to continue to be slow. Southern Africa remains an important area for the study of early human populations because of its size and because it falls within the biogeographic province of early man.

GENERAL CONSIDERATIONS

There has been some tendency in recent years for research to concentrate either on the study of the early rich faunal sites that include limited cultural materials and Upper Pleistocene or Recent sites with abundant traces of archaeological remains. The australopithecine-bearing deposits of Sterkfontein and Swartkrans have produced the earliest acknowledged artifact samples described as early Acheulian (Mason 1961a) and seen as comparable to the Developed Oldowan (Leakey 1971: 274). The artificial origin of other suggested contemporary or earlier finds, notably from Makapan Limeworks (Brain, van Riet Lowe, and Dart 1955; Mason 1962a) and the upper gravel units of the Vaal River (Oakley 1954; Mason 1962b: 59), has been disputed, and the finds from Suurkree need substantiation (Mason 1967a; for discussion see Inskeep 1969: 178). The inferred dating of the Sterkfontein Middle Breccia and the Swartkrans deposits is early Middle Pleistocene (Tobias 1972) and this is then a time measure for the early Acheulian. Occurrences in the Vaal basin at Klipplaatdrif and Three Rivers (Mason 1962a) are considered to be of equivalent antiquity on typological grounds. Younger Acheulian occurrences are known in some measure of association with faunas of the Vaal-Cornelia faunal span which has a suggested correlation with the upper beds at Olduvai Gorge (H. B. S. Cooke i.p.) Examples are the Younger Gravel sites of the Vaal, Cornelia itself, although the main reported artifact occurrence underlies the faunal horizon, and the Elandsfontein (Hopefield) site. The late Acheulian-Fauresmith/MSA interface can be related, on the basis of the Cave of Hearths (H. B. S. Cooke 1962), to the succeeding Florisbad-Vlakkraal faunal span. The Chelmer deposit in Rhodesia and the Maramba River deposit in Zambia (H. B. S. Cooke and Wells 1951) may have similar indirect cultural associations (Bond and Summers 1951) and be of like age. It has become necessary to consider revision of the supposed time range of the Florisbad-Vlakkraal faunal span as on chronometric (Beaumont 1973), geomorphological (Mabbutt 1954), and other combined evidence (Klein i.p.) this is probably between 100,000 and 10,000 years B.P. From this it is apparent that the whole Acheulian complex in Southern Africa lies outside the range of C[14] chronology, and the few finite determinations for Acheulian occurrences should be viewed as minimum ages. This amounts to a not insignificant displacement of the Acheulian/MSA interface relative to previous estimates (J. Deacon 1966). Because of the relationship of the Vaal-Cornelia and Florisbad-Vlakkraal faunal spans to artifact occurrences, they have been described as the handaxe fauna and the MSA fauna, respectively, and their duration deduced from the inferred dating of the cultural entities rather than from biological considerations. As a consequence of the considerations of a longer chronology for Upper Pleistocene cultural entities and a lower extinction rate for mammalian faunas, postulates of "late survivals" of Acheulian industries in central and southern Africa bear reexamination. For more precise chronological data on the terminal Acheulian/MSA interface, chronometric dating methods other than C^{14} will have to be used.

Although the long time range of the Acheulian in southern Africa is evident from relative dating on mammalian faunas, which in turn can in some measure be correlated with the chronometrically dated faunal scales of East Africa, finer calibration of the Acheulian is less easy. As in East Africa, the recognition of multiple stages, actually sequential phase entities in the Acheulian, has been discarded. Broad cultural divisions are the most meaningful, and even here these have to receive fuller description. A lower Acheulian with rarely more than ten flakes removed in the shaping of bifaces and with deep scar beds appears to warrant distinction although there are few acceptable samples (Mason 1962a; M. D. Leakey 1971: 274). Other occurrences have been grouped within the Late or Middle and Late Acheulian (Fauresmith) or Sangoan (Mason 1962a; Inskeep 1969: 175). This parallels at least some views on the East African occurrences (Isaac 1969: 20). To avoid confusion where occurrences of comparable age are referred to the Upper Acheulian in central and East Africa and to the Middle Acheulian in parts of southern Africa, it is convenient here to use only the term Upper Acheulian. These entities have not received fuller description and are in essence sack categories. Studies underway, notably a program of multivariate analysis currently being undertaken by Mason (personal communication), should increase the resolution of them into a series of samples. The Upper Acheulian can only be seen as incorporating considerable interassemblage variability, but with a measure of refinement over the Lower Acheulian. In southern Africa, where dating problems are acute because of the apparent absence of materials suitable for currently available methods of chronometric age determination and the paucity of associated faunal or floral remains for relative dating, the wisdom of retaining broad industrial divisions is very apparent. Finer calibration is a legitimate goal for future research although by no means the only one.

Southern Africa, which for the purposes of this review is defined as south of the equatorial divide and the southern extension of the Rift Valley system, is a stable block (Bond 1963: 603). Erosion and planation have been the dominant geological processes operating with relatively minor change in the landscape achieved in the time range of the whole Pleistocene. Outside the Kalahari basin, centers of internal drainage are not marked, and Pleistocene deposits in general are thin, discontinuous, and not necessarily well exposed. They are mainly limited to fluviatile sequences of gravels, sands, and silts, centers of very localized impeded or internal drainage (pans and vloers, vleis and dambos), cave and cavern fills, mound spring accumulations, and eolian and marine deposits. Unlike East Africa (Isaac 1968: 255), which has been tectonically unstable, there are few exposures of Lower and Middle Pleistocene deposits, and they are not generally favorable to the preservation of primary associations of artifacts, fauna, and any other materials. Chance has played some part in making exposures available, and examples can be cited of the occurrence at Broken Hill (Clark 1959a) exposed by mining, the occurrence at Doornlaagte by quarrying, and, of course, the exposures of gravels in the Vaal basin opened up by diamond digging. Indirectly, modern land-use practices have increased exposures through impairment of the vegetation cover and increase in gully (donga) or eolian action.

The structural stability of southern Africa is also reflected in its biology. In the extreme southwest, the survival of the very ancient forest flora of the Knysna-Humansdorp area, the Cape Flora, and the Karoo Flora all indicate limits of paleoenvironmental change. The flora of the remaining parts of southern Africa is dominated by species belonging to the great tropical flora of Africa (Levyns 1962). This is a mosaic of woodland and grassland savanna of some complexity. All indications are that the general pattern of broad ecological zonation and its diversity has remained constant through the Pleistocene, and, although perturbations in climatic parameters may have affected the distribution of particular species of plants and animals, the whole system appears to have had a high inertia. This is very well illustrated by the continuity in the mammalian fauna between the Middle Pleistocene and the sub-Recent.

The African mammal fauna is notably rich in ungulates. L. H. Wells (1967: 104), for example, has pointed out the need to view extinctions in the antelope fauna between the Middle Pleistocene and the Holocene in dynamic terms with interspecific and intergeneric competition playing an important role. The ecological separation of the grazing ungulates (Gwynne and Bell 1968: 390) is of interest here, and different species can be seen to occupy different microniches within a grazing succession in particular habitats, their relationships being facilitative rather than competitive under stable conditions. This diversity with no single species dominant bespeaks maturity and can be seen in Recent as well as mid-Pleistocene fauna. Homeostatic rather than catastrophic adjustments have been more characteristic through time. Although studies of mid-Pleistocene fauna in southern Africa have been essentially taxonomic and nonquantitative, understandably because of sampling difficulties, the same principles of differential efficiency in utilizing different components in the veld types which structure modern faunal populations have been operative. In southern Africa, as elsewhere in the Ethiopian region, the survival of essentially Pleistocene fauna into the Holocene affords an excellent opportunity for understanding the dynamics of the ecosystems of which past populations were a part.

The stability of paleoenvironments has been stressed here. It does appear to be one of the more striking features of southern Africa in particular, and it does have a bearing on demographic considerations. This does not argue that subtle dislocations that have required adaptive shifts on the part of human populations have not taken place, but they are largely beyond resolution by the present data. These dislocations are likely to have been of low amplitude, with their effects on culture change being felt through coupling to other determinants. This aspect needs stressing so as to encourage more critical and detailed studies of paleoenvironmental factors influencing mid-Pleistocene populations. To be able to best make use of the kinds of paleoenvironmental data available to us, we need to view them in relation to demography, subsistence, technological, and cultural factors.

DEMOGRAPHY

There appear to be two possible approaches to the study of population density and the distribution of Middle Pleistocene hominids. First, there is the direct approach through the study of the distribution and density of archaeological residues. Essentially, this is an approach to the problem from the consideration of settlement patterns. It has been used effectively for short time periods and high density settled communities in limited geographical areas (e.g. Adams 1965).

It is more difficult to control all the variables when considering low density populations of limited archaeological visibility through "deep" time. The second approach can be complementary in that it should provide the theoretical models for empirical testing. It involves the use of analogs to the systemic organization of modern human populations, nonhuman primates, and even carnivores. The inherent danger of analogy in southern Africa, if misused, is that earlier populations will be seen as some hazy kind of Bushmen. Valuable as recent ethnographic studies on particular small social groups in the Kalahari have been, there has been a distressing tendency to make inductive generalizations from the BUSHMEN to the HUNTER-GATHERERS of the tropics, using a very small sample of observations. While there is an urgent need to increase the range of observations of modern hunter-gatherers in southern Africa, this applies equally to nonhuman primate groups and other animals. Interest here, of course, extends beyond simple consideration of determinants of density and dispersal of human populations to aspects such as food and feeding patterns.

The best available data on the distribution of archaeological occurrences in southern Africa are in the *Atlas of African Prehistory* (Clark 1967). This compilation represents a notable achievement, but because of its wide scope, of necessity it suffers from some unevenness in quality of data. Many of the observations recorded are represented by selective and undated finds accumulated in museum collections, and these are difficult to place even within broad industrial divisions. The biface component of the Acheulian has high visibility and is widely recognized; however, samples lacking bifaces or with a low biface component have probably been less reliably reported. The broad subdivisions between pre-Acheulian, Acheulian, and Fauresmith/Sangoan present some problems; for example, the degree to which Lower Acheulian occurrences (see Isaac 1969: 17) and pre-Acheulian plots represent selected collections of artifacts from Upper Acheulian occurrences cannot be adequately determined. The recognition of Fauresmith occurrences in South Africa (Humphreys 1969) and Acheulian and Sangoan occurrences in Rhodesia (C. K. Cooke 1968) has provoked comment in the literature, and this reflects a general lack of precision in the definition of the major industrial divisions at the present time. While a possible future edition of the *Atlas* will afford greater precision, within the strictures of the currently available data the following pattern emerges:
1.   There is a marked increase in the numbers of designated Upper Acheulian sites relative to Lower Acheulian sites.
2.   The Upper Acheulian saw the expansion into the drier western areas.
3.   There is an avoidance of areas underlain by Kalahari sands except on the margins.
4.   The distributions crosscut the broad ecological zonation excluding apparently only the extremes of dry desert and tropical and subtropical forest during the Acheulian *sensu stricto*.

The first point suggests some increase in population through time which would seem to state the obvious. The question is whether this increment is viewed in terms of a linear increase in density through time or as a series of successively reached equilibrium levels. Population densities depend on a number of factors including reproductive and mortality rates, self-regulation of growth, dispersal, competition, and habitat suitability. The archaeological evidence on site distributions primarily reflects dispersal. We may never gain statistically sufficient samples for the computation of mortality patterns because conscious burial and cannibalism do not seem to have been widely practiced. An example of an attempt to calculate mortality age patterns in australopithecine populations is given by Tobias (1972), but it seems questionable that the samples used are natural populations. Certain parameters such as reproductive potential can probably be inferred from modern populations. On physiological grounds a rate of greater than 5 percent can be deemed unlikely, but even at a slightly lower rate the population could double every quarter century (Wrigley 1967: 207). Reproductive success seems less important than behaviorally controlled population self-regulation. The potential for exponential growth was inherent, but it can be assumed that controls regulated this below extreme levels. It is clearly not possible to make a census of mid-Pleistocene populations, but relative estimates of the order of difference between Lower and Upper Acheulian population densities is a possible aim. The relative frequencies of sites suggest a marked difference between the Lower and Upper Acheulian, but the sampling problems are such that reliability is low.

The apparent avoidance of areas underlain by the Kalahari sands may reflect archaeological visibility and inadequate surveys, or it may reflect a real factor related to the availability of permanent standing water. There is an apparent correlation between Acheulian location preferences and water resources that is more marked than in later time ranges. The Power's site on the Vaal is one example and includes large concentrations of artifacts associated with the Younger Gravels unit and extending below present river level. This can be interpreted as a bank-side occupation now being disturbed by river action and clearly is not derived material. The concentration of artifacts is analogous to that at Doornlaagte (Mason 1966), which is situated on the edge of a pan in a gentler sedimentary environment. The Doornlaagte excavation, which included only part of a larger occurrence, exposed an artifact horizon one meter thick and must represent conservatively between ten and twenty thousand artifacts. Such occurrences in themselves are also informative about behavior. Broken Hill and Lochard are examples of dambo associations; Amanzi is a spring depression occupation, and Geelhoutboom a vlei situation. Although the data limit the extension of the argument, it is important to understand the microhabitat preferences of Acheulian populations, such as was attempted at Isimila recently (Hansen and Keller 1971), as this will go part way to explaining dispersal within wider ecological zones.

Archaeological visibility is an important factor when considering the value of large-scale surveys, such as the *Atlas of African Prehistory*, or smaller regional surveys as a basis for gaining relative estimates of density and dispersal of population. For the best explored area of southern Africa, namely South Africa, there is a total of some five hundred sites listed as Acheulian or related industries. These plotted sites have no unit value, some representing tens and others thousands of artifacts, but in total they give of the order of one to two observations for every 10^3 years for a total area of 0.5×10^6 square miles. In theory, at least, the more durable stone artifact products for the whole Middle Pleistocene are recoverable and should relate in some measure to populations. In practice, however, some form of sampling is necessary together with an estimate of its reliability. Some areas of southern Africa are reasonably suitable for this approach. While it may prove impossible to gain other than a low level of precision in population estimates, there is merit in this approach not only in gaining data on variability in forms of occurrences, but also in clarifying some of the sampling difficulties in Lower Palaeolithic research.

DeVore (1963: 311) has characterized hunter-gatherer/foraging human populations as large group-living carnivores and posited an explanation for low human densities relative to the other ground-living primates, such as the baboon, in man's need for hunting space. The estimates of 0.03 to 0.08 persons per 1.0 square mile which he gives for hunter-gatherers in the African savanna is two to three magnitudes lower than that for the baboon in like habitats. It is also an order of magnitude smaller than for large carnivores such as the lion. Because man's hunting propensity is low, it may be too simplistic to relate the relative low density of human population to hunting space. Carnivores such as lions and cheetah take in their own body weight in prey every seven to ten days (Bakkes 1972: 82), but basing an estimate on Gwi hunting (Silberbauer 1965: 30), a figure of seventy to one hundred days would be more appropriate to hunter-gatherers. It can be suggested that human hunters in southern African environments are not in competition with the large carnivores, being less numerous and having a lower kill rate. Overkill due to human predation appears very remote at this level. Although the biomass is reflected in the standing crop ratios of predators to prey, human populations with predation patterns very comparable to those of the large carnivores appear to form a sub-system not directly related to the productivity of the biome. This brings into clearer focus the effects of self-regulated population controls evident in modern population densities at the hunter-gatherer level, which can also be suggested for past populations.

In a model study of Middle/Upper Pleistocene population densities, Lee (1963) used an analogy from recent populations of hunter-gatherers to estimate the population of southern Africa in terms of areas graded on environmental favorability for human occupation. This took into account possible fluctuations in environmental suitability which would receive less emphasis in our present understanding of paleoenvironments. This model draws attention to the large area of southern Africa and its potential importance as a population reservoir in Pleistocene times.

When estimates of population densities are made in numerical terms, these estimates assume, as above, that population density levels are comparable to present day populations at a similar generalized subsistence level in comparable environments. A parallel assumption is that space had the same meaning for population dispersal in the past, and there was an analogous level of uniformity in dispersal patterns. This assumption is probably valid for post-Pleistocene populations with a relative stability linked to intensive broad spectrum resource utilization; however, population fluxes may have been more important in the Middle and Upper Pleistocene populations.

Populations can be dispersed in three main patterns (Garner 1967: 310).

1. Randomly dispersed
2. Clumped
3. Uniformly dispersed

In terms of past human populations, a graded scale can be suggested between random clumping of population units to more uniform nesting or packing of these units in space through time. One end of the scale may approximate the dispersal of early human populations and the other, the more recent populations. If a model of this kind posits more random variability in density of populations in space for the mid- and Upper Pleistocene, then numerical estimates based on modern analogies may be too high. It should be possible to investigate patterning in population dispersal in the archeological record. Discontinuities in the stratigraphic record of the culture in particular areas may evidence this and not be simply due to inadequate sampling or poor archeological visibility. Although this point cannot be elaborated here, uniformitarian principles encourage expectations of continuity and stability of local populations with progressive cultural change through time. This may not be met in the record for the Middle Pleistocene when evidence for the appearance of specific regional adaptations is low or absent.

Although of marginal interest to this paper, the South African australopithecine sites provide a possible example where general inferences can be made on past populations by analogy to carnivore predation patterns. These sites evidence an apparently complex pattern of competition and replacement of one hominid population by another through time. Developed Oldowan/Acheulian populations overlap in time with the robust australopithecine *Paranthropus* population at Swartkrans, where Brain (1970) has suggested that carnivore predation, principally by leopards, has been the main factor in the accumulation of the bone sample. This has implications as yet untested for the other australopithecine occurrences where, hitherto, it has been assumed that the faunal accumulations relate to hominid occupation. That robust australopithecines were a target for carnivore predation in itself would suggest a significant stable population of these hominids. At Swartkrans and indeed the other australopithecine sites, although bovid remains make up the bulk of the fauna, hominids, and Cercopithecoid primates make up a persistent percentage. Carnivore predation goes some way to explaining the richness of sites like Swartkrans in primate fossils. It may also explain features like the higher percentage of juvenile specimens at Swartkrans as compared with Sterkfontein. Tobias (1972) has suggested that this indicates that *Paranthropus* individuals had a lower probability of reaching adulthood than the *A. africanus* individuals represented at Sterkfontein. If body size is taken into account, the *Paranthropus* adults were about twice the size of *A. africanus* adults. Thus, the predominance of *Paranthropus* juveniles at one site and *A. africanus* adults at the other site becomes explicable in terms of selective predation on body size. There would seem to be no need to invoke different natural juvenile mortality rates. This evidence would seem to support Brain's thesis. Swartkrans, and probably the other Transvaal sites then, would seem to fossilize for us an early Pleistocene predator/prey system which can be understood by direct comparison with analogous systems in the present. Leopard predation in the Kruger National Park, for example, shows a high intake of medium and small bovids with a lower level of predation on Cercopithecoid primates. The persistent, if low level, predation on primates has seemingly been responsible for the occurrence of australopithecine fossils in the Transvaal caves, and, importantly, it allows us to see these hominids not simply as fossils for systematic study, but as populations whose densities might be gauged in relation to other elements in the prey system. Further, it is against this background that the appearance of the Lower Acheulian population can be seen in the archeological record.

SUBSISTENCE PATTERNS

In southern Africa occurrences in the time range of the Acheulian that preserve information on foodstuffs and feeding preferences are limited in number. This is because of generally poor conditions of preservation. Only at one site are plant materials preserved. This is the Amanzi Springs (H. J. Deacon 1970; M. J. Wells 1970), where acid, waterlogged conditions have resulted in the preservation of wood and seeds principally. Only the lignin of the cell walls of these woody tissues survives and preservation is clearly very selective. The study of these remains yields information about the microhabitat of the springs rather than any pattern of plant usage. The springs are in an area with a rich geophytic flora, and, as control studies on younger sites show (H. J. Deacon 1972), geophytes are likely to have been the plants of greatest economic importance. Such materials are less resistant to humification and would not be expected to survive at Amanzi Springs. Elsewhere in comparable waterlogged conditions, as for example at Gwisho Springs (post-Pleistocene) and Kalambo Falls, plant materials are similarly preserved, with the notable difference that fruits and seeds in those environments are an important potential foodstuff and, indeed, are represented in the deposits. Here again, however, selective preservation would preclude the appreciation of the full range of plants utilized. The kind of detailed evidence on plant usage that is now becoming available from cave sites of post-Pleistocene and Upper Pleistocene age in southern Africa is unlikely ever to be available for the earlier time ranges. Pollen analysis at its present stage of development has a low resolution and does not appear to offer any immediate solution. Indeed, polleniferous deposits, whether associated with archeological occurrences or not, are rare.

It would seem then that our knowledge of plant utilization is going to depend on the extent to which particular artifact sets can be related to plant food processing and on inferences drawn from a knowledge of available, useable plants in comparable environments. As yet, indigenous plants have been studied for their pharmacological rather than their nutritional value. More definitive studies on availability and usage by present-day human and nonhuman primates in varied habitats are needed. Perhaps, lines of investigation should be aimed less at estimations of the level of dependence on plant foodstuffs in diet and more at possible correlations between tool usage patterns on the one hand, and possible plant usage patterns on the other.

Occurrences associated directly with faunal remains are too few to give any clear indication of hunting capabilities and preferences. The Middle Pleistocene faunas of southern Africa have already received mention concerning relative dating. They are known almost entirely in terms of species lists; interest has been in the systematics so that analyses have been qualitative.

A number of occurrences are known where direct cultural associations are not clear. The Cornelia site excavated by Van Hoepen in 1930 is an example. The fauna-rich horizon, which includes a range of small to large antelopes, two equid species and a hipparion species, four genera of pigs, and two giraffids (H. B. S. Cooke i.p.), overlies an Acheulian horizon in a sequence of valley side silts and clays (Butzer i.p.a.). At present it is impossible to do more than indicate that this rich and varied fauna was contemporary with Acheulian populations. In the case of the Vaal fauna, the associations are again poorly documented, and even in collections from more restricted localities like Pniel, the remains are few, fragmentary, and difficult to relate to the archeology.

The Elandsfontein (Hopefield) site may yet prove to be one of the more informative mid-Pleistocene sites, as it is richly fossiliferous and quantities of artifacts have been found there. The fauna is comparable to that of Cornelia (Hendey 1969, and personal communication), and, in addition to a range of bovids, it includes two equid species, three genera of pigs, the short-necked giraffid, both the black and white rhinos, and two elephant species. This fauna represents natural mortality, carnivore predation, and hunting by Acheulian occupants. A number of carnivores are known from the site, including the lion, a saber-toothed cat, two hyaenids, and a hunting dog. The elephants and rhinos alone can be excluded from possible carnivore predation. The fossils and artifacts are distributed over a two square mile exposure in the sandveld of the southwestern Cape. There is a multiple series of distinct or superimposed scatters of bones and artifacts in a horizon, the elevation of which has been controlled by the water table as the base level of deflation (H. J. Deacon 1964a; for an alternative interpretation, see Mabbutt 1956). Although a number of excavations have been carried out at the site, only one has revealed a convincing association of artifacts and fauna (see Singer and Wymer 1968). This is an anomalous concentration of artifacts with a high biface component in a localized 250 square meter area and associated with a low density scatter of fragmentary bone. Although it is suggested as a butchery site (Singer and Wymer 1968: 67), it does not conform to the high bone density and low artifact frequency pattern suggested for butchery sites (Isaac 1971: 285). The relatively low density of bone could perhaps be due to dispersal by scavengers. As yet, the faunal sample has not been studied in detail, and, thus, it is not informative about hunting practices. The difficulty in interpreting associations in the unconsolidated sand deposit at Elandsfontein is in distinguishing between chance associations and patterned associations. In the instance of the butchery site the artifacts are clearly a discrete association, and their lack of weathering suggests that the occurrence has not been reworked and association of the fauna can be assumed. Elsewhere deflation has uncovered numerous scatters of bone at the site, some in probable association with artifacts, but the evidence is not unequivocal. The interpretation of the fauna poses some difficulties as it includes a range of species (see Hendey 1969) with habitat requirements that are not available in the sandveld at present. Because of the maturity of the southwestern Cape flora, gross environmental change is unlikely, and it may prove that what is represented at Elandsfontein is in the main a fauna related to the exposed shelf during a regressional sea level phase. The fauna of a younger regression phase with an equivalent range of grazers has been well studied by Klein (i.p.).

H. B. S. Cooke (1962) has described the species represented in the fauna from the Cave of Hearths Beds 1 to 3, but quantitative analysis of the available sample is needed. The sample is of limited size for systematic purposes but should be amenable to the informative kinds of analysis pioneered at Makapan Limeworks and now widely used by paleontologists in southern Africa. The Upper Acheulian fauna includes a range of larger antelopes such as the eland, kudu, several alcelaphines, and the waterbuck, as well as smaller antelopes such as the reedbuck and gazelle-like forms (*"Gazella" bondi*). In addition, two equid species, the wide-horned giant buffalo (*Pelorovis* sp.) and the dassie, are represented. This is a very varied and interesting fauna with the species themselves representing a wide range of habitat preferences.

More data are now becoming available for hunting patterns in the later Upper Pleistocene. For example, there are well-studied samples from Kalkbank (Mason, Dart, and Kitching 1958), Witkrans (Clark 1971), Klasies River (Klein i.p.), and Bushman's Rock Shelter (Brain 1969) and all show a comparable emphasis on the hunting of bovids.

Both frequency and age distribution information is necessary if these samples are to be used to trace subtle shifts in hunting competence. At Klasies River, Klein (i.p.) has pointed out that with the exception of the docile eland, the larger bovids are represented predominantly by juveniles. Whatever level of hunting competence this represents, greater competence is unlikely in the Upper Acheulians. Throughout the Middle Pleistocene, medium and large bovids have probably been the principal source of food derived from hunting, with ground game like the hare, dassie, and tortoise in some contributory role.

BEHAVIOR

The markers of behavioral patterning in the Acheulian in southern Africa are almost entirely composed of scatters of stone artifacts. The paucity of paleoenvironmental data and of materials in primary contexts need not be labored further. Problems of dating finds have been generally prominent in discussion of research results, and analyses have been directed at discerning time trends and changes in artifact form, size, and technology. This can be seen in Goodwin's early discussion of handaxe shape in the Montagu Cave sample (Goodwin and van Riet Lowe 1929), and of the size differences between Stellenbosch (Acheulian) and Fauresmith bifaces. Subsequently, Mason (1962a: 224), in his study of the Acheulian occurrences of the Transvaal has used various indices including measures of biface size and shape to characterize Acheulian samples, and again the dorsal preparation of quadrilateral flakes (Mason 1961b: 109) to show technological trends spanning the Middle and Upper Pleistocene. Other more recent studies of single occurrences or smaller series of occurrences in southern Africa for want of a more sophisticated analytical procedure have followed the pattern with the expectation that a trend toward smaller and perhaps broader handaxes is a basis for time ordering (e.g. Fock 1968; Sampson 1972: 58).

Because of the relatively small number and geographical separation of samples, content has received less emphasis. The samples which are stratigraphically superimposed from the Cave of Hearths (Mason 1962a) and Montagu Cave (Keller 1970) apparently show a high level of content similarity, and, thus, variability in artifact content, although recognized (see Mason 1967b: 738), has received little stress. There has been a reluctance to attempt comparisons on content between geographically widely separated sites that are undated. Further, content comparisons have not been facilitated by the adoption of any standard typology. Thus there has not been the same enthusiastic acceptance of activity patterning as an explanation for content variability as in East Africa. The absence of penecontemporaneous series of samples with high content variability demanding explanation either in terms of behavior or some more random processes (Kleindienst 1961; Isaac 1972) is largely the reason for this. Indeed, given the sampling density, data to document the range of content variability in the Acheulian have been lacking. There clearly is variability both in content and in the more subtle stylistic attributes mentioned by Keller (1970), for which satisfactory measures have still to be devised. Because the function of Acheulian artifacts is poorly understood and the evidence of associations between different kinds of artifacts or other materials is minimal, behavioral inferences at this level are few.

Artifact occurrences are, in the main, open sites, with the Cave of Hearths, Montagu, and a third possibility in Wonderwerk Cave notable exceptions. The Montagu Cave Acheulian occupation (Keller 1970; Butzer i.p.b.) is noteworthy because of the nature of the deposits. Both occupation zones are associated with fine and in part laminated sediments and are high in mineral ash content. In this situation, human occupation has contributed significantly to the buildup of the deposits, and there is little doubt that the high ash content of certain horizons represents combusted organic debris. The organic material has probably been chiefly utilized plant waste. Largely artifact-sterile layers, where leaf fall would have been the main contributory source, have a reduced organic component. These occupation residues have some parallel in some post-Pleistocene occurrences in the same mountain belt (e.g. Melkhoutboom and Scott's Cave; see H. J. Deacon 1972), although close identification would seem unwarranted. Montagu Cave, then, evidences fairly intensive and repeated occupation of a cave as does the Cave of Hearths. It should be possible to test how extensive this pattern was in zones like the Cape Folded Belt where the caves are "long lived." As yet, there has been relatively little excavation in large sections of this folded mountain range.

There are a number of open site situations in southern Africa which again show persistent occupation of a particular locality. The Doornlaagte occurrence (Mason 1966) has already been discussed and other examples that could be suggested are Wonderboom in the Transvaal (Mason 1962a: 169), Amanzi (H. J. Deacon 1970), and perhaps Gwelo Koppie in Rhodesia. There are extremely large densities of artifacts in what are layers of undifferentiated multitool thickness. These are clearly not single occupation horizons but are due to multiple occupation over a period when the determination of favorability of a specific locale remained constant. In an ephemeral seasonal pan situation like Doornlaagte, it can be argued that this may have been of relatively short duration. The occupation at Doornlaagte overlies a marly unit indicating lacustrine conditions and is associated with a more sandy marginal facies of a possibly less persistent body of water. The surface of the deposit has a low slope, and the dense packing of the artifacts through a meter thickness strongly suggests they are contained in essentially a lag deposit with a high proportion of the finer sediments removed (H. J. Deacon 1964b; Butzer i.p.a.). These occurrences could be viewed as condensed sequences of penecontemporaneous occupations. Their mode of occurrence precludes study of short term variability, but they are valid samples with a potential for analysis largely untested. A similar, but expanded, sequence may be evidenced at Rooidam in a comparable situation to Doornlaagte (Fock 1968; Butzer 1973).

There are few data available for inferences on group sizes and the range of mobility of groups. Some limits are placed on size by apparent containment within large cave situations and limited open areas. Elandsfontein is the closest approximation to the excavation of a complete occupation area with other completely exposed occurrences for the most part in semiprimary context. Distortion of areas of occupation on compact surfaces through natural processes is perhaps the norm in most southern African situations.

The range of Acheulian groups, as noted by Clark (1970: 100), may be indicated in the sources of raw materials used. For the most part local or widely available materials have been used thus precluding inferences being drawn. Bond's work (1948) at Lochard provided some initial data for consideration, but fuller documentation is lacking and the sampling control is perhaps inadequate (C. K. Cooke 1968). The evidence from the Riet River and Lower Vaal (Humphreys 1970) shows rather restricted use of raw materials local to the sites. For the most part, technologies appear to have been sufficiently adaptable to locally available materials. The Victoria West cores are an outstanding example. Generally the organization was perhaps not geared to a marked degree of selection of materials in relation to ease of working or function.

It is within this limited range of observations and inferences that our present understanding of human behavior in the mid-Pleistocene is set. Although the principal manifestations of behavior, stone artifacts, have been under-studied, the impetus to make these studies more sophisticated will depend on progress in solving some of the problems in sampling and dating and progress in our understanding of paleoecology. More important still is the development of improved theoretical frame works to guide the direction of research and the review of existing data. The limitations of the present concepts are apparent when explanations of change in the cultural record are discussed. A relevant example is the transition between the Acheulian and the Middle Stone Age.

ACHEULIAN TRANSFORMATIONS AND THE ORIGINS OF THE MIDDLE STONE AGE

In the classic tripartite division of the Stone Age in southern Africa, (Goodwin and van Riet Lowe 1929) the Earlier Stone Age, including the Stellenbosch (= Acheulian) and Fauresmith, was succeeded by a complex of variants or variations of cultures belonging to the Middle Stone Age. This early established the concept of a simple succession or group of Earlier Stone Age cultures being followed in time by a more diverse range of industries. The transition from the Earlier Stone Age to the Middle Stone Age was viewed as the possible product of external cultural influences, perhaps deriving from the Mousterian of Europe and North Africa, an explanation in line with the then current concepts of invasion and diffusion. The Fauresmith was seen as closely allied to the Acheulian, but sufficiently distinct to warrant separate industrial status. The possibility was raised that the Fauresmith might be a transitional industry between the Acheulian and the Middle Stone Age.

Subsequent investigators have been reluctant to see the transition from the Acheulian to the Middle Stone Age in terms of exotic influences. A more recent statement makes this clear:

The evidence we have, scattered and unsatisfactory as it is, suggests an unbroken sequence of evolution in artefact making from the Earlier to the Later Acheulian and then a change eliminating the heavy bifaced Earlier Stone Age artefacts, but placing new emphasis on the ancient unifacial flake component at the beginning of the Middle Stone Age (Mason 1962a: 156).

The explanation given for the change or transition to the Middle Stone Age in this example was suggested as dissatisfaction with existing equipment and the desire for improved artifacts. Another view of the autochthonous development of the Middle Stone Age cultures out of the Acheulian laid stress on the transitional character of the Fauresmith and linked it to the Sangoan as two intermediate industries. The Third Pan-African Congress gave formal recognition to this concept (Clark

1957). The Fauresmith and Sangoan industries were seen as falling within an interpluvial phase, when stress on population was high, promoting new patterns of dispersal that, in turn, favored cultural changes leading to the regionally specialized industries of the Middle Stone Age (Clark 1959b: 131).

The original explanatory hypothesis rested heavily on climatic determinism but has been restated recently in modified form (Clark 1970). It retains a stress on the importance of paleoenvironmental changes of the Upper Pleistocene, but is more sophisticated in suggesting a feedback between environmental, demographic, and cultural factors promoting the changes seen in the archeological record between the Upper Acheulian and the Middle Stone Age. This is the most cogent explanation of the processes affecting the populations of the late Middle and early Upper Pleistocene and is discussed further in general terms below.

The distinction between two parallel phyla, the Fauresmith and Sangoan, each with a focus in a different broad ecological zone, has been viewed as evidence for an initial stage of minimally specialized adaptation distinct from the more generalized adaptation of the Acheulian. This view has had to be modified somewhat. The Fauresmith has been suggested as localized in the open grassveld areas of South Africa, but its status as a separate cultural entity from the Acheulian has been questioned. Goodwin and van Riet Lowe (1929) considered the Fauresmith sufficiently distinctive to warrant separate industrial status. The opinion of more recent workers is that there is no industry with a biface component that warrants consideration outside the broad cultural division of the Acheulian (Mason 1962a: 470; Humphreys 1970: 143; Sampson 1972: 52). Occurrences which would have been classified as Fauresmith in the concept of Goodwin and van Riet Lowe, and which have been grouped here within the Upper Acheulian, have been accommodated in divisions like the Later or Final Acheulian (Mason 1962a: 470; Sampson 1972: 59). This terminology simply reflects the view that none of the known occurrences are typologically transitional to the Middle Stone Age. Indeed, it would be difficult to suggest what a transitional industry would look like, apart from the difficulty of holding a concept of intermediate forms, and only one worker has suggested the as yet untested identification of such a transitional industry (Sampson 1972: 280). If a separate entity like the Fauresmith is not acceptable on typological grounds, then different grades of regional adaptation might be considered between the Upper Acheulian *sensu stricto* and a late phase of the Upper Acheulian. If such can be demonstrated, terminological recognition would be required. An alternative is that the younger phases of the Upper Acheulian represent a continuation of the adaptation to the grassland habitats, while new adaptive change is most marked in the Sangoan industries. This is the explanation favored by Clark (1970: 110).

The Sangoan with its apparent crudity in artifacts is the ugly duckling become a swan. It is perceived, then, as an important innovative pattern of adaptation to woodland environments with a technology different from the Acheulian (Clark 1970: 112). The main basis for suggesting the woodland adaptation for the Sangoan is its distribution in equatorial and south central Africa. The core axes, picks, heavy duty scrapers, and small cutting and scraping tools that distinguish it from the Acheulian are presumed to be woodworking tools because of the environmental distribution, although occurrences with the preservation of wooden artifacts are unknown at present. As woodworking is known in the Upper Acheulian at Kalambo Falls, it is a reasonable postulate that a similar or greater reliance on woodworking was present in the succeeding Sangoan. Faunal preservation at Sangoan occurrences is again virtually unknown; Broken Hill is a possible example. The ways in which the Sangoan populations were exploiting their environment are still to be documented.

A further point relates to the dating of the upper phases of the Acheulian and the Sangoan. High reliance has been placed on the finite dating of the Upper Acheulian at Kalambo Falls (Clark 1969: Appendix J), where it has been presumed that the Sangoan falls in a time range of between about 35,000 and 50,000 years B.P. There are a number of age determinations, both finite and infinite, older than 40,000 years B.P. for the Sangoan, and on present experience these are best considered minimal ages. If recent estimates for the age range of Middle Stone Age entities (Beaumont and Vogel 1972: 162) are correct then at least some Sangoan occurrences may be older than 100,000 years. This throws doubt on the expected duration of the Sangoan complex, and efforts to relate its development to paleoenvironmental changes of the Upper Pleistocene become somewhat tenuous (see Clark 1970: 108). There is a view that the Sangoan time range was a period during which tool traditions underwent rapid change with increases in standardization of tool forms and in number of variable toolkits (Clark 1970: 108). This gives to the Sangoan and the contemporary upper phases of the Upper Acheulian a transitional nature, in terms of environmental adaptations if not in terms of artifact forms. Many distinct and regionally scpecialized industrial variants are associated with the superior later Upper Pleistocene tool kits and moreover known fossils of fully modern man

Table 1.   Mean length and breadth/length ratio of handaxes/bifaces

Length in centimeters	100 × breadth over length	Occurrence	Reference
9.2	53	Inhoek	Sampson (1972)
10.2	70	Meirton	Humphreys (1969)
10.6	64	Rooidam	Fock (1968)
11.2 (Min. value)		Elandsfontein	Singer and Crawford (1958)
11.7	57	Waterval	Sampson (1972)
12.2	61	Glen Elliott	Sampson (1972)
12.3	61	Elandskloof	Sampson (1972)
12.1 (median)	60	Three Rivers	Mason (1962a)
12.1 (median)	63	Blaaubank Group 3	Mason (1962a)
12.1 (median)	65	Cave of Hearths	Mason (1962a)
12.6 (median)	65	Wonderboom	Mason (1962a)
13.1 (median)	58	Blaaubank Group 2	Mason (1962a)
13.2 (median)	54	Riverview Estate	Mason (1962a)
14.6	60	Amanzi	Deacon (1970)
14.7	–	Montagu layer 3	Keller (1970)
15.3	–	Wagenmaker Vallei	Malan (1939)
17.4	–	Hangklip	Sampson (1972)
17.5	–	Montagu layer 5	Keller (1970)

Note: The bifaces from these Acheulian sites show a weak tendency for smaller and broader forms to dominate in the youngest samples. The sites of Meirton and Rooidam for example are stratigraphically younger and typologically distinct in the high frequency (up to 70 percent tools) of relatively formalized flake scrapers, from the Upper Acheulian of the Younger Gravels of the Vaal (Riverview Estates sample) and the Doornlaagte site. Both Meirton and Rooidam include relatively short and broad biface forms and, together with the Inhoek site, represent a late phase of the Acheulian in the Vaal Basin. One horizon at the Rooidam site is radiometrically dated (Butzer, personal communication) and this supports its terminal Acheulian designation. The Cave of Hearths sample can be relatively dated to the Florisbad-Vlakkraal faunal span (late Middle–early Upper Pleistocene) and shows a higher median value for length than the Lower Acheulian sample from Three Rivers. These samples however could be distinguished on other criteria such as scar counts. The Three Rivers sample apart the remaining samples could be grouped broadly within the Upper Acheulian of Southern Africa.

follow this transition period (see Clark 1970: 123). Population increases are seen as important in the new adaptation appearing in the Sangoan/late Upper Acheulian, and in the succeeding Middle Stone Age. Support for this is in terms of the increasing density of recorded sites (Clark 1970: 108).

Explanation of the transformation between the Acheulian and Middle Stone Age in southern Africa is a problem related in scale to that of the appearance of the Mousterian in Europe, the Near East, and North Africa. The transition, which is of comparable dating, is, if anything, more abrupt in southern Africa. The explanatory hypothesis analyzed above highlights the lack of empirical data for testing concepts. It may, however, provide a basis for further discussion of the nature of the interplay between demographic, ecological, technological, and social factors in the Acheulian in southern Africa and the contrast with later time.

Our thinking at present seems to be in terms of broad concepts such as degrees of regional adaptation and technological specialization, without our being able to fully comprehend their nature. The long timerange of the Acheulian appears to show homeostatic adjustments between variables such as the density and dispersal of populations, their genetic makeup, and behavioral potentials. The broad cultural divisions recognized within the Acheulian may approximate different equilibrium plateaus. The transition to the Middle Stone Age would seem to be a change of a different order — a result of strong positive feedback between the controlling variables. It may be false to hope that transitional adaptive phases, any more than transitional industries, can be isolated in the archaeological record.

REFERENCES

ADAMS, R. MC. M.
   1965   *Land behind Baghdad.* Chicago: University of Chicago Press..
BAKKER, R. T.
   1972   Anatomical and ecological evidence for endothermy in dinosaurs. *Nature* 238:81–85.
BEAUMONT, PETER B.
   1973   Border Cave — a progress report. *South African Journal of Science* 69:41–46.
BEAUMONT, PETER B., J. C. VOGEL
   1972   On a new radiocarbon chronology for Africa south of the Equator. *African Studies* 31(3):155–182.
BOND, G.
   1948   Rhodesian Stone Age Man and his raw materials. *South African Archaeological Bulletin* 3(11):55–60.
   1963   "Pleistocene environments in Southern Africa," in *African ecology and human evolution.* Edited by F. C. Howell and F. Bourlière. Chicago: Aldine.
BOND, G., R. F. SUMMERS
   1951   The Quaternary succession and archaeology at Chelmer near Bulawayo Southern Rhodesia. *South African Journal of Science* 47(7):200–204.
BRAIN, C. K.
   1969   Faunal remains from Bushman Rock Shelter, Eastern Transvaal. *South African Archaeological Bulletin* 24(2):52–55.
   1970   New finds at the Swartkrans australopithecine site. *Nature* 225-(5238):1112–1119.

BRAIN, C. K., C. VAN RIET LOWE, R. A. DART
 1955   Kafuan stone artefacts in the post-Australopithecine breccia at Makapansgat. *Nature* 175:16–18.
BUTZER, K. W.
 1973   Geological interpretation of Acheulian calc-pan sites at Doornlaagte and Rooidam (Kimberley, South Africa). *Journal of Archaeological Science* 1.
 i.p.a. Geology of the Cornelia Beds, Northeastern Orange Free State.
 i.p.b. "A provisional interpretation of the sedimentary sequence from Montagu Cave (Cape Province) South Africa," in *The archaeology of Montagu Cave*. Edited by C. M. Keller. University of California Publications in Archaeology.
CLARK, J. DESMOND
 1959a Further excavations at Broken Hill, Northern Rhodesia. *Journal of the Royal Anthropological Institute* 89(2).
 1959b *The prehistory of Southern Africa*. Harmondsworth: Pelican.
 1969   *Kalambo Falls prehistoric site*, volume one. Cambridge: Cambridge University Press.
 1970   *The prehistory of Africa*. London: Thames and Hudson.
 1971   Human behavioural differences in Southern Africa during the late Pleistocene. *American Anthropologist* 73(5):1211–1236.
CLARK, J. DESMOND, editor
 1957   Resolutions. *Proceedings of the Third Pan-African Congress on Prehistory*. London: Chatto and Windus.
 1967   *Atlas of African prehistory*. Chicago: University of Chicago Press.
COOKE, C. K.
 1968   The Early Stone Age in Rhodesia. *Arnoldia* 3(39):1–12.
COOKE, H. B. S.
 1958   Observations relating to Quaternary environment in East and Southern Africa. Geological Society of South Africa: Alex du Toit Memorial Lecture Number 5. *Transactions of the Geological Society of South Africa* Annexure to Volume 60.
 1962   "Notes on the faunal material from the Cave of Hearths and Kalkbank," in *Prehistory of the Transvaal*. Edited by R. J. Mason, Appendix 1: 447–453. Johannesburg: University of the Witwatersrand Press.
 i.p.   The fossil mammals of Cornelia, Orange Free State, South Africa. *Memoirs of the National Museum Bloemfontein*.
COOKE, H. B. S., L. H. WELLS
 1951   Fossil remains from Chelmer near Bulawayo, Southern Rhodesia. *South African Journal of Science* 47:207–209.
DEACON, H. J.
 1964a "Report on excavations at Elandsfontein." Unpublished report 1–33.
 1964b "Report on the geology of the Doornlaagte site." Unpublished manuscript.
 1970   The Acheulian occupation at Amanzi Springs, Uitenhage District, Cape Province. *Annals of the Cape Provincial Museums (Natural History)* 8:89–189.

1972 "A review of the post-Pleistocene in South Africa." South African Archaeological Society, Goodwin Series 1:26–45.

DEACON, J.
1966 An annotated list of radiocarbon dates for sub-Saharan Africa. *Annals of the Cape Provincial Museums* 5:5–84.

DEVORE, I.
1963 "A comparison of the ecology and behaviour of monkeys and apes," in *Classification and human evolution*. Edited by S. L. Washburn, 301–319. Viking Fund Publications in Anthropology 37.

FIELDEN, H. W.
1905 The Stone Age of the Zambezi Valley and its relation in time. *Nature* 73:77–78.

FLINT, R. F.
1959a Pleistocene climates in Eastern and Southern Africa. *Bulletin of the Geological Society of America* 70:343–374.
1959b On the basis of Pleistocene correlation in East Africa. *Geological Magazine* 96(4):265–284.

FOCK, G. J.
1968 Rooidam, a sealed site of the First Intermediate. *South African Journal of Science* 64(3):153–159.

GARNER, B. J.
1967 "Models of urban geography and settlement location," in *Models in geography*. Edited by R. J. Chorley and Peter Haggett, 303–360. London: Methuen.

GOODWIN, A. J. H., C. VAN RIET LOWE
1929 The Stone Age cultures of South Africa. *Annals of the South African Museum* 27:1–289.

GWYNNE, M. D., R. H. V. BELL
1968 Selection of vegetation components by grazing ungulates in the Serengeti National Park. *Nature* 230:390–393.

HADDON, A. C.
1906 *Journal of the Royal Anthropological Institute* 36.

HANSEN, CARL L., C. M. KELLER
1971 Environment and activity patterning at Isimila Korongo, Iringa District, Tanzania: a preliminary report. *American Anthropologist* 73(5):1201–1211.

HENDEY, Q. B.
1969 Quaternary vertebrate fossil sites in the south-western Cape Province. *South African Archaeological Bulletin* 24:96–105.

HUMPHREYS, A. J. B.
1969 Later Acheulian or Fauresmith? A contribution. *Annals of the Cape Provincial Museums (Natural History)* 6(10):87–101.
1970 The role of raw material and the concept of the Fauresmith. *South African Archaeological Bulletin* 25:139–144.

INSKEEP, R. R.
1969 Some problems relating to the Early Stone Age in South Africa. *South African Archaeological Bulletin* 24:174–181.

ISAAC, GLYNN L.
1968 Traces of Pleistocene hunters: an East African example, in *Man*

the Hunter. Edited by R. B. Lee and Irven DeVore. Chicago: Aldine.

1969 Studies in early culture in East Africa. *World Archaeology* 1(1): 1–28.

1971 The diet of early man: aspects of archaeological evidence from Lower and Middle Pleistocene sites in Africa. *World Archaeology* 2(3):279–299.

1972 "Early phases of human behaviour: models in Lower Palaeolithic archaeology," in *Models in archaeology.* Edited by David L. Clarke, 167–199. London: Methuen.

JOHNSON, J. P., R. B. YOUNG

1906 The relation of the ancient deposits of the Vaal River to the Palaeolithic period of South Africa. *Transactions of the Geological Sociey of South Africa* 9:53–56.

KELLER, C. M.

1970 Montagu Cave: a preliminary report. *Quaternaria* 13:187–204.

KLEIN, R. G.

i.p. Environment and subsistence of prehistoric man in the Southern Cape, South Africa. *World Archaeology.*

KLEINDIENST, M. R.

1961 Variability within the late Acheulian assemblage in Eastern Africa. *South African Archaeological Bulletin* 16(62):35–52.

1967 "Questions of terminology in regard to the study of Stone Age industries in Eastern Africa: cultural stratigraphic units," in *Background to evolution n Africa.* Edited by W. W. Bishop and J. D. Clark, 821–859. Chicago: University of Chicago Press.

LAMPLUGH, G. W.

1906 Notes on the occurrence of stone implements in the valley of the Zambezi around Victoria Falls. *Journal of the Royal Anthropological Institute* 36:159–169.

LEAKEY, MARY D.

1971 *Olduvai Gorge,* volume three. Cambridge: Cambridge University Press.

LEE, RICHARD B.

1963 The population ecology of man in the early Upper Pleistocene of Southern Africa. *Proceedings of the Prehistoric Society* 29:235–257.

LEVYNS, M. R.

1962 Past plant migrations in South Africa. *Annals of the Cape Provincial Museums* 2:7–10.

MABBUTT, J. A.

1954 Cape Hangklip: a study in coastal geomorphology. *Transactions of the Royal Society of South Africa* 34(1):17–24.

1956 The physiography and surface geology of the Hopefield fossil site. *Transactions of the Royal Society of South Africa* 35(1):21–58.

MASON, R. J.

1961a Australopithecus and the beginning of the Stone Age in South Africa. *South African Archaeological Bulletin* 16(61):8–14.

1961b The Acheulian culture in South Africa. *South African Archaeological Bulletin* 16(63):107–110.
1962a *Prehistory of the Transvaal.* Johannesburg: University of the Witwatersrand Press.
1962b The Earlier Stone Age and the Transvaal. *South African Archaeological Bulletin* 17(Supplement):46–50.
1966 The excavation of Doornlaagte Earlier Stone Age camp, Kimberley District. *Actes du Ve Congrès Panafricain de préhistoire et de l'étude du Quaternaire.* Dakar.
1967a The archaeology of the earliest superficial deposits in the lower Vaal basin near Holpan, Windsorton district. *South African Geographical Journal* 49:39–56.
1967b "Analytical procedures in the Earlier and Middle Stone Age cultures in Southern Africa," in *Background to evolution in Africa.* Edited by W. W. Bishop and J. D. Clark. Chicago: University of Chicago Press.
MASON, R. J., R. A. DART, JAMES W. KITCHING
1958 Bone tools at the Kalkbank Middle Stone Age site and the Makapansgat australopithecine locality, central Transvaal. *South African Archaeological Bulletin* 13(51):85–116.
OAKLEY, KENNETH P.
1954 Study tour of early hominid sites in Southern Africa, 1953. *South African Archaeological Bulletin* 9(35):75–87.
PÉRINGUEY, L.
1911 The Stone Ages of South Africa. *Annals of the South African, Museum* 8.
SAMPSON, C. G.
1972 *The Stone Age industries of the Orange River Scheme and South Africa.* National Museum Bloemfontein Memoir 6.
SILBERBAUER, GEORGE B.
1965 *Bushman survey report.* Gaberones.
SINGER, R., JOHN WYMER
1968 Archaeological investigations at the Saldanha skull site in South Africa. *South African Archaeological Bulletin* 25:63–74.
TOBIAS, P. V.
1972 "Progress and problems in the study of early man in sub-Saharan Africa," in *The functional and evolutionary biology of primates.* Edited by R. Tuttle, 63–93. New York: Aldine-Atherton.
WELLS, L. H.
1967 "Antelopes in the Pleistocene of southern Africa," in *Background to evolution in Africa.* Edited by W. W. Bishop and J. D. Clark, 99–107. Chicago: University of Chicago Press.
WELLS, M. J.
1970 Plant remains from Amanzi Springs. *Annals of the Cape Provincial Museums (Natural History)* 8:191–194.
WRIGLEY, E. A.
1967 "Demographic models in geography," in *Models in geography.* Edited by R. J. Chorley and P. Haggett, 189–215. London: Methuen.

Archeological Occurrences in the Middle Pleistocene of Israel

OFER BAR-YOSEF

ABSTRACT

The geochronological evidences from the coastal plain and the Jordan Valley are reviewed against the geographical background of Israel. The sequence in the Jordan Valley, since it became a closed basin some 2.0–1.7 million years ago reveals a series of limnic formations interrupted by lava flows, tectonic movements, and erosion. Available K/Ar dates with generalized faunal correlations indicate that the site of ʿUbeidiya is at least 0.64–0.68 million years old. The sites of Gesher Benot Yaʿaqov and Maayan Barukh are related to the wet period before the Last Pluvial (defined on the basis of pollen analysis). In the coastal plain within the sequence of eolianites and red loams, the chronological correlations are based on the identification of Tyrrhenian faunas, as well as the sedimentological and palynological studies in Tabun Cave (related to the last pluvial age).

The archeological record, discussed in the second part of the paper, indicates the uneven quality and quantity of the available data. Most of the known and studied assemblages are surface collections, fewer are from old excavations, and those of the more recent excavations (Tabun, Holon, ʿUbeidiya) are not yet published in detail. Non-Acheulian assemblages are not included.

At ʿUbeidiya fourteen different assemblages occurred within a terrestrial-fluviatile cycle (Fi) which is reconstructed as an alluvial fan. This sedimentary unit is intercalated within two limnic units (Li and Lu) demonstrating probably pluvial conditions. The different archeological occurrences are located mainly on the beaches of the old lake, but also on the alluvial fan and within the hilly area. The lithic assemblages include core-choppers, flake tools, spheroids, bifaces and picks in different proportions, but with a clear preference for specific raw materials for each category.

Within the Middle Acheulian, the unique basalt assemblage of Gesher Benot Yaʿaqov is included, where many flake cleavers are present, along with Holon and

I would like to express my sincere thanks to my colleagues, Dr. D. Gilead, Miss N. Goren, Dr. A. Horowitz, Dr. D. Nir, Dr. A. Ronen, and Dr. J. L. Phillips, who read the manuscript and made useful suggestions, and to Mrs. J. Phillips, who edited and typed the manuscript.

The fieldwork on which part of this paper is based was made possible by generous funds of the Israel Academy of Sciences and Humanities and by the Wenner-Gren Foundation for Anthropological Research.

Umm Qatafa. The Upper Acheulian occurrences are divided into four groups of which one probably belongs to an earlier phase and one to a later.

Non-artifactual aspects are also discussed. Locational analysis demonstrates that the Acheulian sites are distributed in many different environmental situations. Some sites are extended and possibly represent repeated occupations, while the small ones are limited to an estimated size of 200–500 square meters, both in caves and open air sites.

It is difficult to evaluate the sources of subsistence, due to lack of faunal quantitative studies; even less is known about hunting habits or possible vegetable foods.

A.   THE GEOLOGICAL BACKGROUND

1.   Introduction

Israel is located in the southwestern corner of Asia and extends over an area of about 400 kilometers in length and about 100 kilometers in width. This territory is naturally divided into three elongated strips, oriented in a north-south direction, which can be further subdivided according to the relatively different climates belonging to each zone. From west to east these are: the coastal plain, which is narrow in the northern part and widens towards the south; the hilly area, dissected by several transverse valleys; and the Jordan Valley, which is part of the Syro-African Rift. Eastward, the Trans-Jordanian plateau stretches into the Syro-Arabian desert (Figure 1).

In a landscape that is built up mainly of sedimentary rocks of the Upper Cretaceous to Tertiary periods, both climate and vegetation vary considerably in relation to the size of the country. Annual precipitation decreases from 1200–1000 millimeters in the Upper Galilee to less than 100 millimeters in the Southern Negev. The same type of decrease occurs from the central coastal plain, which receives 600 millimeters a year, to the lower Jordan Valley, with less than 50 millimeters annual rainfall. The soils within the Mediterranean zone are mainly *terra rossa* and the grey *rendzina* which is typical of the Senon-Eocene chalky areas. In the coastal plain *hamra* (red loam), the product of deteriorated *kurkar* (sandstone) or sand, as well as the alluvial soils, are the most common.

The northern parts of the country are covered with Mediterranean vegetation, mainly the maquis. Eastward and southward Irano-Turanian flora predominate, while the Saharo-Sindian flora is represented in the lower Jordan Valley and parts of the Negev. Enclaves of Sudano-Deccanian flora are found in some oases along the Rift Valley.

The geological research of the Pleistocene was carried out mainly in the Jordan Valley and the coastal plain. These two areas were basically sedimentary basins, modified by tectonic movements, and contain within

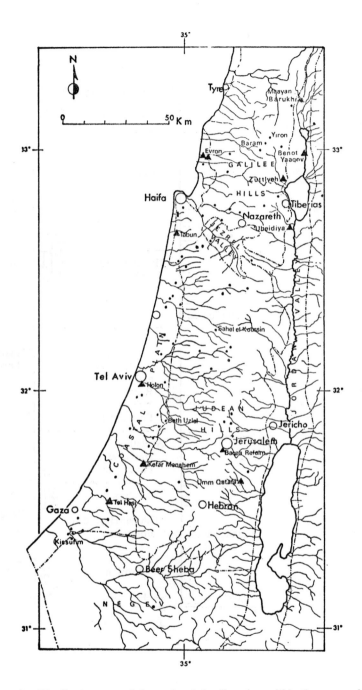

Figure 1. Distribution map of the major Acheulian sites within the geographical regions of Palestine
(triangles = excavated sites, dots = surface collections, circles = modern cities)

Table 1. Geochrological stratigraphy of Israel during the Middle

Years B.P.	Jordan Valley		
	Upper (Hula)		Central
10,000			
			Tabgha Formatio
20,000	Ashmura Formation		
			Lisan Formation
	Dan trav.		
50,000			
	Hasbani Basalt and Hulata Formation		Naharayim basal
100,000			
	Kfar Yuval Travertine and Benot Ya'aqov Formation		Naharayim Formation
	Ayeleth Hashahar Formation		
500,000			tectonic activity
	Yarda Basalt		Yarmuk Basalt
	Mishmar Hayarden Formation		'Ubeidiya Formation
1,000,000			
			Erq el-Ahmar Formation Erosion
	Erosion		
2,000,000	+ + + +		Cover Bas

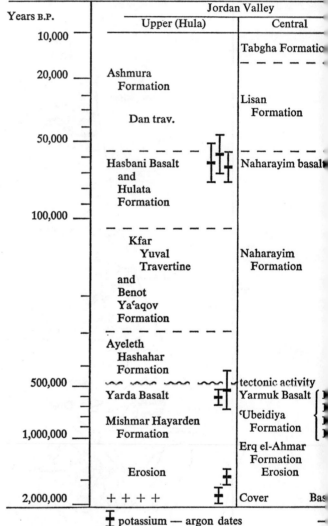

⊥ potassium — argon dates

pes Pleistocene with suggested correlations to the Glacial chronology

ower	Coastal plain	Prehistoric sites	Glacial chronology used in the text	
- — —				
n ormation	M3a			
armar ormation	"Hamra" II M3	Tabun B C	Wurm	Upper Pleistocene
- — —		D E Umm Qatafa		
	T3	F 1 D 2	Riss-Würm (Eem)	
	M2a	Maayan Barukh		
	T2 "Hamra" II	Holon E		Middle Pleistocene
	T1 M2	Gesher Benot Ya'aqov	Riss (Saale) Mindel-Riss (Holstein)	
		Latamne Evron Quarry		
～ ～	"Hamra" I			
	M1a	1-26	Mindel (Elster)	
ora ormation		'Ubeidiya II-24-		Lower
	M1		Villafranchian	
⊢ + + +				

— Formation limits

their deposits some important prehistoric sites. In the mountainous and hilly areas of the Galilee and Judea there are several sites, isolated due to tectonic activity and erosion. There are difficulties in establishing the prehistoric sequence in this region, as well as tracing the geological correlations between the coastal plain and the Jordan Valley.

Table 1 summarizes the major events in each area by mentioning the different geological formations alongside the main sites and the suggested correlations with the Pleistocene glacial chronology.

2.   The Geochronological Evidence from the Jordan Valley

The chronology of the Jordan Valley was established by tectonostratigraphic, palynological, and faunistic studies, and some radiometric dates as well. It is therefore possible to describe the geological history of the Jordan Valley and to set within its framework the archeological occurrences hitherto discovered. (The literature on this subject includes numerous references from which selected ones will be noted.)

Schematically, the long history of the Jordan Valley can be described as consisting of two periods of filling-in. The first period is characterized by invasions of the Mediterranean into a shallow basin through the Jezreel Valley (Esdraelon Valley), by the accumulation of lagoonal and terrestrial formations, and by some limited tectonic dislocations. Several different formations were laid down dating from Miocene through Early Pleistocene as defined by Picard (1943), Schulman (1959), and Horowitz (i.p.). This period terminated with the eruptions of the Cover Basalt, of which the late flows are dated to 1.7–2.0 million years (Table 2). These dates (Table 1) fall within the Matuyama reversal epoch, which is verified by the reversed magnetic polarity of most of these basalt flows (Freund, et al. 1965; Nur and Helsley 1971). The general coverage of the Cover Basalt allowed for the development of drainage systems oriented westward, the relicts of which are known from Bethlehem and the Hameshar Conglomerates in the southern Negev (Garfunkel and Horowitz 1966). The steppe-like, humid conditions which favored the existence of the Bethlehem fauna can be related to this period (see Table 3). It seems that the topographical and climatological situation that can be inferred from the deposits at Bethlehem, as well as from the nature of the faunal assemblage, is different from the relatively high, dissected landscape of today. The absence of paleoarctic elements such as the Cervidae from this assemblage suggests a pre-Glacial Pleistocene date (Hooijer 1958; Clark 1961; Bar-Yosef and Tchernov 1972).

Table 2. Potassium argon dates from the Jordan Valley

Geological unit	Dates in million years	Source
Hasbani basalt	0.073 ± 0.014	a
	0.079 ± 0.013	a
Naharayim basalt	0.064 ± 0.013	a
Yarda basalt	0.64 ± 0.12	b
Yarmuk basalt	0.68 ± 0.05	b
Cover basalt	2.0 ± 0.1	a
	1.7 ± 0.1	a
Intermediate basalt	3.6	c
	4.7 ± 0.2	a
	4.7 ± 0.5	a
	4.9	c
	5.0 ± 0.3	a

Sources: a. G. Siedner, personal communication.
          b. Horowitz, et al. (1973).
          c. Curtis (1965).

The second period in the geological history of the Jordan Valley, which is the major subject of the following pages, begins with the major breakdown of the Jordan graben (Picard 1965), creating the scenario for later events. Henceforth, the development of the Jordan Rift was to be dictated by the accumulation of deposits, endemic tectonics, and erosion within its basin. The same diastrophic movements are responsible for the uplift of the Galilee and the Judean hills.

The geological formations from this period, which extends until the Holocene, are assigned a Lower Pleistocene date (see, for example, Picard 1965); while according to the definition suggested for this symposium, they are mainly Middle and Upper Pleistocene in date. Following the chronological assignment, based on faunal assemblages and the interpretation of the palynological record, most of this second period is post-Villafranchian or Glacial Pleistocene.

The geological data come from boreholes in the Dead Sea basin (Neev and Emery 1967; Horowitz 1968a, i.p.); from the exposures of the ʿUbeidiya formation in the Central Jordan Valley (Picard 1963, 1965; Picard and Baida 1966a, 1966b; Bar-Yosef and Tchernov 1972); from the exposures at Gesher Benot Yaʿaqov, the northern Hula Valley and the boreholes in this basin (Picard 1963, 1965; Schulman 1967; Horowitz 1968b, 1971, i.p.), and are summarized henceforth in the same order.

The cumulative data inform us of a period of erosion following the main faulting phase, and the formation of a system of lakes. The Dead Sea basin was a saline lake at the enclosed southern end of the valley, where the accumulation of the sediments thereafter attained a thickness

Table 3.   Comparison between the faunistic assemblages of Bethlehem, ʿUbeidiya, Latamne, and Gesher Benot Yaʿaqov (from Bar-Yosef and Tchernov 1972)

Bethlehem (Pliocene– Lower Pleistocene)	ʿUbeidiya (Mindel)	Latamne (Mindel/Riss)	Gesher Benot Yaʿaqov (Riss)	Layer numbers
—	*Stegodon* sp.	*Stegodon* cf. *trigonocephalus*	*Stegodon mediterraneus* Hooijer	V
Archidiskodon cf. *planifrons* (F. & C.)	*Archidiskodon* sp.	—	—	
—	—	*Elephas trogontherii* Pohlig	*Elephas trogontherii* Pohlig	II–V
—	—	*Dicerorhinus* cf. *hemitoechus* (Falconer)	—	
Dicerorhinus etruscus (Falconer)	*Dicerorhinus* cf. *etruscus* (Falconer)	—	—	
—	—	—	*Dicerorhinus merckii* (Jäger)	III, V
Hipparion sp.	*Hipparion* sp.	—	—	
—	*Equus stenonis* Cocch.	—	—	
—	—	—	*Equus caballus* L.	II
—	—	*Equus* sp.	—	
—	*Hippopotamus amphibius* (L.)	*Hippopotamus amphibius* (L.)	*Hippopotamus amphibius* (L.)	V
—	—	—	*Sus* cf. *scrofa* L.	unknown
Sus cf. *strozzi* (Meneghini)	*Sus strozzi* (Meneghini)	—	—	
—	*Leptobos* sp.	—	—	
Leptobos sp. nov.?	—	—	—	
—	—	*Bison priscus* (Bojanus)	cf. *Bison priscus* (Bojanus)	V
—	*Bison* ? sp.	—	—	
Gazellospira torticornis (Aymard)	*Gazellospira* sp.	—	—	
—	—	? *Gazella soemmeringi*	—	
—	Oryx-like antelope	—	—	
Giraffa cf. *cameloPardalis* L.	*Giraffa* cf. *camelopardalis* L.	—	—	
—	*Camelus* sp.	*Camelus* sp.	—	
—	*Cervus* cf. *ramosus* Cr. & Job.	—	—	
—	*Cervus philisii* Schaub	—	—	
—	*Cervus senèzensis* Dep.	—	—	
—	—	—	*Cervus* cf. *elaphus* L.	unknown
—	*Dama* sp.	? *Dama mesopotamica* (Brook)	*Dama* cf. *mesopotamica* (Brook)	II

Table 3 (Continued).

Bethlehem (Pliocene– Lower Pleistocene)	'Ubeidiya (Mindel)	Latamne (Mindel/Riss)	Gesher Benot Ya'aqov (Riss)	Layer numbers
—	*Megaceros* sp.	*Megaceros verti- cornis* (Dawk)	—	
—	—	*Crocuta crocuta*	—	
—	*Crocuta* sp.	—	—	
—	*Megantereon megantereon* (Cr. & Job.)	—	—	
Homotherium (?) sp.	—	—	—	
—	*Felis (Lynx)* spp.	—	—	
—	*Enhydrictis ardea* Bravard	—	—	
—	Small mustelid	—	—	
—	*Canis* sp.			
Nyctereutes mega- mastoides (Pomel)	—	—	—	

of about 4 kilometers. According to the fragmentary palynological evidence from the borehole named Melech Sedom 1 (Horowitz 1968a, i.p.), the lower part of the deposits is characterized by pine grains with a small percentage of oak, demonstrating an environment of relatively dry forests; but it was already a pluvial period, taking into account the pollen spectrum above and beyond these layers. According to Horowitz, this situation indicates an early development of the Glacial Pleistocene (Horowitz 1968a, i.p.).

Several exposures of lacustrine deposits, located south of 'Ubeidiya and named Erq el-Ahmar, were suggested to be of the same limnic nature and a part of the 'Ubeidiya Formation (Schulman 1959; Picard and Baida 1966b). Based on a pollen spectrum, Erq el-Ahmar is correlated with the early phases represented in Melech Sedom 1 (Horowitz i.p.) and therefore considered to be the lower member of the 'Ubeidiya Formation (see Table 1). This assignment needs a revision, as the Charophytes are mainly defined as Neogene types (Lipkin, personal communication) and the malacological assemblages contain several extinct species that are absent at 'Ubeidiya (Tchernov, personal communication). It seems that even if the exposures of 'Ubeidiya and Erq el-Ahmar share many sedimentological similarities, the latter exposures deserve the status of a different formation.

The upper part of the 'Ubeidiya Formation consists of the four depositional cycles known from the geological sections of the 'Ubeidiya hill (Picard and Baida 1966a, 1966b; Bar-Yosef and Tchernov 1972).

These cycles designate two fluctuations within the area of an alluvial
fan — from limnic to terrestrial conditions. The relative date suggested by
Haas is based on the general similarity of the mammalian fauna to the
Cromerian fauna and of the rodent assemblage to a phase within the
Biharian succession (Haas 1966, 1968). The general assignment of date
wandered from the later Pliocene (Blanckenhorn and Oppenheim 1927;
Picard 1943), the Lower Pleistocene (Blanckenhorn 1914), Lower Plei-
stocene-Villafranchian (Picard 1952, 1965; Picard and Baida 1966b),
or early Middle Pleistocene, based on an acceptance of the Mindel as a
climato-stratigraphic dating unit (Horowitz 1968b, i.p.; Bar-Yosef and
Tchernov 1972). A potassium-argon date obtained from a basalt flow
on top of the Mishmar Hayarden Formation, near the Bridge of Benot
Ya'aqov and correlated with the 'Ubeidiya Formation (Horowitz i.p.), is
0.64 ± 0.12 million years (Horowitz, et al. 1973). Another basalt flow
near the Yarmuk river gave a date of 0.68 ± 0.05, indicating that the
eruption of lava took place at the same time in several localities.

A preliminary paleomagnetic check gave a normal polarity for the
dated basalt in the Mishmar Hayarden Formation but more paleomagnetic measurements, together with additional K/Ar dates are necessary
for a detailed chronological picture.

The earliest archeological occurrences known in Israel come from this
period. The implementiferous layers of 'Ubeidiya will be discussed below,
but it is worth noting here that even the Mishmar Hayarden Formation
contained several flakes and a few mammal bones under the dated basalt
flow.

The history of the Amora, 'Ubeidiya, and Mishmar Hayarden lakes
ended with a graben movement causing endemic miniature folds and
faults (Picard 1965; and Table 1). It was followed by a period of erosion,
and lacustrine conditions continued to prevail in the Hula Valley as in
the Dead Sea basin. The old Hula lake deposited the Benot Ya'aqov
Formation (Horowitz i.p.), formerly known as the Viviparus Beds or
Lower Lacustrine (Picard 1963, 1965). Based on pollen samples taken
from boreholes and the type section near the Bridge of Benot Ya'aqov,
Horowitz was able to divide this formation into two members, both
characterized by oak forests with some *Fagus* grains. He correlated these
phases with the Early and Late Riss Pluvial (Horowitz i.p.). The site of
Gesher Benot Ya'aqov is found within this formation, which, on the
basis of its fauna, was first suggested by Hooijer to be approximately of
Mindel-Riss age (Hooijer 1959, 1960).

In the Central Jordan Valley both erosion and accumulation of alluvial fans, soils, and screes took place (the Naharayim Formation). This

landscape was partially covered later by basalt flows (which are dated in the northern Jordan Valley to 0.064–0.079 million years [see Table 2]). During the Last Pluvial (Lartet 1869; Picard 1965) the saline Lisan Lake expanded from the southern end and covered almost the whole valley, up to the line between Migdal and Kursi (see Figure 1).

In the Northern Jordan Valley, above the Interpluvial Hulata Formation, the Würmian pluvial is represented by the Ashmura Formation (Horowitz i.p.).

3. The Geochronological Evidence from the Coastal Plain

The stratigraphy of the Coastal Plain was established and discussed in the works of Picard and Avnimelech (1937), Picard (1943), Avnimelech (1938, 1950, 1962), Itzhaki (1961), Reiss and Issar (1961), Issar (1961, 1968), Slatkine and Rohrlich (1964), Kafri and Ecker (1964), Michelson (1968).

Paleogeographic reconstructions suggested by all researchers show the existence of a series of transgressions and regressions represented in the basically sandy sequence of the coastal plain. This sequence overlies a marly one dated to Tertiary through the "Sakiebeds" Late Pliocene or Lower Pleistocene. Generally, the earlier the transgression the farther eastward its remnants are located. The basis for identifying transgressions and regressions is the interpretation of the paleoenvironment in which the different sediments were deposited. Of these, the most common are the *kurkar* (calcareous sandstone in which terrestrial through marine facies were recognized) and the *hamra* which is a paleosol (Yaalon and Dan 1967). Topographically, the *kurkar* form several elongated ridges sub-parallel to the present coast. As a large part of each of the known three-four ridges (counted from west to east) is a type of eolianite *kurkar*, they were assumed to represent sand dunes fossilized after being deposited along old shorelines. However, the study of their stratification showed that each ridge was formed not only through one transgression (see for example, Nir 1970; Ronen 1973). Other types of sediments, such as swampy layers, occur generally between the *kurkar* ridges or in their western flanks. Alluvial deposits are common along wadi courses and between the easternmost *kurkar* ridge and the hilly areas.

As most of the sediments are buried in the subsurface of the coastal plain, which has a low relief, cores from water boreholes served as the main source of information. Marine terraces were detected mainly in the Carmel and at Rosh-Hanikrah (near the Lebanese border).

The depositional history of the coastal plain was accompanied by local tectonic subsidence and dislocations described by several authors (Picard 1943; Avnimelech 1938, 1950, 1962; Itzhaki 1961; Kafri and Ecker 1964; Neev, et al. 1966; Michelson 1968).

Finally, the palynological studies done by Rossignol near Ashdod and Haifa should be mentioned (Rossignol 1962, 1963, 1969). Studying basically transgressive deposits, she determined the type of interpluvial vegetation (grasses and sedges) with some evidence of regressional periods, indicated by the occurrence of Aleppo Pine pollens.

The chronology of the coastal plain is based on paleontological data by which comparisons with the sequence of the West Mediterranean are attempted. Altimetric age determinations were used for the Carmel terraces, as well as beach deposits or abrasion platforms found within or at the foot of the *kurkar* ridges.

The major corner-stones for chronological assigment were as follows:
a.   The identification of Calabrian sediments on the basis of the presence of *Hyalinea balthica* and some other species (see for example, Moshkovitz 1968).
b.   The identification of the Tyrrhenian deposits by the presence of the foraminifer *Marginopora (Amphisorus)*, considered to be a warm water species (Itzhaki 1961; Reiss and Issar 1961; Avnimelech 1962). *Strombus bubonius* was found only in a +2 meter terrace at Rosh-Hanikrah. However, there is as yet no clear three-fold division of the Tyrrhenian which would enable comparisons with the West Mediterranean sequence. The lack of detailed chronology prevents more accurate dating of the prehistoric sites that are related to the Tyrrhenian. Moreover, as the marine fauna of the Eastern Mediterranean originated in the Western Mediterranean, after throrough malacological research it was suggested that most of the different species arrived later in the East (Moshkovitz 1968). This could mean that the Tyrrhenian deposits of Israel should be placed in the Riss-Würm interpluvial.

The prehistoric data of the coastal plain are provided mainly by many surveys and to a lesser extent, excavations. Outstanding are the numerous Acheulian sites and find-spots, in addition to Epi-Paleolithic and Neolithic sites. Rare are Mousterian and Upper Paleolithic sites, most of which are presumably under the sea or within the westernmost *kurkar* ridge. The reason for this phenomenon is their existence during the Würmian regression, when the coastal plain widened westward about 10 kilometers. Analogous data suggest that part of the Lower Paleolithic succession is also buried in the sediments, found today in the subsurface.

Most of the known Acheulian sites are surface finds, usually on the *hamra.* They are limited in their westward distribution and are found from the third *kurkar* ridge eastward (Gilead 1970b). Several sites can be placed in the general stratigraphy of the coastal plain.

At Evron, in the northern coastal plain, two sites are known (Issar and Kafri 1972; Prausnitz 1969; Gilead 1970a). The earliest one (Evron-Quarry) is within a *hamra* deposit related to the regression from the oldest Tyrrhenian shoreline. A small series of handaxes was described as early Middle Acheulian and the faunal remains as of Middle Pleistocene age (Haas 1970). The second site (Evron-Zinad) is stratigraphically higher and its assemblage is considered to be Late (or Upper) Acheulian. It is related to the time of the Tyrrhenian by being behind fossil dunes that contain *Marginopora*. It is probably of Tyrrhenian II age, as the coastal *kurkar* ridge (with *Strombus*) is assigned to Tyrrhenian III.

The site of Holon, near Tel Aviv, is an excavated archeological occurrence within a swampy deposit, intercalated between two *hamra* layers (Yizraeli 1967). A swamp of this type existed when high ground water accumulated behind the ridge of dunes and in the vicinity of the shoreline. As the abrasion platform at the base of the section probably marks Tyrrhenian I, it seems that the site belongs to the regression period, Rissian, as suggested by the excavator, who also defined the lithic assemblage as Middle Acheulian, comparable to Umm Qatafa E.

Another series of finds was located near Kissufim, southeast of Gaza (Ronen, et al. 1972). The difficulties in dating the site are caused by the absence of *Marginopora* from the deposits. On the basis of field observations, the deposits are related to the Tyrrhenian. The industry is defined as Upper Acheulian and is compared to the similar assemblage from Evron.

The only cave site related to sea level fluctuations is the Tabun cave in Mount Carmel (the excavations at Kebarah, 10 kilometers to the south, never reached the lower levels or bedrock). Since the early excavations at Tabun (Garrod and Bate 1937), and especially in the new ones directed by Jelinek, it was noticed that the lower part of the succession is built of sandy deposits (strata G-F-E). Sedimentological analysis (Farrand and Goldberg, in Jelinek et al. i.p.) showed that these deposits are typified by eolian sedimentation, and stratum F particularly is similar to a fossil dune (*kurkar*). The upper part of E becomes silt and D is almost a true loess. The depositional history was explained as an accumulation of a dune in the vicinity of the shoreline (transgression), and a regression of the sea which caused the decrease in supply of sand. The assignment of layers D-C (Mousterian) to pluvial conditions and layers

G-F-E to interpluvial ones is supported by the pollen studies (Horowitz, in Jelinek, et al. i.p.; Horowitz, personal communication). The +39 meter strand-line at the foot of the cave was assigned by Michelson (1968) to Tyrrhenian I, and is now suggested to be of the last Inter-glacial age. But it may easily be that in this *kurkar* ridge, as in westward ones (Ronen 1973), at least two transgressions are represented; one with shoreline deposits and the later one with eolian sands. Acceptance of these results causes the end of the Acheulian of Yabrudian facies to be at the onset of the Last Pluvial.

B.   THE ARCHEOLOGICAL RECORD

1.   *Introduction*

Even a brief survey of the data on the Acheulian sites in Palestine demonstrates its uneven quality and quantity. The material discussed in the works of Garrod and Bate (1937), Neuville (1931, 1951), Stekelis (Stekelis 1960, 1966; Stekelis, et al. 1969), and especially in the com-prehensive work of Gilead (1970a), exhibit the following difficulties:

a.   The source of most of the known sites is surface collections. These collections differ in size and quality, and only in a few sites can more material be obtained.

b.   The excavated sites are few; most of the excavations were carried out long ago, and their collections are spread over many museums and institutions (Umm Qatafa, Tabun, Gesher Benot Ya'aqov, Zuttiyeh). The new excavations are as yet not fully published in a way that would enable detailed comparisons ('Ubeidiya, Holon, Tabun).

c.   The number of earlier sites (defined as Lower or even Middle Acheulian) is limited, while the later ones (Upper or Late Acheulian) are numerous. Apart from emphasizing the different degree of preserva-tion, this phenomenon is probably meaningful in the understanding of the development of the Acheulian. But the lack of most other sources of information (bones, pollen, sedimentological analysis, etc.) leads to typological-technological analysis as the only means of arranging the sites chronologically.

Following the incomplete geological successions (presented above), only a general order of the sites is available. Typological and chronologi-cal considerations show that there are gaps in the Acheulian sequence. In addition, the chronological relationships between the different Upper Acheulian groups, as defined by Gilead (1970a), are still dubious.

Tabun and Yabrud provide the relative dating of the Acheulian of Yabrudian facies, which is stratified below the Mousterian. But the Upper Acheulian open-air sites which form the main bulk of data can be, generally speaking, contemporaneous, showing geographical differences.

The non-handaxe assemblage recovered in Tabun (Tayacian or Tabunian) and Umm Qatafa (Tayacian) are not included in this review. New and larger samples are needed before we can accept or reject any interpretation of the older collections of artifacts. As for the Pre-Aurignacian or Amudian problem, the new excavations at Tabun by Jelinek indicate that the assemblages of layers 13 and 15 in Yabrud Shelter I are different from those at Tabun (Jelinek, et al. i.p.). But as detailed analysis is still in progress, it is preferable to concentrate on the Acheulian sequence.

The available data will be discussed below following the proposed chronological framework (Perrot 1968; Gilead 1970a, 1970b; also see Table 1). However, since the site of 'Ubeidiya provided the largest amount of data to date, it will be discussed at greater length.

2. 'Ubeidiya

The hill of 'Ubeidiya, about 25 acres, lies 3 kilometers south of the Sea of Galilee, on the flanks of the western escarpment of the Jordan Rift. With the aid of heavy machinery, several geological trenches (numbered I–V, K and Ka) were excavated, a total length of about 1100 meters (Picard and Baida 1966a, 1966b; Bar-Yosef and Tchernov 1972). The structure, as observed in these artificial exposures, is of an anticline with several undulations accompanied by several faults. The lowermost layers, at the core of the anticline, have not yet been reached; therefore the base of what is defined as the upper part of the 'Ubeidiya Formation is unknown.

The numerous layers in the trenches were numbered from the observed earliest to the latest ones, and were divided into four cycles (of a total thickness of 154 meters), two limnic and two terrestrial. This division is based on the interpretation of the different lithologies as follows (Picard and Baida 1966a):

a. The Li-cycle, characterized by clays, silts and limestone, terminates with laminated silts, rich with freshwater mollusks and fish remains. One layer contained mammalian bones and some artifacts, and provided the only pollen spectrum analyzed to date (Horowitz in Bar-Yosef and Tchernov, 1972).

b.   The Fi-cycle is made of clays and conglomerates (mainly beach deposits). Most of the archeological finds and faunal remains were obtained from this member.

c.   The Lu-cycle, the upper limnic member, consists of two parts; the lower is basically clay and chalk, while the upper part is a white-greyish-yellow silt series. Only a few artifacts were encountered in this unit.

d.   The Fu-cycle consists mainly of conglomerates, some of which are large basalt boulders. There are no artifacts or mollusks in this member. It is overlain by a neogene block within which the basaltic flow was dated by potassium-argon to 3.6 million years (Curtis 1965).

Picard and Baida attempted to reconstruct the paleoenvironments by interpreting the different lithologies of the numerous layers. Additional data were gained through the analysis of the malacological assemblages, in comparison with the recent ones in the Sea of Galilee (Bar-Yosef and Tchernov 1972; Tchernov 1973). As a result, it seems that a complicated history of an alluvial fan and lake shores is represented. During the first recognized period the lake reached as far as the flanks of the graben's escarpment (Li). Later, the lake receded (Fi), and early man camped on the shores at the edges of the alluvial fan and on mud flats or temporarily dried swamps. From the hilly area, several lithic assemblages were washed and deposited within a wadi infilling. The lake transgressed again (Lu), and then regressed (Fu), this time probably as a result of the beginning of the tectonic activity which finally caused the folding of the formation and the slipping of the Neogene block on top of its younger member (see Figure 2).

The archeological excavations at 'Ubeidiya, carried on since 1960, uncovered fourteen archeological assemblages, mainly within the Fi-cycle. These fourteen assemblages can be divided on the basis of the lithological facies of their occurrence as follows (the numbers in brackets refer to the layer numbers, as explained in Picard and Baida 1966a; and Bar-Yosef and Tchernov 1972):

a.   Within or on top of a swampy layer (II–23, II–24, II–25, II–36, K–20).

b.   On the lake beach and where it passes laterally into the lake or swampy deposit (II–26 = I–15, II–28, I–26d, I–26c, I–26b, I–26a).

c.   Within a fluvial conglomerate (K–29, K–30, III–34).

The most thoroughly excavated area at 'Ubeidiya lies within the stratigraphic limits between II–23 and I–26 (the latter marked in trench II as II–37 to II–39). Its thickness varies from 10 to 19 meters with the passage from terrestrial to lacustrine environment, while the distance along the strike of the layers is about 100 meters. Ten of the above

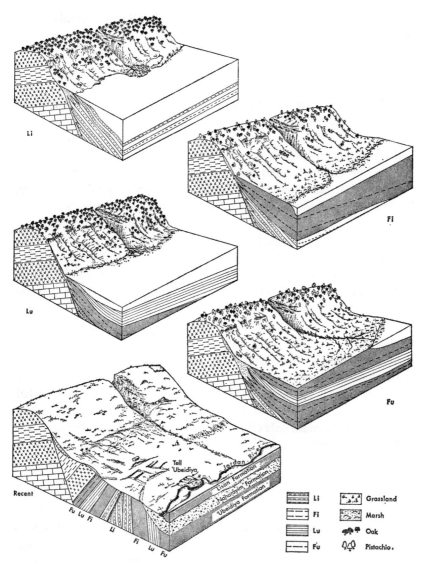

Figure 2. Block diagrams showing four reconstructed ancient landscapes at ʿUbeidiya; the fifth represents the recent situation (from Bar-Yosef and Tchernov 1972)

assemblages are found within this stratigraphic range. Actually, sporadic artifacts were encountered in some of the other layers, reminiscent of the spare finds in FLK, Olduvai Gorge, above the *Zinj.* floor (Leakey 1971: 58–60). This phenomenon seems to indicate the existence of hominids in the vicinity during the time of deposition, although the main site was not discovered.

The sizes of the different assemblages are not uniform. Several contain less than thirty artifacts (II–23, II–28), others 50–100 artifacts (K–20, II–25, II–36, I–26a, I–26a, III–34), and a few between 100–200 artifacts (II–24, I–26b, I–26c). Three assemblages number more than 1000 pieces: I–15, which is a beach deposit and seems to be divided into three concentrations, and K–29 and K–30, which are two stratigraphically and typologically different assemblages embedded in 1.60–1.20 meter thick conglomerates. (These are known in Stekelis 1966, and Stekelis, et al. 1969, as K–5 and K–6 respectively.)

The raw materials used for the manufacture of artifacts are lava (basalt), flint, and limestone. The basalt occurs as pebbles, cobbles, boulders, and scree components; the limestone, as cobbles within the beach and wadi deposits, and the flint in the same environments as small pebbles and cobbles. Early man used each type of rock for different tool types. Choppers and light-duty tools were made of flint, spheroids mainly of limestone, and the handaxe group from basalt, with a few made of flint and limestone. The act of intentional choice is indisputable, as the most common raw material in every lithological facies is basalt; and it is indicated by the predominance of flint artifacts in almost all the assemblages (except for K–30, the handaxe assemblage).

Figure 3 presents the quantitative relationships between nine of the fourteen assemblages. The type categories partially follow the ones used in the reports on Latamne (Clark 1967, 1969) and conform with what has been used in the excavation at 'Ubeidiya. This table should be taken as a preliminary count only (from which utilized cobbles, cores, and debitage are omitted), as detailed study is now under way. In spite of this reservation, it seems that the major typological differences which require some explanation emerge from this figure.

Bifaces are absent from the two stratigraphically earliest assemblages (II–24, K–20). This fact of absence seems to be significant as in II–28. Where there are fewer than thirty artifacts, there is one trihedral. Furthermore, in II–36, where the total number of pieces barely surpasses one hundred, there are several bifaces and trihedrals. Therefore, the absence of these tools from II–24 (of which 195 square meters were excavated) and K–20 seems to be meaningful.

Other quantitative typological differences are shown by the comparison of I–26c, I–26b, I–26a to I–15. Stratigraphically, they are superimposed at the same place, with a depth varying from 5 to 8 meters. Paleoecologically, these are beach deposits passing laterally into a limnic environment. It is hard to estimate the time range between these layers. However, the spheroids which form an important com-

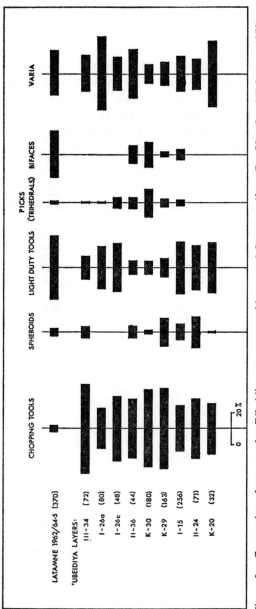

Figure 3. Comparison between the 'Ubeidiya stone assemblages and Latamne (from Bar-Yosef and Tchernov 1972)

ponent in I–15 are absent from I–26a and I–26b. In I–26c, two examples, probably eroded from I–26d, are found. The change from an
assemblage with spheroids to those without spheroids is quite abrupt
and occurs between I–26d and II–36 to I–26c, which lies 0.2–0.5 meters above the aforementioned layers.

It is possible to explain these differences by relating this typological-
quantitative change to the different function of the sites or to seasonality,
but in the author's opinion that is hardly acceptable. However, the spheroids reappear later in a higher layer of Fi, III–34. Comparing the
whole phenomenon to Olduvai (Leakey 1971), it seems that the quantitative importance of spheroids (including subspheroids) is a cultural
feature well pronounced in Developed Oldowan A and B.

Table 4. Mean length of handaxes and the mean value of the thickness to breadth
ratio (from Gilead 1970a; and personal observations)

Site	Mean length (in millimeters)	Mean Th/B
Tabun Ec	84.3	0.510 ± 0.116
Tabun Ed	85.0	0.497 ± 0.114
Tabun F	86.4	0.467 ± 0.085
Beth Uziel	87.2	0.562 ± 0.113
Tabun Eb & Ea	87.6	0.490 ± 0.115
Yiron	89.6	0.523 ± 0.111
Sahel el Koussin	89.7	0.507 ± 0.107
Umm Qatafa DI	93.2	0.496 ± 0.109
Ruhama	93.7	0.475 ± 0.094
Zuttiyeh	93.8	0.567
Evron (Zinnad)	94.4	0.520 ± 0.087
Holon	100.8	0.492
Rephaim — Baqa	102.6	0.581 ± 0.105
Kissufim	105.3	0.490 ± 0.097
Maayan Barukh	114.0	0.488 ± 0.089
Umm Qatafa D2	117.5	0.496 ± 0.085
Umm Qatafa E	135.0	—
ʿUbeidiya K-30	148.8	0.711
Gesher Benot Yaʿaqov V	144.1	0.477 ± 0.080
ʿUbeidiya I-15	153.1	0.702
Latamne	166.6	0.645 ± 0.118

The group of handaxes and picks (including trihedrals) is made on
chunks and pebbles. In this they differ from the same group in EF–HR
at Olduvai (Leakey 1971) or Gesher Benot Yaʿaqov (Stekelis 1960),
where the tools are made on flakes. But the outlines of the handaxes of
K–30 and EF–HR are comparable, since many of them are pointed
(see also Figure 4). A desirable detailed study would be a comparison

at 'Ubeidiya of the handaxe groups of K–30 and I–15, as the two series originate in different environments (the first in the hilly area and the latter from the lake shore). To date the only difference noted is in the use of flint, which in K–30 is about 10 percent and in I–15 amounts to about 25 percent. However, the mean length and the Th/B ratio are very similar in these samples (Table 4).

Summing up the typological evaluations, it seems that there is a considerable similarity between the assemblages of 'Ubeidiya and those of Middle and Upper Bed II at Olduvai (Leakey 1971). The question left open is the extent, chronologically, to which this similarity is meaningful, if at all. If the answer is in the affirmative, even with reservation, and the dates of 0.64 million years and 0.68 million years can be taken as minimal dates, then 'Ubeidiya is earlier than the suggested date (Mindel).

3. Middle and Upper Acheulian

The assignment of an assemblage to the category of Middle or Upper Acheulian is based primarily on technological and typological considerations (following, in general, the definitions used in European and North African literature). The assemblages classified as Middle Acheulian are Gesher Benot Ya'aqov (Stekelis 1960; Gilead 1970a), Umm Qatafa Layer E (Neuville 1931, 1951), and Holon (Yizraeli 1967), all related to the Riss Pluvial. Without arguing about what the different occurrences at 'Ubeidiya should be labeled, it seems obvious that there is a considerable gap between them and the sites mentioned above. This time lapse is evident from the suggested chronology and from the lack of a quantitative typological continuity (Gilead 1970a, 1970b). Two sites are to be placed within this gap: Latamne (in Syria) and Evron-Quarry. While the site of Latamne is well-recorded (Clark 1967, 1969), and dated according to its faunal assemblage (see Table 3), the latter site is known only from brief notes (Issar and Kafri 1972); Prausnitz 1969).

Of the Middle Acheulian sites mentioned above the most unusual occurrence is that of Layer V at Gesher Benot Ya'aqov (Stekelis 1960). There, in a black sandy soil which contains numerous mollusks, bones, and fossil wood, an extremely rich assemblage of handaxes and cleavers appears. Unfortunately, except for limited excavations in 1937, 1951, and 1968, most of the site was destroyed by the public works project which was intended to enlarge the channel of the Jordan River.

The relationship between handaxes and cleavers is about 50 percent to 50 percent (see Figure 4). This makes the assemblage similar to many

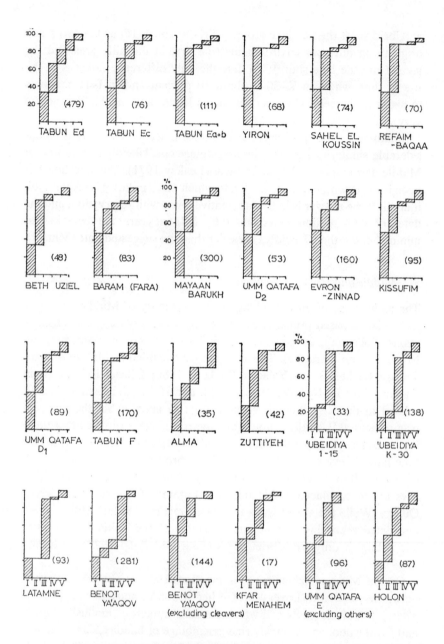

Figure 4.   Cumulative histograms of Acheulian assemblages (after Gilead 1970a):
Group I   — cordiform aspect (amygdaloids, cordiforms, subtriangulars)
Group II — rounded aspect (discoidals, ovaloids, limandes)
Group III — pointed aspect (lanceolates, picks, micoquians)
Group IV — transversal end (cleavers, lageniforms)
Group V   — others

sites in East and North Africa and to several European ones, but different from any other Acheulian site in the Near East. Cleavers are present in other assemblages but they never exceed more than 2 percent of the total bifacial group. An additional exceptional feature is the intensive use of basalt as the raw material (most of the artifacts were made of basalt of a certain lava flow). Basalt is already known from ʿUbeidiya as a raw material for handaxes, but it is never exclusive as at Gesher Benot Yaʿaqov. There are always artifacts made of flint or limestone cobbles, both available in the area of Gesher Benot Yaʿaqov. Even the technique by which the basalt flakes were obtained for the production of cleavers and handaxes — necessitating the use of prepared cores from large boulders — is not known in Palestine before or after this occurrence. The combination of these traits indicates that the assemblage of Gesher Benot Yaʿaqov Layer V is unusual and suggests a cultural connection with Africa. It is worth noting here that the layers above contained a regular Upper Acheulian occurrence, where the whole bifacial group is made of flint.

Of the other two Middle Acheulian assemblages, only Umm Qatafa Layer E was studied in detail (Neuville 1931, 1951; Gilead 1970a), showing a preponderance of lanceolate, cordiform, and amygdaloid handaxes (see Figure 4). Light-duty tools were found with the beginning of the Levallois technique.

At Holon, the industrial picture is much the same. As in Umm Qatafa E, the pointed bifaces form an important group. Other heavy duty tools, such as choppers, are present, as well as light-duty tools, mainly racloirs. There is clear evidence for a slight utilization of the Levallois technique.

The Upper Acheulian has greater cultural variability, comprehensively described by Gilead (1970a, 1970b), who defined the following groups:

a. Maayan Barukh group (MB), represented by the assemblages of the type-locality and Umm Qatafa D₂. Characterized by cordiform and amygdaloid handaxes (about 45 percent), along with ovaloids (about 25 percent), discoids (about 11 percent), cleavers (about 2 percent) and a few pointed forms (about 5 percent).

b. Evron-Kissufim group (EK), the definition of which is based mainly on the assemblages of Evron-Zinnad, Kissufim and Umm Qatafa D₁. Being stratigraphically later, this group is considered to be the continuation of the MB group, with the main change being the decrease in the frequency of ovaloid-discoidal handaxes to 22 percent. Flake tools augment and form approximately 30–60 percent, with frequent utilization of the Levallois technique (Ronen, et al. 1972; Neuville 1951).

c.   Sahel-el-Koussin-Yiron group (SY). The sites grouped under this category are mainly located in the hilly regions. The bifaces are somewhat cruder with the dominance of amygdaloids and discoidals (see Figure 4). Levallois technique is frequent, as in the EK group.

d.   Acheulian of Yabrudian facies (AJ group) is represented best by some of the assemblages of Tabun E. Included also are Abri Zumoffen (Garrod and Kirkbride 1961) and Zuttiyeh. Beside the relative importance of Micoquian bifaces, the flake tools demonstrate a rather Charentian appearance with slight utilization of Levallois technique.

As noted above, the Amudian/Pre-Aurignacian assemblages, although chronologically fitting here, are not discussed because of the lack of new evidence.

4. Technological and Typological Changes through the Palestinian Acheulian

Technological changes through the Acheulian are analyzed in relation to the basic method of handaxe production and the various raw materials. The use of hard or soft hammer, as pronounced in the scars of the biface, is used as a criterion in the French literature to discriminate between the Abbevillian and the Acheulian (see for example, Bordes 1968). Abbevillian handaxes are made by hammerstone exclusively, and the onset of the Acheulian is demarcated by the introduction of the soft hammer technique. As there is a gap between 'Ubeidiya and the Middle Acheulian sites, it is still impossible to ascertain when the soft hammer was introduced into the Palestinian sequence.

Apart from 'Ubeidiya, where a variegated raw material is used (basalt, flint, limestone), and Gesher Benot Ya'aqov Layer V (basalt), most of the Acheulian handaxes in Palestine, with very rare exceptions, are made of flint. Within the flint, two types are designated: the Cenomanian and Eocene flint and the Senonian (known also as "brecciated" flint). The Eocene and Cenomanian flint is generally better than the Senonian one. However, good flint is obtainable throughout Palestine, especially in the mountainous areas. Nowhere are the sources of such flint further than 20 kilometers (or a walking day) from a known site. Therefore, the availability and quality of raw material played only a small role in the process of biface production.

The form and dimensions of handaxes are the expressions of the technical ability of the prehistoric artisan and his tradition. While the technical ability is indicated by the method by which the tool is flaked, and somewhat by its form, the cultural tradition most probably dictates the dominant forms and the use of either flake or chunk as the basic starting point.

According to Gilead (1970a, 1970b), the mean length of handaxes is an aid to placing assemblages within the Acheulian sequence in Palestine. This parameter, presented in decreasing order (Table 4), depicts only the general explicit evolution of the Acheulian handaxe. Undoubtedly, it is meaningful to stress the decrease in the average length of handaxes from the earlier assemblages through the later ones. But, as hinted clearly in the listed indices of refinement (Th/B), it is probably more a matter of raw material choice, the basic piece (chunk or flake), the technical ability of the artisan and his conceptions. The easily checked variable is the basic piece form and a glance at the index at Gesher Benot Ya'aqov V (0.477) versus almost all the Upper Acheulian assemblages shows the difference caused by the use of flakes for biface production. Therefore, a multivariate analysis is required to trace associations and covariations of biface morphological typology, along with other features of their parent assemblages.

A similar problem exists in analyzing the quantitative changes in the handaxe forms (Figure 4). It seems that through the Middle and Upper Acheulian certain morphological traditions can be discerned. Several assemblages kept the pointed form as an important tool group (KM perhaps through EK to AJ group, as defined by Gilead), while others preferred the rounded form (BY, MB, EK[?] to SY group). A somewhat similar phenomenon was noted by Roe in England (Roe 1968).

Flake tools, besides being made on the debitage of handaxes, were also made on flakes obtained from cores (sometimes choppers) by direct percussion. Levallois technique was first introduced in the Middle Acheulian (Umm Qatafa E and Holon) and later characterizes the assemblages termed Upper Acheulian of Levallois facies, such as Kissufim and Evron-Zinnad (Ronen, et al. 1972).

Morphologically (beginning with the 'Ubeidiya assemblages), the commonest types of flake tools are racloirs, denticulates and notches, along with several kinds of retouched flakes. The systematic regularization of the working-edge or the back is known only from the post-'Ubeidiya sites.

Quantitatively, the flake tools are presented in various frequencies in different assemblages. This situation in many cases is due to selective collection. But in carefully excavated samples it seems that flake tools do vary in their proportions. It is expected, in the author's view, that a pattern of assemblage variability similar to the one described for the Late Acheulian in Africa by Kleindienst (1961), will come to light in the Palestinian Upper Acheulian.

C. NON-ARTIFACTUAL ASPECTS OF THE MIDDLE PLEISTOCENE

1. Geographical Distribution and the Situations of Sites

For discussion of the location of a site, the lithological facies of its deposit, its immediate environment and the general regional situation are taken into account. This process is applied for any prehistoric site, but the accuracy of a detailed description, such as for a Lower Paleolithic occurrence, is harder to achieve.

As presented in the geographical-geological review, although Palestine is within the Mediterranean zone, the changes in its landscape following climatic fluctuations were sometimes quite rapid, due to its bordering arid regions. Essentially, the vegetational strips remained the same, but their limits shifted following Pluvial and Interpluvial conditions. Within a rather small country like Palestine, climatic fluctuations could be crucial for early man, as well as considerable tectonic movements and lava eruptions (Jordan Valley, Eastern Galilee, and the Golan Heights).

The main difficulty in a local environmental reconstruction arises from the lack of accurate dating of many sites which would allow placing them within the fragmentary paleoclimatic sequence. The absence of palynological and paleontological data from most of the Acheulian sites makes their position within a reconstructed environment pure guess work.

A glance at the map (Figure 1) shows that the distribution of Acheulian sites covers the whole of Palestine. The most favorable regions were, as in the Upper Pleistocene, the coastal plain, the hilly areas, and the Jordan Valley. The desert region, except for oases, was inhabited only during more humid periods, but as research in it is still in its beginning stages, the number of known sites indicates the state of our data.

Most of the cultural groups within the Acheulian show no special geographical preference, except for one of the Upper Acheulian groups (SY), of which the sites are located in the mountainous and hilly area (Yiron, Baram, Sahel el-Koussin, Rephaim-Baqaa; see Gilead 1970a).

When the situation of the sites is checked in relation to their immediate environment, all possible locations are found. Sites are found on the shores of lakes or swamps, on the banks of wadis, near springs, in mountain passes, on plateaux, and on the edges of intermontane basins. Such a distribution may be used as a basis for possible models interpreting the sites as base camps, ephemeral sites, and seasonal camps. But the fragmentary state of the archeological and faunal evidence may invalidate the reconstruction of cultural activities. It is widely accepted that the number of artifacts and the size of a site may indicate whether it was a base camp or not. Thus, in interpreting the data one may conclude that there were base camps in every region, e.g. Holon in the coastal plain, Umm Qatafa and Yiron in the mountainous region, Maayan Barukh and Gesher Benot Ya'aqov in the Jordan Valley. Of course, within these regions, smaller sites or find-spots were located, which can be interpreted as ephemeral or seasonal camps; but a detailed reconstruction is at present presumptuous.

It may be cautiously pointed out that most of the sites were near water sources, either permanent or ephemeral, a characteristic which is clearer in the earlier sites. In the Jordan Valley the sites are on the shores of a lake ('Ubeidiya I–15, I–26, Gesher Benot Ya'aqov V) or streams ('Ubeidiya K–30, Maayan Barukh, Zuttiyeh). The same is true of the sites on the coastal plain which, like Holon or Evron-Zinnad, were found in swampy deposits or related to wadi courses.

In the hilly zone the sites are on the plateaux or in intermontane basins. The existence of the latter is probably due to karstic activity along with tectonics. In these closed or semi-closed basins were seasonal or permanent swamps (at an altitude of 300–600 meters above sea level). The Valley of Sanur, in the northern Samaria hills, is a recent example of such a swampy basin, rich in vegetation and fauna.

It seems that a hypothetical reconstruction of the nearby environment can prove worthwhile, but for such an essay the data required are found only at 'Ubeidiya, Umm Qatafa, and Tabun. A preliminary reconstruction at 'Ubeidiya indicates that hominid encampments were located on the shores of the lake, but several were in the hilly hinterland (Bar-Yosef and Tchernov 1972). The landscape was variegated, with oak and pistachio forest covering the hills, grassland in the lower areas, and a lake with swampy or stony shores. This is probably the Interpluvial landscape (the Fi-cycle), known better than the Pluvial one where the oak forests were more extended (the Li-cycle). It must be stressed that the conditions called Interpluvial here were more Mediterranean than today, where this part of the Jordan Valley is semi-arid.

The biotopes around Umm Qatafa and Tabun during the late Middle and Upper Acheulian were quite similar (Garrod and Bate 1937; Neuville 1951; Tchernov 1962, 1968a). Judging from the large and small mammals, as well as avifauna, there was a combination of three major biotopes: Mediterranean woodland, Mediterranean grassland, and swampy-steppe areas. In Umm Qatafa the closeness to the desert is indicated by several rock-dwelling species, while at Tabun these are absent.

The site of Umm Qatafa utilized the Judean plateaux near Bethlehem, where there was probably an intermontane basin; but at the same time it was on the edge of the desert. Tabun favored the open forests of Mount Carmel during the Last Interpluvial, with a growing coastal plain as the sea regressed from its shoreline near the cave.

Finally, it is important to evaluate the primary context of each occurrence. Most of the Acheulian assemblages are surface collections or were obtained from conglomerates. Only a few occurrences are in their initial deposit, either in the open ('Ubeidiya, Gesher Benot Ya'aqov, Holon, Evron Quarry and Zinnad, Kissufim), or in caves (Umm Qatafa, Tabun Zuttiyeh). The proximity to the water source in the open-air sites is clearly demonstrated. In several cases not only lake or river shores were inhabited but also mud flats or swampy deposits (which were probably dried seasonally or once every few years). This closeness to water presumably indicates the absence of water bags in the Early and Middle Acheulian. Supporting this conclusion is the fact that many of the handaxes were not manufactured on the living floors and that hunted or butchered animals were brought in.

2.   Types and Size of Sites

It is misleading to compare the number of open-air sites to those in rock shelters and caves. Caves were never numerous in Palestine, the karstic activity of which never reached the state of complexity of that in northern Mediterranean countries. Moreover, open-air sites were discovered due to erosion, public works, and agricultural activities, while cave sites are known only from intentional excavations. Excavations were carried out in complete extant caves, but the existence of ruined caves is an indication that some caves were eroded through the Pleistocene. A fissure filled in with cave deposit found near Jerusalem, in the Judean hills, delivered a microfaunal assemblage dated between 'Ubeidiya and Umm Qatafa (Tchernov 1968b). This is a remnant of a cave probably inhabited by human beings, which was removed by natural agencies, indicating that caves were used as dwelling places during the Middle Pleistocene, earlier than the known Umm Qatafa and Tabun caves.

The size of the living floors within a site is widely accepted as a criterion for the size of the group. An extended open-air site is explained as representing repeated occupations by the same and/or different groups. According to this view, there is almost no difference between the Lower Palaeolithic and the Epi-Palaeolithic sites.

Examples of extended sites are Maayan Barukh and ʿUbeidiya I–15, where several different spatial concentrations were identified (Stekelis and Gilead 1966; Stekelis, et al 1969). Following the recent enlargement of the channel of the Jordan River, it appears that the same distribution was present at Gesher Benot Yaʿaqov Layer V.

The limited floors seem to be better for anthropological evaluation. But except for caves, the definition of the size of a living floor is a matter of estimation. Of the excavated open-air sites, only Latamne and Holon give valuable data. At ʿUbeidiya a cautious estimate may be made, as only one dimension is known (along the strike of the layers), while the other (along the dip) may be estimated approximately. Table 5 offers some tentative figures. If the fragmentary data from ʿUbeidiya is considered on the basis of that of Latamne, with a ratio fo 2 : 3 for the length/width of the living floor, then sizes of an order of 200–500 square meters are arrived at. The size of all the limited floors indicates a small group, and this number is repeated through most of the Palaeolithic in Palestine.

The intensity of activity, as demonstrated by the thickness of the implementiferous layers, changes at the outset of the Upper Acheulian. Perhaps it is related to the use of fire, as shown in Umm Qatafa layers D_2 and D_1 and Tabun layer E. In spite of the lack of details, it is obvious that the number of artifacts increases. A cultural divergence present in the typological aspects, as defined by Gilead (1970a, 1970b), demonstrates the change from Middle to Upper Acheulian. This change, in the author's view, was due to the permanent use of fire and the invention of the water bag.

3. Subsistence Resources

The absence of animal bones from most of the sites and the lack of quantitative studies on the rest make any statement a rough estimate. It is impossible to discuss whether the Acheulians were scavengers or hunters, or both. However, as in other geographic regions, it was concluded that they were both scavengers and hunters, it may be the same in Israel (Butzer 1971; Isaac 1970; Leakey 1971). The lists of mamma-

Table 5.   Average areas of living floor in square meters

Cave site		Open-air sites	
Tabun	540	Latamne 230	
Zuttiyeh	450	ʿUbeidiya * II-24	200
Abu Sif	230	K-20	50
Yabrud I	250	II-36	150
		I-15B	220
		I-15A	2400
		I-26b	540

* Estimated on the basis provided by the excavations at Latamne (Clark 1969).

lian remains from each site furnish some evidence about the close land-scape as well as the potentially edible animals. Of these bones, many were found broken, some undoubtedly by man, although the role of carnivores cannot be excluded.

In ʿUbeidiya the common mammals were the deer and hippopotamus; at Gesher Benot Yaʿaqov they were the elephant and hippopotamus, and at Holon, the elephant, deer, horse, and hippopotamus. At each site there are also smaller mammals, but in the late Middle Pleistocene the latter (deer, gazelle, horse) are dominant. The full list of animals and the total number of bones represented are the result of preservation and subic meters excavated, no less than the result of human activity. Thus, at ʿUbeidiya, on the beach deposits, the number of bones observed increased as the excavation shifted from the wave-washed areas to the muddy deposits. The bones preserved in the gravels of K–30 and K–29 were only the most common elements (hippopotamus and a small deer) in the rich fauna of ʿUbeidiya (Haas 1968). The numerous fish and water turtle remains which are probably part of the natural process of deposition which took place in early man sites located in lake-swamp and riverine environments are another problem to be taken into account.

One butchering site is known from ʿUbeidiya, where an almost complete skeleton of hippopotamus was uncovered with heavy- and light-duty tools around it.

All the mammalian lists (as direct information) as well as the location of many Acheulian sites on Eocene and basaltic soils (as indirect evidence) (Gilead 1970a, 1970b) indicate that man inhabited mainly parkland and grassland areas. These open forest and savannah areas are favored by many herbivores, more so than forested or semi-arid zones.

Except for spheroids, there is no direct information about hunting tools (Clark 1955; Leakey 1971), but wooden spears could have been used, as well as traps. The same guesswork is needed for the evaluation of the vegetal food eaten, on which only indirect evidence (the recent flora and pollen spectra) is obtainable.

SUMMARY

In this essay we have tried to bring together all of the geochronological and archeological data concerning the Middle Pleistocene of Palestine. Since the intensive research on the Middle Pleistocene began only around 1960, it can readily be seen that a great deal of work has been accomplished in the past thirteen years. However, as in all such cases, much more palynological, geochronological and archeological data are needed in order to provide answers to the kinds of questions put forth here.

REFERENCES

ARENSBURG, B., O. BAR-YOSEF
    1967   Yacimiento paleolitico en el valle de Refaim, Jerusalem, Israel. *Ampurias* 29:117–133.

AVNIMELECH, M.
    1938   "Geological observations on the shore near Natania" (in Hebrew), in *Magnes anniversary book*, 248–253. Jerusalem: Hebrew University.
    1950   Contribution to the knowledge of the Quaternary oscillations of the shoreline in Palestine. *Rivista di Scienze Preistoriche* 5:44–56.
    1962   The main trends in the Pleistocene-Holocene history of the Israelian coastal plain. *Quaternaria* 6:479–495.

BAR-YOSEF, O., E. TCHERNOV
    1972   *On the Palaeoecological history of the site of 'Ubeidiya.* Publications of the Israel Academy of Sciences and Humanities.

BLANCKENHORN, M.
    1914   Syrien, Arabien und Mesopotamien. *Handb. region. Geologie* 4. Heidelberg.

BLANCKENHORN, M., P. OPPENHEIM
    1927   Neue beitraege zur kenntnis des Neogens in Syrien und Palastina. *Geologische und Palaeontologische Abhandl. N.F. Jena* 15 (4).

BORDES, F.
    1968   *The Old Stone Age.* London and New York: Weidenfeld and Nicolson.

BUTZER, K.
    1971   *Environment and archaeology* (second edition). Chicago: Aldine-Atherton.

CLARK, J. D.
    1955   The stone ball: its associations and use by prehistoric man in Africa. *Actes du Congrès Panafricain de Préhistoire, Alger, 1952.*

1961   Fractured chert speciments from the Lower Pleistocene Bethlehem levels. *Bulletin of the British Museum* 5:73–99.

1967   The Midle Acheulian occupation site at Latamne, Northern Syria (first paper). *Quaternaria* 9:1–68.

1967   The Middle Acheulian occupation site at Latamne, Northern Syria ria (second paper). *Quaternaria* 10:1–47.

CURTIS, G. H.

1967   "Notes on some Miocene to Pleistocene potassium/argon results" in *Background to evolution in Africa*. Edited by W. W. Bishop and J. D. Clark, 365–369. Chicago: University of Chicago Press.

FREUND, R., M. J. OPPENHEIM, N. SCHULMAN

1965   Direction of magnetism of some basalts in the Jordan Valley and Lower Galilee (Israel). *Israel Journal of Earth Sciences* 14:37–44.

GARFUNKEL, Z., A. HOROWITZ

1966   The Upper Tertiary and Quaternary morphology of the Negev, Israel. *Israel Journal of Earth Sciences* 15:101–117.

GARROD, D. A. E., D. M. A. BATE

1937   *The stone age of Mount Carmel*, volume one. Oxford: Oxford University Press.

GARROD, D. A. E., D. KIRKBRIDE

1961   Excavations of Abri Zumoffen, a Palaeolithic rockshelter near Adlun, in South Lebanon, 1958. *Bulletin Musée de Beyrouth* 16: 7–45.

GILEAD, D.

1970a   "Early Palaeolithic cultures in Israel and the Near East." Unpublished doctoral dissertation (in English), Hebrew University, Jerusalem.

1970b   Handaxe industries in Israel and the Near East. *World Archaeology* 2:1–11.

HAAS, G.

1966   *On the vertebrate fauna of the Lower Pleistocene site 'Ubeidiya*. Publications of the Israel Academy of Sciences and Humanities. Jerusalem.

1968   *On the fauna of 'Ubeidiya*. Proceedings of the Israel Academy of Sciences and Humanities, Section of Sciences 7.

1970   *Metridiochoerus evronensis* n.sp., a new Middle Pleistocene phacochoerid from Israel. *Israel Journal of Zoology* 19:179–181.

HOOIJER, D. A.

1958   An Early Pleistocene mammalian fauna from Bethlehem. *Bulletin of the British Museum* (Natural History, Geology 3:267–292.

1959   Fossil mammals from Jisr Banat Yaqub, south of Lake Huleh, Israel. *Bulletin of the Research Council of Israel* 8G:177–199.

1960   A Stegodon from Israel. *Bulletin of the Research Council of Israel* 9G:104–108.

HOROWITZ, A.

1968a   "Upper Pleistocene-Holocene climate and vegetation of the northern Jordan Valley (Israel)." Unpublished doctoral dissertation (in Hebrew), Hebrew University, Jerusalem.

1968b   "Palynostratigraphy of Melech Sedom 1 borehole." Unpublished report, Geological Survey of Israel.

1971   Climatic and vegetational developments in northeastern Israel during the Upper Pleistocene-Holocene times. *Pollen et Spores* 13:255–278.

i.p.   Development of the Hula basin, Israel. *Israel Journal of Earth Sciences.*

HOROWITZ, A., G. SIEDNER, O. BAR-YOSEF
1973   Radiometric dating of the 'Ubeidiya Formation, Jordan Valley Israel, *Nature* 242:186–187.

ISAAC, G.
1970   The diet of early man: aspects of archaeological evidence from Lower and Middle Pleistocene sites in Africa. *World Archaeology* 2:278–299.

ISSAR, A.
1961   The Plio-Pleistocene geology of the Ashdod area. *Bulletin of the Research Council of Israel* 104:173–182.

1968   Geology of the central coastal plain of Israel. *Israel Journal of Earth-Sciences* 17:16–29.

ISSAR, A., L. PICARD
1961   Sur le Tyrrhénien des côtes d'Israël et du Liban. *Bulletin de l'Association Française pour l'Etude du Quaternaire* 6:35–41.

ISSAR, A., U. KAFRI
1972   Neogene and Pleistocene geology of the Western Galilee coastal plain. *Bulletin of the Geological Survey, Ministry of Development, Israel* 53:1–14.

ITZHAKI, Y.
1961   Pleistocene shore-lines in the coastal plain of Israel. *Bulletin of the Geological Survey, Ministry of Development, Israel* 32:1–9.

JELINEK, A. J., W. R. FARRAND, G. HAAS, A. HOROWITZ, P. GOLDBERG
i.p.   New excavations at the Tabun cave, Mount Carmel, Israel, 1967–1972; a preliminary report.

KAFRI, U., A. ECKER
1964   Neogene and Quaternary subsurface geology and hydrogeology of the Zevulun plain. *Bulletin of the Geological Survey of Israel* 37:1 ff.

KLEINDIENST, M. R.
1961   Components of the East African Acheulian assemblage: an analytic approach. *Acts of the Fourth Pan African Congress of Prehistory* 81–111.

LARTET, L.
1869   *Essai sur la géologie de la Palestine et des contrées avoisinantes, telles que l'Egypte et l'Arabie, comprenant les observations recueillés dans le cours de l'Expédition du Duc de Luynes à la Mer Morte.* Paris: Masson.

LEAKEY, M. D.
1971   *Olduvai Gorge IV. Excavations in Beds I and II; 1960–1963.* Cambridge: Cambridge University Press.

MICHELSON, H.
1968   "The geology of Mount Carmel coastal plain." Unpublished Mas-

ter of Science thesis (in Hebrew), Hebrew University, Department of Geology.

MOSHKOVITZ, S.
1968   "The mollusca in the marine Pliocene and Pleistocene sediments of the south-eastern Mediterranean basin (Cyprus-Israel)." Unpublished doctoral dissertation, Hebrew University, Jerusalem.

NEEV, D., H. E. EDGERTON, G. ALMAGOR, N. BAKLER
1966   Preliminary results of some continuous seismic profiles in the Mediterranean shelf of Israel. *Israel Journal of Earth Sciences* 15:170–178.

NEEV, D., K. O. EMERY
1967   The Dead Sea. *Bulletin of the Geological Survey of Israel* 41.

NEUVILLE, R.
1931   L'Acheulian supérieur de la grotte d'Oumm Qatafa (Palestine). *L'Anthropologie* 41:13–51, 249–263.
1951   *Le Paléolithique et le Mésolithique du Désert de Judée.* Archives de l'Institut de Paléontologie Humaine 24.

NIR, D.
1970   Notes on the Quaternary of the basin of Nahal Shikma. *Studies in the Geography of Israel* 7:1–12 (in Hebrew).

NUR, A., C. E. HELSLEY
1971   Paleomagnetism of Tertiary and Recent lavas of Israel. *Earth and Planetary Science Letters* 10:375–379.

PERROT, J.
1968   *La préhistoire palestinienne.* Supplément au Dictionnaire de la Bible VIII col. 286-446. Paris.

PICARD, L.
1943   Structure and evolution of Palestine. *Bulletin of the Geological Department, Hebrew University, Jerusalem* 4:1–134.
1952   The Pleistocene peat of Lake Hula. *Bulletin of the Research Council of Israel* 2G:147–156.
1963   The Quaternary in the Northern Jordan Valley. *Proceedings of the Israel Academy of Sciences and Humanities* 1(4).
1965   "The geological evolution of the Quaternary in the central-northern Jordan graben, Israel," in *International studies on the Quaternary.* Edited by H. E. Wright, Jr. and D. G. Frey, 337–366.

PICARD, L., M. AVNIMELECH
1937   On the geology of the central coastal plain. *Bulletin of the Geological Department, Hebrew University, Jerusalem* 1:255–299.

PICARD, L., U. BAIDA
1966a *Geological report on the Lower Pleistocene of the 'Ubeidiya excavations.* Publications of the Israel Academy of Sciences and Humanities. Jerusalem.
1966b *Stratigraphic position of the 'Ubeidiya Formation.* Proceedings of the Israel Academy of Sciences and Humanities, Section of Sciences 4.

PRAUSNITZ, M. W.
1969   The sequence of Early to Middle Paleolithic flint industries along the Galilean littoral. *Israel Exploration Journal* 19:129–136.

REISS, Z., A. ISSAR
1961 Subsurface Quaternary correlations in the Tel Aviv region. *Bulletin of the Geological Survey, Ministry of Development, Israel* 32: 10–26.

ROE, D. A.
1968 British Lower and Middle Palaeolithic handaxe groups. *Proceedings of the Prehistoric Society* 34:1–82.
1970 Comments on the results obtained by J. M. Graham. *World Archaeology* 1:339–342.

RONEN, A.
1973 Remarks on the Pleistocene in the Coastal Plain of Israel. *Mitequfat Haeven* 11:43–46 (in Hebrew).

RONEN, A., D. GILEAD, E. SHACHNAI, A. SAUL
1972 Upper Acheulian in the Kissufim region. *Proceedings of the American Philosophical Society* 116:68–96.

ROSSIGNOL, M.
1962 Analyse pollinique de sédiments marins quaternaires en Israël, II: Sédiments pleistocènes. *Pollen et Spores* 4:121–148.
1963 Analyse pollinique de sédiments quaternaires dans la plaine de Haifa — Israël. *Israel Journal of Earth-Sciences* 12:207–214.
1969 Sédimentation palynologique dans le domaine marin quaternaire de Palestine. *Notes et Mémoires sur le Moyen-Orient* 10:1–160.

SCHULMAN, N.
1959 The geology of the central Jordan Valley. *Bulletin of the Research Council of Israel* 8G:63–90.
1967 Remarks on the Quaternary in the northern Jordan Valley. *Israel Journal of Earth Sciences* 16:104–106.

SLATKINE, A., V. ROHRLICH
1964 Sur quelques niveaux marins quaternaires du mont Carmel, Israël. *Israel Journal of Earth Sciences* 13:125–132.

STEKELIS, M.
1960 The Palaeolithic deposits of Jisr Banat Yaqub. *Bulletin of the Research Council of Israel* 8G:63–90.
1966 *Archaeological excavations at 'Ubeidiya, 1960–1963.* Publications of the Israel Academy of Sciences and Humanities. Jerusalem.

STEKELIS, M., O. BAR-YOSEF, T. SCHICK
1969 *Archaeological excavations at 'Ubeidiya, 1964–1966.* Publications of the Israel Academy of Sciences and Humanities. Jerusalem.

STEKELIS, M., D. GILEAD
1966 *Maayan Barukh, a Lower Palaeolithic site in the Upper Galilee.* Centre for Prehistoric Research VIII.

TCHERNOV, E.
1962 Palaeolithic avifauna in Palestine. *Bulletin of the Research Council of Israel* 11B:95–131.
1968a *Succession of rodent faunas during the Upper Pleistocene of Israel. Mammalia depicta.* Hamburg: Verlag Paul Parey.
1968b A Pleistocene faunule from a karst fissure filling near Jerusalem, Israel. *Verhandl. Naturf. Ges. Basel* 79:161–185.
1973 *Pleistocene molluscs of the Jordan Valley.* Publications of the

Israel Academy of Sciences and Humanities. Jerusalem.

YAALON, D. H., J. DAN
1967   "Factors controlling soil formation and distribution in the Mediterranean coastal plain of Israel during the Quaternary," in *Quaternary soils*. Edited by R. B. Morrison and H. E. Wright, 322–338. Desert Research Institute, University of Nevada.

YIZRAELI, T.
1967   A Lower Palaeolithic site at Holon: preliminary report. *Israel Exploration Journal* 17:144–152.

A Comparison of the Late Acheulian Industries of Africa and the Middle East

J. DESMOND CLARK

ABSTRACT

Interpretation of the causes of variation in Paleolithic artifact assemblages is largely dependant on understanding the paleoenvironment in which the makers lived. Pollen and other sources show that the Middle Pleistocene hominids favored a habitat of open savanna/grassland adjacent to water and gallery forest in both Africa and the Middle East, and four major culture areas can be distinguished. Radiometric and paleomagnetic reversal methods of dating begin to show a succession of similar assemblages and changes in the eastern Mediterranean as in Africa, suggesting similar ways of life. Four main variants of the Acheulian techno-complex (including the Developed Oldowan) can be distinguished and these can be seen to interchange, apparently randomly, at different "contemporaneous" localities as well as through time at a single locality. It is suggested that these different tool-kits reflect differences in the sets of activities that evoked them and several possible explanations are given. The Middle Pleistocene cultural assemblages show a general similarity of patterning within the limits of these tool-kits but with infinite variation in the proportions in which the individual artifacts occur. Generally lower percentages of cleavers, a greater use of the Levallois technique and of blades appear to distinguish the eastern Mediterranean and North African culture areas from the rest of Africa in the Middle Pleistocene. There is little formalism of tool-types in the Acheulian, except for the large cutting tools, prior to the time of the Last Interglacial and there is no justification for the concept of a regular developmental sequence of styles and technical refinement.

My sincere thanks are acknowledged here to Glynn Isaac for his valued comments on the draft of this paper; to Ofer Bar-Yosef for putting me right on several matters and for a stimulating introduction to Palestinian archaeology; to Sherwood L. Washburn, Herbert G. Baker, and other colleagues for their helpful advice and discussion; to Jeffrey Bada for the date for Kalambo Falls and to several of the participants in the Symposium, notably Charles Turner and Hilary Deacon, for suggested amendments or additions. The text figures were drawn by Douglas B. Cargo. To all these and to my wife, I express my warm thanks.

INTRODUCTION

Behind any comparative study of stone artifact assemblages is the hope that they will provide understanding of the inferred functional differences in the tools and so of the behavioral differences of their makers. None of these can be understood, however, without taking into account the ecological nature of the habitat exploited by the toolmakers and it is especially important for the prehistorian to know what main plant and animal resources were present and so available for use by the hunting/gathering populations during the Pleistocene when the biomes may often have differed significantly from those of the present day in response to fluctuations in humidity and temperature. The success with which prehistorians can reconstruct hominid behaviour, as it can be deduced from the concentrations of artifacts and associated cultural evidence in primary context on the occupation sites, is directly related to the extent to which the paleoecology can be understood. Since the artifacts themselves are in large part a reflection of the traditional exploitation techniques of the group, it is essential to know what was available to exploit. It is also important to know what kinds of artifacts occur together and with what other sorts of evidence, such as food waste as represented by the associated faunal remains. Equally important is the pattern of dispersal of all such remains on the archeological horizons, whether they be occupation sites with dense concentrations of artifacts and bone, or dispersed, low-density scatters. Similarly, the relationship of this distribution pattern to micro-stratigraphic evidence can show how and, perhaps, why the site is located where it is: its relationship to immediate requirements, for example shade or food resources, either plant or animal, to raw materials for tools and equipment, or to water. Where such paleoecological evidence is lacking, the significance of detailed quantitative and qualitative studies of artifact assemblages may well be questioned and certainly such assemblages cannot be understood except, where they belong in a chronological sequence, as a means of demonstrating changing trends in style and technique through time.

So far as Africa and the Middle East are concerned, the number of sites that already provide this kind of evidence is still very small. Because such localities also are often separated by hundreds or thousands of miles, any attempts to use the empirical evidence they provide for constructing more general models of Middle Pleistocene behavior must at best be considered unproven. Just as ethnography is full of examples of multiple uses for the same type of tool, however, so it is probably true that the further back in time any particular assemblage is located, the more general will be the uses to which the artifacts were put, particularly as the range of equipment types is also increasingly smaller. Although, however, there are many thousands of collections of artifacts, some of impressive proportions, of Acheulian type from Africa and no small number also from the Middle East, most of them are either surface collections or in secondary context from alluvial sediments and so can contribute very little to an understanding of Middle Pleistocene cultural activities, except insofar as the distribution of this widespread industrial or techno-complex is concerned. There are, however, a few sites — most of them, but not all, along the line of the Great Rift Valley — where rapid burial by lacustrine or pyroclastic activities has preserved occupation horizons in primary context and where the composition and distribution of the stone artifact assemblage and associated remains reflect the differing activities of the makers.

For the purposes of this paper the Middle Pleistocene has been taken as that block of time represented by the middle and upper deposits of Bed II, Beds III/IV and the Mesak Beds at Olduvai Gorge and other rock units of comparable age in East Africa. In Europe it is generally taken as starting with the Cromerian Interglacial c. 700,000 B.P.) and ending with the beginning of the Last Interglacial. On the East African radiometric dating evidence, what is thought of as Middle Pleistocene would begin about 1.0–1.5 million years ago and end about 150,000 to 200,000 years B.P. (Isaac 1972). However, since it is the Acheulian and related industrial entities with which we are concerned, it is necessary to look also at some of the latest developments which belong in the Last Interglacial between c. 125,000 and 75,000 B.P.

There are numerous Middle Pleistocene sites in Eurasia but very few undebated assemblages that can be dated to the Lower Pleistocene. On the other hand, the Rift Valley and adjacent parts of the Plateau in East Africa attest a long cultural record represented by the Oldowan Industry and dating back to 2.6, or perhaps to 3.0 million years ago. Possibly tropical Asia may have witnessed a comparable cultural development over this time if the radiometric age of the Djetis beds and the contained hominid is confirmed (Isaac 1972: 409) but, as yet, no early stone artifacts in certain context are known from any Lower Pleistocene sites in Asia. Conceivably this could be due to the circumstances of recovery of the fossils, though it is also probable that some other material, perhaps bamboo, may have been used in southeast

Asia. In Southwest Asia the fractured cherts recovered with a Villa-franchian fauna from the Bethlehem Beds in Israel exhibit character-istics of natural flaking, mostly by pressure (Clark 1961; Hooijer 1958).

In East Africa the Acheulian Industrial Complex is a later develop-ment than the Oldowan and their relationship is best seen in the se-quence at the Olduvai Gorge where the earliest Acheulian assemblage (EF–HR) occurs in Bed II shortly after the faunal break marked by the aeolian tuff, the Lemuta Member, and dating to 1.0–1.5 million years B.P. The Oldowan of Bed I and lower Bed II is stratigraphically and chronologically older than the Acheulian, but in the middle and upper part of Bed II and later, the tradition persists contemporaneously with the Acheulian in a more evolved form known as the Developed Oldowan. This comprises a number of choppers, heavy and light duty scrapers, polyhedrals and spheroids with a small percentage of gen-erally crude handaxe forms. It contrasts with the large cutting tools — the handaxes, cleavers, and knives — of the Acheulian. These two technical traditions sometimes occur separately as they do at Olduvai but it is more usual, in particular at the later Acheulian sites in Africa, to find a range of heavy duty and small scrapers, spheroids, choppers, etc., in the same concentration with the large cutting tools. The African and Middle East assemblages dating to the Middle Pleistocene are, therefore, of three main kinds — those with only large cutting tools (bifaces); those with only flake and chopper artifacts and those where both entities occur together.

These two contemporary and evolving traditions have been inter-preted as the work of two different species of hominids; as evidence of different activity patterns or as reflecting the work of different sexes or age groups of the same population. Except at the beginning of the Middle Pleistocene (c.1.5 million B.P.) when more than one form of hominid may have been present, at least in East Africa, the hominid fossils of the main Middle Pleistocene all appear to belong to different "races" of *Homo erectus* together with, in the later Middle Pleistocene, forms which show morphological development towards the early-*sapiens* type, in particular in Europe (e.g. Vértesszöllös, Swanscombe, and Steinheim). *Homo erectus* fossils occur in direct association with Acheulian industries at Sidi Abderrahman and Rabat in coastal Moroc-co and at Ternifine on the Algerian plateau (Howell 1960; Ennouchi 1969), in Bed IV at the Olduvai Gorge (M.D. Leakey 1971a; Day 1971) and, again, with other Acheulian and Developed Oldowan from the top of Bed II (M.D. Leakey 1971b: 229). The Hazorea fossils are also said to show *Homo erectus* characteristics and are believed to be associated with the Acheulian (Anati and Haas 1967). If Hominid 1470 from Koobi Fora represents one of the earliest *Homo erectus* forms, the lineage is more than 2.6 millions years old in Africa (R.E.F. Leakey 1973). Such and early appearance for *Homo erectus* receives support from the fossils associated with the Djetis fauna in Java where there is a date of 2.0 million years. Populations in the *Homo erectus* pattern appear, therefore, to have persisted over a very long period of time — for some 2 million years or more — before undergoing modification after c. 200,000 years B.P. towards *sapiens* and neanderthaloid forms. Except at the end, morphological changes appear to have been gradual rather than by a series of rapid modifications, followed by periods of no significant change. This is precisely what the stone artifact assemblages and occupation sites show and, although there are infinite variations in the combinations of the various artifact types and techniques, this only helps to emphasize the overall uniformity of the Middle Pleistocene cultural pattern. There are no major differences in the types of artifact found from one end of the Acheulian/"Chopper-Chopping tool" world to the other except in certain poorly known assemblages from sites within the margins of the tropical forest zone in Africa (de Ploey and van Moorsel 1965; Clark 1968). The stylistic developments and refinements that took place after the first appearance of the Acheulian tradition do not reflect regular developmental stages within a cultural continuum so much as random, idiosyncratic changes. Technological developments, such as the Levallois method, that make their appearance after the end of the earlier Acheulian, relate as much to the attributes of the local raw materials used (shape, size, texture, etc.) and other regional preferences as they do to the general level of cultural development at this time; where it was necessary, the Levallois or some technique closely related (e.g. Tachengit) or other (Kombewa) was used. Where cobbles or nodules provided the raw material, the Levallois method appears very late in the record. Although this suggests a fairly high level of technical proficiency, the uniformity of attributes exhibited by the tools and waste that compose the Archeological Occurrences in both Africa and Eurasia imply a basically similar pattern for the way in which the Middle Pleistocene human populations behaved and used their resources. That these resources differed by reason of local availabilty and preferences, cannot be doubted but the Middle Pleistocene industrial pattern suggests to me that the hunting/gathering populations were all doing much the same things. If, indeed, the range of activities was as limited as the stone artifact assemblages suggest, there must, nevertheless, have been room for not a little variation within this pattern as the qualitative and stylistic differences in the composition of the regional tool kits clearly show. Developed Oldowan assemblages from sub-Saharan Africa or Tayacian ones from the Levant, all have a number of technological and typological attributes in common and may stem from similar cultural responses. Acheulian handaxes and cleavers, on the other hand, must surely relate to quite a different set of cultural phenomena which were, nonetheless, related, it would seem, to generally similar sets of activities wherever the Acheulian is found to occur.

Handaxes and cleavers (also the "Knife" of Kleindienst's classification) are almost the only "formal" tools that occur with the Acheulian. The chopper and small tool element, on the other hand, exhibits no such formality prior to those associated with the evolved Acheulian assemblages that belong in the Last Interglacial. Although handaxes and cleavers are made to a general pattern, stylistic variation is considerable between localities as well as through time at the same locality. It is of interest, however, that, especially with the later Acheulian, there is often a preference for one or more particular forms — ovate or lanceolate, for example. We have, as yet, no way of knowing the reason for these stylistic preferences in the "formal tools" in individual assemblages and it could be due to a variety of different causes — for example, local tradition, individual idiosyncratic preferences, or a particular relationship between the form and what it was used on (Isaac 1972) while the changes that can be observed in a succession of cultural horizons at a single locality could result from the changed composition of the hominid group as well as from temporal differences influencing longer term traditional trends or long- or short-term ecological changes.

Radiometric and paleomagnetic dating methods provide the invaluable chronological framework within which the rate of biological and cultural evolution can be measured but we have, as yet, no means of determining relatively short periods of time — of knowing, for example, whether two Archaeological Horizons separated by only a few centimetres of deposit are contemporary within a season or so or whether they are separated by hundreds or thousands of years. Clearly this creates a major impasse in the understanding of the meaning of changes in style or composition in stratified sequences, so that what appears to be contemporary on relative evidence from radiometric dates, sediment studies or fauna may, in fact, be separated by several, perhaps many millennia. At present it seems possible to distinguish with certainty only two main divisions within the Acheulian — an earlier or Lower Acheulian and a later or Upper Acheulian. Certain aggregates may, in the future, be distinguished as a Middle Acheulian but, as yet, the evidence appears to me to be too incomplete or inconclusive to make such a threefold division valid at this time. The Lower Acheulian assemblages are being dealt with in other articles in this volume and are, therefore, covered here only in relation to the later Acheulian industries of Africa and the Middle East.

PALEOENVIRONMENTS OF THE EARLIER MIDDLE PLEISTOCENE IN AFRICA AND THE LEVANT

There is a voluminous literature concerned with local and regional geomorphological and palynological sequences and their interpretations in terms of paleoclimate and environment. Most pollen sequences, however, relate to later Quaternary time from the Last Interglacial (Eemian) through the Last Glacial (Würm/Weichel) and Recent times and there are very few that cover the earlier part of the Quaternary.

North Africa and the Sahara

So far as Africa is concerned, several important studies of spectra from localities in the Sahara (Rossignol and Maley 1969), notably those of Mme. van Campo (1964a) in the high Hoggar in the central Sahara and of Beucher (1967a) from sediments of the hammada du Guir near Beni-Abbés and in the valley of the Saoura in the northwestern Sahara, show what the vegetation was like in the Lower Pleistocene (Villafranchian). In the Hoggar there is evidence for open mixed forest which shows affinities with the Mediterranean forests as well as with the higher altitude open forests of the Middle East (in Iran and the Caucasus), relicts, presumably, of the late Tertiary flora in the Sahara. Tropical African forms are rare. These spectra indicate, therefore, a humid and fairly cold climate; the associated fauna is an archaic one belonging to the tropical savanna (van Campo 1964b).

In the northwestern Sahara, the flora at this time appears to have been predominantly desertic, even halophytic with arboreal elements representing the Mediterranean forests (pine, cedar, oak, etc.), the tropical savanna and a temperate element. The Lower Villafranchian in the Saoura region shows a vegetation of predominantly desertic species with higher altitude elements in which both Mediterranean and Middle East arboreal forms are present but the tropical species are absent. The extent to which allocthonous pollen is represented still has to be determined as it does also for later Quaternary times in the Sahara.

In Kurkur Oasis in the western desert of Egypt (Butzer and Hansen 1968; van Campo et al. 1968) the Villafranchian tufas show a spectrum of 16 percent boreal pollen of Tertiary genera and of the eastern Mediterranean; 7.5 percent subtropical forms of which c. 20 percent are living today on the high plateaux of Ethiopia and tropical East Africa; 22.5 percent of Mediterranean elements; 18 percent of Saharan desertic and halophytic forms; 34 percent grasses with indeterminate affinities and 2 percent hygrophilous elements. Kurkur is outside the Nile drainage today so the Ethiopian pollens are unlikely to have been water transported. A later spectrum shows an increase of xerophytic elements from 18 percent to 42.5 percent and a significant decrease in the tropical, "boreal", and Mediterranean pollen elements.

The Middle Pleistocene vegetation pattern is also known from two localities, the one in the Oued Outoul in the Hoggar (van Campo et al. 1967) and the other in the northwest from the Ougartian sediments in the Saoura valley (Beucher 1967b). In the Hoggar is again found a pattern of tropical and sub-tropical elements in the plains (*Acacia, Cassia, Euphorbia, Combretum,* etc.) with montane elements, partly tropical (e.g. *Podocarpus)* but mostly of Mediterranean (pine, oak, olive, pistachio, etc.) and sub-Mediterranean or desertic type (chenopods, tamarisk, etc.). This montane vegetation still contains, however, genera relating to the Eurasian temperate forests. In the plains the herbaceous element is essentially desertic.

Several climatic oscillations are reported in the Ougartian in the northwest and the floral composition varies in accordance with tendencies towards drier or more humid climatic conditions. The general pattern is one of Saharan herbaceous vegetation with some subtropical tree species, notably *Acacia* species, at lower altitudes and at higher altitudes the Mediterranean forest (pine, cedar, juniper, oak, olive, etc.), together with a less significant Eurasian montane element.

These studies show that the Saharan desertic vegetation, in particular the herbaceous element, predominates in the plains of the Sahara where also by Middle Pleistocene times the dry *Acacia* savanna was becoming important during times when the humidity was greater. The Mediterranean and Eurasiatic forest genera in the mountains represent communities that were isolated during drier periods as they are today but which were able to spread under more humid and cooler conditions when the avaiability of surface water was greatly increased.

The same general pattern is apparent in a number of important studies of later Quaternary and Holocene pollen sequences in the Sahara (Quezel and Martinez 1958, 1962; Faure 1966; Servant and Servant 1970; Alimen et al. 1968; etc). However, it can be demonstrated in much greater detail and amplified by limnological and paleotemperature studies (Servant and Servant 1970).

A Middle Pleistocene tufa from Kurkur Oasis yielded a spectrum with a high percentage of xerophytic pollen (53 percent) and a further diminution in the relict Tertiary forms. This is believed to date to "pluvial" conditions at the beginning of the Middle Pleistocene and, if so, it indicates that these conditions may have related more to lowered temperatures than to any appreciable increase in rainfall.

Apart from the persistence of a diminishing degree of relicts of subtropical Tertiary flora and of the "boreal" higher altitude elements from the Middle East, both of which would appear to suggest more humid conditions during the later Tertiary than were present at any subsequent time in North Africa and the Sahara during the Quaternary), the Lower and Middle Pleistocene vegetation patterns closely parallel those for the late Pleistocene and earlier Holocene. This is a pattern in which the predominantly xerophytic vegetation of the plains was modified by advances of the Mediterranean dry forest, of open *Acacia* parkland and of the tropical and subtropical savannas at times of greater available humidity. Such times occasioned a highly favourable habitat for the large mammalian Ethiopian fauna and, in the more coastal parts of North Africa, of some Holoarctic forms (deer, *Bos,* bear, etc.) of which the *Bos* spread as far south as the central Sahara.

Of course, these palynological studies are correlated with the geomorphology and, where it exists, the prehistory of the localities, some of which have been investigated in considerable detail (Alimen et al. 1969; Chavaillon 1964; Conrad 1969; Rognon 1967; etc.) and show a sequence of four main sedimentary cycles during the Pleistocene. Molluscan evidence and the formation of ferruginous crusts indicate a relatively humid and tropical climate during the Lower Pleistocene in the central Sahara. In the northwest, the climate was more typically Mediterranean and associated with the deposition of carbonates. At the close of the Villafranchian, this was followed by a period of aridity during which the dunefields (ergs) were built up recalling the aeolian tuff (Lemuta) member separating the Lower from the Middle Pleistocene sequence at Olduvai Gorge. The Middle Pleistocene humid periods were similar to but on a more moderate scale than that of the Villafranchian. When the vegetation pattern was re-established, the water courses began to flow again and Acheulian assemblages are found widely dispersed throughout a large part of the desert and North Africa (Conrad 1969: 437-42).

Africa south of the Sahara

Again, there is little direct evidence for vegetation patterns during the Middle Pleistocene but several important geomorphological studies show clearly the nature of the habitat favoured by Acheulian man.

Of particular importance is the work of Bonnefille (1969, 1970a, 1970b, 1972) in Ethiopia. Pollen spectra from silts of the Shungura Formation dating to c. 2.0 million years show floral associations similar to those found in Ethiopia today, namely communities of the woodland savanna, the riverine gallery forest and the montane forest. Spectra show clearly that the paleo environment when these Plio-Pleistocene sediments were laid down was little different from what it is in the Omo valley today but with some indication that the climate was somewhat cooler and more arid. The early hominid habitat here was, therefore, predominantly one of open woodland savanna which is the dominant form in this region today.

A similar environment is projected at this time also for the East Rudolf hominid locality at Koobi Fora (Isaac 1972) on microstratigraphical evidence, while Hay has shown that the paleogeography at Olduvai during Bed I and II times was predominantly arid and similar to that of the western Serengeti today with much grassland, open woodland and saline and freshwater lakes (Hay 1967, 1971). Acheulian occupation sites in upper Bed II and Beds III and IV at Olduvai during the Middle Pleistocene are generally situated close to stream courses or to open water (Hay 1971), as they are also at Olorgesailie. Pollen evidence is absent here but diatoms indicate that the temperature was somewhat cooler (Isaac 1968a).

Two further localities, one on the Ethiopian plateau and the other on the Somalia plateau, show the vegetation pattern in Ethiopia during

the later part of the Middle Pleistocene at a time contemporary with
the Acheulian occupation sites. At Melka Kontouré, grass pollens are
strongly represented (78 percent) and *Acacia* is also present showing
that the habitat was mostly an open one with some thornbush. Gallery
forest was present along the river and montane vegetation was growing on the higher ground close by (Bonnefille et al. 1970). It is probable that the spectrum from the upper Webi Shebeli on the Somalia
plateau associated with an "Oldowan" pebble tool is of comparable
age. It shows that the Ethiopian montane forest, which is present now
only on the higher ridges of the plateau, at that time extended down
also into the river valleys indicating generally cooler temperatures
(Bonnefille et al. 1970).

The pollen evidence from the Acheulian occupation floors at the Kalambo Falls (van Zinderen Bakker, 1969) is also pertinent here since
the radiocarbon ages on the associated wood are all greater than
60,000 years B.P. and a recent isoleucine date obtained for wood from
one of the later Acheulian horizons gives an age of more than 190,000
years (J. L. Bada, personal communication). Further results are under way. The Acheulian wood shows an appreciably greater degree of
racemization than does wood from the overlying sediments with the
Sangoan Industrial Complex. It is apparent, therefore, that not only do
the Kalambo Falls Acheulian occupation floors belong in the later part
of the Middle Pleistocene but there is an important unconformity between the upper and lower beds of the Mkamba Member (Clark
1969).

The Acheulian industry at the Kalambo Falls is associated with two
different vegetation zones. The earlier pollen spectra (Zone U), confirmed by macro remains, show warmer and drier conditions. Riverine
woodland is well represented but the dominant community is a semi-
deciduous forest with *Brachystegia* woodland predominating. This is
replaced by pollen spectra indicating cooler and wetter conditions
(Zone V) with genera representing, perhaps, a difference in altitude of
c. 300 meters above the site. This could be due to a lowering of temperature by some 3°C compared with present-day conditions.

All the available evidence suggests, therefore, that there has been no
catastrophic change in the floristic communities during the Quaternary
and that the Middle and Lower Pleistocene paleoenvironments were not
markedly different from what they are today. The same plant communities were present as are found today in the various localities studied
and climatic changes resulting from long term glacial/interglacial
cycles gave rise, in the tropics and subtropics, to a readjustment of the

616   J. DESMOND CLARK

boundaries of the floristic communities and to the proportionate representation of their main components as they are known today, in
response to cooler or warmer, drier or wetter oscillations. Again, the
much more complete pollen data for the late Quaternary confirm the
view that the Middle Pleistocene patterns are unlikely to have differed
from those of the Upper Pleistocene in any major respects.

*Middle Pleistocene Paleoenvironments and Vegetation Patterns in the
Middle East*

So far as I am aware, only one pollen diagram that may extend back
to include the Great Interglacial and the Riss vegetation patterns has
been published from the Levant. This comes from the core from
borehole K-Jam from the middle of Lake Hula in the basin at the north
end of the Jordan Rift; it is analyzed by Horowitz (1971). The two lower
units in this core (Lower Lacustrine and Main Peat units) of the Hula
Formation are considered by Picard (1965) to belong in the later Middle
Pleistocene on the basis of their relationship to certain volcanics and
of the associated molluscan fauna with the Benot Ya'aqov (Jisr Banat
Yaqub) terrace section at the south end of this basin. More recently, it
has been suggested and accepted by Horowitz on the basis of radiocarbon dates and extrapolations from a second core in Lake Hula (Struiver
1969: 591-2), that the whole of the Hula Formation belongs in the
Later Pleistocene. Farrand (1971: 549) is also in apparent agreement
with this interpretation. If, however, the correlation with the Benot
Ya'aqov formation is correct, then the Middle Pleistocene dating
would seem to be more likely because the Benot Ya'aqov terrace beds
contain an Acheulian which is typologically less developed than the
evolved Acheulian assemblage of the Last Interglacial, and the associated mammalian and molluscan faunas are of Middle Pleistocene type,
according to Hooijer (1959) and Picard (1963). Future work may be expected to show which of these datings is correct. Also, when the detailed
palynology of the four-kilometer-deep borehole Melech Sedom 1 in
the center of the Dead Sea basin referred to by Horowitz, Siedner, and
Bar-Yosef (1973) becomes available, more direct evidence of the sequence of Middle Pleistocene floral communities will become available since this shows an alternating sequence of four more humid
zones separated by drier ones. The third is provisionally correlated
with the Riss and the lower two with the 'Ubeidiya Formation, which
the K/Ar dating (>0.64-0.68) now shows must belong to a period prior
to the Mindel Glaciation.

On the basis of the excellent reconstructions of the paleoecological history of the 'Ubeidiya Formation at the type site and comparison of these with that available from palynology and micro-stratigraphy at several localities of later Pleistocene age both in the Jordan/Dead Sea section of the Rift Valley and from the Palestine coast (Farrand 1971; Rossignol 1963), it is apparent that the composition of the plant communities during the more humid and drier episodes of the Pleistocene did not differ or are unlikely to have differed from each other in any very major respect. Horowitz (1971) and others correlate the warmer and drier episodes with interpluvials/interglacials and colder, humid episodes with pluvials/glacials. During "interpluvials", pollen spectra show very low components of arboreal pollen and very low percentages of oak forest with high values for grass and sedge pollens. By contrast, under "pluvial" conditions there is a high percentage of arboreal pollen and of oak-forest forms with predominantly *Quercus* and low grass and sedge values.

Fossil pollens from the lower part (Harmarmer rock unit) of the later Pleistocene Lisan Lake sediments (Rossignol 1969) and dating between 50,000 and 100,000 B.P. (Farrand 1971: 544) show two wetter zones separated by a drier one. The earlier humid zone is characterized by a dominance of Aleppo pine, fairly abundant grasses, and few xerophytic forms (Chenopods, Compositae, Ephedra). In the succeeding dry zone there is a strong decline in Aleppo pine and grass pollen and an increase in that of the xerophytic plants. In the upper humid zone Aleppo pine again becomes dominant and chenopods and *Artemesia* decrease; there is no change in the Compositae.

The above pollen sequences appear to show that oak forest trees were the dominant form during the maximum of a "pluvial" while pine becomes more important during the interstadials of a glacial. This is confirmed by the evidence and interpretation of the Tenaghi Philippon core from Macedonia in northern Greece (van der Hammen et al. 1971) where it is shown that oak and pistachio dominate in interglacial and postglacial times and pine and herbaceous vegetation in the interstadials.

On the Lebanese coast the molluscan fauna associated with the 6.8 meter Neotyrrhenian (Tyrrhenian III) beach at Naamé is a typical warm water fauna, such as is associated with a tropical climate (Fleisch et al. 1971); a Th230 age determination for this beach has given 90,000 ± 10,000 B.P. (Sanlaville 1971). Pollens associated with this beach at Batroun show a high proportion of trees of Mediterranean species (oak, pistachio, olive, etc.) suggesting a certain humidity which may reflect one of the swings towards wetter conditions during the Last Interglacial (Leroi-Gourhan 1971).

There appears, however, to be a major disagreement in the correlation of the glacial/"pluvial" sequence. Horowitz and others associate the more humid "pluvials" with cooler conditions and so with glacials. Van der Hammen, Wijmstra, and Zagwijn, on the other hand, on the basis of the core from northeastern Greece and others, conclude that the climate during the last glacial was cooler and *drier* than present day climate. During the interglacials, however, humidity and temperature increased allowing for the spread of deciduous oak mixed forest, and steppe vegetation was drastically reduced (van der Hammen et al. 1971: 402 et seq.). Farrand (1971: 561) suggests that the explanation is that northern Greece fell under the influence of the dry continental European air masses while the Levant still enjoyed a Mediterranean climate but with an increase in the winter rainfall. However, Tchernov's study (1968) of the rodent faunas of the Last Interglacial and Acheulian deposits at Oum Qatafa cave in the Judean hills shows a steady trend from more humid, swampy, and steppe conditions with tropical elements in the rodent fauna to an increasingly more arid climate, but one in which forest persisted into the beginning of the Upper Pleistocene.

Evidence from the East African Lakes (summarized in Butzer, Isaac, et al. 1972) confirms the existence of drier and cooler conditions during the Last Glacial, the lake levels being lower and the forest largely replaced by grassland. In the Nile valley the evidence is less clear though Wendorf, Schild, and Said (1970) equate more humid local episodes of winter rain in the later Pleistocene with periods of low Nile floods which are also correlated by Butzer and Hansen (1972) with periods of local wadi activity. Pollen evidence for post-Glacial climate from Anatolia and Palestine, cited by Van Zeist (1969), also demonstrates that cooler, drier steppe conditions were dominant at the end of the Würm and were replaced in the earlier post-Glacial by warmer and more humid conditions favoring the spread of oakpistachio forest.

Correlation of the tropical, Mediterranean, and European glacial sequences aside, there still remains the question of to what extent tectonics in the Rift Valley, as also the changes that took place in Pleistocene sea level, may have affected local climate. The presence of large sheets of water in the Jordan Rift, such as that of the Upper Pleistocene Lisan Lake, can be expected to have contributed to some rise in humidity values and similarly the disappearance of water bodies of this kind as a result of further tectonic movement and vulcanicity must have had a drying effect on the local climate and biome.

Most of the evidence suggests that the climate of the Middle East during the Last Glacial was both cooler by some 5°-7°C and more humid, at times with a rainfall of about 800 millimeters on the uplands; on this basis it can be suggested that the climate of the Middle Pleistocene Glacial periods would probably have been similar. Correspondingly, the interglacials would have been as they are today with much dry steppe vegetation, open deciduous oak and pistachio forest at intermediate elevations, and pine forest on the higher slopes. Interstadials would have been more humid. This, therefore, is the pattern of vegetation communities and changes that provide the essential basis on which any comparison of the cultural assemblages must be based.

Diet

Some vegetable foods would have been more abundant in more humid times than at others and this is likely to have dictated the pattern of occupation. In more arid times, greater local concentrations of plant foods would be likely to lead to larger and essentially seasonal concentrations of men and animals, while more humid conditions can be expected to have led to expanded distributions. Among the most important plant foods would have been grains of cereal grasses, fruits, acorns, pine and pistachio nuts, olives, sedges (Cyperaceae) and other water plants, bark, and gum. Under drier conditions with more restricted groundwater supplies, greater use was made, it might be suggested, of geophytes (tubers, bulbs, rhizomes) and of water plants; the water nut (*Trapa* species) and rhizomes of *Phragmites* reed would have been important sources of food.

It is apparent that in the "interpluvials" the vegetation cover was thicker and more plentiful than is today's, which is the product of desiccation and some 8000 or more years of interference by man and severe overgrazing by his domestic animals. The habitat favored by the human populations in the Near East during the Middle Pleistocene is, therefore, closely similar to that favored by man in North and sub-Saharan Africa, namely an open, herbaceous, and grassland vegetation alternating with areas of deciduous woodland or park savanna where surface water was readily avaiable. Although the individual plants would have been largely different in the Levant and Africa, the hominids must have been exploiting very similar kinds of habitat and similar kinds of resources — acorns, pistachio and other nuts, and fruits in the Levant; grasses in the Levant, North Africa, and the Sahara; and various fruits, roots, tubers, etc. in tropical Africa.

In regard to animal foods, we have several good faunal lists from Acheulian sites in both Africa and the Middle East. The food waste comes from two main kinds of animals — the large game animals (elephant, hippo, rhino, giraffe) which are found more generally singly or in small groups, and the gregarious animals such as *Bos, Equus, Gazelle,* and other antelopes, e.g. hartebeeste. Cervids in Palestine may be expected to have been more generally associated in smaller and some seasonally larger groupings; the same applies to pig. Compared to the food waste on Upper Pleistocene sites, that on Middle Pleistocene sites shows a general lack of specialization but there is, nevertheless, already some evidence to show clear preference for one or more species at some living sites in Africa; for instance *Pelorovis* (twenty-four individuals) and numerous remains of suids at BK II at the top of Bed II at the Olduvai Gorge (M.D. Leaky 1971b: 199); for a small antelope similar to the springbok, *Antidorcas recki,* at SHK II, of closely comparable age and stratigraphic position where a small herd of these animals was found butchered (M.D. Leakey 1971b: 165). At both sites the industry is Developed Oldowan but at TK IV Fish Gully in Beds III/IV, many fish remains are associated with an Acheulian living site (M.D. Leakey 1971b: 283) and the makers of the Acheulian industry on the Olorgesailie living floor at DE/89 concentrated on the giant baboon *(Simopithecus)* (Isaac 1968b).

So far as I know, we do not as yet have individual counts for different animal species at sites in the Middle East which would be significant for showing food preferences, though these have been demonstrated for the Upper Pleistocene in Israel and Cyrenaica (Higgs 1967; Farrand [1971] has summarized some of this evidence). High percentages of large bovids in the food waste correlate with warm and dry conditions ("interpluvial"?), while a high caprine count is associated with cool, moist conditions (=glacial?) (Higgs 1967). Bouchud (1969) finds also that at Qafzeh in the Last Glacial the very dry conditions at the end of the Upper Palaeolithic correlated with a high percentage of *Gazelle,* while the Mousterian, which belongs with a humid and cool episode, has high percentages of deer and ibex as well as of horses, indicating steppe conditions. The Shemsi ("Tayacian"/ "Developed Oldowan" type) industry from Shelter IV at Jabrud in Syria, was also associated with a preponderant number of horse bones, again indicative of steppe conditions at, it is believed, the end of the Riss (Solecki 1968).

It is more usual to find a range of large, medium, and small animal remains on Middle Pleistocene living sites in Africa; the 'Ubeidiya cultural horizons suggest that this is possibly the case also in Palestine. The incompleteness of these remains may be a product of human butchery, food sharing, and eating behavior, but it may also reflect the relative importance of hunting as compared to scavenging as a source of meat. Although all may have been hunted, it might be expected that more regular success would be achieved with the smaller and medium sized and more gregarious animals than with the larger ones. On the other hand, it could be argued that behavioral characteristics of some of the larger animals rendered them easier prey and, certainly, the meat yield per output of energy was considerably greater. When it becomes available, more quantitative data from primary context occupation sites, plotted against distribution scatters, might show which is the more likely explanation for this general incompleteness. A number of sites where single large animals were butchered are known from Africa from this time period (summarized in Clark [1971] and Isaac [1971]) while one of the floors at 'Ubeidiya showed a preponderance of hippopotamus remains (Bar-Yosef and Tchernov 1972: 22), suggesting that in Palestine also the hominid group may have moved temporarily to the site of the kill.

The living floors in the Middle East show the same general mixture of large, medium, and small animals as are found on the African sites. Elephant, hippo, rhino, large, medium, and small bovids, equids and suids together with caprini in Palestine and North Africa, small animals (rodents, tortoise, lizards, etc.), and fish — in fact, a thoroughly varied meat diet is the pattern in the Middle East as in Africa, north and south of the Sahara (Cooke 1963; Haas 1966, 1968; Hooijer 1962). This could imply a generally low level of hunting efficiency and/or a considerable reliance on scavenging in the Middle Pleistocene as opposed to the more specific preferences that can be seen to be present in the Upper Pleistocene. For the hominids of the Middle Pleistocene, it is probable that scavenging was an even more important way of obtaining meat than it was for those of the Upper Pleistocene, or even for some historic and recent populations, since later Pleistocene technology shows several significant developments and refinements over that of the Middle Pleistocene.

CULTURAL PATTERNS EXHIBITED BY ARCHAEOLOGICAL
OCCURRENCES IN AFRICA AND THE MIDDLE EAST IN THE
LATER MIDDLE PLEISTOCENE

Throughout the Mediterranean basin, there is a general similarity between the industrial assemblages from this time range that distinguishes them from those in continental Africa proper. Acheulian assemblages from the Mediterranean floral zone in north Africa, especially the evolved ones dating to the Last Interglacial, show more of a common tradition with those of southern Europe and the Middle East than they do with those from sub-Saharan Africa. In fact, this is probably due to the use of flint and chert and the general size range, though the relationship between north Africa, in particular northeast Africa, and

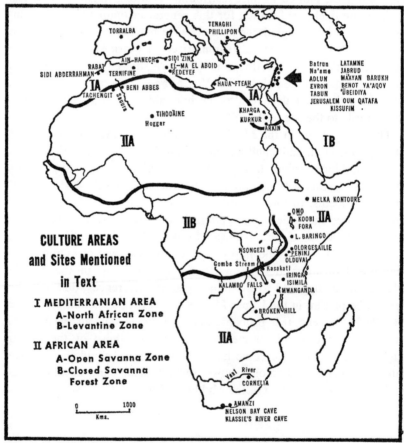

Figure 1. Map of the main Culture Areas identified and the geographical location of the sites referred to in the text

the Levant can be seen even more clearly in the late Pleistocene. The Mediterranean basin, therefore, represents one "Culture Area" within Herskovits' use of the term (1962), divisible into two subregions — the Levantine and Mediterranean North African areas. The rest of Africa forms a second, broad "Culture Area", again with two major subdivisions, one associated more with the eastern, central, and southern dry savanna grasslands and deciduous woodland and the former Saharan grasslands (Tropical Open Savanna Area), and the other more generally, but not always, found in what is now the more heavily tree-covered and humid equatorial zone of West Africa and the Congo basin (Tropical Closed Savanna and Forest Area). Each of these subregions is capable of further subdivision on the basis of local differences in paleoenvironment and stylistic cultural variability. The assemblage compositions in these two main Culture Areas are discussed briefly below for selected sites to show the range in each region. For further details of sites yielding hominid remains see the recent record of these by Isaac (1972). Figure 1 shows the Culture Areas recognized here and the geographical location of the sites referred to in the text.

Sub-Saharan Africa

The culture content of the middle and upper levels of Bed II (M.D. Leakey 1971b) provides the most detailed and complete evidence of continuing industrial tradition during the earlier Middle Pleistocene anywhere in the continent, or, indeed, in the world. The existence of the Acheulian (handaxe/cleaver) tradition contemporaneous with a Developed Oldowan (chopper/small tool) tradition from the beginning of the Middle Pleistocene at c. 1.5 million years is clearly seen at the Olduvai Gorge; the two Acheulian occurrences from the Humbu Formation at Peninj in the Natron basin are of comparable age. These two, large/cutting and small/chopping tool, traditions persist through to the end of Acheulian times in the Last Interglacial. Later assemblages more generally show a blending of these traditions in that the handaxes and/or cleavers are found together with the small tools, while the earlier assemblages are more likely to be found unmixed and so are more readily distinguishable. Possibly this is a reflection of the greater permanence or more regular seasonal use of the later Acheulian sites where the products of several different activities are preserved, mixed together on these occupation floors where the concentration of artifacts is particularly dense. Some confirmation for this is provided by John Yellen's ethno-archeological studies of Bushmen settlement sites in which it is apparent that it is the short term camp sites or special activity camps that provide the most informative evidence of specific activities, while the evidence of those activities becomes inextricably mixed at camps occupied for longer periods and by a larger number of people (Yellen 1973). It is most probable, therefore, that it will be the low density, primary context sites, products of a minimal number of activities or of a single activity, which will provide the best clues as to the functions of different sets of prehistoric stone tools.

More regular re-occupation of camp sites is also evidenced by the stone balls or battered spheroids that are often present on such sites in sub-Saharan Africa if these represent, as the present writer believes, the end-products of prolonged use for pounding and bashing in connection with food preparation and/or tool manufacture, rather than intentional, one-time, manufactured artifacts for use as a bolas or some other such special purpose equipment. Experiment and ethnographic example suggest the former to be the more probable explanation without, of course, excluding secondary use in a more specialized capacity.

Figure 2 compares the tool component of sub-Saharan lithic assemblages arranged in relative order of age with the oldest at the bottom. Tool groupings are those believed to be the most significant for distinguishing variability in Acheulian and Middle Pleistocene aggregates.

The Olduvai EF-HR Acheulian from the upper part of middle Bed II is distinguished by a high percentage of bifaces, only one of which is a cleaver, together with a low percentage of choppers, discoids, and spheroids. The Developed Oldowan B, MNK (main occupation), from the same stratigraphic unit and approximately the same horizon has a high percentage of choppers, spheroids, and battered chunks, approximately the same percentage of heavy and light duty tools, and a very small number (nine) of well made handaxes and one cleaver; these are the earliest found with a Developed Oldowan assemblage (M.D. Leakey 1971b: 150).

The Lower Acheulian (Site RHS) from the Humbu Formation (Natron basin) shows a preponderance of bifaces (handaxes and cleavers) and heavy duty tools and a low percentage of light duty ones. Apart from the greater proportion of heavy duty artifacts this is very like the EF-HR aggregate (Isaac 1967).

The Developed Oldowan assemblages from the top of Bed II TK and BK show high percentages for spheroids and light duty tools, choppers, and a small percentage of bifaces (8.2 percent and 5.3 percent). There are both small and large examples and they show considerable variability in workmanship. The small tools exhibit much secondary retouch as with other Developed Oldowan aggregates (M.D. Leakey 1971b: 184–222). Included here with the Lower Acheulian on account of its resemblance to that from EF-HR is the Acheulian from the site WK in the middle levels of Bed IV (M.D. Leakey 1971 b). It combines a relatively high percentage of handaxes (15.9 percent and cleavers (18.2 percent) with proportionate values of heavy and light duty tools, spheroids, and choppers. This assemblage is presumably older than 700,000 years since paleomagnetic evidence still shows reversed polarity readings up to near the middle of Bed IV, indicating that the Matuyama Reversed Epoch had not yet come to an end (Isaac, personal communication).

The next group of aggregates belongs with the Upper Acheulian. Appreciably more Upper Acheulian sites are known (Clark [editor] 1967) and they show a refinement of technique not present with the earlier aggregates. Four main Acheulian variants have been indentified for East Africa by Kleindienst (1961). Assemblages have been selected here to show that both "conventional" Acheulian (i.e. with 40-60 percent large cutting tools) (Variant A);[1] Developed Oldowan (Variant B); more or less equal combinations of both bifaces and small tools (Variant C); and biface tools with a high percentage of heavy duty equipment (Variant D) belong in this time period — the later Middle Pleistocene. Comparative details for other Upper Acheulian assemblages in East Africa are given by Kleindienst (1961), Howell (1961), and Isaac (1968b), and by Mason (1962) and Keller (1970) for South Africa.

The chronological relationship of most of these assemblages is unknown except, of course, for those at the multi-component sites, but the oldest are probably those from Olorgesailie (between 0.4 and 0.5 million: Isaac 1969), followed by Isimila (0.26 million: Howell et al. 1972), Kalambo Falls (more than 0.19 million: J. L. Bada personal communication), Amanzi (Deacon 1970), Broken Hill (Clark 1959) and Cornelia (Butzer, Clark, and Cooke i.p.) which is probably the latest and probably belongs in the equivalent of the Eemian; though not a primary context site like the others, it is included here to show the late persistence of the Developed Oldowan type of industry.[2]

[1]   In the opinion of the writer the presence of lower values of the Large Cutting Tools showing refinement and soft hammer technique provides sufficient reason for designating such assemblages as Acheulian.

[2]   The artifacts from Cornelia have sometimes been referred to the "Fauresmith Industrial Complex" implying that they belong with a late and evolved stage of the Acheulian. A sealed "Fauresmith" industry from Rooidam, near Kimberley, has recently been dated on calcite by the U/Th method to 115,000 ± 10,000 years B.P. (Butzer, personal communication).

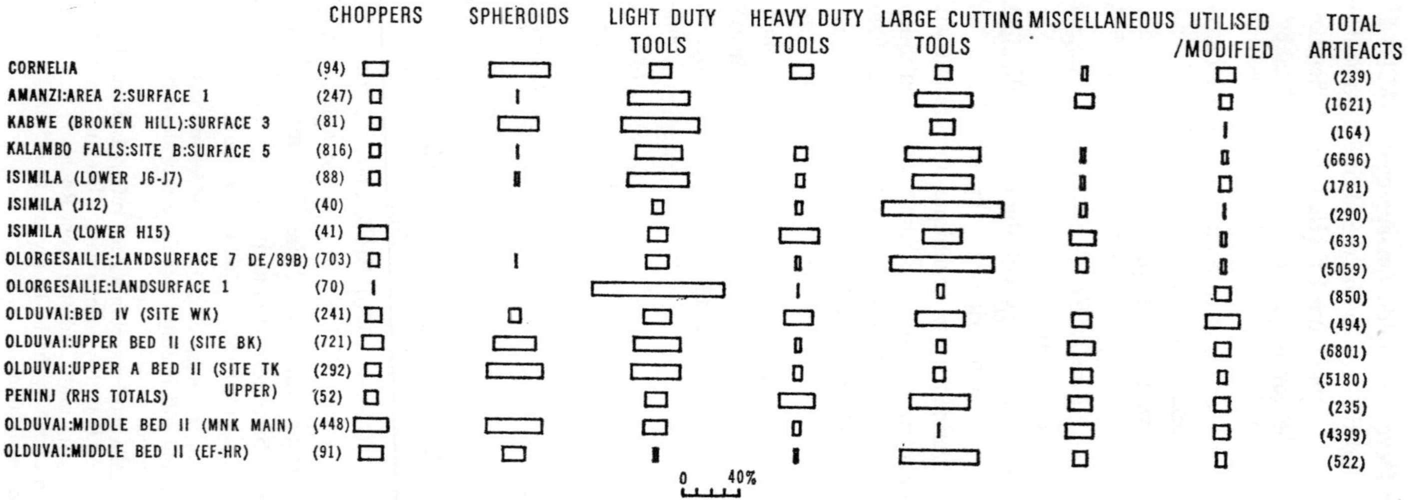

Figure 2. Comparison of the main components of Acheulian and other Middle Pleistocene industrial assemblages in the "Open Savanna" and "Closed Savanna/Forest" Culture Areas of sub-Saharan Africa, showing inter-site variability (For explanatory notes, see Appendix)

A considerable degree of variability in assemblage composition is apparent from Figure 2. This can be well seen repeated at some multi-component sites such as Olduvai and Isimila while at others, for example the Kalambo Falls and Amanzi, the composition of the different aggregates (10 and 9, respectively) varies only within the general range of the components of Variant C (see Figure 5, page 640). The southern slopes of the Atlas mountains and northern part of the Sahara in northwest Africa have some Acheulian industries that are more closely related in raw material, refinement, and technique to those from south of the Sahara, and it is for this reason that the whole of this region has been included in the Tropical Open Savanna Culture Area. Assemblages such as those from the Saoura, Tabelbalat-Tachengit, or Tihodaïne, are clearly comparable to Variants A and C from south of the Sahara (Balout 1967) and at Melka Kontouré, on the plateau in central Ethiopia, a similar range of Variant C and Variant B aggregates is reported by Chavaillon (1971).

The sub-Saharan sites have certain features in common — they are always within a short distance of water, whether it be a stream course, a lake, or a spring; and also near to the sources of the raw material from which most of the tools were made; they are not infrequently sited on sand and most of them represent a fairly dense and discrete concentration of artifacts. Some of them have a quantity of non-artifactual rubble (manuports) mixed with the implements. The classes of artifacts remain the same, though undergoing greater refinement, but the proportions in which the different classes are present on the sites vary considerably even, sometimes, to the total exclusion of some forms. When bone is preserved, it is sometimes found in concentrations with "mixed" Acheulian assemblages (Varian C), but at sites where a single animal or a minimal number of animals were butchered, the artifacts are predominantly choppers and small tools (Variant B) (Clark and Haynes 1969; Isaac 1971). The "Heavy Duty" component (Variant D) is not so well known nor is its connection, if any, with meat processing. The earliest appearance of this Variant is, perhaps, in the Karari industry at East Rudolf dating between 1.3 and 0.9 million years (Harris 1973), and its latest manifestation is probably to be seen in the aggregates from Sangoan Industrial Complex sites (e.g. in the Victoria basin, southern and western Zaïre, and Angola, Ghana, etc.), related, it is thought, to more closed savanna and forest environments in the early Upper Pleistocene.

The technology of these later Middle Pleistocene industries is related to the characteristics of the raw material used for tools. Where this

is found in cobble size, large cutting tools were made in the traditional manner of the "core tool"; where boulders or outcrops provided
the raw material, the technique of primary flaking ranged from direct
anvil (bashing one boulder on another until one or both fractured, as
at the Kalambo Falls) to the proto-Levallois method (as in the Vaal river
basin and the Karoo) and modifications of this, e.g. at Nsongezi in
Uganda. A combination of availability and local idiosyncratic preferences as to size and texture, so leading to tradition, are the most likely
determinants of regional techniques. Texture of raw material does not
appear to be so important as size in influencing technology.

Except on the high veld in South Africa, the Levallois technique is not
nearly as significant a part of Acheulian technology as it is in Europe
or the Near East. This technique does not appear in the Congo basin,
for example, until well on in the "Middle Stone Age" and it is absent or
insignificant in most of the later Acheulian industries south of the Sahara. Exceptions are the late but very interesting Acheulian assemblages from living and factory sites in the Kapthurin beds, Lake Baringo
(M. Leakey et al. 1969). A nearly complete hominid mandible in the
Homo erectus pattern and other remains come from an adjacent and
contemporary site and date to 0.23 million years. Associated with
evolved ovate and Micoquian handaxes, cleavers, a core-axe and
small flake tools and chopper elements were a number of classic,
broad Levallois flakes (26.6 percent) and the cores (72.4 percent) from
which these were struck. The Levallois technique is seen again in several
Upper Acheulian assemblages from the Horn and the northern Sahara.
These industries call to mind the evolved Acheulian with high Levallois
index from Kissufim and other sites in Israel (see below).

Acheulian groups clearly selected their raw material; coarser grained
rocks (lavas, quartzites and sandstones, even gneiss and granite)
for the large cutting and heavy duty tools and the most homogeneous
rocks available for the small tools (silcrete, chert, quartz, indurated
shale, etc.). They used what was locally abundant but the Acheulian
groups also appear to have used perhaps a greater range of raw materials for stone tools than did any other prehistoric group in sub-Saharan Africa at any time before or since; they also appear to have transported raw materials at least 65 kilometers (Bond 1948).

The Mediterranean Culture Area: North Africa

Besides the Algerian plateau, the Atlas range, and the Mediterranean
littoral, this area includes the Nile Valley, at least as far south as Aswan

and the northern oases in the western desert. These are all sites where flint/chert provides most of the raw material but also in this area are the sites in Atlantic Morocco, including those at Casablanca, where the material was predominantly quartzite.

Figure 3 compares the main components of selected Middle Pleistocene assemblages from sites in this Mediterranean Culture Area. Unfortunately, many of the older assemblages from the region are surface collections and, as the small tool element was often considered to be intrusive and not part of the Acheulian complex, it is rarely described. The late Villafranchian site of Ain Hanech in Tunisia provides evidence for the presence of a Developed Oldowan tradition in northwest Africa, but it is not a primary context site and the smaller tool component, if it existed, is lost. It is, however, reported from several sites on the *plateau de Salé* in Morocco where it is associated with pebble choppers and is dated to the Upper Villafranchian (Biberson 1972). The most complete assemblages relating to the earlier Acheulian are those from the Casablanca sites and Rabat and from Ternifine where the association with *Homo erectus* is established.

The STIC Quarry site at Sidi Abderrahman is a primary context site that has a component pattern similar to Variant A from south of the Sahara. It is a stream side site and the sea cannot have been very far distant. The fractured bones of a number of terrestrial mammals are associated with the artifacts in a limestone that forms the basal deposit of the Amirian dune. Animals include hippopotamus, *Rhinoceros simus*, a "forest" elephant, the aurochs, a large taurotragine, hartebeeste, wildebeeste, and horse (Biberson 1961a: 106–11). Marine fauna was not used. The climate is said to have been colder than that of today. The Amirian dune accumulated during a period of low sea level. If the correlation with the Mindel/Glaciation is valid, the occupation site is probably about 0.4 million years old; more probably the Amirian equates with an earlier period of glaciation.

The stone industry, which belongs of Stage III of the Moroccan Acheulian and to our Variant A, shows a preponderance of large cutting tools and a low percentage of light duty flake tools. Pebble tools have been classified here as choppers, and trihedrals as heavy duty picks. Of the large cutting tools, handaxes (298) predominate over cleavers (16). Characteristic handaxe forms are lanceolate, lanceolate accuminate, and chisel ended; the trihedral pick is as characteristic of the Lower Acheulian in North Africa as it is of this culture stage in sub-Saharan Africa and the Middle East. The industry from Ternifine on the Algerian plateau is closely comparable in age and composition

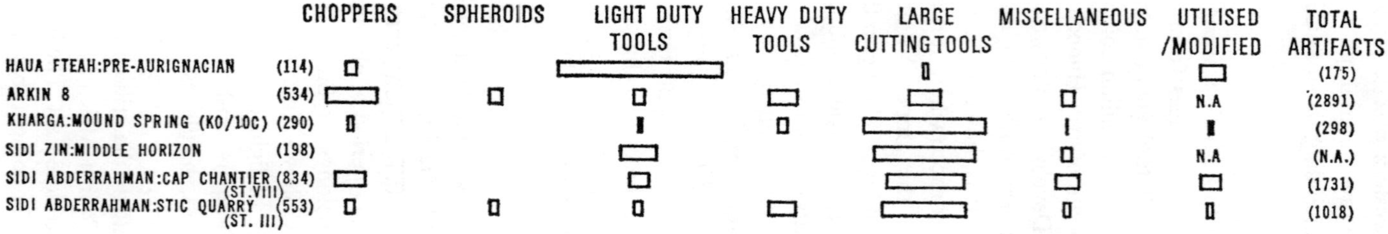

Figure 3. Comparison of the main components of Acheulian and other industrial assemblages of Middle and early Upper Pleistocene age from the North African region of the "Mediterranean" Culture Area, showing inter-site variability (For explanatory notes, see Appendix)

(Balout et al. 1967) but the small tools from this site remain to be described. The other four assemblages shown in Figure 3 belong to a fairly evolved stage of the Upper Acheulian and probably date to Last Interglacial or Riss times.

The evolved Acheulian (Stage 8) from Sidi Abderrahman Extension site belongs with sediments (Tensiftian and Pre-Soltanian) that are equated with the Riss glaciation. The associated fauna is terrestrial and mostly of Ethiopian savanna type. It includes rhinoceros, hippo, horse, hartebeeste, wildebeeste, oryx, a reedbuck, aurochs, gazelles, and ostrich. The dominant forms are the antelopes and the gazelles, rhino, and ostrich (Biberson 1961a: 153). The industry belongs with Variant C and comprises numbers of handaxes, cleavers, and bifacial knives with a smaller light duty flake tool element. Handaxes and knives (428) predominate over cleavers (11) and there are a number of quite small, well made examples of which the triangular and cordiform types are perhaps the most characteristic. The bifacial knives recall examples with the East African Upper Acheulian but are smaller, and they resemble the Quina-type scrapers with the European Mousterian. Flakes show regular retouch as side and end scrapers, points etc., and there are several kinds of blades represented. The raw material for these Moroccan industries is usually hard quartzite which will give longish blades, but it is probable the percentage would have been greater if flint or chert had been available. The spheroid is not represented in this collection but occurs at other sites of comparable age in coastal Morocco. Flakes were detached by direct hard hammer percussion and by the Levallois and disc core methods (Biberson 1961b: 335–80).

At the drying waterhole at Sidi Zin (Gobert 1950) assigned to the Last Interglacial, three industrial levels are represented. The large cutting tools and heavy duty forms are made from large flakes of limestone while the small tool component is made mostly from flint and quartzite. The bottom and top horizons contained chiefly lanceolate and elongate ovate handaxes, pebble choppers, and some informal, light duty flake tools. The middle assemblage, from a paleosol, is characterized by ovate handaxes and U-shaped cleavers, many of them made on large flakes of limestone. With these there occurred a more formally retouched group of light duty scraper forms (Figure 3). These horizons are sealed by a tufa with an informal industry, mostly on flakes and chunks of flint and quartzite, which has been termed "Mousteroid" but which is not at all unlike the Shemsi industry from Jabrud Shelter IV in Syria (see below).

The Mound Spring K.O. 10C at Kharga Oasis (Caton-Thompson 1952: 54–73) has produced from the "eye" what presumably represents a specialized tool-kit relating to specialized activities being carried out in the immediate vicinity of the spring. Unfortunately, fauna is not generally preserved — only one bovid tooth being associated — so it is not known whether very much animal food waste was originally present or not. The industry is made on nodules of flint and is characteristic of the Mediterranean form of evolved Acheulian. Handaxes are mostly lanceolate and elongate ovate, but limande, triangular, and cordiform examples are also characteristic; the cleaver is absent. The small number of heavy duty (core-scrapers) and light duty (scrapers) tools indicate that this assemblage belongs with Variant A. The comparatively small number of waste flakes (191) indicates that the bifaces were made elsewhere and carried onto the site for use; they were not resharpened. Cores for the manufacture of small tools are of the "Clacton" type and the Levallois technique is absent except for one atypical subtriangular core.

The Arkin 8 assemblage comes from the west bank of the Nile almost on the international boundary between Egypt and the Sudan. It is a primary context site of which 64 square meters were excavated (Chmielewski 1968: 111–34). It lay in wadi deposits between the escarpment and the Nile and artifacts were fresh and densely concentrated; natural stones forming a rough semicircle suggest a camping place. The assemblage of handaxes with choppers and heavy duty ("ovate") tools suggests a comparison with Variant D of sub-Saharan Africa, but the predilection for quartz cobbles (76.6 percent) as raw material may have over-emphasized the heavy duty element at this site. Most of the remainder of the artifacts are made from ferricrete sandstone; both raw materials are available locally. The commonest forms for handaxe tools are cordiform, elongate ovate, lanceolate, and triangular. The light duty element includes the normal range of scrapers. The Levallois technique appears to be absent here, but it is present at other and believed later sites (e.g. Arkin 5) in the Nubian section of the Nile valley.

The Acheulian in the Mediterranean Culture Area of North Africa is characterized, therefore, by a preponderance of handaxes in the large cutting tool category, while the cleaver is not nearly so common. The light duty (small, retouched) tool element also generally shows lower values; the spheroids and heavy duty classes, except for the trihedrals (Lower Acheulian) and the choppers, etc. at Arkin 8 and Sidi Zin (Layers 1 and 3) are not an important component of these aggregates.

Handaxe forms show stylistic and chronological similarities to those from the Levant, in particular in the comparable lanceolate and *biseau*-ended forms and the trihedrals of the Lower Acheulian as also in the cordiform, triangular and ovate subclasses with the evolved industries. As yet, the Developed Oldowan (Variant B type) is known only from Ain Hanech where it occurs in a late Villafranchian or evolved Middle Pleistocene context and from the "pre-Mousterian" industry in the tufa at Sidi Zin. Further Variant B assemblages can be expected following excavation of additional sealed Archeological Occurrences.

In the lowest levels at Haua Fteah (McBurney 1967: 75–104) there occurs an aggregate designated Pre-Aurignacian. This represents an industry made on blades and with a small proportion of end scrapers, backed blades, and burins with which there were three broken tip-ends of handaxes and four other small and crude bifaces. The climatic conditions of that time — warmer and probably wetter — were similar to those recorded in the Levant and the age of the industry lies between 50,000 and 80,000 B.P. It is closely comparable to the Amudian from Palestine and both belong in the closing stages of the Last Interglacial.

The Mediterranean Culture Area: the Levant

The Acheulian in the Middle East, together with the Tayacian and Amudian are found in three main regions — the coastal plain, the Ghab/Jordan/Dead Sea Rift, and the high plains and plateaux in the mountains and hilly region separating the two previous regions. The sites are located adjacent to stream courses, lake or pan margins or springs close to the escarpments. Later occupation sites are located in caves and rock shelters as well as in the open. The raw material was predominantly flint with some basalt. There is relationship between the location of sites and the existing favorable or marginally favorable areas for settlement suggesting that this general pattern has been in existence for a very long time (Gilead 1970: 9). The gregarious animals and some larger game appear to have been the more regular sources of meat. Unfortunately most of these species no longer exist in Palestine, but if models for specific sites could be established for the seasonal movements (distances and direction) of the main food animals, they could provide an indication of the possible range of the hominid groups that used them.

Most of what is known about the Acheulian aggregates in the Middle East comes from excavated sites in Palestine (Israel and Jordan) and in

Syria and, although the Acheulian occurs also in southeastern Anatolia (Bostanci 1961), in the Sinai desert (Field 1956: 5–13), Arabia (Field 1956: 97–119), and further east, these are mostly surface collections. The Sinai sites, however, provide a connecting link with those in northeast Africa.

Figure 4 shows the range of industries represented in the Acheulian of the Levant and their relative chronological positions. The composition of the early occupation horizons at 'Ubeidiya in the Jordan Rift and their paleoecological associations are well documented (Stekelis et al. 1969; Bar-Yosef and Tchernov 1972). The Developed Oldowan and Acheulian assemblages from the 'Ubeidiya Formation, which has now been shown to date to before 0.64–0.68 million years (Horowitz et al. 1973) are presumably, therefore, approximately contemporary with the later Lower Acheulian of East Africa and equivalent in age to the earliest stages (I and II) of the Moroccan coastal sequence. An Acheulian and a Developed Oldowan assemblage are included to show the same "parallel phyla" situation as is present in sub-Saharan Africa. While the Developed Oldowan aggregates appear to fall into our Variant B, the Acheulian is not directly comparable to either Variants A or C but is closer to the latter.

Of the nine horizons with artifacts at 'Ubeidiya, three show a significant biface (Acheulian) element and handaxes are present also with one other aggregate. The remaining assemblages belong with the Developed Oldowan tradition. Spheroids are made mostly from limestone, flake tools from flint, bifaces from basalt, and choppers from flint and basalt. The site was adjacent to a fluctuating freshwater lake and marsh with grassland and open woodland on the nearby hillslopes. Rubble is perhaps associated with some of the artifact concentrations and calls to mind the manuport rubble at some of the sub-Saharan sites, referred to above.

The next oldest assemblage is the Acheulian one from a channel sand bank situation on the paleo-Orontes at Latamne in north central Syria (Clark 1967, 1968). This represents a discrete concentration of artifacts in association with a number of large limestone blocks that had been intentionally carried to the site and which might, perhaps, have formed the base of a structure. On the evidence of the related fauna, Hooijer (1959) dates it to the Great Interglacial. This fauna, comprising elephant, rhino, hippo, horse, bison, camel, a giant deer, gazelle, and other antelope, suggests a primarily open environment with gallery forest along the river and woodland steppe on the higher elevations. The paleo-Orontes meandered through its valley with numerous swampy

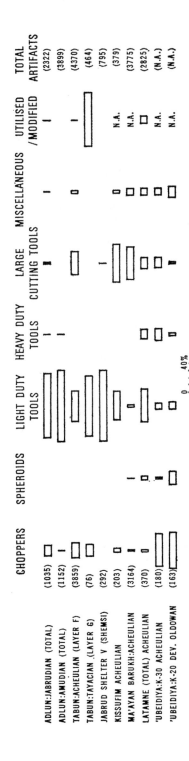

Figure 4. Comparison of the main components of Acheulian and related industrial assemblages of Middle and early Upper Pleistocene age from the Levantine region of the "Mediterranean" Culture Area, showing inter-site variability (For explanatory notes, see Appendix)

lagoons and small pans in much the same way as did the present-day Orontes in the Ghab before the completion of the draining and irrigation project.

The bifaces — almost all handaxes — are comparable to those from the STIC Quarry and Ternifine in North Africa, while the small flake tools are quite typical of the retouched flake element associated with the later Acheulian south of the Sahara. Latamne belongs, therefore, with Variant C. The handaxes were made elsewhere and carried onto the site, while the small tools were made from cores at the site itself. The earlier flint industries, from the channel bank site at Evron in a comparable paleoecological situation and from Holon, both on the coastal plain of Israel, appear to resemble that from Latamne (Prausnitz 1969; and personal observation by kind permission of Dr. Tamar Noy) and so may belong in approximately the same time period.

Typologically later than Latamne but not appreciably so is the Acheulian in the Benot Ya'aqov terrace in the Hula basin of the Jordan Rift. Although the associated fauna is not greatly different from that at Latamne, even though it includes deer and pig, the industry is technologically more advanced. This was first suggested by Gilead (1970) and Bar-Yosef (Bar-Yosef and Tchernov 1972), a view with which I am in agreement after having had the opportunity to examine some of this material through the kindness of Dr. O. Bar-Yosef. It is believed to be Rissian in age (Bar-Yosef and Tchernov 1972: 32). Unfortunately, the assemblages counts are not yet available and cannot, therefore, be included in Figure 4. The assemblage consists predominantly of large cutting tools (handaxes and cleavers) and some flakes, nearly all made from basalt. Handaxes are elongate ovate, ovate, limande, and lanceolate, with some rare lanceolate accuminate forms. The cleavers, like the handaxes, are made on side- and end-struck flakes and the whole appearance of the assemblage is reminiscent of that in lava from the Vaal River Younger Gravels II in South Africa or assemblages in quartzite from Tabelbalat in the Algerian Sahara. For example, the same divergent and convergent cleaver forms, in particular the type with splayed edge, occur at all three localities; and Banot Ya'aqov shows resemblances also to the Acheulian from the Narmada valley in India. Possibly it is the use of basalt that gives this industry a distinctly "African" look. Certainly its appearance is very different from the other later Acheulian assemblages from Palestine that are based on flint. Banot Ya'aqov has also produced a unique bone tool made from a large fragment of elephant long bone and showing percussion flaking of one edge and high polish from use at one pointed end (Stekelis 1960, 1967; and personal observation); other probable bone artifacts occur at this site.

Gilead (1970) has recently reviewed the Late Acheulian of Israel which he divides into four groups arranged chronologically on a typological and attribute basis. Most of the artifacts in these aggregates are made from flint. In the first of the four groups is the site of Ma'ayan Barukh (Stekelis and Gilead 1966), a surface site in the extreme north of Israel. The bifaces are mostly ovates and elongate ovates, cordiform and discoidal handaxes, with a small number of Micoquian examples and seven cleavers. The refinement of retouch is comparable to that seen on Acheulian assemblages in the Maghreb. The second group includes assemblages from cave as well as open sites. That from the silty clay loam in old stream channels at Kissufim (Ronen et al. 1972) south of Gaza is an evolved Upper Acheulian with high percentages of cordiform, almond shaped, ovoid, and discoid handaxes, often of small size. These are associated with flake scrapers and other tools of Jabrudian and Mousterian type and a high Levallois index. Comparable assemblages come from the upper layer at Evron. The high ovate biface element is also found in the Oum Qatafa D^1 assemblage. The high Levallois index is not repeated in the other evolved Acheulian assemblages. Certain more crudely made assemblages, all surface sites, however, in the hills between the coastal plain and the Rift Valley, notably that from Rephaim-Baq'a (Jerusalem) (Stekelis 1948; Arensburg and Bar-Yosef 1967) have a high percentage of discoid handaxes and form Gilead's third group from Israel (Gilead 1970: 116) sites. The industries from Oum Qatafa, E-D, and Holon that lack the Jabrudian flake tool element, represent another variant again (Ronen et al. 1972: 85). However, a similar ovoid to pear-shaped, bifacial component occurs, together with Jabrudian forms in the Upper Acheulian from Tabun, Layer F (Garrod and Bate 1937: 87–9). Comparable evolved Acheulian industries in northwest Africa with diminutive ovate, cordiform, and discoid bifaces are those from El-Ma el Abiod (Balout 1955: 224–31) and Redeyef (Gobert 1958).

The ultimate development of the Acheulian is seen in the Jabrudian in which the scraper component on unprepared flakes is now dominant. This occurs at the type site in Syria (Rust 1950), in Layer E at Tabun where it includes a number of handaxes and cleavers (Garrod and Bate 1937:78–87), at Zuttiyeh (Turville-Petre 1927), and Abri Zumoffen in Lebanon (Garrod and Kirkbride 1961). All these are cave and rock shelter sites and are likely to date to the close of the Last Interglacial or the beginning of the Würm.

Gilead suggests that there is a significant relationship between the mean length of Acheulian bifaces and their age: the later the industry the smaller is the mean length (Gilead 1970: 7). Even though the chronological relationship of some of the assemblages he has used is not precisely known, the general validity of his contention remains; it would be of interest to know whether there is any correlation between scar counts, mean length, and refinement.

In addition to the Acheulian there have been found industries made on flakes, chunks, and cores, without handaxes (Tayacian and Shemsi) and a high proportion of blades (Amudian; Pre-Aurignacian). Their stratigraphic position in relation to the Upper Acheulian and the Jabrudian is clearly shown by the excavations at Oum Qatafa, Tabun, Adlun, and Jabrud Shelters 1 and 4.

The Tayacian/Tabunian (Howell 1959: 15) underlies the Upper Acheulian/Jabrudian at Oum Qatafa (Levels E3-F and G) (Neuville 1951), Tabun (Layer G) (Garrod and Bate 1937: 89–90), and Jabrud Shelter 1 (Solecki 1968) where it is known as the Shemsi industry. At these sites there is unlikely to be any great difference in age between the two complexes, but that from Shelter 4 at Jabrud is older and belongs either in the Last Interglacial or, in my opinion, could easily be older. The Tayacian is a "nondescript" industry with unprepared flakes, chunks, and some cores showing generally crude, informal, and often minimal retouch; choppers are sometimes associated. There is a high percentage of utilized/modified pieces; bifaces appear to be absent, with the exception of one rough example from Jabrud Shelter 4 (Solecki 1968; Figure 7).

The Tayacian/Tabunian is also represented from several open sites associated with the interfluves between two stream courses in broad alluvial plains in the Samaria hills; the usual flake, chunk, and core element is associated again here with choppers (Wreschner 1971). There appears to be a certain reluctance on the part of Middle East archeologists to come to grips with the Tayacian/Tabunian. Admittedly, the number of artifacts on which the descriptions are based is not large, but this "industrial complex" has a very similar appearance to the small tool element in the Upper Acheulian of Africa and, in my opinion, it is the Mediterranean (and European) equivalent of Variant B from the Acheulian Industrial Complex of Africa. In fact, it would surprise me if there were any very great difference in morphology between the Tayacian and the light duty category of artifacts from Latamne.

The Tayacian/Tabunian is not interstratified with the Acheulian at

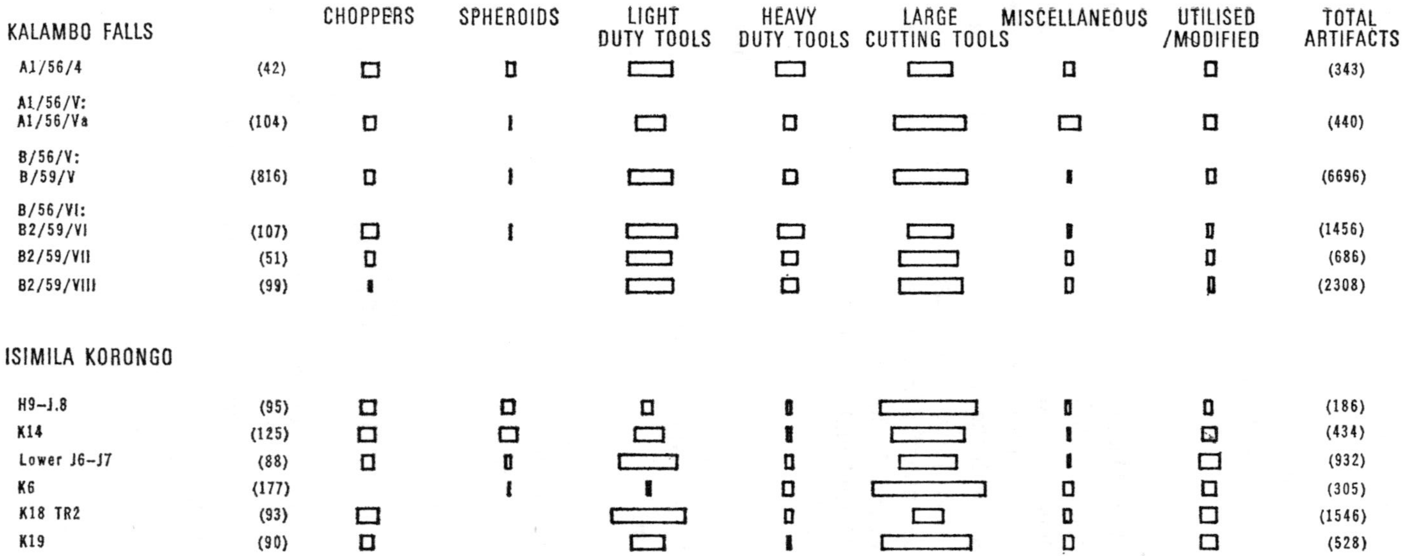

Figure 5. Comparison of the main components of six stratigrapically related Acheulian assemblages (earliest at the bottom) from the Mkamba Member of the Kalambo Falls Formation, Zambia and six from Sandstones 1a, 1b, and 3 from Isimila *korongo*, Tanzania, to show the kind of variability through time that can be expected at a single site (For explanatory notes, see Appendix)

Tabun or Oum Qatafa but the earlier sequence of Acheulian and Tayacian at the latter site is usually considered to antedate the beginning of the Tabun sequence (Neuville 1951: 261), and Farrand shows both Acheulian and Tayacian as existing under both warm and dry and cold and moist conditions (Farrand 1971: 560). If this is so, then it is unlikely that these two traditions are directly related to climate and environment.

There is yet another flaking tradition and industry that makes its appearance in the eastern Mediterranean basin somewhat later than the Tayacian/Tabunian but still prior to the end of the Last Interglacial — the Amudian. It is interstratified with the Jabrudian at Shelter I and again at Tabun but two facies of it occur at the Abri Zumoffen, the lower one in association with the top of the eleven-meter beach and both stratified below the Jabrudian. While the Amudian/Pre-Aurignacian is primarily a blade industry there is also a flake element, some with facetted platforms, and the lower industry has a number (eleven) of pebble choppers (Garrod and Kirkbride 1961). References have already been made to the Libyan Pre-Aurignacian from the Haua Fteah cave.

The Amudian, like the Tayacian, looks at first to be strikingly different from the Upper Acheulian/Jabrudian but the suggestion that they were made by quite different ethnic populations is unwarranted on the existing evidence. Again, it is necessary to await more complete excavation and analysis of occupation concentrations of this kind before the precise relationship to the conventional late Acheulian industries of North Africa and the Levant is known. Already it is apparent that the blade element makes its appearance surprisingly early in some of the Middle East assemblages. For example, blades are present in small numbers as early as the Acheulian industry at Latamne (Clark 1968) and, in some later assemblages, blades are a small but significant component, e.g. Layers D^1 and D^2 at Oum Qatafa (Neuville 1931), Tabun (Garrod and Bate 1937:85–9) and the Shemsi industry from Jabrud (Solecki 1968). This tendency towards blade production, detectable since Great Interglacial times, manifests itself also in the evolved Acheulian in Morocco so that it would not be surprising to find that this represents a general trend throughout the Mediterranean and Atlantic Morocco by Last Interglacial times, a trend which may also have its counterpart in the Levallois blade facies of continental Europe. A blade element is also sometimes present in the northern part of East Africa where blades form 13.4 percent of the unmodified flakes with the evolved Acheulian from the Kapthurin Beds at Lake Baringo (M.

Leakey et al 1969); and again at Hargeisa in northern Somalia 45.2 percent of the waste is blade-like. A significant Levallois element is also present with both these industries (J. D. Clark 1954: 1960–9). This blade element appears to be generally missing from the Acheulian in southern Africa, though large blades are characteristic of the earliest "Middle Stone Age" in the interior of the continent, and the "Middle Stone Age" aggregates that occur *in* and immediately on the eight-meter beach on the south coast of South Africa at Klassie's River and Nelson Bay Cave (Klein 1972), for example, would appear to oc-cupy a comparable stratigraphical position to that of the Jabrudian and Pre-Aurignacian in the eastern Mediterranean.

INDUSTRIAL PATTERNS, DIET, AND BEHAVIOR

Comparing the African and Middle East Acheulian and associated in-dustrial complexes, it is apparent that the settlement sites are to be found in very similar locations — usually close to surface water, whether it be rivers, streams, lakes, or springs. They are localities where, on faunal and pollen evidence, several micro-environments were available for exploitation, suggesting that they were purposely sited in the ecotones. The favored habitat was predominantly dry savanna and steppe with open woodland/forest at no great distance and some form of more closed vegetation — gallery forest — available along the margins of the main water sources.

No significant difference is apparent in the pattern of the occupation sites themselves which are reasonably dense concentrations with clear-ly defined limits. The range of artifactual material these contain indi-cates that several different activities were being carried out at these sites so that the relationship of a specific class or classes of tools to other associated features, including food waste, remains obscure. Con-centrations of natural rubble that can only have been carried onto the site by man occur both in Africa south of the Sahara and probably also in the Middle East at 'Ubeidiya. That they are not known from other sites in the Middle East is, probably, largely an accident of excavation. The purpose or use of this rubble is unknown and various suggestions have been put forward — that it was used to form a platform on swampy ground or to provide a camping place safe from carnivores, that it is the dispersed remains of some kind of shelter or windbreak or of a "larder" constructed to preserve meat from animal scavengers, or that it was for use as missiles, especially at night. The size and pattern of the distribution of the limestone blocks at Latamne lend support to the evidence for some kind of simple building by this time and substantiating evidence comes from Terra Amata (Nice), Kalambo Falls, and the Nile Valley.

Several butchery sites of a single large animal in sub-Saharan Africa show that it is mostly the chopper and light duty tool kit (Variant B) that is associated with this activity, but this does not preclude, though it makes it less likely, that the handaxes and cleavers were an essential part of butchery practices. Although butchery sites with the remains of a single or of several animals are not yet known from the Middle East, there is every reason to suppose that they will be found to occur there and, indeed, one of the K-29/K-30 horizons at 'Ubeidiya may preserve evidence of hippo butchering. This butchery pattern is, of course, well seen again in central Spain at Torralba and Ambrona (Howell 1966: 111–40).

The 'parallel phyla' of Acheulian and Developed Oldowan are present in the earlier part of the Middle Pleistocene in both Africa and the Middle East and continued, through evolved stages of both, into the Last Interglacial. While the composition of the assemblages in the three main culture areas is not the same, the extent to which they vary is no greater, in the writer's opinion, than that which might be expected within the range of a single pattern of behavior if the stone tools found in the different "facies" or Variants that have been recognized are essentially related, as I believe, to the food quest and the particular resources of the biome that were available and used at the time. Whether the assemblages are heavy concentrations or dispersed low density patterns would be determined, therefore, by what it was that was being exploited and for how long, in what quantities and how regularly it was available.

For example, phenomena such as special topographic features naturally concentrating game at favored watering places or the continued presence of groves of fruit-bearing trees might be expected to be used seasonally by hunter-gatherers for as long as they lasted. On the other hand, their disappearance due, perhaps, to higher water levels and flooding, might be expected to lead either to temporary abandonment of the site or to evoke a different set of activities making use of any new resources.

The occurrence of occupation horizons with two quite different "Variants" separated by only a few centimeters of sediments would seem to negate this suggestion. If it can be shown that these few centimeters were deposited in a season or so, then some other explanation must be sought, but I know of no primary context site where the duration of time of this magnitude can be measured and thin layers of sediments that seemingly cover only a very short period of time may, in fact, span many millennia as can now be seen to be the case with the Acheulian at the Kalambo Falls (J.L.Bada, personal communication).

It is also necessary to bear in mind that significant changes in the biome can be brought about by concentrations of large animals such as elephants, while hippos can also effectively change the nature of the riparian vegetation. In as short a time as 300 years, it is estimated (Harold F. Heady, personal communication) that the vegetation cover of a locality can be changed from woodland, through park savanna scrub to grassland and back to woodland again as a result of the activities of elephants and the cycle of changes these bring about in the animal communities that sequentially occupy the area.[3] Similarly a rise of lake level may greatly curtail or eliminate adjacent grass plains and the animals that make use of them, while a fall could have the opposite effect (Sheppe and Osborne 1971). It is not, therefore, difficult to see how relatively short time changes of this kind could affect the nature of the stone tool component of occupation sites if these tools are directly related to the recovery and processing of food. This could, therefore, be one explanation for the alternation of Acheulian and Developed Oldowan/Tayacian assemblages on succeeding horizons at a single location.

The heavy concentration of the large cutting tools on the occupation floors at the Kalambo Falls and the association in this stream bank riparian forest situation of much vegetation in the form of tree trunks, lighter brush, grasses and reeds with, also, clear evidence of fires, makes it necessary to consider whether there might not be a significant connection between handaxes/cleavers and vegetable products for both food and other uses. Several fruits have been recovered with the Acheulian at the Kalambo Falls, mostly from trees that fruit towards the end of the dry season. Unpalatable but nutritious plant foods, such as *Typha* roots, *Trapa* nuts, or waterlily bulbs, could be processed without any elaborate equipment. Another regularly available source of food, but one that would need tools for its collection, could have been the bark of certain trees which is a regular item of diet among chimpan-

[3] Elephants destroy vegetation by ripping off and eating the bark of mature trees, pushing over young trees and trampling seedlings. Preferential selection can bring about the drastic reduction of certain species and, in Uganda, elephants are considered to be a major cause of forest destruction and its replacement by grassland (Buechner and Dawkins 1961).

zees (Izawa and Itani 1966: 102), elephants, and other animals —
and it may well have been used as a matter of course by early hominids also. There are several ethnographic sources that speak of the use
of bark as famine food, in particular the inner bark of pine and birch
eaten by the Scandinavian peoples as late as the end of the nineteenth
century. A traveller in Finland in 1873 records pine trees stripped of
their bark and the finely scraped bark mixed in wooden troughs for
daily use and storage (J.G.D. Clark 1952: 59). Other records of bark
eating are known from Africa.[4] Since it is the inner bark that would
have been used, some kind of implement would have been required to
strip off a sufficient quantity of the bark and to assist in the separation
of the inner from the outer layer. This stripping and separation process
is one possible use to which the large cutting tools of the Acheulian
may have been put, and they would have been equally useful for
stripping bark in search of insects and for cutting out honey. Of course,
this is no more than supposition but, nonetheless, is worthy of serious
consideration. It would be of value also to study the nutritional values
of the various barks and to test by more precise observation and deduction the association of artifacts and resources.

The plant foods of chimpanzees living in savanna woodland in
East Africa could provide an indication of the pattern that might be expected for the early hominids and clearly need to be examined. The
Kyoto University studies in the Kasakati area of Tanzania (Suzuki 1969)
show that a wide range (78) of plants and seven animals are eaten and
that from 8 to 21 plants are used each month. As might be expected,
riverine forest provides most of the plant foods eaten in most months
but, in July to September, towards the close of the dry season, dry
open woodland sources dominate. This is the "hard seed" season (mid-
July to September)[5] when the fruits and hard seeds of *Brachystegia,
Julbernardia*, and the parasitic plant *Philostyles* are the main food
sources. Fruits of *Parinari* and *Strychnos* are also eaten at this time and

---

[4] Besides fruits and nuts, other food sources for African peoples in times of
famine, or as a regular item of diet, are seeds, roots, bark, and gum. For example,
in East Africa the BaGishu eat the green shoots of the mountain bamboo, and
roots (especially *Lannea humilis*) are an important item of food for Karamajong
(Langdale-Brown et al. 1964: 89, 90). In Kenya, the gum from three species of
Acacia is eaten (Seldon 1960). In West Africa and the Sudan, the seeds and pods
of *Pileostigma thonningii* are eaten as are the roots of *Boscia salicifolia* in Zambia
and Mozambique. A number of other fruit trees also have sweet-tasting barks and
roots that are chewed or pounded and mixed with other foods, e.g. the barks of
Antrocaryon micraster, Boscia angustifolia (and the seeds), *Craterispermum ceri-
nanthum*, and *C. laurinum, Ficus capensis* (and aerial roots), *Hexalobus crispi-
florus*, and *Grewia mollis* (chewed with cola) (Irvine 1961: xvii et seq).
[5] Hard seeds of thirteen different trees are used at this time.

Uapaca, Ficus, and *Garcinia* become important in October. Interesting also is the fact that *Brachiaria,* a large-grained grass is also used when it becomes ripe from May to July. The bark of four species of plant is eaten in the Kasakati basin and of two species in the Gombe Stream Reserve.

Of the twenty-nine main plant foods used by the Kasakati chimp population, all except seven are either regularly collected today or used as famine foods by Bantu-speakers in the *miombo* woodlands of south central Africa (e.g. Williamson 1955; Scudder 1962). I have not been able to find references to the remaining seven genera and species, but it is likely that these also may be eaten in rural areas in times of stress since fruits of at least three of them were eaten with no ill effects by the investigating team.

Chimpanzee diet in savanna woodland, therefore, is one of a fair range of plants used in each month (14.4 species) the main concentration, however, being on two to four species, while they are available over a one to two month period. The resources of the gallery forests are utilized mostly during the rainy season. Since chimps are primarily frugivorous, most of their foods are fruits, but more than half of them are dried or half dried fruits and pods that provide an essential source of food in the dry season. Some of these dried seeds have a high (80.5 percent) nutritional value equal to that of soy beans (Suzuki 1969: 118–9).

The savanna chimps are mostly found in mixed nomadic groups of adults and juveniles of both sexes numbering between 10 and 20 individuals on the average (the maximum group size was 43) and the estimated population of the Kasakati basin totaled c.100 individuals. Within the study area of c.2500 square kilometers the chimpanzee occupation was concentrated in only 29 percent of it (that is c.725 square kilometers. Within this area were seven nesting sites which ranged in size between 24 square kilometers and 200 square kilometers with an average of a little over 100 square kilometers so that the average density was just less than one individual for each square kilometer. Such a range is more than four times as great as that observed in semi-deciduous forest (Reynolds and Reynolds 1965: 393-4) and in excess of that for forest savanna mozaic (Goodall 1965: 455–6). Large concentrations occur more often in savanna woodland than in riverine forest, when the group has to move a long distance and when the food supply is concentrated (Suzuki 1969: 135).

Observers of free-ranging chimpanzees stress the continuously changing composition and size of groups and it can be expected that early hominid groups would have had a similar open structure with the composition and size of the bands remaining very fluid. In this connection, Yellen reports that the composition of the Bushman group at Dobe waterhole in the central Kalahari underwent an 80 percent change in the course of a single year, some of the individuals having come from as far as 100 miles away (J.E.Yellen, personal communication).

Of course, the greater importance of meat in the early hominid diet would have introduced important modifications into the model just discussed. Was the Middle Pleistocene pattern, therefore, closer to that of hunter/gatherers in the African savanna today where the population is seasonally more widely dispersed but sometimes concentrated in the woodland during the rains and in small groups centered on the riparian forest and permanent water sources during the dry season? Or was it the reverse of this pattern and nearer to that of the savanna chimpanzee groups?

The apparent absence of any regional specialization in the lithic assemblages before the evolved stage of the Acheulian suggests the probability that there were no major variations in the pattern of hominid behavior during the greater part of the earlier Middle Pleistocene. Although local plant and animal communities varied from region to region, there does not appear to have been sufficient difference between those of one ecosystem and another for hominid behavior to become significantly changed. In fact, adaptation to one main kind of habitat suggests either an inability or a lack of any need to adapt to other kinds of habitat at this time.

The range of animal foods and of raw materials used implies that there were fairly widely ranging groups experimenting with many different foods and materials, making use of whatever happened to be available at the moment, rather than that there was any pattern of regular and deliberate selection of a few particular resources. The use made of plant foods might, therefore, have been similar to that of savanna-dwelling chimpanzee groups where the gallery forest resources are particularly important. This generalized feeding habit would, where meat was concerned, have been complemented by scavenging activities which could account for the range of faunal species on the occupation sites and may well have been a much more important source of meat at this time than is generally admitted. Both scavenging and hunting would, however, require a much closer relationship between animal and hominid movements than occurs with any other primate group. There is good evidence also for deliberate selective hunting by this time as is shown by the sites from the top of Bed II at Olduvai and at Olorgesailie, but both the ability and the need to specialize to the degree seen in the food remains and tool-kits of the Upper Paleolithic and contemporary African "Middle Stone Age" industries are absent from the Lower Paleolithic sites. As yet, we have no opportunity to compare butchery techniques in the different culture areas to determine possible differences. Since it appears most probable that, by this time, meat was the preferred food, the pattern of movement in summer rainfall areas can be expected to have been one of radiation, following the game during the rains and of concentration during the dry season as the game returned to the permanent water and grasses of the home territory. As the remains testify, the meat scavenged or hunted was carried back to the home base and this must have been one of the most significant modifications of any behavioral pattern based primarily on a fruit or vegetable diet. Such behavior would be likely to reduce significantly the number of moves a group would need to make in a year, collected plant food being, similarly, carried into the living area in simple containers. This suggests that the primary consideration for the location of Middle Pleistocene living sites was that they be in areas of maximum game concentration or maximum biomass and that they would be moved in accordance with the movements of the game. It is unlikely that, by this readjustment, hominid intake of plant foods would be much reduced, since the game, being also dependant on many of the same plant sources, would themselves move to them as and where they became available.

One reason for concentrating sites close to water sources was the hominids' need to drink regularly. Another, perhaps equally important reason may have been because these sources supported the vegetation that produced the major plant foods used by man and the larger game animals on which he preyed. Gallery forests and the foods these supported would have formed a dependable reserve that may have been essential to the Middle Pleistocene way of life; a kind of reserve bank that supplied the basic plant staple for man then as it does for the chimpanzee today.

The area over which groups ranged would thus depend upon the local behavior of the game and availability of plant foods. For example, since the distance between the sea and the Jordan Rift is only about 65 kilometers, it would not have been impracticable for there to have been movement of individuals between the groups occupying the coastal plain and those centered in the Rift Valley, though it is probably less likely that whole groups would have alternated in this way unless this was a part of the pattern of seasonal movement of the game animals. In Palestine, if the game movements were at all like those of Europe, it can be expected that deer and other species would have ranged onto the higher ground during the summer and concentrated during the winter and the rains on the low ground when temperatures would have been lower and cover available in the riparian forest (J.G.D. Clark 1972: 28).

CONCLUSIONS

At present, comparisons between Middle Pleistocene industries in Africa and the Levant are possible only at a very general level. Four major Culture Areas where the Acheulian techno-complex is present can be recognized — two in the Mediterranean basin and two in continental Africa. These are distinguished on the basis of the prevailing ecology, food sources, technological and typological characteristics of the industries, and the selection of raw material. Within each of these Culture Areas there are manifest four generalized industrial facies or Variants, A-D, each of which is characterized by quantitative and qualitative differences in the composition of the lithic assemblages. Each Variant exhibits regional differences in the composition of individual aggregates as well as in technique, style, and mean measurements though categories and classes of artifacts remain the same.

These quantitative changes clearly demonstrate a trend towards increasing refinement and specialization through time, but qualitatively it must be stressed that relatively refined examples may occur with the earliest Acheulian assemblages and relatively crude examples with some of the latest. The meaning of this kind of quantitative variability where it is between geologically "contemporary" assemblages is far from clear and is likely to remain so until systematic studies of low density sites are carried out and can provide the opportunity for distinguishing between the cultural products of the different activities. Only in the evolved industries at the end of the long Acheulian tradition is it possible to see any significant differences between those in the Near East and those in Africa. Prior to the Last Interglacial, it is the similarities that are the most characteristic feature of Middle Pleistocene culture and not the differences.

Since activities must relate directly to the territory exploited, there is, at the same time, a great need for more intensive studies of the paleoenvironment of specific primary context occupation sites such as have been carried out at the Olduvai Gorge and 'Ubeidiya as well as for the excavation of the whole of an occupation area on a single horizon and the recovery of the complete distribution pattern of the occupation debris. Prehistorians would, thereby, not only be brought nearer to understanding the relationship between different classes of artifacts and of these to other features of the site, but also could assess the meaning of stratified sequences of interbedded Acheulian and Developed Oldowan/Tayacian assemblages at a single site if some method of assessing short term time intervals can be devised. Possibly this might develop from refinements of the amino acid method of dating (Turekian and Bada 1972) with some form of calibration based upon the extent to which racemization of bone or wood differs between two horizons. No serious attempts have yet been made to apply site catchment methods (Higgs and Vita-Finzi 1972) to Middle Pleistocene sites and clearly herein lies one of the most hopeful approaches for reconstructing the resource potential, for estimating the relative importance of the plant and animal foods and so for constructing models for economic behavior at specific sites.

As yet, the effects of changes in climate and so in environment as they affect the siting, size, and length of occupation, the abundance or absence of bone, and the composition of the lithic assemblages at particular sites are unknown though Farrand's correlation (1971: 560, Table 2) of the Acheulian/Tayacian levels at Jabrud, Tabun, and Oum Qatafa suggest that they were not sufficiently great in the regions enjoying a Mediterranean or tropical climate to change the basic nature of the tool kits.

Lastly, but by no means least important, is the need to extend laboratory studies of wear patterns and organic residues on the edges of unmodified, utilized, and retouched artifacts coming from primary context sites in order to determine whether an artifact may or may not have been used and whether the substance on which it was used was of plant or animal origin. It is clear that the most rewarding studies are those that relate to detailed investigation of the individual primary context horizons where the surviving evidence of the activities and behavior of the occupants, when analyzed by trace element and conventional archeological methods, should lend itself to interpretation once a sufficient body of precise experimental control data becomes available.

APPENDIX: EXPLANATORY NOTES TO FIGURES 2–5

The category groupings of shaped tools shown in these diagrams are those that are considered to be most meaningful for comparing Acheulian and other Middle Pleistocene artifact assemblages from Africa and the Mediter-

ranean basin. They are based upon the typology/terminology established
for the East African Acheulian by Kleindienst (1961) and now widely used
by workers south of the Sahara.

Most of the major tool categories shown here are composed of several
classes of shaped tools as recognized in the original site reports, but in almost all cases these groupings fall naturally within one or other of the
major categories, as indicated below:

Choppers: Various kinds of choppers (side, end, technical), uni-
                      facial (chopping tool), and bifacial.
Spheroids: Polyhedrons, sub-spheroids, and spheroids "globular
                      cores" (Arkin).
"Light duty" tools: Small (i.e. < 10 centimeters) scrapers (various forms)
                      (side, end, nosed, concave, etc.), "points", backed
                      knives, awls, borers, proto-burins, burins, etc.
"Heavy duty" tools: Core-scrapers, picks, core-axes, trihedrals, "other large
                      bifaces".
"Large cutting" tools: Handaxes, cleavers, cleaver flakes, bifacial knives,
                      large (> 10 centimeters) side scrapers.
Miscellaneous: Discoids, modified battered nodules, miscellaneous
                      tools.

The percentages shown are of the total number of shaped tools in the
assemblage (i.e. the figure in brackets after the locality details). The one
exception is the figure for utilized/modified artifacts (including hammerstones, anvils, pieces showing informal utilization and/or modification, etc.)
which is shown as the percentage of all artifacts — shaped tools, utilized/
modified, and unmodified waste.

It will be apparent that some of these aggregates are heavily selected (e.g.
Cornelia, Kissufim, and Ma'ayan Barukh), while others show a lesser amount
of selection (e.g. Sidi Zin and Sidi Abderrahman). In cases where there has
been much selection the small tool and utilized/modified tool classes and
categories, as well, of course, as the unmodified waste, are likely to be
underrepresented. Two further problems relate to "chopping tools" which
might be grouped, on the one hand, with unifacial choppers or with core
scrapers, depending on the edge angle. Chopper values may also be affected
by the classification of certain core forms used by individual authors. A
better term for this category might, therefore, be "core/chopper".

The following assemblages in Figure 2 are classified as Developed
Oldowan — Cornelia; Olorgesailie, Landsurface 1; Olduvai Sites WK, BK,
TK upper, MNK main — the remainder are classified as Acheulian.

Authorities for the assemblage details are as follows:

Figure 2:

Cornelia (Butzer et al. i.p.); Amanzi (Deacon 1970); Kabwe (Broken Hill)
(Clark 1959); Kalambo Falls (Clark 1964); Isimila (Kleindienst 1961);
Olorgesailie, DE89B (Isaac 19668b); Olorgesailie, Landsurface 1 (Klein-
dienst 1961); Olduvai: Bed III (M. D. Leakey 1971a); Olduvai, Bed II (M.
D. Leakey 1971b); Peninj (Isaac 1967).

Figure 3:

Haua Fteah: Pre-Aurignacian (McBurney 19667); Arkin 8 (Chmielewski 1968); Kharga (Caton-Thompson 1952); Sidi Zin (Gobert 1950); Sidi Abderrahman (Biberson 1961b).

Figure 4:

Adlun (Garrod and Kirkbride 1961); Tabun (Garrod and Bate 1937); Jabrud Shelter IV (Solecki 1968); Kissufim (Ronen et al. 1972); Ma'ayan Barukh (Stekelis and Gilead 1966); Latamne (Clark 1968); 'Ubeidiya (Bar-Yosef and Tchernov 1972).

Figure 5:

Kalambo Falls (Clark 1964). Isimila (Kleindienst 1961).

REFERENCES

ALIMEN, H., F. BEUCHER, H. LHOTE, G. DELIBRIAS
   1968   Les gisements néolithiques de Tan-Tartaït et d'In-n-Itinen, Tassili-n-Ajjer (Sahara central). *Bulletin de la Société Préhistorique Française* 65(1):421–457.
ALIMEN, H., H. FAURE, J. CHAVAILLON, M. TAIEB, R. BATTISTINI
   1969   Les études françaises sur le Quaternaire d'Afrique. *Études françaises sur le Quaternaire.* VIII Congrès Internationale de INQUA, Paris:201–214.
ANATI, E., N. HAAS
   1967   The Hazorea Pleistocene site: a preliminary report. *Man* 2(3): 454–456.
ARENSBURG, B., O. BAR-YOSEF
   1967   Yacimiento paleolitico en el valle de Refaim, Jerusalem, Israel. *Ampurias* 29:117–133.
BALOUT, L.
   1955   *Préhistoire de l'Afrique du Nord.* Paris.
   1967   "Procédés d'Analyse et Questions de Terminologie dans l'Étude des Ensembles industriels du Paléolithique inférieur en Afrique du nord," in *Background to evolution in Africa.* Edited by W. W. Bishop and J. D. Clark, 701–735. Chicago.
BALOUT, L., P. BIBERSON, J. TIXIER
   1967   L'Acheuléen de Ternifine (Algérie), gisement de l'Atlanthrope. *L'Anthropologie* 71:217–237.
BAR-YOSEF, O., E. TCHERNOV
   1972   *On the palaeo-ecological history of the site of 'Ubeidiya.* Israel Academy of Sciences and Humanities. 5–35.
BEUCHER, F.
   1967a Quelques éléments de flore pliocène au Sahara nord-occidental.

Comptes rendus de l'Académie des Sciences de Paris 265:1117–1120.

1967b Une flore d'âge Ougartien (seconde partie du Quaternaire moyen) dans les monts d'Ougata (Sahara nord-occidental). *Revue Palaeobotanique et Palynologique, Amsterdam* 2(1-4):291–300.

BIBERSON, P.

1961a *Le cadre paléogéographique de la préhistoire du Maroc atlantique.* Publication Services des Antiquités du Maroc. (16) Rabat.

1961b *Le Paléolithique inférieur du Maroc atlantique.* Publication Service des Antiquités du Maroc. (17) Rabat.

1972   Nouvelles données sur le Pré-Acheuléen (ex-Pebble-Culture) du Villafranchien du Maroc. *Comptes rendus de l'Academie des Sciences de Paris* 271:1972–1974.

BOND, G.

1948   Rhodesian Stone Age man and his raw materials. *South African Archaeological Bulletin* 3(11):55–60.

BONNEFILLE, R.

1969   Indications sur la paléoflore d'un niveau du Quaternaire moyen du site de Melka Kontouré (Ethiopie). *Comptes rendus et Sommaires de la Société Géologique* (7):238–239.
       Comptes rendus de l'Académie des Sciences de Paris 270:924–927.

1970a Résultats de la nouvelle mission de l'Omo (3e campagne, 1969).

1970b Premiers résultats concernant l'analyse pollinique d'échantillons du Pléistocène inférieur de l'Omo (Ethiopie). *Comptes rendus de l'Académie des Sciences de Paris* 270:2430–2433.

1972   "Considérations sur la composition d'une microflore pollinique des formations Plio-Pléistocène de la Basse Vallée de l'Omo (Ethiopie)," in *Palaeoecology of Africa.* Edited by E. M. Van Zinderen Bakker, 7:22–27.

BONNEVILLE, R., N. CHAVAILLON, M. TAIEB

1970   Formations volcano-lacustres quaternaires de la vallée supérieure du Wehi-Shebelli (Ethiopie): données stratigraphiques, préhistoriques et palynologiques. *Comptes rendus de l'Académie des Sciences de Paris* 271:161–164.

BOSTANCI, E. Y.

1961   Researches in south-east Anatolia. The Chellean and Acheulian Industry of Dülük and Kartol. *Anatolia* 6:89–162.

BOUCHUD, J.

1969   Etude paléontologique de la faune du Djébel Qafzeh, Israël. *International Quaternary Association Eighth Congress.* Résumés. Paris, 118.

BUECHNER, H. K., H. C. DAWKINS

1961   Vegetation change induced by elephants and fire in the Murchison Falls National Park, Uganda. *Ecology,* 42:752–766.

BUTZER, K. W., J. D. CLARK, H. B. S. COOKE

i.p.   *The geology, archaeology and fossil mammals of the Cornelia beds.* National Museum, Memoir 8. Bloemfontein.

BUTZER, K. W., C. L. HANSEN

1968   *Desert and river in Nubia: geomorphology and prehistoric en-*

vironments at the Aswan Reservoir. Madison.

1972 Late Pleistocene stratigraphy of the Kom Ombo Plain, Upper Egypt: Comparison with other recent studies near Esna-Edfu. *Bulletin de l'Association Sénégalaise pour l'Étude du Quaternaire.* 35–36:5–14.

BUTZER, K. W., G. L. ISAAC, R. L. RICHARDSON, C. WASHBOURN-KAMAU
1972 Radiocarbon dating of East African lake levels. *Science*, 175: 1069–1076.

CATON-THOMPSON, G.
1952 *Kharga Oasis in prehistory.* London.

CHAVAILLON, J.
1964 *Les formations quaternaires du Sahara nord-occidental.* Publication du Centre de Recherches sur les Zones Arides. C.N.R.S. Sér. Géol. 5 Paris.
1971 *Prehistorical living-floors of Melka Kontouré in Ethiopia.* Eighth Pan-African Congress on Prehistory and Quaternary Studies, Livret-guide.

CHMIELEWSKI, W.
1968 "Early and Middle Palaeolithic sites near Arkin, Sudan," in *The prehistory of Nubia.* Edited by F. Wendorf, 1:110–147. Dallas.

CLARK, J. D.
1954 *The prehistoric cultures of the Horn of Africa.* Cambridge.
1959 Further excavations at Broken Hill, Northern Rhodesia. *Journal of the Royal Anthropological Institute* 89(2):201–232.
1961 Fractured chert specimens from the Lower Pleistocene Bethlehem Beds, Israel. *Bulletin of the British Museum (Natural History) Geology* 5(4):73–90.
1964 The influence of environment in inducing culture change at the Kalambo Falls prehistoric site. *South African Archaeological Bulletin* 19(76):93–101.
1967 The Middle Acheulian occupation site at Latamne, northern Syria (1st paper). *Quaternaria* 9:1–68.
1968 The Middle Acheulian occupation site at Latamne, northern Syria (2nd paper). Further excavations (1965): general results, definitions and interpretation. *Quaternaria* 10:1–72.
1971 Palaeolithic butchery practices, in *Man, settlement and urbanization.* Edited by P. J. Ucko, R. Tringham, and G. W. Dimbleby, 149–156.

CLARK, J. D., editor
1967 *Atlas of African prehistory.* Chicago.
1969 *Kalambo Falls Prehistoric Site, I.* The geology, palaeoecology and detailed stratigraphy of the excavations. Cambridge.

CLARK, J. D., C. V. HAYNES
1969 An elephant butchery site at Mwanganda's village, Karonga, Malawi and its relevance for Palaeolithic archaeology. *World Archaeology* 1(3):390–411.

CLARK, J. G. D.
1952 *Prehistoric Europe: the economic base.* Cambridge.

1972   *Starr Carr: a case study in bioarchaeology.* McCaleb Module in Anthropology 10:1–42. Reading.

CONRAD, G.
1969   L'Evolution continentale post-Hercynienne du Sahara Algérien. Centre de Recherches sur les Zones Arides. CNRS. Série Géologique 10. Paris.

COOKE, H. B. S.
1963   "Pleistocene mammal faunas of Africa with particular reference to southern Africa," in *African ecology and human evolution.* Edited by F. C. Howell and F. Bourlière. Viking Fund Publications in Anthropology 36. New York.

DAY, M.
1971   Post-cranial remains of *Homo erectus* from Bed IV, Olduvai Gorge, Tanzania. *Nature 232:382–387.*

DEACON, H. J.
1970   *The Acheulian occupation at Amanzi Springs, Uitenhage district, Cape Province.* Annals Cape Provincial Museums (Natural History) 8(2). Grahamstown.

DE PLOEY, J., H. VAN MOORSEL
1965   *Contributions à la connaissance chronologique et paléogéographique des gisements préhistoriques des environs de Léopoldville, (Congo.* Studia Universitatis 'Lovanium', Musée de Préhistoire 19. Kinshasa.

ENNOUCHI, E.
1969   Découverte d'un Pithécanthropien au Maroc. *Comptes rendus de l'Académie des Sciences de Paris 269:763–765.*

FARRAND, W. R.
1971   "Late Quaternary palaeo-climates of the eastern Mediterranean area," in *The Late Cenozooic glacial ages.* Edited by K. K. Turekian, 529–563. New Haven.

FAURE, H.
1966   *Reconnaissance géologique des formations sédimentaires post-paléozoiques du Niger oriental.* Mémoire Bulletin de Recherches de Géologie et Mines 47.

FIELD, H.
1956   *Ancient and modern man in southwestern Asia.* Coral Gables, Florida: University of Miami Press.

FLEISCH, H., J. COMATI, P. REYNARD, P. ELOUARD
1971   Gisements à *Strombus bubonius* Link (Tyrrhénien à Naamé [Liban]). *Quaternaria 15:217–238.*

GARROD, D. A. E., D. M. A. BATE
1937   *The Stone Age of Mount Carmel,* volume one. Cambridge.

GARROD, D. A. E., D. KIRKBRIDE
1961   Excavation of the Abri Zumoffen, a Palaeolithic rock-shelter near Adlun, south Lebanon, 1958. *Bulletin du Musée de Beyreuth 16: 7–45.*

GILEAD, D.
1970   Handaxe industries in Israel and the Near East. *World Archaeology 2(1):1–11.*

GOBERT, E. G.
1950 Le gisement paléolithique de Sidi Zin. *Karthago* 1:1–51. Tunis.
1958 L'Acheuléen de Redeyef. *Karthago* 9:3–44. Tunis.

GOODALL, J.
1965 "Chimpanzees of the Gombe Stream Reserve," in *Primate behavior*. Edited by I. DeVore, 425–473. New York.

HAAS, G.
1966 *On the vertebrate fauna of the Lower Pleistocene site 'Ubeidiya.* Israel Academy of Sciences and Humanities.
1968 *On the fauna of 'Ubeidiya.* Proceedings of the Israel Academy of Sciences and Humanities: *Section of Sciences* 7.

HARRIS, J. W. K.
1973 "Archaeological excavations east of Lake Rudolf during the 1972 field season reveal a distinctive new stone industry." Paper presented at Kroeber Society meeting, Berkeley, 12 May, 1973.

HAY, R. L.
1967 "Hominid-Bearing Deposits of Olduvai Gorge," in *Time and stratigraphy in the evolution of man*, 30–42. National Academy of Sciences, Washington, D.C.
1971 "Geologic background of Beds I and II: stratigraphic summary," in *Olduvai Gorge: Excavations in Beds I and II, 1960–1963:* M. D. Leakey, 9–18. Cambridge.

HERSKOVITS, M. J.
1962 *The human factor in changing Africa.* New York.

HIGGS, E. S.
1967 "Environment and chronology: the evidence from mammalian fauna," in *The Haua Fteah (Cyrenaica) and the Stone Age of the southeastern Mediterranean.* C. B. M. McBurney, Cambridge.

HIGGS, E. S., C. VITA-FINZI
1972 "Prehistoric economies: a territorial approach," in *Papers in economic prehistory*. Edited by E. S. Higgs, 27–36. Cambridge.

HOOIJER, D. A.
1958 An early Pleistocene mammalian fauna from Bethlehem. *Bulletin of the British Museum (National History)* Geology 3:267–292.
1959 Fossil mammals from Jisr Banat Yaqub, south of Lake Huleh, Israel. *Bulletin of the Research Council, Israel* 8G, 4:117–199.
1962 "The Middle Pleistocene fauna of the Near East," in *Evolution and hominisation*. Edited by G. Kurth, 81–83. Stuttgart.

HOROWITZ, A.
1971 Climatic and vegetational developments in northeastern Israel during Upper Pleistocene-Holocene times. *Pollen et Spores, Musée National d'Histoire Naturelle, Paris* 13(2):255–278.

HOROWITZ, A., G. SIEDNER, O. BAR-YOSEF
1973 Radiometric dating of the 'Ubeidiya Formation, Jordan Valley, Israel. *Nature* 242:186–187.

HOWELL, F. C.
1959 Upper Pleistocene stratigraphy and early man in the Levant. *Proceedings of the American Philosophical Society* 103(1):1–65.

1960   European and north west African Middle Pleistocene hominines. *Current Anthropology* 1(3):195–232.

1961   Isimila: a Palaeolithic site in Africa. *Scientific American* 205(4): 118–129.

1966   "Observations on the earlier phases of the European Lower Palaeolithic," in *Recent studies in paleoanthropology*. Edited by J. D. Clark and F. C. Howell, 88–201. *American Anthropologist* 68(2).

HOWELL, F. C., G. H. COLE, M. R. KLEINDIENST, B. J. SZABO, K. P. OAKLEY

1972   Uranium-series dating of bone from the Isimila Prehistoric Site, Tanzania. *Nature* 237(5349):51–52.

IRVINE, F. R.

1961   *Woody plants of Ghana with special reference to their uses.* Oxford.

ISAAC, G. L.

1967   "The stratigraphy of the Peninj Group — Early Middle Pleistocene formations west of Lake Natron, Tanzania," in *Background to evolution in Africa*. Edited by W. W. Bishop and J. D. Clark. 229–257. Chicago.

1968a "Traces of Pleistocene hunters: an East African example," in *Man the hunter*. Edited by R. B. Lee and I. De Vore, 253–261. Chicago.

1968b "The Acheulian site complex at Olorgesailie, Kenya: a contribution to the interpretation of Middle Pleistocene culture in East Africa." Unpublished doctoral dissertation, Cambridge University.

1969   Studies of early culture in East Africa. *World Archaeology* 1(1): 1–28.

1971   The diet of early man: aspects of archaeological evidence from Lower and Middle Pleistocene sites in Africa. *World Archaeology* 2:278–298.

1972   "Chronology and the tempo of cultural change during the Pleistocene," in *Calibration of hominoid evolution*. Edited by W. W. Bishop and J. A. Miller, 381–430.

IZAWA, K., J. ITANI

1966   Chimpanzees in Kasakati Basin, Tanganyika. (1) Ecological study in the rainy season, 1963–1964. *Kyoto University African Studies* 1:73–156.

KELLER, C. M.

1970   Montagu Cave: a preliminary report. *Quaternaria* 13:187–204.

KLEIN, R. G.

1972   Preliminary report on the July through September, 1970, Excavations at Nelson Bay Cave, Plettenberg Bay (Cape Province, South Africa). *Palaeoecology of Africa* 6:177–208.

KLEINDIENST, M. R.

1961   Variability within the Late Acheulian Assemblage in eastern Africa. *South African Archaeological Bulletin* 16(62):35–52.

LANGDALE-BROWN, J., H. A. OSMASTON, J. G. WILSON

1964   *The vegetation of Uganda and its bearing on land use.* Kampala.

LEAKEY, M. D.

1971a Discovery of post-cranial remains of *Homo erectus* and associated artifacts in Bed IV at Olduvai Gorge, Tanzania. *Nature* 232:380–387.

1971b *Olduvai Gorge: excavations in Beds I and II, 1960–1963.* Cambridge.

LEAKEY, M., P. V. TOBIAS, J. E. MARTYN, R. E. F. LEAKEY
1969 An Acheulian industry and hominid mandible, Lake Baringo, Kenya. *Proceedings of the Prehistoric Society* 35:48–76.

LEAKEY, R. E. F.
1973 Evidence for an advanced Plio-Pleistocene hominid from East Rudolf, Kenya. *Nature* 242:447–450.

LEROI-GOURHAN, A.
1971 Pollens et terrasses marines au Liban. *Quaternaria* 15:249–260.

MASON, R. J.
1962 *Prehistory of the Transvaal.* Johannesburg: Witwatersrand University Press.

MCBURNEY, C. B. M.
1967 *The Haua Fteah (Cyrenaica) and the Stone Age of the south-east Mediterranean.* Cambridge.

NEUVILLE, R.
1931 L'Acheuléen supérieur de la Grotte d'Oumm-Qatafa (Palestine). *L'Anthropologie* 41(1–2):13–51.

1951 *Le Paléolithique et le Mésolithique du Désert du Judée.* Institut de Paléontologie Humaine, Mémoire 4. Paris.

PICARD, L.
1963 The Quaternary in the northern Jordan Valley. *Proceedings of the Israel Academy of Sciences and Humanities* 1(4):1–34.

1965 *The geological evolution of the Quaternary in the central-northern Jordan graben, Israel.* Geological Society of America Special Papers 84, 337.

PRAUSNITZ, M. W.
1969 The sequence of Early to Middle Palaeolithic flint industries along the Galilean littoral. *Israel Exploration Journal* 19(3):129–138.

QUEZEL, P., C. MARTINEZ
1958 Étude palynologique de deux diatomites du Borku (Territoire du Tchad A.E.F.). *Bulletin de la Société de l'Histoire Naturelle de l'Afrique Noire* 49:230–244.

1962 "Premiers résultats de l'analyse palynologique de sédiments recueillis au Sahara méridional à l'occasion de la Mission Berliet-Tchad," in *Missions Berliet Ténéré-Tchad,* 1:313–321. Paris.

REYNOLDS, V., F. REYNOLDS
1965 "Chimpanzees of the Badongo Forest," in *Primate behavior.* Edited by I. De Vore, 368–424. New York.

ROGNON, P.
1967 *Le massif de l'Atakor et ses bordures (Sahara central).* Centre de recherches sur les zones arides. Série Géologique 9. CNRS. Paris.

RONEN, A., D. GILEAD, E. SHACHAI, A. SAULL
1972 Upper Acheulian in the Kissufim Region. *Proceedings of the American Philosophical Society* 116(1):68–96.

ROSSIGNOL, M.
1963   Analyse pollinique de sédiments quaternaires dans la plaine de Haifa, Israël. *Israel Journal of Earth Science* 12:207.
1969   Une séquence climatique du Pléistocène dans la région de la Mer Morte (Israël). *Pollen et Spores* 11(3):603–614.

ROSSIGNOL, M., J. MALEY
1969   L'Activité hors de France des Palynologues et Paléobotanistes français du Quaternaire. Études françaises dur le Quaternaire, 265–274. *VIII Congrès International de INQUA*. Paris.

RUST, A.
1950   *Die Höhlenfunde von Jabrud (Syrien)*. Neumünster.

SANLAVILLE, P.
1971   Sur le Tyrrhénien libanais. *Quaternaria* 15:239–247.

SCUDDER, T.
1962   *The ecology of the Gwembe Tonga*. Manchester.

SELDON, J.
1960   A guide to East African common Acacias. *Journal of the East African Natural History Society* 23(5, 102):190–197.

SERVANT, M., S. SERVANT
1970   Les formations lacustres et les diatomées du Quaternaire récent du fond de la cuvette tchadienne. *Revue de Géographie physique et de Géologic Dynamique* (2) XII (1):63–76. Paris.

SHEPPE, W., T. OSBORNE
1971   Patterns of use of a flood plain by Zambian mammals. *Ecological Monographs* 41(3):179–205.

SOLECKI, R. S.
1968   "The Shemsi Industry: a Tayacian-related industry at Yabrud, Syria; preliminary report," in *La Préhistoire: problèmes et tendances*. Edited by D. de S. Bordes and F. Bordes, 401–410. CNRS. Paris.

STEKELIS, M.
1948   Rephaim Baqa': a Palaeolithic station in the vicinity of Jerusalem. *Journal of the Palestine Oriental Society* 21:80–97.
1960   The Palaeolithic deposits of Jisr Banat Yaqub. *Bulletin of the Research Council of Israel*. Section G (Geo-Survey) 9G (2–3): 61–87.
1967   Un lissoir en os du Pléistocène moyen de la vallée du Jourdain. *Revista da Faculdade de Letras* 3(10):3–7.

STEKELIS, M., D. GILEAD
1966   Ma'ayan Barukh: a Lower Palaeolithic site in Upper Galilee. *Metqufat Ha-Even* 8:1–23.

STEKELIS, M., O. BAR-YOSEF, T. SCHICK
19669   Archaeological excavatoins at ʿUbeidiya, 1964–1966. *Israel Academy of Sciences and Humanities*, 5–29.

STRUIVER, M.
1969   Yale natural radiocarbon measurements IX. *Radiocarbon* 11:545.

SUZUKI, A.
1969   An ecological study of chimpanzees in a savanna woodland. *Primates: Journal of Primatology* 10(2):103–148.

TCHERNOV, E.
1968   *Succession of rodent faunas during the Upper Pleistocene of Israel.*
       Hamburg: Verlag Paul Parey.
TUREKIAN, K. K., J. L. BADA
1972   "The dating of fossil bones," in *Calibration of hominoid evolution.*
       Edited by W. W. Bishop and J. A. Miller, 171–186. Edinburgh:
       Scottish Academic Press.
TURVILLE-PETRE, F.
1927   *Researches in prehistoric Galilee, 1925–2.* London.
VAN CAMPO, M.
1964a Représentation graphique de spectres polliniques des régions sa-
       hariennes. *Comptes rendus de l'Académie des Sciences de Paris*
       258:1873–1876.
1964b Quelques pollens pleistocènes nouveaux pour le Hoggar. *Comptes
       rendus de l'Académie des Sciences de Paris* 258:1297–1299.
VAN CAMPO, M., P. GUINET, J. COHEN, P. DUTIL
1967   Contribution à l'étude du peuplement végétal quaternaire des
       montagnes sahariennes, III Flore de Oued Outoul (Hoggar). *Pol-
       len et Spores* 9(1):107–120.
VAN CAMPO, M., P. GUINET, J. COHEN
1968   "Fossil pollen from late Tertiary and Middle Pleistocene deposits
       of the Kurker Oasis," in *Desert and river in Nubia.* Edited by
       K. W. Butzer and C. L. Hansen, 515–520. Madison.
VAN DER HAMMEN, T., T. A. WIJMSTRA, W. H. ZAGWIJN
1971   "The floral record of the Late Cenozoic of Europe," in *Late Ce-
       nozoic glacial ages.* Edited by K. K. Turekian, 391–424. New
       Haven.
VAN ZEIST, W.
1969   "Reflections on prehistoric environments in the Near East," in *The
       domestication and exploitation of plants and animals.* Edited by
       P. J. Ucko and G. W. Dimbleby, 35–46. London.
VAN ZINDEREN BAKKER, E. M.
1969   "The Pleistocene vegetation and climate of the Basin," in *Ka-
       lambo Falls prehistoric site,* volume one. Edited by J. D. Clark,
       57–84.
WENDORF, F., R. SCHILD, R. SAID
1970   Egyptian prehistory: some new concepts. *Science* 169:1161–1171.
WILLIAMSON, J.
1955   *Useful plants of Nyasaland.* Zomba: Government Printer.
WRESCHNER, E.
1971   "Bemerkungen zum sogenannten "Tayacien" im mittleren Osten."
       Paper presented at the Eighth International Congress of Proto-
       and Prehistoric Sciences. Belgrade.
YELLEN, J. E.
1973   "Kung Bushman settlement patterns." Paper presented at second
       Meeting of Africanist Archaeologists, Southern Methodist Uni-
       versity, Dallas, Texas.

Acheulean Sites and Stratigraphy in Iberia and the Maghreb

L. G. FREEMAN

ABSTRACT

Acheulean artifact occurrences (in stratigraphic context) from the Iberian Peninsula are discussed in considerable detail. The Sorian sites, Torralba and Ambrona, in cold-indicative deposits, apparently yield the earliest human occupation debris known from the Peninsula (an Acheulean series). The earliest Upper Tagus terrace sites probably accumulated during a subsequent cold period, although at present this stratigraphic complex is inadequately defined. Derived material from an intervening warm phase may be present at San Isidro. The Lower Tagus terrace suite

I wish to express my thanks to Professors Karl W. Butzer and F. Clark Howell for having made available to me otherwise largely inaccessible publications from their personal libraries. Both also read a draft of the discussion of the Torralba and Ambrona occupations. N. Shackleton also provided critical comment. In this paper, evaluation of data from the Iberian Peninsula rests as much on personal familiarity with museum collections, first-hand knowledge of stratigraphic sequences gained in the field, and participation in excavation and tests (Torralba, Ambrona, Castillo), as on an evaluation of published documents. Examinations of Iberian artifact collections over the years have been supported by the University of Chicago Anthropology Department's Lichtstern Fund for Anthropological Research (1962–1963), the Museo Arqueológico Provincial of Oviedo (1962–1963), a Wenner-Gren Foundation Richard Carley Hunt Fellowship (1966), the Patronato de las Cuevas Prehistóricas de Santander (1968–1969), the Ford Foundation (1968–1969) and National Science Foundation Grant GS-2107 to L. G. Freeman and K. W. Butzer for paleoanthropological investigations in Spain (1968–1973). My synthesis of data from the Maghreb relies much more heavily on published primary sources. In this review, I have especially concentrated on Acheulean occurrences in good stratigraphic context, and neglected reported surface collections almost entirely.

There is sufficient accumulated evidence to indicate that the sequence of climatic change during the Pleistocene was far more complex than is usually assumed, and that the standard terminology designating major glacial and interglacial phases has lost most of its meaning for correlation. All designators of the "classical" glacial and interglacial sequence used in this paper are either quotations from the authors or labels used for convenience sake without any stratigraphic implications.

contains nothing demonstrably earlier than the Upper Tagus sequence and the same argument can be made, but only on typological grounds, for Portuguese littoral occurrences. One cave site in Santander contains latest Acheulean materials (two basal occupations at Castillo). Except for the Soria sites, no Acheulean occurrence has been described in sufficient detail, and stratigraphy remains to be verified in the field. The least adequate information is that concerning the Portuguese littoral sites in "raised beaches."

Artifact series from sites in the Maghreb are compared with the Iberian materials. The Torralba/Ambrona series most closely resembles Biberson's Acheulean stages I and II from Sidi-Abderrahman level M, and the collection from Ternifine. The probably (at least partly) later series from Lake Karar and some of the Ternifine pieces are unlike anything known in good context from the Iberian peninsula (except, perhaps, San Isidro). Iberian terrace and beach material is most similar to Biberson's latest "Acheuléen moyen" and his "Acheuléen évolué" (stages VI through VIII). The Sidi Zin assemblages, far better made than their Iberian counterparts, seem most like material from the +15 to +25 meter Manzanares terraces, especially las Delicias.

INTRODUCTION

Surveys of the Paleolithic prehistory of the Iberian Peninsula in languages other than Portuguese and Spanish are lamentably rare, and the last such treatment with any pretense to completeness is the English edition of Obermaier's *El hombre fósil* [Fossil man in Spain], which appeared in 1925. More recent but now outdated summaries in Spanish do exist (Almagro Basch 1954; Pericot García 1942), but none discusses more than a select few Acheulean sites, those often chosen from relatively well-reported surface occurrences of doubtful stratigraphic importance. Since two of the very few earlier Acheulean occupation sites excavated and studied with modern techniques are located in Spain, it is past time for a more thorough synthesis of reported Iberian Acheulean occurrences and a modern assessment of their significance and external and internal relationships. As its primary aim, this paper attempts to fill that need.

All scholars familiar at first hand with both the Spanish Acheulean and its northwest-African counterparts have remarked on the strong resemblance between the Iberian materials and artifact series from the Maghreb. That those resemblances are real, and that the Maghreb and the Iberian Peninsula formed a distinct and interrelated "culture area" during the Lower Paleolithic is in my opinion confirmed beyond doubt. For that reason, a briefer review of Acheulean occurrences from the Maghreb is presented; earlier Pleistocene stratigraphic sequences have been more extensively and completely studied in the Maghreb than in Spain and Portugal, so that the review is suggestive from the standpoint of relative chronologies as well as from that of comparative artifact typology alone. In the present state of knowledge, conclusions derived from this survey can be no more than tentative and general, often partaking more of the nature of enlightened guesses than confirmed scholarly observation. I sincerely hope that the inadequacies of the evidence reviewed may soon be remedied, at least in large part, by renewed field studies and intensified scholarly interchange in international and cross-disciplinary forums such as the one for which this paper was prepared.

1. Torralba / Ambrona
2. Manzanares Terraces
3. Pinedo
4. Alpiarça Sites (Tojal, Vale do Forno)
5. Casal do Monte
6. Aldeia Nova
7. S. of Rio Mira
8. Fortim de Porto Corvo
9. Arrabida
10. Ericeira (S. Julião)
11. Porto de Lobos
12. Cabo Carvoeiro (Peniche)
13. Condeixa
14. la Mealhada
15. Castillo

Figure 1.   Selected Iberian localities mentioned in the text

THE IBERIAN PENINSULA

There are a large number of reported certain or possible occurrences of Acheulean artifactual materials in the Iberian Peninsula. Most are surface finds mentioned briefly in notes or given more extensive monographic treatment (Puente Mocho, Laguna de la Janda, Casal do Monte). A great many are stratified occurrences of derived materials (San Isidro in part, Santo Antão de Tojal), while only three are known to be largely undisturbed stratified occupation residues (Torralba,

Ambrona, Castillo).[1] Recent syntheses of the Iberian Acheulean in secondary sources, with one outstanding exception (Howell 1966), suffer in being derivative and uncritical.

The most important Acheulean occurrences in Iberia are found: (1) in the province of Soria, in north-central Spain; (2) in the Tagus basin, with important concentrations near Madrid and Toledo on the Upper Tagus and from Abrantes to Lisboa on the Lower Tagus; (3) along the Portuguese littoral; and (4) in the Cantabrian province of Santander. The occurrences will be treated in that order.

The Sites in Soria

The sister sites of Torralba and Ambrona are located about 150 kilometers northeast of Madrid in the province of Soria, at elevations of 1115 meters and 1140-43 meters above mean sea level. Torralba, at the edge of the Rio Ambrona-Masegar valley, has been known as a paleontological locality since 1888 and was first excavated by the Marques de Cerralbo in 1909. This early work was unfortunately inadequately published (de Cerralbo 1909, 1911, 1913). The site was then visited (1960) and excavated (1961-1963) under the direction of F. Clark Howell (Howell et al. 1962; Howell 1966; Biberson 1964c, 1968; Biberson and de Aguirre 1965; Butzer 1965; Freeman and Butzer 1966). A monographic report on the work of Howell and his associates is well advanced. Ambrona, less than 2 kilometers northwest of Torralba in the same valley, was discovered and tested by de Cerralbo but a report was never published. Howell rediscovered the site in 1961 and undertook major excavations there in 1962 and 1963. Brief summaries of the recent work are available (Howell et al. 1962; Howell 1966; Biberson et al. 1970).

The Rio Ambrona/Masegar valley dissects the extensive and dry upland plateaus (parameras) of the Sistema Iberica and Cordillera Central. At the time of occupation, the sites were located at the edges of a swampy valley, probably containing a permanent watercourse. At Torralba the major occupation levels were buried by colluvial wash derived from the adjacent valley slopes. The abundance of water in the valley (springs at the base of the slopes, a stream, standing water) and the nutritious, mineral-rich swamp vegetation no doubt attracted numbers of large herbivores and conceivably the valley served as a seasonal

---

[1] Perhaps la Mealhada should be added to this list.

migration route. Game would generally have been far more abundant in the valley bottom than on the waterless uplands.

Butzer has published the Torralba/Ambrona stratigraphic column in some detail (Butzer 1965; Freeman and Butzer 1966). Bedrock consists of unconsolidated Triassic Keuper, which deforms easily when wet; as a result, at least one phase of faulting complicated the stratigraphic situation somewhat. Above the Keuper, Butzer recognizes five depositional units in the Torralba Formation (Lower Complex). At the type-site, they are developed as follows:

a.   Unit I, "Red Colluvium": A calcareous sandy silt or silty sand in a colluvial scree, with cryoclastic components, attaining over 7 meters in thickness locally. Characteristics of this level imply very cold climatic conditions. No pollen or cultural debris.

b.   Unit IIa, "Grey Silts and Sands": A homogeneous silty sand suggesting a well sorted, fluvial valley fill, presumably deposited under cool and moist conditions. No pollen or cultural debris.

c.   Unit IIb, "A Gravel": Five to 30 centimeters of coarse, heterogeneous, cryoclastic subangular gravels between lenses of grey marl or marly sand. This is a colluvial deposit. Stone rings and garlands suggest frequent alternations of temperature around freezing point. Some downslope sliding of gravels and the cultural materials atop them has occurred, but size sorting is not evidenced. The deposits suggest a cold climate with intensive, seasonally concentrated runoff.

d.   Unit IIc, "Lower Grey Colluvium" = "B Gravels": Well stratified gritty sands about a meter thick, intercalated with a few horizons of medium sized, heterogeneous detritus, moved by sliding and rolling. The deposits are not cryoclasic and soil-frost structures do no occur. Butzer interprets the deposits as waterlaid screes from frost-weathering of exposed bedrock on the slopes. The base of the sands and two higher levels show festoons suggestive of solifluction. Climate was cold with seasonally intensive runoff; extensive alpine meadows are indicated by the pollen spectra. There are a total of seven major stratigraphically superimposed cultural horizons in Unit IIc, and there are sometimes several small and isolated lenses of occupation debris in addition to the major continuous cultural layer in a single geological substratum.

e.   Unit IId, "Brown Marl": Up to 90 centimeters of sandy marl with local grit concentrations. The beds indicate a swampy valley fill analogous to modern deposits near active springs. A relatively moist, cool temperate climate is suggested.

f.   Unit IIIa, "Upper Grey Colluvium": Eighty centimeters of material analogous to Unit IIc, except that no gravel strata or cultural materials were recovered. Interpretation like Unit IIc.

g.   Unit IV, "Grey Marl": Up to 50 centimeters of marl formed on alluvial flats of an aggrading floodplain, interrupted at Ambrona by occasional coarse streambed deposits. The marls suggest a moist and fairly temperate climate, and have some characteristics suggesting seasonal waterlogging. Climate was cooler than that at present. Some scattered artifacts and bones occur near the base of this unit.

h.   Unit V, "Reddish Alluvium": About 165 centimeters of coarse alluvial fan deposits including gritty silts and cryoclastic gravels. Climate was drier and quite cold. There is a major occupation level in this unit at Ambrona, but no cultural materials occur at Torralba.

Combined with the botanical and faunal evidence, these alternating cold and temperate deposits can be correlated most convincingly with stadial and interstadial alternations within a major glacial phase. Atop these deposits formed a deep *terra fusca* soil (the "Ambrona soil"). It should be noted that all five depositional units were accumulated during a period of climate cooler than that at present. Howell's suggestion (1966: 120) of an interglacial age for Unit IV is not supported by the evidence. At Torralba, later deposits of the Sahuco Formation (Middle and Upper Complexes) were accumulated following erosion of the Torralba Formation to the north of the remaining site sediments. These consist of alluvial and colluvial deposits that indicate moist, cold conditions. At Ambrona the period of deep *terra fusca* formation is followed by dissection and the deposition of marls containing pollen indicative of interglacial conditions (Butzer 1965, 1971: 458; Freeman and Butzer 1966; Howell 1966). Analysis of the Ambrona site, while well underway, is less advanced than that of Torralba. For that reason, the following discussion is based primarily on observations of materials from the latter site. Although the Ambrona data are unique in some respects, the Lower Occupation in Unit II is broadly comparable with stratigraphically contemporary occupations at Torralba.

POLLEN   Pollen samples from Torralba have been analyzed by J. Menéndez-Amor. Unit I is, unfortunately, largely sterile. Samples within the occupation horizons of Unit II show approximately 50 percent AP, with *Pinus silvestris* dominating the trees. Traces of willow are found in some samples. Almost 40 percent of the total is grass pollen. The rest is composed of *Artemisia,* Caryophyllaceae, Compositae, Chenopodiaceae, and Ericaceae. Sedges are present and may be moderately well represented, probably due to their local abundance in marshes at the site margin. Occasional water plant pollen is reported. In general, the spectra are almost identical to those found today at an elevation of 2,000 meters (about 200 meters above the present altitudinal tree limit) in the Sierra de Guadarrama (Freeman and Butzer 1966: 12). Upper Unit IIIa has spectra with 80-90 percent pine pollen, and some 10 percent Gramineae. Arboreal pollen increases in Unit IV from about 50 percent to nearly 90 percent of the spectra, then declines again to 50 percent. Gramineae, well represented early, decline in the upper samples. Sedges are especially abundant in upper Unit IV, while *Artemisia* and chenopods disappear. Most tree pollen is *Pinus silvestris,* but traces of oak, birch, alder, and willow and one occurrence of *Castanea* are noted. Water plants are also represented. In Unit IV, forests reached the maximum extent ever attained in the Torralba Formation. Even so, the spectra indicate a forest composition comparable to that at elevations of from 1,250 to 1,800 meters today, and thus cooler climatic conditions than those at present. Unit V is essentially sterile in pollen. Especially notable is the occurrence of *Sciadopitys* and haploxylon pine in Unit II deposits. Neither had previously been reported from post-Villafranchian sediments of Spain (Howell 1966; Freeman and Butzer 1966).

Occupation-bearing sediments at Torralba and Ambrona accumulated during a cold climatic phase which itself antedated at least two major warm periods prior to the Holocene. The long core from Padul preserves evidence of a series of three *Artemisia* — Chenopod rich steppes alternating with two major warm-humid woodlands (Florschütz et al. 1971). Butzer suggests a correlation of the lowest Padul steppe phase (Zone G) with the Torralba-Ambrona site deposits (Butzer i.p.).

FAUNA During the 1962/63 field seasons, remains of an estimated minimum of 115 individual animals were recovered *in situ* in the Torralba levels. The greatest estimated minimum number of animals for any level is only 15 (Occupation I). Variations in species composition do occur from level to level, but are no greater than can be expected from sampling error alone; the faunal evidence cannot be used to infer temporal trends or climatic fluctuations. The species list includes *Elephas antiquus, E. trogontherii* (one molar, identified by K. Adam), *Equus caballus, Cervus elaphus,* primitive forms of *Bos primigenius* and *Dama* (the latter more archaic than *D. clactoniana,* according to Aguirre), possibly *Predama, Dicerorhinus hemitoechus,* and traces of *Felis* cf. *leo, Canis* cf. *lupus, Rangifer,* a large cervid provisionally identified as *Euctenoceros* sp., unidentified carnivores, a possible lagomorph and bird remains probably assignable to the families *Anatidae* and *Ciconidae*[2] (Howell et al. 1962; Howell 1966: 121-122; de Aguirre, personal communication). The most abundant remains are those of elephants (31 percent of individuals), although they are always out-numbered by the combined total of individuals of other species in any given level. Horses are next most abundant (21 percent of individuals), followed by cervids (18 percent, excluding *Dama*), bovids (13 percent), *Dama* (6 percent), rhinos (4 percent), and birds (3 percent), with about 2 percent each of *Felis* and other carnivores.[3] The Ambrona fauna is not yet studied in detail, but contains many of the elements from the Torralba list (*Elephas, Equus, Bos, Cervus, Dicerorhinus*, carnivores, Anatidae) as well as grouse, falcons, a macaque, a rodent, a lizard, and a pelobatid toad (Butzer 1971: 460; de Aguirre and Fuentes 1971.). Remains from the occupation in Unit V are predominantly equid bones, with cervids and bovids also present.

STONE ARTIFACTS [4]   The lithic artifact series from the 1961-63 excavations has now been completely analyzed. About 11 percent (102 pieces) of the total series has been so thoroughly altered by geological processes that it can no longer be assigned to deliberate artifact types. The remaining 785 pieces are in mint to negligibly altered condition. Most artifacts are made in chalcedonous flint, about a third as many are made of quartzite, and quartz and limestone are rarely represented. Limestone is better represented than these observations would lead one to expect as a raw material for large implement manufacture. Unre-touched (waste) flakes and debris make up only 22.2 percent of the collection, suggesting that stoneknapping activities were not especially intensive in the areas excavated. Cores make up 5.9 percent of the total, and a variety of types can be recognized (true Levallois cores and flakes are absent). There are abundant retouched and utilized flakes (24.5 percent), but such pieces are outnumbered by deliberately shaped flake tools (33.2 percent), which make up the single largest major artifact category. Bifaces are not well-represented, summing to

---

[2]   Aguirre has added *Capreolus* to this list in a personal communication to Butzer, but a later species list he produced (de Aguirre and Fuentes 1971) makes no reference to this form.
[3]   Earlier, some of the small carnivore remains were diagnosed as mustelids. That identification is now less certain.
[4]   The reader will note differences between this summary and that given by Howell (1966). They exist because I have excluded the Cerralbo collections from consideration, concentrating entirely on the results of Howell's 1961–1963 excavations, and because the 1961 discoveries are not considered when the spatial distribution of recovered materials is crucial to the discussion.

only 7.5 percent of the series or 7.8 percent if broken bits of bifaces are included. Some 2.8 percent of the collection consists of "biface trimming-flakes", though many of these are actually by-products of re-sharpening flake tools and rejuvenating cores. There are several flaked or fractured cobbles (1.7 percent) and some true choppers and chopping tools (0.9 percent). There are also a few hammerstones (0.8 percent) and battered polyhedrals (0.3 percent), and a single disc (0.1 percent).

To maximize comparability with other European assemblages in classifying the flake tool component, an attempt was made to utilize, as far as possible, type definitions and the cumulative graphing technique developed by Bordes (1953a, 1953b, 1961) for application to Lower and Middle Paleolithic assemblages.[5] The attempt entailed some modification of the Bordes type definitions, as had been expected. For present purposes those modifications are largely immaterial. In the following discussion, the seven choppers and chopping tools are incorporated in the flake tool collection as is Bordes' practise, thus raising the total to 267 pieces. Retouched and utilized flakes are excluded from "essential" flake tools (Figure 2).

In the essential flake tool series, there is a single pointlike piece made on what has been called a proto-Levallois flake. This is the only piece which is included in the Index of Levallois types (0.7). Sidescrapers make up 20.5 percent of the collection: about equal numbers of transversal and normal scrapers are represented, while a small number (2.6 percent of flake tools) cannot be assigned to either category. Rare examples of double, canted, alternately retouched, bifacially retouched, and ventral surface scrapers were recovered. Denticulated tools are more abundant, making up some 25.5 percent of the total. There are three tayac points. Notches are quite numerous (10.5 percent). Typical and atypical backed knives make up 6.4 percent of "essential" tools. The series of perforators, endscrapers, and burins in combination is 33.4 percent of flake tools, but almost half of these (14.6 percent) are perforators and becs; the endscrapers and burins are so variable that no meaningful distinction between "typical" and "atypical" specimens can be made. Bordes' Biface Index is moderate (22.1 percent), but it should be remembered that the means of calculating this index necessarily yields a figure much higher than the true proportion of bifaces in the shaped tool series. Usually bifaces are between 5 percent and 15

---

[5] A pointlike piece on a "Proto-Levallois flake" is added to the "essential" series and some types Bordes separates are combined in the graph.

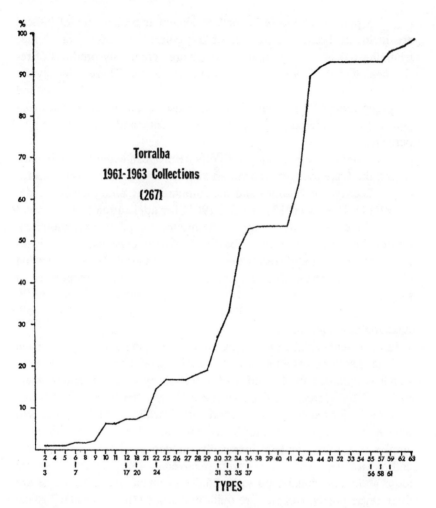

Figure 2. Cumulative percentage graph of "essential flake-tool series" from Torralba

percent of total shaped tools, and they are entirely absent from one occupation.

The bifacial tools (Figures 3-5) are not easy to categorize in classic French terms, and new type-names have had to be devised. However, about 37 percent of the bifaces would be recognized as cleavers or cleaver flakes by most classifiers. A number of the cleavers have tip or butt obliquely skewed to one side, "symmetrical" forms being almost absent. Other kinds of bifaces ("handaxes") include long, thick lanceolate pieces, small ovates, small picks, "screwdriver-ended" bifaces,

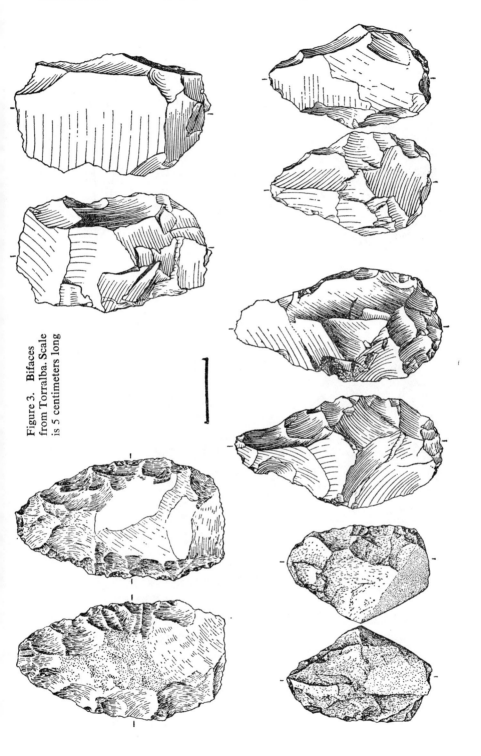

Figure 3. Bifaces from Torralba. Scale is 5 centimeters long

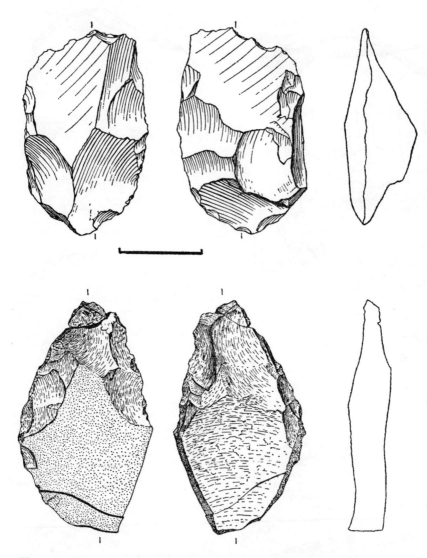

Figure 4.   Bifaces from Torralba. Scale is 5 centimeters long

backed handaxes, and "bifacial knives", as well as a series of minimally trimmed "slab bifaces" in tabular limestone. Soft-hammer technique is sporadically evident. Several observers have commented on the
distinctive African allure of the biface series; this phenomenon could
conceivably be due to independent but convergent development rather
than "phyletic" relationship. Nevertheless, increasing familiarity with
Spanish and North African Acheulean artifacts adds to the strikingly

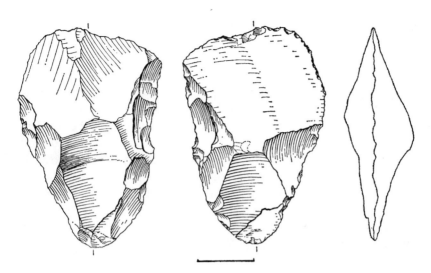

Figure 5.   Cleaver from Torralba. Scale is 5 centimeters long

apparent parallels.[6]

Combining artifacts from all Torralba levels naturally masks differ-ences in level contents. Most occupations are largely indistinguishable in flake tool content, but one stands apart from the rest. There are other levels with as high a proportion of waste and debris (49.2 percent of total artifacts) as that produced by Occupation 8, but none in which

---

[6]   I have always been skeptical about correlations based on artifact typology alone, and continue to believe that they are frequently misleading. Furthermore, until other causes for artifact similarity (restrictions imposed by raw material and tool function, primarily) have been controlled, similarities in artifact typology are as likely to reflect those factors as "phylogenetic" relationship (i.e. information ex-change between intercommunicating social groups with slightly different positions in space and time). I nonetheless feel that the extent and nature of the parallels between the Maghreb and Iberian Acheulean artifact series, involving not one but numerous, probably functionally distinct, implement types made in several raw materials, are so overwhelming as to be sufficient indication that information ex-change within the Iberian-Maghreb regions was conducted on a more intensive and sustained basis than exchange across their boundaries with other neighboring areas. I am the first to admit that inability to specify the kind of information exchange involved or its mechanisms bothers me, but with further intensive research, I am convinced that those mechanisms could be convincingly specified in considerable detail. At present, I am less sure that the use of typology as a basis for long-distance relative chronology is fully justified; good indications of the inadequacy of this approach have been pointed out by Echaide's work (1971) on the Late Paleolithic artifact-assemblage from Budinho. However, at present the artifacts are the only adequately large data set with comparable elements in the Maghreb and Iberia.

674   LESLIE G. FREEMAN

retouched and utilized flakes are so preponderant among shaped tools (58.3 percent).[7]

CHARCOAL AND MACROBOTANICAL REMAINS   Unique conditions of preservation in some Torralba levels permitted survival of a substantial quantity of macrobotanical material. In addition to 232 bits of charcoal of some size, 76 substantial wooden fragments (and hundreds of unidentified bits and pieces) and 31 casts of decayed large wooden objects were recovered during the 1962 and 1963 campaigns. These discoveries were not unexpected: the Museo Arqueológico Nacional, Madrid, houses 28 pieces of wood found by the Marquis de Cerralbo, described by Howell in the Torralba preliminary report (Howell et al. 1962: 34, 36). Identification of macrobotanical remains from the 1962-63 field season was undertaken by Dr. B. F. Kukachka, Wood Products Laboratory, Madison, Wisconsin. Bark and wood of arboreal species as well as unidentified grasses are represented; most of the wood is from conifers, which, when generically identifiable, are usually *Pinus*, often of the *P. silvestris* group. Single specimens of *Salix* (or *Populus*) and birch were recovered.

Fifteen of the larger casts and wooden objects bear convincing marks of deliberate cultural alteration. The pieces in question bear marks of scraping, chopping, and charring. Some seem to be intentionally formed artifacts, mostly blunt-ended wedge or chisel-shaped pieces. There is one cast of a wooden object some 50 centimeters long and 1.5 centimeters thick, with a sharp conical point, interpreted as a spearpoint.

Together, the charring just mentioned and the discovery of abundant flecks of charcoal and bits of carbonized wood provide direct evidence of the use of fire by the prehistoric residents of Torralba. Literally hundreds of near microscopic bits of charcoal were recorded in the field, most so tiny that no attempt was made to collect them. That much of the wood recovered may have been intended as fuel is suggested by the fact that the abundance of wood fragments is directly correlated with the abundance of charcoal in the Torralba levels. Furthermore, there is a tendency for wood and charcoal to cluster together spatially in discrete clumps in several occupations. None of the clumps is an absolutely convincing hearth: no really dense accumulations of charcoal or ash were found; there is no evidence of preliminary preparation of the ground to form a fire receptacle (no depressions, no clusters

[7] This is the level atop which an accumulation of burnt organic material, interpreted as a possible smudge or meat-drying fire, was found.

or rings of stones with high accumulations of charcoal) nor is there evidence of alteration of the ground surface at any point by intense heat. Of course, it is entirely possible to build fires which do not leave such evidence, especially after some exposure to the elements. One accumulation of partially burnt organic material some 2 meters in diameter and 20-30 centimeters deep could have been a smoldering fire or smudge, lit to drive away insects or cure meat, but alternative explanations are possible.[8]

WORKED BONE   During the course of the 1961 field season, Biberson noted that the animal remains from Torralba included a number of bones with clear signs of cutting, charring, and flaking (Howell et al. 1962), and some of the pieces appear to have been intentionally shaped for use as tools (Biberson 1964c: 220-24; Biberson and de Aguirre, 1965). Among the bone artifacts, there is an interesting series of juvenile tusk tips, obliquely bevelled at the point where they were fractured from the shafts of the tusks. These are so similar that they clearly reflect a regular, repetitive pattern of treatment of skeletal material. Other repetitive forms are found as well: chisel-ended pieces on elephant femur diaphyses, elephant ulna picks and sharpened ribs are among them. Some of the flaking and cutting may simply be a by-product of the butchering process, and the charred pieces may result from the roasting of meat, but the faunal collection includes a few pieces which have been extensively altered by flaking to form scraper edges, notches, and other forms with obvious analogies in the lithic artifact inventory. One adult elephant tusk from Ambrona has its tip flaked to a sharp point. The work on such pieces seems inexplicable as a part of the butchering routine. They were probably produced as implements for use in some aspect of the activities undertaken at the site.

PAVEMENTS AND MANUPORTS   All occupation levels at Torralba yielded at least a few unworked large stones (usually limestone chunks, sometimes quartz or quartzite cobbles) which fall outside the expectable size ranges for coarse elements naturally occurring in the sediments. These objects must, at least in large part, have been brought to essentially the locations in which they were discovered by human agency. They need not have been transported any distance: the limestone blocks were probably available close at hand in talus deposits. The manuports (to follow M. Leakey's usage) bear no identifiable marks of use as ham-

[8] Analogous features from Kalambo falls were interpreted as burnt bedding (Clark 1960).

mers, anvils, or cores, but might have served as such for short periods in some cases, especially if the material worked were relatively soft. The number of manuports varies from level to level: most levels produced between 50 and 100 manuports, the minimum number being 14, the maximum 1,758. Where large numbers of unworked stones were recovered, they tended to occur in isolated groups or heaps, and in the earliest occupation they formed a relatively continuous, if somewhat geologically rearranged, pavement on the north side of the occupation level. One boulder in Occupation 7 measured about 75 centimeters in major diameter; it took the efforts of two strong workmen to lift it. A tentative interpretation of the manuports is offered below.

PROPORTIONAL REPRESENTATION OF BODY PARTS   Teeth, tusks, antler bases, and horncores were the most abundantly represented body parts in most Torralba levels. While there are fair numbers of cervical vertebrae, dorsals are far less frequent than they should have been and lumbars are virtually absent. The number of rib fragments found, many of which have been cut, battered, and burned, is but an infinitesimal part of the number expectable. Cranial fragments, exclusive of the upper dentition and bits of maxilla, are very rare, although mandible fragments are far more abundant. The appendicular skeleton is poorly represented, and limb fragments are often flaked, battered, and charred. About 40 percent of the collection consists of fragments too small or altered for species or body part identification, but even if all these were bits of the missing body parts, they are not sufficiently abundant to make up more than a tiny part of the bones in any under-represented category. Most of the unidentifiable bone has been visibly altered by human activity.

The nature of the faunal collection is not as one would expect if the bones were garbage left after on-the-spot meat consumption. The missing body parts are exactly those which bear the bulk of edible material. Some of the bone fragments at the site were obviously shaped and probably used as tools. However, their utility as implements is not a sufficient explanation of the presence of the represented anatomical parts, and most of the bone fragments were clearly not intended for use as tools. It is suggested that the bulk of preserved faunal remains at the site is the useless waste abandoned on the spot when more desirable body parts (for food, hides, or raw material in implement manufacture) were removed to some other locality for further processing.

AGE, SEX, AND SEASONALITY   Sex and gross age estimates have been made for suitable faunal remains from Torralba. These are not sufficiently precise (due to the nature of the remains or to the rates of maturation of the animals in question) to permit inferences about seasonality. Most specimens which could be aged and sexed are elephant bones.

There is an erroneous opinion in the literature that most of the Torralba elephants are young specimens" . . . those most vulnerable to the hunt," and that the same age-skewing exists in the sample of other species (Biberson 1964c: 216). This is simply not the case, at least for the animals recovered during the 1962-63 excavations. Adult specimens make up 70 percent of recognizable individual elephants in that sample, which can be aged with any accuracy, and from the sizes of bone fragments most of the other animals were of adult or subadult stature. Among the elephants are some very robust adult males, at least one of which was probably almost a third taller at the shoulder (15-16 feet) than the largest recorded African elephants. A creature this size might easily have weighed 9000 kilos (or about 10 tons). Smaller, more gracile adult females were also recovered; they are probably at least as abundant as adult males. There are juvenile elephants in the collection (about 30 percent) among which 60 percent are identified from discoveries of the fourth deciduous molar, the remainder having the third milk molar preserved. Among modern Asiatic elephants, D3 is present in three to five year old specimens, and D4 in animals from five to nine years of age. A modern elephant attains about 50 percent of its adult stature by the fifth year, and 60-65 percent by the ninth (Cornwall 1956; Crandall 1964). If these figures can be applied to *Elephas antiquus,* some of the Torralba "babies" might have been as large as a full grown modern specimen. It seems ridiculous to suggest that animals of that size would be especially easy to hunt, all the more so because it is precisely the large juvenile which is considered the least predictable, most dangerous animal by modern hunters. On the basis of the Torralba data, it cannot be maintained that the Acheulean hunters concentrated deliberately or of necessity on the capture of young specimens. In fact, the age and sex makeup of the Torralba specimens (from the 1962-63 excavations) is about what one would expect if the hunters were securing a non-selective sample of all animals in the local herds. Certainly the Torralbans were technologically fully competent to deal effectively with the largest and most dangerous game in their surroundings.

Identifications of Anatidae in Occupation 8 and *Ciconia* in Occupation 6 are suggestive indications of possible seasonality of site use. While members of either taxon may currently winter in the Iberian peninsula, it seems extremely unlikely that they would have done so under much colder climatic conditions. Both kinds of birds might have nested in Central Spain during the warm season, or have died or been killed during migrations in spring or autumn (always assuming that their behavior was analogous to that of their modern relatives). There seems no doubt that the birds are contemporary with the occupation levels although they may not have been hunted by the prehistoric Torralbans. It is tempting, on the basis of the Aves, to suggest that Occupations 6 and 8 took place in the warm season.

ARTIFACT CONSTELLATIONS AND THEIR DISTRIBUTION   There is no evidence of structural remnants, postholes, tentrings, pits, or substantial fireplaces in any Torralba level. At Ambrona, a suggestive pattern of large stones has been noted but is no more convincing as a structure than the huge blocks in Occupation 7 at Torralba. A problematical alignment of long bones and tusks in the same sector (Howell 1966: 128) may also be fortuitous. There is no convincing evidence that the range of activities performed at Ambrona differed in any appreciable way from that at Torralba. No human remains have been recovered from either site. Chipping debris and cores are not abundant enough at any place in either site to suggest that stoneknapping was a substantial component of the activity spectrum. These observations, coupled with the nature of the recovered materials, indicate that both sites served primarily as special hunting camps, where killing and primary butchering of game animals are the only well represented operations attested.

By means of factor analysis, several constellations of similarly varying data categories (animal body parts, stone tools, and vegetal remains) have been recognized. These constellations are characterized as "functional" sets of items used in or produced by distinct sets of activities. One constellation includes choppers, chopping tools, scrapers, elephant tusks, teeth, vertebrae, scapulae, and pelvis and equid teeth, vertebrae, scapulae, and pelvis fragments as well as cervid antler. This constellation seems to reflect coarse rending, meat stripping, and other rough primary butchering activities. Another includes utilized and unretouched flakes and the dense footbones of smaller animals, and is thought to relate to fine slicing and the disarticulation of the joints in question. Two further constellations both include bifacial tools. One consists of elephant skull, perforators, and notches; the other of bovid skull, denticulate tools, and cervid metapodials. These constellations are thought to represent functionally equivalent materials related to the processing of the flesh and cranial contents of elephant and bovid skulls, respectively. The bifacial implements may have served to batter open the convoluted crania (as may the cervid metapodials), while the flake tools could have been used to winkle desirable tidbits out of nooks and crannies. The constellations described were defined by examining raw frequencies of the data categories in each of twelve levels in which materials were sufficiently abundant for meaningful testing. The horizontal position of the pieces was not considered in the Factor Analysis. A later examination of the horizontal distribution of items from each constellation shows a statistically significant tendency for different constellations to be found in different places in all but two of the major occupations. There is no question about the contemporaneity of different constellations in the levels. Often, bones of a single individual animal will be found with several spatial aggregates occupied by material from several different constellations. Differential spatial distributions most probably indicate that distinct butchering operations were performed in different places (Freeman i.p.).

INTERPRETIVE SYNTHESIS   The Torralba/Ambrona site complex is a set of special purpose hunting and preliminary butchering stations along a valley favored by game animals. Probably at one time similar sites interfingered continuously along the valley margins. At Torralba, excavations in level 7 partly overlap with the position of an elephant kill, indicated by the presence of half a carcass in culturally disturbed but still nearly semi-articulated position. At Ambrona, other similar discoveries have been made. Apparently individuals of several species, especially elephants, horses, deer, and cattle, were killed at roughly the same time, and after disarticulation bits of several different animals were processed together in a subsequent stage of butchering and meat preparation. Small animals are almost unrepresented, so that the Torralbans may legitimately be described as "big-game hunters", but within those parameters the hunters were totally non-selective. They cannot be described as specialized elephant hunters, as Biberson has done (1964c), even though the bulk of the meat secured would have been provided by that species. They are better described as purely opportunistic. All animals above a certain size were fair game at Torralba. This may reflect the fact that only animals of a certain size would have been easily visible in the vegetation along the valley bottom. There is no need to assume that the Acheuleans at Torralba and Ambrona only hunted during periods of maximal aggregation of animal herds, either. The number of animals in any occupation is so small and their diversity is so great that the presence of large homogeneous herds of gregarious herbivores needs scarcely be postulated.

Each utilization of the Torralba site seems to have been of extremely short duration — one might almost say ephemeral. Each occupation could very well represent the results of a single hunt, to judge from the fact that parts of several individuals (sometimes from all the individuals represented) were subjected to simultaneous processing in the secondary butchering areas. Given the number of animals represented, this observation strongly supports the inference that the animals were hunted by means of collective drives. Where there is any evidence for the relative position of the actual kill and the locus of secondary butchering of an animal, it seems that the creature was butchered almost where it fell. The fact that several animals were butchered together suggests that several were actually immobilized and killed in close proximity. This suggests that they were probably driven into some natural or artificial obstacle to movement. There is no evidence for traps or pitfalls at either site (in any case the organizational sophistication necessary to construct the requisite number of traps or pitfalls is far beyond that attested prior to Upper Pleniglacial Würm). The most likely natural obstacles which the Ambrona/Masegar valley would have presented are marshy or swampy ground and standing water. Game could easily have been immobilized by miring at either site. (Elephants are notoriously hard to mire because of the large plantar surfaces of their feet, but it can be done). Incidentally, it would have been difficult or impossible to mire game during the cold season after the ground was frozen.

The one convincing weapon from Torralba, a flimsy spear, is scarcely the sort of instrument needed to dispatch a mired elephant. However, once immobilized, the animals could have been stoned to death with reasonable facility. That, I think, explains the local abundance of large manuports in the levels. In fact, some manuport accumulations could be deliberate stockpiles of ammunition made for future eventualities; a social group sophisticated enough to conduct a drive like those suggested would probably have been capable of moving the prey quite precisely in a given direction, taking advantage of the terrain. Stockpiles of raw material for tool manufacture as well as ammunition caches might have been made at several suitable "natural abbatoirs" along the valley. At least some of the charred wooden objects could be firebrands, also fitted for use as weapons in the kill. Similar practices are attested by the ethnographic record (Cloudsley-Thompson 1967: 14). Biberson, Howell, and others have suggested that the finely divided and disseminated charcoal fragments found at both sites might indicate the use of fire in game-drives (Biberson 1964c: 226). Fire is used by contemporary Africans to drive and kill elephants and other game (Cloudsley-Thompson 1967: 12-16), and even though the marshy vegetation of the Ambrona-Masegar valley would have been relatively fire resistant much of the year, enough dead, dry material might have been seasonally available to permit the practice.

In some levels, there are several spatially isolated concentrations of statistically indistinguishable materials, representing multiple synchronous performances of the same set of game processing activities. Often the same body parts of several individuals of different species will be recovered from each such concentration. This situation strongly suggests a relatively egalitarian sharing of the product of the hunt among a series of probably similarly constituted social units — perhaps different teams or individuals who cooperated in the drive. As many as seven lenses, each apparently representing the identical stage in secondary processing of the kill, have been identified in some levels. All are rather small (mean area about 16 square meters), but each may have been produced by a multiperson team. There is no way of estimating the number of team members, of course, or of completely excluding the possibility that, after working in one place for a time, a team might have shifted its locus of activity. Nonetheless, the number of discrete activity loci and the quantity of debris contained in them does suggest cooperation by substantial numbers of people in the hunting and butchering operations. If each locus were the work space of from 1 to 5 people,[9] each team occupying only one locus, the total number of individuals suggested is on the order of 10 to 35. Considering the probable difficulties in game driving in the Ambrona/Masegar valley, I am inclined to think that the larger figure is closer to the minimum number of essential participants in an effective game drive. The degree of cooperation, organization, and planning attested by the Torralba material, if the analysis is correct, certainly demands a highly developed communication system, as complex as articulate speech.

Since most of the meatier body parts were carried away from the site, presumably to some nearby living site, or base camp, it is possible, even likely, that those active in meat processing at the Torralba butchering site did not include the total personnel of a coresident group. Perhaps only active adult and subadult males were involved. In this case, the total population size for the main encampment would have

⁹ I believe that much larger numbers are precluded by the size of the accumulations.

been several (perhaps as much as 4 to 5) times larger than that suggested above.

Even though much meat might have been wasted, an impressive quantity must have been transported away from the site to judge by the missing skeletal parts. In Occupation 7 alone, animals whose carcasses would have yielded at least 30,000 pounds of usable flesh[10] were recovered. Assuming a daily consumption of 5 pounds per man per day, this represents about 6000 man-days of meat rations. Just bearing away so much weight would have presented a small group with severe logistic problems. If each person carried away 100 pounds at a load, 300 loads would have been required to move all the meat: 50 able-bodied men would have to make 6 trips each to carry the lot to the living site. The amount of meat actually utilized might have been considerably smaller than the total available, but the figures still suggest a relatively high group size. Based on such considerations, I am inclined to think that the total size of the cooperating social groups which provided the personnel responsible for the Torralba occupation residues was very large — perhaps on the order of a hundred individuals or more. Such large population aggregates might have been feasible only periodically or seasonally, but it is quite possible, given the undoubted natural wealth of the region in early mid-Pleistocene times, that large human groups were a constant feature of the landscape.

I have no exaggerated hopes that remnants of an Acheulean habitation site will ever be found in the Torralba area. The logical position for such a campsite would be up on the *parameras* overlooking the valley. That location would maximize visibility of movement on the valley floor, and thus facilitate game spotting. Anticipating game movements, hunting parties could descend to the valley floor with greater likelihood of taking animals by surprise. An upland base camp could be sited close enough to the valley margin so that springs would be readily accessible, while human activities in the camp itself would disturb game movements in the valley less than if the living site were located in the valley bottom. If this line of reasoning is correct, it is highly unlikely that the Torralba base camp will ever be discovered, since the *paramera* surfaces have undergone constant erosion throughout the Pleistocene.

[10]   Two adult elephants and one juvenile (12,800 kilos), two red deer (200 kilos), a wild ox (400 kilos), a horse (180 kilos), and a fallow deer (62.5 kilos). The meat weights are 60 percent of live weights given in the literature (see Freeman 1973) or estimated by the author (*Elephas antiquus* weights). I have converted these figures to pounds and rounded off, rather than use a less convenient metric figure (2.25 kilos/man/day) for daily meat consumption.

Sites in the Tagus Drainage

The Tagus River (Spanish *Tajo*, Portuguese *Tejo*), originates in north-central Spain in highlands of the Sistema Iberica and Cordillera Central, and flows west to enter the Atlantic at Lisbon. Extensive suites of Pleistocene alluvial deposits, incorporating abundant faunal and artifactual materials, have been encountered at several localities along the Tagus and its tributaries. The best known Spanish occurrence is the Manzanares-Jarama terrace sequence at Madrid, but another important concentration at Toledo has also received a good deal of attention. In Portugal, the lower Tagus basin and its estuary are the subject of an ample documentation. Regrettably, the literature concerning the three occurrences is as inadequate as it is voluminous.

THE UPPER TAGUS DRAINAGE *Sites in the Manzanares and Jarama terraces* On the southern outskirts of Madrid, remnants of at least three terraces have been recognized along the valleys of the modern Manzanares and Jarama Rivers (Hernández-Pacheco 1928a: 31; Riba 1957: 18-19; Obermaier 1925: 158-163; Vaudour 1969). Terrace elevations of +40 meters, +15-25 meters, and +4—10 meters above present floodplain are indicated, although there is much disagreement among authorities.[11] There may be still higher, culturally sterile, terrace remnants at one or more of the following elevations: + 100-110 meters, +85 meters, or +60-70 meters according to De Terra (1956), Hernández-Pacheco (1928a), and Vaudour (1969). Difference in terrace height has not been given the necessary weight in dating terrace contents in the work of most Spanish authorities who have studied the Manzanares-Jarama materials.

No adequately detailed study of terrace deposits of the Manzanares and Jarama or their likely climatic significance has been published.

---

[11] Disagreement about terrace heights along the Manzanares and Jarama valleys stems in large part from reliance by the authorities on grossly inaccurate estimates of elevation. Most writers did not actually measure terrace heights at all. Gaudry (1895) gave the height of the +40 meter terrace at San Isidro as +60 meters. Oriol Riba calls the same body a +40 to +45 meter terrace. Topographic maps in my possession show the top of the San Isidro sediments as +39 meters above flood-plain, and this agrees with the map published by Pérez (1941).

Another factor contributes to apparent contradictions in the literature. Many authors give the elevation, not of the top of the terrace sediments, but of the top of the erosional bench on which terrace deposits were aggraded. Thus, to Obermaier (1925) and most earlier workers, the San Isidro terrace is at +30 meters, and the floodplain terrace at -2 to -4 meters (below the top of floodplain deposits). While this practice makes considerable sense, it adds a dimension of inconsistency to the literature.

Lacking such evidence, speculation is certainly risky. Nevertheless, there is considerable evidence that terrace aggradation in the Madrid region probably took place under increasingly cold climatic conditions, while downcutting occurred during warmer phases. Each of the three terraces seems to intergrade laterally with colluvial detritus atop a major erosional surface (Riba 1957: 18-19), which could be interpreted as indicating sparse vegetative cover during their formation. Imperatori (1955) has documented major soil flow features (convolutions, pockets) 6 meters below surface in fine deposits of the 40 meter Manzanares terrace in the Usera quarry: these seem convincingly to be cryoturbation phenomena and would indicate intense cold well within the period of terrace aggradation. Last, Gladfelter's detailed study of the drainage basins of Jarama tributaries concludes that "the upper courses of Hesperian rivers aggraded their channels during colder, glacial stages of the Pleistocene, dissecting their channel fills during the waning glacial phases or during more temperate interglacial periods" (Gladfelter 1971: 159). Synchrony between terrace aggradation and the formation of gravel fans and scree detritus is also demonstrable in Gladfelter's research area (Gladfelter 1971: 157). This evidence supports the hypothesis that control for terrace aggradation along the Upper Tagus drainage, including the Manzanares and Jarama terrace sequences, is to be sought in cold-climate phenomena.

The most promising geomorphological work to date in the immediate vicinity of the Manzanares/Jarama sites has been that of Vaudour (1969), who studied terrace deposits and soils in the Lower Henares and the Jarama valley. Terrace gravels Vaudour examined were generally covered with silts or fine colluvium which had been subjected to one or more periods of soil formation (with pedogenesis becoming more complex as terrace height increases). The higher terraces (+50 meters or higher in the Henares, +70 meters or higher in the Upper Jarama) were capped with red fersiallitic soils (Rotlehms) and at least one later generation of brown soils. Lower terraces (+30 meters or lower) lacked red soils, showing only brown soil development. Vaudour equates his +30 meter terraces) terraces with "Riss," terraces from +12 to +20 meters with Würm and the +2-3 meter terrace with the Holocene (Vaudour 1969: 84-91).[12]

[12]   The relationship between the Manzanares and Jarama terrace suites is poorly understood. At the confluence of the two rivers, Hernández-Pacheco gives elevations to base of the Jarama terrace deposits as +12 to 15 meters, +27 to 30 meters, and +50 to 60 meters (Hernández-Pacheco 1928a: 31). Basal heights of the Manzanares terraces between San Isidro and the Madrid-Cáceres-Portugal Railroad bridge are published as +5, +7, +14, and +30 meters by Obermaier (1925: 159–

Past interpretations of the temporal significance of artifactual and faunal materials in the Madrid terraces have relied heavily on gross evaluations of the nature of the sediments in which the stones and bones were found. Spanish paleolithic prehistorians and interested geologists have largely failed to appreciate the fact that changes in the nature of alluvial deposits may simply reflect changes in the position and conditions of an evolving river channel as it meanders across its floodplain rather than climatic factors; even more important, they have usually assumed that a single gross kind of deposit (floodplain silts, for example) formed in all the terraces at the same time, incomprehensible as that may seem. Such assumptions are implicit in work done even as late as the 1950's.

There are well over fifty important occurrences of Paleolithic materials in and on the terraces of the Manzanares and Jarama.[13] The best available survey is still that of Pérez de Barradas (1926). Most stratified occurrences are known from quarries, brickyards, and road or railway cuts, and only a small number of these have ever been collected systematically. The bulk of the artifacts were gathered by quarrymen and donated or sold by them to interested parties. There have been a very few excavations which were reasonably decent for their period, but recovered materials were seldom labelled, and are now usually

---

161). The surface heights of the Manzanares terraces are given in Obermaier as +8 (corresponding to both the +5 and +7 meter erosional benches), +16, and +40 meters. According to Oriol Riba, the same Manzanares terrace surfaces are at +45 meters ("high terrace"), +15 to +25 meters ("middle terrace") and +4 to +12 meters ("low terrace"). Strangely, Riba correlates the +45 meter Manzanares terrace at San Isidro with a +60 to +80 meter Jarama terrace at the confluence of the rivers not far downstream (Riba 1957: 18). Terrace deposits are very discontinuously preserved in this area, so that Riba's judgement can not be based on field observation of the direct correlation of the terraces in question. In the absence of proven major tectonic disturbance, it would seem to me more conservative to equate the San Isidro terrace (base at +30 meters) with the +30 meter (basal elevation) Jarama terrace of Hernández-Pacheco.

De Aguirre mentions a possible "Rotlehm" atop the middle terrace of the Tajo at Campo de Tiro and Buenavista (de Aguirre 1964a: 295); this would be evidence for correlating a red soil horizon with "Eem". However, Martín Aguado does not mention such a horizon, and it is possible that de Aguirre refers to a colluvium like that noted by Vaudour (1969: 90) atop the +12 meter lower Jarama terrace.
[13] The Madrid terraces are incredibly rich sources of Paleolithic material. Pérez notes that some twenty-seven active quarries yielded more than 25,000 artifacts (recognizable as such to the quarrymen) in a single year. The site of El Almendro alone produced 8000 stone tools during one year's exploitation (Pérez de Barradas 1924b: 21). In one site discovered by the author and Sr. José Viloria in 1966 (Huerto de las Lechugas), literally scores of bifaces were seen eroding out of the exposed sections.

found irrevocably mixed with unprovenienced items (even tools from other sites) in museum storage. The deleterious effects of these factors for the attainment of any coherent understanding of sequences of Pleistocene events are self evident. Only the best-documented materials from the Manzanares-Jarama terrace suite merit any further consideration. This, in fact, excludes the bulk of the Jarama terrace material.

THE 40 METER TERRACE   Only one major artifact occurrence from the +40 meter terrace is widely known (Pérez de Barradas 1923, 1924a, 1926).

Already familiar to Casiano de Prado as an important Quaternary faunal locality in the mid-nineteenth century, San Isidro was recognized as a Paleolithic station after 1862, when de Verneuil and Lartet identified a flint cleaver in the possession of a quarryman as a Paleolithic implement (de Verneuil and Lartet 1863: 698-702). The site has been visited by scores of savants in the last century, but very little more is known in detail than was published by the earlier workers, especially Casiano de Prado himself (1864). A full bibliography on San Isidro now numbers over a hundred references. Fortunately, much of the literature available to them was critically synthesized by Wernert and Pérez de Barradas (1921: 3-28; 1925).

For many years, arguments raged over disagreements in the stratigraphic sections presented by different authorities. Even Wernert and Pérez do not seem fully aware that much of this disagreement was due to real differences between the stratigraphic columns accessible to the authors. The San Isidro quarry was huge, and as the standing sediments were cut away, there were inevitable changes in the sedimentary microfacies represented in the visible section. The most important sections in the literature are shown in Table 1. Attempts to reconcile the different strata in detail are pointless. Most of the sections have certain characteristics in common, however. In all cases, the Pleistocene terrace sediments were deposited atop a bench cut to an elevation of 30 meters above the present Manzanares floodplain. Bedrock is a greenish marl (*cayuela*) of Tertiary age with remains of *Anchitherium* and *Mastodon*. Atop this are accumulated up to about 10 meters of what are apparently mostly fluvial sediments, including torrent-borne gravel deposits, current-bedded sands, and flood-plain silts. The sequence of fluvial materials is complex, indicating continuous shifts in channel position during the period of deposition. Local names have been applied to different fluvial microfacies; coarse gravel is called "guijo", fine gravel "garbancillo", and floodplain silts "gredon". These desig-

Table 1. Stratigraphy in San Isidro quarry exposures

Verneuil and Lartet 1863	Casiano de Prado 1864	Obermaier 1916	Pérez 1941 "corte accesoria"	Riba 1957
Humic layer	Humic layer ("canutillo")	Humic layer		Humic layer
				Brown soil ("canutillo")
			Decalcified silts	
Yellow silty sand		Clayey sands Acheulean? 1.5 meters	Yellow or green clayey sandy silts 2.65 meters	Grey-green clayey sands and yellow sands ("gredon")
	Sands			
Reddish silty sand and gravel		Grey reddish sands. Acheulean 7–8 meters	Red sands 0.75–1.25 meters	Coarse sands and brick-red clay
Alternating dark green marls and micaceous sands; the handax level	Grey-blue marls ("gredon")	Grey-blue clay Fauna 0.3–3 meters	White sands with lenses of green clayey-sandy silts at base 4.35 meters	Grey-green sandy clays ("gredon")
				Coarse yellow-reddish sands
Micaceous sands, grey to red or black	Gravels (guijo)	Gravels Fauna, "Chellean" ± 3 meters	Coarse sands and gravels 3.6 meters	Gravels

nations have inappropriately been used as though they have consistent time-stratigraphic significance.

Atop the fluvial sequence Oriol Riba recognizes two laterally derived fine grained colluvial deposits, bracketing a horizon of reddish sands. The layers of fine material are well stratified sandy silts whose fine bedding and inclination seem more appropriate to levee backset beds or channel-side deposits to me. The lower of the two silty "colluvial" beds is said to be formed of locally derived materials, while the upper is described as clearly a soil-flow phenomenon (Riba 1957: 22-37). The latter is a more convincing colluvial deposit than the former. Sometimes apparent solifluction involutions are noted at interfaces between Riba's fine "colluvia" and coarser underlying deposits.

The terrace is capped by a fine sediment popularly called "canutillo" because of its characteristic columnar structure. Sedimentological analysis shows this to be primarily silt with some fine sand, but no appreciable fraction larger than medium sand. Since the 0.05-0.01 millimeter fraction only makes up 30 percent of the material at maximum, Riba calls this deposit a loess-like silt (1957: 41). Possibly aeolian in origin, such fine material is difficult to distinguish from certain lacustrine deposits. Structure of the level as much as sediment size has inclined some workers to consider this deposit a loess. However, the characteristic prismatic or columnar structure, as Riba recognizes, is probably a soil horizon.[14] The so-called colluvial deposits, including the reddish sands, may attain a depth of 4 meters, and the canutillo with the present A horizon is as much as a meter deep. The only soil atop the San Isidro terrace is brown (Vaudour 1969: 91).

The San Isidro collections are widely dispersed and badly identified. Total reliance for statigraphic purposes must be placed on the published attributions of artifacts figured by Verneuil and Lartet (1863), de Prado (1864), Obermaier (1925),[15] and Pérez de Barradas (1941).

[14] Riba identifies the *canutillo* as the deep grey-brown buried A horizon of a fossil para-chernozem (1957: 42). In support, he sites the following characteristics of this deposit: (1) pseudo-mycelium is supposedly present; (2) the canutillo effervesces strongly when treated with HCl; and (3) there is an ash-grey A horizon developed atop the canutillo which is the modern soil. According to Kubiena (1953: 204–205), the first two observations are not characteristic of para-chernozems. The *canutillo* seems more likely to be a B horizon or colloid-rich A/Bh horizon instead.
[15] Unfortunately, Obermaier was inclined to decide relative stratigraphic provenience of artifacts arbitrarily on the basis of their typology. This is typical of all his work in Spain. One "Chellean" biface from San Isidro figured by Obermaier (1925: 81) is an unprovenienced piece collected by Quiroga (Cartailhac 1886: 27). Since Obermaier uses industrial terminology as though it had stratigraphic mean-

Pieces are figured by other authors, but provenience in all those cases seems dubious or is simply not given.

In most exposures, the base of the fluvial deposits at San Isidro consists of up to 3 meters of coarse gravels, or "guijo", the most artifact-rich level in the quarry. Twenty-five lithic artifacts from the guijo are figured by Pérez de Barradas (1941), including 14 true bifaces (4 of these are partial bifaces). Cleavers, lanceolate pic-shaped pieces, small cordiform and narrow-nosed handaxes are represented. Most are asymmetrical in outline, and sometimes lateral margins are nearly denticulated. Artifacts were produced by crudely controlled direct hard hammer percussion. Some pieces from the *guijo* are said to be somewhat rolled but the figured specimens are not heavily altered. The illustrated series is strongly reminiscent of the artifacts from Torralba and Ambrona and is probably to be attributed to the Earlier Acheulean or the early Middle Acheulean (see Figures 6 and 7).

The first artifact recognized at San Isidro is a cleaver-flake with triangular base and excurvate-incurvate sides. The piece is well made by direct hard hammer percussion. The workman who found this piece indicated that it came, not from the *guijo*, but from a sandy level within a deep horizon of alternating dark green silts and sands; beneath this level and atop the Tertiary marl there were at least 2 meters of greyish or reddish micaceous sands (de Verneuil and Lartet 1863: 698-699). This is one of the so-called "gredon" levels at San Isidro (sometimes called *tierra de fundicion),* and it must certainly be later in accumulation than the *guijo* containing Early Middle Acheulean tools. Pérez de Barradas figures two bifaces from the *tierra de fundicion* underlying reddish sands in his sections (Pérez de Barradas 1941: 279-283, 295, 298), and one is clearly a finely made long lanceolate biface trimmed by soft-hammer percussion. Obermaier illustrates one somewhat less well made lanceolate handaxe, an ovate piece with a twisted bit, a partial triangular biface and a nearly rectangular cleaver flake which are attributed to an analogous dark grey-green silt (Obermaier 1925: 84-87, 197). The figured pieces all seem to be essentially unrolled. Judging from the small suite of illustrated pieces, all might be assigned to the Middle Acheulean, or perhaps the Late Acheulean; some are reminiscent of pointed handaxes from the Swanscombe Lower Middle Gravel, but so-called Riss-age deposits in France contain similar tools (Figure 8).

---

ing, his discussion of the stratigraphy of the Madrid Paleolithic localities must be treated with due caution. In contrast, the discussion in Pérez de Barradas (1941) is quite trustworthy.

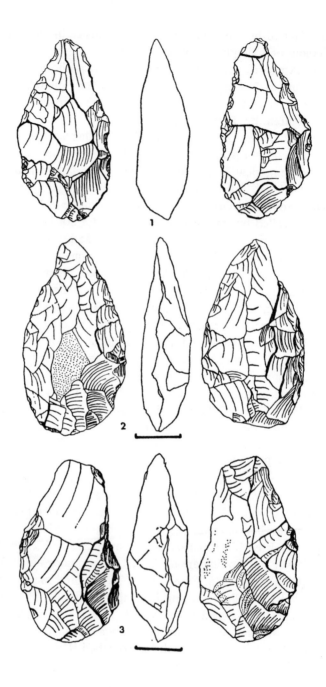

Figure 6.   Bifaces from San Isidro lower level. Number 3 is a chisel-ended piece.
A 5 centimeter scale is sited below each piece for which scale is known. **After**
Obermaier (1925), Pérez (1941)

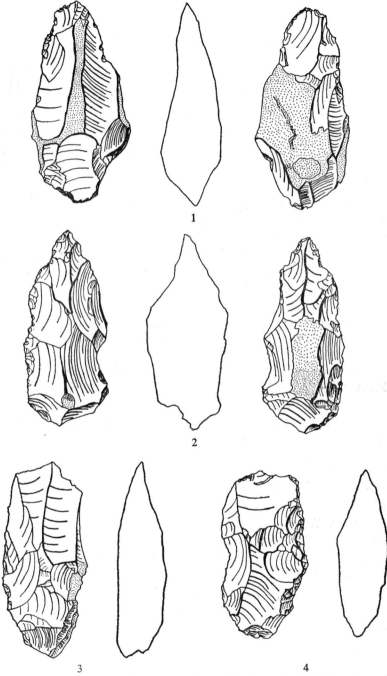

Figure 7.   Bifaces and roughouts from San Isidro lower level. Scale unknown. After Pérez (1941)

692   LESLIE G. FREEMAN

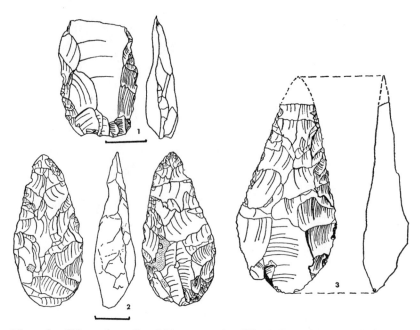

Figure 8.   Bifaces from San Isidro upper level(s). A 5 centimeter scale is sited below each piece for which scale is known. After Obermaier (1925), Pérez (1941).

A series of small implements from the reddish sands is shown by Pérez de Barradas (1941: 300-301). The nine illustrated artifacts are not especially diagnostic, and could easily be found in either Acheulean or Mousterian contexts. No large bifaces are reported from the reddish sands. From the *canutillo* Pérez only reports five nondescript, unrolled flakes which he believes may be Upper Paleolithic (Pérez de Barradas 1941: 299). There are fragments of ceramic in the modern A horizon.

Although abundant faunal materials have been recovered from San Isidro, the bulk of it is insufficiently documented for our purposes. According to Wernert and Pérez, who last reviewed the literature, the following attributions are certain:

From the dark greenish *gredon, Elephas antiquus, Bos, Cervus elaphus* and *Equus;*

From the basal *guijo, Bos* (Wernert and Pérez de Barradas 1925: 65).

By 1941, Pérez himself had discovered *Equus* in the *guijo* and the reddish sands (Pérez de Barradas 1941: 280).

Taken all together, these forms are not particularly useful for stratigraphic correlation. *Elephas antiquus* has the least temporal duration as a species but may be found in sediments dating from the early mid-Pleistocene into the Würm Pleniglacial. The San Isidro elephant does have some peculiarities which show an obvious close relationship with *Elephas antiquus* from Torralba and Ambrona, according to de Aguirre (1969b: 320, 337-338).

In summary, the Pleistocene column at San Isidro includes at least two kinds of deposits. The lower is a fluvial sequence, beginning with coarse channel-bottom sediments containing somewhat abraded Earlier or Early Middle Acheulean artifacts and bones of *Bos* and *Equus* and ending with what may be a series of fine streamside beds or levee deposits which contain Middle or Late Acheulean implements and remains of *Elephas antiquus, Bos, Cervus elaphus,* and *Equus.* This fluvial sequence is thought to have accumulated under increasingly cold conditions related to the onset of a major glacial period. The occurrence of *Elephas antiquus* should indicate that the cold phase in question probably does not fall within the Lower Pleistocene and the typology of Late Middle or Late Acheulean artifacts in sediments accumulated in this sequence suggests that the cold phase is more recent than that attested by deposits of Unit II at Torralba. The upper sequence is possibly an aeolian deposit, which contains only non-diagnostic artifacts. Conceivably there is an intervening colluvial series (the reddish sands and overlying silts), in which derived late Acheulean or Mousterian artifacts and *Equus caballus* are found. The age of the putative colluvial and aeolian deposits cannot be assessed. If only one period of aeolian deposition is responsible for the accumulated sediments it must date from late Weichsel or the postglacial period, since loesslike silts are reported discontinuously atop all terraces at or below 45 meters (except the modern floodplain).

THE 15-25 METER TERRACE This is probably a complex formation, including one platform at about 20-25 meters above present floodplain and another at ca. +15 to +18 meters. The higher part of this series has been examined at Las Delicias (Obermaier and Wernert 1918), Fuente de la Bruja (Pérez de Barradas 1922, 1923), the Tejar de Don Joaquin (Pérez de Barradas 1922, 1923; Pérez de Barradas and Wernert 1921), the Canteras of Domingo Portero (Pérez de Barradas and Wernert 1921), Domingo Martinez (Pérez de Barradas 1922; Pérez de Barradas and Wernert 1921), and some other quarries. The lower series has been studied in cuts at la Gavia (Pérez de Barradas and Wernert 1921), el Almendro (Pérez de Barradas and Wernert 1919; Pérez de Barradas 1923), Lopez Cañamero (Wernert and Pérez de Barradas 1921; Pérez de Barradas 1923), the Plaza del Bonifa (Pérez de Barradas 1924a), Vaquerías del Torero (Pérez de

Barradas 1922, 1923; Wernert and Pérez de Barradas 1921), the Casa del Moreno (Wernert and Pérez de Barradas 1921; Pérez de Barradas 1923; Obermaier and Wernert 1924) and at some less well-reported sites. Whether the quarry at Parador del Sol exposes sediments of this or a more recent terrace is not clear (Obermaier and Wernert 1924). Despite detailed differences between the sediments in these exposures, their industrial and faunal contents are quite similar.

During foundation excavation for a warehouse at the Las Delicias station (Madrid-Portugal railway), workmen revealed terrace sediments reaching 20-25 meters above the Manzanares, and resting atop blue-grey Tertiary clay. Pleistocene deposits start at base with (c) 5-8 centi-meters of waterlaid sands and clays, (b) up to 1.5 meters of dark silts and clays bracketing an apparent occupation floor with abundant li-thic implements, and (a) up to 1.2 meters of clay and modern soil with some flints in the lower 40 centimeters. No faunal remains are reported. Artifacts from (a) are non-diagnostic. The tools from (b) were divided into two groups on purely typological grounds: a lower Acheulean unit and a higher "Early Mousterian" = Mousterian of Acheulean Tradition group (Obermaier and Wernert 1918). Later this attribution was changed and the pieces were assigned to the Mousterian of Acheulean Tradition and 'Sbaikian' complexes (Pérez de Barradas 1926: 66).

In my opinion, based on an examination of the collection in 1966, artifacts from the (b) horizon form a single homogeneous and indivisible aggregate; its assignment to the latest Acheulean is most reasonable, but parallels with the cleaver-flake bearing Mousterian of Acheulean Tradition in Cantabria (Castillo alpha, Pendo 13, Morín 13/14, 15, 16, 17) are very close. The collection includes crude small bifaces (some partial), three cleaver flakes, choppers, chopping tools, and three hand-some fragments of bifacial leaf-shaped pieces. The small tool com-ponent is poorly represented, probably due to selective collecting. It contains simple, bifacially retouched, and double sidescrapers, end-scrapers, perforators, and denticulates. Mousterian disc cores and large and small amorphous cores are relatively abundant. Some of the arti-facts were made by Levallois flaking. Unretouched pieces, many quite large, including chunks and decortication flakes are very abundant. (Obermaier and Wernert noted numerous large fractured flint blocks, which were apparently not saved.) The conclusion that Las Delicias is primarily a workshop seems compelling. Some of the bifaces are broken or seem unfinished, perhaps due to the discovery of flaws in the raw material or accidental breakage during manufacture.

There is no evidence to suggest anything other than the than Early Weichsel age for the main artifact-bearing deposit at Las Delicias. There is somewhat less information on other exposures at this level, but all the illustrated artifacts could well be assignable to the Mousterian of Acheulean Tradition or a latest Acheulean manifestation, and a Weichsel age for collections of this sort seems entirely reasonable.

Exposures in the lower part of the 15-25 meter terrace are somewhat more thoroughly described than those from the upper segment of the terrace. From el Almendro, Pérez and Wernert have discussed Pleistocene sediments deposited atop a 14 meter bench which locally attain a depth of up to 3 meters. The lowest stratum is a stream-laid gravel, as much as two to three meters deep in some sections. An abundant lithic industry and, possibly, remains of *Cervus* were recovered from this horizon. Twenty-five centimeters of sand occur locally atop the basal gravel, and is followed by 60 centimeters of dark-colored sandy gravels. A 12 centimeter soil horizon is developed in fine material capping the section. Neolithic ceramic and bones of *Capra* are reported from the uppermost level, while the underlying strata, especially the basal gravel, contained tools assigned to the "Lower Mousterian" = Mousterian of Acheulean Tradition (Pérez de Barradas and Wernert 1919; Pérez de Barradas 1923; 1926: 75). The illustrated materials, including small cordiform, lanceolate, and triangular bifaces, would justify this attribution. Unfortunately, the Almendro collection seems to have been dispersed or lost except for a very small lot which was revised in 1966. Levallois technique could have been fairly common in the collection, to judge by its prevalence in the remaining series. All the pieces examined are somewhat rolled. Only one small, partial biface in quartzite is preserved. The illustrated series also shows some broken bifaces. The artifacts seen and those illustrated are all of types quite common in Weichsel deposits, and seem most likely to have come from lithic populations of Mousterian of Acheulean Tradition affinities.

At the quarry called Casa del Moreno, in the *termino municipal* of Villaverde on the southeastern edge of Madrid, a 50 meter long section exhibited the following stratigraphy from base to top: (a) basal fine gravels, up to 1.5 meters thick; (b) clayey sediments, locally 30-50 meters in depth, and very similar in color and texture to the tertiary marls, with a whitish sand level at top; (c) the *tierra gredosa*, up to 3-3.5 meters of clays and sands, ending with 50 centimeters of humic earth and modern soil, which contains Neolithic ceramic. The basal gravels contain the bulk of the Paleolithic implements; only slight roll-

696 LESLIE G. FREEMAN

ing and abrasion are noted. The description of the lithics notes nuclei to be most abundant, followed by numerous unretouched flakes, some of large sizes, some small tools and relatively abundant bifaces, including triangular, cordiform, and cleaver-like forms (Wernert and Pérez de Barradas 1921; Pérez de Barradas 1926: 70). The figured artifacts include a variety of pieces, both small and large, whose aspect is decidedly Mousteroid. Some of the small bifaces look unfinished. The collection can undoubtedly be defined as Mousterian, and probably Mousterian of Acheulean Tradition.

Another site with abundant lithic materials is Lopez Cañamero, where a level of red sands and gravels at the base of the alluvial series contained a similar collection of Mousterian implements (Wernert and Pérez de Barradas 1921). The artifact series is again slightly rolled. No point would be served by continuing the list. There are no artifact collections or illustrated series from either segment of the 15-25 meter terrace which have a convincingly pre-Weichsel allure. On the other hand, the terrace must have formed before Upper Paleolithic deposits were common in the landscape.

THE +4 TO +10 METER TERRACE El Sotillo (Wernert and Pérez de Barradas 1930, 1932), el Atajillo (Pérez de Barradas 1922, 1923, 1926: 61), Prado de las Laneros (Pérez de Barradas 1922, 1923, 1924a, 1926: 60), las Carolinas (Wernert and Pérez de Barradas 1921; Obermaier 1917) and la Parra (Pérez de Barradas 1922, 1923, 1926: 58) are among the quarries exposing sediments in this terrace. Sotillo has the richest and best characterized artifact series. The low terrace was 5 meters above modern floodplain at this locality.

Directly atop the Tertiary at Sotillo was a lower gravel level (a), which graded laterally to a reddish sand on the west side of the quarry, and in places was 1.5 meters deep. Level (b), a fine compact current-bedded sand (*arena de miga*), covered the lower gravel where that was represented. Next, some 80 centimeters of quartz sand (c), with tools, were overlain by (d), a 1.6 meters thick deposit of light grey clay sands and fine carbonate-rich silts thought to be aeolian in origin. Level (e) is a reddish sandy gravel, "garbancillo," some 50 centimeters thick, containing archeological materials. Next, 50 to 70 centimeters of supposedly aeolian blackish silt (f), called the "canutillo" containing Neolithic materials below and within the 40 centimeter modern soil horizon ends the Sotillo sequence. Faunal remains reported are the following: from the lower gravels, unidentified rolled tertiary bones; in level (c), *Cervus* sp.; from the garbancillo (e), *Equus* sp., *Cervus* and

Nassa reticulata; from (f), *Cervus* sp. The specimen of *Nassa* was collected in the presence of Wernert and Pérez. This marine species must have been deliberately transported some distance by human agency.

The basal gravels at Sotillo contained a small series of artifacts which may be Mousterian, but some of the tools identified as bifaces are certainly rolled nuclei. The figured pieces include a high proportion of endscrapers, with the types flake-endscraper, flat-nosed scraper, and scraper on a blade shown. Much of the flaking identified as scraper retouch in the report is geological battering and crushing. The basal gravel series might well be Upper Paleolithic, possibly Aurignacian, in affinities. This material is called Upper Chellean by Wernert and Pérez (1930: 60). Level (b) produced a core, wrongly identified as a Chellean or Lower Acheulean biface. The quartz sand horizon (c) contains a blade-rich and obviously Upper Paleolithic (Aurignacian?) artifact series assigned by the authors to a "Precapsian" industrial complex. The "handax" in the scant collection from level (d) is certainly a core, and cannot be used as an Acheulean diagnostic. The so-called "Ibero-Mauritanian Mousterian" in the upper sandy gravel (e) is rich in bifacial leafshaped pieces and has been adduced as evidence for an early prefiguration (or even origin) of the typical Solutrean in the local Spanish Mousterian. The resemblance between the el Sotillo Ibero-Mauritanian Mousterian and the classic Solutrean is entirely explicable, since the collection from level (e) is obviously a rather crude (and somewhat rolled) Middle Solutrean (Wernert and Pérez de Barradas 1932; 1930: 60-68, 93-95, Plates 14-16, 30-34). In extenuation of the errors of the pioneers in Madrileño prehistory, it is only fair to point out that the materials with which they had to deal were terribly atypical in comparison with artifact series normally available to prehistorians: they were, first of all, rather rolled, but, more important, the Madrid collections represent quarry and workshop facies in which large waste and nuclei predominate, while the supposedly finished implements are probably mostly imperfect roughouts, rejected before completion. Most modern prehistorians have accepted the work of their predecessors; they are as hard put to deal with these materials as were Obermaier, Wernert, and Pérez.

Other low terrace sites lead to similar conclusions. In some sites, such as el Atajillo, Prado de las Laneros, and Portazgo, crude but clearly Upper Paleolithic artifacts have been erroneously diagnosed as Mousterian or Lower Paleolithic. In other cases, such as las Carolinas, represented artifacts are mostly quarry or workshop debris which are completely non-diagnostic, so that they cannot be assigned to any Paleolithic facies, but their rudeness has led prehistorians to assign them to Lower or Middle Paleolithic complexes. In no case does any 4-10 meter terrace exposure yield any convincing pre-Mousterian material, and all such exposures probably contain only or almost exclusively Upper Paleolithic collections. A correlation of the Manzanares low terrace with Upper Pleniglacial Würm may logically be suggested.

INTERPRETATIVE SYNTHESIS   The Manzanares/Jarama terrace sequence is fragmentary and inadequately documented.[16] The evidence in hand indicates that the two lowest terrace remnants are to be assigned to the Upper Pleistocene, while the +45 meter terrace is to be considered later Mid-Pleistocene in age. It is suggested that the uppermost (+15 to +25 meter) series of Upper Pleistocene terrace deposits probably accumulated during the Early Würm and Lower Pleniglacial, while the lower series (+4 to +10 meter) accumulated during the Upper Pleniglacial cold phase. Further research on the terrace sequence is clearly necessary to substantiate such correlations, and, hopefully, to distinguish between what seem likely to be two major stages in deposition of what has here been labelled the +15 to +25 meter terrace. There is no known evidence of human occupation in Basal or Lower Pleistocene terrace remnants (+100/110 meter, +85 meter, +60-70 meter terraces) in the Madrid vicinity. The proposed correlation is consonant with the interpretations of Vaudour (1969) and Gladfelter (1971).

Tagus Terraces at Toledo   Although Alía Medina (1945) claimed to have identified four distinct Tagus terraces (17/20, 55/60, 100, and 130 meters) at Toledo, most modern workers were agreed that there are only three (Aranegui 1927; Hernández-Pacheco 1946; Alía Medina and Riba 1957), whose heights above the Tagus floodplain have been given as 86, 52, and 17 meters, respectively (Alía Medina and Riba 1957). To these Martín Aguado has added a new terrace, at 35-40 meters, based on field observation in sectors of the valley where the +52 meter, and +17 meter terraces are also present (this work was

---

[16]   There are a few more extensive faunal lists from the Manzanares terraces, and in some cases elements are mentioned which would be of utility in the climatic and stratigraphic study of the terrace sequence were their provenience given in detail. That is especially true of Imperatori's discovery of *Elephas primigenius*, supposedly from basal gravels of the low terrace at 7.4 kilometers on the Andalusia highway (Riba 1957: 44–46). Unhappily much of the material mentioned in Riba (1957) is from unprovenienced museum collections, and it surprises me that they have been published with stratigraphic attributions. (Most of the Manzanares terrace fauna is in any case relatively banal, and for present purposes is quite limited.)

summarized in Martín Aguado 1963a, 1963b). Various quarries are open in these terraces, and it seems certain that only that at +35-40 meters contains associated fauna and industrial materials. The one dense concentration of stone artifacts is found in quarries at Pinedo, two kilometers upstream from the city of Toledo itself.

According to Martín Aguado's description of an ideal section, Pleistocene sediments at Pinedo rest atop a consolidated red Miocene (?) bed (*alcaen*); the base of the fluvial deposits is ±20 meters above the present floodplain. The surface of the *alcaen* is irregular with numerous depressions or potholes filled with Aguado's "infrabasal" gravels and sands (level 1). Faunal remains from level 1 include abundant bones of *Elephas antiquus,* an indeterminate rhinoceros and the only pieces of *Hippopotamus* reported from the terrace. There are numerous lithic implements, including rolled specimens (Martín Aguado 1963a: 32).

The basal gravels (2) are subdivided: the lower horizon (2a) is mostly gravel of medium to large sizes, containing remains of *Elephas antiquus, Cervus,* and *Bos,* while the upper division (2b) is sandier, with gravels of smaller sizes and remains of *Equus.* Stone tools are abundant throughout level 2 (Martín Aguado 1963a: 32-33).

A layer of current-bedded sands ("intermediate sands" of level 3) truncates level 2b. Level 3 is not certainly known to have yielded artifacts, but fragmentary elephant molars may have been found in the deposit. Atop the intermediate sands are the "Upper Gravels" (4), a sequence of gravels, sands and dark clays, lacking fauna, but with rare artifacts like those from earlier levels. Level 5 is composed of very fine crossbedded sands ("arenas voladoras") which Aguado believes represent dunes, but which more probably are channel-side or levee deposits. No artifacts are reported, but shells of fresh water molluscs and indeterminate bones were recovered (Martín Aguado 1963a: 33-34).

A series of fine silty sediments (level 6) accumulated atop the clearly fluvial sequence. While Riba (1957) has interpreted these as loess, Martín Aguado claims they are fine alluvial deposits (floodplain silts); he does, however, recognize loessic deposition atop the "low" terrace (Martín Aguado 1963a: 35-37). Colluvial deposits (level C) cap the 35-40 meter terrace.

According to Martín Aguado, the infrabasal gravels accumulated during the transition from the Holsteinian to the succeeding cold phase, and from level 2b through the beginning of level 6, the terrace deposits record increasing climatic deterioration equated with the "Riss" gla-

ciation. With the transition from "Riss" to "Eem", the final period
of floodplain-silt deposition was terminated and downcutting began
anew (Martín Aguado 1963a: 38-39; 1963b: 171-172). Aguirre has
challenged this interpretation, on the basis of a study of faunal materials.
He accepts a glacial age for terrace deposits at $+35$ to 40 meters height
at Buenavista (with *Elephas trogontherii, Hippopotamus amphibius,
Bos primigenius, Equus,* and cervids), but assigns the Pinedo fluvial deposits an interglacial ("Holstein") age (de Aguirre 1964a: 296).
Aguirre's argument that terrace deposits on either side of the Toledo
entrenched meander ("torno") formed under distinct climatic regimens
is fundamentally based on an equation of *Elephas antiquus* with warm,
wooded conditions and its absence from the Buenavista sediments. That
point of view cannot be sustained in the face of the undeniable occurrence of this elephant in full glacial deposits at Torralba and Ambrona. Martín Aguado's interpretation would therefore seem the more
reasonable.[17]

The Pinedo artifact series is unique. Thousands of pieces have been
collected from the quarries. Made mostly on quartzite and vein quartz
cobbles, they include a few true bifaces and cleavers, and a great number
of biface roughouts, including a series of characteristic pick-shaped
partial trihedrals. Some of the latter are so sketchily fashioned as to
resemble choppers and chopping tools, and one figured piece (Martín
Aguado 1963a, Plate 22) looks somewhat like an Asturian pick, if
viewed from just one face. Some large flakes and one or two small
ones are figured. Obvious flaws in the raw material can be seen in
Aguado's illustrations of several pieces (Martín Aguado 1963a: Plates
13, 26, 29, 30, 36; 1962: Figure 13), and the crude appearance of the
collection is probably largely a reflection of the fact that many of the
artifacts are incomplete rejects. As was the case for many of the Manzanares occurrences, the Pinedo localities were probably workshops,
immediately adjacent to the streambed sources of raw material for
stone tool manufacture (Figure 9).

THE LOWER TAGUS DRAINAGE   Portuguese terraces of the Tagus from
Abrantes to the river mouth at Lisbon contain abundant testimony of
prehistoric human occupation. Some stratified Acheulean materials are
summarily reported in the literature, but a great many occurrences

[17] Kahlke (n.d.) mentions the presence of *Predama* in the Pinedo strata. If the
provenience of the form is correct, its value as a precise age-indicator must be
quite limited.

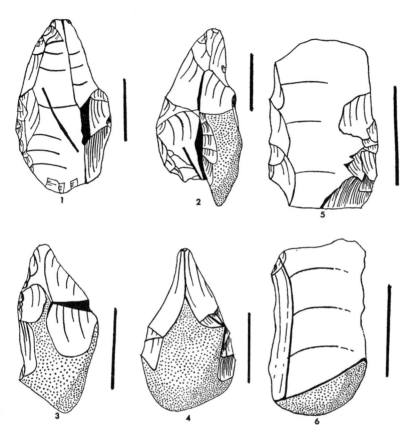

Figure 9.   Pinedo bifaces. A 5 centimeter scale is sited to the right of each piece. Drawn from photographs in Martín Aguado (1963a).

described as Acheulean (including "Chellean") by the authors are really not known well enough to permit secure diagnosis. Basic information concerning the most important Tagus sites was published by Breuil and Zbyszewski (1942, 1945); their pioneer study would benefit from substantial revision.

Dense concentrations of Tagus terrace sites are found in the valleys of the Alpiarça and its tributaries from the town of Alpiarça to Almeirim and there are sporadic occurrences from the Rio Sorraia to the Tagus estuary. The Alpiarça region seems most promising for future investigations.

Breuil and Zbyszewski recognized five major terraces along the lower Tagus (in addition to the present floodplain). Remnants of the highest "Sicilian" terrace (ca. 95-115 meters)[18] are preserved from Vale de Cavalos to the Sorraia valley (Breuil and Zbyszewski 1945: 600). In the vicinity of Condeixa-a-Velha, north of the Tagus, Choffat found a thick travertine, sometimes containing beds of alluvial gravels at base, at an elevation of some 100-110 meters altitude. Seemingly the Condeixa travertines should correlate with the "Sicilian" terrace, although detailed fieldwork is required for verification. Just to the South of Condeixa itself, the tufas are exposed in a ravine, showing the following succession from base to top:

C.1 Jurassic limestone.
C.2 Five to 6 meters of large alluvial gravel cemented into a reddish sand. This level produced a molar of *Elephas,* identified by Deperet as *E. meridionalis,* by Boule and Pohlig as *E. antiquus.*
C.3 About 3 meters of mealy travertine with sand and some gravel, containing remains of *Hippopotamus major* and numerous fragmentary *Helix.*
C.4 Deep travertine bank with lenses of fist-sized and larger rolled cobbles at base, becoming homogeneous and compact at top.

Tufas continue to form in the valley bottom at the present day (Choffat 1898: 1-9).

There are molluscs, numerous vegetal remains and even some feathers in the travertines near Condeixa. On the road from Eira-Pedrinha to N.S. das Dores, an especially rich locality yielded the following molluscs: *Lymnaea auricularia, Bythinia tentaculta, Rumina decollata, Helix barbula,* and *Helix nemoralis.*

All are members of the modern molluscan fauna of the region. The same locality produced several plant species all of which also still survive in the modern flora: *Vitis vinifera, Rubus casius (?), Olea europaea, Laurus nobilis, Quercus pedunculata* or *Q. lusitanica, Alnus glutinosa, Smilax mauritanica,* and *Scolopendrium officinale* (Choffat 1898: 5).

Various authorities have cited the Eira-Pedrinha flora and molluscan fauna as pertaining to the same biotic complex as the *Elephas* and *Hippopotamus* remains. However, that is by no means certain. Choffat specifically states that vegetal remains were recovered at one locality from travertines still in process of formation, and he does not clearly

---

[18]   The designations "Sicilian", "Milazzian", "Tyrrhenian", and "Grimaldian" are those of the authors. I have used them as convenient shorthand labels for formations discussed by Breuil, Zbyszewski, and others, without intending any stratigraphic connotations.

dissociate the Eira-Pedrinha bed from that observation, although he does say that the flora and molluscs were found deep in the road cut (Choffat 1898: 5). It does not at present seem advisable to consider all the Condeixa finds to be contemporaneous on this evidence. The presence of a hippopotamus in the Condeixa travertines seems sufficient indication of an interglacial climate for the time of deposition of the containing level. It is significant that no artifacts have been recovered from the "Sicilian" terrace (Breuil and Zbyszewski 1945: 601).

The high "Milazzian" terrace at 50-70 meters seems to be culturally sterile where it is undisturbed, but solifluction mantles at the base of the 15-35 meter and 10 meter terraces, supposedly derived from the high terrace, contain rolled bifaces and flakes (Breuil and Zbyszewski 1945: 602-604). The proposed correlation of the middle and low terrace solifluction layers with the "Milazzian" terrace gravels seems dubious, to say the least. A middle "Tyrrhenian" terrace with *in situ* industrial and faunal material is found at 15-35 meters above the present floodplain. It is in deposits of this terrace complex that the most satisfactorily documented and convincing Lower Paleolithic occurrences were found (Breuil and Zbyszewski 1945: 604-608). Further fieldwork could probably subdivide the 15-35 meter terrace suite.

The low or "Grimaldian" terrace containing fauna and artifacts is preserved some 8-10 meters above the present Tagus floodplain. At Santo Antão do Tojal, the Grimaldian terrace (on the Rio Trancão) produced bones of *Elephas antiquus and Equus caballus* with a supposedly Middle Paleolithic artifact series (Breuil and Zbyszewski 1942: 56; Zbyszewski 1966: 123). The "Grimaldian" terrace as well as lower terraces developed at $+4$-5 meters seem certainly to postdate the disappearance of the Acheulean industrial complex in Portugal; the supposed derived Acheulean from the low terrace of the Rio Sorraia, east of Benavente, contains no indisputable handaxes and is entirely nondescript (Breuil and Zbyszewski 1945: 608-612; Zbyszewski and da Vega Ferreira 1967).

In the Alpiarça region, there are two major exposures in the 15-35 meter terrace along the left bank of the Tagus and one on the north side of the Atela valley. All are quarries.

The Tojal quarry (Quinta dos Patudos) yielded the stratigraphy shown in Table 2. The lower gravel (level 1) is claimed to be derived from the "Milazzian" terrace by solifluction, and contains supposed "Clactono-Abbevillian" flakes. Only five pieces were found, and the single figured piece is worthless for purposes of diagnosis. An ovate

Table 2.   Stratigraphic columns in three Tagus terrace exposures near Alpiarça; suggested correlations from Breuil and Zbyszewski (1945)

Alto do Freixo Level		Vale do Forno Level		Tojal (Quinta dos Patudos) Level	
9	Gravelly sand ravining lower levels	9	Dune sands	8	Dune sands
8	Red sand	8	Reddish sands, gravels, and grey-yellow micaceous clay	7	Fine, yellowish, micaceous clayey sand
7	Rose sand	7	Yellow-reddish sands and gravels	6	Yellow-ochre sands
6	Grey sand ⟶	6	Green-grey sandy clay ⟶	5	Grey clay with vegetal remains
5	Green-grey sand ⟶	5	Grey clay	4	Greenish-grey clay
4	Grey clay with vegetal remains ⟶	4	Sandy green-grey micaceous clay and clayey sands	3	Gravels
3	Yellow sand	3	Yellow sands and gravels	2	White-yellow sands
2	Grey-white sand	2	Yellow-red gravels and conglomerate ⟶	1	Lower gravel and conglomerate
1	Grey-green clay with vegetal remains ⟶	1	Yellow sands		
Base	Conglomerate ⟶				

biface roughout and several choppers and chopping tools were found in level 2, and a totally nondiagnostic series of crude artifacts from levels 3 and 4 was assigned to the "Middle Acheulean" by the authors. The highest stratum with artifacts of interest to this paper, level 7, produced a series of what may be late Acheulean or even Micoquian tools, including two small lanceolate bifaces. The authors correlate levels 1 through 7 with Elster and Holstein (Breuil and Zbyszewski 1942: 267-293; 1945: 387-415). In the absence of faunal, floral, or sediment studies or absolute dating, the only data available to substantiate this attribution are the artifacts, and they look like pieces found elsewhere in considerably younger deposits.

The Vale do Forno quarry stratigraphy is also shown in Table 2. According to Breuil and Zbyszewski, level 2 with "Clactono-Abbevillian" artifacts should date to Elster, levels 3 through 6 with "Middle" and "Evolved" Acheulean can be correlated with Holstein, while levels 7 and 8 and associated final Acheulean or Micoquian tools are of Riss age. The dune sands capping the sequence would correlate with Würm (Breuil and Zbyszewski 1945: 343-345). The illustrated specimens include a crude biface and partial cleaver flake from level 2, a partial lanceolate or ovate biface, a limande, a very fine parallel sided cleaver flake and some small bifaces from level 5, while levels 7 and 8 yielded a poor partial cleaver and some small bifacial pieces. Numerous choppers, chopping tools and core-like pieces were found in every level. Artifacts from levels 7 and 8 might be found in Final Acheulean or Mousterian of Acheulean Tradition assemblages with equal probability. The collection from the earlier levels could be late Middle Acheulean or Late Acheulean in affinities. In any case, the artifacts are not sufficient evidence for an early mid-Pleistocene (or earlier) age for any part of the Vale do Forno sequence.

The basal conglomerate at the Alto do Freixo has been correlated with the "Mindel gravel" in the other two quarries (Table 2). Levels 4 through 7 yielded tools attributed to the Middle and Final Acheulean (Breuil and Zbyszewski 1945: 417). Three rolled pieces from the conglomerate are figured: they include a chopper/chopping tool and a piece which may be either an amorphous core or a crude biface. Levels 4 through 6 produced some partial bifaces and roughouts, including several quite small pieces and some larger lanceolates, as well as discs or disc cores, choppers, and chopping tools. This collection has a Late Acheulean allure. From level 7 there is an apparent broken cleaver flake, a pick, and several choppers and chopping tools; these pieces could also be Late Acheulean in affinities. The artifact series from the Alto do Freixo is quite similar to that from the other two "middle terrace" quarries.

At Casalinho, East of Alpiarça, crude artifacts including small cores, choppers, and chopping tools have been found eroding from a sandy deposit atop the 50-60 meter terrace (Breuil and Zbyszewski 1945: 329). This site is of considerable potential importance if the artifacts were actually recovered *in situ* from alluvial deposits, since no other occurrence of lithic materials in sediments of the 50-60 meter terrace seems to be documented. However, the pieces are non-diagnostic. At Quinta do Outeiro, North of Alpiarça, similarly undiagnostic arti- facts were recovered from the basal gravels of a 15-20 meter terrace; typically, these deposits are claimed to be of "Mindel" age (Breuil and Zbyszewski 1945: 337). Several amorphous artifacts were found in the basal gravels of the same terrace at Quinta da Goucha (Breuil and Zbyszewski 1945: 433-440). Further South, there are two suggestive occurrences in the Paul Valley. At Quinta de Ramalhais, on the North bank of the Paul, the 20-25 meter terrace is covered by a gravel level which in turn is capped with sands. Although the gravel level is said to contain "Abbevillian" inplements, none is figured and only flakes and flaked cobbles are described. The material from the sands was actually collected from the surface in a vineyard; although the collec- tion is called Acheulean, typical pieces adequate as a basis for such assignment are not figured or described (Breuil and Zbyszweski 1945: 447-51). In a greenish clay capping a terrace at the same elevation on the South bank of the Paul at Corte dos Dois Irmãos, there are arti- facts attributed to the Acheulean, but which may pertain to a later industrial complex (Breuil and Zbyszewski 1945: 451-454). A large series of apparently Late Acheulean implements is reported from the site of Cabeço da Mina (Muge) on the Rio Lamarosa, and some were recovered in apparently acceptable stratigraphic context (Mendes Cor- rêa 1940; Breuil and Zbyszewski 1945: 467-488). Unhappily, there is no indication which of the diagnostic specimens figured were recovered *in situ* and which came from surface collections. At Casal da Mina, there are several terrace remnants on the left bank of the Tagus from Azambuja South to Vila Nova de Rainha. The series has elevations from 15-35 meters and is said to be basically "Tyrrhenian" in age, though an overlay of more recent sediments is noted. At V.N. da Rainha, the base of the terrace deposit consists of greenish clay, and is overlain by pink sands and gravels which in turn are ravined and covered with a solifluction deposit. The pink sands and the solifluction layer yielded numerous small artifacts including scrapers, cores, split cobbles, and chopper/chopping tools. These pieces are rather nondescript, but Breuil and Zbyszewski recognized that they are not characteristic of any Acheulean facies (Breuil and Zbyszweski 1945: 538). In my opinion, they could be Mousterian or even Upper Paleolithic.

There are artifact occurrences in the 8-10 meter terrace (Silha do Bicha, North of Catapereiro, the Monte Borralho canal section, and Monte do Gato on the Rio Sorraia, for example). No horizon of the 8-10 meter terrace system has yet produced convincing Acheulean artifacts, despite the opinion of Breuil and Zbyszewski (1945: 503). to the contrary. All such occurrences can probably be assigned to Mousterian or later industrial complexes (see Zbyszewski 1967).

INTERPRETATIVE SYNTHESIS As is too frequently the case, the most typical and diagnostic Acheulean implements in the Tagus drainage seem to have been found on the present land surface. Such is the case for the handsome bifaces from the Guarda district (Vasco Rodrigues 1959), the better pieces from Cabeço da Mina (Breuil and Zbyszewski 1945: 467-487), and the tools from Casal do Monte (Breuil and Zbyszewski 1942: 54-207). Bifaces found *in situ* are usually poorly finished or incomplete specimens when they are represented at all. The bulk of the stratified collections seems to consist of amorphous pieces, flakes, cores, split pebbles, and chopper/chopping tools. It is suspected that this may reflect the fact that the terrace occurrences are (often redeposited) quarry debris. The surface finds, on the other hand, may represent residues from true living sites, now so eroded as to be unrecognizable.

There is only one possible occurrence of an artifact-bearing stratum in alluvial deposits of the 50-60 meter Tagus terrace (Casalinho). All the obvious Acheulean sites are found in deposits of the 15-35 meter terraces, and in every case where diagnostic artifacts are present, the collections could be assigned to the Late Acheulean; sometimes the pieces seem very modern indeed.

The age of the Tagus terraces is still a matter of speculation. However, the terraces are clearly eustatically controlled and, in at least some cases, are continuous with elevated fossil beaches, which will be discussed below. Faunal remains are rare and poorly reported, while macrobotanical remains from the terraces are mentioned but usually not described. Aside from the Condeixa fauna, there is a mentioned occurrence of *Elephas antiquus* in the "15-35 meter" terrace at Carregado, but the species also occurs in the 8-10 meter terrace at Santo Antão do Tojal, and so is of little use for chronological discrimina-

toni (Breuil and Zbyszewski 1945: 538). While the "15-35 meter terrace" seems likely to be a heterogeneous aggregate of deposits of distinct ages, there is no evidence that any part of the complex antedates the mid-Pleistocene. On the other hand, the fact that the 8-10 meter Tagus terrace contains no convincing Acheulean artifacts suggests that it may date from the later Upper Pleistocene.

Other Portuguese Occurrences

MEALHADA   This extremely important locality on the Rio Certima, North of Coimbra, known since about 1876, was excavated in 1879 and 1880 by Nery Delgado, Ribeiro, and Choffat, and was later the subject of a brief but detailed note by Fontes (Choffat 1898: 8; Harlé 1911: 41; Fontes 1916; Zbyszewski 1966: 118-119). A series of Pleistocene deposits containing mammals, molluscs, plants, and artifacts overlies Tertiary marl bedrock. In simplified section, the sequence begins at base with about 60 centimeters of dark grey to black clay (1) with molluscs at bottom (c), molluscs and plant remains (including tree trunks) in the middle (b), and mammalian remains in the sandier upper section (a). Next, there is a less sandy dark grey clay (2) with rare gravel (1.6 meters), followed by coarse coherent sands (3), some larger elements and stone artifacts (1 meter). The series is completed by about 30 centimeters of gravelly sand (4) with occasional stone tools (Fontes 1916: 9-11, 14). Mammalian remains from 1 (a) include *Elephas antiquus, Hippopotamus major,*[19] *Cervus elaphus,* and *Equus caballus* (Zbyszewski 1966: 119; Fontes 1916: 11). Molluscs from levels 1 (c) and 1 (b) are *Unio* (numerous), *Cyclas* (one valve), *Valvata piscinalis, Planorbis albus, Lymnaea limosa,* and *Lymnaea palustris.* All but the last species is still found in the area, and it is known from France, Spain, and Algeria (Choffat 1898: 8). Level 1 (b) produced seeds of *Trapa bituberculata,*[20] and other vegetal remains identified as *Pinus silvestris, Pinus cembra, Rhododendron, Quercus, Salix cinerea, Betula,* and *Phragmites* (Zbyszewski 1966: p. 119), suggesting warm and relatively moist climate.

The lithic artifacts found in overlying beds, especially the layer of coarse sands (3), include a true biface and four flakes, two at least produced by Levallois technique (Fontes 1916: Figures 4-7). Unfortunately, this locality cannot be directly related at present to a major

---

[19]   Probably *Hippopotamus amphibius?*
[20]   Given by Fontes as *T. natans.*

terrace sequence, and neither flora, fauna, nor the single shaped tool are sufficient grounds for suggesting an approximate age for the sediments.

THE PORTUGUESE LITTORAL Vestiges of raised beaches, fluviatile deposits, and marine abrasional features are preserved at several localities along the Portuguese coast. Lithic artifacts are associated with some of the "beach" deposits. Teixera (1949, 1952) has described nine levels along the northern coast, but lacking extensive sedimentological studies like those begun by Soares de Carvalho (1953, and elsewhere), the significance and interrelationships of these is not understood. Certainly the levels described by Breuil and Zbyszewski (1942, 1945) are too grossly constituted, but at present there is no alternative except to use their schema in discussing the artifact occurrences.

Breuil and Zbyszweski (1942: 348-358; 1945: 592-596) recognized four major marine deposits: a "Grimaldian"[21] complex from 0-12 meters above mean sea level, a "Tyrrhenian" suite from 15-35 meters; a "Milazzian" series from 40-60 meters, and an uppermost "Sicilian" group at 90-100 meters. There are no artifacts in undisturbed deposits of the upper two complexes.

Choffat and Dollfus (1907) described marine faunal collections from three beach levels near the Fortim de Barralha (Cabo d'Espichel). The collection from the 60 meter beach contained *Mactra subtruncata, M. solida, Donax vittatus, Cardium echinatum, Pecten maximus,* and *Mytilus edulis.* The 15 meter level yielded *Mactra solida, Cardium echinatum (?), C. edule, C. norvegicum, Mytilus galloprovincialis, M. edulis, Patella vulgata, P. caerulea, Strongylocentrotus lividus,* and *Pollicipes cornucopia.* In the collection from 6 meters, *Solen marginatus, Tapes pallustra, Venus gallina, Cardium echinatum, C. edule, C. norvegicum, Pectunculus bimaculatus (?), Pecten maximus, Mytilus edulis, Patella vulgata, P. safiensis, P. caerulea, Echinus miliaris* and *Strongylocentrotus lividus* were represented. The 60 meter fauna is characterized as cool temperate, the 15 meter as temperate atlantic, somewhat warmer than the 60 meter assemblage, and the 6 meter collection, with characteristic southern elements, is called warm temperate. Other, less important collections from the region of Porto confirmed this diagnosis (Choffat and Dollfus 1907: 170-173). However, of all the forms in these collections, only one is no longer found on the Portuguese coast, which argues that the climatic differences attested to by the three faunas

[21] See Note 18.

may not be major (Breuil and Zbyszewski 1945: 314). However, the one exotic, *Patella safiensis* = *P. safiana* is now found only on the Moroccan coast and the Mediterranean shores of Algeria (Lecointre 1952: 92) and may be a useful stratigraphic marker. From the 15 meter beach at the Fortim de Barralha, Breuil and Zbyszewski later collected *Helix, Purpura haemastoma,* and *Murex erinaceus* (Breuil and Zbyszewski 1945: 315). These faunas might all be found on the Portuguese littoral under conditions like those of the present day or somewhat warmer.[22]

A molluscan fauna *(Cardium edule, Scrobicularia plana, Mytilus,* unidentified gastropods, and barnacles) is also reported from a cultural horizon of unknown affinities overlain by a consolidated dune on a beach at Areias Gordas (Magoito). Its age was given as final Würm (Breuil and Zbyszewski 1945: 211).

Some relatively typical tools are found in two coastal localities in stratigraphic successions containing identifiable molluscan or plant remains. At the Praia dos Aivados, south of Porto Corvo, the following stratigraphy is noted in the 12-15 meter beach from surface to base:

Level 8.   Modern dune.

Level 7.   Ash-grey sands with post-paleolithic artifacts.

Level 6.   Reddish clayey earth with nondescript small tools (called "Mousterian").

Level 5.   Consolidated dune (ca. 20 meters).

Level 4.   Reddish sands (1.2 meters).

Level 3.   Alternate fine and coarse sands with "Acheulean" (10-12 meters).

Level 2.   Consolidated sands and gravels.

Level 1.   Lumachelle of broken shells. *(Pecten, Mytilus, Ostrea, Anomia ephippium, Tapes, Patella, Balanus, Serpula).* These layers, with rolled cobbles, sit atop a Paleozoic substrate (Zbyszewski 1966: 124). The artifacts from level 3 were examined superficially in 1968 and include some pieces which might possibly have Late Acheulean, or Mousterian of Acheulean Tradition affinities. Just South of the Rio Mira, there are beach deposits at 15-20 meters, with the following strata:

Level 4.   Ash-grey sands with post-Paleolithic artifacts, covered with modern dune sands.

---

[22] It seems likely that the first occurrence of *Purpura haemastoma* and *Patella safiana* in Portuguese littoral sediments reflects the explosive radiation of these molluscs which has been found useful in the dating of strata on the Atlantic coast of Morocco.

Level 3.   Up to 4 meters of grey to yellow sands with artifacts (called "Micoquian").

Level 2.   Grey clayey sands and sandy clays with macro- and micro-botanical remains of *Ericacea, Rhododendron, Pinus, Betula, Salix, Alnus,* and *Castanea.*

Level 1.   Basal conglomerate atop a Paleozoic substrate (Zbyszewski 1966: 124-125).

Artifacts from this locality were seen in 1968, and include pieces appropriate to Late Acheulean contexts, although some of the series might equally well be attributed to the Mousterian of Acheulean Tradition.

Artifacts described as Acheulean were recovered in stratified context at Aleia Nova just west of Vila Real de Santo Antonio (Algarve) almost on the Spanish border. The strata at this site on the 15 meter beach are as follows:

Level 4.   Mixed sands with "Mousterian".

Level 3.   Cross-bedded grey clayey sands and gravels with "Acheulean" (up to 2.5 meters).

Level 2.   Red to grey clayey sands (1.2 meters).

Level 1.   Red sands with grey clay lenses and cobbles, atop the Miocene substrate (Zbyszewski 1966: 125).

At the Fortim de Porto Corvo, an atypical industry recovered from sands atop a +6-8 meter gravel level has been unjustifiably assigned to the Acheulean (Zbyszewski 1966: 123). At Cabo Sines, south of the lighthouse, 10-15 meter beach gravels are overlain by sands and modern dunes. Artifacts are found in both levels below the modern dune sands. Although they are described as Acheulean, at least in part (Zbyszewski 1966: 123), that attribution is also without foundation. The series is nondescript, consisting mostly of chopper/chopping tools, fractured cobbles, and amorphous pieces, most of them quite small. Between the Cabo da Roca, just west of Lisbon, and Peniche (Cabo Cavoeiro) to the north, there are a number of coastal sites wtih lithic artifacts in good stratigraphic context. The importance of the sites at Ericeira has been stressed in the literature. One in particular, San Julião in the 15-20 meter beach, is treated as especially crucial. The sequence, from top to base, is as follows:

Level 10.   Recent dune sand.

Level 9.   Grey sands and "Upper Paleolithic" tools.

Level 8.   Brown sands with "Mousterian".

Level 7.   Cobbles and gravels with "Acheulean" and "Languedocian".

Level 6.   Red sands with gravels at base, filling ravines through all beneath.

Level 5.   Reddish sands with green-grey clay.

Level 4.   Reddish sands with small gravel and "Acheulean".

Level 3.   Rose sands in ravines cutting level 2.

Level 2.   Greenish to sandy-yellowish clays.

Level 1.   3-4 meters of basal grey sands and clays (Breuil and Zbyszewski 1945: 123-135).

Obviously, a complex series of cycles of erosion and deposition is attested to. Starting with the basal level, there are at least three periods of beach, colluvial, or fluvial/estuarine deposition, interrupted by two phases of erosion, all capped by a recent dune. Breuil and Zbyszewski (1945: 136-137) correlated the basal levels with Holstein, level 7 with Eem and the beginnings of Würm, and the upper series to the later Würm and postglacial. However, the evidence which is needed to make the stratigraphy intelligible is really lacking.

Although many artifacts were recovered in intact deposits, they are not clearly distinguished from the surface-collected pieces, nor are they especially diagnostic. The single so-called biface found *in situ* in level 4 looks like a chopper or broken scraper, rather than a true biface. As far as its industrial associations are concerned, San Julião is disappointing.

Further north, at Ribamar, two rather advanced looking Acheulean bifaces or roughouts, as well as some chopper/chopping tools, a disc, and several nondescript flakes and flake tools were found in a sandy deposit filling a ravine in the 20-30 meter raised beach (Breuil and Zbyszewski 1945: 119-120). At the Praia de Santa Cruz, the Praia da Consolaçao and Porto de Lobos, there are atypical artifacts in deposits from 16-35 meters above sea level. None of these sites are especially useful for present purposes, but they provide further evidence of ravining of the "Tyrrhenian" beach and artifact series antedating recent dune deposits (Breuil and Zbyszewski 1945: 69-98). Last, choppers, chopping tools, and possible rolled bifaces were found in basal gravels of a 30-35 meter beach near the mouth of the Rio Minho (Zbyszewski 1966: 117-18).

SYNTHESIS   Lithic artifacts which may be definitely assigned to the Acheulean complex of industries are known on the Portuguese littoral only from the complex series of fossil beaches above 12 meters and below 35 meters in elevation. The evidence at hand suggests that this series is stratigraphically (and thus, temporally) heterogeneous, including periods of erosion as well as deposition, and probably at least one phase of soil development (indicated by the widespread occurrence of reddish silt and sand levels); detailed field and laboratory studies are required before meaningful subdivision of the series will be possible. The poor and probably unrepresentative Acheulean artifact collections from these beaches could be quite late, but speculation on such meager grounds is unwarranted. On present evidence local systematization of the phases of the Pleistocene during which Acheulean assemblages were produced is more immediately to be expected from studies of terrace suite along the Tejo and other major Portuguese rivers than from the inadequately understood record of fossil beaches.

THE MINHO/LOURO TERRACES   In connection with archeological investigations at Budinho, Butzer has evaluated the Pleistocene geomorphic sequence in Southwestern Pontevedra (Spain). His own work and his survey of the literature are directly relevant to understanding the Portuguese terrace and beach sequences and their interrelationships. On the Spanish side of the Minho estuary, he has identified a total of seven terraces, including a floodplain terrace (general level +3 to 10 meters) still inundated by annual high water levels, a Low Terrace (LT) at +22-24 meters, two Middle Terraces at +42-44 meters (MT I) and + 34-36 meters (MT II), and three High Terraces at +76-80 meters (HT I), +65-68 meters (HT II), and +52-59 meters (HT III), as well as several older erosional surfaces of indeterminate stratigraphic significance (Butzer 1967: 92). Tools have been found in beds atop a High Terrace near Lanhelas (Viana 1930) but Butzer tentatively correlates the artifact-bearing deposits with Late Pleistocene colluvium overlying older terrace beds. The terraces themselves seem to be controlled eustatically (Butzer 1967: 94). Regional marine abrasional benches and nips are recognized at +2.5, +6-7, +10-12, +16-17, +23-24, +33-36, and +44-49 meters above mean sea level. No higher marine stage is documented.

The High Terrace complex cannot be directly correlated with shoreline evidence. It is capped by a deep *Rotlehm* paleosol absent from Lower Terrace remnants. Such soils seem not to have formed in the Mediterranean basin since about 80,000 B.P. The +42-44 meter terrace (MT I) is observed to intergrade with the +44-49 meter sea level stand. MT II (+34-36 meters) seems to be linked with a marine stand at +33-36 meters, although direct field connections were not observed. Soils atop the Middle Terraces were poorly developed and later partly denuded.

The Low Terrace at +22-24 meters seems to correlate with a +23-24 meter shore level. Subsequent to deposition, this terrace was dissected and subjected to some tectonic disturbance. In the Middle Louro valley, whose terrace sequence is broadly equivalent with that along the lower Minho, two generations of colluvial material were accumulated after low terrace deposits were faulted. Radiocarbon dates of 26,700 B.P. + 3600,-2500 (I 2174) and 18,000 ± 300 B.P. (I 2175) were obtained for the basal gravel of the Lower Colluvium at the Budinho Paleolithic site. Regardless of the discrepancy between them they are both consonant with a Main Würm age for the deposits, a determination which is in general agreement with other evidence. A Late Würm age was suggested for the Upper Colluvium (Butzer 1967: 89-101). Yet another colluvial horizon, overlying a bench at +2.3 meters at Mougás (North) has been dated as > 39,000 B.P. (I 2177). The bench itself at +2.3 meters is provisionally assigned to the last interglacial, the colluvium to Early Würm (Butzer 1967: 96-97). Butzer points out that if the Low Terrace of the Minho correlates with a +23-24 meter marine base level, presumably prior to the cutting of the +10-12 and +6-7 meter benches which were thought to antedate the Early Würm colluvium at Mougás, the Low Terrace might well predate sealevels now dated 75,000-90,000 B.P. in the Mediterranean basin and coasts of Atlantic Morocco (Butzer 1967: 100).

In his paper for this volume, Butzer proposes a drastically revised system of marine cycles/Pleistocene high sea levels, based on extensive fieldwork in Mallorca. It becomes clear that previously accepted sea level curves incorporate serious errors of oversimplification; there is now conclusive evidence that multiple and chronologically disparate sea levels have converged at identical relative elevations, and that sea level heights are not to be used as unequivocal dating criteria. It follows that the traditional terminology applied to what were formerly thought to be chronologically distinct marine stages must be abandoned. Additionally, the new evidence shows that Pleistocene sea level fluctuations, especially during and prior to the traditional "Tyrrhenian", are far more complex than has been hitherto suspected (Butzer i.p.). Under these circumstances, sea level correlations must be based on other evidence than relative heights, requiring intensive field and laboratory work on a scale not yet available for the Portuguese sea level record. Long-distance correlations between the Portuguese coast and the Mallorquin sequence are bound to be largely meaningless, but assuming that absolute elevations have not been distorted by regional deformation, it is suggestive that no Mallorcan sea level below 35 meters apparent height is earlier than Butzer's Marine cycle V, while all levels between +15 and +35 meters fall in his Marine Cycle W.

The Cantabrian Coast

Reported surface occurrences of Acheulean and Mousterian artifacts (often confused) along Cantabrian beaches are too numerous to cite. Surface scatters of large bifacial implements have also been noted at some distance from the modern littoral, especially near Castillo (Obermaier 1916: 178) and Altamira (González Echegaray 1959). Data published concerning these occurrences are primarily useful as guides to localities where intensive future research may some day prove productive. There is only one Cantabrian site where Acheulean materials are known to occur in stratigraphic context. That site, el Castillo in Santander, Spain, is unique in being the only convincing Acheulean cave occupation in the Iberian Peninsula. Found at about 130 meters above the present Río Pas floodplain in a large residual limestone hum, the Cueva del Castillo is about 10 kilometers from the modern coast as the crow flies.

The Acheulean basal levels at Castillo are overlain by two major Mousterian horizons, four Aurignacian and Perigordian levels, two Magdalenian beds and a layer each of Azilian and Bronze Age materials (Obermaier 1925: 175-177). Only the Mousterian (Freeman 1964, 1970) and Aurignacian/Perigordian artifact series (McCollough 1971) have been described in detail. The most recent (and sketchy) descriptions of the basal complex refer to the existence of two Acheulean horizons (Obermaier 1916) but earlier references are not consistent. Through 1912, the basal levels had not been subdivided, and Breuil and Obermaier described them as a single level of "crude Mousterian" in cave clays containing remains of bear and *Rhinoceros merckii*[23] (Breuil and Obermaier 1913: 3). By 1913, the basal level was diagnosed as Acheulean, and subdivided: the upper part contained true bifaces[24] and many crude limestone artifacts; the lower level contained pieces analogous to the cruder tools in the higher series, and is described as a cave clay rich in *Ursus spelaeus* (Breuil and Ober-

---

[23] The Castillo Acheulean rhino was provisionally called *Rhinoceros tichorhinus* in the earliest report (Breuil and Obermaier 1912: 13).
[24] A large pointed biface labelled as pertaining to Mousterian level alpha is almost certainly the same piece described by Breuil and Obermaier (1914: 234) as having been found in the higher Acheulean horizon. Nevertheless, it has been excluded from my count.

maier 1914: 233-234). In *El hombre fósil*, Obermaier (1916: 178) described the upper level (y) as "Lower Acheulean with typical bifaces, worked on both surfaces. Much worked limestone. Ochre. [Principal fauna: *Cervus elaphus* and *Rhinoceros merckii*]," and the lower horizon (z) as "Clay with rare atypical artifacts and the remains of hearths. [Principal fauna: *Ursus spelaeus* and rarely *Rangifer tarandus*]." *Marmota* was later added to the faunal list from level (z). A reexamination of the faunas by Vaufrey apparently indicated that the identification of *Rangifer* in the lower horizons was incorrect, and that the represented cervid might be *Dama* instead.[25] If so, the Castillo Acheulean deposits could have been accumulated under relatively mild climatic conditions, rather than the full ("Riss") glacial climate suggested by Zeuner (1952: 240). Butzer's new analyses of sediment samples from the Acheulean horizons are also consonant with deposition in rather mild conditions.

The Acheulean horizons are covered by a flowstone layer which, in turn, is overlain by horizons of Charentian Mousterian and cleaver flake rich Mousterian of Acheulean Tradition. The artifact contents of the latter level are statistically indistinguishable in "essential" flake tool series from assemblages in levels 13/14 and 15 at Morin provisionally assigned to Hengelo (González Echegaray and Freeman 1973: 297).[26] High relative numbers of forest-dwelling mammals in the Castillo levels would support their attribution to Hengelo rather than the cooler, dryer Lower Pleniglacial, but that attribution can only be tentative, pending results of Butzer's sediment study. From the artifact series, I judge that the Acheulean deposits are no older than "last interglacial", but whether they are to be assigned to a full interglacial or an Early Würm interstadial cannot be resolved. I personally suspect them to be quite late.

The artifact series I have examined[27] consist of 305 pieces from the upper horizon and 185 from the lower. Shaped tools (excluding cores) are only 32.2 percent of total artifacts, and because of their low num-

[25]   This observation was recorded in an unpublished annotated list of the Castillo faunas made by Vaufrey many years ago. The list is now in the possession of M.-F. Bonifay, who is revising the faunal remains, and who graciously permitted me to use the information.

[26]   At Cueva Morín, two cleaver flake rich Mousterian of Acheulean Tradition horizons (17, 16) are found in late Lower (Würm) Pleniglacial deposits, however (González Echegaray, Freeman, et al. 1971, 1973; Freeman 1964, 1970).

[27]   My diagnosis of the Castillo Acheulean levels is based on the artifact series in the Provincial Prehistoric Museum in Santander. A search for other pieces from these levels in the Institut de Paléontologie Humaine, Paris, in 1962 was fruitless, although some may have escaped my attention.

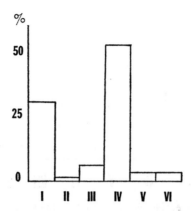

Figure 10. Percentage of total artifacts in the Castillo Acheulean levels (351 Pieces)

Category 1 = Shaped tools.
Category 2 = Levallois Flakes (and points)
Category 3 = Cores.

Category 4 = Unretouched pieces.
Category 5 = Split cobbles.
Category 6 = Geologically crushed pieces.

bers I have combined the two levels for further discussion (Figure 10). Some 54.7 percent of the pieces are unretouched flakes, including very rare blades, and 1.4 percent are Levallois flakes (including one point). Split cobbles are 2.8 percent of pieces, cores are 6 percent and another 2.8 percent have been subjected to heavy (geological) crushing, so that they can no longer be meaningfully typed. Most artifacts are made in quartzite, limestone is abundantly represented, and the shaped tools are generally crude. Much of the waste is rather large, as are many of the flake tools.

The shaped tool series (Figure 11) contains about equal proportions of sidescrapers and denticulated tools (23.9 and 28.3 percent, respectively). In the lower level, denticulates are about three times as abundant as sidescrapers, but the series is small (46 shaped tools), and this disproportion is masked by combining the levels, since sidescrapers are somewhat more abundant than denticulates in the richer upper level. Utilized pieces make up 9.7 percent of the assemblage. Large tools include rabots (1.7 percent), discs (0.9 percent), very abundant choppers and chopping tools (16 percent, with far more chopping tools than choppers) and moderate numbers of bifaces (4.4 percent). The bifaces from the lower level are broken and earlier have passed unrecognized, although they are as frequent as in the upper horizon. The three whole bifaces are rather small (between 18.5 and 25 centimeters long); two are partial cordiforms and one tends toward an irregular

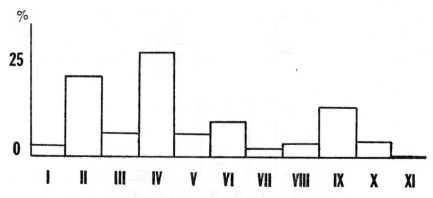

Figure 11.   Percentage of total shaped tools in the Castillo Acheulean levels (113 pieces)

Category 1	Limaces.	Category 7	Rabots.
Category 2	Sidescrapers.	Category 8	Choppers.
Category 3	Notches.	Category 9	Chopping Tools.
Category 4	Denticulates.	Category 10	Bifaces.
Category 5	Other Flake Tools.	Category 11	Discs.
Category 6	Utilized pieces.		

lanceolate shape. Three of the five pieces are limestone, one is ofite, and one is (desilicified) flint. Crude variants of relatively sophisticated tool forms are present in both levels: there are burins in the lower horizon and an endscraper in the upper one. Levallois technique is rare, as are facetted butts.

The overall allure of these two assemblages is vaguely reminiscent of a terribly crude Mousterian of Acheulean Tradition, but the tools are not like any local variant of that facies. The Castillo collections can best be compared in form and workmanship with late French assemblages described by Bordes; the best parallels in proportional representation of the various artifact types are the Pech de l'Azé series of "Riss I" and "Riss II" age (Bordes 1971: especially 7-10).

THE MAGHREB

Acheulean artifact collections from northwestern Africa, between the Sahara and the sea, share striking characteristics with their Iberian counterparts. Pleistocene stratigraphy and the relative chronology of lithic industrial complexes from the Maghreb have received considerable scientific attention, and syntheses of the most salient results of research are easily accessible (Vaufrey 1955; Balout 1958; Alimen

1966). As a result, there is no need in this paper for a comprehensive catalogue and analysis of stratified Acheulean occurrences, and I have been very selective in the material reviewed.

Faunal materials from Acheulean occurrences in the Maghreb are astonishingly abundant and have been competently identified and assessed. For Morocco, the Pleistocene succession of continental and marine cycles has been exceptionally well documented, especially due to Biberson's careful work (1961a, 1964a, 1970, and elsewhere), and may with suitable caution be used as a yardstick for developments in the rest of the Maghreb (Table 3).[28] A comparison with the Iberian sequences yields tentative conclusions about the relative chronology of Acheulean developments across the Mediterraean which could otherwise not be derived.

Amirian Artifact-Bearing Localities

I have excluded from discussion levels and localities whose industrial contents are wholly pre-Acheulean (in the broad sense), although they are briefly mentioned in Table 3. Biberson's terminology for Acheulean stages has been adopted. The earliest true Acheulean in his sense was described by Neuville and Ruhlmann (1941) from the old Schneider quarry working at Sidi Abderrahman.

The ideal stratigraphic sequence they recognized may be summarized, from base to top, as follows:

P.   Pliocene substrate.

O.   Conglomerate of quartzite cobbles: 0.15 meters.

N.   Clayey friable sandstone with fine gravel horizons: 0.60 meters.

M.   Cobble conglomerate in calcareous sandy cement and phosphatic breccia: 0.30 meters. "Clacto-Abbevillian" industry in place atop this level.

L.   Consolidated marly limestone: 0.70 meters.

K.   Fine calcareous limestone: 0.20-0.05 meters.

J.   "Lumachelle" with *Purpura crassilabrum* and *Calyptra trochiformis*: 0.45 meters.

---

[28] Obviously, the Mediterranean littoral faunal sequence is not directly comparable to the Atlantic; different molluscan species are represented in the two areas. It is also true that the "Soltanian" invasion of Atlantic Morocco by European mammalian forms might be later than the arrival of those species in Tunisia and Algeria. The occurrence of "Senegalese" forms in Mediterranean *Strombus* beaches does support their equation with littoral levels bearing Senegalese molluscan forms in Atlantic Morocco and Portugal.

Table 3. Abbreviated Pleistocene stratigraphy for Morocco (after Biberson 1961, 197

	Marine cycle		
Type localities	Typical marine fauna	Date	Name
Schneider quarry at Sidi Abderrahman Shores between +5 and +8 meters	As for Harounian	75,000± to 95,000 years or considerably more	Ouljian
La Cunette Schneider quarry at Sidi Abderrahman From +16 to +18 meters, above a +16 meter platform	*Purpura haemastoma, Patella safiana* "Recent Senegalian fauna"		Harounian
La Cunette Schneider quarry at Sidi Abderrahman Generally between +20 and +28 meters	Earliest appearance of *Purpura haemastoma, Patella safiana.* "Chilo-peruvian" elements disappear gradually. Derived "Sudanese" mammals.	> 200,000 years	Anfatian
Schneider Quarry at Maarif Airport, Tarit I and Tarit II quarries. HIGHEST shoreline about +60 meters	*Purpura (Acanthina) crassilabrum, Calyptra (Trochatella) trochiformis* continue; later "Nordic" elements are added: *Purpura lapillus, Littorina littorea.* Pliocene forms gone.	?	Maarifian
Sidi Messaoud quarries (on a +90 to +95 meter marine platform)	"Chilo-Peruvian fauna" *Purpura (Acanthina) Crassilabrum Calyptra (Trochatella) trochiformis* Pliocene molluscs.	?	Messaoudia

I.   Violet clay with very small cobbles: 0.45 meters.

H.   Dune sandstone with *Helix (Euparypha) pisana:* 13.25 meters.
      Beds D through G accumulated during a later cycle. They fill cuts and caves in the consolidated dune of level H.

G.   Cobble conglomerate with *Purpura haemostoma* and tools: 1 meter.

F.   Soft *Arenicola* sandstone: 0.10 meters.

E.   Conglomerate of very small cobbles in whitish calcareous cement; marine fauna and tools: 1 meter. (Modern interpretations sug-

		Continental cycle		
Name	Date	Typical fauna	Type localities	Industry
Soltanian	10,000± years 32,000± years Base as old as Ouljian	Invasion of European elements. *Cervus* aff. *elaphus, Cervus algeriensis, Sus scrofa, Dicerorhinus kirchbergensis, Ursus arctos,* etc. *Homo sapiens,* "Sudanese" savanna fauna.	La Cunette trench at Sidi Abderrahman	Ibero-Marusian Aterian Mousterian
Presoltanian	Extrapolated	*Homo* spp. "Sudanese" savanna fauna	As for Tensiftian	VIII

Tensiftian	Extrapolated	Evolved *Homo erectus* at Sidi Abderrahman (Grotte des Littorines). "Sudanese" fauna. *Ceratotherium simum, Equus mauritanicus, Alcelaphus probubalis, Connochaetes taurinus, Redunca maupas, Gazella, Hyena.*	Schneider quarry at Sidi Abderrahman; Sidi Abderrahman Extension site	VII VI	Acheulean
Amirian	?	*Homo erectus, Machairodus latidens, Elephas atlanticus, Elephas iolensis, Ceratotherium, Hippopotamus amphibius, Bos, Alcelaphus buselaphus, Equus mauritanicus, Ursos arctos,* and others.	Sidi Abderrahman quarries	V IV III I–II	Acheulean
Saletian	? (Upper Villafranchian)	*Elephas recki.* At Aïn Hanech, analogous formations yielded *Anancus osiris, Stylohipparion libycum, Elephas recki,* and *Omochoerus.*	Salé, near Rabat; Schneider quarry at Maarif Airport		Pre-Acheulean

gest that levels E and F are simply the uppermost sectors of level G).

D. Rose brecciated clayey limestone: 0.75 meters.

C. Degraded dune sandstone: 1.50 meters.

Levels B and A form a continuous capping layer over the sequence, whether or not levels B-G are present.

B. Calcareous crust: 0.02 meters.

A. Red silts: 0.50 meters.

An impoverished mammalian fauna was recovered from the tool-rich horizon at the contact of levels L and M. Unfortunately, it is banal

Table 4.   Mammalian Faunas from selected sites in the Maghreb

Sidi Abderrahman, Ancient Exploitation (M/L contact)	S.T.I.C.	Sidi Abderrahman Grotte des Ours	Ternifine
Ceratotherium simum *Rhinoceros* sp.	*Ceratotherium simum*	*Ceratotherium simum*	*Ceratotherium simum*
	Elephas iolensis	*Elephas iolensis* *Elephas* sp.	*Elephas atlanticus*
Hippopotamus amphibius	*Hippopotamus amphibius*	*Hippopotamus amphibius*	*Hippopotamus amphibius*
	Equus mauritanicus *Bos primigenius*	*Equus mauritanicus*	*Equus mauritanicus* *Bos* sp.
	Alcelaphus buselaphus *Connochaetes taurinus* *Taurotragus derbianus* *T. maroccanus*	*Alcelaphus buselaphus*	*Alcelaphus buselaphus* *Connochaetes taurinus* *Taurotragus* sp.
		Redunca redunca *Gazella atlantica*	*Gazella rufina* *G. cuvieri*
			Camelus thomasi *Camelopardalis giraffa* *Ovis tragelaphus*
			Afrochoerus sp. *Canis anthus*
		Crocuta crocuta	*Crocuta crocuta* *Machairodus latidens* *Hyena striata*
			Felis leo
			Hystrix cristata
		Ursus arctos	Giant baboon *Homo erectus*

(Table 4). Level L is agreed by earlier authors to be a lacustrine formation *sensu lato* (Neuville and Ruhlmann 1941: 43; Lecointre 1952:
8); more specifically the terrestrial mulluscs indicate lagoon deposits:
*Phytra, Leuconia bibersoni, Bulinus, Bithynia, Peringia, Mastusbron-
delii, Euparrypha pisana, E. placenta, Cochlicella conoidea,* and *C. ventricosa* (Neuville and Ruhlmann 1941: 44; Biberson and Jodot 1965:
130-131). To Biberson, this level is to be assigned to the early Amirian,
along with the Acheulean artifact series atop level M.[29] Level K pro-

[29]   The section discussed in my text is a composite of those from the North and
East walls of the Schneider quarry (Neuville and Ruhlmann 1941: 36–43). Levels
C-G are missing from the East wall and levels below J are not represented on the

Sidi Abderrahman Grotte des Littorines	Khebibat	Lake Karar	Sidi Zin
Ceratotherium simum	*Ceratotherium simum*	*Ceratotherium simum*	*Ceratotherium simum*
		Elephas atlanticus	*Elephas atlanticus*
	Hippopotamus amphibius	*Hippopotamus amphibius*	
	Equus mauritanicus	*Equus mauritanicus*	*Equus mauritanicus*
Bos primigenius	*Bos primigenius*	*? Bos primigenius*	*Bos primigenius*
Alcelaphus probubalis	*Alcelaphus buselaphus*	*Alcelaphus buselaphus*	*Alcelaphus buselaphus*
Connochaetes taurinus		*Connochaetes* sp.	*Connochaetes taurinus*
			Taurotragus sp.
	? Bubalus antiquus	*? Bubalus antiquus*	
Hippotragus sp.			
Gazella atlantica	*Gazella atlantica*		*Gazella* sp.
G. dorcas			*Gazella dorcas*
G. cuvieri			*Gazella cuvieri*
			Ovis tragelaphus
	Phacochoerus aethiopicus	*Cervus* cf. *elaphus*	
		Sus scrofa	
Canis anthus			
Crocuta crocuta			
Hyena striata			
Vulpes atlantica			
Mellivora aff. *leucotona*			*Vulpes atlantica*
Monachus albiventer			
Homo sp.	*Homo* sp.		

duced rare molluscs: *Euparypha pisana, Mastus cirtanus, Mastus* cf. *milavianus*. These continental forms indicate a dry, temperate climate (Biberson and Jodot 1965: 131).

The level J lumachelle marks a return of high sea levels. The abundant molluscan fauna includes numerous banal forms (Neuville and Ruhlmann 1941: 45-47), with *Purpura (Acanthina) crassilabrum, Calyptra (Trochatella) trochiformis, Littorina littorea, Purpura lapillus,* and the Pliocene form *Melampus pyramidalis* (Lecointre 1952:

North wall. I have minimized the interpretation given by the authors as it has since been superseded.

83-84).No examples of *Purpura haemostoma* or *Patella safiana* were recovered. The molluscan spectrum is that of a late Maarifian transgressive stage.

The "Grand Dune", level H, contained molluscs appropriate to quite warm and dry temperate climatic conditions: *Euparypha dehnei, E. pisana, Mastus pupa, Mastus jeannoti,* and *Cochlicella ventricosa* (Biberson 1961b: 95; Biberson and Jodot 1965: 132). To Biberson, this dune marks the maximum post-Maarifian marine regression (middle Amirian continental cycle). After some time, the dune was consolidated and karstified, and a following marine transgression deposited levels G through E; both levels G and E contained abundant *Purpura haemostoma* and *Patella safiana* with other (banal) elements (Lecointre 1952: 84); these levels, in turn, are followed by dune deposit Level C) and later, a calcareous crust formed at the top of this horizon. Such crusts have been taken to indicate seasonally heavier-than-modern rainfall, alternating with periods of evaporation (Margat, Raynal, and Taltasse 1954). The calcareous crust and associated "limon rouge" are evidently horizons of a fossil soil, which may antedate the Ouljian marine cycle, although some post-Ouljian crusts are evidently known (Biberson 1961a: 156-157). Margat, Raynal, and Taltase state that such massive calcareous crusts are not associated with Holocene soil development in the region (1954: 28).

The industry from level M has been artificially subdivided on the basis of surface abrasion.[30] Some of the pieces, including mostly choppers and chopping tools, are assigned to the latest Pre-Acheulean, while the fresher specimens are distributed in two Early Acheulean "stages", I and II. Distinctions between the two stages may be arbitrary. Artifacts include choppers and chopping tools, chunky bifacial pieces, trihedral picks, cleavers, and flakes. The bifacial pieces are often made on flakes and most are coarsely worked, but some better finished pieces made with soft-hammer technique are represented (Biberson

---

[30] The assignment of artifacts to different stages of industrial development on the basis of the degree to which they have been subjected to postdepositional alteration, and in particular Biberson's distinction between the latest Pre-Acheulean and the two early phases of Acheulean development (Acheulean stages I and II) in the series from Sidi Abderrahman level M (Biberson 1961b: 132–137) is of dubious validity. I have known it to produce entirely spurious (but seemingly plausible) results. The basis of the distinction of Acheulean stage I from stage II, and of both from the tools assigned to the Evolved Pre-Acheulean should be regarded as speculative, and the definitions of and distinctions between the two Acheulean subdivisions must be subject to future confirmation. All the artifacts within and on level M COULD belong to a single earlier Acheulean industrial complex.

1961b: 155).

Neuville and Ruhlmann figure an interesting artifact series including a convergent denticulate, a large bec, two tip-skewed bifaces and some well finished cleavers and cleaver flakes. Many of the pieces are only summarily worked on the ventral surface. The illustrated artifact series has many obvious close analogies with the Torralba/Ambrona assemblages.

The S.T.I.C. quarry is the locality for Acheulean stage III (the last stage of Biberson's *Acheuléen Ancien*). Atop Cambrian sandstone, there is a conglomerate (F) with *Purpura lapillus* and *Littorina littorea* (the so-called "Nordic" elements of the late Maarifian), overlain by a lumachelle (E) with the same molluscan fauna. Above these levels, there is a deposit of "white vacuolar limestone" (D) with *Euparypha pisana, Cochlicella barbara,* a mammalian fauna (Table 4) and Acheulean artifacts. A deep dune sandstone (C), equivalent to level H at the Sidi-Abderrahman Old Workings, covered by a *limon rouge* with associated calcareous crust (levels A and B), completes the series (Biberson 1961a: 97-99; 1961b: 156-160). The tools from level D comprise choppers and chopping tools, bolas and spheroids, many bifaces and trihedrals, rare cleavers, numerous trimming flakes, some waste flakes, and abundant broken pieces. Lanceolate and nearly lageniform bifaces are shown; there is a tendency for bifaces and trihedrals to have long, narrow points. One tip-skewed piece is illustrated. Duck-billed or "spatulate" bifaces are also mentioned and figured. Some of the cleavers have relatively narrow bits, and ovate or triangular edges (Biberson 1964b: 49-50; 1961b: 179-84). The artifacts include some very fine and symmetrical pieces (Biberson 1961b: 172, Plate 59, number 120); regular patterning is considerably more in evidence than was the case for Stages I and II. Nothing in the Iberian sequence is quite comparable, although there are some (small) spatulate bifaces at Torralba and Ambrona.

The main distinguishing feature which sets Biberson's Stage IV (the earliest Middle Acheulean phase) apart from the Early Acheulean is the appearance of the "prepared core" (Biberson 1961b: 203). While some of the figured pieces might be proto-Levallois cores, it is the presence of regular recognizable nuclei that is the diagnostic of this phase, not the appearance of Levallois technique *sensu stricto,* to judge from the figures. But, since the number of uncontaminated occurrences of artifacts from Early Acheulean contexts is very small indeed, the supposed absence of true cores from "earlier" stages may be due to factors other than their evolutionary position. With the exception of the cores, the other artifacts from Stage IV at Sidi Abderrahman Extension are very similar to tools in the Early Acheulean.

Acheulean Stage V is the last developmental phase found in Amirian sediments. The type site is the Grotte des Ours, a cave hollowed out of the kastified "Grand Dune". Three marine horizons (G_0, G_1, G_2) at the base of the cave fill produced paleontological and archeological materials. Marine shells in these levels include abundant *Purpura haemostoma*. Associated mammalian fossils are listed in Table 4, but it is unfortunately impossible to ascertain the exact provenience of these forms. Artifacts of this stage include the same range of types as earlier levels, but trihedral pieces are lacking and most of the bifaces are quite small. Apiculate and duck-billed pieces are no longer found. Ovate and crude lanceolate bifaces are figured. There are a few cleavers. Stage V has less "character" than the Early Acheulean stages (Biberson 1961b: 221-230). Again, the characteristics Biberson has used to define the stage might well have other than phylogenetic significance.

Ternifine

This site, known since 1870, yielded a large (and, as yet, inadequately described) Acheulean artifact series and a fauna which may best be correlated with Moroccan Amirian faunal complexes. The site is a depression fed by artesian springs. Prehistoric discoveries were made in a basal grey clay horizon and overlying sands. Most noteworthy is the discovery of human remains assignable to *Homo erectus,* and nearly indistinguishable from some specimens of Peking Man (Arambourg 1955, and elsewhere). The only available data for dating purposes are the fossils and the tools, regrettably. The faunal list is shown in Table 4.

For chronological purposes, the occurrence of *Elephas atlanticus* in the Ternifine beds is not especially critical. *Elephas atlanticus* and *Elephas iolensis,* found at Sidi Abderrahman, seem to be broadly contemporary forms with slightly different ecological requirements (Arambourg 1952, 1960).[31] The gazelle is rather suggestive: it is thought to be a forest form (Arambourg 1957: 68). However, there is also an extinct camel in the assemblage. Finds of *Afrochoerus (Notochoerus)* and *Machairodus* suggest respectable antiquity, although sabre-teeth survived fairly late in parts of Europe. As far as I am aware, the giant baboon has not been described, aside from a suggestion that it belongs

[31] Incidentally, there is a tantalizing identification of *Elephas iolensis* in "Level III" (Tayacian?) at Cova Negra near Valencia, Spain (Fletcher Valls 1957: 8, Plate VII; Viñes Masip et al. 1947:29).

to the Mandrill group (Arambourg 1954, 1955, 1956), and is perhaps closely related to *Dinopithecus* or *Gorgopithecus* (Arambourg 1956; Arambourg and Hoffstetter 1963).

The lithic artifacts number over 650. They include choppers, chopping tools, trihedrals, bifaces, cleavers, retouched flake tools, hammerstones, and waste. Only the large tools have been studied in any detail. The bifaces are especially indicative. The series includes amygdaloids (two with skewed tips are figured), thick and very acuminate trihedrals, and spatulate or duck-billed forms, as well as cordiforms. Narrow-nosed, chisel-ended handaxes seem possibly significant for correlation. Most of the cleavers are really cleaver flakes. Ventral retouch on the bifacial pieces is often summary (Balout, Biberson, and Tixier 1967). As will be remembered, these characteristics can be most closely matched in Biberson's Acheulean Stage III from the S.T.I.C. quarry. As was stressed above, the really distinctive forms which characterize this stage are not in the Torralba/Ambrona inventory, although the Iberian series are clearly to be compared with Biberson's Early Acheulean. It is entirely possible that the Ternifine collection is temporally heterogeneous, but if the artifact series is a single, more or less synchronous aggregate, and if its formal characteristics are any indication of age, the collection could even be later than the Torralba/Ambrona assemblages. There are chisel-ended bifaces in the San Isidro lower horizon (see Figure 6), interestingly. These observations are no more than suggestive; it would be very dangerous to attempt refined stratigraphic subdivision of the Early Acheulean on typological grounds.

Tensiftian Artifact-Bearing Localities.

The Grotte des Littorines is one of the numerous cavities in the consolidated "Grand Dune". The basal level filling the cave, level G, is a reworked beach deposit with *Purpura haemostoma*. After partial consolidation, this level was corroded and solution cavities filled with sandy deposits which are laterally continuous with the pink brecciated limestone of basal level D (Biberson 1961a: 149-154; 1961b: 267). These deposits contained a rich fauna (Table 4), a late Middle Acheulean artifact series (Stage VI) and "Sidi Abderrahman Man," two human mandible fragments with teeth (Arambourg and Biberson 1955, 1956). The human remains may be an "evolved" *Homo erectus*, but are so fragmentary that they are best assigned to *Homo* spp. pending further evidence.

The most noteworthy feature of the faunal list is the presence of three gazelle species. One, *Gazella atlantica*, is only known as a fossil. *Gazella dorcas* is presently restricted to arid (semi-desertic) areas. *Gazella cuvieri* is a mountain dweller at present (Arambourg 1957: 50). Arambourg notes that the radiation of antelopes into the Maghreb seems to have occurred during the late Pleistocene (Arambourg 1951: 55).

The collection which typifies Acheulean Stage VI numbers only 254 pieces. It includes choppers and chopping tools, bifaces, cleavers, bifacial sidescrapers, discs, hammers, and utilized and waste flakes. The bifaces are well made, often symmetrical amygdaloid and lanceolate forms. One small proto-cordiform was recovered. Retouch is often extensive, covering both faces of the piece and obliterating the characteristics of the flake on which it was made. Cleavers and cleaver flakes are more hastily finished. A series of cordiform convergent sidescrapers, almost "unifacial bifaces" is also figured. This series would be difficult to distinguish from some Late Acheulean assemblages.

At the Sidi Abderrahman Extension site, a layer of powdery limestone thought to date from the Middle Tensiftian yielded the typeseries for Acheulean Stage VII. Artifacts recovered *in situ* are not abundant. They include chopper/chopping tools and an extremely variable biface series, as well as cleavers and flake tools. The bifaces include gross and archaic looking forms as well as relatively well finished lanceloates, some quite large. Truly diagnostic of this stage are flat oval "limandes," abundant in the powdery limestone horizon. Some are quite small. There are cleaver flakes which are similar to those in the Cantabrian Mousterian. Scrapers, including limaces, are figured, with some true Levallois flakes. In general, parts of this artifact series are strikingly similar to pieces from the +15 to 25 meter terrace sites along the Manzanares.

The Mifsud-Giudice Quarry (Khébibat)

Although no Acheulean artifacts were recovered there, the importance of the Khébibat site is such that it should be mentioned here.

In 1933, fragments of a primitive looking human skull (including bits of maxilla and mandible) were collected from this quarry by J. Marçais (1934). The stratigraphy was later revised in the field by Neuville and Ruhlmann (1944).

The basal level (J) was consolidated sand, probably an ancient dune, atop a platform at present mean sea level. Above this came the following levels:

I.   Semi-consolidated lumachelle with abundant *Littorina obtussata, L. littorea* and *L. saxatilis,* lacking either *Purpura haemastoma* or *Patella safiana* (1 meter). Neither *Calyptra trochiformis* nor *Purpura crassilabrum* was recovered. *Nassa incrassata,* presently found in North Africa only to Mauritania, is noted as well as an abundant banal fauna.

H.   Marine sandstone: 2.20 meters.

G.   Semi-compact lumachelle with fauna like I above.

F.   Consolidated dune sand with some marine shells.

E.   Very compact, cemented lumachelle with *Purpura haemastoma,* less varied molluscan species than I or G (0.70 meters). No *Littorina* was found in this level.

D.   Deep (4.80 meters) consolidated dune with human remains, fauna as in Table 4.

The sequence is continued by a reworked marine conglomerate with *Purpura haemastoma* and *Patella safiana,* a clay, a dune, and *limons rouges* (Neuville and Ruhlmann 1944: 75-77, 85-87). Biberson's correlation (1964a: 518) of level D and the middle Tensiftian seems unassailable on the basis of the sediments and molluscs. The mammalian fauna, on the other hand, is not extremely instructive, but does include an interesting element, the wart-hog, which at present is an open-country dweller.

Sidi Zin

Near Le Kef (Tunisia), this important stratified site was first recognized in 1942, and then excavated by Gobert (1950). Probable Acheulean assemblages were found in three distinct strata beneath a thick calcareous crust. Of all the Maghreb sites dealt with so far, the Sidi Zin levels offer the most insurance against contamination by stratigraphically heterogeneous artifactual materials.

The Lower Level, resting atop sterile sands, is a 20-30 centimeter conglomerate of Calcareous cobbles. The Middle Level is 0.50-0.75 meters of soft grey sandstone. The Upper Level is a thin gravel horizon underlying a "tufa" (better described as simply a crust) up to 1 meter deep (Gobert 1950: 5-9). All four horizons contained fauna (Table 4) but the crust has only *Equus, Alcelaphus, Bos,* and *Ovis,* and no gazelle, while *Elephas* is only present in the Lower Level. Although some other forms are absent from one or another of the artifact-bearing horizons,

their fluctuations do not seem to have climatic or chronological significance. The mammals can be compared to the "Sudanese" savanna
fauna of the Tensiftian and Presoltanian.

The artifacts from the lower level include choppers, chopping
tools, rabots, blunt bifaces, and fine lanceolate handaxes of small
sizes as well as flake tools. Called Micoquian (Gobert 1950: 16),
the assemblage has points of resemblance with Acheulean Stage VI
in Morocco, but the bifaces are extremely fine, small specimens, clearly
more like pieces from the Late Acheulean (Stage VII?). The Middle
Level has a cleaver-flake rich artifact series, including specimens
whose finish and allure is Acheulean in my opinion. Certain of the
artifacts figured can be matched in the Manzanares +15-25 meter
terraces, but many of the "bifaces" are actually unifacial. The Upper
Level is like the Lower, lacking the extensive cleaver-flake suite found
in the intervening horizon. Some artifacts of Mousterian allure, including a crude biface, were recovered from the crust (Gobert 1950:
10-24). The diagnostic forms of the Sudanese savanna fauna are no
longer present in the crust, perhaps suggesting that the age of those
deposits might be correlated with the Moroccan Soltanian.

Ouzidane (Algeria)

Conglomerates at +50-60 meters relative elevation on the right bank
of the Oued Saf-Saf near Tlemcen contain bifacial tools of Middle
or Late Acheulean allure (Vaufrey 1955: 52-54). Unfortunately, the
age of this interesting series cannot be determined on present evidence.

Presoltanian Acheulean Series

Mieg de Boofzheim and Plessis excavated an artifact series at the
Grotte du Rhinoceros, Sidi Abderrahman, which they described as
biface-bearing lower Mousterian (1954). At Cap Chatelier, similar
tools were recovered by Biberson from the "brecciated pink limestone",
attributed to the Presoltanian (Biberson 1961b: 332–385). Over 1700
artifacts were recovered, including the ever-present chopper/chopping
tools, a large flake tool series, bifaces, cleaver flakes, cores, and
waste. The biface series from Cap Chatelier includes ovates, lanceolates,
near discs, and picks as well as small triangular and cordiform pieces.
Some of the bifaces are less than 5 centimeters long. Scrapers are well

represented, and include some bifacially retouched pieces. Cleaver flakes indentical to those from the Cantabrian Mousterian are documented. Biberson (1961b: 335-385) assigns these pieces to the latest Acheulean (Stage VIII). It may be that his classification is correct for the Maghreb, but to me the series is indistinguishable from the Cantabrian Mousterian of Acheulean Tradition (González Echegaray, Freeman, et al. 1971, 1973; Freeman 1964, 1966, 1970). The data from Cap Chatelier and the Grotte du Rhinoceros, combined with other evidence from the Sidi Abderrahman quarries, make the distinction seem purely arbitrary, in that they indicate considerable continuity between the Stage VIII materials and those from earlier and clearly Acheulean collections.

Aïn Fritissa (Morocco)

At this site, a resurgent spring (still active) has deposited a dome of alternating clayey, often ferruginized sand levels, sometimes quite consolidated. Excavations were conducted at the site by Ruhlmann, and Tixier has published his discoveries along with pieces recovered during periodic spring cleanings and surface collections. Unfortunately, the stratigraphic provenience of the artifacts is usually not known. Tixier's excellent publication (1960) makes it obvious that tools of various periods are represented. In addition to fine limandes and lanceolate bifaces, quite similar to pieces from Biberson's Acheulean Stage VII, there are distinctive cleaver flakes like those from Stage VIII and a large series of flake tools, including several Aterian tanged pieces. Renewed excavation at this locality should be rewarding.

Lake Karar (Algeria)

Like Ternifine, prehistoric Lake Karar was a spring-fed basin, but in this case the resulting lake was and still is very small. The lake was formerly some 100 meters in diameter; its maximum dimension is now only some 40 meters. Artifacts, fauna, and worked wood have been gathered from a sandy gravel on the lake bed during periodic dredging of the bottom (Boule 1900).

The faunal list (Table 4) taken alone would seem to indicate a Soltanian age for the materials recovered from the lake-bottom, judging from the presence of *Cervus* and *Sus*. However, the artifact series has more archaic aspects than would be compatible with such a late date. The explanation certainly resides in the fact that neither the artifacts nor the fauna represents a single, short-term accumulation; they are temporally very heterogeneous, contrary to Boule's opinion (1900:18). The earliest artifacts typologically are crude lanceolate, ovate, duck-billed, and bevel-ended bifaces which, if found alone, might well be assigned to Biberson's Stage III; in any case, they seem typologically appropriate to the Early Acheulean (Vaufrey 1955: 74). Better finished forms like Middle and Late Acheulean types and apparently Mousterian artifacts were also recovered and one polished axe was found in the vicinity (but not in lake bottom sediments). The lake has obviously been an attractive and dependable water source for hundreds of millenia.

Synthesis and Critique

A brief and critical summary of this lengthy but still inadequate presentation may hopefully indicate directions for future research.

a.   The Pleistocene natural history and cultural sequence from the Atlantic coast of Morocco has been subject to intense study, and, within limits, is better understood than the Iberian sequences I have surveyed. Much more work needs to be done in both areas, but especially in the Iberian Peninsula. On the other hand, we do not have a single adequately excavated and reported intact Acheulean occupation surface from the Maghreb, and there are certainly sites uniting the requisite conditions for such investigations (Sidi Zin and Aïn Fritissa are both excellent prospects in this regard).

b.   Far more attention must be paid to Portuguese littoral faunas. The presence of *Purpura haemastoma* in the "15 meter" beach level and *Patella safiana* in the "6 meter" beach at Arrabida may be a reflection of the same explosive radiation of these species that occurred during the Anfatian transgression, although temporally the two forms would have reached Portugal somewhat later than Morocco. In any case, the molluscs are a valuable and relatively neglected horizon marker. If the absolute beach elevations have any significance, the presence and position of those molluscs would help confirm that most artifact occurrences along the Portuguese littoral are very recent. Equally pressing is the need for intensive geomorphological and paleontological investigations on both the Iberian and Maghrebian coasts. A concerted attempt to establish regional stratigraphic correlations where they may be discerned, and, equally important, to establish absolute chronologies where possible must be among our primary goals.

c. Acheulean industries from the Iberian Peninsula are most similar to those from the Maghreb, and vice versa. The detailed sequence of industrial development proposed for the best known area within the Maghreb, Atlantic Morocco, can be used as a comparative scale against which the Iberian collections may be ordered. To the extent that the Moroccan scheme reflects purely temporal/phylogenetic development, rather than difference due to chance, raw material choice, the uses of the artifacts or stylistic differences between contemporaneous assemblages, the resultant ordering may be expected to have chronological implications. On the basis of such comparison, the Torralba/Ambrona assemblages (the oldest known in Spain) and the collection from the Sidi Abderrahman Old Workings, Level L/M contact, form a unit. Pre-Acheulean industries precede the Moroccan collections, while such materials are not conclusively known from Iberia.[32] The absence of artifact series in deposits demonstrably earlier than "Amirian" from Spain and Portugal is puzzling, and suggests either that sediments of comparable age have not been identified or studied in Iberia or that the first movement of peoples into the Iberian Peninsula did not occur until quite late. Early artifact collections from France do not resemble the Spanish or Maghreb materials at all closely. In fact, that is true throughout the Acheulean. Improbable though it may seem, this observation suggests that one route of expansion of Acheulean hunters from Africa to the Iberian Peninsula may have been direct, including passage of the Strait of Gibraltar, rather than following the Atlantic Coast. Iberia and North Africa continued to form a distinct "cultural province" at least until Würm.

Materials from the basal levels at San Isidro may have their closest parallels with artifacts from Biberson's Acheulean Stage III. Still crude in appearance, the San Isidro collection contains biface forms which have been said to be somewhat more "evolved" than those from Sidi Abderrahman level L/M contact; however, they are quite close to the Ternifine series, made by *Homo erectus*. Neither the Toledo

---

[32] Such pre-Acheulean industries have been claimed to exist in Spain and Portugal, based on the occurrence of crude choppers and chopping tools in unstratified or undatable contexts. However, such implements persist into the post-Pleistocene period. The "Asturian" complex in Cantabria, dated to 7000–9000 B.P., is an example. An even more striking case is the recognition of a definitely Upper Paleolithic artifact series consisting almost exclusively of chopper/chopping tools, protobiface like forms and flakes at Budinho (Echaide 1971). Such discoveries make it evident that typology alone is insufficient proof of the existence of a pre-Acheulean industrial complex in Iberia.

terrace series nor the Portuguese occurrences are well enough characterized to permit such typological comparisons: they seem to be quarry and workshop debris, by and large. I do not find any indication of considerable antiquity for either the Tejo terrace Acheulean or its coastal counterpart.

Artifacts from the +15-25 meter Manzanares terraces seem roughly similar to types which characterize Biberson's Stage VII, although some could be latest Middle Acheulean. The Castillo Acheulean has no parallels in the Maghreb sequence through Stage VII, but is very probably somewhat later. Stage VIII looks strikingly similar to the Cantabrian cleaver flake rich Mousterian of Acheulean Tradition which persists to Hengelo.

Obviously, typology is a fickle mistress, especially when abused. These suggested comparisons might well prove to be unfounded, should any of the conditions outlined in the first paragraph of this section prove false. Only much further careful investigation of intact occupation sites in good stratigraphic context coupled with intensive regional geomorphological and paleontological work will substantiate or refute the tentative ordering here proposed.[33]

[33]   Both in the Maghreb and Iberia, the most common large Pleistocene mammals are less than ideal as chronological horizon markers. In some cases, detailed studies of the skeletal morphology of a single species, given a large enough sample of individual animals, may reveal progressive changes within the species that are useful for dating purposes in a small region (de Aguirre 1968, 1969a, 1969b), but this evidence can only be used in combination with many other kinds of information. Cross-regional relative chronologies based exclusively on infraspecific variation within a single taxon are unjustifiable, since such variation depends on genetic differences which always reflect many other factors in addition to position in phylogenetic sequence. Claims, for example, that Torralba might be Upper Pleistocene because the subspecies of *Equus caballus* from that site is morphologically similar to skeletal populations known from France at such a late time, are based on an inadequate understanding of the genetic basis of inheritance and the nature of subspecific variation among living animal populations.

Animal populations in France and Spain were separated by topographic barriers to dispersal and gene flow. The effectiveness of those barriers undoubtedly varied from time to time, and it is not likely that breeding populations on either side of the Pyrenees were ever complete reproductive isolates. While some genetic material would have doubtless been interchanged between local breeding populations, adaptation to different ecosystems coupled with the effects of genetic drift would be expected to produce noticeable differences between them. Any expectation that throughout the Pleistocene populations in France and Spain must have been morphologically continuous runs counter to present understandings of the mechanisms of inheritance, the process of evolution, and the nature of the subspecies as an evolving natural unit.

Microfaunas, noticeably more morphologically sensitive to climatic, geographic, and temporal difference than their more mobile and slower maturing larger counterparts, hold more potential for the regional periodization of the Pleistocene,

REFERENCES

ALÍA MEDINA, M.
1945 Notas morfológicas de la región toledana. *Las Ciencias* 10:91–114.
ALÍA MEDINA, M., O. RIBA
1957 *Livret-guide de l'excursion C4: Manzanares et Tolede.* INQUA, V Congrès International, Madrid-Barcelona.
ALIMEN, H.
1966 *Atlas de Préhistoire. Tome II. Préhistoire de l'Afrique.* Paris: N. Boubée.
ALMAGRO BASCH, M.
1954 "El paleolítico español," in *Historia de España.* Edited by R. Menéndez Pidal, 1(1):245–485.
ARAMBOURG, C.
1949 Sur la presence dans la Villafranchienne d'Algérie de vestiges eventuelles d'industrie humaine. *Comptes Rendus de l'Academie des Sciences* 229:66–67.
1951 La succession des faunes mammalogiques en Afrique du Nord au cours du tertiaire et du Quaternaire. *Compte Rendu des Séances de la Société Biogéographique* 241:49–56.
1952 Note préliminaire sur quelques Éléphants fossiles de Berberie. *Bulletin du Muséum, 2e series* 24(4):407–418.
1954 L'Atlanthropus de Ternifine. *Libyca* 2:425–439.
1955 Le gisement de Ternifine et l'Atlanthropus. *Bulletin de la Société Préhistorique Française* 52: 94–95.
1956 Les fouilles du gisement de Ternifine et l'Atlanthropus (1954 à 1956). Congrès Préhistorique de France. *Compte Rendu de la 15e Session*, 171–177.
1957 Observations sur les gazelles fossiles du Pléistocéne supérieur de l'Afrique du Nord. *Bulletin de la Société d'Histoire Naturelle de l'Afrique du Nord* 48:49–81.
1960 Au sujet de *Elephas iolensis* Pomel. *Bulletin d'Archéologie Marocaine* 3:93–105.
ARAMBOURG, C., P. BIBERSON
1955 Découverte de vestiges humains acheuléens dans la carrière de Sidi Abd-er-rahmann, près Casablanca. *Comptes Rendus de l'Academie des Sciences, Paris.* 240:1661–1663.
1956 The fossil human remains from the Paleolithic site of Sidi Abderrahman (Morocco). *American Journal of Physical Anthropology*, n.s. 14(3):467–490.
ARAMBOURG, C., R. HOFFSTETTER
1963 *Le gisement de Ternifine I.* Archives de l'Institut de Paléontologie Humaine, Memoire 32.

but, largely due to the inadequacy of older recovery techniques, are infrequently reported from earlier Pleistocene human occupation levels from Iberia and the Maghreb, and some of the extant finds have gone unanalyzed. There is a pressing need for more work like that of Jaeger (1970) with mammalian microfauna, and for intensified investigations of molluscan fauna like those exemplified by the work of Lecointre, Biberson, and Jodot.

ARANEGUI, P.
1927   Las terrazas cuaternarias del río Tajo entre Aranjuez y Talavera de la Reina. *Boletín de la Real Sociedad Española de Historia Natural* 27:285–290.
BALOUT, L.
1958   *Algérie préhistorique.* Paris: Arts et Metiers Graphiques.
BALOUT, L., P. BIBERSON, J. TIXIER
1967   L'Acheuléen de Ternifine (Algérie), gisement de l'Atlanthrope. *L'anthropologie* 71:217–237.
BALOUT, L., J. TIXIER
1956   L'Acheuléen de Ternifine. *Actes du 15e Congrés préhistorique de France,* 214–218.
BIBERSON, P.
1961a   *Le cadre paléogéographique de la préhistoire du Maroc atlantique.* Publications du Service des Antiquités du Maroc 16.
1961b   *Le Paléolithique inférieur du Maroc atlantique.* Publications du Service des Antiquités du Maroc, Fasc. 17.
1964a   La place des hommes du Paléolithique marocain dans la chronologie du Pléistocene atlantique. *L'anthropologie* 68:475–526.
1964b   Le hachereau dans l'Acheuléen du Maroc Atlantique. *Libyca* 2: 39–61.
1964c   *Torralba et Ambrona. Notes sur deux stations acheuléenes de chasseurs d'éléphants de la Vielle Castille.* Diputacion Provincial de Barcelona, Instituto de Prehistoria y Arqueología Monografías 6:201–248
1968   Les gisements Acheuléens de Torralba et Ambrona (Espagne). Nouvelles Précisions. *L'anthropologie* 72:241–278.
1970   Index cards on the marine and continental cycles of the Moroccan Quaternary. *Quaternaria* 13:1–76.
BIBERSON, P., E. DE AGUIRRE
1965   Expériences de taille d'outils préhistoriques dans des os d'éléphant. *Quaternaria* 7:165–183.
BIBERSON, P., K. W. BUTZER, T. LYNCH (erroneously listed as D. Collins)
1970   *El yacimiento Acheulense de Ambrona.* Universidad de Madrid, Publicaciones del Departamento de Paleontología 10:7–23.
BIBERSON, P., P. JODOT
1965   Faunes de mollusques continentaux du Pléistocène de Casablanca (Maroc). Essai de conclusions paléoclimatiques. *Notes du Service Géologique du Maroc* 25:115–170.
BORDES, F.
1953a   Essai de classification des industries "Moustériennes." *Bulletin de la Société Préhistorique Française* 50:457–466.
1953b   *Recherches sur les limons quaternaires du bassin de la Seine.* Paris: Masson.
1961   *Typologie du Paléolithique ancien et moyen.* Bordeaux: Delmas.
1971   Observations sur l'Acheuléen des grottes en Dordogne. *Munibe* 23:5–23.
BOULE, M.
1900   Étude paléontologique et archéologique sur la station paléolithique

du Lac Karar (Algérie). *L'anthropologie* 11:1–21.

BREUIL, H., H. OBERMAIER
1912 Les premiers travaux de l'Institut de Paléontologie Humaine. *L'anthropologie* 23:1–27.
1913 Institut de Paléontologie Humaine. Travaux exécutés en 1912. *L'anthropologie* 24:1–16.
1914 Institut de Paléontologie Humaine. Travaux de l'année 1913, II: Travaux en Espagne. *L'anthropologie* 25:233–253.

BREUIL, H., G. ZBYSZEWSKI
1942 Contribution à l'étude des industries paléolithiques du Portugal et de leurs rapports avec la géologie du Quaternaire, volume one. *Comunicações dos Serviços Geológicos de Portugal* 23.
1945 Contribution à l'étude des industries paléolithiques du Portugal et de leurs rapports avec la géologie du Quaternaire, volume two. *Comunicações dos Serviços Geológicos de Portugal* 26.

BUTZER, K. W.
i.p. Pleistocene littoral-sedimentary cycles of the Mediterranean basin: a Mallorquin view. *Papers of Burg Wartenstein Symposium* 58.
1965 Acheulean occupation sites at Torralba and Ambrona: their geology. *Science* 150:1718–1722.
1967 Geomorphology and stratigraphy of the Paleolithic site of Budiño (Prov. Pontevedra, Spain). *Eiszeitalter und Gegenwart* 18:82–103.
1971 *Environment and archaeology* (second edition). Chicago: Aldine.

CABRÉ, J., P. WERNERT
1916 *El Paleolítico inferior de Puente Mocho*. Comisión de Investigaciones Paleontológicas y Prehistóricas, Memoria II.

CARTAILHAC, E.
1886 *Les ages préhistoriques de l'Espagne et du Portugal*. Paris: Reinwald.

CHOFFAT, P.
1898 Note sur les tufs de Condeixa et la découverte de l'hippopotame en Portugal. *Communicacões da Direcção des Trabalhos Geológicos de Portugal* 3:1–12.

CHOFFAT, P., G. DOLLFUS
1907 Quelques cordons littoraux marins du Pléistocéne du Portugal. *Communicacões da Commissão do Serviço Geológico de Portugal* 6:158–173.

CLARK, G.
1971 "The Asturian of Cantabria: a re-evaluation." Unpublished Ph.D. dissertation, The University of Chicago.

CLARK, J. D.
1960 Human ecology during Pleistocene and later times in Africa south of the Sahara. *Current Anthropology* 1:307–324.

CLOUDSLEY-THOMPSON, J. L.
1967 *Animal twilight*. London: G. T. Foulis.

CORNWALL, I. W.
1956 *Bones for the archaeologist*. London: Phoenix House.

738   LESLIE G. FREEMAN

CRANDALL, L. S.
1964   *Management of wild mammals in captivity*. Chicago: The University of Chicago Press.
DE AGUIRRE, E.
1964a Los elefantes de las terrazas medias de Toledo y la edad de estos depositos. *Notas y Comunicaciones del Instituto Geológico y Minero de Espana* 76:295–296.
1964b *Las Gándaras de Budiño, Porriño (Pontevedra)*. Excavaciones Arqueológicas en España 31.
1968   Revisión sistemáticade de los Elephantidae por su morfología y morfometría dentaria (primera parte). *Estudios Geológicos* 24: 109–167.
1968   Revisión sistemática de los Elephantidae por su morfología y morfometría dentaria (segunda parte). *Estudios Geológicos* 25: 123–177.
1969b Revisión sistemática de los Elephantidae por su morfología y morformetría dentaria (tercera parte). *Estudios Geológicos* 25: 317–367.
DE AGUIRRE, E., D. COLLINS, J. CUENCA
1964   Perspectivas del paleolítico inferior en España. *Noticiario Arqueológico Hispánico* 6:7–14.
DE AGUIRRE, E., C. FUENTES
1971   *Los vertebrados fósiles de Torralba y Ambrona*. Études sur le Quaternaire dans le Monde. Union Internationale pour l'étude du Quaternaire, VIII Congrès, Paris 1969.
DE CERRALBO, MARQÚES
1909   *El alto Jalón. Descubrimientos arqueológicos*. Madrid: Establecimiento tipográfico Fortanet.
1911   "Páginas de la historia patria." Unpublished manuscript.
1913   Torralba, la plus ancienne station humaine de l'Europe? *Comptes Rendus, XIVeme session, Congrés International d'Anthropologie et d'Archéologie préhistorique*, 277–290.
DE PRADO, C.
1864   *Descripción física y geológica de la Provincia de Madrid*. Madrid: Junta Superior de Estadística.
DE TERRA, H.
1956   "Climatic terraces and the Paleolithic of Spain," in *Libro Homenaje al Conde de la Vega del Sella:* 47–63.
DE VERNEUIL, E., L. LARTET
1863   Note sur un silex taillé trouvé dans le diluvium des environs de Madrid. *Bulletin de la Société Géologique de France* (second series) 20:698–702.
ECHAIDE, M. D.
1971   La industria lítica del yacimiento de Budiño (Pontevedra, España). *Munibe* 23(1):125–154.
ERHART, H.
1956   La genèse des sols en tant que phénomène géologique. Masson, Paris (Second edition 1967).

FLETCHER VALLS, D.
1957   *La Cova Negra de Játiva*. Nota informativa, V INQUA Congress. Diputación Provincial, Valencia.

FLORSCHÜTZ, F., J. MENÉNDEZ-AMOR, T. A. WIJMSTRA
1971   Palynology of a thick Quaternary succession in southern Spain. *Palaeogeography, Palaeoclimatology and Palaeoecology* 10:233–264.

FONTES, J.
1916   Station paléolithique de Mealhada. *Communicações da Commissão do Serviço Geológico* 11:7–15.
1917   Instruments paléolithiques dans la collection de Préhistoire du Service Géologique. *Communicações da Commissão do Serviço Geológico de Portugal* 12:1–16.

FREEMAN, L. G.
i.p.   "The analysis of some occupation floor distributions from Earlier and Middle Paleolithic sites in Spain," in *Behavioral aspects of paleoanthropology*. Edited by Leslie G. Freeman. The Hague: Mouton.
1964   "Mousterian developments in Cantabrian Spain." Unpublished Ph.D. dissertation, The University of Chicago.
1966   The nature of Mousterian facies in Cantabrian Spain. *American Anthropologist* 68(2, 2):230–237.
1970   El Musteriense Cantábrico: nuevas perspectivas. *Ampurias* 31-32: 55–69.
1973   The significance of mammalian faunas from Paleolithic occupations in Cantabrian Spain. *American Antiquity* 38(1):3–44.

FREEMAN, L. G., K. W. BUTZER
1966   The Acheulean station of Torralba (Spain): a progress report. *Quaternaria* 8:9–21.

GAUDRY, A.
1895   Le gisement de San Isidro, près Madrid. *L'anthropologie* 6:615.

GLADFELTER, B.
1971   *Meseta and Campiña landforms in Central Spain*. University of Chicago, Geography Research Paper 130.

GOBERT, E.-G.
1950   Le gisement paléolithique de Sidi Zin. *Karthago* 1:1–64.

GONZÁLEZ ECHEGARAY, J.
1959   El Paleolítico inferior de los alrededores de Altamira. *Altamira* 1958:5–25.

GONZÁLEZ ECHEGARAY, J., L. G. FREEMAN, et al.
1971   *Cueva Morín. Excavaciones 1966–1968*. Santander: Patronato de las Cuevas Prehistoricas.
1973   *Cueva Morín. Excavaciones 1969*. Santander: Patronato de las Cuevas Prehistóricas.

HARLÉ, E.
1911   Les mammifères et oiseaux Quaternaires connus jusqu'ici en Portugal. *Communicaões da Commissão do Serviço Geologico de Portugal* 8:22–85.

HERNÁNDEZ-PACHECO, E.
1928a *Prehistoria del solar Hispano.* Madrid: Real Academia de Ciencias Exactas, Fisicas y Naturales.
1928b *Los cinco rios principales de España y sus terrazas.* Trabajos del Museo Naconal de Ciencias Naturales, Serie Geológica 36.

HERNÁNDEZ-PACHECO, F.
1946   Los materiales terciarios y cuaternarios de los alrededores de Toledo. *Estudios Geográficos:* 225–246.

HOWELL, F. C.
1966   Observations on the earlier phases of the European Lower Paleolithic. *American Anthropologist* 68(2, 2):88–201.

HOWELL, F. C., K. W. BUTZER, E. DE AGUIRRE
1962   Noticia preliminar sobre el emplazamiento acheulense de Torralba (Soria). *Excavaciones Arqueológicas en Espana* 10.

IMPERATORI, L.
1955   Documentos para el estudio del Cuaternario madrileño. Fenómenos de crioturbación en la terraza superior del Manzanares. *Estudios Geológicos* 26:139–143.

JAEGER, J.-J.
1970   Découverte au Djebel Irhoud des premières faunes de rongeurs du Pléistocène inférieur et moyen du Maroc. *Comptes Rendus de l'Academie des Sciences* 270(7):920–923.

KUBIENA, W. L.
1953   *The soils of Europe.* London: Thomas Murby.

LECOINTRE
1952   *Recherches sur le Néogéne et le Quaternaire marins de la côte atlantique du Maroc.* (two volumes). Protectorat de la République Franaise au aroc, Service Géologiqque, Notes et Memoires 99.

MARÇAIS, J.
1934   Découverte de restes humains fossiles dans les grés quaternaires de Rabat (Maroc). *L'anthropologie* 44:579–583.

MARGAT, J., R. RAYNAL, P. TALTASSE
1954   Deux séries d'observations nouvelles sur les croutes au Maroc. *Notes du Service Géologique du Maroc* 10:25–36.

MARTÍN AGUADO, M.
1962   Recientes hallazgos prehistóricos en las graveras de Toledo. *Estudios Geológicos* 18:139–154.
1963a *El yacimiento prehistórico de Pinedo (Toledo) y su industria triedrica.* Toledo: Diputación Provincial.
1963b Consideraciones sobre las terrazas del Tajo en Toledo. *Notas y Comunicaciones del Instituto Geológico y Minero de España* 71: 163–178.

MC COLLOUGH, M.
1971   "Perigordian facies in the Upper Paleolithic of Cantabria." Unpublished Ph.D. dissertation, University of Pennsylvania.

MÉNDES CORRÊA
1940   Novas estações líticas en Muge. *Memorias e Comunicações apresentadas no Congresso do Mundo Português* 1:113–127.

MIEG DE BOOFZHEIM, P., C. PLESSIS
1954 Sidi Abd-er-Rahman. Grotte du Rhinocéros. *Bulletin de la Société de Préhistoire du Maroc*, n.s. 7–8:29–53.
NEUVILLE, R., A. RUHLMANN
1941 *La place du Paléolithique ancien dans le Quaternaire marocain.* Institut des Hautes-Études Marocaines, Collection Hesperis 8.
1944 L'age de l'homme fossile de Rabat. *Bulletin de la Société d'Anthropologie de Paris* (ninth series) 3:74–88.
OBERMAIER, H.
1916 *E hombre fósila* Comisión de Investigaciones Paleontológicas y Prehistóricas, Memoria 9 (first Spanish edition).
1917 *Yacimiento prehistórico de las Carolinas (Madrid).* Comisión de Investigaciones Paleontológicas y Prehistóricas, Memoria 16.
1925 *El hombre fósil.* Comisión de Investigaciones Paleontológicas y Prehistóricas, Memoria 9 (second Spanish edition).
OBERMAIER, H., J. PÉREZ DE BARRADAS
1924 Las diferentes facies del Musteriense español y especialmente del de los yacimientos madrileños. *Revista de la Biblioteca, Archivo y Museo* 1(1):143–177.
1930 Yacimientos paleolíticos del valle del Jarama (Madrid). *Anuario de Prehistoria Madrileña* 1:21–35.
OBERMAIER, H., P. WERNERT
1918 Yacimiento paleolítico de Las Delicias (Madrid). *Memorias de la Real Sociedad de Historia Natural* 9:5–35.
1924 *Yacimientos paleolíticos del valle del Manzanares (Madrid).* Junta Superior de Excavaciones y Antigüedades, Memoria 60.
PÉREZ DE BARRADAS, J.
1922 *Yacimientos Paleolíticos del valle del Manzanares (Madrid).* Junta Superior de Excavaciones y Antigüedades, Memoria 42.
1923 *Yacimientos paleolíticos de los valles del Manzanares y del Jarama (Madrid). Memoria que acerca de los trabajos realizados en 1921–1922.* Junta Superior de Excavaciones y Antigüedades, Memoria 50.
1924a *Yacimientos paleolíticos del valle del Manzanares (Madrid). Memoria que acerca de los trabajos realizados en 1923–1924.* Junta Superior de Excavaciones y Antigüedades, Memoria 64.
1924b Introducción al estudio de la prehistória madrileña. *Revista de la Biblioteca, Archivo y Museo* 1(1):13–35.
1926 *Estudios sobre el terreno cuaternario del valle del Manzanares (Madrid).* Madrid: Ayuntamiento de Madrid.
1941 Nuevas investigaciones sobre el yacimiento de San Isidro (Madrid). *Archivo Español de Arqueología* 14:277–303.
PÉREZ DE BARRADAS, J., P. WERNERT
1919 El Almendro. Nuevo yacimiento cuaternario en el valle del Manzanares. *Boletín de la Sociedad Española de Excursiones* 27:238–269.
1921 El nuevo yacimiento paleolítico de la Gavia (Madrid). *Coleccionismo* 9:55–56.

PERICOT GARCIA, L.
1942   *Historia de España*, volume one. Barcelona: Gallach.

RIBA, O.
1957   *Livret-guide de l'excursion C2: terrasses du Manzanares et du Jarama aux environs de Madrid.* INQUA, V Congrès International, Madrid-Barcelona.

SOARES DE CARVALHO, G.
1953   *A sedimentologia dos depositos detriticos Plio-Quaternarios.* Publicacões do Museu e Laboratorio Minero e Geológico, Universidade de Coimbra, Memorias e Notas 34.

TEIXERA, C.
1949   *Plages anciennes et terrasses fluviaties du littoral du Nord-Ouest de la Péninsule Ibérique.* Boletim do Laboratorio Minero e Geologico, Universidade de Lisboa 17.
1952   Os terraços da parte portuguesa do rio Minho. *Communicacões dos Serviços Geológicos de Portugal* 23:221–246.

TIXIER, J.
1960   Les industries lithiques d'Aïn Fritissa (Maroc oriental). *Bulletin d'Archéologie Marocaine* 3:107–244.

VASCO RODRIGUES, A.
1959   Subsidios para o estudo do Paleolítico no Distrito da Guarda. *Actas e Memorias do I Congresso Nacional de Arqueologia*, 105–108.

VAUDOUR, J.
1969   Données nouvelles et hypothéses sur le Quaternaire de la région de Madrid. *Études et Travaux de "Méditerranée"* 8, 79–92.

VAUFREY, R.
1955   *Préhistoire de lAfrique. Tome I. Maghreb.* Publications de Institut des Hautes Études de Tunis.

VIANA, A.
1930   Estacões palcolíticas do Alto-Minho. *Portucale* 3:189–235.

VIÑES MASIP, G., F. JORDÁ CERDÁ, J. ROYO GÓMEZ
1947   *Estudios sobre las Cuevas Paleoliticas valencianas. Cova-Negra de Bellús.* Valencia. Servicio de Investigación Prehistórica.

WERNERT, P., J. PÉREZ DE BARRADAS
1921   *Yacimientos paleolíticos del valle del Manzanares (Madrid). Memoria acerca de las practicadas en 1919–1920.* Junta superior de Excavaciones y Antigüedades. Memoria 33.
1924   Bosquejo de un estudio sintético sobre el Paleolítico del Valle de Manzanares. *Revista de Archivos, Bibliotecas y Museos* 28:441–465.
1930   El yacimiento paleolítico de El Sotillo (Madrid). *Anuario de Precrítico). Revista de la Biblioteca, Archivo y Museo* 2(5):31–68.
1930   El yacimiento paleolítico de El Sotillo (Madrid) *Anuario de Prehistoria Madrileña* 1:37–95.
1932   El yacimiento paleolítico de El Sotillo (Madrid). Continuación. *Anuario de Prehistoria Madrileña* 2–3:13–60.

ZBYSZEWSKI, G.
1966   Conhecimentos actuais sobre o Paleolítico Português. Associacão dos Arqueólogos Portugueses, *Comemoração do Primeiro Centenário, T II:* 107–133.
ZBYSZEWSKI, G., O. DA VEIGA FERREIRA
1967   Le paléolithique des terrasses du Sorraia à l'est de Benavente. *Comunicações dos Serviços Geológicos de Portugal* 52:95–116.
1969   La station paléolithique da Quinta do Cónego (Cortes, Leiria). *O Arqueologo Português,* third series, 3:7–16.
ZEUNER, F. E.
1952   *Dating the past.* London: Methuen.

Cultural Evolution in France in its Paleoecological Setting During the Middle Pleistocene

HENRY DE LUMLEY

ABSTRACT

Man has lived in Europe since the end of the Lower Pleistocene. There is proof of his presence in the cave of Le Vallonnet (Roquebrune-Cap-Martin, Alpes Maritimes) in a stratigraphic unit dated by its fauna to the Upper Villafranchian (*Allophaiomys* fauna). The deposits are more recent than those of Senèze (greater than 1.5 million years), Valros (greater than 1.4 million years), and Malouteyre-Sinzelles (at 1.3 million years); they are older than Stranska Skala at 0.7 million years. They show a normal magnetization, which could correspond to the Jaramillo episode (0.9–0.95 million years). Apart from several pieces of worked bone, man left behind a tool kit consisting of pebble tools and flakes. There is no trace of fire.

Other sites equally old and approximately the same age as Le Vallonnet have been found in the very high terrace of Grâce at Montières near Amiens, in the very high terrace of Senart near Paris, in the Rhine alluvia of Achenheim and Hangenbieten, on the high terraces of the Têt (Roussillon), of the Rhône, and the Garonne. On these high terraces the tool kit generally consists of pebble tools: choppers, chopping tools, and polyhedrals; there are no bifaces.

In the sediments at Terra Amata, dated to the early Middle Pleistocene about 400,000 years ago, several occupation levels have been discovered, which seem to represent temporary camps. The hearths built at Terra Amata, together with those of Vértesszöllös would seem to be the oldest yet known anywhere in the world. The industry is generally made on pebbles and includes principally choppers often pointed, some chopping tools, rare bifaces (1 percent of the tools) the butts of which are always cortex, some cleavers, and also flake tools: racloirs, Clactonian notches, denticulates, Tayac and Quinson points, etc. The Levallois technique was not employed.

The end of the Middle Pleistocene ("Mindel-Riss" and "Riss") is represented by the sediments of La Caune de l'Arago at Tautavel, and Le Lazaret, Nice. There is evidence for numerous climatic oscillations, and several cultures have been defined: the Acheulian at Le Lazaret, L'Arago, La Grotte du Prince, and Aldène; the Tayacian at L'Arago and La Baume Bonne; the Evenosian at Sainte Anne d'Evenos; and the Pre-Mousterian at Rigabe.

The men of the Middle Pleistocene in Europe (Arago, Lazaret, Orgnac III, Prince, La Chaise, Fontéchevade, Cova Negra, Swanscombe, Ehringsdorf, Vértesszöllös) reveal extensive polymorphism.

In common usage among Quaternary geologists, the Middle Pleistocene includes the "Mindel" (Elster) and the "Riss" (Saale) glaciations (Figures 1-4).* The "Günz-Mindel" (Cromerian) interglacial is also often included, and at times the "Riss-Würm" (Eemian) (Figure 1). These definitions imply a span from about 700,000 or 650,000 years ago to about 120,000 or 80,000 years ago.

Chaline (1969, 1971, 1972) recently suggested that the Middle Pleistocene should start with the beginning of the Günz glaciation (Eburonian?) with the great migratory wave of Eurasian rodents (*Allophaiomys pliocaenicus, Dicrostonyx, Lemmus, Sicista, Cricetus, Allocricetus*) and the arrival of certain elements of the macrofauna, origin of the present one, approximately 1.4 million years ago (Figures 1, 3, and 4).

For E. Bonifay, the Middle Pleistocene is made up of the "Mindel" and the "Mindel-Riss" interglacial. This corresponds in a very general way to the Sicilian cycle *sensu lato*.

In this article, the terms "Günz," "Mindel," "Riss," and "Würm" are not used in a sense that corresponds strictly with glaciations, the beginning and end of which would be clearly defined, and with which the moraines of Penck might be correlated. These are in fact common and convenient terms in use by many French and European geologists. They correspond to fairly long periods, each of which contains several colder oscillations and is characterized by the presence of particular human industries, by particular faunal associations, and above all by the relative degree of paleosol formation on the surface of superficial deposits, especially alluvial terraces.

It is not yet possible to substitute for these classic terms a series of new and clearly-defined biostratigraphic units. However it will be necessary in the future to define such units by choosing outstanding sites which can provide opportunities for the simultaneous exercise of different dating methods on which to base a Quaternary chronology. The evidence will come from stratigraphy which can be tied in with both marine and terrestrial deposits, from paleomagnetism and paleotemperatures, from absolute dating, from microfauna and macrofauna, from pollen and from artifacts.

Sites which fulfill all these criteria and which have actually been studied are still too rare, so we feel that it is preferable to wait for some years before defining such biostratigraphic units within the Quaternary.

In this article, therefore, the classic terms of "Günz," "Mindel," and "Riss" are being used in the full knowledge that they do not each cor-

* See foldout between pp. 748–749

respond to a Great Ice Age but to a series of biostratigraphic units which include several climatic cold periods.

It is also necessary to state that these classic terms do not always receive the same chronological status from different authors (Figure 2). In Figure 3 an attempt has been made to place the periods within the chronological framework of the Quaternary according to the present understanding of many French geologists. The limits of the Middle Pleistocene have also been drawn, following the different interpretations of Quaternary geologists (Figure 1).

According to the definition that we are adopting, the Middle Pleistocene includes the "Günz-Mindel," the "Mindel," and the "Riss." It begins with the Brunhes-Matuyama reversal about 700,000 years ago and ends before the beginning of the "Riss-Würm" interglacial about 120,000 years ago. We divide it here into the very early, early, middle, and late Middle Pleistocene (Figures 3 and 4). It is immediately preceded by the final Lower Pleistocene, which is the equivalent of the very early and lower early Middle Pleistocene of Chaline.

THE FINAL LOWER PLEISTOCENE; "GÜNZ"; THE OLDEST HUMAN INDUSTRIES IN FRANCE

The final Lower Pleistocene, or very early Middle Pleistocene of Chaline, is a period containing several cold climatic oscillations. It corresponds with the "Günz" and lasts from about 1.2 to 0.7 million years ago.

The beginning of the final Lower Pleistocene, or "Günz" was subsequent to the fauna of the classic Upper Villafranchian: Senèze, older than 1.5 million years (Bout 1970: 69); Valros, older than 1.4 million years (Bout 1972: 57); Malouteyre-Sinzelles at 1.3 million years (Bout 1972: 59). Characterized by the arrival in Europe of an *Allophaiomys* associated microfauna, the beginning of the final Lower Pleistocene, or "Günz," would be considerably older than the normal paleomagnetic episode of Jaramillo at 0.9–0.95 million years. This episode is represented at the cave of Le Vallonet, and associated with a well-developed *Allophaiomys* fauna.

The end of the final Lower Pleistocene, or "Günz," would be later than the fauna of Solilhac, which is itself older than 0.7 million years, and earlier than the fauna of Champeix-Coudes which is dated to more than 0.5 million years. It must closely approximate with the Brunhes-Matuyama boundary at 0.7 million years.

The final Lower Pleistocene corresponds to the end of the Matuyama reversed paleomagnetic epoch and includes the short normal episode of Jaramillo at 0.95 to 0.89 million years.

According to Chaline:

... the migration of *Allophaiomys pliocaenicus* and associated species to western Europe marks a very decisive limit between two essentially different groups of fauna. More evolved asiatic migrants come to join the Lower Pleistocene species which continue for some time. Here, then, we have a considerable renewal of fauna which rapidly leads to the establishment of the modern fauna. (1969, 1972:117).

In France, the paleontological deposits which correspond to the first part of the "Günz" ("Eburonian") are numerous: the Le Vallonet cave at Roquebrune-Cap-Martin, the high terrace of Grâce at Montières, Les Valerots at Nuits-Saint-Georges, Balaruc 1 and Mas Rambault near Montpellier, and perhaps the grey Rhine alluvials of Achenheim and Hangenbieten.

This period corresponds in fact with the lower Biharian of Central Europe, the Betfia and Templomhegy phases of Jánossy (this volume); the beginning of the Betfia phase is characterized by the arrival of an *Allophaiomys* fauna. There is evidence for numerous climatic oscillations in Western Europe during this time. Due to pollen studies of the clays from Leffe, southern Alps, Venzo (1965: 381) has distinguished three colder climatic oscillations, which are characterized by the development of pine, spruce, and fir. In the Netherlands, Zagwijn (1963: 67) has distinguished two cold periods in the Kedichem formations: the Eburonian and the Menapian, which are separated by a warmer period, the Waalian. The end of the Waalian corresponds in part to the brief positive episode of Jaramillo (Zagwijn, Montfrans, and Zandstra 1971: 46, Figure 31).

It is probable that after leaving his African cradle, man first appeared in Europe during the final Lower Pleistocene or "Günz": the Vallonet cave, the high terrace at Grâce.

La Grotte du Vallonnet

The cave of Le Vallonnet is situated at Roquebrune-Cap-Martin, near Menton in the Maritime Alps. It consists of a narrow passage which opens after 5 meters onto a small chamber.

Lower Pleistocene Deposits Fragments of stalagmite floor are the chief remains of an infilling which took place before the transgression of the upper Calabrian sea.

Calabrian Transgression The upper Calabrian sea is characterized by a glacioeustatic transgression ("Donau-Günz"). The sea rose to cave level, at the altitude of 108 meters; breakers demolished the former continental deposits, and fragments of the stalagmite floor were broken and rolled. The walls and the ground were eroded by the waves and perforated by lithodomes sponges, (*Cliona*) and sea-urchins. Marine sands rich in foraminifera, fragments of shells and fish remains have been preserved in rock cavities.

The marine fauna is littoral: two species of oysters (*Gryphaea virleti* Desh, and *Gryphaea cucullata* Born) sometimes found stuck to the walls; three species of limpets (*Patella caerulea*, *Patella lusitanica*, and *Patella ferruginea*) to which *Vermetus arenarius*, *Cerithium vulgatum*, *Lithodomus lithophagus*, *Chlamys sp.*, must be added, and the crustaceans *Eriphia spinifrons*, and *Balanus sp.* Fish are usually represented by porcupine fish (*Diodon sp.*) which are closely related to *Diodon acanthodes* Sauvage, known in Pliocene marl in Sicily. Also represented are *Chrysophrys aurata*, *Odontaspis taurus*, and *Myliobati aquila*. The numerous foraminifera are evidence of a truly littoral environment and show definite Tertiary affinities (*Dorothia gibbosa*, *Asterigerina planorbis*, etc.).

The isotopic composition $^{18}0/^{16}0$ of the seashell carbonates seems to indicate that the sea was much warmer than now.

Final Lower Pleistocene Deposits ("Günz") The sea withdrew during a period of glaciation and never returned to the Le Vallonnet cave level (upper Calabrian regression).

Three series of layers, C, B II, and B 1, are essentially made up of clayey sands which contain angular stones and pebbles from the Roquebrune conglomerate. The presence of frost-shattered stones and pebbles which have been broken by frost in Beds B II and B 1 lead to the conclusion that at least part of the infilling was deposited during a cold climate. This infilling has suffered much alteration and part decalcification of the surface after deposition.

Post-Villafranchian Deposits After the final Lower Pleistocene, a violent gullying washed away the infilling of the passage and the front part of the first chamber. A channel pointing towards the entrance of the cave was hollowed out of the top of those levels which had stayed intact in the bottom of the cave. The channel was filled up with a red colluvial clay (Bed A). A thick stalagmitic floor later filled in the entrance of this chamber and protected what was left of the infilling from subsequent erosion. The isotopic composition $^{18}O/^{16}O$ of the calcium carbonates of this floor shows that it was formed during a colder period than the present, perhaps at the end of the final Lower Pleistocene.

FAUNA   Fauna discovered in the final Lower Pleistocene ("Günz") levels is extremely rich and relatively well-preserved; it permits precise dating of the site. A great number of species is included:

Primates	Cynomorph	*Macacus sp.*
Fissiped carnivores	Canidae	*Canis sp.*
	Felidae	*Felis sp.*
		Acinonyx pardinendis
	Ursidae	*Ursus sp.*
	Hyaenidae	*Crocuta perrieri*
Pinniped carnivores	Phocidae	*Monachus albiventer*
Artiodactyls	Hippopotamidae	*Hippopotamus sp.*
	Suidae	*Sus sp.*
	Bovidae	*Bos sp.*
		Leptobos sp.
	Cervidae	Several archaic cervids recalling Upper Villafranchian forms
	Capridae	An archaic caprid recalling Upper Villafranchian forms
Perissodactyls	Rhinocerotidae	*Dicerorhinus struscus*
	Equidae	*Equus stenonis*
Proboscidians	Elephantidae	*Elephas meridionalis*
Cetaceans		*Balaena sp.*
Rodents		*Hystrix major*
		Allophaiomys cf. *pliocaenicus*, micro-to-nicaloid and pitymo-gregaloid morphotypes
		Ungaromys nanus
		Glis minor
		Eliomys cf. *quercinus* helleri
		Apodemus mystacinus
		Mus sp. with Asiatic affinities
Insectivores		cf. *Asoriculus sp.*
Reptiles		*Testudo sp.*

The presence of the meridional or southern elephant, and the absence of the mastodon are evidence that this fauna dates from the end of the Villafranchian. The presence of large forms of canid, felid, and bovid, however, already announce the Middle Pleistocene fauna.

The microto-nivaloid and pitymo-gregaloid morphotypes of *Allophaiomys pliocaenicus* are integral parts of the assemblage at the site of Les Valerots, Nuits-Saint-Georges (Côte d'Or) which is, according to Chaline, attributable to the very early Middle Pleistocene.

The same age is confirmed by the presence at Le Vallonet of three species common to the two infillings of the cave: *Ungaromys nanus*, *Glis minor*, and *Eliomys quercinus*. The fact that the site is situated in the Mediterranean biogeographical zone is shown by the presence of the Mediterranean field mouse *Apodemus mystacinus* and an insectivore of the *Asoriculus* type.

According to Chaline (1971: 68) the cold and sparsely wooded steppe of Burgundy (Les Valerots) would correspond to barren steppe with locally wooded patches in the Mediterranean zone (Le Vallonnet).

FLORA   Preliminary pollen analysis by Renault-Miskovsky and Girard shows evidence for a lightly wooded steppe with clusters of trees: pine, birch, and Atlantic oak.

PALEOMAGNETISM   The magnetization of the infilling measured by Poutiers and Fernex (1972) is fairly stable and normal.

DATING   The site of Le Vallonnet can be reasonably dated (Figure 4). The macrofauna allows the statement that it is later than Senèze (older than 1.5 million years), than Valros (older than 1.4 million years) and than Malouteyre-Sinzelles (1.3 million years). The *Allophaiomys* microfauna shows that it is contemporaneous with the sites of Balaruc I and Mas Rambault near Montpellier, with Les Valerots at Nuits-Saint-Georges, and with the high terrace of Grâce at Montières. Le Vallonnet can be placed even more precisely into the second half of the Betfia phase of the lower Biharian of Jánossy owing to the evolutionary stage of *Allophaiomys pliocaenicus* (microto-nivaloid and pitymo-gregaloid morphotypes). It is therefore considerably earlier than the site of Stranska Skala, near Brno in Moravia, which probably belongs to the Tarkö phase of the upper Biharian and which probably coincides with the Brunhes-Matuyama boundary at 0.7 million years, according to the evidence presented by Kukla (this volume). From the faunal evidence therefore, the site of Le Vallonnet can be placed between 1.3 and 0.7 million years.

As Poutiers and Fernex (1972) have demonstrated that the magnetization of the infilling is fairly stable and normal, it must either be attributed to the Brunhes Epoch, younger than 0.7 million years, or to the brief normal episode of Jaramillo between 0.9 and 0.95 million years, or to the Oldowan between 1.7 and 1.85 million years. The faunal evidence would not support attribution to either the Brunhes Epoch or the Olduvai Event. Therefore the Le Vallonnet deposits, which show normal magnetization, are likely to date from the Jaramillo episode, between 0.9 and 0.95 million years.

INDUSTRY   An industry has been discovered in the final Lower Pleistocene deposits. The artifacts include flakes, tools made on pebbles — choppers, rostrocarinates, pebble tools, and worked bones.

Waste flakes and tools made on pebbles had been abandoned in the middle of the small chamber; large mammal bones, on the other hand, had generally been pushed back against the wall. Man had brought shed antlers, which are generally found in groups into the cave. Subsequently some of them seem to have been intentionally cut.

Upper Villafranchian man, who came to take refuge in the Vallonnet cave as in a lair, does not seem to have known fire, and the arrangement of the living site seems to have been very simple. His hunting technique must have been rudimentary: he brought a great number of old animals into the cave, probably ill or dead ones. He even transported partly decomposed fragments of whale carcasses stranded on a nearby beach.

Le Vallonnet is certainly the oldest dated site in Europe in which evidence of man's presence has been shown.

The Uppermost Terrace of Grâce at Montières (Amiens)

In the Somme valley, the uppermost alluvial deposits of Grâce can be dated to the final Lower Pleistocene (Bourdier 1969: 186; Bourdier, Chaline, and Puissegur 1969). They consist of about 5 meters of periglacial gravel, the summit of which dominates the Somme valley at about 55 meters above Montières, a suburb of Amiens. This gravel is covered by a thick layer of river sands and silt.

The presence of an archaic equid tooth of the *stenonis* type, and a microfauna which includes *Allophaiomys pliocaenicus* suggests dating the terrace to the final Lower Pleistocene.

In 1958, Bourdier and Agache discovered a flint tool retouched by man and some flakes obviously retouched, *in situ* in the gravels. These objects are contemporary with the Le Vallonnet tools.

The Uppermost Terrace of Sénart (Paris Region)

In the Seine valley, the uppermost terrace of Sénart is greatly altered and can be dated to the final Lower Pleistocene. Bourdier and Orliac found two polyhedral pieces similar to those from the high terraces of the Têt valley on the plain of Roussillon (Bourdier 1969: 187).

The High Terraces of Roussillon

The Roussillon plain stretches from the Corbières Massif in the north to the Pyrenées in the south and west; it is bordered by the Mediterranean in the east. Three small coastal streams cross it: the northernmost Agly, the Têt, and the southernmost Tech.

Between Prades and Perpignan, the Têt valley contains a remarkable succession of Quaternary terraces, principally on the left bank cut into the Pliocene formations and covered with paleosols. These terraces are often preserved in the form of small outliers which crown residual buttes; more rarely they take the form of extensive sheets slightly inclined to the east. These Quaternary formations possess sufficiently marked characteristics to distinguish four phases of deposition:

To the west of the plain, the HIGH LEVELS reach more than 200 meters above sea level, their altitude descending to 15 meters above sea level near the coast. They are covered with well-developed and highly leached, fersiallitic soils.

The MEDIUM LEVELS extend from 100 to 10 meters above sea level, from west to east. They are covered by moderately leached fersiallitic soils.

The LOWER LEVELS are visible from 45 to 2 meters above sea level on the edge of the pool of Salses. They are covered by slightly leached, fersiallitic soils still preserving carbonates.

The VERY LOW LEVELS may be seen along the Têt valley where they sometimes emerge from under the modern alluvial deposits of the middle valley. They are covered with brown soils.

The high levels can be dated from the beginning of the final Lower Pleistocene (Günz). Archaic industries, of quartz, or more rarely quartzite, have been discovered on these terraces. A few pieces have been found *in situ*. They indicate a pebble industry including some polyhedrals, choppers, and rare chopping tools (de Lumley 1969b: 151).

The High Terrace of the Rhône

At the confluence of the Rhône and the Gard, south of the Gardon, at an altitude of 60 to 70 meters, the alluvial deposits from the Rhône form an immense flat surface, the "costière Nîmoise," dated to the final Lower Pleistocene (Günz) by local geologists. To the north of the village of Montfrin, the site of Le Bois des Orgnes has produced a series of pebble tools: choppers, some of which are very altered and extremely windworn; they would appear to be penecontemporaneous with the deposition of the terrace (de Lumley 1971: 124; Meignen 1972: 3).

80-Meter Terrace of the Garonne

The 80-meter terrace of the Garonne is generally dated to the final Lower Pleistocene. Near Mondavezan to the north-west of Cazères (Haute Garonne), Breuil and Méroc (1950) found pebble tools, rolled and patinated, probably contemporary with the deposition of the terrace.

The Rhine Alluvium of Achenheim and Hangenbieten

The two sites, Achenheim and Hangenbieten, situated in Alsace west of Strasbourg (Bas-Rhin) present very important stratigraphical sections, which may be seen in some quarries being exploited for the extraction of loess and sand or gravel (Thévenin 1972):

1.   Alluvial deposits from the Rhine: an old terrace, that of Hangenbieten-Mundolsheim, consists of Rhine alluvials (mud and grey sand) with a warm fauna ("pre-Mindel," probably "Günz").
2.   Red sand from the Vosges and yellow sandy silt: these sands contain small spermophile burrows ("Mindel").
3.   A stage of incision: a 25-meter depression cut into the Rhein deposits and Vosges sands.
4.   "Limon rouge" from the plateaux ("Mindel-Riss").
5.   Lower older loess forming the interlocking tiers of Achenheim ("Riss I").
6.   Interstadial lehm ("Inter-Riss I-II").
7.   Middle older loess, lower part ("Riss II").
8.   Interstadial lehm ("Inter-Riss II-III").
9.   Middle older loess, upper part ("Riss III").
10.   Interglacial lehm ("Riss-Würm").
11.   Upper older loess and younger loess ("Würm").
12.   Fluvio-lacustrine accumulation ("Post-glacial").

The small burrows found in the red Vosges sands contain the remains of a large spermophile (*Citellus* cf. *dietrichi*) and owl pellets (*Arvicola* cf. *mosbachensis, Microtus arvalis, Microtus ratticeps, Microtus gregalis, Sorex* cf. *araneus*) which allow the dating of these sands to a cold phase of the "late Mindel" (Chaline and Thévenin 1972). The red Vosges sands have also provided remains of a small wolf, a deer, a reindeer, and the tooth of an equid.

The Rhine alluvials which lie below are therefore "pre-Mindel" and could date from the "Günz" (final Lower Pleistocene).

These deposits have yielded some worked tools: a pebble with a single flake scar in the sand quarry of Hurst at Achenheim and a pebble with two flakes removed from the sand quarry of Jeuch-Wallan at Hangenbieten (Werner, Millot, and von Eller 1962; Thévenin 1972).

THE VERY EARLY MIDDLE PLEISTOCENE;
"GÜNZ-MINDEL";
THE OLDEST INDUSTRY CONTAINING BIFACIAL TOOLS

The very early Middle Pleistocene ("Günz-Mindel" or Cromerian) is a period of increased warmth which is said to have lasted from 0.7 to 0.65 million years approximately. It corresponds with the beginning of the Brunhes normal epoch. Zagwijn, van Montfrans and Zandstra (1971) have recently brought to light several climatic oscillations within this period including a cold episode. In the mediterranean Languedoc, this period is characterized by substantial volcanic activity: Agde 0.73, Saint-Thibery 0.68, Vias 0.67, Roque-Haute 0.64 million years (Bout 1972: 57).

Some small irregular bifaces, rolled and fractured, were discovered by d'Ault de Mesnil in the reddish-brown gravels containing *Hippopotamus amphibius major, Rhinoceros* and *Equus stenonis,* from the highest terrace of the Somme at Abbeville, which dates from the "Günz-Mindel." These are the oldest bifacial tools currently known in Europe (pre-Abbevillian).

EARLY MIDDLE PLEISTOCENE; "MINDEL";
FIRST ORGANIZED CAMPS IN THE OPEN AIR AND THE
APPEARANCE OF FIRE

The early Middle Pleistocene ("Mindelian" or "Elsterian") is the glacial period said to have lasted from 0.64 to 0.3 million years. It corresponds to the first half of the period of normal magnetization of Brunhes. In Germany, the Netherlands, and England, it is generally subdivided into two major cold periods (Elster I and II) separated by a substantial warm period, the Cortonian. At Leffe, south of the Alps, Venzo (1965: 381) has shown in his pollen studies, two major cold oscillations and a minor third one in deposits probably attributable to this period. In France, the early Middle Pleistocene is characterized:

... by the appearance of true *Microtus* and *Pitymys* which have evolved from *Allophaiomys pliocaenicus* and by the disappearance of many elements of the Lower Pleistocene (*Mimomys, Ungaromys, Glirulus, Hypolagus, Beremendia*). The fauna, except for some archaic elements which continue (*Pliomys, Allocricetus*) is very similar to that of the present, the fossil spiecies being represented by more primitive sub-species (Chaline 1972).

Abbeville

At Abbeville, the reddish-brown gravel from the uppermost terrace of the Somme is topped by whitish marly sands with calcium carbonate concretions, rich in fauna, in which d'Ault de Mesnil found a few handaxes. These were hardly rolled, if at all, and have a grey patina; they were later used by Breuil to establish the Abbevillian type industry.

FAUNA   Very abundant fauna allows the site to be dated to the early Middle Pleistocene (very end of the "Günz-Mindel") according to Bourdier (1969: 192) or to an early interstadial of the "Mindel." It includes one single molar of an advanced *Elephas meridionalis*, of the sub-species *cromerensis*; molars of *Elephas trogontherii*, *E. antiquus*, and *E. primigenius* all show archaic characteristics as in the Forest Bed at Cromer; the numerous *Rhinoceros* molars most probably belong in the main to *Rhinoceros etruscus* according to Pontier; the *Rhinoceros leptorhinus*, a close relative of *Rh. etruscus* and of *Rh. mercki*, is rare in this deposit. The *Elasmotherium*, the giant rhinoceros of the Asiatic Quaternary, with a single long horn and molars showing folded enamel, existed at Abbeville according to Gaudry (cited by d'Ault). If we leave aside its doubtful existence in the Rhine valley, mentioned by d'Archiac, Abbeville is the only west European site to contain the *Elasmotherium*. It is difficult to suppose that Gaudry was in error because, six years before he studied the d'Ault collection, he and Boule had written a detailed monograph on the Russian *Elasmotherium* fossils. The equids include *Equus (stenonis) robustus*, *Equus caballus*, and a small asinine equid, most probably *Equus hydruntinus* (Stehlin and Graziosi). The cervids show some archaic elements: *Cervus soli-hacus, Cervus (Megaceros) belgrandi, Cervus (Dama) somonensis.* The latter persists up to the full Middle Pleistocene ("Mindel-Riss") at Menchecourt near Abbeville, a locality which supplied the type of the species. But, besides these archaic cervids, there were probably "recent" species: *Cervus elaphus, Cervus canadensis, Capreolus ca-preolus.* Pontier admits the existence of *Bos etruscus, Bos elatus* of the Villafranchian, and *Bison priscus* of which Commont has studied a complete skull; according to Kurtén (1968) it appeared in Europe during the final Lower Pleistocene ("Günz II") and seemed to be a steppe animal, like *Elasmotherium* or *Equus hydruntinus*; its presence agrees with the evidence from the flora. Among the carnivores, Gaudry has found a similarity between *Hyaena* cf. *crocuta* and *Hyaena brevirostris,* a species as large as a lion which has been found in the early Quaternary of Süssenborn, in Germany. Commont found a canine and incisors of *Machairodus latidens.* The *Sus scrofa* is said to be represented by an archaic form; d'Ault mentions a small ursid and the great beaver, *Trogontherium.*

INDUSTRY   The industry collected by d'Ault de Mesnil includes rough handaxes, usually with an untrimmed butt and sinuous lateral edges. They have been worked with a stone hammer. Flake tools are uncharacteristic. Pebble tools have not been preserved.

Abbevillian industries have also been discovered in France in a Marne terrace at Chelles, Seine and Marne, and on the high terraces of the Garonne.

The Cave of Escale

The Escale cave is siuated in the low valley of the Durance, near the village of Saint-Estève-Janson. Discovered in 1960 during the building of the Saint-Estève canal by Electricité de France, it has been excavated by E. Bonifay.

STRATIGRAPHY   The Quaternary deposits which can at present be recognized reach a thickness of 20 to 25 meters. They are made up of cryoclastic scree, silty loess, a limestone with plant remains, and a reworked Miocene gravel. They can be subdivided into three episodes corresponding to colder climates and separated by interstadial beds which were deposited under a temperate or warm-temperate climatic regime. The stratigraphy is as follows from bottom to top.

Bed A3 (1-2 Meters Thick)   These beds correspond to a temperate interstadial or an interglacial. Pebbles which have not been frost shattered are embedded in a matrix of reddish clay.

Beds A2 and A1 (2-3 Meters Thick)   Here angular scree represents a glacial stage ("middle Mindel" of E. Bonifay). The climate was probably cold and very wet, causing an intense frost shattering and the deposition of rubble. The following phases can be distinguished within this cold stage:
a.   a less cold and more dry phase towards the bottom,
b.   a cold and very wet phase as evidenced by the rubble, and
c.   a warmer and very wet phase at the top, which caused severe channelling of the underlying levels of rubble.

Beds B6, B5, B4, B3, B2 (1.5-2.5 Meters Thick)   These deposits correspond to a warm and very wet interstadial (penultimate "Mindelian" interstadial of E. Bonifay). There is a complete absence of frost action; the sediments deposited in the cave have undergone severe alteration but not intense reddening. The deposits are generally clay-like with highly altered pebbles.

Beds F, E, C, B1 (3-7 Meters Thick)   This angular rubble can be equated with a glacial stage before the last "Mindelian" stage of E. Bonifay. Sedimentological studies provide evidence for the following climatic phases:
a.   cold and very wet, with a cold season contrasting with a warm or hot season. The sediments are comopsed of elements of cryoclastic origin mingled with wind transported materials (Beds B1 and C),
b.   a fairly cold and wet phase resulting in heavily cryoclastic deposits which alternate with loess, probably not from a notably hot season (Beds D, E), and
c.   a fairly cool and wet phase just before the beginning of the interstadial, allowing for the washing of the scree laid down previously.

Bed G (1.5-3 Meters Thick)   These deposits correspond to a temperate and wet interstadial (last "Mindelian" interstadial of E. Bonifay), which caused non-cryoclastic eboulis to be deposited in a red clay matrix. Pebbles underwent heavy alteration. Within the cave, these red breccias are succeeded by travertines (G[1]) which incorporate heaps of vegetable remains, in particular large quantities of *Celtis* seeds: these *Celtis* limestones sometimes reach a thickness of 2 meters. The fauna is temperate.

Beds L, K, J, I, H (4-7 Meters Thick)   This angular scree corresponds to a glacial stage ("upper Mindelian" of E. Bonifay). The sedimentology provides evidence of the following phases:
a.   a very cold and wet phase as shown by intense cryoclastic action; the fauna is very cold (lower part and base of Bed H),
b.   a more temperate phase resulting in the reworking of the reddened sediments and a very brief return of "temperate" faunal elements (middle part of Bed H: red scree),
c.   a very cold and quite dry phase, but with less intensive evidence of leaching; possibly due to cryonivation; less intensive frost-weathering (upper part of Bed H), and
d.   at the top is evidence for a cold and probably quite wet phase; there is an alternation of dry cold seasons with cold, wetter ones. Wind transported materials were laid down in the cave and cemented as very hard fine sandstone (hardened loess) alternating with moderately frost shattered breccia (Beds L, K, J, I).

Red clay (Several Meters Thick)   This was deposited, according to E. Bonifay, during the "Mindel-Riss" interglacial.

The faunas confirm the paleoclimatic data and demonstrate, according to M. F. Bonifay an alternation between cold to very cold faunas (*Hemitragus, Gulo, Vulpes praeglacialis*) and warm faunas (*Megaceros, Testudo,* Suids, Cynomorph monkey). According to the faunal evidence, these deposits can perhaps be dated to the beginning of the Middle Pleistocene.

FAUNA   The fauna is very rich in levels B to H inclusive. It is comprised of the following species:

Primates		Cynomorph (cf. *Semnopithecus*)
Carnivores	Canidae	*Canis etruscus* f. major
		Vulpes vulpes L. *jansoni* M. F. Bonifay
		Vulpes praeglacialis Kormos
		cf. *Cuon stehlini* Thenius
	Felidae	*Lynx spelaea* M. Boule
		Jansofelis vaufreyi M. F. Bonifay
	Ursidae	*Ursus deningeri* v. Reich
	Hyaenidae	*Hyaena prisca* M. de Serres
	Mustelidae	*Meles sp.*
		Mustela palerminea Petenyi
		Gulo gulo schlosseri Kormos

Artiodactyls	*Hemitragus jemlahicus bonali* H. and St.
	Megaceros sp.
	Sus sp.
Perissodactyls	*Dicerorhinus sp.*
Lagomorphs	*Leporidae* ind.
Rodents	*Sciurus sp.*
	Eliomys quercinus helleri
	Clethrionomys glareolus
	Pliomys episcopalis
	Pitymys subterraneus
	Microtus agrestis jansoni J. Chaline
	Microtus brecciensis mediterraneus
	Arvicola mosbachensis
	Apodemus sylvaticus
	Allocricetus bursae duranciensis
	J. Chaline
Insectivores	*Talpa* cf. *europaea*
	Sorex sp.
	Crocidura sp.

Bats
Extremely numerous birds
Reptiles (numerous tortoise)
Amphibians

It is necessary to note the disappearance of certain characteristic Villa-franchian elements which still existed at the beginning of the Middle Pleistocene, such as *Rhinoceros etruscus, Elephas meridionalis, Equus stenonis,* and the Machairodonts. Certain species such as *Ursus deningeri, Cuon* cf. *stehlini,* and *Megaceros* can be recognized in the early Middle Pleistocene deposits of Germany. The particular character of the large mammal fauna of the cave of Escale is underlined by the presence of *Hyaena prisca, Hemitragus jemlahicus bonali,* and a highly unusual brachygnathous feline *Jansofelis vaufreyi. Hemitragus jemlahicus bonali* together with *Canis etruscus* were the most numerous species.

The presence of *Lynx spelaea* and *Vulpes vulpes jansoni* heralds the faunas of the upper Middle Pleistocene.

The association of *Pliomys episcopalis* and *Allocricetus bursae duranciensis* is characteristic of the European Middle Pleistocene faunas. The absence of *Castillomys crusafonti, Mimomys,* and *Allophaiomys* places these deposits after those dated to the final Lower Pleistocene.

According to Jánossy, the microfauna can be compared with those from the sites of lower Tarkö, Tiraspol, Stranska Skala. This allows the site to be placed in the first part of the lower Tarkö phase (upper Biharian) of Jánossy, that is to say, at the beginning of the Middle Pleistocene.

The infilling of the cave of Escale, being contemporary with that of Stranska Skala, would therefore be dated to about 700,000 years ago.

The microfauna suggests either a landscape of arid woodland steppe, or forest, depending at which level it is found. According to Chaline (1972: 284) a layer of ashes corresponding with the disappearance of forest species is undoubted evidence of a forest fire.

Terra Amata

The site of Terra Amata is situated at Nice on the western slopes of Mount Boron, 300 meters from the commercial port, at the corner of Boulevard Carnot and the blind alley of Terra Amata. In October of 1965, large earth-moving works led to the discovery of prehistoric occupation floors, and a rescue excavation was undertaken from 28 January to 5 July 1966.

STRATIGRAPHY   The quaternary sediments reach 10 meters in thickness and rest on a shelf of cretaceous rock: Turonian limestone and Cenomanian marl.

Pliocene   A small deposit of yellowy-grey muddy sands (Sections V and XXIII) was discovered to the southwest of the site. Stuck against the Turonian limestone, its summit was situated between an altitude of 19 and 20.5 meters. This isolated deposit was covered by recent colluvials. The study of foraminifera (Blanc Vernet 1969; Randrianascolo 1972) has allowed it to be dated to the end of the Pliocene.

Microfauna is limited to banal species from shallow waters, with a prevalence of *Rotaliidae, Elphidiidae, Nonionidae*; some species show evidence for brackish waters: *Ammonia beccarii, A. beccarii tepida, Protelphidium paralium*. The presence of *Discorbidae, Cibicides, Planorbulines* suggests the existence of aquatic plants. However a fairly large proportion of planktonic species (16 percent) shows that this tidal flat must have been very much open to the sea.

Early Middle Pleistocene ("Mindel")   The Quaternary deposits of the early Middle Pleistocene, which are the best developed may be subdivided into four units or cycles, of which the first three (A, B, and C_1) each begin with a transgressive marine beach, covered with sediments largely of eolian origin (marine regression) (Figure 5).* These beaches, situated at the same altitude, probably correspond to minor interstadials at the very end of the early Middle Pleistocene ("Mindel"). They are

* See foldout between pp. 764–765

earlier than the middle Middle Pleistocene beach ("Mindel-Riss") the shoreline of which may be found a few hundred meters away in Le Lazaret Cave.

STRATIGRAPHIC UNIT A: This is represented by three types of deposits: (1) Aa — a littoral marine deposit corresponding to a positive oscillation of the sea, (2) Ab — loess-like deposits corresponding to a regression of the sea, and (3) Ac — altered sediments corresponding to a warm period.

Stratigraphic Unit Aa: This is made up of littoral marine deposits, which rest on a large abrasion surface, slightly inclined to the sea and at an altitude of 23 to 25 meters. It starts with a line of large pebbles perforated by marine organisms. These boulders are overlaid by a series of gravel beds and beach ridges stacked one against the other. At 26 meters a wave-cut notch indicates the relative altitude of the sea. The storm beach of this sea has been preserved between 28.95 and 29.6 meters. These marine deposits are composed of fine sandy sediments which contain a high percentage of coarse sand.

Stratigraphic Unit Ab: The Ab beach is covered by sandy loess-like silt of a pale green olive color, which was most probably deposited during a cold dry period. When it has not been altered it presents a continuous structure. Elsewhere in the zone where alteration has taken place, it passes progressively from a polyhedral structure, to a prismatic structure with pseudomyceliums.

Stratigraphic Unit Ac: These eolian deposits are altered by a soil, in major part truncated, reddish yellow at the top, where the compact, clayey illuviation horizon exhibits prismatic macrostructure and blocky microstructure. The lower part of this soil has small white concretions. A substantial calcareous crust is developed at the base of the sandy silts, and even within the Turonian calcareous marls. This soil probably corresponds to a warm and humid climate. The top of this soil is affected by calcretion, a paleosol, covering Unit B. Calcareous concretions formed among the structural aggregates.

STRATIGRAPHIC UNIT B: As in the preceding unit, three types of deposits may be distinguished here: (1) Ba — littoral, marine deposits corresponding to a positive oscillation of the sea, (2) Bb — loess-like deposits corresponding to a regression of the sea, and (3) Bc — altered sediments corresponding to a warm period.

Stratigraphic Unit Ba: This beach lies disconformably on that of Unit A towards the south and hollows out the pale green olive loess-like silts and the soil which is above them towards the north. A step, cut by breakers into the former deposits gives us reason to believe that the altitude of the corresponding sea front was 26 meters. A storm beach is preserved between 27 and 27.8 meters.

Stratigraphic Unit Bb: The Ba beach is covered by loess-like silt, pale brown in color and up to 2 meters thick; this probably corresponds to a new cold and dry period. At the base these deposits are mixed with marine sands, much of it coarse. Above, the coarse sands become rarer and the sediments are composed of clayey silt which is fairly rich in fine sands.

Stratigraphic Unit Bc: The surface of the deposits of Stratigraphic Unit B, particularly the loessic silts, has been altered, but the clayey illuvial horizon has completely disappeared. Calcium concretions corresponding to a paleosol Ca-horizon, have formed among the structural aggregates of an even older paleosol, formed at the surface of Stratigraphic Unit A.

STRATIGRAPHIC UNIT c1: As in the preceding units, three types of deposits may be distinguished: (1) C1a — littoral marine deposits corresponding to a positive oscillation of the sea, (2) C1b — dunes and loess-like silt corresponding to a regression of the sea, and (3) C1c — altered sediments corresponding to a new optimum climate.

Stratigraphic Unit C1a: The shoreline deposits of the C1a cycle correspond to a new transgression which has cut into the previous Quaternary deposits, a broad erosion platform slightly inclined towards the sea and situated between an altitude of 24.25 and 26.5 meters. This beach comes to an end on the mainland with a series of beach ridges stacked one against the other. A notch cut into the beach between 25.6 and 26.1 meters by the breaking waves is an indication of the corresponding altitude of the sea. The oldest episodes (M7 to P4a) are composed of beds of pebbles enveloped in silty, clayrich sands, which alternate with beds of silty-clay sands. These silty-clay sands are at times very rich in organic matter, the sediments being dark in color.

Above, there is a beach ridge of pebbles (P3 to P1s).

At the top, and thicker towards the south, a substantial layer of coarse white sand (SB) of peculiar structure terminates the marine series. No doubt this corresponds to a calmer phase of the sea and announces the beginning of a new regression.

Two kinds of oysters, *Gryphaea virleti* and *Gryphaea cucullata*, were discovered on this beach. Hitherto, their presence had been considered as characteristic of the beginning of the Quaternary.

Stratigraphic Unit C1b: At the beginning of a new regression, the wind, sweeping over the large sand surfaces which were no longer reached by the sea, deposited a dune some ways back from the beach ridge. The dune is brownish-yellow at the top, light grey at the base and is up to 1 meter thick (DH-DZ6). These dune deposits are made up of silty-clay sands. From the base to the top of the dune, an increase in the percentage of fine elements (silt-clay) and a decrease of sands, especially coarse sands, may be noticed.

These deposits are locally topped by colluvial silts which suggest a rapid sedimentation of elements that may have been washed off older deposits. They consist of reddish or greyish-red earth to the north, greenish to the south, and present a continuous structure with a polyhedric tendency. These deposits are rich in pseudomycelium and the lines of calcium carbonate emphasize the stratification. They contain a few coarse calcium carbonate and marly elements, black and very altered. During excavation, a fauna containing in particular *Cyclostoma elegans, Bulimus decollatus, Helix,* and some charcoal was discovered in these deposits. Heavy erosion subsequently truncated the dune and the overlying colluvium, as well as the older loess-like silts (Bb) of the B unit.

Stratigraphic Unit C1c: A weak soil, red brown or very pale brown, later formed on the eroded surface. It presents a different structure according to whether it is formed from the loess-like silts of the regressive Bb unit, or on the dune and the colluvium of the regressive C1b. On the loess-like silts of the regressive Bb unit, the clay accumulation horizon is composed of a plastic clay of prismatic structure, brown-red at the top, red at the bottom. On the dune and the colluvium of the regressive C1b unit, it is composed of clay silt with a polyhedric structure, brown-grey with flecks of rust color, grey, and brown. Rich in pseudomycelium especially at the top, it present a hydromorphous aspect at the bottom.

This soil, which contains at its base many terrestrial gasteropods, in particular *Cyclostoma elegans* and *Bulimus decollatus,* most likely corresponds to a temperate climate.

STRATIGRAPHIC UNIT C2: Unlike the three preceding ones, the C2 unit does not begin with a transgressive marine beach, at least at Terra Amata. It is possible however that a small positive oscillation of the sea, less important than the preceding ones, did not reach the altitude of this site.

The pale brown paleosol of C1c, the colluvium and the dune of Unit C1b are directly covered with pale yellow loess-like silt, more than 2 meters thick, which appears to have been brought there by the wind during a new cold and dry period dating from the early Middle Pleistocene (very end of the "Mindel"). In fact this is a sandy clay silt, very poor in coarse sands, very pale brown or yellow in color, and which feels like loess. It has a continuous structure which is increasingly polyhedric towards the top. The sand is fine and relatively well-sorted.

These sediments have been enriched later in calcium carbonate, during the formation of the "Mindel-Riss" soil. They are found in fact at the level of the calcium carbonate accumulation of the paleosol. Units hardened by calcium carbonates serve to emphasize bedding characteristics.

Middle Middle Pleistocene ("Mindel-Riss" Paleosol)   This is characterized by a substantial soil reaching up to 2.5 meters in thickness. In spite of the absence of upper horizons, a clay B horizon and calcareous Cca horizons can be recognized.

The clayey B horizon is very thick and well-developed. Dark red brown to brown red, with greenish specks at the top, it becomes brown yellow at its base. The coarse elements are very much altered, the clay content is above 40 percent at the top; it decreases towards the middle and becomes high again at the base. This horizon is completely decalcified.

The associated calcium carbonate horizon consists at its surface, of a well-crystallized calcareous crust up to 10 centimeters thick, while at the base there is a yellowish-white horizon containing large lime concretions. Towards the northwest of the site, the crust laterally becomes a calcium carbonate deposit interstratified in the loess-like silt, where it emphasizes bedding characteristics which show pronounced dips towards the southeast.

Upper Middle Pleistocene ("Riss")   These deposits are represented by yellow loess-like silt which is preserved only in the southern zone.

"Riss-Würm"   This soil has been almost entirely eroded away. Only the lower part of the clay accumulation zone and the calcium carbonate deposit have been preserved in the southeastern zone of the section.

"Würm"   A wide thalweg cut into the Quaternary deposits before the last glaciation was probably filled in at the end of the "Würm" by brown clayey earth.

Post-Glacial   Red colluvial clay lies disconformably up to 3 meters thick on the Quaternary deposits. It dates from the great periods of deforestation and contains fragments of Roman pottery. A reddish soil, very poorly developed, has formed later on the surface of this colluvial clay which came from older paleosols.

FAUNA FROM STRATIGRAPHIC UNIT C1   Abundant fauna has been found on the prehistoric occupation levels in the units C1a and C1b:

Canis lupus
Sus scrofa, large
Capra ibex
Bos primigenius
Cervus elaphus
Rhinoceros mercki
Elephas meridionalis, evolved
Rabbits
Various rodents
Birds
Testudo

DATING   The fauna recalls that of sites attributed by Jánossy to the upper Tarkö phase (final Biharian): Tarkö upper bed, Vértesszöllös, Mosbach (Figure 4).

The three transgressive beaches at Terra Amata, that is, the three Stratigraphic Units Aa, Ba, and C1a, may correspond respectively to the three temperate climatic phases of Shackleton, numbered 15, 13, and 11 and dated 600,000–550,000, 500,000–480,000, and 450,000–380,000 years ago (cf. Shackleton, this volume). The occupation horizons uncovered at Terra Amata in the stratigraphic unit C1a would then date to between 450,000 and 380,000 years. It should be remembered that the occupation horizons at Torre in Pietra, the industry of which resembles that of Terra Amata, have been dated to 430,000 years by the potassium argon method. The early Acheulian industry at Terra Amata also has similarities with those discovered on the occupation floors of Torralba and Ambrona in Spain and associated with an early Middle Pleistocene fauna. According to Aguirré, Elephas antiquus of Torralba is at an evolutionary stage close to the elephant of Cava Molinario (Cava Bianca, Cava Nera) near Rome, a site which is dated to 420,000 years.

INDUSTRY[1]   Several superimposed occupation floors have been discovered at Terra Amata beneath the last beach ridge, within the ridge itself and in the dune which tops it. Beneath the last beach ridge and

[1]   No attempt has been made to translate the symbols used for indices, or in most cases the names of artifact types, etc. Readers unfamiliar with these indices and terms are referred to de Lumley (1969, 1971); or to the writings of Bordes (e.g. La typologie du paléolithique ancien et moyen, 1961. Bordeaux: Delmas), Editors.

within it, the stone industry consists chiefly of worked pebbles (70.6 percent). On the dune above the beach, worked pebbles represent only 7.8 percent, and a greater number of tools have been made on flakes. Nevertheless there are some considerable similarities among the industries of the different occupation levels.

Levallois technique is not represented (IL = 0.1 percent) and blades are rare (ILam = 3.3 percent). Flakes with a plain butt are frequent, whereas those with a facetted butt are extremely rare (IF = 2.6 percent and IFs = 0.9 percent). Flakes with cortex butt are very frequent (ITc = 62.2 percent) due to the raw material used and the great number of tools made on pebbles. Most of the flakes are in fact blanks from choppers.

The classic set of tools ("micro-industrie") is worked either on flakes (92.2 percent in the dune and 70.6 percent in the beach) or on pebbles (7.8 percent in the dune, 29.4 percent in the beach). *Racloirs* are numerous (IRess = 54.9 percent of the small tools in the dune, 46 percent of those in the beach) but they represent only 45.1 percent of the entire tool assemblage in the dune, and 17 percent in the beach. Tools with convergent retouched edges, which are rare in the beach (IRc = 2 percent) are a little more numerous in the dune (IRc = 4 percent). The *racloirs* have often been prepared by retouch called *"surélevé"* or retouch called *"écailleuse scalariforme"*.

Notched pieces (35.3 percent and 40.9 percent) as well as denticulates are relatively numerous. Tools with Clactonian notches are more abundant in the beach (14 percent) than in the dune (7.8 percent). The presence of Tayac points, Quinson points, and protolimaces should be mentioned.

Pebble tools ("macro-industrie") are common and are characteristic of the tools discovered on the Terra Amata occupations floors (17.5 percent in the dune and 62.5 percent in the beach). They are mainly represented by various types of choppers. Chopping tools are few in the beach (5.9 percent) and become very rare in the dune. Pointed choppers and unifacial picks (pointed unifacial pebbles) are very characteristic. They not unnoticeable in the beach, but they become rare in the dune.

Bifaces are extremely rare (1 percent of tools). There is always an untrimmed cortex butt and very often a transverse cutting edge. They are shaped by large trimming scars and their edges show no sign of regularization by secondary retouch.

Finally let us mention a few cleavers, nearly always prepared on split pebbles, occasionally on flakes.

Table 1

		Assemblage from layer C1a Transgressive phase		Assemblage from layer C1b Regressive phase
		Clayey silts with pebble lenses	Beach ridge	Dune
Proportions among the totality of flakes	Levallois index	0.7	0.0	0.0
	Plain platform index	19.9	11.0	17.6
	Faceted platform index (incl.)	2.0	0.5	2.5
	Dihedral platform index	1.0	0.5	1.6
	Facetted platform index (restricted)	1.0	0.0	0.9
	Talons nuls index [1]	34.1	53.6	40.5
	Cortex platform index	43.9	34.9	39.9
	Blade index	4.2	2.0	3.0
Proportions in relation to the series comprised of small tools, pebble tools, and pebbles with a single scar	Small tools on flakes	6.1	3.5	47.0
	Small tools on pebbles	5.4	1.5	4.0
	Small tools on flakes and on pebbles	11.5	5.1	51.0
	Pebble tools	29.2	8.6	11.0
	Pebbles with a single scar	51.7	86.3	37.0
Proportions in relation to the series comprised of small tools and pebble tools	Small tools on flakes	12.6	25.8	74.6
	Small tools on pebbles	11.3	11.3	6.3
	Small tools on flake segment and on pebbles	23.9	37.1	80.9
	Pebble tools	60.6	62.9	17.5
Proportions in relation to the series comprised of small tools on flakes and on pebbles	*Racloirs* (≈side scrapers)	44.4	47.8	54.9
	Plain *racloirs*	25.9	39.1	31.4
	Double *racloirs*	0.0	4.3	7.8
	Convergent *racloirs*	0.0	4.3	3.9
	Transverse *racloirs*	18.5	0.0	0.0
	Bifacially trimmed *racloirs*	0.0	0.0	11.7
	Tools of Upper Paleolithic varieties	7.4	4.3	1.9
	Grattoirs (end scrapers)	0.0	4.3	0.0
	Burins	7.4	0.0	1.9
	Perçoirs (awls, borers)	0.0	0.0	0.0
	Knives with retouched backs	0.0	0.0	0.0
	Notches and denticulates	44.4	43.4	33.3
	Notches	22.2	13.0	11.7
	Denticulates	22.2	30.4	21.6
	Denticulated *racloirs*	7.4	8.7	11.7
	Tools showing a Clactonian notch	14.8	13.0	7.8

Proportions in	Choppers	88.6	87.2	17.5
relation to the	Chopping tools	9.1	10.2	0.0
series comprised	Bifaces	0.5	0.5	1.6
of pebble tools	Cleavers	2.2	0.0	0.0
Proportions among the choppers	Pointed choppers	27.0	33.5	9.0

Pebbles with only one flake scar, convex, and with no cutting edge are very plentiful. Classed among the tools, they represent more than 30 percent of the total. They were probably used for hammering or percussion.

Bone implements are rare: a shaft of elephant bone, pointed by percussion; bones of which the point had been hardened by fire; a fragment, the extremity of which is shiny from use; an awl, some *racloirs* on long bones. (See Table 1.)

HUMAN FOOTPRINT   Apart from coprolites, the only direct trace that man has left is a right foot print 24 centimeters long, discovered in the dune and unfortunately difficult to interpret. With the help of a formula to establish the size of an individual, constructed by L. Pales, C. Chippaux, and H. Pineau, we may presume that the human being who left his foot print in the dune sand of Terra Amata measured 1.56 meters. But we do not know if it was a child, adolescent, or adult.

LIVING SITES   It does not seem as though there was a permanent camp at Terra Amata, at least in the dune. The living sites were probably occupied for only a few days each. In fact, in each level, flakes have been found side by side, which fit together, at the very spot where they fell as they were being removed from the core. The Acheulian nomads came, set up their shelter, made their tools, and left before they had much time to trample down the soil beneath their feet. Most of the camps correspond to brief seasonal halts made in the spring. This last point has been established from the evidence of the human coprolites which were discovered near the structures, and which contain pollen. They were studied by J. L. de Beaulieu, who found that the pollen all belong to plants which flower at the end of spring or the beginning of summer.

On arrival, a temporary hut was built, supported by poles or pegs, traces of which have been found during excavation. The outline of the structure is defined by blocks of stone which held the sides of the hut to the ground. This is also apparent from the distribution of tools and culinary remains that littered the occupation areas. The structures, always oval in shape, probably measured from 7 to 15 meters long by 4 to 6 meters wide. One of the oldest structures was surrounded by a line of large boulders, 30 centimeters in diameter, sometimes piled one on the other, and circumscribing a thick layer of organic matter and ashes (Figure 6).* The hut floor was in places paved with pebbles, or covered with skins which have occasionally left their imprint. The hearths were built in the center of the hut, either on soil which had been paved beforehand with pebbles, or in a small hollow dug in the sand, 30 to 50 centimeters in diameter. To protect the fire from drafts, a small wall of stones or pebbles was built, always on the northeast, the side of the prevailing winds. The hearths which have been discovered in the dune structure seem to indicate small fires. Those in the earlier structures on the beach were certainly larger if we may judge by the large quantities of charcoal and ashes found. The hearths of Terra Amata are, together with those of Vértesszöllös, the oldest known in the world. The fires which had been lit in the small hollows of 30 to 50 centimeters in diameter dug into the dune, remind one of those described by Laszlo Vertès from the Vértesszöllös excavation in Hungary, also dating to the early Middle Pleistocene (upper Tarkő phase).

The fact that he had the idea of protecting his hearths by a low stone wall leads us to suppose that the shelter that prehistoric man had set up was not free from draughts and therefore was most probably made from branches.

Inside the huts, small working areas bear witness to the exact place where the artisan made his tools. In the center of the workshop, an empty zone, without flakes, corresponds to the place where he sat on the ground or on a block of stone. All around lie waste flakes, which can be fitted together around their core to reconstitute the original pebble.

Labastide d'Anjou

In a terrace of the valley of the Fresquel, Aude basin, dated to the early Middle Pleistocene ("Mindel") at the site of Labastide d'Anjou, L. Méroc, and subsequently A. Tavoso have discovered and studied an industry very similar to that of Terra Amata: many choppers, rare chopping tools, a few picks, and some handaxes.

Montmaurin Caves

Excavations of the Montmaurin caves, undertaken by L. Méroc, have

* See foldout between pp. 764–765

led to separate discoveries in the shelter of La Terrasse, and in La Niche. At the base of the sequences are Middle Pleistocene deposits containing fauna incuding *Rhinoceros mercki*, and an associated quartzite industry. According to L. Méroc, these deposits are very close in time to a breccia with *Machairodus* in the classic cave of Montmaurin, studied earlier by M. Boule.

The mandible discovered at La Niche somewhat resembles those of Mauer and L'Arago and would thus probably date from the early Middle Pleistocene ("Mindel").

Cave of La Nauterie

The karst of La Nauterie, in the Romieu (Gers) region, is filled by substantial Quaternary deposits, attributed by Prat and Thibault to the "Mindel," "Mindel-Riss," "Riss," and the "Würm."

Beds 2, 3, 4, and 5	Würm
Bed 6	Riss III
Bed 7	Riss II
Bed 8	Riss I
Beds 10, 11, and 12	Mindel-Riss
Beds 13 and 14	Mindel
Bed 15	Günz?

Beds 13 and 14, attributed to the "Mindel" (early Middle Pleistocene), contain an archaic fauna with, among others, an equid of stenonian character, and *Dicerorhinus etruscus*.

Beds 10 to 12, attributed to the "Mindel-Riss" (middle Middle Pleistocene) are richest in fauna, with an overwhelming majority of bones from *Ursus deningeri* (95 percent), *Equus caballus mosbachensis*, *Hystrix sp.*

In Bed 14, dated to the "Mindel," a flint flake was discovered.

MIDDLE MIDDLE PLEISTOCENE; "MINDEL-RISS"; APPEARANCE OF THE LEVALLOIS TECHNIQUE

The middle Middle Pleistocene ("Mindel-Riss," Holstein, or Hoxnian) is a period which may have lasted from 350,000 to 300,000 years ago (phase 9 of Shackleton). It is essentially a time of returning warmth, during which it is still possible to trace numerous minor oscillations. In particular, several climatic zones have been distinguished in England from the pollen diagrams of Hoxne and Nechelles (a town near Birmingham). In southern mediterranean France, it is particularly characterized by the formation of important brownish-red soils on top of terrestial alluvia (moderately leached, fersialitic soil).

In La Grotte du Lazaret, Nice, the transgressive sea of the "Mindel-Riss" (sometimes called Milazzian, Tyrrhenian I, or Paleotyrrhenian) has left behind on the bedrock a beach of large rolled pebbles perforated by lithophages. The isotopic composition of the oxygen of the carbonates of the sea shells from this beach seems to indicate two sets of beaches, one of which corresponds to a fairly warm climate (δ $^{18}0/^{16}0 = -2$) and the other a less temperate climate (δ $^{18}0/^{16}0 = -1$ to 0). The "Mindel-Riss" interglacial lasted a very long time and incorporated minor climatic oscillations. The least temperate periods seem to have happened at the very end of the "Mindel-Riss" as shown by values of $\delta = -1$, for the beach at Le Lazaret which is situated immediately below the "Riss 1" deposits.

The substantial climatic improvement of the middle Middle Pleistocene interglacial is shown by the migration of *Hystrix* cf *major* as far as Burgundy, at Perrières near Dijon. During this long period, the line of *Microtus brecciensis* changes, according to A. Chaline (1972: 121) from the evolutionary stage *mediterraneus* to that of *orgnacensis*; the line of *Allocricetus bursae* changes from the sub-species *duranciensis* to that of *correzensis* via the intermediate *pyrenaicus*. The macrofauna is characterized by the reappearance of some species and the abundance of cervids. The evolution of the majority of the species present can be traced into the late Middle Pleistocene and the Upper Pleistocene.

The Cave of Mas des Caves at Lunel Viel

The cave of Mas des Caves is situated less than 1 kilometer to the northwest of Lunel Viel, near Montpellier. Its original entrance has been filled in, and today's artificial opening is at the bottom of a quarry. It was excavated in 1928 by Jules de Christol, followed by Marcel de Serres, Dubreuil, and Adrien Jeanjean. In 1962, E. Bonifay opened up a new excavation.

STRATIGRAPHY   The Quaternary infilling dates from the middle Middle Pleistocene ("Mindel," "Mindel-Riss," and "Riss"). According to E.

Bonifay, the lower series can be dated to the "Mindel." It consists mainly of very large altered blocks fallen from the roof, and of clay and sterile sands. The upper unit, nearly 4.5 meters thick, in which 14 layers have been recognized, is made up of shingle, yellow sands, and red varved silt. It may date from the "Mindel-Riss" interglacial or the very beginning of "Riss."

FAUNA   This is plentiful and well-preserved. It contains the following species:

Fissiped carnivores	Canidae	*Cuon priscus* Thenius
		Canis lupus lunellensis
		M. F. Bonifay
		Vulpes vulpes Linné
	Felidae	*Felis monspessulana* M. F. Bonifay
		Felis (Panthera) lunellensis
		M. F. Bonifay
		Felis spelaea Goldfuss
		Felis (Lynx) cf. *pardina*
		Felis (Lynx) spelaea M. Boule
	Ursidae	*Ursus deningeri* Von Reichenau
	Hyaenidae	*Hyaena prisca* de Serres
		Crocuta spelaea intermedia de Serres
	Mustelidae	*Mustela palerminea* Petenyi
		Lutra sp.
		Meles thorali spelaeus
Pinniped carnivores		*Phoca sp.*
Artiodactyls	Suidae	*Sus sp.*
	Bovidae	*Bos primigenius* Boj.
		Bison sp.
	Cervidae	*Cervus elaphus* Linné
		Capreolus cf. *süssenbornensis*
		Euctenoceros mediterraneus M. F. Bonifay
Perissodactyls	Rhinocerotidae	*Dicerorhinus etruscus* Falconer
	Equidae	*Equus caballus* Linné
		Equus hydruntinus Regalia
Rodents		Quite rare
Lagomorphs		Abundant
		Talpa sp.
Insectivores		*Erinaceus sp.*
Bats		Quite rare
Birds		*Bufo*
Amphibians		*Testudo*
Reptiles		

This fauna is characterized by the arrival of numerous temperate species, most of which were to continue to evolve during the whole of the late Middle Pleistocene and the Upper Pleistocene: *Cervus elaphus, Equus caballus, Equus hydruntinus, Crocuta spelaea, Felis spelaea,* and the large bovids. Besides these new arrivals, endemic forms persisted which died out elsewhere: *Hyaena prisca, Meles thorali spelaeus, Euctenoceros mediterraneus, Dicerorhinus etruscus,* and several forms from the early Middle Pleistocene such as *Canis lupus lunellensis* and *Felis (Lynx) spelaea* which were to survive until the present.

This fauna is perhaps similar to that discovered at the sites of La Caune de l'Arago, Uppony, and Heppenloch, which correspond to the Uppony phase (early Oldenburgian) of Jánossy.

FLORA Fossil flora in the form of charcoal, grass stalks, leaf prints, and seeds is being studied. The presence of seeds from *Celtis sp.* is to be noted.

INDUSTRY The stone industry is fairly homogeneous. It consists chiefly of worked pebbles: choppers and chopping tools; *racloirs*, denticulates, and becs. The presence of protolevallois flakes should be noted. There are bones which show signs of having been used as a chisel or point, or retouched, as well as bone splinters which show traces of intentional rectilinear incisions. The site shows traces of human arrangement, and there is evidence of certain structures: prepared hearths, boulders set in a line forming a boundary which cuts across the cave, bedding of foliage shown by the accumulation of plant refuse: grass stalks, twigs, and leaves from trees, *Celtis* seeds.

The Early Acheulian of the Somme Valley

The only Acheulian industries which probably date from the "Mindel-Riss" interglacial (Borde's early Acheulian) are those discovered either in the solifluction formed at the base of the section of the Rue de Cagny, in the suburb of St. Acheul at Amiens, or in the stratified gravel at the base of the section of Cagny-la-Garenne, or in the middle terrace of the Somme at Montières-les-Amiens. The handaxes with untrimmed butts and sinuous lateral edges are still very frequent; the ficron has made its appearance at Rue de Cagny, the limande at Cagny-la-Garenne and at Montières-les-Amiens. The flake industry is not well-known.

La Caune de l'Arago

The cave of Arago is situated in the eastern Pyrenees, north of the Roussillon plain near the small village of Tautavel, 19 kilometers north-west of Perpignan.

STRATIGRAPHY   The Quaternary infilling consists mainly of a layer several meters thick of sand and yellow sandy silt, mostly of eolian origin (eolian sands, loess-like silt) which suggest a dry cold climate perhaps corresponding to the very beginning of the penultimate glaciation ("Riss"). In these eolian deposits, two principal series may be distinguished; they are separated by a substantial hardpan colored by iron and manganese hydroxides, which might correspond to a less arid and more temperate climatic oscillation. In the upper series, the presence of many channels cut into the silt suggest brief, wetter periods. The deposits of La Caune de l'Arago has many analogies with Stratigraphic Unit B ("Riss I"?) at the cave of La Baume Bonne.

FAUNA   The fauna is abundant and well-preserved, with many species represented:

Carnivores	Canidae	*Canis lupus*
	Felidae	*Felis (Panthera) pardus*
		Felis spelaea
	Ursidae	*Ursus sp.*
	Mustelidae	*Meles meles*
Artiodactyls	Suidae	*Sus scrofa*
	Bovidae	*Bos primigenius*
	Cervidae	*Cervus elaphus*
		Rangifer tarandus
	Capridae	*Capra ibex*
Perissodactyls	Rhinocerotidae	*Rhinoceros mercki*
		Rhinoceros hemithecus
	Equidae	*Equus caballus* cf. *mosbachensis*
Probiscidians		*Elephas antiquus*
		Castor fiber
Rodents	Lagomorphs	*Oryctolagus cuniculus cuniculus*
	Gliridae	*Eliomys quercinus helleri*
	Arvicolidae	*Dolomys (Pliomys) lenki*
		Microtus brecciensis orgnacensis
Birds		*Cricetulus (Allocricetus) bursae*
		pyrenaicus
Reptiles		*Testudo sp.*

The presence of an archaic horse, somewhat similar to the one at La Micoque (Prat 1968), of a small wolf, a large panther, remains of rodents now extinct (*Eliomys quercinus helleri, Microtus brecciensis orgnacensis, Dolomys (Pliomys) lenki),* taken together with the particular evolutionary stage reached by *Cricetulus (Allocricetus) bursae pyrenaicus* (Chaline 1971) allow the site to be dated, as with Mas des Caves at Lunel Viel, to the middle Middle Pleistocene (see Figure 4), Uppony phase (early Oldenburgian of Jánossy). The great frequency of horse and rhinoceros should be noted, as it shows the expansion of steppe conditions also suggested by the great thickness of the eolian deposits. The presence of reindeer in middle Middle Pleistocene deposits is also noteworthy.

INDUSTRY   The stone tools left behind by the paleolithic hunters on the various occupation levels of La Grotte de l'Arago are very numerous: more than 100,000 objects have been uncovered. At almost every level they are similar to an early Tayacian but several layers at the top of the sediments contain a middle Acheulian industry.

The *Tayacian* industry (Figures 7 through 10) is usually in quartz, more rarely in flint, and occasionally in quartzite. The debitage is not Levallois (IL = 4.2 percent). The indices of faceting (IF = 16.3 percent; IFs = 6.4 percent) and the blade indices (ILam = 3.6 percent) are very low. Particularly characteristic is the moderate proportion of *racloirs* (IRess = 41 percent), comprised in particular of plain and transverse *racloirs*, the very high proportion of tools with retouch called "*surélevé*" (18.3 percent), the presence of retouch called "*écailleuse scalariforme*," the relative abundance of Tayac points, Quinson points, Clactonian notches, denticulates and *becs* with Clactonian notches, the presence of protolimaces: all these give this industry resemblances to the Tayacian or proto-Charentian of La Baume Bonne and La Micoque. Pebble tools are abundant: choppers, chopping tools, and some polyhedrals; but bifaces are extremely rare: less than one biface to one thousand retouched tools. The presence of micro-choppers and micro-chopping tools recalls an earlier industry called the Buda industry, from Vértesszöllös in Hungary.

The MIDDLE ACHEULIAN assemblage (Figures 11 and 12), made mostly of schist, is one with Levallois debitage. The *racloirs*, of which the percentage is fairly high, were often made by means of a flat retouch; the kind of retouch called "*surélevé*" was, on the other hand, very little used. The most numerous types of bifaces are amygdaloid, oval, or lanceolate.

LATE MIDDLE PLEISTOCENE; "RISS"; DIVERSIFICATION OF PREHISTORIC CULTURES; FIRST SIGNS OF RITUAL

The late Middle Pleistocene ("Riss," "Saale," "Gipping," "Wolstonian") was a period of glaciation probably lasting from about 200,000 to 120,000 years ago. The reversed episodes of Levantine (311-293 × 10^3 years), Jamaica (215-198 × 10^3 years), and Blake (114-108 ×

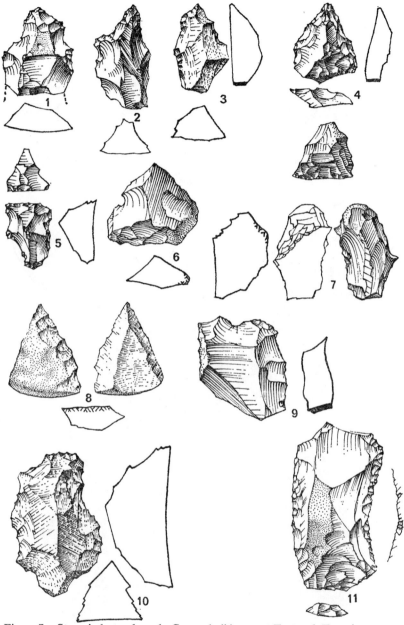

Figure 7.   Stone industry from la Caune de l'Arago at Tautevel. Tayacian

1–3.   Tayac points
4.   A point with retouch called *"surélevé"*.
5.   Denticulate and *"bec"*.
6.   Clactonian notch.
7.   Convergent *"racloir"*.
8.   Denticulate.

9.   A Clactonian notch adjacent to a simple, convex sidescraper edge.
10.   Denticulate.
11.   Double *"racloir"*.

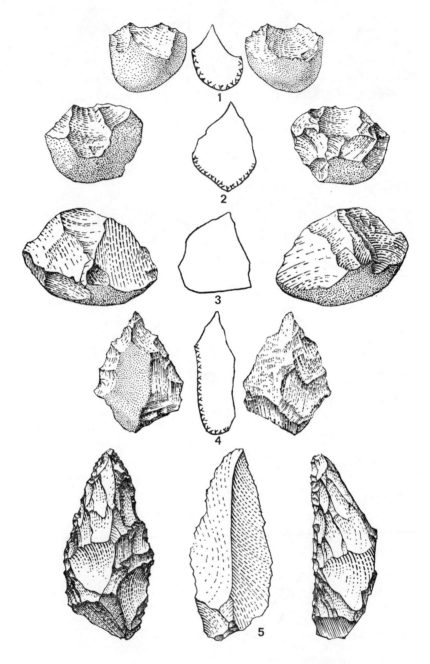

Figure 8.   Stone industry from la Caune de l'Arago at Tautavel. Tayacian.
1–3.   Micro-chopping tools.
4.   Tayac point.
5.   Quinson point.

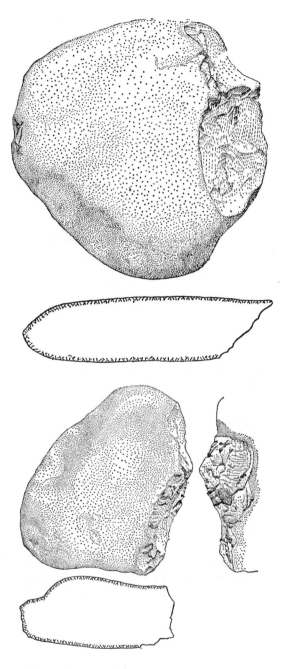

Figure 9.   Stone industry from la Caune de l'Arago at Tautavel. Tayacian.
1.   Chopper.

Figure 10.   Stone industry from la Caune de l'Arago at Tautavel. Tayacian.
1.   Chopper.

10^3 years) events have still not been traced in the continental deposits of the Late Pleistocene.

Three cold periods during the late Middle Pleistocene ("Riss"), which were separated by long interstadials have been shown by the sedimentological study of the caves and rock shelters in southeastern (Lazaret) and southwestern France (La Micoque, Le Pech de l'Azé) and by the study of alluvial deposits in the Seine basin and the Somme valley. These three cold phases could well correspond with the three colder phases 8, middle 7, and 6 of Shackleton, dating approximately to 300,000-250,0000 years, 240,000 years, and 200,000-120,000 years ago. Furthermore, there is evidence for a substantial contemporary marine transgression.

Chaline has pointed out that this period is characterized by fauna which includes a large part of the "Wurmian" species, sometimes represented by a distinct subspecies, and some archaic species such as *Pliomys lenki*, *Allocricetus bursae*, and *Microtus brecciensis*.

The late Middle Pleistocene effectively corresponds with the Solymar phase of Jánossy. Cave deposits dated to the "Riss" are relatively frequent in the southern mediterranean region: Le Lazaret, L'Observatoire, Rigabe, La Baume Bonne, Orgnac 3, Aldène, and in the southwest, Le Pech de l'Azé II, La Micoque, and Combe-Grenal.

La Grotte du Lazaret

Le Lazaret cave is situated in Nice on the western slopes of Mount Boron.

STRATIGRAPHY   In Le Lazaret, the continental deposits of the "Riss" which lie above the "Mindel-Riss" beach reach nearly 6 meters in depth (Figure 14).

"Riss I"   The first stage of this (Beds XXVI to XX) is characterized by a relatively cold and humid climate. There is evidence of a drier oscillation, phase C, in the middle of this period; it is marked by a momentary interruption of the allochthonous clay deposits. Six principal phases may be distinguished in "Riss I."

Phase A: After the retreat of the "Mindel-Riss" sea, the beach was covered by a fairly thin stalagmitic floor (Bed XXVI). It is evidence for a humid and still temperate climate.

Phase B: A cold, humid climate helped to bring about a thermoclastic exfoliation of the walls, resulting in thick frost-riven scree containing large boulders (Bed XXIV). Large quantities of colluvial clay, most probably from an old altered red soil ("Mindel-Riss" paleosol?), formed on the slopes of Mount Boron, penetrated the cave, and got mixed with the scree. These clay flows show that the climate was humid.

Phase C: The climate then became drier. The deposition of clay inside the cave stopped; the only deposition was caused by the mechanical phenomena due to the alternating frost and thaw, which allowed a layer of large blocks enveloped in a cryoclastic scree with a very small number of fine elements to be laid down (Bed XXIII).

Phase D: A new cold and very humid climatic phase then resulted in the deposition of a cryoclastic scree with great boulders, the effect of frost, flooded in a bed of red clay from the outside, the effect of humidity (Bed XXII).

Phase E: A thin and discontinuous sheet of stalagmite (5 millimeters thick) is evidence of a small, relatively temperate and humid oscillation, during which sedimentation of all kinds was interrupted (Bed XXI bis).

Phase F: A thick layer of plastic clay, red, homogeneous and compact, more than one meter thick, seals off the "Riss I" levels (Beds XXI and XX). In these layers of clay, calcium carbonate elements are rare; frost action is nonexistent. This clay was brought into the cave during a very humid period.

"Inter-Riss I-II"   This is characterized by substantial phenomena of corrosion and alteration. The rare pebbles of the underlying beds are decomposed and appear in the form of whitish chalk nodules. This temperate climatic period could correspond to the temperate episode between phases 8 and 7 of Shackleton dated approximately to 250,000.

"Riss II"   These levels (Beds XIX to VIII) are essentially composed of thick cryoclastic scree, very much frost-shattered, which in certain beds (XII) includes very large boulders. These deposits incline towards the interior of the cave and correspond in part, to a mass of scree sliding down the slopes of Mount Boron, perhaps under the effect of solifluction. Clay and clay-sand lenses are interstratified in the mass of the infilling. The second stage, like the first, is therefore characterized by a relatively cold and humid climate.

Phase A: Beds XIX to XIV can be attributed to phase A. In this unit, clayey scree alternates with layers of clay containing rare stones.
Bed XIX: clayey scree
Bed XVIII: clay with scree

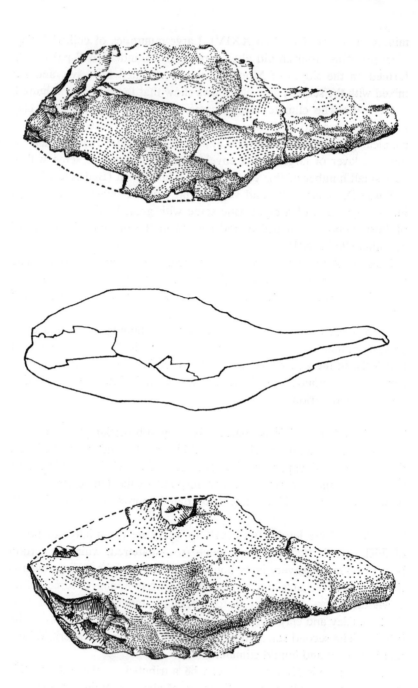

Figure 11.   Stone industry from la Caune de l'Arago at Tautavel. Middle Acheulian.

1.   Lanceolate biface

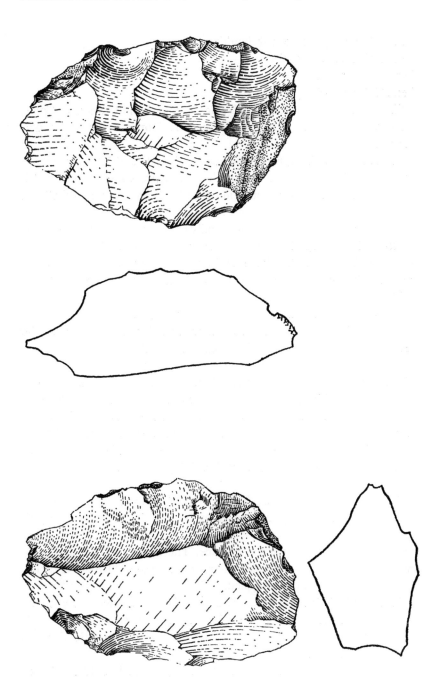

Figure 12.   Stone industry from la Caune de l'Arago at Tautavel. Middle
Acheulian
1.   Amygdaloid biface

Bed XVII: clayey scree with boulders
Bed XVI: clay with pebbles
Bed XV: clayey scree
Bed XIV: clay with pebbles

These layers were formed during a cold humid climate. Colder periods (clayey scree) alternated with more humid periods (clay with pebbles).

Phase B: This phase, which includes Beds XIII and XII is essentially composed of a mass of fallen boulders, sometimes huge, enveloped in dark brown clay. It corresponds most probably to a less humid climate than that of Phase A but probably a little colder.

Phase C: These are deposits essentially made up of angular scree (Beds XI to VIII) enveloped in red or brown red clay. The climate remained very wet but from the decrease in the percentage of pebbles and boulders, it may be assumed that the climate had become a little less cold.

Phase D: During this last phase of "Riss II," a very moist and not very cold climate led to the formation of substantial layers of clay (Beds VII to V) most probably of extraneous origin.

"Inter-Riss II-III"   The beds dated from "Riss II" underwent alteration after deposition; in particular, stones in Beds VII to V which are extremely corroded and most often appear in the form of whitish nodules looking like chalk. This period of temperate climate could correspond to the temperate episode between phases 7 and 6 of Shackleton, dated approximately to 220,000 to 200,000 years ago.

"Riss III"   These deposits, Beds IV to V, consist of angular scree enveloped in sandy clay, carried along by trickling water. It probably corresponds to a fairly cold and very moist climate, certainly much more continental than the present one. The series of "Riss III" sediments appear much more homogeneous than those of "Riss I" and "II". Three phases can be distinguished:

Phase A: This is represented by Beds IV and III, angular scree consisting of small and medium size elements, enveloped in a clay matrix of brown-red color. The percentage of boulders seems a little higher at the base of Bed IV.

Phase B: Bed II was deposited during a much colder climate; boulders are more frequent.

Phase C: A moist and not very cold period at the end of "Riss III" favored the deposition of thin-bedded, clayey-sandy silts.

FAUNA   The fauna of these levels is well-preserved and abundant. The "Riss III" fauna is best known. It includes the following species:

Carnivores	Canidae	*Canis lupus*
		Vulpes vulpes
	Felidae	*Felis (Lynx) spelaea*
		Felis (Panthera) pardus lunellensis
	Ursidae	*Ursus arctos*
Artiodactyls	Suidae	*Sus scrofa*
	Bovidae	*Bos primigenius*
	Cervidae	*Cervus elaphus*
		Dama sp. large
	Capridae	*Capra ibex*
		Rupicapra rupicapra
Perissodactyls	Equidae	*Equus caballus pivetaui*
Proboscidians		*Elephas antiquus*
Lagomorphs		*Oryctolagus cuniculus cuniculus*
Rodents	Sciuridae	*Marmota marmota*
	Gliridae	*Eliomys quercinus helleri*
	Cricetidae	*Cricetus cricetus*
	Arvicolidae	*Dolomys (Pliomys) lenki*
		Clethriomys clareolus
		Microtus (Microtus) subterraneus
		Arvicola sp.
	Muridae	*Apodemus sylvaticus*

The presence of an archaic horse and a large panther, the evolutionary stage of the wolf, the remains of a field-mouse now extinct, *Dolomys (Pliomys) lenki*, confirm that this is effectively a "pre-Würm" fauna (late Middle Pleistocene or "Riss").

Deer, forest animals, are very much more numerous than horses, which are grass-land animals. The relative abundance of cervids leads us to think that it was then wetter than today in the Maritime Alps, which agrees with the information given by the sediments. In the "Riss III" levels, the wolf, the chamois, the marmot, the abundance of ibex, the presence of the ptarmigan among the birds, the alpine accentor, the alpine chough, and the Great Snowy Owl (*Nyctea scandiaca*) show that the climate of the Mediterranean coast at the end of the "Riss" was distinctly more severe than it is today. In the levels that indicate a relatively cold climate, ibex are more frequent than deer. The reverse is true in beds which were deposited during a more temperate climate.

FLORA   Pollen analysis allows a reconstitution of the coastal forest landscape at the end of the late Middle Pleistocene (end of the "Riss") when the Scots pine predominated. In the moister valleys, the white oak, birch, elm, and hazel developed.

PALEOTEMPERATURES   The $^{18}0/^{16}0$ ratio determined on molluscs from "Riss III" deposits is evidence, on the one hand that the water was fresher than it is today (four grams of salt less per liter of water); on the other, it shows a mean temperature during the warm season of six degrees below that measured today.

The comparison of results obtained by the study of the fauna and flora, by analysis of sediments and isotopic analysis of carbonates, allows a reconstruction of the landscape of the Nice region at the end of "Riss III." The climatic conditions of the coast around Nice were certainly colder and more continental than they are today; they must have been like those found today at an altitude of about 1,000 meters in the southern Alps: cold, temperate, and relatively dry much of the year, wetter in autumn and winter, sunny in summer.

The Cave of La Baume Bonne

At La Baume Bonne, Quinson, Basses Alpes, the late Middle Pleistocene ("Riss") deposits correspond to three stadials separated by altered soils.

Unit B   This unit, probably dating to the first stadial of the "Riss" seems to have started with a dry climate which favored the deposit of substantial layers of sand, without cryoclastic elements. This was followed by a cold moist climate during which a large quantity of cryoclastic rubble was deposited. Fauna of "Riss I" levels inlcudes a great number of ibex, a large horse and a large bovid.

"Inter-Riss I-II"   During a long, warm, and probably dry period, intensive alteration affected the "Riss I" deposits. The upper part, rich in iron and manganese, forms a fairly hard crust.

Unit C   Moisture increased considerably at the beginning of this stage, probably dated to "Riss II," sufficiently to provide a circulation of water in the karst and a washing of the cave. There is only a small amount of the previous infilling left stuck against the northern wall of the site. A period slightly less moist, but very cold, persists during the whole time of the deposition of the beds during the second stage of the "Riss." In these levels, all the pebbles are extremely frost-shattered, showing that the cold was very intense. Water, rich in CO_2 and with a great dissolving capacity, slowly decalcified the entire sediments.

A warming up of the temperature towards the middle of "Riss II" is marked by a break in sedimentation, a slight alteration, and a small crust of manganese (Bed I). Finally, the growing humidity caused a new channelling towards the end of the second stadial of the "Riss," forming a deep gully in the southern zone of the cave and emptying nearly the whole of the shelter.

The "Riss II" fauna has completely disappeared.

"Inter-Riss II-III"   The series of levels corresponding to the second stadial was very much altered during this interstadial, and there is evidence of a real diagenesis of sediments. A crust of iron and manganese (Bed G) up to 20 meters thick seals off the former infilling. Part of the manganese has been released and is deposited in the form of spherical nodules or small plates in the mass of the sediments.

Unit D   This unit, dating probably to "Riss III" rests disconformably on the preceding units. The beginning was marked, as in "Riss II" by a very moist period during which a new scouring of the cave took place. The "Riss III" deposits show traces of a very severe climate, both cold and wet. All pebbles and consolidated sandstone tools are very frost-shattered.

In fact the "Riss III" deposits include five series of beds, each of which fills a gully hollowed out of the unit immediately below. The deposits which accumulated in these gullies were each in turn subjected to solifluction; flints and pebbles were pushed up vertically. Between the deposition of each of these five units, an increase of moisture favored the hollowing out of channels. Decalcification by cold water rich in CO_2 must have gone on during the whole of "Riss III." At the end of this period, a considerable increase in moisture caused substantial gullies in the underlying levels.

Fauna of the "Riss III" levels is nearly always decalcified. However, there are ibex bones and the astragalus of a Merck rhinoceros within the section of consolidated and non-decalcified breccia.

The Site of Orgnac III

The site of Orgnac III, Orgnac-l'Avon, Ardèche, is in the form of an elliptic cavity with an area of 600 meters square filled up to the lapias level. The stratigraphy described by J. Combier shows certain analogies with those of Le Lazaret Cave.

First Sedimentary Unit   This is marked by the deposition of beds of angular pebbles, alternating with fine strata of clayey micaceous sands which are sub-horizontal and continuous. Red sandy clay with a few rare stones is evidence of the warming up of the climate and dates most probably from an interstadial of the "Riss."

Second Sedimentary Unit   The principal collapse of the rock-shelter occurred during the beginning of this unit. The deposits consist of a 4-meter-thick layer of cryoclastic scree enveloped in red and brown clay. Layers of dry angular stony material are visible especially at the base and in the upper part. Clay deposits on the other hand are predominant in the middle. The stratigraphy of this second unit is similar to the infilling which, at Le Lazaret, is attributed to "Riss II."

The microfauna determined by Chaline would seem to confirm the age of the second unit as the middle of the "Riss."

The mammal fauna includes aurochs, horse, red deer, *Rhinoceros mercki, Rhinoceros hemitoecus,* wild boar, and beaver; carnivores are rare.

In spite of the presence of some rodents typical of a forest landscape *(Apodemus sylvaticus, Eliomys quercinus),* the predominance of *Microtus mediterraneus* and the presence of *Cricetulus (Allocricetus) bursae* and *Dolomys (Pliomys) lenki* suggest a fairly open landscape, similar to the steppe. This recalls the associations found in the beds of La Caune de l'Arago and the lower levels at La Baume Bonne.

The Cave of Aldène

In the cave of Aldène, Cesseras, Hérault, there is a remnant of sediments at the entrance, stuck against the north wall, which probably date to the "Riss." Excavations by Barral and Simone in 1971 and 1972 were undertaken in order to define the stratigraphy:

A_1 Stalagmite floor
A_2 Very hardened red breccia
B   Beige colored breccia with coarse elements, cemented by a heavily concreted sandy silt
C   Red colluvial clay
D   Eboulis subjected to alteration and cemented by beige colored silt
E   Beige colored silt with thin clay lenses
F   Gravel with altered elements cemented by red clay with sandy lenses

G Compact clayey silt
H Stalagmite floor with *Helix*
I Bed of small pebbles encased in iron and manganese oxide
J Quartz sand cemented by brown-red clayey silt
K Reddish clayey silt
L Deposition of aluminium and lime phosphates

An Acheulian industry and a fauna rich in bears appear at several levels.

Rodents discovered in levels B and C confirm the attribution to the "Riss": *Dolomys (Pliomys) lenki, Cricetulus (Allocricetus) bursae* (migratory hamster), *Dicrostonyx torquatus* (artic lemming). The evolutionary stage reached by these different species enables Chaline to place beds B and C in the middle of the "Riss" when a very severe climate must have obtained, shown notably by the migration of the arctic lemming which originates from the northern zone.

The Cave of Rigabe

In Rigabe cave, Artigues, Vas, a thick layer of deposits dates from the "Riss." (E. Bonifay 1962.)

"Riss II" sediments These are represented by Beds S to N which consist of altered cryoclastic scree together with colluvial clay.

"Inter Riss II-III" This is characterized by an important alteration of the "Riss II" infilling.

"Riss III" sediments These are made up of cryoclastic scree giving evidence of cool, moist climate which may be compared with the "Riss III" climate of Le Lazaret cave.

These levels are very rich in fauna, including a great number of cervids, bovids, ibex, horse, hyaena, and Merck's rhinoceros.

CULTURES OF THE LATE MIDDLE PLEISTOCENE ("RISS")

Four industrial groups have been distinguished during this period:
1. Acheulian: This group derived from the lower Acheulian of the "Mindel-Riss"; it lasted during the whole of "Riss," "Riss-Würm," and

continued during the first "Würm" stadial. The middle Acheulian may be dated to "Riss I" and "II," the upper Acheulian to "Riss III," and the final Acheulian to "Riss-Würm" and the beginning of "Würm."
2.   Tayacian: This group derived from the Clactonian or the Buda of "Mindel-Riss," it also lasted during the whole of the "Riss" glaciation. It is a forerunner of the Charentian.
3.   Evenosian: This group is found within the "Riss," and seems to be on the Clactonian line of Clacton, and could be the forerunner of some denticulated Mousterian industries of the "Würm."
4.   Pre-Mousterian: This group could be the forerunner of either the typical Mousterian or the Charentian from Ferrassie.

ACHEULIAN   Several classification schemes for the French Acheulian have been suggested. Breuil founded his on stratigraphy much more than on typology. On the other hand, Bordes has based it on typology. We adopt the latter method. (See Table 2.)

Table 2

Commont	Breuil	Bordes	Chronology
Upper Acheulian	Acheulian VII Acheulian VI	Final Acheulian	"Würm I" and "Riss-Würm"
	Acheulian V	Upper Acheulian	"Upper Riss"
Acheulian	Acheulian IV	Middle Acheulian	"Lower and Middle Riss"
Chellean	Acheulian III Acheulian II Acheulian I	Lower Acheulian	"Mindel-Riss"

The Middle Acheulian   This is well-represented in the Somme valley at Cagny-la-Garenne, in La Rue de Cagny and the Bultel Tellier quarry ("l'Atelier Commont"). Bordes has distinguished a primitive middle Acheulian. The first was discovered in the solifluction gravel at Cagny-la-Garenne and in the sands of La Rue de Cagny, situated below the reddish-brown sands. It dates therefore from the very beginning of the "Riss." The evolved middle Acheulian was discovered in the reddish-brown sands of Cagny-la-Garenne and "l'Atelier Commont", as well as in the basal scree of older loess I and II at Cagny-la-Garenne. It dates from the very beginning of the "Riss."
   Bifacial tools of Abbevillian type, with unworked cortex butt are not very numerous. Ficrons are frequent in the primitive middle Acheulian,

which also includes limandes, amygdaloids, lageniforms, and elongated cordiforms. In the evolved middle Acheulian there is a high percentage of limandes at the Rue de Cagny (c:2); lanceolates and cordiforms are predominant at L'Atelier Commont.

The Levallois technique seems to have been discovered at the beginning of the "Riss," and we can distinguish a middle Acheulian with Levallois technique at Cagny-la-Garenne and a middle Acheulian without Levallois technique at L'Atelier Commont.

In the southwest, the middle Acheulian has been discovered in the Charente valley, in "Riss I and II" deposits at the cave of Pech de l'Azé, Carsac, Dordogne, and in the clay silt sands of "Riss I and II" of the Adour basin, Chalosse, and Pays Basque. The "Chalossian" is a middle Acheulian dated to "Riss II" by Thibault at Nantet and Montsoué, central Chalosse. The middle Acheulian tools of the Garonne are often worked on quartzite pebbles.

In southeastern France, the upper beds of La Caune de l'Arago (Figures 11 and 12), Le Lazaret, and L'Observatoire have also supplied middle Acheulian industries

Upper Acheulian Sites which provide upper Acheulian industries are frequent and to be found all over France. In the Somme valley at Cagny-la-Garenne, the Seine basin at Tillet and Houppeville, they are most often found in the scree at the base of the older loess III (beginning of "Riss III"). Cave sediments dated from "Riss III" which correspond to a fairly, severe climate also supply upper Acheulian tools: La Chaise and Combe Grenal in the southwest, Aldène, Orgnac III, and Le Lazaret in the southeast.

In northern France, the upper Acheulian industries often contain beautifully made bifacial tools, often lanceolate or micoquian. The Levallois technique is fully developed. Flake tools, often on Levallois flakes are numerous and, if the bifacial tools are discounted, it is nearly impossible to distinguish this industry from some Mousterian ones of the "Würm." The Acheulian of the Charente valley is similar to that in the north.

The upper Acheulian of "Riss III" from the cave of La Chaise in Charente, and from Combe-Grenal in Dordogne, studied by Bordes, has a rather particular appearance. It is very rich in well-made flake tools and poor in handaxes (5-8 percent). The latter are most often amygdaloid and sometimes backed, in which case they resemble east European forms. In the sandy silts ("Riss III") of central Chalosse, Bouheben, Nantes, and the Chalosse de Pouillon, Thibault has discovered

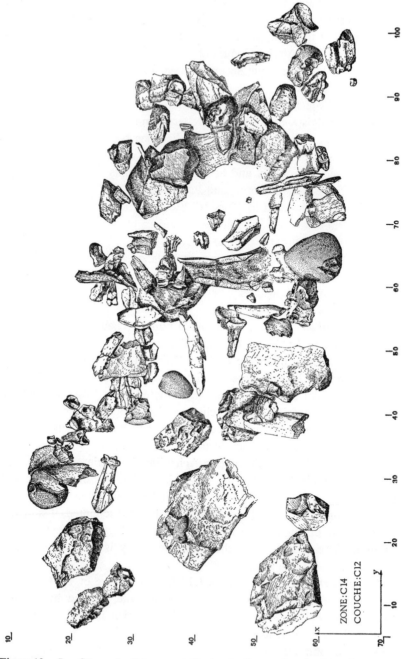

Figure 13.   La Caune de l'Arago at Tautavel. Occupation horizon from bed C12 (zone C 14) on which the human pre-Neanderthal mandible of Arago II was discovered.

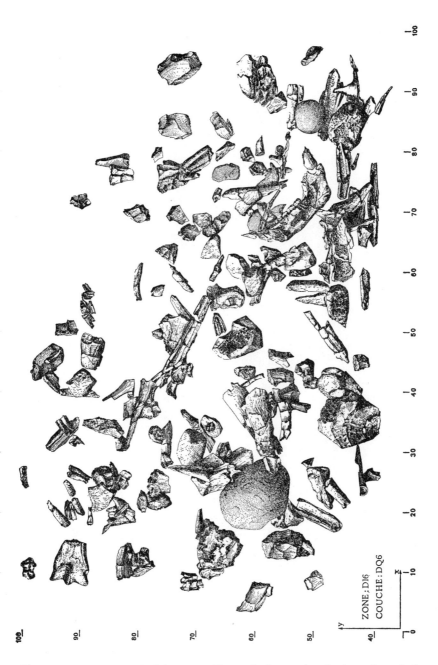

Figure 14. La Caune de l'Arago at Tautavel. Occupation horizon from bed DQ6 (zone D 16) on which the human pre-Neanderthal mandible of Arago XIII was discovered.

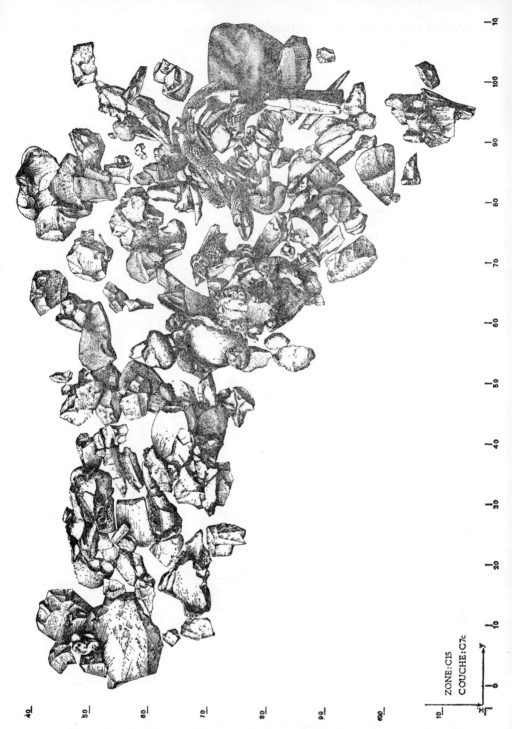

ZONE:C15
COUCHE:C7c

Figure 15. La Caune de l'Arago at Tautavel. Occupation horizon from bed C7c (zone C 15) on which the human pre-Neanderthal skull of Arago XXI was discovered.

an industry of Acheulian facies which recalls that of Combe-Grennal and La Chaise.

In the cave of Le Lazaret, Nice, the deposits of the penultimate glaciation are made up of 6 meters of frost-shattered scree, enveloped in colluvial red clay. This unit corresponds to a moist and very cold climate, with frequently alternating frost and thaw. Two warmer periods ("Inter-Riss") favored the formation of two soils showing signs of alteration: the frost action stopped and the calcium carbonate decomposed. Thus the stratigraphy is divided into three distinct sections probably equivalent to the three major stadials of the penultimate glaciation ("Riss I, II, and III"). The industry of the "Riss III" deposits may be considered as being upper Acheulian with a debitage that is only weakly Levallois (see Figures 15, 16 and Plates 4, 5, 6). It is rich in *racloirs*, poor in *"couteaux à dos retouchés"* and in upper paleolithic type tools. It is characterized by a large proportion of worked pebbles, especially choppers. The relatively abundant bifacial tools are usually of lanceolate type and occasionally have an untrimmed cortex butt.

The upper Acheulian of Le Lazaret (Figures 15, 16 and Plates 4, 5, 6) can be included in the mediterranean Acheulian group: l'Observatoire, La Grotte du Prince, Aldène, Torralba, Torre in Pietra, Imola, etc. It is distinct however from the upper Acheulian group scattered across Provence and mediterranean Languedoc at some distance from the mediterranean coast. This latter is characterized by a dominant Levallois debitage, a relative abundance of the upper paleolithic type tools and a small proportion of worked pebbles: Les Sablons, Cros-de-Peyrolles, Fontarèche.

At Orgnac III (Ardèche), "Riss III" deposits contain an upper Acheulian industry with amygdaloid bifaces and cleavers. This is associated at the base of the unit with a flake industry which is not of Levallois technique. At the top it is associated with Levallois flakes.

Final Acheulian or Micoquian This started during the last interglacial and lasted through the whole of the first "Würmian" stadial. It presents numerous typological and technological facies.

The northern Micoquian includes large lanceolate bifacial tools, and Micoquian ones associated with an industry with Levallois debitage and of Levallois facies at Le Tillet in the grey series; and at Houppeville in the reddish-brown series. The Micoquian of Grainfollet, Brittany, contains a small percentage of lanceolate or Micoquian bifaces associated with a flake industry of weakly Levallois technique, quite rich in *racloirs* which have often been obtained by the retouch called *"écailleuse scalariforme."*

The final Acheulian of Micoquian type of the Largue valley in the Basses Alpes at Plan de Gondran, Saint-Laurent, Le Clos, and Sylvabelle, is derived directly from the upper Acheulian of the Mediterranean. The Acheulian type bifaces (bifacial backed scrapers, lanceolate, micoquian, lanceolate, ficrons, amygdaloids, naviforms) are always more numerous than Mousterian bifacial tools: cordiforms and subtriangulars. However, the retouch technique on certain of these tools which are shaped by small flakes and convex on one side, and by large flaking on the other, undoubtedly introduces the Mousterian of Acheulian tradition. This Micoquian industry generally with a Levallois facies, has as its characteristics the fact that it is made on Levallois flakes, a high percentage of *racloirs*, a large proportion of tools with retouched convergent edges, a larger number of denticulates than upper paleolithic type tools, a small percentage of *"couteaux à dos,"* the presence of tools with a thinned base, and burin blows at the distal end of convergent *racloirs* or *"racloirs déjetés,"* a small proportion of pieces with retouch called *"écailleuse scalariforme"* or of Charentian type.

TAYACIAN   Parallel with the Acheulian, there is another culture, the Tayacian, which also lasted the whole of the "Riss": La Micoque ("Riss I, II, III"), La Baume Bonne ("Riss I, II, III"), La Caune de l'Arago ("Riss I") (see Figures 7 through 10). This industral complex is characterized by the very reduced quantity of Levallois flaking, the very small number of blades, a large percentage of simple *racloirs*, both convex and transverse, the predominance of tools with Quina retouch, relative abundance of Tayac points, Quinson points, Clactonian notches, the presence of proto-limaces derived from *"racloirs surélevés doubles"* with convergent edges. Chopping tools are rare, but choppers are abundant. Handaxes are very rare but sometimes beautifully worked as at La Baume Bonne and L'Arago. They are absent at La Micoque. At La Caune de l'Arago, Tautavel, pebble tools are very frequent: choppers, chopping tools, and some polyhedral tools. The presence of micro-choppers and micro-chopping tools has similarities with the older industry at Vértesszöllös in Hungary, called the Buda industry (see Figure 8, Numbers 1 to 3).

The evolution of the Tayacian industries was marked during the course of time by a progressive decrease of the percentage of Clactonian notches, denticulates, *becs* made by adjacent Clactonian notches. These traits were concomitant with an increase of the percentage of

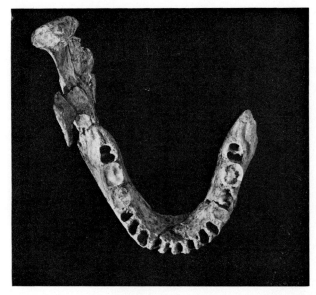

Plate 1.   La Caune de l'Arago at Tautavel. The human pre-Neanderthal mandible of Arago II. Scale two-third.

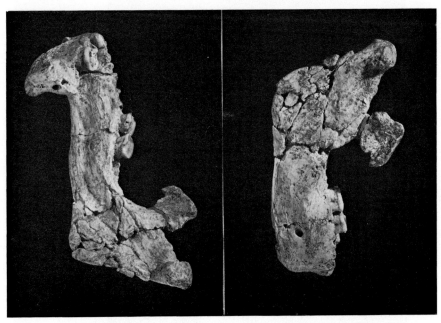

Plate 2.   La Caune de l'Arago at Tautavel. The human pre-Neanderthal mandible of Arago II. Scale two-third.

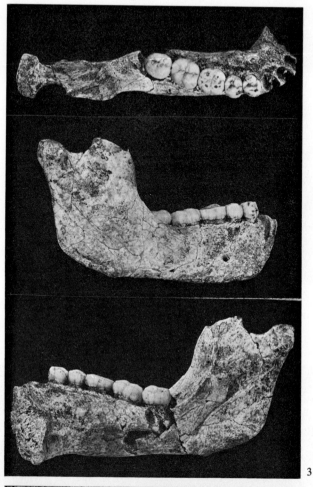

3

4

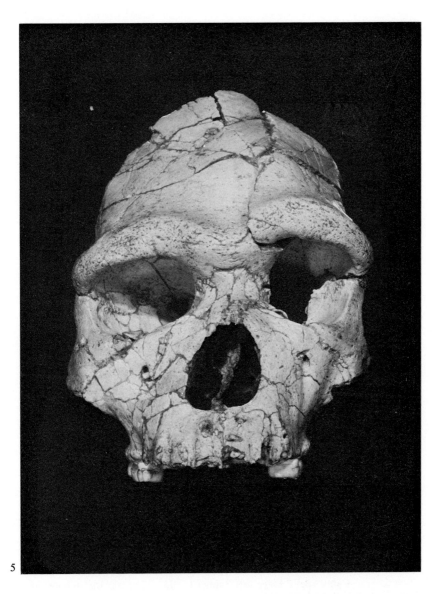

5

Plate 3.　La Caune de l'Arago at Tautavel. The human pre-Neanderthal mandible of Arago XIII. Scale one-half.

Plate 4.　La Caune de l'Arago at Tautavel. The skull of Tautavel man had been left on an occupation horizon together with stone tools and fragments of bone from rhinoceros, horse, aurochs, deer, ibex, and lion. The posterior section of the skull (parietals and occipital) is missing which suggests that the skull was discarded after the flesh had been removed. A schist flake is visible inside the cranial cavity. Scale one-half.

Plate 5.　La Caune de l'Arago at Tautaval. Front view of the human pre-Neanderthal skull. Scale two-third.

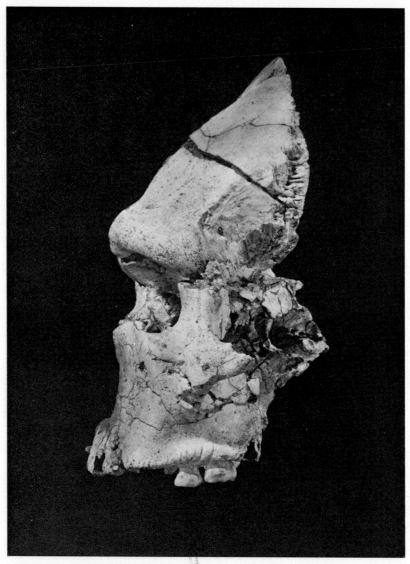

Plate 6. La Caune de l'Arago at Tautavel. Side view of the human pre-Neanderthal skull. Scale two-third.

racloirs, and in particular simple convex or transverse *racloirs* and "*tranchoirs*." Bifacial tools are more often lanceolate than in the "Riss III" deposits. The Micoquian bifaces and the backed pseudo-biface appear at the end of the last stadial of the "Riss." It is during this period that the Tayacians worked real leaf-shaped points at La Baume Bonne. The Tayacian, a very promising culture, acted as a ferment on several others. It was widespread outside France: High Lodge, England, and Venosa, southern Italy. From the beginning of "Würm I" it branched out into several groups: para-Charentian, atypical Charentian, of Quina type; it can therefore be defined as a "proto-Charentian."

EVENOSIAN A very different culture from the Tayacian, but often confused with it, the Evenosian has been found in deposits from the end of the "Riss": Sainte-Anne-d'Evenos (Var), Les Trecassats, *série* I (Vaucluse), La Braïsse I and II (Basses Alpes), Frenillot, Grand Muscat and Pouderouses (Hérault), Fontéchevade (Charente). It is characterized by a non-Levallois flaking technique, and it was often made on natural flakes. It includes a very small percentage of *racloirs* and a fairly large proportion of tools of the upper paleolithic type such as *grattoirs* and burins, multiple Clactonian notches, *becs* with adjacent notches, truncations, spheroids, chopping tools obtained by the removal of large flakes, but choppers and handaxes are absent. The Evenosian from the "Riss" seems to be in the line of the Clactonian of Clacton, and might be the forerunner of some Mousterian industries with denticulates, as the eastern Tayacian is of the Charentian.

The chief differences between the Tayacian and the Evenosian are summarized in Table 3.

Pre-Mousterian of the "Riss"

In the layers attributed to the "Riss" at the cave of Rigabe (Var) and la Baume des Peyrards (Vaucluse), a pre-Mousterian industry is characterized by being on flakes of Levallois technique, by a large number of Levallois flakes not made into tools, by a fairly high proportion of *racloirs* and tools with retouched convergent edges, and by the presence of retouch called "*écailleuse scalariforme*." These industries are forerunners of either the typical Mousterian or of the Charentian of La Ferrassie.

Conditions of Life during the Late Middle Pleistocene ("Riss")

The cultures of this period, Acheulian, Tayacian, Evenosian, pre-

Table 3

Tayacian	Evenosian
Tools generally formed by the trimming of well-struck flakes.	Tools often made on natural flakes.
Racloirs numerous and well-made.	*Racloirs* rare and poorly formed.
Transverse *racloirs* numerous.	Transverse *racloirs* absent or rare.
Racloirs dejetés of "High Lodge" type are numerous.	*Racloirs dejetés* of High Lodge type are absent or rare.
Limaces or *proto-limaces* are present.	*Limaces* and *proto-limaces* are absent.
Retouch of the form called *écailleuse scalariforme* is common.	Retouch *écailleuse scalariforme* is absent.
Tools of Upper Paleolithic types present in moderate amounts.	High proportions of Upper Paleolithic forms.
Clactonian notches of the variety termed *surélevé* are rare.	Clactonian notches *surélevé* are numerous.
Truncated flakes are rare or absent.	Truncated flakes numerous.
Tayac points numerous.	Tayac points rare or absent.
Choppers common, chopping tools rare.	Chopping tools common, choppers rare.
Boules polyhédriques (spheroids) absent.	*Boules polyhédriques* common.
Bifaces present but rare.	Bifaces absent.

Mousterian, correspond to distinct ethnic groups who lived side by side for many tens of thousands of years without ever losing their autonomy. They evolved slowly during the whole of this time, apparently unaware of each other. Reciprocal influences are rare.

People usually settled on river banks, on well-exposed hill slopes, on loess plains or in caves. Sometimes they built primitive settlements or camps on sandy permeable ground which remained firm and relatively dry underfoot, even in a wet climate as at Les Sablons, Cros de Peyrolles, and Fontarèche. The middle Acheulian "l'Atelier Commont" appears as a rounded structure, 25 meters square (about 5 by 5 meters). In the caves, the living areas were arranged to make them more comfortable. At La Baume Bonne, oval huts up to 5 meters by 2.5 meters wide were set up, which were paved with pebbles as a protection against moisture. At Rigabe, a fireplace had been built: a wall of dry stones defined the hearth.

Excavations in the "Riss III" deposits of Le Lazaret have produced evidence for a large structure 11 meters long by 3.5 meters wide, which had been built near the entrance of the cave by the upper Acheulians (Figure 17). The doors of the hut faced the interior of the cave, and a small wall of dry stones near the entrance protected the living area from winds coming from the sea. From the scrupulously careful study of the stone industry and bone remains, and their distribution on the hut floor, it is possible to reconstruct partially the interior arrangement of the structure, which was divided into two rooms. In the back, two small fires had been lit directly on the ground. Round these, Acheulian hunters had put bedding made of seaweed covered with skins, as witnessed by the shells which had been attached to the seaweed and the ungual phalanges from carnivores.

These people had therefore reached a sophisticated level of culture. When they left Le Lazaret after the winter sojourn, they put a wolf's skull just behind the cave entrance after having removed the brain through a hole 5 centimeters in diameter, cut into the right parietal. It is possible that by this gesture they sought to acquire some of the wolf's power.

At La Caune de l'Arago, the anterior part of a human skull lay upside down on a very rich prehistoric living site, skull-cap down, jaw bone in the air (see Plates 2 and 4). It had been left by man in the midst of a heap of rhinoceros, horse, auroch, deer, and ibex bones. The flesh had been stripped away before it was left there, and the back part of the skull had been removed. A flake was found in the skull cavity. It is not impossible that the skull may have been opened in order to extract the brain perhaps during ritual proceedings.

Hominids of the Middle Pleistocene ("Mindel-Riss") and the Late Middle Pleistocene ("Riss")

Human remains dating from the middle Pleistocene and the late Middle Pleistocene discovered in France are still fairly rare.

GROTTE DU PRINCE (VINTIMILLE): a pelvis associated with an Acheulian industry.

GROTTE DU LAZARET (NICE): the right parietal of a child and 2 teeth associated with an Acheulian industry.

ORGNAC III: 2 teeth associated with an Acheulian industry.

LA CAUNE DE L'ARAGO: 14 isolated teeth, phalanges, fragments of parietal, 1 mandible with 6 teeth in place (Arago II) (see Plates 1 and 2), a half mandible with 5 teeth (Arago XIII) (Plate 3), the anterior part of an adult skull (Arago XXI) (Plates 5 and 6) associated with a Tayacian industry.

LA CHAISE, BOURGEOIS DELAUNAY CAVE SHELTER: a skull cap, frontal and parietal bones, occipital, temporal, mandible and fragment of maxilla with 3 molars.

LA CHAISE, GROTTE SUARD: fragment of skull cap (frontal and parietal), a temporal, a child's frontal with its mandible, 1 incisor, 1 canine, 1 premolar.

GROTTE DE FONTÉCHEVADE: skull cap, fragment of mandible and a radius, associated with an Evenosian industry.

The recent discoveries, particularly those of La Caune de l'Arago, at Tautavel, have allowed us to gain some fresh knowledge of these people.

The only complete skull that we know in France from the "Riss" is that found at Tautavel (see Plates 5 and 6). It may be compared with that of Steinheim man. Measurements of the curvature of the frontal bone give evidence for a flatness of the skull comparable with or greater than the majority of Neanderthals. The forehead however is not as flat as that found in some classic archanthropines, the Pithecanthropines and Sinanthropines for example. There is no sagittal crest.

In examining the relative proportions of the frontal bone of Tautavel man, a longitudinal development is to be observed, greater than on most of the Neanderthals; it seems smaller however transversely. A pronounced post-orbital narrowing can be noticed. From above, the post-orbital narrowing is easily distinguishable. It is distinctly more pronounced than that of the Neanderthal skulls and comparable with that of Steinheim. It is less pronounced however than that of the Sinanthropines and Pithecanthropines.

Unlike modern man, the frontal bosses in the Neanderthal adult are weakly developed; they are completely absent from the frontal of Tautavel man, as in Steinheim man. The lateral crests of the frontal bone are prominent and very high. The temporal fossae of the frontal bone are vast and deeper than those on the Steinheim and Neanderthal skulls.

The supraorbital torus is very pronounced. A superciliary arcade and a supraorbital arcade can be distinguished, running superiorly and latterly: the *sulcus supraorbitalis*. The supraorbital trigone is not separated off from the supraorbital arcade. The strongest region of the torus is approximately 30 millimeters from the mid line as in Steinheim man. The glabella is depressed in comparison with the torus, as in Steinheim man. The torus therefore does not constitute a continuous ridge as in Neanderthals, but it is comparable to that present in Steinheim man. The depression present over the supraorbital torus is shallow. It is less pronounced than on the frontal bone of Steinheim man. The supraglabellar depression is well-defined.

The frontal sinuses are visible on X-ray photographs. They are very small. Their size is not connected with the strong development of the torus.

Orbits are large, low, and rectangular, much lower than those of the classic Neanderthals; the apertures resemble those of Steinheim. The interorbital distance is very large; it is comparable with or slightly superior to the largest measurements found in Neanderthals.

Prognathism is very pronounced, the face clearly projecting in front of the brain case. This aspect is further emphasized by a pronounced alveolar prognathism. The upper maxilla is massive and robust. The anterior aspect is nearly flat and, as in Neanderthals, has no canine fosse. It must be mentioned however that a slight depression is noticeable in the La Ferrassie specimen. In Steinheim man, the canine fossa is deep and marked. In the classic archanthropines, it exists apparently in Sinanthropus but is absent in Pithecanthropus IV.

The palate is deep.

The alveolar arcade is somewhat upsiloid, sockets of the two premolars and three molars pass through a straight line. The individual had lost his two second premolars during his lifetime, and their sockets are partially resorbed. M2 is the largest tooth and M3 is relatively small: M1<M2>M3. The occlusal aspect of the molars is relatively simple and there is no cingulum.

There is a very pronounced external mandibular ridge. It merges with the exterior alveolar line, is very well-developed at the level of the sockets of M1 and M3. The same kind of ridge may be observed in Steinheim man, and it also exists in certain Neanderthals, as for example, La Ferrassie. On the internal aspect, the frontal crest is relatively pronounced. The frontal depressions are not discernible. Vascular traces are few, but the superior longitudinal sinus can be distinguished.

The bulging of the frontal pole must have been particularly developed to conform with the great distance between the orbits. A preliminary examination of the endocranium shows that the third frontal convolution was well-developed and the area of Broca must have been very pronounced. The endocranial volume must have been relatively small, certainly smaller than that found in the average classic Neanderthal but somewhat greater than that of Steinheim.

Furthermore, the discovery of a number of pre-Neanderthal parietals from western Europe allows some very useful comparisons. The examination of these bones produces evidence of two types of pre-Neanderthal individuals among the "Riss" population, in which the stage of hominization of the skull differs somewhat: Le Lazaret man with whom the fossils from La Chaise and Steinheim may be associated and Cova Negra man with whom the Fontéchevade and Swanscombe fossils may be grouped. Le Lazaret man, like La Chaise and Steinheim, is characterized by a long parietal bone in which the asterion is posteriorly situated, which indicates a poorly developed occipital rotation. The man from Cova Negra, like the Fontéchevade and Swanscombe specimens on the other hand, is characterized by a short, almost square bone on which the asterion is located in a lower, more anterior position, which would indicate a greater rotation of the occipital. As a direct consequence of this difference in rotation, the temporal margin is, on the parietal bone from Le Lazaret, as in some Pithecanthropines, longer than the sagittal margin; whereas on the Cova Negra parietal, as on certain pre-Neanderthals from western Europe (Fontéchevade, Swanscombe) the temporal margin is distinctly shorter than the sagittal margin. This characteristic is to be found in most Neanderthals and in modern man.

A comparison of the height ratio of the sagittal and bregma-lambda chords shows that the child from Le Lazaret compares with the adult from La Chaise as a modern nine-year-old would to a modern adult. It also shows that the Cova Negra parietal bone resembles modern man more closely than La Chaise. The maximum height of the Le Lazaret parietal bone is comparable to or slightly less than that of Neanderthals; that of Cova Negra on the other hand, is greater than that of the Neanderthals: it falls within the range of variation of present-day man and approximates to that of Swanscombe. Further, when examined from the anterior aspect, the Le Lazaret parietal bone like that of La Chaise, has a weakly rounded curvature in the transverse plane; in contrast, the Cova Negra parietal is markedly rounded in the transverse plane. The two parietals from Le Lazaret and La Chaise therefore seem less evolved than those of the Neanderthals; the Cova Negra parietal seems to possess certain characteristics more evolved than those of the Neanderthals. These observations are confirmed by the study of the peri-biparietal spheres, within which the parietals are inscribed using the bregma, lambda, and frontoparietal points. Delattre and Fenart (1960) have shown that the phenomenon of ontogenetic rounding of the human biparietal arch has been responsible for the placing on this same sphere of two other points: the asterion and the internal incisoral point. In the pongidae, these two points are always situated outside the sphere because of the negative rotation of the back of their skull during growth.

Some descriptive geometric constructions allow us to place these points in relation to the peri-biparietal sphere. In the Neanderthals (Krapina Pa 1), the asterion and the internal incisoral bridge are situated either on the sphere, or inside it, as in modern man. The same disposition can be found in Cova Negra man, whose skull rounding had thus reached the evolutionary stage of the Neanderthals and modern man. On the Le Lazaret parietal however, the asterion is situated outside the sphere, which allows us to conclude that skull rounding is less evolved and that less positive rotation took place during ontogenesis.

The disposition of the meningeal vessels gives further evidence for the feeble occipital rotation of the parietal bone of Le Lazaret: the bregmatic and lambdatic branches are parallel and run superiorly whereas on the Cova Negra parietal these two branches are more horizontally directed and present a fan-like aspect diverging posteriorly as in modern man. In the same way, the difference in skull rotation of these two hominids explains why at the encephalic level the general direction of the Sylvian fissure is very oblique in the Le Lazaret brain and almost horizontal on that of Cova Negra.

The rare pre-Neanderthal mandibles on the other hand give evidence of a certain homogeneity among the "Riss" hominids. The very different size of mandible suggests a substantial sexual dimorphism: Arago XIII (Plate 3) and Mauer belonging to males, and Arago II (Plates 1 and 2), Montmaurin and Asych to females. Their dimensions are large: the mandible (external bicondylar diameter) in particular for Arago XIII, is of great width. Their alveolar arcades built above the basilar arcade are convex anteriorly; their symphyses are receding, the mental trigones are absent, digastric fossae are situated only on the lower part of the bone, their genio-glossal fossae are deep, their *torus transversus inferior* and the marginal swellings are very thick, and their lateral prominences are pronounced. But what is most remarkable, in particular in Arago XIII and Mauer, is the development of the alveolar planum and of the internal oblique line, the very low position of the superior genial fossa and the mental foraminae. (See Table 4.)

Table 4

	Mauer	Montmaurin	Arago II	Arago XIII	Banolas
Total length	122 mm	111 mm	108 mm	124.5 mm	107 mm
Total width	132 mm	133.5 mm	128 mm	158 mm	110 mm
Mandibular index	92.4	83.1	84.4	78.8	97.3
Thickness of lateral protruberance	21 mm	16 mm	17.3 mm	25 mm	16 mm
Robusticity index [a]	55.9	54.2	48.5	68.5	55.4
Basal component	31.6	45.2	31.5	22.5	50.8
Alveolar component: Symphysial angle	93°	98°	103°	106°	89°

[a] at chin cavity level.

Their rami are high and very wide; their condyles are of large dimensions; their coronoid proceses are very short and low; the sigmoid
notches are weakly expressed and their lowest points are posteriorly
situated. The pharyngial crest is very salient and the triangular planum
pronounced. Their retro-molar triangles are vast, their retro-molar
grooves are wide and deep. In Arago II and Mauer, the rami are vertical in relation to the body of the mandible, and remarkably wide. In
Arago XIII and Montmaurin the rami are slightly inclined. The position of the alveolar component of the mandible of Arago II is like that
of the Montmaurin fossil; and the Arago XIII like that of Mauer. A
mandibular depression suggesting a slight bony chin may be observed
on Arago II; it is lacking on Arago XIII as on Mauer and Montmaurin.
The dimensions of the teeth vary greatly. Some are of medium size and
belong to female mandibles (Arago II, Montmaurin, Asych); others of
very large size belong to male type mandibles (Arago XIII and Mauer
for example). The molar cusp pattern is not very archaic. In their
overall dimensions and morphology the European pre-Neanderthal
mandibles present a certain homogeneity; in a number of characteristics
however, they seem to differ from the mandibles of the Pithecanthropines who lived during the Middle Pleistocene on the other side of the
Mediterranean in Africa and Southeast Asia: Atlanthropus, Pithecanthropus, and Sinanthropus.

In the light of all these observations, the pre-Neanderthals of western
Europe show:

1. ARCHAIC CHARACTERISTICS which allow us to consider that they
are at an evolutionary stage near that of Archanthropus (*Homo
erectus*): marked prognathism, very developed sub-orbital tori, marked
post-orbital narrowing, frontal flattening, and in the mandible a
strongly developed alveolar planum and internal oblique line, with very
low positioning of the superior genial fossa;

2. CHARACTERISTICS WHICH DISTINGUISH them from African and Asian
archanthropines, such as less pronounced supratoral sulcus, less pronounced post-orbital narrowing and absence of a sagittal crest; and

3. CHARACTERISTICS WHICH SOMETIMES RESEMBLE the west European
classical Neanderthals, such as an absence of a canine cavity in the
man of Tautavel.

Much polymorphism must have existed in the populations of western Europe during the Middle Pleistocene. Thus the skull of Tautavel
man may be compared with that of Steinheim in the marked post-
orbital narrowing, in the disposition of the torus and the supratoral
sulcus, in the configuration of the orbits and in the small skull capacity.

Other characteristics which underline differences are the morphology of the maxilla and absence of a canine fossa.

In the study of the parietal bones we have been able to show several individuals whose skull development differed. To the Le Lazaret specimen whose skull rounding was apparently incomplete, it is possible to add the Middle Pleistocene fossils from La Chaise, Tautavel, and Steinheim. To the man of Cova Negra, whose skull rounding was complete, it is possible to add those of Fontéchevade and of Swanscombe.

To conclude, from many morphological characteristics, the west European pre-Neanderthal seem to belong to the same evolutionary stage as the Archanthropines of Africa and Asia. They could however, be situated on a parallel evolutionary branch or subphylum, which would strengthen the hypothesis that several human groups evolved independently on different continents: that is, independent evolution of subgroups. In the same way that the polycentric origin of modern man can be allowed, a polycentric origin of the paleoanthropines (Neanderthals) can be imagined.

REFERENCES

BLANC-VERNET, L.
1969 Contributions à l'étude des Foraminifères de Méditerranée. *Recueil de Travaux de la Station Marine d'Endoume.*
BONIFAY, E.
1962 *Les terrains quaternaires dans le Sud Est de la France.* Travaux de l'Institut de Préhistoire de l'Université de Bordeaux 2.
1968 "Stratigraphie et industrie lithique de la grotte du Mas des Caves à Lunel-Viel (Herault)," in *La Préhistoire: problèmes et tendances,* 37–46. Paris: C.N.R.S.
BONIFAY, M. F.
1969 "Faunes quaternaires de France," in *Etudes sur le Quaternaire,*
1971 *Carnivores quaternaires du Sud-Est de la France.* Mémoires du Museum de l'Histoire Naturelle, n.s., série C, Tome XXI, fasc. 2. 127–142. Paris: VIII° Congrès INQUA 1969.
BOURDIER, F.
1969 Étude comparée des dépôts quaternaires des bassins de la Seine et de la Somme. *Bulletin d'Information de Géologues du Bassin de Paris* 21:169–231.
BOURDIER, F., J. CHALINE, J. J. PUISSEGUR
1969 Données nouvelles sur les Mollusques et les Micromammifères quaternaires des régions d'Amiens et de Paris. *Comptes rendus des séances de l'Académie des Sciences,* série D, 268:266–269.
BOUT, P.
1970 Problèmes du volcanisme, V. *Revue d'Auvergne* 84:29–73.
1972 Problèmes du volcanisme, VII. *Revue d'Auvergne* 86:53-79.

BREUIL, H., L. MEROC
1950   Les terrasses de la Haute Garonne et leurs quartzites. *Préhistoire* 11:1–15.

CHALINE, J.
1969   "Les rongeurs du Pleistocène moyen et supérieur de France (systématique, biostratigraphie, paléoclimatologie)." Unpublished doctoral thesis, Dijon. C.N.R.S. number: AO 3377.
1971   La microfaune du Vallonnet (A.M.) et le problème des correlations micro-macromammifères à la limite pleistocène inférieur-moyen. *Bulletin du Musée d'Anthropologie Préhistorique de Monaco* 17:66–69.
1972   *Le Quaternaire. L'histoire humaine dans son environnement.* Paris: Doin.

CHALINE, J., A. THÉVENIN
1972   Deux terriers de spermophiles dans les sables vosgiens d'Achenheim et l'âge des industries sous-jacentes sur galets brisés du Bas-Rhin. *Revue Archéologique de l'Est* 23:205–216.

DELATTRE, A., R. FENART
1960   *L'hominisation du crâne.* Paris: C.N.R.S.

DE LUMLEY, H.
1966   Les fouilles de Terra Amata à Nice, Premiers résultats. *Bulletin du Musée d'Anthropologie Préhistorique de Monaco* 13:29–51.
1969a   A paleolithic camp at Nice. *Scientific American* 220:42–50.
1969b   "Les civilisations préhistoriques en France. Correlations avec la chronologie quaternaire," in *Etudes Françaises sur le Quaternaire,* 151–169. Paris: VIII° Congrès INQUA 1969. Supplement au Bulletin de l'Association Française pour l'étude du Quaternaire.
1969c   *Le paléolithique inférieur et moyen du Midi méditerranéen dans son cadre geologique,* volume one: *Ligurie-Provence.* Gallia-Préhistoire 5.
1971   *Le paléolithique inférieur et moyen du Midi méditerranéen dans son cadre géologique,* volume two: *Languedoc, Roussillon, Catalogna.* Gallia-Préhistoire 5.
1971   Découverte de l'homme de l'Arago. *Le courrier du CNRS* 2:16–20.

DE LUMLEY, H., et al.
1969   *Une cabane acheuléenne dans la grotte du Lazaret (Nice).* Mémoires de la Société Préhistorique Française 7.

DE LUMLEY, H., M.-A. DE LUMLEY
1971   Découverte des restes humains antenéandertaliens dâtés du début du Riss à la Caune de l'Arago (Tautavel, Pyrenées-Orientales). *Comptes rendus de l'Académie des Sciences de Paris,* série D, 272:1739–1742.

KURTÉN, B.
1968   *Pleistocene mammals of Europe.* Chicago: Aldine.

LETOLLE, R., H. DE LUMLEY, C. VERGNAUD-GRAZZINI
1971   Composition isotopique de carbonate organogènes quaternaires de Méditerranée occidentale: essai d'interprétation climatique. *Comp-*

tes rendus de séances de l'Académie des Sciences, série D, 273: 2225–2228.

MEIGNEN, L.
1972 "Le paléolithique inférieur et moyen de la basse vallée du Gard dans son cadre géologique." Unpublished doctoral thesis, University of Paris.

MISKOVSKY, J.C.
1970 "Stratigraphie et paléoclimatologie du Quaternaire du Midi méditerranéen d'après l'étude sedimentologique du remplissage des grottes et abris sous-roche. (Ligurie, Provence, Bas-Languedoc, Roussillon, Catalogne.)" Unpublished doctoral thesis, University of Paris.

POUTIERS, J., P. FERNEX
1972 "Quelques remarques sur la stratigraphie et les propriétés magnetiques de dépôts quaternaires de la Côte d'Azur," in *Colloque sur l'étude du remplissage détritique, chimique et biologique des grottes pour servir à la reconstitution de l'environnement au Quaternaire.* Nice: Association Française pour l'étude du Quaternaire.

PRAT, F.
1968 "Recherches sur les Equidés pléistocènes de France." Unpublished thesis, University of Bordeaux.

PRAT, F., C. THIBAULT
i.p. "Gisement pleistocène de Nauterie à la Romieu (Gers). Note preliminaire," in *Colloque sur l'étude du remplissage détritique, chimique et biologique des grottes pour servir à la reconstitution de l'environnement au Quaternaire.* Nice: Association Française pour l'étude du Quaternaire.

RANDRIANASOLO, A.
1972 "Étude des foraminifères du Pliocène du Mont Boron et du Quaternaire de la region de Nice (Alpes Maritimes)." Unpublished doctoral thesis, University of Provence.

SHACKLETON, N. J., N. D. OPDYKE
1973 Oxygen isotope and palaeomagnetic stratigraphy of equatorial Pacific core V 28-238: oxygen isotope temperatures and ice volumes on a 10^5 year and 10^6 year scale. *Journal of Quaternary Research* 3:39–55.

THÉVENIN, A.
1972 Du paléolithique ancien au néolithique dans l'est de la France: actualité de recherches. *Revue Archéologique de l'Est* 23:163–204.

VENZO, S.
1965 "The Plio-Pleistocene boundary in Italy, in *Subcommission on the Lower Boundary of the Pleistocene,* volume one. Lodz: Report of the VIth International Congress on Quaternary, Warsaw.

WERNER, P., G. MILLOT, J. P. VON ELLER
1962 Un "pebble-tool" des alluvions rhénanes de la carrière Hurst à Achenheim. *Bulletin Service carte géologique Alsace-Lorraine* 15:29–36.

ZAGWIJN, W. H.
1963   Pollen-analytic investigations in the Tiglian of the Netherlands. *Mededelingen van de geologische Stichting,* n.s. 16:49–71.
ZAGWIJN, W. H., H. M. VAN MONTFRANS, J. G. ZANDSTRA
1971   Subdivision of the "Cromerian" in the Netherlands: pollen-analysis, paleomagnetism and sedimentary petrology. *Geologie en Mijnbouw* 50:41–58.

Middle Pleistocene Hominids

D. R. PILBEAM

ABSTRACT

Paleoanthropologists have interpreted human evolution during the Pleistocene in terms of a number of "phases". Early Pleistocene and earliest Middle Pleistocene hominids fall into at least two groups that apparently represent distinct species; the robust-toothed *Australopithecus boisei* and more advanced *Homo habilis* (or early *Homo* sp.). These differ cranially, dentally, and postcranially. Middle Pleistocene hominids can be classified in *Homo erectus*, specimens of which seem to be generally younger than early *Homo* sp. Later Middle Pleistocene and Late Pleistocene hominids are generally classified as neanderthaloids or archaic *Homo sapiens*, and are generally younger than most *Homo erectus* and older than most modern *Homo sapiens*.

Hypothetical frameworks for interpreting human evolution have rarely been made very explicit. Anthropologists have tended to view evolution as regular and gradual, although hominid phylogeny may in fact have been characterized by lengthy periods of stasis; they have divided on the one hand into advocates of widespread evolution in which most populations contributed to later generations, and on the other into those who believe it more likely that major evolutionary changes were usually due to change in populations that were relatively restricted geographically.

The *Homo* lineage apparently exhibits phases of relatively little change, particularly in dental and gnathic morphology, and, to a lesser extent, in endocranial volume. There are also periods during which change was faster. Such a phase during the Late Pleistocene may reflect relatively rapid dispersal of modern *Homo sapiens* populations.

The pattern of morphological change may suggest that hominid behavior was quite stable for lengthy time periods. This might perhaps be reflected in the archaeological record of the Oldowan and Acheulean. The Late Pleistocene hominid morphological changes very broadly parallel an acceleration of technological change, and may reflect changes in communicative and cognitive abilities.

INTRODUCTION, BACKGROUND, AND THE "GENERAL CONSENSUS"

It is difficult to articulate a "traditional" or "consensus" view of Pleistocene hominid evolution. However, it has been quite widely agreed that the hominids underwent a series of changes during the late Cenozoic which can be conveniently analyzed as "phases" or "stages" (Aram-bourg and Hoffstetter 1963; Piveteau 1957; Clark 1964; Brace 1967; Pilbeam 1972a).

Late Pliocene and early Pleistocene hominids have been assigned to one or more species lineages of *Australopithecus;* one of these lineages has also been classified as an early species of the genus *Homo, Homo habilis* (L. Leakey, Tobias, and Napier 1964; Pilbeam 1972a). Many believe that this lineage is represented in Middle Pleistocene times as *Homo erectus,* populations of which in turn evolved toward the end of the Middle Pleistocene into early populations of *Homo sapiens* (variously known as "neanderthalers," "neanderthaloids," "archaic *Homo sapiens*," and so forth). Individuals exhibiting quite "modern" (that is, similar to living *Homo sapiens*) morphological features, particularly in the skull, appear sporadically in the later parts of the Middle Pleisto-cene (Bordes, ed. 1972). Whether or not they are sampled from entire populations that are equally modern is unknown; evidence for such populations only becomes fully convincing after about 40,000 years (Clark 1964; Oakley 1964; Butzer 1971).

These phases of human evolution are generally described in terms of the degree of development of particular functional complexes. Thus, *Australopithecus* species are characterized at least by the following characteristics. In comparison with apes, their brains are larger with re-spect to body weight, different in external morphology, and probably internally reorganized (Holloway 1972). Neurocrania are either sub-spherical, with rounded occipital and frontal regions and small supra-orbital tori (so-called "gracile" *Australopithecus, A. africanus,* or *Homo africanus),* or longer and lower, with rather more angulated occipitals, flatter frontals, and more pronounced tori (so called "robust" *Australo-pithecus,* or *Paranthropus, A. robustus, A. boisei, P. robustus,* or *P. boisei*) (Tobias 1967a). Relative to apes of equivalent body weight, cheek teeth are large, and cranial and gnathic structures involved in mastication are robust, reflecting well-developed and powerful chewing muscles (Pilbeam 1972a; Tobias 1967a). There is some evidence to suggest that differences between the various species of *Australopithecus* in cheek tooth area and brain volume are to a marked degree allomet-rically related to differences in body weight. Incisors and canines are small relative to cheek teeth, particularly in the larger species (Robin-son 1956). Postcranial remains indicate that *Australopithecus* species were bipeds, though some, at least, were apparently not identical to those hominids generally assigned to *Homo* (R. Leakey, Mungai, and Walker 1972). Body proportions may also have differed from those of *Homo* (R. Leakey 1973a). (However, in Robinson's opinion [1972], South African gracile *Australopithecus* [according to Robinson *Homo africanus*] resembles later *Homo* postcranially.)

The earliest populations that are generally placed in *Homo* are those of *H. erectus,* known best from east and southeast Asia. Classically, *H. erectus* has been defined by the following complex of traits (Clark 1964). Average population brain volumes are substantially larger than those of *Australopithecus.* Neurocrania are long and low, with angulated occipitals and relatively flattened frontals, moderate to large supraorbital tori, and thickened vault bones (involving the outer and inner tables as well as the diploë) (Weidenreich 1943). Molars and premolars are smaller than in *Australopithecus,* both absolutely and relative to body weight, while anterior teeth are absolutely as large and, relative to cheek teeth, larger than those of the earlier genus (Weidenreich 1936, 1937).

Postcranially, *Homo erectus* resembles *Homo sapiens* more closely than any *Australopithecus* species, although there appear to be some differences between certain samples of the two *Homo* species. In particular, *H. erectus* long bones from Choukoutien exhibit a thickening of the cortex and narrowing of the medulla (paralleling the thickening of the tables in the skull), as the femur from Olduvai does to a certain extent (Weidenreich 1941; Day 1971; Day and Molleson 1973).

Populations intermediate in certain morphological features (dentition, neurocranial shape, endocranial volume) between *Homo erectus* and *Australopithecus africanus* have in the past decade been recovered in Kenya (R. Leakey 1970, 1971, 1972a, 1972b, 1973a, 1973b), Tanzania (L. Leakey, Tobias, and Napier, 1964; Tobias 1965), and Ethiopia (Howell 1969; Coppens 1970a, 1970b, 1971) in late Pliocene and early Pleistocene deposits. They may also be sampled in South Africa (Clarke and Howell 1972) and Indonesia (Tobias and von Koenigswald 1964). Variously classified as *Homo habilis, Australopithecus habilis, H. africanus, Homo* species, and so forth, their exact phylogenetic position will be difficult to determine until *H. erectus* and *A. africanus* samples can be more firmly dated. Brain volumes fall between those of *Australopithecus* and *Homo erectus* (Tobias 1971a; Pilbeam 1969, 1970; Pilbeam and Vaisnys 1974); neurocranial shape is similarly intermediate (if allometry is taken into account), as are tooth morphologies and proportions.

Early or archaic *Homo sapiens* (neanderthalers, etc.) are really well known only after about 70,000 years, especially in Europe (Clark 1964;

Von Koenigswald 1958). Earlier, in the second half of the Middle Pleistocene, the record is much patchier and dating quite insecure. Individuals or populations resembling *Homo erectus*, archaic *Homo sapiens*, and even to some extent modern *Homo sapiens*, are present between 70,000 and perhaps 600,000 years, though whether or not they are contemporaneous is unknown. Archaic *Homo sapiens* is characterized by brain volumes similar to those of modern man (larger than *Homo erectus*); long, low neurocrania with rather sharply rounded occipital regions; prominent, though variable, supraorbital tori; generally rather thinner vault bones than those of (at least Asian) *H. erectus;* incisors that are larger relative to cheek teeth than those of modern man; and postcranials quite similar to those of recent *H. sapiens* (although some of the neanderthalers of Europe and Southwest Asia differed in certain poorly understood ways) (Coon 1962).

Modern man differs skeletally from earlier hominids mainly in having a subspherical neurocranium, with rounded occipital and vaulted frontal regions, moderate to absent supraorbital tori, and a flexed basicranium (Lieberman and Crelin 1971; Lieberman, Crelin, and Klatt 1972; Lieberman 1974; Pilbeam 1972a).

General trends in late Cenozoic hominid evolution (in the sense of there simply being changes through time, irrespective of rate or its constancy) can be briefly summarized as follows. Primitive bipedalism gave way to the more advanced type characteristic of *Homo;* stature and body weight also increased. Brain volume enlarged, presumably as the brain was internally reorganized. Some, though by no means all, of the brain size expansion was related to increasing body weight. Average neurocranial morphology changed, from subspherical, to ovoid, to elongated with flattened frontals and angulated occipitals; it then "filled" while remaining elongated, and finally became subspherical again. Whether or not these changes in shape correspond to actual changes in a phyletic line is one of paleoanthropology's more interesting problems. Vault thickness fluctuated, like that of long bone cortex. Cheek teeth (apparently) became steadily reduced. Incisors and canines followed a less regular course, first increasing somewhat, then later decreasing (the size increase may have been correlated with a gain in body weight). Proportions of the anterior and posterior teeth shifted in a complex way, probably because the two parts of the dentition responded to different selection pressures.

This "general consensus" view of late Cenozoic hominid evolution has traditionally (Birdsell 1972; Brace, Nelson, and Korn 1971; Coon 1962; Weiner 1971) been projected against the chronological backdrop of an Alpine glacial sequence (Würm, Riss, Mindel, and Günz). Although the Alpine region is not a good one on which to base a regional stratigraphic column (Flint 1971), the lithological and chronostratigraphic units in the Alps have been extended on a virtually worldwide basis; attempts were made to squeeze stratigraphic columns in other regions into a quadriglacial (or quadripluvial) sequence, with or without the Alpine nomenclature (Movius 1944; Coon 1962). This has had unfortunate results, particularly for the relative dating of hominids. It became widely accepted that the four glacials fell within the Pleistocene Epoch, which included at its base a marine unit, the Calabrian Stage, defined first in southern Italy (Flint 1971). Continental deposits of Early Pleistocene age, placed in the Villafranchian Stage, were thought to correlate wholly or partially with the Calabrian. Earlier workers were rarely in agreement as to the exact position of Villafranchian or Calabrian age beds relative to the Alpine glacial sequence. The Villafranchian was seen sometimes as pre-glacial, or as containing the earliest glacial (Howells 1967) and perhaps interglacial too (Weiner 1971; Coon 1962). The Middle Pleistocene (post-Villafranchian) has traditionally commenced with either the "first" (Clark 1964) or "second" glacial (Day 1965; Movius 1944) and terminated at the beginning of the last interglacial.

Australopithecus species are confined mostly or entirely to the Pliocene and early Pleistocene (Bishop and Miller 1972). *Homo erectus* remains from Asia are widely interpreted as of earlier Middle Pleistocene age (Hooijer 1968; Kahlke 1968) as are those from North (Coon 1962) and east Africa (Isaac 1967; M. Leakey 1971a). Fully modern man does not appear on a wide scale until well into the Late Pleistocene (Bordes, ed. 1972). A majority of scholars see the later stages of human evolution as essentially a rather straightforward affair, with early *Homo* types evolving from populations perhaps resembling *Australopithecus africanus,* these in turn evolving into *Homo erectus* and then to *Homo sapiens.* In general, it is assumed that only one species of hominid was present after the early Middle Pleistocene, although this might have been highly variable. Not all populations of the lineage at one time level are thought to have given rise to populations at the next; occasionally, groups probably evolved in isolation for relatively long periods of time (Clark 1964; Coon 1962; Pilbeam 1972a). However, there are other equally strongly held, albeit minority, views. Thus, extreme "unilineal" views of human evolution would place most individual fossils or populations within the lineage leading to modern man, few segments of which became geographically isolated without descendants (Brace 1967; Brace, Nelson, and Korn 1971).

"Multilineal" theories, where stages may overlap and populations become isolated for varying lengths of time, divide conveniently and arbitrarily into two types: "presapiens" and "preneanderthalers" (McCown and Kennedy 1972). Each sees most groups of archaic *Homo sapiens* as playing only a minor role in the emergence of modern man; they differ in the time depth to which they trace the last common ancestor of the two groups. The "general consensus" as I have outlined it above would place the split relatively late in the Middle Pleistocene, and can be termed a "preneanderthal" interpretation (Clark 1964; Howell 1951, 1952, 1957). However, some workers (Vallois 1954) prefer to locate the divergence further back in time, and would include some or all of the remains from Swanscombe, Steinheim, Vértesszöllös, and Mauer in a "presapiens" stock isolated from that which led to archaic *Homo sapiens* populations. Advocates of the most extreme presapiens theories would place not only archaic *Homo sapiens* populations on a side branch, but *Homo erectus* too, although L. Leakey (1972), for one, suggests the possibility of some hybridization between modern and archaic types. (In fact, the degree of isolation of the lineages or sublineages is rarely specified.)

One major drawback to many of these theories is that they center predominantly around Europe, which is unlikely to have been THE center of later hominid evolution (Pilbeam 1972a).

FOSSILS AND FRAMEWORKS

In this section I want to discuss the extent to which theoretical expectations influence our interpretation of the fossil data, and try to outline tentative frameworks against which hominid fossils can be evaluated. Paleoanthropology has, like any other science, a wide range of theoretical perspectives from which the data are viewed. Unlike most other sciences, paleoanthropology has been lax in overtly stating its hypotheses, which have instead remained implicit or poorly articulated. Only when hypotheses are stated explicitly and in detail is it possible to test them adequately. To do so requires the formulation of a set of explicit mathematical (or quantitative) hypotheses which correspand to the verbal hypotheses and are devised to illuminate, evaluate, sort, and rank them (Pilbeam and Vaisnys 1974).

Before any kind of meaningful biological conclusions can be drawn from the hominid fossil record, the remains themselves must be sorted into lineages. Elsewhere (Pilbeam 1972b), I have suggested a minimum set of conditions to be met before such sorting can be realistically undertaken. First, material should be conveniently and comprehensively distributed in time and space. (This condition is rarely satisfied in paleontology, and certainly not in the case of Hominidae.) Second, remains should be well-dated. Clearly, interpretations will differ radically depending upon relative positions and absolute ages of fossils. Third, sample sizes should be adequate for quantitative analyses. Fourth, the biological meaning of the characters under analysis ought to be understood; in general, this requires an understanding of the functional anatomy of teeth, muscles, bones, and joints. These last points are of considerable importance, and relatively little attention has been paid to them until rather recently.

Fossils in a sample, or in a number of more or less contemporaneous samples, are sorted into groups on the basis of their similarities and differences. Some idea of the distribution of characters within living species can be obtained and, by analogy, extended to the fossil record in order to discriminate "species" at a particular time level. Knowledge of the functional meaning of a specific character is clearly of great importance in evaluating variation in fossils. For example, suppose a set of fossils from one general time horizon segregates into those with prominent supraorbital tori and those lacking them entirely, with no intermediates. We might by analogy point out that chimpanzees possess such structures, while they are at best poorly developed in orangutans; the two species are only moderately variable, and there is no overlap for this trait. Further, we might believe that the differences between these two species can be explained functionally in terms of the relative disposition of calvaria and face, and degree of development of the masticatory apparatus (Biegert 1963). We would conclude that the differences between the two hominid brow types (ridged versus smooth) were statistically and biologically meaningful. (Of course, if the sample could be segregated into the same groups using other traits, that is, if character discontinuities were concordant, then we should feel on still safer ground.)

Interpretation of similarities and differences is also important in linking "species" groupings at different time levels into species lineages. If there is little phyletic change through time in a lineage (statis), then there are few problems. However, if temporally distinct samples are different, problems as to the interpretation of the differences arise again, and it is important to understand not only statistical distributions, but biological meaning too.

Paleoanthropologists have paid relatively little attention in the past to the influence of size upon shape. Within species, between species, and within evolving lineages, in order to maintain "functional efficiency," shape may change in response to changing scale, a phenomenon known as allometry (Giles 1956; Cock 1966; Gould 1966, 1971). It is rare among animals for shape to remain constant over a range of sizes. If attention is not paid to this, particularly in phyletic studies, problems can result. For example, *Australopithecus africanus* and *Homo sapiens* have braincases of a similar shape: high and subspherical, with rounded occipital regions and steep frontals. However, the absolute brainsize of *H. sapiens* is three times that of *A. africanus;* presumably body weights also differed considerably; Robinson (1972) estimates *A. africanus* at between 40 and 60 pounds, From what we know of cranial allometry in related mammal species (among African pongids, for example), with increasing size we would expect relative flattening of the skull, angulation of the occipital region, and so forth. It is then at least as plausible to view forms with somewhat longer and flatter crania, such as *Homo habilis* and *Homo erectus,* as logical results of increasing the size of an *A. africanus* type of skull (without implying a necessary phyletic relationship), than to assume that hominid skulls would have remained subspherical as they underwent major size changes.

Paleontologists have often tended to interpret the fossil record in terms of an evolutionary process aptly termed "phyletic gradualism" (Eldredge and Gould 1972). In this view, new species arise by the modification of ancestral populations. The transformation is even and slow, and it involves large numbers, if not all, of the ancestral species. The transformation occurs over all or most of the ancestral species' range. If the assumptions are correct, then the fossil record should consist of long, continuously graded sequences exhibiting steady change, breaks which are due to "imperfections" in the record.

However, Eldredge and Gould (1972) point out that the theory of allopatric speciation, derived from population biology, can be applied to the paleontological record and can often lead to a different set of expectations. New species can arise by the splitting of lineages. They may evolve rapidly, and generally a small subpopulation of the ancestral form will give rise to a new species. New species will often originate in a small part of an ancestral species' range, generally in a peripheral isolated area. In consequence, local sequences ought to show breaks, due to invasion of new species, and transitional forms will be difficult to locate. This view of phyletic change its authors term "punctuated equilibria": long periods of relative statis, dotted with bursts of speciation, rapid change, migration, mixing, and replacement. Presumably, such population changes operate at the infraspecies as well as the species level.

Of course, we should expect evolutionary events to be explicable by combining features of both models, which probably represent extremes of a continuum of processes. Many paleoanthopologists are phyletic gradualists and expect to derive from the fossil record evidence for a slow, steady transformation of hominid populations involving most, if not all, of a species at a particular time level. Such expectations can profoundly affect interpretations of new hominids. Thus, the late Pliocene hominids from East Rudolf (R. Leakey 1973a, 1973b, and personal communication), with brains as large as Middle Pleistocene *Homo erectus,* are a little difficult to interpret within a phyletic gradualist model without invoking two species lineages. They pose much less of a problem for punctuated equilibria hypotheses. Here, as elsewhere in paleoanthropology, unless we are careful, the "cloven hoofprint of theory" can mold our view of the data right from the start (Eldredge and Gould 1972).

How then should we visualize evolution of the *Homo* lineage(s) during the late Cenozoic? At any given time level, the species probably consisted of a series of allopatric populations, isolated more or less by a variety of barriers to gene flow. Population genetic studies (Yellen and Harpending 1972) of living hunters and gatherers suggest that within a broad geographical area any particular breeding group (band) might exhibit a relatively high degree of genetic heterogeneity, while widely separated groups would be relatively homogeneous. Within a particular geographical area, however, changes through time would be due to a variety of factors: local evolution, total replacement by populations from elsewhere, invasion with hybridization, and varying degree of invasion, replacement, hybridization, and local evolution.

Some local population continuity through time would be expected; it can indeed be rather well documented for Middle and Upper Pleistocene sub-Saharan African and Indonesian hominids (Pilbeam 1972 a). Geographical continuities through time could be established, theoretically, by statistical means (providing that univariate and multivariate measures of "distance" between individuals and populations reflect genetic similarities and differences). Thus, suppose at time T_1, there are populations *a* in area A and *b* in area B, and at T_2, populations *a'* in A and *b'* in B. If there is geographical population continuity through time, *a* and *a'* should be more similar than *a* and *b,'* and *b* and *b'* more similar than *b* and *a'*. Small samples unfortunately make it difficult, though not impossible, to test such models for hominids.

Divergence of hominid populations to the species level would be difficult to prove, for the presence of intermediates (hybrids) between two populations may or may not mean that they are separate species. Thus, intermediate and intergrading populations between yellow and chacma baboons are used to argue that the two are subspecies (Jolly 1966). Between anubis and hamadryas baboons, the intermediates are found only in a narrow "hybrid zone," and therefore are thought to imply that separate species exist (Kummer 1968). In Simpson's sense (1961: 153), neither species is seen as contributing significantly to the other's evolutionary future.

Another interesting aspect of the probable structure of early hominid populations has been discussed by Van Valen (1966: 380, 381).

Consider a species that is divided, by extrinsic barriers and regional adaptation, into more or less separate ... subspecies. For reasons directly or indirectly related to their somewhat different adaptations, some of these subspecies are on the average more similar to their ancestors in some respects than are other subspecies. A subspecies relatively primitive in one feature may be relatively specialized in others. ... However, it is further assumed that there is sufficient gene flow between adjacent subspecies to prevent the development of reproductive isolation and perhaps ... to introduce advantageous genes or gene complexes from one subspecies to another.

Now consider the likely course of evolution in such a species. Speciation, extinction, or merging of subspecies may or may not occur. ... Assume sufficient gene flow so that speciation has not occurred ... but not an amount sufficient to overwhelm the subspecific differences. If the species continues to exist, it will eventually happen that it will be on the average so distinct from its condition at the arbitrary starting time, that taxonomists will call it a different species. ... The advance may have been at different rates in different subspecies. ... It is even conceivable that one subspecies at the later time may be less advanced ... than another subspecies at the earlier time.

Looking at single subspecies and ignoring their ages, a taxonomist would probably put one or more subspecies of the later [time-successive] species into the earlier species, or vice versa. This is to say that, when phyletic evolution is examined in such fine grain ... equal positions on the evolutionary grades used to demarcate [time-successive] species may well occur at somewhat different times in different subspecies, which nevertheless may continuously retain an interconnected gene pool.

Detecting migration, hybridization, or replacement from the fossil record alone is very difficult. Take the case of Middle Pleistocene hominids, for example. They have been subdivided by those advocating "presapiens" theories into two lineages: *erectus*-like (including samples from Kabuh and Notopuro Beds in Java, Choukoutien Locality 1, etc.) and *sapiens*-like (Mauer, Vértesszöllös, Steinheim, Swanscombe, and so forth) (Pilbeam 1972a). Phyletic relationships between these two groups will depend first on their chronological positions; the "*sapiens*-like" set may, for example, be mostly younger than the "*erectus*-like" group. If the two sets were generally coeval, and displayed nonoverlapping morphologies, it might still be hard to demonstrate that only one set of populations (the *sapiens*-like ones, say) were ancestral to modern man, to the exclusion of *erectus*-like groups; that is, that the the lineages might be different at the species level. Evidence from Australia, for example, suggests a mingling of "archaic" and "modern" groups in the Late Pleistocene (Thorne 1971). Until we have analyzed much more thoroughly data already in hand, or, probably, until we have more data, it will be hard to choose among a variety of replacement-hybridization models.

THE STRATIGRAPHIC SETTING

Since our main purpose is to discuss Middle Pleistocene stratigraphy, what is said here will be brief and provisional. However, as indicated in the preceding section, absolute and relative dating of fossils is fundamental to an educated comprehension of their meaning.

A wide variety of stratigraphic schemes have been proposed for the last 2 to 3 million years (Broecker and van Donk 1970; Butzer 1971; Cooke 1972; Emiliani 1966; 1968; Evans 1971; Flint 1971; Kukla 1970; van der Hammen, Wijmstra, and Zagwijn 1971; Wolstedt 1966; to name but nine). None of these authors agrees precisely with any of the others; most are probably about equally acceptable; and, no doubt, none is absolutely correct. However, all are useful advances beyond the four glacial-pluvial schemes still utilized so widely in many anthropological textbooks. (Of course, there is a variety of these frameworks too, but most of them agree in the belief that the last three glacials fall within the last 400,000 years or so.)

Evidence from a variety of sources, including deep-sea cores (Emiliani 1966; Broecker and van Donk 1970; Kent, Opdyke, and Ewing 1971; McIntyre, Ruddiman, and Jantzen 1972; Keany and Kennett, 1972; Kennett and Huddleston 1972; Imbrie and Kipp 1971; Hunkins; Bé, Opdyke, and Mathieu 1971; Broecker 1971), pollen analyses of finegrained continental sediments (van der Hammen, Wijmstra, and Zagwijn 1971; Wright 1972; Shackleton and Turner 1967; Turner and West 1968), loess deposits (Kukla 1970), and fluctuating lake levels (Shuey 1972), points to the existence of many more glacial cycles (climatic fluctuations from warmer than present [interglacial] to significantly colder than present [glacial] conditions, with mean durations of somewhat under 100,000 years) than are suggested by quadriglacial schemes. Clearly, the "four major" glaciations (in the sense of the terms Mindel, Riss, Elster, Saale, and so forth) include more than one glacial cycle. Equally clearly, there are potentially many ways of grouping >N glacial cycles into N glaciations, and problems of correlation undoubtedly arise because groupings tend to vary from one worker to another (Shotton 1967; Flint 1971).

The paleoclimatic evidence listed above suggests that there have been about eight glacial cycles within the Brunhes normal polarity epoch, which began around 700,000 years ago. (Cox 1972; Dalrymple 1972; Opdyke 1972). It has been assumed that climatic fluctuations deduced from different evidence, for example, from deep-sea cores, raised beaches, and loess profiles (Broecker and van Donk 1970; Kukla 1970; Kukla and Koci 1972), are synchronous, although this has not really been adequately demonstrated except for the Weichsel-Holocene and possibly the Saale-Eem transitions.

It is also often assumed that a good correlation has been proven between climatic fluctuations as inferred from geological evidence and cyclic changes in the time-space distribution of solar energy as calculated by Milankovitch and others (Broecker, et al. 1968; Broecker and van Donk 1970; Imbrie and Kipp 1971; Milankovitch 1930; Vernekar 1968), although this remains to be demonstrated with certainty (Flint 1971; Shackleton 1971; Saltzman and Vernekar 1971).

What follows is an attempt to put approximate ages on some of the stratigraphic units and localities that have a bearing on hominid phylogeny.

Europe

The stratigraphy of northwest Europe is known in some detail in the Netherlands, Germany, and England. Data come mainly from pollen-analytical and mineralogical studies of borings from fine-grained sediments, although geomorphological information has aslo been used. In the Netherlands, a sequence of predominantly cold (c) and predominantly warm (w) stratigraphic units has been defined covering the Late Pliocene and Early Pleistocene (van der Hammen, Wijmstra, and Zagwijn 1971). They are, from the youngest: Weichsel (c), Eem (w), Saale (c), Holstein (w), Elster (c), Cromer (w), Menap (c), Waal (w), Eburon (c), Tiglian (w), and Pretiglian (c). Older units contain more than one glacial cycle. It is probable that the full complexity of mid-Pleistocene climatic events is not reflected in this scheme.

Even the last glacial cycle has yet to be calibrated unambiguously. It is likely that the Eem began around 125,000 years ago; however, its duration is a matter of some debate. It is perhaps unlikely that it lasted 50,000 years (Shackleton 1969), as has become widely assumed; rather, the later part of the generally warm period between around 125,000 and 75,000 years probably represents major interstadials that fall, by definition, in the early Weichsel (Brørup and Odderade in the Netherlands, Drama and Elevtheroupolis in Greece) (van der Hammen, Wijmstra, and Zagwijn 1971; Broecker and Ku 1969; Dansgaard, et al. 1971; Johnsen, et al. 1972; Mörner 1972; Sancetta, et al. 1972). It is distinctly possible that the term "Eem" has been used for different parts of the generally warm period between 125,000 and 75,000 years ago.

The Saale was thought to be a complex cold unit, separated in Central Europe into Drenthe and Warthe phases. The less cool phase between these advances has supposedly been dated by a KAr age of 145,000 ± 25,000 years (Evans 1971; Frechen and Lippolt 1965). According to Evans (1971) the Holstein interglacial is represented by beds at Kempen-Krefeld in the Middle Rhine region, dated between 145,000 ± 25,000 and 220,000 ± 40,000 years ago. However, van der Hammen, Wijmstra, and Zagwijn (1971) estimate the age of the Holstein in the Netherlands at around 300,000 years, which seems more likely. Evidence from Germany and Czechoslovakia (Kukla 1970; Dücker 1969) indicates two warm phases between supposedly Elster and Saale age deposits. It is thus quite likely that different interglacials have been called Holstein, and there is no certainty that hominids of supposedly Holstein age are in fact contemporaneous.

According to van der Hammen, Wijmstra, and Zagwijn (1971) and Butzer (1971), the Elster cold phase falls between about 300,000 and a little under 400,000 years ago. Evans (1971), presumably bracketing a somewhat different combination of glacials, dates the complex from <350,000 ± 20,000 to around 220,000 ± 40,000 years ago.

The predominantly warm "Cromer complex" spans at least two interglacials in East Anglia (Funnell and West 1962; West and Wilson 1966) between Baventian and Lowestoftian. In the Netherlands, van Montfrans and Hospers (1969) and Zagwijn, van Montfrans, and Zandstra (1971) have shown that the "Cromerian" there contains at least three, and possible four, interglacials between Elster and Menap. The youngest has an age of around 400,000 years; the oldest falls just before what is apparently the Matuyama-Brunhes boundary, and would in that case be a little over 700,000 years (Cox 1972; Dalrymple 1972; van Montfrans 1971; Opdyke 1972). The inferred age of the Menap (>700,000 years) does not necessarily imply that the Baventian, nor its supposed Alpine correlate the Gunz, is of equivalent age (Shackleton 1971). It should be noted here that the ages of the Alpine glacial and interglacial complexes are unknown (Richmond 1970; Flint 1971).

The boundary between mainly warm Waal and predominantly cool Menap is characterized by a polarity reversal which may correlate with the beginning of the Jaramillo normal polarity event(s), which would imply a date of around 1 million years (van Montfrans 1971; Dalrymple 1972; Fleck, et al. 1972). A supposedly Waal age fauna from Sainzelles in France is capped by basalt KAr dated at 1.3. million years (Azzaroli 1970). Normal polarity in the late Tiglian and early Eburon may represent Olduvai and/or Gilsa normal events, suggesting ages between 1.86 and 1.6 million years (van Montfrans 1971; Dalrymple 1972; Opdyke 1972). A fauna at Le Coupet in France, dated at a little under 2 million years. (Curtis 1967; Bout 1969), has been broadly correlated with the Eburon in the Netherlands (Azzaroli 1970); another from Roca Neyra in France has been interpreted as a tentative equivalent of the Pretiglian (Azzaroli 1970), which would thus be dated at around 2.5 million years (Curtis 1967; Savage and Curtis 1970; Tobien 1970; Bout 1968).

According to Azzaroli (1970), Bout (1969), and Savage and Curtis (1970), European Villafranchian faunas range in age from well over 3 million years to under 2 million years. Azzaroli's Upper Villafranchian B runs to around 1 million years and would terminate presumably with the Menap, if correlations and "dates" are approximately correct; the Upper Villafranchian A, correlating with the Tiglian, would thus terminate at around 1.75 million years (Azzaroli 1970). Howell (1966) and others would place Eburon and Waal age faunas after the Villafranchian, equivalent at least in part to the Biharian biostratigraphic unit in central Europe (Kurtén 1968; Kretzoi and Vértes 1965).

Such differences of opinion are probably due to a number of factors other than the purely definitional: identification of faunal elements, their correlation, the association of faunas with chronostratigraphic units, and others.

If the base of the Pleistocene is drawn at the base of the Italian marine Calabrian Stage, then it can be dated at around 1.75 million years (Flint 1965, 1971; Selli 1967; Berggren, et al. 1967; Nakagawa, Niitsuma, and Elmi 1971; Hays and Berggren 1971; Poag 1972), considerably later than the beginning of the continental Villafranchian land mammal Stage. Only Azzaroli's Upper Villafranchian B (circa 1.75 to 1 milion years) overlaps with Calabrian time. If the Pleistocene has to be subdivided into Lower, Middle, and Upper segments, as good a Lower-Middle boundary as any would be 700,000 to around 1 million years, (somewhere between "Cromer" age and pre-Menap faunas).

Southeast Asia

Important hominid-bearing deposits in Java fall into a series of lithostratigraphic units (van Bemmelen 1949; van Heekeren 1957); Putjangan, Kabuh, and Notopuro Beds, corresponding broadly with Djetis, Trinil, and Ngandong faunas. Attempts have been made, unsuccesfully, to tie this sequence to a quadriglacial scheme (Movius 1944). Faunal elements from low in the Putjangan Beds (von Koenigswald 1970) suggest a possible correlation with Tiglian age faunas in Europe, though such long distance correlations are inevitably suspect. Dates from Kabuh Beds at Sangiran, and from sediments of the Muriah volcanic complex 80 kilometers north of Trinil supposedly containing a Trinil fauna, range from 500,000 to 900,000 years with large margins of error; the Kabuh Beds at Sangiran alone are probably 700,000 to about 1 million years (von Koenigswald 1968; von Koenigswald and Ghosh 1973; Isaac 1972; Jacob 1972; Day and Molleson 1973). Putjangan Beds have been dated at Modjokerto (Jacob 1972a) to 1.9 ± 0.4 million years and at Kedung Brubus (Day and Molleson 1973) to 1.91 million years. It is thus likely that faunas of the Putjangan Beds overlap those of the European Upper Villafranchian, at least Azzaroli's (1970) Upper Villafranchian B faunas. Trinil and later faunas would then be European Middle Pleistocene correlatives, at the latest.

East Asia

The classic hominid site, Locality 1 at Choukoutien near Peking, has been correlated with European Elster (Kurtén and Vasari 1960) and Holstein (Kahlke 1968) units. However, it may be over-optimistic to attempt to fit non-European deposits into a simplistic four glacial framework (Hooijer 1968). Locality 1 has also been correlated with late Trinil faunas in Java (Kahlke 1968; Hooijer 1968) and would thus be dated to around 600,000 ± 100,000 years if the Indonesian ages reviewed above are approximately correct. Kretzoi and Vértes (1965) have recently suggested a correlation between Locality 1 and faunas of the Templomhegy Phase of the Central European Biharian Stage. A fauna of this age from Stránská Skálá in Czechoslovakia has been correlated with the soil of loess cycle I at Cerveny Kopec near Brno, five kilometers to the east (Kukla 1970). The soil was apparently formed just after a reversed-normal polarity change (Matuyama-Brunhes boundary?), which would imply an age of around 700,000 years (Cox 1972; Dalrymple 1972).

Faunas from hominid sites near Lantian in east central China (Aigner 1972; Chow, et al. 1965) correlate with Djetis faunas (Kungwangling) and with those from Trinil and Choukoutien Locality 1 (Chenchiawo). Thus, Chinese hominid-bearing sites probably span the time covered by the major Indonesian localities.

East Africa

The "gosamer of climatic succession" (Bishop 1968) has long dominated African stratigraphy. Recent progress on calibration of Late Pliocene and Early Pleistocene east African sediments and their contained faunas (Maglio 1970; Cooke and Maglio 1972) suggests that firm correlations with Eurasia may soon be possible. Hay (1967) and Maglio (1972) have proposed local and regional biostratigraphic and chronostratigraphic units that can be dated, in some cases very accurately. Maglio's (1972) *Metridiochoerus* faunal zone at East Rudolf correlates with Hay's (1967) East African Faunal Assemblage 3 at Olduvai (Bed I and lower Bed II), and with faunas above tuff F of the Shungura Formation, Omo (Brown 1972; Howell 1972); the probable age of these faunas is around 1.9 to 1.6 million years. The succeeding East Rudolf *Loxodonta* faunal zone (Maglio 1972) correlates with faunas from Olduvai middle and upper Bed II, and

Peninj (Isaac 1967; M. Leakey 1971a; Howell 1972; Curtis and Hay 1972); ages range from around 1.6 to about 1 million years. These faunas have been called Middle Pleistocene, as opposed to Lower Pleistocene (M. D. Leakey 1971a; Isaac 1967). Evidently, they correlate with European Upper Villafranchian B faunas (Azzaroli 1970), or with earliest Middle Pleistocene (Mosbachian, Biharian) faunas (Howell 1966).

The term "Middle Pleistocene" seems to have been applied to chronostratigraphic units beginning both around 1 million years (Azzaroli 1970) and around 1.75 million years ago. (Howell 1966; Hooijer 1968; M. D. Leakey 1971a; Isaac 1967). If, in fact, faunas similar to those of the European Middle Pleistocene (in Azzaroli's sense) occur in Asia and Africa prior to 1 million years ago, it is interesting to speculate on what this might mean in terms of the migrations and distribution of faunal elements, particularly Hominidae.

It is probably best to use local stratigraphic terminology until correlation and calibration are more precise.

THE HOMINID RECORD

What follows is a brief regional description and discussion of the hominid record in terms of a particular stratigraphic framework. It needs to be reemphasized that the correlations proposed above are very likely partially or wholly wrong, and represent but one of a number of subequally plausible schemes. If the temporal framework changes, so too will interpretations of the fossils.

In east Africa, large-toothed, rugged-skulled *Australopithecus boisei* is present in deposits at Omo (Shungura Formation) (Howell 1969, 1972; Coppens 1970a, 1970b, 1971), Olduvai (L. Leakey 1959; Tobias 1967a), East Rudolf (R. Leakey 1970, 1971, 1972a, 1972b, 1973a; R. Leakey, Mungai, and Walker 1971), and Peninj (L. Leakey and M. D. Leakey 1964; Tobias 1966). Geological age ranges from perhaps 1 million to at least 2 million years (Howell 1972); teeth and jaws from the Shungura Formation below tuff F and the East Rudolf *Mesochoerus limnetes* zone suggest that this lineage may have persisted, relatively unchanged (at least dentally and gnathically) from around 3 million years. Postcranial remains of *A. boisei* suggest a rugged from, markedly sexually dimorphic, capable of bipedal locomotion but not identical to species of *Homo* (R. Leakey 1971, 1972a, 1973a; R. Leakey, Mungai, and Walker 1972; Day

1969a). It is of interest to note the long period of apparent stasis for this lineage.

At least one other lineage is represented in east Africa during this range of time, one with smaller dental and gnathic dimensions. The occlusal morphology of this lineage differs from that in *A. boisei* and the anterior teeth are relatively larger and cheek teeth smaller than in the robust australopithecine (L. Leakey, Tobias, and Napier 1964; Tobias 1965, 1966; Robinson 1965, 1972; R. Leakey 1971, 1972b; Pilbeam and Zwell 1972). Teeth and jaws are well represented at Omo (Shungura and Usno Formations), Olduvai, and East Rudolf. Dental arcade shape is variable; at both Olduvai and East Rudolf two shapes (U- and V-) seem to occur (R. Leakey 1971, 1972a). Whether these are dichotomous or continuously varying types cannot be determined yet, although the most parsimonious hypothesis at present is that one variable lineage of small-toothed hominids is being sampled. Teeth and jaws of this lineage can be traced back to at least 3 million years at East Rudolf (R. Leakey 1973a, 1973b) even further at the Shungura Formation (Howell 1969; Coppens 1970a; Brown 1972). More recently, similar materials have been found as young as perhaps 1 million years at East Rudolf *(Loxodonta africana* faunal zone), where they are essentially similar to mandibles described elsewhere as *Homo erectus* (R. Leakey 1972a, 1973b). Thus, the lineage is *Homo*-like in jaws and teeth for a surprisingly long period of time.

Cranial remains of the same lineage have been recovered from Bed I and lower and middle Bed II at Olduvai Gorge (age range circa 1.9 to 1.5 million years) (Tobias 1964, 1971a; L. Leakey and M. D. Leakey 1964; L. Leakey, Tobias, and Napier 1964; L. Leakey 1966; M. Leakey, Clarke, and L. S. B. Leakey 1971). The material, together with some of the Olduvai dental and mandibular remains, has been labeled *Homo habilis*. Here we will refer to it, for the moment, as early *Homo* sp. Four sufficiently complete cranial specimens are known, yielding a mean endocranial volume of around 650 cubic centimeters; vault bones are thin, and the calvariae longer and somewhat lower than in the smaller *Australopithecus africanus*, with more sloping frontals and slightly better developed supraorbital tori. Parietal bones are markedly elongated. Morphologically rather similar crania have been recovered from the *Mesochoerus* faunal zone at East Rudolf, having probable ages of a little under 3 million years (R. Leakey 1973a, 1973b). They are larger than those at Olduvai (over 800 cubic centimeters) and differ in certain features (parietal shape). Whether or not they are from the same lineage is debatable, but tentatively it can be assumed that they are. (Again, this is an excellent example of the way in which interpretations would differ between proponents of "phyletic gradualism" or "punctuated equilibria" models.) The cranial evidence, like dental and gnathic, perhaps implies a lengthy period of stasis for this lineage too (at least in east Africa), from around 3 to 1.5 million years or less.

Postcranial remains that are very reminiscent of *Homo* have been reported from the *Metridiochoerus* and *Loxodonta* zones at East Rudolf (R. Leakey 1971, 1972a; R. Leakey, Mungai, and Walker 1972). Recently, they have been recorded from the older *Mesochoerus* zone too (R. Leakey 1973a, 1973b). It seems plausible to associate the cranial, dental, mandibular, and postcranial *Homo* material in a single lineage.

Thus, at least two lineages of hominids lived synchronously and (probably) sympatrically in east Africa for close to 2 million years. Although data are still inadequate, it is distinctly possible that both remained relatively unchanged throughout that time, implying successful adaptations to stable niches.

The ancestors of the two lineages are unknown, and must presumably have lived during the earlier Pliocene (4 to 5 million years B.P.). A form similar to South African *A. africanus* would make a plausible ancestor, cranially and postcranially. However, until the older South African sites can be dated, and until early Pliocene east African hominids have been recovered, exact relationships must remain speculative.

East African material that has been or can be assigned to *Homo erectus* is known from Olduvai Gorge (upper Bed II and Bed IV) and is between 1 million and perhaps 500,000 years old (M. D. Leakey 1971a, 1971b). Hominid 9 from upper Bed II (900,000 to 1 million years) has a number of characteristics of Asian *H. erectus* – thick vault bones, massive supraorbital torus, sloping frontal, angulated occipital (L. Leakey 1961; M. D. Leakey 1971a); endocranial volume is 1000 cubic centimeters (Tobias 1971a). Skull fragments of hominid 12 from Oldivai Bed IV (L. Leakey and M. D. Leakey 1964) have been tentatively asigned to the same species (M. D. Leakey 1971a), although the brain was apparently considerably smaller (Holloway 1973). Fragmentary or eroded mandibular and dental remains from Olduvai may also represent *H. erectus* (M. D. Leakey 1971a). Postcranial remains (Day 1971) (innominate and femur) of hominid 28 from Bed IV, estimated to be around 800,000 to 700,000 years old, resemble homologous parts of *H. erectus* from Choukoutien and have been tentatively assigned to that species (Day and Molleson 1973).

Later Middle Pleistocene and early Upper Pleistocene hominid remains in east Africa (falling between about 500,000 and 50,000 years) are sparse (Tobias 1968). Mandibles from the Kapthurin Formation of the Baringo Basin in Kenya (M. Leakey, Martyn, and Leakey 1969), and Dire-Dawa in Ethiopia resemble those of earlier east African forms. Cranial remains from Eyasi in Tanzania and Broken Hill in Zambia are similar to those of earlier hominids (Olduvai hominid 9), as well as the approximately contemporary neanderthals of Europe. These "neanderthaloids" seem to have evolved locally from earlier *H. erectus* populations (Tobias 1968).

Essentially, the east African hominids can be treated in two segments, one between 3 and about 1 to 1.5 million years (early *Homo* sp.), the other younger than about 1 million years (*H. erectus;* archaic *H. sapiens* or *H.s. rhodesiensis*). The relationship between these segments is hard to ascertain at present. Some have suggested the migration of *H. erectus* into east Africa around 1 million years ago, while others have argued in favor of local evolution.

Hominids from Kanjera in Kenya (five individuals) (L. Leakey 1935; Tobias 1968) and the Kibish Formation of the Omo basin, Ethiopia (three individuals) (Day 1969b) apparently differ from contemporaneous east African neanderthaloids. Some of the remains (Omo II and III) are rather archaic looking; others (Kanjera I, Omo I) resemble modern *Homo sapiens* in having delicately built facial skeletons, relatively steep frontals, and moderate brow ridges. The age of the material is uncertain, but probably exceeds 50,000 years (Oakley 1964; Butzer 1969, 1971; Butzer, Brown, and Thurber 1969). This material can be interpreted in a variety of ways. It may represent a cranially variable population that overlapped both neanderthaloid and modern ranges; alternatively, the more modern individuals from the two sites may be sampled from relatively advanced populations. Most would derive these more modern specimens from neanderthaloid populations (Tobias 1961, 1968; Brothwell 1963a), though some would link them with the Lower and early Middle Pleistocene *Homo* sp. (L. Leakey 1972). Clearly, the pattern in east Africa is complex, and it is not yet possible to choose between a number of alternative hypotheses.

The same can be said of other parts of the world. In South Africa, an early *Homo*-like hominid may be represented at Swartkrans, although age is uncertain (Clarke and Howell 1972). Mid- or Late

Pleistocene specimens from Saldanha (Singer 1954) and the Cave of Hearths at Makapansgat (Tobias 1971b) resemble the neanderthaloids further north. Modern *Homo sapiens* may occur relatively early (Vogel and Beaumont 1972; Singer and Smith 1969), although what is probably the oldest well-dated early modern man comes from Florisbad (Drennan 1937; Galloway 1937; Tobias 1968), and is probably older than 40,000 years old (Bada, Protsch, and Schroeder 1973; Butzer, personal communication)

In North Africa and southwest Asia, only relative dates are available at present (Maglio i.p.); probably no hominids older than about 800,000 years are known, although archeological material may document hominid occupation before that time (Biberson 1967). A series of Algerian and Moroccan hominids, known mainly from dental and gnathic remains, spans the time from perhaps about 800,000 years to the Upper Pleistocene, apparently documenting the "transition" from *Homo erectus* to archaic *Homo sapiens* (Tobias 1968). Cranial remains from Ternifine (Arambourg and Hoffstetter 1963) and Thoma's Quarry, Casablanca (Ennouchi 1968, 1972) are said to resemble *H. erectus*. In southwest Asia, these phases of hominid evolution may be represented by material from Hazorea in Israel (Anati and Haas 1967).

Later Pleistocene localities at Jebel Irhoud in Morocco, Haua Fteah in Libya (Tobias 1968), a number of sites in Israel and Lebanon (Tabūn, Skhūl, Zuttiyeh, Djebel Qafzeh, Amud, Ksar'Akil), and Shanidar in Iraq (McCown and Keith 1939; Suzuki and Takai 1970: Solecki 1963) have yielded hominid remains resembling both sub-Saharan archaic hominids and European neanderthals, yet exhibiting some features recalling modern *Homo sapiens* (Tobias 1967b). It is not clear whether specimens are being sampled from one highly variable morphologically intermediate population (McCown and Keith 1939) or two such populations, one being more archaic (Tabūn, Amud, Shanidar) the other more modern (Djebel Qafzeh, Skhūl) (Brothwell 1961, 1963b; Howell 1958; Howells 1970; Vallois and Vandermeersch 1972). As noted, a similar problem arose with interpretation of the east African material. Answers to such questions hinge on obtaining better absolute and relative dates and more complete samples like those from Djebel Qafzeh (Vandermeersch 1966, 1969, 1972).

Fossil hominid sites are unknown for much of central and southern Asia; however, China and southeast Asia are quite well represented. The Chinese archeological and paleoanthropological record begins in late- or post-Villafranchian deposits (Chang 1968; Aigner 1972); the earliest hominid-bearing locality at Lantian (Kungwangling) probably correlates with European sites dated at around 1 to 1.5 million years. A skull cap and maxilla (Woo 1965) from Kungwangling in east central China comes from deposits of this age (Aigner 1972). The specimen has very thick vault bones (outer and inner tables are thickened especially, rather than the diploë); supraorbital tori are well developed. Endocranial volume is in the range of 750 to 800 cubic centimeters.

Up to 1966, almost fifty individuals had been recovered from Locality 1 at Choukoutien (Weidenreich 1936, 1937, 1941, 1943), represented mostly by cranial and dental remains. Jaws and teeth resemble those of approximately contemporaneous hominids from Africa and Java. Cranial volumes are larger than those from Lantian, averaging around 1050 cubic centimeters for seven estimates (Tobias 1971a); it is quite likely that this reflects a real increase through time though an unknown but probably small fraction might be due to greater body size. Vault bones were somewhat thinner than those of the Lantian specimens, frontals better filled, and brow ridges less massive. A number of postcranial remains are known from Choukoutien (Weidenreich 1941); femora resemble that of Olduvai hominid 28 (Day 1971; Day and Molleson 1973). A fully bipedal hominid was clearly represented, but one differing from modern man in certain (poorly understood) features. Stature was small (estimated at around 154 centimeters for males and 141.5 centimeters for females) and body weight moderate (approximately 55 kilograms for males).

Few later Pleistocene Chinese hominids are known (Chang 1962). Those from Ma-pa (Woo and Peng 1959) and Ch'ang-yang in southern China, and Ting-ts'un in the north, are supposedly of "last interglacial" age or older. They are said to be neanderthaloid, and have been described as intermediate between local *H. erectus* and *H. sapiens.*

Hominids from Java are known from the Putjangan, Kabuh, and Notopuro Beds of Java. Hominid material from Trinil and Sangiran recovered before 1940 is not of absolutely certain provenance (Hooijer 1951). However, the hominids may be broadly grouped into older Djetis and younger Trinil samples, the former spanning the time from around 1.5 million years or more to perhaps 1 million or 900,000 years. (Pilbeam 1972a). Dental and mandibular remains from the Putjangan beds have been assigned to various taxa *(Meganthropus palaeojavanicus, Pithecanthropus robustus, Homo modjokertensis).* It seems probable that they can be grouped into one lineage, particularly if it is realized that a considerable time span may be involved (Tobias and von Koenigswald 1964; von Koenigswald 1955, 1970; Weidenreich 1945; Marks 1953; Sartano 1961). Two crania are known, one an infant, the other adult. Both indicate actual or extrapolated adult endocranial volumes of less than 800 cubic centimeters (Weidenreich 1945; von Koenigswald 1968, 1970; Tobias 1971a). The adult (skull IV) has thick vault bones, and an angulated occipital; in comparable parts it is broadly similar to the Lantian (Kungwangling) skullcap.

Asian crania of the period around 1.5 ± 0.5 million years thus share certain features (capacities around 800 cubic centimeters, thick vault bones, etc.). Dentally and gnathically these specimens resemble both Late Pliocene and Early Pleistocene *Homo* sp. and *Homo erectus* from east Africa (Tobias and von Koenigswald 1964); cranially they resemble *Homo* sp. in volume (600–850 cubic centimeters) but *Homo erectus* (Olduvai hominid 9, for example) in morphology. The meaning of these similarities and differences depends closely on more precise dating of the Indonesian hominids in particular.

Since 1963, hominids have been recovered from the Kabuh Beds at Sangiran at an encouraging rate. Five crania are known, together with isolated teeth and a mandible (Tobias 1971a; Sartano 1968, 1970; Jacob 1966); recently, elusive and important basicranial fragments have been retrieved (Jacob 1972b, 1972c). Kabuh Beds at Trinil yielded the original *Homo erectus* calvaria, several femora, and isolated teeth. The Trinil bone beds may preserve fossils of widely varying age (van Heekeren 1957); thus, there is some doubt about the relationship of postcranial material and the Trinil skullcap of *Homo erectus* (Day and Molleson 1973). The six Trinil age crania (from Trinil and Sangiran) resemble those from Choukoutien, although they are somewhat smaller (mean volume around 900 cubic centimeters) (Tobias 1971a). The Trinil femora are indistinguishable from modern *Homo sapiens*, differing somewhat from those of Choukoutien and Olduvai hominid 28. It is possible that they may not represent *H. erectus* (Day and Molleson 1973), although it should be remembered that "modern" femora are known from Pliocene levels at East Rudolf (Leakey 1973a, 1973b).

Later Indonesian hominids are known from the poorly dated Notopuro Beds. The associated Ngandong fauna is an impoverished Trinil fauna with some more modern elements. Eleven hominid calvariae and two tibiae are known from Ngandong in central Java (Weidenreich 1951). Morphologically the crania resemble earlier Javanese

832   D. R. PILBEAM

hominids, and about the only significant difference is in endocranial volume, a sample of six individuals from Ngandong averaging 1100 cubic centimeters. The tibiae are modern-looking (Weidenreich 1951; Jacob 1967).

It seems likely then that *Homo erectus*-like populations were present in Java from around 1.5 million years to less than 500,000 years. Other than a modest increase in brain volume and some reduction in tooth size, relatively little change seems to have occurred.

The earliest modern man in the southeast Asia region is known from Niah in Borneo, dated at 40,000 years (Brothwell 1960). The Niah skull is lightly built, resembling some Australian crania. The oldest Australian human remains, from Lake Mungo in New South Wales (Thorne 1971; Bowler, Thorne, and Polach 1972), date from almost 30,000 years (Barbetti and Allen 1972), and appear fully modern. Other Australian remains, however, are considerably more archaic looking (Macintosh 1965; Macintosh and Larnach 1972); for example, the large sample from Kow Swamp in Victoria dated at around 10,000 years (Thorne and Macumber 1972). Crania from this site have thick vaults, low frontals with prominent tori, massive faces, and robust mandibles. It is possible that these hominids are a continuation of the archaic forms represented earlier in Java. It is a further possibility that Australian Aborigines represent a mixing of this lineage with more modern types that first appeared in southeast Asia around 40,000 years ago (Thorne 1971). More material, well-dated, should clarify this point, and also help to throw light on the more general problem of the transition from archaic to modern *Homo sapiens* populations. What happened in Australia during the past 30,000 or 40,000 years may well resemble what occured in most parts of the Old World between perhaps 100,000 and 30,000 years ago, and could therefore be used as a "model" for such events.

If hominids were present in Europe during the Villafranchian, they were there in very low numbers. Deposits at Vallonet in France record human occupation possibly during the Jamarillo normal event (Upper Villafranchian B) (Howell 1959, 1966). A fragment of a possibly human tooth from Přezletic in Czechoslovakia is probably early "Cromerian" (Fejfar 1969). Other "Cromerian" age hominid sites (about 400,000 to 600,000 years) are Mauer in Germany (Howell 1960; Kurtén 1968), Vértesszöllös in Hungary (Kretzoi and Vértes 1965), and possibly Petralona in Greece (Hemmer 1972). These specimens sample populations that are quite probably no older than those that have classically been termed *Homo erectus* (Choukoutien

Locality 1, Kabuh and Putjangan Beds, Olduvai Bed II and lower Bed IV, Ternifine) and may be significantly younger than most of the latter.

In a number of features, the European hominids are more advanced than *H. erectus;* thus, the occipital from Vértesszöllös (Thoma 1972a) and the Petralona cranium (Kanellis and Marinos 1969) have both been seen as intermediate between *H. erectus* and *H. sapiens*. The Vértesszöllös occipital, in particular, resembles *H. sapiens;* in fact, in some features it appears more "modern" even than the later neanderthals (Thoma 1966, 1972b; Wolpoff 1971). Whether or not this implies that more than one European species lineage is being sampled (one more archaic, the other more advanced) would be hard to demonstrate with such meager samples; it seems unlikely, although different infraspecific populations may be involved.

Hominid remains from interglacial deposits at Swanscombe in England and Steinheim in Germany have been dated to the Holstein or equivalent interglacial(s). Possible ages range around 300,000 years, and they are probably considerably younger than the "Cromerian" age hominids (Howell 1960, 1966; Bordes 1968). These two specimens have been discussed and evaluated extensively (Howell 1960; Ovey 1964); some (Vallois 1954) have seen one (Swanscombe, generally) or both (L. Leakey 1972) as morphologically modern and distinctively different from neanderthals or *Homo erectus*. However more recent multivariate analyses indicate that Swanscombe and Steinheim, although different from some of the west European Weichsel neanderthalers (La Chapelle, for example), are certainly not modern (Weiner and Campbell 1964).

Hominids of Saale (or its probable equivalent) age and earlier have been recovered in France: Arago, La Chaise (Grotte Suard and Grotte-abri Bourgeois-Delaunay), Le Lazaret, Montmaurin, Orgnac-l' Aven, and La Rafette (Howell 1960; Piveteau 1967, 1970, 1972; Debénath and Piveteau 1969; H. de Lumley and M. A. de Lumley 1971, 1972; Bouvier and Rousseau 1972; Constable 1973). From somewhat younger, post-Saale deposits in France, Germany, Italy, and Czechoslovakia come specimens from Fontéchevade, Malarnaud, Monsempron, Ehringsdorf, Taubach, Saccopastore, Quinzano, and Gánovce. Specimens from Bañolas in Spain and Krapina, Yugoslavia have also been placed in the last interglacial or in early Weichsel interstadials. All these specimens can probably be dated between 125,000 and 75,000 years, although it is difficult to assign more precise ages to any of the specimens (Brace 1964; Clark 1964; Guenther 1959, 1964;

Jelinek 1969; Pilbeam 1972a; Sergi 1958; Vallois 1949; Vlček 1955). The samples from Ehringsdorf and Krapina, together with the Saale age specimens from France, exhibit considerable cranial variability (for example, in parietal and frontal morphology). Whether more than one lineage is being sampled is hard to say (Behm-Blancke 1958; Brace 1964; Jelinek 1969; Ozegović 1958; Schaefer 1959). The frontal fragment Fontéchevade 4 (Fontéchevade I), which apparently lacks a supraorbital torus entirely, has been used to support "presapiens" theories (Vallois 1949, 1954, 1958). It should be pointed out that Fontéchevade 5 (II) is not especially modern in morphology (Weiner and Campbell 1964).

With the limited data available at present, I doubt that it is possible to decide for sure how many populations are sampled in Europe during the warmer phases before the main Weichsel glacial (around 70,000 years).

PATTERNS IN HOMINID EVOLUTION

I want to start this final section with two quotes that represent rather divergent opinions; most views would range somewhere in between. They are selected to illustrate some of the reasons for disagreement.

The textbooks . . . suggest that *Homo sapiens* stems from *Homo erectus*; this view can no longer be sustained. The time interval between Java and Peking man in Asia, or the Olduvai form of *Homo erectus* in Tanzania, and the appearance of *Homo sapiens* over a wide area from Europe and east Africa, is far too short. Moreover, there is a growing body of evidence showing that in the Lower Pleistocene and the beginning of the Middle Pleistocene there existed another species . . . *Homo habilis*. The morphology of this species and in particular of the occipital bone, the parietals, the articulation for the mandible, the mandibular arcade, and the teeth all strongly suggest an ancestral stage to *Homo sapiens*. . . . We must now consider that *Homo habilis* was leading to *Homo sapiens* with *Homo erectus* as a contemporary side branch.

If we conclude that *Homo sapiens* was already present in the Middle Pleistocene [Vértesszöllös, Kanjera, Steinheim, Swanscombe, Fontéchevade, Omo-Kibish Fm.] and was contemporary with *Homo erectus,* we are forced to reconsider the origin of such strange Upper Pleistocene hominids as classical Neanderthal man in Europe, Rhodesian man in Africa, and Solo man in Asia. These hominids all combine some features reminiscent of *Homo sapiens* and others suggestive of *Homo erectus.* Is it not possible that they are all variants of the result of cross-breeding between *Homo sapiens* and *Homo erectus?* (L. Leakey 1972: 27).

Why *must* we believe that no fossil population as a whole can have given rise to the next one directly? Why *must* we assume that evolution only occurred when a small population became isolated? Why, indeed, *must* we assume that fossil hominid populations were polytypic? ... Why must we assume that hominids of the *erectus* species ... were temporarily and repeatedly separated from each other long enough for major differentiation to take place? ... It is possible to suggest that the wide-ranging foraging activities of hominid groups from the Australopithecines on would have prevented any kind of isolation of a major or protracted sort (Brace 1968: 31).

Given the same set of data, why should interpretations differ so much? First, the data are relatively meager and therefore open to many interpretations. Second, chronologies can differ radically. I have outlined one particular stratigraphic scheme in section C, but as I emphasized there it is unlikely to be correct in all or even most details, and any absolute or relative changes in chronology could alter an interpretation to a great or lesser extent. (Suppose, for example, the older Asian *Homo erectus* and the European hominids from Vértesszöllös, Mauer, Swanscombe, and Steinheim were contemporaries, rather than being separated by several hundred thousand years as might also be possible. Interpretations would almost certainly be affected.) Third, disagreements will arise over the meaning of similarities and differences. Fourth, the theoretical perspectives from which the fossils are viewed may differ; the most obvious contrasts are between models invoking "phyletic gradualism" on the one hand and "punctuated equilibria" on the other. Finally, and this is perhaps the most subtle and important point, hypothetical frameworks are very rarely articulated explicitly and at length.

Few paleoanthropologists are now typologists; most realize that fossils represent individuals that were once part of genetically variable populations that were themselves part of a network of groups linked by gene flow across wide areas. At all time levels, local populations would have expanded or contracted, replacing others or being replaced, generally by processes of fusion, absorption, and hybridization. The populations involved might have been genetically very similar; less frequently, populations would have been genetically — and morphologically — different, having shared only a remote ancestry. In some cases, the differences between populations might have been so great as to preclude interbreeding, or keep it at a phylogenetically insignificant level. When fossils are providing the information about populations, such distinctions are of course often difficult to make.

Most of human evolution during the past 2 million years or more (excluding the *A. boisei* lineage) probably involved population shifts, changes, and mergers that remained at the infraspecies level. In interpreting the Pleistocene hominid fossil record, then, we are looking in much finer grain than is the case for almost any other group. Hence, we should expect disagreements over interpretation, for "*Homo* will probably furnish the first well-studied case of the evolution of several subspecies in geological time" (Van Valen 1966).

In order to review briefly the late Pliocene and Pleistocene fossil record of *Homo*, I want to look at four different time segments, each of which seems to have been a period of relative stasis, and between which there are discontinuities; the periods are (approximately) from 3 to 1.5 million years, 1.5 million to 500,000 years, 500,000 to 50,000 years, and 50,000 years to the present.

During the first phase, hominids were present in Africa, and possibly elsewhere in the Old World tropics and subtropics (Java, China, presumably India too, probably not Europe). Hominids were certainly present in Asia early in the second phase, and probably in Europe too, although the first evidence that hominids could cope with cold climate conditions in higher latitudes comes only late in the second phase. (However, the evidence against earlier cold climate adaptations is largely negative.) After 500,000 years, hominids were distributed widely in the Old World, excluding Australia. The extents to which hominid population distributions and densities fluctuated with climatic changes, especially in temperate regions, are unknown (although presumably information on such patterns could be obtained from archeological data and from large mammal distributions). Colonization of non-open habitats such as forest, and marginal areas like Australia and the Americas, seems to have followed the widespread emergence of populations of modern *Homo sapiens* after about 40,000 years.

Hominids throughout this whole range of time very closely resembled *Homo sapiens* postcranially, and were apparently fully bipedal; this strengthens their inclusion in *Homo*. Populations between 3 and 2 million years may have ranged in height between 135 and 157.5 centimeters. By one million to 500,000 years, hominids were closer to modern stature, populations averaging 152.5 to 167.5 centimeters or more.

Brain size may well have been rather stable from 3 to 1.5 million years, with population means varying between perhaps 600 and 800 cubic centimeters. Between 1.5 and 1 million years, mean values may well still not have exceeded 800 or 900 cubic centimeters; around 1 million to 700,000 years, larger volumes occur, ranging up to 1000 cubic centimeters. After about 500,000 years, hominid populations have mean volumes in the range of living *Homo sapiens*. These increases in brain size, and their relationship to body size changes, cannot be understood more fully until better data are available. However, it does look as though brain and body weights during this time might have been allometrically related, with an exponent equal to or exceeding unity; such a relationship would imply very strong selection in favor of brain expansion over and above that related to increased stature (Gould 1971). There is no way of knowing whether the increase was regular or episodic.

Internal brain structure certainly changed during this time period, with shifts in neuron and glial cell density and morphology, and the development of new interconnections (Holloway 1972). Internal shifts can only be detected by the paleontologist from the imperfect evidence of external brain morphology available in the form of endocasts. Holloway has shown that australopithecines were advanced relative to living pongids; his work on *Homo* material is awaited with great interest.

Cranial shape and morphology also changed radically through time. From 3 to 1.5 million years, crania were longer and lower than those of *Australopithecus africanus* (which makes, as discussed before, an excellent pre-*Homo* model, even if known specimens are too young to represent actual ancestors), yet with rounded occipitals and moderate brow ridges; vault bones were thin. From 1.5 to 1 million years, hominids, even those with endocranial volumes around 800 cubic centimeters, had thick-boned calvariae, with flatter frontals, bigger brow ridges, and rather more angulated occipitals. Such forms are known from crania only in Asia at present; their presence in Africa is uncertain, although there is a hint that they may have been represented in the *Loxodonta* faunal zone at East Rudolf (R. Leakey 1973a).

What is the relationship between the earlier *Homo* sp. and this early *Homo erectus*? Is one the ancestor of the other? How should we then explain the changes in skull shape — by invoking allometry? Why the thickening of vault bones? Alternatively, is there solid evidence for the coexistence of two "Homo" lineages, for instance in east Africa, differing in cranial morphology? At what level ought these lineages, should they exist, be classified — as subspecies or species? The number of questions is almost endless, and inversely proportional to the amount of data.

After about 1 million years ago, later *Homo erectus*, with larger brains, are found in Asia and east and north Africa; there is no more evidence than from the earlier *erectus* period for the coexistence of cranially divergent hominid populations (although the data are admittedly meager).

Populations with rather *erectus*-like crania continue until late in the Pleistocene (in sub-Saharan Africa and southeast Asia, for example); in Australia, the Kow Swamp sample may represent the latest of such archaic-looking groups. However, from perhaps 400,000 years on (Vértesszöllös), crania with non-*erectus* features turn up in increasing numbers, especially in Europe. Occipitals were on the average somewhat more rounded, and brow ridges rather less prominent. There seems little reason not to derive such forms from earlier *Homo erectus* types (assuming that relative dating is correct). Although there may be direct continuity (excluding *erectus*) between forms such as Vértesszöllös, Steinheim, and so forth, and pre-*erectus* early *Homo* sp., it is not a connection documented by actual fossils. The evolution of modern human-type crania, with high vaults, rounded occipitals, and high frontals with only moderate supraorbital tori, is poorly understood. Likely ancestors would presumably have resembled neanderthalers of one sort or another, with equally large, but differently packaged, brains in long, low calvariae. Why should such a skull shorten and change shape so drastically? Various explanations have been proposed, generally focusing on reductions in dental and facial size with putative shifts in climatic or cultural selection factors (Brace 1964, 1967; Brose and Wolpoff 1971). An alternative explanation is that the alteration in shape is linked to changes in basicranial morphology.

In modern man the basicranium anterior to the foramen magnum is arched; the human newborn basicranium is not flexed, the curvature developing after the age of about two years as the pharynx forms (by "dropping" the larynx). Nonhuman primates also have nonflexed or flat basicrania and lack pharynxes (Lieberman and Crelin 1971). Depressingly few fossil hominids preserve the basicranial region intact, but those few *Australopithecus* and *Homo erectus* that are known resemble nonhuman primates (Lieberman 1974). The Steinheim cranium, although damaged, distorted, and imperfectly prepared, may well have had an "intermediate" basicranial morphology, as apparently had the complete cranium from Broken Hill in

Zambia (Kramp 1936; Lieberman 1974). Presumably, their pharyngeal morphologies were also "intermediate." Hominids with modern, though robust, crania (for example, Skhūl V) are the oldest known at present to have fully modern basicranial and, presumably, pharyngeal morphologies (Lieberman 1974). Basicranial flexion may be an important factor, although probably not the only one, in the phylogenetic shortening of the modern human cranium, which in turn affected overall cranial shape. If basicranial flexion is controlled by pharyngeal development, and if a pharynx is crucial to the evolution of fully modern vocal language, then one can hypothesize fairly strong selection pressure for behaviors which could result in rapid morphological change.

Although fossils with certain "modern" features do probably turn up rather early in the fossil record (the Vértesszöllös occipital, Fontéchevade 4 and Kanjera I frontals, Omo-Kibish Formation I cranium), it is by no means certain that any of these had entirely "modern" skulls — the Kanjera I occipital, for example, is strongly curved as in other early hominid (Tobias 1959) — nor do they necessarily represent whole populations of equally "modern" individuals. Good evidence for the first such populations does not occur until 40,000 to 50,000 years.

The dentition and jaws changed relatively little during long periods of time. Thus, the maxilla of hominid 1470 (R. Leakey 1973b) from East Rudolf (circa 3 million years) and that of *Homo erectus* IV (Tobias and von Koenigswald 1964) from the Putjangan Beds of Sangiran (circa 1.25 million years or more) are very similar. Mandibles from the *Loxodonta* faunal zone at East Rudolf bear striking resemblances to mandibles half as young again. This broad continuity through time and across space differs from the heterogeneity and change to be seen in the cranium; for this reason it is rash to utilize only dental or gnathic information in assessing population relationships.

Evolutionary changes seem to have been quite rapid around 1.25 million ± 250,000 years, at least in terms of brain volume and cranial changes, and similarly accelerated around 75,000 ± 25,000 years. These periods may have been times of general change across many populations, presumably in response to selection pressures that acted in a similarly widespread manner. Alternatively, and perhaps more likely (at least in the more recent case), the change might have been relatively localized, and spread by shifting and hybridizing populations. As I suggested above, modern *sapiens* populations may have evolved in and spread from a relatively restricted part of the total species range, around 50,000 to 100,000 years ago. The precise geographical location, if in a temperate region, would presumably have shifted with fluctuating climates and habitats. Supports for such a thesis would come in the form of evidence for very rapid change in different geographical areas, the coexistence of archaic and modern populations, and indications of hybridization in early modern populations in regions outside the area of original evolution. At present, we have insufficient data to test this hypothesis in areas other than Australia, and even there the evidence can be interpreted in other ways (Thorne 1971).

Inferences about hominid behavior and population adaptations can be drawn from analyses of archeological data, and can also flow from a better understanding of functional anatomy. The archeological record suggests that human technological skills may not have changed significantly for a very considerable period after the inception of stone toolmaking (Isaac 1972). It is interesting therefore to note that hominid brain volumes changed relatively little for close to 1.5 million years after that event. The pace of technological and morphological change seems to have remained low even as recently as 300,000 or 400,000 years.

The emergence of *Homo sapiens* populations coincides with a period of more rapid cultural change that accelerated still more during the dispersal (or widespread evolution) around 40,000 to 50,000 years ago of fully modern *Homo sapiens* (Isaac 1972; Bordes 1972). If the morphological changes discussed above can indeed be linked to the evolution of more efficient cognitive and communicative systems, then it should eventually be possible to associate individual behavioral changes as inferred from paleontological data with the results of hominid behavior deduced from the archeological record.

REFERENCES

AIGNER, J. S.
1972   Relative dating of north Chinese faunal and cultural complexes. *Arctic Anthropology* 9:36–79.
ANATI, E., N. HAAS
1967   The Hazorea Pleistocene site: a preliminary report. *Man* 2:454–456.
ARAMBOURG, C., R. HOFFSTETTER
1963   *Le gisement de Ternifine*. Archives de l'Institut de Paléontologie Humaine Memoires 32.

AZZAROLI, A.
1970 Villafranchian correlations based on large mammals. *Giornale di Geologia* 35:111–131.
BADA, J. L., R. PROTSCH, R. A. SCHROEDER
1973 The racemisation reaction of isoleucine used as a palaeotemperature indicator. *Nature* 241:394–395.
BARBETTI, M., H. ALLEN
1972 Prehistoric man at Lake Mungo, Australia, by 32,000 years B.P. *Nature* 240:46–48.
BEHM-BLANCKE, G.
1958 "Umwelt, Kultur und Morphologie des eeminterglazialen Menschen von Ehringsdorf bei Weimar," in *Hundert Jahre Neanderthaler.* Edited by G. H. R. von Koenigswald, 141–150. Utrecht: Kemink en Zoon.
BERGGREN, W. A., J. D. PHILLIPS, A. BERTELS, D. WALL
1967 Late Piocene-Pleistocene stratigraphy in deep sea cores from the south-central North Atlantic. *Nature* 216:253–255.
BIBERSON, P.
1967 "Some aspects of the Lower Palaeolithic of northwest Africa," in *Background to evolution in Africa.* Edited by W. W. Bishop and J. D. Clark, 447–476. Chicago: University of Chicago Press.
BIEGERT, J.
1963 "The evaluation of characteristics of the skull, hands, and feet for primate taxonomy," in *Classification and human evolution.* Edited by S. L. Washburn, 116–145. Chicago: Aldine.
BIRDSELL, J. B.
1972 *Human evolution.* Chicago: Rand McNally.
BISHOP, W. W.
1968 Means of correlation of Quaternary successions in East Africa. *International Association for Quaternary Research* 8:161–172.
BISHOP, W. W., J. A. MILLER, editors
1972 *Calibration of hominoid evolution.* Toronto: University Press.
BORDES, F.
1968 *The Old Stone Age.* London: Weidenfield and Nicholson.
1972 Physical evolution and technological evolution in man: a parallelism. *World Archaeology* 3:1–5.
BORDES, F., editor
1972 *The origin of Homo sapiens.* Paris: UNESCO.
BOUT, P.
1968 La limite Pliocene-Quaternaire en Europe occidentale. *Bulletin de l'Association francaise pour l'étude du Quaternaire* 1:55–78.
1969 Datations absolues de quelques formations volcaniques d'Auvergne et du Velay et chronologie du Quaternaire Européen. *Revue d'Auvergne* 83:267–280.
BOUVIER, J. M., J. M. ROUSSEAU
1972 Fragment cranien humain d'age Rissien (?) des alluvions de la Dordogne. *L'Anthropologie* 76:325–330.
BOWLER, J. M., A. G. THORNE, H. A. POLACH
1972 Pleistocene man in Australia: age and significance of the Mungo

skeleton. *Nature* 240:48–50.

BRACE, C. L.

1964   A consideration of hominid catastrophism. *Current Anthropology* 5:3–43.

1967   *The stages of human evolution.* Englewood Cliffs: Prentice-Hall.

1968   Comment on "The Pleistocene epoch and the evolution of man." *Current Anthropology* 9:30–31.

BRACE, C. L., H. NELSON, N. KORN

1971   *Atlas of fossil man.* New York: Holt, Rinehart and Winston.

BROECKER, W. S.

1971   "Calcite accumulation rates and glacial to interglacial changes in oceanic mixing," in *Late Cenozoic Glacial Ages.* Edited by K. K. Turekian, 239–266. New Haven: Yale University Press.

BROECKER, W. S., T-L. KU

1969   Caribbean cores P6304-8 and P6304-9: new analysis of absolute chronology. *Science* 166:404–406.

BROECKER, W. S., D. L. THURBER, J. GODDARD, T-L. KU, R. K. MATTHEWS, K. J. MESOLELLA

1968   Milankovitch hypothesis supported by precise dating of coral reefs and deep-sea sediments. *Science* 159:297–300.

BROECKER, W. S., J. VAN DONK

1970   Insolation changes, ice volumes, and the O^{18} record in deep-sea cores. *Reviews of Geophysics and Space Physics* 8:169–198.

BROSE, D. S., M. H. WOLPOFF

1971   Early Upper Paleolithic man and late Middle Paleolithic tools. *American Anthropologist* 73:1156–1194.

BROTHWELL, D. R.

1960   Upper Pleistocene human skull from Niah Caves, Sarawak. *Sarawak Museum Journal* 9:323–349.

1961   The people of Mount Carmel. *Prehistoric Society Proceedings* 27: 155–159.

1963a Evidence of early population change in central and southern Africa: doubts and problems. *Man* 132:101–104.

1963b Where and when did man become wise? *Discovery* (June):10–14.

BROWN, F. H.

1972   "Radiometric dating of sedimentary formations in the lower Omo Valley, Ethiopia," in *Calibration of hominoid evolution.* Edited by W. W. Bishop and J. A. Miller, 273–288. Edinburgh: Scottish Academic Press.

BUTZER, K. W.

1969   Geological interpretation of two Pleistocene hominid sites in the Lower Omo Basin. *Nature* 222:1133–1135.

1971   *Environment and archeology* (second edition). Chicago: Aldine-Atherton.

BUTZER, K. W., F. H. BROWN, D. L. THURBER

1969   Horizontal sediments of the lower Omo Valley: the Kibish Formation. *Quaternaria* 11:15–30.

CHANG, K-C.

1962   New evidence on fossil man in China. *Science* 136:749–760.

1968   *The archaeology of ancient China* (revised edition). New Haven: Yale University Press.

CHOW, M. M., C-K. HU, Y-C. LEE
1965   Mammalian fossils associated with the hominid skull cap of Lantian, Shensi. *Scientia Sinica* 14:1037–1048.

CLARK, W. E. LE GROS
1964   *The fossil evidence for human evolution* (second edition). Chicago: University of Chicago Press.

CLARKE, R. J., F. C. HOWELL
1972   Affinities of the Swartkrans 847 hominid cranium. *American Journal of Physical Anthropology* 37:319–336.

COCK, A. G.
1966   Genetical aspects of metrical growth and form in animals. *Quarterly Review of Biology* 41:131–190.

CONSTABLE, G.
1973   *The Neanderthals.* New York: Time-Life.

COOKE, H. B. S.
1972   Pleistocene chronology: long or short? *Maritime Sediments* 8:1–12.

COOKE, H. B. S., V. J. MAGLIO
1972   "Plio-Pleistocene stratigraphy in east Africa in relation to proboscidean and suid evolution," in *Calibration of hominoid evolution.* Edited by W. W. Bishop and J. A. Miller, 303–330. Edinburgh: Scottish Academic Press.

COON, C. S.
1962   *The origin of races.* New York: Knopf.

COPPENS, Y.
1970a   Localisation dans le temps et dans l'espace des restes d'Hominidés des formations plio-pléistocènes de l'Omo (Ethiopie). *Comptes rendus des séances de l'Académie des Sciences* 271:1968–1971.
1970b   Les restes d'Hominidés des séries inférieures et moyennes des formations plio-villafranchiennes de l'Omo en Ethiopie. *Comptes rendus des séances de l'Académie des Sciences* 271:2286–2289.
1971   Les restes d'Hominidés des séries supérieures des formations plio-villafranchiennes de l'Omo en Ethiopie. *Comptes rendus des séances de l'Académie des Sciences* 272:36–39.

COX, A.
1972   "Geomagnetic reversals — their frequency, their origin and some problems of correlation," in *Calibration of hominoid evolution.* Edited by W. W. Bishop and J. A. Miller, 93–106, Edinburgh: Scottish Academic Press.

CURTIS, G. H.
1967   "Notes on some Miocene to Pleistocene potassium/argon results," in *Background to evolution in Africa.* Edited by W. W. Bishop and J. D. Clark, 365–370. Chicago: University of Chicago Press.

CURTIS, G. H., R. L. HAY
1972   "Further geological studies and potassium-argon dating at Olduvai Gorge and Ngorongoro Crater," in *Calibration of hominoid evolution.* Edited by W. W. Bishop and J. A. Miller, 289–302. Edinburgh: Scottish Academic Press.

DALRYMPLE, G. B.
1972 "Potassium-argon dating of geomagnetic reversals and North American glaciations," in *Calibration of hominoid evolution*. Edited by W. W. Bishop and J. A. Miller, 107–134. Edinburgh: Scottish Academic Press.

DANSGAARD, W., S. J. JOHNSEN, H. B. CLAUSEN, C. C. LANGWAY
1971 "Climatic record revealed by the Camp Century ice core," in *Late Cenozoic glacial ages*. Edited by K. K. Turekian, 37–56. New Haven: Yale University Press.

DAY, M. H.
1965 *Guide to fossil man*. London: Cassell.
1969a Femoral fragment of a robust australopithecine from Olduvai Gorge, Tanzania. *Nature* 221:230–233.
1969b Omo human skeletal remains. *Nature* 222:1135–1138.
1971 Postcranial remains of *Homo erectus* from Bed IV, Olduvai Gorge, Tanzania. *Nature* 232:383–387.

DAY, M. H., T. I. MOLLESON
1973 "The Trinil femora," in *Human evolution*. Edited by M. H. Day, 127–154. London: Taylor and Francis.

DEBÉNATH, A., J. PIVETEAU
1969 Nouvelles découvertes de restes humain fossiles à La Chaise-de-Vouthon (Charente). Position stratigraphique des restes humains de la La Chaise (abri Bourgeois-Delaunay). *Comptes rendus des séances de l'Academie des sciences* 269:24–28.

DE LUMLEY, H., M. A. DE LUMLEY
1971 Découvertes de restes humains anténéandertaliens datés du début du Riss à la Canne de l'Arago (Tautavel, Pyrénées-Orientales). *Comptes rendus des séances de l'Académie des sciences* 272: 1739–1746.
1972 "Les prédécesseurs de l'homme moderne dans le Midi méditerranéen," in *The origin of Homo sapiens*. Edited by F. Bordes, 46–48. Paris: UNESCO.

DRENNAN, M. R.
1937 The Florisbad skull and brain cast. *Royal Society of South Africa Transactions* 25:103–114.

DÜCKER, A.
1969 Der Ablauf der Holstein-warmzeit in Westholstein. *Eiszeitalter und Gegenwart* 20:46–57.

ELDREDGE, N., S. J. GOULD
1972 "Punctuated equilibria: an alternative to phyletic gradualism," in *Model in paleobiology*. Edited by T. J. M. Schopf, 82–115. San Francisco: Freeman, Cooper.

EMILIANI, C.
1966 Paleotemperature analysis of Caribbean cores P6304-8 and P6304-9 and a generalized temperature curve for the past 425,000 years. *Journal of Geology* 74:109–126.
1968 The Pleistocene epoch and the evolution of man. *Current Anthropology* 9:27–47.

ENNOUCHI, E.
1968 Un nouvel archanthropien au Maroc. *Annales de Paléontologie* 56:95–107.
1972 Nouvelle découverte d'un archanthropien au Maroc. *Comptes rendus des séances de l'Académie des sciences* 274:3088–3090.

EVANS, P.
1971 "Towards a Pleistocene time-scale," in *The Phanerozoic Time-Scale*. Edited by W. B. Harland and E. H. Francis, 35–38. Geological Society of London, Special Publication 5.

FEJFAR, O.
1969 Human remains from the early Pleistocene in Czechoslovakia. *Current Anthropology* 10:170–173.

FLECK, R. J., J. H. MERCER, A. E. M. NAIRN, D. N. PETERSON
1972 Chronology of late Pliocene and early Pleistocene glacial and magnetic events in southern Argentina. *Earth and Planetary Science Letters* 16:15–22.

FLINT, R F.
1965 *The Pliocene-Pleistocene boundary*. Geological Society of America, Special Paper 84.
1971 *Glacial and Quaternary geology*. New York: Wiley.

FRECHEN, J., H. J. LIPPOLT
1965 Kalium-argon-daten zum Alter des Laacher vulkanismus, der Rheinterrassen und der Eiszeiten. *Eiszeitalter und Gegenwart* 16: 5–30.

FUNNEL, B. M., R. G. WEST
1962 The Early Pleistocene of Easton Bavents, Suffolk. *Quarterly Journal of the Geological Society of London* 118:125–141.

GALLOWAY, A.
1937 The nature and status of the Florisbad skull as revealed by its non-metrical features. *American Journal of Physical Anthropology* 23:1–16.

GILES, E.
1956 Cranial allometry in the great apes. *Human Biology* 28:43–58.

GOULD, S. J.
1966 Allometry and size in ontogeny and phylogeny. *Biological Reviews* 41:587–640.
1971 Geometric similarity in allometric growth: a contribution to the problem of scaling in the evolution of size. *The American Naturalist* 105:113–136.

GUENTHER, E. W.
1959 Zur Altersdatierung der diluvialen Fundstelle von Krapina in Kroatien. *Bericht über die 6 Tagung der Deutschen Gesellschaft für Anthropologie*, 202–208.
1964 Zur Altersdatierung der "Homo"-Fundschicht von Ehringsdorf bei Weimar. *Zeitschrift für Morphologie und Anthropologie* 56: 23–32.

HAY, R. L.
1967 "Revised stratigraphy of Olduvai Gorge," in *Background to*

evolution in Africa. Edited by W. W. Bishop and J. D. Clark, 221–228. Chicago: University of Chicago Press.

HAYS, J. D., W. A. BERGGREN
1971 "Quaternary boundaries and correlations," in *Micropalaeontology of oceans.* Edited by B. M. Funnell and W. R. Riedel, 669–691. Cambridge: Cambridge University Press.

HEMMER, H.
1972 Notes sur la position phylétique de l'homme de Petralona. *L'Anthropologie* 76:155–162.

HOLLOWAY, R. L.
1972 "Australopithecine endocasts, brain evolution in the Hominoidea, and a model of hominid evolution," in *The functional and evolutionary biology of primates.* Edited by R. H. Tuttle, 185–203. Chicago: Aldine-Atherton.
1973 New endocranial values for the East African early hominids. *Nature* 243:97–99.

HOOIJER, D. A.
1951 The geological age of Pithecanthropus, Meganthropus and Gigantopithecus. *American Journal oof Physical Anthropology* 9: 265–281.
1968 "The Middle Pleistocene fauna of Java," in *Evolution and hominisation* (second edition). Edited by G. Kurth, 86–90. Stuttgart: Fischer.

HOWELL, F. C.
1951 The place of neanderthal man in human evolution. *American Journal of Physical Anthropology,* n.s. 9:379–416.
1952 Pleistocene glacial ecology and the evolution of "classic neanderthal" man. *Southwestern Journal of Anthropology* 8:377–410.
1957 The evolutionary significance of variation and varieties of "neanderthal" man. *Quarterly Review of Biology* 32:330–347.
1958 "Upper Pleistocene men of the southwest Asian Mousterian," in *Hundert Jahre Neanderthaler.* Edited by G. H. R. von Koenigswald, 185–198. Utrecht: Kemink en Zoon.
1959 The Villafranchian and human origins. *Science* 130:831–844.
1960 European and northwest African Middle Pleistocene hominids. *Current Anthropology* 1:195–232.
1966 Observations on the earlier phases of the European Lower Paleolithic. *American Anthropologist* 68 (2,2): 88–201.
1969 Remains of Hominidae from Pliocene/Pleistocene formations in the lower Omo basin, Ethiopia. *Nature* 223:1234–1239.
1972 "Pliocene/Pleistocene Hominidae in eastern Africa — absolute and relative ages," in *Calibration of hominoid evolution.* Edited by W. W. Bishop and J. A. Miller, 331–368. Edinburgh: Scottish Academic Press.

HOWELLS, W. W.
1967 *Mankind in the making.* New York: Doubleday.
1970 Mount Carmel man: morphological relationships. *Proceedings of the Eighth International Congress of Anthropological and Ethnological Sciences* 1:269–272.

HUNKINS, K., A. W. H. BÉ, N. D. OPDYKE, G. MATHIEU
1971 "The late Cenozoic history of the Arctic ocean," in *Late Ceno-zoic glacial ages*. Edited by K. K. Turekian, 215–238. New Haven: Yale University Press.

IMBRIE, J., N. G. KIPP
1971 "A new micropaleontological method for quantitative paleoclima-tology: application to a late Pleistocene Caribbean core," in *Late Cenozoic glacial ages*. Edited by K. K. Turekian, 71–182. New Haven: Yale University Press.

ISAAC, G. L.
1967 "The stratigraphy of the Peninj Group — early Middle Pleistocene formation west of Lake Natron, Tanzania," in *Background to evolution in Africa*. Edited by W. W. Bishop and J. D. Clark, 229–257. Chicago: University of Chicago Press.
1972 "Chronology and the tempo of cultural change during the Pleisto-cene," in *Calibration of hominoid evolution*. Edited by W. W. Bishop and J. A. Mliler, 381–430. Edinburgh: Scottish Academic Press.

JACOB, T.
1966 The skull cap of *Pithecanthropus erectus*. *American Journal of Physical Anthropology* 25:243–260.
1967 *The racial history of the Indonesian region*. Utrecht: Kemink en Zoon.
1972a The absolute date of the Djetis beds at Modjokerto. *Antiquity* 46:148.
1972b The problem of head-hunting and brain eating among Pleistocene men in Indonesia. *Archaeology and Physical Anthropology in Oceania* 7:81–91.
1972c New hominid finds in Indonesia and their affinities. *Mankind* 8:176–181.

JELINEK, J.
1969 Neanderthal man and *Homo sapiens* in central and eastern Europe. *Current Anthropology* 10:475–503.

JOHNSEN, S. J., W. DANSGAARD, H. B. CLAUSEN, C. C. LANGWAY
1972 Oxygen isotope profiles through the Atlantic and Greenland ice sheets. *Nature* 235:429–434.

JOLLY, C. J.
1966 Introduction to the Cercopithecoidea, with notes on their use as laboratory animals. *Symposia of the Zoological Society of London* 17:427–457.

KAHLKE, H. D.
1968 "Zur relativen Chronologie ostasiatischer Mittelpleistozän-Faunen und Hominoidea-Funde," in *Evolution und Hominisation* (second edition). Edited by G. Kurth, 91–118. Stuttgart: Fischer.

KANELLIS, A., G. MARINOS
1969 Die Höhle von Petralona. *Proceedings of the Fourth International Congress of Speleology in Yugoslavia* 4–5:355–362.

848   D. R. PILBEAM

KEANY, J., J. P. KENNETT
1972 Pliocene-early Pleistocene paleoclimatic history recorded in Antarctic-Subantarctic deep-sea cores. *Deep-Sea Research* 19:529–548.

KENNETT, J. P., P. HUDDLESTON
1972 Late Pleistocene paleoclimatology, foraminiferal biostratigraphy and tephrochronology, western Gulf of Mexico. *Quaternary Research* 2:38–69.

KENT, D., N. D. OPDYKE, M. EWING
1971 Climate change in the north Pacific using ice-rafted detritus as a climatic indicator. *Geological Society of America Bulletin* 82:2741–2754.

KRAMP, P.
1936 Die topographischen Vehältnisse der menschlichen Schädelbasis. *Anthropologisches Anzeiger* 12:112–130.

KRETZOI, M., L. VÉRTES
1965 Upper Biharian (Intermindel) pebble-industry occupation site in western Hungary. *Current Anthropology* 6:74–87.

KUKLA, J.
1970 Correlations between loesses and deep-sea sediments. *Geologiska Föreningens Förhandlingar* 92:148–180.

KUKLA, J., A. KOČÍ
1972 End of the last interglacial in the loess record. *Quaternary Research* 2:374–383.

KUMMER, H.
1968 *Social organization of hamadryas baboons.* Bibliotheca Primatologica 6.

KURTÉN, B.
1968 *Pleistocene mammals of Europe.* Chicago: Aldine.

KURTÉN, B., Y. VASARI
1960 *On the date of Peking man.* Commentationes Biologicae 23 (7).

LEAKEY, L. S. B.
1935 *The Stone Age races of Kenya.* Oxford: Oxford University Press.
1959 A new fossil skull from Olduvai. *Nature* 184:491–493.
1961 New finds at Olduvai Gorge. *Nature* 189:649–650.
1966 *Homo habilis, Homo erectus* and the australopithecines. *Nature* 209:1279–1281.
1972 "Homo sapiens in the Middle Pleistocene and the evidence of Homo sapiens' evolution," in *The origin of Homo sapiens.* Edited by F. Bordes, 25–29. Paris: UNESCO.

LEAKEY, L. S. B., M. D. LEAKEY
1964 Recent discoveries of fossil hominids in Tanganyika: at Olduvai and near Lake Natron. *Nature* 202:5–7.

LEAKEY, L. S. B., P. V. TOBIAS, J. R. NAPIER
1964 A new species of the genus *Homo* from Olduvai Gorge. *Nature* 202:7–9.

LEAKEY, MARGARET, J. E. MARTYN, R. E. F. LEAKEY
1969 An Acheulean industry with prepared core technique and the

discovery of a contemporary hominid mandible at Lake Baringo, Kenya. *Prehistoric Society Proceedings* 35:48–76.

LEAKEY, M. D.
1971a *Olduvai Gorge*, volume three: *Excavations in Beds I and II, 1960–1963*. Cambridge: Cambridge University Press.
1971b Discovery of postcranial remains of *Homo erectus* and associated artefacts in Bed IV at Olduvai Gorge, Tanzania. *Nature* 232: 380–383.

LEAKEY, M. D., R. J. CLARKE, L. S. B. LEAKEY
1971 New hominid skull from Bed I, Olduvai Gorge, Tanzania. *Nature* 232:308–312.

LEAKEY, R. E. F.
1970 Fauna and artefacts from a new Plio-Pleistocene locality near Lake Rudolf in Kenya. *Nature* 226:223–224.
1971 Further evidence of Lower Pleistocene hominids from East Rudolf, North Kenya. *Nature* 231:241–245.
1972a Further evidence of Lower Pleistocene hominids from East Rudolf, North Kenya, 1971. *Nature* 237:264–269.
1972b New fossil evidence of the evolution of man. *Social Biology* 19: 99–114.
1973a Further evidence of Lower Pleistocene hominids from East Rudolf, North Kenya, 1972. *Nature* 242:170–173.
1973b Evidence for an advanced Plio-Pleistocene hominid from East Rudolf, Kenya. *Nature* 242:447–450.

LEAKEY, R. E. F., J. M. MUNGAI, A. C. WALKER
1971 New australopithecines from East Rudolf, Kenya. *American Journal of Physical Anthropology* 35:175–186.
1972 New australopithecines from East Rudolf, Kenya (II). *American Journal of Physical Anthropology* 366:235–252.

LIEBERMAN, P.
1974 "On the evolution of language: a unified view," in *Antecedents of man and after*, volume one: *Primates: functional morphology and evolution*. Edited by Russell Tuttle. World Anthropology Series. The Hague: Mouton.

LIEBERMAN, P., E. S. CRELIN
1971 On the speech of Neanderthal man. *Linguistic Inquiry* 2:203–222.

LIEBERMAN, P., E. S. CRELIN, D. H. KLATT
1972 Phonetic ability and related anatomy of the newborn and adult human, Neanderthal man and the chimpanzee. *American Anthropologist* 74:287–307.

MACINTOSH, N. W. G.
1965 "The physical aspect of man in Australia," in *Aboriginal man in Australia*. Edited by R. M. Berndt and C. H. Berndt, 29–70. Sydney: Angus and Robertson.

MACINTOSH, N. W. G., S. L. LARNACH
1972 The persistence of *Homo erectus* traits in Australian Aboriginal crania. *Archaeology and Physical Anthropology in Oceania* 7:1–7.

MAGLIO, V. J.
1970 Early Elephantidae of Africa and a tentative correlation of Afri-

can Plio-Pleistocene deposits. *Nature* 225:328–332.
1972   Vertbrate faunas and chronology of hominid-bearing sediments east of Lake Rudolf, Kenya. *Nature* 239:379–385.
i.p.   Origin and evolution of the Elephantidae. *American Philosophical Society Transactions.*

MARKS, P.
1953   Preliminary note on the discovery of a new jaw of *Meganthropus* von Koenigswald in the lower Middle Pleistocene of Sangiran, Central Java. *Indonesian Journal of Natural Science* 109:26–33.

MCCOWN, T. D., A. KEITH
1939   *The Stone Age of Mount Carmel,* volume two. Oxford: Oxford University Press.

MCCOWN, T., K. A. R. KENNEDY
1972   *Climbing man's family tree.* Englewood Cliffs: Prentice-Hall.

MCINTYRE, A., W. F. RUDDIMAN, R. JANTZEN
1972   Southward penetrations of the North Atlantic polar front: faunal and floral evidence of large-scale surface water mass movements over the last 225,000 years. *Deep-Sea Research* 19:61–77.

MILANKOVITCH, M.
1930   Mathematische Klimalehre und astronomische Theorie der Klimaschwankungen. *Handbuch der Klimatologie* 1:1–176.

MÖRNER, N-A.
1972   When will the present interglacial end? *Quaternary Research* 2:341–349.

MOVIUS, H. L., JR.
1944   *Early man and Pleistocene stratigraphy in southern and eastern Asia.* Papers of the Peabody Museum of American archaeology and Ethnology 19 (3).

NAKAGAWA, H., N. NIITSUMA, C. ELMI
1971   Pliocene and Pleistocene magnetic stratigraphy in Le Castella area, southern Italy: a preliminary report. *Quaternary Research* 1:360–368.

OAKLEY, K. P.
1964   *Frameworks for dating fossil man.* Chicago: Aldine.

OPDYKE, N. D.
1972   Paleomagnetism of deep-sea cores. *Reviews of Geophysics and Space Physics* 10:213–249.

OVEY, C. D., editor
1964   *The Swanscombe skull.* Royal Anthropological Institute Occasional Paper 20.

OZEGOVIĆ, F.
1958   "Die Bedeutung der Entdeckung des Diluvialen Menschen von Krapina in Kroatien," in *Hundert Jahre Neanderthaler.* Edited by G. H. R. von Koenigswald, 27–31. Utrecht: Kemink en Zoon.

PILBEAM, D.
1969   Early Hominidae and cranial capacity. *Nature* 224:386.
1970   Early hominids and cranial capacity (continued). *Nature* 225: 747–748.

1972a *The ascent of man.* New York: Macmillan.

1972b "Evolutionary changes in the hominoid dentition through geological time," in *Calibration of hominoid evolution.* Edited by W. W. Bishop and J. A. Miller, 369–380. Edinburgh: Scottish Academic Press.

PILBEAM, D., J. R. VAISNYS

1974 "Hypothesis testing in paleoanthropology," in *Antecedents of man and after,* volume two: *Paleoanthropology, morphology, and Paleoecology.* Edited by Russell Tuttle. World Anthropology Series. The Hague: Mouton.

PILBEAM, D., M. ZWELL

1972 Sexual dimorphism and the single species hypothesis. *Yearbook of Physical Anthropology.*

PIVETEAU, J.

1957 *Traité de paléontologie,* volume seven. Paris: Masson.

1967 Un pariétal humain de la Grotte du Lazaret. *Annales de Paléontologie* 53:167–199.

1970 Les Grottes de la Chaise (Charente). *Annales de Paléontologie* 56:175–225.

1972 "Une découverte de A. Debenath," in *The origin of Homo sapiens.* Edited by F. Bordes, 57. Paris: UNESCO.

POAG, C. W.

1972 Correlation of early Quaternary events in the U.S. Gulf Coast. *Quaternary Research* 2:447–469.

RICHMOND, G. M.

1970 Comparison of the Quaternary stratigraphy of the Alps and Rocky Mountains. *Quaternary Research* 1:3–28.

ROBINSON, J. T.

1956 *The dentition of the Australopithecinae.* Transvaal Museum Memoir 9.

1965 *Homo "habilis"* and the australopithecines. *Nature* 205:121–124.

1972 *Early hominid posture and locomotion.* Chicago: University of Chicago Press.

SALTZMAN, B., A. D. VERNEKAR

1971 Notes on the effect of earth orbital radiation variations on climate. *Journal of Geophysical Research* 76:4195–4197.

SANCETTA, C., J. IMBRIE, N. G. KIPP, A. MCINTYRE, W. F. RUDDIMAN

1972 Climatic record in north Atlantic deep-sea core V23-82: comparison of the last and present interglacials based on quantitative time series. *Quaternary Research* 2:363–367.

SARTANO, S.

1961 *Notes on a new find of a Pithecanthropus mandible.* Publikasi Teknik Seri Paleontologi 2.

1968 Early man in Java: Pithecanthropus skull VII, a male specimen of Pithecanthropus erectus (I). *Koninklijke Nederlandse Akademie van Wetenschappen,* series B, 71:396–422.

1970 Observations on a new skull of Pithecanthropus erectus (Pithecanthropus VIII) from Sangiran, Central Java. *Koninklijke Nederlandse Akademie van Wetenschappen,* series B, 74:185–194.

SAVAGE, D. E., G. H. CURTIS
  1970 *The Villafranchian Stage-Age and its radiometric dating.* Geological Society of America, Special Paper 124.

SCHAEFER, U.
  1959 Die Stellung der Skelette aus Krapina im Rahmen der Neandertaler des Riss-Würm-Interglazials und des Würm-Glazials. *Bericht Uber die 6 Tagung der Deutschen Gesellschaft für Anthropologie,* 209–214.

SELLI, R.
  1967 "The Pliocene-Pleistocene boundary in Italian marine sections and its relationship to continental stratigraphies," in *Progress in oceanography,* volume four. Edited by M. Sears, 67–86. New York: Pergamon.

SERGI, S.
  1958 "Die Neandertalischen Palaeanthropen in Italien," in *Hundert Jahre Neanderthaler.* Edited by G. H. R. von Koenigswald, 38–51. Utrecht: Kemink en Zoon.

SHACKLETON, N. J.
  1969 The last interglacial in the marine and terrestrial records. *Proceedings of the Royal Society of London,* series B, 174:135–154.
  1971 "Notes on Pleistocene radiometric age-determinations itemized in this volume," in *The Phanerozoic time-scale.* Edited by W. B. Harland and E. H. Francis, 35–38. Geological Society of London, Special Publication 5.

SHACKLETON, N. J., C. TURNER
  1967 Correlation between marine and terrestrial Pleistocene successions. *Nature* 216:1079–1082.

SHOTTON, F. W.
  1967 The problems and contributions of methods of absolute dating within the Pleistocene period. *Quarterly Journal of the Geological Society of London* 122:356–383.

SHUEY, R. T.
  1972 Paleomagnetic and paleoclimatic implications of a deep core from Pleistocene Lake Bonneville. *American Geophysical Union Transactions* 53:356.

SIMPSON, G. G.
  1961 *Principles of animal taxonomy.* New York: Columbia University Press.

SINGER, R.
  1954 The Saldanha skull from Hopefield, South Africa. *American Journal of Physical Anthropology* 12:345–362.

SINGER, R., P. SMITH
  1969 Some human remains associated with the Middle Stone Age deposits at Klasies River, South Africa. *American Journal of Physical Anthropology* 31:256.

SOLECKI, R.
  1963 Prehistory in Shanidar Valley, northern Iraq. *Science* 139:179–193.

SUZUKI, H., F. TAKAI, *editors*
1970   *The Amud man and his cave site.* Tokyo: University of Tokyo.

THOMA, A.
1966   L'occipital de l'homme Mindélian de Vértesszöllös. *L'Anthropologie* 70:495–534.
1972a Cranial capacity, taxonomical and phylogenetical status of Vértesszöllös man. *Journal of Human Evolution* 1:511–512.
1972b On Vértesszöllös man. *Nature* 236:464–465.

THORNE, A. G.
1971   Mungo and Kow Swamp: morphological variation in Pleistocene Australians. *Mankind* 8:85–89.

THORNE, A. G., P. G. MACUMBER
1972   Discoveries of late Pleistocene man at Kow Swamp, Australia. *Nature* 238:316–319.

TOBIAS, P. V.
1959   Studies on the occipital bone in Africa, V: The occipital curvature in fossil man and the light it throws on the morphogenesis of the Bushman. *American Journal of Physical Anthropology* 17:1–12.
1961   New evidence and new views on the evolution of man in Africa. *South African Journal of Science* 57:25–38.
1964   The Olduvai Bed I hominine with special reference to its cranial capacity. *Nature* 202:3–4.
1965   Early man in east Africa. *Science* 149:22–33.
1966   The distinctiveness of *Homo habilis. Nature* 209:953–957.
1967a *Olduvai Gorge,* volume two: *The cranium and maxillary dentition of Australopithecus (Zinjanthropus) boisei.* Cambridge: Cambridge University Press.
1967b "The hominid skeletal remains of Haua Fteah," in *The Haua Fteah (Cyrenaica).* Edited by C. B. M. McBurney, 338–380. Cambridge: Cambridge University Press.
1968   "Middle and early Upper Pleistocene members of the genus Homo in Africa," in *Evolution und Hominisation* (second edition). Edited by G. Kurth, 176–194. Stuttgart: Fischer.
1971a *The brain in hominid evolution.* New York: Columbia University Press.
1971b Human skeletal remains from the Cave of Hearths, Makapansgat, northern Transvaal. *American Journal of Physical Anthropology* 34:335–368.

TOBIAS, P. V., G. H. R. VON KOENIGSWALD
1964   A comparison between the Olduvai hominines and those of Java and some implications for hominid phylogeny. *Nature* 204:515–518.

TOBIEN, H.
1970   Biostratigraphy of the mammalian faunas at the Pliocene-Pleistocene boundary in middle and western Europe. *Palaeogeography, Palaeoclimatology, Palaeoecology* 8:77–93.

TURNER, C., R. G. WEST
1968   The subdivision and zonation of interglacial periods. *Eiszeitalter und Gegenwart* 19:93–101.

VALLOIS, H. V.
1949   The Fontéchevade fossil men. *America Journal of Physical Anthropology* 7:339–362.
1954   Neandertals and presapiens. *The Journal of the Royal Anthropological Institute* 84:2–20.
1958   *La Grotte de Fontéchevade II. Anthropologie.* Archives de l'Institut de Paléontologie Humaine 29.

VALLOIS, H. V., B. VANDERMEERSCH
1972   Le crâne moustérien de Qafzeh (Homo VI). *L'Antropologie* 76: 71–96.

VAN BEMMELEN, R. W.
1949   *The geology of Indonesia.* The Hague: Nijhoff.

VAN DER HAMMEN, T., T. A. WIJMSTRA, W. H. ZAGWIJN
1971   "The floral record of the Late Cenozoic of Europe," in *Late Cenozoic Glacial Ages.* Edited by K. K. Turekian, 391–424. New Haven: Yale University Press.

VANDERMEERSCH, B.
1966   Nouvelles découvertes de restes humains dans les couches Levalloiso-Moustériennes du gisement de Qafzeh (Israël). *Comptes Rendus des séances de l'Académie des Sciences* 262:1434–1436.
1969   Les nouveaux squelettes moustériens decouvertes à Qafzeh (Israël) et leur signification. *Comptes rendus des séances de l'Académie des Sciences* 268:2562–2565.
1972   "Récentes découvertes de squelettes humains à Qafzeh (Israël): essai d'interprétation," in *The origin of Homo sapiens.* Edited by F. Bordes, 49–54. Paris: UNESCO.

VAN HEEKEREN, H. R.
1957   *The Stone Age of Indonesia.* The Hague: Nijhoff.

VAN MONTFRANS, H. M.
1971   Palaeomagnetic dating in the North Sea basin. *Earth and Planetary Science Letters* 11:226–235.

VAN MONTFRANS, H. M., J. HOSPERS
1969   A preliminary report on the stratigraphical position of the Matuyama-Brunhes geomagnetic field reversal in the Quaternary sediments of the Netherlands. *Geologie en Mijnbouw* 48:565–572.

VAN VALEN, L.
1966   On discussing human races. *Perspectives in Biology and Medicine* 9:377–383.

VERNEKAR, A. D.
1968   *Long-period global variations of incoming solar radiation.* Hartford: Travelers Research Center.

VLČEK, E.
1955   The fossil man of Gánovce, Czechoslovakia. *Journal of the Royal Anthropological Institute* 85:163–171.

VOGEL, J. C., P. B. BEAUMONT
1972   Revised radiocarbon chronology for the Stone Age in South Africa. *Nature* 237:50–51.

VON KOENIGSWALD, G. H. R.
1955   Meganthropus and the Australopithecinae. *Proceedings of the*

Third Pan-African Congress on Prehistory, 158–160.

1968   "Das absolute Alter des Pithecanthropus erectus Dubois," in *Evolution und Hominisation* (second edition). Edited by G. Kurth, 195–203. Stuttgart: Fischer.

1970   Java: prae-Trinil man. *Proceedings of the Eighth International Congress of Anthropological and Ethnological Sciences* 1:104–105.

VON KOENIGSWALD, G. H. R., *editor*

1958   *Hundert Jahre Neanderthaler.* Utrecht: Kemink en Zoon.

VON KOENIGSWALD, G. H. R., A. K. GHOSH

1973   Stone implements from the Trinil Beds of Sangiran, Central Java. I. *Koninklijke Nederlandse Akademie van Wetenschappen,* series B, 76:1–17.

WEIDENREICH, F.

1936   The mandibles of *Sinanthropus pekinensis:* a comparative study. *Palaeontologica Sinica,* series D, 7.

1937   The dentition of *Sinanthropus pekinensis:* a comparative odontography of the hominids. *Palaeontologica Sinica,* n.s. D, 1.

1941   The extremity bones of *Sinanthropus pekinensis. Palaeontologica Sinica,* n.s. D, 5.

1943   The skull of *Sinanthropus pekinensis:* a comparative study on a primitive hominid skull. *Palaeontologica Sinica,* n.s. D, 10.

1945   Giant early man from Java and South China. *Anthropological Papers of the American Museum of Natural History* 40:1–134.

1951   Morphology of Solo man. *Anthropological Papers of the American Museum of Natural History* 43:205–290.

WEINER, J. S.

1971   *The natural history of man.* New York: Universe.

WEINER, J. S., B. G. CAMPBELL

1964   "The taxonomic status of the Swanscombe skull," in *The Swanscombe skull.* Edited by C. D. Ovey, 175–209. Royal Anthropological Institute Occasional Paper 20. London.

WEST, R. G., D. G. WILSON

1966   Cromer Forest Bed Series. *Nature* 209:497–498.

WOLPOFF, M. H.

1971   Is Vértesszöllös II an occipital of European *Homo erectus? Nature* 232:567–568.

WOLSTEDT, P.

1966   Der Ablauf des Eiszeitalters. *Eiszeitalter und Gegenwart* 17:153–158.

WOO, J.-K.

1965   Preliminary report on a skull of *Sinanthropus lantianensis* of Lantian, Shensi. *Scientia Sinica* 14:1032–1035.

WOO, J.-K., R.-C. PENG

1959   Fossil human skull of early paleoanthropic stage found at Mapa, Shaoquan, Kwangtung Province. *Vertebrata Palasiatica* 3:176–182.

WRIGHT, H. E.

1972   Interglacial and postglacial climates: the pollen record. *Quaternary Research* 2:274–282.

YELLEN, J., H. HARPENDING
   1972   Hunter-gatherer populations and archaeological inference. *World Archaeology* 4:244–253.
ZAGWIJN, W. H., H. M. VAN MONTFRANS, J. G. ZANDSTRA
   1971   Subdivision of the "Cromerian" in the Netherlands; pollen-analysis, palaeomagnetism and sedimentary petrology. *Geologie en Mijnbouw* 50:41–58.

Geological and Ecological Perspectives on the Middle Pleistocene

KARL W. BUTZER

THE MID-PLEISTOCENE "PROBLEM": HISTORICAL BACKGROUND

The mid-Pleistocene time range, no matter how defined, has long presented a peculiar set of problems in terms of stratigraphic definition, paleoecological characterization, and archeological resolution. These problems can best be appreciated in their historical background and the structure of this symposium was, in fact, directed to a complex of issues that finds its origins in the development of Pleistocene studies over the past century. It is against this background that the import and significance of the symposium contributions can best be understood and evaluated.

Time-stratigraphic subdivisions are generally introduced as a matter of convenience. In the case of Europe, where basic Pleistocene concepts evolved during the late nineteenth and early twentieth centuries, Pleistocene subdivisions were first formally considered by the International Quaternary Association meetings of 1932, in Leningrad. Available for discussion at that time were four or five Alpine glaciations, three major Fennoscandinavian glaciations, a number of paleosols, and disparate paleobiological evidence, including a rudimentary faunal zonation (for an overview of the state of the art in the 1920's, see Woldstedt 1929). The Leningrad Congress chose to define the penultimate glacial and penultimate interglacial as "Middle Pleistocene," relegating earlier glacials and interglacials to the "Lower Pleistocene." By the late 1950's the cumulative growth of information from the major world continents presented a far more complex picture of multiple, cold "glacials" and fostered a wide range of professional disagreement (see Woldstedt 1958, for the critical overview most representative of the period). Successive attempts at Pleistocene subdivision since 1958 (see Butzer 1971a: Table 4) have sought new grounds for agreement by emphasizing one or other regional litho- or bio-stratigraphic sequence. At the same time the Pleistocene was "growing longer," since the 1948 International Geological Congress in London had effectively recommended inclusion of most of the marine Calabrian in the Pleistocene and thus, implicitly, added much of the continental Villafranchian to the base of the Pleistocene column. It now appeared that a long "non-glacial" Pleistocene, characterized by alternating cold and warm phases, preceded the development of the first ice sheets in Scandinavia and the Alps. The development of potassium-argon dating compounded this problem in the early 1960's by demonstrating that all earlier estimates of the absolute duration of the Pleistocene had been grossly incorrect, and that accepted Pleistocene deposits at Olduvai were almost 2 million years old (see Evernden and Curtis 1965).

Far from nearing resolution, the state of stratigraphic confusion has been increased in recent years as new avenues of research are followed up and the body of factual information grows at an exponential rate. In part this confusion has been a result of parochialism or disciplinary particularism, whereby leading researchers have assumed their own corpus of data to be complete and correct, without making a thorough appraisal as to why intraregional or interregional contradictions persisted. In part, too, the fault has been that of synthesizers who neglected to keep abreast of current research or who failed to grasp the nature of the underlying problems, hiding their own ignorance behind dogmatic statements or smart stratigraphic legalisms. In the meantime, regional or disciplinary research continues in a conceptual vacuum, with increasingly divergent results and seemingly insurmountable problems of correlation between high- and low-latitude continents and between the sea and the land. In default of an objective reexamination of criteria and results, the beginning student of the Pleistocene is faced by an almost insurmountable morass of unintegrated and seemingly contradictory data, an unlimited number of alternative stratigraphic frameworks, and a nomenclature so debased as to be worse than useless.

Thus the mid-Pleistocene "problem" concerns that core of the Pleistocene lying before the span of reasonably resolved stratigraphic detail and ecological understanding of the late Pleistocene, and after the Plio-Pleistocene transition. This "problem" is more than a matter of suitable time-stratigraphic framework or nomenclature. Involved, too, are matters of fundamental understanding as to the nature of the mid-Pleistocene. Was there ever a "non-glacial" Pleistocene, i.e. a protracted span of early Pleistocene time without formation of significant ice caps on the landmasses of Eurasia and North America? Was the wave-length and amplitude of climatic cycles in the mid-Pleistocene constant and comparable to the late Pleistocene interglacial-glacial sequence? Were any of the demonstrable mid-Pleistocene warm intervals interstadials rather than interglacials? Are reconstructions of late Pleistocene, glacial-age climate or vegetation relevant for earlier glacials as well? Were mid-Pleistocene climatic oscillations of sufficient amplitude to leave a tangible record in the tropics as well as in higher latitudes? How were worldwide climatic anomalies reflected in distinct climatic provinces and regional litho- or bio-stratigraphic sequences? All these questions and corollary issues are as central to the mid-Pleistocene "problem" as are an adequate definitions of stratigraphic boundaries and the exact number of cold-warm climatic cycles.

Finally, there is the whole sphere of biological events, including faunal evolution and dispersals as well as the complex issues involving the hominization process. These themes are discussed more fully in the parallel evaluation of Glynn Isaac, but two points may be made here.

First, it deserves emphasis that biostratigraphic zonation was from the beginning tied in with evolving concepts of mid-Pleistocene resolution. However, the advent of chronometric yardsticks began to reveal that faunal horizons are not everywhere synchronous. Thus, contrary to widespread, earlier expectations, biostratigraphic units could no longer serve as markers for the entire timespace continuum of the mid-Pleistocene universe. Clearly, it had become necessary to reappraise the mid-Pleistocene faunal record from more sophisticated evolutionary, ecological, and zoo-geographical perspectives.

Second, it may be called to mind that subdivisions of the Old Stone Age or Paleolithic followed closely upon litho- and biostratigraphic delimitation within the Pleistocene. Consequently the Lower Paleolithic was widely equated with the Middle Pleistocene and, ultimately, with both the Lower and Middle Pleistocene. Stage concepts and temporal implications were commonly attached to industrial variants of the Lower Paleolithic such as "Abbevillian," Acheulian, "Clactonian," "Tayacian," or their Asiatic counterparts. Then, criteria for subdividing the Acheulian came under fire, while the mid-Pleistocene time range began to stretch from a few tens of thousands of years to a half million years or more. It became evident that the Acheulian, whatever it represented, spanned a million years and three continents, thus defying any ethnohistorical concept of a sociocultural group (Butzer 1971a: Chapter 26). Cultural change as well as human biological evolution during the mid-Pleistocene were now seen to be surprisingly slow. During the last two years, the archeological and paleontological evidence from East Rudolf has even pushed the origins of man back to 2.5 million years. Consequently the nature of mid-Pleistocene hominization requires intensive, multidisciplinary scrutiny. It is here that new stratigraphic and paleoecological approaches also promise to be particularly rewarding.

THE MID-PLEISTOCENE "PROBLEM:" SYMPOSIUM CONTRIBUTIONS

Several of the symposium papers synthesized the results of specialized approaches to the study of unusually long Pleistocene records. These subdisciplinary techniques included deep-sea core analyses, glacial-eustatic stratigraphy, alluvial geomorphology, loess investigations, and palynology. Each method contributed its own partial picture of mid-Pleistocene events and so provided new insights for a more comprehensive understanding.

The Deep-Sea Core Records

Shackleton (this volume) has provided an incisive analysis of the deep-sea core records, and his detailed oxygen isotope record for equatorial Pacific core V28–238 covers at least the past 800,000 years, as calibrated by the Brunhes-Matuyama paleomagnetic reversal. The 22 stages identified are paralleled by those of other cores, such as V23–100 from the tropical Atlantic, and reflect changes in ocean isotopic composition caused by the waxing and waning of ice sheets on the northern hemisphere continents. In very broad terms, Shackleton's stage 1 can be identified with the Holocene, his stages 2 to 4 with what is conventionally described as the Last Glacial in continental records, and stage 5 with the "Last Interglacial." Only the very beginning of stage 5 appears to correspond to the classical "Eemian" pollen profiles (Turner, this volume) and this brief phase marks the only segment of core V28–238 that argues for a greater melting of the residual ice masses than experienced during Holocene times. Shackleton (in discussion) argues that the stage 5/6 boundary would conform most appropriately to the conventional Middle/Upper Pleistocene boundary.

Turning to the earlier record of core V28–238 it is apparent that cyclic glacial-interglacial alternations extend back at least to stage 22, some 800,000 years ago. The amplitude of variation between maximum glaciation and maximum deglaciation varies in detail, but remained basically comparable through time, suggesting some fundamental constraints to the planetary glacial-interglacial pendulum. However, there was no strict periodicity, and the wave length of the superimposed fluctuations expressed by Shackleton's stage units is by no means constant. Several conclusions can be drawn from evaluation of this data: (1) Apparent glacial-interglacial oscillations extend backwards in time for at least 800,000 years. (2) At the very least nine such "cold" stages can be identified prior to the Upper Pleistocene, with a variable duration of about 18,000 to 67,000 years, compared with 23,000 to 73,000 years for the "warm" stages. (3) In its detail, each glacial and inter-glacial hemicycle was different, so that one cannot speak of repetitive climatic events. This is underscored by the variations in wind strength deduced from eolian components in cores off West Africa. (4) Correlation of Shackleton's multiple deep-sea units with existing, continental time-stratigraphic schemes is impossible, although cautious comparisons with detailed lithostratigraphic sequences — defined with some measure of radiometric control, do appear to be possible. (5) The absence of any striking events or discontinuities in the lower half of core V28–238 suggests that an arbitrary, radiometric or paleomagnetic datum must be chosen for the Lower/Middle Pleistocene boundary. Shackleton (in discussion) suggests the Brunhes-Matuyama reversal for this purpose, on account of its ready worldwide applicability.

Glacial-Eustatic Stratigraphy

The complexity of the glacial-eustatic curve derived on Mallorca (Butzer, this volume) is approximately comparable to that of the deep-sea isotopic record, bearing in mind that the littoral sedimentary cycles of Mallorca provide only a minimal level of resolution and that the time axis is increasingly distorted prior to 250,000 B.P. As Shackleton (this volume) points out, the deep-sea isotopic record may also be read as a trace of glacial-eustatic changes of world sea level. Gross comparisons between V28–238 and the Mallorquin data can be made back to marine hemicycle W2 and deep-sea stage 9. Beyond that the incomplete nature of and lack of isotopic dating or paleomagnetic data for the Mallorquin curve limit its general evaluation. However, a general measure of support is given to the conclusions offered above in regard to the deep-sea evidence. On a worldwide basis, glacio-eustatic sea levels offer a relative stratigraphic tool for distinguishing glacial and interglacial alternations, but they are seldom suitable for specific time-stratigraphic purposes. Even on a regional basis, bio- or time-stratigraphic concepts such as Tyrrhenian or Monastirian offer no assistance in correlation and are often no more than a source of confusion.

The European Glacials

Although no conference paper specifically dealt with glacial geology, due to the inability of Lüttig to attend, the papers of Brunnacker, Gladfelter, and Kukla touch on this theme from several points of view. As emphasized by Brunnacker (this volume), the state of resolution of the till and outwash stratigraphies in the Alpine piedmonts and the North European Plain is incomplete, contradictory at the scale of interregional comparisons, and unsuitable for time-stratigraphic applicability.

Nonetheless, most global stratigraphic schemes ultimately fall back on terminologies derived from a modified or amplified version of Penck's scheme of Günz, Mindel, Riss, and Würm. Consequently Brunnacker (in discussion) explained the rationale of the original, Penckian four-glacial scheme, its weaknesses, subsequent modifications, and invalid application to biostratigraphic horizons. These pertinent historical insights will be developed by Brunnacker in a separate paper, and can only be summarized here.

During the first decade of the twentieth century Penck defined his four Alpine glaciations on the basis of a composite of criteria (*glaziale Serie*): (a) vertically superposed ground moraines and their surface expression, (b) horizontally arranged arcs of terminal and recessional moraines, and (c) vertically and horizontally differentiated glaciofluvial terraces. Each glaciation was defined from a different piedmont ice lobe. These lobate formations were poorly interdigitated, and no complete or reliable direct correlation was ever established downstream along the Danube River. As a result, correlation of the incomplete sequences of pre-Würmian features from lobe to lobe remained controversial, so that not even the basic four-fold scheme has been successfully established through the northern Alpine piedmont. In the 1920's, Soergel found there were more than four alluvial terraces along the Saale drainage of Thuringia. These were arbitrarily designated Günz, Mindel, Riss, and Würm, with additional I, II, or III subdivisions introduced as deemed necessary to accommodate all terraces present. This unacceptable "correlation" of terrace system and glacial sequence was then tenuously linked to certain macrofaunal horizons. Consequently, the subsequent popularization of the G-M-R-W bio- and time-stratigraphic scheme by Zeuner and others has little in common with Penck's original definition. Further complications were introduced shortly thereafter when Eberl added a pre-Günzian glacial complex (Donau I, II, III), using other criteria of definition than did Penck. Finally, in the early 1950's, Schaefer identified an even earlier Biber "glacial."

At this point the Alpine terminologies applied by various workers through much of Europe and even in Morocco had become quite meaningless. Recent fieldwork in each of the type-areas is therefore directed towards establishing local litho-stratigraphic units to which the original Penckian terminology MAY ultimately be applicable.

Cold-Climate Alluvial Terraces

Since both the glacial stratigraphy and terminology have proved to be of little or no value for resolution of the mid-Pleistocene record, other lines of evidence have been intensively followed up by Brunnacker and his students among the alluvia and loesses of the lower Rhine Valley, and by Kukla and his associates in the loess of Czechoslovakia and eastern Austria. A unique sequence of Plio-Pleistocene deposits has already been established for the Netherlands, documenting progressive impoverishment of thermophile species among the Dutch flora during successive early cold intervals (van der Hammen, et al. 1971). However, a more complete mid-Pleistocene record is preserved a little further upstream among excellent surface exposures near Cologne and in the Neuwied Basin. Here Brunnacker (this volume) has demonstrated repetitive cycles of cold-climate alluviation or loess accumulation, alternating with warmer episodes of soil formation. Seven such cycles have occurred since the Brunhes-Matuyama geomagnetic reversal of 700,000 B.P. Syngenetic ice-wedge casts indicative of permafrost first appear ca. 700,000 B.P. and are associated with all alluvia and loesses — except for those of the second of these cycles. No permafrost is indicated in earlier deposits, but icerafted debris first appears at the base of the oldest Main Terrace, which appears to date from the Jaramillo geomagnetic event almost 900,000 B.P.

Unfortunately the early Pleistocene record of the Lower Rhine is not now satisfactorily correlated with the geomagnetic chronology, probably as a result of undetected breaks and inconsistencies in the Netherlands sequence (Brunnacker and Kukla, discussion comments). In any event, cold-climate phases sufficiently severe to decimate the Netherlands flora begin with the end of the Pliocene, severe winter freezing of Rhine and its affluents is verified for the cold intervals since 900,000 B.P., and permafrost characterized most cold hemicycles since 700,000 B.P. Brunnacker consequently suggests that the Lower/Middle Pleistocene boundary be set at the base of the first truly cold alluvium that straddles the Brunhes-Matuyama boundary. Problematic is the smaller number of major alluvial and loess cycles in the Lower Rhine (seven) than in the deep-sea record (eight) since 700,000 B.P.

The deep-sea and Rhine evidence of increasing and surprisingly dramatic cold during the early Pleistocene finds support in the pollen record of Villarroya (Remy 1958) and the faunal record of the French Massif Central (Bout, this volume). In fact, Bout recognizes frost-weathered slope deposits and cryoturbated basin beds in successive sedimentary units as old as 1.9 million B.P., although clear indications for permafrost are lacking.

The Loess Record

Perhaps the longest and most complete continental record presently available for the mid-Pleistocene has been studied in unusual detail in the relatively dry lowlands of Moravia (Kukla, this volume). Here eolian loess, hillwash, soil horizons, and ecologically-sensitive snail assemblages prove the existence of eight complete cycles of glacial-age loess and interglacial soils within the last 700,000 years. Including the Krems profile of Lower Austria, it further appears that a minimum of eight additional loess cycles span the preceding million years back to the Olduvai geomagnetic event. This picture of complexity matches that of the deep-sea record and further illustrates the degree to which the till sequences are incomplete and therefore unsuitable for Pleistocene subdivision. This composite, normative loess profile also warns against simple intercorrelations of loess cycles in more humid parts of Europe where the record is generally incomplete and snail faunas have commonly been leached out. Finally, the history of interpretation of even these Czechoslovak and Austrian loess sections shows the impracticability of any reliable external correlations without radiometric dating or geomagnetic marker horizons. Kukla (this volume, and discussion) gives six possibilities to define the Lower/Middle Pleistocene boundary, all linked either directly or indirectly to the Brunhes-Matuyama boundary or the Jaramillo event.

Palynology and the Interglacial Record

Turner's critical re-evaluation of the northwest European pollen horizons (this volume) shows beyond question that the mid-Pleistocene interglacial record is rather more complex than hitherto assumed. The Holsteinian interglacial, accepted as the antepenultimate warm phase, is fortunately rather distinctive and the uniform and welldefined vegetational succession can be readily identified. With the Holsteinian as a datum, there are AT LEAST two pre-Holsteinian interglacials younger than the Brunhes-Matuyama boundary and at least one interglacial between the Holsteinian and Eemian. Including the Holocene, this gives a minimum of six interglacial horizons within the last 700,000 years. Presumably further work will eliminate the remaining, apparent discrepancies between mid-Pleistocene records based on various categories of information. Of special interest are Turner's estimates of the duration of the Holsteinian as 17,000–25,000 and the Eemian as 9,000–11,000 years. This suggests that the palynologically defined interglacials occupied only a portion of the much longer minimum-glaciation intervals represented by the odd numbered deep-sea stages of Shackleton (this volume). In fact, the Eemian interglacial appears to have coincided with the maximum deglaciation indicated for the initial stages only of Shackleton's stage 5 (e).

Although Turner (in discussion) indicated that eradication of the last Pliocene floral elements (following the Waalian interglacial horizon of the Netherlands) would be a logical palynological criterion to define a Lower/Middle Pleistocene boundary, he concluded that a biostratigraphic boundary linked to the Brunhes-Matuyama geomagnetic reversal would be of more universal applicability.

THE MID-PLEISTOCENE RECORD IN HIGHER LATITUDES

The preceding review of the conference contributions allows a number of general conclusions concerning the Pleistocene record in higher latitudes:

a. The European interglacial and Rhine alluvial records indicate a minimum of six, the Czechoslovakian loess a total of eight cold-warm cycles since the Brunhes-Matuyama geomagnetic reversal. Since eight comparable cycles are also indicated in both the Pacific and Atlantic deep-sea cores, this must be seen as evidence for eight glacial intervals of hemispheric or global significance during the past 700,000 years.

b.   With possible exception of the designation Würm, that can probably be applied to the last glacial complex, the till or outwash stratigraphies are hopelessly inadequate to provide a valid or practicable nomenclature for the preceding seven glacials.

c.   At least five of the glacials since 700,000 B.P. were sufficiently severe to produce permafrost conditions in midlatitude Europe. For the lower Rhine Basin this implies a mean temperature depression of at the very least 11° C. Consequently the "glacial Pleistocene" unquestionably extends back to the Brunhes-Matuyama boundary.

d.   An uncertain but nonetheless substantial number of cold-warm cycles can be recognized prior to 700,000 B.P., although the severity of the cold intervals did not match that of glacial phases during the Brunhes normal polarity epoch.

e.   Each cold hemicycle prior to 700,000 B.P. appears to have led to floral decimations in western Europe while providing an environment suitable for loess accumulation in east-central Europe. Furthemore, the deep-sea record indicates extensive glaciation for at least the later of these cold phases. The available evidence could in fact be interpreted with recourse to repeated cold impulses characterized by a progressive intensification of climatic stress.

In view of our present understanding of the mid-Pleistocene record in higher latitudes, two major lines of argumentation can be introduced to propose that the Lower/Middle Pleistocene boundary be linked to the Brunhes-Matuyama geomagnetic reversal by one or other set of criteria. In particular:

1.   Whether or not it can ultimately be demonstrated that the Matuyama epoch saw high-latitude climatic oscillations of increasing amplitude, only by 700,000 B.P. were the cold intervals sufficiently severe to bring permafrost to mid-latitude Europe. It can therefore be argued that the major climatic oscillations of the Brunhes epoch were of glacial-inter-glacial amplitude. Thus a variety of paleoclimatic criteria can be mustered to argue for a Lower/Middle Pleistocene boundary about 700,000 years ago.

2.   The experiences of several decades of unsatisfactory boundary definitions show that practicable stratigraphic boundaries must be tied to chronometric horizons, despite established geological tradition favoring bio-, litho-, or climato-stratigraphic markers or discontinuities. In addition, a geomagnetic reversal or event can be identified in a diverse range of sediments not amenable to radiometric dating, thus providing optimal opportunities for valid, worldwide correlation.

If the responsible commission of the International Quaternary Asso-

ciation could propose a geologically acceptable Lower/Middle Pleistocene boundary, usefully linked to the Brunhes-Matuyama reversal, it
would be of great practical value for interregional and intercontinental
correlation. At the regional or subdisciplinary level it would remain
possible or preferable to employ local or specific boundary criteria within the spirit of a more general definition.

MID-PLEISTOCENE RECORDS OF TROPICAL AFRICA

The preceding discussion was deliberately limited to higher latitudes,
where time-stratigraphic concepts and definitions have traditionally been
developed. However, the potassium-argon chronology of sediments,
faunas, and archeology in the Eastern Rift of Tanzania, Kenya, and
Ethiopia is unrivalled and stratigraphic generalizations can no longer be
carried out in ignorance of the tropical Pleistocene. It will accordingly
be necessary to examine the Pleistocene record of tropical Africa, the
only low-latitude subcontinent with suitable stratigraphic data.

Several cautions must be stated before discussing the African evidence.
There are no continuous sequences, let alone cores of organic data for
the mid-Pleistocene, despite isolated and discontinuous pollen information from Ethiopia (Melka-Kontoure, Omo Basin) and Zambia (Kalambo Falls). The faunas of tropical Africa even now retain a high proportion of Pliocene elements and the Ethiopian faunal province provides
no useful temperature-sensitive forms (Maglio, this volume). Again,
fossil faunal assemblages commonly include woodland, grassland, and
riverine/lacustrine forms, and few quantitative analyses of total assemblages are available. Altogether, therefore, there is little biological evidence, throwing the major weight of paleoecological evaluation to sedimentology which, like all other single lines of evidence, is not uncondi-
tionally reliable. Additionally, modern ecological "balances" and climatic "stability" in East Africa are precarious and difficult to define. So,
for example, a non-outlet lake such as Lake Rudolf was 15 meters
higher than today in 1896 and 5 meters lower in 1955, while the range
of fluctuation for the past two millenia is greater than 40 meters (Butzer
1971b, and in discussion).

The only record of mid-Pleistocene cold in East Africa comes from
ancient weathered and dissected moraines in the high mountains. The
longest sequence is provided by Mt. Kilimanjaro, where four periods of
glaciation are verified and the second of which was older than 460,000
B.P. (Downie 1964; Evernden and Curtis 1965). In South Africa there

is some evidence for several episodes of accelerated frost-weathering during the early to mid-Pleistocene time range (Butzer 1973). H. Deacon (this volume, and in discussion) points out that the thermophile Knysna rainforest sets considerable restraints on the amplitude of thermal fluctuations during the South African Pleistocene. However, thermophile Pliocene elements in the Colchian and Hyrcanian forests of the Black and Caspian Sea littorals survived Pleistocene periglacial conditions, so that the problem may be one of identifying suitable refuges (Butzer and Helgren 1972).

The longest and most complete sequence available from East Africa is that of Olduvai Gorge (Hay 1972; Leakey, Hay, et al. 1972; also Hay in Evernden and Curtis 1965, and Leakey, this volume). Unfortunately the long-term meso-environmental trends through time cannot be rigorously interpreted due to tectonic modifications of the basin floor and major changes in orographic expression of the nearby volcanic peaks. However the incompletely studied, detailed facies alternations of the middle and upper part of the Olduvai column do seem to imply shorter term environmental changes.

Perhaps equally informative for these purposes is the far more incomplete record of the Omo-Rudolf Basin. A possible model for Pleistocene climatic variation in East Africa is provided by the evidence for repeated high-level lakes during the past 12,000 years (Butzer, Isaac, et al. 1972). One high level of Lake Rudolf involved a transgression of 60 to 80 meters from shortly before 9500 B.P. to a little after 7100 B.P. A second transgression of some 60 to 70 meters was accomplished in a few centuries after 6600 B.P., terminating perhaps 4000 B.P. but followed by a brief positive oscillation of similar amplitude shortly before 3200 B.P. These three transgressions of 60 to 80 meters within a 7,000 year span had a duration of 1 to 3 millenia and with a cumulative thickness of 21 meters constitute Member IV of the Kibish Formation (Butzer i.p.a, and in discussion). Probably comparable is the record of Member III (45 meters thick, shortly before 37,000 B.P.) with two transgressions, Member II (22.5 meters thick, date uncertain) with a single transgression, and Member I (over 26 meters thick, ca. 130,000 B.P.?) with two or more transgressions. Consequently, most of the later Pleistocene has experienced a moisture regime comparable to that of the present day, although there have been repeated, relatively brief periods of conspicuous lake expansion at long intervals. These moister intervals included one or more high-lake events, each lasting a few millenia. If the earliest verified high Rudolf lake level of Kibish age dates from the terminal Middle Pleistocene, the question arises whether similar events occurred before this. Possible deposits in the center of the Omo Basin may well have been destroyed by repeated mid-Pleistocene faulting. However, a sedimentary record to this effect is also lacking from the more stable northwestern half of the basin, and Bonnefille (1972) has shown that mid-Pleistocene deposits of Melka-Kontoure were laid down when the Ethiopian uplands were drier than today. It is therefore possible, but by no means certain, that Lake Rudolf was generally low from 130,000 B.P. to about 0.8 million B.P., when the last of the Plio-Pleistocene Omo Group deposits were laid down. The available evidence presently suggests that Lake Rudolf was somewhat deeper than today for most of the time from 4.5 or 5 million B.P. until 0.8 million B.P. Long-term trends of lake level reflected both on hydrological changes and ongoing tectonic deformation, but an argument can be made that the amplitude of variation was reduced and that the duration of short and long-term fluctuations was greater than during the later Pleistocene (Butzer i.p.a, and in discussion).

The Omo-Rudolf record, seen in conjunction with the evidence for multiple, mid-Pleistocene glaciation of Mt. Kilimanjaro, cautions against overgeneralization that the East African mid-Pleistocene was paleoclimatically uneventful. However, the magnitude of the changes implied should also not be over-emphasized. As Isaac (this volume) convincingly argues, the complex vertical and horizontal zonation of ecological opportunities in East Africa practically assures the survival of all basic eco-niches through climatic vicissitudes of the scale indicated in the later Pleistocene record. The points to be made here are that environmental changes have occurred throughout the East African Pleistocene, that the details and rationale of these changes are still obscure, but that the scale of any such changes was insufficient to change the fundamental ecological mosaic. The full range of moisture fluctuations of the past 5 million years has probably been experienced within the 10,000 years of Holocene time. In view of the pollen and faunal record of the Holocene we can therefore assume a lack of permanent ecological repercussions for Pleistocene wet-dry fluctuations. Furthermore, Pleistocene thermal variations have left no tangible record away from the high mountains, and it must similarly be assumed that any such changes did not seriously affect the complex patterns of ecological opportunities.

Turning to southern Africa, the evidence is somewhat less satisfactory due to the absence of adequate radiometric controls, and the resulting lack of a stratigraphic framework. Unlike East Africa, where topographic and edaphic variation is pronounced, southern Africa is rather more uniform (Deacon, this volume), so that any significant environmental changes would necessarily have initiated wholesale zonal eco-shifts. Possible hints as to magnitude and wave length of mid-Pleistocene variation are given by a recent evaluation of late Pleistocene paleo-climates (Van Zinderen Bakker and Butzer 1973). Mid-Pleistocene sequences are presently available from the Vaal River (Butzer, Helgren, et al. 1973), the Gaap Escarpment (Butzer i.p.b), and the southeastern Cape coast (Butzer and Helgren 1972). These all indicate significant, long-term changes in stream competence or spring and eolian activity. So, for example, four or more tufa-accretion cycles of the Gaap are hardly explicable without a rainfall of at least 600 to 800 millimeters (compared with 300 to 400 today). Similarly, the coastal Knysna rainforest was subject to both semiarid planation and laterite formation during Plio-Pleistocene-times. In the interior, short-term climatic oscillations were super-imposed upon long-term trends, as is illustrated by the mixed lacustrine and subaerial sedimentary sequences at the Acheulian sites of Doornlaagte and Rooidam (Butzer 1974).

At the very least, this recent South African evidence suggests that mid-Pleistocene environmental patterns were far from stable or predictable. However, there are no useful temporal frameworks and inter-regional correlations are difficult or impossible. No realistic estimate can be made as to the number of major climatic cycles recorded in southern Africa, and the broad trends suggested here cannot now be linked with any global events.

Altogether, the mid-Pleistocene record of tropical Africa remains incoherent, despite some promising local sequences. There is no paucity of evidence for change as such, but the nature and patterns of such changes are still problematical. Many more years of fieldwork will be necessary before it can be decided whether or not regional climato-stratigraphies can indeed be established, and it is highly doubtful even now that major climatic changes can be simply followed from one climatic province to another. Consequently, the tropical African record does not yet contribute much towards an understanding of the mid-Pleistocene. However, it does clearly show that the climatic cycles of higher latitudes are presently of little or no value in analyzing mid-Pleistocene records of the tropical continents. This strengthens the conference's plea for a radiometric-geomagnetic definition of intra-Pleistocene stratigraphic boundaries.

MIDDLE PLEISTOCENE ECO-ZONATION AND ARCHEOLOGICAL CONTEXTS

The basic eco-zonation of Europe, Africa, and North America during the maximum of the Last Glacial is understood or at least amenable to analysis (see Butzer 1971a: chapters 18–22). By contrast, such information is either very scarce or non-existent for the glacials or interglacials of the Middle Pleistocene. Frenzel (1968a, 1968b) has attempted to reconstruct the vegetation of mid-latitude Eurasia during the Penultimate ("Saale") glacial and the Holsteinian as well as Eemian interglacials. His data is of uneven quality from one area to another, reflecting on the quantity and quality of the available pollen data and other lines of inference. Nonetheless, Frenzel's partial reconstructions do provide working hypotheses of considerable heuristic value.

At the specific level of application to archeological problems, continental reconstructions are of more questionable value. The level of temporal resolution of any reconstruction is necessarily low since there seldom are adequate data to fix pieces of information in a strictly contemporaneous picture of a single phase of a glacial or interglacial. In fact stratigraphic control is so poor and mid-Pleistocene climatic cycles so many that much of the data is best considered to be of uncertain age. Yet Gladfelter and Turner (this volume) have both shown how complex the course of a cold or warm sedimentary or pollen sequence can be. Furthermore, the archeological record shows that even multiple occupations at any one site-complex span only brief intervals of time that coincide with a single set of ecological determinants. Consequently large-scale time-space reconstructions are utopian if not undesirable goals at our present level of understanding of the Middle Pleistocene.

A good part of recent geo-archeological research in mid-Pleistocene time ranges has concentrated on local litho-stratigraphic work. Despite initial misgivings by most workers involved, it is becoming increasingly apparent that such "floating" geological contexts are, in default of radiometric opportunities, a successful means of approaching stratigraphic problems of the Middle Pleistocene. Floating stratigraphies also encourage a pragmatic interpretation of site contexts in terms of depositional environments and regional settings. If there are geological deficiencies to be lamented, these are first and foremost a reflection of the "general" geologist's lack of familiarity with sedimentological and pedological techniques or his inability to study sedimentary and geomorphological contexts at the level of detail that other scientists necessarily bring to bear on archeological sites.

REFERENCES

BONNEFILLE, RAYMONDE
1972   "Associations polliniques actuelles et quaternaires en Ethiopie (vallées de l'Awash et de l'Omo)." Unpublished D.Sc. thesis, University of Paris.

BUTZER, K. W.
1971a   *Environment and archeology: an ecological approach to prehistory.* Chicago: Aldine-Atherton.
1971b   *Recent history of an Ethiopian delta: the Omo River and the level of Lake Rudolf.* University of Chicago Department of Geography, Research Paper 136:1–184.
1973   Pleistocene "periglacial" phenomena in southern Africa. *Boreas* 2:1–11.
1974   Geological interpretation of Acheulian calcpan sites at Doornlaagte and Rooidam (Kimberley, South Africa). *Journal of Archaeological Science* 1:1–25.
i.p.a   The Mursi, Nkalabong and Kibish Formations, Lower Omo Basin: stratigraphy and interpretation. *Prehistoric Archeology and Ecology* 3.
i.p.b   Paleo-Ecology of South African australopithecines: Taung revisited. *Current Anthropology* 15.

BUTZER, K. W., D. M. HELGREN
1972   Late Cenozoic evolution of the Cape Coast between Knysna and Cape St. Francis, South Africa. *Quaternary Research* 2:143–169.

BUTZER, K. W., D. H. HELGREN, G. J. FOCK, R. STUCKENRATH
1973   Alluvial terraces of the lower Vaal River, South Africa: a reappraisal and reinvestigation. *Journal of Geology* 81:341–362.

BUTZER, K. W., G. L. ISAAC, J. L. RICHARDSON, C. K. WASHBOURN-KAMAU
1972   Radiocarbon dating of East African lake levels. *Science* 175:1069–1076.

DOWNIE, C.
1964   Glaciations of Mt. Kilimanjaro, Northeast Tanganyika. *Bulletin, Geological Society of America* 75:1–16.

EVERNDEN, J. F., G. H. CURTIS
1965   The potassium-argon dating of late Cenozoic rocks in East Africa and Italy. *Current Anthropology* 6:343–385.

FRENZEL, BURKHARD
1968a   The Pleistocene vegetation of northern Eurasia. *Science* 161:637–649.
1968b   Grundzüge der Pleistozänen Vegetationsgeschichte Nord-Eurasiens. Wiesbaden: F. Steiner.

HAY, R. L.
1972   "Geologic background of Beds I and II: stratigraphic summary," in *Excavation in Beds I and II, Olduvai Gorge,* volume three.

HAMMEN, T. VAN DER, T. A. WIJMSTRA, W. ZAGWIJN
1971   "The floral record of the late cenozoic of Europe," in *Late Cenozoic Glacial Ages.* Edited by K. K. Turekian, 391–424. New Haven; Yale Unversity Press.

Edited by M. D. Leakey, 9-18. Cambridge: Cambridge University Press.

LEAKEY, M. D., R. L. HAY, R. PROTSCH, *et al.*
  1972   Stratigraphy, archaeology and age of the Ndutu and Naisiusiu Beds, Olduvai Gorge, Tanzania. *World Archaeology* 3:328–341.

REMY, HORST
  1958   Zur Flora und Fauna der Villafranca-Schichten von Villarroya Prov. Logrono, Spanien. *Eiszeitalter und Gegenwart* 9:83–103.

VAN ZINDEREN BAKKER, E. M., K. W. BUTZER
  1973   Quaternary environmental changes in southern Africa. *Soil Science* 116:236–248.

WOLDSTEDT, PAUL
  1929   *Das Eiszeitalter.* Stuttgart: F. Enke.
  1958   *Das Eiszeitalter,* volume two: *Europa, Vorderasien und Nordafrika im Eiszeitalter.* Stuttgart: F. Enke.

ZAGWIJN, W. H.
  1963   Pollen-analytic investigations in the Tiglian of the Netherlands. *Mededelingen van de Geologische Stichting,* n.s. 16:49–71.

Sorting out the Muddle in the Middle: An Anthropologist's Post-Conference Appraisal

GLYNN LL. ISAAC

Reporting a conference in which eighteen assorted earth-scientists, paleontologists and archeologists actively discussed the mid-Pleistocene for ten days is rather like the problem of providing an intelligible radio commentary on a football game. In order to understand the interactions themselves, one has to be present at the arena — so I will not try to give an account of the exchanges as such, but will try to formulate an anthropologist's view of the configurations which emerged.

The jig-saw puzzle metaphor used in the preface is perhaps again expressive. My concern in this appraisal is with the fits and joins which were established round the table, and with the glimpses of pattern that we all gained, rather than with an account of how and by whom the pieces were moved.

One of the most important lessons that we all seemed to learn by working on the puzzle together was that the scale of the mid-Pleistocene picture is far larger than has usually been recognised. Instead of having to fit our fragments of evidence into a frame formed by a few hundred thousand years, we are free to move them about within a span of time approaching a million years. Many of the pieces of evidence make much better evolutionary sense when they are not forced into misleading juxtaposition with other pieces. The change in our perception of the scale of the puzzle also affects our awareness of how many pieces we still lack before we can perceive even the outlines of the environmental and evolutionary history of the period.

The scale and complexity of the record

One of the major causes of over-simplification in Pleistocene studies is the fragmentary nature of the record. Given relatively simple versions of Quaternary history, of the kind often proposed by the pioneers of our disciplines, it has been possible to fit the small fragments to them with the illusory impression that by fitting them one is confirming the initial model. Labels for elements in such simplified sequences then come to give a misleading sense of security and precision.

Shackleton laid before the symposium clear evidence from oxygen isotope analysis of deep-sea sediments, that since the Brunhes-Matuyama polarity change there have been AT LEAST eight interglacials, each separated by more prolonged periods of fluctuating ice accumulation on the northern continents. Since the non-interglacial intervals do not group together into definable "macro-glacials," terrestrial stratigraphers can finally lay to rest the time-honored four-fold climato-stratigraphic scheme of Gunz, Mindel, Riss, and Würm, plus correlatives. Given the more or less repetitive nature of glacial advances every 100,000 years or so, sections showing evidence of warm and/or cold paleoenvironments cannot be dated by assignment to one of a small number of named, climatic events. In order to choose the appropriate oscillation one has to have geophysical, biostratigraphic, or other evidence; and then of course, it is this other evidence rather than climate that is dating the section. Particular hazards exist with the dating procedure aptly described by Kukla as the "famous count-from-top" method, since many sections contain hidden gaps.

There were lengthy discussions of the intricacies of European mid-Pleistocene stratigraphy and aspects of these are summarized by Karl Butzer in his appraisal. Suffice it to say here, that it emerged that the most complete sections available concur with the ocean core evidence in indicating many more interglacials than are allowed for in the classic four-fold scheme. Examples of such sections are the calcic loesses of Central Europe (Kukla, this volume), the Rhine sequences of "terraces," loesses, and soils (Brunnacker, this volume), and the Netherlands basin sequence (van der Hammen, Wijmstra, and Zagwijn 1971). In view of the importance of the latter, it is regrettable that circumstances prevented attendance by a representative from the Netherlands in spite of an invitation.

Charles Turner, who in the event was the only palynologist present, showed that this discipline too confirms the existence of more botanically distinctive interglacials than was formerly admitted. Discussion emphasized the possibility that distinct sequential interglacials were, under conditions of less than optimal correlation criteria, being lumped into categories such as "Eemian," "Holstein," or "Cromerian."

Karl Butzer showed that well-preserved and carefully studied coastal sequences may contain evidence of far more sea level fluctuations than are allowed for in conventional schemes.

It emerged clearly from the discussions that it is highly dangerous for paleoanthropologists to date hominid remains or archeological sites by means of labels such as Mindel, Holstein, Riss II, etc. These labels cover heterogeneous sets of climatic events, strata, and fossil assemblages. Sites should only be grouped and correlated by reference to specified biostratigraphic criteria and/or geophysical data. Once this has been done, climatic episodicity may add precision to chronological placement within a stage, a zone, a land mammal age, or a polarity epoch. Evidently the "gossamer of climatic correlation" (Bishop 1968) has been no less of an obstruction to the development of mid-Pleistocene stratigraphy in Europe than it was proved to be fifteen years ago in Africa (Cooke 1958; Flint 1959).

Europe and Africa compared

The symposium devoted some discussion to the contrast between the character of the mid-Pleistocene record in temperate Europe and in Africa. Mary Leakey, Glynn Isaac, and Karl Butzer all emphasized that long, quasi-continuous sections in East Africa do NOT as yet show the kinds of climatic oscillations that are so conspicuous in the temperate zone. This is not of course at all the same as saying that environmental fluctuations did not occur, but we may need deep bore-holes into water-logged sediments in order to resolve and record them. Hilary Deacon and Glynn Isaac both emphasized the fact that the complex mosaics of biotopes in Africa probably acted as a buffer which prevented climatic fluctuations from decimating the Lower Pleistocene biota, as occurred in Europe. Presumably in this regard the tropics were a more stable environmental cradle for early stages of human evolution and cultural development.

The Brunhes-Matuyama boundary and the colonization of the temperate zone

From the contributions and discussions there emerged a strong awareness of the existence of one, and only one, global phenomenon in mid-Pleistocene time which can as yet be recognized in all continents and used to establish time-equivalences. This is the change of geomagnetic polarity which occurred approximately 700,000 years ago. It would

be hard to over-emphasize the importance of this for both biostratigraphy and paleoanthropology. Indeed a consensus opinion developed
at the symposium that the lower limit of the formal Middle Pleistocene
sub-division of geological time should be linked to this opportunely
placed geophysical event. (See Appendix II.)

The recognition of this time-plane in various key European sections
and in East African sections allows for the first time a fully objective
assessment of the chronological relations of the hominid fossils and
the cultural record in these two continents.

Continuing with the work begun during the 1971 Wenner-Gren
symposium on Calibration of Hominoid Evolution (Bishop and Miller
1971), this conference pooled its expertise in order to compile correlation charts illustrating what is now known about time relationships in
the mid-Pleistocene, and these are presented with commentaries in
Appendix I. It is clear that given the paucity of isotopic age determinations in the middle range of Pleistocene time, the Brunhes-Matuyama
boundary provides a crucial datum point. As Kukla put it, "in addition
to count-from-top, we have count-from-Brunhes."

The implication of the evidence as it now stands is that there are
relatively abundant fossil and artifactual traces of man in Equatorial
Africa well back in the Matuyama, and probably also in the Gauss
Epoch (greater than 2.4 million years) (see Leakey, and Isaac, this
volume); while in the cool temperate zone all traces seem to be of
Brunhes age. The Mauer mandible follows closely on the polarity
change, and may be the oldest currently known and dated trace in
temperate Eurasia. (See Brunnacker, this volume). Archeological sites
such as 'Ubeidiya and Vallonet which are in the Mediterranean basin,
and which are probably of late Matuyama age (Bar-Yosef and de
Lumley, this volume) appear to me as possible examples of pioneer
stages in the expansion of man's ecological range from the tropics to
the boreal zones.

The implications of a very few K/Ar dates from Java are that some
of the hominids are appreciably greater than 700,000 years old. (See
Pilbeam, this volume.) Part of the Chinese series may also be as old as
this. The application of paleomagnetic studies to the deposits in Java
and China is a matter of urgency.

Changing mammal faunas

Until recently sequential evolutionary changes in biota, especially
mammal faunas, provided the main interconnecting thread that allowed

fragmentary Quaternary sedimentary sequences to be linked together into geological history. Within the confines of natural regions this has usually worked fairly well. However, the advent of geophysical methods for the recognitions of time equivalences shows that many equations between regions that once seemed reasonable on the basis of matching faunas need to be adjusted.

Mammalian paleontology was represented in the symposium by the contributions of Jean-Jacques Jaeger, Denès Jánossy, Kahlke, and Vincent Maglio. Regrettably Dr. Kahlke could not be present at the meetings. These papers have different coverage, but they overlap in a way which throws some features in Pleistocene paleontology into sharp relief.

Jánossy's contribution is primarily concerned with the seriation of micromammal faunas in Europe, but he is able to look outward and make suggestions about relations with Asia and with the Mediterranean. Jaeger concerned himself with the total faunal sequence of northwest Africa including the largely endemic micromammals. Kahlke indexed the main macromammal faunas of Europe and Asia and made suggestions on their seriation and correlation. Maglio provided the only treatment of the fossil record for sub-Saharan Africa and also offered a review of information on the relationships between the Palearctic, Ethiopian, and Sivo-Malay biogeographic provinces.

From these contributions and discussions of them, a number of significant generalizations emerged very clearly. First, there have been very different amounts of change in different regions during the span of Pleistocene time. In the tropics in general, and Africa in particular, stable mammal faunal configuration had been achieved by the end of the Pliocene and faunistic changes since then have been comparatively slight. By contrast the faunas of temperate Europe and Asia have undergone drastic change involving reduction in diversity and marked modification to many characteristic provincial forms. The difference shows particularly clearly in the micromammals: in Africa, changes between Pliocene and modern faunas is subtle and hard to detect, whereas for the same time range in Europe major alterations in composition and readily measurable shifts in morphology are clearly evident. These developments seem to have occurred progressively through time, so that a fairly detailed system of micromammal stratigraphic zones can be proposed for Europe.

A second point to emerge was that the estimation of time relationships between biostratigraphic divisions in different, widely spaced regions poses severe problems if it has to depend on faunal evidence alone. Errors can be large. For example, geophysical dating now shows that the faunas designated as early Middle Pleistocene by biostratigraphers in East Africa are actually almost three quarters of a million years older than early Middle Pleistocene (Biharian) faunas in Europe. The relative and absolute ages of faunas in separate biogeographic provinces which have not been adequately calibrated by geophysics are still very uncertain. For instance, the age of the Djetis fauna in Java should probably not be more precisely stated than 1.2 ± 0.5 million years.

The paleontological data of course is not of importance only for correlation and the estimation of time relationships. On the contrary, those interested in evolution and the history of life will be much better off when geophysics takes over the role of timekeeper leaving paleobiologists free to examine the process of change without being involved in the circularity of using observed differences to gauge dates. Jánossy's report on European microfauna has important ecological implications, as well as providing a framework of biostratigraphic zones. Discussion at the symposium showed that there are local biographic complexities to the record which could not be treated in his brief summary paper. Also the process of speciation may have geographic and ecological dimensions so that in addition to their chronological aspect, stages or subspecies which broadly characterize particular zones may turn out to have rather complex but ecologically informative distributions in space and time.

As Maglio pointed out the distinct biogeographic provinces of the Old World were differentiated through combined effects of ecological contrasts and partial isolation. Yet limited faunal interchange between provinces is evident in the record. This may incidentally provide an opportunity for inferring time relations between regions, but faunal interchange is really of more interest as a process in evolutionary and biological change than as a dating method. The available data tabulated by Kahlke and Maglio shows comparatively high intercontinental mobility for carnivores and elephants. Perhaps the spread of the human species will be better understood when other histories of ecological and geographic expansion have been worked out and when the full biogeographic context of human origins is better known.

The establishment of the Acheulian industrial pattern

It also emerged that the Acheulian pattern of stone industries, that is to say industries including numerous bifaces and in some cases cleavers, began to be made in Africa well back in the Matuyama Epoch, perhaps as much as 1.4 million years ago. (See Isaac and Leakey, this volume.) In Atlantic and Mediterranean Europe, industries of this kind are absent or extremely rare until about half-way through the Brunhes Epoch, at which time sites such as Torre in Pietra, Terra Amata, and Torralba document the establishment of the pattern there also.

In Central Europe, Continental Asia, and East Asia, as has long been recognized, occasional bifaces are found in some assemblages, but the Acheulian pattern of stone tools was never established. The group avoided decisive discussion of this ancient and long-lasting culture-geographic differentiation, perhaps largely because of our current ignorance of the function of bifaces, even in areas where they are abundant. (See Clark, and Isaac, this volume.)

Human evolution

Detailed discussion of the morphology of hominid fossils and their evolutionary significance lay beyond the scope and ambitions of the symposium; but David Pilbeam presented a very effective survey of some of the alternative hypotheses, and of some new ways of looking at the record. He suggested that we need to consider the possibility that there were long periods of stasis: that is to say, periods during which there are regional and temporal variations on a theme, but no marked progressive changes. One such period may have lasted from about three million years ago to around the beginning of the Middle Pleistocene (1 million years to .7 million years). Another possible period of stasis covers the central span of the Middle Pleistocene and in Pilbeam's suggestion, following Lieberman and others, only came to an end with spread, some 30,000 to 100,000 years ago, of genes determining a flexure in the basicranium. It has been suggested that this flexure reflects the dropping of the larynx and the expansion of competence for articulate speech.

The concept of stasis was found by some members of the group to have possible analogues in archeology. Mary Leakey reported that during perhaps the span of half a million years, represented by Upper Bed II to Bed IV, she could find little evidence of systematic progressive change in the sites, or in the artifact assemblages. Other records are perhaps subject to similar interpretation.

Abiding uncertainty about the relative and absolute age of most

Middle Pleistocene hominid fossils has been a great hindrance in the formulation and testing of adequate evolutionary hypotheses. Therefore one useful achievement of the symposium was perhaps the compilation of a chart which expressed the state of information on this question. (See Appendix IA). In this chart it can be seen that many important fossils are represented by range lines indicative of wide margins of uncertainty regarding their age. In Europe, the Middle Pleistocene hominid remains can only be dated by reference to rather broad biostratigraphic divisions. One set including Mauer and Vértesszöllös are of "Biharian" age (see Jánossy and Kukla, this volume). Another set that includes Arago, Swanscombe, Montmaurin, etc. belong in terminal Biharian, or post-Biharian, but pre-Upper Pleistocene, time. Within each of these wide brackets, the fossils float with their age relations being uncertain.

Archeology and adaptation

The issues involved in the study of developments in human behavior during the middle range of Pleistocene time are complex. However, the conference provided a very valuable forum for exchange of ideas and information amongst the small group of archeologists present, and between them and the natural scientists.

Several archeologists stressed that they felt that our understanding of adaptation can only be as good as the best worked out case studies of archeological traces of human activity in relation to a reconstructed, local paleoenvironment. Examples of this kind which were discussed included Vértesszöllös, Terra Amata, Torralba, 'Ubeidiya, Latamne, and Olduvai. All of these and many other research projects have involved close collaboration between archeologists and natural scientists. Clues to human adaptive patterns come from a wide range of evidence, such as the choice of site location, food refuse, indicators of seasonality, and the disposition of structures and artifacts. In many cases it is as yet very difficult to distinguish between separate but superimposed occupation episodes, or to assess the duration of occupation. These are problems with which the archeologists badly need help from natural scientists. Terra Amata emerged from de Lumley's reports of it as one of the mid-Pleistocene sites where resolution of individual, short-term occupation episodes may be optimal.

The case studies provide interpretations of early human livelihoods and activity in relation to reconstructions of many facets of environment, including geography, topography, vegetation, fauna, climate, and seasonality. With the movement away from narrow historicism, we now recognize that such working models of life in the past have considerable interest and importance for evolutionary theory, even when the site is floating in chronology and its age is known only in rather vague terms. At the present stage of studies the scope and quality of the evidence is worth more than chronological precision.

There was some amusing, but significant discussion about the role of pachyderms in modifying the paleoenvironmental record. Charles Turner reported an instance from Britain in which the incidence of grass pollens in the mud of an interglacial pond was apparently greatly inflated by high concentrations of hippopotamus dung. Desmond Clark mentioned evidence from Africa suggestive of the fact that elephants induce quasi-cyclic changes in vegetation by converting woodland to grassland, whereupon their numbers are reduced and regeneration of vegetation begins.

Several participants reported a tendency for mid-Pleistocene sites to be located in or very close to stream beds. There was some discussion of criteria for distinguishing stream-determined configurations from human ones. Karl Butzer made a plea for the presentation of comprehensive data on particle size, form, and disposition when this matter is an issue.

Glynn Isaac raised in his contribution the question of possible patterned differences in the density of bone refuse. One such possible pattern concerns differences between sites dominated by bifaces, and those with other predominant tool forms. Another allegedly possible contrast involved an impression of greater bone densities on sites in the temperate zone than on sites in the tropics. During discussion, Karl Butzer stressed that interpretations of this kind are extremely dangerous, until allowance has been made for differences in preservation. It was, however, agreed that it was important that comparative data be compiled concerning bone refuse, expressed both in terms of minimum numbers of individuals and density by weight (i.e. number and weight per meter square).

There exists a widespread notion that big game hunting began during the Middle Pleistocene and that it had profound, formative influence on human evolution. It emerged from contribution and discussion that the contrast between Middle and Lower Pleistocene bone refuse patterns is not at all marked and that one should therefore regard this kind of interpretation as an oversimplification.

The participants scanned the record for traces of intensive use of marine foods in the Middle Pleistocene, but found that all known examples seem to date from the late Pleistocene or Holocene. Fresh water fish remains were reported from sites at 'Ubeidiya and Olduvai, with land snails also at some of the latter. There was some discussion of the abiding problem of assessing the composition and importance of vegetable foods in early prehistory. Even rare sites like Choukoutien or Kalambo Falls which preserve macroscopic traces, do not do so in a way which has any quantitative significance. Desmond Clark urged the value of making indirect assessments from the study of site location in relation to plant food resources.

The antiquity of fire as a part of man's adaptive mechanism was briefly considered. Traces are present at most of the important early sites in the temperate zone (e.g. Choukoutien, Vértesszöllös, Terra Amata, and Torralba), but we do not know its antiquity in Africa, except that its use was established by the time of the Kalambo Acheulian, perhaps at about 200,000 years ago. We now know that the absence of traces does not mean ignorance of fire since charcoal is unstable under tropical conditions of ground-water leaching. Presumably addition of fire to man's technological repertoire was part of the background to the colonization of the temperate zone in the early Brunhes epoch.

Artifacts

Artifacts, and in particular flaked stone artifacts, are the principal documentation that comes down to us of the cultural rule systems and skills of mid-Pleistocene men. As such, archeologists are determined to squeeze from their stones as much interpretative blood as possible, and as a consequence, the studies have become intricate, with numerous classificatory categories being counted and many attributes being measured. Some participants felt that there is a danger of obscuring what in some cases are simple intrinsic structures in industries, by the elaborateness of the description. Others felt that, provided that one is prudent in one's interpretation, the retention of elaborate categorizations need not be unrealistic.

It emerged from the contributions and from the discussions, that over large tracts of the Old World, there is a certain similarity to the structure of variation amongst stone artifact assemblages. Thus in almost all areas where some mid-Pleistocene industries are dominated by bifaces and qualify for designation as "classic Acheulian," others which show every sign of being contemporary and essentially sympatric, have only very few bifaces and are dominated by a range of small scrapers, denticulates, small pointed tool forms, and various other types. In the Early and early Middle Pleistocene of East Africa, the second series of industries is sometimes known as the Developed Oldowan (see Leakey and Isaac, this volume), while amongst later mid-Pleistocene industries of Africa, Kleindienst formerly suggested the term "Acheulian type B" (see Clark, and Isaac, this volume, for discussion and references). In the Middle East, in early Upper Pleistocene industries, the principal non-biface dominated series are termed "Jabrudian," "Amudian," etc. (see Bar-Yosef, and Clark, this volume). In Europe, numerous names have been given to Middle Pleistocene industries which are not classic Acheulian industries: Clactonian, Tayacian, Evenossian, etc. (See de Lumley, this volume.) In all these regions there is active debate amongst the archeologists regarding the best lines of explanation for the observed patterns of variation and differentiation. Some favor the idea that each industrial pattern was the habitual product of a distinct cultural and ethnic group, which over hundreds of thousands of years propagated its traditions separately from the traditions of other cultural groups. In some cases each tradition is believed by some workers to be associated with a separate genetic system: a species or sub-species of man. Other archeologists favor the idea that recurrent differences in the need for certain artifact types could give rise to situations in which they were sometimes abundant, sometimes rare. This has come to be known as the activity facies explanation of variability.

In addition, I myself have made a plea for the notion that there is a lot of free play between stone tools and adaptation: that a wide variety of forms and assemblage compositions would equally well fulfill the needs of mobile non-agricultural peoples; and that we could expect a great deal of recurrent variation through drifts in local norms. Protagonists of all these points of view were present and the issues were raised in discussion, but time did not allow the matter to be thrashed out. It is in fact fairly clear that the questions cannot be resolved with the data now in hand. One interesting suggestion did emerge: namely, that more attention should be paid to the morphology of types held in common between assemblage types. Where the forms are similar, in spite of different percentage incidence, that might favor activity facies explanation; where different, perhaps the parallel phyla explanation.

The stratigraphers sought to know from the archeologists whether there are any culture-stratigraphic zonation patterns that might be of use to them. The archeologists replied in effect that great caution is necessary; old ideas about an inevitable surge of progressive refinement of artifacts through the Pleistocene had proved unrealistic. In long continuous sections such as at Olduvai, it was possible to demonstrate very long periods within which fluctuation rather than systematic change occurred. However, even in this case there were some trends, notably a slow rise in the incidence of small scrapers. (See Leakey, this volume.) Some participants felt that certain apparent trends might prove to be general. These include perhaps, first, a rise in the number of formalized tool types, and in the degree of formalization; second, a rise in the tendency for distinct geographically differentiated cultural systems to develop. If they are real at all, these trends are weak. They may allow sets of well documented assemblages to be zoned, but dating a site from the morphology of individual tool forms, or from assumptions about the history of assemblage characteristics, remains dangerous and undesirable.

When some of the earth scientists asked what archeologists were able to say about the evolution of society, Ofer Bar-Yosef pointed out that if one did not look at changes in the artifacts, there was a misleading sameness to the size and character of the archeological sites from two million years ago right down to the end of the Pleistocene! Clearly there were limits on the scale of societies which lived by foraging, so that development in size is seldom manifested in the Pleistocene record. However the subtle and erratic changes in artifacts, with eventual increases in the degree of formalization and regional differentiation are surely symptomatic of profound changes in the degree of elaboration of cultural systems as a whole.

The influence of raw material on artifact morphology and on similarities and differences amongst assemblages emerged as an important and controversial topic. Thus there were lively exchanges over the question of whether resemblances between the "Acheulian" of Spain and Africa were more likely to be due to the use of similar materials or to intermittent movement to and fro across the Straights of Gibraltar. In another context, Henri de Lumley reported that one observed characteristic of "Tayacian" industries was the use of difficult raw materials. From these discussions there emerged a clear need for closer investigation of the relationships between "fracture-mechanics," "typology," and "function."

Conclusion

Discussions repeatedly led us to fresh awareness of the great scale and complexity of environmental and evolutionary events during the Middle

Pleistocene. Amongst these the symposium identified intricate patterns of climatic change, which must surely have affected human evolution, but whose effect is not yet clearly resolved.

An invigorating vein which ran through the contributions and which pervaded the discussions was a concern with understanding the process of change as opposed to mere narrative history. This will surely have a salutary effect on both methods and results.

The glimpse afforded by the symposium of the state of our ignorance of the mid-Pleistocene encouraged humility; but there are also signs of solid progress being made. Amongst the most tangible of these is the recognition of the Brunhes-Matuyama time plane, and the ability which this gives us to interrelate evolutionary changes in far-flung regions, and to chart the colonization of the temperate zone by a species with tropical origins.

REFERENCES

BISHOP, W. W.
    1968   Means of correlation of Quaternary successions in East Africa. *Proceedings VII Congress, International Association for Quaternary Research* 8:161–172. Salt Lake City: University of Utah Press.

COOKE, H. B. S.
    1958   *Observations relating to Quaternary environments in east and southern Africa.* Alex I. Du Toit Memorial Lecture 5. *Geological Society of South Africa*, Annexure to volume 60.

FLINT, R. F.
    1959   On the basis of Pleistocene correlation in East Africa. *Geological Magazine* 96:265–284.

VAN DER HAMMEN, T., T. A. WIJMSTRA, W. G. ZAGWIJN
    1971   "The floral record of the late Cenozoic of Europe," in *Late Cenozoic Glacial Ages.* Edited by K. Turekian, 391–424. New Haven: Yale University Press.

Correlation Charts Compiled
at the Symposium

APPENDIX 1

The presence round the table of expert stratigraphers familiar with many important regional sequences offered a unique opportunity for the compilation of charts showing informed opinion regarding the age of various hominid fossils and sites that had been considered at the meeting.

Data were collected on the blackboard. A plot of the suggested position was prepared for revision and annotation at the conference. All those present helped as appropriate, with D. Pilbeam and G. Isaac taking responsibility for transposing the initial patchwork into two diagrams with commentaries. Barbara Isaac has redrawn the figures.

The charts are concerned more with estimates of the age limits BETWEEN WHICH the paleoanthropological document probably lies, rather than with what in most cases would be a misleadingly exact date. That is to say, each line on the diagrams suggests the range of uncertainty about age.

The assessment of the Symposium regarding uncertainties over the ages of selected hominid fossils in the range 2.0 to 0.1 million years[1]

Southern Africa

There are virtually no isotopic dates so that age estimates all depend on faunal correlations and general geological considerations. The various Transvaal australopithecine sites may range in date from about

---

[1] Notes and comments compiled by G. Isaac and D. Pilbeam.

three million to one million years. Swartkrans, Kromdraai, and Sterkfontein Extension which have often been referred to as Middle Pleistocene, are perhaps of late Lower Pleistocene age in the sense of this
Symposium.

The ages of the Broken Hill and Elandsfontein crania remain uncertain within wide ranges. It has often been assumed that they are
Upper Pleistocene, but the fauna associated with both is in many ways
best regarded as Middle Pleistocene (Klein 1973; Butzer 1973). Recent C[14] results give ages of 40,570 ± 000 and 40,570 ± 000 BP respectively for fauna associated with the crania, but new racemisation
tests are not consistent with these dates (Protsch 1973; Bada, personal
communication to J. D. Clark).

Eastern Africa

More than one hundred well dated hominid fossils have been recovered
from early Pleistocene deposits in eastern Africa (i.e. ~ 2.0 - 1.5 million years). Only selected specimens can be shown on the chart. For
information on dating, see Curtis and Hay (1972), Leakey for Olduvai
(this volume), Isaac for Peninj (this volume), Brock and Isaac for
East Rudolf (i.p.), Howell (1969), and Brown (1972) for Omo.

From the time range ~ 1.5 to 0.1 million years there are fewer
fossils, and those that are known are less well dated. Olduvai Hominid
9 from LLK II is well back in the Matuyama Reversed Epoch, while
various hominid fossils from Bed IV (e.g. Hominids 2, 28 and 12) are
all very close on one side or other of the Brunhes/Matuyama boundary
at about 0.7 million years.

The Kanjera cranial material and the Kapthurin mandible are of
presumed Brunhes age, but little precision is possible. Two contradictory K/Ar results have been obtained for the Kapthurin Formation;
an underlying lava gives 0.23, while sanidines from tuffs in a basal
unit give about 0.66 million years (Bishop 1972:230-231). The mandible is in any case in the upper part of the formation and therefore
younger than either unit for which the determinations were run.

The Eyasi partial cranium should be regarded as undated. Although
widely accepted, the evidence for an Upper Pleistocene age is very
slender.

The Kibish Formation partial crania (Leakey, Butzer, and Day
1969) are most likely to be end Middle Pleistocene, or very early
Upper Pleistocene. The Th/U measurements are indicative of an age

of 0.13 million years, which is a very reasonable estimate albeit unconfirmed (Butzer, Brown, and Thurber 1969).

The geological interpretations on which an age of 1.1 million years was attributed to the Chesowanja hominid fossil have proven to be erroneous (Hill, Walker, and Bishop, personal communication). The fossil can therefore only be loosely dated on the basis of faunal associations.

North Africa

The only geophysical age determinations are Th/U measurements on marine shells (Jaeger, Freeman, this volume). On the basis of fauna, Ain Hanech is the oldest site, followed by Ternifine. Both are immediately "post-Villafranchian". Jaeger estimates that a gap of at least 0.3 million years separates Ternifine from the next oldest localities.

The localities of Temara and Rabat are attributed to the pre-Soltanian local stage. This stage is apparently bracketed by dates of 0.145 to 0.125 million years for the preceding stage (Jaeger, this volume). The sites of Sale and Sidi Abderahman are earlier but can only be dated by extrapolation.

Western Asia

K/Ar dates for basalt flows date part of the 'Ubeidiya Formation and its contained distinctive mollusc fauna. The archeological sites at 'Ubeidiya itself may be of a similar age or somewhat older than the basalts (see Bar-Yosef, this volume). The 'Ubeidiya fauna was considered probably to be of an age equivalent to the very earliest stage of the Biharian (Jánossy, this volume) or Lower Pleistocene, i.e. 0.7 to 1.5 million years (Maglio, this volume). The fauna from Latamne seems to be of late Biharian or early post-Biharian age equivalence.

In a number of sites, Acheulian industries and various non-Acheulian industries can be shown to be of "last interglacial" age, i.e. 0.08 to 0.1 million years.

Eastern Asia

In Java, Djetis faunas are unlikely to be any older than around 1.5 million years (Maglio 1973) thus the K/Ar dates with large error figures (Pilbeam, this volume) are presumably maxima. Ngandong faunas are unlikely to be as young as, or younger than about 0.1 million years (Maglio, personal communication). Thus the Javanese hominids probably range in age from 1.5 million years or else to perhaps considerably more than 0.1 million years.

Although difficult to correlate with European faunas, that from Choukoutien Locality I in China is of late Biharian age, probably falling around 0.4 to 0.6 million years. A racemisation age of 0.3 million years is probably a minimum. The localities at Lantian are about the same age (Aigner 1972; Pilbeam, this volume), while Kungwangling at Lantian is older and broadly correlative with Djetis faunas, therefore being up to 1.5 million years old. Earlier uranium-series dates for locality I gave age-ranges of 175-300,000 years for the upper levels, and 180,000 to greater than 500,000 years for the lower (Cherdyntsev 1961).

Europe

Post-Villafranchian and pre-last glacial age faunas in Europe can be divided into Biharian and post-Biharian phases. The hominids have been dated for the most part by faunal means; they subdivide into two age groups, Biharian and post-Biharian. Within each group, sites are ordered solely on the basis of faunal evidence (Jánossy, de Lumley, Kahlke, this volume). The early sites apparently fall in the order Mauer, Vértesszöllös, Montmaurin. The published Th/U measure-

---

Key to the Charts

– – – – – – –	Range of uncertainty for a site or fossil.
ACHEULIAN (ETC.)	Duration during which an industrial pattern is estimated to been in operation.
□	A K/Ar date associated with a site or fossil.
○	A Th/U "date" associated with a site or fossil.
◇	A protein racemisation age estimate.
△	A C[14] date age estimate.

Paleomagnetic data are crucial to arguments in many cases but cannot easily be shown on the chart.

The polarity time scale along the margin is simplified from that of Cox in *Science* 63:237–245 (1969), with the name Olduvai Event being transferred on account of its priority to what was termed the Gilsa Event. (See Gromme and Hay in *Earth and Planetary Science Letters* 10:179–185 (1971.)

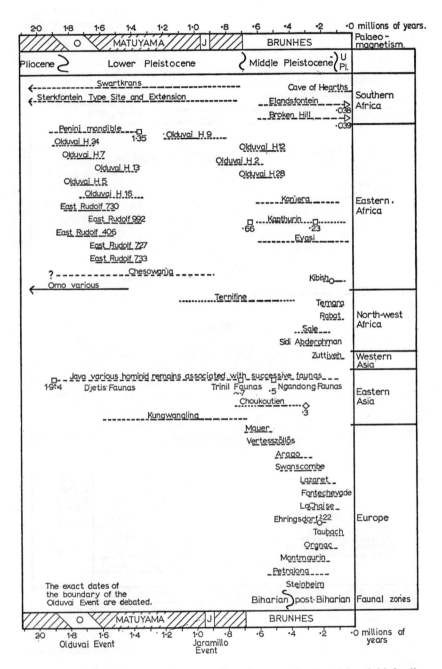

Figure 1.   Ranges of uncertainty regarding the age of selected hominid fossils ~ 2.0 to .01 million years

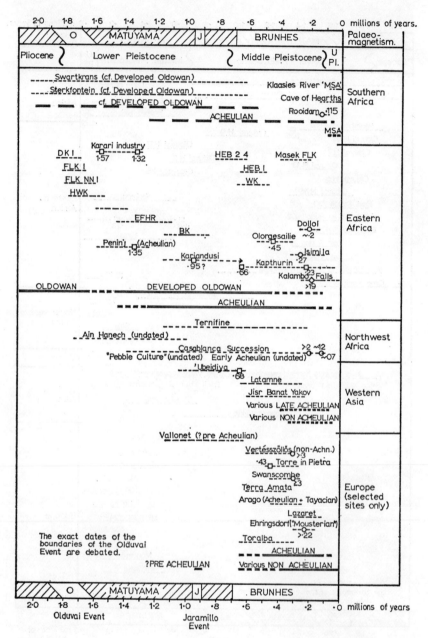

Figure 2.   Ranges of uncertainty regarding the ages of selected archeological sites and industries

ments on travertines at Vértesszöllös are best regarded as minimum ages.

The second group of sites, all apparently younger than about 0.4 million years cannot be ordered precisely, although the seriation shown here is considered the most probable. Sites in southern France which record periods of raised sea level can be correlated tentatively with the deep-sea record of isotopic fluctuations (Shackleton, this volume). Thus Terra Amata, Arago, Lazaret and other archeological and hominid sites can be fitted with some confidence between around 0.45 million years and 0.1 million years. Petralona may be older than Swanscombe and Arago. A Th/U measurement on bone from the upper middle gravel at Swanscombe indicates an age in excess of 0.3 million years (Gladfelter, personal communication). The Steinheim skull site (Brunnacker, personal communication) need not have been of the same age as the faunal site; the position of the hominid is therefore equivocal. Th/U measurements on travertines at Taubach show the hominid teeth to be around 0.125 million years; travertines at Ehringsdorf are all older than 0.22 million years (Broecker, Goddard, Mania, and Kukla 1973).

The assessment of the Sympo*ium regarding the ages of selected archeological sites and stone industries.

This chart is presented as a supplement to Figure 1, which summarized information and uncertainty regarding the ages of hominid fossils. Much of the information and logic is held in common between the two charts and is not repeated in this commentary.

Southern Africa

The only geophysical dates concern post-Acheulian and post mid-Pleistocene industries. A late Acheulian industry, or Acheulian derivative, has been "dated" to 0.11 million years at Rooidam by the Uranium series method (Butzer 1974). Industries believed to be post-Acheulian (i.e. Middle Stone Age etc.) are associated with last-interglacial high sea levels for which age estimates of 0.125 to 0.075 million years seem reasonable (Deacon and Butzer, information to the Symposium; See also Wymer and Singer 1972; Klein 1974; Beaumont and Vogel 1972). The Swartkrans and Sterkfontein industries have been classified as Developed Oldowan by M. D. Leakey (1970), and Sterkfontein as Acheulian (Robinson and Mason 1962). Faunal evidence suggests an age of at least a million years for these.

Eastern Africa

A long series of geophysical dates span a range from greater than two million years to about 0.2 million eyars. After about 1.4 million years, industries of classic Acheulian aspect occur in the succession along with others of differing aspect for which M. D. Leakey's label "Developed Oldowan" is used here. The Kalambo Falls carbon dates of 60,000 for the Upper Acheulian have commonly been used as a standard of reference in African paleoanthropological chronology. J. D. Clark reported to the symposium that amino acid racemisation determinations on organic materials from Kalambo may be indicative of an age approaching 0.2 million years. If confirmed, extensive revisions to chronology will be necessary. For further information on dating and interpretation, see M. D. Leakey and G. Ll. Isaac in this volume.

Northwest Africa

Geophysical dates are only available from the upper part of the succession. Ain Hanech is regarded by Jaeger (this volume) as immediately "post-Villafranchian". The early part of the pre-Acheulian and the Lower Acheulian succession is undated.

Western Asia

A geophysical date is now available for lavas at the top of the 'Ubeidiya Formation which suggests that 'Ubeidiya Acheulian is at least 0.68 million years old (see Bar-Yosef, this volume). Various late Acheulian industries and non-Acheulian industries such as the Jabrudian are associated with the last major marine transgressions and its correlatives. Ages of 0.07 to 0.125 million years for these seem reasonable estimates. Between these, sites such as Latamne, Jisr Banat Yakov, etc., float without precise dating.

Europe

Very few geophysical dates are available, the oldest secure date being the Torre in Pietra Acheulian at $\leqslant$ 0.43 million years (see Isaac 1972).

On the basis of faunistic evidence the Grotte du Vallonet seems likely to be between 1.3 and 0.7 million years (see de Lumley, this volume). Vértesszöllös is of full "Biharian" age and is therefore likely to be older than ~ 0.4 million years. Most other well known sites are probably "post-Biharian" in age and their position in the range ~ 0.4 to ~ 0.1 million years is based on estimations. Deposits of this entire time range contain industries of both Acheulian and non-Acheulian aspect (Tayacian, Clactonian, Evenossian, and pre-Mousterian or Mousterian). On the chart, only non-Acheulian industries are given designation.

Only a small selection of sites discussed are shown: these are indicative of the degree of uncertainty, but do not represent the full complexity of known sites, etc. Other dates shown are as follows:
1. Vértesszöllös, greater than 0.3 million years (see Isaac 1972 for references and discussion).
2. Swanscombe, ⩾ 0.3 million years (report by Gladfelter to the Symposium of an unpublished Th/U result.).
3. Ehringsdorf, greater than 0.22 million years (Uranium series determinations reported by Kukla; see Broecker, Goddard, Mania, and Kukla 1973).

REFERENCES

AIGNER, J. S.
1972 Relative dating of north Chinese faunal and cultural complexes. *Arctic Anthropology* 9:36–79.
BEAUMONT, P. B., J. C. VOGEL
1972 On a new radiocarbon chronology for Africa south of the Equator. *African Studies* 31(3):155–182.
BISHOP, W. W.
1972 "Stratigraphic succession 'versus' calibration in East Africa," in *Calibration of hominoid evolution*. Edited by W. W. Bishop and J. A. Miller, 219–246. Edinburgh: Scottish Academic Press.
BROCK, A., G. LL. ISAAC
i.p. Palaeomagnetic stratigraphy and chronology of hominid-bearing sediments east of Lake Rudolf, Kenya. *Nature*.
BROECKER, GODDARD, MANIA, KUKLA
1973 Manuscript in preparation.
BROWN, F. H.
1972 "Radiometric dating of sedimentary formations in the lower Omo Valley, Ethiopia," in *Calibration of hominoid evolution*. Edited by W. W. Bishop and J. A. Miller, 273–287. Edinburgh: Scottish Academic Press.

BUTZER, K. W.
   1973   Re-evaluation of the geology of the Elandsfontein (Hopefield)
          site, southwestern Cape. *South African Journal of Science* 69:
          234–238.
   1974   Geological interpretation of Acheulian calcpan sites at Doorn-
          laagte and Rooidam (Kimberley, South Africa). *Journal of Ar-
          chaeological Science* 1:1–25.
BUTZER, K. W., BROWN, F. H., D. L. THURBER
   1969   Horizontal sediments of the lower Omo Valley: the Kibish For-
          mation. *Quaternaria* 11:15–29.
CHERDYNTSEV, V. V.
   1961   "Absolute age determination of Quaternary fossil bones by means
          of heavy elements isotopes relations," in *Problems of anthropo-
          gene geology*, 85–95. Moscow: Nauk.
CURTIS, G. H., R. L. HAY
   1972   "Further geological studies and potassium-argon dating at Oldu-
          vai Gorge and Ngorongoro Crater," in *Calibration of hominoid
          evolution*. Edited by W. W. Bishop and J. A. Miller, 289–302.
          Edinburgh: Scottish Academic Press.
HOWELL, F. C.
   1969   Remains of Hominidae from Pliocene/Pleistocene formations in
          the lower Omo basin, Ethiopia. *Naure* 223:1234-1239.
ISAAC, G. LL.
   1972   "Chronology and the tempo of cultural change during the Plei-
          stocene," in *Calibration of hominoid evolution*. Edited by W. W.
          Bishop and J. A. Miller, 381–430. Edinburgh: Scottish Academic
          Press.
KLEIN, R. G.
   1972   The Late Quaternary mammalian fauna of Nelson Bay Cave
          (Cape Province, South Africa): its implications for magafaunal
          extinctions and environmental and cultural change. *Quaternary
          Research* 2:135–142.
   1973   On the geological antiquity oof Rhodesian man. *Nature* 244:311–
          312.
   1974   Environment and subsistence of prehistoric man in the southern
          Cape Province, South Africa. *World Archaeology* 5:249–284.
LEAKEY, M. D.
   1970   Stone age artifacts from Swartkrans. *Nature* 225:1222–1225.
LEAKEY, R. E. F., K. W. BUTZER, M. H. DAY
   1969   Early *Homo sapiens* remains from the Omo River region of
          south-west Ethiopia. *Nature* 222:1132–1138.
MAGLIO, V. J.
   1973   Origin and evolution of the Elephantidae. *American Philosophical
          Society Transactions*.
PROTSCH, R. R. R.
   1973   "The dating of Upper Pleistocene sub-Saharan fossil hominids
          and their place in human evolution: with morphological and
          archaeological implications." Unpublished doctoral dissertation.
          University of California at Los Angeles.

ROBINSON, J. T., R. J. MASON

   1962   Australopithecines and artefacts at Sterkfontein. *South African Archaeological Bulletin* 17:87–125.

WYMER, J. J., R. SINGER

   1972   "Middle Stone Age occupational settlements on the Tzitzikama coast, eastern Cape Province, South Africa," in *Man, settlement and urbanism.* Edited by P. J. Ucko, R. Tringham, and C. W. Dimbleby, 207–210. London: Duckworth.

Delimitation of the Geologic Time Term "Middle Pleistocene"

APPENDIX 2

During the discussion sessions at Burg Wartenstein, there was tacit agreement that each person should define what he or she meant by the term "Middle Pleistocene" but that we would not engage in legalistic disputes over different usages. However in a session towards the close of the meeting, the question was formally discussed. It emerged that in spite of initial differences, wide agreement had developed amongst participants. On the basis of the consensus at the conference table, Karl Butzer and Glynn Isaac drew up the following memorandum. This is being communicated to appropriate stratigraphic tribunals such as INQUA, together with the list of those participants who have specifically expressed their wish to endorse the proposition. There have been no dissenters.

MEMORANDUM

It was the sense of the participants at the Burg Wartenstein Symposium 58, entitled "Stratigraphy and Patterns of Cultural Change in the Middle Pleistocene" that:
1. The beginning of the Middle Pleistocene should be so defined as to either coincide with or be closely linked to the boundary between the Matuyama Reversed Epoch and the Bruhnes Normal Epoch of paleomagnetic chronology.
Clearly in view of the short time which has elapsed since the establishment of paleomagnetic reversal chronology, this is a proposal without formal precedents. However, in view of the great difficulties

experienced in Pleistocene studies with regard to the recognition of time equivalences between separate bio-geographic provinces, we urge that advantage be taken of this unique global criterion. The following arguments can be advanced in favour of the proposal:

a.   It is particularly difficult to assess time equivalences in the middle range of Pleistocene time because only in a very few regions has it yet proved possible to date fossil faunas, fossil floras, and climatic events of this age, by means of isotopic determinations. The time span lies beyond the capabilities of the C^{14} method, and other methods such as potassium argon, thorium uranium, and amino acid dating, are only rarely, and with difficulties, applicable.

b.   The Bruhnes-Matuyama boundary can be recognized on all continents and in oceanic sediments. In each region, sections can surely be found where the relationship between the paleomagnetic boundary and provincial bio-stratigraphic and time-stratigraphic entities can be determined, thereby extending the value of the criterion beyond those sediments on which magnetic determinations have been, or can be made.

c.   Coincidentally in several regions, the Bruhnes-Matuyama boundary rather closely coincides with the lower limit of stratigraphic divisions now assigned to the "Middle Pleistocene." Thus in the Netherlands the Bruhnes-Matuyama boundary has been determined to fall within the early part of the "Cromerian" bio-stratigraphic entity. In Central Europe it has been determined to relate to early stages of the "Biharian" bio-stratigraphic entity.

On the other hand, there are regions where this criterion will necessitate drastic changes in the current usage of geologic-time nomenclature (e.g. East Africa). However, since we now know there are major discrepancies in the time equivalence of current usages, no useful definition of a bounding time-plane can be made without involving revision in some regions.

2.   The end of the Middle Pleistocene should be so defined as to coincide with the beginning of the last interglacial transgression or an equivalent, stratigraphically definable event. (The position of this time-plane is clearly far more difficult to determine in many provincial sequences, but it nonetheless seems the best available boundary. Various chronological evidences converge to indicate a date of about 125,000 years for the proposed boundary, but this value should not be specifically incorporated into the definition.)

It goes beyond the intentions and competence of this group to determine how the intentions of this proposal can best be reconciled with the normal procedures of international stratigraphic commissions, but we strongly urge that a way be found to implement them. In particular we feel that advantage should be taken of the Bruhnes-Matuyama polarity change as a boundary criterion.

Biographical Notes

OFER BAR-YOSEF was born in Jerusalem in 1937, and received his B.A. (1963), M.A. (1965), and Ph.D. (1971) from the Hebrew University, Jerusalem. Lecturer in Prehistory in the Institute of Archaeology (1970). Excavated with M. Stekelis in Ein Gev (1963–1964), surveyed prehistoric sites on the coastal plain of Israel (1965–1966), excavated with E. Tchernov at Hayonim Cave, Galilee (1965–1971) and at 'Ubeidiya, Jordan Valley (1967–1974). Published works include (with E. Tchernov) *On the palaeoecological history of the site of 'Ubeidiya.* (Publications of the Israel Academy of Sciences and Humanities. Jerusalem, 1972.)

PIERRE BOUT was born in Paris in 1906. His positions include Docteur ès Sciences Naturelles, ex-Maître de Recherche at the CNRS (Centre National de la Recherche Scientifique), and Chargé de Cours on the Faculté des Lettres de Clermont-Ferrand (France) at the Institut de Géographie. His thesis (1960) was on "Le Villafranchien du Velay et du Bassin hydrographique moyen et supérieur de l'Allier" and some publications representative of his later work are "Étude stratigraphique et paléogéographique du gisemant de mammifères fossiles pléistocène moyen de Solilhac, près Le Puy-en-Velay (Haute Loire), France" *Geologie en Mijnbouw,* 1964) and "Absolute ages of some volcanic formations in the Auvergne and Velay areas and chronology of the European Pleistocene" (*Palaeogeography, Palaeoclimatology, Palaeoecology,* 1970).

KARL BRUNNACKER was born in 1921 in Castell/Unterfranken Germany.

From 1946 to 1950 he studied Geology at the University of Erlangen and received his Ph.D. in 1950 from the University of Erlangen. From 1950 to 1963 he worked as Wissenschaftlicher Mitarbeiter at the Bayerisches Geologisches Landesamt, Bodenkunde und Quartärgeologie (Habilitation: Technical University of Munich, in Geology and Soil Science, 1958). In 1963 he was appointed to the Lehrstuhl für Eiszeitenforschung at the University of Colohne, and in 1968 was elected Corresponding Member of the German Archeological Institute. About 150 works by Dr. Brunnacker have been published.

ELIZABETH K. BUTZER was born in Germany in 1935. In 1955 she graduated from the Gymnasial Abitur, Liebfrauenschule in Bonn, received her Educational Certificate in 1957 from the Pedagogische Akademie (Bonn), and taught elementary school from 1957 to 1959. She has worked as a field assistant to K. W. Butzer in Spain and Africa. In 1974 she received a B.A. (Honors Anthropology) from the University of Illinois and is currently working toward the M.A. in geography.

KARL W. BUTZER was born in Germany in 1934. He received his B.Sc. (Honors Mathematics) from McGill University in 1954 and his M.Sc. (Meteorology) in 1955. In 1957 he received his Dr. rer. nat. (Physical Geography) from the University of Bonn. He was Assistant and Associate Professor of Geography at the University of Wisconsin from 1959 to 1966 since which time he has been Professor of Anthropology and Geography at the University of Chicago. He received an award from the Association of American Geographers in 1968 for his work, *Environment and archeology*, cited as an Outstanding Geographical Synthesis. Dr. Butzer has authored some one hundred papers as well as six works and monographs, and as editor (with L. G. Freeman of *Prehistoric archeology and ecology* (first volume 1972). He has carried out geological and geoarcheological research in Egypt, Spain, Ethiopia, and South Africa since 1956.

J. DESMOND CLARK was born in England in 1916. He received his B.A. and Ph.D. in Archeology from Cambridge University in 1937 and 1950. He served during the war in Africa, and was Director of the Rhodes-Livingstone Museum in Zambia from 1937 to 1961. Since then he has been a Professor of Anthropology at the University of California at Berkeley. His archeological fieldwork has been extensive; most parts of central and southern Africa, Angola, Syria, the Sahara (Niger), and the Sudan. A Fellow of the British Academy and of the American

Academy of Arts and Sciences, he is also a Member of the Permanent Committee of the Pan-African Congress on Prehistory and Quaternary Studies and, in 1971–1972, was a Guggenheim Fellow. Some 200 papers by Dr. Clark on archeological subjects have been published in scientific journals in Africa, Britain, and the U.S.A. Books include: *The Kalambo Falls prehistoric site, The prehistory of Africa, The atlas of African prehistory* (compiler), *Background to evolution in Africa* (edited with W. W. Bishop), and volumes on the prehistory of Zambia, the Horn, Angola, and southern Africa. Dr. Clark is currently editor for the first volume of the *Cambridge history of Africa*.

HILARY JOHN DEACON was born in Cape Town, South Africa, in 1936. He studied at the University of Cape Town, receiving there his B.Sc. in Geology and Archeology, B.A. (Honors) in Archeology (1962), and M.A. in Archeology (1966). In 1967–1968, he held a British Council Scholarship, Institute of Archaeology, University of London. Positions he has held include: (1963–1969) Professional Officer and Senior Professional Officer (Archaeology) Albany Museum, Grahamstown; (1969–1971) Deputy Director, Albany Museum, Grahamstown; (1971–present) Senior Lecturer in Archaeology, University of Stellenbosch. Mr. Deacon's major interests in his field are the prehistory of sub-Saharan Africa and environmental archeology in southern Africa.

HENRY DE LUMLEY, born in 1934 in Marseille, received his Licence ès-Sciences Naturelles at Marseille in 1955 and his Doctorat ès-Sciences Naturalles (Géologie) at Paris in 1965. He is currently Maître de Recherche at the CNRS (Centre National de la Recherche Scientifique) and a professor at the Université de Provence and at the Université Aix-Marseille in Marseille. He has about 140 published works on the geology of the Quaternary, the Lower and Middle Paleolithic, human paleontology, and paleoecology. In addition, Dr. de Lumley is known for his excavations in the caves of Vallonnet, Lazaret, Baume Bonne, Hortus, and Arago in the south of France.

LESLIE G. FREEMAN was born in 1935 in the United States. Educated at the University of Chicago, he is now Associate Professor of Anthropology there. He is the author of numerous articles on paleolithic prehistory. He assisted F. Clark Howell at the excavation of Torralba and Ambrona, two Acheulean sites in north-central Spain and, with J. González Echegaray, jointly directed excavations at Cueva Morin, on the Spanish north coast, which have been the subject of a multi-volume monograph.

BRUCE G. GLADFELTER received his Ph.D. from the University of Chicago in 1970. Since then he has been an Assistant Professor at the University of Illinois at Chicago Circle in the Department of Geography. Pleistocene field research which he has done includes work in central Spain (1967, 1969) and England (1970, Clacton; 1972, Hoxne). Publications by Dr. Gladfelter include *Meseta and Campiña landforms in central Spain: a geomorphology of the Alto Henares Basin* (University of Chicago Department of Geography Research Paper 130, 1971) and *Excavation of the Clactonian industry at Clacton-on-Sea, Essex, England* (Proceedings of the Prehistoric Society, 1974).

ANNE BARBARA ISAAC, born in 1936 in England, was educated there. She took an honors degree in English at Cambridge University (1958). Thereafter, she spent two years at the Sheffield City Museum and one year at the Institute of Archaeology in London. At present, she works with Glynn Isaac, and has co-authored several publications with him.

GLYNN LLWELYN ISAAC was born in 1937 in Cape Town and educated there as far as his first degree in Zoology and Geology (1958). He took and honors degree in Pleistocene Archaeology at Cambridge University (1961) and was recruited into East African Prehistory by Louis Leakey (1961–1965). In 1969, his Ph.D. was granted by Cambridge University for a thesis on Olorgesailie. Now he teaches at the University of California at Berkeley while continuing field research in East Africa. Representative works by Dr. Isaac are "Studies of early culture in East Africa" (*World Archaeology*, 1969) and "Chronology and the tempo of cultural change during the Pleistocene" (in *Calibration of hominoid evolution*, edited by Bishop and Miller, 1972).

JEAN-JACQUES JAEGER was born in 1944 in France. Educational background: Élève à l'École Normale Supérieure, ULM (Paris, 1963–1967); Licencié ès Sciences biologiques (Paris, 1965); Licencié ès Sciences de Sciences de la Terre (Strasbourg, 1966); Agrégation Sciences Biologiques (Paris, 1967). At present, he is an Assistant agrégé at the Université des Sciences et Techniques du Languedoc at Montpellier. Numerous publications include the following articles in the *Comptes Rendus de l'Academie des Sciences*, Paris: "Les Rongeurs du Pleistocène moyen de Ternifine (Algérie)," 1969; "Découverte au Jebel Irhoud des premières faunes de Rongeurs du Pleistocène inférieur et moyen du Maroc," 1970; "Les Micromammifères du Villafranchien inférieur du Lac Ichkeul (Tunisie): données stratigraphiques et biogéographiques nouvelles," 1971.

DÉNES JÁNOSSY was born in 1926 and received his teacher's diploma in Natural Sciences and Chemistry in Budapest in 1948. He has worked steadily at the Natural History Museum in Budapest, beginning in 1946 as Conservator, becoming in 1952 Curator of Vertebrate Paleontology, in 1961 Deputy Keeper, and in 1970 Keeper of the Paleontology Department. Since 1954, he has given lectures in archeology and geology at the University of Sciences. In 1959, he was a Candidate of Sciences and in 1968 he became Doctor of Sciences. In 1970, he received first prize in Natural Sciences from the Ministry of Culture. Dr. Jánossy has been a participant and lecturer at various international conferences in England, France, Germany, Czechoslovakia, Poland, and the U.S.S.R. and is also a member of the International Committee on the Plio-Pleistocene Boundary. Over forty-five works by Dr. Jánossy have been published.

HANS-DIETRICH KAHLKE, born in 1924, now lives in the German Democratic Republic. He studied at the Guilford Technical College (Surrey), Cambridge University (Extramural Studies), the University of Jena, and the University of Berlin. He is presently the director of the Institute of Quaternary Paleontology at Weimar. Dr. Kahlke is the author of more than 100 papers and books on Quaternary paleontology and archeology.

GEORGE J. KUKLA was born in 1930 in Prague and received his RnDr. from Charles University there. He has worked in mineral prospecting in Europe, South and Central America, and Ceylon. From 1958 to 1970, as a Research Associate of the Czechoslovak Academy of Sciences, he studied the stratigraphy of paleolithic sites, caves, and loess exposures, using paleomagnetic methods. The National Science Foundation awarded him the Senior Foreign Scientist Fellowship in 1970, and since 1971 he has been Senior Research Associate at Lamont Doherty Observatory, Columbia University. Publications by Dr. Kukla include "Correlation between loesses and deep sea sediments" (in *Geol. Fören. Stockholm Förh*, 1970) and "When and how will the present interglacial end?" (in *Quaternary Research*, 1972).

MARY DOUGLAS LEAKEY was born in London and became interested in prehistory as a child in southern France where her family lived. She married Louis Seymour Bazett Leakey in 1936 and came to live in East Africa in 1938. Since 1960, she directed excavations at Olduvai Gorge.

VINCENT JOSEPH MAGLIO was born in 1942 in New York City. He received his B.A. in biology from Queens College, CUNY, in 1965; his M.A. from Harvard University in 1967; and his Ph.D. from Harvard University in 1971; and has done field research in East African paleontology since 1966. His interests include the evolution of functional anatomical systems, faunal evolution in Africa, and Pliocene-Pleistocene correlations. Representative publications: "Early Elephantidae of Africa and a tentative correlation of African Plio-Pleistocene deposits" (in *Nature*, 1970), "Plio-Pleistocene stratigraphy in East Africa in relation to proboscidean and suid evolution" (in *Calibration of hominid evolution*, edited by Bishop and Miller, 1972), and "Vertebrate faunas and chronology of hominid-bearing sediments east of Lake Rudolf, Kenya" (in *Nature*, 1972).

DAVID PILBEAM was born in England in 1940 and educated at Cambridge (B.A., M.A.) and Yale (Ph.D.). At present, he is Associate Professor of Anthropology at Yale University, and his research interests include human and non-human primate evolution, primate behavior and ecology, functional anatomy, numerical analysis and methodology, and methodology. Dr. Pilbeam has published various papers on human and non-human primate evolution, biochemical evolution, behavior, stratigraphy, and numerical methodology, as well as *The evolution of man* (Thames and Hudson, 1970) and *The ascent of man* (Macmillan, 1972).

NICHOLAS JOHN SHACKLETON, born in 1937 in London, spent his early childhood in East Africa. He received his degree in Geology and Physics from Cambridge in 1961 and his Ph.D. from Cambridge in 1967 for his thesis, "The measurement of palaeotemperatures in the Quaternary era." Since 1961, he has been a member of the Cambridge University Sub-Department of Quaternary Research and his present position is Assistant Director of Research. Dr. Shackleton has published various papers on the Quaternary period.

CHARLES TURNER completed his post-graduate and post-doctoral studies on the Middle Pleistocene of East Anglia at the Sub-Department of Quaternary Research, Cambridge University (1962–1968). From 1968 to 1970, he was a lecturer in Geography at Birkbeck College, University of London, and since then has been a Staff Tutor in Earth Sciences on the Faculty of Science, Open University. Publications include: "Correlation between marine and terrestrial Pleistocene successions" (with N.

After the Australopithecines

Stratigraphy, Ecology, and Culture Change in the Middle Pleistocene

Editors

KARL W. BUTZER
GLYNN LL. ISAAC

Assisted by

ELIZABETH BUTZER
BARBARA ISAAC

MOUTON PUBLISHERS · THE HAGUE · PARIS
DISTRIBUTED IN THE USA AND CANADA BY ALDINE, CHICAGO

Shackleton, in *Nature*, 1967), "The subdivision and zonation of inter-glacial periods" (with R. G. West, in *Eiszeitalter und Gegenwart*, 1968), and "The Middle Pleistocene deposits at Marks Tey, Essex" (*Phil. Trans. Roy. Soc.* London, 1970).

091216